Nietzsche and the Problem of Subjectivity

Nietzsche Today

Volume 5

Nietzsche and the Problem of Subjectivity

Edited by
João Constâncio, Maria João Mayer Branco
and Bartholomew Ryan

DE GRUYTER

ISBN 978-3-11-055470-0
e-ISBN (PDF) 978-3-11-040820-1
e-ISBN (EPUB) 978-3-11-040840-9
ISSN 2191-5741

Library of Congress Cataloging-in-Publication Data
A CIP catalog record for this book has been applied for at the Library of Congress

Bibliographic information published by the Deutsche Nationalbibliothek
The Deutsche Nationalbibliothek lists this publication in the Deutsche Nationalbibliografie; detailed bibliographic data are available in the Internet at http://dnb.dnb.de.

© 2017 Walter de Gruyter GmbH, Berlin/Boston
This volume is text- and page-identical with the hardback published in 2015.
Typesetting: Lumina Datamatics
Printing and binding: CPI books GmbH, Leck
♾ Printed on acid-free paper
Printed in Germany

www.degruyter.com

Acknowledgements

The editors wish to express their gratitude to the following institutions:

–Fundação para a Ciência e Tecnologia (FCT), which funded the research project "Nietzsche and the Contemporary Debate on the Self", PTDC/FIL-FIL/111444/2009. The book reflects the research that was undertaken within this project for three and a half years.

–Instituto de Filosofia da Nova (IFILNOVA) and Faculdade de Ciências Sociais e Humanas (FCSH)/Universidade Nova de Lisboa (UNL). We are particularly grateful for the institutional support to our Nietzsche International Lab (NIL). For more information on NIL, see http://www.nietzschelab.com

The editors also wish to express their gratitude to the following scholars who belong to NIL and have contributed to this volume with much more than just a text for one of the chapters:

Pietro Gori, Paolo Stellino, Benedetta Zavatta, Marta Faustino, Luís Sousa.

Contents

References, Citations, and Abbreviations —— XI

João Constâncio, Maria João Mayer Branco and Bartholomew Ryan
Introduction to *Nietzsche and the Problem of Subjectivity* —— 1

Part I: Tradition and Context

Isabelle Wienand
1   Writing from a First-Person Perspective: Nietzsche's Use of the Cartesian Model —— 49

David Wollenberg
2   Power, Affect, Knowledge: Nietzsche on Spinoza —— 65

Nikolaos Loukidelis and Christopher Brinkmann
3   Leibnizian Ideas in Nietzsche's Philosophy: On Force, Monads, Perspectivism, and the Subject —— 95

Paul Katsafanas
4   Kant and Nietzsche on Self-Knowledge —— 110

Luís de Sousa and Marta Faustino
5   Nietzsche and Schopenhauer on the 'Self' and the 'Subject' —— 131

Pietro Gori
6   Psychology without a Soul, Philosophy without an I. Nietzsche and 19th Century Psychophysics (Fechner, Lange, Mach) —— 166

Anthony Jensen
7   Helmholtz, Lange, and Unconscious Symbols of the Self —— 196

Giuliano Campioni
8   Nietzsche and "the French Psychologists": Stendhal, Taine, Ribot, Bourget —— 219

Maria Cristina Fornari
9   Social Ties and the Emergence of the Individual: Nietzsche and the English Perspective —— 234

Benedetta Zavatta
10   "Know Yourself" And "Become What You Are". The Development of Character in Nietzsche and Emerson —— 254

Part II: The Crisis of the Subject

João Constâncio
11   Nietzsche on Decentered Subjectivity or, the Existential Crisis of the Modern Subject —— 279

Bartholomew Ryan
12   The Plurality of the Subject in Nietzsche and Kierkegaard: Confronting Nihilism with Masks, Faith and *Amor Fati* —— 317

John Richardson
13   Nietzsche vs. Heidegger on the Self: Which I Am I? —— 343

Sebastian Gardner
14   Nietzsche and Freud: The 'I' and its Drives —— 367

Yannick Souladié
15   Nietzsche, Deleuze: Desubjectification and Will to Power —— 394

Keith Ansell-Pearson
16   Questions of the Subject in Nietzsche and Foucault: A Reading of *Dawn* —— 411

Jaanus Sooväli
17   Gapping the Subject: Nietzsche and Derrida —— 436

Maria João Mayer Branco
18   Questioning Introspection: Nietzsche and Wittgenstein on 'The Peculiar Grammar of the Word "I"' —— 454

Werner Stegmaier
19 Subjects as Temporal Clues to Orientation: Nietzsche and Luhmann on Subjectivity —— 487

Sofia Miguens
20 Three Senses of Selfless Consciousness. Nietzsche and Dennett on Mind, Language and Body —— 511

Part III: Current Debates – From Embodiment and Consciousness to Agency

Mattia Riccardi
21 Nietzsche on the Embodiment of Mind and Self —— 533

Paolo Stellino
22 Self-Knowledge, Genealogy, Evolution —— 550

Brian Leiter
23 Moralities Are *a Sign-Languages of the Affects* —— 574

Ken Gemes and Imogen Le Patourel
24 Nietzsche on Consciousness, Unity, and the Self —— 597

Herman Siemens
25 Nietzsche's Socio-Physiology of the Self —— 629

Robert B. Pippin
26 The Expressivist Nietzsche —— 654

Complete Bibliography —— 668

List of Contributors/Affiliations —— 695

Index —— 697

References, Citations, and Abbreviations

All German quotations of Nietzsche's writings are from the following editions:

BAW   Nietzsche, Friedrich (1933–1940) *Historisch-kritische Gesamtausgabe*, Hans Joachim Mette/Carl Koch/Karl Schlechta (eds.), Munich: C.H. Beck'sche Verlagsbuchhandlung. Reprinted as: *Frühe Schriften 1854–1869*, Munich: DTV 1994.

KSA   Nietzsche, Friedrich (1980) *Sämtliche Werke. Kritische Studienausgabe in 15 Bänden*, Giorgio Colli/Mazzino Montinari (eds.), Munich/Berlin/New York: DTV/De Gruyter.

KSB   Nietzsche, Friedrich (1986) *Sämtliche Briefe. Kritische Studienausgabe in 8 Bänden*, Giorgio Colli/Mazzino Montinari (eds.), Munich/Berlin/New York: DTV/De Gruyter.

KGB   Nietzsche, Friedrich (1975–) *Briefwechsel. Kritische Gesamtausgabe*, established by Giorgio Colli and Mazzino Montinari, continued by Norbert Miller and Annemarie Pieper, Berlin/New York: De Gruyter.

KGW   Nietzsche, Friedrich (1967–) *Werke Kritische Gesamtausgabe*, established by Giorgio Colli and Mazzino Montinari, continued by Wolfgang Müller-Lauter and Karl Pestalozzi (eds.), Berlin/New York: De Gruyter.

References to published or titled texts by Nietzsche follow the standard abbreviations, which are given below. The German abbreviations are used when a text is quoted in German; the English abbreviations, when a text is quoted in English translation.

Unless otherwise stated, the cited translations are the following:

Works by Nietzsche

Nietzsche, Friedrich (1966) *The Birth of Tragedy*, ed./transl. Kaufmann, W., New York: Random House.

Nietzsche, Friedrich (1967) *On the Genealogy of Morals*, ed./transl. Kaufmann, W., New York: Random House.

Nietzsche, Friedrich (1983) *Untimely Meditations*, transl. Hollingdale, R.J., Cambridge/London/New York/New Rochelle/Melbourne/Sydney: Cambridge University Press.

Nietzsche, Friedrich (1986) *Human, All Too Human*, ed./transl. Hollingdale, R.J., Cambridge: Cambridge University Press. Nietzsche, Friedrich (1989) *Description of Ancient Rhetoric*, in: *F. Nietzsche on Rhetoric and Language*, ed. & transl. by Gilman, S.L./Blair, C./Parent, D.J., New York: Oxford University Press, pp. 2 ff.

Nietzsche, Friedrich (1989) *The History of Greek Eloquence*, in: *F. Nietzsche on Rhetoric and Language*, ed. & transl. by Gilman, S.L./Blair, C./Parent, D.J., New York: Oxford University Press, pp. 213 ff.

Nietzsche, Friedrich (1996) *Selected Letters of Friedrich Nietzsche*, Indianapolis: Hackett.

Nietzsche, Friedrich (1996c) *Selected Letters of Friedrich Nietzsche*, ed. and trans. Christopher Middleton, Chicago: University of Chicago Press. [reprint]

Nietzsche, Friedrich (1997) *Daybreak*, ed. Clark, M./Leiter, B., transl. Hollingdale, R.J., Cambridge: Cambridge University Press.
Nietzsche, Friedrich (1998) *Philosophy in the Tragic Age of the Greeks*, ed./transl. Cowan, M., Washington: A Gateway Edition.
Nietzsche, Friedrich (1999) *On Truth and Lying in a Non-Moral Sense*, in: Nietzsche, F., *The Birth of Tragedy and Other Writings*, ed. Guess, R./Speirs, R., transl. Speirs, R., Cambridge: Cambridge University Press, pp. 139–153.
Nietzsche, Friedrich (2001) *The Gay Science*, ed. Williams, B., transl. Nauckhoff, J., Cambridge: Cambridge University Press.
Nietzsche, Friedrich (2002) *Beyond Good and Evil*, ed. Horstmann, R-P./Norman, J., transl. Norman, J., Cambridge: Cambridge University Press.
Nietzsche, Friedrich (2005) *The Anti-Christ, Ecce Homo, Twilight of the Idols and Other Writings*, ed. Ridley, A./Norman, J., transl. Norman, J., Cambridge: Cambridge University Press.
Nietzsche, Friedrich (2005) *The Case of Wagner*, in Nietzsche, F., *The Anti-Christ, Ecce Homo, Twilight of the Idols and Other Writings*, ed. Ridley, A./Norman, J., transl. Norman, J., Cambridge: Cambridge University Press, pp. 231–262.
Nietzsche, Friedrich (2005) *Nietzsche contra Wagner*, in Nietzsche, F., *The Anti-Christ, Ecce Homo, Twilight of the Idols and Other Writings*, ed. Ridley, A./Norman, J., transl. Norman, J., Cambridge: Cambridge University Press, pp. 263–282.
Nietzsche, Friedrich (2006) *Thus Spoke Zarathustra*, ed. Del Caro, A./Pippin, R., transl. Del Caro, A., Cambridge: Cambridge University Press.

Occasionally, some of the authors have chosen to quote from the following translations:

Nietzsche, Friedrich (1954) *Twilight of the Idols*, ed./transl. Kaufmann, W., in: *The Portable Nietzsche*, New York: Viking Penguin.
Nietzsche, Friedrich (1974) *The Gay Science*, ed./transl. Kaufmann, W., New York: Random House.
Nietzsche, Friedrich (1966) *Thus Spoke Zarathustra*, ed./transl. Kaufmann, W., New York: Random House.
Nietzsche, Friedrich (1966) *Beyond Good and Evil*, ed./transl. Kaufmann, W., New York: Random House.
Nietzsche, Friedrich (1987) *Beyond Good and Evil*, trans. R.J. Hollingdale, London: Penguin.
Nietzsche, Friedrich (1992) *Ecce Homo*, trans. R.J. Hollingdale. London: Penguin.
Nietzsche, Friedrich (1996) *Beyond Good and Evil*, ed./transl. Smith, D., Oxford: Oxford University Press.
Nietzsche, Friedrich (1998) *Twilight of the Idols*, Oxford: Oxford University Press.
Nietzsche, Friedrich (2003) *Thus spoke Zarathustra*, trans. T. Wayne, New-York: Algora Publishing.
Nietzsche, Friedrich (2011) *Dawn: Thoughts on the Presumptions of Morality*, Stanford: Stanford University Press.
Nietzsche, Friedrich (2012) *Ecce Homo. How To Become What You Are*, trans. D. Large, Oxford: Oxford University Press.
Nietzsche, Friedrich (2013) *Human, All Too Human: Volume Two*, trans. Gary Handwerk, Stanford: Stanford University Press.

Translations from the *Nachlass* are from the following editions:

WEN   Nietzsche, Friedrich (2009) *Writings from the Early Notebooks*, ed. Geuss, R./ Nehamas, A., transl. Löb, L., Cambridge: Cambridge University Press.
WLN   Nietzsche, Friedrich (2003) *Writings from the Late Notebooks*, ed. Bittner, R., transl. Sturge, K., Cambridge: Cambridge University Press.
WP   Nietzsche, Friedrich (1967) *The Will to Power*, ed. Kaufmann, W., transl. Kaufmann, W./Hollingdale, R.J., New York: Random House.

Notes from the *Nachlass* not available in WEN, WLN, or WP have been translated by either the editors or the authors.

References to the *Nachlass* are given as follows: NL year, note, KSA volume, pages; e.g., NL 1885, 31[31], KSA 11: 367–369. References to a translation are added after the references to the KSA, e.g. NL 1885, KSA 11, 31[131] = WLN, 10. Sections or chapters that are not numbered but given a title in Nietzsche's text are quoted accordingly: e.g. EH, Why I am so Clever 9. A few authors abbreviate these titles: e.g. EH Clever 9. A few of the authors have added the KSA page references to the abbreviated references to English translations: e.g. BGE 43, KSA 5: 60.

Abbreviations of Nietzsche's works in German

AC	*Der Antichrist. Fluch auf das Christenthum*
DD	*Dionysos-Dithyramben*
EH	*Ecce homo. Wie man wird, was man ist*
	EH klug *Warum ich so klug bin*
FW	*Die fröhliche Wissenschaft*
GD	*Götzen-Dämmerung oder Wie man mit dem Hammer philosophirt*
	GD Irrthümer *Die vier grossen Irrthümer*
GM	*Zur Genealogie der Moral. Eine Streitschrift*
GT	*Die Geburt der Tragödie*
GT Versuch	*Die Geburt der Tragödie, Versuch einer Selbstkritik*
JGB	*Jenseits von Gut und Böse. Vorspiel einer Philosophie der Zukunft*
M	*Morgenröthe. Gedanken über die moralischen Vorurtheile*
MA	*Menschliches, Allzumenschliches. Ein Buch für freie Geister*
NL	*Nachgelassene Fragmente/Notate/Aufzeichnungen Nietzsches*
NW	*Nietzsche contra Wagner. Aktenstücke eines Psychologen*
PHG	*Die Philosophie im tragischen Zeitalter der Griechen*
UB	*Unzeitgemässe Betrachtungen*
VM	*(MA II) Vermischte Meinungen und Sprüche*
WA	*Der Fall Wagner. Ein Musikanten-Problem*
WL	*Wahrheit und Lüge im aussermoralischen Sinne*
WB	*Richard Wagner in Bayreuth*

WS	*Der Wanderer und sein Schatten*	
Z	*Also Sprach Zarathustra. Ein Buch für Alle und Keinen*	
	Z I Verächtern	Von den Verächtern des Leibes
	Z II Tugendhaften	Von den Tugendhaften

Abbreviations of Nietzsche's works in English

A	*The Antichrist*	
AOM	(HH II) *Assorted Opinions and Maxims*	
BGE	*Beyond Good and Evil. Prelude to a Philosophy of the Future*	
BT	*The Birth of Tragedy*	
BT Attempt	*The Birth of Tragedy, Attempt At a Self-Criticism*	
CW	*The Case of Wagner*	
D	*Daybreak*	
DD	*Dithyrambs of Dionysus*	
DS	(UM I) *David Strauss*	
EH	*Ecce Homo. How One Becomes What One Is*	
	EH BGE	Beyond Good and Evil
	EH Clever	Why I am so Clever
	EH CW	The Case of Wagner
	EH GM	Genealogy of Morals
	EH Wise	Why I am so Wise
GM	*On the Genealogy of Morals. A Polemic*	
GS	*The Gay Science*	
HH	*Human, All Too Human*	
HL	(UM II) *On the Use and Disadvantage of History for Life*	
NCW	*Nietzsche contra Wagner. Out of the Files of a Psychologist*	
NL	*Nietzsche's Posthumous Notebooks*	
PTAG	*Philosophy in the Tragic Age of the Greeks*	
RWB	(UM IV) *Richard Wagner in Bayreuth*	
SE	(UM III) *Schopenhauer as Educator*	
TI	*Twilight of the Idols. How To Philosophize with a Hammer*	
	TI Ancients	What I Owe the Ancients
	TI Errors	The Four Great Errors
	TI Morality	Morality as Anti-Nature
	TI Reason	"Reason" in Philosophy
	TI Socrates	The Problem of Socrates
	TI Skirmishes	Skirmishes of an Untimely Man
TL	*On Truth and Lying in a Non-Moral Sense*	
UM	*Untimely Meditations*	
WS	(HH II) *The Wanderer and His Shadow*	
Z	*Thus Spoke Zarathustra*	
	Z IV Cry	The Cry of Distress
	Z III Wanderer	The Wanderer
NB	*Nietzsche's Library/Nietzsche-Bibliothek*	

Abbreviations of works by other authors

AA   Kant, Immanuel (1900–) *Gesammelte Schriften*, ed. the Royal Prussian, subsequently German, then Berlin-Brandenburg Academy of Sciences, 29 vols., Berlin: Reimer, subsequently De Gruyter.

AR   Liebmann, Otto (1880) *Zur Analysis der Wirklichkeit: Eine Erörterung der Grundprobleme der Philosophie [On the Analysis of Reality]*, 2nd edition, Strassburg: Trübner.

AT   Descartes, René (1996) *Œuvres*, ed. Adam, Ch./Tannery, P., 11 vols., Paris: J. Vrin.

BLBK Wittgenstein, Ludwig (1998) "The Blue Book", in: *Preliminary Studies for the "Philosophical Investigations", Generally Known as The Blue and Brown Books*, Oxford, UK: Blackwell. [2nd edition 1969]

CD   Freud, Sigmund (1961) *Civilization and its Discontents* [1934], in: *Standard Edition of the Complete Psychological Works of Sigmund Freud*, transl. under the general editorship of James Strachey, in collaboration with Anna Freud, assisted by Alix Strachey and Alan Tyson, vol. 21, London: Hogarth Press and Institute of Psycho-Analysis, pp. 57–145.

CL   Emerson, Ralph Waldo, (1904a) *The Conduct of Life*, in: *The Complete Works*, Concord Edition, vol. 6, Boston Mass.: Houghton Mifflin.

CPR   Kant, Immanuel (1998) *Critique of Pure Reason*, ed./transl. Guyer, P./Wood, A.W., Cambridge: Cambridge University Press.

CV   Wittgenstein, Ludwig (1998) *Culture and Value*, Oxford: Blackwell.

De Anima   Aristotle (1986), *Aristotle in Twenty-Three Volumes. VIII On the Soul, Parva Naturalia, On Breath*, ed. W. S. Hett, Cambridge, Mass./London: Harvard University Press/Loeb Classical Library

E   Emerson, Ralph Waldo (1883), Essays: First and Second Series, Boston Mass.: Houghton Mifflin.

Ethics   Spinoza, Baruch de (1985) *Ethics*. In *Collected Works of Spinoza*, ed. and trans. Edwin Curley, Princeton: Princeton University Press.

FL   Emerson, Ralph Waldo (1862) *Die Führung des Lebens*, transl. Mühlberg, E.S. von, Leipzig: Steinacker.

FR   Schopenhauer, Arthur (1974) *On the Fourfold Root of the Principle of Sufficient Reason*, transl. Payne, E.F.J., La Salle, IL: Open Court.

Freud, SE   Freud, Sigmund (1953–74) *Standard Edition of the Complete Psychological Works of Sigmund Freud*, 24 vols., transl. under the general editorship of James Strachey, in collaboration with Anna Freud, assisted by Alix Strachey and Alan Tyson, London: Hogarth Press and Institute of Psycho-Analysis.

KpV   Kant, Immanuel (1913) *Kritik der praktischen Vernunft*, in: Immanuel Kant, *Gesammelte Schriften*, ed. the Royal Prussian, subsequently German, then Berlin-Brandenburg Academy of Sciences, vol. 5, Berlin: Reimer, subsequently De Gruyter, 1–163.

KrV   Kant, Immanuel (1911) *Kritik der reinen Vernunft*, in: Immanuel Kant, *Gesammelte Schriften*, ed. the Royal Prussian, subsequently German, then Berlin-Brandenburg Academy of Sciences, vols. 3 and 4, Berlin: Reimer, subsequently De Gruyter, 1–552 and 1–252.

KU	Kant, Immanuel (1913) *Kritik der Urteilskraft*, in: Immanuel Kant, *Gesammelte Schriften*, ed. the Royal Prussian, subsequently German, then Berlin-Brandenburg Academy of Sciences, vol. 5, Berlin: Reimer, subsequently De Gruyter, 165–485.
LSA	Emerson, Ralph Waldo (1904b) Letters and Social Aims, in: *The Complete Works*, Concord Edition, vol. 8, Boston Mass.: Houghton Mifflin.
Mon	Leibniz, Gottfried Wilhelm (1714) *Les principes de la philosophie ou la monadologie [Monadology]*, in: Gottfried Wilhelm Leibniz, *Philosophische Schriften*, vol. 1, ed. Holz, H.H., Frankfurt a.M.: Suhrkamp, 438–483. [French text and German translation]
NBs	Wittgenstein, Ludwig (1998) *Notebooks 1914–1916*, ed. Anscombe, G.E.M./Wright, G.H. von, transl. Anscombe, G.E.M, Oxford, UK: Blackwell. [2nd edition 1979]
NE	Emerson, Ralph Waldo (1876) *Neue Essays (Letters and Social Aims)*, transl. Schmidt, J., Stuttgart: Auerbach.
Nic. Ethics	Aristotle (1986), *Aristotle in Twenty-Three Volumes*. XIX *Nichomachean Ethics*, ed. H. Rackham, Cambridge, Mass./London: Harvard University Press/Loeb Classical Library
NS	Leibniz, Gottfried Wilhelm ([1695], 1996) *Système nouveau de la nature et de la communication des substances, aussi bien que de l'union qu'il y a entre l' âme et le corps [New System]*, in: Gottfried Wilhelm Leibniz, *Philosophische Schriften*, vol. 1, ed. Holz, H.H., Frankfurt a.M.: Suhrkamp, 200–226. [French text and German translation]
OAFP	Leibniz, Gottfried Wilhelm ([1694], 1996) *De primae philosophiae emendatione, et de notione substantiae [On the Advancement of First Philosophy]*, in: Gottfried Wilhelm Leibniz, *Philosophische Schriften*, vol. 1, ed. Holz, H.H., Frankfurt a.M.: Suhrkamp, 194–200. [Latin text and German translation]
OARC	Drossbach, Maximilian (1884) *Über die scheinbaren und die wirklichen Ursachen des Geschehens in der Welt [On the Apparent and the Real Causes of Becoming in the World]*, Halle: Pfeffer.
PEFW	Schopenhauer, Arthur (1999) *Prize Essay on the Freedom of the Will*, ed. Zöller, G., transl. Payne, E.F.J., Cambridge: Cambridge University Press.
PI	Wittgenstein, Ludwig (1958) *Philosophical Investigations*, transl. Anscombe, G.E.M., 2nd edition, Oxford, UK: Blackwell.
PR	Wittgenstein, Ludwig (1998) *Philosophical Remarks*, ed. Rhees, R., transl. Hargreaves, R./White, R., Oxford, UK: Blackwell. [2nd edition 1975]
RAW	Teichmüller G. (1882) *Die wirkliche und die scheinbare Welt: Neue Grundlegung der Metaphysik [The Real and the Apparent World]*, Breslau: Koebner.
RPP	Wittgenstein, Ludwig (1998) *Remarks on the Philosophy of Psychology, Volume I*, ed. Anscombe, G.E.M./Wright, G.H. von, transl. Anscombe, G.E.M., Oxford, UK: Blackwell. [1st pub. 1980]
SKS	Kierkegaard, Søren (2013) *Søren Kierkegaards Skrifter*, 28 text volumes and 28 commentary volumes, ed. Cappelørn, N.J./Garff, J./Knuden, J./Kondrup, J./McKinnon, A., Copenhagen: Gad.
SuZ	Heidegger, Martin (1976) [1927] *Sein und Zeit*, Tübingen: Niemeyer. [Gesamtausgabe, vol. 2, Frankfurt a.M.: Klostermann 1977]

TF	Liebmann, Otto (1882) *Gedanken und Tatsachen: Philosophische Abhandlungen, Aphorismen und Studien [Thoughts and Facts]*, Stuttgart: Trübner.
TLP	Wittgenstein, Ludwig (2001) *Tractatus Logico-Philosophicus*, transl. Pears, D.F./ McGuinness, B.F. with an introduction by Bertrand Russell, London/New York: Routledge.
TP	Spinoza, Baruch de (2000) *Political Treatise*, trans. Samuel Shirley, Indianapolis/ Cambridge: Hackett.
TTP	Spinoza, Baruch de (2004) *Spinoza's Theologico-Political Treatise*, trans. Martin D. Yaffe, Newburyport, MA: Focus Publishing.
V	Emerson, Ralph Waldo (1858) *Versuche* (*Essays*: first and second series), transl. Fabricius, G., Hannover: Carl Meyer.
WWR I	Schopenhauer, Arthur (1958) *The World as Will and Representation, vol. I*, transl. Payne, E.F.J., New York: Dover.
WWR II	Schopenhauer, Arthur (1958) *The World as Will and Representation, vol. II*, transl. Payne, E.F.J., New York: Dover.
WWV I	Schopenhauer, Arthur (1949) *Die Welt als Wille und Vorstellung Erster Band*, in Arthur Schopenhauer (1946–1950), *Sämtliche Werke*, vol. 2, ed. Hübscher, A., 7 vols., Wiesbaden: Brockhaus.
WWV II	Schopenhauer, Arthur (1949) *Die Welt als Wille und Vorstellung Zweiter Band*, in Arthur Schopenhauer (1946–1950), *Sämtliche Werke*, vol. 3, ed. Hübscher, A., 7 vols., Wiesbaden: Brockhaus.

João Constâncio, Maria João Mayer Branco and Bartholomew Ryan
Introduction to *Nietzsche and the Problem of Subjectivity*

This book resulted from a research project which assumed that subjectivity remains a valid philosophical problem today, and that Nietzsche's thought is deeply concerned with this problem. In modern philosophy, from Descartes through to Schopenhauer and beyond, the "problem of subjectivity", as we called it in the title of our book, is first of all a theoretical question about the nature of human consciousness, and particularly about human *self*-consciousness. Already for Descartes the question, "what is consciousness?", becomes the question whether the 'I' or 'Self' that we articulate in our self-consciousness is 'a subject', an underlying, permanent reality that is the thinker of our thoughts, the knower of our knowledge, and the agent or doer of our deeds. Belief in such a subject can be equated with Descartes' belief in the existence of a *res cogitans*. Although he does not use the term 'subject', his 'thinking substance' is indeed supposed to be the 'subject' that underlies all manifestations of the *cogito*, the 'I think'. The reason why Descartes is so easily led from consciousness to self-consciousness is certainly because asking about consciousness involves a self-reflexive movement whereby one becomes (explicitly) conscious of one's consciousness. Paradoxically, our consciousness is unconscious most of the time, for we are not conscious of it *as such*, and so in our everyday dealings with the world we tend not to look at things as things that are given to our consciousness, while we also tend not to look at our consciousness as any sort of kernel or core of our being. But in acquiring consciousness of our consciousness we are led naturally to think of ourselves as 'thinking beings' and 'subjects', precisely as Descartes did.

However, it is well known that Nietzsche radically rejected the Cartesian subject and the dualism it entails. It is also well known that he rejected Schopenhauer's replacement of the Cartesian subject with an unconscious 'will' or individual 'character', and of course Nietzsche also rejected Kant's conception of a purely 'logical' – but still permanent – subject, a 'transcendental I of apperception' positioned at the centre of our subjectivity. If the problem of subjectivity is simply the question whether there is in some sense a 'subject', it seems that nothing much needs to be written about "Nietzsche and the problem of subjectivity". He rejected the notion of a subject, he considered the subject a 'fiction', and the only question seems to be whether we should understand this as implying that Nietzsche is a physicalist who reduces the first-personal, subjective perspective to 'physiological' processes in the brain, or the first postmodernist, the first thinker to denounce the subject as an ideological fiction and tool of domination, which is now 'dead'.

We think, however, that this is a hasty conclusion, and that this volume shows that there is much more to Nietzsche's approach to the problem of subjectivity, as well as to the problem of subjectivity itself, than the preceding paragraph suggests. First, becoming conscious of consciousness in a subjective way, that is, 'first-personally', or 'phenomenologically', and then asking what consciousness 'is', that is, asking what is the nature of consciousness as manifested not only objectively, but also subjectively, raises a panoply of theoretical questions that cannot be reduced to the question about the *existence* of an underlying and unifying 'subject'. Nietzsche deals with these questions, and indeed he seems to have been fascinated by them.

There is, for example, the question of dualism. As many scholars have noted, criticising dualism and developing a non-dualistic conception of consciousness is a major concern for Nietzsche. Especially in his posthumous notebooks, he seems to have worked out a quite sophisticated 'adualistic' conception of consciousness, in fact a post-Spinozistic 'double aspect' conception of the body-soul relationship. This conception involves a very interesting distinction between 'self' (*Selbst*) and 'I' (*Ich*), which seems to dislocate our identity from the 'surface' of consciousness to the 'depths' of the 'body'.

But, to take another example, there is also the question of epiphenomenalism – i.e. the question whether consciousness is causally efficacious or not. This is also a crucial issue, which leads to the problem of free-will, and which has been extensively discussed in the literature on Nietzsche in recent years. Several of the articles included in this collection are new contributions to the scholarship on this issue (see, for example, chapters 6 and 7). Embodiment is another related issue, which Nietzsche also tackles (see, in particular, chapter 21), and which was also a major theme of Schopenhauer's philosophy, Nietzsche's 'master' (see chapter 5). Note that in the first volume of Schopenhauer's *World as Will* and Representation embodiment is a question that clearly belongs to the problem of subjectivity, for he conceives of embodiment as our *first-personal* experience of being a body.

The question whether consciousness is adaptive or why has it been selected and preserved in the course of human evolution is also another crucial issue for Nietzsche. Perhaps his most important reflection on consciousness is, or at least includes, an 'extravagant conjecture' about the evolutionary nature of consciousness (see GS 354). Issues of rationality are of paramount importance for Nietzsche as well. His well-known focus on 'power' is to a great extent a reflection on the limits of human reason, particularly of reason as conceived of by modern philosophy precisely in the context of its development as a philosophy of subjectivity and the subject. For Nietzsche, the ultimate question seems to be whether rationality has any power over us, or the use of reason at the level of consciousness is just the 'surface' of unconscious power-relations among 'drives', 'affects', and 'instincts' that really decide what we do and are.

This last issue is an important part of Nietzsche's concern with the *value* of consciousness, which means (at least prima facie) his concern with the "overestimation of consciousness" (GS 11) in modern philosophy and modern culture. But his concern is in fact much wider than this. Nietzsche sees Descartes' dualism and the overestimation of consciousness in modern philosophy as a modern reformulation of Plato's old "error", the "invention of pure spirit and the Good in itself" (BGE Preface), as well as of Christianity's faith in the immortal 'soul' (BGE 54). As noted below (see chapter 11), Nietzsche believes that the question of the relationship between consciousness and the drives, instincts, and affects is a very old question. It lies at the heart of the modern approach to consciousness, but it was already a crucial question for Socrates and Plato, who formulated it in terms of an opposition between "instinct and reason" (BGE 191). In a few key-passages, Nietzsche rephrases this as an opposition between instinct and language, or between our purely instinctual life and our social life as language-users (BGE 268, GS 354), as well as an opposition between our 'affects' and our conscious thoughts, this being (he argues) a key opposition for the understanding of morality (e.g. BGE 187, BGE 198, GS 333). In Nietzsche's writings, the question of consciousness is closely linked with the question of agency (see, for example, chapters 14, 23, 24, and 26).

Moreover, in one of Nietzsche's most central texts on the problem of subjectivity – namely, aphorism 12 of *Beyond Good and Evil*, where he clarifies his position as a critique and rejection of what he terms the "atomism of the soul" – Nietzsche can be said to also reject any form of eliminism, and he is quite explicit:

> Between you and me, there is absolutely no need to give up "the soul" itself, and relinquish one of the oldest and most venerable hypotheses – as often happens with naturalists: given their clumsiness, they barely need to touch "the soul" to lose it. But the path lies open for new versions and sophistications of the soul hypothesis – and concepts like the "mortal soul" and the "soul as subject-multiplicity" and the "soul as a society constructed out of drives and affects" want henceforth to have civil rights in the realm of science. (BGE 12)

This passage becomes particularly important if one considers, firstly, the fact that where Nietzsche says 'soul' he could have said 'subject', as he takes the term 'subject' to be no more than a scholarly and modern term for the older, pre-modern concepts of 'soul' and 'spirit' (NL 1885, 36[36], KSA 11: 565–566); and secondly, the fact that here he most clearly offers a non-eliminist *alternative* to the modern model of an underlying and unifying 'subject' of our thoughts and actions. He proposes that all 'atomistic' models of subjectivity, whether Cartesian, Kantian, broadly Christian or Platonic or of any other sort, be replaced with the conception of a 'subject-multiplicity' (*Subjekts-Vielheit*). What this means is, of course, open to interpretation, but it is certain that Nietzsche equates this subjective multiplicity, or this 'subject' which is in fact a 'multiplicity', not only with a mortal subject, a 'mortal soul', but also with the "soul as a society constructed out of drives and affects" (BGE 12). Several of the chapters below explore this idea of multiplicity (see, for example, chapters 8, 12, 18), or revise traditional notions of self-referentiality, reflexivity, and intentionality in the light of it (see, for example, chapters 11 and 13).

The issue of multiplicity in Nietzsche involves also his famous 'perspectivism'. In modern philosophy, the discovery of the first-personal, subjective realm of consciousness, of self-referential consciousness, or of consciousness of consciousness, leads to the idealist thesis that "the world is my representation" (WWR I §1), as Schopenhauer famously put it. The world becomes 'phenomenon', a 'phenomenal world'. In *Human, All Too Human*, Nietzsche seems to radicalise rather than discard modern phenomenalism, as he claims that Schopenhauer's 'world = representation' should be amended and replaced with 'world = error' (HH I 19). Also in *The Gay Science*'s aphorism on consciousness, Nietzsche asserts that what we call 'world' is merely a 'surface- and sign-world', a 'false' world of 'generalities', a world, as it were, constructed by our consciousness' linguistic conceptualisations. And yet he locates these linguistic conceptualisations and constructions of our 'surface- and sign-world' in the always already *social* milieu of 'communication'. That is most likely the reason why he writes that his conception of consciousness leads not only to a 'true phenomenalism', but also to a true 'perspectivism' (GS 354). Nietzsche's world = error is not the merely subjective world of solipsism – i.e., it is not the world as *my* representation –, but rather a social world where a multiplicity of perspectives communicate with each other, impact on each other, modify each other. We may call this a world of 'intersubjectivity', but we have to bear in mind that part of Nietzsche's point is that the perspectival world of social communications – or the world constituted by a non-solipsistic consciousness, which is in fact a social *Verbindungsnetz*, "a net connecting one person with another" (GS 354) – should not be seen as an aggregate of fixed, permanent, unifying 'subjects'. The multiple perspectives that emerge and interact within a realm of social communications do not belong to 'subjects', as they are not rooted in any substance or underlying reality (see chapter 19 for a radical exploration of the idea that there are no substances if the world is constructed by a multiplicity of perspectives). However, the relationship between Nietzsche's social conception of consciousness and the issues of intersubjectivity, social identity, reciprocal recognition etc. remain a largely open question (see chapters 9, 11, and 25). The same goes for Nietzsche's relationship with idealism in general. Is his 'true phenomenalism and perspectivism' still a form of idealism, despite his usual self-presentation as an anti-idealist (e.g. BGE 15, BGE 39, BGE 210, GS 372, TI Ancients 2)? In a note from 1882, for example, Nietzsche speaks of his own kind of "idealism" ("*Meine Art von 'Idealismus'*", NL 1882, 21[3], KSA 9: 685), and defines it as an "idealism" (which he puts in quotation marks) which results from the belief that every sensation "contains an evaluation [*Werthschätzung*]" and every evaluation "fantasises and invents [*phantasirt und erfindet*]" (NL 1882, 21[3], KSA 9: 685).

But Nietzsche's conception of a 'true phenomenalism and perspectivism' has another major implication for the way in which he can be said to deal with the problem of subjectivity. The problem of subjectivity is after all the question about what is it and what does it imply to exist as a being that is first-personally conscious of itself. But this question is naive if it is not, in part, a question about what one can *know* about oneself from the first-person experience of oneself. The question about *self-knowledge* is a crucial part of the problem of subjectivity, as several chapters in this book show (see, for example, chapters 4, 7, 10, 11, 22, 26). As we shall discuss in just a moment (when we discuss the individual chapters in more detail), Nietzsche has a fundamentally sceptic view of self-knowledge, and in his terminology this means that he believes that one's 'inner world' is a 'phenomenal world', just as the external world. Or, in other words, his 'true phenomenalism and perspectivism' applies both to first-personal, subjective knowledge and to third-personal, objective knowledge. Paul Katsafanas (chapter 4) and Paolo Stellino (chapter 22) argue that Nietzsche seeks in 'genealogy' a new, non-introspective way of obtaining self-knowledge; Robert B. Pippin (chapter 26) argues that although Nietzsche is indeed sceptical about self-observation *qua* introspection and rejects it, he develops an 'expressivist' account of the self of self-knowledge, one which entails that what is expressed *in* our actions is a source of (retrospective) self-knowledge.

We thus have a quite impressive list of questions and problems involved in what we call the problem of subjectivity, namely: the nature of consciousness; the existence or non-existence of the subject as a substance; dualism; the self (perhaps as something distinct from the I); epiphenomenalism; embodiment; evolution; rationality (vs. power); the relationship between consciousness and the drives, affects, and instincts; agency; multiplicity (vs. 'the atomism of the soul'); self-referentiality, reflexivity; intentionality; perspectivism and phenomenalism; communication, language and conceptualisation; intersubjectivity; idealism; self-knowledge. That Nietzsche was fascinated by these questions and problems is especially clear from his notebooks. However, in the books that he actually published, including those he left prepared for publication before his mental collapse, he presents his theoretical positions on the problem of subjectivity in an extremely fragmented and condensed fashion – sometimes even *en passant* – and, most importantly, he often seems to take great care to embed them in a *practical* context, indeed in a context which may be called 'existential', or perhaps 'practical-existential'. The question about what is it and what does it imply to exist as a being that is first-personally conscious of itself is also an existential, or practical-existential, question, and several of the chapters of this volume highlight precisely this dimension of the problem of subjectivity (see chapters 8 to 13). Here the problem becomes, at least for Nietzsche, a much more local problem, that is, a matter of describing and diagnosing a particular existential situation, namely the existential situation of modern human beings faced with the 'death of God' and 'nihilism', or what is it and what does it imply to exist as a being that is first-personally conscious of itself in this practical-existential situation. Perhaps the whole of twentieth-century philosophy can be characterised as involving a crisis of the modern conception of the subject that is intrinsically connected with a broader practical-existential situation, such that even the problems that seem more purely theoretical in philosophy (such as epiphenomenalism or embodiment) are in fact embedded in a context which is ultimately normative.

This crisis of the modern subject and the whole philosophical question of modernity and postmodernity – and particularly the question whether Nietzsche is still a modern or already a postmodern philosopher – are the theme of Part II of the book. Part I focuses on 'tradition and context', that is, on Nietzsche's sources, as well as on the philosophical comparison between his views on the problem of subjectivity and the views of some of the most important philosophers that preceded him in the modern era. We believe that the ten chapters that compose Part I come as close as possible to giving a comprehensive view of the relevant 'tradition and context'. Part III focuses on philosophical debates and questions of Nietzsche scholarship that are being discussed today, and that belong to the constellation of problems which we have subsumed under the title "Nietzsche and the Problem of Subjectivity".

We feel particularly proud for having brought together in this volume some of the best scholars from two traditions of Nietzsche scholarship that only rarely communicate with each other: broadly speaking, the 'Anglophone' and 'Continental' traditions. Let us now briefly consider each chapter of the book individually.

Part I: Tradition and Context

The first chapter is **Isabelle Wienand**'s "Writing from a First-Person Perspective: Nietzsche's Use of the Cartesian Model". As the title suggests, this chapter interrogates the importance of Descartes for the development of Nietzsche's conception of subjectivity by focusing on an affinity between Nietzsche and Descartes which is rarely mentioned or at least rarely valued as particularly relevant, which is the fact that they both write from a first-person (or first-personal) perspective, that is, from a *subjective* perspective. When scholars and philosophers consider the relation between Nietzsche and Descartes, they usually focus on Nietzsche's rejection of Descartes substantialisation of the 'I', but not on the fact that in writing he, too, like Descartes, adopts the perspective of an 'I' (or, as Wienand puts it, of an *ich* although not of an *Ich* with a capital letter). Wienand also tries to show that Nietzsche's well-known rejection of Descartes' *res cogitans* may be just the surface of a more fundamental affinity between the two, such that Cartesian subjectivity may in fact be a helpful resource to understanding Nietzsche's conception of the Self – or at least of the 'I' (the *ich*) that writes his philosophy. In the first part of the chapter, Wienand highlights, in particular, that there is an important continuity between Descartes conception of the union of soul and body in *The Passions of the Soul* (1649) and Nietzsche's naturalistic account of agency, a continuity which Nietzsche makes explicit when in *The Antichrist* he praises the temerity of Descartes' theory of animals (A 14). In modern philosophy, this was the first theory to entail a naturalistic conception of animals as 'machines', or of animality as a mechanism and hence as a matter of internal organisation. Friedrich Albert Lange, in his *History of Materialism* (one of the books that influenced Nietzsche's philosophical development most decisively), underlines the fact that Descartes' conception of animals as machines played a crucial role in the history of materialism, and particularly in the development of the naturalistic conception of human psychology in terms of 'animal psychology' and 'physiology' (e.g. in De la Mattrie's conception of the *homo natura* as *l'homme machine*). In the second part of the chapter, Wienand explores her interpretation of the affinity between Nietzsche and Descartes by arguing that *Ecce Homo* has Descartes' *Discourse on Method* as its '(anti-)model'. In *Ecce Homo*, Nietzsche radicalises Descartes' adoption of the first-personal perspective by never allowing his discourse to leave the subjective realm of the first-personal, and he radicalises Descartes naturalism not only by emphasising the context-bound nature of his 'I' (*ich*) but also by adding the fabric of the instincts to Descartes' narrative of the subject as a free spirit.

In chapter 2, "Power, Affect, Knowledge: Nietzsche on Spinoza", **David Wollenberg** begins by examining Nietzsche's historical contact with Spinoza's philosophy, highlighting what topics interested him the most. On this basis, he then explores more precisely both where Nietzsche saw Spinoza as a 'precursor' and where he felt it necessary to part ways. Nietzsche's collected remarks evidence a sustained reflection on Spinoza's philosophy, although one that evolved over time, and that has a crucial turning-point when Nietzsche reads Kuno Fisher's *Geschichte der neuern Philosophie: Baruch Spinoza* in 1881. As is well established, it was this reading that prompted the famous postcard to Overbeck where Nietzsche calls Spinoza his 'precursor'. Wollenberg then focuses, specifically, on how Spinoza's philosophy draws a linkage from the striving for power to the affirmation of being (basically because the affect corresponding to an increase in power is joy, and the affect corresponding to a decrease in power is sadness), and on how studying Nietzsche's reaction to this linkage in Spinoza helps us understand the linkage for Nietzsche himself. As Wollenberg underlines, there are fundamentally two themes in Spinoza that are of the greatest concern to Nietzsche: (a) the identification of virtue and power, and in particular the power of the affects; and (b) the identification of the most powerful affects with understanding and affirmation, particularly Spinoza's 'intellectual love of God'. Thus, the chapter connects questions of psychology and power to broader existential issues, but uses this "wider lens" (as Wollenberg calls it) in order to make clearer how Nietzsche is particularly drawn to Spinoza's model of human subjectivity as being constituted by "an agonistic conflict of affects, where one affect can only be supplanted by a stronger one". This concept of an internal struggle of the affects and the idea, as Fischer puts it, that the "affects are the power expressions of human nature" are crucial for Nietzsche's development of the hypothesis of the 'will to power' as a psychological hypothesis, and hence also for his whole conception and critique of human subjectivity. It is important to note that, according to Wollenberg, when Nietzsche assumes (or at least appears to assume) that Spinoza "posited an independent subject who could freely and intentionally perform the task of displacing the passionate with the reasonable affects", Nietzsche is in fact just mis-reading or mis-remembering Fischer's account of Spinoza's conception of subjectivity. Therefore, the affinity between Nietzsche and Spinoza regarding their conception of subjectivity goes even deeper than Nietzsche acknowledges (which does not prevent their differences on such issues as rationality and affirmation – or love of the world – from remaining as significant as Nietzsche tries to make them).

Nikolaos Loukidelis' and **Christopher Brinkmann**'s chapter, "Leibnizian Ideas in Nietzsche's Philosophy: On Force, Monads, Perspectivism, and the Subject", considers the relationship between Nietzsche and Leibniz by mapping the influence of three nineteenth-century philosophers on Nietzsche that defended Leibnizian ideas and made Nietzsche acquainted with the fundamental aspects of Leibniz's thought. These are Otto Liebmann, Maximilian Drossbach, and Gustav Teichmüller. Otto Liebmann seems to have been crucial for the development of Nietzsche's conception of *force*, and hence indirectly for his reconception of the will not only in terms of an inner force of the human organism, but also as a multiplicity of 'wills to power'. Liebmann sides with Leibniz in his defence of 'dynamism' and his opposition to 'corpuscular theory'—a dynamism which assumes the existence of 'centres of force with no extension', thereby rejecting the reduction of causality to external relations of 'collision and pressure'. Whereas Nietzsche's knowledge and use of these ideas—and particularly of the notion of 'action at a distance', *actio in distans*, *Wirkung in die Ferne*—is usually associated with his reading of and about Boscovich, Loukidelis and Brinkmann show the importance of Liebmann (and indirectly of Leibniz) in this respect. Liebmann is also Nietzsche's source in another crucial aspect of Nietzsche's relation to Leibniz with regard to the problem of subjectivity. It was through Liebmann that Nietzsche became acquainted with what he calls Leibniz's "incomparable insight" that "consciousness is merely an *accidens* of representation and *not* its necessary and essential attribute" (GS 357). Maximilian Drossbach, on the other hand, developed Leibniz's conception of 'monads' in a way that influenced Nietzsche's conception of drives (*Triebe*) as 'wills to power'. In his notebooks, Nietzsche acknowledged that "we can speak of atoms and monads in a relative sense" (NL 1887, 11[73], KSA 13: 36). The crucial point, however, is that drives as forces and quasi-monads have sensations (*Empfindungen*) and representations (*Vorstellungen*), but since "consciousness is merely an *accidens* of representation and *not* its necessary and essential attribute" (GS 357), that does not imply that drives have consciousness. On the contrary, consciousness, according to Nietzsche, emerges from *unconscious* drives: conscious mental states are "*only a certain behaviour of the drives towards one another*" (GS 333), "thinking is only a relation between these drives" (BGE 36). And this is indeed a crucial point (which Loukidelis and Brinkmann do not explore). Leibniz's monadological model and the way he distinguishes representation (or sensation and perception) from consciousness (or apperception) allow Nietzsche to conceive of the unconscious *as mental*, thereby avoiding the kind of 'property dualism' which interprets the difference between unconsciousness and consciousness as identical with the difference between the physiological and the psychological. And, as Loukidelis and Brinkmann show, Gustav Teichmüller's influence on Nietzsche results mainly from the way in which the former developed a related aspect of Leibniz's thought: perspective and perspectivism. Monads are perspectives (each is a 'living mirror of the universe', or a 'point-of-view' over the whole), hence conceiving of reality in terms of a multiplicity of monads entails conceiving of it in perspectival terms, or as a multiplicity of perspectives. Again, for Nietzsche (especially for the Nietzsche of the notebooks), this entails conceiving of the *drives* as quasi-monadological forces that develop their own perspectives on the universe and thus contribute decisively for constituting the world of our experience, what Nietzsche calls "the world *that is relevant to us*" (BGE 34), or the "phenomenal world". Thus, as Loukidelis and Brinkmann conclude, Nietzsche's so-called 'continuum model' – that is, his 'adualistic' conception of consciousness as continuous with unconscious processes that can either be described as organic, physiological, or as mental, psychological[1] – has been greatly influenced by the Leibnizian ideas of Otto Liebmann on force, Maximilian Drossbach on monads, and Gustav Teichmüller on perspectivism.

Paul Katsafanas' chapter, "Nietzsche and Kant on Self-Knowledge", is much less about Kant's possible influence on Nietzsche's conception and criticism of self-knowledge than about fundamental affinities between the two thinkers. Identifying these affinities – but also differences between Kant and Nietzsche – gives a great contribution to the clarification of the context in which Nietzsche writes about self-knowledge, as well as to the clarification of his substantive views. Katsafanas' main point is the rejection of the prejudice according to which Kant and Nietzsche have diametrically opposed views of self-knowledge because Kant argues for the complete transparency of our minds and Nietzsche for complete opacity. Katsafanas claims that the differences between Kant and Nietzsche on self-knowledge are subtler and more interesting than traditionally assumed. Kant recognises two distinct forms of self-knowledge: introspection, which gives us knowledge of our sensations, and apperception, which is knowledge of our own activities. Kant acknowledges that both modes of self-knowledge can be error-ridden and are particularly prone to being distorted by selfish motives; thus, neither is guaranteed to provide us with comprehensive self-knowledge. Nietzsche departs from Kant in arguing that these two modes of self-knowledge (a) are not distinct and (b) are far more limited than Kant acknowledges. In addition, Nietzsche departs from Kant in arguing that we can acquire self-knowledge by looking away from ourselves. With his typical clarity, Katsafanas provides a brief sketch of the ways in which this is so, and highlights, in particular, how Nietzsche argues that genealogy enables a form of self-knowledge: it helps us to identify some of the subtle factors shaping our actions as well as the influence of our current conceptual repertoires on our perceptions and understandings of our actions.

In their chapter, "Nietzsche and Schopenhauer on the 'Self' and the 'Subject'", **Luís de Sousa** and **Marta Faustino** argue that Schopenhauer's

---

1 See Abel (2001), Abel (2012: 501ff.); see also Constâncio (2011).

influence on Nietzsche's critique of the traditional conception of the subject, as well as on his new account of subjectivity, remains largely unexplored.[2] Schopenhauer was one of the first philosophers in the Western tradition to systematically criticise the Cartesian conception of the subject in terms that pointed towards a naturalistic redefinition of our identity as human beings. He rejected the Cartesian, dualistic assumption that personal identity consists in our rational self-consciousness, and replaced it with the hypothesis that our innermost being is in fact 'the body', 'the organism' with its conative nature – the organic body as 'will'. Thus Sousa and Faustino argue that when Nietzsche equates the 'Self' (*Selbst*) with the body (Z I, On the Despisers of the Body), he is in fact refashioning Schopenhauer's conception of our innermost being as the 'will' of our organic body. Likewise, they argue that when Nietzsche presents the 'I' or 'ego' – that is, the 'subject' – as a mere construction, a projection, a fiction, or an illusion of self-consciousness, he again remains on solid Schopenhauerian ground. The same goes for Nietzsche's conception of reason and the intellect (or conceptual consciousness) as 'tools' of unconscious drives and affects, as well as for his deflationary conception of consciousness as a mere 'surface' of such unconscious processes. Thus, Sousa and Faustino conclude that in this regard Nietzsche's principal departure from Schopenhauer consists in his replacement of the latter's conception of the 'will' as a substance and a unity with the conception of a *multiplicity or plurality* of unconscious and fluid, insubstantial drives and affects. One of the novelties of Sousa and Faustino's article lies in their discussion of Schopenhauer's and Nietzsche's expressivism. Schopenhauer gives an 'expressivist' account of action insofar as he conceives of action as expressive of 'will', in fact as expressive of what he calls 'character', which is anything but a neutral substratum, a 'subject' in both the Cartesian and the Kantian tradition. Nietzsche's expressivism is a radicalisation of Schopenhauer's insofar as it replaces the notion of an 'unchangeable character' being expressed in our actions with the notion that what is expressed in action is basically the strength or weakness of a changeable organisation of drives and affects. But Nietzsche's expressivism may even be more radically different from Schopenhauer's than this formulation suggests. For Nietzsche's version implies (as Robert B. Pippin argues) that what is 'expressed' in our actions does not exist at all within us *before* or *independently* of being expressed in our actions.[3]

---

[2] According to Sousa and Faustino, Janaway (1991) and Constâncio (2011) are the main exceptions.
[3] See Pippin (2010), as well as Pippin's chapter in this volume.

The next chapter, **Pietro Gori**'s "Psychology without a Soul, Philosophy without an I: Nietzsche and 19th Century Psychophysics (Fechner, Lange, Mach)", focuses on how Nietzsche's way of posing the problem of subjectivity is rooted in a nineteenth-century context in which many other German authors and scholars were attempting to establish, or at least dreamed of establishing, a scientific psychology compatible with naturalism. Thus the chapter considers, in particular, how Nietzsche's thought relates to Fechner's, Lange's, and Mach's, but also takes into account and depicts a broader context. This is the context not only of Fechner's attempt to found 'psychophysics' with the publication of the two volumes of his *Elemente der Psychophysik* (1860), but also of Emil du Bois-Reymond's conferences on *The Boundaries of the Knowledge* of Nature (1872) and *The World's Seven Puzzles* (1880), as well as of a 'return to Kant' that created a first wave of naturalistic, science-oriented neo-Kantianism. Gori highlights Fechner's role in this context because the idea of a 'psychophysics' was groundbreaking for naturalism in its time, and although Nietzsche may have been acquainted with it only via Lange and others, he seems to have wanted to evoke it in his redefinition of philosophy as "physio-psychology" in *Beyond Good and Evil* (BGE 23). Fechner's project made monism for the first time scientifically, or at least scholarly, acceptable in the field of psychology (hence the 'physics' in 'psychophysics'), and particularly a monism based on Spinoza's ontological 'parallelism', that is, in his *double aspect* conception of the relation between the physical and the psychical. This conception – that is, the thesis that the physical and the psychical are two aspects, or two equally admissible *descriptions*, of one and the same reality – also plays a decisive role in Lange's neo-Kantianism, as well as in Mach's scientific psychology. Both Lange and Mach attempt what Franz Brentano termed a 'psychology without a soul' – that is, without a *substantive* soul, without an entity called 'soul', a *res cogitans*. They both see the so-called 'soul' as nothing more than a first-personal description of a physical reality. According to Gori, a "psychology without a soul" is what Nietzsche's naturalisation of thought processes and his critique of the Cartesian subject are all about. Moreover, although Mach seems not to have read Nietzsche and there is no evidence that Nietzsche's reading of Mach changed his views in any way (for Nietzsche did not read Mach before 1886), it is interesting to note how their common inspiration, Lange, led them both from a 'psychology without a soul' to an even more radical 'philosophy without an I'. When in BGE 16 Nietzsche asks the "metaphysical question" whether it is possible to speak of the I as the cause of our thoughts, the implied answer, Gori argues, is that the I can*not* be a cause of our thoughts. The so-called 'I' is in fact a mere 'regulative fiction' or (in Mach's terminology) a mere 'ideal unity' wholly devoid of efficacy or causal power.

Thus Pietro Gori's chapter introduces in full force the heatedly debated question of *epiphenomenalism*. His position supports (mostly with historical arguments) that of Mattia Riccardi's.[4] They both claim that, according to Nietzsche, our first-order consciousness can be efficacious, but our high-order consciousness cannot. Self-consciousness either *qua* consciousness of our conscious states, or *qua* consciousness of being the 'I' that could ideally give unity to a multiplicity of first-order conscious states, is epiphenomenal. For Gori, in particular, it is Nietzsche's assertion that the so-called 'I' is merely a 'regulative fiction'–or merely a grammatical construction and hence one of the "prejudices of reason" (TI Reason 5)–that entails that he is an epiphenomenalist regarding self-consciousness. For Nietzsche, Gori claims, our first-personal conception of the so-called 'I' should be reduced to an epiphenomenon of "physiological processes located beneath it".

However, Gori's chapter also introduces another crucial theme that complicates matters with regard to the issue of epiphenomenalism. This other theme is Lange's fundamentally *sceptical* version of the 'double aspect' approach to the problem of subjectivity, a theme which is in fact the centrepiece of the chapter that comes after Gori's, Anthony Jensen's article on "Helmholtz, Lange, and Unconscious Symbols of the Self". Lange's skepsis is first of all about introspective self-knowledge, or in his own terms, "self-observation" (*Selbstbeobachtung*). Its main idea is that the results of self-observation are by nature linguistic constructs, such that self-observation is in principle inferior to external, third-personal observation and the whole field of psychology is hence problematic. Here is one of Lange's main formulations of his view:

> In psychology we can undertake no dissections, can weigh and measure nothing, can exhibit no preparations. Names like thinking, feeling, willing are mere names. Who will point out exactly what corresponds to them? Shall we make definitions? A treacherous element! They are of no use, at least for any exact comparisons. And with what are we to connect our observations? With what measure shall we measure? In this groping in the dark it is only childish prejudice or the clairvoyant impulse of the metaphysician that is sure of finding anything. (Lange 1881: 136/Lange 2006 [1875]: 354)

The creation of a name, especially a classificatory name, tends always to make believe that there is some sort of entity, or a "true unity" (*eine wahre Einheit*), that corresponds to it, even when nothing like that unity can be actually observed:

> [...] psychological analysis often shows clearly how little what is denoted by a single word forms a true unity. What is, for instance, the "courage" of the sailor in the storm, and then

---

4 See Riccardi (forthcoming).

on the other hand in regard to supposed ghostly apparitions? What is "memory", what is "ratiocination", having regard for the various forms and spheres of their effects? Almost all these psychological notions give us a word by means of which a portion of the phenomenon of human life is very imperfectly classified. With this classification is combined the metaphysical delusion of a common substantial basis of these phenomena, and this delusion must be destroyed. (Lange 1881: 137–138/Lange 2006 [1875]: 355–356)

In proposing that scientific psychology be henceforth developed as a 'psychology without a soul', Lange is certainly implying (as Gori emphasises) that 'soul' is just another word to which nothing actually observed corresponds (or is just a collective name for the *not really* observable realm of first-personal experience), and therefore psychology should become a fundamentally physiological research of *physical* realities.[5] As Lange remarks, the kernel of scientific method is the establishment of observations that remove the influence of what is personal, or "neutralise the subjectivity of the researcher" (Lange 2006 [1875]: 387, see Lange 1881: 177). Even without further considerations, this fact immediately entails the scientific superiority of external observation over self-observation (which is intrinsically subjective, first-personal). But the sceptical point is precisely that it is so delusional to think that one can observe and investigate 'the soul' as a non-physical substance as it is to think that one can really observe the brain in such a way as to establish with certainty "the localisation of the mental faculties" (Lange 1881: 138/Lange 2006 [1875]: 356). The point of departure of psychology is the subjective, the first-personal, which means that its point of departure is necessarily a muddled bunch of linguistic constructs (or, in Nietzsche's unforgettable formulation in D 119, "a more or less fantastic commentary on an unknown, perhaps unknowable, but felt text"). What physiology, or 'psychophysics', or 'scientific psychology' tries to do is to find physical and hence truly observable realities that may correspond to such linguistic constructs. But, for this reason, it will always have to remain a 'groping in the dark'. Or, to put it in terms of Lange's 'double aspect' approach, the physical and the psychical are indeed two aspects, or two equally admissible descriptions, of one and the same reality, but the former is necessarily based on the latter, and hence the former will never overcome the failures and distortions of the latter.

---

[5] Lange is indeed clear about the fact that one cannot truly observe 'the soul', and hence the latter is only a word: "in the few phenomena which so far have been made accessible to more precise observation, there is not the smallest occasion to assume a soul in any very definite sense at all" (Lange 1881: 167–8/Lange 2006 [1875]: 381). He is equally clear about 'the will': "when we speak of 'will', we only add a comprehensive word for a group of vital phenomena" (Lange 1881: 148/Lange 2006 [1875]: 365). The influence of these passages in, for example, BGE 12 and BGE 19 can hardly be overestimated.

A scientific description of events in the brain (even if it is as successful as such descriptions can be nowadays) is at best only less arbitrary than a description of mental events in folk-psychology, or in philosophy.

Anthony Jensen's article emphasises this sceptical side of Lange's thought – and of course its influence on Nietzsche. Jensen's argument is that Nietzsche takes sides with Lange in the latter's disagreement with Herman Ludwig von Helmholtz, and this constitutes a perhaps small, but nonetheless crucial nuance of his views on the problem of subjectivity, particularly of his conception of consciousness and his view of the relationship between the conscious and unconscious aspects of subjectivity. Through Lange's influential critique of Helmholtz, Jensen argues, Nietzsche came to realise that the usual naturalistic designations of sub-conscious activity – drives, instincts, urges, desires, power-quanta, etc. – are not actually referential. They are just a series of antirealist symbolic representations that can be useful and informative but never demonstrative. All epistemological descriptions of the causes of mental processes – whether physiological or first-personal – necessarily distort the genuine character of whatever reality stands outside of our conceptualisation of it. Helmholtz's view was that we can only know 'signs' of external objects, but no such problem arises with regard to what is supposedly given through the internal sense within us. As Jensen puts it, Helmholtz "was an anti-realist about external objects, but a common-sense empirical realist about our knowledge of the function of the senses; Lange, on the other hand, was a thorough-going anti-realist both about external objects and about the internal subjective world through which those external objects are cognized". The inner world of willing, feeling, and thinking is as opaque as the external world of spatial objects, or as Nietzsche puts it several times in the notebooks, the inner world is no less a 'phenomenal' world, a world of interpretation and linguistic construction, than the external world, and therefore our philosophical 'phenomenalism' should be extended to the inner world.[6]

Thus, the first major implication of Jensen's paper is that although the naturalistic drive of the first generation of neo-Kantianism was indeed crucial for Nietzsche's development – as emphasised not only by Gori's treatment of German 'psychophysics', but also (in other respects) by Wollenberg's treatment of Kuno Fischer and Loukidelis' and Brinkmann's treatment of Otto Liebmann, Maximilian Drossbach, and Gustav Teichmüller –, the sceptical drive of Lange's version of neo-Kantianism was no less influential in Nietzsche's development.

---

6 See NL 1885, 2[131], KSA 12: 129–132, NL 1885, 2[204], KSA 12: 167, NL 1887, 11[113], KSA 13: 53–54, NL 1888, 14[152], KSA 13: 333–335, NL 1888, 15[90], KSA 13: 458–460.

And this realisation may also contribute to the clarification of his relation to the philosophers treated in Wienand's, Katsafanas' and Sousa's and Faustino's chapters. Nietzsche is more of a naturalist than Descartes, Kant, and Schopenhauer, but he is also more of a sceptic. He develops several naturalistic aspects of their thought (as well as of Spinoza's and Leibniz's), but this seems to have led him to a scepticism that they would certainly reject, particularly regarding the problem of subjectivity.

However, Jensen's main claim is another one, namely that Nietzsche's adoption of Langean scepticism entails the rejection of the two interpretations of the relationship between consciousness and unconsciousness that have dominated Nietzsche scholarship in recent years. These are the 'kind-epiphenomenalism' of Brian Leiter et al. and the 'last-link' interpretation of Günter Abel. The latter is also epitomised, according to Jensen, in Constâncio (2011). According to 'kind-epiphenomenalism', consciousness is not causally efficacious because (put simply) it is a mere epiphenomenon of unconscious events, either physiological or psychological; in Mattia Riccardi's version, as we saw above, only self-consciousness is considered epiphenomenal, first-order conscious mental states are not. By contrast, the 'last link' interpretation considers conscious mental states to be causally efficacious in bi-directional chains of causations. Such states are conceptualisations of unconscious processes and hence 'last links' in causal chains that run from the unconscious to the conceptualised, but in adding conceptualisations and therefore a whole new representational framework to these chains they become 'first links' in new causal chains that run from the conscious to the unconscious. Their power is limited (as Constâncio 2011 emphasises in many ways), but they are not powerless. The problem, according to Jensen, is that given Nietzsche's Langean scepticism regarding self-knowledge, it should be clear that he does not understand his own descriptions of subjectivity as referential designations whose truth or falsity rests on their adequation to a world-itself. Instead, his various descriptions are to be taken as symbols or signs ('words', 'names') whose expression indicates the momentary arrangement of a subject's dynamic disposition. Consequently, an historical awareness of a person's subjective expressions over time becomes the necessary condition of a symbolic understanding that is meaningful, even if not demonstrative. The consequence of this, according to Jensen, is that "both the epiphenomenal and last-link interpretations are mistakenly worried about the relations of things and processes which are actually not things or processes at all, but only a relation of symbols whose order and ascribed relations is itself only the result of an historical process of overwriting and reinterpreting by means of symbols". Or, as he also puts it: "even those naturalistic subjective facticities that are said to underlay our conscious activity must be considered signs, symbols, and anti-realist designations for something we know not what". Thus, given Nietzsche's anti-realist (and indeed sceptical) view of the internal subjective world, he cannot have held either an epiphenomenal or a last-link interpretation of the relationship between consciousness and unconsciousness.

Although Constâncio's 2011 paper on Nietzsche and Schopenhauer on consciousness does not mention Lange as Nietzsche's main influence in this respect, it does not fail to mention Nietzsche's scepticism regarding proper knowledge of the inner world. One of the main ideas of the paper (following Josef Simon and Werner Stegmaier)[7] is that given that thoughts are 'signs' (e.g. NL 1880 6[253], KSA 9: 263), then thoughts about our thoughts, including Nietzsche's thoughts about consciousness and the relationship between consciousness and unconsciousness, are also 'signs', and even such apparently simple concepts as 'I', 'drive' or 'consciousness' are therefore linguistic constructs, not names designating entities that one might actually be able to observe inside oneself. This is, however, an *epistemological* point. It may be correct to say, as Jensen claims, that Nietzsche's "descriptions of subjectivity" should not be understood as "referential designations whose truth or falsity rests on their adequation to a world-itself". But it is a fact that Nietzsche attempts such "descriptions of subjectivity", and hence the question remains as to whether they describe the relationship between consciousness and unconsciousness in terms of some sort of 'kind-epiphenomenalism' or in terms of a 'last link' with limited power within the organism. (Similarly, Paul Katsafanas' assertion that Nietzsche replaces introspective self-knowledge with genealogical self-knowledge is not at all refuted by the fact that Nietzsche endorses Lange's scepticism regarding self-knowledge. This endorsement entails only that genealogy is for Nietzsche a very tentative, modest form of 'knowledge' – a 'groping in the dark', a work of interpretation in which one orientates oneself by nothing more than 'signs' and 'symptoms' of hidden, subterranean processes).

Constâncio's chapter in this volume is not at all about the debate on epiphenomenalism or mental causation. But it includes (albeit almost as an aside) a critique of Mattia Riccardi's claim that self-consciousness is epiphenomenal for Nietzsche. Within the context of his interpretation of GS 354, Constâncio argues that Nietzsche's evolutionary perspective entails that self-consciousness is adaptive, and since no feature of a species can be adaptive without having causal powers, self-consciousness cannot be epiphenomenal, or inefficacious. According to Constâncio, Nietzsche's claim that consciousness is 'superfluous' means only that consciousness is not a necessary condition of individual organic func-

---

7 Cf. Simon (1984) and Stegmaier (2000).

tions. But the addition of consciousness to these functions, and particularly of self-consciousness, has made a huge difference in the evolution of the human species: it has *caused*, and continues to *cause*, the development of society and social interaction as we know them. In a brief note, Constâncio also reiterates the argument that since Nietzsche regards consciousness as a 'tool' of drives, affects, and instincts, he cannot have conceived of it as causally inert. If some x is a tool, inefficaciousness cannot belong to x as a property.[8] Constâncio's 2011 paper on Nietzsche and Schopenhauer also included another argument. There are passages in which Nietzsche *seems* to be saying that conscious thoughts can never be 'causes' or that there is no mental causation at all. But, in fact, these passages mean something else, namely that conscious thoughts cannot be equated with *mechanistic* causes, conscious thoughts do not 'cause' actions the way a billiard ball causes the movement of another billiard ball. But conscious thoughts are 'power-claims'. They are not sufficient for action, but as power-claims occurring within complex and organised constellations of other power-claims (called 'human organisms'), conscious thoughts exert some degree of limited power over us, thereby *contributing* to our actions (but not 'causing' them in isolation from unconscious drives, affects, and instincts). No doubt, there is in Nietzsche a critique of the 'overestimation of consciousness', but it does not entail epiphenomenalism.[9] A fourth argument that we consider to be decisive in favour of 'last link' interpretations vs. epiphenomenalism is one of the arguments proposed by Paul Katsafanas in his 2005 paper on Nietzsche's theory of mind, namely that Nietzsche considers consciousness (including self-consciousness) to be *dangerous* to the healthy functioning of human organisms. As Katsafanas puts it, "if a thing is dangerous, then it surely *does something*".[10]

---

8 Jensen agrees that epiphenomenalism is inconsistent with the tool metaphor, but he believes that, on the other hand, last-link readings are inconsistent with the mirror metaphor (GS 354 and Constâncio 2011). But the latter is not the case. The mirror metaphor describes consciousness precisely as a last link in a causal chain that runs from the unconscious to conceptualisation; the tool metaphor describes consciousness (the 'mirror') as a *first link* in a new causal chain that runs from conceptualisation to action. As mentioned above, what Jensen terms "last-link readings" involves this sort of bi-directional causal chain. (Nietzsche's conception of such causal chains is further complicated by the fact that he wants to avoid mechanistic models and emphasises that whatever may look like an isolated 'cause' in a causal chain is in fact only *one* 'power-claim' interacting and occurring simultaneously with a multiplicity of other 'power-claims', and hence having its power limited by these other 'power-claims', 'centres of force', 'power-quanta', etc.)
9 See also Ken Gemes' chapter in this volume. See NL 1883–84, 24[2], KSA 10: 643–644, NL 1888, 14[146], KSA 13: 330–331; GS 11, GS 354.
10 See Katsafanas (2005: 1). See, in particular, GS 11 and GS 354.

In fact, by expanding on this last argument we are led easily into a unifying theme among the next (and last) three chapters of Part I of this volume. In one of the passages where Nietzsche writes that consciousness is "a danger", he adds that "he who lives among the most conscious Europeans even knows it is a sickness" (GS 354). The idea that consciousness is a sickness, and particularly that the intellectual elite of Nietzsche's age suffers from excessive consciousness, is a crucial idea of Dostoevsky's *Notes from the Underground*[11] – and, more generally, a crucial idea in many nineteenth-century authors and cultural critics that concern themselves with such themes as decadence, nihilism, or the death of God. This is a sure sign that Nietzsche's focus on subjectivity, and particularly on consciousness, should not be interpreted as essentially theoretical, but rather as *practical-existential*. Besides naturalism and scepticism, *existentialism* should be considered a third crucial tendency in Nietzsche, and Giuliano Campioni's, Maria Cristina Fornari's, and Benedetta Zavatta's chapters highlight precisely different aspects of Nietzsche's practical-existential approach to the problem of subjectivity.

Giuliano Campioni's chapter is one of the most illuminating and surprising of this collection as regards Nietzsche's sources on subjectivity. Titled "Nietzsche and 'the French Psychologists': Stendhal, Taine, Ribot, Bourget", the chapter focuses on Nietzsche relation to these four authors, and aims to clarify why Nietzsche has them in mind (although not only them) when in dealing with the problem of subjectivity he praises "the French Psychologists" (e.g. BGE 218, HH I Preface 8, EH, Why I am so Clever 3). More generally, his chapter aims to clarify in which sense and under the influence of which authors and ideas Nietzsche characterises all of his works from *Beyond Good and Evil* onwards as works of "a psychologist". (The fact that he always writes in the first-person, or from a subjective perspective, as Isabelle Wienand's chapter accentuates, is obviously a point to be taken in consideration here). Campioni suggests that Nietzsche only started to see himself as "a psychologist" after reading (during the Winter of 1883) Paul Bourget's *Essais de psychologie contemporaine*. Stendhal and Dostoevsky may be for him the greatest psychologists, the only ones he regards as comparable to himself, but Bourget seems to be his model as an author writing from the perspective of 'a psychologist'. This has several implications. Firstly, it confirms Nietzsche's anti-metaphysical conception of 'psychology' – but with a twist. Nietzsche sees Bourget's psychology as expressive of the 'Latin spirit', and therefore as an alternative to the metaphysical mystifications typical of the 'German spirit'. But what moves a 'Latin' psychology like Bourget's

---

11 See Dillinger (2012).

is typically "a *pleasure* to deny and dismember, as well as some careful cruelty which knows how to use the knife with confidence and elegance, even when the heart bleeds" (BGE 210). A 'Latin' psychology like Bourget's is anti-metaphysical, but not necessarily scientific and constructive in its aims. Its main focus is *self-critique*, therefore its perspective remains first-personal, subjective, and its 'objectivity' is often expressed by an *I* (as in Bourget's and Nietzsche's writings) because it basically consists in a debunking of *self*-deceptions, including the metaphysical self-deceptions that posit the 'I' as a unity and a substance. Secondly, this anti-metaphysical, self-critical 'psychology' is not at all solipsistic. If Nietzsche's psychology is modelled on Bourget's, then it is a kind of cultural critique. There is no doubt that Nietzsche's 'psychology' deals with the same cultural themes as Bourget's: nihilism, *décadence*, modern art, in sum: the whole "European consciousness" (BGE 259), and not just the individual consciousness. Ultimately, that is why Nietzschean psychology is in fact a 'genealogy'. However, none of this aims to suggest that Nietzsche is not interested in naturalism and the kind of scientific (or proto-scientific) psychology that he found in the likes of Lange or Mach. In fact, he cultivated his interest in this kind of psychology by becoming an avid reader not only of German but also of French authors, particularly Taine and Ribot, but also others. The point is that his interest in scientific psychology, including French scientific psychology, is subordinated to his interest in practical-existential 'psychology'. This is particularly clear, as Campioni shows, in Nietzsche's approach to one of the themes that interests him the most in such 'French psychologists' as Stendhal, Taine, Ribot, and Bourget: the theme of psychological *multiplicity*, which is closely related to the theme of psychological *opacity*. Nietzsche's critique of the "atomism of the soul" (BGE 12), Campioni claims, is closely related to a psychological theory that can be traced back to Stendhal's correspondence, Taine's *De l'intelligence*, Bourget's essays as well as novels, and Ribot's scientific research on the delicate mechanisms behind the formation and disintegration of personality: the theory of the '*petits faits*' or '*petits faits vrais*', according to which the so-called 'I' is in fact *composed of a multiplicity* of 'small facts', and these facts are for the most part unconscious, contradictory, difficult to decipher, and ultimately opaque. Like Bourget's, Nietzsche's principal aim in taking up this theory is not so much to develop it further as a *theory*. Campioni's argument warrants the conclusion that Nietzsche is first and foremost interested in using the theory for the more important task of describing and diagnosing the European human being's existential situation in the age of the death of God, nihilism, and *décadence*.

Maria Cristina Fornari's chapter, "Social Ties and the Emergence of the Individual: Nietzsche and the English Perspective", explores the way in which Nietzsche's engagement with the problem of subjectivity was influenced by another kind of source: the 'Englishmen'. For Nietzsche, this term has a much wider meaning than in common usage. The 'Englishmen' refers to all European Darwinists, evolutionists, and utilitarians, in fact to the perspective that all of them seem to have in common (the "English perspective", as Fornari terms it). Among the 'Englishmen' who have influenced Nietzsche the most there is his friend Paul Rée, a young Prussian. Nietzsche's main source of inspiration (both positive and critical) is perhaps Herbert Spencer. Although Fornari's approach is mostly focused on establishing Nietzsche's sources, she is able to show not only that there is one theme that dominates Nietzsche's engagement with the Darwinists, evolutionists, and utilitarians, but also that for Nietzsche that theme has a crucially practical-existential dimension, or is not a merely theoretical problem. As Fornari's title suggests, this theme is the individual and its 'social ties' – or individuality and the relationship between individual and community. Nietzsche's treatment of this theme from *Human, All Too Human* onwards (and especially after meeting Rée) shows that his diatribes against Darwinists and evolutionists in general are merely a surface of "intense confrontation and fruitful dialogue", as Fornari puts it. Nietzsche is undoubtedly an evolutionist and a Darwinist of some sort, for he clearly believes not only in evolution, but also in the kind of blind mechanism that 'natural selection' is all about. But his attitude towards utilitarianism is something else. What Fornari's article clearly shows is that Nietzsche's critique of the 'English perspective' is in fact a critique of the *moral or normative presuppositions* of this perspective, such that what he rejects in Darwinism and evolutionism is not so much their main theoretical hypotheses as rather the utilitarian valuations that embed those hypotheses within the 'English perspective'. Nietzsche's views on 'adaptation' are a good example of all of this. He rejects 'adaptation' for presupposing that the altruism of merely passive, reactive individuals is *good* because it is *useful* for the whole, the community. The 'English' conception of adaptation is fundamentally normative, and Nietzsche focuses precisely on its normative implications. In the light of these implications, the non-utilitarian nature of the values and achievements of higher individuals' becomes morally suspect, while the utilitarian values of the 'herd' pass for the only possible values – for morality itself. Or, in other words, the 'English perspective' transforms Darwinian evolutionism into an ideological weapon that thwarts the individual's possibilities of self-creation and spiritual self-enhancement. Against this, and from a practical-existential perspective, indeed from a normative one, Nietzsche develops (in slightly different ways across time) an alternative evolutionary notion of individuality and the relationship between individual and community which is highly relevant for the study of his views on the problem of subjectivity. Fornari underlines, in particular, how the theme of subjective multiplicity dovetails with this evolutionary perspective. The 'individual' is in fact shown to be a "dividuum" (HH I 57) composed of a multiplicity of 'drives' that *evolve* and have *evolved* across time; the gregarious individual whose subjective multiplicity organises itself as a social self that conforms to the community and becomes a mere "function of the herd" (GS 116) is the rule; but this does not in any way exclude the possibility of 'higher types', 'free-spirits', 'overmen', 'sovereign individuals' that become exceptionally individual by taking upon themselves, synthesising, and combining in a unique way a great multiplicity of perspectives made possible by the multiplicity of their drives.

The last chapter of Part I is **Benedetta Zavatta**'s "'Know Yourself' and 'Become What You Are'. The Development of Character in Nietzsche and Emerson". The theme of 'character' is an important dimension of Nietzsche's treatment of the problem of subjectivity. Zavatta's chapter aims to show how Emerson's conception of character crucially influenced Nietzsche from his youth through to his latest writings. From very early on, Nietzsche was interested in the connection between character and fate, but also in the individual's capacity to change at least some aspects or elements of its character, and hence of what would otherwise be its predestined fate. Nietzsche's reading of Emerson played, in particular, a decisive role in the way he eventually came to reject Schopenhauer's thesis of the immutability or unchangeability of character. Emerson gave Nietzsche the notion of a character that is able to expand indefinitely over time. On the other hand, Nietzsche's conception of how character changes and expands opposes Emerson's in one important respect. Nietzsche rejects the notion that agents can change their character (i.e. their 'temperament', the ultimate association of 'drives' that constitute them, the distinctive bundle of *affective*, and primarily *unconscious*, features and dispositions that make them unique) by conscious deliberation, as if agents possessed a metaphysical faculty, the 'will', by means of which they could simply and directly effectuate, for example, the project of 'giving style' to their character. People change, Zavatta argues, by developing an 'aspirational' or 'ideal' Self, but such a Self can only have motivational force if it is an *affective* idealisation *of one's subconscious drives* (e.g. NL 1880, 7[95], KSA 9: 336–337, NL 1881, 11[18], KSA 9: 448). Conscious purposes play a secondary role in processes of self-creation – or, as GS 360 indicates, their force is merely 'catalytic'. In fact, their efficaciousness depends on their being much more than ends of isolated 'intentions'. As an emancipatory, liberating process of 'becoming what one is' – as idealised by Emerson's 'heroic' model of character development –, self-creation is to a large extent a matter of 'discipline' and continuous 'experimentation'. Like Emerson, and again influenced by him, Nietzsche sees the capacity for this kind of 'great liberation' as the privilege of a rare few. Only the rare few are capable of what

Emerson terms 'intellectual nomadism', the capacity some people have to turn every kind of circumstances, no matter how painful, to their advantage, as if every event could be a means to the expansion of character, or to affirmation and spiritual growth and power. Such 'nomadism' is, for Emerson and for Nietzsche, the precondition of the capacity to develop the kind of Self one may term 'Dionysian', or, as Zavatta also puts it, 'a nomadic and imperialist Ego, which aims to expand its power beyond the boundaries imposed by the limited time-span of its existence'.

Part II: The Crisis of the Subject

João Constâncio's chapter, "Nietzsche on Decentered Subjectivity or, the Existential Crisis of the Modern Subject", is to some extent an introduction to Part II of this volume. The main point of his chapter is that Nietzsche's writings describe a deep crisis of modern subjectivity. Constâncio argues that Nietzsche's theoretical conception of a 'decentered subject', i.e., of a non-transparent, opaque "subject-multiplicity", as Nietzsche terms it in BGE 12 – radically modifies the modern conception of the subject, but neither does Nietzsche proclaim the death of the subject, nor is his approach to the problem of subjectivity chiefly theoretical. Nietzsche's Langean scepticism regarding self-knowledge makes him discard the aspiration to present a foundational, privileged 'theory' of subjectivity, absolutely freed of self-deception and capable of declaring all other theories to be self-deceived. Nietzsche's views are, instead, heuristic hypotheses ('regulative fictions' in his terminology) which allow him to reflect upon, describe, and diagnose the *existential* situation of his age. Nietzsche's approach to the problem of subjectivity is perhaps best labelled as 'practical-existential', and the way he treats the problem can even be said to anticipate some of the chief tenets of twentieth-century existentialism. Focusing first on *Beyond Good and Evil*, Constâncio tries to show that the reason why Nietzsche makes the point that the problem of subjectivity should be traced back to the Greeks and especially to Plato's dualistic 'errors' is because the crisis of the modern subject that he wants to describe belongs to the wider crisis of the transcendent, metaphysical *values* which Plato and his 'errors' created or, in other words, to the crisis Nietzsche calls 'the death of God'. Nietzsche's not chiefly theoretical, but rather practical-existential description of modern subjectivity in terms of its (a) plasticity, (b) dividedness, (c) lack of hierarchic organisation, (d) problematic self-referentiality, (e) undeterminedness, and (f) self-deceptiveness serves a normative project, as it aims to contribute to the "struggle against nihilism" (NL 1886, 5[50], KSA 12: 201–204, NL 1886, 7[31], KSA 12: 306) and, in particular, against the modern experience of fragmentation, disintegration, contradictoriness, 'weakness' and 'paralysis of will' caused by the death of God. In the last section of his article, Constâncio focuses on Book V of *The Gay Science*, and tries to illuminate not just the theoretical (and evolutionary) but also the practical-existential dimension of aphorism 354 by exploring its contextual connection with aphorism 356. Consciousness emerges from this analysis as a "connecting-net" (GS 354) of a society of "actors" (GS 356). In late modernity, when one becomes truly conscious of one's consciousness, one discovers oneself as an actor among actors – and certainly not as Descartes' *res cogitans* and pure *cogito*. Or, in other words, one discovers that one's subjectivity and indeed intersubjectivity is very far from constituting a Hegelian, emancipated, free world of reciprocal 'recognition'. Instead one discovers one's decentred subjectivity and decentred intersubjectivity in a world of atomised and yet massified *misrecognition*. This shows, according to Constâncio, that Nietzsche's take on subjectivity and intersubjectivity anticipates not only Camus or Sartre, but also Lacan, and it involves a critical engagement not only with Descartes, Kant, or Schopenhauer, but also (even if unintentionally) with German Idealism. Constâncio's main point, however, is that not only is this critical engagement a practical-existential engagement, but it also aims to *prevent* that the death of God causes some sort of 'death of the subject' (or death of the 'spirit'). Nietzsche modifies but does not eliminate either the first-personal perspective of the 'I' of consciousness or the social perspective of intersubjectivity because his ultimate task is to provoke a first-personal, *subjectivised* experience of the existential crisis of the modern subject. That is why at least in this respect he can still be said to belong to modernity and modern philosophy – and not yet to postmodernity.

The contribution by **Bartholomew Ryan** is called "The Plurality of the Subject in Nietzsche and Kierkegaard: Confronting Nihilism with Masks, Faith and *Amor Fati*". While Kierkegaard belongs to a generation earlier than Nietzsche, he is not a source of Nietzsche's thought, and in fact his reception (like Nietzsche's) is mostly posthumous. That is the first reason why Ryan's analysis of the relationship between Nietzsche and Kierkegaard fits into Part II of this book. But, secondly, in exploring this relationship one immediately enters the discussion of the 'crisis of the subject', as well as the discussion of fundamentally practical-existential issues rather than simply theoretical. There has been much written on Kierkegaard and Nietzsche by world famous philosophers and commentators (with the forerunners being Georg Brandes, Georg Lukács, Karl Löwith and Karl Jaspers) for the obvious reason in that they epitomise the philosopher of suspicion *par excellence* in the wake of Hegelian philosophy, the birth of modern democracy and nationalism, and the beginning of mass media, the scientific age and a secular society. Ryan acknowledges the previous work done by philosophers and scholars up until now, but seeks to show in this chapter that in fact the subjectivity that Kierkegaard and Nietzsche are grappling with in the age of modernism and beyond is a subjectivity that is transformed into a plurality rather than being nothing at all or unified. This chapter becomes very interesting in that it can be read both as a penetrating dialogue between Nietzsche and Kierkegaard bringing them closer together; but also as a subtle critique of them and critique of our understanding of them – in that Kierkegaard's "purity of heart to will one thing" and objective to unify the self as subject, and Nietzsche's destruction of all values and truths about the existence of subjectivity, turns the elusive self as subject into a plurality and disunity. Thus, we may think of Kierkegaard's Johannes Climacus' motto "truth is subjectivity" – truth being Climacus' "wound of negativity" – as applying to both Nietzsche and Kierkegaard. Probably the most important difference between Nietzsche and Kierkegaard (born thirty-one years before Nietzsche) is their relationship to Christianity and appraisal of Socrates and Christ as prototypes for living passionately and thinking dangerously. But this great difference helps shed light on our understanding of the crisis of subjectivity in why Nietzsche was so vehemently against Socrates and Christ, and why and how Kierkegaard was so determined to renew an extremely passionate *Imitatione Christi* and awaken a new Socrates for the present age. This idea of Christianity and these figures under scrutiny provide the basis for the transformation of subjectivity into a plurality for Kierkegaard's and Nietzsche's future readers. In this chapter, we can think again of the many points of contact between Kierkegaard and Nietzsche via experiencing the plurality of the subject, such as, for example, in their celebration of existential passion in their striking depictions of a Dionysian and Christ-like existence; their anti-system stance and unrelenting critique of modern philosophy; the creation of masks and multiple voices; the attack against the bourgeoisie of emerging democratic society and the established church; their increasingly solitary existence; their call for honesty; their humour, irony and wit; and finally their stylistic positioning as dramatic-poetic thinkers at odds with academic philosophical writing.

In the next chapter, "Nietzsche vs. Heidegger on the Self: Which I Am I?", **John Richardson** argues that although Nietzsche and Heidegger are both famous critics of our usual (they claim) conception of ourselves as subjects, each also offers a positive account of what's really there, where we take a subject to be. As regards Heidegger, Richardson focuses only on *Being and Time*, and thus only on the 'existential' aspect of that book that involves a conception of the 'I'. As regards Nietzsche, Richardson develops a view perhaps epitomised by D 115 (though he does not quote this particular passage). Here Nietzsche claims that there is no 'I' or 'ego', but the *opinion* that we form of ourselves *as if* there existed the "so-called ego" is nonetheless "a fellow worker in the construction of our character and our destiny" (D 115). Our self-understanding as an 'I' does not entail the existence of an entity that could be theoretically investigated and termed 'the I', but our practical-existential relation to ourselves involves that we conceive of ourselves as an 'I' or self.[12] Or, in Richardson's own terms, although Nietzsche clearly rejects a "core view of the self", that is, the conception of the self as a "core or center of me, by comparison with which some of the things 'I am' are secondary", he holds a *reflexive view of the self* according to which "my self lies in how I am 'towards myself', i.e. reflexively refer to myself". This view of the self, Richardson argues, is the one Nietzsche and Heidegger (in *Being and Time*) have in common, though in different forms.[13] What they both reject in their critiques of subjectivity is the particular version of the 'core view' that posits the 'subject', or the 'I of consciousness', as the core 'me', or 'true self'. But they both insist on our capacity to 'self-relate' as the capacity that makes us selves, and they both insist that this self-relating happens primarily (though certainly not exclusively) 'beneath' consciousness. Moreover, they both agree, according to Richardson, that "this non-linguistic and non-conscious referring is still a matter of *intentionality*: a meaning or intending of some content", and in fact they both agree, also, that "there is a way we 'mean' or 'view' ourselves that is prior to awareness and words". That is why, again for both, the self-reflexive view of the self is not just descriptive, but also 'formative', that is: it always involves a self-referring directed at a not-yet-formed-self, at an 'aspirational self' – a self that one needs to 'create' and 'become'. Thus, the main difference between Nietzsche and Heidegger is the difference between the former's naturalism and the latter's phenomenological transcendentalism. For Nietzsche the task of achieving selfhood involves something different from, and in fact something more than, attuning oneself with a pre-given or inbuilt trans-

---

[12] As Richardson points out, this view is also developed by Gardner (2009) as the view that Nietzsche's has a 'theoretical conception of the self' as 'fictive' but in his 'practical thought' he still relies on a (non-theoretical) conception of the self. The 'fiction' is part of our practical-existential experience of ourselves – that is, of our first-personal and hence 'subjective' view of ourselves.

[13] Such a view, as Richardson remarks, can also be ascribed to Fichte, Nozik, or Vellemen, among many others. Ultimately, it is the view, as Richardson puts it, that "the self *is* [...] how it views itself". But the fact that this view originates in Fichte should be particularly emphasised, as this fact establishes a link between Nietzsche and German Idealism which is usually neglected. Gardner and Constâncio briefly allude to this link in their respective chapters. See also Pippin's chapter for an 'expressivist' account of Nietzsche's (unintended) affinity with German Idealism, particularly with Hegel.

cendental. Facing one's mortality and guilt – understood as, so to speak, suprahistorical and supra-personal structures of one's existence qua *Dasein* – is not enough. The task of achieving selfhood is for Nietzsche much more "historically and personally local", as Richardson writes. It involves dealing with one's biological and social constitution. On the other hand, however, there is even so another important affinity between Nietzsche and Heidegger on the self: they both equate the task of achieving selfhood with a sort of authenticity that entails freeing oneself from a social identity which stifles individuality and is fostered by the sociability of consciousness. A Nietzschean 'free spirit' can only achieve an individual self by freeing himself/herself from the 'herd', very much like in *Being and Time* authentic care (for oneself and others) entails freeing oneself from the everyday inauthenticity of the '*they*' (*das Man*). In both cases (it is crucial to emphasise it again), authenticity is *not* tantamount to identifying oneself with a core or 'true' self, especially *not* if this is interpreted as the subject of consciousness.

Sebastian Gardner's chapter, "Nietzsche and Freud: The 'I' and its Drives", focuses on the differences of Nietzsche and Freud, which receive much less attention than their points of similarity. In the first part of his chapter, Gardner tries to show that, though the concept of drive is of central importance for both thinkers, Nietzsche and Freud conceive human psychology in very different terms. In the second part of his chapter, Gardner tries to show that their differences emerge also and most sharply in the context of value. Here, those differences reflect a fundamental philosophical disagreement concerning the extent to which naturalisation can satisfy our axiological needs. Although Gardner basically considers the points of similarity between Nietzsche and Freud a matter of common knowledge, it is important to highlight them here, as he also briefly does. First, Nietzsche is an obvious precursor of naturalistic depth psychology, and Nietzsche and Freud have, as Gardner puts it, a "shared naturalistic emancipatory ambition". For their thought is centred on the idea of diagnosis and therapy, and they both aim at a "naturalistic reconstrual of human personality" that might ameliorate our condition by disabusing us of "rationalistic prejudices". Secondly, if the concept of drive is crucial for both, this means that they both "impute *a division within the human subject*" (our italics), as Gardner writes. This is the main reason why Freud's thought belongs to the 'crisis of the subject' and should be compared with Nietzsche's in Part II of this volume. Nietzsche's and Freud's drive model divides the subject between the ends that he/she pursues as a conscious agent and the hidden, unconscious ends that he/she pursues as 'drive' – and, most importantly, makes the latter the ultimate cause of the former. The "agent *qua* executor of reasons for action" is just (according to Nietzsche's preferred metaphors) a "surface" and a "tool" of the "agent *qua* bearer or vehicle or medium of drive". So why do they differ so much with regard to the concept of drive, as Gardner claims? Gardner's argument is complex, and this is not the place to discuss it in detail. His main claims are the following. Firstly, Nietzsche does not try to develop, as Freud does, a scientific theory and a clear, coherent model of human subjectivity and agency. Secondly, there is in Nietzsche a "rub" between his "theoretical dissolution of the self" and his practical (or one should perhaps say, 'practical-existential') concept of an aspirational self, what Gardner terms "his ethical ideal of substantial individuality". Finally, in contrast to Freud, Nietzsche is in fact an anti-realist in regard to drives: his drive model, his talk of drives "is all metaphors [*es ist Alles Bilderrede*]" (D 119) (and this is, of course, another way of expressing the Langean scepticism discussed in Gori's, Jensen's, and Constâncio's chapters). As regards the second part of Gardner's chapter and his claim that in the context of value Nietzsche and Freud differ even more than at the theoretical level, his main point is that Freud's project is basically a project of full naturalisation embedded in a utilitarianism (or hedonism) he sees no reason to question, while Nietzsche's philosophy is precisely about a need for meaning and a modern crisis of meaning which he believes cannot be in any way solved by the faith in science and naturalism (for the latter faith only perpetuates the predominance of the 'will to truth' and hence does not create new, affirmative values). Nietzsche believes, on the contrary, that a utilitarianism (or hedonism) such as Freud's has to be questioned within such a crisis of meaning. Though Gardner's treatment of these tensions is fundamentally aporetic, it seems to us to warrant the conclusion that Freud's approach to the problem of subjectivity is quintessentially modern, while Nietzsche's conception of the problem of subjectivity in practical-existential terms expresses a true sense of crisis and questions all sorts of modern hopes of individual and collective emancipation and self-determination. Gardner ends his chapter by claiming (although rather tentatively) that "there is in Nietzsche an echo of Kant's 'primacy of practical reason' and of Fichte's *Thathandlung*" and hence "a recognizably transcendentalist residue". And yet Nietzsche seems indeed to question quite radically the emancipatory hopes of the subject of such a *Thathandlung*.

Yannick Souladié's chapter, "Nietzsche, Deleuze: Desubjectification and Will to Power", examines essentially two aspects of the relationship between Nietzsche and Deleuze that evince how the former influenced the latter's view of the problem of subjectivity. In the first part of his chapter, Souladié focuses on Deleuze's interest in Nietzsche's self-presentations in his last works. Instead of isolating himself from the world as a subject, Nietzsche inserts his own figure in his books, but he does it in a way that does not fixate him as a subject/author of the book and, on the contrary, displays a true process of 'desubjectification'. Nietzsche's self-presentations are at the same time self-abolitions. Most likely, no other thinker goes as far as Deleuze in ascribing to Nietzsche a radical rejection, elimination even, of the subject. As Souladié points out, for Deleuze conceiving of a "subject", particularly of a subject as author of a book, is as wrong as "fabricating a beneficent God to explain geological movements". For Deleuze, the art of writing is the art of desubjectification *par excellence*, and Nietzsche seems to him to be *par excellence* the (non-)author who is aware of this. In writing, Nietzsche shows that 'he' is in fact not a 'subject', but rather a 'complexity of forces', sheer 'multiplicity' in the midst of 'life' and as part of 'life'. According to Souladié's Deleuzian interpretation, this is what it means to philosophise alongside "the guiding thread of the body". In philosophising, that is in writing his works, Nietzsche can be said to engage in a process of desubjectification because he writes as a 'body' (not as a subject) that opens itself up to the multiplicity of the world by discovering within himself a multiplicity of voices. Nietzsche's activity of writing/philosophising is a merging with the world, which culminates in Nietzsche's complete dissolution, that is, in his madness. In the second part of his chapter, Souladié tries to show that Nietzsche also enacts this process of desubjectification, or of simultaneous self-affirmation and self-abolition, in his non-biographic works. Souladié's main example is Nietzsche's exposition of the "hypothesis" of the "will to power" in BGE 36. According to Souladié, this crucial aphorism does not really present the will to power as a *mere* hypothesis, but rather as "an affirmation" which criticises identity, substance and the subject-object dichotomy. The will to power aims to enable a new unifying relationship with the world which overcomes the distinction between the philosophical subject and its 'object world'. Such an affirmation, according to Souladié, "is neither dogmatic, nor simply hypothetical: it is problematic". It is not dogmatic because Nietzsche does not simply assert it as a logician demonstrates a claim or a scientist asserts a proposition about the objective world; but it is not just a hypothesis like any other because it is (supposed to be) Nietzsche's direct expression of his most intimate experience as a body (or as a multiplicity), such that its suprapersonal implications result precisely from the fact that the expression of one's most intimate, personal experience cannot fail to have a suprapersonal relevance. But then the will to power remains indeed 'problematic'–for its affirmation remains rooted in the *merely* personal. Thus, the question that one should perhaps ask Deleuze–and all Deleuzians–is whether all of this is really substantiallly different from the claim that Nietzsche does *not* eliminate the first-personal and subjective and only redescribes it as a "subject-multiplicity" (BGE 12) whose conscious states are surfaces, tools, and mirrors of unconscious drives and affects.

Keith Ansell-Pearson's chapter, "Questions of the Subject in Nietzsche and Foucault: A Reading of *Dawn*", interrogates the relationship between Nietzsche and Foucault by exploring the latter's conception of 'care of the self' and 'ethical resistance', as well as the former's text of 1881, *Dawn*, and its affinities with the themes of Foucault's so-called 'ethical turn'. The usual post-modern interpretation of Nietzsche – including Foucault's – claims that Nietzsche deconstructs and dissolves the subject. But, Ansell-Pearson argues, this raises at least two problems: "(a) how do we explain Nietzsche's appeal, running throughout his writings, to our becoming those that we are (unique, singular, incomparable, *self-creating, self-legislating*)? (b) how do we account for the interest in the self and the subject shown by Foucault in what we now call his late writings?" In dealing with these two questions, Ansell-Pearson begins by analysing the way in which Foucault appropriated Nietzsche for the ends of anti-humanism in the early and middle periods of his thought, i.e., up to the point of his late writing and so-called ethical turn. As an anti-humanist thinker, Foucault's interest in the concept of the subject is in dissolving and destroying it by showing how it is engendered (as a 'subject of knowledge') by repressive, or controlling social practices. As Ansell-Pearson writes, "The key claim is that there is no *given* subject of knowledge": there is no 'human nature', no 'human being', no fixed human identity, and in this sense 'man' *qua* subject of knowledge should by now be declared as dead as God. At this point, Nietzsche is particularly important for Foucault as the teacher of a 'passion for knowledge' (*Leidenschaft der Erkenntnis*) that shows us how to abandon the positing of solid identities and engage in a radical experimentation with ourselves – an experimentation allegedly freed from the prejudice of a fixed subject. However, as Ansell-Pearson emphasises, Foucault's ethical turn shifts the focus of his attention "from the production of the subject through regimes of power-knowledge to how the subject produces itself through a form of ethical life and involving technologies of the self". In this new context, the reconception of the subject or self not as a substance but rather as an activity, and in fact as a self-reflexive activity, becomes relevant and acceptable. Foucault's "care of the self" entails the conception of a self-reflexive self capable of "critically examining the processes of its own constitution and bringing about changes in them". In the last part of his chapter, Ansell-Pearson explores the possibility that Foucault may not have seen how *Dawn* (or *Daybreak*, as the most common translation goes) epitomises Nietzsche's own concern not only with the care of the self and the technologies of the self, but also, as Ansell-Pearson puts it, with "ethical resistance to normalization and the biopolitical tendencies of modernity". Thus Ansell-Pearson highlights Nietzsche's appeal to 'creativity' (instead of 'authenticity') as involving the project of creating and becoming a self (or as involving a 'formative' view of a reflexive self, to borrow Richardson' terminology used above). But in his (very Foucaultian) reading of *Dawn*, Ansell-Pearson is especially interested in showing that, for Nietzsche, becoming a self in this sense is fundamentally not so much about preserving a subjective independence from an abstract 'herd' as is about *resisting*, as a unique individual, the disciplining effects and the communitarian tyranny typical of modern "commercial society" (D 174). This is the context in which Nietzsche develops his own ethic of self-cultivation – an ethic which, according to Ansell-Pearson, is obviously concerned with cultivating one's character as a multiplicity of 'drives' (e.g. D 560), but which is no less concerned with a sort of Stoic resistance and care of the self modelled on Epictetus and starkly opposed to the Christian, particularly Pascalian hatred of the ego.

Jaanus Sooväli's chapter, "Gapping the Subject: Nietzsche and Derrida", discusses both thinkers' interpretation of the concept of the subject by focussing not only on how Nietzsche influenced Derrida in this respect, but also on how Derrida's deconstruction of the subject may be said to be a development of Nietzsche's. Sooväli begins by raising the question as to why Derrida quotes Nietzsche more than any other philosopher – almost always in decisive moments – and yet he has only written a few short independent texts on Nietzsche. In certain respects, Nietzsche goes well beyond Freud, Heidegger, or Husserl in the direction of Derrida's thought. Sooväli's answer to his own question is that Nietzsche, with his multiple voices and philosophical perspectives, is himself a paradigm of self-deconstruction. Nietzsche does not need to be deconstructed – he deconstructs himself. However, Sooväli's further point is that neither Derrida's nor Nietzsche's deconstruction of the subject aims to remove or eliminate the concept of the subject (although this is a common objection raised against both). Their aim is to radically change its interpretation. In order to show that this is so, Sooväli focuses on BGE 16. Here, he claims, it is clear that Derrida is right in pointing out that already for Nietzsche "the subject is always inscribed in language". They both try to show that no mental state and no concept is ever directly *present*. There are always other mental states and concepts that 'construct' them, and therefore the conditions of their possibility always presuppose a detour, a mediation, a relation to these other mental states and concepts. The subject is always already "caught in differential relationships that exclude simple self-presence and are governed by language", and that is why "the subject is a 'function' of (or is 'produced' by) language". According to Sooväli, this is the main point in which Nietzsche has directly and explicitly influenced Derrida's conceptions of *différance*. It is certainly interesting to note that if this is so, then Nietzsche's influence on Derrida is rooted in the way his Langean scepticism regarding self-knowledge shows subjectivity and language to be intertwined. Moreover, if all of this is so, Nietzsche's affinity with Derrida is found in the same aspect of his philosophy as his affinity with Wittgenstein, as Maria João Mayer Branco emphasises in the next chapter. In fact, that same aspect of Nietzsche's philosophy is also the one that immediately connects his approach to the problem of subjectivity with that of two other author who might otherwise have little in common: Niklas Luhmann and Daniel Dennett. The last three chapters of Part II focus on the crisis of the modern subject as evinced in the philosophical relationship between Nietzsche and these three authors: Ludwig Wittgenstein, Niklas Luhmann and Daniel Dennett.

Maria João Mayer Branco's chapter, "Questioning Introspection: Nietzsche and Wittgenstein on 'The Peculiar Grammar of the Word "I"'", is one of the most extensive discussions of language and intersubjectivity in the collection, and it aims to show that there is a crucial affinity between Nietzsche's and Wittgenstein's rejection of introspection. By exploring their 'anti-Cartesianism' and the way they both question the *cogito*'s epistemological immediacy, transparency, and interiority, Branco tries to clarify the reasons why both Nietzsche and Wittgenstein claim that first-personal, subjective self-knowledge is an indirect, mediated access of the 'I' to itself in which language plays a decisive role. They both criticise the kind of ontological conception of the subject that transforms the self into a metaphysical, concealed and inexpressible substance completely transparent to itself and detached from the public, intersubjective world in which it lives. Thus, they both argue, though in different ways, that one of the chief failings of Cartesianism is the fact that it does not acknowledge that the individual subject only becomes an individual subject by using a language and, hence, it is always already connected with and actually belongs to an intersubjective space of linguistic conceptualisation. Moreover, they both converge in rejecting traditional referentialist views of language, particularly of the kind that entails that words for inner states and an inner 'I' designate, describe, or simply refer to an observable reality. Consequently, both Nietzsche and Wittgenstein convert the Cartesian ontology of the ego and its epistemological claims into a linguistic or grammatical question. After establishing that the Cartesian conception of the self is a point of departure that is common to Nietzsche's and Wittgenstein's analyses of subjectivity and self-knowledge, Branco elucidates Nietzsche's and Wittgenstein's criticisms of Cartesianism. In the section on Nietzsche, she focuses mainly on *Daybreak*, *Beyond Good and Evil*, *Twilight of the Idols* and *The Gay Science*, and in section on Wittgenstein she focuses on the famous 'private language argument' (PI, Part I, §§ 243–315), as well as on crucial passages from the *Blue Book*. Branco points out that the (first-personal) experience of pain or suffering is not only a crucial example and focus of analysis for Wittgenstein, but also for Nietzsche. He, too, realises that "the knowledge acquired through suffering" (D 114) seems to be the best instance of first-personal self-knowledge. Suffering "separates", as Nietzsche claims (BGE 270), it distinguishes and it awakens a "silent arrogance" in the sufferer, as well as the "certainty" that he knows what nobody else can know (BGE 270, D 114). Nevertheless, however valuable and "noble" (BGE 270) this state may be, it demands "relief" (D 114). Even the sufferer, Branco argues, cannot know himself introspectively, and in fact his pain releases in him the "*need to communicate*" (GS 354). For (the later) Wittgenstein, too, even pain is not at all an argument in favour of introspective knowledge. The meaning of such words as 'pain' and 'I' is learned and lies in their use within intersubjective forms of life, such that they always already presuppose a language that could not have been created by a single individual and, therefore, could never have been a 'private' language. Thus, both Nietzsche and Wittgenstein believe that becoming conscious of oneself through pain should in fact make us realise the opaque nature of our so-called self-consciousness. Self-reflexive suffering (and particularly the kind of 'great suffering' which is so important for Nietzsche) is not so much an experience where the truth about who we are reveals itself as rather an experience where we lose track of what such 'truth' might signify. On the other hand, the fact that, as Nietzsche and Wittgenstein agree, self-reflexive suffering can promote the 'need to communicate' suggests that alternative forms of non-introspective self-knowledge are thinkable. According to Branco, for both Nietzsche and Wittgenstein the 'I' is not really incommunicable, and further research on Wittgenstein's expressivist account of sensation may come to contribute decisively for clarifying Nietzsche's position on self-knowledge. For Nietzsche's critique of Descartes' *cogito* is indeed not eliminist, and it involves a conception of an *inner* 'pathos of distance' (BGE 257), which should be interpreted in the light of Nietzsche's conception of consciousness as a "net connecting one person with another" (GS 354).

Werner Stegmaier's chapter, "Subjects as Temporal Clues to Orientation: Nietzsche and Luhmann on Subjectivity", is an extremely original exploration of the affinity between Nietzsche and Luhmann regarding the problem of subjectivity, particularly of the way in which both thinkers converge not only in identifying the most fundamental paradoxes involved in the modern philosophical concept of the subject, but also in trying to make these paradoxes productive for the progress of their thought. According to Stegmaier, Nietzsche and Luhmann are particularly interested in the 'subject' as a concept that in the Enlightenment fulfilled the function of liberating "the individual from his bond to God and his traditional social relationships, thus radically handing him back to himself–as autonomous thinker". In order to fulfil this function, the concept of the subject had to become paradoxical, as it had to posit every human being as simultaneously unequal *and* equal to every other human being. This paradox was made even deeper by the scientific, that is, *objectifying*, approach to subjectivity in modern philosophy. This approach converts the subject into its opposite, namely an 'object' of inquiry. By adopting this objectifying approach and positing a transcendental subject–a subject that is 'me' and yet is a universal subject constituted by theoretical and practical structures supposedly common to all – modern transcendental philosophy falls into paradox. According to Stegmaier, in the twentieth century Husserl's transcendental phenomenology is especially paradigmatic of this paradoxical nature of transcendental philosophy. Nietzsche and Luhmann, by contrast, expose the paradoxical nature of transcendental philosophy, indeed of every philosophy of the subject in general. They both argue that if a concept leads to paradox its claim to refer to something real outside of itself (its referentiality) has to be questioned. In particular, they both show that there is no reason to assume that the word 'subject' designates some sort of really observable and describable entity. No real answer to the question of what is 'subjectivity' can be expected, for nothing 'corresponds' to the word 'subject'. As Stegmaier puts it – in one of the strongest, most forcible postmodern denials of the subject in this volume – "the concept of the subject is a means for description, not an object of description". Nietzsche and Luhmann converge in this, according to Stegmaier: "instead of asking what a 'subject' is, they looked for the *function* or functions the concept has fulfilled in European philosophy – functions which in the meantime may already have changed and become superfluous". But Stegmaier also believes that Nietzsche's and Luhmann's efforts to dissolve the concept of the subject by showing its paradoxical nature do not end in a cul-de-sac. As mentioned, Stegmaier supposes paradoxes to be productive. Thus, he argues that the paradoxes of subjectivity make Nietzsche replace the concept of the subject with the concept of 'perspective', or rather 'perspectives'. Nietzsche does this by showing (a) that 'subject', 'I', 'consciousness', 'agent' (or 'doer'), etc. are mere linguistic constructions, and (b) they were constructed in order to fulfil a social function, namely to "create unity and order over time in the chaos of ideas of individuals and among individuals" (and hence to make society possible). Realising this makes Nietzsche free the subject from any transcendental a prioris and *construe* a new conception of the subject, namely the subject as a unique *perspective* radically separated from all other 'subjects' (or perspectives) and unable to reach them in their 'subjectivity'. Similarly, Luhmann replaces the concepts of subject and perspective with the concept of *observation* (the concept of an impersonal and yet self-referential observation that autopoetically *constructs* social reality as a linguistic realm of social communications). Stegmaier's ultimate aim seems to be the interpretation of both Nietzsche's 'perspectives' and Luhmann's 'observation' in terms of his own philosophy of 'orientation'.

Sofia Miguens' chapter, "Three Senses of Selfless Consciousness: Nietzsche and Dennett on Mind, Language and Body", considers philosophical affinities between Nietzsche and Dennett – and, more generally, between Nietzsche and contemporary philosophy of mind – by assessing some of Nietzsche's views on mind, language, body, consciousness and the self in the context of contemporary debates. The chapter can also be read as a discussion of Daniel Dennett's idea of a 'dismantling of the Cartesian Theatre' and the general idea of a 'selfless consciousness'. The chapter is divided in three parts, each of which discusses a different meaning of 'selfless consciousness'. In Part 1 (*Vielheit* and *Intermittenzen*), Miguens considers what role natural language may play in consciousness. Miguens focuses on GS 354, an aphorism that Dennett quotes more than once in his work on consciousness, and she tries to assess Nietzsche's proposal (according to which consciousness developed under the pressure of the need for communication) by appealing to Dennett's conception of the status of the self and the role of high-order mental states in his functionalist models of consciousness (*Brainstorms*, 1978 and *Consciousness Explained*, 1991). The main point that Miguens makes is that Nietzsche and Dennett converge in intertwining consciousness and language – and, therefore, consciousness and publicity (for language, in contrast with a brain, or a body, is public and shared). In addition, Miguens shows that Nietzsche and Dennett also converge in understanding consciousness as intermittent, as well as in identifying different levels of awareness, including sub-personal awareness. Only at the 'surface level' of language and conceptualisation are there conscious mental states – and particularly, a 'self' and *proper* consciousness *qua* self-consciousness. The intertwinement of consciousness and language is indeed what leads to the conclusion (both for Nietzsche and for Dennett) that there definitely is no 'Cartesian natural unity or centre stage'. In Part 2 (*Unterseelen*), Miguens dovetails Nietzsche's idea of 'sub-souls' with Dennett's engagement with Antonio Damasio's objections to classic, dis-embodied (and, as it were, 'dis-embrained') functionalism. Retracting from this kind of functionalism, Dennett credits Nietzsche as an inspiration for the idea that evolution embodies information in all parts of the body. In Part 3 (Is that all? *Warheit* and *Wissenschaft*), Miguens draws some conclusions regarding the fruitfulness of comparing Nietzsche and Dennett. It seems to us important to ponder over what she has to say in this section, for it raises key general questions about what is at stake in this present volume.

Miguens' main point is that we should sharply separate treatments of consciousness, mind, body, self, language, etc. that belong to philosophy of mind and cognition from treatments that belong to metaphysics, epistemology, moral philosophy or, more generally, treatments that involve *content* and hence questions of value and of truth. As soon as, for example, Nietzsche explores the hypothesis that (proper) consciousness *qua* conceptual and linguistic consciousness 'falsifies', he stands immediately outside of the field in which a comparison with Dennett's functionalism makes sense. Or, to take another example, when Nietzsche reflects on the *value* for the 'affirmation of life' either of something like the Cartesian theatre or of something like a selfless consciousness, he is no longer in any possible dialogue with psychology, or cognitive science, or Dennett's philosophy of mind.

This raises two main questions. First, there is the question of the so-called 'analytic Nietzsche'. Does the trend that transforms Nietzsche into an analytic philosopher make sense? Nietzsche may easily be considered an 'analytic' philosopher in a very broad sense: he is not 'irrational', and he makes claims and at least sometimes presents arguments to underpin them. But (Miguens suggests) he does not belong to the analytic tradition in the same way as, say, Frege or even Husserl (who weren't born much later than Nietzsche) do. And one of the reasons for this is precisely that in the analytic tradition thoughts tend not to be considered to be 'mental states', that is, analytic philosophers tend to assume, as Miguens puts it, that "the appropriate units for pursuing an investigation on thought-world relations are propositions or judgements, *and not selves*". The second question Miguens' final thoughts raise is whether it is "really the same author continental and analytical philosophers are interested in when they are interested in Nietzsche, *in particular where a critique of the subject is concerned*". Most likely, a Deleuzian, say, is mostly interested in Nietzsche's axiological stance towards the problem of subjectivity, whereas an analytical philosopher will most likely be interested either in embodiment or in Nietzsche's evolutionary conjectures about consciousness, or in his psychological theory of motivation. Is Nietzsche really able to make them communicate?

As regards the 'analytic Nietzsche', we believe that though it is certainly wrong to assimilate Nietzsche too much to the analytic tradition – particularly if that entails losing focus on the practical-existential dimension of his writings –, recent scholarship that manages to relate current analytic debates with Nietzsche thought has proven much more interesting than might be expected. Moreover, even if Nietzsche can be said not to belong to the tradition that assumes that 'propositions are facts', his anti-realism about concepts (or about both moral and epistemic norms, as Brian Leiter puts it in his chapter) is certainly relevant for the analytic tradition today. Finally, we believe that this volume is itself a contribution, even if a modest one, to the promotion of fruitful philosophical dialogues not only between anglophone and continental Nietzsche scholars, but also between 'analytics' and 'continentals'. That Nietzsche's writings are able to mediate the latter kind of dialogue is indeed surprising – but it seems to be a fact.

Part III: Current Debates – From Embodiment and Consciousness to Agency

The aim of **Mattia Riccardi**'s chapter, "Nietzsche on the Embodiment of Mind and Self", is (as the title suggests) to work out in some detail Nietzsche's view on the embodiment of mind and self. In order to do so, Riccardi makes use of an important distinction in contemporary philosophy of mind, namely Barry Dainton's distinction between 'effective embodiment' and 'phenomenal embodiment'. The mind is said to be 'effectively embodied' when it is said to depend *de facto* on the kind of body it happens to have. As many passages in Nietzsche's published and unpublished writings show, Nietzsche clearly believes the mind to be effectively embodied, and as at least a few key-passages (such as Z I, On the Despisers of the Body) show, he also believes the 'self' (*Selbst*) to be effectively embodied. But a mind is said to be 'phenomenally embodied' only if it can be said to be present to itself as embodied, that is, (as Riccardi puts it) to experience its own mental life "as in some sense shaped by the kind of body it happens to have. Here, the relevant dimension is purely phenomenological" – here, what is at stake is purely the first-personal, subjective experience that a mind has of itself, and particularly the reflexivity that is thought to justify our talk of a 'self'. Riccardi's thesis is that Nietzsche believes that although we are effectively embodied, we lack phenomenal embodiment. But Riccardi qualifies this claim in an important respect. He acknowledges that Nietzsche follows Schopenhauer in arguing that the body is the only 'immediate object' in our experience – that is to say, in defending that besides having third-personal knowledge of our body, we also have a first-personal, subjective experience precisely of our embodiment in *this* body, which distinguishes it from any other spatial object in our experience. According to Riccardi, the problem, however, is that Nietzsche believes that in spite of the fact that we have first-personal, subjective, phenomenal access to our our own body, it is also a fact that such access is fundamentally defective, such that our body as phenomenally given is in truth a "*terra incognita*" (NL 1882, 5[31], KSA 10: 225) or, as Riccardi writes, "we lack epistemic access to a certain range of facts concerning the way in which the body shapes mind and self". In particular, we lack, from a phenomenal point of view, epistemic access to the way in which our body is supposed to shape our "propositionally articulated conscious attitudes (like beliefs, desires, emotions, volitions, etc.)", and therefore we lack phenomenal embodiment *with respect to this class of psychological states* (albeit not with respect to all classes of psychological states). Thus the problem is again the defectiveness of introspection and its intrinsic entanglement with language. Our introspective access to our propositionally articulated conscious attitudes is mediated by language and indeed itself propositional, so that it causes us not only to remain "unknown to ourselves" (GM Preface 1) but also to think of ourselves as if we were disembodied minds and selves. As Riccardi puts it, "Nietzsche takes what is usually called the *Cartesian* picture of mind and self to accurately capture the conception we naïvely form of ourselves as thinkers and agents". This sort of phenomenal (although not effective) disembodiment is particularly clear, as well as particularly stark, with respect to our self-understanding as an 'I' or 'self'. In self-referentially employing the word 'I' and using it to give unity to the whole of our mental life, we have no sense of how our bodies effectively shape the states in which we do that and thus we fall into the pseudo-disembodied experience of ourselves that typically originates our self-conception as 'souls' or 'subjects'. Therefore, according to Riccardi Nietzsche's conception of our *effective* embodiment is fundamentally objective or third-personal, and it belongs to Nietzsche's rejection of the Cartesian illusions that our lack of phenomenal embodiment typically promotes. Nietzsche's conception of 'drives' and his thesis that 'body' and 'soul' are just different ways of describing the same reality (basically the reality of the drives) are third-personal and aim to account for our effective embodiment. Like Sofia Miguens, Riccardi analyses Nietzsche's conception of a "subject-multiplicity" (BGE 12) and explores his views on effective embodiment by comparing them to Dennett's and other functionalist views.

Paolo Stellino's chapter, "Self-knowledge, Genealogy, Evolution", can be said to begin by exploring a crucial idea also discussed in Paul Katsafanas' chapter. Although Nietzsche's position regarding self-knowledge is admittedly sceptical (which means, to say it once more, that it is basically 'Langean'), he nevertheless believes that there is a non-negligible difference between direct and indirect self-knowledge – or between first-personal, subjective, introspective self-knowledge and third-personal, objective, scientific self-knowledge –, such that the latter can be attained, at least to some extent or to a certain degree, *if* it is understood and undertaken not only as physiology and psychology but also, and most crucially, as 'genealogy'. This move from introspective psychology to physio-psychology *qua* genealogy has, however, an introspective starting point, that is, a starting point in (first-personal) self-knowledge. It is self-knowledge that lets us know that there is no self-knowledge, as Stellino paradoxically puts it. In other words, it is by introspection that one discovers that introspective self-knowledge is impossible and we need an alternative method to probe the hidden depths of our psychological or subjective life. Nietzsche's scepticism regarding self-knowledge is what leads to the development of the genealogical method as we need a better or truer method of self-observation. (Not by accident, the *Genealogy* of Morality begins precisely with the assertion that "we are unknown to ourselves", GM Preface 1). Stellino explores this idea by investigating the evolutionary dimension of genealogy and comparing Nietzsche's use of it for self-knowledge with recent attempts to provide evolutionary and genealogical critiques of morality. Stellino focuses, in particular, on Ruse (1986) and Joyce (2006) and their respective attempts to defend evolutionary anti-realist account in metaethics.

Brian Leiter's chapter, "Moralities Are a *Sign-Language* of the Affects", is an excellent example of how Nietzsche's view of subjectivity (or his use of psychology as an explanatory idiom) can contribute to the most sophisticated debates of contemporary moral psychology and philosophy of the emotions. Leiter offers an interpretation and partial defence of Nietzsche's idea that moralities and moral judgements are 'sign-languages' or 'symptoms' of our affects, that is, they are *caused* by our emotions or feelings, and these are causes whose existence "can be correctly inferred from the symptom or sign", as Leiter puts it in his reconstruction of Nietzsche's view. According to this reconstruction, moral judgements result from the interaction of two kinds of affective responses: first, a 'basic affect' of inclination towards or aversion from certain acts, and then a further affective response (the 'meta-affect', or 'moral affect') to that basic affect, that is, either an inclination towards or an aversion away from a basic affect. Leiter argues that Nietzsche views basic affects (basic inclinations towards X and aversions away from Y) as *non-cognitive*, that is, as identifiable solely by their phenomenal character – by how they feel to the subject who experiences the affect; by contrast, meta-affects such as guilt and shame sometimes incorporate a *cognitive* component like belief. Leiter ascribes this view to Nietzsche by exploring Katsafanas' (2013) interpretation of drives as *dispositions to have affective responses under certain conditions*. The same drive has the potential to give rise to different moral feelings depending on the circumstances, but the causal root of a moral judgement (the "motivational oomph or push") is always the qualitatively distinctive *feel* of an affect and this affect is always a way in which a drive responds to given circumstances (or what it feels like for us to respond to these circumstances while being driven by a given drive X). That is why moralities and moral judgements are 'sign-languages' or 'symptoms' of our affects. In addition, Leiter tries to show that this view is compatible with his previous reading of Nietzsche, particularly with what he terms Nietzsche's "Doctrine of Types" (Leiter 2002: 8–10), by arguing that Nietzsche believes that the psychological component of a person's type consists of drives and a person is always constituted by a relatively stable set and association of drives. In accordance with Nietzsche's Lamarckianism, sets and associations of drives tend to be stable even when they are culturally acquired character traits. As Leiter points out, in the early twenty-first century, we know that characterological traits are not inherited (for they have no gene), but behavioural genetics has established that they are *heritable*, which means that they can be said to "mimick the Lamarckian result". If this is so and therefore, as Leiter argues, at least the kernel of Nietzsche's outdated Lamarckianism can be reformulated and made plausible by means of our contemporary distinction between inheritance and heritability, then moralities and moral judgements can indeed be said to be 'sign-languages' and 'symptoms' caused by 'type-facts' about persons, as it will become plausible to conceive of them as ultimately rooted not only in strictly biological type-facts, but also in stable sets and associations of drives. Or, in other words, by updating and indeed replacing Nietzsche's Lamarckianism with a plausible (and still 'Nietzschean') psychology of drives, we can see that moral judgements are caused by "affects and meta-affects, which are the joint product of nature and culture", as Leiter puts it. The chapter concludes with a discussion of philosophical and empirical psychological reasons for thinking that Nietzsche's account of moral judgement is correct. In this context, Leiter's discussion of Nietzsche's moral 'anti-realism' (an anti-realism which, in fact, concerns both moral and epistemic norms) seems to us to make particularly clear how Nietzsche's psychology and his view of the problem of subjectivity crucially underpin his reflections on such themes as morality and nihilism.

Ken Gemes' and **Imogen Le Patourel**'s chapter, "Nietzsche on Consciousness, Unity, and the Self", seems to us to be an important attempt to provide a state-of-the-art critical update on some of the key issues of this volume: what is Nietzsche's view of consciousness and its relation to the drives and their unconsciousness, and how does Nietzsche conceive of the self and its unity, that is, its wholeness, or completeness. In Part 1 of their chapter, Gemes and Le Patourel argue that Nietzsche makes a "pronounced distinction between the self and the I or ego". They claim that he is sceptical about the I or ego – that is, about the I or ego of consciousness –, but not about the self that is formed at the level of unconscious drives. As regards the I, Nietzsche sometimes seems to be sceptical about the very *existence* of the I or ego, but his considered view "involves only scepticism about its importance for self, action and agency". As for the self, Nietzsche sees it as "the core of one's agency", and yet he locates it primarily in the unconscious, namely as the result of the activity the drives and the way they interrelate. However, Gemes and Le Patourel discuss two alternative views of the self as a primarily unconscious interrelation of the drives. What they call 'the egalitarian version' entails that any given collection of drives constituting an individual organism is a self. The 'elitist version', by contrast, entails that only a few individual organisms are truly 'selves', that is, genuine selfhood presupposes a unified set of drives that only a few individuals are really able to achieve. According to Gemes and Le Patourel, Nietzsche favours the elitist version and equates the process of 'becoming what one is' and being a genuine individual with the process of achieving internal unity and order at the unconscious level of drives. Most importantly, Gemes and Le Patourel interpret this unity and order as imposed by a predominant drive. Genuine selfhood is possible only because certain drives can predominate over all other drives within the organism, in fact only because a given 'master drive' can do this by supplying a creative vocation or task and marshalling one's capacities in the service of this creative vocation or task (and hence in the service of certain values). Nietzsche ascribes a secondary role to consciousness in this kind of process, and this is the essential meaning of his critique of the overestimation of consciousness, or his "largely deflationary account of the role of consciousness", as Gemes and Le Patourel put it. Part 2 of their chapter discusses this way of interpreting the unity of self. The 'predominance model' – according to which unity is achieved when a master drive organises or sublimates the other drives into hierarchical relations to itself – has an alternative, namely the model proposed by Paul Katsafanas, according to which unity should be seen as a harmony between the drives and conscious reflection. Gemes and Le Patourel argue that Nietzsche is a "champion of agonal struggle and the great sceptic of the power and function of conscious reflection", and therefore "should not be domesticated [...] as an apologist for a traditional valorisation of harmony between instincts and reason". They conclude that the predominance model best captures Nietzsche's position, as it entails that "it is always the drives rather than consciousness that are the root causal determinants of our actions and the formation of the self, and that where consciousness does have a role, it is essentially as a tool of the drives". Note, this view involves the rejection of epiphenomenalism, while it also involves the rejection of the traditional overestimation of consciousness, especially of the view that the I of consciousness is a knower and doer that can stay above the drives and control them by reflecting upon them.

Herman Siemens' chapter, "Nietzsche's Socio-Physiology of the Self", examines Nietzsche's thought on the social and historical sources of the self as a counter-argument against the liberal concept of the individual. In specific, the chapter takes issue with the notion of the asocial, antecedently individuated person to which the liberal notion of freedom, as the right to choose one's concept of the good, is attached. Nietzsche, Siemens argues, offers both a powerful critique of the asocial, antecedently individuated concept of personhood, and an alternative counter-conception of personhood and sovereignty. On the critical side are arguments to the effect that the individual or person is inseparable from its ends or values, which in turn are socially constituted, and that our capacities as individuals, especially for sovereign agency, are the product of a long social history and pre-history. On the positive side is the constructive counter-claim that the maintenance and cultivation of our capacities for productive, autonomous agency is dependent on relations of measured antagonism both between and within us as individuals, or rather: as '*dividua*'. Siemens reconstructs these arguments along four main lines of thought: on the social origins and character of (self-)consciousness (§ 1); on the (pre-)history and social constitution of our capacities as sovereign individuals (§ 2); on the social origins of moral phenomena, understood as internalisations of communal norms (§ 3); on Nietzsche's physiological destruction of the substantial moral subject, coupled with the physiological reconstruction of the subject as '*dividuum*' (§ 4). The texts discussed come mainly from the *Nachlass* of 1880–1882 (KSA 9), where Nietzsche develops a socio-physiology of the self. These texts allow Siemens to interrogate the rationale for the typically Nietzschean 'category mistake' of discussing moral and political issues in physiological terms. Nietzsche's physiological discourse is understood as part of his programme to naturalise morality and serves to deflate moral concepts by exposing the metaphysical errors on which they are based. It also enables Nietzsche to reconstruct the historical emergence of the individual from the social 'organism' in a way that avoids substance ontology in favour of processes modelled on organic life. In this regard, he also develops a prescriptive alternative to the liberal concept of freedom that turns on radically individual self-legislation, grounded in processes of self-regulation that enable each individual as *unicum* to meet its conditions of existence. And against the Socratic ideal of inner harmony, Nietzschean sovereignty involves the maintenance of maximal but measured inner antagonism through relations of measured outer antagonism with equals.

In the last chapter of this collection, "The Expressivist Nietzsche", **Robert B. Pippin** engages in an important attempt to clarify in detail some of the polemic views that he put forward in his book, *Nietzsche, Psychology* & First Philosophy. There he had tried to interpret in a new way the important passage of *Beyond Good and Evil* where Nietzsche claims that his writings make "psychology" once again "the queen of the sciences", and so once more the "path to the fundamental problems" (BGE 23). Pippin's argument was, and remains, that the French *moralistes* (particularly Pascal, La Rochefoucauld, and above all Montaigne) are the main inspiration of Nietzsche's conception of 'psychology', and that this conception leads to a characterisation of Nietzsche's conception of agency as 'expressivist'. Pippin's attempt to align Nietzsche with that tradition aims, first of all, to make the point that Nietzsche "is unquestionably better understood as a French *moraliste* than the German metaphysician of Heidegger's influential lectures from the 1930s and 1940s". Secondly, Pippin's aim is to reject the view according to which Nietzsche's conception of psychology is fundamentally naturalistic.

Our volume, particularly in Part I, shows that the sources of Nietzsche's conception of 'psychology' are rather multifarious. Although it is certainly right that Nietzsche identifies with Montaigne or La Rochefoucauld in their way of doing 'psychology', (i) Descartes also remains important for him (as shown in Isabelle Wienand's chapter), (ii) the French 'psychologists' include for him the likes of Stendhal and Bourget (as shown by Giuliano Campioni's chapter), (iii) the scientific, naturalistic psychology of his time is perhaps less important than that of Montaigne or Bourget, but is nonetheless quite important (as shown Pietro Gori's, Maria Cristina Fornari's and again Giuliano Campioni's chapters), (iv) neo-Kantianism (from Schopenhauer to Teichmüller and others) is another major influence; and (v) Friedrich A. Lange is perhaps his most important source and influence. Interestingly, this work on Nietzsche's sources, and especially the way several of the authors highlight Lange's role, either directly (as in Anthony Jensen's and João Constâncio's chapters) or indirectly (as in Maria João Mayer Branco's), confirms the kernel of Pippin's main claim, namely that Nietzsche's psychology is fundamentally focused on the critique of introspection and more generally, as he puts it, on "the problem of self-knowledge and the relation between that problem and knowledge of others' actions and words, and especially the unique kind of difficulty one faces in attempting to know such things as why one (or anyone) did what one did, what it actually was that one (or anyone) did; what one (or some other) truly values; why one values what one does; could one come to know what sort of a life one might truly affirm, and if so how?" Neither the natural sciences nor a metaphysics of the basic structure of the soul can provide such self- and other-knowledge, and this for several reasons, according to Pippin: "partly because it is neither empirical nor a priori knowledge, partly because the soul is not an object in the usual sense, but mostly because in his treatments such putative self- and other-knowledge is almost always an expression of some self-deception that must be overcome". This focus on self-deception is what ultimately unites Nietzsche and the French *moralistes*, and it is also the reason why they know, as Nietzsche knows, that in order to attain any glimpse of self- and other-knowledge what is needed is not so much a scientific 'method' and general 'theory' of the soul as rather the ability to find "ways to characterize how the human soul typically works (how such questions as those above are posed and pursued) in ways true to the unstable, variable, situation dependent, self-interested contexts in which they arise". And this is what leads to Nietzsche's 'expressivism'. The main idea is that self- and other-knowledge results from what is expressed *in* our own deeds and the deeds of others. Introspective knowledge of our own ex ante formulations of intention is not really knowledge. Without such formulations and the 'mindedness' they entail there would be no difference between human deeds and merely material events (e.g. bodily movements), but such formulations are only provisional and tell us nothing about what we really 'are', that is, about what really matters to us, what we are really committed to doing, and hence defines us. Only the action, only what is expressed in the deed after it has happened, reveals what we are or (perhaps more precisely) allows for an interpretation and retrospective reconstruction that can be tentatively equated with self- or other-knowledge.

Thus, Nietzsche is still committed to the distinction between action (or deed) and event, but he is able to make this distinction in a way that is different from voluntarism, spontaneity theories, and intention-causal theories. According to Pippin, this different way of making the distinction involves conceiving of the intentional intelligibility as "the domain of value, self-subsumption under norms", and conceiving of such intelligibility as depending on what is expressed *in* actions that are public involves, in turn, conceiving of human valuing as basically "collective, sustained over time, mediated in many institutional, religious and artistic practices, and inherited; *very rarely* open to revision". In other words, intentional intelligibility is intersubjective. But, if so, then we might add that the first-personal – the 'subjective' involved in that 'inter-subjectivity' – remains relevant, such that Nietzsche's 'psychology', as well as his 'perspectivism', can still be said to remain within the boundaries of the problem that modern philosophy has so forcibly *posed*: the problem of subjectivity.

References

Abel, Günter (2001) "Bewußtsein – Sprache – Natur. Nietzsches Philosophie des Geistes", in: *Nietzsche-Studien* 30, 1–43.
Abel, Günter (2012) "Die Aktualität der Wissenschaftsphilosophie Nietzsches", in: H. Heit, G. Abel and M. Brusotti (eds.), *Nietzsches Wissenschaftsphilosophie*, Berlin/Boston: De Gruyter, 481–530.
Constâncio, João (2011) "On Consciousness. Nietzsche's Departure from Schopenhauer", in: *Nietzsche-Studien* 40, 1–42.
Dillinger, Jakob (2012) "Bewusstsein als Krankheit. Eine Anspielung auf Dostojewskij in Die fröhliche Wissenschaft Nr. 354?", in: *Nietzsche-Studien* 41, 333–343.
Gardner, Sebastian (2009) "Nietzsche, the Self, and the Disunity of Philosophical Reason", in: K. Gemes and S. May (eds.), *Nietzsche on Freedom and Autonomy*, Oxford: Oxford University Press, 1–31.
Janaway, Christopher (1991) "Nietzsche, the Self, and Schopenhauer", in: Keith Ansell Pearson (ed.), *Nietzsche and Modern German Thought*, London: Routledge, 119–142.
Joyce, Richard (2006) *The Evolution of Morality*, Cambridge, MA: MIT Press.
Katsafanas, Paul (2005) "Nietzsche's Theory of Mind: Consciousness and Conceptualization", in: *European Journal of Philosophy* 13, 1–31.
Katsafanas, Paul (2013) "Nietzsche's Philosophical Psychology", in: K. Gemes and J. Richardson (eds.), *The Oxford Handbook of Nietzsche*, Oxford: Oxford University Press, 727–755.
Lange, Friedrich Albert (1881) [1875] *The History of Materialism and Criticism of its Present Importance*, vol. 3/3, English translation by Ernest Chester Thomas, Boston: Houghton, Mifflin & Co.
Lange, Friedrich Albert (2006) [1875] *Geschichte des Materialismus und Kritik seiner Bedeutung in der Gegenwart*, Book II, Leipzig: Elibron Classics.
Leiter, Brian (2002) *Nietzsche on Morality*, London/New York: Routledge.

Pippin, Robert B. (2010) *Nietzsche, Psychology, and First Philosophy*, Chicago/London: University of Chicago Press.
Riccardi, Mattia (forthcoming) "Nietzsche on the Superficiality of Consciousness", in: M. Dries (ed.), *Nietzsche on Consciousness and the Embodied Mind*, Berlin/Boston: De Gruyter.
Ruse, Michael (1986) *Taking Darwin Seriously*, New York: Blackwell.
Simon, Josef (1984) "Das Problem des Bewusstseins bei Nietzsche und der traditionelle Bewusstseinsbegriff", in: M. Djuric and J. Simon (eds.), *Zur Aktualität Nietzsches*, vol. 2, Würzburg: Königshausen & Neumann, 17–33.
Stegmaier, Werner (2000) "Nietzsches Zeichen", in: *Nietzsche-Studien* 29, 41–69.

Part I: **Tradition and Context**

Isabelle Wienand
1 Writing from a First-Person Perspective: Nietzsche's Use of the Cartesian Model

Introduction[1]

This paper aims to clarify the notion of subject or Self in Nietzsche's philosophy. There are indeed many methods to apply in order to achieve this goal. One fruitful way to understand the status of *ich* in Nietzsche's writings is to work out the converging points and differences with prevailing conceptions of the Self in modern philosophy. My suggestion consists in showing that Nietzsche's sense of the Self bears recognisable features that we find in particular in Descartes' thoughts. Some interesting points can be drawn from this analogy. First, Descartes' thoughts about the immediate and clear knowledge of the *Cogito* serve as a basis against which Nietzsche develops his idea of the Self; and second, the Cartesian writing from the first-person perspective is an (anti-)model for Nietzsche's autobiographical texts. There are of course important differences between both thinkers and the purpose of my contribution is not to minimize them. However, Nietzsche's critique of the conscious subject qua *Cogito* does not preclude the relevance of considering Cartesian subjectivity as a significant model to better capture Nietzsche's conception of the Self. At the same time, Descartes constitutes a helpful model and source in understanding what Nietzsche wants to achieve in writing in the first-person. I argue that reading the *Discourse on the Method* (1637) helps us determine to which purpose Nietzsche is writing about himself, for example in the new Prefaces to the second edition of *Daybreak* (1886) and *The Gay Science* (1887). Ultimately, this paper is part of a larger concern to illustrate with arguments other than Heidegger's[2] and Lampert's[3] that it makes sense to study and to teach Nietzsche within the tradition of modern philosophy, in order to understand and evaluate accordingly what Nietzsche says about the Self.

---

[1] The article is a revised version of a paper I gave at the department of philosophy of the Universidade Nova de Lisboa in January 2012. I am very grateful to the organisers, João Constâncio and Maria João Mayer Branco for inviting me to contribute to their research project on Nietzsche's conception of the Self, as well as to the participants of the Nietzsche International Lab (NIL) for their valuable comments. I am also very appreciative of the linguistic improvements Bartholomew Ryan has made.
[2] Heidegger 1961, vol. 2: 141–192, in particular the section entitled "Der innere Zusammenhang der Grundstellung von Descartes und Nietzsche", 189–192.
[3] Lampert 1993: 143–271.

The paper has two parts. Part 1 considers Nietzsche's critique of the *Cogito* and of other Cartesian concepts. I show that Cartesian subjectivity is a helpful resource to understand Nietzsche's conception of the Self. Part 2 focuses on the first-person perspective in the *Discourse on the Method*. I stress its importance as a (anti-)model for Nietzsche's self-presentation. I conclude by suggesting that the philosophical autobiography which Nietzsche seems to offer to his readers in his late text *Ecce homo* (1888) narrates the *ich* both as a fate, determined by historical, familial, physiological factors, and as something entirely new and independent. In this sense, Nietzsche completes the Cartesian narrative of the subject as a free spirit by adding a fundamental component to the Self: the fabric of the instincts.

1 Thinking about the Self

We should approach Nietzsche's conception of the Self with more caution, that is, we should refrain from believing that his contribution to the understanding of the Self is unprecedented in the history of modern philosophy. However, my claim is neither that Nietzsche's philosophy is – without Nietzsche knowing it – a variation of Descartes' metaphysics of subjectivity.[4] Nor that Nietzsche's philosophy helps us understand early modern philosophy.[5]

Nietzsche is well known for making use of the first-person perspective in his philosophical writings in a way that seems in many regards novel and unique. By doing so, he achieves a radical turn in the way philosophy has been conceived, written and read, but also in so far as he brings thought and existence into a radically new combination. Nietzsche makes us conscious of the ordinary features of our life, our habits, our experiences and our dreams, which not only play a decisive role upon the conditions of the emergence of certain types of

---

[4] See for instance the influential reading of Heidegger in Heidegger 1961, vol. 2: 189: "Nietzsche's comment to the Cartesian 'cogito ergo sum' is in all respects the proof that he misjudges [*verkennt*] the inner essential historical [*wesengeschichtlichen*] connection of his own metaphysical position with Descartes'." (My translation)

[5] Lampert 1993: 2: "Bacon, Descartes, and Nietzsche mutually illuminate one another. Bacon and Descartes, often enough considered in some sense the fathers of modern philosophy, seem to me to share in all essentials the view of philosophy set out in Nietzsche's three pronouncements. Confirmation of Nietzsche's three principles is beautifully accessible in their writings; they are 'Nietzschean' philosophers, legislators who mastered an esoteric style and whose thoughts are among the greatest modern events. Nietzsche's pronouncements provide entry to their writings, and their writings reciprocate: reflection on them and their revolutionary consequences prepares the reader to enter Nietzsche's writings with a clear sense of what is possible for a philosopher."

thoughts, feelings and habits. They also constitute the very matrix of the elaboration of the philosophers' ideas, which seem to be disconnected from everyday life. Nietzsche suspects that the most abstract and disinterested thoughts are not generated by the universal power of understanding alone and are not of a selfless origin, as it is usually imagined. Thinking is not a process that engages only the intellectual part of the thinker. It is always embedded in the fabric of the Self. Henceforth, Nietzsche suggests that philosophy is not only an intellectual contribution to the advancement of truth, but also entails at its very basis a not fully conscious attempt to make sense of one's own existence. As he writes at the beginning of *Beyond Good and Evil* (1886), the domain of philosophy offers a particular opportunity for the philosopher to enterprise a kind of unintentional self-narration:

> It has gradually become clear to me what every great philosophy has hitherto been: a confession on the part of its author and a kind of involuntary and unconscious memoir [...] (BGE 6)[6]

The first chapter of *Beyond Good and Evil*, from which the above passage is quoted, focuses upon the prejudices of the philosophers. Nietzsche identifies in the very principles of the discipline of philosophy a series of preconceived ideas, of blind beliefs, and of atavistic convictions: "On the Prejudices of Philosophers" serves the function of discrediting the truth claim of these foundational principles and of displaying the flaws in their assumptions. This first chapter also serves the more positive purpose of defining anew what philosophy should be about (psychology),[7] how philosophers of the future should be "attempters" (*Versucher*[8]), and of laying down new foundational principles (the idea of will to power[9]).

---

[6] KSA 5: 19: "Allmählich hat sich mir herausgestellt, was jede grosse Philosophie bisher war: nämlich das Selbstbekenntnis ihres Urhebers und eine Art ungewollter und unvermerkter mémoires [...]."
[7] See BGE 23/JGB 23, KSA 5: 38: "All psychology has hitherto remained anchored to moral prejudices and timidities [*moralischen Vorurtheilen und Befürchtungen*]: it has not ventured into the depths. To conceive it as morphology and the development-theory of the will to power [Entwicklungslehre des Willens zur Macht], as I conceive it – has never yet so much entered the mind of anyone else [...]."
[8] See BGE 42/JGB 42, KSA 5: 59: "A new species of philosopher is appearing: I venture to baptise these philosophers with a name not without danger [*nicht ungefährlichen Namen*] in it. As I divine them [...] these philosophers of the future might rightly, but perhaps wrongly, be described as attempters [Versucher]." See also the ninth chapter of BGE, "What is noble?" (*Was ist vornehm?*).
[9] BGE 36/JGB 36, KSA 5: 54–55: "The world seen from within, the world described and defined according to its 'intelligible character' – it would be 'will to power' and nothing else."

In *Beyond Good and Evil* Descartes is presented as holding the naive belief, according to which one has an immediate and indubitable access to oneself. Nietzsche dismisses the Cartesian thesis as unwarranted on the grounds that Descartes does not demonstrate that the existence and the nature of the mind can be known with indubitable certainty (see *Meditations*, in particular the Second Meditation, AT VII: 23–34). Descartes does not convincingly show that the *Cogito* is the fundamental experience of the existence of the ego, i.e. the ultimate proof against sceptic arguments. In §16 of *Beyond Good and Evil* Nietzsche refers implicitly to the Cartesian *Cogito*-experience without naming it when he writes:

> There are still harmless self-observers who believe "immediate certainties" exist, for example "I think" [...]. (BGE 16)[10]

One could quote *ad libitum* other passages from *Beyond Good and Evil* – e.g. BGE 54, BGE 191 as well as from the *Nachlass* notes from August–September 1885,[11] in which Nietzsche rejects the Cartesian experience of the evidence of the *res cogitans*. As Robert Rethy aptly writes:

> In fact, in a closely connected series of notes written in August-September 1885, and thus contemporaneous with *Jenseits von Gut und Böse*, Nietzsche speaks more explicitly of "going beyond" mere Cartesian doubt, emphasizing the moral-practical restrictions to that doubt. Descartes, he writes, "ist mir nicht radikal genug" [...] In being "vorsichtiger" [than Descartes], Nietzsche is still philosophizing in the spirit of Descartes, but doing the latters' work "better" than he himself did or could do. [...] Descartes's "superficiality" or "Leichtfertigkeit" consists, then, not in doubting, but in not doubting enough, in being literally "leicht fertig mit dem Zweifel." It is Descartes' own greatest achievement, his method that is the tool that triumphs over science itself, by posing the question of the value of the highest values. In this sense [...] Nietzsche is Descartes' heir, the latter's "new organon" of method destroying the very edifice for the construction of which it was devised – the edifice of modern science. (Rethy 1976: 294–295)

Nietzsche recognises that thoughts come to consciousness. Yet it is, as he claims, a logical error to attribute them to the thinking substance, the intellectual subject qua the origin of thoughts. He contests that the emergence of thoughts can be simply explained in terms of causality: the conscious 'I' cannot

---

10 KSA 5: 29: "Es giebt immer noch harmlose Selbst-Beobachter, welche glauben, dass es 'unmittelbare Gewissheiten' gebe, zum Beispiel 'ich denke' [...]."
11 NL 40[10], KSA 11: 632: "– Descartes is not radical enough for me. In face of his demand [*Verlangen*] to have something for certain and 'I do not want to be deceived', it was necessary to ask 'why not?' In short, moral prejudices (or reasons of utility) in favour of certainty [*Gewißheit*] against appearance [*Schein*] ..." (My translation) See also NL 1885, 40[20], 40[22], 40[23], 40[24], KSA 11: 637–641.

be related as the cause of thoughts with certainty and immediate evidence. Therefore, the proof of the existence of the *res cogitans* is "the fact of a very strong belief", as he writes in a *Nachlass* note dated from autumn 1887:

> "There is thinking: therefore there is something that thinks" [*Es wird gedacht: folglich giebt es Denkendes*]: this is the upshot of all Descartes' argumentation. But that means positing our belief in the concept of substance already as "true a priori": – that, when there is thinking, there ought to be something "that thinks", is simply an expression of our grammatical habit which adds a doer to every deed. In short, here already a logical-metaphysical postulate is being made – and not just a statement … On the path followed by Descartes one does not reach something absolutely certain, but only the fact of a very strong belief
>
> If one reduces the proposition to "There is thinking, therefore there are thoughts", one has a mere tautology: and precisely that what is in question, namely the "reality of the thought" is not alluded to – that is, the "apparent reality" [*Scheinbarkeit*] of thought cannot be rejected in this way. But what Descartes wanted was that the thought have not only an apparent reality, but a reality in itself. (NL 1887, 10[158], KSA 12: 549)[12]

Nikolaos Loukidelis brings to our attention that what Nietzsche knew from the canonical works of Descartes (*Discours de la méthode*, *Meditationes*, *Principia Philosophiae*) was most probably from secondary sources.[13] One should also bear in mind that Nietzsche had read neither the Sixth Meditation, nor *The Passions of the Soul* (1649), nor the correspondence with Elisabeth of Bohemia and the French diplomat Pierre Chanut – these being precisely the texts in which Descartes elaborates a non-dualistic account of self-consciousness (see Descartes 2015).

As we know, the claim that both substances form a union and interact with one another (see the Sixth Meditation and the letters from and to Elisabeth from

---

[12] NL 1887, 10[158], KSA 12: 549: "'Es wird gedacht: folglich giebt es Denkendes': darauf läuft die argumentatio des Cartesius hinaus. Aber das heißt, unsern Glauben an den Substanzbegriff schon als 'wahr a priori' ansetzen: daß, wenn gedacht wird, es etwas geben muß, 'das denkt', ist aber einfach eine Formulirung unserer grammatischen Gewöhnung, welche zu einem Thun einen Thäter setzt. Kurz, es wird hier bereits ein logisch-metaphysisches Postulat gemacht – und nicht nur constatirt … Auf dem Wege des Cartesius kommt man nicht zu etwas absolut Gewissem, sondern nur zu einem Faktum eines sehr starken Glaubens Reduzirt man den Satz auf 'es wird gedacht, folglich giebt es Gedanken' so hat man eine bloße Tautologie: und gerade das, was in Frage steht die 'Realität des Gedankens' ist nicht berührt, – nämlich in dieser Form ist die 'Scheinbarkeit' des Gedankens nicht abzuweisen. Was aber Cartesius wollte, ist, daß der Gedanke nicht nur eine scheinbare Realität hat, sondern an sich."
[13] Loukidelis brings further evidence that Nietzsche read the *Meditations* via Ueberweg's *Grundriss der Geschichte der Philosophie*, 3. Teil (*Die Neuzeit*), also from A. Spir, *Denken und Wirklichkeit. Versuch einer Erneuerung der kritischen Philosophie*, 1877, from E. Dühring, *Natürliche Dialektik*, 1865. See Loukidelis 2005: 300 – 309, here in particular 303 – 306.

May and June 1643[14]), and that the soul's desire of knowledge is explained in terms of a passion (*admiration*), and finally that the soul can only have an indirect control over the body's power. Descartes also recognises in the Treatise on the passions that we do have a limited knowledge of bodily movements.[15] Bearing this in mind, it is possible to conjecture that the Cartesian account of the Self as a union of soul and body, which can only be perceived in a confused way through the senses, is not as foreign to Nietzsche's account of the Self as one could expect. Admittedly, my point is speculative, as there is to my knowledge no document indicating that Nietzsche did read the *Passions de l'âme*. Moreover Nietzsche might have disagreed with the *Passions*, had he read it.

A less hypothetical point about the relevance of going back to Descartes in order to understand Nietzsche's conception of the Self better is the fact that, despite the greater disagreement from 1885 onward of Nietzsche with Descartes' epistemology, Nietzsche praises in *The Antichrist* the temerity of Descartes' theory of animals. In Nietzsche's eyes the French scientist has paved the way for a better understanding of the body as a self-regulated machine.[16]

> We have learned better. We have become more modest in every respect. We no longer trace the origin of man in the "spirit", in the "divinity", we have placed him back among the animals. [...] As regards the animals, Descartes was the first who, with a boldness worthy of reverence, ventured to think of the animal as a machine: our whole science of physiology is devoted to proving this proposition. Nor, logically, do we exclude man, as even Descartes did [...]. (A 14)[17]

The details of Descartes' use of the model of the automaton for his physiology cannot be explained in this article.[18] It is however important to keep in mind that the debate in early modern philosophy about the status of animals was ongoing,

---

14 See AT III: 660–668, 683–685, 690–695. For an English translation of the full correspondence between Descartes and Elisabeth, see Shapiro 2007. For the letters from 1643 on the union between soul and body, see in particular pp. 59–71.
15 See for instance Brown 2006, Canziani 1999: 67–91 and Wienand/Ribordy 2013: 142–159.
16 See in particular G. Campioni, "Nietzsche, Descartes und der französische Geist" in: Campioni 2009: 40–45.
17 KSA 6: 180: "Wir haben umgelernt. Wir sind in allen Stücken bescheidner geworden. Wir leiten den Menschen nicht mehr vom 'Geist', von der 'Gottheit' ab, wir haben ihn unter die Thiere zurückgestellt. [...] Was die Thiere betrifft, so hat zuerst Descartes, mit verehrungswürdiger Kühnheit, den Gedanken gewagt, das Thier als machina zu verstehn: unsre ganze Physiologie bemüht sich um den Beweis dieses Satzes. Auch stellen wir logischer Weise den Menschen nicht bei Seite, wie noch Descartes that [...]."
18 See F. de Buzon's illuminating essay "L'homme et le langage chez Montaigne et Descartes" (De Buzon 1992: 451–466).

since Montaigne had argued that the difference between animals and humans was not of essence, but of degree (see Montaigne 1962: 415–466). In the fifth Part of the *Discourse*,[19] Descartes reacts against Montaigne by claiming that animals cannot speak mainly because they are deprived of a mind.[20] Nietzsche shows a distinct interest for his own thinking on physiology, in particular on the issue whether the naturalist account is adequate to explaining how human beings act.[21]

Finally, one can add that both Descartes and Nietzsche think about their own Self in a similar way. We recognise in both the awareness with which they perceive their double task of *dismissing* the very principles of almost the entire tradition of philosophy and *setting* up new ones. Thus, Nietzsche and Descartes present themselves as *ego contra omnes*: both are in a permanent conflict with the scholastic tradition in the case of Descartes, and with modern philosophy in the case of Nietzsche.[22] *Ego* supra omnes, they present themselves also as the first thinkers who have overcome their teachers and their own prejudices.

Summing up, Descartes' metaphysics and epistemology constitute an important source for Nietzsche in working out a more "careful", less "superficial" account of the Self. Similarly, Cartesian physiology permits him to develop his naturalistic account of agency. As for Descartes' psychology, it is not attested that Nietzsche was familiar with it. Had he been, it is possible that he would have agreed with the Cartesian claim of the union of soul and body as well as with his analysis of the phenomenon of the passions.

2 Writing from the first-person perspective

Descartes is an important (anti-)model for the tradition of writing philosophy in the first-person. However, the *Discourse* does not inaugurate this literary form in

---

19 See this famous passage from the *Discourse* (AT VI: 57): "For it is quite remarkable that there are no men so dull-witted [*hébétés*] or stupid – and this includes even madmen [*insensés*] – that they are incapable of arranging various words together and forming an utterance from them in order to make their thoughts understood [*fassent entendre leurs pensées*]; whereas there is no other animal, however perfect and well-endowed [*heureusement né*] it may be, that can do the like." See also the commentary of Gilson, in: Gilson 1925: 423–429. (Translations of Descartes according to Descarte (2008), unless otherwise indicated).
20 See for example Des Chene 2001.
21 On this question, see the clarifying chapter of Robert Pippin, "'L'agir est tout'. Nietzsche et le sujet", in Pippin 2006: 141–175.
22 See A. Camus, "Nietzsche et le nihilisme" in: Camus 1951: 92: "Instead of the methodical doubt, Nietzsche has practiced the methodical negation, the careful [*appliquée*] destruction of all that still hides [*masque*] nihilism from itself [...] He has written, in his own way the *Discourse on the method* of his time [...]." (My translation)

philosophy, as Etienne Gilson reminds us in his commentary,[23] as Montaigne's *Essays* exerted a determining influence upon the autobiographical form of the *Discours*, and also on Nietzsche.[24]

Other more contemporary sources, such as the literary circles around the celebrated writer Guez de Balzac (1597–1654) which Descartes frequented before leaving for Amsterdam, are also important to consult in order to have a more precise picture of Descartes, the "most eloquent philosopher of recent times". Descartes construes the *Discourse*, i.e. initially the "histoire de [son] esprit"[25] by making use of existing literary models, such as the model of the *honnête homme*.[26] For de Balzac, telling "the history of one's spirit" means presenting in a literary form "the adventures" and the heroic feats of one single man against the age-old tradition of Aristotelianism. This "histoire" not only *describes* to the readers the marvellous deeds of a single thinker, as a "picture" (*tableau*) does;[27] but it also serves an *instructive* purpose as a "fable" does (see *Discourse* I, AT VI: 4[28]). The reader could be inspired to follow or not the ways in which Descartes has tried to conduct his philosopher's life.[29]

---

[23] Gilson reminds us that the meaning of "histoire" as a genuine self-portrait is to be found in Montaigne's (Montaigne 1962:922–980) See Gilson's commentary (Descartes 1925: 98).

[24] See Pippin 2006: 21–59 and Vivarelli 1994: 79–101.

[25] See the letter of de Balzac to Descartes, 30 March 1628 (AT I: 570–571): "Besides, Monsieur, I beg you to remember *L'histoire de votre esprit*. All your friends are waiting for it, and you have promised it to me in presence of Pater Clitophon, whom we called Monsieur de Gersan in common language. He will take pleasure in reading your various adventures [*aventures*], which take place on the average and highest level of air [*dans la moyenne et dans la plus haute région de l'air*], in considering your achievements against the people of the School [*les gens de l'Ecole*], as well as the path you have followed, the progress you have made in the truth of things, etc." (My translation)

[26] See Cavaillé 1994: 349–367, in particular 362–367.

[27] See *Discourse* I, AT VI: 4: "I shall be glad, nevertheless, to reveal in this discourse what paths I have followed, and to represent my life in it as if in a picture, so that everyone may judge it for himself; and thus, learning from public response the opinions held of it, I shall add a new means of self-instruction to those I am accustomed to using."

[28] See E. Gilson (Descartes 1925: 98–99): "A fable [*fable*] is a story [*récit*] which contains for the reader a moral dimension [*moralité*] from which some will profit, but whose conclusions will not have the universal nor necessary character of moral precepts in the strict sense. The phrase ["comme une fable"] announces an instructive story, as a fable ought to be [*fabula docet*], that is, neither more (as morality would be) nor less (as a narrative story would be) than a fable." (My translation)

[29] Descartes does not think nor wish that his method to conduct one's spirit should be followed by anybody. As Gilson writes (Descartes 1925: 100), Descartes does not advise a universal use of the sceptical method: "Descartes means it seriously when he limits his ambitions to 'be useful for

De Balzac's letter is a precious source for the genesis of the *Discourse*. It reminds us that the literariness of the *Discourse* does not preclude the honesty of its author. The "fable" of Descartes' life is a frank and honest account of how to proceed in order to teach, entertain and touch the reader (*docere, delectare et movere*) – the main duties of classic Ciceronian rhetoric. Here is an example:

> My present aim, then, is not to teach the method which everyone must follow in order to direct his reason correctly, but only to reveal how I have tried to direct my own. One who presumes to give precepts must think himself more skilful than those to whom he gives them; and if he makes the slightest mistake, he may be blamed. But I am presenting this work only as a history [*histoire*], or, if you prefer, a fable [*fable*] in which, among certain examples worthy of imitation, you will perhaps also find many others that it would be right not to follow; and so I hope it will be useful for some without being harmful to any, and that everyone will be grateful to me for my frankness [*franchise*]. (*Discourse* I, AT VI: 4)[30]

For our discussion, the epistolary witnessing of de Balzac underlines the importance of the first-person perspective not only *in*, but also *of* Descartes' philosophy. The writing subject (*je*) is not only the explicit point of view of Descartes' writings.[31] It also illustrates the metaphysical relevance of the 'I' as the fundamental instance on which the certainty of existence is experienced. As we saw in Part 1, the *cogito, ergo sum* is the principle upon which the *res cogitans* is established as the absolute certitude of the existence of oneself and of other thinking selves.

We find a similar pattern in Nietzsche's texts, in particular in the Prefaces from 1886 and after. The self-narrative accounts do not serve primarily to give the reader autobiographical details about Nietzsche.[32] In the Prefaces to the

---

some without being harmful to any'; he invites everyone to read him, but he does not invite everyone to imitate him." (My translation)

30 See the remarks by Georges Cantecor on Descartes' "frankness", cited by Gilson (Descartes 1925: 99): "A writer who narrates his past can be in good faith [*de bonne foi*] and nevertheless deceive himself [*se duper lui-même*], forget important facts, put the facts which he remembers in a wrong [*factice*] order, transfer more recent preoccupations to the past reporter, etc. Every intellectual or sentimental autobiography is prone to such mistakes; and one does not see why Descartes' story alone would be exempt from these mistakes." (My translation)

31 Consider for instance the First Meditation I, AT VII: 18: "I am here quite alone, and at last I will devote myself sincerely and without reservation to the general demolition of my opinions"; and *The Passions of the Soul* I §1, AT XI: 327–328: "And yet the teachings of the ancients about the passions are so meagre [*si peu de chose*] and for the most part so implausible [*si peu croyable*] that I cannot hope to approach the truth except by departing from the paths [*chemins*] they have followed."

32 See Ijsseling 1997: 140–156.

second edition of *Daybreak* and *The Gay Science*, Nietzsche adapts the account of his solitary life to the history of the genesis of his books:

> At that time I undertook something not everyone may undertake: I descended into the depths, I tunnelled into the foundations, I commenced an investigation and digging out of an ancient faith [...]. (D Preface 2)[33]

In other words, Nietzsche does not narrate the biographical details of his existence ("But let us leave Herr Nietzsche: what is it to us that Herr Nietzsche has become well (*gesund*) again?", GS Preface 2). Yet in a similar way as in the *Discourse* (e.g. AT VI: 4), Nietzsche reconstructs and organises some events of his *vita* according to the main topics discussed in *Daybreak* and *The Gay Science* (e.g. morality, the question of health, and the event of the death of God). The purpose of this self-referential account is not only to confer a greater credibility and historical veracity to his philosophical works, but also to illustrate his idea that philosophy transforms existence. These late Prefaces should therefore be read as autobiographical in the sense that they shed light on the complex relation between existence and philosophy.

One should also not forget that the first edition of *Human, All Too Human* I (1878) was prefaced with a passage of the third part of the later Latin translation of the *Discourse* – the third part focuses upon the maxims of the *morale par provision*. The Latin edition was published in 1644 with the title *Dissertatio de Methodo Recte regendæ rationis, & veritatis in scientiis ivestigandæ* (see AT VI: 517–720). This motto is a key passage in as much as Nietzsche uses this Cartesian self-narration in order to situate himself against, or to compare himself with the French model. Here is the famous concluding passage of Descartes' prudent morality:

> I decided to review the various occupations which men have in this life, in order to try to choose the best. Without wishing to say anything about the occupations of others, I thought I could do no better than to continue with the very one I was engaged in, and devote my life to cultivating my reason and advancing as far as I could in the knowledge of the truth, following the method I had felt such extreme contentment that I did not think one could enjoy any sweeter or purer one in this life. Every day I discovered by its means truths which, it seemed to me, were quite important and were generally unknown by other men; and the satisfaction they gave me so filled my mind that nothing else mattered to me. (*Discourse* III, AT VI: 27)[34]

---

[33] KSA 3: 12: "Damals unternahm ich Etwas, das nicht Jedermanns Sache sein dürfte: ich stieg in die Tiefe, ich bohrte in den Grund, ich begann ein altes Vertrauen zu untersuchen und anzugraben [...]."

[34] The German translation of the Latin edition of the *Discourse*, which Nietzsche uses "in place of a Preface", differs slightly from the French original (see footnote 36). It reads as follows

In his interpretation, Rethy[35] rightly suggests that in contrast to Descartes, Nietzsche does not care about a provisory abode while reconstructing the principles of philosophy, as he describes the free spirit as a homeless wanderer (see HH I 638). Probably the most important common point in both self-narratives is the euphoria in the search for truth, the "passion for knowledge" (*Leidenschaft der Erkenntnis*). In this regard, Descartes appears as an example of the free spirit. He writes that seeking knowledge has yielded "the fruits which I had already tasted on this path [and they] were such that, according to my judgment, nothing more agreeable and more innocent could be found in this life".[36] In *Human, All Too Human*, the importance of and pleasure in seeking knowledge ("Pleasure in Knowledge", HH I 252) is a recurrent motive (e.g. HH I 107, 197, 200, 225, 253, 292, 500).[37]

To sum up, Descartes' *Discours* offers a helpful model in interpreting Nietzsche's use of the first-person perspective. In particular, the citation of a passage from the third part of the *Discours* in the first edition of *Human, All Too Human* clearly stresses the importance of the model of the French solitary philosopher in exile. Descartes appears as a free spirit for his "Leidenschaft der Erkenntnis". In the late Prefaces from 1886 onwards, Nietzsche seems to share a similar concern, in as much as the narration of oneself is a kind of argument to demonstrate the transforming power of philosophy.

(KSA 2: 11): "An Stelle einer Vorrede '–eine Zeit lang erwog ich die verschiedenen Beschäftigungen, denen sich die Menschen in diesem Leben überlassen und machte den Versuch, die beste von ihnen auszuwählen. Aber es thut nicht noth, hier zu erzählen, auf was für Gedanken ich dabei kam: genug, dass für meinen Theil mir Nichts besser erschien, als wenn ich streng bei meinem Vorhaben verbliebe, das heisst: wenn ich die ganze Frist des Lebens darauf verwendete, meine Vernunft auszubilden und den Spuren der Wahrheit in der Art und Weise, welche ich mir vorgesetzt hatte, nachzugehen. Denn die Früchte, welche ich auf diesem Wege schon gekostet hatte, waren der Art, dass nach meinem Urtheile in diesem Leben nichts Angenehmeres, nichts Unschuldigeres gefunden werden kann; zudem liess mich jeder Tag, seit ich jene Art der Betrachtung zu Hülfe nahm, etwas Neues entdecken, das immer von einigem Gewichte und durchaus nicht allgemein bekannt war. Da wurde endlich meine Seele so voll von Freudigkeit, dass alle übrigen Dinge ihr Nichts mehr anthun konnten.' Aus dem Lateinischen des Cartesius."

35 Rethy 1976: 289–297 and 294–295.

36 My translation. The French original diverges slightly from the Latin translation: In the French text, Descartes speaks of the "extreme contentments" whereas the Latin edition speaks of the "fruits" of his method of enquiry (*fructus hujus methodi*; see Rethy 1976: 292–293). Here the French original: "J'avais éprouvé de si extrêmes contentements, depuis que j'avais commencé à me servir de cette méthode, que je ne croyais pas qu'on en pût recevoir de plus doux, ni de plus innocents en cette vie [...]." (AT VI: 27)

37 See G. Campioni 2009: 37–39.

However, the emphasis seems to be elsewhere in Nietzsche's autobiography *Ecce Homo*. This posthumous text does not stress so much the transfigurative virtue of philosophy for human life. It is rather the inalterable character of his existence, its destiny (*Verhängniss*) which Nietzsche narrates in his emphatic *vita*:

> The fortunateness of my existence, its uniqueness perhaps, lies in its fatality: to express it in the form of a riddle, as my father I have already died, as my mother I still live and grow old. (EH, Why I am so Wise 1)[38]

In this passage, Nietzsche seems to emphasize the weight of his parents' fate upon his existence. *Prima facie*, this recourse to apparently historical elements of his life distinguishes Nietzsche from Descartes. Whereas Descartes does not consider the presentation of his familial background as appropriate information to understanding his "histoire de [son] esprit",[39] Nietzsche is very loquacious and ambivalent about the determining importance of his parents, in particular of his father for his life (e.g. EH, Why I am so Wise 3–5). On the one hand, Nietzsche considers himself as having inherited heavily from his father (e.g. "I consider the fact that I had such a father as a great privilege [*Vorrecht*]", §3; "I have never understood the art of arousing enmity towards myself [*gegen mich einzunehmen*]–this too I owe to my incomparable father", §4; "In yet another point I am merely my father once more", §5). On the other hand, he refutes the idea that children are akin to their parents. Nietzsche writes in the same chapter "Why I am so Wise" §3 that

> One is least related to one's parents: it would the most extreme sign of vulgarity to be related to one's parents. Higher natures have their origins infinitely farther back, and with them much had to be assembled, saved and hoarded.[40]

In this apparent self-contradicting description of himself, Nietzsche seems to struggle with the task to describe what he, as a philosopher, is in the most

---

38 KSA 6: 264: "Das Glück meines Daseins, seine Einzigkeit vielleicht, liegt in seinem Verhängniss: ich bin, um es in Räthselform auszudrücken, als mein Vater bereits gestorben, als meine Mutter lebe ich noch und werde alt."
39 Descartes refers to his childhood only twice in the *Discours*: "From my childhood I have been nourished upon letters" (AT VI: 5); "a religion in which by God's grace I had been instructed from my childhood" (AT VI: 23). There is no explicit mention of his parents or family in the *Discours*.
40 KSA 6: 268–269: "Man ist am wenigsten mit seinen Eltern verwandt: es wäre das äusserste Zeichen von Gemeinheit, seinen Eltern verwandt zu sein. Die höheren Naturen haben ihren Ursprung unendlich weiter zurück, auf sie hin hat am längsten gesammelt, gespart, gehäuft werden müssen."

genuine way: both a result of hereditary processes and the exact opposite of a kind of genetic influence, both the son of his parents, of his time and era, and the late heir of antecedents, not related by blood. The perfect formulation for this revised genealogy is: "Setting aside the fact that I am a *décadent*, I am also its antithesis [*Gegensatz*]" (§2). In other words, Nietzsche writes both the "histoire de [son] esprit" and the constitution of his instincts (e.g. "my sureness of instinct" [*Instinkt-Sicherheit*], §6; "to attack [*Angreifen*] is among my instincts", §7). By doing so, Nietzsche contends that the Cartesian self-narrative is incomplete. For Nietzsche, the *Discourse* does not sufficiently explain the genesis of the spirit; it does not give a proper account of how Descartes became a philosopher. Put differently – and as mentioned at the beginning of this article – Nietzsche stresses that the highest achievements of the philosopher are not purely of a spiritual nature, but are also rooted in the fabric of the instincts:

> Thus in fact does that long period of sickness seem to me now: I discovered life as it were anew, myself included, I tasted all good and petty things in a way that others could not easily taste them – I made out of my will to health, to life, my philosophy ... For pay heed to this: it was in the years of my lowest vitality that I ceased to be a pessimist: the instinct for self-recovery forbade to me a philosophy of indigence and discouragement ... (EH, Why I am so Wise 2)[41]

Thus, writing in the first-person for the Nietzsche of *Ecce Homo* is a serious philosophical issue. By defining himself as both a decadent and the exact opposite of it, Nietzsche suggests that the narrator of his own life always incorporates second-, third- person and impersonal perspectives into his autobiography. The *ich* is composed out of many less well-known, less conscious layers that the self-narration attempts to articulate into a coherent narrative.

Despite the obvious fact that Descartes' intellectual autobiography is not a recapitulation of his works, but a self-presentation to inaugurate his scientific career, we can perhaps draw a last interesting view shared by both thinkers. The non-transparency of the notion of the Self, as Nietzsche has repeatedly shown – particularly in *Beyond Good and Evil* – against the Cartesian evidence of the *Cogito*, does not however lead Nietzsche to dismiss the Self as being inoperable. For both authors, the sense of oneself remains fundamental in the philosophical

---

[41] KSA 6: 266–267: "So in der That erscheint mir jetzt jene lange Krankheits-Zeit: ich entdeckte das Leben gleichsam neu, mich selber eingerechnet, ich schmeckte alle guten und selbst kleinen Dinge, wie sie Andre nicht leicht schmecken könnten, – ich machte aus meinem Willen zur Gesundheit, zum Leben, meine Philosophie ... Denn man gebe Acht darauf: die Jahre meiner niedrigsten Vitalität waren es, wo ich aufhörte, Pessimist zu sein: der Instinkt der Selbst-Wiederherstellung verbot mir eine Philosophie der Armuth und Entmuthigung ..."

task of writing from the first-person perspective. Consequently it would be more prudent to conclude that for Nietzsche the *ich*, albeit entailing different and even contradicting identities, nevertheless exists as a constitutive instance. One should refrain from generalising Nietzsche's critique of the *Cogito* as being a "falsification" (*Fälschung*) (BGE 17/JGB 17)[42] to his own conception of the Self. One should also not reduce Descartes' conception of the subject to the Cartesian *Cogito*.[43] In this way, one would perhaps be less tempted to oppose Nietzsche to Descartes, but rather to see – as Jean-Luc Marion suggests – in Descartes a thinker to whom Nietzsche comes back time and again, in order to "find his own path of thought" (*pour trouver [son] propre chemin de pensée*).[44]

Conclusion

The aim of the paper was to work out the relevance of Descartes for our understanding of Nietzsche's notion of the Self. Descartes' "superficiality" is a useful criticism for understanding Nietzsche's less transparent notion of the Self. Nietzsche was probably wrong to think that Descartes was "superficial", but he was right to see in Descartes a valuable (anti-)model to think and write about the Self. The general aim of this contribution is evidently not to claim that Descartes is the only thinker one should read to understand Nietzsche better. The recent work done in the *Nietzsche-Forschung* on the relationship between Nietzsche and Kant shows this eloquently.[45] The point was to suggest that reading Descartes' works again for his sake, but also for the sake of clarifying Nietzsche's conception of the Self is a worthwhile detour.

---

[42] BGE 17/JGB 17, KSA 5: 31: "As for the superstition [*Aberglauben*] of the logicians, I shall never tire of underlining a concise little fact which these superstitious people are loath to admit – namely, that a thought comes when 'it' wants, not when 'I' want; so that it is a falsification of the facts [*Fälschung des Thatbestandes*] to say: the subject 'I' is the condition of the predicate 'think'. It thinks: but that this 'it' is precisely that famous old 'I' is, to put it mildly, only an assumption, an assertion, above all not an 'immediate certainty' [*nur eine Annahme, eine Behauptung, vor Allem keine 'unmittelbare Gewissheit'*]."
[43] See in particular J.-L. Marion's recent book, *Sur la pensée passive de Descartes* (Marion 2013: 135–176).
[44] Marion 2013: 12.
[45] See for instance Branco 2013: 497–512, Constâncio 2013: 475–495, Hill 2003, Himmelmann 2005, Riccardi 2010: 333–351 and Siemens 2013: 419–437.

References

Branco, Maria João Mayer (2013) "Musicofobia, musicofilia e filosofia: Kant e Nietzsche sobre a música", in: *Kriterion: Revista de Filosofia* 54/128, 497–512.
Brown, Deborah J. (2006) *Descartes and the Passionate Mind*, Cambridge: Cambridge University Press.
Buzon, Frédéric de (1992) "L'homme et le langage chez Montaigne et Descartes", in: *Revue philosophique de la France et de l'étranger* 1, 451–466.
Campioni, Giuliano (2009) *Der französische Nietzsche*, trans. R. Müller-Buck and L. Schröder, Berlin/New York: De Gruyter.
Camus, Albert (1951) *L'homme révolté*, Paris: Gallimard.
Canziani, G. (1999) "La métaphysique et la vie. Le sujet psychosomatique chez Descartes", in: K. Sang Ong-Van-Cung (ed.), *Descartes et la question du sujet*, Paris: Presses Universitaires de France, 67–91.
Cavaillé, J.-P. (1994) "'Le plus éloquent philosophe des derniers temps'. Les stratégies d'auteur de René Descartes", in: *Annales. Histoire, Sciences Sociales* 49/2, 349–367.
Constâncio, João (2013) "'Quem tem razão, Kant ou Stendhal?' uma reflexão sobre a crítica de Nietzsche à estética de Kant", in: *Kriterion: Revista de Filosofia* 54/128, 475–495.
Descartes, René (1925) *Discours de la méthode*, ed. E. Gilson, Paris: Vrin.
Descartes, René (2008) *The Philosophical Writings of Descartes*, trans. J. Cottingham, R. Stoothoof and D. Murdoch, 3 vols., Cambridge:Cambridge University Press.
Descartes, René (2015) *Der Briefwechsel mit Elisabeth von der Pfalz* [und mit Christina von Schweden sowie Pierre Chanut], French-German, ed. I. Wienand and O. Ribordy, trans. I. Wienand and O. Ribordy, B. Wirz with the collaboration of A. Schiffhauer, Hamburg: Meiner.
Des Chene, D. (2001) *Spirits and Clocks. Machines and Organism in Descartes*, Ithaca: Cornell University Press.
Gilson, E. (1925) Commentaire in: *René Descartes. Discours de la méthode*, Paris: Beauchesne.
Heidegger, Martin (1961) *Nietzsche*, 2 vols., Pfullingen: Neske.
Hill, R. Kevin (2003) *Nietzsche's Critiques: The Kantian Foundations of his Thought*, Oxford: Oxford University Press.
Himmelmann, Beatrix (ed.) (2005) *Kant und Nietzsche im Widerstreit*, Berlin/New York: De Gruyter.
Ijsseling, I. (1997) *Over Voorwoorden. Hegel, Kierkegaard, Nietzsche*, Amsterdam: Boom.
Lampert, L. (1993) *Nietzsche and Modern Times: A Study of Bacon, Descartes, and Nietzsche*, New Haven: Yale University Press.
Loukidelis, N. (2005) "Quellen von Nietzsches Verständnis und Kritik des Cartesischen *cogito, ergo sum*", in: *Nietzsche-Studien* 34, 300–309.
Marion, J.-L. (2013) *Sur la pensée passive de Descartes*, Paris: PUF.
Montaigne, Michel de (1962) *Œuvres complètes*, ed. M. Rat, Paris: Gallimard.
Pippin, Robert B. (2006) *Nietzsche, moraliste français. La conception nietzschéenne d'une psychologie philosophique*, trans. I. Wienand, Paris: Odile Jacob.
Rethy, R. (1976) "The Descartes Motto to the First Edition of *Menschliches, Allzumenschliches*", in: *Nietzsche-Studien* 5, 289–297.
Riccardi, Mattia (2010) "Nietzsche's critique of Kant's thing in itself", in: *Nietzsche-Studien* 39, 333–351.

Shapiro, L. (ed.) (2007) *The Correspondence between Princess Elisabeth of Bohemia and René Descartes*, Chicago: University of Chicago Press.
Siemens, H.W. (2013) "Travando uma Guerra contra a Guerra: Nietzsche contra Kant acerca do conflito", in: *Kriterion: Revista de Filosofia* 54/128, 419–437.
Vivarelli, Vivetta (1994) "Montaigne und der freie Geist", in: *Nietzsche-Studien* 23, 79–101.
Wienand, I./Ribordy, O (2013) "Public and Private Objections to the Cartesian Thesis of Mind-Body Union: The Divergent Replies in Descartes' Letters", in: *Society and Politics* 7, 2/14, 142–159.

David Wollenberg
2 Power, Affect, Knowledge: Nietzsche on Spinoza

Spinoza is not a philosopher who many readers immediately associate with Nietzsche. The two may even appear as bookends to the rationalist enlightenment project. Spinoza once asked, "who but a desperate and insane person would want to say farewell rashly to reason?"[1]; Nietzsche is sometimes considered to have made precisely such a valediction.[2] Spinoza wrote his great work, the *Ethics*, in a 'geometric order', a tightly-constructed philosophic system of propositions and demonstrations; Nietzsche consistently attacked such systems as manifestations of calcified thinking and even intellectual cowardice.[3] Spinoza's political thinking calls for the creation of a strong, even absolute, state; Zarathustra refers to the state as "the coldest of all cold monsters".[4]

However despite these differences and others, Nietzsche embraced Spinoza as a fellow member of "*die ersten Aristokraten in der Geschichte des Geistes*".[5] He consistently included Spinoza in the lists he made of predecessors to his own thought and impact, found in both published and unpublished writings.[6] He even states that Spinoza's blood flows through his own veins.[7] An 1881 postcard to his friend Franz Overbeck expresses his recognition of this affinity in the most emphatic terms of all:

> I am utterly amazed, utterly enchanted! I have a *precursor*, and what a precursor! I hardly knew Spinoza: that I should have turned to him just *now*, was inspired by "instinct." Not only is his over-all tendency like mine – making understanding [*Erkenntnis*] the *most powerful* affect – but in five main points of his doctrine I recognize myself; this most unusual and

---

[1] Spinoza, *Theological-Political Treatise* (henceforth: TTP), ch. 15
[2] A classic exemplar of this view is Habermas 1987. For discussion and critique of this view, see Pippin 1996: 252ff.
[3] He even included Spinoza himself in such attacks (see TI Skirmishes 23).
[4] Moreover, Spinoza's state is preferably a democracy, whereas for Nietzsche democracy is a decadent form of political organization. TTP, chs. 16–20; *Political Treatise* (TP, ch. 2). Nietzsche, Z I, On the New Idols; HH I 472; KSB 8, nr. 1128 (09.10.1888). [Translations from published works by Kaufmann unless otherwise indicated. Translations from Spinoza's *Ethics* by Edwin Curley, trans. *Ethics* (New York: Penguin, 1996) unless otherwise indicated.]
[5] NL 1881 15[17], KSA 9: 642.
[6] For example, see NL 1884 25[454], KSA 11: 134; NL 1881 26[432], KSA 11: 266; AOM 408. These lists of precursors vary in their constituents, but Spinoza is consistently included.
[7] NL 1881 15[17], KSA 9: 642; NL 1881 12[52], KSA 9: 585.

loneliest thinker is closest to me precisely in these matters: he denies the freedom of the will, teleology, the moral world-order, the unegoistic, and evil. Even though the divergences are admittedly tremendous, they are due more to the difference in time, culture, and science. *In summa*: my lonesomeness [*Einsamkeit*], which, as on very high mountains, often made it hard for me to breathe and made my blood rush out, is now at least a twosomeness [*Zweisamkeit*].[8]

This is not to imply that Nietzsche did not have criticisms of Spinoza as well: he did, and they grew more frequent and harsher as the years went on. But these criticisms indicate a thoughtful engagement rather than a summary dismissal. Spinoza remained an important foil for Nietzsche's thought throughout the latter's final productive decade, and it is often in their disagreements that we find the most revealing comments of all.[9] And yet despite the torrent of new Nietzsche scholarship produced each year, the relationship of these two great thinkers remains surprisingly underexplored.[10]

In this chapter, I will first briefly examine Nietzsche's historical contact with Spinoza's philosophy, highlighting what topics interested him the most. I will then explore more precisely both where Nietzsche saw Spinoza as a precursor and where he felt it necessary to part ways. As anyone familiar with his corpus might expect, Nietzsche's views on Spinoza are found in scattered remarks in both the published and unpublished writings, rather than in sustained expositions or polemics.[11] In what follows I hope to show that these remarks, at first sight disparate and unconnected, in fact show tremendous coherence and in composite evidence a sustained reflection on Spinoza's philosophy and its consequences (although Nietzsche's sympathy to that philosophy was to change over time). Spinoza's geometric method systematically unites various sub-disciplines of philosophy – metaphysics, epistemology, ethics, etc. – and I will argue here that exploring Nietzsche's responses to Spinoza enables us to gain a better sense of how these themes are connected for Nietzsche as well. Specifically, Spinoza's philosophy draws a linkage from the striving for power to the affirmation of being itself, two themes also core to Nietzsche's thinking, though rarely explicitly linked by him.

---

[8] KSB 6, nr. 135 (30.07.1881); Nietzsche 1982: 92; translation modified.
[9] An excellent example of this is NL 1886/1887 5[71], KSA 12: 211–217, discussed below. One contemporary who did recognize the Spinoza connection early on was Nietzsche's friend Peter Gast, who compared the two at Nietzsche's funeral. See Gawoll 2001: 50.
[10] I discuss some of this literature in Wollenberg 2013. Some of the older literature on the subject is also discussed in Wurzer 1975.
[11] There are about 65 mentions of Spinoza's name in the KSA, in addition to passages where Spinozan terms of art are mentioned or imitated (e.g. *deus sive natura*, *sub specie aeternitatis*, *amor dei intellectualis*, etc.). The most detailed of these appear in the *Nachlass*, as will be discussed.

As the postcard to Overbeck indicates, the initial point of interest for Nietzsche is not Spinoza's metaphysics (in the sense Spinoza would call the *natura naturans*, 'naturing nature') but rather the power of the affects, and especially the role of will, passions, and understanding in human subjectivity. But in what follows I will show that what begins as an *Auseinandersetzung* about the power of the human affects results in a wide-ranging critique that ends in Nietzsche's articulation of their ultimately conflicting existential visions, a divergence that can be characterized in two terms: *amor dei* and *amor fati*.

The Nietzsche-Spinoza relationship touches on many complex issues, and in this chapter I can only touch briefly on many of them. My goal here is to explore this relationship in its breadth rather than the issues at stake in their depth, as I wish to sketch a sufficiently high-level overview of Nietzsche's entire engagement with Spinoza such that the reader can see the full spectrum – and connectedness – of its themes. Consequently, I will generally refrain from engaging with the scholarly literatures and debates that surround many of the individual philosophical issues at stake, all of which deserve extensive treatment on their own but to which I cannot do full justice without taking us too far afield from the present discussion. In a future book-length study of these two thinkers, I will be further exploring the ramifications of all these issues in more adequate detail. But I believe that for a brief treatment such as this one, taking a wider lens will be revealing: showing how Nietzsche connects questions of psychology and power to broader existential issues in regards to Spinoza allows us to better understand how Nietzsche connects them in his own philosophy as well.

1 Nietzsche's contact with Spinoza's philosophy

Nietzsche mentions Spinoza in his notebooks as early as 1872, the year *Birth of Tragedy* is published, and continues to do so for the remainder of his productive years, with Spinoza's name appearing in nearly every published work from *Human, All Too Human* (1878) until *Twilight of the Idols* and *Antichrist* (1888).[12] But as I have argued in greater detail elsewhere, there is no evidence that Nietzsche ever actually read Spinoza's texts directly: his knowledge appears to have been entirely mediated by secondary literature and conversations with others.[13]

---

[12] The only exceptions are *Zarathustra* and the two Wagner books.
[13] Wollenberg 2013. For Kuno Fischer as Nietzsche's primary source, see also Brobjer 2008: 77ff. and Scandella 2012: 308–332.

We can divide Nietzsche's contact with Spinoza into three periods. During the first period, which extends from 1872 until 1881, Nietzsche's comments on Spinoza are brief (usually just a few words), reveal no specific knowledge of Spinoza's thought beyond what an educated person of the day would know, and are positive in an uncritical way: Spinoza is the "purest sage" and the "knowing genius".[14] During this period Nietzsche would have had exposure to Spinoza's ideas via many of his readings including Goethe, Schopenhauer, Lange, Afrikan Spir, and Eugen Dühring, among others. In addition to his documented correspondence with Overbeck, Spinoza's name was also likely to have arisen in his conversations with Paul Rée and Lou-Andreas Salomé during this period.[15] But the closest we come in this period to an 'engagement' with Spinoza's actual ideas is the occasional recording of an individual quote, such as in 1876 when Nietzsche jots down the famous line from the *Ethics*, "a free man thinks of nothing less than of death, and his wisdom is a meditation on life, not on death".[16] (No commentary from Nietzsche accompanies, however.)

A second period is inaugurated with Nietzsche's reading of Kuno Fisher's *Geschichte der neuern Philosophie: Baruch Spinoza* in 1881. It was this reading that prompted the excited postcard to Overbeck quoted above (Overbeck having sent him the book, upon Nietzsche's request, earlier that year).[17] As the postcard indicates, Nietzsche read enthusiastically, and his notes from this reading of Fischer surpass in extent the total of all his previous comments on Spinoza by far. But for the first time, Nietzsche's remarks also turn critical in a substantive way. Far more than the postcard itself indicates, Nietzsche's notes also express great reservations about the man he has just called his precursor. I will return to these notes in greater detail below. But I wish to point out here that nearly all of Nietzsche's notes from this reading stem from one chapter of Fischer, the

---

14 HH I 157, HH I 475. See also D 497.
15 For further discussion of Nietzsche's contact with Spinoza in these early years, see Wurzer 1975: 38, 52, 68, 88, 141. KSB 5, nr. 291. Gunter Abel believes that Rée's book *Ursprung der moralischen Empfindungen* is the early Nietzsche's primary source for knowledge of Spinoza (Abel 1984: 49).
16 *Ethics* IVP67. NL 1876 19[68], KSA 8: 346. I speculate that Nietzsche took this line from Harold Høffding's *Philosophy of Religion*, Part IV.D. Høffding is also the source of the pseudo-Spinozistic formulation *sympathia malevolens* used in *Genealogy*, GM II 6 (the phrase is not used by Spinoza himself). Similarly in HH I 93 there is a single line from Spinoza's *Political Treatise* (TP II.7), the likely source of which is Schopenhauer's *Parerga and Paralipomena* §124.
17 KSB 6, nr. 123 (8.07.1881). Fischer 1865. Scandella (2012) shows that this was the edition of Fischer that Nietzsche utilized. [References to Kuno Fischer are to his 1865 edition of the *Geschichte der neuern Philosophie, 1 bd., 2 teil: Baruch Spinoza*; translations my own.]

twenty-second, which concerns themes of Spinoza's psychology: the affects, human will, virtue, and power.[18]

Nietzsche appears particularly drawn to Spinoza's model of human subjectivity as being constituted by an agonistic conflict of affects, where one affect can only be supplanted by a stronger one. Active affects of understanding will only drive human action insofar as these overpower the passions, and therefore, to again quote the postcard, a thinker must make "understanding the *most powerful* affect". When Nietzsche brings up Spinoza in *Gay Science* §333, written shortly after first reading Fischer, it is precisely to discuss this concept of an internal struggle of the affects. Similarly, in the years that follow 1881, substantive discussions of Spinoza in the *Nachlaß* consistently address this same topic of the affects.[19]

Nietzsche's receptivity to Spinoza's theory of the affects seems especially apropos in 1881, coming as it did during his writing of the *Gay Science*. That work, together with his two previous works *Human, All Too Human* and *Daybreak*, seek to unearth the genuine motivations for human behavior, which may be far more egoistic, unreasonable, amoral, or even immoral than we credit them as being. But in the years following *Zarathustra*, Nietzsche's writings about human behavior clearly broaden in scope from a psychology of individual motivations to what we might call an archaeology of societal *Weltanschauungen*.[20] It is in this context that a third period of Nietzsche's relationship with Spinoza begins, a phase that is inaugurated when, in Winter 1885–86, Nietzsche asks himself this question in his notebook:

> I saw no one who had ventured a critique of moral value-feelings: and I soon turned my back on the meager attempts made to arrive at a description of the origin of these feelings

---

[18] At first glance, Nietzsche's postcard indicates a familiarity with a wider range of topics: the freedom of the will, teleology, the moral world-order, the unegoistic, and evil. But in fact this list appears to be a paraphrase of a single sentence in Fischer's conclusion, where Fischer remarks that Spinoza denies freedom, the difference between good and evil, self-consciousness, moral ends, and ends in general (Fischer 1865: 550).

[19] Judging from his notes during these years, Nietzsche appears to have mis-read or mis-remembered Fischer as saying that Spinoza posited an independent subject who could freely and intentionally perform the task of displacing the passionate with the reasonable affects. An 1884 note, for example, talks about Spinoza's hypocrisy in saying one could overcome the passions, or have the knowledge to will knowledge. This complaint would persist in Nietzsche's mind, eventually finding published form in BGE 198, which complains of Spinoza's "naïvely advocated destruction of the affects through their analysis and vivisection". See e.g. NL 1884 26[285], KSA 11: 226; NL 1885/1886 2[83], KSA 12:101–103; NL 1888 14[92], KSA 13: 268–270; NL 1888 18[16], KSA 13:536–537.

[20] Foucault's essay "Nietzsche, Genealogy, History" remains the classic treatment of this latter methodology. Published in Foucault 1984: 76–100.

(as by the English and German Darwinists). How can Spinoza's position, his denial and rejection of moral value judgments, be explained? (Was it a consequence of a theodicy?)[21]

In his few remaining productive years following this note, Nietzsche will turn to Spinoza with renewed interest, reading about him in the works of, among others, Liebmann, Lecky, and Höffding. Most importantly, he undertakes a second, fuller reading of Kuno Fischer,[22] which provides the greatest scholarly interest.[23] The notes Nietzsche takes during this second reading of Fischer cover a much broader swath of topics than those of his first, and are sourced from a greater number of chapters including ones concerning including Spinoza's notion of *Deus sive natura* (God *or* nature), teleology, reason, and imagination. Nonetheless, once again, the chapter that draws Nietzsche's greatest interest in terms of quantity and richness of notes is the twenty-second, on the power of the affects. Spinoza's greatest contribution, Nietzsche indicates, is in his understanding of the affects as the power expressions of human nature.[24] Understanding the 'soul' as a fluctuating array of desires, or in Nietzsche's terms a "social structure of drives and affects", has far-reaching consequences for our understanding of action, morality, and the overall orientation toward the world that Spinoza and Nietzsche call *amor dei* and *amor fati*, respectively.[25] Of the three periods, the third is where Nietzsche is least sympathetic to Spinoza. It is nonetheless the most interesting and that wherein Nietzsche offers his most wide-ranging commentary on the epistemological, ontological, and psychological themes of Spinoza's philosophy.

Rather than speculate about what in Spinoza interested Nietzsche given our contemporary understanding of the former's philosophy, I suggest that the more productive approach would be to turn to Nietzsche's notes themselves.[26] In what follows, I will primarily focus on those notes following his second reading of

---

21 NL 1885/1886 2[161], KSA 12: 144. Translation by Kaufmann modified. In this chapter I will not directly address the critique of morality, but see Wollenberg (2013) for further treatment.
22 For a fuller discussion of these late readings, see Wurzer 1975: 128ff.
23 In the case of the others mentioned, we must rely primarily on marginal notes and underlining, a task that presents obvious hermeneutical difficulties. With Fischer, Nietzsche takes longer, more comprehensive notes this second time around than he does in 1881.
24 Fischer, perhaps influencing Nietzsche, expresses the belief that Spinoza's theory of the passions is the *Meisterstück* of his entire philosophy (Fischer 1865: 408).
25 *Ethics* IIIP57; BGE 12.
26 Most scholars, however, have taken the first approach and ignored Fischer. See e.g. Yovel 1992, Schacht 1995, and Della Rocca 2008, all of whom discuss the Nietzsche-Spinoza relationship without any discussion of Fischer's influence. The one exception of note is Scandella (2012), but as that author notes, his study is meant to be more "preliminary" in nature, i.e. more focused on proving that Fischer was Nietzsche's primary source for Spinoza, than is the present chapter.

Fischer, which constitute his most extensive treatment of Spinoza by far.[27] These notes cover many themes, not always in an orderly fashion. I believe we can group nearly all of them as falling into two broad, interdependent categories[28]: 1) the identification of virtue and power, and in particular the power of the affects; and 2) the identification of the most powerful affects with understanding and affirmation, particularly in Spinoza's 'intellectual love of God'. I will structure the remainder of this chapter around these two themes. (And henceforth by 'Spinoza' I will mean specifically Fischer's Spinoza, without commentary as to the accuracy of his interpretation.[29])

2 Nietzsche's engagement with Spinoza

2.1 Virtue and power

In Nietzsche's 1887 notes, he summarizes Spinoza's virtue theory as follows:

> The natural-egoistic perspective: virtue and power are identical. It does not abjure, it desires, it struggles not against but for nature; it is not the annihilation, but the emancipation, of the most powerful affects. Good is what furthers our power: evil the opposite. Virtue follows from the striving toward self-preservation.[30]

There is much in these few dense sentences that needs to be unpacked. To do so, let us take a step back and look at Spinoza's philosophy of power to which Nietzsche's comments relate.

Spinoza first presents a closed, mechanical universe, strictly determined by cause-and-effect, and shorn of *teloi* or a freely-intervening, super-natural God.

---

27 See KSA 12, 7[4]. This long note includes comments about thinkers beyond Spinoza as well, especially Kant, primarily derived from his readings in Chur in the summer of 1887. These reflect an interest in similar themes, especially the relation of *Erkenntnis* and activity.
28 The most significant group of comments that do not fall directly into these two categories relate to the conscience and form the basis for the discussion in *Genealogy*, GM II 15. However I believe even these remarks are not entirely unconnected to the connection between understanding and affirmation, as I discuss in Wollenberg 2013.
29 To assist the reader, who will likely be more familiar with – and have easier access to – the *Ethics* itself than to Fischer's work, I will frequently directly cite propositions of the *Ethics* to which Fischer is referring. My doing so should not be understood as an attempt to cite the 'actual' Spinoza in contrast to Fischer's, but rather as an aid to the reader who wishes to follow Fischer's discussion by means of Spinoza's text.
30 NL 1887 7[4], KSA 12: 259–270.

He then declares that he will present man as being no different from other individual things in this universe, treating "human actions and appetites just as if it were a question of lines, planes, and bodies".[31] All things are thus essentially understood within the context of deterministic nature. His presentation could be characterized in words that Nietzsche once used for his own philosophy: "the de-anthropomorphizing of nature and the re-naturalizing of man".[32]

Individuals – human and otherwise – are defined for Spinoza not by their component parts (which can be replaced without an essential loss of identity[33]) but rather by a fundamental striving often referred to in the literature as the *conatus*.[34] To quote Spinoza's own definition, "each thing, so much as is in it, strives to persevere in its being".[35] This doctrine should not be understood as one of self-preservation in an entirely reactive sense, i.e. as merely a response to threats: as Fischer emphasizes, this tendency is both "the preservation of our being and the increase of our power".[36] All human behavior expresses a constant striving to increase the *potentia agendi*, the power of acting. And since for Spinoza the human individual is equally mind and body, this includes the *potentia cogitandi* as well: even our ideas and imaginations should be understood fully as expressions of this striving.[37]

The conatus doctrine characterizes all individual things in nature, i.e. it is as much a physical principle as a psychological one. If human beings appear to be acting differently than other natural things, this is due not to some qualita-

---

[31] *Ethics* IIIPref.
[32] "*die Entmenschung der Natur und dann die Vernatürlichung des Menschen*" (NL 1881 11[211], KSA 9: 525; See also GS 109). Their affinity in this project was noted by Nietzsche himself, who in a note describes his own position as "*chaos* sive natura: von der *Entmenschlichung der Natur*" (NL 1881 11[197], KSA 9: 519). I will return to this idea of "*chaos* sive natura" below.
[33] *Ethics* IIP13L4. The converse is true as well: Spinoza gives the example of a Spanish poet who, despite maintaining an effectively identical body, could no longer be considered the same individual following a psychological affliction that altered him dramatically (*Ethics* IVP37S). In Spinoza there is another element of individuality that he calls the ratio of motion and rest (see *Ethics* IIP13L1 and what follows) but there is no evidence that Nietzsche read this part of Fischer's discussion.
[34] From the Latin, *Conatus ... nihil est praeter ipsius rei actualem essentiam* ("The striving ... is nothing but the actual essence of the thing") (*Ethics* EIIIP7).
[35] *Ethics* IIIP6. The Latin "*quantum in se est*" is translated by Curley as "as far as it can by its own power". I have tried above to be closer to Fischer's more literal translation, "*ein jedes Ding, so viel an ihm ist, strebt in seinem Sein zu beharren*" (Fischer 1865: 352).
[36] Fischer 1865: 502.
[37] *Ethics* IIP21, IIIP12, IIIP54. Fischer translates *potentia* with a variety of German terms including *Macht*, *Kraft*, *Fähigkeit*, and *Vermögen*. It appears to me that he uses the German terms interchangeably.

tive difference in the human soul, but rather to the more complex nature of human bodies. A consequence of this more complex nature is that the conatus of a human being can be expressed in an incredibly diverse range of psychological or affective forms. The full gamut of affects that characterize human life – love, remorse, scorn, gratitude, etc. – follows as a more intricate manifestation of the fundamental striving.[38] As Fischer puts this point, the "affects are the power expressions of human nature".[39] Nietzsche's greatest interest in Spinoza centers on this theme. Fischer, in the chapter of his book that Nietzsche twice read so carefully, goes to great length expounding how the range of emotions in all their apparent heterogeneity in fact follow from this one *Grundform* of affect, namely the striving for an increase in power.[40]

This *Grundform* of affect corresponding to an increase in power is defined as *joy*. Its reverse, the decrease in power, *sadness*. These affects of joy and sadness express the *transition* from one state to another, not those posterior states themselves. Thus, men do not strive toward joy as an end, but rather toward increased power, and experience joy in their increasing it.[41] What complicates one's continual experience of joy is that one's striving is continually hindered and deflected by one's external encounters (other individuals are all simultaneously striving in this same manner). As in Newtonian mechanics, the interactions of striving individuals can result in a determinative reaction by each.[42] To the degree that an individual is consequently determined as a result of such encounters with external forces, rather than acting as the adequate cause of his own actions, he is said to be suffering passions.[43] Spinoza calls this condition servitude or slavery (*Knechtschaft*).[44] Passions can be, though are not necessarily, sad, i.e. indicative of a decrease in one's power of acting. All genuine 'activity', by contrast, expresses the individual's own striving for power, rather than determination by external forces, and is necessarily joyous.[45]

---

38 So for example 'love' is defined as "joy with an accompanying idea of an external cause" (*Ethics* IIIP13C). The appendix to *Ethics* III presents a laundry list of such extrapolations from the fundamental striving.
39 Fischer 1865: 485. Compare to KSA 12, 10[133].
40 Fischer 1865: 502.
41 Fischer 1865: 354ff.
42 Fischer 1865: 337ff. In the heart of the *Ethics*'s discussion of the human mind, Spinoza engages in a long digression on the mechanics of bodily interactions (following *Ethics* IIP13).
43 Fischer 1865: 350ff. Because one is necessarily only a part of nature, Spinoza is clear that all individuals necessarily must suffer some passions (*Ethics* IVP4).
44 I compare Spinoza's slavery with the case of Nietzsche's slaves in GM in Wollenberg 2013.
45 Fischer 1865: 382; *Ethics* IIIP59.

To the degree one is active rather than passive, one's striving can be entitled *virtuous*.[46] As Fischer writes, "in Spinoza there is no other virtue besides capability [*Tüchtigkeit*] or power [*Macht*]. Its opposite is not vice, but powerlessness ... But if virtue is the greatest power, so is it necessarily the object of the strongest desire ... because there is nothing that is as desire-worthy as it."[47] This concept of virtue provides a criterion by which to ground a naturalistic value standard: that which increases our actual power of acting is objectively good.

Such a virtue theory obviously stands in sharp contrast to the dominant ideologies of Spinoza's day, which posited virtue in meekness. Fischer contrasts Spinoza's order of values to traditional ones in even more explicit terms than does Spinoza himself, terms that will be immediately recognizable to readers of Nietzsche:

> Good or bad [in Spinoza's sense] are those affects which either advance or inhibit human power [*Macht*]. They are as real as the capacity [*Vermögen*] of human nature. Good and evil, in the sense of customary morality, are arbitrary, and therefore imaginary and unclear representations. Thus the judgments of this morality, which speaks always only about good and evil actions, are baseless and vacuous, because they create their predicates from the imagination and attribute to phenomena what does not in fact accord with them.[48]

These latter values of good and evil are imaginary, and in their most common form, theological, are the subject of attack by both Spinoza and Nietzsche. These latter values entail imperfection in the world, i.e. that the world would be better if it were somehow other than how it is. By positing standards of value external to the world, they are necessarily world denying. But Spinoza, like Nietzsche, is not "beyond good and bad"; the values of good and bad correlate to an actual increase in the power of acting.[49] And because such an increase is defined according to objective, naturalistic standards, rather than any product of the human *imaginaire*, living virtuously in Spinoza's sense necessarily involves an affirmation of the world as it is.[50]

---

46 *Ethics* IVD8; Fischer 1865: 506.
47 Fischer 1865: 483. Fischer even goes so far as to say that, for Spinoza, this virtue is our end [*Zweck*], a disputable claim but one that may explain Nietzsche's insistence of Spinoza's inconsistency on this matter. See Fischer 1865: 484; BGE 13.
48 Fischer 1865: 510.
49 GM I 17. Although Nietzsche is admittedly not always consistent on the matter, he at least sometimes attests that "there is nothing to life that has value, except the degree of power" (NL 1886/1887 5[71], KSA 12: 211–217).
50 There can be no affirmation of evil, for evil is nothing. The world could not be otherwise than it is and thus has no imperfections. As such, the idea of evil has no positive component to it (Fischer 1865: 208–210).

In broad strokes Nietzsche was sympathetic to this picture. In the *Genealogy*, of course, he himself famously contrasts the noble, world-affirming values of good and bad with the slavish, world-denying values of good and evil.[51] As with Spinoza, such values are considered expressive of our natures, not the product of a free choice.[52] It is essentially characteristic of the weak to affirm not this world but a 'better' one, and to posit their weakness as a voluntary choice rather than as a determined expression of who, and what, they essentially are. And again like Spinoza, Nietzsche connects power with happiness and activity, and elsewhere in this period with virtue as well.[53]

For readers of this book, Spinoza's focus on individuals' essential striving to increase in power will likely be evocative of Nietzsche's own claims about an essential will to power. Like Spinoza, Nietzsche at times presents will to power as the fundamental impulse underlying the change in all things, human or otherwise, while at other times he presents it as a monocausal physiological (or psychological) explanation for human action.[54] Did Nietzsche take an interest in Spinoza's affect theory because he saw it as a proto-form of his own philosophy of power? Any comparison of the two doctrines is obviously complicated by the fact that in his published works, Nietzsche's discussions of will to power tend to be oblique and relatively sparse, and it is thus challenging to exposit the theory with the nuance Nietzsche may have intended by it.[55] The most sustained expositions come from the late notebooks, especially those of 1888, where Nietzsche offers relatively lengthy reflections on what it would mean to understand will to power as being the *Grundform* of a variety of phenomena, including knowledge, art, morality, life, etc. Given Nietzsche's interest specifically in Spinoza's affec-

---

[51] This is not to imply that Nietzsche simply associates himself with the nobles' position. I have discussed the apparent avenues of influence of Fischer on the *Genealogy* in Wollenberg 2013.
[52] GM I 13.
[53] GM I 10, NL 1887 10[32], KSA 12: 472. I would especially draw the reader's attention to NL 1887/1888 11[54], KSA 13: 24–27, where Nietzsche offers a preface to a work entitled "Von der Herrschaft der Tugend. Wie man der Tugend zur Herrschaft verhilft. Ein tractatus politicus von Friedrich Nietzsche". Not only is *tractatus politicus* the name of one of Spinoza's works, but in this preface Nietzsche contrasts his own view with those who view the world *sub specie boni*, a teleological position the refutation of which Nietzsche associates with Spinoza in the notes following his second reading of Fischer.
[54] For the former, see NL 1885 38[12], KSA 11: 610–611. For the latter, consider e.g. BGE 13.
[55] Despite the great association of Nietzsche with the phrase 'will to power', Nietzsche's statements concerning it in his published works are admittedly complex, often marked by ironic overtones, and beyond what I can discuss here. For a discussion of this complexity see Pippin 1999: 97f. However in his late notebooks Nietzsche does make more extended efforts to extrapolate the notion, and it is these efforts that are illuminating for our purposes here.

tive psychology, the most fitting place to make a comparison of the two authors would be Nietzsche's passage exploring will to power as a psychological principle. Nietzsche lays out his thoughts there as follows:

> That the will to power is the primitive affect-form, that all other affects are its elaborations [*Ausgestaltung*]:
>
> That it is a substantial elucidation to posit power instead of individual happiness as that toward which all living things are supposed to be striving: "a thing strives toward power, toward increase of power" – pleasure [*Lust*] is only a symptom of the feeling of achieved power, a consciousness of difference –
>
> – a thing does not strive toward pleasure, but rather pleasure occurs, when what one strives for is achieved: pleasure accompanies, pleasure is not the motive …
>
> That all impelling force is will to power, that there are no other additional physical, dynamic, or psychological forces.[56]

Laid out in these terms, Nietzsche's doctrine sounds very similar to Spinoza's. Both take a monocausal view of the striving to increase power as the fundamental human affect, with all other affects following therefrom. Both understand joy as the affect corresponding to an actual increase in power (Fischer himself using the German *Lust* to translate Spinoza's *laetitia*[57]). And yet Nietzsche follows this train of thought by, of all things, an attack on Spinoza's understanding of causal determinism:

> In our science, where the concept of cause and effect is reduced to an equality-relation, with the ambition to prove that on each side lies the same quantity of force, the driving force is missing [*felht die treibende kraft*] … It is a simple matter of experience that change never ceases: intrinsically we do not have the least ground to understand that one change must follow upon another. On the contrary, an achieved condition would appear forced to preserve itself, if it did not have in it the capacity [*Vermögen*] to seek to not preserve itself …
>
> Spinoza's principle of self-preservation should put a halt to all change: but the principle is false, the opposite is true. With all living things it is quite clear to show that they act not to preserve themselves, but to become *more* …[58]

How should we understand Nietzsche's criticism of Spinoza here? Nietzsche knows that Spinoza's *conatus* includes more than a static notion of self-preser-

---

[56] NL 1888 14[121], KSA 13: 300. Ellipses in original. The phrase in quotes is not attributed. Compare BGE 36 for a similar extrapolation regarding the affects.
[57] E.g. Fischer 1865: 432. Other times Fischer uses *Freude*. (His choice of which word to use in any instance appears arbitrary.)
[58] NL 1888 14[121], KSA 13: 300–301. Ellipses in original.

vation; he had himself written in his notebook a quote from Fischer, "what we do, we do to preserve *and increase* our power".[59] Moreover, the latter part of this note, attacking the possibility of a genuine understanding of cause-and-effect as well as the principle of self-preservation, appears at first glance to be almost a non sequitur unrelated to the earlier part of the note concerned with elaborating human psychology as a manifestation of the will to power.

However, when we take a more holistic view of Nietzsche's comments on Spinoza we see that this is very much *not* a non-sequitur. The notes show that over the years Nietzsche had engaged in serious reflections on Spinoza's theory of the affects and its consequences. By at least 1887 if not earlier, Nietzsche shows particular interest in the way that striving for power is intricately linked for Spinoza with a striving for understanding, and specifically for understanding cause and effect. For Spinoza, this understanding leads to a position of affirmation called *amor dei intellectualis*. As we will see, Nietzsche also proceeds from the will to power to an affirmative position, what he terms *amor fati*, and it is in the light of Spinoza's philosophy that Nietzsche navigates his path from the former to the latter.

2.2 Power, rationality, and affirmation

To understand Nietzsche's critique we need to more carefully explore Spinoza's theory of power in order to see the implications of Spinoza's affect theory on his claims about rationality and knowledge. Doing so will allow us to bridge the lacuna in the line of reasoning in the fragment quoted above, and see how Nietzsche connected Spinoza's affect theory to much broader themes about knowledge and life.

To quote again from Nietzsche's notes following his second reading of Fischer:

> The idiosyncratic thinker reveals himself: Understanding [*Erkenntnis*] becomes master over all the other affects; it is stronger. "Our true activity consists in our thinking nature, in reasonable contemplation. The desire for activity = the desire to live reasonably."[60]

For Nietzsche, where Spinoza specifically goes wrong in his theory of power is in this assertion, namely that true human activity is expressed in reasonable understanding (in Fischer's translation *Erkenntnis*).[61] We must therefore dig a

---

59 Fischer 1865: 484; NL 1887 7[4], KSA 12: 259–270; emphasis added.
60 NL 1887 7[4], KSA 12: 259–270. Quotation marks in original.
61 Nietzsche complained even in 1881, "*Wie phantasirt Spinoza über der Vernunft!*" (NL 1881 11[132], KSA 9: 490). Fischer uses the words *Vernunft*, *Verstand*, and *Erkenntnis* fairly inter-

little deeper into Spinoza's claim. Why must the 'free man', the model of human life, be essentially rational for Spinoza? As Nietzsche's note records, activity, understanding, and power are all linked for Spinoza. If the premise of Spinoza's virtue theory obtains, that the most valuable affects are by definition the most powerful ones, then Spinoza's case for rationality depends on his ultimately being able to show that the active, reasonable affects are indeed the strongest. Fischer explains this point well while simultaneously posing the question that Nietzsche also seizes upon:

> Our activity is our capability [*Tüchtigkeit*], our virtue ... Our true activity consists in our thinking, in reasonable reflection [*Betrachtung*]. The desire for activity is equally the desire to live reasonably and to act, to not affirm anything except the reasonable life both for ourselves and for others. ... Thus the ethical life follows necessarily from the active affects. ... The active affects will necessarily overthrow the passions when they are more powerful than those are, because each essence, thus also human nature, strives to be as powerful as possible. ... Spinoza's ethical teaching therefore depends on this point. The question of concern is: are the active affects more powerful than the passions?[62]

It is this final question that bothers Nietzsche so much about Spinoza's thought: why does rational thought *necessarily* imply an increase in power? In his 1881 notes to Fischer, he understands Spinoza to be providing a somewhat utilitarian answer to this question: reasonable behavior engages with the world in a manner more beneficial to us than does passionate behavior. As he writes in his notebook, people "cannot be more united than when they live reasonably. They cannot be more powerful than when they agree completely".[63] Though Spinoza believes we are always striving for power, the presence of passions inhibits the capability of our striving by deviating it toward the foolish pursuit of transient and imaginary goods.[64] But reasonable understanding, insofar as we can achieve it, allows us to escape this condition, and to will what is truly good for us given our natures. For the lone individual, reason weakens the power of the passions,

---

changeably, with a tendency to use "*adäquate Erkenntnis*" to describe the highest use of reason. In NL 1887 7[4], KSA 12: 259–270 Nietzsche generally uses *Erkenntnis*, and to avoid using inconsistent terminology myself I will follow his lead.

62 Fischer 1865: 383–384.
63 NL 1881 11[193], KSA 9: 517–518.
64 Because reason is not independent from will, it is not the case that we judge with our reason that something is good, and therefore will it (or fail to will it because of some kind of akrasia). Rather, "we judge something to be good because we strive for it, will it, want it, and desire it" (*Ethics* IIIP9). Therefore insofar as our striving is inhibited by passions, our judgments of what truly constitute our true goods become misdirected.

which toss men about "like waves on the sea".[65] For human society, moreover, reason leads men to be harmonious with one another, and society is at its most powerful when its members are united in common purpose. (Hence Spinoza's philosophy may be egoistical but it is not necessarily on that account megalomaniacal.)[66] Because Spinoza's virtue theory is oriented around increasing one's power of action, the more beneficial outcomes of these reasonable engagements with the world would by themselves indicate why Spinoza would consider reason more valuable than the passions. Reason estimates according to valuations of what is truly good and bad for us; the passions, on the other hand, by imaginary valuations of 'good and evil'. An increase in one's understanding of the world as it is thus necessitates a striving for preservation and power more in accordance with one's true good. And so, because the mind necessarily strives to increase power, the mind's activity will be in accordance with reason. It is only passions that impede this striving, and lead to irrational, detrimental behavior.

But Nietzsche's 1887 notes focus on a second, more fundamental reason why Spinoza links activity and reason, one more ontological than utilitarian. As Nietzsche notes, in Spinoza's view "the highest good is the understanding of the unity of our intellect with the universe".[67] For Spinoza, reasonable ideas are possible because the human mind is a mode of God's infinite power of thinking.[68] As such, there is a certain harmony between the order of rational ideas and the order of things. The mind's rational production of ideas tracks the same causal logic that underlies the efficient causality of nature itself. Because both rational ideas and the order of things follow in parallel fashion from God's essence, for a thing *to be* necessarily means for that thing *to be intelligible*.

The mind genuinely *acts* insofar as its ideas truly express this power of thinking, which, following from a true understanding of nature, is inherently reasonable. The order of nature follows fixed and eternal laws; rational thinking

---

65 *Ethics* IIIP59S. Spinoza discusses the power of reason against the passions especially in *Ethics* V P1–20.
66 These social benefits to living reasonably are especially discussed in the latter half of *Ethics* IV, as well scattered places in the political writings (e.g. the preface to the *Theological-Political Treatise*, TTP).
67 NL 1887 7[4], KSA 12: 259–270. Emphasis in original.
68 To quote Spinoza's own words, "when we say that the human mind perceives this or that, we are saying nothing but that God ... insofar as he is explained through the nature of the human mind ... has this or that idea" (*Ethics* IIP11C). See also IIP43S; Fischer 1865: 428ff. Spinoza himself recognizes the difficulty of this idea and asks his reader's forbearance for not immediately explaining this idea sufficiently (*Ethics* IIP11S). I must ask the same of mine. For a more detailed study of Spinoza's modal metaphysics than I will offer here, see Melamed 2013.

is expressed in adequate understanding of those laws and therefore of God's infinite and eternal essence.[69] It is only the interference of passions that inhibits this thinking and leads to unreasonable imagination.[70] But passions – and this is a fundamental principle for Spinoza – do not express anything positive of the mind's essence. They are an adventitious hindrance to the power of thinking that has resulted from an external encounter.[71] As Fischer puts this relation between reason, power, and activity:

> My capability [*Tüchtigkeit*] is manifest in that which I, with my own force [*Kraft*] alone, perform, my weakness in that which others bring about with me or in me. Therefore human virtue consists in understanding. Understanding is virtue, virtue is power [*Macht*], power is nature, which as its own law obeys no one and acts on its own force [*Kraft*]. So the understanding follows from human nature as it fulfills its law. The human being, insofar as he thinks clearly and distinctly, acts according to the capacity [*Vermögen*] of its nature exactly as virtuously as does the sun in its shining.[72]

The mind's reasonable understanding of the world is essentially virtuous and therefore necessarily joyous. Reason is thus qualitatively different from, and necessarily superior to, the passions.[73]

Because the themes of rationality and affirmation are so tightly linked in Nietzsche's response to Spinoza, I will proceed immediately to Fischer's presentation of the latter, and then discuss Nietzsche's response to both themes together. For as Nietzsche joined them in his notes,

> Spinoza believes he understood everything absolutely. In doing so, he has the greatest feeling of power [...] The consciousness of this "understanding" persists [*hält bei ihm an*]: a love of God results from it, a joy in existence as it is, in all existence.[74]

---

69 As Spinoza boldly declares in *Ethics* IIP47. See especially Fischer 1865: 316ff.
70 See Fischer 1865: 495ff. For a contemporary account of Spinoza's theory of imagination (and knowledge more broadly) see Wilson 2007: 89–141.
71 Fischer 1865: 350ff.
72 Fischer 1865: 506–507.
73 There are of course more nuances to Spinoza's theory than I have laid out here: if active affects of reason were *ipso facto* more powerful than the passions, then the latter would pose minimal threat to reasonable life, and a book like the *Ethics* would not be necessary. But just as strong men can be overwhelmed by a group of weaker men, so too can reasonable affects come to be inhibited by passions. The development of the mind is not a progressive *Aufhebung* from passion to reason but rather an endless agonistic struggle. Opposed affects, oriented toward conflicting goods, cannot mutually persist unchanged alongside one another. One must eliminate the other, and it is the strength of the affect – not necessarily its correspondence with truth – that makes it victorious. The victory of reason is by no means inevitable. The *Ethics* is a tool to help bring about such a victory.
74 NL 1887 7[4], KSA 12: 259–270.

Spinoza's primary ethical claim is that the greatest good for mankind is in the activity of reason, specifically in the love of God and affirmation of being that follows from the mind's intuitive understanding of God's essence. As discussed above, rational understanding for Spinoza is inherently joyous, and because we seek increased power we *necessarily* affirm and will the product of ratiocination, which is increased knowledge of the world. As Fischer summarizes this, "the act of understanding implies the act of willing in itself".[75] Conversely, any understanding of the world other than a rational one is necessarily world-denying, an affirmation of the objects of imagination. The passions have no positive element to them and therefore any attempted affirmation of passionate ideas reflects an affirmation of nothing. Such an affirmation of non-rational ideas would thus constitute, to use a non-Spinozan term, nihilism.

In rational thinking one understands that all of nature has been necessarily determined to be exactly as it is; as such there is nothing about the world that the mind strives to negate. Counter to those thinkers (including Descartes[76]) who claim that the will is wider than the intellect, and that we are ultimately free to will independently from what the intellect presents, Spinoza claims that will and intellect are identical. Will is nothing but the mind's striving for power, and given that increased understanding implies an increased power of thinking, we inherently will the fruits of reasonable thought. (Only passions inhibit or deflect this willing.) In striving for an understanding of nature, one therefore also strives at the same time to be, as Nietzsche once put it, "only a yes-sayer".[77] Rationality is inherently affirmative because to understand the world is to will it.

Understanding is a joyous activity, and because in Spinoza's jargon "joy with the accompanying idea of an external cause" defines love, an understanding of the 'eternal essence' of God or nature can be characterized as *amor dei intellectualis*.[78] Spinoza's affirmative stance toward being rests on this founda-

---

75 Fischer 1865: 480. Now the mind, to be sure, is capable of both rational ideas and also confused ideas caused by the senses and other influences. Experience, because of its randomness, can lead to such confused ideas. Illusion and self-deception thus express a kind of deformed will, the situation Spinoza terms slavery.

76 Descartes's position is in my opinion more in line with our everyday intuitions than is Spinoza's. "The intellect ... enable[s] me to perceive the ideas which are subjects for possible judgments ... the will simply consists in our ability ... to affirm or deny, to pursue or avoid ... when the intellect puts something forward for affirmation or denial or pursuit or avoidance." "Fourth Meditation", in Descartes 2007, II: 39–40.

77 GS 276. This is the first aphorism of GS IV, written immediately after Nietzsche's 1881 reading of Fischer.

78 Fischer records this thought in Spinoza's own Latin: "*Amor dei intellectualis sive cognitio aeternae essentiae*" (Fischer 1865: 544).

tion. As one understands God, one loves God, and moreover this intellectual love of God, effectively synonymous with the highest use of reason, is man's greatest good.[79] To quote Fischer's words on this matter: "We are one with the eternal order of things when we affirm its necessity; we affirm it as soon as we understand [einsehen] it. Thus is our love of God most firmly grounded on our understanding of God, that is, that the human intellect is one with the whole."[80] Such love is, in the famous phrase, *sub specie aeternitatis*: it affirms things not in terms of the durational, sensuous relationship we might have with them, but as we rationally understand them to follow from the necessity of God's eternal nature.[81] A life that follows from such love of God is the greatest (really the only truly good) life a person can live. Because it knows and affirms the world as it is in its innermost necessity, it is the life of the free man, for such a person is free of the passions that confuse the mind and lead to imaginations that the world could be otherwise than how it is.

Following each of his readings of Fischer, Nietzsche recorded comments about how for Spinoza rational ideas are both qualitatively different from, and unambiguously better than, passionate ones. However, his critique, to which we now turn, does not rest on a simplistic dichotomy: Spinoza the 'rationalist' who rejects the passions versus Nietzsche the 'irrationalist' who rejects reason *tout court*. Rather, for Nietzsche, Spinoza has fundamentally mischaracterized what reason (and therefore affirmation) entails.

Nietzsche's reception of Spinoza's rationalism trends increasingly unsympathetic over the course of the 1880s, with comments that become more fleshed out and, I believe, more interesting, as the years go on. Early in the decade, around the end of what I have called the first period of Nietzsche's engagement with Spinoza, his tone toward Spinoza's rationalism is consistently positive, and he praises Spinoza precisely for his commitment to *Erkenntnis*. *Daybreak* (1881) praises men of understanding like Spinoza for adding beauty to the world, and the 1881 postcard to Overbeck asserts an affinity with Spinoza precisely in a mutual tendency to make understanding the most powerful affect.[82] By contrast, only a half-decade later, in the 'third period', he criticizes Spinoza for too naively linking understanding with happiness.[83] In his latter Fischer notes of 1887, he records quotes with strong claims about the power of reason only to

---

79 See especially *Ethics* VP15, VP20.
80 Fischer 1865: 178.
81 See especially *Ethics* VP29.
82 D 550; KSB 6, nr. 135.
83 NL 1885/1887 2[131], KSA 12: 129–132.

follow them by multiple exclamation marks and strongly pejorative commentary.[84] In these latter years, one increasingly finds Nietzsche describing Spinoza and his thought with terms like "poison-brewer" and "hocus pocus".[85]

But much more interesting than the trend toward negativity is the dramatically widening *scope* of Nietzsche's comments about Spinoza from the second to the third period. What characterizes the comments of the second period is that they look at questions of knowledge and rationality in the light of individual motivations.[86] In the third period, by contrast, Nietzsche connects Spinoza's thinking about rationality to much broader themes of metaphysics and one's essential orientation toward the world. What is important about these later comments, far more than their negative tone, is that they recognize that a metaphysical psychology underlies Spinoza's affect theory. Spinoza's psychology is grounded in his ontology, and thus his views on rationality have, for Nietzsche, troubling implications for what is involved in world affirmation.

Following the second reading of Fischer, Nietzsche offers synthesized reflections on Spinoza's linking of power, understanding, and the affirmative stance toward being the latter calls *amor dei intellectualis*:

> Spinoza believes he understood everything absolutely. In doing so, he has the greatest feeling of power. This drive had overwhelmed and obliterated all other drives. The consciousness of this "understanding" does not stop with it: a kind of "love of God" results therefrom, a joy in existence as it is, in all existence. From where do all moods arise, sadness, fear, hate, envy? From one source: from our love of transient things. With this love [i.e. of God], the entire category of such desires [i.e. for particular things] vanishes. [...]
>
> When, in the last account, everything happens by virtue of the divine power, so is everything perfect in its way, so is there nothing ugly [*Übel*] in the nature of things; if man is

---

84 NL 1887 7[4], KSA 12: 259–270.
85 BGE 5, BGE 25. This trend occurs in the context of a broader transformation in Nietzsche that distinguishes the so-called positivistic period of the turn of the 1880s from the post-Zarathustra period, a development beyond the scope of this chapter. Let it suffice to say here that this general trend should not be understood as a dichotomy, with the early period simply celebrating rationalism while the latter disdains it. Both periods indicate a complex relationship to reason that deflates its capability while recognizing its centrality for life nonetheless. For more discussion see Magnus/Higgins 1996: 21–68.
86 For example, in *Gay Science* (1882), Nietzsche attacks supposedly sober rationalists as in fact hiding inner passions; he dismisses as "error" those who believe that "in science one possessed and loved something unselfish, harmless, self-sufficient, and truly innocent, in which man's evil impulses had no part whatever–the main motive of Spinoza who felt divine when attaining knowledge." GS 37, GS 57. See also, for example, NL 1883 7[131], KSA 10: 286;NL 1883 8[17], KSA 10: 340; NL 1884 26[3], KSA 11:151; NL 1884 26[280], KSA 11: 223–224; all of which concern individuals seeking truth, certainty, and understanding.

entirely unfree, so is there nothing evil in the nature of the human will; so are ugliness and evil not in things, but rather only in the human imagination.[87]

Although one can occasionally find similar-sounding comments from Nietzsche himself,[88] he goes on in this note to deride Spinoza's so-called affirmation as in fact a kind of world denial. He writes that Spinoza's dismissal of transient things is a "disdainful rejection" of life's goods, while what Spinoza calls the clear thinking of reason is disparaged as a "perpetual slander of everything, in order to bring unity to the highest heights in clear thinking".[89] Such comments are in line with the general trend in which Spinoza has transformed from being the "purest sage" to being naïve, hateful, engaged in self-mockery, and offering a consumptive philosophy.

But is Nietzsche's characterization of Spinoza's stance toward existence, as evidenced in the above quote, so truly different from what Nietzsche will himself praise in his own name less than two years later?

> Such a spirit who has *become free* stands amid the cosmos with a joyous and trusting fatalism, in the *faith* [*Glauben*] that only the particular is loathsome, and that all is redeemed and affirmed in the whole – *he does not negate any more*. Such a faith, however, is the highest of all possible faiths: I have baptized it with the name of *Dionysus*.[90]

Such formulations offering deep praise for affirmation as the goal of thinking are frequent in the late Nietzsche, and in them we find another hint of Spinozan influence. As he puts it in a late note, "the highest condition that a philosopher can reach: standing Dionysically to existence [*Dasein*] – : my formula for that is *amor fati*".[91]

We thus have two formulae for the highest goal of philosophy and hence for human life: *amor dei* and *amor fati*. Both thinkers identify freedom with the affir-

---

[87] NL 1887 7[4], KSA 12: 259–270.
[88] Most obviously GS 276: "I want to learn more and more to see as beautiful what is necessary in things … I do not want to wage war against what is ugly. I do not want to accuse; I do not even want to accuse those who accuse. *Looking away* shall be my only negation."
[89] NL 1887 7[4], KSA 12: 259–270 ("*beständige Verleumdung von Allem, um Eins in die Höchste Höhe zu bringen*").
[90] TI Skirmishes 49. This position is specifically attributed to Goethe, although Nietzsche remarks that Spinoza helped him achieve it. (In Nietzsche's final few years we find a number of notes in which Spinoza is referred to as the *Heilige Goethes*: NL 1887/1888 11[138], KSA 13: 63–65; NL 1888 12[1], KSA 13: 195–211; see also, NL 1887 10[170], KSA 12: 558.) One should not make too much of the contrast of 'freedom' (in this quote) and "entirely unfree" (in the previous): for Spinoza, a recognition that there is no escape from the determinism of causal nature is part of what characterizes the 'free man' (see the end of *Ethics* IV). See Pfeffer 1972: 159ff.
[91] NL 1888 16[32], KSA 13: 492.

mation of fatalism and the rejection of teleology.⁹² Both recognize a kind of 'redemption' as it were in the whole rather than in the particular.⁹³ Both are even willing to utilize the language of divinity in their positions, despite their mutual attacks on traditional religion. And it appears indisputable that Nietzsche's coinage is indebted to his reading of Spinoza.⁹⁴ How are we then to distinguish *amor fati* from *amor dei*? Much as with conatus and will to power, we once again find here a position of Nietzsche's that on its surface appears similar to Spinoza's, but which Nietzsche takes pains to distinguish from his precursor's.

To understand Nietzsche's critique of *amor dei intellectualis*, let us first discuss how he saw the object of Spinoza's love and then how he saw the character of the love itself. Regarding the *Deus* that is loved, Nietzsche in his final years makes increasingly frequent attacks on the premises that underlie Spinoza's God. While he realizes that this God is not the God of Christianity, and that Spinoza is quite overtly intending to show the impossibility of such a king of the universe, Nietzsche believes that Spinoza has nevertheless not fully escaped the trappings of the theological mindset after all. The forward line of this critique attacks Spinoza for putting forward a 'God' that is capable of infinitely novel production because infinitely powerful. Nietzsche sees this as a sign that Spinoza still possesses the yearnings that motivated the traditional metaphysics that the latter had ostensibly tried to escape.⁹⁵ Nietzsche considers it a contradiction in terms to declare that the universe has the power to bring about infinitely new things. If the universe is already the sum of all power, always active and everywhere at its complete perfection, then by definition there is no outside source from which to draw force and bring about something essentially new.

> The world, even if it is no longer a God, is still supposed to be capable of the divine power of creation, the power of infinite transformations; it is supposed to constantly prevent

---

92 Joan Stambaugh points out that for Nietzsche there is more than one kind of fatalism for Nietzsche. *Amor fati* comes closer to what he called "Russian fatalism", in which one understands one's own existence as a piece of fate, rather than "Turkish fatalism", which denotes more of a divine dispensation of destiny, and from which one can run away, at least for a time. See Stambaugh 1994: 79–81. Nietzsche links Spinoza's position with "Russian fatalism" at GM II 15.
93 Spinoza at times uses the term *beatitudo* (e.g. *Ethics* IP49S), Nietzsche *Erlösung* (e.g. Z II, On Redemption).
94 The term *amor fati*, which Nietzsche invented, is introduced in the first paragraph of GS IV, Nietzsche's first writing after reading Fischer. Wurzer argues convincingly that the term must be understood as a reaction to that reading (see Wurzer 1975: 80–86). See also Yovel 1992: 104.
95 Spinoza claims that the power of nature is infinite, something Nietzsche specifically rejects: "*Das Maß der All-Kraft* ist bestimmt, nicht 'Unendliches' " (NL 1881 11[202], KSA 9: 523). See also NL 1884 25[299], KSA 11: 87. For Spinoza see *Ethics* IP34 with *Ethics* IP8, IP16.

itself from returning to any of its old forms; it is supposed to possess not only the intention but the *means* of avoiding any repetition; to that end, it is supposed to control every one of its movements at every moment so as to escape goals, final states, repetitions – and whatever else may follow from such an unforgivably insane way of thinking and desiring. It is still the old religious way of thinking and desiring, a kind of longing to believe that *in some way* the world is after all like the old beloved, infinite, boundlessly creative God – that in some ways "the old God still lives" – that longing of Spinoza which was expressed in the words "*deus sive natura*" (he even felt "*natura sive deus*"). What, then, is the law and belief with which the decisive change, the recently attained preponderance of the scientific spirit over the religious, God-inventing spirit, is most clearly formulated? Is it not: the world, as force, may not be thought of as unlimited, for it *cannot* be so thought of; we forbid ourselves the concept of an infinite force as incompatible with the concept "force." Thus – the world also lacks the capacity for eternal novelty.[96]

Against the infinitely powerful God (and human understanding thereof) that Spinoza posits, which Nietzsche understood to be a unity because synonymous with the singular substance that is nature as a whole, Nietzsche puts forward a theory of nature as chaos, what he in his notes even calls *chaos* sive natura.[97] In this idea Nietzsche attempts to rid the world of the quality of logical necessity, that one event must necessarily follow upon another. Nature does not act by following laws. Such a concept is only the legacy of our religious heritage ('law' having a moral aftertaste) and a grammar that we cannot escape (the insistence of a 'doer' in any action).[98]

But since these metaphysical themes require a book-length study in their own right, we must leave them not fully explored and return to our major themes of understanding and affirmation. This attack on nature-as-infinite-substance has implications not only for abstract ontology but for human epistemology as well. To describe the world as chaos as Nietzsche does is to deny the possibility of *Erkenntnis* in Spinoza's sense. For Spinoza *Erkenntnis* follows from the mind being a mode of God's infinite intellect, a position Nietzsche describes as Spinoza

---

[96] NL 1885 36[15], KSA 11: 556–557 (translation Kaufmann/Hollingdale); see also NL 1886 2[145], KSA 12: 138; NL 1886 2[158], KSA 12: 143; NL 1887 10[138], KSA 12: 535–536.

[97] NL 1881 11[197], KSA 9: 519–520. See also GS 109; NL 1881 11[157], KSA 9: 502; NL 1881 11[225], KSA 9: 528, among others. Greg Whitlock argues that this worldview "completely inverts the metaphysics of Spinoza" (see Whitlock 1996: 207), a position aligned with NL 1886/1887 5[71], KSA 12: 211–217, where Nietzsche describes his position as antipodal to pantheism.

[98] NL 1885 36[18], KSA 11: 559; NL 1888 14[79], KSA 13: 257–259; NL 1888 14[122], KSA 13: 301–303. The connection between grammar and our false ideas of action is a one Nietzsche makes a few times. See e.g. BGE Preface 20; NL 1885 35[35], KSA 11: 526; NL 1885 40[23], KSA 11: 639–640; NL 1887 10[158], KSA 12: 549.

"deifying his drive" [*seinen Trieb* vergöttert].⁹⁹ Spinoza's theory demands not merely that we understand individual things, but that we understand them as modes of God's infinite and eternal essence, such that individual cases can only be understood in the light of a more fundamental truth. For Spinoza, the logical order of nature enables man's rational thinking. The intellectual love of God is "*ein Accord in der Harmonie des Ganzen*".¹⁰⁰ God's eternal truths are expressed most clearly in mathematical (or geometric) knowledge. But to identify the world as chaos is to deny any such enduring reality to modes as well. Basic building blocks of mathematical knowledge for Spinoza, such as lines, planes, and bodies, etc. do not truly exist for Nietzsche; they are images, albeit ones necessary for life, that humans have imposed on this chaos of nature.¹⁰¹ Knowledge in Spinoza's sense becomes impossible in Nietzsche's scheme. For Nietzsche, nature is not a harmonious organization, nor does it have any logical essence that can be understood adequately. To quote a late note, "the world is not an organism, but rather chaos: the development of 'intellectuality' is an instrument for the relative preservation of the organization [of man]."¹⁰²

While Nietzsche may agree with Spinoza's underlying premise that the will to knowledge follows from a striving for power,¹⁰³ Nietzsche understands the will to power's expression in *erkennen* as meaning "not 'to understand' but to schematize – to impose upon chaos as much regularity and form as our practical needs require".¹⁰⁴ In other words, what we call *Erkenntnis* is only a contrivance in which we impose as much form and regularity on the flux as is practicably possible.¹⁰⁵ Such understanding is not the logical outcome of a mind expressing God's infinite attribute of thought but rather a tool resulting from a need to make the world intelligible and calculable: "the development of reason is adjustment, invention, with the aim of making similar, equal".¹⁰⁶ If there are no enduring things in nature, and all understanding only schematization of chaos, then "the concept of

---

99 NL 1887 7[4], KSA 12: 259–270.
100 Fischer 1865: 544.
101 See e.g. GS 112, BGE 4.
102 NL 1888 11[74], KSA 13: 37. Thinking of the universe as an 'organism' is a position Nietzsche associates with efforts to consider the universe as coherent in total and capable of endless novelty of production, a position he attributes to Spinoza as mentioned above (see NL 1881 11[213], KSA 9: 525; BGE 4).
103 Fischer calls it "a necessary consequence of our desire" (Fischer 1865: 544).
104 NL 1888 14[152], KSA 13: 333–335. See also NL 1888 14[93], KSA 13: 270–271; NL 1888 14[122], KSA 13: 301–303.
105 NL 1888 14[152], KSA 13: 333–335.
106 NL 1888 14[152], KSA 13: 333–335. Nietzsche may be attacking Spinoza's position at NL 1887 10[90], KSA 12: 507–508 as well.

causality is completely useless ... [and] interpretation by causality a deception".[107] That our experience of events appears to have a formulable character in no way implies that any law of necessity rules over them; necessity itself is only an interpretation arising from our perception of successive events. [108]

And if knowledge of causality, which serves as the base for Spinoza's geometric model of rational understanding, is an impossibility, then Spinoza's theory of affirmation become consequently untenable. For Spinoza *amor* emerges from rationality.[109] An increase in knowledge is joyous, and this joy manifests as love of God, the cause of this joy. In attacking the possibility of *Deus sive natura*, Nietzsche attacks the possibility of such an understanding, and with it of Spinoza's *amor dei*, as well. Nietzsche believes the epistemology that this position demands, much like the ontology behind it, to be an atavism of the theological mindset. It is the legacy of religious (especially Christian) thinking that leads Spinoza to posit the possibility of adequate knowledge in a rational capacity grounded in God's infinity.[110]

Nietzsche recognizes that in dropping the intellectual component of *amor*, both the character and the object of *amor* must be conceived entirely differently. For Spinoza, *amor dei* results from the mind's adequate understanding of God's infinite and eternal essence. The mind is a mode of God's infinite thinking, and as such it shares in God's eternity (Nietzsche describes this position as "bringing unity to the highest heights".)[111] In such an understanding, the mind conceives the world not in the transient nature of its individual components, as individual minds encounter them sensually in duration, but *sub specie aeternitatis*, as God conceives them in their eternity.[112] Nietzsche, by contrast, puts forward instead what he calls *amor fati*. In discussing this position, he does not entirely shy away from the language of divinity himself. In an 1882 letter to Overbeck he equates *amor fati* with a "fatalistic 'submission to God'", and as quoted above

---

[107] NL 1888 14[98], KSA 13: 274–276.
[108] Nietzsche praises Hume's insight on this matter (NL 1885/1886 2[83], KSA 12: 101–103; NL 1887 9[91], KSA 12: 383–387). We cannot discuss here the obvious tension in Nietzsche's position, that nature is known as unknowable chaos. A good discussion of the problem can be found in chapter 11 of Rosen 1989.
[109] *Ethics* VP32, Fischer 1865: 519ff. Love is joy with the accompanying idea of an external cause (*Ethics* IIP13S).
[110] NL 1886/1887 5[71], KSA 12: 211–217. Although it may sound ironic to say that Spinoza's thinking is a continuation of Christian thought, given Spinoza's Jewish lineage, Nietzsche's poem *An Spinoza* makes clear that he sees Spinoza's philosophy as very much anti-Jewish (NL 1884 28[49], KSA 11: 319).
[111] NL 1887 7[4], KSA 12: 259–270.
[112] *Ethics* VP33.

he describes *amor fati* as "standing Dionysically to existence".¹¹³ But if Nietzsche refrains from using Spinoza's terminology of *amor dei*, it is no doubt in part because *chaos sive natura* attempts to turn Spinoza's *deus* doctrine on its head. Given an ontology of chaos, such unity as is implied by the term *Deus* becomes impossible. The mind has no adequate knowledge of nature's essence. Consequently, there is no unified perspective of nature's eternity in which the mind can transcend duration. *Amor fati* is love on the plane of duration, a love of fate, a love of what has come before and of what is to come. If Nietzsche can use the word 'eternal' at all to describe the object of this love, if there is anything one can truly affirm beyond transience and perishability, then it is within the horizon of duration that such eternity must be located. In other words, eternity must become sempiternity. God must become a circle.¹¹⁴

Conclusion: Spinoza's longing

While it may be tempting to conclude that Nietzsche's critique of Spinoza's affect theory ultimately rests on these underlying metaphysical disagreements, Nietzsche has another concern which I believe he considered equally fundamental. In the paragraph about God's infinity quoted in section II above, Spinoza's position is characterized not as an error in logic or argumentation but as a "longing". Such statements about Spinoza's hidden desires and intentions, for which it is difficult for the scholarly reader to argue *pro* or *contra*, find frequent manifestation in Nietzsche's later characterizations of his 'precursor'. Spinoza had claimed that nature's causal necessity is the quintessential object of knowledge; but for Nietzsche on the other hand, "necessity is not a fact, but rather an interpretation".¹¹⁵ And as an interpretation, such claims tell us something about the interpreter who makes them: Spinoza's God should in fact be understood "*sub specie Spinozae*".¹¹⁶ That is to say, even more than in metaphysical disputations, Nietzsche is interested in exploring the way in which the differences between his and Spinoza's positions boil down to distinctions in their own affective constitutions, i.e. to what motivated their two contrasting visions of philosophical *amor*.¹¹⁷ Behind the maligning of Spinoza's metaphysics is quite fre-

---

113 KSB 6, nr. 236, NL 1888 16[32], KSA 13: 492–493.
114 BGE 56.
115 NL 1887 9[91], KSA 12. 383–387; NL 1888 14[98], KSA 13: 274–276.
116 A 17.
117 As Nietzsche implies to be generally the rule among philosophers at BGE 6.

quently animadversion against Spinoza himself as the thinker of those metaphysics. Nietzsche characterizes Spinoza's philosophy as an expression of his "basic instinct, which was logical".[118] Spinoza believed that one understood the world adequately insofar as one understood God's essence. In fact, Nietzsche claims, Spinoza was "deifying his drive", imposing a rational order onto the chaos of nature and then apotheosizing it.[119]

Nietzsche reads Spinoza as follows: we will power, therefore we will knowledge, therefore we will eternity. This is because knowledge is first and foremost a knowledge of nature's necessity, i.e. that deterministic, unchanging laws of cause-and-effect essentially define all change, and that we achieve the most fundamental knowledge when we look past the changing to the unchanging. Spinoza is not the only thinker guilty of locating truth in the unchanging, but he is the paradigmatic example of it. "[Philosophers] think that they show their *respect* for a subject when they de-historicize it, *sub specie aeterni* – when they turn it into a mummy", as Nietzsche writes in *Twilight of the Idols*. "[They say that] whatever has being does not become; whatever becomes does not have being."[120] Nietzsche attributes such an instinct to these thinkers' affective constitutions and specifically to a "fear of everything changing", a charge he throws against Spinoza more than once in the latter years.[121] A characteristic passage:

> That which has been feared the most, the cause of the most powerful passions (pride, lust) has been treated by men with the greatest amount of hostility and eliminated from the "true" world. Thus they have eliminated the affects one by one – posited God as the antithesis of evil, that is, placed reality in the negation of desires and affects (i.e., in nothingness).
>
> In the same way they have hated the irrational, the arbitrary, the accidental (as the causes of countless physical passions). As a consequence, they negated this element in being-in-itself and conceived it as absolute "rationality" and "purposiveness."
>
> In the same way, they have feared change, transitoriness: this expresses a gloomy [*gedrückte*] soul, full of mistrust and bad experience (the case of Spinoza: an opposite kind of man would account change a stimulus).[122]

It is from this psychologically driven 'fear of change' that Spinoza found the truth of beings: not in their durational existence as we encounter them, but "*sub specie aeternitatis*", under the aspect of eternity. Such attacks, ascribing

---

[118] NL 1886/1887 5[71], KSA 12: 211–217.
[119] NL 1887 7[4], KSA 12: 259–270.
[120] TI Reason 1.
[121] NL 1887 9[160], KSA 12: 430; NL 1888 18[16], KSA 13: 536–537.
[122] NL 1888 18[16], KSA 13: 536–537 (Kaufmann translation modified).

Spinoza's philosophy to his fears and weaknesses, are ubiquitous in Nietzsche's later writings about his 'precursor'. Spinoza's philosophy is at times attributed to his consumption; it is even maligned as vampiric and lacking in blood.[123] And perhaps Nietzsche thought that such an attitude was, in its way, appropriate: Spinoza claims one's ideas express one's power of thinking, and so it is only poetic justice for Nietzsche to attack those ideas as expressive of a weak constitution.

From a mixture of fear and naïveté, Spinoza ascribed the highest value to the *Ewig-Gliechbeibenden*, the "eternal constant".[124] His *amor dei* involved affirmation of things not in their perishability, but in an unchanging necessity they supposedly expressed. In his *amor dei* Spinoza believed that the mind achieved a kind of eternity, and thus the truest self-preservation of all.[125] The *Ethics* emphasizes the eternity of the mind, not the body.[126] ("But what is *amor*, what *deus*, if there is not a drop of blood in them?", Nietzsche protests.[127]) It was his weakness, his "condition of distress", that led Spinoza to develop a philosophy hostile to change and expressive of a striving for self-preservation.[128]

With this framework of Spinoza's 'fear of change' in mind, we are in a position to close the lacuna in the note quoted in section I above, in which Nietzsche's writing jumped from the affects as power expressions of human nature to an attack on knowledge of cause-and-effect and Spinoza's claims about self-preservation.[129] Spinoza's principle may be, much like Nietzsche's, that one strives for increased power. But for Spinoza, the highest expression of this striving is in the mind's achievement of ideas *sub specie aeternitatis*. Understood in this light, 'self-preservation' re-emerges on a higher plane than the mere preservation of the corporeal self. As the mind strives for power, it necessarily strives also for an understanding of God's infinite essence, that is to say that it strives to overcome durational transience and to achieve unchanging eternity by means of eternal ideas. Man's difficulties and struggles all stem from passions, the result of encounters with the world during the duration of our life.

---

123 GS 349, GS 372. For a list of such comments see Stegmaier 2004: 112.
124 NL 1887 9[26], KSA 12: 348.
125 *Ethics* VP22–23ff.
126 Fischer 1865: 525ff. In Spinoza's own words, "the human mind cannot be absolutely destroyed with the body, but something remains which is eternal" (*Ethics* EVP23).
127 GS 372.
128 GS 349.
129 Nietzsche links will to power and Spinoza's claims about self-preservation in another place as well, *Beyond Good and Evil*, where he somewhat obliquely chides Spinoza for inconsistency in this matter (BGE 13).

We find our blessedness by contrast in eternity, in which our mind is one with a God that we have never essentially encountered, only thought. If we accept that all things are striving for eternity in this way, we can see why Nietzsche would suppose that "Spinoza's principle of self-preservation should put a halt to all change": an achievement of this unchanging eternity (were it possible) would be the end point of such striving.[130] That Spinoza willed such an end point was a sign of an underlying fear, even of a vengeful mindset, against durational becoming.[131]

As such, Nietzsche believed, Spinoza's affirmation was a species of world denial, affirming a 'true' world that exists in uneasy relationship with the world that we actually encounter.[132] Such an ascription, to use language that Nietzsche employs elsewhere, is an imposing of the character of 'being' upon becoming.[133] In contrast, Nietzsche sought to affirm change itself, to posit the value of the "briefest and most transient".[134] This affirmation of change Nietzsche calls his "innermost nature", *amor fati*.[135] Such a position – the endorsement of unreason and change, of danger, of perishing – he believes characteristic of a strong and playful nature, one that he himself had but that the consumptive Spinoza did not.[136]

And so to conclude what has been a whirlwind tour through a series of complex themes. Though Spinoza didn't claim that he had (or could) entirely escape the passions that generally afflict human life *sub specie durationis*, he believed that in those moments of *amor dei* he had escaped the negation of the world that follows from passionate desires. In these moments of adequate understanding the ideas of the mind were eternal because selfsame with God's eternal ideas. Man's rational understanding is a moment of God's infinite intellect.[137] For Nietzsche, the mind is not capable of active affects entailing such an adequate understanding of nature. As such, the reasonable knowledge of God is

---

130 NL 1888 14[121], KSA 13: 300–301.
131 On the vengeful nature of such willing, see Z II, On Redemption. Nietzsche attributes the spirit of revenge to Spinoza on a few occasions, including NL 1884 26[285], KSA 11: 226 and NL 1884 28[49], KSA 11: 161.
132 In the original version of TI's short aphorism "How the true world finally became an error", it is Spinoza, not Plato, who personifies the oldest form of the error: "reasonable, simple, factual, *sub specie Spinozae*. A circumlocution for the sentence, 'I, Spinoza, *am* the truth.'" (KSA 14: 415).
133 NL 1886/1887 7[54], KSA 12: 312.
134 NL 1887 9[26], KSA 12: 348.
135 NCW, Epilogue 1; EH CW 4.
136 NL 1888 16[55], KSA 13: 504; NL 1888 18[16], KSA 13: 536–537.
137 Fischer 1865: 544.

impossible, and with it Spinoza's *amor dei* as well, which is grounded in the knowledge that "every moment [has] a logical necessity".[138] In Nietzsche's view, to devalue the passions and instead aim to attain a 'reasonable' condition, as Spinoza tells his readers to do, is delusional.[139] Nietzsche believes that an attempt to live 'Spinozistically' is to disparage the actual world. Such 'love' is not world-affirmation but "the last, thinnest, and emptiest ... brain afflictions of [a] sick web-spinner".[140]

But if Spinoza could have responded to Nietzsche, he would likely have said that his successor's affirmation rang hollow in its own way. By declaring nature to be chaos, and knowledge little more than schematization, Nietzsche can say *that* he affirms, but not truly *what* he affirms. By positing *chaos* sive natura, Nietzsche makes adequate knowledge of any kind impossible.[141] In other words, Nietzsche says that Spinoza's *amor dei* is empty, but Spinoza would respond that Nietzsche's *amor fati* is blind.

References

Abel, Günter (1984) *Nietzsche: Die Dynamik der Willen zur Macht und die ewige Wiederkehr.* Berlin/New York: De Gruyter.
Brobjer, Thomas (2008) *Nietzsche's Philosophical Context*, Urbana: University of Illinois Press.
Della Rocca, Michael (2008) *Spinoza*, London: Routledge.
Descartes, René (2007) *The Philosophical Writings of Descartes*, trans. J. Cottingham, R. Stoothoof and D. Murdoch, 3 vols., Cambridge: Cambridge University Press.
Fischer, Kuno (1865) *Geschichte der neuern Philosophie, 1 bd., 2 teil: Baruch Spinoza*, Heidelberg: Bassermann.
Foucault, Michel (1984) *The Foucault Reader*, ed. Paul Rabinow, New York: Pantheon Books.
Gawoll, Hans-Jürgen (2001) "Nietzsche und der Geist Spinozas", in: *Nietzsche-Studien* 30, 44–61.
Habermas, Jürgen (1987) *Philosophical Discourse of Modernity*, trans. Frederick Lawrence, Cambridge, MA: MIT Press.

---

138 NL 1886/1887 5[71], KSA 12: 211–217.
139 See NL 1881 11[132], KSA 9: 490; NL 1881 11[193], KSA 9: 517–518.
140 TI Reason 4. Although Spinoza is not named in this passage, he is clearly the target intended, as evidenced by the attacks on *causa sui* and the concept of "God" described, and by the term web-spinner, an insult Nietzsche levies against Spinoza (BGE 25; TI Skirmishes 23).
141 One might ask whether the chaotic worldview does not also make knowledge or affirmation of the eternal recurrence impossible. Nietzsche answers this, in my opinion somewhat unsatisfactorily, as follows: "The 'chaos of the universe' as the exclusion of any teleological activity is not contrary to the idea of the cycle: the latter is just an unreasonable necessity, without any formal ethical aesthetic consideration." NL 1881 11[225], KSA 9: 528.

Magnus, Bernd/Higgins, Kathleen M. (1996) "Nietzsche's Works and Their Themes", in: Bernd Magnus and Kathleen Marie Higgins (eds.), *Cambridge Companion to Nietzsche* (Cambridge: Cambridge University Press).
Melamed, Yitzhak (2013) *Spinoza's Metaphysics: Substance and Thought*, Oxford: Oxford University Press.
Nietzsche, Friedrich (1982) *The Portable Nietzsche*, ed. W. Kaufmann, New York: Viking.
Pfeffer, Rose (1972) *Nietzsche: Disciple of Dionysus*, Lewisburg: Bucknell University Press.
Pippin, Robert B. (1996) "Nietzsche's Alleged Farewell", in: Bernd Magnus and Kathleen Marie Higgins (eds.), *Cambridge Companion to Nietzsche*, Cambridge: Cambridge University Press, 252–278.
Pippin, Robert B. (1999) *Modernism as a Philosophical Problem*, Oxford: Blackwell.
Rosen, Stanley (1989) *The Ancients and the Moderns: Rethinking Modernity*, New Haven: Yale Press.
Scandella, Maurizio (2012) "Did Nietzsche Read Spinoza? Some Preliminary Notes on the Nietzsche-Spinoza Problem, Kuno Fischer, and Other Sources", in: *Nietzsche-Studien* 41, 308–332.
Schacht, Richard (1995) *Making Sense of Nietzsche*, Urbana: University of Illinois Press.
Spinoza, Baruch de (1996) *Ethics*, trans. Edwin Curley, New York: Penguin.
Stambaugh, Joan (1994) *The Other Nietzsche*, Albany: SUNY Press.
Stegmaier, Werner (2004) "'Philosophischer Idealismus' und die 'Musik des Lebens': zu Nietzsches Umgang mit Paradoxien", in: *Nietzsche-Studien* 33, 90–128.
Whitlock, Greg (1996) "Roger Boscovich, Spinoza, and Nietzsche: The Untold Story", in: *Nietzsche-Studien* 25, 200–220.
Wilson, Margaret D. (2007) "Spinoza's Theory of Knowledge", in: Don Garret (ed.), *Cambridge Companion to Spinoza*, Cambridge: Cambridge University Press, 89–141.
Wollenberg, David (2013) "Nietzsche, Spinoza, and the Moral Affects", in: *Journal of the History of Philosophy* 51(4), 617–649.
Wurzer, William (1975) *Nietzsche und Spinoza* (Monographien zur philosophischen Forschung, vol. 141), Meisenheim am Glan: Anton Hain.
Yovel, Yirmiyahu (1992) *Spinoza and Other Heretics*, vol. 2., Princeton: Princeton University Press.

Nikolaos Loukidelis and Christopher Brinkmann
3 Leibnizian Ideas in Nietzsche's Philosophy: On Force, Monads, Perspectivism, and the Subject

1 Introduction

What do Leibniz, the hard-line metaphysician of the Baroque era, and Nietzsche, the destroyer of metaphysics, have in common? This could certainly be a central question for a reader of the present paper who does not have any specific information on the relationship between the two philosophers, but nevertheless possesses a good overview of the history of Western thought.

Before taking a closer look at the impact that Leibnizian thinking had on Nietzsche we would first like to remind the suspicious reader that a general historical approach to philosophy which strictly divides periods and groups of thinkers tends to oversimplify things. On these terms, the reader in question can put emphasis on the fact that Leibniz lived before Nietzsche and that Nietzsche lived after Kant, and consequently point out that Leibniz, not having the chance to get acquainted with Kant's critical project, inevitably constructed a naive and to a great extent fantastic metaphysics, while Nietzsche, who was well schooled in Kantian thinking, ended up radicalizing it and totally rejecting metaphysics.

This account overlooks many important aspects of Leibniz's and Nietzsche's work and intentions. Leibniz was not at all a blind follower of the scholastic tradition. In his own famous remarks, he noted that this tradition certainly had a profound effect on him, but he discovered modern science "while still being quite young"[1] (NS § 2) and this encounter freed him from the "yoke of Aristotle" (NS § 3). The influence that modern science has exercised on Leibniz becomes particularly evident, if one examines his concept of *substance*. According to a scholastic tradition that was prevalent during the seventeenth century the activity of a substance was caused due to a mere potentiality [*potentia nuda*] which inhered in it and was provoked by a stimulus (OAFP § 2). Leibniz opposes this notion by developing a dynamical concept of substance. Its potentiality is not a passive but an active one (it includes a striving aspect) and is developed by itself. But even the explanations of modern dynamics are inadequate, because it is wrong to postu-

---

[1] All translations from the French, Latin and German are our own.

late that movement [*mouvement*] can only be caused by a collision of bodies [*choc des corps*] regardless of any inner causality (NS § 18), and at this point Leibniz goes back to the tradition of Aristotelian substantiality and its entelechy.

Elements of Leibniz's thinking as stated before are to be found in Nietzsche. Although not a scientist himself, he had great interest in modern physics and his concept of the "will to power" is partly inspired by contemporary developments in this field. He also sees that simple mechanics cannot be solely based on the phenomenon of pressure and collision [*Druck und Stoß*] and introduces his concept of "will to power" in order to fill that gap[2]:

> The triumphant concept of "force", with which our physicists have eliminated God from the World, needs supplementing: it must be ascribed an inner world which I call "will to power", i.e., an insatiable craving to manifest power; or to employ, exercise power, as a creative drive, etc. The physicists cannot eliminate "action at a distance" [*Wirkung in die Ferne*] from their principles, nor a force of repulsion (or attraction). There is no help for it: one must understand all motion, all "appearances", all "laws" as mere symptoms of inner events, and use the human analogy consistently to the end. (NL 1885, 36[31], KSA 11: 563 = WLN, 26–27, modified)[3]

The relationship between Nietzsche and Leibniz is an issue that has been given various treatments.[4] These treatments illuminate many aspects, but fail to deal with a methodological problem of great importance. Nietzsche owes his knowledge of the philosophical tradition (apart from Greek antiquity and a few exceptions) not to an independent study of the writings of the classics of this field, but to his occupation with the philosophy of the late nineteenth century.[5] This

---

[2] There are of course further similarities between Leibniz and Nietzsche. In the course of this paper I am going to discuss in detail (apart from the concept of force) two of these similarities: the monadological model and perspectivism.
[3] We have been following here the reading of KGW IX/4: 26 (Notebook W I 4): "mit dem unsere Physiker Gott aus der Welt geschafft haben" and not Montinari's reading: "mit dem unsere Physiker Gott und die Welt geschafft haben".
[4] The most extensive and significant ones are Kaulbach 1979 (cf. Kaulbach 1980: 49ff.) and Abel 1998, e.g. p. 12f., 280ff. (cf. Abel 2012: 503ff.). Interesting, and in many cases important, remarks are also to be found in Müller-Lauter 1971, especially p. 32f. (cf. Müller-Lauter 1999: 23f.), Figl 1982, mainly p. 86ff. (with reference to more literature on Leibniz and Nietzsche), Simon 1984: 17ff., Poellner 1995, e.g. p. 222ff., 277ff., Gerhardt 1996, e.g. p. 50f., Schlimgen 1999, especially p. 32ff., Sleinis 1999, Günzel 2001, Riccardi 2009, especially p. 214, Bornedal 2010, e.g. p. 136f., Springmann 2010: 59ff., Constâncio 2011, e.g. p. 19, Anderson 2012: 63f., 68f., Fleming 2012: 340f.
[5] Even if Nietzsche presents himself as untimely and often states that he does not bother to read the works of his inferior contemporaries, he was in fact immensely interested in the literary, scientific and cultural developments produced by his own generation.

means that for spotting the specific philosophical context in which Nietzsche's work is to be located, the appeal to the original text of the great philosophers should not be regarded as the first priority. Rather, one has to track down the account, to which Nietzsche relates *directly*, and this is exactly the point where secondary literature on Leibniz and Nietzsche does not really help us.[6] To trace some important sources is a main task of this paper. At the same time and on this basis we are going to state the contribution of Leibnizian thinking to some of Nietzsche's central themes.

2 The influence of Otto Liebmann, Maximilian Drossbach and Gustav Teichmüller

Interest in the philosophy of Leibniz grew immensely after the publication of studies by Bertrand Russell, Louis Couturat and Ernst Cassirer at the beginning of the twentieth century.[7] Even if nothing comparable occurred in the nineteenth century, one can't say that Leibniz was a neglected philosopher during this period. Many thinkers had a good or even high opinion of him and incorporated Leibnizian elements in their thought. In this section I will highlight some basic references to Leibniz in the works of Otto Liebmann, Maximilian Drossbach and Gustav Teichmüller, references that shaped Nietzsche's understanding of this philosophical classic. I do not intend here to go into historical details, such as to deal for example with chronological questions (when exactly did Nietzsche read what? etc.) or annotations on books that Nietzsche owned and are still being kept among what is left of his personal library in Weimar. For the purposes of this paper, we can say that Nietzsche has studied – in the true sense of the word – the books which we are going to discuss.

2.1 Otto Liebmann and the concept of force

Otto Liebmann (1840–1912) has secured a place in the history of thought as one of the leading neo-Kantians. This characterization is certainly not wrong, but at the same time not entirely correct, because Liebmann criticizes Kant often and openly, and to a much greater extent than other neo-Kantians. Even in his most known (though certainly not his best) work *Kant* and the Epigones [*Kant* und die

---

6 For some minor exceptions, see 2.1 and 2.2.
7 Russell 1900, Couturat 1901, Cassirer 1902.

Epigonen], chapters of which end mostly with the famous: "Therefore we must go back to Kant", we find apart from a very positive appraisal of many doctrines of Kant's theoretical philosophy a severe criticism of the notion of the thing-in-itself.

Liebmann regards Leibniz in many cases as a predecessor of Kant. Both philosophers for example support "dynamism" and are opposed to the "corpuscular theory" (AR, 311). They assume the existence of "centres of force with no extension" [*unausgedehnte Kraftcentra*] (ibid.), whereas Descartes accepts only "collision and pressure" [*Stoß und Druck*] as "the only causes of motion" (AR, 310). Liebmann takes the side of Leibniz and Kant and develops his own theory on the nature of *actio in distans*:

> It has been said that the term "action at a distance" is an anthropomorphism. And it is, indeed! Its prototype given to us in inner experience is the power of the will, partly directly and partly indirectly; directly, by being conscious of moving our heavy limbs through our will; indirectly, by giving our muscles through our will the necessary tension, with which we resist to an invisible, merely *felt* drag. But this openly admitted anthropomorphism as such is by no means reprehensible, by no means wrong, but perhaps quite inevitable, maybe even objectively right. More specifically, the following can be said about the genesis and crystallisation of this mysterious term: A natural analogy imposes it on us at various moments. (TF, 66)[8]

At this point, we can easily give a good example of the value of examining Nietzsche's sources. Friedrich Kaulbach, perhaps the most important commentator on the relationship between Nietzsche and Leibniz, rightly points out that the famous notebook entry NL 1885, 36[31], which was cited above and which emphasizes that we should trust the analogy between our own will (according to Nietzsche that is essentially will to power) and motion in the outer world, entails a connection to "the dynamical natural philosophy, which has received essential impulses from Leibniz" (Kaulbach 1979: 136; cf. Springmann 2010: 62f.).[9]

---

[8] "Man hat gesagt, der Begriff der Wirkung in die Ferne sei ein Anthropomorphismus. Und das ist er allerdings! Sein in der inneren Erfahrung gegebenes Urbild ist die Willenskraft, und zwar theils direct, theils indirect; direct, indem wir das Bewusstsein haben, durch unseren Willen unsere schweren Gliedmaßen in Bewegung zu versetzen; indirect, indem wir durch den Willen unsere Muskeln diejenige Spannung verleihen, vermöge welcher einem unsichtbaren, nur *gefühlten* Zuge Widerstand entgegengesetzt wird. Aber dieser offen eingestandene Anthropomorphismus als solcher ist noch keineswegs tadelnswerth, keineswegs falsch, sondern vielleicht ganz unvermeidlich, vielleicht sogar materiell richtig. Genauer kann über die Genesis und die Objectivirung dieses mysteriösen Begriffs Folgendes gesagt werden: Eine natürliche Analogie drängt ihn uns bei den verschiedensten Gelegenheiten auf."

[9] It is true that Leibniz had objections to the notion of an action at a distance (cf. for example Liebmann's remarks and quotes from the correspondence between Leibniz and Clarke in TF, 68ff.). This point is connected to his critique of Newton, but shouldn't be overemphasized,

However the key to this note is only given, if we consider that Nietzsche speaks in favor of the "analogy of man" (NL 1885, 36[31], KSA 11: 563) after having read Liebmann's *Thoughts and Facts*.[10] The same applies to Nietzsche's extensive use of the idea that "all movements, all 'phenomena', all 'laws' [are] only [...] symptoms of an inner event" (NL 1885, 36[31], KSA 11: 563), which is inspired from Liebmann's suggestion that "the change of the spatial constellation [*räumlichen Constellation*]" is "nothing else than a mere symptom of an inner event that can't be spatially perceived" [*eines innerlichen, räumlich nicht wahrnehmbaren Geschehens*] (TF, 85).[11] Liebmann's epistemology of physics which combines original philosophical analysis with deep specialized knowledge was of great importance to the late Nietzsche.

2.2 Maximilian Drossbach and the monadological model

Maximilian Drossbach (1810–1884) was a manufacturer and a non-academic philosopher, who published several books.[12] We know that Nietzsche has read at least one of them: *On the Apparent and the Real Causes of Becoming in the World* [*Über die scheinbaren und die wirklichen Ursachen des Geschehens in der Welt*].[13] Clearly this book had an impact on him. The many elements of Leibni-

---

because there are important similarities between Leibniz' and Newton's views on the dynamical nature of matter. A further Leibnizian element that can be found in NL 1885, 36[31] is the analogy between man and other beings. This point will become more evident in 2.2.

10 Kaulbach is nevertheless one of the very few scholars, who discuss the question of the sources of Nietzsche's understanding of Leibniz. He regards it as an important one (even if he admits that he can't answer it) and suggests that it is possible that Nietzsche owes his knowledge of Leibniz' monadological model to his reading of Kuno Fischer's history of modern philosophy (Kaulbach 1980: 51). He also mentions a speech of the physiologist Du Bois-Reymond (Du Bois-Reymond 1974 [1870]) on Leibniz and his influence on the natural sciences. Kaulbach's hints are quite helpful, since it is very probable that Nietzsche has read both, but unfortunately no one has yet really proved it. Volker Gerhardt refers to three more contemporary authors: Friedrich Albert Lange, Eugen Dühring and African Spir (Lange 1866, Lange (1974) [1873], Dühring 1873, Spir 1877), but can't explain through these references how Leibnizian concepts reached Nietzsche's thought, because the accounts of Leibniz found there are rather critical (Gerhardt 1996: 50).

11 For further relevant passages, see Loukidelis 2007: 391ff.; cf. also Riccardi 2009, e. g. p. 122ff., 136f.

12 For a list of these books, see OARC, V.

13 It is probable that Nietzsche has read more books from Drossbach. Scholarship on the relationship between Nietzsche and Drossbach is still in its early stages. For the existing literature on the subject, see Loukidelis 2014: 229 and add to the items mentioned there Riccardi 2014: 256ff.

zian thought that it contains drove him to formulate important aspects of the concept of will to power. According to Drossbach:

a) The world consists of countless simple beings [*Wesen*] that interact and form connections.
b) Some beings are more complex and more developed than others.
c) Despite that all beings function in the same way: they have sensations [*Empfindungen*] and representations [*Vorstellungen*], although they are not identical but of a different nature.
d) "Lower" beings have a rudimentary form of consciousness, whereas "higher" possess a clearer one.[14]

These statements bare striking similarities to the monadological model that one finds in Nietzsche's notebook entries on the will to power.[15] He often speaks of beings that long to expand their field of influence, that interact with other entities and form complexes consisting of a plurality of will-to-power-quanta [*Willen-zur-Macht-Quanta*]. There are of course not only similarities but also differences to the monads as conceived by Leibniz. It is well known that these are windowless [*sans fenêtre*], whereas the will-to-power-quanta continually interact.[16] Moreover, Nietzsche's quanta always change. As he puts it in a remarkable note: "Constant elementary units, atoms, monads do not exist" [*es giebt keine*

---

14 Some textual evidence: "The sensations and representations emerge regardless of whether the being is conscious [*bewusst*] of them or not. We as humans also have a lot of representations without being conscious of them [...]. The beings at the lowest levels of their connection also generate sensations and representations as the beings at the highest level [...], but the representation is more incomplete, darker in the one case as in the other." (OARC, 35f.; "Die Empfindungen und Vorstellungen entstehen unabhängig davon, ob das Wesen ihrer klar bewusst wird oder nicht. Auch wir Menschen haben viele Vorstellungen, ohne ihrer bewusst zu sein [...]. Die Wesen auf den niedrigsten Stufen ihrer Verbindung erzeugen ebenso Empfindungen und Vorstellungen, wie die auf der höchsten [...], nur dass die Vorstellung im ersteren Falle unvollkommener, dunkler ist, als im anderen Falle."). "LEIBNIZ is right: All beings are analogous. What emerges within man [*im bewussten Menschengebilde*] in a distinct way is available in all beings [*Gebilden*], but is not yet developed, cannot distinctly be known." (OARC, 46; "LEIBNIZ hat Recht: Alle Wesen sind analogisch. Was im bewussten Menschengebilde deutlich hervortritt, das ist in allen Gebilden ebenfalls vorhanden, nur noch nicht entwickelt, nicht deutlich erkennbar")
15 Literature on Nietzsche and Drossbach mentions that the latter was very much influenced by Leibniz and states implicitly or explicitly that Nietzsche owes his knowledge of the monadological model to him, but doesn't actually deal with the relationship between Nietzsche and Leibniz.
16 Drossbach points out that "the real beings are thoroughly open [...] [and] can be reached from all sides", whereas Leibnizian monads are "closed, windowless, endless small houses" (OARC, 92).

dauerhaften letzten Einheiten, keine Atome, keine Monaden] (NL 1887–1888, 11[73], KSA 13: 36 = WLN, 212–213).

At this point an important question emerges: is it really justifiable to speak of monads as far as Nietzsche is concerned? The answer is yes, provided of course that one doesn't forget the differences we have already mentioned and pays proper attention to a sentence found in the very same note from which we quoted above: "We can speak of atoms and monads in a relative sense" [*Relativ, dürfen wir von Atomen und Monaden reden*] (NL 1887–1888, 11[73], KSA 13: 36). Let me cite this sentence in its context:

> – a quantum of power, a becoming [*ein Werden*], inasmuch as nothing in it has the character of "being"; inasmuch as
>
> – the means of expression that language offers are of no use to express becoming: it's part of our *inescapable need* for preservation that we constantly posit a cruder world of the permanent, [*die eine gröbere Welt von Bleibend⟨em⟩*], of "things" etc. In relative terms, we may speak of atoms and monads: and it's certain that the *smallest world is, as regards permanence, the most permanent* ... (NL 1887–1888, 11[73], KSA 13: 36 = WLN, 212–213)

One main idea of this passage (and of numerous other remarks to be found in Nietzsche's oeuvre) is that language cannot depict reality, but only a mere schema of it, conceived in simplifying categories (unity, constancy etc.): Becoming is always richer than our conception of it. Nietzsche accepts however that it is legitimate to use concepts,[17] if we are careful enough to know their limits. Let us take the concept of the body for example. The body *is a unit in a relative sense*. This means that it is not immortal, it changes, but it also has a plurality of organs that interact with each other as parts of *one* system, *one* organism (which is itself a part of a larger context, *nature*). It would be absurd to expand Nietzsche's critique of abstract metaphysical notions to all concepts. Apart from the fact that it would extremely weaken his philosophical enterprise, this isn't his intention at all.

2.3 Gustav Teichmüller and perspectivism

Gustav Teichmüller (1832–1888) came to Basel in 1868 as a professor of philosophy, where Nietzsche became acquainted with him. The next station in his

---

[17] In the note cited above he goes so far as to say that the same atom (the constancy of which he has already severely criticized!) "will be the longest lasting in the end" (NL 1887–1888, 11[73], KSA 13: 36).

career was Dorpat. He arrived there in 1871 and remained until his death in 1888. Even though Nietzsche had read several books of Teichmüller, the most relevant was his encounter with his main philosophical work: *The Real and the Apparent World. A New Grounding of Metaphysics* [*Die wirkliche und die scheinbare Welt. Neue Grundlegung der Metaphysik*].[18]

In this work one encounters a thinker that comes to results similar to Leibniz's by using a different argumentation (RAW, 138). One of the most important doctrines that Teichmüller shares with Leibniz is *perspectivism*. He sees the importance of the latter's conception of a simple substance as "a perpetual living mirror of the universe" [*un miroir vivant perpetuel de l' univers*] (Mon § 56[19]; cf. RAW, 242), but has strong objections to the fact that Leibniz (and Aristotle) do not take into consideration the eminent role of *space* and *time* in the mirroring process and support therefore a misleading notion of objectivity (RAW, 242f.).[20] Apart from this, it is interesting to see that Teichmüller does not define his perspectivism only in epistemological terms, but also includes the *vital interests* of the human and the animal world:

---

[18] In this paper I won't deal with the general relationship between Nietzsche and Teichmüller. For further information on this topic see the almost complete bibliography in Loukidelis 2014: 227. For Teichmüller and Nietzsche on perspectivism cf. e.g. Small 2001: 41ff.

[19] The next paragraph of the *Monadology* (§ 57) is the one containing the well-known example of the "one and the same city, which viewed from different aspects appears to be totally different and is quasi multiplied *perspectively*".

[20] "If Leibniz had elaborated his thought that the monad is a mirror of the universe [*ein Spiegel des Universums*] and depicts it perspectively, and related it to the idea of time and space, he would have had to search and find why this image can't be an objective, but only a perspective one and that the forms of space and time constitute the perspective character of the image, while he and his solely objective view remained in a certain way faithful to the Aristotelian conception and acknowledged only the mere worldly relative nature of time and space, since both categories mean nothing outside the world. But the perspective origin was not acknowledged by Aristotle and Leibniz and they therefore always referred both forms to the things themselves despite the inexplicable ideality of these forms, which they of course must have noticed." (RAW, 242f.; "Hätte Leibniz [...] seinen Gedanken, dass die Monade ein Spiegel des Universums sei und dasselbe perspectivisch abbilde, weiter durchdacht und auf die Idee von Zeit und Raum bezogen, so hätte er suchen und finden müssen, warum dies Bild kein objectives, sondern nur ein perspectivisches sein könne und dass die Formen von Raum und Zeit grade den perspectivischen Character des Bildes ausmachten, während er in seiner bloss objectiven Betrachtung gewissermassen bei der Aristelischen Auffassung stehen blieb und nur die bloss innerweltliche relative Natur der Zeit und des Raumes erkannte, da beide Kategorien ausserhalb der Welt nichts bedeuten. Den perspectivischen Ursprung aber bemerkten Aristoteles und Leibniz nicht und sie bezogen beide Formen desshalb immer auf die Dinge selbst trotz der unerklärlichen Idealität dieser Formen, die ihnen freilich auffallen musste.")

If we stood on the sun, the Copernican world view would be given to us apparently; since we're standing on earth, the Ptolemaic doctrine appears to be true; if we stood on Venus or Jupiter we would get a different perspective conception of the world each time. The mouse whines, if caught by the cat, the cat however is very pleased about it. If the party of progress praises a law, the conservatives will be downcast, and just the other way round. In short, the perception of things is always related to a certain view and is therefore perspective. (RAW, 185)[21]

Perspectivism is also for Nietzsche a doctrine which pays tribute to more than the intellectual aspects of man's life. However, he goes much further than Teichmüller who only casually mentions the examples of cat and mouse and the opposite parties, and affirms that the vital interests, which manifest themselves in our minds as *drives*, play an important role in *constituting the world of experience*. In this way he is trying to replace the traditional theory of knowledge with a "perspective theory of affects" [*Perspektiven-Lehre der Affekte*] (NL 1887, 9[8], KSA 12: 342). This is a remarkable attempt to combine anthropology and transcendental philosophy[22] and thus overcome the polarity between nature and reason.

2.4 Teichmüller, Drossbach, Liebmann and Nietzsche's concept of the subject

In the previous sections we have reconstructed the influence of Liebmann, Teichmüller and Drossbach on Nietzsche's concepts of power, (elementary) units and perspective. We are now going to show that the same concepts play an eminent role in Nietzsche's understanding of the subject. Let us take a first example from the following psychological analysis, in which we can find *mutatis mutandis* Teichmüller's perspectivism and Drossbach's beings:

> From each of our fundamental drives comes a perspectival valuation of everything that happens and is experienced [*eine verschiedne perspektivische Abschätzung alles Geschehens und Erlebens*]. Each of these drives feels restrained, or fostered, flattered, in respect to each

---

21 "Wenn wir nun auf der Sonne ständen, so wäre die Kopernikanische Weltauffassung für uns durch den Schein gegeben; da wir auf der Erde stehen, so ist der Schein für die Ptolomäische Lehre; ständen wir auf der Venus oder dem Jupiter, so würden wir jedesmal eine verschiedene perspectivische Auffassung der Welt gewinnen. Die Maus jammert, wenn sie von der Katze ergriffen wird; die Katze aber ist darüber sehr befriedigt. Wenn die Fortschrittspartei ein Gesetz lobt, so sind die Conservativen niedergeschlagen, und umgekehrt. Kurz die Auffassung der Dinge wird hier immer auf einen bestimmten Standpunkt bezogen und ist also perspectivisch."
22 Kant can also be considered as a philosopher of perspectivism. See e.g. Kaulbach 1990: 11ff.

of the others; each has its own law of development (its up and down, its tempo, etc.) – and one approaches death as the other rises./

Man as a multiplicity of "wills to power": each one with a multiplicity of means of expression and forms. The individual *supposed* [*angeblichen*] "passions" [*Leidenschaften*] (e.g. man is cruel) are merely *fictitious unities*: that which enters consciousness from the differential fundamental drives as *of the same kind* becomes, through a synthesising fiction, a "being" [*Wesen*] or "faculty" [*Vermögen*] – a passion. (NL 1885–86, 1[58], KSA 12: 25 = WLN, 60)

The dialectical figure, which we pointed out in section 2.2, is present in this note, too. On the one hand, Nietzsche criticizes the notion of a constant psychological unit, but on the other hand, he doesn't abandon the project of describing our inner life with the means of language (which, as mentioned above, project dogmatic categories onto the world of becoming) – *simply because such a life exists*. Hence he emphasizes e.g. "that our world of desires and passions is the only thing 'given' as real" (BGE 36), that our drives philosophize (BGE 6) and that "the degree and type of a person's sexuality [*Geschlechtlichkeit*] reaches up into the furthermost peaks [*letzten Gipfel*] of their spirit" (BGE 75). Numerous remarks of Nietzsche on human psychology and physiology and on the conduct of life depart from the reality of our bodily functions and our passions.[23] They constitute a basic pillar of the affirmative aspect of his philosophy, an aspect that is often neglected by scholars occupied too much with merely expounding Nietzsche's criticisms of the metaphysical tradition.

In section 2.1, we have seen that Liebmann stresses the analogy between human will and its results (bodily movements, muscle tension) on the one hand and action at a distance and motion in the outer world on the other. It is therefore natural that his conception of the subject should somehow entail the same analogy. We can find more details in a relevant passage of *On the Analysis of Reality*. After having praised the "psychological discovery" of Leibniz "that 'to *have* representations' and 'to *be* conscious of them' is not at all the same thing" (AR, 212), Liebmann asks himself:

> Where is all the knowledge of the scholars, the entire life experience of the individual, from which within a short time interval after all only a disappearing minimum is and can be present in the light-district of consciousness? Could the immense mass of my personal thoughts-supply be radically destroyed, be canceled entirely, since I am only conscious of a highly limited selection of them? (AR, 212)[24]

---

[23] This reality is according to Nietzsche at the same time an *interpretation*. This is a crucial point that requires a special treatment, which we can't offer in this paper.
[24] "Wo steckt denn das ganze Wissen des Gelehrten, die ganze Lebenserfahrung des Individuums, von der innerhalb eines kurzen Zeitintervalls ja doch nur ein verschwindenes Minimum

And here is his answer:

> Obviously not! [...] [T]he forgotten representations are indeed not in consciousness, but in the soul; not free but latent; not ἐνεργείᾳ, but δυνάμει within me; as tension forces, though not as living forces; enough, they are "des connaissances virtuelles" and can be converted under favorable conditions into "connaissances actuelles", just as the virtual speed and tension force of a compressed coil spring is converted after the removal of the inhibitory pressure to actual speed and living force. (AR, 212f.)[25]

It is plain to see that Liebmann goes back to Leibniz, in order to answer his question, and Nietzsche follows him, when he for example states that: "'Our inner world is much richer, more comprehensive, more hidden', we feel with Leibniz [*so empfinden wir mit Leibnitz*]" (GS 357). This is also the case when Nietzsche refers to Leibniz' "incomparable insight" that "consciousness [*Bewusstheit*] is merely an *accident* of representation [*Accidens der Vorstellung*] and *not* its necessary and essential attribute" (GS 357), which is in fact a paraphrase of one of Liebmann's remarks.[26]

3 Concluding remarks

In this paper, we have given a sketch of the influence that three to a great extent Leibnizian thinkers of the nineteenth century have exercised on Nietzsche and an account of aspects of the latter's philosophy, which were formed to a considerable degree under this influence. It would not be an exaggeration to say that Nietzsche's relationship to Leibniz has been of great importance in shaping central Nietzschean ideas, and that therefore a full-length account is badly needed. Here is a list of points which should be taken into consideration and discussed:

---

im Lichtbezirk des Bewußtseins gegenwärtig ist und sein kann? Soll etwa die unübersehbare Masse meines persönlichen Gedankenvorraths radical vernichtet, gänzlich annulirt sein, solange ich mir nur einer höchst beschränkten Auswahl davon *bewußt* bin?"
25 "[D]ie vergessenen Vorstellungen sind zwar nicht im Bewußtsein, wohl aber in der Seele; zwar nicht frei, aber latent; zwar nicht ἐνεργείᾳ, aber δυνάμει in mir; als Spannkräfte, wiewohl nicht als lebendige Kräfte; genug, sie sind – 'des connaissances *virtuelles*' und können sich unter günstigen Bedingungen in 'connaissances *actuelles*' umwandeln, wie die virtuelle Geschwindigkeit und Spannkraft einer gedrückten Spiralfeder sich bei Aufhebung des hemmenden Druckes in actuelle Geschwindigkeit und lebendige Kraft umwandelt."
26 Cf.: According to Liebmann's account, Leibniz conceived "consciousness [...] [as] an accident of representation [*Accidens der Vorstellung*]" (AR, 213). For more details on the subject see Loukidelis 2006, Loukidelis 2013: 17ff.

1. Liebmann, Drossbach and Teichmüller are of course important sources of Nietzsche's understanding of Leibniz, but they are surely not the only ones. Future scholarship needs to focus on further literature that Nietzsche has read.[27] Moreover, the reader of this paper should not assume that we have exhausted the Leibnizian potential of the three thinkers mentioned above. There are many passages on Leibniz in Liebmann's "On the analysis of reality" and *Thoughts and Facts*, in Drossbach's *On the Apparent and the Real Causes of Becoming in the World* and in Teichmüller's *The Real and the Apparent World* which we haven't discussed and which have to be examined, in order that scholarship obtains an even clearer picture of the Leibnizian elements in Nietzsche's thought.

2. In this paper, we emphasized the similarities between Leibniz and Nietzsche, but also between Nietzsche and Liebmann, and Drossbach and Teichmüller. Two reasons were primarily our guide. On the one hand, Nietzsche tends to severely criticize other philosophers, even if they have exercised an important influence on him. Thus, we had to stress the untold, well-concealed story. On the other hand, if one compares two thinkers, it is more fruitful from the point of view of systematic philosophy to produce some strong points. (It is an aim of this paper to stimulate systematic thought in scholarship on Leibniz and Nietzsche.) However, a full account of the relationship between Nietzsche and Leibniz should name and analyze all their differences.[28]

3. A basic issue in Nietzsche's understanding of the world is the absence of distinction between inorganic and organic structures. According to this understanding both structures are characterized not only by a visible activity, but also by an inner world. This point that is known in Nietzsche scholarship as the *continuum principle* or *continuum model*[29] has the advantage that it fills the problematic gap between the inorganic and the organic world, since these two worlds are considered to be of similar nature. It would be interesting though to see whether contemporary natural philosophy can accept this Leibnizian-Nietzschean doctrine and its metaphysical presuppositions.

---

[27] Apart from the hints of Kaulbach and Gerhardt (see 2.1) it should be noted that a possible source is Friedrich Überweg's history of modern philosophy (Überweg 1866; the chapter on Leibniz is to be found on p. 88ff.).

[28] On the differences between Leibniz and Nietzsche cf. 2.2., Figl 1982: 88, Springmann 2010: 61ff. On Nietzsche's critique of Drossbach and Teichmüller see e.g. Loukidelis 2013: 39ff.

[29] Cf. e.g. Constâncio 2011: 26, Abel 2012: 501ff.

4. A further interesting point is connected to the fact that Karl Otto Apel introduces his notion of the "body a priori" [*Leibapriori*] referring to Leibniz. He of course admits that "the historical Leibniz [...] doesn't overcome the Platonic-Cartesian division of the spheres of body and soul or of subject and object" (Apel 1975: 267). However, we can find here incoherence in the thought of Leibniz if we ask the following question: Should the body of a monad taken as a point of view be treated equally with the objectively given world of bodies? (Apel 1975: 267f.) Apel answers this question by affirming the philosophical priority of the body: "If human knowledge is an *a priori* perspective, the *a priori* of the 'intellectus' is not enough, it seems rather that we need something like a 'body a priori'" (Apel 1975: 268). This is a thought that we certainly find in Nietzsche's work together with its application to practical philosophy. Considering and analyzing Nietzsche's extensive remarks on the subject (which go hand in hand with his reflection on the conduct of life of an individual)[30] could lead scholars to a *monadological philosophy of life*, the exposition of which is a chapter yet unwritten in Nietzsche scholarship.[31]
5. Comparative studies on Nietzsche and Descartes or Spinoza have shown the importance of both eminent rationalists for Nietzsche. A closer look at linking Nietzsche and Leibniz could reveal that the latter is *the decisive figure*, if we want to understand certain aspects of the former's relationship to rationalism and to reconstruct some key concepts of his philosophy.

References

Abel, Günter (1998) *Die Dynamik der Willen zur Macht und die ewige Wiederkehr*, 2nd edition, Berlin/New York: De Gruyter.
Abel, Günter (2012) "Die Aktualität der Wissenschaftsphilosophie Nietzsches", in: H. Heit, G. Abel and M. Brusotti (eds.), *Nietzsches Wissenschaftsphilosophie*, Berlin/Boston: De Gruyter, 481–530.
Anderson, R. Lanier (2012) "The Will to Power in Science and Philosophy", in: H. Heit, G. Abel and M. Brusotti (eds.), *Nietzsches Wissenschaftsphilosophie*, Berlin/Boston: De Gruyter, 55–72.
Apel, Karl-Otto (1975) "Das Leibapriori der Erkenntnis: Eine erkenntnisanthropologische Betrachtung im Anschluß an Leibnizens Monadenlehre", in: H.-G. Gadamer and P. Vogler

---

30 On Nietzsche and the conduct of life see Gödde/Loukidelis 2016.
31 The term *monadologische Lebensphilosophie* is only briefly mentioned in an essay of Jürgen Habermas on Nietzsche's epistemology (Habermas 1985: 525).

(eds.), *Neue Anthropologie. Siebenter Band: Philosophische Anthropologie. Zweiter Teil*, Munich/Stuttgart: DTV/Thieme, 264–288.

Bornedal, Peter (2010) *The Surface and the Abyss*, Berlin: De Gruyter.

Cassirer, Ernst (1902) *Leibniz' System in seinen wissenschaftlichen Grundlagen*, Marburg: Elwert'sche Buchhandlung.

Constâncio, João (2011) "On Consciousness. Nietzsche's Departure from Schopenhauer", in: *Nietzsche-Studien* 40, 1–42.

Couturat, Louis (1901) *La logique de Leibniz d'après des documents inédits*, Paris: Alcan.

Du Bois-Reymond, E. (1974) [1870] "Leibnizische Gedanken in der neueren Naturwissenschaft", in: S. Wollgast (ed.), *Vorträge über Philosophie und Gesellschaft*, Hamburg: Meiner, 25–53.

Dühring, Eugen (1873) *Kritische Geschichte der Philosophie von ihren Anfängen bis zur Gegenwart*, 2nd edition, Berlin: Heimann's.

Figl, Johann (1982) *Interpretation als philosophisches Prinzip: Friedrich Nietzsches universale Theorie der Auslegung im späten Nachlass*, Berlin/New York: De Gruyter.

Fleming, Marie (2012) "Nietzsche on Science and Consciousness", in: H. Heit, G. Abel and M. Brusotti (eds.), *Nietzsches Wissenschaftsphilosophie*, Berlin/Boston: De Gruyter, 333–344.

Gerhardt, Volker (1996) *Vom Willen zur Macht: Anthropologie und Metaphysik der Macht am exemplarischen Fall Friedrich Nietzsches*, Berlin/New York: De Gruyter.

Gödde, G./Loukidelis, N. (eds.) (2016) *Nietzsche und die Lebenskunst*, Stuttgart/Weimar: Metzler.

Günzel, Stephan (2001) "Leibniz heute noch gefährlich: Die Theodizee als moderne Denkfigur – Über das implizite und explizite Fortwirken von Leibniz bei Nietzsche", in: H. Poser (ed.), *Nihil sine ratione – Mensch, Natur und Technik im Wirken von G.W. Leibniz (VII. Internationaler Leibniz-Kongress)*, Berlin: Gottfried Wilhelm Leibniz Gesellschaft, 434–440.

Habermas, Jürgen (1985) "Nachwort (1968): Zu Nietzsches Erkenntnistheorie", in: *Zur Logik der Sozialwissenschaften*, Suhrkamp, Frankfurt a.M., 505–528.

Kaulbach, Friedrich (1979) "Nietzsche und der monadologische Gedanke", in: *Nietzsche-Studien* 8, 127–156.

Kaulbach, Friedrich (1980) *Nietzsches Idee einer Experimentalphilosophie*, Cologne: Böhlau.

Kaulbach, Friedrich (1990) *Philosophie des Perspektivismus: Erster Teil. Wahrheit und Perspektive bei Kant, Hegel und Nietzsche*, Tübingen: Mohr.

Lange, Friedrich Albert (1866) *Geschichte des Materialismus und Kritik seiner Bedeutung in der Gegenwart*, Iserlohn: Baedeker.

Lange, Friedrich Albert (1974) [1873] *Geschichte des Materialismus und Kritik seiner Bedeutung in der Gegenwart*, Erstes Buch, Frankfurt a.M.: Suhrkamp [Reprint of 2nd edition, Iserlohn: Baedeker 1873].

Liebmann, Otto (1865) *Kant und die Epigonen: Eine kritische Abhandlung*, Stuttgart: Schober.

Loukidelis, Nikolaos (2006) "Nachweis aus Otto Liebmann, *Zur Analysis der Wirklichkeit*", in: *Nietzsche-Studien* 35, 302–303.

Loukidelis, Nikolaos (2007) "Nachweise aus Otto Liebmann, *Gedanken und Thatsachen* (1882)", in: *Nietzsche-Studien* 36, 391–396.

Loukidelis, Nikolaos (2013) *Es denkt: Ein Kommentar zum Aphorismus 17 aus "Jenseits von Gut und Böse"*, Würzburg: Königshausen & Neumann.

Loukidelis, Nikolaos (2014) "Nietzsche und die 'Logiker'", in: H. Heit and L. Heller (eds.), *Handbuch Nietzsche und die Wissenschaften*, Berlin/Boston: De Gruyter, 222–241.

Müller-Lauter, Wolfgang (1971) *Nietzsche. Seine Philosophie der Gegensätze und die Gegensätze seiner Philosophie*, Berlin/New York: De Gruyter.
Müller-Lauter, Wolfgang (1999) "Das Problem des Gegensatzes in der Philosophie", in: *Über Werden und Wille zur Macht. Nietzsche-Interpretationen I*, Berlin/New York: De Gruyter, 1–24.
Poellner, Peter (1995) *Nietzsche and Metaphysics*, New York: Oxford University Press.
Riccardi, Mattia (2009) *"Der faule Fleck des Kantischen Kriticismus". Erscheinung und Ding an sich bei Nietzsche* (Beiträge zu Friedrich Nietzsche, vol. 14), Basel: Schwabe.
Riccardi, Mattia (2014) "Nietzsche und die Erkenntnistheorie und Metaphysik", in: H. Heit and L. Heller (eds.), *Handbuch Nietzsche und die Wissenschaften*, Berlin/Boston: De Gruyter, 242–264.
Russell, B. (1900) *A Critical Exposition of the Philosophy of Leibniz*, Cambridge: Cambridge University Press.
Schlimgen, Erwin (1999) *Nietzsches Theorie des Bewusstseins*, Berlin/New York: De Gruyter.
Simon, Josef (1984) "Das Problem des Bewusstseins bei Nietzsche und der traditionelle Bewusstseinsbegriff", in: M. Djuric and J. Simon (eds.), *Zur Aktualität Nietzsches*, vol. 2, Würzburg: Königshausen & Neumann, 17–33.
Sleinis, E.E. (1999) "Between Nietzsche and Leibniz: Perpectivism and Irrationalism", in: B.E. Babich and R.S. Cohen (eds.), *Nietzsche, Theories of Knowledge, and Critical Theory. Nietzsche and the Sciences I*, Dordrecht/Boston/London: Kluwer, 67–76.
Small, Robin (2001) *Nietzsche in Context*, Aldershot/Burlington/Singapore/Sydney: Ashgate.
Spir, Afrikan (1877) *Denken und Wirklichkeit. Versuch einer Erneuerung der kritischen Philosophie, Erster Band. Das Unbedingte*, Leipzig: Findel.
Springmann, Simon (2010) *Macht und Organisation: Die Machtkonzeption bei Friedrich Nietzsche und in der mikropolitischen Organisationstheorie*, Berlin: Duncker & Humblot.
Überweg, Friedrich (1866) *Grundriss der Geschichte der Philosophie von Thales bis auf die Gegenwart. Dritter Theil. Die Neuzeit*, Berlin: Mittler & Sohn.

Paul Katsafanas
4 Kant and Nietzsche on Self-Knowledge

A typical view of Kant and Nietzsche on self-knowledge might go something like this: Kant thinks that our mental lives are entirely transparent to us, whereas Nietzsche claims that the mind is utterly opaque. Kant believes that we usually know what we are doing and why, placing great faith in our introspective capacities; Nietzsche believes, to put it in his own words, that "actions are *never* what they appear to be [...] all actions are essentially unknown" (D 116). In short: Kant and Nietzsche are antipodes, the one emphasizing self-knowledge and the other self-ignorance.

A closer examination of Kant and Nietzsche reveals that this picture is misleading on several levels. Kant does not embrace the naïve claim that our minds are transparent to us; he is alive to the possibility of unconscious, inaccessible, hidden, and repressed mental contents. And while Nietzsche firmly maintains that there is no hope of rendering *all* mental content conscious, he does think that there are certain routes that bring us to greater self-knowledge.

In this essay, I pursue a more nuanced account of the differences between Kant and Nietzsche on self-knowledge. I examine the *kinds* of self-knowledge that they recognize, the *extent* to which self-knowledge is possible, and the best *routes* to attaining it. The essay falls into three sections. Section One examines Kant's claim that there are two capacities for self-knowledge, which he terms "inner sense" [*innerer Sinn*] and "apperception" [*Apperzeption*]. Neither of these capacities is immune to error, and neither provides us with comprehensive knowledge of our mental economies. Section Two argues that Nietzsche agrees with Kant that these two capacities yield some self-knowledge. Yet Nietzsche is far more pessimistic about their prospects; given the complexities of our mental economies, these capacities give us at best a rudimentary knowledge of our mental lives. Nonetheless, the differences between Kant and Nietzsche on these points are a matter of degree rather than of kind.

Section Three introduces what is, in my view, a more important difference between Kant and Nietzsche. Nietzsche argues that we can attain self-knowledge by – as he puts it – looking away from ourselves. I argue that this is the real point of departure between the two thinkers; it marks Nietzsche's most profound break with Kant on the topic of self-knowledge. In addition, I contend that in examining Kant and Nietzsche's views on self-knowledge, we can see a profound shift in ways of regarding our mental lives. Although Kant recognizes the possibility of self-deception and acknowledges that the mind is in certain respects opaque, he clings to the premodern idea that opacity is – or at least *should be* – correctible. Nietzsche, on the other hand, treats opacity as ineliminable and sees the traditional routes to self-knowledge as misdirected.

1 Kant on self-knowledge

Kant famously writes,

> The **I think** must be **able** to accompany all my representations: for otherwise something would be represented in me that could not be thought at all, which is as much as to say that the representation would either be impossible or else at least would be nothing to me. (CPR B 131–132)[1]

The claim that the "I think" must be capable of accompanying all representations might suggest that all representations are self-conscious or at least self-consciously accessible. Moreover, Kant claims that "maxims" – specifications of what we are doing and why – are the object of moral assessment, which might suggest that he thinks we can have certain knowledge of our motives for acting. And he gives self-consciousness pride of place, writing that

> The fact that the human being can have the "I" in his representations [i.e., is self-conscious] raises him infinitely above all other living beings on earth. Because of this he is a *person* [...] i.e., through rank and dignity an entirely different being from *things,* such as irrational animals, with which one can do as one likes. (*Anthropology*, AA 7: 127)

Given the prominence and preeminence of self-consciousness in Kant's writings, it is tempting to assume that he takes our mental lives to be transparent to us.

However, this is a mistake. Kant quite bluntly asserts that "the depths of the human heart are unfathomable" (*Metaphysics* of Morals, AA 6: 447).[2] He writes that "it is absolutely impossible by means of experience to make out with complete certainty a single case in which the aim of an action otherwise in conformity with duty rested simply in moral grounds" (*Groundwork*, AA 4: 407). In other words, it is absolutely impossible to know, with complete certainty, whether I have acted on the motive that I take myself to have acted upon. Indeed, when I

---

[1] I cite Kant's works by the volume and page number of the Berlin Akademie Ausgabe, *Kants gesammelte Schriften*, hereafter abbreviated AA, except for the *Critique of Pure Reason* (hereafter CPR), which is cited by A/B version page numbers.

[2] He continues, "Who knows himself well enough to say, when he feels the incentive to fulfill his duty, whether it proceeds entirely from the representation of the law or whether there are not many other sensible impulses contributing to it that look to one's advantage (or to avoiding what is detrimental) and that, in other circumstances, could just as well serve vice?" (*Metaphysics* of Morals, AA 6: 447).

think I have discovered the motive for my action, this "discovery" is often an invention: in a line that sounds decidedly Nietzschean, Kant writes, "without noticing it, we suppose we are discovering within ourselves what we ourselves have put there" (*Anthropology*, AA 7: 133). Our alleged self-knowledge often turns up only distortions, confabulations, and errors. Thus, Kant writes

> the field of sensuous intuitions and sensations of which we are not conscious, even though we can undoubtedly conclude that we have them, that is *obscure* representations in the human being (and also in animals) is immense. Clear representations, on the other hand, contain only infinitely few points of this field that lie open to consciousness; so that as it were only a few places on the vast *map* of our mind are *illuminated*. (*Anthropology*, AA 7: 135)

So Kant is at once deeply committed to the importance of self-consciousness and skeptical about its extent. To see why this is so, we need to investigate the way in which Kant thinks we achieve self-knowledge. There are two paths to self-knowledge, each with its own peculiar limitations.

1.1 Two kinds of self-knowledge

Kant claims that there are two sources of self-knowledge: inner sense [*innerer Sinn*] and apperception [*Apperzeption*].[3] Inner sense is what we would today call introspection: it is "consciousness of what we undergo as we are affected by the play of our own thoughts" (*Anthropology*, AA 7: 161). It provides us with knowledge of our own sensations. Kant believes that it is a form of perception: he writes that inner sense is "a mere faculty of perception" (*Anthropology*, AA 7: 45).

But we also have a second source of self-knowledge:

> Man ... who knows the rest of nature solely through the senses, knows himself also through pure apperception; and this, indeed, in acts and inner determinations which he cannot regard as impressions of the senses. (CPR A 546/B 574)

Apperception is knowledge of our own activity. Kant's idea, here, is that we do not attain knowledge of our own judgments and actions through inner sense. Take a typical case: I decide to walk to my office to do some work. I set out; the action is underway. I needn't observe myself or attempt to introspect my motives in order to determine what I am doing; I know, without needing to resort to the observation of sensory states, that I am walking to my office in order to do some work. It seems natural to say: I know what I am doing because my action is a

---

3 See CPR A 107, B 132, B 152–159, and *Anthropology*, AA 7, Section 24.

product of my *decision*, my "inner determination", to walk to my office. In short, it seems that I sometimes know that I am A-ing precisely because I have made a decision to A. It is in this way that apperception is non-sensory.

Kant makes it clear that these two forms of self-knowledge are distinct; neither can be reduced to the other. He complains that "the terms *inner sense* and *apperception* are normally taken by psychologists to be synonymous, despite the fact that the first alone should indicate a psychological (applied) consciousness, and the second merely a logical (pure) consciousness" (*Anthropology*, AA 7: 142). In the following passage, he explains why the conflation of apperception and inner sense is an error:

> Inner sense is not pure apperception, consciousness of what the human being *does*, since, this belongs to the faculty of thinking. Rather, it is consciousness of what he *undergoes*, insofar as he is affected by the play of his own thoughts. It rests on inner intuition … There is then only *one* inner sense, because the human being does not have different organs for sensing himself inwardly … (*Anthropology*, AA 7: 161)

So Kant draws a sharp distinction between the way in which we know our own judgments and their products, on the one hand, and the way we know our sensations and appetites, on the other. Apperception is a power of thinking; inner sense is a mode of sense-perception. Moreover, these passages emphasize that inner sense pertains to the passive – to what we *undergo*. Apperception pertains to the active, to what we *do*.

These distinctions between activity and passivity play an important role not only in Kant's moral theory, but in his analysis of the mind:

> in regard to the state of its representations, my mind is either *active* and exhibits a faculty (*facultas*) or it is *passive* and consists in *receptivity (receptivitas)*. A cognition joins both together … Representations in regard to which the mind behaves passively, and by means of which the subject is therefore *affected* … belong to the *sensuous* cognitive faculty. But ideas that comprise a sheer *activity* (thinking) belong to the *intellectual* cognitive faculty. (*Anthropology*, AA 7: 140)

Apperception and inner sense fall on opposite sides of this divide.

In sum, then, inner sense is a type of perception directed at our sensations. Apperception is a consciousness of our own activity, and is non-sensory.

1.2 The limitations and failures of self-knowledge

Above, we noted that Kant believes that self-knowledge often fails: "it is absolutely impossible by means of experience to make out with complete certainty a single case in which the aim of an action otherwise in conformity with duty rested simply in moral grounds" (*Groundwork*, AA 4: 407). He reiterates this point elsewhere, writing:

> even a human being's inner experience of himself does not allow him so to fathom the depths of his heart as to be able to attain, through self-observation, an entirely reliable cognition of the basis of the maxims which he professes, and of their purity and stability. (*Religion*, AA 6: 63)

Notice that Kant does not limit failures of self-knowledge to sensations, the province of inner sense; these passages emphasize that knowledge of our own actions – the realm of apperception – can also fail. Let's start, though, with the problems of inner sense.

Inner sense can fail due to the intrinsic limitations of perceptual capacities. It faces all the vulnerabilities of more familiar forms of perception, such as vision. In particular, for Kant perception provides us with access to appearances rather than things-in-themselves. He writes,

> experience (empirical cognition), inner no less than outer, is only the cognition of objects as the *appear* to us, not as they *are* (considered in themselves alone). For what kind of sensible intuition there will be depends not merely on the constitution of the object of the representation, but also on the constitution of the subject and its receptivity. (*Anthropology*, AA 7: 141)

The way in which an object appears to me depends not only on the nature of the object but also on the nature of my cognitive capacities. I see the object before me as a brown oblong table; but these colors, shapes, and classifications need not be attributes of the object as it is independently of perception. Just so with my inner states: I perceive myself as resentful of Fred's success, but this may diverge from my actual motives. As Kant puts it, inner sense "represents to consciousness even our own selves only as we appear to ourselves, not as we are in ourselves. For we intuit ourselves only as we are inwardly *affected*" (CPR B 153). So inner sense is susceptible to all the problems that plague outward sense perception.

A second mode of failure for inner sense arises not from the intrinsic limitations of the faculty, but from an extrinsic factor: pressures toward self-deception. Kant writes that "one is never more easily deceived than in what promotes a good opinion of oneself" (*Religion*, AA 6: 68). Suppose I engage in behavior that might be appropriately described either as impressing Robert or belittling Claire; I am more likely to interpret myself as acting on the former, praiseworthy motive rather than the latter, disagreeable motive. After all, the former interpretation enables me to preserve a positive image of myself. As Kant puts it, "We like to flatter ourselves by falsely attributing to ourselves a nobler motive, whereas in fact we can never, even by the most strenuous self-examination, get entirely behind our covert incentives" (*Groundwork*, AA 4: 407). Put simply, "the human being has from nature a propensity to dissemble" (AA 25: 1197), and this shows up in our interpretations of ourselves.

So failures of inner sense can be traced both to the intrinsic limitations of perception and to extrinsic interferences. Consider how this might apply to apperception. Apperception is non-sensory, so it cannot be directly affected by the ordinary limitations of perceptual systems. However, it can be influenced by them at one remove. Take an external analogue: if poor vision leads me to perceive the shadow as a threatening person, I may judge that I ought to run away in order to escape from danger. I will have apperceptive knowledge of this judgment and the resultant action. In one way, no error infects this judgment: I know that I am running away in order to escape danger. In another way, there is an error: there is no danger from which to escape. Just so with self-knowledge. I have inner awareness of my motive for impressing Robert but not for belittling Claire. As a result, I decide to act in a way that will impress Robert, but fail to notice that it also comes at Claire's expense. The error begins with inner sense but resounds into the domain of apperception.

Additionally, the pressure toward self-deception can infect apperception as easily as inner sense, leading me to misrepresent my own grounds for action. Suppose we alter the above example slightly: I have inner awareness of both motives, but decide to act on the praiseworthy one. Out of a desire to think well of myself, I ignore the effects of the disagreeable motive and take myself to be acting only on the praiseworthy ones. Nonetheless, external observers would describe me as influenced by the disagreeable motive. Here, my decision is not fully transparent to me; self-deception has led me astray.

Thus, apperception can be misled by failures of inner sense and pressures toward self-deception. Might apperception also suffer from intrinsic limitations? Kant isn't explicit about this, but we can envision one way in which it might. Suppose our apperceptive knowledge results from the fact that our decisions determine our actions. For example, I have apperceptive knowledge that I am walking to my office because I have decided to perform this action and the decision has caused the action. If our decisions play a less important role than Kant thinks – if our decisions *contribute to* but do not *fully determine* the nature of our actions – then apperceptive knowledge might be limited. I will argue, below, that this is exactly the possibility that Nietzsche explores.

2 Nietzsche on self-knowledge

In this section, I will argue that while Nietzsche acknowledges that both introspection and apperception can provide us with some degree of self-knowledge, he is less impressed than Kant with their powers.[4] Nietzsche argues that the limitations of these capacities are far more complex and pervasive than Kant acknowledges. It's not just that we miss hidden motives and are misled by self-deception; the problems are much deeper, to the extent that we often completely misunderstand our actions. The same point applies to apperception: while Kant acknowledges that our choices sometimes have facets of which we are unaware, Nietzsche adds that our choices play a much less important role in the production of our actions than we suppose, and accordingly provide us with less extensive knowledge of what we are doing. Thus, the acts issuing from our decisions can be as obscure as the acts of others.

2.1 Nietzsche on introspection or inner sense

As we saw above, Kant believes that the main limitations on inner sense arise through the pressures of self-deception. Nietzsche certainly agrees that self-serving interpretations of attitudes are ubiquitous and constitute a danger for those seeking self-knowledge. For example, he writes,

> *Self-observation.* – Man is very well defended against himself, against being reconnoitered and besieged by himself, he is usually able to perceive of himself only his outer walls. The actual fortress is inaccessible, even invisible to him, unless his friends and enemies play the traitor and conduct him in by a secret path. (HH I 491)

However, there is an important difference between Nietzsche and Kant on this point. Kant's emphasis on self-deception suggests that, were self-deception absent, there would be no great obstacles to self-knowledge; inner sense, cleared of the distortions of self-deception, would provide us with generally accurate and reasonably comprehensive knowledge of ourselves, just as perception provides us with generally accurate and reasonably comprehensive knowledge of the external world.

Nietzsche rejects this assumption. The idea that we *deceive ourselves* about our motives implies that we have some dim cognizance of our actual motives, but hide them from ourselves. Take the case that concerns Kant: although I present myself as acting for beneficent reasons, I am actually motivated by self-interest. If this is to count as a case of self-deception, I must have at least some

---

[4] Of course, Nietzsche doesn't use the Kantian terms "inner sense" and "apperception". However, he does discuss the capacities picked out by these Kantian terms: introspection and the knowledge resulting from judgment.

inkling that I am actually motivated by self-interest. Otherwise it would be a mere error; no *deception* would be involved.

Nietzsche thinks that in many cases we lack even this dim awareness of our hidden motives. He claims that it is a "universal madness" to think that we generally know what we are doing. For "the opposite is precisely the naked reality demonstrated daily and hourly from time immemorial! [...] actions are *never* what they appear to be [...] all actions are essentially unknown" (D 116). For example, consider the scientists and philosophers discussed in the *Genealogy*, who Nietzsche presents as motivated by the ascetic ideal. His claim is *not* that these individuals secretly know that they are motivated by asceticism and deceive themselves about this; instead, his claim is that although scientists and philosophers may never have given a thought to asceticism, they are nonetheless motivated by it. There is no *deception* involved here; there is just an error. (The ascetic priests are different – they, Nietzsche emphasizes, are not just in error but self-deceived.)

So the problem for Kant is self-deception. The problem for Nietzsche is different and more complex. There are a number of factors rendering self-knowledge difficult. First, the influences of motives on thought are so pervasive and so complex that even honest attempts to know oneself will often fail (D 116, GM Preface 1). If each action were motivated by one or several desires and affects, then it would be easy enough to identify them. However, Nietzsche believes that the etiology of our actions is far more complex than this.

For one thing, we tend to attribute our actions to coarse, forceful motives such as lust, anger, love, pity, and so on. Yet Nietzsche believes that these are not the factors that have the most decisive influence on us. He writes that "the milder, middle degrees [of our affects], not to speak of the lower degrees which are continually in play, elude us, and yet it is they which weave the web of our character and destiny" (D 115). Some of these mild motives will be minute affective reactions; others will involve external environmental factors. For example, in *Ecce Homo*, Nietzsche claims that the most important factors in his own development were ones that might wholly escape notice:

> these small things – nutrition, place, climate, recreation, the whole casuistry of selfishness – are inconceivably more important than everything one has taken to be important so far. (EH Clever 10)

So Nietzsche's point is that we tend to overlook the effects of apparently inconsequential factors such as minute, mild affects, climate and diet; yet it is just these states that have a decisive influence on our actions.

More generally, for Nietzsche there is no definite set of motives prompting action: no matter how deeply we investigate, no matter how many motives we uncover for an action, we can always find a deeper layer. This is part of what Nietzsche means when he writes,

> Cause and effect: there is probably never such a duality; in truth a *continuum* faces us, from which we isolate a few pieces, just as we always perceive a movement only as isolated points, i.e. do not really see, but infer ... (GS 112, emphasis added)

Our attempts to ascertain the motives for our actions amount to nothing more than isolations of a few points on a continuum. We may find one, two, or thirty motives for an action, but there will always be more; there will always be different ways of understanding the causes, finer discriminations among the motives, different classifications or descriptions of them, and different prioritizations of them. Thus, Nietzsche writes,

> Everything which enters consciousness is the last link in a chain, a closure. It is just an illusion that one thought is the immediate cause of another thought. The events which are actually connected are played out below our consciousness: the series and sequences of feelings, thoughts, etc., that appear are symptoms of what actually happens! – Below every thought lies an affect. *Every thought*, every feeling, every will is *not* born of one particular drive but is a *total state*, a whole surface of the whole consciousness, and results from how the power of *all* the drives that constitute us is fixed at that moment – thus, the power of the drive that dominates just now as well as of the drives obeying or resisting. The next thought is a sign of how the total power situation has now shifted again. (KSA 12, 1[61] = WLN, 60)

Our actions are products of our "total state" (*Gesamtzustand*), yet this total state cannot be adequately captured by talk of discrete motives, or discrete causes and effects.[5] Nietzsche's claim, here, is that trying to find a discrete cause for an action is analogous to trying to find one for a historical event. Take, for example, the First World War. We can isolate certain events – an assassination, a treaty, an ultimatum – but each of these is only one point in an enormously complex series of events, and each acquires its importance only as part of a much broader context. Moreover, there are very different ways of framing the causal history of this event. One explanation of the First World War might focus on the actions of a few great individuals, another on economic forces, another on spiritual malaise, another or a desire for meaningful direction, another on political machinations, another on imperialism, another on nationalism, another on delays in diplomatic communications. Each of these stories might be extremely informative; thinking that one of them must be uniquely correct (or maximally informative) would be decidedly

---

5 Constâncio (2011) provides an especially lucid analysis of this point in his discussion of the "continuum model".

odd. Nietzsche's point is that just the same reasoning applies to actions. Different specifications of motives, different description of causal histories will highlight different features of the agent's mental economy, and each will be incomplete. Other stories highlighting different features will always be possible.

This brings us to a closely related point involving language and concepts. I have argued elsewhere that Nietzsche understands conscious states as linguistically or conceptually articulated (Katsafanas 2005; see also Constâncio 2011). Whereas unconscious states and processes have definite, structured content, this content is articulated in a nonconceptual form. States become conscious when their content is translated into a conceptual form. If this is correct, then the very way in which we become conscious of mental activities is constrained by our linguistic and conceptual resources. If I lack the concept *ressentiment*, for example, I cannot be conscious of my *ressentiment* as *ressentiment* (I may be conscious of it as a vague ache, or as jealousy, or as envy, but not as *ressentiment*). Nietzsche claims that we lack concepts for most of the mild motives of the sort mentioned in D 115 (quoted above). It follows that our ability to bring these motives to consciousness is severely limited. I will return to this point below in Section Three, arguing that it generates a deep obstacle to self-knowledge.

For all of these reasons, Nietzsche thinks that the obstacles to self-knowledge extend far beyond self-deception. Indeed, he doubts that we can achieve self-knowledge at all:

> We are necessarily strangers to ourselves, we do not comprehend ourselves, we *have* to misunderstand ourselves, for us the law 'each is furthest from himself' applies to all eternity. (GM Preface 1)

We are *necessarily* [*nothwendig*] strangers to ourselves – this is not a contingent state that might be overcome by further acts of introspection. For introspection provides only a modicum of self-knowledge, and misses much of the complexity of our mental economies.

2.2 Nietzsche on apperception

What about the second form of self-knowledge, apperception? Again, Nietzsche is less impressed than Kant with its prospects. It's true that I can attain *some* knowledge of what I am doing by deciding, judging, and so forth. But Nietzsche emphasizes that the *content* of these judgments and decisions is not as transparent to us as Kant believes.

Consider a representative passage. BGE 32 remarks that moral theories that emphasize conscious intentions – and this would include Kant's theory – involve "the first attempt at self-knowledge". However, these theories err by positing "the intention as the whole origin and prehistory of an action". Today, Nietzsche suggests, we should move past this, noting that "everything about [the action] that is intentional, everything about it that can be seen, known, 'conscious', still belongs to its surface and skin – which, like every skin, betrays something but conceals even more. In short, we believe that the intention is merely a sign and symptom that still requires interpretation" (BGE 32).

In short, conscious decisions and intentions are superficial. But why? The problem is that background drives and affects shape the course of conscious deliberation in ways that the agent typically fails to recognize. Nietzsche believes conscious thought is "secretly guided and channeled" by the agent's drives (BGE 3); when an agent steps back from and reflects upon a drive, the agent's "intellect is only the blind instrument of *another drive*" (D 109). I have argued elsewhere that drives affect perceptual saliences, the ways in which we classify or categorize experiences, the manner in which we frame decisions, and the ways in which the agent's decision progresses (see Katsafanas 2013). For example, suppose I decide to help Megan and take myself to be doing so out of compassion. Deliberating on the case, I might have the following conscious thoughts: I will offer Megan assistance, because I pity her unfortunate state. For Nietzsche, there is much more going on in the background.

First, I may be ignoring or failing to detect the presence of other motives, such as a desire to ingratiate myself with Megan or to impress a bystander (these are the sorts of concerns that occupy Kant, as we saw above). In this vein, Nietzsche remarks that "the will to overcome an affect is ultimately only the will of another, or several other, affects" (BGE 117). My reflective thought may be driven by background motives.

Second, and more importantly, I may be ignorant of the way in which my motives are affecting my perception of the situation. Nietzsche claims that a drive will "emphasize certain features and lines in what is foreign, in every piece of the 'external world', retouching and falsifying the whole to suit itself" (BGE 230). This point is repeated in other passages:

> From each of our basic drives there is a different perspectival valuation [*perspektivische Abschätzung*] of all events and experiences. (KSA 12, 1[58])

> There is no doubt that all sense perceptions are wholly permeated with *value-judgments* ... [*gänzlich durchsetzt sind mit* Wethurtheilen ...] (KSA 12, 2[95])

If my view of the world is structured by motives that I fail to detect, then my reflective deliberations – which, after all, take place in the context of this structured view – will have presuppositions, biases, and distortions that escape my notice. To give a simple example: I may perceive Megan as in an unfortunate state precisely because I actually resent her success; I may see her as in need of pity precisely because I secretly envy her. An observer with different motives would see the situation quite differently.[6]

Third, I may misunderstand the nature of the emotion that I am expressing. I take pity to be a state aimed at helping those in need, whereas Nietzsche suggests that it can constitute a covert attempt to extend my power over others (see D 132–138, GS 338, GM III 14, BGE 260). Thus, even if I manage to *identify* one of my motives, I may not *understand* it.

Fourth, all of this complexity only scratches the surface. For surely it is a mistake to claim, with Kant, that there is a *unique* or *single* reason for my action. As discussed in the prior section, Nietzsche believes that rather than attributing actions to discrete causes, we should see them as emanations from the "total state" of our mental economy. Conscious decisions, thoughts, and motives are one part of this total state, but only a small part. For example, once I have recognized that my pity for Megan constitutes an attempt to express my power over her, I can cut still deeper, asking why I am motivated to express my power in just this way, why pity in particular seems fitted here. Doing so would reveal even more of the "total state" of my mental economy.

This is just a quick and simplified example, but we can already see what bothers Nietzsche about the Kantian analysis of apperceptive knowledge. Kant is perfectly right that our decisions and judgments provide us with some self-knowledge. But Nietzsche draws attention to the fact that we are often ignorant of the true nature of our decisions and judgments. My decisions, influenced by the factors discussed above, have many layers of complexity that elude ordinary awareness. So they, too, provide no sure route to self-knowledge.

In addition, these reflections entail that there is no clean distinction between apperception and introspection. I may have apperceptive knowledge that I am acting so as to help Claire, but understanding what this actually means requires extended introspection, self-observation, and analysis. So the claim that we can neatly partition "doings" and "undergoings" comes to seem too simple. As Nietzsche puts it,

> "I have no idea what I am *doing*! I have no idea what I *ought to do*!" – you are right, but be sure of this: *you are being done!* [du wirst gethan!] at every moment! Mankind has in all ages confused the active and the passive: it is their everlasting grammatical blunder. (D 120)

---

6 I have analyzed this point at length in Katsafanas (2013) and Katsafanas (2015).

When we think we are doing, we are also being done. Each doing is also an undergoing, and Kant's clean divisions of our mental lives are, in Nietzsche's view, too superficial.

3 The paths to self-knowledge

We have seen that Kant and Nietzsche agree that there are two routes to self-knowledge: introspection and judgment (or inner sense and apperception). Kant acknowledges that both kinds of self-knowledge can be compromised by errors and pressures toward self-deception. Nietzsche agrees, but is far more skeptical: he sees introspection and apperception as intrinsically flawed, capable of providing us only with a selective and partial picture of our inner lives. Moreover, he gives us reasons for doubting that these capacities can be isolated from one another.

At this point, then, it might seem that Nietzsche's main advance over Kant is simply that he advocates a more realistic account of the limitations of human knowledge. However, a further difference arises when we consider the ways in which Kant and Nietzsche think we can correct the deficiencies of introspection and apperception. Given the different obstacles that the two thinkers acknowledge for self-knowledge, it stands to reason that they will identify different routes to its attainment. Below, I treat their accounts in turn.

3.1 Kant: Introspection and conscience

Kant claims that "the **First Command** of all Duties to Oneself" is to know oneself (*Metaphysics* of Morals, AA 6: 441). As he puts it,

> This command is "*know* (scrutinize, fathom) *yourself*," not in terms of your natural perfection (your fitness or unfitness for all sorts of discretionary or even commanded ends) but rather in terms of your moral perfection in relation to your duty. That is, know your heart – whether it is good or evil, whether the source of your actions is pure or impure, and what can be imputed to you as belonging originally to the *substance* of a human being or as derived (acquired or developed) and belonging to your moral *condition*. (*Metaphysics* of Morals, AA 6: 441)

In other words, the first duty to myself is to discover the propensities, dispositions, motives, and desires that bear on the moral standing of my actions. It's easy to see why Kant thinks that this is an important duty: in order to fulfill the demands of morality, I must act on the appropriate maxims.[7] But, as we saw in Section One, I cannot know what maxims I am acting upon without knowing my own propensities, dispositions, motives, and desires. Striving to fulfill the demands of morality therefore requires striving to know myself. [8]

But how, given the impediments to self-knowledge discussed above, am I to do so? Kant's proposal is straightforward: "only the descent into the hell of self-cognition can pave the way to godliness" (*Metaphysics* of Morals, AA 6: 441). That is, the best hope for self-knowledge is engaging in extensive acts of introspection, attempting to discover whether any covert or hidden motives might be influencing one's judgments.

Of course, there is a potential problem: we saw, above, that self-deception can lead introspection astray. How is further introspection to help, then? Won't the further acts of introspection be misled by the very same motives? If "one is never more easily deceived than in what promotes a good opinion of oneself" (*Religion*, AA 6: 68), then why would extensive introspection be likely to yield accurate verdicts? Suppose, for example, that I want to determine whether my dealings with Megan have been influenced by selfish motives. Regardless of how much I introspect, it seems that I will be influenced by the desire to acquit myself of selfishness.

Kant's response to this concern rests on the idea that while I can never be certain that I have overcome all traces of self-deception, I can be certain that I have rigorously attempted to do so. To see this, consider his analysis of conscience. Conscience is the unerring certainty that one has given one's best effort to subject oneself to scrutiny. Kant writes,

> an *erring* conscience is an absurdity. For while I can indeed be mistaken at times in my objective judgment as to whether something is a duty or not, *I cannot be mistaken in my subjective judgment as to whether I have submitted it to my practical* reason (here in its role as judge) for such a judgment; for if I could be mistaken in that, I would have made no practical judgment at all, and in that case there would be neither truth nor error. (*Metaphysics* of Morals, AA 6: 401, emphasis added)

Kant emphasizes that I can be mistaken about whether something is my duty. However, I cannot be mistaken about whether I have attempted to determine what my duty is. This is the sense in which conscience is unerring.

---

[7] In particular, I must act only on those maxims that pass the Categorical Imperative test.
[8] For a helpful discussion of this aspect of Kant's view, see Ware (2009). Notice also that there is an interesting difference between Kant and Nietzsche on this point: whereas Kant claims that we have a moral commitment to seeking self-knowledge, Nietzsche warns us that seeking self-knowledge is ruinous for most individuals (EH Clever 9).

The same point applies to self-knowledge. I am trying to do my duty, and accordingly descend into the "hell" of introspection, examining my motives. I can be mistaken about what my motives are. But conscience provides me with an unerring knowledge of whether I have done my best to discern what my motives are. While I may not succeed in garnering accurate self-knowledge, I cannot fail to know whether I have genuinely tried to do so.

So Kant's picture is relatively simple: the problem is self-deception; the solution is trying to detect the self-deception through honest and comprehensive acts of introspection. There are risks here: Kant claims that "nothing is more harmful to a human being than being a precise observer of himself" (AA 25: 252). For "all self-scrutinizers fall into the gloomiest hypochondria" (AA 25: 863).[9] Confronted with my own selfish, morally deficient motives, I may be unable to maintain a positive image of myself. Nonetheless, this is the risk that must be weighed against the rewards of attaining self-knowledge.

3.2 Nietzsche: Looking away from oneself

Kant claims that we can attain self-knowledge via conscientious introspection because he believes that the chief obstacle to self-knowledge is self-deception; conscience and further introspection, he hopes, can remove that obstacle. Nietzsche, of course, is less sanguine. As we saw above, the obstacles to self-knowledge extend much further than self-deception; introspection has intrinsic limitations. It's not that we have an adequate capacity that has, unfortunately, gone astray due to a corrupt character. Instead, we have an inadequate capacity, unsuited to its goal. Further exercises of this capacity are unlikely to help.

Additionally, Nietzsche rejects the Kantian claim that deliverances of conscience have a special epistemic standing. The sense that one has given one's best effort to introspection may be erroneous. Nietzsche's dismissive attitude toward conscience is perhaps clearest in WS 38, where he writes, "The bite of conscience, like the bite of a dog into stone, is a stupidity." Elsewhere, he bemoans the fact that most individuals' "intellectual conscience"–which would be an affect that motivates one to believe only that for which there is good evidence–is severely lacking (GS 2). More generally, Nietzsche explicitly distances conscience from justification: one's conscience is nothing more than another feeling whose content is shaped by epistemically irrelevant factors (cf. GM II 24). As he puts it in WS 52, "The content of our conscience is everything that was reg-

---

9 These passages are quoted in Wood (2003).

ularly demanded of us without reason during our childhood, by persons whom we respected or feared."

So neither further acts of introspection nor reliance on conscience will be particularly helpful in attaining comprehensive self-knowledge. How, then, should we proceed? Nietzsche writes that "the psychologist must look away from *himself* in order to see at all" (TI Arrows and Epigrams 35). The same point is echoed in the Preface of the *Genealogy*, where Nietzsche emphasizes that we have never *sought* ourselves – and then presents genealogy as a route to self-knowledge. On the face of it, this is an astonishing claim. I want to attain knowledge of myself, yet I am told to look away from myself in order to do so. How can looking at something *other* than the object I want to understand help? What might Nietzsche have in mind?

If the *Genealogy* is any indication, then looking away from oneself to attain self-knowledge involves looking at genealogies. So let's consider how genealogy might uncover facts that are relevant for self-knowledge.

We can start with the most obvious possibility. Nietzsche famously remarks,

> Direct self-observation [*unmittelbare Selbstbeobachtung*] is not nearly sufficient for us to know ourselves: we require history, for the past continues to flow within us in a hundred waves. (HH II 223)

Commentators often interpret this passage as claiming that motives or forces present in the deep recesses of the past still persist in the present. For example, the ascetic priests embraced the values of humility, inoffensiveness, and compassion out of *ressentiment*; so, somehow, when I embrace those values today, I am still doing so out of *ressentiment*.

If this claim were true, genealogy would be a good path to self-knowledge. Unfortunately, though, the claim is completely implausible. The fact that one type of person in a completely distinct social, cultural, and historical setting embraced a value because they experienced a certain affect does not entail that I, in circumstances that could hardly be more different, must embrace the same value out of the same affect. Consider just how *ahistorical* such a claim would be – it would entail that there are timeless, ineluctable relationships between affects and values. This hardly seems consistent with Nietzsche's analysis of the way in which affects such as bad conscience, reverence, envy, so on have been tethered to different values over time. So Nietzsche must mean something else when he claims that the past flows through us in a hundred waves.

In fact, I think Nietzsche identifies two ways in which genealogy is relevant for self-knowledge. Let's start with the more straightforward one. Above, we saw that one of Nietzsche's concerns about self-knowledge is that mild and unnoticed motives play a decisive role in shaping our lives, yet elude introspection.

We miss the subtle influences upon action, for we cannot detect them in the moment of choice. Genealogy, though, can uncover them. By examining long stretches of human behavior rather than isolate moments of choice, we are able to detect the effects of these subtle, mild influences.

An image may help. Consider the kinds of explanations that arise in geology. I ask why a canyon stretches before me in the alluvial plain. The geologist tells me that the slight yet constant pressure of rain and wind has, over millennia, chiseled the canyon. Rain and wind appear to be very mild and almost unnoticeable features when compared to the resilience of stone. If I were simply to examine the rocky landscape for a moment, I would never suspect that such slight forces would yield such dramatic results. And yet, taking a longer view, I see that they do. The power of this mild cause cannot be understood without studying long stretches of time. Just so, Nietzsche thinks, with our own psychologies. We focus on the crude, momentary eruptions of force: the strong passions, the conscious decisions, the resolutions of will. And we overlook the host of minute forces that shape us in far more profound ways.

These are just the kinds of factors that genealogy and history can reveal. For example, rather than attributing our drive toward knowledge to an independent thirst for truth, we can see how it was shaped by ascetic tendencies. Or rather than seeing a philosophical system as driven by a pure urge to get at the truth, we can see it as springing from factors that the philosopher fails to recognize: "Gradually, it has become clear to me what every great philosophy so far has been: namely, the personal confession of its author and a kind of involuntary and unconscious memoir" (BGE 6). History and genealogy can help to reveal the presence of various drives, in part by showing how these drives motivate patterns of behavior that might be visible only in the long term.

So one way in which I can learn something about myself by looking away from myself is by detecting – either in historical characters, or even in my own history – gradual shapings of behavior that result from apparently minor factors. But this is not the only way in which genealogy is relevant; let's turn to the second and more complex point.

Put briefly, genealogy helps us discover unnoticed aspects of the conceptual scheme through which we experience and interpret the world. This point is very difficult and requires careful explication; I address it in more detail in Katsafanas (in progress). However, let me sketch the view here.

In the *Genealogy*, Nietzsche is at pains to emphasize the way in which one conception of agency supplanted another. For example, he writes:

> Just as the common people separates lightning from its flash and takes the latter to be a *deed*, something performed by a subject, which is called lightning, popular morality sepa-

rates strength from the manifestations of strength, as though there were an indifferent substratum behind the strong person which had the *freedom* to manifest strength or not. But there is no such substratum; there is no "being" behind the deed, its effect and what becomes of it; "the doer" is invented as an afterthought, – the doing is everything. (GM I 13)

Here, Nietzsche draws attention to the way in which our modern conception of agency treats the agent as distinct from what he does. At its most extreme, this is the libertarian conception of free will, which holds that the agent is to be identified with a characterless and utterly undetermined capacity for choice. The ancient conception, Nietzsche suggests, does not recognize this distinction: the agent's character is given by the nature of the agent's action, by what the agent actually does. The agent of antiquity does not take himself to be distinct from his past, his social relationships, and his community, nor does he see his actions as things that might or might not express his character; put simply, he *is* his deeds and relationships. (These accounts of agency obviously require far more explication than I can provide here.)[10]

Nietzsche's concern is not whether any particular philosopher (or ordinary agent) explicitly adopts just these thoughts about agency. Rather, he is concerned with the way that an agent who internalizes something like this sense of agency will experience his action. To the extent that I tacitly adopt the modern conception of agency, I will tend to experience my choices as wholly undetermined by and unreflective of my character. I will tend to see punctual moments of conscious choice as of overriding importance. I will tend to see myself as self-defining and isolated from my environment.

In this manner, the way in which I experience my action depends upon the conception of agency that I tacitly adopt. For example, we moderns are perennially tempted to say, with Kant, that our experience of deliberation commits us to taking ourselves to be free: we cannot engage in genuine deliberation without presupposing that we are free to determine our forthcoming action.[11] But Nietzsche's point is that just this sort of experience is historically contingent. It is not a datum, not a starting point, but a link in a complex story. Genealogy helps me to see that my conception of agency is *optional:* it supplanted an early form, and could be supplanted by another. Genealogy thus helps me to see that the conceptual scheme through which I view the world structures my perception of the world.

---

10 For more extended analyses of these matters, see Taylor (1992) and Williams (1993).
11 Kant claims that human choice "can indeed be *affected* but not *determined* by impulses [...] *Freedom* of choice is this independence from being determined by sensible impulses" (*Metaphysics* of Morals, AA 6: 213–214). Elsewhere, he writes that the will is "a faculty of determining oneself from oneself, independently of necessitation by sensible impulses" (CPR A 534/B 562).

This is part of what Nietzsche draws attention to in BGE 16, when he denies that there are any immediate certainties:

> There are still harmless self-observers who believe that there are "immediate certainties"; for example, "I think," or as the superstition of Schopenhauer put it, "I will"; as though knowledge here got hold of its object purely and nakedly as "the thing in it self" without any falsification on the part of either the subject or the object. But that "immediate certainty," as well as "absolute knowledge" and the "thing in itself," involve a *contradictio adjecto*. I shall repeat a hundred times; we really ought to free our selves from the seduction of words! Let the people suppose that knowledge means knowing things entirely; the philosopher must say to himself: When I analyze the process that is expressed in the sentence, "I think," I find a whole series of daring assertions that would be difficult, perhaps impossible, to prove; for example, that it is I who think, that there must necessarily be something that thinks, that thinking is an activity and operation on the part of a being who is thought of as a cause, that there is an "ego," and, finally, that it is already determined what is to be designated by thinking – that I know what thinking is. [...] In place of the "immediate certainty" in which the people may believe in the case at hand, the philosopher thus finds a series of metaphysical questions presented to him, truly searching questions of the intellect; to wit: "From where do I get the concept of thing? Why do I believe in cause and effect? What gives me the right to speak of an ego, and even of an ego as cause, and finally ego as the cause of thought?" (BGE 16)

Here, Nietzsche points to the way in which apparently simple inner perceptions – perceptions of the fact that I am thinking, for example – have a host of presuppositions about the nature of agency, thinking, subjectivity, causality, and thinghood. Were my concept of agency different, Nietzsche emphasizes, I would not perceive my own thinking in the same way. My current conceptual repertoire influences even the most basic perceptions. And part of what genealogy does is uncovers these facts about the nature of my conceptual scheme.

The parallel, in Kant, would be knowledge of the Categories. The *Critique of Pure Reason* uncovers the conceptual structure of (so Kant claims) all self-conscious cognition. Precisely because this conceptual structure is intrinsic to all self-conscious cognition, it is not self-knowledge in the ordinary sense: uncovering this structure gives me knowledge not of my own idiosyncratic mental economy, but of the shared mental economies of all rational creatures. But suppose Kant is wrong: suppose the conceptual structure of conscious thought varies across different agents. Suppose, for example, that there is nothing inevitable about the experience of choice as undetermined by desire. Then a historical reconstruction of the ways in which certain conceptual schemes have come to seem inevitable will help us to see that these schemes are, in fact, contingent. And this will show us that Kant is more right than he realizes when he writes that "Without noticing what we are doing, we suppose we are discovering within us what we ourselves have put there" (*Anthropology*, AA 7: 133). For here Kant has in mind the instilling of false motives and desires within ourselves. But for Nietzsche our self-invention goes far beyond this: the very conceptual schemes through which we experience the world, the schemes which structure our most basic understandings of ourselves and our relations to the world, are historically fluid. This is precisely the way in which the past flows through us in a hundred waves. And this is precisely the kind of self-knowledge that can be attained only by looking away from oneself.

4 Conclusion

Kant recognizes two distinct forms of self-knowledge: introspection and apperception. Introspection acquaints us with the sides of ourselves that Kant characterizes as passive: our sensations, affects, and so on. Apperception is knowledge of our own activities. It is a form of knowledge that arises from the fact that we in some sense create that which we know. Both modes of self-knowledge can go astray, and are particularly prone to being distorted be selfish motives; thus, neither is guaranteed to provide us with comprehensive self-knowledge.

I have argued that Nietzsche agrees with some aspects of this model. He, too, sees introspection and judgment as providing us with a limited degree of self-knowledge. However, he sees these capacities as far more limited than Kant acknowledges. In part, this is due to our psychic complexity: Nietzsche believes that it is a mistake to treat our actions as caused by discrete motives, decisions, and judgments. Instead, our actions are emanations from the "total state" of the organism. Introspection and judgment can do no more than scratch the surface of this total state, identifying only the most forceful and obvious motives while neglecting the many subtle, apparently minor influences.

But this disagreement over the scope of self-knowledge is not the deepest difference between Kant and Nietzsche. In Section Three, I argued that whereas Kant recognizes two forms of self-knowledge, Nietzsche seems to posit three. In particular, Nietzsche claims that we can acquire self-knowledge by *looking away* from ourselves. Section Three provided a brief sketch of two ways in which this might be so. In particular, genealogy enables us to identify some of the subtle factors shaping our actions as well as the influence of our current conceptual repertoires on our perceptions and understandings of our actions. For Nietzsche's point is that the very way in which we conceptualize our deliberations, motives, and actions is influenced by our current conceptual scheme.[12]

---

[12] I owe great thanks to Maria João Branco, João Constâncio, Marta Faustino, Pietro Gori, Maria Filomena Molder, Paolo Stellino, Benedetta Zavatta, and other participants in the Nietzsche

References

Constâncio, João (2011) "On Consciousness. Nietzsche's Departure from Schopenhauer", in: *Nietzsche-Studien* 40, 1–42.
Kant, Immanuel (1996) *The Metaphysics of Morals*, ed. Mary Gregor, New York: Cambridge University Press.
Kant, Immanuel (1998) *Groundwork of the Metaphysics of Morals*, ed. Mary Gregor, New York: Cambridge University Press.
Kant, Immanuel (1999a) *Critique of Pure Reason*, eds. Paul Guyer and Allen Wood, New York: Cambridge University Press.
Kant, Immanuel (1999b) *Critique of Practical Reason*, eds. Paul Guyer and Allen Wood, New York: Cambridge University Press.
Kant, Immanuel (1999c) *Religion within the Boundaries of Mere Reason*, eds. Allen Wood and George di Giovanni, New York: Cambridge University Press.
Kant, Immanuel (2006) *Anthropology from a Pragmatic Point of View*, ed. Robert Louden, New York: Cambridge University Press.
Katsafanas, Paul (2005) "Nietzsche's Theory of Mind: Consciousness and Conceptualization", in: *European Journal of Philosophy* 13, 1–31.
Katsafanas, Paul (2013) "Nietzsche's Philosophical Psychology", in: K. Gemes and J. Richardson (eds.), *The Oxford Handbook of Nietzsche*, Oxford: Oxford University Press, 727–755.
Katsafanas, Paul (2015) "Value, Affect, Drive", in: Peter Kail and Manuel Dries (eds.), *Nietzsche on Mind and Nature*. Oxford: Oxford University Press. 163–188.
Katsafanas, Paul (in progress) "The Moral Significance of Perceptual Experience".
Taylor, Charles (1992) *Sources of the Self: The Making of the Modern Identity*, Cambridge: Harvard University Press.
Ware, Owen (2009) "The Duty of Self-Knowledge", in: *Philosophy and Phenomenological Research* 79(3), 671–698.
Williams, Bernard (1993) *Shame and Necessity*, Berkeley/Los Angeles: University of California Press.
Wood, Allen (2003) "Kant and the Problem of Human Nature", in Allen Wood (ed.), *Essays on Kant's Anthropology*, Cambridge: Cambridge University Press.

International Lab, who offered many helpful comments and critiques during a presentation of this paper at the Universidade Nova de Lisboa.

Luís de Sousa and Marta Faustino
5 Nietzsche and Schopenhauer on the 'Self' and the 'Subject'

1

Nietzsche is known, amongst other things, for being one of the first philosophers in the Western tradition to deconstruct the traditional image of the self. On the one hand, Nietzsche seems to do away with the notion of the 'self' altogether if by 'self' we understand something essentially linked to consciousness or reason. On the other hand, a more moderate interpretation would hold that what Nietzsche calls into question is not the 'self', but only the image of it as the center of consciousness and reason, that is, the 'subject' in the traditional sense. According to this line of thought, if it is at all legitimate to talk about our 'self', it is as something that lies deep beneath the threshold of consciousness, at the level of our most fundamental and unconscious drives. Thus, Nietzsche's new image of the self forms the basis of his more general assault on consciousness and reason. For the latter, far from having the value ascribed to them, deceive us by concealing the inner depths of our being. In fact, according to Nietzsche, they should be taken as surface-phenomena and as tools of those inner drives and instincts that most properly constitute our self.

As much as these ideas may seem revolutionary, the present article aims to show that they are better grasped and understood in the light of Schopenhauer's ideas concerning the subject and the self. Schopenhauer was one of the first philosophers to introduce a fundamental change in the direction philosophy took after Descartes. For Schopenhauer, our innermost essence does not lie in a so-called theoretical soul and our rational consciousness is at best only a part – and a minor one – of our true self, which is much better grasped when we take into account our organic body and in particular its willing, drive-like nature.

It is to Schopenhauer that we must look, then, if we want to trace out one of the most important sources – if not the most important one – of Nietzsche's insights concerning the self and kin concepts such as the mind, the body and the will. We will find that even when Nietzsche is making claims that are arguably opposed to those of Schopenhauer, he is in fact still working within an essentially Schopenhauerian framework, even if in many respects he does go beyond it. The present article will thus also aim to show that Nietzsche's thoughts concerning the 'self' and the 'subject' are better seen as a development, radicalization and, in some respects, recasting and overcoming of Schopenhauer's thought.

The argument will be developed in the three following sections. In section 2, we will be concerned with showing that Nietzsche's critique of the cogito is, in a great measure, a reinstatement of Schopenhauer's (and also Kant's) critique. This will be meant to demonstrate that Nietzsche's critique does not amount to a rejection of the idea of the self, but only to a rejection of the identification of the self with the subject. In section 3, we will move to Nietzsche's positive account of selfhood and argue that Schopenhauer's account is his starting-point. Finally, in section 4 we will analyze Schopenhauer's and Nietzsche's accounts of character and draw the consequences of their new conception of selfhood to their theories of action. It shall become clear that, also in this respect, Nietzsche is better understood when seen in the light of Schopenhauer's insights on the matter.

2

For a long time it was a very common and widespread idea that Nietzsche totally rejected modern conceptions of subjectivity and selfhood. In other words, he was taken as a thinker who rejected the idea that we are selves. This idea fitted well with the portrayal of Nietzsche as a post-modernist *avant la lettre*. In the last two decades this picture was challenged by Robert Pippin among others. Pippin (1999) argued that Nietzsche should be seen as part of the development and radicalization of modernity's own self-critique. If by modernity in the philosophical sense one understands the movement originally initiated by Descartes, all modern philosophy can be read as an evolving critique of its own presuppositions. Thus, Nietzsche could be seen as fitting into the modern tradition, even perhaps as its culmination, in the sense that he too develops and radicalizes modernity's critique of Descartes.

When dealing with the topic of the 'subject' and the 'self' in Nietzsche it is vital to carefully distinguish his critique of the Cartesian cogito from his own account of the self. In other words, his critique of the I to be found mainly among his published writings in a few aphorisms from *Beyond Good and Evil*, should not be taken as an outright rejection of the idea of the self, perhaps along the lines of David Hume. We will aim to show that evidence can be found that Schopenhauer might have provided a model for Nietzsche's accounts of the subject or 'I' and the embodied self. For in Schopenhauer there is a clear distinction between the subject of cognition, our conscious 'I', and what we are at bottom, which is the embodied subject of willing or, more simply, the will. In this sense, Schopenhauer can be seen as Nietzsche's precursor in the radicalization and culmination of modern philosophy's self-critique.

Concerning the I or the ego, the following passage shows clearly how Nietzsche conceives of his relation with modern philosophy:

> So what is really going on with the whole of modern philosophy? Since Descartes (and, in fact, in spite of him more than because of him) all the philosophers have been out to assassinate the old concept of the soul, under the guise of critiquing the concepts of subject and predicate. In other words, they have been out to assassinate the fundamental presupposition of the Christian doctrine. As a sort of epistemological skepticism, modern philosophy is, covertly or overtly, *anti-Christian* (although, to state the point for more subtle ears, by no means anti-religious). People used to believe in "the soul" as they believed in grammar and the grammatical subject: people said that "I" was a condition and "think" was a predicate and conditioned – thinking is an activity, and a subject *must* be thought of as its cause. Now, with admirable tenacity and cunning, people are wondering whether they can get out of this net – wondering whether the reverse might be true: that "think" is the condition and "I" is conditioned, in which case "I" would be a synthesis that only gets *produced* through thought itself. *Kant* essentially wanted to prove that the subject cannot be proven on the basis of the subject – and neither can the object. The possibility that the subject (and therefore "the soul") has a *merely apparent existence* might not always have been foreign to him, this thought that, in the form of the Vedanta philosophy, has already arisen on earth once before and with enormous power. (BGE 54)

According to Nietzsche, modern philosophy is essentially anti-Cartesian philosophy in the sense that it aims to "assassinate the old concept of the soul". Although he does not mention it explicitly here, he has in mind the idea that "assassinating" the concept of the soul means to deny that the essence of the human being (his self) lies solely in his consciousness or in his thinking.

Even though Schopenhauer does not seem to figure anywhere in this passage, he may provide a kind of missing link between Kant and Vedanta philosophy. Both constitute arguably the greatest influences on Schopenhauer's thought, as he himself recognizes when he cites them not only as his direct sources and influences, but also among the few predecessors of his own work (WWR I, xv). And Nietzsche was of course well aware of that.[1]

---

[1] A posthumous fragment containing an earlier version of the aphorism quoted above ends with Nietzsche suggesting that *The Birth of Tragedy* involves a "new", "even if preliminary" expression of the "apparent existence" (*Scheinexistenz*) of the subject (NL 1885, 40[16], KSA 11: 635–636). Given that Nietzsche's position in his first work can be roughly described as Schopenhauerian, we can read this suggestion as Nietzsche's acknowledgement of Schopenhauer's influence on BGE 54. Moreover, according to Schlimgen (1999: 41), Nietzsche's source for this aphorism and its conflation of Kant and Vedanta philosophy was none other than Paul Deussen's *Das System* des Vedanta. Besides being a reputed orientalist, Deussen was himself an avowed Schopenhauerian: he edited Schopenhauer's collected works and founded the *Schopenhauer*

For Schopenhauer, the subject is the ultimate basis or presupposition of all cognitive functions of consciousness. Not only all consciousness is consciousness of an object, but also all consciousness is dependent on a subject. The subject forms the point of unity of all cognitive acts. However, despite being the essential condition of all consciousness, the subject is unable to know itself as such. Since every object presupposes a subject, the subject of consciousness would have to be detached from itself, as it were, in order to achieve self-knowledge.[2] Yet, even if this were possible, the subject would not know itself as *subject*, but only as another object. As Kant, before Schopenhauer, has expressed it, whenever the (transcendental) subject attempts to know itself, it ends up going around in a constant circle.[3] The subject is elusive by definition, for it is always presupposed in the very act of grasping itself. Thus, the subject is the unobjectified and unobjectifiable presupposition of cognition and therefore cannot know itself as such, that is, as a subject of *consciousness*.

Schopenhauer's thesis is best read as a reinstatement of Kant's central claim in the Paralogisms' chapter of the *Critique of Pure Reason*. Here, Kant argues that all propositions drawn from the "sole text" of rational psychology, from the "I think", are analytic. In other words, these propositions make explicit the concept of consciousness, the conditions under which there can be something like a transcendental I, the conditions of subjectivity. These conditions are, for instance, the transcendental I functioning as the ultimate subject of thoughts, its numerical identity, its being distinguishable in principle from any kind of object, etc. Kant's great lesson is precisely that we cannot understand these conditions of subjectivity as if they were predicates of an object, i.e., as if they permitted us to cognize the properties of a real object called "I".

According to Schopenhauer, although the subject is one of the essential components of the "world as representation", being one of its essential poles, it

---

Gesellschaft and the Schopenhauer Jahrbuch. For an interpretation of BGE 54 see also Itaparica (2014).
2 See FR, 208: "Consequently there is no *knowledge* of *knowing*, since this would require that the subject separated itself from knowing and yet knew that knowing; and this is impossible".
3 CPR B 404/A 346: "Through this I, or He, or It (the thing), which thinks, nothing further is represented than a transcendental subject of thoughts = x, which is recognized only through the thoughts that are its predicates, and about which, in abstraction, we can never have even the least concept; because of which we therefore turn in a constant circle, since we must always already avail ourselves of the representation of it all times in order to judge anything about it; we cannot separate ourselves from this inconvenience, because the consciousness in itself is not even a representation distinguishing a particular object, but rather a form of representation in general, insofar as it is to be called cognition; for of it alone can I say that through it I think anything."

does not figure in it as one object among others. Rather the essential forms of knowing are not applicable to it, as it stands outside space, time and causality and, as a result, is non-individual. That is, the subject as such cannot be identified with any knowing individual, person or body: "It is whole and undivided in every representing being" (WWR I, 5).

For Schopenhauer, the subject of cognition should not to be understood as a soul and much less as a substance. To begin with, the subject has a thoroughly functional role. That is, it is a mere correlate of objects and nothing else beyond its relation to the latter. Secondly, according to Schopenhauer, the soul is itself an illegitimate concept inasmuch as it is created surreptitiously by postulating and hypostasizing a cause of such subjective phenomena as thinking and willing (WWR I, 489ff.). Schopenhauer criticizes this procedure on the grounds that it entails an application of the principle of sufficient reason to the subject, whereas its validity is confined to the relation between objects only. Furthermore, according to Schopenhauer, it was only in the context of academic philosophy that the concept of the soul was taken as a substance. In fact, Schopenhauer argues, the concept of substance is a pseudo-genus, whose only true species is matter. According to him, its creation served only to subsume the concept of the soul as one of its species, besides matter, in order to demonstrate the former's alleged immaterial and imperishable character and therefore its immortality.

We will now claim that Nietzsche's attack on the subject occurs along the lines of Schopenhauer's (and Kant's) attack and like the latter does not entail *per se* a rejection of selfhood.

In the passage quoted above, the main idea Nietzsche attributes to Vedanta philosophy, that is, that of the "illusory existence of the soul", provides, in fact, a good summary of Schopenhauer's own thesis, that the subject of cognition as such is a mere phenomenon. It is unknowable and non-individual and therefore does not provide us with criteria for self-identification.

Even though Nietzsche's arguments for conceiving of the subject as an illusion differ from the ones presented by Schopenhauer, their respective conclusions are fairly in line with each other. Both put seriously into question the alleged evidence of the Cartesian cogito insofar as this is understood as an immediate insight into the nature of our self as that of a thinking being. Let us now look at one of Nietzsche's most explicit statements on the topic from his published writings:

<blockquote>
As far as the superstitions of the logicians are concerned: I will not stop emphasizing a tiny little fact that these superstitious men are loath to admit: that a thought comes when "it" wants, and not when "I" want. It is, therefore, a *falsification* of the facts to say that the subject "I" is the condition of the predicate "think." It thinks: but to say the "it" is just that
</blockquote>

> famous old "I" – well that is just an assumption or opinion, to put it mildly, and by no means an "immediate certainty." In fact, there is already too much packed into the "it thinks": even the "it" contains an *interpretation* of the process, and does not belong to the process itself. People are following grammatical habits here in drawing conclusions, reasoning that "thinking is an activity, behind every activity something is active, therefore –." (BGE 17)

When one compares his various statements on this topic, one concludes that for Nietzsche the subject is something projected as it were behind the stream of consciousness, functioning as its point of unity. According to Nietzsche, we are led into this by a sort of "transcendental illusion" concerning the fundamental form of grammar, the subject-predicate form.[4] Belief in the subject-predicate distinction is, according to Nietzsche, the strongest and most ancient of all our beliefs. It is our "*Ur-glaube*":

> That we have a right to *distinguish* between subject and predicate, between cause and effect – that is our strongest belief; in fact, at bottom even the belief in cause and effect itself, in conditio and conditionatum, is merely an individual case of the first and general belief, our primeval belief in subject and predicate (as the assertion that every effect is a doing and that every conditioned presupposes something that conditions, every doing a doer, in short a subject). Might not this belief in the concept of subject and predicate be a great stupidity? (NL 1886, 4[8], KSA 12: 181–182 = WLN, 104)

We commit the "transcendental" mistake of conceiving of things as mirroring our fundamental grammatical-logical forms of comprehension. At bottom, this was what Kant had already criticized in his "Paralogisms" as a confusion between the logical and the real subject of thought. From the fact that the "I" must be the ultimate subject of every thought and for that reason cannot be thought otherwise than as a subject we conclude mistakenly that it must be also the ultimate substrate of all thoughts, that is, a thinking substance or being.[5] To this idea Nietzsche adds that to think of something as a subject of something else is not only to think of it as its substrate, but also as its cause. This is the reason why for Nietzsche the critique of the concept of substance and causality falls into one with his critique of the ego.[6] In both cases, the problem is the

---

[4] For the critique of the subject-predicate structure as the fundamental form of thinking, see, for instance, GS 354; BGE Preface 20, 35, 54; GM I 13; TI Reason 5; NL 1886–1887, 4[8], KSA 12: 182; NL 1887, 35[35], KSA 12: 526.

[5] For an account of Nietzsche's appropriation of the *Paralogisms* see Hill (2003: 180ff.).

[6] Cf. for example NL 1887, 10[19], KSA 12: 465: "Der *Substanz*begriff eine Folge des *Subjekts*begriffs: *nicht* umgekehrt! Geben wir die Seele, 'das Subjekt' preis, so fehlt die Voraussetzung für eine 'Substanz' überhaupt."

same: we tend to hypostasize the subject-object form of grammar and presuppose in every process a substrate as its cause. This connection is made explicit by Nietzsche not only in the passage here under discussion but also in many others where he links his critique of the ego to his more general critique of the concepts of substance and cause. In fact, sometimes Nietzsche goes as far as thinking that we created our general concepts of cause and effect, of substance and accident by way of a false analogy with the ego: "it [language] believes in the 'I', in the I as being, in the I as substance, and it *projects* this belief in the I-substance onto all things – that is how it creates the concept of *thing* in the first place ... Being is imagined under everything, *pushed under everything* – as a cause; the concept of 'being' is only derived from the concept of I ..." (TI Reason 5; see also GS 127; TI Errors 3; NL 1885, 38[3], KSA 11: 597–598; NL 1887, 10[19], KSA 12: 405; NL 1887, 35[35], KSA 12: 526; NL 1885–1886, 2[83], KSA 12: 101–102; NL 1887, 9[63], KSA 12: 369; NL 1887, 9[98], KSA 12: 391; NL 1888, 14[79], KSA 13:258–259)[7]

All this means, regarding the ego, that to posit a subject of thoughts is also to posit something that causes thoughts. But, for Nietzsche, the only thing to which we have some sort of phenomenal access is the stream of consciousness. We are not able to catch the alleged causality at work here. This is clearly evinced by the fact that "a thought comes when 'it' wants, and not when 'I' want". Far from conveying us any substantial knowledge, all talk of ourselves as subjects of consciousness ends up being tautological. The only thing that is legitimate to say about consciousness is that "there is thinking" or "there are thoughts" (WP 484/NL 1887, 10[158], KSA 12: 549).

With Schopenhauer, and Kant before him, we could say that the subject of cognition was not a real being, a thing-in-itself and therefore not an imperishable substance. As we already saw, the consequence for Schopenhauer was that the subject was reduced to its functional character as the subjective correlate and condition of perceptions and thoughts. This also entailed that the subject as such can never be turned into an object, being therefore unknowable. Thus, Schopenhauer concluded that the subject, taken as such, is in fact completely anonymous, which is one of the points Nietzsche is trying to make in the previous passage. *Es denkt*, that is, *it thinks* means that *no one* in particular is doing the thinking. We ourselves *are not* the thinkers. The "it" does not specify a self. The difference between Schopenhauer and Nietzsche in this respect seems to lie

---

[7] In fact, in TI Errors 3 Nietzsche goes further than this and asserts that belief in causality and the ego originates in the belief in ourselves as agents, that is, in our will as causal efficacious. See below section 4 of this article.

merely in the fact that whereas the former still allows talk of the subject understood as a necessary condition of consciousness, Nietzsche wants to point out that the need to assume a subject of thinking is based on an illegitimate analogy with grammar, which distinguishes a subject from a predicate. However, this is not the whole story as the talk of "transcendental illusion" could suggest. Even though the fundamental form of our representations – the grammatical distinction between subject and predicate – has no correspondence to the "things in themselves", for Nietzsche this form is "transcendental" not only because without it we wouldn't be able to represent anything at all (for Kant as for Schopenhauer), but mainly because without it we wouldn't even be able to *survive*. Thus, *a priori* synthetic judgments are false, but nevertheless necessary, for "the conditions of life might include error" (GS 121). As much as Nietzsche thinks that the I is invented and totally illusory, he also recognizes it as a necessary and indispensable illusion for beings like us:

> What separates me most deeply from the metaphysicians is: I don't concede that the "I" is what thinks. Instead, I take the *I itself to be a construction of thinking*, of the same rank as "matter", "thing", "substance", "individual", "purpose", "number": in other words to be only a *regulative fiction* with the help of which a kind of constancy and thus "knowability" is inserted to, *invented into,* a world of becoming. [...] It is only thinking that posits the I: but up to now philosophers have believed, like the "common people", that in "*I* think" there lay something or other of unmediated certainty and that this "I" was the given cause of thinking, in analogy with which we "understood" all other causal relations. However habituated and indispensable this fiction may now be, that in no way disproves its having been invented: something can be a condition of life and *nevertheless be false*. (NL 1885, 35[35], KSA 11: 526 = WLN, 20 – 21)[8]

3

We shall now show that Nietzsche's 'modern' critique of the cogito does not entail a direct rejection of the notion of the self. We shall see that in this respect he follows Schopenhauer's model in that the cogito should be replaced by the idea of an unconscious, embodied and drive-like self. It cannot be denied that Nietzsche corrects and develops Schopenhauer's account of the self. However, it will become clear by the end of this section how much both his critique of the cogito and his new account of selfhood are indebted to Schopenhauer.

---

[8] Cf. also BGE 4; NL 1881, 11[270], KSA 9: 544 – 545; NL 1885, 38[3], KSA 11: 598; NL 1886 – 1887, 7[63], KSA 12: 318.

3.1

We will start by outlining Schopenhauer's move from his account of the subject of cognition to his account of the self as will. Although Schopenhauer assents to Kant's critique of Descartes' cogito, he intends in another respect to go beyond Kant. There is a sense in which Schopenhauer allows the subject to become an object for itself, claiming that it is possible for it to gather substantive knowledge about its own self. But, and here lies the crux of the matter, this self-knowledge does not concern the "transcendental subject", that is, the ultimate subject of perception and thought. According to Schopenhauer, the subject comes to know its own self exclusively as will or, as he also puts it, as "subject of willing". Whereas propositions concerning the subject of cognition are analytic, the proposition "I will" is a genuine expression of synthetic, that is, substantive, albeit empirical, self-knowledge.[9] It is, in fact, to this latter form of awareness that Schopenhauer applies the concept "self-consciousness". From a systematic point of view, Schopenhauer's "self-consciousness" corresponds to Kant's "inner sense". But, whereas Kant, following previous modern philosophers, took inner sense as an act of introspection whereby our soul becomes an object for itself,[10] for Schopenhauer we are not aware of ourselves as souls at all, but as an embodied will.[11]

It should be taken into account that what Schopenhauer labels "will" comprises much more than mere episodes of willing in the common sense of the word. Willing is a label for the whole domain of feeling (*Gefühl*). Besides what we usually call by that name, episodes of will comprise pleasures, pains, emotions, in sum, all our inner affective life:

> Everyone who observes his own self-consciousness will soon become aware that its object is at all times his own willing. By this, however, we must understand not merely the definite acts of will that lead at once to deeds, and the explicit decisions together with the actions resulting from them. On the contrary, whoever is capable of grasping in any way that which is essential, in spite of the different modifications of degree and kind, will have no hesitation in reckoning as manifestations of willing all desiring, striving, wishing, longing, yearning, hoping, loving, rejoicing, exulting and the like, as well as the feeling of

---

9 FR, 211: "Starting from knowledge we can say that 'I know' is a an analytical proposition, whereas 'I will' is a synthetical, and moreover a posteriori, that is to say, is given by experience, here by 'inner experience' (in other words, in time alone)."
10 An example of this can be found in CPR B 399–400/A 341–342.
11 And as a matter of fact Schopenhauer thinks that 'inner sense' is an inadequate designation of our self-consciousness. See, for instance, PEFW, 9–10.

> unwillingness or repugnance, detesting, fleeing, fearing, being angry, hating, mourning, suffering, in short, all affects and passions. For these are only movements more or less weak or strong, stirrings at one moment violent and stormy, at another mild and faint, of our own will that is either checked or given its way, satisfied or unsatisfied. (PEFW, 10–11)

As mentioned, what Schopenhauer has in view with the term "will" should not be taken as a purely mental state. Schopenhauer does more than simply replace Kant's object of inner sense, i.e. the soul, by another type of object, the will. For, according to Schopenhauer, willing is essentially linked to the awareness we have of ourselves as bodies – our embodied self-consciousness. In other words, not only self-consciousness corresponds to a privileged access to ourselves but also to a first-person experience of our own body. Self-consciousness is, thus, essentially linked to our bodily nature. According to Schopenhauer, the body is given to us in two thoroughly different ways. From the point of view of an outer observer, our body is a representation, that is, an object in space and time and subject to causal laws. On the other hand, each of us has inner access to his or her own body. According to Schopenhauer, this inner awareness of our body is tantamount to an awareness of our *will*:

> To the subject of knowing, who appears as an individual only through his identity with the body, this body is given in two entirely different ways. It is given in intelligent perception as representation, as an object among objects, liable to the laws of these objects. But it is also given in quite a different way, namely as what is known immediately to everyone, and is denoted by the word *will*. (WWR I, §18, 100)

In fact, according to Schopenhauer, the distinction between consciousness of will and consciousness of the body is a mere abstraction. We have no consciousness of willing whatsoever apart from the first-personal consciousness of our body:

> Finally, the knowledge I have of my will, although an immediate knowledge, cannot be separated from that of my body. […] the body is the condition of knowledge of my will. Accordingly, I cannot really imagine this will without my body. (WWR I, §18, 101–102)

When viewed from an ontological point of view, body and will form an identity in Schopenhauer's scheme of things. What we, from an external perspective, call body is – if viewed inwardly – will.

Clear evidence that the distinction between the subject (called "ego" by Nietzsche) and the self is not only absolutely crucial for Nietzsche, but also significantly inspired by Schopenhauer's ideas, can be found in Zarathustra's speech "On the Despisers of the Body". In fact, the whole speech seems intended as a criticism of Schopenhauer on Schopenhauer's own terms. Let us focus for now on the aspects under discussion in this section.

Against those that "despise the body", that is, those that in one way or the other view the soul as our innermost essence and therefore distinguish it absolutely from the body Zarathustra claims: "But the awakened, the knowing one says: body am I through and through, and nothing besides; and soul is just a word for something on the body". Then, a few lines below, Zarathustra says of the body that "it does not say I, but *does* I", implying thereby a distinction between the conscious part of the body (the soul), which is able to say I, and its basis, the body as a whole or totality. Although the body, as the basis of consciousness, cannot say "I", it lies "behind" our "thoughts and feelings" and it "is called self" (Z I, On the Despisers of the Body).

The thesis Nietzsche is arguing against in this passage is the same Schopenhauer has tried to reject, namely, the dominant Cartesian idea that one's true self lies in the *res cogitans*, the domain of reason and consciousness, that the latter is characterized by self-transparency and consequently that introspection provides us access to the innermost essence of subjectivity. But, whereas Schopenhauer still basis his account of the self on the alleged privilege of bodily inner awareness, Nietzsche is clearly opposed to any form of foundationalism. He does not claim any evidence for his thesis on the self from any kind of immediate or primordial certainty (cf. BGE 16, 19, 34, 281; GS 127). We already had the opportunity to see an important aspect of this critique when we discussed his critique of the cogito or the "I think". A similar criticism applies to the Schopenhauerian "I will" (BGE 16).[12]

It should be borne in mind, though, that Nietzsche's critique of immediate certainties does not imply that the realm of the body does not enjoy a certain privilege, at least when compared with that of the so-called "soul". Despite the fact that this topic does not get much discussion in his published writings, we can find some significant passages concerning it throughout his late notebooks. In these[13] Nietzsche suggests that in fact some kind of methodological priority should be granted to the body:

> The phenomenon of the *body* is the richer, clearer, more graspable phenomenon: to be given methodological priority, without drawing any consequences about its ultimate significance. (NL 1886–1887, 5[56], KSA 12: 205–206 = WLN, 113)

---

[12] For an analysis of Nietzsche's critique of self-observation, immediate certainties and the problem of its accuracy as a critique of Schopenhauer's theory of self-consciousness cf. Constâncio (2013).

[13] Cf. NL 1884, 26[374, 432], KSA 11: 249, 266; NL 1884, 27[27], KSA 11: 282f.; NL 1885, 36[35], KSA 11: 565; NL 1885, 37[4], KSA 11: 576–579; NL 1885, 39[13], KSA 11: 623f.; NL 1885, 40[21], KSA 11: 638–639; NL 1885, 42[3], KSA 11: 692–695; NL 1885–1886, 2[68, 70, 91], KSA 12: 92f., 106; NL 1886–1887, 5[56], KSA 12: 205f.

In other passage from his notebooks Nietzsche mentions that it is "essential to start from the body and to use it as a guiding thread. It is the far richer phenomenon, and can be observed more distinctly. Belief in the body is better established than belief in the mind" (NL 1885, 40[15], KSA 11: 635 = WLN, 43; see also NL 1885, 36[35], KSA 11: 565; NL 1885, 37[4], KSA 11: 576–579; NL 1885–1886, 2[102], KSA 12: 112).[14] In order to justify the body's methodological priority Nietzsche reverses Descartes' evil spirit argument. If "spirit", argues Nietzsche, can deceive us about the most unshakable belief we have–the belief that we possess a body, more than that, that we are a body–then it could also deceive us about its own nature and existence as "spirit" (NL 1885, 36[36], KSA 11: 565–566; see also BGE 34).

Despite the fact that Nietzsche does not rely on an immediate certainty to disclose the "essence" or "inner nature" of the body, his account of it shows a number of striking similarities with the one presented by his "educator".[15] As is well-known, although the status of the so-called power ontology is problematic, when Nietzsche comes to a more narrow determination of our organic body he says that it has the same reality of our inner world of drives and affects (JGB 36; see also NL 1885, 34[123], KSA 11: 461–462; NL 1885, 37[4], KSA 11: 577). Sometimes Nietzsche also characterizes the drives and affects that constitute the body as "souls" and our body as a "society constructed out of many 'souls'" (BGE 19). It may come as surprising that Nietzsche resorts to the old concept of "soul" to characterize the body's plurality. However, according to him it is not necessary to forsake the soul hypothesis (BGE 12). Instead, he wants to transform the way it is traditionally understood. The "souls" that, according to Nietzsche, make up our bodies and thereby ourselves are characterized by him in various ways: as "under-wills" (BGE 19), as "under-souls" (BGE 19), as mortal souls (BGE 12), and as "wills to power" (NL 1885–1886, 1[58], KSA 12: 25). Furthermore, they form "a society constructed out of drives and affects" (BGE 12).

We can see that, in contrast to Schopenhauer, for whom the body objectifies an essentially unified will, Nietzsche thinks our body or organism is essentially plural, being made up of manifold beings. As opposed to the illusory unity of our conscious ego, the body displays "a tremendous *multiplicity* [...]" (NL 1885–1886, 2[91], KSA 12: 106 = WLN, 77; see also NL 1885, 37[4], KSA 11: 577). Furthermore, Nietzsche is adamant that these under-wills are not atomic beings. They are nothing fixed or substantial that could exist independently: "*No subject-atoms. The sphere of the subject constantly becoming larger or smaller–*

---

14 On the body as guiding thread see Wotling (1995: 83–108).
15 On Nietzsche and Schopenhauer as philosophers of the body see Salaquarda (2007).

the centre of the system constantly *shifting* [...]" (NL 1887, 9[98], KSA 12: 391–392 = WLN, 158–159; cf. also BGE 12). He says also that these "under-wills" are centers and even dynamic *quanta* of the will to power: "*there is no will*: there are points of will constantly augmenting or losing their power" (NL 1887–1888, 11[73], KSA 13: 36–37 = WLN, 212–213; see also NL 1885, 37[4], KSA 11: 576–579).

Nietzsche portrays the relation amongst the various centers of the will to power, or amongst the various "under-wills" or "under-souls" that make up our body, by means of political metaphors. This can be already seen in his talk of a "society" of drives and affects or "souls". For Nietzsche, the "political" nature of this relation implies that there is competition, even conflict amongst the drives, but at the same time certain types of organization, coordination and hierarchy among them, essentially dependent upon determinate temporary arrangements ensuing from their conflict.[16]

Nietzsche's term of art for the nature of these conflicting drives, the "will to power", seems, of course, to have been explicitly devised as opposed to and a surrogate for Schopenhauer's will. Schopenhauer uses the suffix "to life" to designate the "will". According to him, what the will aims at is essentially its own conservation, as shown by the instinct of self-preservation and the sexual instinct. For this reason, Schopenhauer says that "will" and "will to life" are synonymous expressions (WWR I, §54, 275). However, according to Nietzsche, "life" falls short of describing the basic aim of any living being, since every living thing does "everything it can *not* to preserve itself but to become *more*" (NL 1888, 14[121], KSA 13: 300 = WLN, 256–257; see also BGE 259), that is, to grow, to expand itself, to overcome others, to dominate, in short, to increase its power. Self-preservation would then be only a particular consequence or side-effect of the will to power and by no means life's central striving goal or aim:

> Psychologists should think twice before positioning the drive for self-preservation as the cardinal drive of an organic being. Above all, a living thing wants to *discharge* its strength – life itself is will to power – : self-preservation is only one of the indirect and most frequent *consequences* of this. (BGE 13; see also GS 349)

As a consequence, Nietzsche conceives the human being as an endless flux of creation, destruction, evolution, change and transformation, produced by an eternal struggle among different and opposing forces (wills) which fight for their own growth, enhancement and power over all the others. According to Nietzsche, the human being is, thus, at each moment, the result of the eternal

---

[16] For an account of Nietzsche's political model for understanding the self, see Herman Siemens' chapter in this book.

struggle among the forces that constitute him, the expression of the relations of commandment and submission within him, the reflex of the hierarchies that are established, destroyed and again re-established or transformed in the organism that he is.

3.2

This conception of the human being as body and the latter as an interplay of power-relations among drives and affects entails for Nietzsche a significant revaluation of the nature and role of consciousness. According to him, consciousness is only a small part of bodily existence itself. In the language of Zarathustra, consciousness is a "small reason" when compared to the body's "great reason" (Z I, On the Despisers of the Body). We would like to show now that here, too, Nietzsche is developing Schopenhauer's thesis of the secondary and accidental nature of consciousness in relation to that of the body or will.[17]

Based on the identity of body and will, Schopenhauer ascribes to the will organic functions such as digestion and breathing (WWR I, §23, 115). In fact, for Schopenhauer, the will is the underlying agent of all organic functions and causal events, even mechanical ones. However, we should bear in mind that Schopenhauer does not want us to think that organic functions are a product of voluntary action. The latter is only the case when the will is guided by consciousness. Schopenhauer wants to show that precisely the opposite obtains, that is, that, contrary to common acceptance, activity of the will does not presuppose consciousness or reason. Only animals – and even they only to a certain measure – conduct their action according to representations. Being conducted by consciousness is an accidental feature of the will. For Schopenhauer, the will, and that is to say the self, must be conceived in its innermost essence as unconscious.[18] In fact, for Schopenhauer, it is of paramount importance to distinguish the will as something conative, drive-like, unconscious, blind and irrational from the intellect and, in particular, from the rational intellect, which possesses the exact opposite set of features. This is already implied in Schopenhauer's idea of the composite nature of self-consciousness. In the latter the subject of cognition comes to some sort of identity with the subject of willing, even though

---

17 For a thorough analysis and comparison of Schopenhauer's and Nietzsche's accounts of consciousness, cf. Constâncio (2011) and Janaway (1991).
18 On the will's "blindness" see, for example, WWR I, §19, 105–106; §23, 114–115; WWR II, ch. XIX, 201; ch. XX, 252; ch. XXII, 277; ch. XXIII, 293; ch. XXVII, 345–348.

both are completely heterogeneous and should be carefully distinguished. To illustrate this relation, Schopenhauer likens the ego to a plant. The *root* is the will, whereas the intellect is the corona, that is, its efflorescence, the ego being the rhizome, the "indifference point" between both (WWR II, ch. XIX, 202–203). This propels also Schopenhauer's criticism of the traditional conception of the subject as an irreducible unity of cognition and willing, where the cognitive function is taken as primary and willing as a mode of cognition. In fact, according to Schopenhauer the opposite holds. The ego exists only as a compositum and, Schopenhauer claims, our unconscious, conative, drive-like and irrational part is the essential one. It constitutes our innermost being in opposition to our conscious mind, which is a more secondary and accidental part of what we are. It is, in a word, our "true self".

Schopenhauer models the relation between consciousness and will on the relation between organism and brain. Just as the organism is the whole of our organic life and the brain is just one of its organs, an appendix that serves to regulate its relations with the outer world – Schopenhauer even calls it a parasite of the organism (WWR II, ch. XIX, 244) –, consciousness must be seen as a secondary and accidental feature of our being. Kant's unity of consciousness, that is, the subject of cognition, is generated by an operation in which the brain assembles all its cognitive acts in one point. This fixed point, which traverses time and succession for as long as the organism lives, has, however, a status similar to that of a convex mirror's focus (WWR II, ch. XXII, 277). According to Schopenhauer, "the theoretical ego" is itself only a transitory state of the will as the metaphysical basis of the whole organism (WWR II, ch. XX, 250; WWR II, ch. XXII, 277).

Since the intellect is part of the organism, where it appears objectified by the brain, it takes part in the overall economy of the organism as well. The natural function of the brain is, thus, to serve the conservation and reproduction of the organism and thereby to serve the "will to life". From this Schopenhauer concludes that cognition remains for the most part at the service of the will and consists in knowledge of relations between objects and ultimately between objects and the organism itself. In other words, the intellect is only a tool of the will, as Schopenhauer also says. This can even lead to the will exerting control over the intellect. For example, the will can forbid certain thoughts to the intellect (WWR II, ch. XIX, 208) and keep its ultimate intentions hidden from the latter (WWR II, ch. XIX, 209) lest they do not damage the good opinion we have of ourselves. In general, we do not know what we desire or fear (WWR II, ch. XIX, 209) and sometimes we can be wrong about the real motive of our actions (WWR II, ch. XIX, 210).

As mentioned, Nietzsche too devalues consciousness as a consequence of his conception of the self as body: "we are in the phase of modesty of consciousness" (WP 676/NL 1883–1884, 24[16], KSA 10: 654). For Nietzsche, consciousness is also a surface (D 125)[19] and a mirror (GS 354)[20] of the realm of the complex, unknown and for the most part unknowable inner processes of the organism. This makes it a secondary, accidental, "superfluous" (GS 354) and parasite-like component of what we are, something we could in principle entirely do without:

> For we could think, feel, will and remember, and we could also "act" in every possible sense of the term, and yet none of all this would have to "enter our consciousness" (as one says figuratively). All of life would be possible without, as it were, seeing itself in a mirror [...] (GS 354).

In fact, according to Nietzsche, not only "all of life" *would be* possible without consciousness, but most of it *is in fact* possible and happens without the interference of consciousness: "and still today, the predominant part of our lives actually unfolds without this mirroring" (GS 354). As a result, "our so-called consciousness" is nothing but "a more or less fantastic commentary on an unknown, perhaps unknowable, but felt text" (D 119). That of which we become aware – "that for which alone we have consciousness and words" (D 115) – is thus only a very small part, the most extreme and extravagant one, "the superlative degrees of these processes and drives" (D 115; cf. also GS 11). Since we tend to neglect or disregard that for which we have no words, the image we have of ourselves is necessarily vague, incomplete and illusory: we are unaware of the "milder, middle degrees, not to speak of the lower degrees which are continually in play", and hence we have no knowledge of precisely those elements which most decisively work on "the construction of our character and destiny" (D 115). Concerning self-observation and self-consciousness, Nietzsche is, thus, a thoroughgoing phenomenalist[21]: "One must not look for phenomenalism in the wrong place: nothing is more phenomenal (or, more clearly:) nothing is so much deception as this inner world which we observe with the famous 'inner sense'" (WP 478/NL 1888, 14[152], KSA 13: 334–335).

In this respect, it is natural to consider Nietzsche as being more radical than Schopenhauer. After all, Schopenhauer is thought to claim knowledge of the thing-in-itself as will precisely through inner awareness of the body. However,

---

[19] Cf. also GS 354, D 121.
[20] Cf. also EH Clever 9; NL 1883, 12[33], KSA 10: 406; NL 1883–1884, 24[16], KSA 10: 653; NL 1885–1886, 1[61], KSA 12: 26.
[21] On Nietzsche's phenomenalism of self-consciousness cf. Abel (2001) and Schlimgen (1999: 70ff.).

we should not let ourselves be misled by that claim. The fact that for Schopenhauer we have a more immediate access to reality through inner awareness does not mean that such access is unconditioned. Firstly, according to Schopenhauer, we do not know our will as such, that is, "as a whole". We are aware of it solely through time, that is, in succession. At each moment we know only our singular acts of will, that is, we know our will only in slices, as it were. But more important than this last feature is the fact that the will is conceived as something essentially foreign to consciousness. In fact, the essential "opaque" character of the self is one of Schopenhauer's most pervasive and influential insights – one that is absolutely decisive for understanding Nietzsche's Schopenhauerian heritage – although it is too often neglected in superficial accounts of his philosophy.²²

Besides being a "surface" and a "mirror", consciousness is also for Nietzsche, as it was already for Schopenhauer, a "tool" (D 109)²³ of subconscious and hidden processes and that means a tool of the body as a whole (the body understood as a society, interplay and struggle of drives). In the famous analogy from *Zarathustra*, the body is a "great reason", that is, "a multiplicity with one sense, a war and a peace, one herd and one shepherd"; reason in the traditional sense – i.e., reasoning as a conscious activity of the I of consciousness, reasoning as an activity of the "soul", or "mind" – is nothing but a "small reason", "a small work- and plaything of your great reason" (Z I, On the Despisers of the Body²⁴). This is a thesis that Nietzsche insistently repeats throughout his work, both in the published books and in the posthumous notes. In a fragment from 1885, for example, Nietzsche writes the following:

> If *I* have something of a unity within me, it certainly doesn't lie in the conscious I and in feeling, willing, thinking, but somewhere else: in the sustaining, appropriating, expelling, watchful prudence of my whole organism, of which my conscious self is only a tool. (NL 1885, 34[46], KSA 11: 434 = WLN, 2–3)²⁵

---

22 For a thorough comparison between Nietzsche's and Schopenhauer's accounts of inner observation see Constâncio (2013).
23 Cf. also GM II 16; NL 1880, 6[130], KSA 9: 229; NL 1885, 34[46], KSA 11: 434; NL 1885, 40[38], KSA 11: 647; NL 1885–1886, 1[124], KSA 12: 40.
24 For a thorough interpretation of this passage cf. especially Gerhardt (2006).
25 Cf. also D 119; GS 354; BGE 3, BGE 191; NL 1881, 11[243], KSA 9: 533; NL 1884, 27[19], KSA 11: 279; NL 1885, 40[38], KSA 11: 647; NL 1885, 37[4], KSA 11: 576 = WLN, 29–31: "We find it ill-considered that precisely human consciousness has for so long been regarded as the highest stage of organic development and as the most astonishing of all earthly things, indeed as their blossoming and 'goal'. In fact, what is more astonishing is the *body*: there is no end to one's admiration for how the human *body* has become possible; how such a prodigious alliance of living beings,

According to Nietzsche, our conscious aims and goals are merely means for attaining altogether different, unknown, unconscious and higher goals. The latter concern the "life of the drives", that is, our organic life, of which we remain for the most part unaware:

> Ultimately, we understand the conscious ego itself only as a tool in the service of a higher, comprehensive intellect; and then we are able to ask whether all conscious willing, all conscious purposes, all evaluations are not perhaps only means through which something essentially different from what appears in consciousness is to be achieved. (NL 1883–1884, 24[16], KSA 10: 654 = WP 676)

Despite the differences in their conception of consciousness, both authors see consciousness as a mediator of the "inner life" of the drives and the outside world: "It's essential that one makes no mistake about the role of 'consciousness': *what developed it* is our *relationship with the 'external world'* " (NL 1887–1888, 11[145], KSA 13: 67 = WLN, 228). According to Schopenhauer, consciousness emerged as the medium of motives. For, in order for certain organisms to survive, it was necessary for the organism to guide its activity by representations of outer objects and not just by stimuli. Animal species would not have survived if their activity were not guided by motives. Consciousness arose as function of the organism's need of survival in a competitive environment and its activity betrays this genesis everywhere. For Nietzsche too consciousness emerged only because of its usefulness to the economy of life: "*consciousness exists to the extent that consciousness is useful*" (NL 1885–1886, 2[95], KSA 12: 108 = WLN, 78). However, Nietzsche's hypothesis for the emergence of consciousness, laid down in GS 354, is in its details very different from the one presented by Schopenhauer. For Nietzsche it was the need to communicate that generated consciousness, the latter being, thus, an essentially intersubjective phenomenon ("for only as a social animal did man learn to become conscious of himself" [GS 354]), whereas for Schopenhauer it is an essentially individual phenomenon – in fact, it is only because we (and animals) are conscious beings that we are also individuals at all.[26]

---

each dependent and subservient and yet in a certain sense also commanding and acting out of its own will, can live, grow, and for a while prevail, as a whole – and we can see this does *not* occur due to consciousness! For this 'miracle of miracles', consciousness is just a 'tool' and nothing more – a tool in the same sense that the stomach is a tool."

[26] The different accounts of the origin of consciousness provided by both authors can be surely traced back to their different understandings of the phenomenon: for Nietzsche consciousness is linked to the ability to employ symbols and in particular language and concepts, whereas for Schopenhauer there is consciousness whenever perceptive representation occurs. Nietzsche's

3.3

There is finally something to be said about the way each philosopher understands the nature of consciousness in relation to our bodily, unconscious side. As we have seen, consciousness is a tool of the will (Schopenhauer) or a tool of the body as a "great reason", that is, a tool of the drives (Nietzsche). But what is exactly the status of this tool? Does it form a continuum with the "life of the drives" or is it something altogether different from it?

The status and nature of the intellect in Schopenhauer is somewhat ambiguous. On the one hand, the intellect is itself will, that is, it objectifies the will as "will to know" (WWR II, ch. XX, 258–259). On the other hand, there is a qualitative difference between intellect and will. Schopenhauer assumes that with the intellect something essentially new comes to the world as opposed to the will: "The world now shows its second side; hitherto mere *will*, it is now at the same time *representation*, object of the knowing subject" (WWR I, §27, 150). Contrarily to the will, which is characterized as something with an active and striving nature, but also as "unconscious" and "irrational", the intellect is, by itself, passive, "indifferent" (WWR II, ch. XIX, 208), a "*vis inertiae*" (WWR II, ch. XIX, 213) and, as such, apt to become "the cold and indifferent spectator, the mere guide and counselor of the will" (WWR II, ch. XXII, 277–278). Thus, according to Schopenhauer, there is on the one hand intellect, which is isolated from the will and has no trace of it, and on the other hand will, which is totally blind and devoid of intellect. The former is subordinated to the latter like the hammer to the smith, and the realms are as different and apart as a hammer and a smith (cf. WWR II, §19, 225).

In this sense, Schopenhauer can still be said to maintain a certain form of dualism between, on the one hand, the will and, on the other hand, the intellect. Nietzsche rejects this dualism by denying its two basic assumptions, namely, that the will is blind and that the intellect is impervious to the will.[27] According to Nietzsche, life is a continuum in all its possible domains and ways of manifestation, which means that nothing is really separated from anything else and that the properties of each thing differ from one another not essentially but only in a

---

account of the origin of consciousness is a vast subject that would require separate treatment. For that reason we will not develop it further. For an account of the linguistic and symbolic nature of consciousness see Abel (2001), Constâncio (2011, 2012) and Katsafanas (2005).

[27] For the following discussion we are indebted to João Constâncio. For his account of the difference between Nietzschean drives and affects and Schopenhauer's will see Constâncio (2011).

matter of degree.[28] In this sense, and contrary to what might seem at first sight, the characterization of reason or the intellect as a "small reason" which belongs to a greater reason, namely the body, is already a refusal of Schopenhauer's essential separation and distinction of two different domains. Firstly, the intellect belongs to a certain form of unity which, itself and as a whole is already *rational*; secondly, because it belongs to this greater unit it can never be totally separated or distinguished from it, but rather shares with it its bodily, instinctual, drive-like nature.

It is important to look a bit closer into this thesis, as it might not be at first sight evident. How indeed can Nietzsche attribute "intelligence" to the body? As a first clarification one can say that the body is intelligent inasmuch as it is a whole or totality organized, oriented and directed towards certain aims or goals. Once the traditional ruling and commanding powers of (small) reason over the body have been undermined, it must be assumed that the body itself entails a certain inherent form of intelligence which is responsible for its (self-)organization, orientation, direction and meaning, and consequently also for its behaviors, decisions and actions. In short, Nietzsche materializes in the body the competences and powers that have traditionally been ascribed to the intellect and, therefore, we can say with Gerhardt that for Nietzsche the body becomes "the fully present actuality which realizes itself in its own sense of direction and action" (2006: 284).

It is important to note that, in Nietzsche's worldview, not only the body is this "great reason" totally self-organized and self-oriented, but also each and every drive that constitutes it is already in some sense "intelligent" – and by no means "blind" as Schopenhauer would have it. This is so because every instinct or drive entails (even if unconsciously) a certain form of evaluation and is thus naturally oriented towards a certain end or value. A drive without a goal or value simply does not exist:

> If only it were possible to *live* without evaluating, without having aversions and partialities! – for all aversion is dependent on an evaluation, likewise all partiality. A drive to something or away from something divorced from a feeling one is desiring the beneficial or avoiding the harmful, a drive without some kind of knowing evaluation of the worth of its objective, does not exist in man. (HH I 32)[29]

All the drives that constitute us are thus guided by some value, and the goals and values that we as individuals pursue are the result of the internal struggle

---

28 This position is usually designated as Nietzsche's "a-dualism". See Abel (2001) and Constâncio (2011).
29 On this topic cf. especially Richardson (2004: 70–78) and Janaway (2007: 202–222).

among the drives, expressing the victory of one drive or a complex of drives over others.[30] It is true that Schopenhauer does not deny that drives or instincts pursue some form of goal or end of their own, even if unconsciously, and thus far his account of the instincts would not be much different from Nietzsche's. The fact that drives and instincts have goals or ends would not indeed *by itself* imply that they are not simply blind and mechanical forces towards something, such as, for example, gravity or growth. What makes Nietzsche's account different from Schopenhauer's in this regard is that for Nietzsche those goals, aims and values that drives pursue are the expression of "some kind of *knowing* evaluation" (HH I 32),[31] that is, the result of a certain (minimal) form of perceptual perspective or interpretation, "a perspectival evaluation of everything that happens and is experienced" (NL 1885–1886, 1[58], KSA 12: 25 = WLN, 59–60), and therefore of some kind of *intelligence*. Drives manifest intelligence insofar as in their pursuit of power and command – in the pursuit of their own goals or values – they perceive each other, interpret the ongoing power-relations among them and evaluate the outer world in order to accomplish their own aims and satisfy their needs, that is, to impose their own perspectives, values and power-claims over all the others:

> It is our needs *which interpret the world*: our drives and their for and against. Every drive is a kind of lust for domination, each has its perspective, which it would like to impose as a norm on all the other drives. (NL 1886–1887, 7[60], KSA 12: 315 = WLN, 139; cf. also D 119)

Far from being blind, drives and instincts are thus rather, from the Nietzschean perspective, "clever" or "intelligent" perspectives or evaluations and, in fact, "the most intelligent type of intelligence discovered so far" (BGE 218).[32]

It should be noted that, in this respect, Nietzsche's characterization of the plurality of beings that constitutes us as "souls" is anything but innocent.

---

[30] Nietzsche often uses political metaphors to describe the hierarchical power-relations among the drives. Cf. for ex. BGE 6; NL 1885, 37[4], KSA 11: 576; NL 1885, 40[21], KSA 11: 638; NL 1885, 40[42], KSA 11: 650.

[31] That's why they are called "under-souls" and the body described as a "society constructed out of many 'souls'" (BGE 19), that is, a unity composed by multiple and opposing perspectives and interpretations.

[32] Cf. also NL 1885, 37[4], KSA 11: 576 = WLN, 29–31: "The magnificent binding together of the most diverse life, the ordering and arrangement of the higher and lower activities, the thousandfold obedience which is not blind, even less mechanical, but a selecting, shrewd, considerate, even resistant obedience – measured by intellectual standards, this whole phenomenon 'body' is as superior to our consciousness, our 'mind', our conscious thinking, feeling, willing, as algebra is superior to the times tables."

Nietzsche does not share Schopenhauer's conception of the unconscious. For Schopenhauer, the will's unconsciousness has a thoroughly negative character. The will is unconscious in the sense of being opposed to consciousness. "Unconscious" means, for Schopenhauer, lack of consciousness (*bewusstlos*). Nietzsche, on the contrary, takes up Leibniz' hypothesis of "unconscious perceptions"[33] extending it both to feelings and the will. As opposed to Schopenhauer, Leibniz' "incomparable insight" entails that "consciousness [*Bewußtheit*] is merely an *accidens* of the power of representation [*Vorstellung*] and not its necessary and essential attribute; so that what we call consciousness [*Bewußtsein*] constitutes only one state of our spiritual and psychic world (perhaps a sick state) and by no means the whole of it" (GS 357). In other words, whereas Schopenhauer equated representation with consciousness, Nietzsche, following Leibniz, thinks that our inner unconscious organic life is representational, even if at the same time unconscious. Thus, in arguing that the nature of the beings that make up our body is "*of the same kind*, all feeling, thinking, willing" (NL 1885, 40[21], KSA 11: 629 = WLN, 43–44), Nietzsche is not claiming that there are so many centers of consciousness.[34] Instead they are precisely something that feels, thinks and wills unconsciously, that is, without "seeing itself in the mirror" (GS 354).

Since from the Nietzschean perspective it is our needs and drives that interpret the world, that are responsible for the values and goals we pursue, and also that determine our global character as individuals, there is no act, decision or thought that could be independent or even thinkable independent of those drives, instincts and affects that constitute us. More concretely and against Schopenhauer, just as the will is not totally devoid of some form of intellect, the intellect cannot be severed from the will either:

> Just as feeling – and indeed many feelings – must be recognized as ingredients of the will, thought must be as well. In every act of will there is a commandeering thought, – and we really should not believe this thought can be divorced from the "willing", as if some will would then be left over! (BGE 19)

---

[33] For Nietzsche's references to Leibniz' doctrine see GS 354 and GS 357.
[34] It is true that in one aphorism from his notebooks he entertains the idea: "And for us, even those smallest living beings which constitute our body (more correctly: for whose interaction the thing we call 'body' is the best simile –) are not soul-atoms, but rather something growing, struggling, reproducing and dying off again: so that their number alters unsteadily, and our living, like all living, is at once an incessant dying. There are thus in man as many 'consciousnesses' as – at every moment of his existence – there are beings which constitute his body." (NL 1885, 37[4], KSA 11: 576 = WLN, 29–31) However we think passages like this are better construed as meaning that every center is representative, instead of every center being fully conscious.

Intellect and will are thus not separate and independent domains but rather interconnected parts of the same continuum whose history and development depends on the perpetual play and games of forces between drives, instincts and affects. Far from being detached from the activity of drives, consciousness, knowledge and all the productions of the intellect are thus rather the result of the final "agreement" between them. As Nietzsche explains in *The Gay Science*, we tend to think "that *intelligere* must be something conciliatory, just, and good, something essentially opposed to the instincts", when in fact "*it is only a certain behaviour of the drives towards one another*" (GS 333). Before one thought arises, Nietzsche writes in the same aphorism, each drive must have presented its own perspective on the object, a struggle between different drive-perspectives must have occurred, and finally some sort of "appeasement", "concession" or "ultimate reconciliation" among them must have been achieved, in order for a thought to become conscious (cf. GS 333).[35] As we shall see below, it is along the same lines that Nietzsche conceives the processes involved in human action and behavior.

4

The new conception of the 'subject' and the 'self' that results from the Schopenhauerian and Nietzschean critiques of the *cogito* is also reflected in both Schopenhauer's and Nietzsche's theories of action. More concretely, the dismissal of reason from the center of subjectivity and the relegation of consciousness to a secondary, superficial and parasite-like level implies the destruction of the traditional agent and the conception of an alternative model of agency, as well as the reformulation of related notions like motivation, freedom and responsibility.

Schopenhauer's account of action issues directly from what can be called his "inverted dualism", as exposed above. Accordingly, for Schopenhauer, actions are, in a way, a product of two kinds of factors. One of them springs directly from our intellectual side, that is, from consciousness, cognition and reason. The other one expresses our affective and conative nature, that is, our inner drives and instincts, our will or character. Motives for action proper belong to the intellectual component of action, they hinge upon consciousness and therefore upon the subject of cognition. They are outer objects of intuitive perception or abstract objects, that is, concepts, judgments, thoughts in general.

---

[35] Cf. also BGE 36: "[...] thinking is only a relation between these drives [...]".

The character, on the other hand, corresponds to the irrational, conative and drive-like side of actions. It should be kept in mind that although actions issue from the interplay of these two factors, it is the character that is primary and makes up what we at bottom are, our 'inner nature', as Schopenhauer says.

Following Kant, Schopenhauer distinguishes between the intelligible and the empirical character. Those constant features and qualities that can be ascertained in everyone's behavior constitute precisely what is called the empirical character. But, according to Schopenhauer, we are only able to ascertain the character empirically because it is an appearance of its intelligible counterpart, that is, of the character considered as a thing-in-itself free from the forms of phenomena: space, time (change), and causality. If the empirical character were not a manifestation of an intelligible one, its unity would be only contingent. The intelligible character is, then, the *a priori* unity of the self that is gradually expressed and revealed in the series of actions that composes our life-course. It is this unity of the intelligible character that, once restored empirically, appears as empirical character.

Since the intelligible character is not subject to time or change, the empirical character can be said to be inborn and constant, which means that human beings have a fixed character throughout their lives. Variations in the observable behavior of the same human individual are not due to changes in character, but rather to changes in the knowledge of circumstances (to changes in motives, that is, in the intellectual component of action). Being inborn, fixed and unchangeable, the character amounts to an individual essence which completely determines what the individual is and does. Even though the presentation of different motives (different aims or purposes) to the intellect is an important and even necessary component of every action, the choice of a particular motive is, however, always already predetermined by each particular character, since the character cannot decide against its own inner nature.

Throughout the animal kingdom, specimens of the same animal species share the same character. They (re)act in pretty much the same way to the same circumstances, showing very few signs of individuality. But the human species is a bit different. Human action is not predictable in the same manner. Because they are rational, humans are able to survey various motives simultaneously and choose one among them. For the same reason, in humans there may be a conflict of motives. This is frequently interpreted as a sign that humans are free to choose a course of action independently of their animal nature, of the general character of the human species. However, Schopenhauer wants us to note that the "mechanism" of rational deliberation is not all that different from the one that drives animals towards perceptive motives. In both cases, which motive will in the end prevail depends, first and foremost, on the nature of the character.

In this respect, the main difference between humans and animals is that the former have individual characters alongside the character of their respective species. In other words, the laws that rule human action differ according to the individual in question. Since animals are devoid of reason, there is, in them, no gap between desire and action. Their desires are at once a manifestation of the character of their species and tend to turn immediately into action. Human beings, on the other hand, possess an individual character besides a general character of the human species. Human desire is a manifestation of the character of species as well, but only those actions that are consciously resolved upon by each unique human being are a sure sign of their respective individual character. This is also the reason why humans can desire many contradictory and conflicting things. However, we can only draw conclusions concerning an individual's unique character from those desires that have been effectively converted into deeds. Our life-course mirrors, as it were, our otherwise unknown intelligible character. Through our past life we get a glimpse of our unique individual nature.[36]

A similar view has been ascribed to Nietzsche by influential scholars like Brian Leiter. According to Leiter, Nietzsche endorses fatalism throughout his whole productive life, on the basis of the assumption that "the basic character of each individual's life is fixed in advance in virtue of an individual's nature, that is, the largely immutable physiological and psychological facts that make the person who he is" (Leiter 1998: 219). Nietzsche's "fatalism" would be different from both classical fatalism and classical determinism, in the sense that it wouldn't entail that all the facts of human life are necessary, but only that the particular nature or essence of any individual decisively circumscribes all its possible trajectories. Whereas the circumstances in which one finds oneself are not predetermined, the "natural facts" about a person would causally determine the way in which the person responds or reacts to those circumstances.[37]

This looks like a restatement of Schopenhauer's immutable character and, in fact, there are plenty of Nietzsche's texts which do seem to support this view. Already in *Human, All Too Human*, for example, Nietzsche says that "every man is himself a piece of fate; when he thinks to resist fate [...], it is precisely fate that is here fulfilling itself" (WS 61). In *Beyond Good and Evil*, Nietzsche repeats that "at our foundation, 'at the very bottom', there is certainly something that

---

36 For Schopenhauer's theory of character and action see FR §42, §43; WWR I, §18, §20, §26, §28, §55, §70; PEFW, "The Will before the consciousness of other things", 42f., 49f. For a standard study on the topic see also Atwell (1990) as well as Janaway (1989: 208–247).
37 Cf. Leiter (1998: 224–225).

will not learn, a brick wall of spiritual *fatum*" (BGE 231). And in *Twilight of the Idols* the same idea is expressed: "An individual is a piece of fate, from the front and from the back; an individual is one more law, one more necessity imposed on everything that is coming and going to be" (TI, Morality as Anti-Nature 6).

Passages like these, together with his well-known critique of the "free will" (cf. for example D 124; GS 127; GM I 13; BGE 21; TI Errors 7), do indeed make Nietzsche appear more radically fatalist or determinist than Schopenhauer himself. On the other hand, however, the picture of Nietzsche as a thoroughgoing fatalist fits uneasily with other passages where Nietzsche explicitly denies determinism (BGE 21), speaks of his own conception of freedom (TI, Skirmishes of an Untimely Man 38), or urges the individual to create himself (GS 335) or become the "gardener" of his own character (D 560). One must thus assume that even though Nietzsche accepted part of Schopenhauer's account of human action, he was not totally content with its final result and still struggled to grant some degree of freedom, though limited and restrained, to individual characters and actions.[38] We won't be able to deal here in detail with Nietzsche's account of freedom nor with the polemics surrounding the possibility of self-creation, but by way of a contrast between Schopenhauer's and Nietzsche's accounts of the character and their repercussions in their theories of action we shall be able to show that Nietzsche's determinism must, at least, be qualified, and must not be identified with the one defended by Schopenhauer.

Nietzsche's most enlightening text regarding both the influence and the overcoming of Schopenhauer concerning human action is, perhaps, section 13 of the first essay of the *Genealogy of Morality*. In this passage, Nietzsche famously states the following:

> A quantum of force is just such a quantum of drive, will, action, in fact it is nothing but this driving, willing and acting, and only the seduction of language (and the fundamental errors of reason petrified within it), which construes and misconstrues all actions as conditional upon an agency, a "subject", can make it appear otherwise. And just as the common people separates a lightning from its flash and takes the latter to be a *deed*, something per-

---

[38] It must be noted that also Schopenhauer felt the need to make some notion of freedom compatible with his otherwise strict determinism, in order to explain people's feeling of guilt and responsibility. He does this by claiming that even though individuals are not responsible for their actions – for each action is necessary –, they are nevertheless responsible for what they *are*, that is, for their character. Hence one of Schopenhauer's mottos: "freedom does not lie in action, but in being" (cf. for ex. PEFW, 87). Schopenhauer terms this kind of freedom, which precedes existence and lies outside space and time, "intelligible freedom". In *Human, All Too Human* Nietzsche calls this theory a "fable" and the idea of an "intelligible freedom" a "fantastic concept" (HH I 39).

formed by a subject, which is called lightning, popular morality separates strength from the manifestations of strength, as though there were an indifferent substratum behind the person which had the *freedom* to manifest strength or not. But there is no such substratum; there is no "being" behind the deed, its effect and what becomes of it; "the doer" is invented as an after-thought, – the doing is everything. (GM I 13)

This is one of Nietzsche's most significant passages on the criticism of the "agent" conceived as an indifferent substance or substratum standing behind actions as their intentional cause and assuming full responsibility for them as a "free subject". According to Nietzsche in this passage as in many others, such an agent is illusory, a mere construction added to the deed, since, in fact, "*both doing and doer are fictions*" (NL 1887–1888, 11[113], KSA 13: 53 = WLN, 221–222). That is, there is no doer behind the deed, as if doer and deed were two different and independent things and the former were the cause of the latter. Quite emphatically, Nietzsche stresses that there is only doing and that to think an action as an effect of an acting subject is as fantastic and "imaginary" (TI Errors 4) as thinking a lightning as cause of a flash. Now, does this mean that Nietzsche totally abolishes the notions of doer or agent, thus abandoning any possible conception of "agency"? Or is this still compatible with some form of agency, amounting rather to a deep reformulation of what is involved in human action?

Robert Pippin has convincingly shown that the latter is the case.[39] On account of precisely this passage, Pippin argues that Nietzsche can be included in the "brotherhood of modern anti-Cartesians", like Hegel, Wittgenstein or Heidegger, who have opposed themselves to metaphysical dualism and escaped intentionalism or causal accounts of action through what he calls an "expressivist" model of agency.[40] In a very summarized form, this model defends that an agent cannot be conceived in independence from the action, since it is the action that constitutes the agent as the one he properly is. In other words, it is not the agent who intentionally causes or determines the action, but the action that determines the agent, furthermore expressing it. Implied is the idea that an action cannot but express the individual who performs it, independently of the conception the individual has about himself or about his actions. That is, independently of the intention or purpose the individual thought he had for performing a certain action, it is only the action that, once performed, can show the individual which were his real purposes or intentions and, consequently, also who he really is. Far from being the effect of a doer, the deed shall thus rather

---

39 Cf. Pippin (2010: 67–84), as well as his article in this volume.
40 Cf. Pippin (2010: 77).

be conceived as its expression or manifestation. Accordingly, Nietzsche does not deny that there is a doer, but only that this doer can be conceived as something separate or independent from the deed: in Pippin's expression, "it is 'in' the deed".[41] This naturally implies, on the one hand, that the individual never reaches complete knowledge of his motivation for action beforehand (no matter how clear might his purposes seem to him) and, on the other hand, that he has no real possibility of a free, independent and indifferent choice between different paths of action (since the action must always express who he is).

Once again, a quick look at another aspect of Schopenhauer's theory of action might help to understand Nietzsche's "expressivist" account. In fact, it is even surprising that among that "brotherhood of modern anti-Cartesians" who defended a similar account of action, Pippin does not mention Schopenhauer. From an epistemological point of view, there can hardly be a stronger proponent of this account than Schopenhauer and it seems probable that Nietzsche took his insight directly from him. It is true, as we shall see, that Nietzsche's radicalization of Schopenhauer's theory of action also implies a deep transformation of the latter's expressivism, so that in the end we are, in fact, faced with two fundamentally different expressivisms. This notwithstanding, it seems undeniable that also in this respect Schopenhauer should be seen as Nietzsche's precursor. We will first look at their epistemological common ground, so that we can then move to what most fundamentally distinguishes them.

Schopenhauer's theory of action depends on a crucial thesis which, though already mentioned, shall now be looked at more carefully, namely, the correspondence between willing and bodily action. As we have seen, Schopenhauer defends an identity between body and will, which are, in fact, simply two perspectives of the same phenomenon: what one calls the body, from an external perspective, is the will from an inner one. And the best way to grasp this identity is precisely by looking at the relation between willing and bodily action. According to Schopenhauer, an act of will should not be taken as a (mental) cause of the movement of the body. The act of will and the corresponding act of the body are, instead, one and the same thing, although seen from two different perspectives: what the act of will is subjectively appears objectively, in space and time, as an act of the body:

> Every true act of his will is also at once and inevitably a movement of his body; he cannot actually will the act without at the same time being aware that it appears as a movement of

---

[41] Pippin (2010: 75). Pippin borrows the expression from Zarathustra's speech "On the Virtuous" (cf. 2010: 76).

the body. The act of will and the action of the body are not two different states objectively known, connected by the bond of causality; they do not stand in the relation of cause and effect, but are one and the same thing, though given in two entirely different ways, first quite directly, and then in perception for the understanding. The action of the body is nothing but the act of will objectified, i.e., translated into perception. (WWR I, §18, 100)

What is at stake here is that (true) willing is essentially linked to action, that is, true willing cannot but *express* itself in actions. Thus, just as for Nietzsche, one can only get acquainted with one's willing and one's character *a posteriori*, through the deeds in which it is expressed. In this sense, also Schopenhauer could have said that there is no doer or that "the doing is everything". What Schopenhauer is pointing out is that willing to which no action corresponds is no real willing. For the same reason, one cannot say one truly wills something without actually carrying it out:

> Resolutions of the will relating to the future are mere deliberations of reason about what will be willed at some time, not real acts of will. Only the carrying out stamps the resolve; till then, it is always a mere intention that can be altered; it exists only in reason, in the abstract. Only in reflection are willing and acting different; in reality they are one. (WWR I, §18, 100–101)

It is precisely in the light of this aspect of Schopenhauer's theory of action that Nietzsche's account of agency must be understood. The above quoted passage from the *Genealogy of Morality* is a clear example of the way Nietzsche both appropriates Schopenhauer's insights and at the same time manages to use them against him. One of the main targets of this passage is the idea that behind persons or even things in general a substratum different from their manifestations could be thought. This is precisely Schopenhauer's view: acts of will are neither a cause nor even something different from the corresponding acts of the body. Similarly, the character is not a lifeless something behind deeds, acting as their cause. The character is, rather, objectified, mirrored or expressed by its deeds.

Nietzsche radicalizes Schopenhauer's account by claiming that aims and purposes are not causes at all, but rather symptoms of our inner states. In fact, when Nietzsche rejects the will, what he is calling into question is precisely the idea that conscious motives, aims and purposes can by themselves be the cause of actions, not to speak of explaining them. Despite the pervasiveness and primitiveness of this belief – so that the very concept of causality, including the idea of an "I" as cause of its thoughts, has been deduced from it (TI Errors 3) – for Nietzsche "the belief in the will as the cause of effects is the belief in forces that work by magic" (GS 127; cf. also M 130; BGE 19; TI Reason 5; NL 1887, 9[98], KSA 12: 391). According to Nietzsche, what we construe as a final cause is in fact an effect of the inner struggle between the drives that compose our self. That is, also in action it is the perpetual game of forces between instincts, drives and affects which is at play and determines it, according to the hierarchy which is at each time established in the organism. According to Nietzsche in *Beyond Good and Evil*, what is peculiar to action is a certain feeling of power, freedom or command, which gives one the illusion of having freely chosen something, of being in conditions to perform it and of being itself the sole cause and reason of it. The fact is, however, that the individual who is commanding is *at the same time* the one who is obeying – or better: that in the "society constructed out of many 'souls'" (BGE 19) which we are, there is always part of us commanding and part of us obeying, particularly when we are performing a given action. Thus, the sense of a unitary agency as well as the pleasure and feeling of power that the individual might experience while performing an action arises when he identifies himself both with the one that wills, the one that commands and the one that successfully accomplishes the action: in Nietzsche's analogy, "what happens here is what happens in every well-constructed and happy community: the ruling class identifies itself with the successes of the community" (BGE 19).

Despite the differences in their conceptions of the self or the agent (be it conceived as a unitary substratum or as a coordination and organization of multiple drives and affects), what is at stake here for both authors is the refusal of any intellectualist theory of action, according to which knowledge or conscious motives or purposes would be sufficient to determine the action. Independently of the degree of efficacy one might want to attribute to Nietzsche's conscious states,[42] it is clear that both agree that an action cannot be explained or understood with recourse to conscious motives alone. According to Schopenhauer, actions and therefore particular acts of will are subject to the principle of sufficient reason – because it is always possible to ask why someone did this or that –, but, on the other hand, the subject of willing or willing as such and as a whole is groundless, for it is not conditioned by such reasons. As we saw, even though conscious, rational motives are a necessary component of every action, it is irrationality, the character that ultimately determines the action. Nietzsche

---

[42] Against the epiphenomenalism generally attributed to Nietzsche (ex. Leiter 2002), it has been convincingly argued by authors like Paul Katsafanas (2005) and João Constâncio (2011) that even though conscious mental states are not causally efficacious in the strong sense of the term, they nevertheless have a share in the global economy of the organism, thus having an impact and influencing the "total state" that precedes a thought or an action. Thus, despite the fact that the power of the totality of the instincts will always be greater than any conscious mental state and that the power of the latter will always be limited and indirect, it would be erroneous to assume that consciousness has no efficacy whatsoever.

seems to go one step further by claiming that the whole process which leads one to perform a certain action, including the real and decisive "conflict of motives", happens subconsciously, without one being aware of it, so that the real process as well as the real motivation of one's actions remains totally concealed (D 129). It is in this sense that for Nietzsche, as well as for Schopenhauer, there is no free agent in the sense of an indifferent cause of actions which could act one way or another. In Pippin's wording, actions are rather, for both, a mere expression of those hidden and concealed processes which are thoroughly unconscious and can only become visible and recognizable through the deed and after it has been accomplished.

However – and here lies the crux of the difference between both authors' expressivisms –, Schopenhauer still separates the deeds from what they somehow express, namely the agent, the character. In other words, he still conceives the character as something that exists in and by itself independently of the way it is objectified, mirrored or expressed in its deeds so that in a way he still separates the 'lightning' from the 'flash'. According to Nietzsche, however, not only the doer can in no way be separated from the deed, but there *is* no doer, that is, there is no will, no character, no substratum, no *being* behind the deeds. The doer is rather constituted *by* the deed and *in* the deed, having no existence *before* or *behind* it. Note how this difference is decisive and makes Nietzsche's expressivism radically different from Schopenhauer's. Whereas for Schopenhauer it is the pre-existing and fixed character that expresses itself as a whole in each action of an individual, for Nietzsche the character does not pre-exist the action at all but is rather constituted *in the moment of acting*, as part of the action itself. The doer is (expressed) "in" the deed in the sense that only then, in the deed, it is effectively realized.[43]

In this sense, one could say that Nietzsche keeps from the Schopenhauerian theory of character only the empirical one, that is, the character *as expressed in actions*, without its intelligible and immutable counterpart. Nietzsche's refusal of Schopenhauer's intelligible character follows, in turn, directly from his conception of the self as a dynamic organization of multiple drives and affects. That is, Nietzsche still believes that, as individuals, we have a "character", but whereas Schopenhauer conceives of it as a permanent and unchangeable substance or essence which determines our behavior and actions from birth until death, Nietzsche conceives of it as an ever-changing and evolving unity, depending on the above mentioned struggle between our drives and instincts and on the kind of organization and "order of rank" that is established among

---

43 Cf. Pippin (2010: 80ff.).

them *when and while actions occur*. Since those drives and instincts are, as we have seen in the previous section, minimal forms of evaluative perspectives which constantly interact with the external world – thus constantly affecting and being affected by it – and furthermore fight for their own power and dominance over all the others, their internal organization and direction is by no means fixed and eternal, as Schopenhauer would have it, but rather dynamical, relational and thoroughly temporary or provisory. As a consequence and against Schopenhauer, for Nietzsche one's identity is by no means fixed and pre-given, but rather progresses over time as the result of a continuous interpretation and reinterpretation of what one does in the course of one's life. This implies that the constitution of one's identity is, on the one hand, necessarily retrospective and, on the other hand, an ongoing, constantly revisable and potentially endless process.[44]

Thus, even though in a broad sense both authors can be said to be committed to an expressivist model of action, their expressivisms differ in two fundamental respects. First, whereas for Schopenhauer it is the intelligible character that expresses itself in actions, thus allowing the individual to learn what he or she necessarily and eternally is, for Nietzsche the action is simply the expression of the organization and hierarchy of forces that is constituted at the moment of acting, which was not necessarily the same in the previous action, and will not likely remain the same after the action is completed. Note that this does not imply a total arbitrariness or instability of the character. Even though Nietzsche rejects Schopenhauer's immutability of character, he does recognize a certain stability and coherence in characters throughout time. Provided that the circumstances do not radically change, the transformations that are constantly occurring are generally minor and do not provoke a radical change in actions and behaviors (HH I 41). This is the reason why Nietzsche can speak about "types" of human beings, such as "the weak", "the strong", "the slaves", "the masters", "the healthy", "the sick", "the herd animals", "the higher men", and so on. Those are, precisely, certain configurations and organizations of drives and instincts that correspond to particular ways of acting, thinking and evaluating, which, despite minor changes and evolution, tend to remain stable in the course of one's life.[45]

Secondly, and as a consequence, whereas for Schopenhauer the action cannot but express what we always already are and will be, for Nietzsche it is

---

[44] For the interpretative and progressive nature of one's identity in Nietzsche see Pippin (2010: 79ff.). Cf. also Nehamas (1985: 170 – 199).
[45] Cf. Constâncio (2014: 167 – 168) and Richardson (1996: 52ff.).

actually the action which, in time, determines what we are and shall become. In other words, whereas for Schopenhauer all my future possible actions are *a priori* determined by my nature, my essence, my character, for Nietzsche, character is, itself, a work in progress, something that does not exist as a whole beforehand but is rather being constructed and slightly changed at every moment and with every action. It is in this sense that there is no doer *behind* the deed, as if one could distinguish the substance, the *substratum*, from its expressions or manifestations in the action, as Schopenhauer still endorses. For Nietzsche, the doer is rather constituted by and through the action, which is the reason why it cannot be conceived independent of it nor even be distinguished from it: the doer *is* the sum of its expressions – and nothing before, beyond or behind them.

It follows then from what has just been revealed that the picture Leiter presents from Nietzsche is really more Schopenhauerian than Nietzschean.[46] If it is true, on the one hand, that also for Nietzsche the range of possibilities of action for a human being are limited and determined by some "natural facts" about him or her; on the other hand, these "natural facts" do not amount to an absolutely immutable nature or essence which would once and for all determine who one is and what one will do, in the sense of Schopenhauer. The relative constancy and stability of the character throughout one's limited length of life might indeed give the impression of immutability, thus also justifying Nietzsche's more fatalist claims quoted at the beginning of this section. However, as Nietzsche writes in an aphorism from *Human, All Too Human* against the thesis of the "unalterable character", it is precisely the brevity of our life that misleads us in this respect: "if one imagines a man of eighty-thousand years, however, one would have in him a character totally alterable" (HH I 41). Indeed, the fact that the individual is a "work in progress", in the sense explained above, shall not be underestimated. Even though the individual is not free to act in total independence or indifference to his own peculiar configuration of drives and instincts or change this configuration when or as he pleases, the fact is that this configuration *is* indeed constantly being affected and thus changed by all kind of experiences, actions and thoughts an individual under-

---

[46] With this we by no means intend to present a refutation of Leiter's whole thesis in "The Paradox of Fatalism and Self-Creation in Nietzsche" (1998). That would require, among other things, a discussion of Nietzsche's theory of self-creation in connection with Schopenhauer's doctrine of the "acquisition of character", from which we totally abstained in this paper. The only point of criticism here is, as explained above, Leiter's attribution of a Schopenhauerian-like "essence" or "nature" to Nietzschean characters.

goes. And, in a certain sense, this makes an individual's future open. The openness of his or her future is so limited and narrow that this might seem just a little modification of Schopenhauer's deterministic view. Nietzsche himself claimed to be a "nuance" (EH CW 4) and, as we tried to show, in what concerns his relation to Schopenhauer's account of the 'subject' and the 'self', he is, in fact, just a nuance. But in this as in many other respects, it is a significant one.

References

Abel, Günter (2001) "Bewußtsein–Sprache–Natur. Nietzsches Philosophie des Geistes", in: *Nietzsche-Studien* 30, 1–43.
Atwell, John E. (1990) *Schopenhauer, the Human Character*, Philadelphia: Tempel University Press.
Atwell, John E. (1995) *Schopenhauer on the Character of the World: The Metaphysics of Will*, Berkeley/Los Angeles: University of California Press.
Constâncio, João (2011) "On Consciousness. Nietzsche's Departure from Schopenhauer", in: *Nietzsche-Studien* 40, 1–42.
Constâncio, João (2012) "Consciousness, Communication, and Self-Expression. Towards an Interpretation of Aphorism 354 of Nietzsche's The Gay Science", in: J. Constâncio and M.J. Mayer Branco (eds.), *As the Spider Spins: Essays on Nietzsche's Critique and Use of Language*, Berlin/Boston: De Gruyter, 197–231.
Constâncio, João (2013) "On Nietzsche's Conception of Philosophy in *Beyond Good and Evil*: Reassessing Schopenhauer's Relevance", in: M.E. Born and A. Pichler (eds.), *Texturen des Denkens: Nietzsches Inszenierung der Philosophie in "Jenseits von Gut und Böse"*, Berlin/Boston: De Gruyter, 145–164.
Constâncio, João (2014) "'O que somos livres para fazer?' Reflexão sobre o problema da subjectividade em Nietzsche", in: Scarlett Marton, Maria João Mayer Branco and João Constâncio (eds.), *Sujeito, Décadence e Arte. Nietzsche e a Modernidade*, Lisbon/Rio de Janeiro: Tinta-da-China, 159–196.
Emden, Christian J. (2005) *Nietzsche on Language, Consciousness and the Body*, Chicago: University of Illinois Press.
Gardner, Sebastian (2009) "Nietzsche, the Self, and the Disunity of Philosophical Reason", in: K. Gemes and S. May (eds.), *Nietzsche on Freedom and Autonomy*, Oxford: Oxford University Press, 1–31.
Gerhardt, Volker (2006) "The Body, the Self and the Ego", in: Keith Ansell Pearson (ed.), *A Companion to Nietzsche*, Oxford: Blackwell, 273–296.
Hill, R. Kevin (2003) *Nietzsche's Critiques: The Kantian Foundations of his Thought*, Oxford: Oxford University Press.
Itaparica, André Luís Mota (2014) "Crítica da modernidade e conceito de subjectividade em Nietzsche", in: Scarlett Marton, Maria João Mayer Branco and João Constâncio (eds.), *Sujeito, décadence e arte. Nietzsche a modernidade*, Lisbon/Rio de Janeiro: Tinta da China, 39–60.
Janaway, Christopher (1989) *Self and World in Schopenhauer's Philosophy*, New York/Oxford: Oxford University Press.

Janaway, Christopher (1991) "Nietzsche, the Self, and Schopenhauer", in: Keith Ansell Pearson (ed.), *Nietzsche and Modern German Thought*, London: Routledge, 119–142.
Janaway, Christopher (2007) *Beyond Selflessness. Reading Nietzsche's Genealogy*, Oxford: Oxford University Press.
Katsafanas, Paul (2005) "Nietzsche's Theory of Mind: Consciousness and Conceptualization", in: *European Journal of Philosophy* 13, 1–31.
Leiter, Brian (1998) "The Paradox of Fatalism and Self-Creation in Nietzsche", in: Christopher Janaway (ed.), *Willing and Nothingness. Schopenhauer as Nietzsche's Educator*, New York/Oxford: Oxford University Press, 217–257.
Leiter, Brian (2002) *Nietzsche on Morality*, London/New York: Routledge.
Nehamas, Alexander (1985) *Nietzsche: Life as Literature*, Cambridge, MA: Harvard University Press.
Pippin, Robert (1999) *Modernism as a Philosophical Problem: On the Dissatisfactions of European High Culture*, rev. edition, Malden, MA: Blackwell.
Pippin, Robert B. (2010) *Nietzsche, Psychology, and First Philosophy*, Chicago/London: University of Chicago Press.
Richardson, John (1996) *Nietzsche's System*, New York/Oxford: Oxford University Press.
Richardson, John (2004) *Nietzsche's New Darwinism*, New York/Oxford: Oxford University Press.
Salaquarda, Jorg (2007) "Leib bin ich ganz und gar… Zum dritten Weg bei Schopenhauer und Nietzsche", in: Konstantin Broese, Matthias Koßler and Barbara Salaquarda (eds.), *Die Deutung der Welt. Jorg Salaquardas Schriften zu Arthur Schopenhauer*, Würzburg: Königshausen & Neumann.
Schlimgen, Erwin (1999) *Nietzsches Theorie des Bewußtseins*, Berlin: De Gruyter.
Wotling, Patrick (1995) *Nietzsche et le Problème de la Civilisation*, Paris: PUF.

Pietro Gori
6 Psychology without a Soul, Philosophy without an I

Nietzsche and 19th Century Psychophysics (Fechner, Lange, Mach)

1 Introduction

Nietzsche's view of the problem of subjectivity – and particularly of the "I" *qua* subject – has an important role in his thought, and is, for this reason, extensively discussed in the secondary literature. As with other themes in Nietzsche's philosophy, its interpretation is deeply problematic, mostly because it is not always clear whether and to what extent Nietzsche is committed to a rejection of the I.

The I becomes a particularly important object of investigation in Nietzsche's late writings, because it is one of the distinctive elements of the Western worldview and its metaphysics of substance. Nietzsche's most significant reflections on the I – which he sees as the question on the substantial referent of psychic phenomena – occur in the first book of *Beyond Good and Evil*, devoted to the "prejudices of philosophers". Nietzsche then deals with that topic in *Twilight of the Idols*, "'Reason' in Philosophy", 5. In that section he blames the "basic presuppositions [...] of *reason*" for clearing the way to a "crudely fetishistic mindset. It sees doers and deeds all over: [...] it believes in the 'I', in the I as being, in the I as substance, and it *projects* this belief in the I-substance onto all things. [...] Being is imagined in everything – *pushed under everything* – as a cause." In these pages, Nietzsche is clearly taking a stand against all philosophical approaches that still make an uncritical use of the I and are therefore unable to give up the commonsensical view of the I. Thus, Nietzsche calls into question the legitimacy of using the proposition "I think" as an immediate certainty (BGE 16).[1] Nietzsche argues that in order to be able to discuss this issue, one would have to answer

> a set of bold claims that are difficult to establish – for instance, that I am the one who is thinking, that there must be something that is thinking in the first place, that thinking is an activity and the effect of a being who is considered the cause, that there is an "I" and

---

[1] P. Bornedal (2010, ch. 3) has recently dealt with Nietzsche and Kant's critique of Descartes' "I think". See also Loukidelis 2005.

finally, that it has already been determined what is meant by thinking, – that I *know* what thinking is. (BGE 16)

Moreover, since if we split the proposition "I think" into its two constituent parts,[2] we notice that the usual conception of the I stems from a non-philosophical account of both of them, and it bears with it traces of a naive metaphysics. Thus, Nietzsche concludes:

> In place of that "immediate certainty" which may, in this case, win the faith of the people, the philosopher gets handed a whole assortment of metaphysical questions, genuinely probing intellectual questions of conscience, such as: "Where do I get the concept of thinking from? Why do I believe in causes and effects? What gives me the right to speak about an I, and, for that matter, about an I as cause, and, finally, about an I as the cause of thoughts?" (BGE 16)

The kind of problems raised by Nietzsche is clear, but that does not make the questions less problematic, especially when one takes into account the fact (which was never denied by Nietzsche, but who on the contrary was well aware of it) that the notion of the I plays an important role in the common and immediate representation of acts of thought, and is, therefore, the indispensable basis of individual actions (practical and moral). This framework becomes even more complex when the question of the I is extended to include that of the soul, and we move from a classical problem for philosophy and psychology to more delicate issues concerning religion in general and Christianity in particular. Nietzsche explicitly connects these different levels in BGE 54, where he reflects on the I and stresses that in Descartes' time it was impossible to account for thinking without ascribing a cause to it, but modern philosophy eventually overcame this limitation:

> Since Descartes [...] all the philosophers have been out to assassinate the old concept of the soul, under the guise of critiquing the concepts of subject and predicate. In other words, they have been out to assassinate the fundamental presupposition of the Christian doctrine. As a sort of epistemological skepticism, modern philosophy is, covertly or overtly, *anti-Christian* [...]. People used to believe in "the soul" as they believed in grammar and the grammatical subject: people said that "I" was a condition and "think" was a predicate and conditioned – thinking is an activity, and a subject *must* be thought of as its cause. Now, with admirable tenacity and cunning, people are wondering whether

---

[2] Nietzsche devotes special attention to this dualism, especially in the years following *Beyond Good and Evil*. See in particular GM I 13 and its preparatory note, NL 1886, 7[1], KSA 12: 247–250. Below I will refer to both texts. See also TI Errors 3, which incorporates and unifies the observations made in BGE and GM. Nietzsche's view of the relation between doer and deed is thoroughly discussed in Pippin 2010, chapter 4.

they can get out of this net – wondering whether the reverse might be true: that "think" is the condition and "I" is conditioned, in which case "I" would be a synthesis that only gets *produced* through thought itself. (BGE 54)

In this passage, Nietzsche sees the soul as a religious interpretation of a fundamental psychological principle. This view was most probably influenced by a contemporary debate that included Friedrich A. Lange as one of the contenders.[3] The I of which Nietzsche speaks in BGE 16 does not differ from the soul discussed by Lange in his *History of Materialism*, (where Nietzsche found a detailed, updated exposition of the latest publications in psychology), nor is it different from what the Austrian physicist Ernst Mach called, in the same years, the "supposed psychic unity" that science claimed to be able to locate within the brain.[4] Mach, in particular, stresses the dependence of philosophical and scientific knowledge on a religious tradition of thought and deplores the fact that science insists on seeking a "seat of the soul" (*Seele*) in the ganglia of the brain, thereby failing to raise the hypothesis that no substantial entity of that kind actually exists.

The main problem that Mach addresses is the relation between body and I (matter and spirit) or, more generally, between the physical and the psychical – an issue widely debated in the nineteenth century and which has in Gustav Fechner's psychophysics one of its main points of reference. Indeed, Mach's investigations presuppose Fechner's results, which Mach intended to develop into a *neutral monism*. He thought that it provided an anti-metaphysical solution to the mind-body problem (see below sec. 4). Lange also relies on Fechner in his attack on the limitations of the explanations of the body/soul relation provided both by the materialism and the physiology of sense organs typical of psychology. In Lange's time, psychology was still engaged in seeking a substantial basis for its main object of study and, for this reason, remained in a "pre-scientific" stage of research (see below sec. 3). No wonder, then, that both Lange and Mach, taking a hint from Franz Brentano, raised the possibility of establishing a "psychology without a soul" and tried to show, in particular, that that position could be defended without resort to paradoxical formulations. Thus, they became spokesmen for a goal of considerable philosophical significance, that is,

---

[3] Lange's influence on Nietzsche's thought has been clearly demonstrated by Salaquarda 1978 and Stack 1983, and later confirmed by several studies from the *Quellen-Forschung*.

[4] Mach 1914: 26. The discussion concerning science's research on the self as an indivisible unit that forms the basis of mental processes is already present in *Beiträge zur Analyse der Empfindungen*, published in 1886 and purchased by Nietzsche probably in the same year (see Mach 1886: 19 n. 13). I will deal with Mach's view of the I in both section 4 and 5.

the fact that contemporary psychology no longer needed to refer to a substantial ground of psychic functions (without at the same time seeing its object of investigation vanish) is what brought about its liberation from the old scholastic metaphysics.

In this paper, I shall hence give an account of the nineteenth-century debate on the I and soul in order to address the problem of the subject as raised by Nietzsche in BGE 16. I shall first draw from that debate some elements that contextualize the "metaphysical questions" mentioned by Nietzsche in BGE 16 (that is, whether and on what basis is it possible to speak of the I as the cause of thoughts); and then, on that basis, I shall turn from psychology to philosophy and discuss Nietzsche's criticism of the subject and his view of what might be called a "philosophy without an I".

2 Towards a psychology without soul

If one wants to give a general and synthetic overview of psychological research as it was carried out in Germany in the second half of the nineteenth century, it should be pointed out as its main feature the intention of giving psychology the status of a real science, that is a mathematically founded discipline, which is able to furnish the tools to measure the object under investigation. The problem of the scientific foundation of psychology arose at that time due to Kant's reflections in the *Critique of Pure Reason* regarding the issue of the psychological knowledge of the soul as a substance and the philosophical problem related to it of the "community of the soul with the organic body".[5] The attempt of authors active in the first half of the nineteenth century to solve or at least circumvent the difficulties noted by Kant gave rise to multiple solutions, the most effective and most significant of which can be ascribed to Johann Friedrich Herbart and Gustav Fechner. The former had developed a system of mathematical computability of the soul, while the second is the father of psychophysics, a discipline based on a neutral assessment of physical and psychic events, focusing in particular on the possibility of measuring sensations.[6] The contribution of both researchers was undoubtedly important, especially since it constituted a reference for further investigations. These were, however, characterized by an addi-

---

[5] I. Kant, CPR A 384, A 392–393 and B 427. On Kant's position regarding the possibility of the existence of any "psychophysical problem", see Martinelli 1999: 9–19.
[6] On Herbart and Fechner see especially Banks 2003, chapters 3 and 6; Leary 1980, Sachs-Hombach 1993, Heidelberger 1996.

tional feature. In particular they had in view the rejection of those metaphysical principles that still characterized psychological studies, for the sake of a more honest "return to Kant". Since the mid-nineteenth century in philosophical and scientific domains people felt the need to return to Kant's epistemology and relinquish the idealist philosophy of nature and, with it, the metaphysical and speculative interpretation of Kant's thought. Authors who belong to the school of neo-Kantianism – such as Friedrich Lange and Otto Liebmann – and to whom we owe a first reception of Fechner's ideas, have privileged scientific themes in the work of Kant, particularly those relating to problems of psychology and anthropology. They tried, first of all, to grasp Kant's lesson without relapsing into the errors of previous interpreters. Secondly, they kept their investigation up-to-date as much as possible by relying on the most recent results of scientific knowledge.[7]

A further characteristic feature of German psychology, directly linked with the intention of establishing its scientific foundation, concerns the interest in the physiological investigation of sense organs. Given the difficulty of applying an exact method of investigation to a non-ascertainable object as the soul, reference to the bodily dimension appeared to be an essential step to provide psychology with a solid foundation. More than anyone else, Herbart struggled with problems relating to the establishment of a scientific study of the soul. At first he rejected Johannes Müller's influential idea that "no one is a psychologist without being a physiologist" (Müller 1822: 45). Herbart gave physiology a subordinate role, privileging instead a purely mathematical quantification of the entities studied by psychology. Herbart's intention of avoiding any form of measurement proved, however, untenable in the eyes of scientists of the time: the mathematical model should, in fact, be applied to anything, that is, the intended quantification could not subsist without measurement. On the other hand, such measurement could be applied to nothing else but sensations, a fact inconsistent with Herbart's theoretical assumptions. Thus, his proposal ultimately failed because of its purely speculative character. Studies continued in the direction of an experimental psychology that could enable an effective measurement of the soul. A further step on this course was made by Fechner, who proposed a scientific procedure to determine quantitatively the relation between psychic experience and measurable external stimulus. More simply, Fechner resorted to the physiology of sense organs to measure sensations, on the assumption that these are nothing but physical evidence of psychic phenomena.[8]

---

7 Cf. Lehmann 1987 and Martinelli 1999:52–53.
8 For a more extensive and comprehensive reconstruction of this process, see Guzzardi 2010, in particular chapter 2.

It was Ernst Mach himself who pointed out this transition in one of the writings in which he demonstrated to adhere, at least in the beginning, to Fechnerian psychophysics. He observed that "the part of the life of the soul which is immediately connected to the organism's physical phenomena has become in recent times accessible to exact research. I mean the sensations" (Mach 1863: 204). Mach emphasized what we said above, namely the fact that in psychology one cannot talk about "exact research" with reference to Herbart's mere mathematical quantification; rather, it was necessary for research to make use of processes aimed at the measurement of sensations, and therefore Herbart's mathematical psychology could be accepted only in the light of Fechner's psychophysics.

At the same time, however, Mach noticed the inadequacy of Fechner's solution. The latter still pursued the analysis of material phenomena involved in psychic phenomena with the purpose of locating a "seat of the soul". As we shall restate later, Mach radicalized Fechner's project, criticizing him for upholding a position that was still metaphysical. Conversely, Mach observes that the route taken by psychological research in its development goes in the direction of the soul's disappearance inside the nervous system. Nothing remains of the soul except its final effect, the fact that it is a principle able to give unity to the manifold, whereas its complete redefinition on the basis of the body leads to a "psychology without a soul" as its necessary outcome.[9]

In the following paragraphs, I will have to show in more detail what was hitherto only hinted at. For the moment, I am interested in showing how the outcome of Mach's considerations regarding the route taken by psychology up to the time of Fechner fits perfectly in the context of nineteenth-century science, which clearly shares with psychology the sense of a lack of metaphysical foundations. The conception for which psychology would be ready to abandon the reference to a substantial and spiritual soul, which cannot be identified except as a mathematical concept built on purely theoretical terms out of the system of relations linking psychical events to physical ones, corresponds to the most general position of science in the late nineteenth century, engaged in freeing itself from animistic and mythological conceptions that had their origin in the

---

[9] This conclusion is presented by Mach in his *Knowledge and Error* (1905), which I will deal with in section 5. Before him, the idea of a "psychology without a soul" had been expressed by Lange, in the second edition of the *History of Materialism* (1975), taking over what was previously written by Brentano in his *Psychologie vom empirischen Standpunkt* (1874, vol. 1: 76). In the next section I will deal with Lange's reconstruction of the development of scientific psychology and, thus, with the development of the line of reasoning that led him to support such a position.

worldview of common sense.¹⁰ More generally, during the nineteenth century, Western thought underwent a radical transformation, witnessing the collapse of the principles on which its knowledge was built. For those who are acquainted with Nietzsche, this can be easily understood by thinking of the "death of God": a formula with which he identifies the disorientation of his age, whose foundations lie beyond the religious and moral level. Metaphors aside, and remaining within the field of natural science, we may say that physical investigations at that time revealed a much less definite and unchangeable reality than what was believed. To these investigations were added mathematical studies, which in the nineteenth century undermined the foundations of Newtonian physics and reshaped the descriptive scope of the Euclidean system, on the basis of which the former stood. The emergence of Riemann's geometry, for example, made clear that the previously adopted model was not as "truthful" as it was previously believed. In fact, it says nothing about reality, merely describing it by means of a scientifically effective and "economic" system. Without expanding on a topic that deserves a thoroughly different treatment, I think it is important to emphasize the sense of disorientation experienced by scientists of those times, with which, however, they dealt in a positive way, turning it into a stimulus for a reconfiguration of the process of investigation of their own disciplines. This process culminated, for example, in Poincaré's conventionalism, as well as in Mach's studies on the economic character of scientific knowledge, which marked the beginning of twentieth-century research on matter and space.

An author who shortly after the mid-nineteenth century became the spokesman for the explanatory problem of modern epistemology was Emil du Bois-Reymond with his two conferences in 1872 and 1880 respectively: *The Boundaries of the Knowledge of Nature* and *The World's Seven Puzzles*. The former is famous for the way it ends, with an "*Ignorabimus!*" that does not leave room for the possibility of surpassing certain cognitive limits and solving certain problems posed by natural reality. One of these problems concerns the discourse relative to knowledge of psychic phenomena, particularly regarding their relation to the material dimension – what, in modern terms, we would label the mind-body problem. Du Bois-Reymond argues in particular that "consciousness [i.e. any mental process] cannot be explained by its material conditions" and that "it will never be explainable [...] on the basis of such conditions" (Du Bois-Reymond 1886: 117), and continues carrying out a detailed analysis of the histor-

---

10 As is well known, Mach was among the forerunners of that position. His work on *Mechanics in its historical-critical development* (1883) was a landmark for contemporary epistemology and for the philosophy of science in the early twentieth century. For more on this, see Blackmore 1972.

ical development of the debate on the relation between body and soul (*Leib und Seele*). His conclusion in this regard is that, since there was no progress in the understanding of mental processes on the basis of their material states, they should be considered, as much as the relation between matter and force, an insurmountable limit of our knowledge of nature (Du Bois-Reymond 1886: 125).

Du Bois-Reymond's reflections aroused great interest at the time, and references to his conferences can be found in different writings coming from the field of natural history and physiology.[11] They are an important sign of the cultural context within which scientific psychology evolved. The latter has precisely expressed the demand to be defined on a new basis, freeing itself from the remnants of an age-old metaphysics that surreptitiously attempted to introduce something that it could not specify, much less quantify or measure.

3 Friedrich Lange on the brain, soul and scientific psychology

Much of the elements considered above can be found in the examination carried out by Friedrich Lange in two chapters added to the second edition of the History of Materialism, published in 1875: *Brain and Soul* and *Scientific Psychology*.[12] The first of these opens with a discussion of the difficulty of putting forward any argument regarding the relation between brain and soul that is not contradicted by facts. However, the difficulty is not regarded by Lange as resulting solely from the futility of the studies of the period. Rather, he argues that the greatest problem is a theoretical one, consisting in particular in the fact that we have not yet been able to formulate a non-animistic hypothesis about the nature of the brain's activity. Having no other reference points on the basis of which to structure their own investigations, Lange explains:

---

[11] On the debate regarding Du Bois-Reymond's warning, see Bayertz/Gerhard/Jaeschke 2007. A copy of the two conferences presented by Du Bois-Reymond in 1872 and 1880 can be found in Nietzsche's library (cf. G. Campioni et al. 2003: 202), although there is no record that he effectively read them. Thomas Brobjer has reported this fact, relating Nietzsche's interest in the work of Du Bois-Reymond to his knowledge of the writings of Richard Avenarius and Mach, which according to Brobjer were "three of the most important philosophers of science from that period", and whose contribution is particularly linked to the development and transformation of nineteenth-century positivism (see Brobjer 2008: 92).

[12] These chapters are included in the third part of the second volume, which is devoted to the way in which the natural sciences have addressed issues relating to *man and soul*.

> Even educated men constantly fall back again, as if it were from despair, upon the theories, long since refuted by the facts, of a localisation of the cerebral activity according to the various functions of the intellect and the emotions. We have, it is true, repeatedly expressed ourselves against the view that the mere continuance of obsolete opinions is so great a hindrance to science as is commonly supposed; but here it does in fact appear as though the phantom of the soul showing itself on the ruins of Scholasticism continually confuses the whole question.
>
> We could easily show that this ghost [...] plays a great part amongst the men who consider themselves entirely free from it, amongst our Materialistic leaders; nay, their whole conception of the way in which we must conceive the cerebral activity is essentially dominated by the popular conceptions which were formerly held as to the mythical faculties of the soul. (Lange 1881: 113)

Therefore, the progress of psychology collides with traces of scholastic ideas: the idea that an explanation of psychical phenomena is only possible on the basis of the identification of a substantial foundation of the latter. According to Lange, the materialistic view of nature conceives the soul always as something existing on its own, a "ghost" (*Gespenst*) that populates our brain. Right from the outset, Lange expresses himself critically against this view of things, recognizing the liberation from the old metaphysics of substance precisely as the starting point on which a psychology, wanting to conform to natural science, should be based. In this, however, he acknowledges a fundamental difficulty, pointing out how some attempts in that direction have gone astray. This is the case of phrenology, which begins with the basically correct idea that the commonly accepted faculties of the soul are in fact abstractions (Lange 1881: 113), only to end up on the tendency to fall back on localization. Lange's final comment is that phrenology, while being in principle aimed at going "beyond the standpoint of the spectral soul", ultimately multiplies brain functions and assigns a subject to each of them. In this way, it "ends by peopling the whole skull with specters", failing to meet its founders' original intentions (Lange 1881: 125).[13]

---

[13] The quoted passage continues in this way: "[Phrenology] falls back to the naive standpoint, which will not be content without putting a machinist to sit in the ingenious machine of our body to guide the whole." This metaphor closely recalls the observation made by Nietzsche in GS 360 where he complains about our tendency to personification and to look for an active cause underlying purely physiological events. In particular, Nietzsche points out, we tend to conceive our will as a "*driving* cause", but in doing so we mistake "the helmsman for the steam". This passage is of particular interest for the present discussion, because it appears in an example that Lange gives slightly below in the chapter on *Brain and Soul*. In fact, in GS 360, Nietzsche describes the cause of acting according to a purpose as "a small accident in accordance with which this quantum 'discharges' itself in one particular way: the match versus the powder keg". Thus, a few

Phrenology proves to be, therefore, absolutely unscientific, but precisely for this reason it serves for Lange as an example of the "irresistible tendency to personification" which represents the real danger in studies on brain and soul. The fact that up to his time phrenology has not been able to provide a good explanation of the relation between the brain and psychic functions springs, according to Lange, from the tendency to make use of abstract ideas, personifying them, instead of limiting oneself, as much as possible, to an understanding of reality (Lange 1881: 125). Thus, Lange's argument moves towards physiology as a discipline that makes use of the bodily dimension to explain psychic phenomena without going beyond the level of the reflex movements of the nerves. The discussion of this position, focused in particular on the figure of Johannes Müller, allows Lange to highlight a very important element for philosophical reflection on the scientific description of man. Even the physiological explanation of psychic phenomena is characterized by a fundamental difficulty, since reducing the psychical to the physical proves itself to be, as a matter of fact, impossible. Sensations, for example, are by no means something whose origin can be traced: researchers simply assume that they exist on the basis of physical signals in their bodies (Lange 1881: 128–130). The reason why a complete reduction of psychic phenomena to the bodily dimension is not possible is because the former phenomena *do not exist* at all. In fact, Lange remarks that the concepts used by psychology are nothing other than the product of a purely theoretical classification. They do not specify something real in itself. It is therefore useless to look for their bodily counterpart, because the physiological substrate of the faculties of the soul is not univocally linked to them. In other words, it does not exist as a true "seat" of these faculties in the body. Lange observes:

> Above all, we must be clear that in all the paragraphs of the ancient scholastic psychology there is nowhere mention of things that we may ever expect to find again in the elements of the cerebral functions. It is with them as much as if one tries to find the various activities of a locomotive, so far as they can be externally observed [...] In our whole traditional psychology the actions of men are classified, without any regard to the elements of their origin, according to certain relations to life and its aims, and indeed in such a way that the mere psychological analysis often shows clearly how little what is denoted by a single word forms a true unity. [...] Almost all these psychological notions give us a word by

---

pages after the discussion of phrenology, looking at the actual cause of a reaction in humans, Lange writes: "The living force for the transmitting process is ready prepared in the nerve, as that of muscular contraction in the muscles; it can only be set free by the infinitely feeble impulse of the light-wave, as the elastic forces of a barrel of powder by the glimmering spark" (Lange 1881: 157). Considering that the fifth book of GS was composed in 1886, it is not implausible to think that Lange was a direct source of §360.

means of which a portion of the phenomena of human life is very imperfectly classified. With this classification is combined the metaphysical delusion of a common substantial basis of these phenomena, and this delusion must be destroyed. (Lange 1881: 137–138)

This final remark from this passage is of particular significance, because it identifies the point of division between scientific research and metaphysical explanation. This point is represented by the "mortal leap" that is taken when one ascribes an ontological value to a logical scheme aimed at description and calculation. In the case at hand, psychology provides a classification of psychical phenomena with a view to their study, to which is added, however, at a later stage ("pushed under" [*untergeschoben*], as Nietzsche would say) a substantial cause, as if that classification were a determination of the reality of things. Setting this problem aside, Lange nevertheless acknowledges a positive role to physiology in the advancement of scientific psychology. The latter, in particular, represents a step forward compared to the materialistic view, which remained tied to the intention of circumscribing a physical basis for the "faculties of the soul".[14] In addition, Lange remarks that true progress in brain studies consists in being able to refer the primal basis of psychical functions back to the physiological dimension, without the need to add mythical causes as explanations of these functions.[15]

Although recognizing that metaphysics has lost its *raison d'être* in psychological studies, a number of problems concerning the mind-body relation remain, nevertheless, unsolved. In particular, the difficulty in explaining some psychical phenomena arising from the physical substrate seems to lead research to an insurmountable limit. Although studies of the period began to spread the idea that there was nothing to investigate once all the "symptoms" of a given phenomenon[16] were specified, there remains the feeling, nevertheless, that something is left unexplained, that some aspects concerning sensations have not been taken into

---

14 Lange writes: "If the 'muscular sense' or the 'will-impulse' is hypostasized in the sense of this old psychology as a 'faculty', which is served by a greater or lesser portion of the brain, then on the materialistic view the 'faculty of the soul' is destroyed together with the corresponding part of the brain [...]. If, on the contrary, we keep strictly in view that from the standpoint of physiology, even in the production of a conscious impulse of will, we have to do with an organic process like every other, that the 'faculty' of psychology is only a name, with which the possibility of the process is apparently elevated to a special thing, [...] then we cannot at all see why even the 'terminus' of a psychical line or the place of origin of a 'faculty', like any other part of the brain, may not be replaced in its activity by new lines." (Lange 1881: 147)
15 See Lange 1881: 152–157. Lange's observations concerning this point refer to Wilhelm Wundt's *Grundzüge der physiologischen Psychologie* (1874).
16 That is, when it has been traced to nerve currents and states of tension, see Lange 1881: 159–160.

account. Referring implicitly to Du Bois-Reymond – and thereby showing how much his warning was present in the eyes of scholars of the time – Lange notes that

> the co-operation of very many, and, individually considered, extraordinarily feeble nerve impulses, must give us the key to the physiological understanding of thinking, and the form of this co-operation is the characteristic feature of each individual function. What in this remains unexplained – the manner, the external, natural phenomenon – is at the same time an internal one for the thinking subject: that is the point which altogether overpasses the limits of the knowledge of nature. (Lange 1881: 161)

The reconstruction developed by Lange on the debate concerning the relation between brain and soul in nineteenth-century German psychology shows that this discipline was moving towards a scientific account of the problem, understood in the sense of a complete emancipation from the metaphysical traces of scholastic metaphysics. At this point, Lange addresses the problem of the scientific foundation of psychology mentioning (most critically) Herbart's position, who was the first to attempt a mathematization of psychology. Lange notes that the idea of a "mathematical psychology" is certainly promising, but it does not constitute a sufficient step forward towards a genuine emancipation from metaphysics. And thus the risk is to become deeply disappointed, as in the case of phrenology, if one wants to believe "that Herbart with his differential equations has as thoroughly mastered the world of ideas, as Kopernicus and Kepler the world of the planets" (Lange 1881: 162). I will not go into the multiple aspects of Lange's critique of Herbart. What interests me is solely to stress the reason why mathematical theory represented an important phase, although not sufficient and definitive, in the development of scientific psychology. In remarking that Herbart's view is still based on metaphysical principles, Lange notes that it constitutes a first step towards a new modality of psychological investigation. "Herbart's school", he writes, "forms for Germany an important link in the epoch of transition, although here science is only beginning painfully to struggle free of metaphysics" (Lange 1881: 167–168). The contribution of Herbart and the authors related to him consists in having opened a path of research, which, however, fails because of its willingness to resort by any means to the concept of an absolutely simple soul, a concept that in principle can only be posited, but in no way further determined. Conversely, Lange remarks, "in the few phenomena which so far have been made accessible to more precise observation, there is not the smallest occasion to assume a soul in any very definite sense at all" (Lange 1881: 167–168). Hence he concludes that psychology's true progress should consist in the complete liberation from the metaphysics of substance and thus in the rejection of those accessory and unnecessary hypotheses which Herbart still seems to be willing to admit:

"But does not psychology then mean the doctrine of the soul? How, then, is a science conceivable which leaves it doubtful whether it has any object at all?" Well, here we have again a charming example of the confusion of name and thing. We have a traditional name for a considerable but by no means accurately defined group of phenomena. This name has come down from a time when the present requirements of strict science were unknown. Shall we reject the name because the object of science has been changed? That were unpractical pedantry. Calmly assume, then, a psychology without a soul! And yet the name will still be useful, so long as we have something to study that is not completely covered by any other science. (Lange 1881: 168)

The direction of Lange's investigation cannot fail to recall some of Nietzsche's observations.[17] In fact, the rejection of all substantialistic hypotheses implies showing how much the progress of research had rendered the former useless, thus revealing above all its purely illusory character. Nevertheless – and this is worth noting if one wants to understand Nietzsche's later statements about the soul – Lange also claims that there is no harm in preserving the concept of soul as the object of psychological investigation, provided that it is defined in non-metaphysical terms.

Lange's idea that "scientific psychology" should be adapted to the principles of naturalistic studies and look no further than to what can actually be observed and measured is conveyed by Fechner's work in particular, to whom Lange is indebted and an obvious supporter (see Martinelli 1999: 52–56). A defense of Fechner's psychophysics is particularly clear in the critical remarks that Lange makes to Herbart, focused mainly on the character to be assigned to sensations and more generally on the idea, located in the sections of the *History of Materialism* examined thus far, of the relation between the physical and psychic sphere. Fechner's monistic model, which considers the physical and the psychical as two aspects of a single reality, is also referred to by Ernst Mach. As we shall see in the next two paragraphs, Mach shares with Lange the idea of founding a "psychology without soul", but goes a step further than Fechner's theory, giving rise to the anti-metaphysical direction, which will prove decisive for twentieth century's studies in both psychology and physiology.

4 The relation between the physical and the psychical

Psychophysics was born as a discipline with the publication of the two volumes of *Elements of Psychophysics* by Fechner (1860), and it is therefore to him that

---

[17] He was in fact influenced by Lange in many aspects, as is fully demonstrated in Salaquarda 1978 and Stack 1983 and subsequently in a lot of critical literature on Nietzsche's sources.

we owe its principles. The aspect that I would like to emphasize at the end of this discussion concerns the position in which Fechner takes on the relation between body and soul, which of course constitutes the theoretical background that forms the basis of the positive contribution of psychophysics, consisting in the measurement of the relation between physical and psychic in the area of research devoted to human sensation. In the beginning of his main work, Fechner defines psychophysics as the "exact doctrine of the functionally dependent relations of body and soul [*Körper und Seele*] or, more generally, of the material and the mental, of the physical and psychological worlds" (Fechner 1966: 7). From this definition it can already be seen that the study of the relation between body and soul is not dealt with according to the traditional perspective, which treats them as two distinct and separate entities. Fechner aims to investigate "functional relations" between the physical and the psychical on the basis of a Spinozist ontology that takes them as two aspects of one and the same reality. Thus, he considers that there are no metaphysical differences among what may be designated as "material and spiritual world" (or physical and psychical). At the basis of both domains there is only one substance.[18] This monistic vision represents obviously a step forward in psychological studies when contrasted with the scholastic metaphysics deplored by Lange. Fechner gets rid of the idea of the soul as a substance having ontological autonomy from the body and thus renders meaningless any attempt at locating a seat of that alleged spiritual entity in the brain or in any other part of the organism. However, psychophysics is still characterized by its metaphysical foundation, represented by the way in which the substantial unity, to which both the psychical and the physical are referred, is defined. The Spinozist or Schellingian character of Fechner's conception represents perhaps the only aspect that prevents his system from serving as a model for a "science of the soul". There remains in its foundation an unresolved element, whose nature cannot be investigated and is therefore by no means describable or quantifiable.

This is the aspect on which Mach's critique of Fechner is focused. In *The Analysis of Sensations* (first published in 1886 as *Beiträge zur Analyse der Empfindungen*) Mach proposes a possible solution for the determination of the relation of the physical to the psychical, without falling into the difficulties raised by psychophysics, but maintaining, at the same time, its fundamental monistic structure. Mach's proposal is known under the name of "neutral monism" and

---

[18] For a discussion of the general characteristics of Fechner's psychophysics, see Martinelli 1999: 40ff., in addition to the already mentioned Banks 2003, chapter 6, and Heidelberger 1996.

consists in admitting as the only reality that of the "elements".[19] The latter comprise, for example, colors, sounds, temperatures, pressures ("ultimate component parts [of reality investigated scientifically] which hitherto we have been unable to subdivide any further"; Mach 1914: 5–6). These elements do not possess any characteristic *in themselves*; they may be described in physical as well as in psychical terms depending on the dimension that in each case we are referring to (be it constituted by physical objects outside us–*Körper*–or by our own body–*Leib*). Mach, moreover, adds that the elements specifically related to individual corporality are described as "sensations" and that, since it is not possible for us to relate to them except through our own body, the terms "sensations" and "elements" are synonymous in most of the cases.[20]

It may be immediately noticed that Mach's definition avoids the metaphysical difficulty in which psychophysics is involved by taking the elements as a non-identifiable and especially non-definitive substrate. These are, indeed, the components to which phenomena studied on an exclusively methodological basis can be traced by the researcher, without the latter being necessarily committed to accept their ontological status. Mach stresses pointedly that his research path leaves always open the possibility that the "simple", to which in each case one arrives, is susceptible to further division. Therefore, its elements cannot be incorporated in any substantialist model, even if one were to think of an atomical system whose components do not present qualitative features of their own.

Thus, the moment Mach formulates his "principle of complete parallelism of the psychical and physical" (Mach 1914: 60), he claims for himself a position superior to that of Fechner, in an explicitly "anti-metaphysical" sense. Thanks to his conception of the elements, Mach says that the view he advocates

> is different from Fechner's conception of the physical and psychical as two different aspects of one and the same reality. In the first place, our view has no metaphysical background, but corresponds only to the generalized expression of experiences. Again, we refuse to distinguish two different aspects of an unknown *tertium quid*; the elements given in experience, whose connexion we are investigating, are always the same, and are of only one nature, though they appear, according to the nature of the connexion, at one moment as physical and at another as psychical elements. (Mach 1914: 61)

---

19 The name was used for the first time by Bertrand Russell to refer to the orientation which would be inaugurated by Mach and was common to a large number of philosophers and scientists living in the beginning of the twentieth century (see Banks 2003: 136).
20 This equation has generated quite a few misunderstandings over the years. For a detailed discussion of the theme of the "elements" in Mach, see Banks 2003.

Mach rejects the metaphysical foundation of Fechner's psychophysics, but agrees with the idea of overcoming the distinction between a corporeal and a spiritual world, focusing as well on the *functional* dimension of the relation between both domains. Since there is no physical or psychic phenomena, but only a physical or psychic *interpretation* of them, it does not make sense, in scientific research terms, to take into account anything else except the mode in which the elements are assembled. By focusing in turn on *relatively* more stable connections, it is possible to define the "metaphysical concepts of 'body' and 'I' (matter and soul)" (Mach 1914: 40), which in Mach's system clearly lose the metaphysical sense of an independent subsistence of their component elements.

5 The I as "ideal unity"

In the light of these observations, it is possible to address the specific issue of the I in Mach. He defines, first of all, psychic unity as the combination of sensations that refer to the individual bodily dimension (*Leib*), thus depriving the former of any determination beyond that complex of dispositions and feelings:

> That complex of memories, moods, and feelings, joined to a particular body (the human body), which is called the "I" or "Ego", manifests itself as relatively permanent. I may be engaged upon this or that subject, I may be quiet and cheerful, excited and ill-humored. Yet, pathological cases apart, enough durable features remain to identify the ego. Of course, the ego also is only of relative permanency. The apparent permanency of the ego consists chiefly in the single fact of its continuity, in the slowness of its changes. (Mach 1914: 3)

According to this perspective, the I is not anything beyond the multiplicity of elements that are related to the body (*Leib*); its origin is purely logical and derives from the demand of unity for the purpose of recognition. By means of the determination of a *soul* (Mach relates psychological unity explicitly to this notion), it is, in fact, possible to identify a person as such while observing her changes. The need to orient itself leads the intellect to build a unitary reference which may be used to give a name to the most persistent content of a complex of sensations. There is nothing beyond this purely practical process. The I, as well as the physical bodies (*Körper*), lose for Mach their traditional metaphysical value since it is not possible to identify a real and material substrate that remains once an object is deprived of all its properties.[21] Both the bodies and the

---

[21] What is at stake here is the classical problem of the thing-in-itself, which Mach explicitly rejects as a useless and illusory notion. See Mach 1914: 6 and 30n.

I are simply a thought-construction. They are "only makeshifts, designed for provisional orientation and for definite *practical* ends" (Mach 1914: 13).

In his analysis of the I, Mach pays particular attention to the ontological primacy of the elements in what concerns the purely nominal unitary complex of notions developed by the intellect. Thus, the fundamental psychological concept is then to be defined starting from the formation of an "ideal mental-economic unity", whose function is to bring together "elements that are most intimately connected with pleasure and pain". "The delimitation of the ego", continues Mach, "is instinctively effected, is rendered familiar, and possibly becomes fixed through heredity" (Mach 1914: 22–23). On a strictly ontological basis, the complete dependence of the I from the elements demonstrates the illusory character of "its" metaphysical value. The elements, in fact, represent the "material" that, once connected, constitutes the individual soul; without the former there would be nothing to delimit:

> The primary fact is not the ego, but the elements (sensations). [...] The elements constitute the I. I have the sensation green, signifies that the element green occurs in a given complex of other elements (sensations, memories). When I cease to have the sensation green, when I die, then the elements no longer occur in the ordinary, familiar association. That is all. Only an ideal mental-economical unity, not a real unity, has ceased to exist. (Mach 1914: 23–24)

On the basis of Mach's monistic conception, it is not therefore possible, from a metaphysical point of view, to "save" the I (Mach famously argued that "*das Ich ist unrettbar*" – "the I is unsavable"; Mach 1914: 24). In fact, the I is lost in the (impermanent) connections between elements and it is thus necessary to abandon any pretension of ascribing an autonomous existence to it. In other words, once it is acknowledged that the subject is composed of sensations, it is impossible to want to maintain the integrity of the alleged psychical unity, as has been done in the past by science. The latter, Mach remarks, driven by the habit of "treating the unanalyzed ego-complex as an indiscernible unity", has attempted first to separate "the nervous system [...] from the body 'as the seat of the sensations'", and then turned to the brain and "selected [it] as the organ best fitted for this end" (Mach 1914: 26). Finally, science admitted the existence of a single *point* as seat of the soul, which was obviously not able to locate (Mach 1914: 26–27).[22] While sustaining a radical critique of scientific research of

---

[22] Mach's remark is highly reminiscent of Lange's reconstruction, who focused at length on science's claim to locate a "seat" of the soul. We should notice also that after this paragraph Mach quotes a passage from Lichtenberg: "In his philosophical notes Lichtenberg says: 'We become conscious of certain representations that are not dependent upon us; of others that we

his day, Mach is aware, nevertheless, of the need to distinguish two domains of discourse, safeguarding the I's value as a reference notion, which is not possible to relinquish on the merely practical level. "In spite of all this", Mach admits conclusively, "the Ego is what is most important and most constant for my instinctive conceptions. It is the bond that holds all my experiences together, and the source of all my activity" (Mach 1914: 357). The consequence of this development is a new vision of the world in which "the antithesis between ego and world, between sensation (appearance) and thing [...] vanishes and we have simply to deal with the connection of elements" (Mach 1914: 14).

The reference to the illusory nature of the distinction between appearance and reality forms the point of departure of a section in *Knowledge and Error* (1905), in which Mach summarizes his own position concerning the I, using strong Nietzschean tones. Mach begins with the observation that, at the basis of the philosophical conception of the dualism between phenomenon and thing-in-itself, there lurks the view of common sense, which confounds "findings under the most various conditions with findings under very definite and specific conditions" (Mach 1976: 7). He continues:

> The weird and unknowable "thing-in-itself" behind appearances [*Erscheinung*] is the ordinary object's unmistakable twin, having lost all other significance. After misconstruing the boundary between the internal and external and thereby imposing the stamp of appearance [*Schein*] on the ego's entire content, have we any further need for an unknowable something outside the confines that the ego can never transcend? Is it any more than a relapse into ordinary thought to see some solid core behind "delusive" appearances? (Mach 1976: 7)[23]

---

at least think are dependent upon us. Where is the border-line? We know only of the existence of our sensations, presentations and thoughts. We should say, *It thinks*, just as we say, *It lightens*. It is going too far to say *cogito*, if we translate cogito by I *think*. The assumption, or postulation, of the ego is a mere practical necessity'" (Mach 1914: 28. This quote is present already in the first edition of Mach's work, Mach 1886: 20). This passage is the implicit point of reference of aphorism 17 of *Beyond Good and Evil*, in which Nietzsche carries further his critique of Descartes' I *think*, reflecting on the necessity of referring to an impersonal subject, that is, to the activity of thought itself, without having necessarily to *create* a subject underlying this event (see Loukidelis 2013). Thus, Lichtenberg seems to be a common source for both authors' reflections and this passage in particular constitutes a point of contact between Mach's psychological reflections and passages from Nietzsche's text.

23 As a confirmation of the Nietzschean character of Mach's thought and language, one should compare this passage with the final part of BGE 17, in which Nietzsche claims that "grammatical habits" mislead us into believing that thought is an activity, that every activity is produced by an agent, and as a result into postulating an ego as a cause of thought. Nietzsche continues: "Following the same basic scheme, the older atomism looked behind every 'force' that produces

Mach's anti-metaphysical position is well illustrated here. He thoroughly rejects any reference to a "thing-in-itself" inasmuch as it is beyond the reach of our understanding and thus superfluous (Mach 1914: 30n). Insofar as it is a mere illusory concept, it is also useless. Everything that we can know remains within the horizon of our ego. Moreover, Mach does not even admit the need to postulate such a metaphysical substrate in order to give meaning to what is observable. In his view, this is the difference between scientific knowledge and common sense. The latter is constitutively characterized by errors and "appearance".[24] Contextualizing his discourse in the field of psychology, Mach criticizes the pretension, still obvious in the science of his time, of seeking a substantial element beneath psychical phenomena. If one were to admit the principle of parallelism between the physical and the psychical domain, one would see how "the question as to appearance and reality loses its sense" (Mach 1976: 7). In fact, "elements like red, green, hot, cold and the rest, are physical and mental in virtue of their dependence on both external and internal circumstances" and "the only possible further question of interest concerns their functional interdependence, in the mathematical sense". Thus, continues Mach, "if we look at the restricted ego without prejudice, it too turns out to be a functional connection between these elements" (Mach 1976: 7–8). Mach is particularly clear on this point: "We need no unknown and unknowable something" to place beneath the ego's activity. "Yet there is something all but unexplored standing behind the ego, namely our body; but every new observation in physiology and psychology makes the ego better known to us" (Mach 1976: 8).

In the light of Lange's remarks examined in paragraph 2, these conclusions by Mach do not seem to require further explanation. In fact, they are in agreement with the perspective presented in the *History of Materialism*, which envisions the development of psychological studies progressing in the direction of a complete liberation from the traditional metaphysical conception. If psychology wants to establish itself as science, it should free itself from the need to find a

---

effects for that little lump of matter in which the force resides, and out of which the effects are produced, which is to say: the atom. More rigorous minds finally learned how to make do without that bit of 'residual earth'". With this comparison, it is certainly not our intention to argue for a direct influence between both authors (in this case, an influence of Nietzsche on Mach), but rather to highlight the agreement of their thought, which is accounted for by a contextualization of their ideas in a common cultural background.

24 Even in this point the similarities with Nietzsche's way of thinking are evident. The most important aspects are the fact that both stress the superfluousness of the "thing-in-itself" and the fact that they both reject as nonsensical the distinction between appearance and reality (see e.g. Mach 1976, ch. 1 and TI, How the 'true world' finally became a fable).

permanent material principle as a substrate of the soul. Any contrary attempt represents a step back from the position that holds to the *functional* character of all scientific notions.

Thus, with a sentence that sounds very similar to Nietzsche's remarks in BGE 54 and GM I 13 in which he rejects the distinction between agent and action in psychical phenomena, Mach continues to claim that "one who still needs an observing and acting subject has failed to see that he could have saved himself the whole trouble of the enquiry [of the reciprocal dependence of representations], for he has now gone full circle" (Mach 1976: 8). Finally, in perfect alignment with Lange, Mach takes Herbart's position into account, pointing out how the progress of psychology entails overcoming its chief limitation, that is, the fact of not having been able to take the decisive step towards a science free of metaphysical references:

> It was Herbart's main merit to have examined the processes of ideas as such, yet even he spoiled his whole psychology by starting from the assumption that the soul is simple. Only lately have we begun to accept a psychology without soul. (Mach 1976: 8)

6 The I as a "regulative fiction"

The considerations developed in the previous paragraphs present the context of Nietzsche's position towards the fundamental psychic unity. The discussion of Lange's and Mach's ideas is all the more useful in understanding some aspects of Nietzsche's critique of his contemporaries' conception of the ego since he had direct knowledge of both authors' work. In Lange's case, the debt is especially relevant as is now widely demonstrated in the critical literature. However, the same cannot be said of Mach. He is not mentioned in any of Nietzsche's writings and it is not possible to trace back to him any passage, be it published or unpublished. Despite this, it is possible to note a deep affinity regarding some epistemological positions, probably a sign of a common background of references.[25]

Nietzsche's point of view regarding the problem of the I is especially similar to Mach's critical approach to metaphysical knowledge. In fact, Nietzsche focuses on the purely fictional nature that characterizes the ego, with emphasis on the general characteristics of the activity of thought, which he describes in purely physiological terms. The I is considered as the product of a secondary activity of thought – that of logic – which intervenes in ascribing a subject to a process that is constitutively free of it:

---

[25] For a discussion of the relation between Nietzsche and Mach, see Gori 2009 and 2012.

> What separates me most deeply from the metaphysicians is: I don't concede that the "I" is what thinks. Instead, I take the I itself to be a construction of thinking, of the same rank as "matter", "thing", "substance", "individual", "purpose", "number"; in other words to be only a regulative fiction with the help of which a kind of constancy and thus "knowability" is inserted into, invented into, a world of becoming. [...] It is only thinking that posits the I: but up to now philosophers have believed, like the "common people", that in "I think" there lay something or other of unmediated certainty and that this "I" was the given cause of thinking. (NL 1885, 35 [35], KSA 11: 526 = WLN, 20 – 21)

The I, as a product of thought, is nothing more than a conceptual entity whose value is limited to practical usefulness with a view to a categorization of the world and to its purely logical organization. Moreover, according to this perspective, the I belongs to the sphere of those substantial elements to which one is used to attributing absolute existence and whose origin lies in the translation of the outside world into a language that can be understood and used by our intellect.[26] Basically this is the same as Mach's idea according to which, as we have already seen, the I and the body are concepts that fulfill purely practical needs. It is not possible to locate any autonomous and absolutely permanent entity underneath them. Furthermore, Nietzsche agrees implicitly with Mach in admitting that the individual unity that holds together the multiplicity of perceptions, affects and sentiments which we refer to our body derives from a purely intellectual operation.[27] Besides, this operation conforms to the tendency of admitting being in a reality characterized by becoming and is, therefore, indicative of a purely metaphysical perspective, as Lange had already pointed out.

Nietzsche's reflections are not limited to the latter point. In his view, the I has a feature that distinguishes it from other substantial entities that arise from the simplification of a chaotic multiplicity through isolation of fixed and uniform forms. In order to give unity to feelings, perceptions and memories, one looks for something that is able to act as a source of such dispositions – as their "cause". The unification of the multiplicity of sensations is made through identi-

---

[26] This is the case of the material atom, which Nietzsche, in BGE 12, directly compares with the notion of the soul in as much as both concepts are generated by a fundamental "metaphysical need". On the adaptive value of substantialist notions see also GS 110 and 111.
[27] In a notebook from 1887 – 1888, Nietzsche points out in a more explicit way this dependence of the purely fictitious notion of the I from logic, demonstrating in particular the *need* of its admission in order that the human being be theoretically imposed upon the world. In fragment NL 1887, 9[89], KSA 12: 382, in particular, he speaks of the I as that "which is not touched by becoming", restating that the acknowledgement of individual subjectivity does not correspond to the description of a content that can be actually isolated, but instead leads in a more simple way to delimit a fictitious permanent core to which sensations and modifications ascribable to the sphere of inner sense can be referred.

fication of a spiritual entity, whose delimitation is not made otherwise than from its ability to act and for this reason it has no sense wanting to ascribe an existential value to it, as if it were possible to indicate and describe that from which an action springs in instances where all that is possible to ascertain are the effects of the action itself. In Nietzsche's interpretation, the subject is nothing but a creation of the activity of representation, an erroneous simplification generated by thinking that one can "designate as such the force which posits, invents, thinks, as distinct from all individual positing, inventing, thinking" (NL 1885, 2[152], KSA 12: 141 = WLN, 91).[28] We are moving within the general perspective that is synthetically expressed in Nietzsche's conclusion in GM I 13, according to which "there is no 'being' behind the deed, its effect and what becomes of it; 'the doer' is invented as an afterthought, – the doing is everything". If we apply this remark to the case of psychic phenomena, it is easy to see how it answers the question of the relation between body and mind (or, as has been previously defined, body-soul). Nietzsche reflects particularly on thought, noticing that it is not distinguished from the physiological activity that determines it and that as a result there is no subject-object dualism to substantiate it. There is no author of thoughts. The latter arise from the organism's inner processes. In the same way, there is no subject distinct from the sensations generated by our perceptive faculty: they appear spontaneously to us and only

---

28 The will to find a subject-agent located beneath the unfolding of events is a theme on which Nietzsche has insisted at length, deploring in particular the human being's tendency to anthropomorphize natural dynamics. This is evident, for example, in the case of the interpretation of the link between cause and effect. The latter is the model of a purely necessary dynamic, which, however, is commonly described in terms of human agency, even intentional one. The tendency, that is, is to project in things a familiar model of activity that ascribes subjective characteristics to the force that moves material reality. (See NL 1885, 2[83], KSA 12: 101–103 and NL 1888, 14[95], KSA 13: 273). This aspect was already pointed out by Lange in the pages of his *History of Materialism*, when he claims that force is "personified immediately" in the idea of matter, since we represent it "as an outflow of matter, as it were its tool. [...] What is anthropomorphic in the idea of matter still belongs at bottom to the notion of matter, to which, as to every subject, we transfer a part of our *ego*." (Lange 1880: 380) This observation may be compared directly with the following note by Nietzsche, in which is still manifested the tendency, common to Lange (1881: 156), to dismiss as "mythological" every explanation that claims to ascertain substantial entities beneath psychic phenomena: "'Cause' and 'effect': calculated psychologically, this is the belief which expresses itself in the verb, in active and passive, doing and being done to. In other words: it is preceded by the separation of what happens into a doing and a being done to, by the supposition of something that does. Belief in the doer is behind it: as if once all doing were subtracted from the 'doer', the doer itself would remain over. Here we are always prompted by the 'notion of I': all that happens has been interpreted as doing: with the mythology that a being corresponding to the 'I' – – " (NL 1886–1887, 7[1], KSA 12: 249–250 = WLN, 129).

afterwards do they enter consciousness and are, thus, organized and understood. It is only at this point that the I's "regulative fiction" steps in. The latter is nothing but a logical support for the categorization of sensations (that are thus related to an unitary substrate), its usefulness being as undeniable as is its ontological inconsistency.

Nietzsche's most explicit discussion of the physiological conception of thought can be found in two fragments from 1884–1885, whose degree of development leaves us wondering if he intended to prepare them for publishing or even include them in *Beyond Good and Evil*. The first of the two notes contains also a draft for a title: *That which is involuntary in thought*. It reads:

> A thought emerges, often mixed and obscured by a crowd of thoughts. We take it out, purify it, put it on its feet and see how it *walks* – all this very swiftly! […] The origin of thought is concealed from us; it is highly probable that it is a *symptom* of a more extensive condition like every feeling: that precisely this one and no other comes, that it comes with more or less brightness […], in all this something of a total-condition is expressed. (NL 1884, 26[92], KSA 11: 173–174)

Nietzsche is of course referring to a form of conscious thought, which he considers a simple *sign* of an activity that takes place at a "pre-psychological" level.[29] However, when we speak of a psychological level we refer to something that arises from a much wider process, occurring at the depths, at the organic level, and of course in a manner absolutely devoid of intentionality. The origin of thought remains, therefore, unknown to us, not revealing itself at a conscious level, whereas everything we are aware of "is merely a surface- and sign-world" (GS 354), i.e. a *superficial* effect of the activity of the drives that constitute the inner dynamics of the organism.[30] This discussion is reprised and developed in the second note, written in 1885:

---

[29] For an in-depth and exhaustive discussion of the issue of thinking and consciousness in Nietzsche, see Lupo 2006 (in particular p. 107ff.). On this topic see also Abel 2001, Emden 2005.

[30] This claim of a "superficial" character of consciousness leads to the open debate on whether Nietzsche defends a strong epiphenomenalism or not. Such a view is developed in Leiter (2002) and in Riccardi (forthcoming), while Katsafanas (2005) argues against the strong epiphenomenalist reading. In his thorough study on Nietzsche's dealing with consciousness from 1880 to 1888, Lupo (2006) also argues that Nietzsche rejects a metaphysical view of consciousness (as a *faculty*), but accepts an epiphenomenal view of it (even if not a strong one). In this section I basically follow Lupo, since it seems to me that his view is the most coherent with Nietzsche's statements from the *Nachlaß* 1884–1885. Nevertheless, it is not my intention to intervene in that debate, and even less to say a final word on the question of the causal efficacy of consciousness (also discussed in Constancio 2011), which I think exceeds the aims of this paper.

In the form in which it comes, a thought is a sign with many meanings, requiring interpretation or, more precisely, an arbitrary narrowing and restriction before it finally becomes clear. It arises in me – where from? How? I don't know. It comes, independently of my will, usually circled about and clouded by a crowd of feelings, desires, aversions, and by other thoughts, often enough scarcely distinguishable from a "willing" or "feeling". [...] It is drawn out of this crowd, cleaned, set on its feet, watched as it stands there, moves about, all this at an amazing speed yet without any sense of haste. Who does all this I don't know, and I am certainly more observer than author of the process. [...] The origin of the thought remains hidden; in all probability it is only the symptom of a much more comprehensive state. (NL 1885, 38[1], KSA 11: 598–596 = WLN, 34–25)[31]

As we can see, Nietzsche restates the same idea in a more extensive form, namely that the process that generates thought takes place beneath consciousness, preceding the formation of a psychological or even logical dimension. By tracing cognitive processes back to their physiological foundation, he notes the absolute absence of a subject who could consciously –*voluntarily*– steer their occurrence.

What occurs in the case of thought is nothing more than the necessary occurrence of chemical and physical events whose outcome reaches our consciousness when the process reaches its end. Nietzsche refrains from any form of ontological commitment that could supply an answer to the question concerning the author of this activity. His suspension of judgment with regard to it is supported by the idea that we can remain simple spectators of the outcome of this unconscious process and that our intervention is reduced only to isolating the final thought from the "pulsional", instinctive mass from which it proceeds. The main error of Logic, to which is due the misunderstanding concerning the character of thought and the subsequent invention of an I, consists, thus, in this

---

[31] It may be useful to say a few words to put this fragment into context. In fact, it appears in a very interesting section of the *Nachlaß* (group 38 of 1885), since many of its ideas appeared later in the group of paragraphs 15–19 of *Beyond Good and Evil*. In NL 1885, 38[3], KSA 11: 597–598, for example, one can find a retrieval of the fragment relative to the belief in the I as a cause of thought and as a immediate certainty (this note is clearly a preparation for BGE 16, as well as for the one which precedes it): "– thought is posited by the I; however hitherto one believed like the populace that in the 'I think' there is something immediately certain and that this 'I' is a given *cause* of thought, in analogy to which we can understand all other causal relations." It is no coincidence that immediately preceding it there is a note on logical thinking, where the idea of *regulative fiction* reappears, and that immediately after it there is a passage concerning "truth" (one should note that BGE 16 ends with the question: "but why insist on the truth?"). And again, flipping through the notebook of 1885, one can read a note on the subject of "will" that is a preparation for BGE 19, in which issues concerning the problem of the subject as the author of his own actions reappear.

attribution of an author/agent guiding the articulation of an absolutely natural dynamics. Thus, Nietzsche goes in the direction of a naturalization of thought processes, moving in the opposite direction to the practice of the anthropomorphic spiritualization of nature so harshly criticized by Lange, for example.

Stripped of the ontological value traditionally ascribed to it by psychology and of its autonomy from the chain of sensations, the I reveals its logical-fictional character, adopted for the purpose of ordering the flow of perceptions – a conclusion that, as we have seen, matches perfectly, either in its perspective as well as in its terms, that of Mach. According to this naturalization of thought, Nietzsche takes his argument to extremes and a few years later writes a note in his notebook, which suggests the complete exclusion of the subject-act dualism as a fiction:

> "Thinking", as posited by the theorists of knowledge, simply doesn't occur: it is a quite arbitrary fiction achieved by selecting one element from the process and subtracting all the others, an artificial trimming for the purpose of intelligibility …
>
> The "mind", something that thinks: maybe even "the mind absolute, pure, unmixed" – this conception is a derivative, second consequence of the false self-observation that believes in "thinking": here first an act is imagined that doesn't occur, "thinking", and secondly a subject-substratum is imagined in which every act of this thinking, and nothing else, originates; i.e., both doing and doer are fictions. (NL 1887–1888, 11[113], KSA 13: 54 = WLN, 222)

In this passage Nietzsche is, of course, referring to a form of conscious thought, the culmination of a chain of processes enacted at a physiological level, of which only the final outcome can be apprehended. Both agents in this relation are the product of the translation of physiological dynamics in a language we can understand. Thus, they are mutually dependent on a logical level, and, as is the case with the "true" and "apparent" world spoken of in *Twilight of the Idols*, the elimination of the one entails the elimination of the other. In fact, there is no 'thinking' except as the ceaseless articulation of drives and instincts in the organism, just as there is no 'mind', a subject identifiable as '*something that thinks*'. Mind and thought can be defined only in relation to each other; once the former's ontological inconsistency is revealed, the latter loses meaning as well. Dualism is, therefore, overcome. In fact, it is completely eliminated.

7 Philosophy without an "I"

In light of these remarks, it is possible to observe a certain affinity between, on the one hand, Nietzsche's reflections on thought and the "I" and, on the other hand, the position of those who, in his time, argued for the possibility of founding a scientific psychology. In general, Nietzsche shares the tendency to set himself free from a system of thought that claims to be able to find substantial entities everywhere, as if only with reference to them it were possible to achieve knowledge of a particular event. In contrast, philosophy for Nietzsche should go beyond ancient metaphysics and learn to do without those reference points that are as useful as they are illusory. The I is precisely one of those entities that we can only define as an "ideal unity" of our thoughts, and therefore something that can only result from the psychic activity it is supposed to cause. Nietzsche thus agrees with both Lange and Mach, who complained that scientific research should not aim at finding a "seat of the soul" and envisioned a new psychology that acknowledged the ontological inconsistency of its object of research. Accordingly, Nietzsche dissolves the I/subject in the depths of the physiological processes located beneath it, and in fact reduces it to them.[32] He does not think that the development of philosophy should lead to the (absolute) rejection of the I as a reference for human agency, but he definitely rejects the "prejudice of reason" which claims that the I is a substantial entity. One may still refer to the I, but only if one stresses its purely logical character, i.e., sees it as an "ideal unity" or "regulative fiction" that results from an interpretation of the physiological processes out of which conscious thought in his various forms arises (NL 1883, 9[41], KSA 10: 358).[33] As we read in Nietzsche's writings (chiefly in his notebooks), conscious thought is only the final moment of a long chain of

---

[32] Nietzsche's view of the reduction of mental states to bodily states (see NL 1883, 9[41], KSA 10: 358) deserves a separate discussion, and we should first focus on the fact the he never provided a clear definition of what he meant by the term "body" (*Leib*). Without going into an issue that deserves a much more thorough treatment, I shall merely quote Luca Lupo's observations on this subject: "The notion of body held by Nietzsche is problematic, not univocal, and not reducible to a form of positivist materialism nor to a form of vitalism: in the place of the term 'body', philosophers employ the much more cautions phrase 'what we call body' and say of the latter that it is a 'symbol' pointing to a specific activity, that is, to the cooperation of a multitude of beings. Nietzsche thinks of the body as a field of forces, an organized entity, plural and multiple, in a word: *system of relations*" (Lupo 2006: 133). See also Gerhardt 2006.

[33] In a note from 1885 Nietzsche stresses our erroneous giving an ontological value to this interpretation. He particularly argues that the proposition "I think" is a falsification of a natural process, and we mistake the result of that process for its cause. Whereas thought produces the I, we nonetheless see this I as the author of psychic phenomena: "*The chronological order reversed. The 'external world' affects us: the effect is telegraphed into our brain, there arranged, given shape and traced back to its cause: then the cause is projected, and only then does the fact enter our consciousness. That is, the world of appearances appears to us as a cause only once 'it' has exerted its effect and the effect has been processed. That is, we are constantly reversing the order of what happens.* – While 'I' see, *it is already seeing something different*" (NL 1885, 34[54], KSA 11: 437 = WLN, 4).

events that take place at an unconscious level, and the positing of a subject as the author of thought is due to our inability to order correctly the relation between cause and effect.[34]

We are thus thrown back to the starting point of this research, that is, to Nietzsche's critique of the "I think" in BGE and his remark that it is "a *falsification* of the facts to say that the subject 'I' is the condition of the predicate 'think'" (BGE 17). According to Nietzsche, we should replace this Cartesian "immediate certainty" with the idea that thought comes without an external subject willing it, and therefore we should say "it thinks" rather than "I think" ("*Es denkt*" rather than "*Ich denke*").[35] This would represent a considerable progress in philosophy, for it would entail our final release from that "metaphysical need" that prevails both in the scientific as well as in the religious sphere, a need that compels us to trace reality back to absolute foundations, no matter whether material (atoms) or spiritual (souls).

We can now provide an answer to the question initially raised – whether Nietzsche thinks that a "philosophy without an I" is actually possible. If we take the I as a remnant of a metaphysics of substance, that possibility does not strike us as so paradoxical. Philosophy should indeed get rid of this substantial notion, all the more so if philosophy wants to become truly "anti-christian" (BGE 54). But this task is limited to a very specific epistemic context and thus to a particular kind of I. More specifically, it does not involve a rejection of the I as a fundamental reference for the self-understanding of the subject as agent. In other words, the answer to the question whether the soul (i.e. the principle of human agency) disappears along with the I of psychology and philosophy (i.e. the cause of thoughts) is negative. Nietzsche's critique of the I is quite radical, but it does not prohibit the human being from referring to its own subjectivity – provided, however, that the latter is conceived of in a different way, that is, stripped from its metaphysical surface.

This is what we can infer, for example, from BGE 12. Here, Nietzsche criticizes the "atomistic need", and claims that alongside the principle of materialistic atomism "we must also put an end to that other and more disastrous atomism, the one Christianity has taught best and longest, the *atomism of the*

---

[34] The reversal of the causal order of particular events, which Nietzsche finds peculiar to human beings, is one of the main topics of TI, The Four Great Errors. In §3 of that section Nietzsche particularly deals with the *error of a false causation* by making reference to the problem of "the I (the 'subject') as cause" and claiming that it is owing to the "oldest and most enduring psychology" that the "world become a multitude of doers" and "a doer ('subject') pushed its way under all events".

[35] A detailed discussion of BGE 17 is provided in Loukidelis 2013.

soul [*Seelen-Atomistik*]", that is "the belief that the 'soul is something indestructible, eternal, indivisible'" (BGE 12). Nietzsche, however, does not stop at this point, but goes on to observe that "there is absolutely no need to give up 'the soul' itself, and relinquish one of the oldest and most venerable hypotheses [...]" (BGE 12). This passage is not in contradiction with what we stated above. Nietzsche's reasoning is in many respects close to that of Lange: he underlines, like Lange, the need to *reformulate* the concept of soul. The old conception of the soul as "a monad, an *atomon*" is to be replaced with a soul that becomes "mortal" and loses its substantial character by becoming a mere "subject-multiplicity", a sheer plurality of "drives and affects".

Thus the soul remains a subjective point of reference, and it retains, as such, the practical value that it had for the human being.[36] This is Nietzsche's view in *Twilight of the Idols*. The analysis of the "eternal idols", which are the truths established by the tradition (see EH, Twilight of the Idols 1), aims to abolish their value as absolutes, but not–as is often believed–to completely withdraw them from the practical plane. A closer look shows that Nietzsche focuses on how the faith in the epistemic legitimacy of knowledge created the "decadent" as a specific human type.[37] Therefore, is aim is not to reject the principles of our self-understanding–which are, after all, necessarily references for our agency–, but rather to "revaluate" them and promote the emergence of a new humanity, particularly of a new type of theoretical, intellectual human being. The possibility of a "philosophy without I" means, in sum, that behind the notion of an "I" there is a particular world-interpretation which needs to be reshaped in order for the human being to refer to the world and to itself in a new–revaluated–way.

References

Abel, Günter (2001) "Bewußtsein–Sprache–Natur. Nietzsches Philosophie des Geistes", in: *Nietzsche-Studien* 30, 1–43.
Banks, Erik C. (2003) *Ernst Mach's World Elements. A Study in Natural Philosophy*, Dodrecht: Kluwer.
Bayertz, K./Gerhard, M./Jaeschke, W., (eds.) (2007) *Weltanschauung, Philosophie und Naturwissenschaft im 19. Jahrhundert*, vol. 3: *Der Ignorabimus-Streit*, Hamburg: Meiner.
Blackmore, John T. (1972) *Ernst Mach. His Work, Life, and Influence*, Berkeley/Los Angeles: University of California Press.

---

[36] As we have seen, Mach states the same view in speaking of the economic utility of the concepts of body and I for scientific investigation.
[37] See Gori/Piazzesi 2012: 17ff..

Bornedal, Peter (2010) *The Surface and the Abyss*, Berlin: De Gruyter.
Brentano, Franz (1874) *Psychologie vom empirischen Standpunkt*, Leipzig: Dunker & Humblot.
Brobjer, Thomas (2008) *Nietzsche's Philosophical Context: An Intellectual Biography*, Urbana: University of Illinois Press.
Campioni, G./D'Iorio, P./Fornari, M.C./Fronterotta, F./Orsucci, A. (eds.), in collab. with Müller-Buck, Renate (2003) *Nietzsches persönliche Bibliothek*, Berlin: De Gruyter.
Constâncio, João (2011) "On Consciousness. Nietzsche's Departure from Schopenhauer", in: *Nietzsche-Studien* 40, 1–42.
Du Bois-Reymond, Emile (1886) "Über die Grenzen des Naturerkennens", in *Reden von Emil Du Bois-Reymond*, Leipzig: Veit, 106–130.
Emden, Christian J. (2005) *Nietzsche on Language, Consciousness and the Body*, Chicago: University of Illinois Press.
Fechner, Gustav (1966) [1860] *Elements of Psychophysics*, vol. 1, Engl. trans., New York: Holt, Rinehart and Winston.
Gerhardt, Volker (2006) "The Body, the Self and the Ego", in: Keith Ansell Pearson (ed.), *A Companion to Nietzsche*, Oxford: Blackwell, 273–296.
Gori, Pietro (2009) "The Usefulness of Substances. Knowledge, Metaphysics and Science in Nietzsche and Mach", in: *Nietzsche-Studien* 38, 111–155.
Gori, Pietro (2012) "Nietzsche as Phenomenalist?", in Helmut Heit, Günter Abel and Marco Brusotti (eds.), *Nietzsches Wissenschaftsphilosophie*, Berlin/Boston: De Gruyter, 345–356.
GORI, Pietro/PIAZZESI (2012) Chiara, Crepuscolo degli idoli, Introduzione, traduzione e commento, Roma: Carocci.
Guzzardi, Luca (2010) *Lo sguardo muto delle cose*, Milan: Raffaello Cortina.
Heidelberger, Michael (1996) *Die innere Seite der Natur: Gustav Theodor Fechners wissenschaftlich-philosophische Weltauffassung*, Frankfurt a.M.: Klosterman.
Katsafanas, Paul (2005) "Nietzsche's Theory of Mind: Consciousness and Conceptualization", in: *European Journal of Philosophy* 13, 1–31.
Lange, Friedrich Albert (1880) [1875] *The History of Materialism and Criticism of its Present Importance*, vol. 2/3, English translation by Ernest Chester Thomas, Boston: Houghton, Mifflin & Co.
Lange, Friedrich Albert (1881) [1875] *The History of Materialism and Criticism of its Present Importance*, vol. 3/3, English translation by Ernest Chester Thomas, Boston: Houghton, Mifflin & Co.
Leary, David E. (1980) "The Historical Foundations of Herbart's Mathematization of Psychology", in: *Journal of the History of Behavioral Sciences* 16, 150–163.
Lehmann, Gerhard (1987) "Kant im Spätidealismus und die Anfänge der neukantische Bewegung", in: Hans L. Ollig (ed.), *Materialien zur Neukantianismus-Diskussion*, Darmstadt: WBG, 44–65.
Leiter, Brian (2002) *Nietzsche on Morality*, London/New York: Routledge.
Loukidelis, Nikolaos (2005) "Quellen von Nietzsches Verständnis und Kritik des Cartesischen *cogito, ergo sum*", in: *Nietzsche-Studien* 34, 300–309.
Loukidelis, Nikolaos (2013) *Es denkt: Ein Kommentar zum Aphorismus 17 aus "Jenseits von Gut und Böse"*, Würzburg: Königshausen & Neumann.
Lupo, Luca (2006) *Le Colombe dello Scettico. Riflessioni di Nietzsche sulla Coscienza negli anni 1880–1888*. Pisa: ETS.
Mach, Ernst (1863) "Vorträge über Psychophysik", in *Österreichische Zeitschrift für praktische Heilkunde* 9, 146–148, 277–279, 294–298, 316–318, 335–338, 352–354, 362–366.

Mach, Ernst (1886) *Beiträge zur Analyse der Empfindungen*, Jena: Fischer.
Mach, Ernst (1914) *The Analysis of Sensations*, Eng. trans. Chicago/London: Open Court.
Mach, Ernst (1976) [1905] *Knowledge and Error. Sketches on the Psychology of Enquiry*, Eng. trans., Drodrecht: Reidel.
Martinelli, Riccardo (1999) *Misurare l'anima. Filosofia e psicofisica da Kant a Carnap*, Macerata: Quodlibet.
Müller, Johannes (1822) *Dissertatio inauguralis physiologica sistens Commentarios de Phoronomia Animalium*, Bonn: Thormann.
Pippin, Robert (2010) *Nietzsche, Psychology, and First Philosophy*, Chicago: Chicago University Press.
Riccardi, Mattia (forthcoming) "Nietzsche on the Superficiality of Consciousness", in: Manuel Dries (ed.), *Nietzsche on Consciousness and the Embodied Mind*, Berlin/Boston: De Gruyter.
Sachs-Hombach, Klaus (1993) *Der Geist als Maschine. Herbarts Grund legung der naturwissenschaftlichen Psychologie*, in: Jörg F. Maas (ed.), *Das sichtbare Denken*, Amsterdam: Rodopi, 91–111.
Salaquarda, Jorg (1978) "Nietzsche und Lange", in: *Nietzsche-Studien* 7, 236–253.
Stack, George (1983) *Lange and Nietzsche*, Berlin: De Gruyter.

Anthony Jensen
7 Helmholtz, Lange, and Unconscious Symbols of the Self[1]

Two main lines of Nietzsche-interpretation about the relationship between consciousness and unconscious processes have become dominant over the past decade.[2] Brian Leiter argues that Nietzsche holds a "kind-epiphenomenal" theory of mind, i.e., that both the ideational and unconscious factors that manifest themselves in human agency should carry the status of a convenient but ultimately misleading terminology for what are actually the determinations of physiognomic "type-facts" (Leiter 2002: 87–92). A property of consciousness is kind-epiphenomenal, for Leiter, insofar as its instrumentality can only be defined in relation to some other set of natural properties, which in Nietzsche's case are predominately discussed in embodied or physiognomic terms (Leiter 2002: 91). The other major line of interpretation is perhaps best represented by Günter Abel, who demonstrates how consciousness does add something to unconscious processes for Nietzsche, something which cannot be explained solely by reference to physical processes: namely, concepts. Not to be mistaken for a deterministic mechanism, consciousness is a sort of last link on a continuum chain which adds conceptual content to the competitive play of drives (Abel 2001). Conscious concepts simplify, abbreviate, and indeed falsify the neuro-stimulations that are processed at an unconscious level. Insofar as they do, consciousness cannot be considered just a different name for physical pro-

---

[1] A version of this paper was presented to the Universidade Nova de Lisboa in January, 2013. I would like to thank the participants of that talk for their insightful criticisms and suggestions.
[2] Although Nietzsche is often considered one of the philosophical forerunners to twentieth-century theories of the Unconscious, there is no single complete or comprehensive articulation of what his view actually was anywhere in his writing. Indeed, when one compares the 236 occasions that Nietzsche mentions 'Unbewusstsein' or one of its cognates (Unbewusstheit, das Unbewusste), verbalizations (unbewusstwerden), or adjectivals (unbewusst) to the 673 mentions of 'Bewusstsein' and its related terms, one gets the impression that he had no systematic doctrine of the unconscious in the way of his philosophical and psychological successors. More often, though not always, Nietzsche's 'unconscious' is introduced as an antipodal notion to one or another traditional conceptions of consciousness as a substantial aspect of the self. This is partly attributable to both the non-systematic character of Nietzsche's writing generally and the substantial development in Nietzsche's thinking over his career. But the lack of single comprehensive doctrine of the unconscious is partly attributable, as well, to Nietzsche's idiosyncratic presentation of the unconscious.

cesses. Both interpretations can assemble a wealth of evidence from Nietzsche's corpus, and both have their forerunners and new converts.³

João Constâncio joins those who argue against the epiphenomenalist view (Constâncio 2011). His approach to understanding Nietzsche's view involves the elucidation of Nietzsche's historical context, an approach that seems to me entirely necessary given how closely Nietzsche tends to pose his arguments in (too-often unacknowledged) dialogue with other thinkers. Constâncio rightly sees Schopenhauer as a particularly informative background on which and against which Nietzsche's views on subjectivity come clear, or at least clearer. Although divergent in fundamental ways, Nietzsche adapts Schopenhauer's view that what that last-link consciousness adds to unconscious expressions is a representational framework that allows us to comprehend in conceptual symbols what was formerly only unconsciously efficacious. Nietzsche's view of the relation of conscious and unconscious aspects of the person marks a "departure that, in several decisive points, also retains Schopenhauer's position *as its point of departure*" (Constâncio 2011: 3).⁴ But one cannot discuss every influence on Nietzsche in a single article, and I think Constâncio would be the first to agree that filling in the historical record would only aid scholars in constructing a more comprehensive account.

In my outline here of the influence of the proto Neo-Kantians, what emerges is a rather different picture than either the 'kind-epiphenomenal' reading or the 'last link' interpretation of the relationship between consciousness and unconsciousness.⁵ One sometimes underestimates how prominently the first generation of Neo-Kantians figured in Nietzsche's early reading, authors like Kuno

---

3 Among many papers that address this theme, see Katsafanas 2005, Acampora 2006, Janaway 2006, Poellner 2006; and the fine collection of papers in Gemes/May 2009.
4 My own article on the relation between Nietzsche and Schopenhauer with respect to the self, which I submitted a few months before Constâncio (2011) to a collection to be published by Manuel Dries, argued a similar thesis by concentrating on the possibility of 'freeing' the self from the unconscious dictates of drives, affects, and instincts. My thesis then was that Nietzsche's rejection of Schopenhauer on this dissolution from the unconscious facticities of selfhood – a *Selbstverleugnung* – was one of the most important motivations for the development of his perspectival theory of judgment and both aesthetical and ethical value. Those doctrines emerge only after a fundamental engagement with Schopenhauer's vision of the possibility of an 'ecstatic' self.
5 Classifying these thinkers is admittedly not without its hazards, since the term itself would have been anachronistic at that time. Moreover, of the thinkers I list, only Lange has any claim to the Marburg school – none has any direct connection to Southwest Neo-Kantianism. For my own argument as to why these thinkers mark the essential transition between mid-century German materialism and the more popular 'schools' of Neo-Kantianism, see my encyclopedia article: http://www.iep.utm.edu/neo-kant/. For an argument that the earlier thinkers actually have more right to the claim of Neo-Kantian than either the Marburg or Southwest schools, see Köhnke 1986.

Fischer, Otto Liebmann, Friedrich Ueberweg, and Eduard Zeller, who actually wrote to Nietzsche about philological matters.[6] The influence of peripheral figures like Müller, Boscovich, Spir, Gerber, and Mach is also crucial. Above all, and especially with respect to epistemological matters and the formation of Nietzsche's naturalism, stands the influence of Hermann Ludwig von Helmholtz and Friedrich Albert Lange, the latter of whom was also a student of Nietzsche's mentor, Friedrich Ritschl.[7] My major aim in this paper is to show how a well-known disagreement between Helmholtz and Lange of itself informed a small but crucial nuance of Nietzsche's view of the relationship between the conscious and unconscious aspects of subjectivity. I claim that through specifically Lange's influential critique of Helmholtz, Nietzsche came to realize that the usual naturalistic designations of sub-conscious activity – drives, instincts, urges, desires, power-quanta, etc. – are not actually referential, but a series of anti-realist symbolic representations that can be useful and informative but never demonstrative. The consequence of this is that both the epiphenomenal and last-link interpretations are mistakenly worried about the relations of things and processes which are actually not things or processes at all, but only a relation of symbols whose order and ascribed relations are themselves only the result of an historical process of overwriting and reinterpreting by means of symbols.

1 Outline of the Nietzschean unconscious

Consistent with his view of pervasive becoming, there are for Nietzsche no static substantial 'things' in reality. There can therefore be no substantial 'self' so

---

[6] A happy exception is Peter Bornedal (2010). Bornedal does very fine work of contextualizing Nietzsche's epistemology in the context of his reading of the early Neo-Kantians. For alternative descriptions, see also R. Kevin Hill (2003: 13–19); and Michael Steven Green (2002: 36–53). Green's account of Nietzsche's reading of Afrikan Spir is illuminating, especially with respect to the Spir's disagreement with Helmholtz concerning the nature of force. See Green 2002: 73, 80–83. Brief but informative discussions on Helmholtz and Lange in connection with Nietzsche can also be found in Robin Small (2001: 47–62, 156–159). For a discussion of Nietzsche's reading generally, see Thomas H. Brobjer (2008).

[7] Indeed, it is not an exaggeration to say that one of the very earliest books to present a comprehensive articulation of Nietzsche as a genuine philosopher – by that I mean Hans Vaihinger's 1902 *Nietzsche als Philosoph* – understood Nietzsche within an explicitly Neo-Kantian framework. Two works by Vaihinger are dedicated to understanding Nietzsche within the tradition of Neo-Kantianism. First, the last twenty pages of his masterwork, *Die Philosophie des Als Ob: System der theoretischen, praktischen und religiösen Fiktionen der Menschheit* (Vaihinger 1922). Second, Vaihinger's *Nietzsche als Philosoph* (1902).

much as temporary states that can be classified as either conscious or unconscious according to whether we have a conceptual awareness of them. Consciousness is no single thing; on the contrary, "Es giebt also im Menschen so viele 'Bewußtseins' als es Wesen giebt, [...]" (NL June–July 1885, 37[4], KSA 11: 577). What lies beneath conscious states can thus be no single metaphysical will, as Schopenhauer claims, but a multiplicity of process drives: 'Triebe', or the synonymous 'Instinkte', 'Affekte', and 'unbewusste Motiven'–"eines Gesellschaftsbaus vieler 'Seelen'" (JGB 19, KSA 5: 33). The Triebe themselves are not substances–not "Seelen-Atome, vielmehr als etwas Wachsendes, Kämpfendes, Sich-Vermehrendes und Wieder-Absterbendes: [...]" (NL June–July 1885, 37[4], KSA 11: 577). They are positively described as power-seeking process-drives within agonistically relational substructures: "Machtansprueche" (JGB 22, KSA 5: 37) or "Herrschafts-Verhaeltnissen" (JGB 19, KSA 5: 34).

Nietzsche characterized the relationship between these conscious and unconscious aspects of the self with a diverse array of metaphors. Among other things, conscious states are said to be 'mirrors' [Spiegel] of unconscious states (see, for examples, FW 354, KSA 3: 590; and MA I 132, KSA 2: 126); or 'surfaces' [Oberflächen] of unconscious states (see, for examples, M 125, KSA 3: 116; EH klug 9, KSA 6: 294; and NL Summer 1883, 12[33], KSA 10: 406); or 'relations' [Verhalten] of unconscious states (see, for examples, FW 333, KSA 3: 559; and JGB 36, KSA 5: 55); or, in encomium to Leibniz, an "Accidens der Vorstellung" (FW 357, KSA 3: 598); or a 'highest level' of organic development (NL June–July 1885, 37[4], KSA 11: 576); or a "Verbindungsnetz zwischen Mensch und Mensch" (FW 354, KSA 3: 591); or even a dangerous development of unconscious states that gives the false impression of something "Bleibendes, Ewiges, Letztes, Ursprünglichstes!" (FW 11, KSA 3: 382f.); or a sort of 'polyp of our being' that results from unconscious 'nutriments' (M 119, KSA 3: 111). In pronounced rejection of the Cartesian Ego and in equally pronounced alignment with Schopenhauer's views, Nietzsche thinks conscious activity can be regarded as 'tools' [Werkzeuge], 'playthings' [Spielzeuge] or 'organs' [Organe] of unconscious states (see, for examples, M 109, KSA 3: 98; FW 99, KSA 3: 454; Z I Verächtern, KSA 4: 39; GM II 16, KSA 5: 322; NL Fall 1880, 6[31], KSA 9: 200; NL Fall 1880, 6[130], KSA 9: 229; NL Summer–Fall 1884, 27[26], KSA 11: 282; NL April–June 1885, 34[46], KSA 11: 434; NL June–July 1885, 37[4], KSA 11: 576f.; NL August–September 1885, 40[38], KSA 11: 647f.).[8]

---

8 Constâncio (2011: 11) differentiates tool and organ. I think this unnecessary both because the context of the passages is synonymous for both and because Nietzsche would obviously have known that 'organon' means 'tool' in Greek.

Some of these images have inconsistent meaning-extensions, even within the same passage (FW 354 is especially problematic in this respect). When we attempt to predicate a working relationship between the unconscious and conscious aspects of the self on the basis of those metaphors, the inconsistency of itself seems to be what gives license to the two divergent streams of interpretations mentioned earlier. If consciousness is the 'surface' or 'Oberfläche' of something, then it is spatially contiguous with that thing; however, if it is a 'mirror' or 'Spiegel' then it must be spatially distinct from the thing reflected. More problematically, the notion of consciousness as a 'Werkzeug' of the unconscious drives would, by its usual denotation, indicate two entities, one controlling and one controlled in order to accomplish what ends the controller seeks, and seeks intentionally. Like a carpenter who uses a hammer to pound a nail, Nietzsche implies that the drives 'use' conscious concepts in order to get what they 'want'.[9] However, such an image seemingly instills a causal power to a substance, which is an unsustainable assumption for Nietzsche insofar as he problematizes causation generally (see, for examples, M 121, KSA 3: 115; FW 112, KSA 3: 472f.; FW 127, KSA 3: 482f.; JGB 21, KSA 5: 35f.; GD Irrthümer 3–8 generally; NL Fall 1887, 9[91](65), KSA 12: 383–387)[10] and causal relations among the inner constituents of selfhood specifically (see, for examples, GD Irrthümer 3, KSA 6: 90f.; FW 127, KSA 3: 482f.; JGB 3, KSA 5: 17f.; JGB 16, KSA 5: 29–34; NL April–June 1885, 34[46], KSA 11: 434; NL Fall 1885–Fall 1886, 2[139], KSA 12: 135f.; NL September–October 1888, 22[22], KSA 13: 592f.; NL Winter 1883–1884, 24[21], KSA 10: 658). Consequently, the epiphenomenal reading is inconsistent if Nietzsche earnestly thought of the relationship in causal terms; the last-link reading is inconsistent if conscious activity is nothing more than a reflection of unconscious factors.

The inconsistency of his imagery of itself begs the question as to how Nietzsche thought we can *know* the self really is comprised of one sort of relation or another. Schopenhauer, famously, has perhaps more confidence than any other philosopher in the power of intuitive self-observation, and Nietzsche perhaps the least.[11] The self is, for Schopenhauer, an object of experience among other objects of experience; and yet the one object in the world whose apprehension can also be immediate when it avoids the typical mediation

---

9 Constâncio (2011: 19) emphasizes this quasi-perceptual ability of drives to discern their ends. On this, see also Wotling 2011: 74–78.
10 For a discussion, see Poellner 2000: 51–57; Constâncio 2011: 28.
11 Although Constâncio does not discuss this issue in his (2011), he does at length in his (2013).

involved in subject-object dichotomies – since we are both "ein Erkennendes und ein Erkanntes" (WWV II, sec 19; 4: 235)[12] – by means of intuitive insight into the internal workings of Will. We represent the body phenomenally, in terms of space, time, and causality. But when we look inside ourselves, such mediation falls away: "Von sich weiß Jeder unmittelbar, von allem Andern nur sehr mittelbar" (WWV II, sec 18; 4: 224). And what we immediately apprehend – though cannot be said to understand since that requires mediation by the forms of cognition – is that the striving, urging, driving Will is the reality of which conscious intellectual life is merely the represented objectification (WWV II, sec. 20; See also WWV I, secs. 18 & 19).

This is one position of Schopenhauer's that Nietzsche never held either with respect to the terminology of 'objectification' or to the more general thesis about non-cognitive self-apprehension. A row of passages from *Daybreak* make this clear. "Wir sind Alle nicht Das, als was wir nach den Zuständen erscheinen, für die wir allein Bewusstsein und Worte [...] haben" (M 115, KSA 3: 107). "Die Handlungen sind niemals Das, als was sie uns erscheinen! [...] mit der inneren Welt steht es ebenso!" (M 116, KSA 3: 109). We are, as the famous preface to the *Genealogy* of Morals would also claim, "unknown to ourselves, we knowers" (GM Preface 1, KSA 5: 247).

Here a familiar problem in Nietzsche-studies arises. On the one hand, Nietzsche seems to preclude the possibility of knowing a phenomenon in the usual way, and, on the other, proceeds to talk in seemingly dogmatic and sometimes hyperbolic ways about that same phenomenon. We are told that the organism is itself a relation of drives, that consciousness is a mirror, surface, or tool of unconscious factors, and yet are also told that we cannot understand what the inner world really is. Were Nietzsche a dogmatic realist in the mode of Aristotle or, closer to home, the German materialist philosophers like Vogt, Molescott, or Czolbe, then his claims about the character of what lies under the surface of consciousness must surely be regarded with skepticism in light of his critique of the limits of knowledge. And of course Nietzsche never appeals to the kind of mystical apprehension of the inner nature of the self that Schopenhauer employs. What recourse does Nietzsche have, then, to define the relationship between the conscious and unconscious aspects of the self? Here is where I think closer attention to the philosophical framework of the proto Neo-Kantians can help.

---

12 References to Schopenhauer are to the *Zürcher Ausgabe*, 10 vols., edited by Arthur Hübscher et al. (Zurich: Diogenes, 1977).

2 Physiognomy by Helmholtz and Lange

Nietzsche's immediate reaction to reading Friedrich Albert Lange's *Geschichte des Materialismus* (1866) was to declare it "without a doubt the most significant philosophical work to have appeared in the last hundred years" (Letter to Muschacke, November 2006, KSB 2: 184).[13] In a letter to Gersdorff following his first reading, Nietzsche notes with approval three theses concluded by Lange:

1. Die Sinnenwelt ist das Produkt unsrer Organisation;
2. unsre sichtbaren (körperlichen) Organe sind gleich allen andern Teilen der Erscheinungswelt nur Bilder eines unbekannten Gegenstandes;
3. unsre wirkliche Organisation bleibt uns daher ebenso unbekannt wie die wirklichen Außendinge. Wir haben stets nur das Product von Beiden vor uns.[14]

---

[13] The most comprehensive work on the relation between Nietzsche and Lange is the well-known monograph by George J. Stack, *Lange and Nietzsche* (1983). While the work is rightly regarded as classic for the new ground it broke, it nevertheless addresses Lange in a peculiarly idealistic light and underestimates Lange's place in the formation of Neo-Kantianism. For one example, Stack mentions Hermann Cohen only twice, and Natorp not at all. On both occasions, Stack claims that Lange's view of Kant was influenced by Cohen, especially between 1866–1875. This ignores entirely the fact that Cohen's first commentary on the subject, *Kant's Theorie der Erfahrung* only appeared in 1871 (before that he had mostly been interested in Plato, myth, and culture), that by that time Lange's *Geschichte des Materialismus* had been in print for five years, and the fact that Lange influenced Cohen far more than vice versa. A less comprehensive, though more historically-informed vision of the relationship can be found in Salaquarda 1978: 236–253.

[14] Letter to Carl von Gersdorff, End of August, 1866; KSB 2: 160. Nietzsche is quoting from F.A. Lange, *Geschichte des Materialismus und Kritik seiner Bedeutung in der Gegenwart* (Iserlohn: J. Baedeker, 1866), 493. My own citations are to Lange, *Geschichte des Materialismus und Kritik seiner Bedeutung in der Gegenwart*, 2 vols., edited by Hermann Cohen (Leipzig: J. Baedeker, 1902 [1866]). The quotation here is thus to Lange 1902 [1866], vol. 2: 423. Although this letter is quite early, Nietzsche never 'broke' with Lange's thought at any point in his career as he did with other influences. That Nietzsche was still thinking about precisely this passage of Lange into his mature writings, see NL Winter 1883–1884, 24[35], KSA 10: 663. Dating the waves of Lange's influence is made difficult, however, when we note that Nietzsche's original copy of his book is missing from his personal library. The copy found today in Weimar is the 1887 edition. So while we can determine that Nietzsche read Lange from early to late, we cannot know precisely to what extent Nietzsche was reading Lange during the composition of his middle works, which is especially unfortunate in the case of *Daybreak*. There is, however, evidence of renewed interest in early Neo-Kantianism generally at that time. See Nietzsche to Overbeck, 20/21 August 1881, KSB 6: 116–118.

To contextualize the meaning of these three theses, though, we must first turn to Lange's teacher, Herman Ludwig von Helmholtz,[15] whom I call a proto Neo-Kantian insofar as he understood it as his task to ground the basic insights of transcendental idealism in the best findings of neuro-physiognomy. The opening paragraph of his lecture "Über das Sehen des Menschen" is dedicated to Kant: "Ihm wünschen wir in Denkmal zu setzen, welches fortan verkünden soll, dass unsere Zeit und diese Stadt eine dankbare und ehrende Erinnerung für Männer hat, denen sie wissenschaftlichen Fortschritt und Belehrung verdankt."[16] What the physiognomy of the senses tell us, at base, is that the radically particular, unique, non-repeatable, and personally-contextualized electrico-chemical impressions upon the nervous systems of we "bits of dust on the surface of the planet" do not and cannot match the general, common, often-repeated, and inter-subjectively valid concepts and words that comprise conscious cognition and communication (Helmholtz 1995: 366).[17] In 1870, shortly before the composition of his 'On Truth and Lies', Nietzsche was led to call this Schopenhauerian-Helmholtzian observation about observation, "die wunderbarste", something about which he was in "genaue Übereinstimmung".[18] But more the scientist than Schopenhauer, Helmholtz's experiments with stereoscopic visual illusions led him to deny through science rather than philosophy the nearly-ubiquitous presumption that visual objects "*are always imagined as being present in the field of vision as would have to be there in order to produce the same impression on the nervous mechanism*" (Helmholtz 1962 [1867], vol. 3: 2; emphasis original). The nervous system in no way reproduces what electro-chemical information registers for the sense organs because of some influence of real external objects, but processes information in a way ready-made for conscious conceptualization. This basic insight led Helmholtz to naturalize Kant's theory of experience as an aggregate product of the interaction between the world and one's subjective facticities. Where Kant considered the categories of the mind as that which both enabled experience and precluded the possibility of understanding an object 'in-itself', Helmholtz considered sense physiognomy to

---

15 For Lange's admiration of Helmholtz's naturalistic ground of Kant's transcendental aesthetic, see Lange 1902 [1866], vol. 2: 409: "Einer der erfolgreichsten Forscher, Helmholtz, hat sich der Anschauungen Kants als eines heuristischen Princips bedient und dabei doch nur mit Bewusstsein und Consequenz denselben Weg verfolgt, auf welchem auch Andre dazu gelangten, den Mechanismus der Sinnesthätigkeit unserm Verständniss näher zu bringen."
16 Herman von Helmholtz, "Über das Sehen des Menschen", in Helmholtz 1904: 79.
17 The similarity to the opening image of Nietzsche's *On Truth and Lie in an Extramoral Sense* is striking. See Bornedal 2010: 29.
18 Nietzsche to Carl von Gersdorff, 12.12.1870, KSB 3: 161.

have the same function of enabling phenomenal knowledge but precluding all inferences about noumena.¹⁹ The senses, rather than just the mind, are imbued *a priori* with a tendency to supply form where there is none, to classify and categorize the welter of experience into recognizable patterns.

> Our apperceptions and ideas are *effects* wrought on our nervous system and our consciousness by the objects that are thus apprehended and conceived. Each effect, as to its nature, quite necessarily depends both on the nature of what causes the effect and on that of the person on whom the effect is produced. To expect to obtain an idea which would reproduce the nature of the thing conceived, that is, which would be true in an absolute sense, would mean to expect an effect which would be perfectly independent of the nature of the thing on which the effect was produced; which would be an obvious absurdity. Our human ideas, therefore, and all ideas of any conceivable intelligent creature must be images of objects whose mode is essentially codependent on the nature of the consciousness which has the idea, and is conditioned also by its idiosyncrasies. (Helmholtz 1962 [1867], vol. 3: 19)

As the eyes have slowly evolved to register and process into sensations those stimulations which serve some practical importance, so too does conscious cognition allow us to comprehend objects only in ways that serve a practical, albeit unconscious use for that organism. In that sense, there is no question about either a 'subject-free' apprehension of an external object or even the accurate correspondence between the world and our ideas of it. "Our ideas of things *cannot* be anything but symbols", Helmholtz writes, "natural signs for things which we learn how to use in order to regulate our movements and actions" (Helmholtz 1962 [1867], vol. 3: 19; emphasis original).²⁰ The properties which we commonly understand objects to possess are simply phenomenal affects of the constitutive function of our sense physiognomy. Nothing can be dogmatically asserted about the world as it stands outside that physiognomy (Helmholtz 1962 [1867], vol. 3: 20). The mediation between subject and object is therefore an entirely symbolic process rather than a designatory or referential one.²¹

---

19 See, for example, his 1878 address for the anniversary celebration of the University of Berlin, reprinted as "The Facts of Perception", in Helmholtz 1977: 119f.
20 Nietzsche comes very close to rephrasing Helmholtz, when he notes, "A thought, no less than a word, is only a sign: one cannot speak of a congruity between the thought and the real. The real is some kind of drive-movement" (NL 1880, 6[253], KSA 9: 263). This would seem to suggest that Nietzsche is closer to Helmholtz than Lange, a view which it seems to me Werner Stegmaier holds in his "Nietzsches Zeichen" (2000: 50). I think, as we shall see, that Nietzsche is in fact more closely aligned with Lange.
21 The influence of Helmholtz's claim here runs through Lange, as we will see; but it became thematic, too, for the critico-positivists like Mach, to whom Nietzsche had a complimentary copy of

Like Helmholtz, Lange treats language and concept formation as a process of naturalistic *Zeichen*-construction, which operates for the sake of an organism's greater success in navigating reality.[22] The sciences, for him as well, fail to designate reality simply, but offer an exceedingly useful set of symbols with which we can make sense of that reality within the scope of our "*Kreis der Erfahrung*".[23] Lange, however, would radicalize Helmholtz's observations about the phenomenal limits of representation.[24] His simple but crucial observation on method places him in clear opposition to Helmholtz: "[W]ir bemerken, dass derselbe Mechanismus, welcher sonach unsre sämmtlichen Empfindungen hervorbringt, jedenfalls auch unsre Vorstellung von der Materie erzeugt" (Lange 1902 [1866], vol. 2: 410; emphasis original). Precisely the same phenomenal symbolism that attends every physiognomic observation of an external object accompanies self-observations as well.[25] Consequently, self-observation yields no less a phenomenal surface than does either thinking an external object (Kant) or perceiving it (Helmholtz). Lange continues,

> Will ich meine Gedanken noch einmal denken, so rufe ich jene Empfindungen in den Sprachwerkzeugen hervor, welche wir oben gleichsam als den Körper des Gedankens kennen lernten. Ich empfinde sie so äusserlich, als jede andre Empfindung, und was Geist, Inhalt, Bedeutung dieses Complexes feinster Empfindungen betrifft, so verhält es sich damit nicht anders, als mit dem ästhetischen Werth einer *Zeichnung*. (Lange 1902 [1866], vol. 2: 384f.; my emphasis)

Genealogie of Morals sent (see Nietzsche to Naumann, 08.11.1887, KSB 8: 188), and Ferdinand Avenarius, with whom Nietzsche corresponded regularly (see Nietzsche to Avenarius, 10.09.1887, KSB 8: 146; Nietzsche to Avenarius, 14.01.1888, KSB 8: 229; Nietzsche to Avenarius, 20.07.1888, KSB 8: 359; the three letters from Nietzsche to Avenarius, 10.12.1888, KSB 8: 516–519; and two letters from Nietzsche to Avenarius of 22.12.1888, KSB 8: 544). Helmholtz's physiognomic observations were key to both branches of Neo-Kantian philosophy, and formed the very basis of Ernst Cassirer's *Philosophie der symbolischen Formen* (1923–29).

22 For Lange's rephrasing of Helmholtz's position on concept formation, see Lange 1902 [1866], vol. 2: 139–153, 408–425. For a rehearsal of Lange's position on language, see also Stack 1983: 138.

23 Cf. Lange 1902 [1866], vol. 2: 420–427. See also Stack 1983: 134.

24 Two of the direct influences on Lange in this respect, and thereby indirectly on Nietzsche, were Emil Du Bois-Reymond and Johannes Müller. For the Du Bois-Reymond, see Lange 1902 [1866], vol. 2: 160–163; for Müller, see Lange 1902 [1866], vol. 2: 412–415.

25 Another of Nietzsche's preferred authors came to the same conclusion. Maximilian Drosbach, whom Nietzsche began to read only in 1885, eloquently summarizes "Der subjectivist hat Recht, dass die Erscheinungswelt bloss subjective Vorstellung, Product seines Vorstellens ist, aber Unrecht wenn er nun doch behauptet, sie sei wahrnehmbar, sie sei Object seines Wahnehmens." (Drossbach 1884: 61)

Just as Helmholtz was able to show that our scientific knowledge of external objects is necessarily composed of fragmentary symbols whose truth value is a function of their practical import to creatures physiologically composed as we are, so did Lange extend that same insight into the character of the consciousness of the subject who so construes that world. Said otherwise, Helmholtz was an anti-realist about external objects, but a commonsense empirical realist about our knowledge of the function of the senses; Lange, on the other hand, was a thorough-going anti-realist both about external objects and about the internal subjective world through which those external objects are cognized. For both men, the objects of which we have experience present themselves to our consciousnesses as rough approximations, as symbols. But only for Lange are the subjective faculties through which we determine those objects as objects-for-us – insofar as we consider them through the very same forms of subjectivity that we perceive all other objects – understood as symbols-for-us rather than things at all.

This leaves Lange with a more consistent perspectivism than Helmholtz.[26] Truth is true not in itself but only for us. By 'for us', Lange means nothing like post-modernist relativism wherein truth is reduced to a matter of taste or choice, but in reference to the transcendental conditions for having an experience at all. For Kant, the transcendental involved pure intuitions and the categories of the understanding which were universal for all rational agents. For Helmholtz, more personalized physiognomic factors were added as transcendental conditions of experience. What is new in Lange is the observation that while there must be *some* transcendental conditions that constitute possible experience, what precisely these unconscious bases are in-themselves – whether in fact they are universal or particular – must remain unknown to conscious representation. Since consciousness always symbolizes, abbreviates, and abstracts from experience what is needed for the type-facts of a particular organism, any conscious representation of consciousness or the unconsciousness must, too, be considered merely a symbolic abbreviation. Talk of "menschliches Wesens und seines Elementes" is thus permitted only insofar as we acknowledge that the character of that designation is "hypothetisch", a "Voraussetzung", an "Abstraction", a "Fiction", precisely "so lange sie als solche im Bewusstsein bleibt".[27]

---

[26] "Denn gerade durch die Abstraction von der vollen, mannigfach zusammengesetzten Wirklichkeit sind auch andre Wissenschaften dazu gelangt, den Charakter der Exactheit zu erhalten. Exact ist ein für allemal für uns, die wir die Unendlichkeit der Naturwirkungen nicht zu übersehen vermögen, nur Dasjenige, was wir selbst exact machen. Alle absoluten Wahrheiten sind falsch; Relationen dagegen können genau sein." (Lange 1902 [1866], vol. 2: 455).

[27] This and the preceding at Lange 1902 [1866], vol. 2: 455.

3 Consequences for Nietzsche's view of self

The very passage that Nietzsche so enthusiastically recommended to Gersdorff, one of few extended quotations that Nietzsche would *ever* transcribe in correspondence, is the precise one where Lange definitively broke from Helmholtz, adding to Helmholtz's physiognomic theory of symbolization of objects the recognition that the subjective mechanism which symbolizes those objects is itself only knowable as an abbreviated symbol. So when Nietzsche demands that consciousness and its relation to our body be treated physiognomically (see, for example, HH I 10, KSA 2: 30; D 202, KSA 3: 176–178; NL Summer–Fall 1884, 26[432], KSA 11: 266; NL June–July 1885, 37[4], KSA 11: 576ff.; NL August–September 1885, 40[21], KSA 11: 638f.), it goes without saying he means something beyond the typical naturalistic rehearsal that in place of a soul or ego or transcendent self we should restrict our discussions to naturalistically-warranted compositions of drives, quantities of power, instincts, affects, etc. He may well also have in mind something beyond Helmholtz's exhortation to consider outer experience as constituted by physiognomic affects. What I wish to suggest is that Nietzsche accepts Lange's programmatic claim that even those naturalistic subjective facticities that are said to underlay our conscious activity must be considered signs, symbols, and anti-realist designations for something we know not what. And precisely insofar as we have *conscious concepts* of Triebe, Instinkte, Affekte, and the rest, those terms would necessarily be considered mere abbreviated symbolic surfaces and not designations referencing a real relation within subjectivity. He says just this by way of elucidating to Gersdorff the thrust of Lange's theory:

> Also das wahre Wesen der Dinge, das Ding an sich, ist uns nicht nur unbekannt, sondern es ist auch der Begriff desselben nicht mehr und nicht weniger als die letzte Ausgeburt eines von unsrer Organisation bedingten Gegensatzes, von dem wir nicht wissen, ob er außerhalb unsrer Erfahrung irgend eine Bedeutung hat. (Letter to Gersdorff, End of August 1866, KSB 2: 160)

The task now is to see whether the mature Nietzsche did hold this position or whether his expression to Gersdorf was just youthful exuberance.[28] During the

---

[28] I would like to thank Mattia Riccardi for drawing my attention to BGE 15 in this respect. On the surface, Nietzsche's claim that – "sense organs are *not* appearances in the way idealist philosophy uses that term: as such they certainly could not be causes!" – would seem to indicate that Nietzsche did indeed move away from Lange's position in his later writings. However, this is misleading. BGE 15 ridicules idealism for holding that the organs productive of knowledge would be

composition of *Die fröhliche Wissenschaft*, Nietzsche adopts Helmholtz's position that what we think of as experiential objects are naught more than symbols: "dass Alles was bewusst wird, ebendamit flach, dünn, relative-dumm, generell, Zeichen Heerden-Merkzeichen wird, dass mit allem Bewusstwerden eine grosse gründliche Verderbniss, Fälschung, Veroberflächlichung und Generalisation verbunden ist" (FW 354, KSA 3: 593).[29] And in a passage from precisely the same years, Nietzsche goes on to make the specific addendum that Lange himself had issued against Helmholtz: "Unsre Sinnesorgane als Ursachen der Außenwelt? Aber sie selber sind ja auch erst Wirkungen unsrer 'Sinne'" (NL Winter 1883–1884, 24[35], KSA 10: 663). Evidence like this strongly suggests that as much as the sense organs are for Lange, for Nietzsche are drives, urges, passions, etc. merely interpretive symbols for only the surface of what ineluctable processes occur within our skin. Those very factors which we say lead us to consciously 'symbolize' the world are, considered in their own turn, nothing more than symbols of some conscious process, ideations of a mind composed of drives and urges that are themselves nothing but the product of the ideations of a mind. Of what lies beyond our conscious symbol-forming, Nietzsche claims we cannot, by definition, be conscious. "Die unbekannte Welt des 'Subjects'. – Das, was den Menschen so schwer zu begreifen fällt, ist ihre Unwissenheit über sich selber, von den ältesten Zeiten bis jetzt!" (M 116, KSA 3: 108. See also NL June–July 1885, 37[4], KSA 11: 578).

Our hypothesis is given additional weight by virtue of the fact that the individual natural-physiognomic designations Nietzsche himself employs are elsewhere admitted to be just abbreviated or symbolic ways of thinking that do not adequate to reality (NL June–July 1885, 37[4], KSA 11: 578). Of his Lieblingswort 'Affekte', Nietzsche himself claims: "**Der Glaube** an **'Affekte'.** Affekte sind eine Construktion des Intellekts, eine Erdichtung von Ursachen, die es nicht giebt" (NL Winter 1883–1884, 24[20], KSA 10: 657; emphasis original). Of nerve-impulses, Nietzsche writes with the same 'als-ob'/'es sei' expressions that Hans Vaihinger would adopt:

---

nothing more than ideas, and thus not efficacious. It says nothing, however, about how we must *think* about those organs. Nietzsche is certainly not an idealist in the sense that he thinks objects are nothing more or less than ideational projections. My position is that Nietzsche thinks those objects are real; the manner in which they are *represented* to the knower, however, must reckon the representational capacities of that knower. Thus I read BGE 15 as a critical remark about the ideal character of objects, whereas my argument here concerns how we represent those objects.

29 Nietzsche continued to esteem Helmholtz into his mature period, even if he took Lange's side of their debate. He even asked his publisher to send a complimentary copy of *Zur Genealogie der Moral* to Helmholtz. See Nietzsche to Naumann, 08.11.1887, KSB 8: 188.

Selbst das Verhältnisss eines Nervenreizes zu dem hervorgebrachten Bilde ist an sich kein nothwendiges; wenn aber eben dasselbe Bild Millionen Mal hervorgebracht und durch viele menschengeschlechter hindurch vererbt ist [...], so bekommt es endlich für den Menschen dieselbe Bedeutung, als ob es das einzig nothwendige Bild sei und als ob jenes Verhhältniss des ursprünglichen Nervenreizes zu dem hergebrachten Bilde ein strenges Causalitätsverhältniss sei; wie ein Traum, ewig wiederholt [...]. Aber das Hart- und Starr-Werden einer Metapher verbürgt durchaus nichts für die Nothwendigkeit und ausschliessliche Berechtigung dieser Metapher. (WL 1, KSA 1: 884)

Of drives, he writes in *Daybreak*:

Wie weit Einer seine Selbstkenntniss auch treiben mag, Nichts kann doch unvollständiger sein, als das Bild der gesammten Triebe, die sein Wesen constituiren. Kaum dass er die gröberen beim Namen nennen kann: ihre Zahl und Stärke, ihre Ebbe und Fluth, ihr Spiel und Widerspiel unter einander, und vor Allem die Gesetze ihrer Ernährung bleiben ihm ganz unbekannt. (M 119; KSA 3: 111)

Of his designation of the self as a 'society' of drives or souls, he writes:

Der Begriff "Individuum" "Person" enthält eine große Erleichterung für das naturalistische Denken [...] Thatsächlich stecken dort Vorurtheile: wir haben leider keine Worte, um das wirklich Vorhandene, nämlich die Intensitäts-grade auf dem Wege zum Individuum, zur "Person" bezeichnen. [...] Ich habe einmal den Ausdruck "viele sterbliche Seelen" gebraucht ... (NL August–September 1885, 40[8], KSA 11: 631f.)

The same goes even for his usage of the designation 'Will to Power'. The phrase is for Nietzsche a symbol for what is itself ineluctable, and not the referential designation of an actuality. Even if there are some empirical traces that would point to its existence, this evidence could only be an interpretable surface, an abbreviation of diverse experiences in a single word-group, precisely what Lange calls 'figurative truths'. That Nietzsche shares this view, we see him admit: "Es giebt keinen 'Willen'; das ist nur eine vereinfachende Conzeption des Verstandes" (NL Winter 1883–1884, 24[34], KSA 10: 663).[30] 'Will' is a meaningful and convenient designation for a group of superficially similar surface-appearances, but nothing that identifies exactly a genuinely-real referent. Such designations are "eigentlich Worte allein für superlativistsche Grade dieser Vorgänge

---

[30] For a discussion, see Müller-Lauter 1999: 73ff. Stack (1983: 292–298), I find, is largely correct with having found this parallel with Lange. However, I think he takes an unnecessary step into the *Standpunkt des Ideals* by treating what I consider Nietzsche's anti-realism or symbolic descriptions as 'myths'. See his (1983), 293f. His term, I find, carries too much cultural and pedagogical baggage. It also misleadingly attributes a sort of conscious freedom enjoyed by the creator of myths, who can choose to fashion the myth in any way he/she would like. The symbols Nietzsche uses, however, are in no less necessary than how the eye abbreviates, orders, and forms visual experience.

und Triebe [...]" (D 115, KSA 3: 107). The designations are "eine blasse, dünne und äußerst ungenaue Werth- und Kraft-Vorstellung [...]" (NL June–July 1885, 37[4], KSA 11: 578). They are all just "Namen für extreme Zustände [...]" (D 115, KSA 3: 107). Anything below that threshold of superficial *Schein* is entirely unknown.

So there is good evidence that Nietzsche held both the terminology and the spirit of Lange's claims about the limits of self-knowledge into his mature writing. Moreover, the anti-realist view I ascribe to Nietzsche has interpretive advantages.[31] Acknowledging the symbolic character of Nietzsche's descriptions of the inner world allows us to navigate more surely through the inconsistent metaphors he employs when discussing the relationship between the aspects of our inner world. The images of tools and surfaces, though informative, are inconsistent when we consider them as real objects, the former of which, when applied to the 'real' constituents of 'inner life', implies a causal relation, while the latter of which rejects it. Considered as symbolic surfaces whose referent is ineluctable, however, we are unburdened from taking their implied predicate extensions as realist descriptions of their interrelations. It prevents us, too, from balking at the oft-noted awkwardness with which Nietzsche so freely discusses the 'reasons', 'causes', 'symptoms', 'grounds', etc., that led agents and even cultures to their historical actions, despite the fact that he problematizes that same sort of psychologizing (see for example, FW 335, KSA 3: 562f.). Their descriptive value rests in their presenting rough, abbreviated symbols capable of informing and elucidating to a relatively greater degree. But they cannot be considered descriptions whose truth value rests on their adequation to the real world.

Apart from the interpretive advantage, the global anti-realism I ascribe to Nietzsche makes good philosophical sense as well. It seems both unwarranted and, indeed, inconsistent that Nietzsche's epistemological critiques should apply to external objects but not to the internal. If Nietzsche's principle objection to the possibility of 'knowing' objects is that conceptualization is a kind of falsifying abbreviation that transforms objects into phenomenal appearances according to some kind of need (e.g. FW 354, KSA 11: 464), then I neither see any evidence nor any intuitive reason to think that Nietzsche only attributed his perspectivism to external objects, stopping short of the unconscious constituents of the self. Why should we be confident, in other words, that we have reached the 'real' inner objects that constitute selfhood when we talk of relations, drives, quanta, etc., when Nietzsche actually thinks all words and desig-

---

31 Among accounts which examine Nietzsche's use of symbols in more detail than I can here, see especially Simon 1995, Cox 1997, Abel 1999, Abel 2004: 72–104, Stegmaier 2008.

nations will fail to adequately articulate the range of experiences that impresses itself upon us? To ignore this is not only to ignore Lange's crucial influence, but to impute an unnecessary inconsistency into Nietzsche's epistemology.

4 Equivocal symbols of the self

'Last-link' interpreters of Nietzsche's theory of mind recognize that thinking is a construction of signs. This active construction is in fact what distinguishes consciousness from unconscious activities, which is the key to their claim that consciousness is something more than epiphenomenal. Constâncio holds a similar view of the necessity of thinking in terms of signs and symbols, but makes an important and to my mind correct step beyond these in recognizing that the act of thinking of the self as a symbol-constructing thing will yield the consequence that the self is itself nothing but a symbol for something whose actual character we cannot represent. Constâncio writes, "[A] conscious mental state is a particular constellation of conceptual representations within an open system of signs. As 'surface', it is, as we saw, a 'total state' – but this means that it expresses *in signs* the total state of the organism" (Constâncio 2011: 31). He continues, "All concepts are signs, and even the description of consciousness as a relation of signs is itself a relation of signs – and not an adequate picture or a copy of something that actually exists and has in itself the properties with which it is represented in our thoughts" (Constâncio 2011: 32). With this I wholly agree, and would only add the historical remark that Lange had both precedence and influence on this exact view.

Yet there is an intriguing consequence to Nietzsche's use of symbols to articulate the relation between the unconscious and conscious, even insofar as we agree with Constâncio to say *that* consciousness is itself a symbolic representation. That consequence is one that Lange sensed well – in fact, he states it on the very same page that Nietzsche copied over to Gersdorff. Lange writes "Es ist einstweilen ganz gleichgültig, ob die Erscheinungen der Sinnenwelt auf die Vorstellung oder auf den Mechanismus der Organe zurückgeführt worden, wenn sie sich nur als Producte unsrer Organisation im weitesten Sinne des Wortes erweisen" (Lange 1902 [1866], vol. 2: 423). Lange rightly recognized here that it was immaterial to argue that the relation of the unconscious to the conscious elements of our subjective constitution should be considered in any definitive way, precisely because that arrangement can never be considered to obtain in the world beyond our subjective representation of it. Since, as we saw, for Nietzsche, too, the designations we use are symbols whose arrangement is of our own making, it is of no ontological consequence whether we designate their relationship as epiphenomenal or as a last link. Each of these terms is still an unconscious interpretation of that which interprets unconsciously. We can therefore never hold confidence that our descriptions of our inner entities or even processes – *much less then relationships we predicate them into* – correspond to the way the world is independently of those descriptions.

Nietzsche confirms precisely this. "The mental as the ability to be master through symbols [*Zeichen*] of a huge quantity of facts." And thus we have the Helmholtzian claim. But what comes in the next sentence is purely Lange. "*This mental world, this symbol-world, is itself sheer 'appearance and deception'* ['Schein und Trug'], *just as every 'thing of appearance' already is.*"[32] This means that drives, instincts, urges, power-wills, and so forth, are not things or processes whose relationships to each other or to consciousness – whether we symbolize them as tool, a mirror, a continuum, or a polyp – is something scholars should be asking about in earnestness. Such mistakes what Nietzsche considers a symbolic construction about the mental life for a discovery whose actual relations require elucidation, something tantamount to calculating the effects of road friction on a car's gas mileage by feeling the smoothness of a map. Thus when scholars even as considerate as Constâncio think that, "[A]n organism *is* its drives or instincts, and there is no intelligible 'in itself' beyond that" (Constâncio 2011: 18), or "that at every moment the 'total state' of the organism *is* a cluster of perspectival relations" (Constâncio 2011: 25),[33] and proceed, as both camps do, to wonder about what sorts of relationship those drives and instincts stand in, they're all missing a key Nietzschean point – one that Nietzsche took directly from Lange: "Wenn Jemand ein Ding hinter einem Busche versteckt, es eben dort wieder sucht und auch findet, so ist an diesem Suchen und Finden nicht viel zu rühmen [...]" (WL 1, KSA 1: 883).

In keeping with Lange's critique of Helmholtz, if all such designations are merely superficial symbols for something unknown, then questions about their *actual* relations in one way or the other are in fact moot. It is not a question of how things relate, but how we symbolically represent them as relating. Along my reading, if the symbols Nietzsche employs to describe the self commit him to

---

[32] NL April–June 1885, 34[131], KSA 11: 464. See also NL Summer 1886–Spring 1887, 6[11], KSA 12: 237: "Die erfinderische Kraft [...] arbeitete im Dienst des Bedürfnisses, nämlich von Sicherheit, von schneller Verständlichkeit auf Grund von Zeichen und Klängen, von Abkürzungsmitteln [...]."

[33] I thank Constâncio for personally clarifying his intention in this respect. Both in his (2011) and (2013) paper, the latter of which was not available at the time I composed the present article, Constâncio argues for the symbolic status of any designation of our mental contents in a way that brings our positions much closer.

inconsistent views – as is the case with his usage of 'Werkzeug', 'Spiegel', etc. –, then it only underscores how his words stand as symbols and do not designate realities to which we might predicate any particular interactive relationships. The symbols are not symbols *of* anything, but expressions of how a particular agent is led to represent the self.

5 What Nietzsche adds to Lange

For Lange and Nietzsche both, the conditions for the possibility of conscious awareness of an object renders that object a mere symbol, sign, abbreviation, or convenient fiction for something of whose nature as it stands beyond our conscious awareness we are, by definition, not consciously aware. Provided that the relation between unconscious and conscious can only be demarcated in consciousness by symbols, which themselves are an unconscious product of a symbol-constructing set of faculties that are themselves only represented symbolically, it seems for both that complete ignorance of what 'we really are' is a foregone conclusion. Nietzsche seems to confirm this himself. "Der Gedanke ist ebensowohl wie das Wort, nur ein Zeichen: von *irgend einer* Congruenz des Gedankens und des Wirklichen kann nicht die Rede sein. Das Wirkliche ist irgend eine Trieb-bewegung" (NL Fall 1880, 6[253], KSA 9: 263; my emphasis).[34]

To remold Constâncio's phrase, Nietzsche's departs here from Lange, but also retains Lange's position *as its point of departure*. A passage in *Human, All Too Human* makes clear there is another path beyond what Lange envisioned. Although "to observe the self immediate observation [*unmittelbare Selbstbeobachtung*] is not nearly sufficient for us to know ourselves", (and we should by now know why), this is not the only means of observation.

> [W]e require history [*Geschichte*] since the past flows inside us in a hundred waves; we ourselves are, indeed, nothing but that which at every moment we sense of this continued flowing [*Fortströmen*]. It may even be said that here too, when we desire to descend into the river of what seems to be our own most intimate and personal being, there applies the dictum of Heraclitus: we cannot step into the same river twice. (HH II 223, KSA 2: 477)[35]

---

34 Note, too, that Nietzsche speaks of this relation with intentional ambiguity: it is 'some sort' of relation, which I take to mean he acknowledges the application of his own claim about symbols in the preceding sentence to apply to the mechanism by which we seem to construct those symbols.
35 The draft of this passage from 1876/1877 makes even clearer this same thought. "Die moralische Selbstbeobachtung genügt jetzt keineswegs, Historie und die Kenntniß der zurückgeblie-

Part of the reason why cognitive representation constructs abbreviated symbols rather than static definitions for static things is that neither the subject nor object is itself static (HL 1, KSA 1: 250; GM Preface 1, KSA 5: 247).[36] Neither language nor concepts, to speak in the merest generalizations, can 'handle' reality as it truly is since it is always flowing, and so the ineluctable unconscious self constructs formalizing abbreviations in order to better navigate the world and achieve the satisfaction of its drives and instincts. As the contingent facts of an organism shift over time in response to its growth within a particular environment, so do the symbols take on a perspectival character relative to its 'type facts'. Thus whatever anything is, it can never be designated by an absolute or, to our purpose here, immutable descriptive judgment. Historical judgment, however, as a process of re-writing, re-interpreting the signs used to designate objects and constitute their meaning for agents roughly like us, is suited to this task.

> [D]ass etwas Vorhandenes, irgendwie Zu-Stande-Gekommenes immer wieder von einer ihm überlegenen Macht auf neue Ansichten ausgelegt, neu in Beschlag genommen, zu einem neuen Nutzen umgebildet und umgerichtet wird; dass alles Geschehen in der organischen Welt ein Überwältigen, Herrwerden und dass wiederum alles Überwältigen und Herrwerden ein Neu-Interpretieren, ein Zurechtmachen ist, bei dem der bisherige "Sinn" und "Zweck" nothwendig verdunkelt oder ganz ausgelöscht werden muss. (GM II 12, KSA 5: 313f.)

Subjective facticities, whatever they are, are something in existence. As such our symbolic designations of them are continually reinterpreted anew according to the power aims that are dominant at a particular temporal moment. With words that echo Lange's physiognomy precisely, Nietzsche continues:

> Wenn mann die Nützlichkeit von irgend welchem physiologischen Organ (oder auch einer Rechts-Institution, einer gesellschaftlichen Sitte, eines politischen Brauchs, einer Form in den Künsten oder im religiösen Cultus) noch so gut begriffen hat, so hat man damit noch nichts in Betreff seiner Entstehung begriffen [...] Aber alle Zwecke, alle Nützlichkeiten sind

---

benen Völkerschaften gehört dazu, um die verwickelten Motive unseres Handelns kennen zu lernen. In ihnen spielt <sich> die ganze Geschichte der Menschheit ab, ale ihre großen Irrthümer und falschen Vorstellungen sind mit eingeflochten; weil wir diese nicht mehr theilen, suchen wir sie auch nicht mehr in den Motiven unserer Handl<ungen>, aber als Stimmung Farbe Oberton erklingen sie mit darin." (NL End 1876–Summer 1877, 23[48], KSA 8: 421) Notice that Nietzsche actively chose to omit 'moralische' in the published version, which perhaps indicates that he reconsidered how widely this thinking extended.

36 Although I will not address them here, other reasons involve the complexity and particularity of external objects.

nur Anzeichen davon, dass ein Wille zur Macht über etwas weniger Mächtiges Herr geworden ist und ihm von sich aus den Sinn einer Funktion aufgeprägt hat; und die ganze Geschichte eines "Dings", eines Organs, eines Brauchs kann dergestalt eine fortgesetzte Zeichen-Kette von immer neuen Interpretationen und Zurechtmachungen sein [...]. (GM II 12, KSA 5: 314)

What I think Nietzsche means by the *historical* observation of things and selfhood both is that it, unlike static observation, marks not what the signs of selfhood are but how they change over time, that is, how agents over time construct and express new symbols to stand for what reality does not disclose to cognition simply. There are no single correct, timeless set of symbols for expressing that ineluctable something, even while *some* general set of symbols is necessary for the possibility of communicating anything at all. This is just where Nietzsche's idiosyncratic vision of historiography comes into play.[37] As a diagnostician who reads the passing issuance of signs over time – in short, a genealogical historian – Nietzsche considers himself in position to read how symbolic expressions reflect kinds of life, reflect, that is to say, what drives, affects, urges, and instincts are actually being expressed within the *act* of representation, within the act of constructing the signs.[38]

Only a naïve historian thinks the designations he records as having been used by past peoples actually refers correspondentially to really-existent things external to either their descriptions or else his record of their descriptions.[39] 'Punishment', for an example from the *Genealogie*, is a single word that stands as a conceptual abbreviation intended to designate a multifaceted and temporally-shifting phenomenon. The genealogical historian's task is to show how accidental, disjointed, and transitional that term is, how it references nothing real outside the mind of the historian, and how even historians' own interpretations of that term are themselves equally accidental, disjointed, and transitional. 'Punishment' is revealed to be a symbol that expresses a range of inner forces

---

[37] For my interpretation of Nietzsche's later historiography, see Chapters 6 & 7 of my *Nietzsche's Philosophy of History* (2013).
[38] This 'expressivist' interpretation of Nietzsche's notion of subjectivity is gaining popularity due principally to the work of Robert B. Pippin. For fuller accounts than I can give here, see his *The Persistence of Subjectivity: On the Kantian Aftermath* (2005), Chapter 14; and the fuller expression in his *Nietzsche, Psychology, and First Philosophy* (2010), Chapter 4.
[39] Notebook reflections from 1882 on a translation of Emerson's *Versuche* (V) (1858) reflect an important influence on Nietzsche's thinking about the self as a historical project that is only represented historically. See NL Beginning of 1882, 17[1–4], KSA 9: 666; especially the first entry: "In every activity is the abbreviated history of all becoming. ego." Much has been written on Emerson's influence on Nietzsche. For a brief summary, see Brobjer 2008: 22–25.

that constitute an historiographical interpretation (GM II 13, KSA 5: 316ff.). The same holds for those symbolic tokens commonly employed to designate our inner selves: 'instincts', 'drives', etc. Those aspects of our inner life, admittedly just convenient words for something about which we cannot talk, cannot be described as such but constantly *express* themselves in all the actions of agents throughout history.

Symbolic designations like 'soul' or 'brain' or even 'drives' are interesting, therefore, not for their referentiality, but insofar as they reveal something important about the kind of life that would seek to express the ineluctable in that way. So, too, with the Hegelian-Hartmannian 'Geist', or with the reductive materialists' phrenological 'brain' – what kind of life would express things thus? And so, too, with Nietzsche's various naturalistic symbols: what kind of life will historians ascribe to those who use symbols like 'drives', 'instincts', 'wills', 'forces', 'energies', 'powers', 'continuums', and so on. Are the symbols expressions of health or of decay? None of these terms articulates the in-itself of reality, either inside or outside the skin, as Lange and I think Constâncio would have claimed. But by their expression over time we apprehend something crucial about the ones doing the expressing. Since historical observation stands as a dynamic record of the changing symbols utilized by individuals and cultures to navigate their world as they manifest their inner selves outwardly through language, we get a sense, though no demonstration, of the great play of perspectives, the endless expressions of wills to power within symbols. No aspect of the self, whether conscious or unconscious, is comprehensible in-itself without the falsifying mediation of cognition; but a gradual, continual unmasking occurs through its active expression in its various deeds and is made evident to careful genealogical observation, as if "euer Selbst in der Handlung sei, wie die Mutter im Kinde ist" (Z II Tugendhaften; KSA 4: 123). That expression of the mother is nothing isolatable and describable as a thing in the child, but a sort of dynamic of feeling that transmogrifies over time in ways more or less pronounced as the child develops throughout her life and expresses that inner development in outward actions. Those who watched carefully the development of the child, her actions over time, would read those actions as meaningful symbolic expressions of some inner core, the identity of which is neither isolatable nor describable as such, but which always gives a sense of what underlies it. So too does history, as the sum of expressions of subjectivity, and historiography, as an instantiation of the record of those symbols expressed within symbols, grants at least insight into the relation between unconsciousness and consciousness, if never an adequate realist description of the actual interrelation of the conscious and unconscious aspects of the self. "Aber es giebt kein solches Substrat; es giebt kein 'Sein' hinter dem Thun, Wirken, Werden; 'der Thäter'", indeed any doer in the sense of a chain, a surface, a tool, or a mirror, "ist zum Thun bloss hinzugedichtet, – das Thun ist Alles" (GM I 13, KSA 5: 279).

References

Abel, Günter (1999) *Sprache, Zeichen, Interpretation*, Frankfurt a.M.: Suhrkamp.
Abel, Günter (2001) "Bewußtsein – Sprache – Natur. Nietzsches Philosophie des Geistes", in: *Nietzsche-Studien* 30, 1–43.
Abel, Günter (2004) *Zeichen der Wirklichkeit*, Frankfurt a.M.: Suhrkamp.
Acampora, Christa Davis (2006) "Naturalism and Nietzsche's Moral Psychology", in: Keith Ansell-Pearson (ed.), *A Companion to Nietzsche*, Oxford: Blackwell, 314–333.
Bornedal, Peter (2010) *Surface and the Abyss: Nietzsche as Philosopher of Mind and Knowledge*, Berlin/New York: De Gruyter.
Brobjer, Thomas (2008) *Nietzsche's Philosophical Context*, Urbana: University of Illinois Press.
Constâncio, João (2011) "On Consciousness. Nietzsche's Departure from Schopenhauer", in: *Nietzsche-Studien* 40, 1–42.
Constâncio, João (2013) "On Nietzsche's Conception of Philosophy in *Beyond Good and Evil*: Reassessing Schopenhauer's Relevance", in: M.E. Born and A. Pichler (eds.), *Texturen des Denkens: Nietzsches Inszenierung der Philosophie in "Jenseits von Gut und Böse"*, Berlin/Boston: De Gruyter, 145–164.
Cox, Christoph (1997) "The 'Subject' of Nietzsche's Perspectivism", in: *Journal of the History of Philosophy* 35(2), 269–291.
Drossbach, Maximilian (1884) *Über die scheinbaren und die wirklichen Ursachen des Geschehens in der Welt*, Halle: C.E.M. Pfeffer.
Gemes, Ken/May, Simon (eds.) (2009) *Nietzsche on Freedom and Autonomy*, Oxford/New York: Oxford University Press.
Green, Michael Steven (2002) *Nietzsche and the Transcendental Tradition*, Urbana: University of Illinois Press.
Helmholtz, Herman von (1904) *Populäre Vorträge*, ed. Daniel Shumway, Boston: Heath & Co.
Helmholtz, Herman von (1962) [1867] *Treatise on Physiological Optics*, 3 vols., trans. James P.C. Southall, 3rd edition, New York: Dover.
Helmholtz, Herman von (1977) *Epistemological Writings: The Paul Hertz/Moritz Schlick Centenary Edition of 1921*, trans. Malcolm F. Lowe, Dordrecht/Boston: D. Reidel.
Helmholtz, Herman von (1995) *Science and Culture: Popular and Philosophical Lectures*, ed. D. Cahan, Chicago: University of Chicago Press.
Hill, R. Kevin (2003) *Nietzsche's Critiques: The Kantian Foundations of his Thought*, Oxford: Oxford University Press.
Janaway, Christopher (2006) "Nietzsche on Free Will, Autonomy, and the Sovereign Individual", in: *Aristotelian Society Supplementary Volume* 80, 339–357.
Jensen, Anthony (2013) *Nietzsche's Philosophy of History*, Cambridge: Cambridge University Press.
Katsafanas, Paul (2005) "Nietzsche's Theory of Mind: Consciousness and Conceptualization", in: *European Journal of Philosophy* 13, 1–31.
Köhnke, K.C. (1986) *Entstehung und Aufstieg des Neukantianismus: Die deutsche Universitätsphilosophie zwischen Idealismus und Positivismus*, Frankfurt a.M.: Suhrkamp.

Lange, Friedrich Albert (1902) [1866] *Geschichte des Materialismus und Kritik seiner Bedeutung in der Gegenwart*, 2 vols., ed. Hermann Cohen, Leipzig: J. Baedeker.
Leiter, Brian (2002) *Nietzsche on Morality*, London/New York: Routledge.
Müller-Lauter, Wolfgang (1999) *Über Freiheit und Chaos*, Berlin/New York: De Gruyter.
Pippin, Robert B. (2005) *The Persistence of Subjectivity: On the Kantian Aftermath*, Cambridge: Cambridge University Press.
Pippin, Robert B. (2010) *Nietzsche, Psychology, and First Philosophy*, Chicago/London: University of Chicago Press.
Poellner, Peter (2000) *Nietzsche and Metaphysics*, Oxford: Oxford University Press.
Poellner, Peter (2006) "Phenomenology and Science in Nietzsche", in: Keith Ansell-Pearson (ed.), *A Companion to Nietzsche*, Oxford: Blackwell, 297–313.
Salaquarda, Jörg (1978) "Nietzsche und Lange", in: *Nietzsche-Studien* 7, 236–253.
Schopenhauer, Arthur (1977) *Zürcher Ausgabe*, 10 vols., ed. Arthur Hübscher et al., Zurich: Diogenes.
Simon, Josef (1995) "Verstehen ohne Interpretation?: Zeichen und Verstehen bei Hegel und Nietzsche", in: *Distanz im Verstehen: Zeichen und Interpretationen II*, Frankfurt a.M.: Suhrkamp.
Small, Robin (2001) *Nietzsche in Context*, Aldershot/Burlington: Ashgate.
Stack, George J. (1983) *Lange and Nietzsche*, Berlin/New York: DeGruyter.
Stegmaier, Werner (2000) "Nietzsches Zeichen", in: *Nietzsche-Studien* 29, 41–69.
Stegmaier, Werner (2008) *Philosophie der Orientierung*, Berlin/New York: De Gruyter.
Vaihinger, Hans (1916) *Nietzsche als Philosoph*, 4th edition, Berlin: Reuther & Reichard.
Vaihinger, Hans (1922) *Die Philosophie des Als Ob: System der theoretischen, praktischen und religiösen Fiktionen der Menschheit*, 7th edition, Leipzig: Meiner.
Wotling, Patrick (2011) "What Language do Drives Speak?", in: J. Constâncio and M.J. Mayer Branco (eds.), *Nietzsche on Instinct and Language*, Berlin/New York: De Gruyter.

Giuliano Campioni
8 Nietzsche and "the French Psychologists": Stendhal, Taine, Ribot, Bourget

In his journey to Cosmopolis (NL 1884, 28[52], KSA 11: 320), which started in Nice during the winter 1883, Nietzsche is in close contact with the contemporary French culture and discovers a new "psychology", which offers him recently developed possibilities of "dangerous knowledge" (BGE 23). This new psychology is to be considered more and more "the queen of the sciences", so that "the rest of the sciences exist to serve and prepare for it. Because, from now on, psychology is again the way to the fundamental problems" (BGE 23). Nietzsche believes himself to be a part of the "charming company" of "the latest Frenchmen": "I cannot imagine another century in history where you could cobble together such a list of inquisitive and, at the same time, delicate psychologists as you can with contemporary Paris", he writes (EH, Why I am so Clever 3). In fact, Nietzsche feels he is more radical and more coherent then they are, because he is a critic of the metaphysical and moral residues still present in their positions. He describes himself, on several occasions, as an "unparalleled psychologist", the first psychologist among philosophers (EH, Why I am a Destiny 6). This can be acknowledged by careful readers who are able to read him "as good philologists read their Horace" (EH, Why I Write Such Good Books 5). All of Nietzsche's works from *Beyond Good and Evil* onwards are works of "a psychologist". The term is often present in sketches of titles (see, for example, the several alternative titles for *Twilight of the Idols* in NL 1888, 22[6] KSA 13: 586.) *Beyond Good and Evil* is "a *critique of modernity*", in which "psychology is applied with avowed hardness and cruelty" (EH BGE 2); *On the Genealogy of Morals* shows "the psychology of Christianity" (first essay), "the psychology of the *conscience*" (second essay), and the psychology of the ascetic ideal and *décadence* (third essay), which Nietzsche himself calls "a psychologist's three crucial preparatory works for a revaluation of all values" (EH GM); *The Antichrist* contains the psychology of Christ against the grossness of Renan *in psychologicis*; *The Case of Wagner* describes the psychology of the artist of decadence and the comedian; and the writings collected in *Nietzsche contra Wagner* are, according to the subtitle, the "the files of a psychologist": here, "the psychologist speaks" against the musician.

The term "psychologist" is strongly emphasized in Nietzsche's writings after his reading of Paul Bourget's *Essais de psychologie contemporaine* during the winter of 1883. For the philosopher, "psychology" seems to be the expression of a radically alternative tradition and practice of knowledge, incompatible with the German spirit. Psychology is characterized by the "*passion of knowledge*", that "critical discipline and every habit that leads to cleanliness and rigor in matters of the spirit", a "*pleasure* in saying no, in dissecting, and in a certain level-headed cruelty that knows how to guide a knife with assurance and subtlety, even when the heart is bleeding" (BGE 210). All of this is incompatible with the idealistic mendaciousness and metaphysical mystification that characterizes the German spirit: "The French psychologists – and where else are there still psychologists today?" (BGE 218), and "But where today are there psychologists? In France, certainly; perhaps in Russia; definitely not in Germany" (HH I Preface 8). "Russia" is an implicit reference to "the eminent psychologist" Dostoevsky ("regarding the insight of analysis, none could stay at his level, even in most modern Paris" – Letter to Emily Fynn, around 04.03.1887, KSB Bd. 8: 39). Nietzsche "discovers" the Russian writer in French translations ("translated into French, for heaven's sake, not in German!" – Letter to Brandes, 20.10.1888 KSB Bd. 8: 457), and refers to him, following the French critics, in connection to psychological analysis about *ressentiment* and the "underground" man, and again to outline the figure of Christ as "idiot" (NL 1888, 15[9] KSA 13: 409).

Nietzsche uses Bourget – the French "psychologist" he feels especially close to – against the German spirit. In Bourget, Nietzsche found the terms of comparison between *l'esprit latin* (of which Descartes, with his *Discours de la méthode,* is the constant and strongest exemplification) and *l'esprit germanique* (the romantic "becoming"). On one hand, we have "the ordering and deductive method that preferably uses analysis, simplification and succession; and on the other hand, there is the very vision of things, being complex and synthetic, disordered and divining, which embraces several objects together" (Bourget 1885b [NB], p. 258)[1]. Racine, Abbé Prevost and Descartes seem to consider

> [...] life as a defined reality, fixed and clear in its lines; while in the eyes of Shakespeare, Goethe and Carlyle, this same life is something mobile and indeterminate, perhaps a dream, always in the act of creation and dissolution. The first of these two methods has been particularly developed by the peoples of the Latin-Greek tradition, and they have their logic and beautiful clarity thanks to it. The second one gave its best fruits with the Germans and the British, deriving from it their charm and depth [...]. (Bourget 1885b [NB], p. 258)

The mixture of elements from these two different cultural traditions, whose "metaphysics" proceeded from a physiological background – from "an initial

---

[1] Translations from French to English by the editors.

and constituent cause" –, produced the most interesting "cases" of *décadence*, complex and hybrid natures: from Baudelaire to Amiel. Paris – the "capital city of the nineteenth century" – is the experimental laboratory of new values and forms of life, the capital city where – distant from the *rabies nationalis* – those hybrids individuals are born that herald a new European.

Nietzsche accepts the characterization offered by Bourget of the Latin and Germanic spirit, making it more complex and nuanced, in particular the comparison between the clarity that achieves a definite shape and the chaotic darkness that relates to the anxiety of becoming. The last word, in this direction, is entrusted to *Ecce Homo* – the autobiography written to "destroy and root out every myth about me" (NL 1888–1889, 25[6], KSA 13: 639). Here the anti-German stance becomes the preliminary background of the necessary "cleansing" of thought: the Germans "never went through a seventeenth century of hard self-examination as the French did – a La Rochefoucauld, a Descartes has a hundred times more integrity than the best of the Germans, – they have not produced a psychologist to this day" (EH CW 3).

The copy of *Nouveaux Essais* in Nietzsche's library [NB] has many traces of being read by him. Bourget (like other French contemporaries who have later dealt with Nietzsche, such as Faguet, De Roberty, Brunetiere, Fouillée, Bourdeau etc.) is unaware of having contributed so strongly to the plot of Nietzsche's writings, in particular of having been such an important point reference in the latter's polemic against the German spirit. Bourget will know of Nietzsche only superficially from 1893 on – already in the phase of his militant traditionalism and nationalism –, when Mrs. Bourget gives her husband a very brief summary of Nietzsche's thought (significantly, the German philosopher had sent a copy of *Beyond Good and Evil* via his editor to the address of the French writer: see the letter to Naumann, 02.08.1886 KSB Bd. 7: 216). It is strange but emblematic that in the final edition of the *Essais*, published by Plon in 1899 as the first volume of the *Oeuvres complètes*, Bourget placed Nietzsche within the German tradition (as a passionate Wagnerian, he probably associated Nietzsche mostly with the metaphysics of the artist of *The Birth of Tragedy*). This is the tradition of the big systems (the "taste to think in terms of large classes"), the tradition farthest removed from the clear and distinct spirit of analysis. In fact, in a sentence from the first edition Bourget now adds Nietzsche's name alongside Hartmann and Schelling: "This is a very significant sketch, in a few lines, of the method that generated so many systems, from Schelling's system to those of Hartmann and Nietzsche, through Hegel and Schopenhauer" (Bourget 1993: 393).

Of course, before Bourget, Nietzsche had encountered Stendhal, the French psychologist who was dearest to him. About him Nietzsche declares only passionate support, as the most natural heir of that will of clarity (the will to explain "easily, reasonably, mathematically": *De l'amour*, first preface, 1826) that pushes analytical passion to the extreme. This "passion of knowledge" is in fact modelled on *l'amour-passion* outlined by Stendhal, particularly in *De l'amour*, which Nietzsche knew well. And this "psychologist"-free-spirit, too, "goes against the German taste" (BGE 39). "*Pour être bon philosophe*–this last great psychologist says–*il faut etre sec, clair, sans illusion. A banquier, qui a fait fortunes, a une partie du caractère requis pour faire des découvertes en philosophie, c'est-à-dire pour voir clair dans ce qui est*" (BGE 39). "And occasionally when I praise Stendhal as a deep psychologist, German university professors ask me how to spell the name" (EH CW 3).

The autobiographical reconstruction aside–similar to the reconstruction regarding Schopenhauer and Dostoevsky ("Stendhal, one of the best accidents in my life–because all the epochal events of my life came to me by chance and not through anybody's recommendation–is completely invaluable", EH, Why I am so Clever 3)–, it should be noted that Nietzsche only acquired a passionate interest in Stendhal in 1879, after having read the German translation of Taine's *Histoire de la Littérature anglaise*. Nietzsche will remain faithful to Stendhal until–Stendhal "who has perhaps had the most thoughtful eyes and ears of all Frenchmen of *this* century" (GS 95). The reading of Stendhal as a psychologist is strongly linked to the rediscovery of Taine and the valorization of *Beylisme*, also taken from Paul Bourget. Towards the end of Taine's Preface to his *Histoire*, Nietzsche must have read an enthusiastic judgment on Stendhal as a psychologist capable of "*analyse intime*" and of "*admirables divinations*". According to Taine, Stendhal was still obscure and paradoxical to most contemporary readers because of his original talent and "premature ideas" ("he has been considered dry and excentric, thus remaining isolated"). "He clarified the most complicated internal mechanisms, [...] he dealt with feelings as it must be done, namely as a naturalist and as a physicist, making classifications and evaluating the forces" (Taine 1878: 31).

And Taine concludes with the metaphor of philology as careful and patient reading:

> No one has better taught to open one's eyes and see, see the men around and the present life, and then to red the ancient and authentic documents, to read beyond the white and black on pages, to see under the old press, under the hazy outline of a text the exact feeling, the movement of ideas, the mood in which it had been written. (Taine 1878: 31)

Taine can be defined as the first true, enthusiastic disciple of Stendhal, and Nietzsche evaluates him as such: "Another student of Stendhal is *Taine*, the first living historian of today" (NL 1885, 38[5], KSA 11: 599).

In Paul Bourget, however, there is from the beginning an ambiguity regarding his own practice as a "psychologist", and Nietzsche detected it well in his criticism of the novel *André Cornelis*, which seems to be tyrannized by Dostoevsky's spirit.² This ambiguity gradually dissolves the impassive scientific analysis into traditionalism, which is precisely what happens with Bourget's turn from the psychological novel to the moralistic novel and then to the *roman à thèse*, the novel-thesis (*Le Disciple*, of 1889, sensationally marks the turning point.) The search for remedies for the "moral disease" of society – which Bourget had at first only described as a psychologist – will eventually prevail. In 1896 he writes in an article: "After analyzing the moral illnesses, the *duty* of the writer is to indicate remedies" (*Gazette de France*, 17 June 1896).

Developing seeds that were present since the beginning as restless "*nostalgies de la croix*", Bourget gets to the healing of the "social disease" by prescribing, as the only remedy, the Catholic religion and traditional values:

> Psychology is to ethics like anatomy to therapeutics ... a long investigation into the moral illnesses forced me to recognize the truth proclaimed by teachers with an authority far superior than mine, like Balzac, Le Play and Taine: that, for individuals as well for society, Christianity is now the only and necessary condition of health or healing. (Bourget 1993, "Préface de 1899": 442)

Thus he writes in the introduction to the second edition (1899) of his successful *Essais*. The judgment of the Danish cosmopolitan critic Georg Brandes was exemplary. Brandes praised "the security and the depth of psychological analysis" of Bourget and found inside *L'étape* (the pro-clerical novel of 1902, which was radically critical towards modernity, and supported by the *Action française*) the presence of prejudiced positions, giving to this novel a flavor of falseness. The consummate novelist was replaced by the high Catholic prelate. Brandes writes that the novel

> [...] is sometimes silly and becomes a sermon, it often drifts into marginal considerations that interpret and explain the plot, so that the reader does not fail to see the moral point. [...] No great man and no bishop could have given this kind of perspective such seductive and safe form. No Catholic *pamphlet* of this level has been published since the time of Joseph de Maistre, and it is even fun to see now the most elegant and melancholic expert and professional of the adultery in the role of a papal Zouave (1902).³

Nietzsche develops the notions of *décadence* and "physiology of art" in his active confrontation with French "psychology", therefore away from all sorts of

---

2 "*Aber es scheint, daß der Geist Dostoiewskys diesen Pariser Romanciers keine Ruhe läßt?*", "but it seems that Dostoevsky's spirit does not let go of these Parisian novelists", letter to Hyppolite Taine, 04.07.1887 KSB Bd. 8: 106, editors' translation.
3 Brandes, *Paul Bourget*, "Frankrig", in Brandes 1906: 78ff.

moralistic evaluation. He thought that the tradition and energy of the "free spirits"–the spirits opposed to the widespread and fatal "disease of the will"– lived in the followers of Stendhal (the "*rougistes*"), in Paris-*Cosmopolis*. This is shown, for example, in the letter from 11 March 1885 which he sends to Resa von Schirnhofer in Paris, and in which he invites the lady to look for the "*Rougistes*":

> There seems to be in France some sort of Stendhal-enthusiasts, I was told of some who call themselves "*Rougistes.*" I would like to ask you to scout around a little bit for them: you could, for example, try to find a new edition of *Le rouge et le noir* with a preface from a certain Mr. Chapron, if I heard correctly. Where did this fine hen (he has died) lay her eggs? There are no voluminous that he might have written. And try to make the acquaintance of the *liveliest* disciple of Stendhal, Mr. Paul Bourget, and tell me which essays he wrote recently (here in Nice I showed you his collection of essays on *psychologie contemporaine*.) As I see it, he is really the true disciple of that genius the French people only discovered forty years too late (among the Germans, I am the first to have discovered him, and without having taken a cue from France). The other famous exponents of the literature of this century, for example Sainte-Beuve and Renan, are too sweetish and wavering for me; but everything that is ironic, hard, sublimely wicked, like Mérimée,–oh what a delicious flavor for my palate! (KSB Bd.7: 18)

The expression "*rougistes*" should in fact be traced back to Léon Chapron (a friend of Bourget and editor, before his death, of a new edition of Stendhal's novel), who had the idea of founding "*un dîner des 'Rougistes'*"–that is, of "*amateurs passionnés de Rouge et Noir*" (Bourget 1889: 262). Nietzsche must have gotten the information he sends to the student Resa von Schirnhofer from Bourget's review, either directly or indirectly.

Nietzsche identifies in Stendhal, as psychologist and analyst, as he was read in those years, the most vivid representative of a strong line that started from the *idéologues*. Taine is the privileged inheritor of this tradition, or "*l'audacieux briseur des idoles de la métaphysique officielle*", according to Bourget's judgment,–and that image is significant for Nietzsche. Due to a few traits of his scientific nihilism, Taine seems able to cope with the European "disease of the will", which is epitomized by the voluptuous dilettantism of Renan ("*ce mal de douter même de son doute*"), but also by the plebeian and shameless curiosity of the romantic Sainte-Beuve (who also belongs to the "populace of the weak-will" and is therefore an opponent of Stendhal: NL 1884, 26[379], KSA 11: 251), indeed by every histrionic and demagogic bad taste, by the idealism of weakness.[4]

---

[4] The sarcastic, unforgiving, characterization of the "psychologist" Sainte-Beuve (who "so neugierig ist, so aushorcherisch, so lüstern wie er; Heimlichkeiten schnüffelnd, wie er; instinktiv die Bekanntschaft mit Menschen von Unten und Hintenher suchend, nicht viel anders als es die Hunde unter einander machen, die ja auch auf ihre Art Psychologen sind)", NL 1887–1888, 11[9],

8 Nietzsche and "the French Psychologists": Stendhal, Taine, Ribot, Bourget

There is no doubt that the image Nietzsche has of Taine owes much to the portrait drawn by Bourget: sound energy of character, invincible rigor in his internal discipline, scientific asceticism ("*la sincerité implacable de la pensée*") and, ultimately, a radical and courageous nihilism. In the Third Essay of *On the Genealogy of Morals* Nietzsche is mainly referring to Taine when he emphasizes the "intellectual cleanness" of "these hard, strict, abstinent, heroic spirits who make up the glory of our time" (GM III 24), the extreme representatives of the last mask of the ascetic ideal, the faith in "truth" and science. "Taine is the man of truth, he is veracity in person" – Renan himself said it, according to Brandes. Nietzsche took from Taine and Bourget the psychological theory – which he mentions several times from 1885 on – of the "*petits faits*" or "*petits faits vrais*". Once again, we must go back to Stendhal, the French writer who sees the novel as "*living psychology*" (Taine) and uses the expression "*petits faits vrais*". Already in the preface to *De l'intelligence,* Taine shows that "le *moi*" is made up of a series of "*small facts*". Psychology becomes a science of facts, of "*petits faits*". The dissolution of the classic subject and of the soul as "*atomon*" ("*c'est à l'âme que la science va se prendre ...*") is the central theme of the new psychological science. This is Bourget's commentary on Taine's psychology:

> "It turns to the soul, equipped with accurate and insightful tools of which three hundred years of experience have proved the correctness and measured the capacity. It brings an art, a moral, a politics, a new religion, and our concern today is to look for them!"[5] With what confidence he assigns the ideal goal of all research to the "discovery of the small facts, well-chosen, relevant, meaningful, largely detailed and meticulously known!"[6] It clear why the new generation of that time – whose deep faith he expressed through formulas that were precise like mathematical axioms and vibrant like the verses of a hymn – recognized him as the initiator, the man who saw the promised land and was telling in advance its regenerations and mysterious delights! (Bourget 1883: 217–218)

Nietzsche thinks that it is possible that the death of the soul-*atomon*–as the expression of a metaphysical need–does not lead to the sunset of the *soul*

KSA 13: 11 and NL 1885, 35[43]KSA 11: 529 derives, to a great extent, from Barbey d'Aurevilly, who speaks of "ce fureteur et ce friand littéraire qui mettait sa fine langue à tout [...]". See also TI Skirmishes 3, where the influence of the Goncourt is closer: cf. Goncourt 1887 [NB], vol. II: 66, 90, 103. The passages about Sainte-Beuve have signs of having been read by Nietzsche. But before adopting so starkly the stance of critical distance, Nietzsche had asked for and had read Ida Overbeck's translation of a few essays that Sainte-Beuve published with the publisher Schmeitzner, titled *Menschen des 18. Jahrhunderts,* and he had considered "something really worth mentioning" (*sehr Beachtenswerthes*) a review of Sainte-Beuve by George Sand that he read in her *Histoire de ma vie* (Letter to Franz Overbeck, 28.04.1880, KSB, Bd. 6: 17).

5 Taine, *L'Histoire de la littérature anglaise*, III: 611.
6 Taine 1870 I: 2.

hypothesis, but rather to the opening of a road towards "new versions and refinements" of this hypothesis: "concepts like the 'mortal soul' and 'soul as subject-multiplicity' and 'soul as a society constructed out of drives and affects' want henceforth to have civil rights in the realm of science" (BGE 12). Here, once again, Nietzsche agrees with Bourget's analysis and the new French psychology. In distancing himself from "classical" psychology and metaphysics he does not fall into a physiological-materialistic reductionism:

> Assuming that the small facts that constitute the *I* could be studied through the procedures of the experimental method and, consequently, that physiology is a science, Taine distances himself from the materialistic school, which precisely reduces the entire study of the soul to a simple chapter of physiology. Taine has seen very well that a phenomenon of consciousness, an idea for example, is the cause of another series of phenomena of consciousness, whatever the corresponding physiological change be. Therefore, even if we consider the soul as a simple function of the brain, we should however study the inner life as inner life and, from the point of view of thought, as thought. [...] From the point of view of Taine, the psychologist is interested in everything that belongs to the existence of man and can be documented. From the way to decorate a room and prepare a table, to the way to pray to God and to honor the dead, there is nothing that does not deserve to be looked at, commented on, interpreted, for there is nothing in which man does not commit something of his inner being (Bourget 1883: 218–219).

According to Nietzsche, "the human soul and its limits", its history and unexhausted possibilities, are "the predestined hunting grounds" for the psychologist (BGE 45). Bourget speaks of an "act of faith in this dark and painful, yet adorable and inexplicable reality which is the human Soul" in his preface to the *Nouveaux Essais* (Bourget 1885a: VII)[7] and in the *Essais*:

> The work of the psychologist [...] is to highlight a distinctive feature of the course of a disease of the soul. It can also be said that in the depths of every beautiful literary work lies hidden the affirmation of a great psychological truth, as in the depths of every beautiful work of painting or sculpture lies hidden a great anatomical truth (Bourget 1883: 147–148).

The French contemporary psychology (especially Ribot) studied the delicate mechanisms that allow the construction and maintenance of the *person*. This assumes that a person is complicated and fragile construction that can become a partial ruin at any given moment in time. The separated stones are the starting point for a new building that then rises quickly side by side with the old one. And Nietzsche writes: "In general, one should not presuppose that there are

---

[7] This is underlined by Nietzsche in the copy that exists in his personal library.

many human beings who are 'persons'. And in fact some are *several* persons, the great majority are *none*." (NL 1887, 10[59], KSA 12: 491–492) He thus underlines many times "the weakness of the will, the insecurity", and even the split of the "I" in "a multiplicity of 'persons'" (NL 1888, 14[113], KSA 13, 290). The widespread practice of hypnotism, conceived as a kind of "moral vivisection", allows the recovery of a side of our psychic life that is unknown to our consciousness, and thus the recovery of a psychic richness that is usually hidden by the affirmation of personal consciousness. It also provides the psychologist with a tool to wrest the unconscious from the hands of the physiologists, without making it a mystically dark entity. The psychological investigation becomes a process of analysis that is able to consider the subject as a whole, without sacrificing the observation either of its organic or of its psychic side. That also permits the reconstruction of illness and convalescence, or rather the observation of the history of their evolution. It is a kind of genealogy of a plural history: hence the affinity and often the interchangeability, in Nietzsche, of the terms "genealogist", "psychologist", "physiologist". The "moral vivisection" changes the traditional observational standards, for the overcoming of the unidimensionality of psychic life dissolves the very concept of "psychological individual": what we can read in psychic is in fact a multiplicity of stories, a multiplicity of organizations, such that valuations of health and sickness are revealed in their merely conventional/social character.[8] The central theme is the clash–heightened by civilization–between the human being and its environment. This is an important aspect of Taine's pessimism, who dreams of periods of strong energy, in the image of the healthy "beasts of prey" of the Renaissance. As for Bourget, the focus of his analysis is the disagreement between the environment and his own ideal, a disagreement which expresses the romantic weakness and discomfort of the modern world. For Bourget, Flaubert epitomizes this extreme powerlessness, this incapacity to withstand and live through the contrast between reality and ideal, this being physiologically "organized for unhappiness"[9]:

> The effect is moral crisis and torture for the heart. But the use of the word "unhealthy" is inaccurate, if it intends an opposition between a natural, normal state of the soul–a healthy one–and a corrupt, artificial one–a "unhealthy" state of the soul. Properly speaking, there are no diseases of the body, doctors say: there are only physiological states, being woeful or good, but all of them normal when you consider the human body as an apparatus in which a certain quantity of evolving matter is combined. Equally, there is

---

[8] On these notions, see Remo Bodei's original analysis (2002).
[9] See Flaubert's letter to Maxime du Camp, Croisset, 07.04.1846. Quoted by Bourget 1883: 138.

neither sickness nor health of the soul, for the non-metaphysical observer there are only psychological states: in our pain and faculties, in our virtues and vices, in our volitions and sacrifices, he sees nothing more than changing combinations, but fatal and therefore normal, obedient to the well-known laws of the association of ideas (Bourget 1883, *Essais*: 12).

There is nothing real within the *I* "*sauf la file de ses événements*;"; the *I* is nothing but the composition and decomposition of feelings, perceptions, impulses, "a stream and a bundle of nerve vibrations": "*Le moi visible est incomparablement plus petit que le moi obscur*" (H. Taine 1870: 7). The psychological reality is multiplicity. Our conscious personality – or rather, the consciousness that each of us has of his/her current state as connected to previous states – is just a small portion of our personality, if compared to that one which remains sunk within us: "*nous sommes obscurs à nous-même, notre vraie personne s'agite, s'ingénie, s'accroît, dépérit en nous à notre insu*" (Paul Bourget 1885: 142). And repeatedly – and with particular strength at the beginning of the *Genealogy* – Nietzsche declares: "We are unknown to ourselves, we men of knowledge, unknown ourselves to ourselves" (GM Preface 1).[10]

The theory of the "*petits faits vrais*" – the basis of all these psychological theories – is expressed in several of Stendhal's letters, which are quoted by Bourget (*Réflexions sur l'art du roman*: 266). We are reminded also of the title from a late novel by Bourget called *De petits faits vrais* (1930), which from the *motto* and the preface onwards specifically evokes the "*table des Beylistes*". When Nietzsche tells stories or narrates significant events that define a character or a situation, he often uses Stendhal's expression, sometimes with irony. Taine explicitly reveals his source: "*Le perfectionnement nouveau consiste à laisser là l'a priori, la philosophie pure et déductive, les méthodes mathématiques [...] C'est ce qui fait la littérature depuis Balzac et les observateurs détail significatif; c'est la théorie du petit fait (Stendhal).*" (Taine 1907, tome III: 315)

Bourget shows that pessimism is "the last word of the whole work" of Taine. The same could be said of the "naturalists", who build their novels of analysis and their literature of investigation accumulating "*documents significatifs*" and "*documents humains*". The powerlessness against "*les forces trop écrasantes*" is the result of a determinism with no escape. The very definition of Taine's theory envelops in itself "the germ of the darkest and most hopeless nihilism" (Bourget

---

10 See also Taine's position, even if he privileges the chemical-combinatory element over the genetical-dynamical: "the idea of an *I* is a product: many materials diversely elaborated contribute to its formation [...], no matter how close we can be to ourselves we can still be wrong in many ways with regard to our *I*" (Taine 1870.t. 2: 191).

1883: 235). Nietzsche reacts against this "fatalism of '*petits faits*' (*ce petit faitalisme*, as I call it)" (GM III 24) that characterizes each positivism that kneels in front of the "*petits faits*": it is an extreme form of asceticism, a religion of science that expresses confidence in the future and a sense of decadence. Nietzsche writes: "People suffer in Paris as if hit by cold Autumn winds, as if by a frost of great disillusions, as if the Winter had arrived, the last, final Winter" (NL 1885, 35[34], KSA 11: 525).[11] "The best fruit of science is the cold resignation that, pacifying and preparing the soul, reduces one's suffering to bodily pain" – Bourget wrote, quoting Taine.[12]

Nietzsche's critique is especially addressed to the tyrannical theory of the *milieu* and Taine's alleged "objectivity", which hides his preference for "strong and expressive types, also more for those who enjoy than for the puritans" (NL 1884, 26[348] KSA 11: 241). But Nietzsche certainly finds points of agreement with Taine: perfect health as a balance of forces (Goethe is the example), the valorization of Greek culture, an admiration for the "monsters of strength", from the "*condottieri*" of the Renaissance to Napoleon, etc.

Bourget's *Essais* – which influenced Nietzsche's judgments on Stendhal and Taine – also helped him define a number of issues of the crisis of his time through the exploration of central and symptomatic characters. From his "journey to Cosmopolis" – the Parisian culture expressed by a fashionable psychologist – Nietzsche evaluates the literary trends as symptoms of a more general state of health of an entire civilization.

In his analysis of "French psychology", an important role is played by the *romanciers*. Reading novels and short stories, Nietzsche develops many useful ideas for the analysis of the social crisis and crisis of values. Reading the critics he knows so well, he also discovers the affinity between the multiform French *décadence* and the "case" of Wagner.

These are the years when Nietzsche opposes the intentions of his critical philology, physiology, and genealogy to any form of predetermined, fixed, and prejudiced interpretation that refuses the patient work of deciphering. He proposes that one reads the forces that pass through the text, the forces that constitute it: to read well, to read slowly, with "caution, patience, subtlety. Philology as *ephexis* in interpretation: whether it concerns books, newspaper articles, destinies, or facts about the weather", he writes in *The Anti-Christ* (A 52). This is a "will to know", a will to go deep and stand in front of the various manifestations

---

[11] See also TI, Skirmishes of an Untimely Man 7.
[12] Bourget 1883, cit. pp. 234–235. See Taine 1877: 267.

of the complexity of the real by reading the signs of vitality and decadence of a culture, by deciphering its hieroglyphics without falsifying their sense.

This is the difference between the "psychology" of Taine ("the procedures of psychological anatomy of a researcher who looks at literature as a sign" as Bourget puts it), and the "psychology" of those collect for the sake of collecting, for the sake of idle curiosity, for example the *Colportage-Psychologie* of the Goncourt brothers, which is an expression of weakness of will and impotence (TI Skirmishes 7).

The contemporary French novel, even that of the "little *romanciers* of newspapers" and chance *boulevardiers de Paris*", is a tool for psychological analysis of the best Frenchmen, the heirs of the "old, multiform *moralistic* culture" (BGE 254), as well as a sign of the times. Nietzsche makes explicit reference to the novels of the Goncourt brothers (*Charles Demailly*; *Renée Mauperin*; *Manette Salomon*; *La Faustin*) and those of Paul Bourget (in particular *Un crime d'amour* and *André Cornelis*). The copies kept in Weimar bear numerous signs of having been read by Nietzsche. Paul Bourget is particularly aware of *"reprendre cette tradition du roman d'analyse"* which dates back to the French moralists. *La princesse of Cléves* by M.me Lafayette, *Adolphe* by Benjamin Constant, *Volupté* by Sainte-Beuve and *Dominique* of Fromentin are some of the masterpieces recognized even by Nietzsche.

Bourget writes in the Introduction to his *Essais* (1883: V–VI): "Here the artistic procedures are analyzed only as signs [...] I did not try either to discuss talents, or paint characters. My ambition was to prepare some useful notes for the historian of moral life of the second half of the French nineteenth century." Significantly, Bourget had started in 1872 with an essay on Spinoza where it is already possible to see the *romancier* interested in the analysis of the passions of love, the "psychologist" who, following Taine and Sainte-Beuve, wants to refer philosophical doctrines back to human, personal feelings: *"poèmes métaphysiques ne sont qu'une transformation suprême, comme l'efflorescence idéale de notre sensibilité."*[13] The range of his interests included the "scientific" analysis of the passions and determinism. he writes: "L'Ethique *figure parmi les ouvrages qui doivent demeurer en psychologie.*" Spinoza, in Bourget's particular, "positivist" reading, is present in the "psychologist" Taine. Bourget will only reject him in the *Disciple,* in the name of "tradition" and morality. Adrien Sixte, the determinist "master", refers to Spinoza: he desired *"étudier les sentiments humains comme le mathématicien etudie ses figures de géometrie"*. In *Physiologie*

---

[13] P. Bourget, *Le roman d'amour de Spinoza*, <<Renaissance>> 28 December 1872, in: Bourget 1912: 213.

de l' amour modern, Bourget will still find himself playing with Spinoza's *Ethics*, sometimes developing arguments *more geometrico* and citing the philosopher's analysis of jealousy (*Ethics*, III, prop. XXXV, Scholium).

As a novelist, Bourget gets his first and strong impetus from Balzac: the novel as a diagnosis of the evils of French society, the novel as an essay of psychology and sociology. For Nietzsche and Bourget, Paris and the *"vie parisienne"* represent the center of *décadence* and the privileged place of its analysis. And even the extreme will to critique (up to "vivisection") is *"une débauche comme une autre"* (*Cosmopolis*), an expression of decay and physiological weariness: reality crumbles, spontaneous life is replaced with reflection and abstract thinking. There is a direct relationship between the Bouget's "psychology" and Balzac's "physiologies" of the inhabitants of the metropolis, as both aim to grasp symptoms of psychological and physiological weariness. Balzac is an *"anatomiste"* accustomed to the halls of dissection, but according to Taine he also knows, like no one else, how to depict as *"les monstres grandioses"* and the new *"bête de proie, petites ou grandes"*. In *Notes sur Paris. Vie et opinions de M. Frédéric-Thomas Graindorge*, Taine becomes an emulator of Balzac and exercises the idleness of a psychologist (*"Pour moi, je vais dans le monde comme au théâtre, plus volontiers qu'au théâtre"*) (Taine 1877: 21) with the pessimistic analysis of the forms of life of the big city and the various masks of modern society. These images of the physiological weariness and decay of the big city quickly become commonplace in literature and, generally, in the analysis of the growing "degeneration" that Nietzsche analyzed in terms also influenced by Charles Feré, the physician of Bicêtre known for his contributions to "animal magnetism" (i.e., hypnotism) and suggestion. He also collaborated in Ribot's *Revue Philosophique*.

"The Parisian as the European extreme" (NL 1883/84, 24[25] KSA 10: 659) proliferates in Nietzsche's reading, to the point of becoming a stereotype: from Bourget's *Essais* ("the modern man, as we see him walking back and forth along the *boulevards* of Paris with his thinner members, the excessively expressive appearance of his face, his excessively acute eyes, shows clear signs of depleted blood, of reduced energy of muscles, of exaggerated nervousness. The moralist recognizes in this the work of vice. But vice is often the product of a combination of feeling with thought: it is interpreted and amplified by thought in such a way that, after a short time of confusion, the whole substance of animal life is absorbed"; Bourget 1883: 152) to the description given by the Goncourt brothers in *Renée Mauperin* (chap. XXX). Denoisel, the Parisian par excellence (*"marveilleusement formé au grand art de vivre par la pratique de la vie parisienne, il était l'homme de cette vie: il en avait les instincts, les sens, le génie"*, *"rompu à toutes les expériences de Paris"*) is compared to the savage who *"triomphe de la nature dans une forêt vierge"*). (Goncourt 1864: 176) This image comes from Balzac's metaphor that compared Paris to a "virgin forest". Nietzsche makes explicit reference to this novel in a posthumous fragment from Spring–Autumn 1884 (NL 1884, 25[112] KSA 11: 42).

Paris looks like a "greenhouse", a metaphor that appears many times in Nietzsche's writings. In such a "greenhouse" many human plants are produced in artificial conditions, even tropical ones. In Paris, Taine wrote,

> chaque amour-propre devient colossal trop de travail et trop de plaisirs: Paris est une serre surchauffée, aromatique et empestée, et au terreau âcre et concentré, qui brûle ou durcit l'homme [...] Le public est blasé, il faut crier trop haut pour qu'il écoute. Chaque artiste est comme un charlatan que la concurrence trop âpre oblige à forcer sa voix (Taine 1877: 133–135).

The expression ("*serre*"/"greenhouse") returns in the *Preface* of Edmond de Goncourt's novel *La Faustin*: "*je veux faire un roman qui sera simplement une étude psychologique et physiologique de jeune fille, grandie élevée et dans la serre chaude d'une capital, un roman bâti sur des documents humains*". (Edmond de Goncourt 1882: II)

Paris, the great experimental laboratory of values, necessarily produces waste material of great interest for the "psychologist:" the decadents, the extreme products of an age of transition, unable to rule and order the multiple contradictory instincts that constitute them as children of modernity. Nietzsche analyzes and fights the multiform expressions of a *décadence* which is historically defined, and which involves discomfort and rejection of the "average" man: *décadence* as exoticism, as cosmopolitanism, as the cult of the innocent and the primitive, as the religion of suffering, as Tolstoyism, as Wagnerism as an opiate, as Buddhism, etc. Many of these guises of *décadence* are represented in the "figures" of the superior man in the fourth part of *Zarathustra*.

The issues discussed here – which are central for the last Nietzsche – are popularized by the naturalist and decadent literature of the fashionable novels, in Bourget's successful *Essais*, clinical cases from the big city. Multiple and plural souls are the protagonists of Bourget's novels: already *L'irréparable* (1884) is presented as a study of the multiplicity of the I. This novel includes an implicit reference to Ribot, who appers as a professor of psychology (the author of a work called "De la dissociation des idées, *où il a étudié les maladies de la volonté*") and explains to Bourget his theories about the complexity of the *I* as a complexity of the body, and thus the relationship between the *I* and the unconscious (Bourget 1928: 3–4). In Bourget, we find the loss of a center, the lack of a dominant instinct capable of giving order, the "disease of the will" as *le mal du siècle*: the evaluation of an entire generation. There is the generalized feeling that one is living in a period of radical crisis of values, in a society sentenced to death.

In Nietzsche, the ambivalent attitude toward *décadence* points to the will to a "great health", which is to contain "the sick character-traits of the century, but counterbalancing them with a superabundant, plastic, restoring force" (NL 1885–1886, 2[81] KSA 12: 100).

> This fate falls henceforth on Europe, that her strongest children arrive late and rarely to their spring–, that in most cases they perish already young, already disgusted, wintered, darkened, precisely because they have drunk to the last drop, with all the passion of their strength, the cup of disappointment – and that is today the cup of *knowledge*: and they would not be the strongest if they were not the most disappointed! For this is the test of their strength: only through the whole disease of our time can they come to *their* health. *Late* spring is their mark [...]. (NL 1887, 6[24], KSA 12: 241–242)

References

Bodei, Remo (2002) *Destini personali. L'età della colonizzazione delle coscienze*, Milan: Feltrinelli.
Bourget, Paul (1883) *Essais de psychologie contemporaine*, Paris: Lemerre.
Bourget, Paul (1885a) *Nouveaux Essais de psychologie contemporaine*, Paris: Lemerre.
Bourget, Paul (1885b) "Amiel", in: *Nouveaux Essais*, Paris: Lemerre, 251–304.
Bourget, Paul (1889) "Réflexions sur l'art du roman", in: *Études et Portraits* I, Paris: Lemerre, 261–279.
Bourget, Paul (1912) *Pages de critique et de doctrine*, tome I, Paris: Plon.
Bourget, Paul (1928) *L'irréparable*, Paris: Plon.
Bourget, Paul (1930) *De petits faits vrais*, Paris: Plon.
Bourget, Paul (1993) *Essais de psychologie contemporaine. Etudes littéraires*, ed. A. Guyaux, Paris: Gallimard.
Brandes, Georg (1906) *Samlede Skrifter*, tome XVI, Copenhagen: Gyldendal.
Goncourt, Edmond and Jules de (1864) *Renée Mauperin*, Paris: Charpentier.
Goncourt, Edmond and Jules de (1887) *Journal*, vol. II, Paris: Charpentier.
Goncourt, Edmond de (1882) *La Faustin*, Paris: G. Charpentier.
Stendhal (Henri Beyle) (1857) *De l'amour*, Paris: Michel Lévy.
Taine, Hippolyte (1863–1864) *Histoire de la littérature anglaise*, vol. 4, Paris: Hachette.
Taine, Hippolyte (1870) *De l'intelligence*, vol. 2, Paris: Hachette.
Taine, Hippolyte (1877) *Notes sur Paris. Vie et opinions de M. Frédéric-Thomas Graindorge*, Paris: Hachette.
Taine, Hyppolite (1878) *Geschichte der englischen Literatur*. Erster Band: *Die Anfänge und die Renaissance-Zeit der englischen Literatur*. Bearbeitet und mit Anmerkungen versehen von Leopold Katscher, Leipzig: E. J. Günther [BN].
Taine, Hippolyte (1907) *Sa vie et sa correspondance*, 4 Bde., hg. von Victor Giraud, Paris: Hachette.

Maria Cristina Fornari

9 Social Ties and the Emergence of the Individual: Nietzsche and the English Perspective

1 Introduction

Nietzsche's reading of the "Englishmen" (the Darwinists, evolutionists and utilitarians who were so popular in the European philosophical scene at the time) has been well established by recent literature.[1] Yet the importance of the "Englishmen" is perhaps not sufficiently emphasized, because people continue to put too much faith in Nietzsche's own declarations of hostility towards the debates of this "philosophy of merchants" which, rather than progress on a theoretical and moral path, is content with sanctioning what exists and proclaiming as absolute and originary the gregarious values of the herd. In fact, however, contact with English philosophy – in particular Spencer and the constellation of authors associated with him – changes Nietzsche's perspective about the nature and origin of morality, but also plays a role in his elaboration of the notions of subject, individual and human "type", as I will try to show.

Early on Nietzsche is led down the path of the new Anglo-Saxon philosophy by Paul Rée, a young Prussian whom he considers "an Englishman" due to his empiricism and scientific passion. From 1875 onwards – around the time their friendship began – Nietzsche dropped his philological focus and developed a passion for scientific and anthropological readings, which were much more effective and concrete than the metaphysical mists of traditional German philosophy. The primordial Darwinian man, with his wealth of ancestral behaviours and needs, comes to replace the transcendental subject or Schopenhauer's individual genius. For a short period, Nietzsche's joint reflections with Paul Rée even made him conceive of morality as originating in its usefulness for the social group, and of the individual as the safeguarder of the group itself.

But this historical conception of the individual soon gave way to more theoretical considerations. In light of the awareness of the I as a prism and as a com-

---

[1] Cf., for example, Moore 2002, Fornari 2006, Brobjer 2008.

pound, instead of a monolithic and irreducible core, Nietzsche reflects upon the world of drives that constitute it, and that either strengthen or destroy it. He is helped here by Herbert Spencer who, with his doctrine of an individual perfectly adapted to the environment, conceives a new type of human being, established in drives that Spencer himself (and not nature, as he would have us believe) considers essential for the development of mass society: altruism, goodness and benevolence.[2]

Spencer's theory has a heuristic significance that Nietzsche unveils brilliantly: the hypothesis that is taken in advance – that nature's goal is to increase life – aims to promote values that could nourish an already weakened modernity. Nietzsche does not accept this individual, so determined as to possess fixed altruistic devices even in the species' organic structure; so homogeneous and interchangeable as to constitute a useful member of a collective body; so other-directed as to aspire to a future society in which the goal of the individual and that of the community will coincide in a state of perfect harmony and happiness. These are the results of the application of Spencer's evolutionism to the newly formed French sociology (Espinas, Fouillée, Guyau), which effectively extends the paradigms of biology and physiology to politics and state theory.

Nietzsche recognizes in this depersonalization the main moral tendency of his time, and does not cease to fight it as a symptom of vital exhaustion. In order to create a contrast with the gregarious individual – who is unable to acknowledge the relativity of his own scale of values –, Nietzsche gives shape to a plural subject that continuously creates the table of his own values and priorities. The *Overman* – who is able to sustain in himself many perspectives – counterbalances the human type outlined by evolutionism.

English philosophy (taken *lato sensu*) is therefore far from marginal in Nietzsche's reflections with regard to the formation of the individual and the subject. As is often the case with Nietzsche, what at first glance looks like a moment of pure opposition is actually the result of an intense confrontation and fruitful dialogue with his own references.

---

[2] "The value of altruism is *not* the outcome of science, but instead men of science are misled by the ruling instinct of today into believing that science confirms the desire of their instinct (see Spencer)": NL Winter 1880–1881, 8[35], KSA 9: 390, continued in NL Spring–Autumn 1881, 11[98], KSA 9: 476: "In every instant in the conditions of a being countless ways of its *development* are open: the ruling instinct does not approve any of them except the one which is on the way to its ideal. Thus, the image Spencer makes of the future of man does not constitute a scientific necessity, but is instead a *desire* drawn from current ideals."

2 Individual and community

The first meaning of *subjectivity* that deserves to be taken into account and which Nietzsche is engaged with since the early years is without doubt the one that refers to *individuality*. The dialectic between individual and community was always among Nietzsche's key interests even before *Human, All Too Human*. After having abandoned the idealistic projects shared with Richard Wagner for a rebirth of myth through art – which aimed to promote a community centred on the figure of the genius –,[3] Nietzsche reconsiders the individual-community relationship in light of a naturalistic and evolutionary dynamics, particularly from the anthropological perspective which emerged in the 1870s, and which is known to Nietzsche through the reading of, amongst others, Bagehot, Tylor, Lubbock, and Carey.[4] Without excluding the validity of the Darwinian hypothesis, according to which the social instinct predominates and paves the way for the altruistic drives, Nietzsche considers that the relation between the individual and the tribe or group is explained by the latter's need for self-preservation, and he conceives the writing of the table of moral values as something designed for this purpose.[5] Just as happens in most animal groups, the individual cannot rely on his own individual experiences if it is to survive in a world that is hostile and difficult to cope with. Since idiosyncratic behaviour puts the whole community in danger, it is only natural that the individual that attempts to go alone wounds up being stigmatized and ostracized.

However, in one of the rare fragments explicitly devoted to Darwinism, Nietzsche already acknowledges the risks associated with the fixity of a type:

> *On Darwinism.* The more the human being has a sense of community, sympathetic affections, the more he is attached to his tribe: and the tribe is best preserved where individuals

---

[3] On these issues cf., above all, Campioni 1979, Barbera/Campioni 2010.
[4] In Nietzsche's library (henceforth: NB): J. Lubbock, *Die Entstehung der Civilisation und der Urzustand des Menschengeschlechts*, Jena 1875. On Bagehot and Carey see *infra*, notes 8 and 12. As regards E.B. Tylor, Nietzsche had at least consulted *Die Anfänge der Cultur*, Leipzig 1873, at the library of the University of Basel in June 1875.
[5] "The unegoistic drive is perhaps a late development of the social instinct; in any event, the inverse is not true. The social instinct arises from the constraint exerted from interest for another being (the slave for his master, the soldier for his leader) or from fear, with its recognition that we need to cooperate so that we do not perish individually. This feeling, inherited, arises later, without the original motive coming at the same time to consciousness; it has become a need that looks out for an opportunity to become active. To care for others, for a community, for an issue (like science) appears then to be unegoistic, but at bottom it was not" (NL Spring – Summer 1877, 23[32], KSA 8: 415).

are more devoted to it. Here good and courageous customs are reinforced, here the subordination of the individual is learned, the character is educated and strengthened. – But here the danger of stability, stultification, is great. Untethered, much more insecure and *weaker* individuals that try new and many things are those on which progress depends: countless among them perish without consequence, but in general they loosen things up and in this way they weaken from time to time the stabile element, they introduce something new in a place that has grown weaker. The new element will be gradually assimilated by the collective, which on the whole remains intact. The degenerative natures, the slight degenerations are of paramount importance. Wherever progress should occur, a weakening must have preceded it. (NL 1875, 12[22], KSA 8: 257)[6]

Nietzsche is already convinced here, as he will be more and more as time goes by (up to the *Anti-Darwin* fragments from 1888),[7] that the determinant principle is not the struggle for existence. Rather, in addition to the necessary stability of the social group, the presence of weak and degenerative elements, which are able to accommodate and assimilate the infection of the new, is even more necessary for some sort of evolution (which Nietzsche calls the "ability to reach higher goals"):

The weaker nature, as well as the nobler, at least freer one, makes possible all progress. A people that has in any way grown weaker and disintegrates, but that on the whole is still strong: that people can receive and assimilate the infection of the new. Likewise the individual person: the problem of education is to bestow on an individual so much firmness and strength that he, as a whole, cannot be brought from his path. But then the teacher has to inflict wounds on him: and if thus the pain, the need, has arisen, something new and noble can be inoculated here. The total force will accept this in itself and thus be ennobled. (NL 1875, 12[22], KSA 8: 257)

Similarly, in his *Physics and Politics*,[8] after illustrating the ways in which groups gain stability,[9] Bagehot denounced the danger inherent in the fixity of custom:

---

[6] In a subsequent note, this fragment is given the title: "On the value of inflicting wounds" and refers to the significant aphorism 224 of *Human, All Too Human*: "Ennoblement through degeneration".

[7] These are the two long notes NL 1888, 14[123] and 14[133], KSA 13: 303 and 315, from the Spring of 1888 that are preparatory to the eponymous section of *Twilight of the Idols* (TI, Skirmishes of an Untimely Man 14).

[8] In NB the German translation with the title *Der Ursprung der Nationen. Betrachtungen über den Einfluss der natürlichen Zuchtwahl und der Vererbung auf die Bildung politischer Gemeinwesen* (Bagehot 1874). At the end of 1879, Nietzsche was still asking his publisher to inform him of "all that exists in German from Bagehot" (letter to Ernst Schmeitzner, 28.12.1879, KSB 5, 474).

[9] "Man, being the strongest of all animals, differs from the rest; he was obliged to be his own domesticator; he had to tame himself. And the way in which it happened was, that the most obedient, the tamest tribes are, at the first stage in the real struggle of life, the strongest and the conquerors. All are very wild then; the animal vigour, the savage virtue of the race has died out in none; and all have enough of it. But what makes one tribe – one incipient tribe, one bit of a tribe –

> What is most evident is not the difficulty of getting a fixed law, but getting out of a fixed law; not of cementing (as upon a former occasion I phrased it) a cake of custom, but of breaking the cake of custom; not of making the first preservative habit, but of breaking through it, and reaching something better. (Bagehot 2007: 40)[10]

The history of modern civilization does not begin until after this emancipation.

Even for the U.S. economist Henry Carey, society consists of combinations resulting from the existence of differences, from the presence of different individualities among the individuals that compose it. The more perfect the proportion to each other is (which Carey defines in chemical terms as "the law of definite proportions"), the more the ability increases to coordinate efforts. Carey's point of view–similar to that of Mill, which Nietzsche criticized as typical of a "market society"[11]–aimed at a "gregarious" cohesion, in which the human purpose of engaging in commercial exchanges might accomplish the highest union of man with his fellow man.[12]

Therefore, already by the time of *Human, All Too Human*, Nietzsche is interested in the development of single individuals, for whom, however, permanence in a stable structure seems to be a necessary requirement. If it is true that, as part of a whole, we share its living conditions and assimilate its experiences and judgements, and even if we feel that our existence is supremely and maximally justified only as function of a whole,[13] it does not follow that we necessarily have to live subjugated to the collective body. The interesting hypothesis Nietzsche will put forward shortly thereafter, prompted by the reading of Wilhelm Roux,[14] goes in the opposite direction. The ties and judgements acquired in the social context are, according to this hypothesis, the force that *propels* the emergence of the individual, once a supervenient change turns these ties and judgements inapplicable to a new context.[15]

---

to differ from another is their relative faculty of coherence." (Bagehot 2007: 39; German trans.: Bagehot 1874: 61)

10 This passage is missing from the German translation.

11 See D 174 and D 175.

12 See H.C. Carey, *Lehrbuch der Volkswirtschaft und Socialwissenschaft*, 2nd edition, Vienna 1870, NB. *Die Grundlagen der Socialwissenschaft*, Munich 1863 (which Nietzsche certainly knew: see Fornari 2009: 320).

13 Cf. NL Spring–Autumn 1881, 11[185], KSA 9: 513.

14 W. Roux, *Der Kampf der Theile im Organismus. Ein Beitrag zur Vervollständigung der mechanischen Zweckmässigkeitslehre* (Roux 1881), NB (lost). See for example NL Spring–Summer 1883, 7[98], KSA 10: 275, again from Roux: "All states and communities are something *lower* to the individual, but nonetheless necessary forms of his *higher cultivation*."

15 Commenting on some brief passages by Spinoza drawn from the sixth volume of the *Geschichte der neueren Philosophie* by Kuno Fischer (1880), Nietzsche, regarding the instinct of

When social ties collapse, a conflict breaks out among everything we had assimilated. It is then that

> the human being must suffer all the way down inside himself the effects of the social organism, must atone for what does not serve a purpose in the conditions of existence and in the judgments and experiences that were suitable *for the whole*, and finally comes to create *his own possibility of existence as an individual*, through a reorganization, assimilation and excretion of instincts in himself. For the most part these *experiment-individuals* perish. (NL Spring-Autumn 1881, 11[182], KSA 9: 509)

This "awakened individual" who, in self-defence, aspired to assimilate the opinions of the ruling ones, has found motives for his liberation precisely in his submission to the community. In the community, he learns self-respect, he proves now to be ready to fight "for his own existence, for his new taste, for his relatively *unique* position in relation to everything – deems it better than the overall taste and despises the latter. He wants to dominate" (NL Spring – Autumn 1881, 11[156], KSA 9: 500), although he is destined to succumb to the anarchy of drives that he still does not know how to control. Therefore, his inclusion in a collective organism is vital as this represents "a preliminary stage of egoism, not its opposite" (NL Spring – Autumn 1881, 11[185], KSA 9: 513).

This interesting hypothesis is not further developed. Only seldom will Nietzsche speak of the collective organism in positive terms as conducive to the birth of the individual, developing instead a dialectic of strong opposition between them, as we shall see.[16] However, Nietzsche has difficulties in defining

---

preservation, states: "On the contrary, I: the primitive egoism, the herd instinct, are older than the 'will to self-preservation.' First the human being is developed as a *function*: from here, the individual is, in turn, detached as a result, in that he, *as a function*, comes to KNOW and incorporates progressively countless conditions of the *whole*, of the organism" (NL Spring – Autumn 1881, 11[193], KSA 9: 517).

16 We should bear in mind, however, the fragment 11[286] from November 1887 – March 1888, in which, under the rubric "Morphology of *self-esteem*", Nietzsche clearly summarizes this path: "First viewpoint: to what extent *feelings of sympathy and community* are the lower, preparatory stage at a time when personal self-esteem and individual initiative in evaluation are not yet possible. Second viewpoint: to what extent the *height of collective self-esteem*, pride in the distinction of the *clan* [...] is a school for individual self-reliance; that is, in so far as it compels the individual to *represent* the pride of the whole ... He has to speak and act with extreme respect for himself in so far as he represents the community in his own person ... Also when the individual feels like the *instrument* and *mouthpiece of the deity*. Third viewpoint: to what extent these forms of *depersonalization* in fact give the person a tremendous importance, in so far as higher powers employ him; religious awe before oneself the condition of the prophet and poet. Fourth viewpoint: to what extent responsibility for the whole *trains* the individual to, and *permits* him, a broad view, a stern and terrible hand, a circumspection and coolness, a grandeur of bearing and gesture, which he

theoretically this individual, and regards it rather as a "pragmatical" representation of multiple instincts.[17] This occurs especially after being critically challenged, from the early 1880s onwards, by the fixity of type decreed both by English psychology and philosophy, whose scientific method and anti-metaphysical outlook greatly interested him. The "plural individual"–the individual "beyond I and You"–is what Nietzsche will oppose to the egoistic perspective of the gregarious man as a perspective unable to acknowledge the need for multiple perspectives.

3 A plural subject

In *Human, All Too Human*, Nietzsche chooses to avail himself, in his philosophical and moral investigations, of the "advantages of psychological observation".[18] In the process of unmasking ideals, values and hardened behaviours, the subject and the individual are unveiled in their real emotional and instinctual elements. For example, many aphorisms are dedicated to compassion – one of the most important themes in Schopenhauer's ethics–, and their aim is to reveal compassion as the outcome of the play of drives, and hence as anything but a proof of the altruistic character of the human soul.[19]

On the basis of the conflict of drives, the painful alienation of the ascetic is also explained. In his irrepressible thirst for power, he exercises his tyranny upon himself, in the absence of other objects, by sacrificing a part of himself to himself, in a challenge in which he is both victim and torturer. What in him seems altruism and sublime sacrifice is nothing but the expression of a self-division of the "I", which tyrannically demands something from itself.[20]

---

would not permit himself on his own behalf. *In summa:* collective self-esteem is the great preparatory school for personal sovereignty." But a last consideration is enough to mark the distance: "The noble class is that which inherits this training" (NL 1887–1888, 11[286] KSA 13: 111, Kaufmann's translation).

[17] The individual, once emerged from the crowd with his idiosyncratic taste, is forced to discover himself as "ephemeral", unable to stop the flux of his instincts. Nietzsche realizes that "there is no individual, that in the more fleeting of instants he is something different from the next, and that his conditions of existence are that of an immense number of individuals" (cf. NL Spring – Autumn 1881, 11[156], KSA 9: 500).

[18] See HH 35 and HH 36.

[19] Cf. HH 50, 103; cf. also D 133.

[20] Isaiah Berlin's retrieval of this dynamic is interesting. As is well known, he views it as one of the possible degenerations of the concept of positive liberty. Cf. Berlin 1958.

In the relevant aphorism from *Human, All Too Human* called "Morality as the self-division of man", we find Nietzsche opposing the prejudice of the unitary "I" and describing, in accordance with the latest models of scientific psychology, various levels of personality in conflict, thereby evincing signs of a striking modernity:

> the I is not the position of a being in regard to several others (instincts, thoughts, etc.). The ego is rather a plurality of personal forces, of which sometimes one, sometimes the other, comes to the fore as *ego* and looks to the others as a subject to an influential and determinant outside world. The subject bounces around, it is likely that we feel the degrees of forces and instincts as proximity and distance and interpret as a landscape and surface what in fact is a plurality of degrees of quantity. (NL Autumn 1880, 6[70], KSA 9: 211)

Nietzsche had already taken an interesting cue from Friedrich Albert Lange, who, quoting from Goethe's *Morphology*, had brought his conclusions near "the standpoint to which all our recent discoveries are forcibly carrying us":

> "Every living thing" he teaches "is not a single thing, but a plurality, even in so far as it appears to us as an individual, it still remains a collection of living independent beings, which in idea and disposition are the same, but phenomenally may become the same or similar, other or dissimilar. Those beings are partly connected from their origin, partly find each other and combine. They divorce themselves and seek themselves again, and so effect an endless production in all ways and in all directions. The more imperfect the creature is, the more are these parts the same or similar, and the more they resemble the whole". (Lange 1887 [1875]: 579–580; Eng. trans. of the 1875 edition: Lange 1881: 38)

Nietzsche, for whom "in morality man treats himself not as *individuum* but as *dividuum*" (HH 57), shows his interest in this passage by drawing a visible line at the margin of the first paragraph.[21]

Among the first to acknowledge the fragmentation and changeable nature of the *moi* is also Hippolyte Taine, lauded by Nietzsche. Taine wrote in his *De l'intelligence* (1870):

> man as whole appears as a hierarchy of centres of sensation and impulses, each with their initiative, their functions and their sphere, under the government of a more perfect centre that receives from them local data, sends them general injunctions and does not differ from them except for its more complex organization, its wider action and its higher rank. (Taine 1914 [1870], I: 8, editors' translation).

---

[21] Nietzsche also marks the reference to Virchow, which follows immediately, as one who "must be counted among the men who, by means of positive research and a theory full of sagacity, have helped us to understand the relation among beings whose intimate community forms the 'individual'" (Lange 1887 [1875]: 580).

and:

> From this [psychological] point of view, one realizes that the self has no reality, except the series of its events; that these, although having different aspects, have the same nature and may be all reduced to sensations; that sensation for itself, when considered from the outside and by that indirect way called external perception, may be reduced to a group of molecular movements. A flux and a bundle of sensations and impulses, which, viewed from the other side, are also a flux and a bundle of nervous vibrations: that is the spirit. (Taine 1914 [1870], I: 7, editors' translation)

For Taine, the *moi* is nothing but a metaphysical ghost, a bundle of relations that should not be substantialized, one of the mere 'verbal entities' that have entered almost all regions of nature, in particular the two extremes of science:

> in psychology with the notion of the self and its faculties; in the preliminary parts of physics with the notion of matter and its primitive forces. Hitherto, this illusion has obstructed psychology, especially in France; one has applied oneself to observe the pure self; one has attempted to see in the faculties "the causes which produce the soul's phenomena"; one has studied reason, the faculty which produces ideas of the infinite and discovers necessary truths; and the will, the faculty which produces free resolutions. One has, thus, made nothing but a science of words. (Taine 1914 [1870], I: 346–348)

In Taine we can easily recognize strong echoes of Hume and an obvious debt to James Stuart Mill, in particular to his *System* of Logic. Taine urges a return to Condillac and Mill and his English successors as the way to progressively attain a rigorous science of the facts.[22]

Even consciousness, the most mysterious of the organic phenomena, is for Taine explained by the flux of sensations, and its description is not far from

---

[22] There is a profound convergence of interests between Taine and English philosophy. Already in 1882, Taine endorses Locke, Berkeley and Hume for having provided metaphysics with a psychology, but a major turning point occurs when he becomes aware of John Stuart Mill: "In Europe, at present, the scene is empty. The Germans adapt and reshape the old French materialism. The French listen from habit, but somewhat wearily and distractedly, to the scraps of melody and eloquent commonplace which their instructors have repeated to them for the last thirty years. In this deep silence, and from these dull mediocrities, a master comes forward to speak. Nothing of the sort has been seen since Hegel" (Taine 1864: 7–8; Eng. trans.: Taine 1870: viii–ix). This study was later published in the third part of *Histoire de la littérature anglaise*, which exists in Nietzsche's library (NB) in a German translation; *Geschichte der englischen Literatur*, Leipzig 1878–80.

The Spencerian Alfred Fouillée argued for the persistence of the subject, a more or less latent consciousness in the apparent fragmentation of the I, explained by the play of sensations, images and thoughts, which are, however, submitted to the final "centralizing" action of the brain (La science sociale contemporaine, Paris 1880, NB, p. 218ff.).

Nietzsche's, as a domain from which we perceive only the higher levels: "peaks illuminated in a continent whose depths remain in the shadow" (Taine 1914 [1870], I: 283)[23] Nietzsche will later become acquainted with studies on changes of personality conducted with great success by French physiological psychology (especially Bernard, Ribot and Féré).[24] From the latter emerges more and more the conception of a plural "I" that can be lived as unitary only in an exceptional and fictitious way. By analysing psychopathological disorders of personality, these studies contribute to a new definition of consciousness and the subject. The latter are regarded as an outcome of a dynamic equilibrium, always on the verge of disintegration. The I, a synthetical function *par excellence*, is now an unstable compound, continually threatened by fragmentation, and its "normality" is just the outcome of a temporary compromise between the energies at play.

Consciousness and subjectivity itself, as investigated from the point of view of scientific psychology, result from a full admission of their biological and material conditioning. Interesting attempts at an interpretation of what was later labelled the *mind-body problem* take shape here. This was a problem which Taine and Alexander Bain, for example, did not believe to be that difficult to solve. Arguments in favour of two substances – a material and an immaterial substance that might be able to connect with each other in a vague and indefinite way – were no longer compatible with science and a clear way of thinking.[25]

In the early 1880 s, Nietzsche moves along a similar path. Reflecting on the nature and origin of morality (his main interest at the time), he then seems to abandon the merely descriptive (or, should we say, socio-anthropological) investigation typical of *Human, All Too Human* in favour of a "physiology of

---

23 Also interesting is the passage on p. 352, in which Taine compares the groups of rudimentary sensations, of which we are not conscious, to "rudimentary souls", and "just as the nervous apparatus is a system of organs in different states of complexity, so the *psychological individual would be a system of souls in different stages of development*" (italics mine). Compare with BGE 19, where the body is defined by Nietzsche as a "society constructed out of many souls".
24 "It was also through the direct or indirect mediation of these readings that the German philosopher arrived at the plural structure of the 'I,' at the genealogical construction of the subject, at in the search for a 'new centre.' Psychological reality is multiple: its strong dynamism does not lead to a spontaneous harmony between its parts, being rather the outcome of a hegemonic activity of one of the parts over the others. Nietzsche could thus reach the conclusion that the source of the will lies in biological actions accomplished in the most profound intimacy of our tissues: to such an extent it is true to say that the former is we ourselves" (Campioni 2001: 46).
25 See A. Bain, *Mind and Body* (1873); German trans. *Geist* und *Körper. Die Theorien über ihre gegenseitigen Beziehungen*, Leipzig 1874, NB, p. 158. Still in Nietzsche's library (NB), A. Bain, *Erziehung als Wissenschaft*, Leipzig 1880, with numerous underscores.

morality", which is inseparable from his relation to English philosophy, especially Spencer's evolutionism.

The confrontation with Spencer, which begins in the Spring of 1880 with the careful reading of *The Base of Ethics* in German translation,[26] leads Nietzsche to a more overtly biological account of moral issues – particularly through the idea of an individual adapted to the environment and perfectly suited to the purposes of the species –, as well as to a reflection on the complex world of the instincts or drives (*Triebe*). For Nietzsche, these drives are not characterized by their being directed towards the achievement of well-defined goals, but rather by their having a movement and direction which cannot be clearly determined.

Spencer, a "glorifier of the purposiveness of selection" (Spring – Autumn 1881, 11[43], KSA 9: 457), believes he knows the favourable circumstances for the development of an organic being. His modern temperament ("Mr. Herbert Spencer is a *décadent*"),[27] which celebrates the altruistic and benevolent instinct, has given life to a version of the "type-man" that discards as "non-adaptive" the whole world of multiple drives which impel the individual in too many directions and fail to be justified as useful.[28] Spencer's adaptation mutilates those characteristics of the individual that, not finding an immediate purpose, may *eventually* yield the most beautiful results; whereas it is clear that the purpose of the individual is for Nietzsche only "*a hypothesis*, a more or less arbitrary *program*", on the basis of the brief and casual knowledge he has of his own self.[29] Nietzsche warns us that man understands only a little of himself and nothing is more incomplete than our knowledge of the drives that constitute our nature. The individual will hardly be able to name them – their number and strength, their ebb and flow, their reciprocal interplay amongst each other, all of that remains completely unknown.[30]

It will be with a direct look at the "uneconomical" unfolding of the drives that Nietzsche will therefore pursue his investigations regarding the individual

---

[26] *Die Tatsache der Ethik* (Spencer 1879), NB. Also by Spencer, Nietzsche had already acquired, in August 1875, *Einleitung in das Studium der Sociologie*, Leipzig 1875. For an in-depth analysis of Nietzsche's relation to Spencer's evolutionism allow me to refer to my (2006).
[27] TI, Skirmishes of an Untimely Man 37.
[28] "'Useful-harmful!' 'Utilitarian!' Behind these empty words lies the prejudice that the direction in which the human (or even animal, plant) is to be developed has been settled. As if thousands of developments, beginning at any point, were not possible! As if the decision on which is the best, the highest, was not a mere matter of taste" (NL Spring – Autumn 1881, 11 [106], KSA 9: 479).
[29] Cf. NL Autumn 1880, 6[148], KSA 9: 234; NL Spring – Autumn 1881, 11[73], KSA 9: 469; NL Spring 1880 – Spring 1881, 10[D60], KSA 9: 426; NL Spring – Autumn 1881, 11[37], KSA 9: 559.
[30] See D 119; NL Autumn 1880, 6[18], KSA 9: 197.

and subjectivity.³¹ His reflection is, as mentioned, influenced by the contemporary debate that in those years was being intensified and transformed, due not only to the contribution of psychology, but also to the latest studies on the nature of protoplasm and cellular organisms.

Although he often professed his ignorance,³² Nietzsche actually shows some knowledge of the latest developments in science and is ready to address the most recent questions, though always with a view to their transposition into the philosophical and moral field. Suffice to think of his reading of the biologist Karl Semper, whose monograph from 1880 moves in the direction of a refutation of Spencer's teleology – a refutation that Nietzsche immediately adopts; or of his reading of Wilhelm Roux (already mentioned above), who replaced the idea of adaptation to the environment with the idea of an evolution of organic parts according to an "internal principle", taking place in the form of a constant struggle for space and nourishment.³³ It is perhaps no coincidence that one of the most explicit definitions of "will to power" – as a constant activity of formation and transformation with no preformed purpose or predetermined outcome – is located in a paragraph of the *Genealogy* that calls Spencer into question, particularly his concept of "adaptation" (GM II 12).

Thus, "will to power" is the name Nietzsche gives to our appropriative and interpretative processes, to the "subject" supposed to initiate new acts of creation and ordering of the world. But how can the notion of the "subject" be restored in the dynamics of the *Wille zur Macht*? Already for Foucault, as is well known, the greatest strength of Nietzsche's project lies in not aspiring to a *refoundation* of the subject,³⁴ which ceases to be conceived as a simple and immutable essence. Every individual is nothing but a changing unit of organization, and even the individual body [*Leib*] is merely an activity that posits asymmetries and differences.³⁵

---

31 On these topics the study of A. Orsucci (1992) is essential.
32 "Said in secret: the little work I can do with my eyes is now turned, almost exclusively, to studies of physiology and medicine (of which I know so little! – and there are many things that I must truly *know!*)" (letter to F. Overbeck, 20/21.08.1881, KSB 6: 116).
33 K. Semper, *Die natürlichen Existenzbedingungen der Thiere. Zweiter und Erster Theil*, Leipzig 1880 (NB); W. Roux, *Der Kampf der Theile im Organismus* (Roux 1881).
34 "Where the soul pretends unification or the self fabricates a coherent unity, the genealogist sets out to study the beginning – numberless beginnings whose faint traces and hints of color are readily seen by an historical eye. The analysis of descent permits the dissociation of the self, its recognition and displacement as an empty synthesis, in liberating a profusion of lost events." (Foucault 1971: 145 – 172; Eng. trans.: Foucault 1977: 145 – 146).
35 "We have forbidden ourselves today to fable of 'unity', of 'soul,' of 'person': with such hypotheses one makes the problem more difficult, that much is clear. And even those tiny living

The definition of this new subjectivity is the focus of numerous research interests that emphasize Nietzsche's attempts to undermine traditional psychology. The latter is an ally of metaphysics and morals, because it preserves the principle of identity and the "subject" as the centre of gravity of action and evaluation.[36] The destruction of this alliance, with which morality has infected and affected the experience of the self, is an essential step for the achievement of the transvaluation of values and the *Overman*.[37] One possible hypothesis is that the Overman represents no more than a *Lebensform* opposed to the overwhelming power of the herd-instinct – a form of life capable of breaking with instinctual atavisms and reorganising its cognitive and perceptual apparatuses around new and unusual perspectives.

4 A functional subject

Whereas psychology and morality want a free and responsible subject, sociology on the other hand wants it adapted and functional. In the light of positivist ideas, evolutionist and utilitarian English and organicist sociologists, supporters of Spencerism (Alfred Fouillée, Jean-Marie Guyau, Alfred Espinas) seeking general well-being, impose alleged "natural" purposes on the individual by integrating it in collective structures and turning it into a useful function of the whole, rather than aspiring to the real emancipation of the individual.

This view was also supported by biology, by now aware of the gregarious nature of tissues and cells. This idea of "colonial" formations, in which the individual element was a function of the survival of the whole, suggested that such a model could also be transferred to the social and political dimensions.

---

creatures, which constitute our body (more correctly: what we call 'body' is the best simile of their interaction –), are not for us soul-atoms, but rather something that grows, fights, reproduces and dies again: so that their number is variably changing, and our life is like all life a constant dying. There is in man so many 'consciousnesses' as there are beings that, at every moment of its existence, constitute his body." (NL 1884–1885, 37[4], KSA 11: 576) Thus Klossowski: "But what then is the *identity* of the self? It seems to depend on the *irreversible history* of the body, a linkage of causes and effects. But this linkage is pure appearance. The body is constantly being modified so as to form one and the same physiognomy; and it is only when the resources for the body's rejuvenation are impoverished that the person becomes fixed, and its *'character'* hardens" (Klossowski 1975: 54–55; Eng. trans.: Klossowski 1997: 29).

36 See, amongst others, Schrift 2001, Acampora 2006, Piazzesi 2007.

37 See Piazzesi 2007: 275. See Acampora 2006: 325: "Nietzsche's reflection upon, and ultimate rejection of, at least certain kinds of evolutionary thesis reflect his concern to reconceptualize the human subject".

Nietzsche, who is well aware of this literature,[38] notes that "today it seems *to do everyone good* when they hear that society is on the way to *adapting* the individual to general requirements, and that *the happiness and at the same time the sacrifice of the individual* lies in feeling himself to be a useful member and instrument of the whole" (D 132), even if there are disagreements about the type of organism to which the individual should be adapted – whether it should be the state, the nation, a people or a economic community:

> there is also a wonderful and fair sounding unanimity in the demand that the ego has to deny itself until, in the form of adaptation to the whole, it again acquires its firmly set circle of rights and duties – until it has become something quite novel and different. What is wanted – whether this is admitted or not – is nothing less than a fundamental remoulding, indeed weakening and abolition of the *individual*: one never tires of enumerating and indicting all that is evil and inimical, prodigal, costly, extravagant in the form individual existence has assumed hitherto, one hopes to manage more cheaply, more safely, more equitably, more uniformly if there exist only *large bodies and their members*. Everything that in any way corresponds to this body- and membership-building drive and its ancillary drives is felt to be *good*, this is the *moral undercurrent* of our age; individual empathy and social feeling here play into one another's hands. (D 132)[39]

The lowering of the individual in some collective concept, its placement in an organism in which it can hide and find shelter is equivalent to a removal of its peculiar characteristics:

> As soon as we want to determine the purpose of man, we start with a concept of man. But there are only individuals. From those previously known, the concept can be obtained by removing the individual element – thus, to establish the purpose of man would be to prevent individuals from becoming individual and instruct them to become general. Is not every individual, conversely, the attempt to achieve a higher genus than man by means of his most individual things? My morality would be to take the general character more and more away from man and specialize him, make him incomprehensible to others to a certain degree (and therefore turn him into an object of experience, of wonder and instruction for them). (NL 1880, 6[158], KSA 9: 237)

The utilitarian imperative "act always in the more useful manner for the community" – with which John Stuart Mill, for example, has distorted the Kantian

---

38 In Nietzsche's Library (NB) one can find *John Stuart Mill's Gesammelte Werke. Autorisierte Uebersetzung unter Redaktion von Theodor Gomperz*, Leipzig 1869–1875, vols. I, IX–XII; A. Espinas, *Des sociétés animales* (Espinas 1878); A. Fouillée, *La science sociale contemporaine* (Fouillée 1880); J. M. Guyau, *Esquisse d'une morale sans obligation ni sanction*, Paris 1885 (lost); and *L'irréligion de l'avenir. Étude sociologique*, Paris 1887. Espinas and Fouillée have been instrumental in Nietzsche's critique of organicist sociology.
39 See also GS 119.

imperative and concealed the *Golden Rule* – is intended only for a fully homogeneous community of individuals with the same needs and enough means to satisfy them. It is an imperative for present society, a completely useless abstraction, and Nietzsche asserts: "it is the antithesis of *my* tendency, the greatest possible number of changing and heterogeneous organisms, which, having reached a state of ripeness and rottenness, drop their fruit; even though most of the individuals perish, it is the few that matter" (NL Spring–Autumn 1881, 11[222], KSA 9: 527).

The herd-instinct, which in my view is a notion that Nietzsche develops while reading Spencer, is a set of atavistic structures which first nature and then culture help to increase, with obvious repercussions in the political and social spheres. Chronologically, the first occasion that the terms *Heerde* (herd) and *Hornvieh* (horned cattle)[40] appear is when Nietzsche is engaged in reading a few pages from *Die Tatsache der Ethik*, in which Spencer contends with Hobbes and his doctrine that obligations are derived solely from the coercive power of the law. According to Spencer, Hobbes fails to see that the law is summoned only *ex post* in order to sanction a harmonious natural state towards which human conduct tends spontaneously. Everything depends on a fluid exchange, in which each individual is guided by the others and unknowingly contributes to the common good: the Hobbesian State displays thus its artificiality by contrast with a spontaneous non-violent harmony.[41] It is here that Nietzsche writes at the bottom of the page *Hornvieh* and *Heerde*,[42] demonstrating his strong indignation against the prejudiced idea of natural harmony as goal and result of the evolutionary path.

The object of the new social science, to which Nietzsche objects, is therefore the individual body endowed with life: between the body and society there is a relation of isomorphism. Relations between the individual and community are

---

40 The term *Heerdenthier* appears only in a fragment from 1873 (NL 1873, 29[149], KSA 7: 695) and in VM 233, but in a different sense.

41 Similarly Guyau, beginning as a fervent Spencerian, developed a doctrine according to which life, a force with expansive character, drives us in the direction of others up to the point of owning itself. Ethics should simply limit itself to recognizing man's natural tendency towards socialization in a natural moral progress in which injunctions of categorical imperatives and religious dogmas will no longer have reason to exist: "A positive and scientific morality [...] cannot but give the individual this commandment: develop your life in all directions, be as much as possible an individual rich in intensive and extensive energy; be, therefore, the most *social* and *sociable* being." Whereas Nietzsche instead will say meaningfully: "Cultivate all your forces – but this means cultivate anarchy! Perish!" (NL Autumn 1880, 6[159], KSA 9: 237)

42 Cf. Spencer 1879: 57–58 (NB).

modelled on those between the organism and its component parts. Each element concurs naturally to the good of the organism, and the organism as a whole exists only through the action of the parts in a "*conspiration universelle et incessante*"[43] dictated by life. This should not cancel the individual element, because for Spencer living units do not lose and cannot lose their individual awareness; whereas for Fouillée "an evolution occurs in the opposite direction which is no less incontestable than the other and that is characterized by the growing autonomy of the individual; we tend to diversity and decentralization as much as to unity and centralization".[44] For Nietzsche, a statement like this is little more than a subterfuge.[45]

The animosity that Nietzsche clearly expresses against English psychology and its derivations is due to the fact that he thinks that there is great danger in the idea of an adaptive model of the relation between individual and environment. For Nietzsche, adaptation is synonymous with reactivity, passivity; whereas what emerges more and more for him is the idea of a struggle – internal and external – of the organism, a consequence of the relational dynamics and powerful activities of every form of life.

In opposition to the morality of altruism and sacrifice of the individual for the benefit of the species, Nietzsche's demand is therefore to "produce beings that stand above the whole species 'man': and to this goal sacrifice themselves and their fellow". Whereas morality seems for Nietzsche to find a limit in the preservation of a "type" through homogenization and levelling down, "the other movement: my movement: is, on the contrary, sharpening of all contradictions and divisions, the elimination of equality, the creation of the super-powerful. The first movement produced the last man. *Mine* the overman". "Not 'mankind' but '*overman*' is the goal!",[46] clarifies Nietzsche, thereby pointing out "Comte's misunderstanding" and one of the focal points of his philosophical goals.

---

43 Cf. Espinas 1878: 58 (NB).
44 Fouillée 1880: 249. Underlined by Nietzsche who adds, to the side, "*falsch*" (false).
45 "The 'growing autonomy of the individual': these Parisian philosophers such as Fouillée speak of this; they ought to take a look at the *race moutonnière* to which they belong! Open your eyes, you sociologists of the future! The individual has grown strong under *opposite* conditions; what you describe is the most extreme weakening and impoverishment of mankind; you even desire it and employ to that end the whole mendacious apparatus of the old ideal! you are so constituted that you actually regard your herd-animal needs as an ideal! A complete lack of psychological integrity!" (NL November 1887 – March 1888, 11[137], KSA 13: 63, Kaufmann's translation)
46 See NL Spring–Summer 1883, 7[21], KSA 10: 244 (in polemic with Dühring); NL July 1882–Winter 1883/1884, 1[36], KSA 10: 19; NL Summer–Autumn 1884, 26[232], KSA 11: 210. Numerous fragments confirm that Nietzsche feels himself to be "in opposition to the *morality of equality*": a "new hierarchy of spirit" that sanctions inequality among men, creators, higher

5 'Beyond me and you'

The position reached by Nietzsche – the deduction of all affects from "will to power" organizing itself in temporary hierarchies and constituting the movement of *life* – represents a sharp antithesis to the dichotomous type of philosophy and traditional psychology. Falsification regarding the I plays a central role in the story that the latter tells:

> The psychological error out of which the antithetical concepts "moral" and "immoral" arose is: "selfless," "unegoistic," "self-denying" – all unreal, imaginary.
> False dogmatism regarding the "ego": it is taken in an atomistic sense, in a false antithesis to the "non-ego"; at the same time, pried out of becoming, as something that is a being. The *false substantialization of the* ego: (in the faith in individual immortality) this is made into an article of faith, especially under the influence of *religio-moral training*. After this artificial separation of the ego, and the declaration that it exists in and for itself, one confronted a value antithesis that seemed irrefutable: the single ego and the tremendous non-ego. It seemed evident that the value of the single ego could lie only in relating itself to the tremendous "non-ego" – being subject to it and existing for its sake. – Here the herd instincts were decisive: nothing is so contrary to this instinct as the sovereignty of the individual. But if the ego is conceived as something in and for itself, then its value must lie in self-negation. (NL Autumn 1887, 10[57], KSA 12: 485, Kaufmann's translation)

The false autonomy granted to the individual as *atomon* is therefore used by the herd instincts, which loathe its independence and transfer its purposes to something else. This is the *enormous falsification in psychologicis* of current morality, from which stems the worst slander against egoistic instincts and real motives of action.

But what to say of individualism itself? Nietzsche warns us that the latter is a modest and still unconscious form of "will to power",

> here it seems sufficient to the individual to get free from an overpowering domination by society (whether that of the state or of the church). He does not oppose them as a person but only as an individual; he represents all individuals against the totality. That means: he instinctively posits himself as equal to all other individuals; what he gains in this struggle he gains for himself not as a person but as a representative of individuals against the totality.

---

men, is in fact necessary (see NL Summer – Autumn 1884, 26[143] and 26[258], KSA 11: 187 and 217) and will constitute for Nietzsche an antidote to nihilism. The need for a "new hierarchical order" is expressed in the title or subtitle of numerous fragments from the Summer of 1883 up to the beginning of 1888.

> Socialism is merely a means of agitation employed by individualism: it grasps that, to attain anything, one must organise oneself to a collective action, to a 'power.' But what it desires is not a social order as the goal of the individual but a social order as a means for making possible many individuals: this is the instinct of socialists about which they frequently deceive themselves [...]. The preaching of altruistic morality in the service of individual egoism: one of the most common lies of the nineteenth century. (NL Autumn 1887, 10[82], KSA 12: 502, Kaufmann's translation)

The gregarious individual embodies the most short-sighted and extreme form of egoism, in which the perspective of an *I*, artificially constructed out of the given social values, tries to impose itself as the only one that is valid and possible.[47] Moreover, the so-called individualist still has not understood which false representation of himself hides behind his needs and desires. A way out of this dead-end seems to be the synthetic man, the *man that combines*, the one who is able to take upon himself the plurality of perspectives, aware of the fact that "the highest man, if such a concept be allowed, would be the man who represented the antithetical character of existence most strongly, as its glory and sole justification".[48]

The individual is only a sum of sensations, judgements, conscious errors, a *faith*, a small fragment of the real life-system or multiple fragments gathered together by thought and imagination, a unity that does not last. However, the new subject discloses itself as power that is fulfilled in its wanting itself always as contradiction, discontinuity, becoming, chaos: an awareness of being an epiphenomenon of a "real life-system", "the tree's bud" (and "what do we know about what may become of us in the interest of the tree?").[49]

> *Let us stop feeling ourselves to be such imaginary egos! one is this imaginary ego!* Let us gradually learn *to get rid of the alleged individual!* Discover the errors of the ego! Perceive *egoism* as mistake! Do not conceive altruism as its opposite. That would be love for other alleged individuals! No! Let us go BEYOND "me" and "you"! FEEL COSMICALLY! (NL Spring–Autumn 1881, 11[7], KSA 9: 442)

---

47 "The will to one morality thus proves to be the tyranny of the type to which this one morality is tailored, over the other types: it is annihilation or standardization in favor of the prevailing type" (NL Autumn 1887, 9[173], KSA 12: 437 = WLN, 170).
48 Cf. NL Autumn 1887, 9[119], 10[17] and 10[111], KSA 12: 403, 462 and 519; WP 881. "Nietzsche speaks explicitly of the fact that the I is also involved in the dissolution of all values; the irony of the overman [*Übermensch*] must be directed towards the I as well [...]. What is at stake here is far more generally an ideal of life and wisdom that ends up pointing to a plural subject, as a goal of moral perfection, able to experience its own interpretation of the world without the need of believing it "true" in the metaphysical sense of the world, that is, in the sense of being rooted in a certain and unshakable foundation" (Vattimo 2000: 190–191).
49 Cf. NL Spring–Autumn 1881, 11[7], KSA 9: 442.

This is the difficult imperative Nietzsche delivers to us for a new, possible human condition, in which living and fruitful contradictions co-exist and in which last and definitive values, with their load of violence, are no longer allowed.

References

Acampora, Christa Davis (2006) "Naturalism and Nietzsche's Moral Psychology", in: Keith Ansell-Pearson (ed.), *A Companion to Nietzsche*, Oxford: Blackwell, 314–333.
Acampora, Christa Davis (2008) "Forgetting the subject", in: S.V. Hicks and A. Rosenberg (eds.), *Reading Nietzsche at the Margins*, West Lafayette: Purdue University Press, 34–56.
Bagehot, Walter (1874) *Der Ursprung der Nationen. Betrachtungen über den Einfluss der natürlichen Zuchtwahl und der Vererbung auf die Bildung politischer Gemeinwesen*, Leipzig: F.A. Brockhaus.
Bagehot, Walter (2007) *Physics and Politics. Or Thoughts on the Application of the Principles of 'Natural Selection' and 'Inheritance' to Political Society*, New York: Cosimo.
Barbera, S./Campioni, G. (2010) *Il genio tiranno. Ragione e dominio nell'ideologia dell'Ottocento: Wagner, Nietzsche, Renan*, Pisa: ETS.
Berlin, Isaiah (1958) "Two Concepts of Liberty", in: I. Berlin (1969), *Four Essays on Liberty*, Oxford: Oxford University Press.
Brobjer, Thomas (2008) *Nietzsche and the English: The Influence of British and American Thinking on His Philosophy*, New York: Humanity Books.
Campioni, Giuliano (1979) "Individuo e comunità nel giovane Nietzsche", in: *Prassi e teoria*, 1, 145–177.
Campioni, Giuliano (2001) *Les lectures françaises de Nietzsche*, Paris: PUF.
Campioni, G./D'Iorio, P./Fornari, M.C./Fronterotta, F./Orsucci, A. (eds.), in collab. with Müller-Buck, Renate (2003) *Nietzsches persönliche Bibliothek*, Berlin: De Gruyter.
Espinas, Alfred (1878) *Des sociétés animales*, Paris: G. Baillière.
Fischer, Kuno (1880) *Geschichte der neuern Philosophie, Bd. 6, 3.* neu bearbeitete Auflage / München: F. Basserman.
Fornari, Maria Cristina (2006) *La morale evolutiva del gregge. Nietzsche legge Spencer e Mill*, Pisa: ETS. [German translation Wiesbaden 2009]
Fornari, Maria Cristina (2009) "Beiträge zur Quellenforschung", in: *Nietzsche-Studien* 38, 320.
Foucault, Michel (1971) "Nietzsche, La généalogie, l'histoire", in: *Hommage à Jean Hyppolite*, Paris: PUF, 145–172.
Foucault, Michel (1977) "Nietzsche, Genealogy, History", in: D.F. Bouchard (ed.), *Language, Counter-Memory, and Practice: Selected Essays and Interviews*, Ithaca: Cornell University Press, 145–164.
Fouillée, Alfred (1880) *La science sociale contemporaine*, Paris: Hachette.
Klossowski, Pierre (1975) *Nietzsche et le cercle vicieux*, Paris: Mercure de France.
Klossowski, Pierre (1997) *Nietzsche and the Vicious Circle*, Chicago: University of Chicago Press.
Lange, Friedrich Albert (1881) *History of Materialism*, Eng. trans., vol. III, Boston: Houghton Mifflin.
Lange, Friedrich Albert (1887) [1875] *Geschichte des Materialismus*, 2nd edition, Iserlohn/Leipzig: J. Baedeker.

Moore, G. (2002) "Nietzsche, Spencer and the Ethics of Evolution", in: *The Journal of Nietzsche Studies* 23, 1–20.
Orsucci, A. (1992) *Dalla biologia cellulare alle scienze dello spirito. Aspetti del dibattito sull'individualità nell'Ottocento tedesco*, Bologna: Il Mulino.
Piazzesi, C. (2007) "Pathos der Distanz et transformation de l'expérience de soi chez le dernier Nietzsche", in: *Nietzsche-Studien* 36, 258–295.
Roux, Wilhelm (1881) *Der Kampf der Theile im Organismus. Ein Beitrag zur Vervollständigung der mechanischen Zweckmässigkeitslehre*, Leipzig: W. Engelmann.
Schrift, A.D. (2001) "Rethinking the Subject: Or How One Becomes-Other than What One Is", in: Richard Schacht (ed.), *Nietzsche's Postmoralism. Essays on Nietzsche's Prelude to Philosophy's Future*, Cambridge: Cambridge University Press, 47–62.
Spencer, Herbert (1879) *Die Tatsache der Ethik*, Stuttgart: Schweizerbart.
Taine, Hippolyte (1864) *Le positivisme anglais. Étude sur Stuart Mill*, Paris: Baillière.
Taine, Hippolyte (1870) *English Positivism. A Study on John Stuart Mill*, London: Williams and Norgate.
Taine, Hippolyte (1914) [1870] *De l'intelligence*, 3rd edition, Paris: Hachette.
Vattimo, Gianni (2000) "La saggezza del superuomo", in: G. Vattimo (ed.), *Dialogo con Nietzsche. Saggi 1961–2000*, Milan: Garzanti.

Benedetta Zavatta

10 "Know Yourself" and "Become What You Are"

The Development of Character in Nietzsche and Emerson

A central notion for understanding the Emerson-Nietzsche relation is the notion of character. Character development is the ultimate goal of both authors' ethics: the criteria according to which one judges things as good or bad and decides how to relate with others.

The word character can be used to denote multiple concepts. First of all, a character is a distinctive element that makes a thing unique. For instance, Nietzsche speaks of "the character of existence" (NL 1888, KSA 13, 17[3] my translation), or "the character of life" (NL 1875, KSA 8, 5[188] my translation) signifying the distinctive feature that reveals the essence of life or existence. Applied to an individual, character indicates the distinctive bundle of features that makes him/her unique.

The term character is also used to mean "moral character", namely the virtue of fortitude and firmness in facing troubles, or the virtue of "resoluteness" in pursuing one's own goals or affirming one's own point of view.

A person of character is thus a person who courageously affirms her originality, copes even with the most terrible events without falling to the ground, and pursues his/her goals under any circumstances, overcoming all obstacles.

Conversely, "to have no character" is an expression that denotes either a lack of distinctiveness or originality, i.e. the tendency to be driven by others, and/or a lack of resoluteness, i.e. indecisiveness. A man without character is what Nietzsche would call "a weak personality", while a man of character is called "a strong personality".

For instance, Nietzsche uses the word character in this second sense when he deplores the "lack of character and strength [*Mangel an Charakter und Kraft*] in David Strauss" (DS 7). David Strauss, like every other human being, was characterized by a unique mixture of talents and defects, propensities and aversions. But he lacked character in the sense that he had not been able to give an "appropriate" form to this bundle of properties.

The expression "character development" or "character formation" indicates precisely the path that brings from character (1) to character (2). How should this process be accounted for? Is it a work to be carried out or a destiny to be fulfilled? And how is character (2) related to character (1)?

These questions arose in Nietzsche very early, when he was still a student at *Schulpforta*. They remained at the centre of his philosophy until his last writings and were answered in different ways in different times of his life, also because they are strictly related to the issues of fatalism and agency that Nietzsche interpreted differently over time.

Undoubtedly, Nietzsche found important inspiration in the use of character in Goethe's philosophy, where the notion of *Bildung* is absolutely central. Using a metaphor taken from the natural world, Goethe describes the process of character formation as self-cultivation. Character (1) is the seed that, by receiving appropriate care, germinates, grows, and becomes character (2). However, the American essayist Ralph Waldo Emerson was also an important source for Nietzsche in this regard. Nietzsche began reading Emerson at a very young age and returned to his writings in many crucial moments of his life. In fact, Emerson's thought was already engrained in German philosophy, to the extent that he was called in Germany "the American Goethe" (and inevitably dismissed by the argument: "why should we need Emerson if we already have Goethe?").[1] Emerson's interpretation of Goethe's theory of character, however, presents some features that are totally foreign to the German *Geist* and can be considered as distinctively American. These peculiarities were exactly the features that Nietzsche appreciated the most and most eagerly assimilated in his philosophy.

1 Temperament and character

In an autobiographical note from May 1861, Nietzsche reflects about the development of character in the following terms:

> Although the seeds of our moral and spiritual dispositions are already present in us, and the fundamental character is, so to say, inborn in each of us, nonetheless the form, both moral and spiritual, that we acquire as adults is the effect of external circumstances that touch us in different ways, sometimes more deeply, sometimes more superficially (BAW 1: 276, my translation).[2]

---

[1] Goethe's work became immediately popular in the United States precisely because of Goethe's strong emphasis on the close connection between knowledge and practice: "The pages of *The Dial* abounded in references to Goethe's ideas and writings. No author occupied the cultivated New England mind as much as he did" (Frothingham 1959: 57). By contrast, German idealism had no strong attraction for American intellectuals and it was considered as "wonderful specimens of intellectual gymnastics" (Wellek 1965: 171).

[2] "Denn wenn auch die Keime zu den geistigen und sittlichen Anlagen schon in uns verborgen liegen, und der Grundcharackter jedem Menschen gleichsam angeboren ist, so pflegen doch erst

In other words, Nietzsche assumes that character is the result of the influence exerted by (unpredictable) events on *an (equally unpredictable) bundle* of spiritual and moral dispositions that are inborn in us. This view substantially resembles that of Goethe in the *Metamorphosis of Plants*. According to Goethe, the natural realm is ruled by two competing forces: on the one hand, an inner necessity drives each organism to grow until all potentialities of its nature are fulfilled; and on the other hand, external circumstances offer resistance to this process and constrain growth. The final shape that the organism will take is determined by the interplay of these two opposite forces, the internal and the external one. This view will be confirmed and further developed by Nietzsche in two school essays written in the following year, *Fate and History* and *Freedom* of the *Will and Fate*, in which the influence of Emerson is clearly detectable.[3] Emerson deals with the issue of character formation in the essay *Fate* belonging to the collection *The Conduct of Life*, which Nietzsche discovered and began reading in 1862. Emerson substantially picks up on Goethe's framework and states: "In science we have to consider two things: power and circumstance.... Once we thought positive power was all. Now we learn that negative power, or circumstance, is half" (Emerson 1904a: 14–15, 1862: 9–10). Each organism is driven by an inner force to grow and develop itself: "Life is a search after power", i.e. every living being, from plant to man, tends to put into act its own potential. This expansive process is however limited by circumstances. The form of each being will thus result from the interplay between its internal force and environmental pressure. This same interpretative framework can also be applied to human beings, whose character will be the product of the interaction between an inner drive to grow and expand their power, and the pressure exerted by circumstances.

However, Emerson understands "circumstances" as not only external conditions, but also and most importantly as internal constrains. Innate and acquired inner dispositions are even more powerful and disruptive in the course of our life than catastrophes like earthquakes or floods, because they affect our thinking unconsciously and are therefore very difficult to recognize and oppose. In Emerson's time the theories of Spurzheim, the founder of modern phrenology, and the Belgian astronomer Quetelet, who studied correla-

---

die äußern einwirkenden Verhältnisse, die in bunter Mannigfaltikeit den Menschen bald tiefer, bald flüchtiger berühren, ihn so zu gestalten, wie er als Mann sowohl in sittlicher als geistiger Beziehung auftritt" (BAW 1: 276).

3 Nietzsche was so powerfully struck by his reading of this collection that in 1863 he planned to make a summary of the book for his friends with extracts from all of the essays (BAW 2: 221).

tions between environmental factors and human disposition to crime, were very fashionable (Richardson 1995: 468). Drawing on Hippocrates' ancient theory of body fluids and their influence on man's temperament, thinking and behaviour, Spurzheim and Quetelet came to the conclusion that physical characteristics, as the form and dimension of the skull, reveal inborn natural dispositions. Although rejecting their simplistic formulations, Emerson used their views, together with Lamarck's theory of inheritance of acquired traits, to support the assumption that some attitudes and dispositions are inborn in the individual, and inevitably influence its thinking and behaviour. With a beautiful metaphor he states that our ancestors' qualities constitute "the variety of notes for that new piece of music that our life is" (Emerson 1904a: 10). In other words, he thinks that each individual comes to life with a natural endowment which cannot be changed, but only conveniently utilized. This constitution inevitably influences one's own approach to life, and all one's own thinking and behaviour.

Endorsing Emerson's view, the young Nietzsche observes an amazing correspondence between people's character and their good or bad fortune. Some people continuously complain about misfortune, while others seems to be happy everywhere and under all circumstances. Thus he advances the hypothesis that events are not good or bad in themselves, but people make them such through the interpretation that their character suggests. While pessimistic people colour all events with a moody, melancholy tint, happy and joyous people see everything through rose-coloured glasses. In *Fate and History*, focusing on this topic, Nietzsche asks himself:

> Do we not encounter everything in the mirror of our personality? And do not events provide, as it were, only the key of our history while the strength and weakness with which it affects us depends merely on our temperament? Ask gifted doctors, Emerson says, how much temperament decides, and what, in general, it does not decide? (BAW 2: 58, my translation)[4]

Ultimately, Nietzsche asks himself: "Can a tone, in general, touch us if there is no corresponding string in us?" (BAW 2: 61 my translation). He explores Emerson's view in further detail in an essay from 1864, called *On Moods (Über Stimmungen)*. Nietzsche observes how, amazingly, sensations that are generated in us when making a new experience seem to correspond to our pre-existing internal moods. He explains this fact by assuming that, from the wide variety of external data, one selects only those that can be most easily processed. These

---

4 See Emerson 1858: 308, 1862: 6. See also Stack 1992: 87.

are the data that better fit one's own pre-existent cognitive framework. The soul is, by contrast, not even touched by experiences that it cannot assimilate (BAW 2: 407). In other words, Nietzsche concludes that, in a way, one's own *Stimmung* "predisposes" one to be touched by some sensations instead of others and thus also "attracts" good or bad fortune.[5]

However, determinism is not Emerson's last word. He states: "a man's fortunes are the fruits of his character" (Emerson 1904a: 41), but character is not a given. Emerson defines it as "nature in its highest form", or nature perfected. In other words, character is the result of a *voluntary* work done on one's own "nature" (temperament and inborn dispositions) with the aim of perfecting and enhancing it. According to Emerson, there are two opposite principles in nature, namely spirit and matter. Man participates from both principles. Insofar as he is matter, i.e. nature, he is determined, but insofar as he is spirit, he is free, and indefinitely free. In other words, Emerson maintains that one can indefinitely rework the rough material that one has received from nature. Thus, on the one hand, it is true that one's fortune or misfortune is determined by one's character. But, on the other hand, it is also true that it is up to the individual to work on its character or not, namely to be a person that interprets everything to her own advantage or one that succumbs under the pressure of "adverse fate".

Ultimately, according to Emerson, human beings are not absolutely free, i.e. free to choose or change the (internal and external) circumstances under which

---

[5] Emerson states: "How a man thinks, so he is, and how a man chooses, so he is, and so is its nature. A man is a method, a progressive arrangement: a <u>selecting principle</u> gathering <u>his like to him</u> wherever he goes. He takes only <u>his own out of the multiplicity that sweeps and circles round him</u>" (Emerson 1883: 136–137, 1858: 107, underlined and marked in the margin by Nietzsche). This view is further developed by Nietzsche in his mature works, where beliefs and actions are taken as symptom of one's own character. The strong connection between one's own character and the events of one's own life is also the basis for Nietzsche's *amor fati*. Zarathustra says: "I am a wanderer and a mountain climber ... I do not like the plains and it seems I cannot sit still for long./And whatever may come to me now as destiny and experience – it will involve wandering and mountain climbing: ultimately one experiences only oneself./The time has passed in which accidents could still befall me, and what *could* fall to me now that is not already my own?/It merely returns, it finally comes home to me – my own self and everything in it that has long been abroad and scattered among all things and accidents" (Z III Wanderer, Nietzsche 2006: 121). If Zarathustra is a wanderer, i.e. ones that loves putting everything into question, and a mountain climber, i.e. ones that loves taking hard paths, he will find in every argument a stimulus to revise his view and move on towards a further truth, continuously overcoming his previous statements. This is not fortuitous, but necessary. When Zarathustra states that nothing is casual, he is not admitting a "providential plan". Simply the organism, i.e. the individual as a multiplicity of drives, interprets data from outside according to its peculiar internal configuration. Thus all events are *necessarily* linked to the person to whom they befall as, in a way, they are produced by him.

they live and act. However, they are free to choose whether to directly oppose these circumstances, and thus be defeated, or to interpret them to their own advantage. The secret of great men's success consists precisely in the fact that they did not stupidly oppose necessity, but learned how to profit from it: "The water drowns whip and sailor like a grain of dust. But learn to swim, trim your bark, and the wave which drowned it will be cloven by it and carry it like its own foam, a plume and a power" (Emerson 1904a: 34). This is the very lesson of American pioneers: to make a virtue out of necessity.

Nietzsche appreciated very much Emerson's "typically American mindset" according to which, eventually, "The good remains, the worst goes by [*das Gute bleibt, das Böse vergeht*]" (BAW 2: 222, my translation, see Emerson 1862: 14) and "the good is only the most subtle evolution of evil" (BAW 2: 59, my translation, see Emerson 1862: 25). Nietzsche copied these maxims about the power of the individual to turn adverse or bad circumstances into good ones in a notebook from 1863, together with a passage from Emerson's essay *Power*: "All successful men ... were causationists [*Kausalisten* in the German translation]. The mind that is parallel with the laws of nature will be in the current of events and strong with their strength" (BAW 2: 261, my translation, see Emerson 1862: 54).[6]

Nietzsche agrees that, in order to be successful, one should not oppose necessity. Rather, one should recognize it and accept it. However, this acceptance is not a passive surrender. Rather, it represents the precondition for the individual to deploy all his power. For what concerns character development, one should cultivate one's drives as a patient and skilful gardener, and make use of them "productively and profitably" (D 560). In other words, one should "survey all the strengths and weakness" that one's nature "has to offer and then fit them into an artistic plan until each appears as art and reason and even weakness delight the eye; [...] only then is a human being at all tolerable to behold!" (GS 290). In his copy of *The Conduct of Life* Nietzsche heavily underlined the following passage, which will become a major inspiration of his later writings: "For if Fate is so prevailing, man also is a part of it, and can confront fate with fate" (Emerson 1904a: 24, 1862: 17). In other words, once a person has learnt how to artistically 'dispose' of the hard facts of her life, she becomes a "piece of fate" and acquires the invincible power of a force of Nature.[7]

---

[6] See Emerson 1862: 37–38, 1904a: 54, 56. Nietzsche copied two series of extracts from Emerson's essays *Beauty* and *Power*. Some extracts appear in both series, with slight differences. These extract series are not included in the KGW, thus see BAW 2: 257–261.

[7] Emerson states that the individual who has learnt how to exploit his natural endowment at best is no longer dependent from circumstances, but "appears to share the life of things, and to

However, the seventeen-year-old Pforta student immediately found out the weak point of Emerson's argument and, in his second school essay from spring 1862, called *Freedom* of the *Will and Fate*, observed that "freedom of the will" is nothing but "freedom of thought" and both of them are "limited [*beschränkt*]" (BAW 2: 60, my translation). In other words, Nietzsche immediately put into question Emerson's notion of "voluntary deliberation" and doubted that the skill to change oneself can be "learned" or voluntarily developed. Rather, Nietzsche suspects that the process of *Bildung* or character formation is determined by a complex net of causes and cannot be voluntarily and purposively achieved.

2 Does character change?

By the end of 1865 Nietzsche began reading Schopenhauer, and this reading played a very decisive role in maturing his philosophical vocation. Very soon, however, Nietzsche rejected Schopenhauer's metaphysics of the will as void of any scientific value. The reading of Emerson did not directly influence Nietzsche's criticism of Schopenhauer's metaphysics, as for instance the reading of Lange did. However, Emerson provided Nietzsche with a relevant countermodel to Schopenhauer's ethics and, in particular, to his approach to character, thus importantly contributing to the development of Nietzsche's mature view on this issue.

According to Schopenhauer, character is the "essence" or "inner moving force" of a human body, or organism. The character of each individual is "a unique combination of three basic incentives [of human action], namely, egoism [*Egoismus*], compassion [*Mitleid*], and malice [*Bosheit*]" (WWR I, 301). They are incentives or drives that mix in different degrees in each individual organism, and their relation to one another in each individual organism is precisely a

---

be an expression of the same laws which control the tides and the sun, numbers and quantities" (Emerson 1883: 90–91, 1858: 337–338). A mature individual expresses the same huge power of nature, because he has understood the necessity of its laws and knows how to profit from them. Such an individual has become "an agent and playfellow of the original laws of the world" (Emerson 1883: 93, 1858: 339, marked with lines in the margin). This is the case of Zarathustra, who as a creator (i.e. interpreter of events) has gained the right to sit at the gaming-table of the gods (Z III, The Seven Seals 3). He wants to exploit the power of "lightning" (Z IV, On the Higher Man 7) and learn how to skate on ice in order to "go faster", "drink from all glasses" and wash himself even with "dirty water" (Z II On Human Prudence, see Emerson 1862: 41, 1858: 335).

person's "character"–her "intelligible", individual, innate, and unchangeable character: "Beneath the changeable mantle of his years, his relationships, even of his knowledge and outlook, there lurks, like a crab in its shell, the identical and intrinsic human being, wholly unalterable and always the same" (Schopenhauer 2009: 70).[8]

Discussing the theory of immutability of character, Nietzsche states that "Schopenhauer was wrong on this, as on almost everything" (KSB 6 nr. 40, my translation), and explained Schopenhauer's erroneous conclusion in terms of "the brevity of human life", which provide humans with just a partial perspective on things:

> That the character is unalterable is not in the strict sense true; this favorite proposition means rather no more than that, during the brief lifetime of a man, the effective motives are unable to scratch deeply enough to erase the imprinted script of many millennia. If one imagines a man of eighty-thousand years, however, one would have in him a character totally alterable: so that an abundance of different individuals would evolve out of him one after the other (HH I 41).

Just like Schopenhauer, Nietzsche conceives character as a relation of drives. However, differently from Schopenhauer, Nietzsche does not think of drives as immutable properties. Drives are rather intended as interpretative processes acquired through one's interaction with the external world. Therefore, character cannot be intended as an immutable, pre-existing essence or substance. Rather, Nietzsche seems to set no limits to the possibility of character being altered. "To become who one is" is a regulative ideal that gives rise to a never-ending development aimed at indefinitely increasing one's power. The only limit is that imposed by the brevity of human life, namely by the fact that every human being, in his brief life-span, can be affected just by a limited number of circumstances. Admitting the possibility of expanding experience beyond this temporal limit we could imagine "a character totally alterable". In other words, we can expect that out of the same individual totally different personalities will develop.

Emerson was very influential in Nietzsche's rejection of Schopenhauer's thesis of the immutability of character and, specifically, in the development of

---

[8] In fairness to Schopenhauer, his conception of character is more complex than most accounts suggest, for it includes the idea that one may fail or succeed in "acquiring" one's character. While a person's deliberations are not "determined by motives distinctly known", her actions remain inauthentic, that is, not really her own, not really the actions that her unchangeable, intelligible character would choose if it had distinct knowledge of those motives (see WWR I, 304ff.). I thank João Constâncio for his help on this point.

the aforementioned aphorism. Consistently with his American mindset, Emerson conceives character as indefinitely expanding:

> The changes which break up at short intervals the prosperity of men are advertisements of a nature whose law is growth. Every soul is by this intrinsic necessity quitting its whole system of things, its friends and home and laws and faith, as the shellfish crawls out of its beautiful but stony case, because it no longer admits his growth, and slowly forms a new house (Emerson 1883: 119–120, 1858: 94).

According to Emerson, indefinite growth is the law of nature: "there is no end in nature, but every end is a beginning; … there is always another dawn risen on mid-noon, and under every deep a lower deep opens" (Emerson 1883: 309). Individuals are no exception to this law and their character, as "a self-evolving circle", passes "from a ring imperceptibly small, … to new and larger circles, and that without end" (Emerson 1883: 304). Contrary to Schopenhauer's crab, Emerson's shellfish escapes its shell when it becomes too small to contain it. In other words, the inner force that drives each individual to grow and increase its power causes the individual to escape the indurated form of his character every time he feels the necessity to move further.

Endorsing Emerson's stance, Nietzsche concludes that people can indefinitely change their character over time. However, in contrast to Emerson, Nietzsche underlines that those changes are not purposively achieved, but are produced by a complex net of causes. In other words, Nietzsche cannot say with Emerson "be yourself", because one cannot develop one's character simply by will. Starting from *Human, All Too Human* Nietzsche rejects the notion of intentional agency and, consequently, also rules out the possibility of voluntarily shaping one's own character. Bringing to its last consequences Schopenhauer's assumption that everything in the empirical world is linked to a net of causes,[9]

---

[9] Schopenhauer does not negate the human capacity of acting morally under deliberation, but he refuses the idea of free will intended as "the possibility to do otherwise" under the same circumstances. As people make in every moment the only possible decisions that they could make, they are not to be held responsible for their actions. At this point, in order to preserve the notion of responsibility that is the pillar of every kind of morality, Schopenhauer is forced to introduce a metaphysical essence as *prima causa*. Besides the empirical character, which is involved in the net of causality as any other empirical object, Schopenhauer postulates the existence of an intelligible character, which is instead free. Similarly to Plato's myth of Er, Schopenhauer's argument is based on the assumption that, as everyone has chosen their character (or *daimon*) freely, one can blame only oneself for the consequences of such a choice, namely for one's destiny. Nietzsche strongly opposes Schopenhauer's notion of intelligible character and defines it as nothing but a "fable" (HH I 39). In other words, he argues that Schopenhauer arbitrarily introduces such a notion to deny the inevitable conclusion that every strict mind would have drawn

Nietzsche concludes that "man can be made accountable for nothing, not for his nature, nor for his motives, nor for his actions, nor for the effects he produces" (HH I 39). Therefore, man is accountable neither for engaging nor for not engaging in the process of self-perfection. While, according to Emerson, the individual has a moral commitment with regard to itself and its fellow human beings, namely to discover his vocation and pursue it at all costs; for Nietzsche, "the individual is a piece of fate, from the front and from the back, one more law, one more necessity for all that is coming and shall be" (TI, Morality as Anti-Nature 6). In other words, none of man's deeds, included "giving style" (see GS 290) to his character, are the result of an intentional, deliberate choice, but a spontaneous one, i.e. an unintentional outcome of one's own internal organization of drives.

How does Nietzsche account for the process of character-formation? As mentioned, from a theoretical point of view Nietzsche states that any characteristic (*Eigenschaft*) that the individual has inherited or acquired is *in principio* alterable. However, people do not shape their character by consciously designing an "ideal" and then acting in accordance with it. In other words, people do not change themselves by conscious deliberation, as there is no metaphysical faculty, such as will, that can direct the project of "giving style" to one's own character. Rather, the "schema of how we should be"–that can be also called "aspirational Self"–is an involuntary and unconscious output of one's own drives (NL 1880, KSA 9, 7[95]).[10] Drives are goal-oriented–and it is precisely based on the result they are aimed at that they are selected–but in a sub-conscious way (Richardson 2004: 96). This is why the process of character development appears as "unintentional". As Constâncio (2012) keenly observes, in order to adapt successfully to the environment, the individual needs to transform itself and therefore needs a "sketch" of the final product. But this schema is provided by the drives, and only thereafter translated into a conscious purpose: "Ideals of this sort are the anticipatory hopes of our drives, and nothing else. As surely as we have drives, they also lay out in our fantasy a sort of schema of ourselves, a schema of how we should be in order to satisfy our drives–this is idealising!" (NL 1880, KSA 9, 7[95]). Furthermore, Nietzsche underscores the neces-

---

from the observation of empirical causality (AOM 33). Rejecting the notion of *causa sui* (free cause), Nietzsche states that the chain of empirical causality cannot be broken and everything in nature is part of a whole.

10 See Constâncio 2012. What Nietzsche calls "schema" can be thought of as a "very general image" or a "sketch" that provides "not only the guideline, but the moving force itself" (NL 1881, KSA 9, 11[18]).

sity to reconfigure the importance of purposes in determining one's action. Purposes are not the moving force of our action, but the "catalytic force".[11] If action is to be regarded as a "discharge of force", the purpose can at best determine the direction of this discharging. In other words, a purpose is "something quite insignificant, mostly a small accident" compared to its effect. Nietzsche suggests that we conceive of a purpose as a match that, interacting with a powder keg, triggers an explosion (that is, the action) or, still better, as the helmsman of a ship – a helmsman that determines no more than the direction of a trip, while the moving force is provided by the steam (GS 360).[12]

3 Liberate what you are

Ultimately, from the years of *Human, All Too Human* onwards, Nietzsche is in favour of a strict determinism and explicitly rejects both the notion of will as a metaphysical faculty that causes our action and the notion of moral responsibility therewith connected. He thus accounts for the process of "becoming who one is" as a self-selection of drives, aimed at specifying "who one is" (Richardson 2004: 96).[13] While social selection selects drives with a view to the prosperity of a group, self-selection favours the drives that are aimed at expressing one's own peculiarity. Although intentions and purposes are, at best, just directing forces of this process, nonetheless freedom should be admitted as a regulative hypothesis. In other words, in everyday life a person cannot do otherwise than think of herself as free. She should think she is free to choose between drinking or not drinking a glass of water, even if, in reality, it is her "commanding" drive that decides. Similarly, for what concerns character building, the individual thinks of itself as free. Obviously, not free to change directly its inner dispositions (be courageous, be open-minded, etc.), but at least free to choose the most suitable conditions to which expose himself in order to provoke these changes.

---

[11] The idea of "catalytic force" has been suggested to Nietzsche by Julius Robert Meyer: "A force is 'catalytic' insofar as it stands in no kind of quantitative relationship to the intended effect. An avalanche falls into the valley; a gust of wind or the beat of a bird's wing is the 'catalytic force' that gives the signal for the fall and brings about the extensive destruction" (Meyer 1845: 80, see Abel 1998: 43–49, Constâncio (forthcoming).

[12] Note that this entails that *rational* purposes may have some sort of (limited) power within the organism and, therefore, Nietzsche's psychology of drives is not an "irrationalist's" refusal of reason: see Constâncio (forthcoming).

[13] "The key to becoming myself is to select my values, i.e. the goals or dispositions that – in making my behavior – specify 'who I am'" (Richardson 2004: 96).

Nietzsche insists a lot on the "discipline" which the individual should undergo in order to "become who he is", or fully develop his character. This process is articulated into two parts: a *pars destruens* and a *pars construens*. First of all, the individual should analyse the influences to which he has been subjected since his young age. Family, education, society as well as religion and morality have imposed some beliefs, ideas and values upon him that he has unconsciously interiorized and now feels as instincts. The first step to "become who one is" is to recognize these alien instincts and remove them. Once freed from the pressures to conform to the values and beliefs of the group in which he has grown up, the individual can start exploring his own "conditions of existence" (see NL 1881 KSA 9, 11[46], 11[59]), namely the values and beliefs that he needs in order to flourish as a unique and peculiar being. In order to achieve this purpose, he should break with his habits and test the effect of different conditions on himself, namely change his diet, the weather, his readings, etc. The more conditions he experiments with, the deeper he shall unfold and realize himself.[14] How much Emerson was influential in the articulation of this project is proven by Nietzsche's note on the last page of the *Essays*:

> To proceed from the smallest/nearest 1) The whole discernable interconnection in which a single person is born and raised. 2) The habitual rhythm of our thoughts, feelings, our intellectual requirements and nourishment. 3) *Attempts* at transformation: to begin with, break with your habits (for example, your diet). To lean intellectually once on one's adversaries, to try to live in their air; to journey, in every sense "unsettled and fugitive"–for a time. To ruminate from time to time over one's experiences, repose. 4) *Attempts* at the ideal *composition* and later at the ideal *life* (NL 1881, KSA 9, 13[20], my translation, see also NL 1881, KSA 9, 11[258]).

The American essayist underlines that the internal circumstances which silently affect one's own thinking and behaviour do not consist only of the set of inborn dispositions that follow from temperament or have been inherited from ancestors. Society exerts on each of his member a very strong pressure that begins from the

---

14 In *Ecce Homo* Nietzsche explains "how he has become who he is", namely how his character has developed from birth to the present moment. Nietzsche speaks about the circumstances of his birth, his family, and the main influences that affected his life (as the reading of Schopenhauer or the friendship with Wagner). Then he tells how he became aware of these influences and got rid of them. At this point, he began the path of realization of his potential. He accepted things he could not change, such as his poor health, and turned it into an advantage. The periodic illnesses to which he was subjected were used as opportunities for a more careful self-observation, or a way to experience *décadence*, or again as an opportunity for tuning his sensibility. Then Nietzsche explored the habits most suitable to his constitution. Periodically he broke with his routine and tested new conditions.

first infancy. Not only direct education, but also and above all social models and stereotypes shape one's own worldview and even the idea one makes of oneself. From simply growing up in a certain family and society, one internalizes a specific model of virtue and behaviour, and quite naturally tends to conform to it. Society assigns to each individual a role to perform, a mask that over time makes one incapable of recognizing one's real face. Against the threat of conformism, Emerson claims the uniqueness of every human being and exhorts everyone to "be oneself", namely to find and pursue one's own true Self.

> Society everywhere is in conspiracy against the manhood of every one of its members ... The virtue in most request is conformity. Self-reliance is its aversion.... Whoso would be a man, must be a nonconformist. He who would gather immortal palms must not be hindered by the name of goodness, but must explore if it be goodness (Emerson 1883: 51–52).

In Emerson's project of character development, the notion of vocation plays a key role. According to Emerson, each individual has a peculiar talent to express. In some "happy moments" the individual has an insight into this talent, as he finds activities that he can perform easier and better than others. These are the moments in which his "true Self" manifests itself. The individual should revere such insights and trust the truth they let him see. Once he has found his vocation, he should pursue it with iron determination, disregarding other people's praise or blame. Emerson's self-reliance can be defined as "the wish to be oneself, to live as one thinks best, to take chances deviantly, to pursue one's special vocation, to define oneself as different from others, to follow the line of one's distinctiveness without deflection". The goal is not "self-aggrandizement", but simply defending one's own dignity as a human being (Kateb 1995: 32). However, as the individual can indefinitely rework the rough material that it received from nature, the process of unfolding one's true Self has to be thought as virtually never-ending: "Our life is an apprenticeship to the truth that around every circle another can be drawn; that there is no end in nature, but every end is a beginning; that there is always another dawn risen on mid-noon, and under every deep a lower deep opens ... Step by step we scale this mysterious ladder; the steps are actions, the new prospect is power" (Emerson 1883: 301–305).

Nietzsche was profoundly fascinated by Emerson's "heroic" model of character development as a liberation of one's own "true Self" from the pressures imposed by the "herd". From the third *Untimely Meditation* onwards he thought of the philosopher as an independent thinker, who does not fear to challenge the authority of institutions in which he has grown, and heroically bear isolation and misunderstanding in order to express his own originality. Nietzsche further developed this ideal in the figure of the free spirit, who removes external influences from his mind and now "thinks differently from what, on the basis of his origin, environment, his class and profession, or on the basis of the dominant views of the age, would have been expected of him" (HH I 225). The achievement of independence from dominant truths and values, as well as from other people's praise or blame, represents also the first part of the path towards the "Overman" (Z I, Prologue 3) that Zarathustra presents to his friends.

Zarathustra's teachings on the "Overman" should be seen as nothing but another way to present the project of character development. For each individual the Overman is a regulative ideal that expresses one's own "not yet attained, but attainable Self" (Cavell 1990: 12). In Emersonian terms, it expresses one's own true Self, or full potential. However, such a true Self or potential is not set once and for all. It is not to be thought of as something that one has to discover and achieve. Therefore the path towards the Overman is presented as a never-ending process of *Selbt-Überwindung*, in which there is always a further potentiality to express, or a further result to be achieved. In other terms, there is not a true Self that the individual should discover and fulfil. From the same individual, a multiplicity of individuals can potentially develop.

4 Intellectual nomadism

For both Nietzsche and Emerson the processes of "knowing oneself" and that of "becoming who one is", i.e. realizing one's own potential, goes hand in hand. In other words, one cannot know "who one is" through introspection, but only by testing oneself in practice. Emerson wrote in the essay *Fate*: "A man's power is hooped in by a necessity which, by many experiments, he touches on every side until he learns its arc" (Emerson 1904a: 19–20). In other words, one gets to know oneself only by acting in the world, by relating to others, by dealing with the events that befall one. The more circumstances one experiences, the better one shall know oneself, and the bigger the part of one's potential that one will express. On the back cover of Emerson's *Essays* Nietzsche wrote: "Suck out your circumstances and contingencies – and move onto other! It is not enough to be *one* man. That would imply calling for you to limit yourselves! But go from one to another!" (NL 1881, KSA 9, 13[3] my translation).

In fact, Emerson recognizes that the "driving force" that leads towards character development is not equally strong in everyone. Some individuals have been endowed with more energy than others. They will thus be more prepared and happier than others to experiment with new conditions:

> In proportion to the vigor of the individual, these revolutions are frequent, <u>until in some happier mind</u> [*in einem glückseligeren Geisten*] <u>they are incessant</u> and all worldly relations <u>hang very loosely about him, becoming as it were a transparent fluid membrane</u> through

which the living form is seen, and not, as in most men, an <u>indurated</u> heterogeneous fabric of many dates and of no settled character, in which the man is imprisoned. Then there can be enlargement, and the man of to-day scarcely recognizes the man of yesterday. And such should be the outward biography of man in time, <u>a putting off of dead circumstances</u> day by day, as he renews his raiment day by day (Emerson 1883: 120, 1858: 94–95).[15]

The propensity to change and the capacity to profit from every circumstance is called by Emerson "intellectual nomadism". In 1882 Nietzsche copied in his notebook of extracts from the *Essays* the definition of such an attitude. "Intellectual nomadism [*geistiger Nomadentum*] is the gift of objectivity or the gift to find everywhere a feast for the eyes. Every human being, every thing is my discovery, my possession: the love, which makes him alive for everything, *smooths* his forehead" (NL 1882, KSA 9, 17[13] my translation). Nietzsche recognizes this attitude as typical of the wanderer, who "takes pleasure in change and transience" (HH I 638, see also AOM 211). Insofar as the man devoted to knowledge has abandoned the belief in eternal truths he is similar to a wanderer, i.e. a traveller who is conscious that his voyage has no final destination. This fact does not deprive the journey of its value, nor the wanderer of his enthusiasm. Each stage of the never-ending voyage of knowledge (i.e. each experience) is rather recognized as worth living for. Emerson's spiritual attitude to nomadism corresponds to what Nietzsche defines as "skepticism of strength".[16] It characterizes all "great spirits", such as Zarathustra, who can neither be satisfied with any truth for long with, nor renounce exploring themselves further (A 54).

For the individual for whom knowledge is the highest aim, every circumstance, even the worst one, is welcomed as an opportunity to experience life and himself further. As the passage from Emerson's essay *History* that Nietzsche put as a motto of *The Gay Science* says: "To the poet, to the philosopher, all things are friendly and sacred, all events profitable, all days holy, all men divine." The poet-philosopher which Nietzsche is referring to is the Troubadour,

---

15 Nietzsche heavily underlined this passage and put many vertical signs at the margin. We can find a reference to this passage in NL 1878, KSA 8, 32[12].

16 The "skepticism of weakness" is, by contrast, embodied by the "shadow", which is the pessimist counterpart of the wanderer. The shadow says: "all is the same, nothing is worth it, searching does not help" (Z IV Cry). In other words, while the wanderer takes pleasure in change and transience, the shadow sees such transience as a proof that human achievements are worthless. This attitude essentially coincides with nihilism, which deprives the world of meaning and value. Nietzsche traces back this "refusal to take a stance" to a disease and degeneration of the will or, in other words, to a weak organization of internal drives (BGE 208). In a weak type that endorses skepticism, thinking is paralyzed, as all perspectives are seen as void of value.

whose typical association of wisdom and cheerfulness is called *gaya scienza*.[17] Emerson describes exemplarily the "gay science [*heitere Wissenschaft*]" of Provençal culture as the awareness that all things are interconnected. This view makes the poet-philosopher recognize their higher necessity and love them as they are. Thus, while most people's pleasure is always "tinged with pain", i.e. ruined by the awareness that no pleasure lasts forever, the poet-philosopher's pains are instead "edged with pleasure" (Emerson 1904b: 37, 1876: 36), because he can recognize their utility from the point of view of self-knowledge and character development.[18]

Both Emerson and Nietzsche often criticize modern society for providing the individual with too much comfort and, most of the times, also with ready-made choices. He is thus deprived both of the possibility of truly knowing himself and of that of becoming "what he is".[19] Facing demanding situations is very important in order to fully develop one's potential. Only a real and stinging necessity causes the individual to find hidden resources and develop new skills. Emerson states: "In general, every evil to which we do not succumb is a benefactor" (Emerson 1883: 114, 1858: 89, heavily underlined and marked on the margin by Nietzsche) and Nietzsche echoes him as follows: "What does not kill me, makes me stronger" (TI, Maxims and Arrows 8). [20]

Against all pessimists, who see in suffering an argument against life, Nietzsche endorses Emerson's cheerfulness, the capacity to gratefully welcome every experience as an opportunity to increase one's wisdom. Nietzsche wrote on the title page of Emerson's *Essays* the following note:

---

[17] Nietzsche considered Provençal culture as a "luminous point" (NL 1884, KSA 11, 25[419], my translation) in world history and, longing for its restoration, decided to entitle the book he was writing "*die fröhliche Wissenschaft* (la gaya scienza)". In a letter to Rohde, who had assumed that the adjective "gay [*fröhlich*]" referred to his recovered health, Nietzsche explains that the title of his work refers to the Troubadours' poetic culture, or "*gaya scienza*" (KSB 6 nr. 345). The lyrics of the *Troubadours*, dealing with the topics of heroism and love, exalted aristocratic and chivalric values. See Campioni 2010.
[18] Nietzsche bought the *Neue Essays*, the German translation of Emerson's *Letters and Social Aims*, in April 1876 and promptly read it. See KSB 5 nr. 529.
[19] Nietzsche copied down the following passage from Emerson's essay *Self-Reliance* in his notebook of extracts from 1882: "Our housekeeping is mendicant, our arts, our occupations, our marriages – we have not chosen, but society has chosen for us. We shun the rugged battle of fate, where our inner strength is born" (NL 1882, KSA 9, 17 [39], my translation, see Emerson 1858: 57, 1883: 75). See also: "Our strength grows out of our weakness. The indignation which arms itself with secret forces does not awaken until we are pricked and stung and sorely assailed" (Emerson 1858: 89, my translation).
[20] See also GS 19 and WB 6.

> The capacity for pain is an outstanding sustainer [*Erhalter*], a kind of assurance of life: *this is what has preserved pain* [*dies ist es, was der Schmerz erhalten hat*]: it is as useful as joy – not to say too much. I laugh at the enumeration of pains and afflictions through which pessimism wants to prove itself – Hamlet and Schopenhauer and Voltaire and Leopardi and Byron. Life is something that ought not be, if it can be sustained just in this way! – you say. I laugh at this "ought" and thereby position myself for life, in order to help, so that out of pain arises as rich a life as is possible – security, prudence, patience, wisdom, variety [*Abwechselung*], every subtle nuances of bright and dark, bitter and sweet – in all we are indebted to pain, and an entire canon of beauty, sublimity [*Erhebung*], divinity is possible only in a world of deeper and more variable and diversified pain. That which lets you judge life cannot be justice [*Gerechtigkeit*] – because justice would know that pain and adversity – – – Friends! We must increase the pain in the world if we want to increase the joy [*Lust*] and the wisdom (NL 1881, KSA 9, 13[4]).[21]

While Schopenhauer and other pessimists recommend the liberation of man *from* desire in order to liberate him also from the painful frustration that striving for something provokes, Emerson aims at the liberation of man *through* desire: the desire to discover and fulfil one's own potential. Such a process is hard and demanding, for knowledge progresses only through experience, and experience, in turn, necessarily involves suffering and pain. However, pain and suffering are redeemed by the higher value of the goal that one pursues. Ultimately, endorsing Emerson's stance, Nietzsche states that for the individual who considers life as an experiment aimed at increasing his knowledge and power, troubles and suffering are much more valuable than comfort and contentment. *Amor fati* is precisely the attitude of he who no longer struggles to change things but sees all of them as part of his "personal providence" (GS 277).

5 A Dyonisian Self

From the time of *Human, All Too Human* onwards, Nietzsche considers historical knowledge as essential for the process of knowing oneself: "Direct self-observation is not nearly sufficient for us to know ourselves: we require history, for the past continues to flow within us in a hundred waves; we ourselves are, indeed, nothing but that which at every moment we experience of this continued flowing [*Fortströmen*]" (AOM 223).[22] What is Nietzsche's conception of history

---

[21] See also GS 318.
[22] At the time of the *Untimely Meditations*, Nietzsche was so concerned with exalting originality as a disruptive power against the authority of tradition and dominant opinion that he strongly devalued historical knowledge. Schopenhauer, or Nietzsche's ideal philosopher, is portrayed as

here? Clearly, he is not referring to the impersonal and objective narration of events canonized by German historicism as "scientific". Rather, Nietzsche seems to refer to a sort of subjective, emotional sharing of experiences: "… we ourselves are … nothing but that which at every moment we experience of this continued flowing". This statement implies that, according to the mood of the moment, we sympathise with this or that event in history, which tells us what we are, i.e. reveals us a part of ourselves. In other words, according to our present interest, we instinctively select some facts from the flow of history which our soul resounds with particularly intensity. Then we re-live these moments internally, drawing from them the same sensations that we would have had through a first-hand experience. These experiences, as those we made first-personally, contribute to our self-knowledge.[23]

Nietzsche compares this kind of experience to a voyage, because it leads to the discovery of new ways of life, new perspectives from which to look at things:

> He who, after long practice in this art of travel, has become a hundred-eyed Argos, will in the end be attended everywhere by his *Io* – I mean his *ego* – and will rediscover the adventurous travels of this *ego* in process of becoming and transformation in Egypt and Greece, Byzantium and Rome, France and Germany, in the age of the nomadic or of the settled nations, in the Renaissance and the Reformation, at home and abroad, indeed in the sea, the forests, in the plants and in the mountains. – Thus self-knowledge will become universal knowledge with regard to all that is past (AOM 223).

How much the reading of Emerson influenced the development of Nietzsche's view is revealed in some passages from the essay *History* that he copied in his notebook of extracts from Emerson's *Essays* in 1882[24] and by the marginal notes written on the first page of the essay *History*. At the beginning of this essay

---

one who, disregarding tradition, see things "for the first time", i.e. express his judgment independently, without relying on the opinions of others. He has acquired most of his knowledge "out of himself" (SE 7) similarly to Heraclitus, whose eye flamed toward its inward centre and had no need of other men (PTAG 8). See Campioni 1987: 211.

23 As Nietzsche had already stated in the second *Untimely Meditation*, one's own right to turn to history is proportional to one's own need for it. Therefore, one can turn to history only insofar as one is driven by the need of knowing who he is. Just in this way the consideration of the past is not an idle past-time, or a burden that weighs on the present, but becomes real nourishment. See Zavatta 2013.

24 "I want to live all history in my own person [*die ganze Geschichte in eigner Person durchleben*] and appropriate all power and glory, without bowing down in front of a king or any other greatness [*irgend einer Größe*]" (NL 1882, KSA 9, 17[4] my translation); "The creative instinct of the mind betrays itself in the use we make of history: there is *only* biography. Everybody must know *his* whole task [*seine ganze Aufgabe*] – The unplanned, wild, meaningless [*planlose rohe widersin-*

Emerson presents the metaphysical basis of his conception of history – namely, the notion of an "Oversoul" containing the souls of all past, present, and future human beings. Emerson holds that the individual can enter into union with this "Oversoul" by freeing itself from its subjectivity and accessing a higher dimension of being. In these moments of mystical ecstasy man feels one with all other men, whether living or dead, despite their temporal and spatial separation.

> There is one mind common to all individual men. Every man is an inlet to the same and to all of the same. He that is once admitted to the right of reason is made a freeman of the whole estate. What Plato has thought, he may think; what a saint has felt, he may feel; what at any time has befallen any man, he can understand. Who hath access to this <u>universal mind</u> is a party to all that is or can be done, for this is the only and sovereign agent (Emerson 1883: 9, 1858: 1).

Nietzsche commented in the margin of this passage: "No! But it is an ideal! [*Nein! Aber es ist ein Ideal!*], my translation". In other words, Nietzsche rejects Emerson's "Oversoul" as a metaphysical entity, but nonetheless admits it as an ideal. The ideal of Nietzsche's man of knowledge is precisely that of "sharing" mankind's experience in order to increase his experience beyond the narrow boundaries imposed by his individual life-span. This ideal is further clarified by the note Nietzsche wrote at the top of the page: "Oh our greed! I feel nothing of selflessness, but rather an all-desiring self, which through many individuals – just as it sees with its eyes and grasps with its hands, is also a self that holds fast to the whole past and does not want to lose anything which could in principle belong to it" (NL 1881, KSA 9, 13[7]). Already at the time of the second *Untimely Meditation* Nietzsche was dreaming of an "infinitely powerful nature", which could "draw to itself and incorporate into itself all the past, its own and that most foreign to it, and as it were transform it into blood" (HL 1). For such an infinitely powerful nature there would be no limit to the amount of stimuli that it would be able to assimilate, and its soul would contain the whole of universal history. Exploring this perspective further, Nietzsche wrote on the frontispiece of Emerson's *Essays*: "Do you want to become an impartial, universal eye? Then you shall have to do it as an individual that has gone through *many* individuals and whose latest individual *requires* all previous ones as functions" (NL 1881, KSA 9, 13[5] my translation).[25] During this sort of "emotional sharing" and

---

nige] must disappear and be replaced with the Here and the Now" (NL 1882, KSA 9, 17[5] my translation).

25 These marginal notes are developed in NL 1881, KSA 9, 11[65], [119], [141], [197] and finally resulted in GS 249. See also AOM 17. In the following years, namely from 1884 onwards, Nietzsche turns Emerson's conviction that history has to be read and explained from a personal point of

experience of mankind as such, the individual is far from being a pure, disembodied eye of the world that contemplates without being affected. Rather, from the men of the past, the individual gains a hundred hands through which it touch things and a hundred skins through which it is affected by them. In fact, by multiplying its senses, the individual also increases the amount of suffering and joy that it experiences. This feeling is what should be called historical *sense* (see GS 337).

It is thus thanks to the reading of Emerson that Nietzsche began redefining the notion of objectivity from a "disinterested" view of things to a sum of many intensely *interested* perspectives. This notion is exhaustively presented in *On the Genealogy* of Morals as follows: "There is *only* a perspectival seeing, *only* a perspectival 'knowing,': the *more* affects we are able to put into words about a thing, *the more* eyes, various eyes we are able to use for the same thing, the more complete will be our 'concept' of the thing, our 'objectivity'" (GM III 12). In other words, Nietzsche recognizes that all perspectives involve an interest. This interest–born, in turn, from a need–determines the focus of the perspective. Objectivity as a lack of perspective is impossible–it lies beyond the human capacities. However, this notion can be preserved as an ideal to which one can get closer by adding more and more perspectives on the same thing. But a perspective cannot be created for the sake of intellectual play. Each perspective arises according to a specific condition of existence. Thus, to generate different perspectives, one needs to cultivate within oneself "different individuals" as internal "functions". They will provide so many worldviews as conditions of existence. Ultimately, the greatest desire of the man of knowledge is not the immortality of the soul, but rather to gather into himself a multitude of mortal souls, which become his "internal functions".

6 The imperialist Ego

The affinity between Nietzsche's and Emerson's approaches to the notion of character, and their emphasis on character development as the highest and only real good for the individual, can be explained through their common debt to

---

view, or relived empathetically in one's own soul, into the much stronger thesis that present man contains in himself, under the form of instincts, all the past judgments and deeds of his ancestors. The awareness of being heir is accompanied by a feeling of proudness. Nietzsche declares himself proud of humanity, proud that the blood that flows through his veins is the same as that of Plato, Pascal, Spinoza, and Goethe (NL 1881, KSA 9, 12[52], see also NL 1881, KSA 9, 15[17]).

Goethe's philosophy. However, the ideal of harmonious personality typical of Weimar classicism is turned by Emerson and Nietzsche into a nomadic and imperialist Ego, which aims to expand its power beyond the boundaries imposed by the limited time-span of its existence. In other words, the plastic drive that characterizes Goethe's ideal of form is put to the service of an *expansive* force that leads towards a greater and greater enhancement of power. The stronger the synthetic "plastic power" (HL 1), the wider the horizon that the individual can embrace. Thus, on the one hand, Nietzsche and Emerson insist on the idea of building individuality and strengthening the *ego* against the threats of modern society, mainly conformism and selfless morality.[26] On the other hand, they insist on the necessity of expanding one's experience (through intellectual nomadism, through history, etc.), in order to fully explore one's potential. And, as this potential is not set once for all, but *in principio* unlimited, there is no limit to the experiences that the man striving for power would like to make. Such an approach leads to the grateful acceptance of life as it is and to welcoming all meetings and events as an opportunity for character building. It leads to a propensity for experimenting and for taking pleasure in change and transience. Finally, it leads to a revaluation of history as an invaluable repository of experiences from which the present man can and should profit.[27] Whereas in Emerson the desire to enlarge one's own horizon beyond the limits imposed by individuality culminates in ecstatic moments in which one merges

---

[26] In Nietzsche's "morality of the mature individual", where character development is the highest good both for the individual and for society, compassion is regarded as a form of weakness, namely as a "morbid" indulging in sorrow (D 134), or inability to resist stimuli (see EH Wise 4) that ruins both the individual and society.

[27] In the portrait of the American essayist sketched in *Twilight of the Idols*, Nietzsche praises Emerson precisely for his inexhaustible energy, which led him to periodically change his mindset and explore new points of view, appreciating every perspective as valuable, and every circumstance as useful: "Emerson ... just does not know how old he already is and how young he still will be – he could apply Lope de Vega's saying to himself: '*Yo me sucedo a mi mismo*'. His spirit always find reasons to be satisfied and even grateful" (TI, Skirmishes of an Untimely Man 13). Nietzsche applies to himself the formula "*yo me sucedo a mi mismo* (I am my own successor)" in a note from 1887 (NL 1887, KSA 13, 11[22]), while in a letter to Carl Fuchs from the same period he tells his friend: "I do not know how old I am already and how young I still will be" (KSB 8, nr. 963, my translation). Although he was almost at the end of his lucid life, he felt the need to put everything into question once again, all his values, truths, and habits, in order to pass into a "new and higher form of being" (KSB 8, nr. 963, my translation). In other words, he still felt powerfully within himself the drive towards further development of his character. In the second part of his letter to Carl Fuchs, Nietzsche says that the German people accuse him of eccentricity just because they do not understand what his centre is. In other words, they do not understand that he does not aim at self-consistency, but at developing his character further and further.

with the Oversoul, the Dionysian Self theorized by Nietzsche can be thought of as an individual which contains within himself many other individuals as his functions.[28]

References

Abel, Günter (1998) *Nietzsche. Die Dynamik der Willen zur Macht und die ewige Wiederkehr*, Berlin/New York: De Gruyter.
Campioni, Giuliano (1987) "'Wohin man reisen muss': Über Nietzsches Aphorismus 223 aus Vermischte Meinungen und Sprüche" in: *Nietzsche-Studien* 16, 209–226.
Campioni, Giuliano (2010) "Gaya scienza und gai saber in Nietzsches Philosophie", in: Chiara Piazzesi, Giuliano Campioni and Patrick Wotling (eds.), *Letture della Gaia Scienza – Lectures du Gai Savoir*, Pisa: ETS, 15–38.
Cavell, Stanley (1990) *Conditions Handsome and Unhandsome: The Constitution of Emersonian Perfectionism*, Chicago/London: University of Chicago Press.
Constâncio, João (2012) "A Sort of Schema of Ourselves: On Nietzsche's 'Ideal' and 'Concept' of Freedom", in: *Nietzsche-Studien* 41, 127–162.
Constâncio, João (forthcoming) "Nietzsche on Consciousness, Will, and Choice: Another Look at Nietzschean Freedom", in: Manuel Dries (ed.), *Nietzsche on Consciousness and the Embodied Mind*, Berlin/Boston: De Gruyter.
Emerson, Ralph Waldo (1858) *Versuche (Essays: First and Second Series)*, translated by G. Fabricius, Hannover: Carl Meyer.
Emerson, Ralph Waldo (1862) *Die Führung des Lebens*, translated by E. S. von Mühlberg, Leipzig: Steinacker.
Emerson, Ralph Waldo (1876) *Neue Essays (Letters and Social Aims)*, translated by J. Schmidt, Stuttgart: Auerbach.
Emerson, Ralph Waldo (1883) *Essays: First and Second Series*, Boston Mass.: Houghton Mifflin.
Emerson, Ralph Waldo (1904a) "The Conduct of Life", in: *The Complete Works*, Concord Edition, vol. 6, Boston Mass.: Houghton Mifflin.
Emerson, Ralph Waldo (1904b) "Letters and Social Aims", in: *The Complete Works*, Concord Edition, vol. 8, Boston Mass.: Houghton Mifflin.
Frothingham, Octavius B. (1959) *Transcendentalism in New England*, New York: Harper & Brothers. [Reprint of: New York, Putnam's Sons 1876].
Kateb, Georg (1995) *Emerson and Self-reliance*, Thousand Oaks: Sage.
Meyer, Julius Robert (1845) *Die organische Bewegung im Zusammenhang mit dem Stoffwechsel*, Heilbronn: C. Drechsler'sche Buchhandlung.

---

[28] At the end of his life, when dementia came upon him, Nietzsche convinced himself that he had successfully gathered within himself all the experience and power of the men who lived before him: "What is disagreeable and offends my modesty is that at bottom I am every name in history" (KSB 8 nr. 1256, my translation).

Richardson, John (2004) *Nietzsche's New Darwinism*, New York/Oxford: Oxford University Press.

Richardson, Robert D. (1995) *Emerson: The Mind on Fire*, Berkeley/Los Angeles/London: University of California Press.

Schopenhauer, Arthur (2009) *The Two Fundamental Problems of Ethics*, ed. Cristopher Janaway (The Cambridge Edition of the Works of Schopenhauer), Cambridge: Cambridge University Press.

Stack, George (1992) *Nietzsche and Emerson. An elective affinity*, Athens: Ohio University Press.

Wellek, René (1965) *Confrontations: Studies in the Intellectual and Literary Relations Between Germany, England, and the United States During the Nineteenth Century*, Princeton, NJ: Princeton University Press.

Zavatta, Benedetta (2013) "Historical Sense as Vice and Virtue in Nietzsche's Reading of Emerson", in: *Journal of Nietzsche Studies* 44(3), 372–397.

Part II: **The Crisis of the Subject**

João Constâncio
11 Nietzsche on Decentered Subjectivity or, the Existential Crisis of the Modern Subject

1 Introduction

In a note from 1885, Nietzsche points out that "subject" is no more than a scholarly and modern term for the older, pre-modern concepts of "soul" and "spirit" (NL 1885 36[36], KSA 11: 565). Similarly, in his Preface to *Beyond Good and Evil*, he asserts that in modernity "the soul-superstition [...] still causes trouble as the superstition of the subject or I" (BGE Preface). Although Nietzsche's knowledge of modern philosophy was far from perfect, he was very well aware of what was modern and old in modern philosophy. If we look at *Beyond Good and Evil* and *The Gay Science* as the two published works in which Nietzsche raises the problem of subjectivity in a most clear and incisive way,[1] our first impression may well be that he raises the problem in a very modern way, namely as a theoretical question about the nature of consciousness, and especially about the nature of conscious thought as manifested in a *cogito*, i.e., in the self-consciousness of an 'I think' (e.g. BGE 17, BGE 54, GS 354, GS 357). But we can also observe that he is keen to suggest that Descartes' dualism is merely a modern reformulation of Plato's old "error", the "invention of pure spirit and the Good in itself" (BGE Preface), as well as of Christianity's faith in the immortal "soul" (BGE 54). Moreover, Nietzsche believes that at the heart of the modern question about the subject and the nature of consciousness, there lies the old question about the relationship between consciousness and the "drives" (*Triebe*) or "instincts" (*Instinkte*), an old question which Socrates and Plato formulated in terms of an opposition between "instinct and reason" (BGE 191). In a few key-passages, Nietzsche rephrases this as an opposition between instinct and language, or between our purely instinctual life and our social life as language-users (BGE 268, GS 354), as well as an opposition between our "affects" and our conscious thoughts, this being (he argues) a key opposition for the understanding of morality (e.g. BGE 187, BGE 198, GS 333).[2] In fact, one of Nietzsche's main

---

[1] Book V of *The Gay Science* is particularly relevant. Given that Nietzsche wrote and published it after *Beyond Good and Evil*, I shall refer to *The Gay Science* as if it came later than *Beyond Good and Evil* in the chronology of Nietzsche's works.
[2] See Constâncio/Branco (2011).

(anti-dualist) contentions is that these oppositions express developments along a continuum, such that they are all ultimately illusory. Consciousness is not really 'opposed' to the drives, the instincts, or the affects, but is rather a mere result and surface-manifestation of developments and movements that occur in the unconscious depths of our instinctual and affective life. Every conscious mental state is "*only a certain behavior of the drives towards one another*" (GS 333), "thinking is only a relation between these drives" (BGE 36). As I have argued elsewhere, this is the key-idea behind Nietzsche's metaphorical conception of consciousness as 'surface', 'mirror', and 'tool'.[3]

Thus, in both *Beyond Good and Evil* and *The Gay Science* Nietzsche seems to be engaged in a theoretical discussion of the problem of subjectivity, all the more so since he explicitly highlights continuities and discontinuities between his views and those of the main figures of modern philosophy, particularly in Descartes (BGE 16, BGE 17, BGE 54), Spinoza (BGE 198, GS 333), Leibniz (GS 354, GS 357), Kant (BGE 54), and Schopenhauer (BGE 16, GS 99). He does not mention Hegel (or Fichte) in this connection, but he praises Hegel for having introduced the idea of development (and hence of evolution, history, and becoming) in the history of modern philosophy (GS 357). This idea is crucial in the most important aphorism that Nietzsche wrote on the problem of consciousness, which is aphorism 354 from Book V of *The Gay Science*. It is here where Nietzsche puts forward an *evolutionary* account of consciousness. Given that he concludes that consciousness "is really just a net connecting one person with another", such that "consciousness actually belongs not to man's existence as an individual but rather to the community- and herd-aspects of his nature" (GS 354), what he has to say here about consciousness must surely be discussed in connection with Fichte's and Hegel's thesis that the 'I' of consciousness results from reciprocal 'recognition' (*Anerkennung*) and, therefore, from social interaction.[4]

However, given that Nietzsche has an extremely deflationary view of the 'I' of consciousness and does not shy away from declaring that the 'subject' of modern philosophy is (both as knower and as agent) merely a fiction,[5] many readers of Nietzsche consider that he not only influenced Barthes' notion of a 'death of the author' or Foucault's notion of a 'death of man' but also explicitly defended something like a postmodern 'death of the subject'. Whether this is so

---

[3] See Constâncio (2011a); see also Abel (2001) and Lupo (2006).
[4] On Nietzsche's social conception of the 'Self', see Herman Siemens' chapter in this volume.
[5] See BGE 34; TI Errors 3; NL 1885, 35[35], KSA 11: 526; NL 1885, 38[4], KSA 11: 598; NL 1887, 9[91], KSA 11: 383–387; NL 1887 9[108], KSA 11: 398; NL 1887 19[19]; NL 1888 14[79], KSA 13: 257–259.

or not belongs to the wider question as to whether Nietzsche's thought represents a complete break with modernity and the Enlightenment project (as he himself seems to suggest) or only radicalises the demands of this project and in calling for a 'revaluation of all values' still holds on to the emancipatory dreams of modernity. The full discussion of this wider question is, however, well beyond the scope of this chapter, for it involves discussing Nietzsche's notions of rationality, objectivity, science, truth, his political views, etc.

The main point of this chapter is that Nietzsche's writings describe a very deep crisis of modern subjectivity and radically modify the modern conception of the subject by introducing the notion of a 'decentered subject' (i.e., of a non-transparent, opaque "subject-multiplicity", as Nietzsche terms it in BGE 12) – but Nietzsche does not proclaim the death of the subject, he does not abandon or reject the idea of subjectivity, he does not even eliminate either the first-personal perspective of the 'I' of consciousness or social perspective of intersubjectivity, and therefore his thought, at least in this respect, can still be said to belong to modernity and modern philosophy. In making this point, I shall also argue that the reason why Nietzsche points out that the problem of subjectivity should be traced back to the Greeks and especially to Plato's dualistic 'errors' is because the crisis of the modern subject that he wants to describe belongs to the wider crisis of the transcendent, metaphysical *values* which Plato and his 'errors' created or, in other words, to the crisis Nietzsche calls 'the death of God'.

Since I shall be focusing almost exclusively on *Beyond Good and Evil* and *The Gay Science*, one first objection may spring to mind immediately. In both works, Nietzsche explicitly declares that he is not interested in theoretical discussions of the problem of subjectivity, particularly in the modern sense of a question about the nature of consciousness. This could indicate that his approach to the problem of subjectivity is one of postmodern rejection. In *Beyond Good and Evil* he writes:

> In all seriousness, there is something touching and awe-inspiring about the innocence that, to this day, lets a thinker place himself in front of consciousness with the request that it please give him *honest* answers: for example, whether or not it is "real", and why it so resolutely keeps the external world at arm's length, and other questions like that. The belief in "immediate certainties" is a *moral* naiveté that does credit to us philosophers: but – we should stop being "merely moral," for once! (BGE 34)

And in *The Gay Science*, precisely in the all-important aphorism about consciousness in Book V (GS 354), he adds:

> As one might guess, it is not the opposition between subject and object which concerns me here; I leave that distinction to those epistemologists who have got tangled up in the snares of grammar (of folk metaphysics). (GS 354)

The passage from *Beyond Good and Evil* reiterates Nietzsche's frequent claim that there are no "immediate certainties" about consciousness (e.g. BGE 16). This is his usual argument against introspection, self-observation, or self-knowledge as first-personal knowledge.[6] We are fundamentally "unknown to ourselves" (GM Preface 1), for (a) our self-consciousness only lets us know about "the ultimate reconciliation scenes and final accounts" (GS 333) of long, unconscious processes and struggles occurring within ourselves, and (b) our first-personal access even to these 'final accounts' – i.e., to consciousness as a mere 'surface' of unconscious drives and affects – is conditioned by language and, according to Nietzsche's (basically Neo-Kantian) views on language, this makes all self-knowledge merely "a more or less fantastic commentary on an unknown, perhaps unknowable, but felt text" (D 119). For Nietzsche, words and concepts are 'invented' signs, which can offer no more than anthropomorphic, symbolic interpretations of given phenomena, according to the principle that new names "create new 'things'" (GS 58). Thus, if there is any reason to claim, as modern philosophy claims, that the 'external world' is a 'phenomenal world' (a 'representation', in Schopenhauer's language), there is all the more reason to follow Friedrich A. Lange's scepticism and claim that also the so-called 'inner world' is merely 'phenomenal' – a world which can be said to be "given" (BGE 36), but which is always already given in perspective and symbolically and, hence, as fundamentally unfathomable.[7]

The passage from *The Gay Science* extends this argument. 'Subject' and 'object' are merely words: no less than other similar words, such as 'conscious-

---

[6] See Paul Katsafanas', Anthony Jensen's, Maria João Mayer Branco's, and Paolo Stellino's chapters in this volume.

[7] The skeptic argument according to which we have no 'immediate certainties' about our inner world and are fundamentally 'unknown' to ourselves because our inner access to ourselves is mediated by language (i.e., by such signs as 'consciousness', 'I', 'agent', 'drive', 'affect', 'desire', etc.) is an argument with which Nietzsche became acquainted quite early in his readings of Lange's *History of Materialism*, and which he has in mind when he claims (as he often does in the *Nachlass*) that we should extend our 'phenomenalism' to the inner world (NL 1885, 2[131], KSA 12: 129–132; NL 1885, 2[204], KSA 12: 166–167; NL 1887, 11[113], KSA 13: 53–54; NL 1888, 14[152], KSA 13: 333–335; NL 1888, 15[90], KSA 13: 458–460). See also D 116; see Stegmaier (2000) and Constâncio (2011a) on how Nietzsche also expresses his Langean skepticism by claiming that all our thoughts, including those about our inner world, are merely 'signs'. Nietzsche's criticism of Descartes' and Schopenhauer's conception of introspection (or 'self-observation' and 'self-knowledge') as knowledge of a 'thing in-itself' makes the same point. See BGE 16 and Constâncio (2013). On Lange and his influence on Nietzsche's skepticism regarding self-knowledge, see Anthony Jensen's chapter in this volume. His chapter, as well as an exchange of emails with him, inspired an important part of this chapter.

ness', 'I', 'agent', 'drive', 'affect', etc., the words 'subject' and 'object' make believe that they designate observed, immediately given 'things', when in fact they 'create' these 'things'. Moreover, these two words have a particularly strong rhetorical and persuasive force because they were first invented to express the basic structure of Indo-European languages: they are grammatical words that entangle us in the "snares of grammar" (GS 354). We see ourselves as 'subjects' because grammar seduces us into believing that since "thinking is an activity" and "behind every activity something is active" (BGE 17), there must be an 'I' that thinks, "an I as cause of thoughts" (BGE 16). Or, put slightly differently, we see ourselves as 'subjects' because grammar "construes and misconstrues all forms of activity as conditional upon an agency, a 'subject'" (GM I 13). The first-personal approach to the question about the nature of consciousness – the 'problem of subjectivity' as a theoretical question about the 'subject' of self-observation or introspection, as well as about the external world as the 'object' of that subject's knowledge – is hence only a modern development of our entanglement in the 'snares of language'.[8]

Thus Nietzsche's Langean scepticism regarding self-knowledge seems to justify a rejection of the typically modern, subjective, first-personal approach to subjectivity and consciousness, as well as its replacement with an objective, third-personal perspective. In *Beyond Good and Evil*, the term "physiopsychology" (BGE 23) seems to designate precisely this third-personal perspective. Psychology is to become physiology. In *The Gay Science* 354, Nietzsche's evolutionary account of consciousness also seems to be wholly third-personal and dispense with subjective self-observation or introspection. All of this seems to confirm that Nietzsche is no longer a modern philosopher and his influence on postmodern thinking results from the fact that he is already 'postmodern' in his approach to subjectivity and consciousness.

There are, however, two insurmountable problems with this conclusion. (a) Firstly, Nietzsche's writings abound in clear indications that he never actually abandoned the first-personal perspective. In *Beyond Good and Evil* 12, he explicitly criticises the naturalistic elimination of the old and venerable 'hypothesis of the soul'. Given their "clumsiness", naturalists "barely need to touch 'the soul' to lose it" (BGE 12), whereas Nietzsche wants to preserve it. Moreover, the

---

8 Besides GS 354, BGE 17 and GM I 13, see also BGE Preface, BGE 16, 34, 54, TI Reason 5; in the posthumous notes, see NL 1880, 10[D67], KSA 9: 428, NL 1885, 35[35], KSA 11: 526, NL 1885, 36[26], KSA 11: 562, NL 1885, 40[11], KSA 11: 632–633, NL 1885, 40[16], KSA 11: 635–636, NL 1885, 40[20], KSA 11: 637–638, NL 1885, 40[31], KSA 11: 644, NL 1885, 40[39], KSA 11: 648–649, NL 1887, 9[144], KSA 12: 417, NL 1888, 14[122], KSA 13: 301–303. See Constâncio (2011b).

first main assumption of the all-important hypothesis of the will to power is that "our world of desires and passions is the only thing 'given' as real" (BGE 36). Here as elsewhere, Nietzsche uses his introspective knowledge of the inner world of 'desires and passions' in order to undertake his critique of introspective self-knowledge. Therefore, his point in such passages as BGE 16 is that *when we introspect* we find in ourselves no 'immediate certainties' that might allow us to obtain introspective knowledge of what we ultimately are. The point is the opaqueness, or non-transparency of the first-personal perspective – it is not to call for its elimination. (Thus Nietzsche's unconscious 'drives' and 'wills to power' cannot be observed from a first-personal perspective, but they are nonetheless theoretically posited *from the vantage point of this perspective*).

(b) Secondly, not only is Nietzsche's Neo-Kantian, Langean scepticism based on a first-personal perspective – and particularly on a first-personal perspective that discovers our inner world to be saturated with linguistic constructions and empty of purely observational contents –, but such a scepticism also intends to cast doubt over the objective, third-personal approach to the problem of consciousness. The point is that *both* when one takes the subjective approach *and* when one takes the objective approach one cannot avoid using words that *purport* to report on what can be first-personally observed and yet only *construct* (or 'invent', 'create') a particular view of what our inner world is. As I have argued elsewhere, from very early on Nietzsche follows Schopenhauer in claiming that, if one is to engage in a theoretical search for the nature of subjectivity and particularly of consciousness, one has to consider the subjective and the objective perspectives as complementary, and not as rival, incompatible perspectives. Nietzsche does not privilege the objective over the subjective perspective. He uses them both, on the Schopenhauerian assumption that they complement each other.[9]

There is, however, a simpler, and more plausible, explanation for the fact that both in *Beyond Good and Evil* and *The Gay Science* Nietzsche states that he is not interested in the typically modern way of posing the problem of subjectivity. What Nietzsche rejects is (a) the *purely theoretical* approach typical of modern philosophy, and (b) the *naive optimism* typical of that approach. In posing the problem of subjectivity, modern philosophy is content with placing itself in front of consciousness with the request that it please provide honest answers about the ultimate nature of consciousness and the 'I' of consciousness. How does Nietzsche's approach differ from this?

---

9 See Constâncio (2011a).

11 Nietzsche on Decentered Subjectivity — **285**

(a) First, there are two reasons why Nietzsche can be said to pose the problem of subjectivity in a way which is not only theoretical, but also practical. (i) Besides wanting to inquire about the nature of consciousness, Nietzsche wants to *describe and indeed to diagnose the European experience of consciousness in late modernity*. His aim is to describe how the death of God has affected our first-personal relation to ourselves, our consciousness of ourselves, our subjectivity. He believes that the human being is "the sick animal" (GM III 28, etc.); in *Beyond Good and Evil* and *The Gay Science*, he inquires as to whether the death of God has made the disease of the human being even worse, and how. Thus his model of a decentered subjectivity and a 'subject-multiplicity' is by far not a merely theoretical hypothesis, but rather a model that both serves a description and already reflects an experience of fragmentation, disintegration, contradictoriness, 'weakness' and 'paralysis of will' caused by the death of God. No Cartesian, Kantian, Schopenhauerian, or Hegelian conception of the 'subject' can account for this experience. (ii) But, of course, Nietzsche does not just concern himself with the diagnosis of the modern human being's *décadence*. His problem is also the cure, his concern is also the development of a normative project of 'affirmation of life' and, as he puts it in the *Nachlass*, "struggle against nihilism" (NL 1886, 5[50], KSA 12: 202, NL 1886, 7[31], KSA 12: 306). This is the second reason why his model of a decentered subjectivity and a 'subject-multiplicity' is not merely theoretical. It both serves and already reflects a normative project.

(b) Nietzsche replaces the theoretical optimism of modern philosophy with a Langean scepticism, and his version of this scepticism is, again, no longer merely theoretical, but also practical. He believes that if philosophers now re-enact the Cartesian procedure of becoming conscious of their consciousness, what they will find in themselves will not be an unshakeably certain principle upon which they can build a metaphysics and figure out the purpose of their existence and their place in the universe, but rather an opaqueness and undeterminedness which the death of God has made much more serious than it ever was. Consciousness of one's consciousness has become tantamount to a first-personal knowledge of nihilism, particularly of a modern nihilistic lack of belief and disorientation. And pointing this out implies, in a way, the *opposite* of an elimination of subjectivity – the opposite both of the physicalist elimination of the first-personal and of the postmodern, posthuman, Althusserian reduction of the world to 'processes without a subject'. Nietzsche still takes the problem of subjectivity seriously because in fact there is hardly anything that he takes more seriously than his own *subjectivised awareness* of the modern human being's lack of purpose, lack of meaning, lack of a place in a universe newly discovered as purposeless and chaotic (an 'infinite nothing', etc.). Nietzsche's philosophy is not just the site of a theoretical crisis of the modern subject. Much more importantly, it is the site of the existential crisis of the modern subject – or, better still, the site of the *subjectivisation* of this crisis. Thus, when Nietzsche demands "that psychology again be recognised as queen of the sciences" and thus become again "the path to the fundamental problems" (BGE 23), these "fundamental problems" that he has in mind are the existential problems of modern human beings in European late modernity.[10]

2 Subjectivity as an existential problem in *Beyond Good and Evil*

In Part One of *Beyond Good and Evil*, Nietzsche begins by introducing the problem of subjectivity in a way which seems to be basically theoretical. He puts forward the idea that our conscious thoughts are a multiplicity of mental states which emerge involuntarily from a multiplicity of unconscious processes of feeling, willing, and thinking, and are hence neither caused, nor controlled by an 'I' (BGE 17). He claims that the 'I' is thus a mere "synthetic concept" (BGE 19), in fact a synthetic concept which is not the 'condition' of our thinking, but rather 'conditioned' by our thinking, i.e. an after-thought and synthesis which already presupposes a multiplicity of thoughts and whose existence as some sort of entity is merely "apparent" (BGE 17, BGE 54). And this is what seems to lead to his rejection of the "atomism of the soul" and the conclusion that if there is ever some sort of unity to our mental life it can only be that of a "subject-multiplicity" (BGE 12), never that of a permanent, fixed, substantial, indivisible subject or 'I' (or of the "soul" as an underlying "*atomon*", BGE 12). The so-called 'I' of consciousness is not really the centre and ultimate presupposition of the multiplicity of our conscious thoughts, this multiplicity cannot be said to 'belong' to an 'I', and our sense of self depends on the unconscious coordination and hierarchisation of our "drives and affects" (BGE 12), that is, on the 'body' as a 'society of many souls', a society of "under-wills" and "under-souls" (BGE 19).

---

[10] See Pippin (2010). Pippin is right in linking Nietzsche's conception of psychology with La Rochefoucauld and other French moralists. But it should also be linked with other Frenchman, namely with such 'psychologists' as Taine and Bourget. In Bourget's case, it is particularly clear how psychology and the diagnosis of European *décadence* and nihilism go hand in hand. See Giuliano Campioni's chapter in this volume. See also Pippin's chapter in this volume, as well as the editors' remarks in the Introduction.

As long as these remain coordinated and hierarchised, there is a 'self', there is 'unity' understood as "*organization* and *connected activity*" (NL 1885–1886, 2[87], KSA 12: 104 = WLN, 76). This was already Nietzsche's view in his *Zarathustra*, where he conceived of the 'I' of consciousness as a mere tool or play-thing of an unconscious 'Self', i.e., of the 'Self' that results from the organisation and connected activity of our body (Z I, On the Despisers of the Body). The decentered subjectivity of a subject-multiplicity is, therefore, not incompatible with forms of integrated subjectivity and agency.

However, if we look at *Beyond Good and Evil* as a whole, these aphorisms that focus on the 'I' of consciousness and seem much more theoretical than practical come to light as belonging to the wider project of describing and diagnosing the present condition of a *collective* 'consciousness'. From the start, Nietzsche's main theme (even when he deals with 'the prejudices of the philosophers') is "the European consciousness" (BGE 259). His concern is always with "the European spirit" (BGE 188, BGE 253), "the European soul" (BGE 245, BGE 254), also with the "European taste" (BGE 245, BGE 253) and "the European will" (BGE 201) – or, in sum, with what characterises "European culture" (BGE 202, BGE 250), especially in his own day and in the future. His reflection on many "peoples and fatherlands" also belongs to this project.

And he says this much in the Preface. *Beyond Good and Evil* is not so much about the "the soul-superstition" or "the superstition of the subject or I" as rather about the "magnificent tension of spirit in Europe, the likes of which the earth has never known" – a tension which has indeed its remote origin in Plato's "invention of pure spirit and the Good in itself", but which is, more precisely, the tension issuing from "the struggle against Plato" (BGE Preface). This means the struggle against the will to a metaphysical truth, to a 'true world' as a world which can only be reached by 'pure spirit' and which human beings are supposed to value unconditionally for being identical with 'the good in itself'. As the *Genealogy of Morality* will explain, this will to (a metaphysical) truth is the "kernel" (GM III 27) of an "ascetic ideal" that projects all positive value onto a transcendent realm of absolute truth and, thus, makes the nothingness of such a transcendent world appear as if it were something, while also making the reality of our perspectival, immanent world appear is if it were nothing. In *Beyond Good and Evil*, Nietzsche defines 'nihilism' as the attitude of a will to truth that prefers "an assured nothing" to "an uncertain something" (BGE 10). And he focuses on the present and the future of what he calls in his notebooks "the struggle against nihilism" (NL 1886, 5[50] KSA 12: 202, NL 1886, 7[31], KSA 12: 306). The nature of the struggle has changed. Plato's transcendent world of absolute truth and value is no longer credible – his error has been "overcome" (BGE Preface), that is, "God is dead", as Nietzsche had announced in the first edition of *The Gay Science* (GS 108, GS 125, etc.). That does not mean that the "struggle against nihilism" is over, nor does it mean that it has ceased to be a "struggle against Plato", for what is at stake is still a struggle against the devaluation of *this* world. But now the struggle is against the "extreme nihilism" (NL 1887 9[35], KSA 12: 351) resulting from the death of God.

The problem of subjectivity is hence a fundamental problem of *Beyond Good and Evil*, but only because the 'tension' of the struggle against nihilism is a *spiritual* tension. There will be no struggle unless the 'European consciousness' remains *subjectivised* – or, in Nietzsche's own terms, unless 'the spirit' in Europe remains capable of experiencing *itself* "as 'need'" (BGE Preface). At the most fundamental level, the problem of subjectivity in *Beyond Good and Evil* is this self-referentiality of spirit in Europe. Can the European spirit remain aware of itself as spirit and feel the need for a spiritual struggle against nihilism? And can the European consciousness, soul, spirit, will, taste remain some sort of self-referential *subject* in this context?

Already in the Preface, Nietzsche suggests that a fundamental divide between the masses and the spiritual elite of Europe is an important aspect of the question at stake. Given that Plato's transcendent world of absolute truth and value is no longer credible, Europe now "breathes a sigh of relief after this nightmare, and at least can enjoy a healthier – well – sleep" (BGE Preface). This sleep may be very satisfying for the great majority of people living in Europe, but Nietzsche claims to belong to those few who are the heirs of "all the force cultivated" for centuries through the struggle against Plato, against the ascetic ideal, against nihilism. And these few, the cultural elite of Europe, are the ones "*whose task is wakefulness itself*" (BGE Preface). These few cannot sleep – or, better still, the question is precisely whether they, too, will fall asleep in bovine satisfaction, or will instead reveal themselves as "*good Europeans* and free, *very free spirits*" capable of maintaining awake "the whole need of spirit and the whole tension of its bow" (BGE Preface). "Perhaps", Nietzsche concludes, they have "the arrow too, the task, and – who knows? the goal ..." (BGE Preface).

Thus, for Nietzsche, the options are clear. Either the European elite is strong enough to continue the spiritual struggle against nihilism and shoots at the goal of continuing it with bow and arrow, or the future of humanity in Europe will belong to the 'last man', i.e., to the post-metaphysical, self-satisfied, petty human being (or post-human being) who cares only for comfort and has no spirit. If the future is the triumph of "the universal, green pasture happiness of the herd, with security, safety, contentment, and an easier life for all" (BGE 44), then the death of God will have caused another, even more terrible death: the death of the 'spirit', the death of "high spirituality" in Europe, the death of European culture, taste, will, soul, consciousness – the *death of the European subject*.

Nietzsche does not call for the 'death of the subject'. On the contrary, one of his most fundamental concerns is to *prevent* this death, particularly in Europe (or 'the West'). One only has to search for the words 'spirit' (*Geist*) and 'spirituality' (*Geistigkeit*) throughout *Beyond Good and Evil* to confirm that Nietzsche's concern with 'the spirit as need' and 'wakefulness itself' pervades the whole book. Given that Nietzsche proposes that the Christian conception of the soul, as well as all forms of the modern, Cartesian conception of an atomistic subject, be replaced with the hypothesis of a "subject-multiplicity" (BGE 12), let us now consider how throughout *Beyond Good and Evil* Nietzsche uses this hypothesis not only to describe the situation of modern human beings in late modernity in Europe but also to express his views on what can and should be done in that situation – his normative exhortations to the cultural elite.

We may begin by observing that in *Beyond Good and Evil* Nietzsche seems almost obsessed with one important aspect of that situation. He believes that there is a particular 'instinct' which is becoming dominant in late modernity – the "herd-instinct" (BGE 191–203, 260, 268). He realises how offensive is it to describe the massification of culture in late modernity in terms of a herd-instinct ("we are considered almost sinful for constantly using expressions like 'herd,' and 'herd instinct' with direct reference to people of 'modern ideas'", BGE 202), but he cannot help it, for "this is where our new insights happen to lie" (BGE 202). His main concern is that the dominance of the herd-instinct not only creates a type of human being devoid of spirit, but even outlaws and erases the possibility of "high spirituality" and "free spirits":

> For his part, the herd man of today's Europe gives himself the appearance of being the only permissible type of man and glorifies those characteristics that make him tame, easy-going and useful to the herd as the true human virtues, namely: public spirit, goodwill, consideration, industry, moderation, modesty, clemency, and pity. (BGE 199)

'Herd-morality' (or "morality of timidity", BGE 201, or "slave-morality", BGE 260) sees "the preservation of the community" (or "herd utility") as the only thing of value (BGE 201). Nietzsche might see nothing wrong in this 'herd morality' and the predominance of "public spirit, goodwill, consideration, industry, moderation, modesty, clemency, and pity" if this predominance did not tend to radically repress and label as "evil" everything that appears to threaten the survival of the community:

> A high, independent spiritedness, a will to stand alone, even an excellent faculty of reason, will be perceived as a threat. Everything that raises the individual over the herd and frightens the neighbour will henceforth be called *evil*; the proper, modest, unobtrusive, equalising attitude and the *mediocrity* of desires acquire moral names and honours. (BGE 201)

Nietzsche's replacement of the "atomism of the soul" (BGE 12) with the alternative hypothesis of a "subject-multiplicity" is at least implicitly presupposed in these passages. Firstly, because Nietzsche's conviction that the modern human being is being moulded and tailored (or "cultivated and disciplined", as his refrain goes) by socialisation, i.e. by custom and morality, presupposes a *plastic* subject – and hence the opposite of the permanent, fixed, substantial, indivisible subject of psychological atomism. Throughout *Beyond Good and Evil* Nietzsche emphasises the plasticity of his subject-multiplicity. In aphorism 268, for example, he states that the "structure" of a person's soul and "what the soul sees as its conditions of life, its genuine needs" are best revealed by "a person's valuations", and these are a shifting, changing, plastic "rank order" of values, which depends on "sensations" and, therefore, on a person's environment:

> What group of sensations in a soul will be the first to wake up, start speaking, and making demands is decisive for the whole rank order of its values, and will ultimately determine its table of goods. (BGE 268)

If this were not so, a "natural, all-too-natural *progressus in simile*" could not be observed in late modernity in Europe, i.e. the great majority of people would not be involved (as Nietzsche believes they are) in the process of "becoming increasingly similar, ordinary, average, herd-like, – increasingly *base*!" (BGE 268). Who a person is, is ultimately synonymous with the "order of rank" in which "the innermost drives of his nature stand with respect to each other" (BGE 6). Without a *multiplicity* of drives and their different goals or values, there would be no such "order of rank", and without the plasticity of this kind of "structure" no "*progressus in simile*", no massification of the modern human being could ever take place. Moreover, lability to sensation or feeling (*Empfindung*) and the plasticity of the plural structure of the subject are also part of the explanation of the opposite process. No one could ever become exceptional and different from the others at the level of 'spirit' (i.e., 'noble' instead of 'base') without "profound suffering": "order of rank is almost determined by just *how* deeply people can suffer [...] Profound suffering makes you noble; it separates" (BGE 270).[11]

But, secondly, and most importantly, Nietzsche's hypothesis of a subject-multiplicity is implicitly presupposed in his views on massification because these views presuppose (not only a plastic but also) a *divided* 'subject'. Nietzsche's idea is that the 'herd-instinct' *represses and predominates over* the other instincts or drives.[12] These other instincts are first of all the "animal

---

11 See also BGE 225.
12 On the predominance of drives over other drives, see Ken Gemes' chapter in this volume.

instincts" (GM II 22), the "old instincts" of the hunter-gatherer – "all those instincts of wild, free, prowling man" (GM II 16) –, also known (from the perspective of conventional morality) as "the bad drives" (BGE 23). These cause "affects of hatred, envy, greed, and power-lust", which are, however, according to Nietzsche, "the conditioning affects of life" (BGE 23). The 'bad drives' belong to the species and cannot be eradicated. But, contrary to common opinion, Nietzsche does not preach a return to the pre-social predominance of the 'old instincts' or the 'bad drives'. For he considers that the human being only became 'interesting' as a result of socialisation and, especially, of the development of the ascetic ideal (GM I 6, GM II 16, GM II 22), which should, therefore, not be simply or unconditionally lambasted. The Preface of *Beyond Good and Evil*, in particular, makes very clear (as we saw) that what is important (or interesting) for Nietzsche is the "tension of spirit in Europe", not brute animality. His problem is rather that he believes the repression of the 'bad drives' to be a repression of precisely those drives whose 'spiritualisation' (*Vergeistigung*) is needed for and is at stake in the struggle against nihilism. 'High spirituality' requires levels of courage and strength to stand alone and be independent that can only come from the spiritualisation of "all those instincts of wild, free, prowling man" (GM II 16). What makes herd-morality label as 'bad' even the most spiritual manifestations of these instincts is its fear of individuality and its (perhaps illusory) need to cultivate mediocrity for the sake of the community's preservation:

> When the highest and strongest drives erupt in passion, driving the individual up and out and far above the average, over the depths of the herd conscience, the self-esteem of the community is destroyed – its faith in itself, its backbone, as it were, is broken: as a result, these are the very drives that will be denounced and slandered the most. (BGE 201)

Throughout the whole of *Beyond Good and Evil* Nietzsche dissects the dividedness of the modern human being. He believes that this dividedness is, to a great extent, shared by every modern human being. In late modernity, everyone is "a heap of contradictions", as Nietzsche writes in his notebooks (NL 1887, 9[183], KSA 12: 446). Christian morality has divided human beings by preaching "obedience" to Church and State, thereby helping impose the predominance of the herd-instinct (BGE 61, BGE 199). Pity (or compassion) has been instrumental in this respect. Pity divides you by making you feel the other's suffering (as Schopenhauer taught), such that it not only "doubles" your "woes" (BGE 30), ruins your "independence" of spirit (BGE 41) and deepens your "self-hatred" (BGE 222), but also promotes the interiorisation of the herd-instinct by most naturally becoming "pity for social 'distress,' for 'society'" (BGE 225). This is clearly Nietzsche's main concern in his raging against Jesuitism (BGE Preface) as a "religion of pity" (BGE 206), and also the reason why he thinks that "the *democratic* movement is the heir to Christianity" (BGE 202). The democratic movement (or "democratic Enlightenment", BGE Preface) is ultimately based on Christian pity for "the creature in the human being" (BGE 225): it promotes even further the interiorisation of the herd-instinct by institutionalising the modern ideal of "equal rights", and leads to "socialist pity" (BGE 21) and the illusory idealisation of "a future state of society where 'the exploitative character' will fall away" (BGE 259).

If anything excuses Nietzsche for his reactionary politics – and especially for his rhetorical excesses aimed at modern pity for the "sick and injured" or for "the grumbling, dejected, rebellious slave strata who strive for dominance" (BGE 225) – is the fact that he seems to have truly believed that modernity's overestimation of comfort and its aversion to suffering, especially to 'profound suffering', might eventually erase 'the spirit' from the face of the earth and result in the sweeping triumph of the nihilism of 'last men'. The level of self-alienation already accomplished by the predominance of the herd-instinct over the other 'animal instincts' functioned, for him, as a clear sign of such terrifying danger.[13]

But Nietzsche's dissection of the internal division of the modern human being goes much deeper than this. 'Slave morality', either in the form of Christian morality or in any other secular form, divides modern souls between their allegiance to the 'herd' and their allegiance to other, non-gregarious animal instincts, but also between the egalitarian 'table of goods' of that morality and the aristocratic 'tables of goods' of older, pre-Christian moralities, whose traces remain (as cultural inheritances, as it were) in the soul of the modern human being. After claiming that there are two basic types of morality, "slave morality" and "master morality", Nietzsche writes:

> I will immediately add that in all higher and more mixed cultures, attempts to negotiate between these moralities also appear, although more frequently the two are confused and there are mutual misunderstandings. In fact, you sometimes find them sharply juxtaposed – inside the same person even, within a single soul. (BGE 260)

---

[13] In BGE 212, for example, he writes that "equal rights" could end up as "equal wrongs" because they might wage "a joint war on everything rare, strange, privileged, on the higher man, higher soul, higher duty, higher responsibility, on creative power and mastery" (BGE 212). On the 'last man' theme ("we see how humanity is becoming smaller, how you are making it smaller!") and on the abolishment of suffering as the implicit aim of modern pity and modern ideology of equal rights, see, for example, BGE 225: "you want, if possible (and no 'if possible' is crazier) *to abolish suffering*. [...] The discipline of suffering, of great suffering – don't you know that this discipline has been the sole cause of every enhancement in humanity so far?"

Perhaps no one can consistently embrace one of the basic types of morality and do away with the other: "we modern men are determined by a *diversity* of morals; our actions shine with different colours in turn, they are rarely unambiguous, – and it happens often enough that we perform *multicoloured* actions" (BGE 215).

This is the proper context of Nietzsche's constant talk of 'atavisms' and hereditariness, particularly of his belief that not only genetic traits, but also 'memes' (as we now say) pass on from generation to generation: "What a man's forefathers liked doing the most, and the most often, cannot be wiped from his soul [...] It is utterly impossible that a person might fail to have the qualities and propensities of his elders and ancestors in his body" (BGE 264). But the problem here is not that a person can do nothing but repeat what previous generations have done (an absurd claim, particularly in late modernity); the problem is rather that no matter how different, even exceptional a person becomes in a given direction, for example by virtue of education and culture, that same person will still remain a *contradictory* 'subject-multiplicity': "In our very popular, which is to say vulgar age, 'education' and 'culture' essentially *have* to be the art of deception – to deceive about lineage, about the inherited vulgarity in body and soul" (BGE 264). Even if one has a strong "instinct for rank" (BGE 263), that is, an 'instinct of reverence' that lets one have noble reverence for one's own soul (for "*the noble soul has reverence for itself*", BGE 287), in modernity one will not fail to also have (in a lesser or greater degree) an "instinct of submissiveness" (BGE 261). The 'base' and the 'noble' coexist in the modern 'European consciousness'. Or, more precisely, all thoughts of a modern 'European consciousness' are merely 'surfaces' of struggles among a multiplicity of contradictory, inherited instincts, so that even the consciousness of a philosopher is "not *opposed* to instinct in any decisive sense – most of a philosopher's conscious thought is secretly directed and forced into determinate channels by the instincts" (BGE 3).

According to Nietzsche's diagnosis, one of the main reasons why this is a characteristically modern and European phenomenon which can only be found to a lesser degree in other ages and cultures is because modern Europe has strongly developed a unique "historical sense". Thanks to the development of this sense, we now "have secret entrances everywhere, like no noble age has ever had, and, above all, access to the labyrinths of unfinished cultures and to every half-barbarism that has ever existed on earth" (BGE 224). Nietzsche claims that this is "an ignoble sense" (BGE 223), that is, "a sense and instinct for everything, a taste and tongue for everything" (BGE 223). Given the human plasticity and lability to sensation, the development of such a sense cannot fail to create the greatest contradictoriness among the instincts. The spirit is often capable of turning this "to its advantage" (BGE 223, BGE 224) – but always at the peril of disintegration.

This is an important part of what Nietzsche means by his characterisation of modernity as 'decadent'. Modernity is "an age of disintegration" (BGE 200), an age in which the pre-modern "types", however "sturdy and hard", have been disintegrating at a "kind of *tropical* tempo", so that "variation, whether as deviation (into something higher, finer, rarer) or as degeneration and monstrosity" has "come onto the scene in the greatest abundance and splendour" (BGE 262). Thus passages such as this one indicate Nietzsche's *ambivalent* evaluation of multiplicity. 'Multiplicity' is another word for *complexity*. The rejection of the 'atomism of the soul' entails that the human soul is not something simple (i.e., indivisible or monadic), but rather complex (*vielfaches*, BGE 291). What we have seen so far about the complexity of the modern soul is that it (a) involves plasticity; (b) involves dividedness and indeed struggle among a multiplicity of elements (sc. drives, affects, instincts, conscious and unconscious thoughts, desires, passions, etc.), (c) involves different possibilities of organisation, connected activity, 'order of rank' among a multiplicity of elements; (d) involves self-referentiality, or reflexivity. What Nietzsche values in the human being (and finds 'interesting') would be impossible without complexity: the 'tension' of the spirit, its "power to invent and dissimulate" (BGE 44), the kind of reflexivity that makes it expand and engenders an "inner [...] pathos of distance" (BGE 257), its ability to "gaze with many eyes and consciences from the heights into every distance, from the depths up to every height, from the corner onto every expanse" (BGE 211), its capacity to grow by questioning itself, especially by 'revaluing' its own values and creating new ones (BGE 212). But complexity is also the seed of 'decadence' (or *décadence*, as Nietzsche usually writes, apparently in honour of Paul Bourget, Charles Féré, and other French writers who have shaped his views on this topic). Nietzsche often construes the idea of *décadence* as a lack of organisation, hierarchy, and order in a whole – for example, in a book, or in a musical composition, but most importantly in a person's psychology. In *On the Genealogy* of Morality, he describes how the human being's entrance in society shattered the animal health which it enjoyed as a hunter-gatherer, disorganised his instincts, and introduced in human history the internal dividedness between 'herd' and individual animality described above. And here Nietzsche makes very clear how the development of spiritual self-referentiality played a crucial role:

> the poor things were reduced to relying on thinking, inference, calculation, and the connecting of cause with effect, that is, to relying on their "consciousness", that most impoverished and error-prone organ! [...] The whole inner world, originally stretched thinly as though between two layers of skin, was expanded and extended itself and gained depth, breadth and height in proportion to the degree that the external discharge of man's instincts was *obstructed*. (GM II 16)

In *Twilight of the Idols*, Nietzsche defines d*écadence* is a disarray of the instincts which drives people to feel that they have to fight their instincts ("to have to fight the instincts – that is the formula for decadence: as long as life is ascending, happiness is equal to instinct", TI Socrates 11). In *The Anti-Christ*, he adds the idea that d*écadence* is a disarray of the instincts which even drives people to *prefer* what is harmful to what is really beneficial for themselves ("I call an animal, a species, an individual corrupt when it loses its instincts, when it chooses, when it prefers things that will harm it", A 6).

In *Beyond Good and Evil* Nietzsche's expresses the idea of *décadence* by writing that (due mostly to the hyper-development of the historical sense) the modern human being is an inner "chaos":

> the past of every form and way of life, of cultures that used to lie side by side or on top of each other, radiates into us, we "modern souls". At this point, our instincts are running back everywhere and we ourselves are a type of chaos (BGE 224).

One important aphorism – focused specifically on the German soul in modernity – emphasises how the kind of 'chaos' Nietzsche has in mind entails inner contradictoriness: in the German soul "the noblest stands right next to the most base", "the German soul is multiple, it originates in different places and is more piled up and pieced together than actually constructed", "the German soul has passages going this way and that, it has caves, hiding places and dungeons; its disorder has much of the charm of the mysterious; the German is an expert on the secret paths to chaos". Therefore, one should establish as a fact "the contradictory nature at the base of the German soul" (BGE 244).

However, Nietzsche is also clear about his ambivalent evaluation of complexity, even of contradictoriness. He conveys the idea of self-referentiality or reflexivity by reconceiving it in terms of a relationship between creature and creator: "in human beings, *creature* and *creator* are combined" (BGE 225). Self-creation is an important part of our lives. In observing ourselves and questioning what we are and revaluing our values, we constantly recreate ourselves.[14] Our 'chaos' represents a constant danger of disintegration, but also represents the fragmented material for the enlargement and ennoblement of our spirit:

> In human beings, *creature* and *creator* are combined: in humans there is material, fragments, abundance, clay, dirt, nonsense, chaos; but in humans there is also creator, maker,

---

14 On this sense of 'self-creation' (as a not necessarily conscious, or fully conscious, process based on self-observation and revaluation, particularly revaluation of one's 'aspirational self', or ideal 'schema' of ourselves), see Benedetta Zavatta's and especially John Richardson's chapter in this volume.

hammer-hardness, spectator-divinity and seventh day: – do you understand this contrast? (BGE 225)

But the way Nietzsche understands self-referentiality and self-creation entails another fundamental characteristic of human subjectivity and its complexity – a characteristic which brings us back to Nietzsche's scepticism regarding self-knowledge. The "material, fragments, abundance, clay, dirt, nonsense, chaos" which we observe in ourselves and on the basis of which we constantly recreate ourselves cannot be simply observed, known, directly accessed as the object of some sort of "immediate certainty", for we, humans, are fundamentally "unknown to ourselves" (GM Preface 1). Besides (a) plasticity, (b) dividedness, (c) hierarchic organisation, and (d) self-referentiality, the complex subjectivity of Nietzsche's 'subject-multiplicity' is also characterised by its (e) *undeterminedness*. In one of *Beyond Good and Evil*'s most famous sayings Nietzsche declares that "human being is the still undetermined animal" (BGE 62). That this claim should be interpreted in connection with Nietzsche's (basically Langean) scepticism regarding self-knowledge, becomes clear in the aphorism where he writes that "the human being is a complex [*vielfaches*], hypocritical, artificial, and opaque animal" (BGE 291), and only the invention of "good conscience" and the "lengthy falsification" we call "morality" have made possible for him to "enjoy his soul as something *simple* [*einfach*], for once" (BGE 291). The undeterminedness of the human being lies in its 'soul', spirit, consciousness, in its complex, reflexive subjectivity. Every look inside the soul discovers only its opaqueness; the belief in inner 'immediate certainties' is actually no more than an instance of self-deception; in fact, all our thoughts about our thoughts and, more generally, all our self-reflexive attempts to give determinedness to our undeterminedness involve some degree of self-deception, and are hence 'hypocritical' and 'artificial' to some extent. This holds even for the deepest, most considerate philosophies – and, of course, even for Nietzsche's own philosophy. No matter how deep one digs inside oneself, one is still using language to stop at a given surface and *conceal* from oneself a deeper level of meaning. The "cave" every philosopher digs in search for some truth has always "an even deeper cave behind it" (BGE 289), every word that he uses in the search for some truth – especially when he questions himself and speaks about himself – "is also a mask", i.e. a tool of self-deception:

> Every philosophy is a foreground philosophy – that is a hermit's judgment: "There is something arbitrary in *his* stopping here, looking back, looking around, in his not digging any deeper *here*, and putting his spade away – there is also something suspicious about it." Every philosophy *conceals* a philosophy too: every opinion is also a hiding place, every word is also a mask. (BGE 289)

There is an obvious paradox in these claims. The 'hermit' watches the philosophers digging their caves and denounces their self-deception; he sees further than them, he spots the deeper cave behind every cave they dig – and yet, if he is able to do that, then surely he, too, is a philosopher (not to mention the fact that "a philosopher was always a hermit first", BGE 289). If his claim that *all* philosophers deceive themselves is true, then he, too, is deceiving himself while making this claim – for making such a claim is what typically counts as being a philosopher. The paradox becomes even more obvious if we remember that the 'hermit' is, of course, the *philosopher* Nietzsche.

Nietzsche delights in this kind of paradox. He *wants* to make the bold and paradoxical claim that given the fundamental undeterminedness of human subjectivity, there is always an element of self-deception in all attempts at self-knowledge. And this brings us back to the passage where Nietzsche rejects the theoretical approach to the problem of subjectivity. Only "innocence" and "moral naiveté" can account for the approach of a thinker who places himself "in front of consciousness with the request that it please give him *honest* answers" (BGE 34). In asking whether consciousness is "real", or why consciousness "so resolutely keeps the external world at arm's length" (BGE 34), such a thinker discovers important aspects of the soul's fundamental undeterminedness, but if he believes that this undeterminedness can be overcome, he is certainly unaware of the fundamental self-deceptiveness of self-knowledge. Given the nature of human subjectivity – its (a) plasticity, (b) dividedness, (c) hierarchic organisation, (d) self-referentiality, (e) undeterminedness, and especially its (f) self-deceptiveness –, consciousness cannot possibly give 'honest' answers about itself.

But the paradox is, again, obvious. Nietzsche's knowledge of the nature of human subjectivity (that is, of a, b, c, d, e, and f) lets him know that the nature of human subjectivity cannot be known. Or, in other words, Nietzsche's scepticism regarding self-knowledge involves a (first-personal) theory about the nature of human subjectivity, and therefore involves self-knowledge, in fact precisely the kind of (first-personal) self-knowledge that his scepticism claims to be impossible.

It is always very difficult, perhaps impossible, to articulate sceptic views (such as Nietzsche's views on self-deception and self-knowledge) without falling into paradox, perhaps even into outright contradiction. If we apply the principle of charity and try to construe Nietzsche's views in the least paradoxical and contradictory way, our first move should be to ascribe to his views a much more modest epistemic status than that of a 'theory', or of 'knowledge'. Nietzsche does not claim 'knowledge' about self-knowledge, i.e. he does not claim to possess proper 'knowledge' about the impossibility of self-knowledge, and he does not claim to possess a foundational, privileged 'theory' of subjectivity, absolutely freed of self-deception and capable of declaring all other theories to be self-deceived. Nietzsche's views are, instead, *heuristic hypotheses* ("regulative fictions" in his terminology) which allow him to reflect upon and diagnose the *existential situation* of his age.

In *Beyond Good and Evil*, Nietzsche drives his efforts of cultural reflection and diagnosis to a kind of climax in Part Six ("We, Scholars"), where he deals not so much with the 'disease' that afflicts *most* people in late modernity (the predominance of the 'herd-instinct' etc) as rather with the specific form which that same 'disease', the 'European disease', takes among the cultural (or spiritual) *elite*. This he calls "paralysis of the will" (BGE 208).

Among the cultural elite, everyone is more or less a sceptic, for "when a philosopher these days makes it known that he is not a sceptic, [...] everyone gets upset" (BGE 208). The reason for this, Nietzsche suggests, is not that everyone lives in possession of a well-grounded sceptic philosophy, but only that the "paralysis of the will" makes everyone a sceptic. A paralysed will feels most comfortable living in scepticism, so that it will fear anything that shakes its scepticism. Or, in other words, scepticism is "the most spiritual expression of a certain complex physiological condition" which Nietzsche calls "paralysis of the will" and "which in layman's terms is called weak nerves or a sickly constitution" (BGE 208). Such a paralysis and sickly constitution means that people "no longer have any sense of independence in decision-making, or the bold feeling of pleasure in willing" (BGE 208). And this lack of independence, boldness, and pleasure in willing has many forms and manifests itself in many ways: "most of what presents itself in the shop windows these days as 'objectivity,' for instance, or 'scientifically,' 'l'art pour l'art,' or 'pure, will-less knowing,' is only dressed-up scepticism and paralysis of the will, – I will vouch for this diagnosis of the European disease" (BGE 208).

Nietzsche explicitly dovetails this 'diagnosis' with the problem of *nihilism* (and, therefore, with the 'death of God'). He suggests that what the paralysed, sceptic will of the European spiritual elite fears the most is the kind of revolutionary, perhaps literally destructive, explosive nihilism one reads about in Russian novels: "a dynamite of the spirit, perhaps a newly discovered Russian *nihiline*, a pessimism *bonae voluntatis* that does not just *say* No or *will* No, but – the very thought is terrible! – *does* No" (BGE 208). For Nietzsche, the nihilism one should really fear the most is the opposite of this explosive Russian nihilism, namely the one which manifests itself as a paralysis of the will – the kind of sceptic, pessimistic nihilism which culminates in the bovine happiness of 'last men'.

Against *this* kind of nihilism Nietzsche puts forward the idea of "another, stronger type of scepticism" (BGE 209) – *his* type of scepticism, his type of 'dynamite'. This should be "a harsher and more dangerous new type of scepticism", "the scepticism of a bold masculinity" (BGE 209). Nietzsche clearly sees it as an *affirmative* kind of scepticism (and not as "hostile to life", not as a "negation of life", in which case it would be just another form of nihilistic scepticism), and he clearly sees it as something *spiritual* – at bottom a radical engagement with the task of revaluing all values and thus entering into "the enormous, practically untouched realm of dangerous knowledge" (BGE 23). But, most importantly, Nietzsche sees it as a form of "dangerous freedom" (BGE 209), a form of affirmative and spiritual freedom (or the freedom of a 'free spirit') that overcomes the 'paralysis of the will' *not by a theoretical refutation of scepticism*, but by an act (or a series of acts) of *sheer, arbitrary, bold choice, decision, 'will'*.

Nietzsche characterises this 'will' in two basic ways. Firstly, he presents it as a recuperation and new spiritualisation of the 'old instincts' or, put differently, as a metamorphosis of the 'bad drives' into a willingness to 'command' and indeed 'legislate' in the realm of the spirit – ultimately, in the realm of *value*. This is what is at stake in the famous passage in which Nietzsche claims that

> true *philosophers are commanders and legislators*: they say "That is how it should be!" they are the ones who first determine the "where to?" and "what for?" of people, which puts at their disposal the preliminary labor of all philosophical labourers, all those who overwhelm the past. True philosophers reach for the future with a creative hand and everything that is and was becomes a means, a tool, a hammer for them. Their "knowing" is *creating*, their creating is a legislating, their will to truth is – *will to power*. (BGE 211)

Secondly, Nietzsche conceives of the new will capable of overcoming the 'European disease' as a will that might be able to achieve 'greatness' by giving *unity and wholeness* to the dispersed, sickly divided, disorganised multiplicity of the modern subject. In aphorism 212, Nietzsche presents this conception as his "ideal" (BGE 212), but makes clear that this is a *local* ideal: an ideal – or an idea of "greatness" – which fits the present times by simply inverting what predominates in these times, but which would therefore be inadequate in other times. Nietzsche explicitly mentions the sixteenth century and the age of Socrates as examples of other times in which other ideals would be appropriate: the ideal of equal rights may have been right for the sixteenth century and the ideal of Socratic irony may have been right for Socrates and his time. Philosophers' ideals, Nietzsche claims, should express their opposition to the age in which they live – that is, should express the fact that they are philosophers *because* their enemy is the ideal of their age, i.e., because, as philosophers, they are by definition "the bad conscience of their age" (BGE 212). Thus, Nietzsche's ideal of an affirmative, commanding, legislating, creative 'will to power' is the exact opposite both of the lack of individual will typical of those human beings in whom the herd-instinct predominates and of the sceptical paralysis of the will typical of the cultural elite of modern Europe.[15] The ideal of such a will involves aristocratic and individualist values ("being noble, wanting to be for yourself, the ability to be different, standing alone and needing to live by your own fists", BGE 212), which Nietzsche considers to be most opposed to the values of his age. (Note, however, that he adopts these aristocratic and individualist values strategically and for the sake of the future of humanity and the European spirit – which paradoxically entails a commitment to humanist and communal values). But, most importantly, he uses his conception of subjective multiplicity to construe such a will as a will that achieves "greatness" by achieving "unity in multiplicity" (BGE 212) – that is, as a will that manifests "the ability to be just as multiple as whole, just as wide as full" (BGE 212).

That is how Nietzsche expects the spirit to turn multiplicity "to its advantage" (BGE 223, BGE 224). In the age where the development of the historical sense and especially the absence of belief prompted by the death of God have made the human spirit and subjectivity more plastic than ever, more divided than ever, more disorganised than ever, more reflexive and more undetermined than ever – or self-referential and undetermined to the point of paralysis – , such an extreme disunity may still become a new form of great *spiritual* unity. In late modernity, only that would count for Nietzsche as the development of a 'genuine Self'.[16] The possibility of a spontaneous, non-reflexive, organic unity comparable to the health of other animals (or to our pre-social ancestors') is forever lost for us. According to Nietzsche, something like an integrated subjectivity and a genuine, first-personal relation to a unifying 'Self' is still possible, although only as the result of a spiritual process of 'self-creation' – and although only in non-foundationalist, non-transparent terms.[17]

But, to repeat, this development of genuine Self in this sense is not supposed to result from new knowledge, but rather from a new subjective attitude, which is involved in Nietzsche's new scepticism:

---

[15] As Nietzsche puts it in BGE 212: "Today, the will is weakened and diluted by the tastes and virtues of the times, and nothing is as timely as weakness of will: this is why precisely strength of will and the hardness and capacity for long-term resolutions must belong to the concept of 'greatness', in the philosopher's ideal."

[16] On Nietzsche's conception of a 'genuine Self', see Gemes 2009.

[17] As Elliot L. Jurist puts it (in a book which was inspirational for this chapter), Nietzsche "denies the possibility of any conventional notion of unified agency" and has indeed a model of "decentered subjectivity", just like Lacan (see below) – but "still, Nietzsche defends what legitimately can be termed a sense of integrated agency, wherein the self can achieve coherence and determination, although not transparency" (Jurist 2000: 212).

This scepticism despises and nevertheless appropriates; it undermines and takes possession; *it does not believe but does not die out on this account*; it gives the spirit a dangerous freedom, but is severe on the heart. (BGE 209, my emphasis)

In this respect, Nietzsche is truly a precursor of existentialism. Affirming life in the face of nihilism (i.e., in the face of the absurdity, or meaninglessness, that results from the death of God), and affirming it by sheer decision and not on the basis of philosophical knowledge or wisdom – that involves an 'existentialist' conception of freedom and is the 'existentialist' stance *par excellence*.

3 Consciousness in *The Gay Science* 354

Let us now turn to the other main text considered in this chapter: *The Gay Science*, particularly aphorism 354 of Book V, which is perhaps Nietzsche's main aphorism on consciousness.[18]

Here, Nietzsche's procedure seems clear. He asks a theoretical question, and in order to answer it puts forward what he calls an "extravagant conjecture" (GS 354). The question reads: "*To what end* does consciousness exist at all when it is basically superfluous?". This is asked as a typical evolutionary question. Given that "man, like every living creature, is constantly thinking but does not know it"; given that conscious thinking is only the "surface" of most of our thinking, or "only the smallest part of it, let's say the shallowest, worst part"; and given that we can not only think unconsciously, but also "feel, will, remember, and also 'act' in every sense of the term" without becoming conscious of any of that, our consciousness does indeed seem to be "basically superfluous" (GS 354). So why has it been selected in the course of human evolution? Where does its evolutionary value lie? Why did it develop and why was it eventually preserved as a characteristic of our species? Nietzsche's 'extravagant conjecture' is that "*consciousness in general has developed under the pressure of the need to communicate*" (GS 354). He explains this by writing the following:

[...] as the most endangered animal, [man] *needed* help and protection, he needed his equals; he had to express his neediness and be able to make himself understood – and to do so, he first needed "consciousness", i.e. even to "know" what distressed him, to "know" how he felt, to "know" what he thought. (GS 354)

---

[18] This section is in part a reformulation and abridgment of Constâncio (2012).

The conception of consciousness involved in this important passage accords with a posthumous note where Nietzsche defines "consciousness" (*Bewußtheit*) as a "*Wissen um ein Wissen*" (NL 1880, 10[F101], KSA 9: 438), i.e. as reflexive "knowledge" (*Wissen*) about what one already "knows" unconsciously.[19] This is, of course, the idea implied in the metaphorical image of consciousness as a "mirror", which Nietzsche employs at the beginning of aphorism 354. Consciousness is the human organism's ability to "see itself in the mirror" (GS 354), i.e. to know about or become aware of its own thinking, feeling, willing, remembering, and acting, which would otherwise remain unconscious.[20]

Pace Mattia Riccardi, the question why has this 'mirroring', or reflexive consciousness, been preserved in the course of human evolution cannot in any way entail the epiphenomenal nature of human consciousness, and in fact it does not even raise the question whether human consciousness is epiphenomenal.[21] In saying that human consciousness is "basically superfluous" Nietzsche's point is not that reflexive knowledge is never efficacious, or that knowing that one knows is always outside of the causal chains that explain our actions, or that knowing that one is thinking, feeling, willing, remembering, or acting changes nothing in what we actually do. Nietzsche's point is rather (a) that all organic functions of which we can become conscious (as for example thinking, feeling,

---

19 In explaining this definition, Nietzsche explicitly states that "the most usual form of knowing [*Wissen*] is the one without consciousness [*Bewußtheit*]" (NL 1880, 10[F101], KSA 9: 438).
20 In Constâncio (2011a), I showed how Nietzsche's use of this mirror metaphor comes from Schopenhauer. But the conception of self-reflection as a becoming conscious of such organic functions as thinking, feeling, etc. can be traced back to Aristotle (*Nic. ethics* IX, 1170a–b). Aristotle points out that we become conscious of being alive, or conscious "that we are", because while seeing we perceive that we see, while hearing and walking we perceive that we hear and walk, and while perceiving and thinking we perceive that we perceive and think. But there are two important differences between Aristotle and Nietzsche: (a) Aristotle speaks of "perception" or "perceiving" (αἰσθάνεσθαι) and does not actually have a word for 'consciousness'; (b) Aristotle remarks that *whenever we see* we perceive that we see, etc. – while Nietzsche's idea is precisely that most of the time we see without becoming truly conscious that we are seeing, i.e., without 'monitoring' our own consciousness, or without becoming *conscious of our consciousness*.
21 See Riccardi (forthcoming). I use the term 'epiphenomenal' in its strongest sense, so as to imply that consciousness is so completely dependent on its unconscious causes that it can only be considered causally irrelevant (or 'superfluous'). But note that if Riccardi's epiphenomenalism, as well as Leiter's, means only that although 'consciousness is not causally efficacious in its own right' (Leiter 2002: 92), representations acquired in self-conscious mental states can 'become party to causally relevant psycho-physical mechanisms beneath the level of consciousness – which is to say, their causal power derives from their being "internalized", not from their being self-conscious' (Leiter 2014: 73), then their views are, in the end, very similar to my own view of consciousness (and particularly of 'incorporation') in Constâncio (2011).

willing, remembering, and acting) can take place *either with or without* consciousness, and (b) this raises the question why was consciousness ever selected in the course of human evolution. The fact that all organic functions can take place without consciousness does not entail that consciousness is causally inert, that is: it does not entail that the emergence or supervenience of mental events makes no causal difference – it does not entail that such a supervenience is a by-product of physical events and stands aside from the physical causal chains that lead to our actions. In fact, (c) Nietzsche assumes that consciousness is adaptive, i.e., has brought a decisive reproductive advantage to the species, and (d) he argues (or at least speculates) that consciousness is adaptive in the sense of 'group adaptive' (as the evolutionary jargon goes), i.e., not necessarily beneficial and even often harmful for individuals as such, but crucial for the natural selection of a group and hence for the preservation of a species. This is precisely what is implied in the passage just quoted above: man as individual was "the most endangered animal", and consciousness came to the rescue not only because it allowed him "to 'know' what distressed him, to 'know' how he felt, to 'know' what he thought", but also, and crucially, because it allowed him to communicate his needs among "his equals" (GS 354), that is, it allowed him to build a whole new type of communities – communities based on conscious communication. (e) Hence, far from being 'epiphenomenal', or 'inefficacious', consciousness is for Nietzsche one of the crucial causes of the development of society as we know it (and therefore of all social inter*action* as we know it). Or, in other words, consciousness is 'superfluous' only in the sense of not being a necessary condition of individual organic functions. In the evolution of the human species it has not been at all 'superfluous', nor is it at all 'superfluous' in the daily weaving of the reality which counts for us as most real: our social reality.[22]

---

22 To be precise, Mattia Riccardi's argument is that although our first-order consciousness can be efficacious, high-order consciousness – i.e., self-consciousness *qua* consciousness of our conscious states (also known as 'monitoring consciousness' or 'HOT', 'higher-order thought') – is always epiphenomenal. In other words, in GS 354 'consciousness' means 'self-consciousness', and Nietzsche's 'superfluousness claim' means that self-consciousness is never efficacious in its own right. But in order to make this plausible as an interpretation of GS 354, Riccardi would have to show that Nietzsche believes that self-consciousness is not adaptive and was never involved in the *causal* development of human society – which seems to me to be the exact opposite of what Nietzsche is saying. In Constâncio 2011a, my main argument against interpreting Nietzsche as an epiphenomenalist was that he conceives of consciousness as *a tool* of the drives and affects. The notion that some *x* is a tool seems to me to rule out that inefficaciousness can belong to *x* as a property. Note that the kind of tool that Nietzsche has in mind is continuous with the drives and affects – it is not a tool like the hammer, but rather like the hand: "consciousness is the hand with

Another misconception is that Nietzsche believes that consciousness consists in, or is identical to, the communication of needs among equals. Nietzsche does argue that the evolutionary value of consciousness lies in the fact that it "has allowed human beings to communicate *their needs* through communication-signs" (GS 354). But this is only the reason why consciousness was naturally selected – it does not entail that *all* communication through communication-signs is communication of needs. Nietzsche explicitly makes the point that in the course of human evolution and history the development of the ability to communicate needs among equals or in society has eventually produced a "surplus", *ein Ueberschuss* (GS 354). He writes: "where need and distress have for a long time forced people to communicate, to understand each other swiftly and subtly, there finally exists a surplus of this power and art of expression, a faculty, so to speak, which has slowly accumulated and now waits for an heir to spend it lavishly" (GS 354).

Moreover, although Nietzsche's conception of consciousness in this crucial aphorism entails that reflexive knowledge is a necessary condition of consciousness – particularly as a 'high order', reflexive knowledge of one's needs –, it does not equate consciousness with reflexive knowledge, as if the latter were the *only* necessary condition of consciousness. It is often overlooked that Nietzsche's characterisation of consciousness in GS 354 also involves its conception in terms of *intentionality*. By 'intentionality' I mean one's human ability to 'mean' *qua* an ability to posit a content, that is, to direct one's mind toward something, and ultimately to reach out to something outside of oneself.[23] Nietzsche focuses, in particular, on our ability to transform the insideness of our sensations into an outsideness. He writes:

---

which the organism reaches out furthest: it must be a firm hand" (NL 1885, 34[131], KSA 11: 464). Interestingly, the metaphor of the hand as a tool and of the soul as a hand comes from Aristotle: "the soul, then, is like a hand; for the hand is a tool which employs other tools" (*De Anima* III, 432a1 – 2, my translation).

[23] I use the term 'intentionality' in the phenomenological sense developed first by Brentano and then by Husserl and Heidegger. 'Intentionality' taken in this sense has nothing to do with 'intentions' in the usual sense of the word. See, for example, Heidegger (1985: 29): "*Intentio* literally means *directing-itself-toward*. Every lived experience, every psychic comportment, directs itself toward something. Representing is a representing of something, recalling is a recalling of something, judging is a judging about something, presuming, expecting, hoping, loving, hating – of something". See also, for example, Richardson (2012: 48 – 49, 55ff.). As Richardson puts it in his interpretation of Heidegger's *Dasein*, intentionality is ultimately what "gives as a 'there' [*Da*], as a world or space of experience" (Richardson 2012: 58).

[...] our becoming conscious of our sense impressions [*Sinneseindrücke*] in ourselves, our power to fix them and as it were place them outside of ourselves, has increased in proportion to the need to convey them *to others* by means of signs. (GS 354, translation modified)

When, for example, my retina is affected by a new sense impression, my brain allows me to see not the retina being affected by a new sense impression, but an object *outside* of myself. My 'consciousness' is first of all this ability to extend beyond myself, to orient myself towards the horizon or circle of my sensations (e.g. towards the visual horizon produced by my retina) in such a way that that horizon appears to me as if it were independent of my sense organs, as if it stood outside my body and had nothing to do with an inner state of my body. Although, as Nietzsche explains in *Daybreak*, I cannot but live imprisoned within my sensations – within a "concentric circle", as he puts it, which is "peculiar" to my body and has my body as its "mid-point" (D 117) –, my consciousness makes me experience such a 'concentric circle' as an 'outside'.

Thus, consciousness, according to Nietzsche, is (a) reflexive knowledge, but is reflexive knowledge as (b) an *intentional* 'knowing that one knows' – that is, one which creates an 'outside of us', and hence a distinction between an 'inner-' and an 'external-world'. The further point is that (c) we need *concepts* in order to become conscious of something outside of us (that is, in order to 'mean' something). I need the concept 'bird' in order to see a bird *as a bird*; I need the concept 'room' in order to see the space around me *as a room*. Otherwise I shall be merely aware of sense impressions – or, to put it differently, merely aware of an 'image' (*Bild*) which I do not really differentiate from myself, or which I place neither inside nor outside of myself. My awareness rises to the level of consciousness in the proper sense of the world only when I manage to use *general representations* (or "generalities", GS 354) to 'fix' an interpretation of my sense impressions, e.g. when I manage to interpret an image within my visual horizon as 'a bird', or conceptualise the sensorial horizon where I am now standing and moving as 'a room'.

Our "animal consciousness" (GS 354) is properly human – or *is* consciousness in the proper sense of the world – when it becomes reflexive, intentional, and conceptual consciousness. But this means also that the properly human consciousness is *linguistic*: "conscious thinking *takes place in words, that is, in communication-signs*" (GS 354). We only become 'conscious' in the proper, human sense of the word when we 'fix' our 'sense impressions' and 'place them outside of ourselves' by using concepts – but the use of concepts presupposes the use of language (and that is why "the development of language and the development of consciousness [...] go hand in hand", GS 354). Put differently, our merely animal awareness (our unconscious, lower order thinking, feeling, willing, remembering, and acting) only becomes 'consciousness' in the proper, human sense of the word when it is supplemented by the kind of conceptualisation that presupposes 'communication-signs', and hence the whole social and linguistic milieu of communication. When Nietzsche writes that consciousness "has increased in proportion to the need to convey [our sense impressions] *to others* by means of signs", he is not just saying that communication has fostered the development of subtler and more complex concepts. He is saying *that*, but he is also making the much more radical point that reflexivity, intentionality, and conceptualisation belong to the social realm of communication. There is an inescapably *public dimension* in human reflexivity, intentionality, and conceptualisation – in human consciousness. No matter how isolated we are or feel, our consciousness is always based on our immersion in the milieu of communication, all our concepts refer back to social contexts and public meanings, all our conscious thoughts are implicitly related to a drive to communicate, and in fact they all keep us more or less implicitly connected to others at all times.

Thus Nietzsche's definition of consciousness in GS 354 should not come as a surprise: "Consciousness is really just a net connecting one person with another" (GS 354) or (in a more literal translation), "consciousness is really just a connecting-net [*Verbindungsnetz*] that links one person to another" (GS 354). For Nietzsche, 'consciousness' in the proper sense of the word is not something that individual human organisms produce, so to speak, spontaneously by themselves alone. As a 'connecting-net', consciousness is fundamentally relational and communal. Put differently, Nietzsche's view of consciousness implies a radical 'connectivism' according to which consciousness is a 'systemic' event that only arises within social, intersubjective spaces. It emerges from a multiplicity of connections that are social, and not merely organic and individual. Or, to put it in yet another way, conscious thoughts that occur within an individual human organism are really just part of – or a link within – a social milieu of sign-communication (and most likely this milieu is, in turn, just part of – or a link within – an even larger milieu of communication which includes non-conscious communication). Therefore, "consciousness actually belongs not to man's existence as an individual but rather to the community- and herd-aspects of his nature" (GS 354).

This brings us back to two of the crucial themes that we encountered in *Beyond Good and Evil*: the herd-instinct and Nietzsche's Langean scepticism regarding self-knowledge. These two themes now appear combined. Since language is composed of 'communication-signs', and since our properly human, reflexive, intentional, conceptual consciousness depends on language, as conscious beings we are always already entangled in the realm of communication. In fact, our consciousness tends to serve the herd-instinct and its predominance, as if it were fundamentally a tool of this instinct (and ultimately of 'the genius of the species'). For not only does it foster our ability to convey our needs to others and seek protection among our equals, but also develops in us a self-understanding which is relative to our existence as elements of a net of communication, not as autonomous individuals. When we introspect and consciously access our individual inner world, what we find in there is not individual at all, but rather linguistic and therefore public, 'herd-like':

> each of us, even with the best will in the world to understand ourselves as individually as possible, "to know ourselves", will always bring to consciousness precisely that in ourselves which is "non-individual", that which is "average"; due to the nature of consciousness – to the "genius of the species" governing it – our thoughts themselves are continually as it were outvoted and translated back into the herd perspective. (GS 354)

We are capable of self-consciousness, that is, capable of becoming conscious of ourselves as an individual 'Self'; more generally, we have the ability, as human organisms, to become reflexively conscious of a great multiplicity of inner organic functions, such as thinking, feeling, willing, or remembering. It can also count as a fact that we have a 'sense of Self' and usually believe those organic functions to be unified around a 'Self' (even if there is no reason to assume that they must always be unified). In this sense we can be said to be capable of 'self-consciousness', that is, capable of becoming conscious of ourselves as an individual 'Self'. At least since Descartes, we tend to interpret this as a becoming conscious of an 'I', the so-called 'I of consciousness'. Nietzsche's point is, once again, that (a) our access to our inner states is mediated by language – it is not an 'immediate certainty' of ourselves, or a Cartesian presence of ourselves to ourselves, but merely an interpretation of ourselves in terms of words and concepts; (b) words develop as 'communication-signs', and the concepts which they 'fix' are 'generalities' whose meanings belong to the social milieu of communication (to the 'herd'); (c) it follows that our self-understanding and self-consciousness in terms of words and concepts is not knowledge of our individuality, and should, on the contrary, be considered a process which makes us *less* individual, i.e., more like the others with whom we inhabit a given milieu of communication, more 'non-individual', more 'average' (or "base", as Nietzsche had already argued in BGE 268).

All of this seems to put together a fairly coherent and interesting *theoretical* position regarding the problem of subjectivity. Nietzsche terms it a "true phenomenalism and perspectivism" – one which defends that "the world of which we can become conscious is merely a surface- and sign-world" (GS 354), and which includes in this "surface- and sign-world" both the outer and the inner world. For "everything which enters consciousness thereby *becomes* shallow, thin, relatively stupid, general, a sign, a herd-mark" (GS 354). Thus *The Gay*

Science completes Nietzsche's theoretical reconception of human subjectivity as a decentered subjectivity.

'Decentered subjectivity' (as well as 'decentered agency') is an expression usually associated with a particular theory of the subject, namely in Jacques Lacan. As Elliot L. Jurist puts it, it is true that Lacan was not "directly influenced by Nietzsche" (Jurist 2000: 10) – and moreover, Lacanians usually "identify Lacan as an important alternative to Nietzschean-influenced poststructuralist thinking" and its "rejectionist stance against the subject" (Jurist 2000: 270) –, but it should nonetheless be clear that Lacan's "psychoanalytic theory [of the subject] expounds the notion of decentered agency in a way that constitutes one vision of Nietzschean agency" (Jurist 2000: 10). So far, I have used the expression 'decentered subjectivity' to refer to the lack of centre of Nietzsche's 'subject-multiplicity' – a lack which accounts for the modern experience of first-personal fragmentation, disintegration, contradictoriness, 'weakness' and 'paralysis of will'. But there is more to the idea of decenteredness than this. For the idea of decenteredness also involves the Langean skepsis that we have encountered throughout this paper: when I introspect and observe the multiplicity of my drives, affects, thoughts, passions, desires, etc., I cannot find any real centre in this multiplicity because I cannot find anything there but the *words* that the 'symbolic order' (or 'the herd') has anonymously developed in order to make communication (and indeed society) possible. Every thought about myself is always already an interpretation of myself in terms of such 'communication-signs' as 'I', 'thought', 'desire', 'feeling' (for no really observable reality corresponds to them). Ultimately, what I find inside myself when I introspect is not at all the 'I' as the centre of my inner world, but merely *a name* that fixes my social or symbolic identity without meaning anything truly individual, i.e., truly not-applicable to another subjective multiplicity. By means of a joke, the Lacanian philosopher Slavoj Žižek conveys this sense of 'decentered subjectivity' very well:

> We all know the old joke referring to the enigma of who really wrote Shakespeare's plays: "Not William Shakespeare, but someone else with the same name." This is what Lacan means by the "decentered subject"; this is how a subject relates to the name that fixes its symbolic identity: John Smith is (always, by definition, in its very notion) not John Smith, but someone else with the same name. (Žižek 2012: 422)

Taken in isolation, aphorism 354 of *The Gay Science* can hardly be interpreted as something other than a theoretical treatment of the problem of consciousness. When Nietzsche writes that he leaves the distinction between subject and object for the epistemologists, he does not seem to be saying that he is not interested in theories of subjectivity. He can surely be taken to be saying that his theory of consciousness supersedes the distinction between subject and object and is, therefore, preferable to any theory based on that distinction.

But, if one looks at the context in which the aphorism appears, things immediately become slightly different. A thorough 'contextual interpretation' of the aphorism (to use Werner Stegmaier's term of art) might offer us not only a slightly, but even a radically different picture.[24] To conclude this chapter, I shall try to illuminate the practical and existential dimension of aphorism 354 by exploring its contextual connection with aphorism 356. This shall also make clearer how Nietzsche's view of consciousness and decentered subjectivity in *The Gay Science* involves the theme of intersubjectivity.

4 (Inter-)subjectivity as an existential problem in *The Gay Science*

Aphorism 356 of *The Gay Science* is Nietzsche's greatest attempt to describe modern societies as societies of *actors* – societies where everyone plays a role and wears 'masks'.

The aphorism is titled, "*The extent to which things will become ever more "artistic" in Europe*" (GS 356), which suggests that in a society of actors everyone is in a sense an artist, for everyone is constantly performing and deceiving, everyone is constantly composing their own 'masks', their own personal identities and characters, and in fact creating illusions – for themselves and for others. Although the aphorism seems to evaluate this only negatively, it is not a secret to anyone that creating one's own 'mask' and living as an artist of one's life – indeed as "a poet" of one's life (GS 299), is an important part of Nietzsche's ideal of free-spiritedness. So, why does Nietzsche censor here what he usually praises?

The explanation seems to be that he believes that in modern Europe people are becoming more and more 'artistic' *in the wrong way*. Firstly, the role they play as actors of real life is basically the role prescribed by "their so-called profession" (GS 356). Secondly, and contrary to real artists, they have no distance from their role. There are always "many other roles they may have been *able* to

---

24 See Stegmaier 2012. Stegmaier's 'contextual' approach drives him to the conclusion that even Nietzsche's talk of a "true phenomenalism and perspectivism" should not be taken in a theoretical sense (according to Stegmaier, Nietzsche has no theories, only "footholds" for "orientation"): see Stegmaier 2012: 280 – 285; see also Stegmaier's chapter in this volume.

play", but now "it's too late" – now "the role has actually *become* character; and artifice, nature" (GS 356). There even seems to be a rule here: if one is unable to keep one's distance from one's role and lets one's role become habitual, it will eventually become second-nature, or "every time man starts to discover the extent to which he is playing a role and the extent to which he *can* be an actor, he *becomes* an actor" (GS 356), that is, he becomes the role he is playing. This is what happened to the Greeks, Nietzsche claims: "When the Greeks had fully accepted this *faith in roles* – the faith of *artistes*, if you will – they underwent, as is well known, step by step an odd metamorphosis that is not in every respect worth of imitation: *they really became actors*" (GS 356). Therefore, modern Europe is now on the cusp of repeating the fate that brought down the ancient Greek civilisation – for "it was not, as innocents tend to say, Greek culture that conquered Rome, but the *graeculus histrio* [the little Greek actor]" (GS 356). And this is already a third point: in modern Europe, people are becoming more and more "artistic" in the wrong way also because in becoming their professional roles – and in having to do this in order to "make a living" (GS 356) – they have become individualistic to the point of making society impossible: "*We are no longer material for a society*, this is a timely truth".

The way in which Nietzsche makes this third point conflicts with most interpretations of his thought as individualist. Here he seems to lament the fact that "we are no longer material for a society" – and further reflection on the aphorism as whole only confirms this. His interpretation of the differences between the Middle Ages and Modernity seems to praise the former as a time of community and to censor the latter as a time of individualism. In the Middle Ages, he claims, people believed that their social roles were not individual choices, but simply what they were predestined for:

> With the help of this faith, estates, guilds, and inherited trade privileges were able to establish those monsters, the broad-based social pyramids that distinguished the Middle Ages and to which one can credit at least one thing: durability (and durability is a first-rank value on earth). (GS 356)

By contrast, in the modern age, like in all "truly democratic ages", people "unlearn this faith" (GS 356), i.e. this faith in a hierarchic and predestined social order. All of this has the consequence that a certain type of human being becomes extinct: "the great architects", i.e. the designers of social institutions capable of lasting "millennia" as wholes in which people develop "the basic faith that man has worth and sense only in so far as he is *a stone in a great edifice*" (GS 356). In modernity, "we are no longer material for a society" because a society requires precisely that man be "*firm* above all, a 'stone' ... above all not an actor!" (GS 356). Modernity is dominated by the same democratic faith as "the

Periclean age", that is, by "the American faith which is increasingly becoming the European faith as well", the faith in the individual – the faith "where the individual is convinced he can do just about anything and *is up to playing any role*; and everyone experiments with himself, improvises, experiments again, enjoys experimenting, where all nature ends and becomes art ..." (GS 356).

This whole argument is, however, highly redolent of Jacob Burckhardt's theses on the differences between the Middle Ages and the Italian Renaissance – and this suggests that what Nietzsche is really driving at is an *ambivalent* appraisal of Modernity. In the Middle Ages, Burckhardt argued, "man was conscious of himself only as a member of a race, people, party, family or corporation – only through some general category" (Burckhardt 1990 [1878]: 98). The Italian Renaissance involved a radical break with the Middle Ages because it involved a radical development of *individuality*, of the "*uomo singolare*" or "*uomo unico*": "man became a *spiritual individual*, and recognised himself as such"; very high degrees of "intellectual freedom and independence" flourished for the first time in history. Burckhardt calls this kind of freedom a condition in which man attains a "feeling of his own *sovereignty*".[25] This is, of course, the inspiration of Nietzsche's idealisation of the "sovereign individual" (GM II 2). And Burckhardt's eulogy of the typical Renaissance sovereign individual as "*il uomo universale*" – the individual who gives unity and style to the greatest possible multiplicity or complexity in himself – is the inspiration of Nietzsche's conception of greatness as "unity in multiplicity", or "wholeness in manifoldness" (*Ganzheit im Vielen*, BGE 212), which I mentioned above. Thus in aphorism 356 of *The Gay Science* Nietzsche is most likely agreeing with Burckhardt's conclusion: "excessive individualism" is as admirable as is dangerous for a society (Burckhardt 1990 [1878]: 289).

If this is right, then aphorism 356 does indeed express a typical Nietzschean ambivalence: Modernity as a democratic age of the individual is at the same time an age of extreme *décadence* and an age of great promise – an age in which most people will tend to become more and more 'artistic' in the wrong way, but also in which people can, more than ever before, become 'artistic' in the right way, that is, as 'sovereign individuals', as 'commanders and legislators', as creators of new values. The double-edged nature of times of crisis where traditional values and beliefs breakdown – as well as Nietzsche's ambivalent appraisal of such times – was already clearly expressed in *Beyond Good Evil*, particularly in aphorism 262:

> [In such times] the "individual" is left standing there, forced to give himself laws, forced to rely on his own arts and wiles of self-preservation, self-enhancement, self-redemption.

---

25 Burckhardt (1990) [1878]: 66, 98ff., 289, 359 n. 32.

> There is nothing but new whys and hows; there are no longer any shared formulas; misunderstanding is allied with disregard; decay, ruin, and the highest desires are horribly entwined (BGE 262).

After the death of God, in the age of post-metaphysical nihilism, all of this is true more than ever before: the collapse of Christianity (and the whole 'ascetic ideal') has forced people, as never before, to ask whether "existence has any meaning at all" (GS 357); and as never before, people feel the *need for meaning or purpose*. According to Nietzsche (as is well known), we tend to live by the belief that "any meaning at all is better than no meaning at all" (GM III 28), and our will has developed such a *"horror vacui"* (GM III 1) that it "prefers to will *nothingness*, than *not* will" (GM III 1, GM III 28), that is, prefers to fill the "emptiness" that surrounds it with a fictitious idea of an overriding purpose than live without no purpose at all, "like a leaf in the breeze, the plaything of the absurd, of 'nonsense'" (GM III 28). The fact that after the death of God "new whys and hows" abound everywhere and each individual "is up to playing any role" is a symptom of such a need for meaning. The collapse of belief – or of all "shared formulas" – has atomised society to an unprecedented degree and threatens, if not with complete dissolution, at least with the loss of 'spirit' described above in the section on *Beyond Good and Evil*. How the creation of new values (or 'new laws') could restore our ability to be "stones" and "material for a society" (GS 356) is hard to see. But Nietzsche's 'struggle against nihilism' – particularly in the form of a struggle against the nihilism of 'last men' – surely involves the prospect of restoring such an ability, and is therefore not so 'individualist' as usually supposed.

It is not difficult to see how all of this should redefine the interpretation of the aphorism on consciousness (as well as of the points we considered in the section on *Beyond Good and Evil*). (a) Firstly, consciousness now appears as the 'connecting-net' of a society of actors. In late modernity, when one becomes truly conscious of one's consciousness, one discovers oneself as an actor among actors – and certainly not as Descartes' *res cogitans* and pure *cogito*. (b) Secondly, the idea that "consciousness actually belongs not to man's existence as an individual but rather to the community- and herd-aspects of his nature" (GS 354) – or that we can only bring to consciousness "precisely that in ourselves which is 'non-individual', that which is 'average'" (GS 354) – should now be reinterpreted as meaning that what one can bring to consciousness, either in one's interaction with others or in one's interaction with oneself, is always a 'mask' – or, at least, is never a personal identity wholly independent or disconnected from one's symbolic identity as 'John Smith'. (c) The overwhelming massification of society which Nietzsche believes to be taking place in modern Europe (the growing predominance of the 'herd-instinct', etc.) should also be reinterpreted in this light:

people become more and more 'average' and similar to each other *by becoming their social* roles, by fully identifying with their symbolic identities, by believing in the names that the 'herd' gives them, by interacting with each other as actors who have lost their ability to distance themselves from their masks. (d) Accordingly, the 'surface- and sign-world' made possible by consciousness – i.e., by a "connecting-net that links one person to another" (GS 354) – is far from being a Hegelian, emancipated, free world of reciprocal 'recognition'. On Nietzsche's view, it is rather an atomised and yet massified world of *misrecognition*.[26]

It should, however, not be forgotten that Nietzsche highlights the fact that the development of language and consciousness has created "a surplus" of the "power and art of expression" (GS 354). He balances his claim that people are becoming less and less individual with the claim that never before in the history of humanity was there a greater accumulated quantity of such a 'surplus'. This quantity can now be spent "lavishly" (GS 354) in heightened forms of individual self-consciousness and self-creation (or of individual 'will to power' *qua* spiritual will to self-expression). But, as aphorism 356 suggests, Nietzsche is far from valuing individualism unconditionally. Ultimately, his concern is the typically *modern* concern with humanity being able or unable to become again "material for a society" (GS 356), or, put differently, the typically modern project of attempting to rescue human history from "the gruesome rule of chance and nonsense" and thus "teach humanity its future as its *will*, as dependent on a human will" (BGE 203). His faith in individual self-creation is hence a faith in "a new type of philosopher and commander" (BGE 203) that could help accomplish the modern project not only of individual but also of collective self-determination or emancipation.[27] Nietzsche does not abandon the modern project, even if his overall tendency is to underscore how the death of God has transformed it into a much harder, perhaps quixotic, project. (e) Becoming truly self-conscious in late modernity – truly conscious of one's consciousness – is indeed tantamount to becoming conscious of nihilism and the death of God, or to acquiring a subjectivised awareness of the modern human being's lack of meaning. In this context, 'self-creation' will have much more to do with a hard, probably quixotic and tragic 'struggle against nihilism' than with the aesthetic and unconcerned self-fashioning usually associated to that project. In any case, inner dividedness, decenteredness, undeterminedness, and non-transparency to oneself will be part of any efforts of self-creation, as much as misrecognition in a society of actors will be part of any efforts to

---

26 On Nietzsche on recognition and misrecognition, see Constâncio (2015).
27 For the definition of the modern project as the project of "an individually and collectively self-determining life", see Pippin 1999: 3.

restore a sense of community, indeed a sense of care for our collective destiny as a species (or for the future of "humanity" as something "supra-personal", RWB 4).

Given all this, one should conclude not only that Nietzsche's treatment of consciousness and the problem of subjectivity has a strong existential dimension, but also that it really anticipates the existentialist approach to the question of existence. As Hannah Arendt remarks, for Sartre and Camus the problem of existence is the (Nietzschean) problem that "man is never identical with himself as a thing is identical with itself. An inkpot is always an inkpot. Man is his life and his actions, which are never finished until the very moment of his death. He *is* his existence" (Arendt 1994 [1946]: 191). Losing all distance towards one's role and mask in a society of actors, and thus losing not only one's ability to identify the openness of existence, but also one's power to change it (or to 'self-creation') – that is precisely what Sartre and Camus termed *l'esprit sérieux*:

> *L'esprit sérieux*, which is the original sin according to the new [French, existential] philosophy, may be equated with respectability. The "serious" man is one who thinks of himself *as* president of his business, *as* a member of the legion of Honour, *as* a member of the faculty, but also *as* father, *as* husband, or as any other half-natural, half-social function. For by so doing he agrees to the identification of himself with an arbitrary function which society has bestowed. [...] Since everyone knows well enough in his own heart that he is not identical with his function, *l'esprit sérieux* indicates also bad faith in the sense of pretending. (Arendt 1994 [1946]: 190–191)

This 'pretending' is certainly no less complicated for Nietzsche than for Sartre or Camus. Nietzsche's Langean scepticism entails that no one is ever transparent to oneself, no one ever inhabits an inner space of full honesty and transparent sincerity on the basis of which a purely false, insincere mask could be built. The human being is indeed never identical with itself as an inkpot is identical with itself – and this non-identity with itself goes so far as to entail that one cannot ever remove all masks and present oneself either to others *or to oneself* without some mask. Even when a man does not encourage a mask of himself "to wander around, in his place, through the hearts and heads of his friends", a mask of him "will be there all the same" (BGE 40); even within his own heart and head he finds only his masks. His becoming conscious of his consciousness as such is tantamount to becoming conscious of his non-identity with himself – and indeed of the impossibility of becoming self-reflexively transparent to himself. In the age of 'extreme nihilism' this is also tantamount to experiencing himself in terms of the most extreme undeterminedness, i.e. as undetermined 'chaos'.

And yet Nietzsche – in the spirit of Kant, Fichte, and Hegel – does not cease to subjectivise his individual existence with the search for the "most final and most certain reasons pro and con" (GS 2), that is, with the task of giving determinedness to his 'I' by asking for reasons to think and act in one way and not in any other.[28] Although his consciousness of his existence has become a subjectivised awareness of the modern lack of meaning or purpose, and although he knows (as we saw in the section on *Beyond Good and Evil*) that his 'will' to affirmation is not motivated by a theoretical refutation of pessimism or nihilism, he still cherishes his 'contempt' for those who stand in the midst of "the whole marvellous uncertainty and ambiguity of existence *without questioning*" (GS 2). He stands there questioning – and his attempts to look affirmatively at the "uncertainty and ambiguity of existence", his efforts to replace the nihilistic sense of "straying through an infinite nothing" (GS 125) with the sense of being an "argonaut" (GS 382) facing "a new dawn" and sailing into an "open sea" (GS 343), can hardly be equated with the postmodern rejection of 'grand narratives'. And, most importantly (to emphasise again the main point of this chapter), his questioning and affirmative stance in the face of nihilism and "the whole marvellous uncertainty and ambiguity of existence" is everything but a renunciation of the idea of subjectivity (and inter-subjectivity); on the contrary, that stance implies that he sees his philosophy as the site in which the existential crisis of the modern subject is not only theoretically identified, but also first-personally discovered as a practical problem – the site in which the existential crisis of the modern subject is *subjectivised*.

References

Abel, Günter (2001) "Bewußtsein – Sprache – Natur. Nietzsches Philosophie des Geistes", in: *Nietzsche-Studien* 30, 1–43.
Arendt, Hannah (1994) [1946] "French Existentialism", in: *Essays in Understanding 1930–1954*, New York: Harcourt, 188–193.
Burckhardt, Jacob (1990) [1878] *The Civilization of the Renaissance in Italy*, London: Penguin.
Constâncio, João/Branco, Maria João Mayer (eds.) (2011) *Nietzsche on Instinct and Language*, Berlin/Boston: De Gruyter.
Constâncio, João (2011a) "On Consciousness. Nietzsche's Departure from Schopenhauer", in: *Nietzsche-Studien* 40, 1–42.
Constâncio, João (2011b) "Instinct and Language in Nietzsche's *Beyond Good and Evil*", in: J. Constâncio and M.J.M. Branco (eds.), *Nietzsche on Instinct and Language*, Berlin/Boston: De Gruyter, 80–116.

---

28 On the thesis that Kant, Fichte, and Hegel have in common the notion that our asking for reasons is the source of our self-consciousness (or of our conscious self-understanding as an 'I'), see Rödl (2007).

Constâncio, João (2012) "Consciousness, Communication, and Self-Expression. Towards an Interpretation of Aphorism 354 of Nietzsche's The Gay Science", in: J. Constâncio and M.J. Mayer Branco (eds.), *As the Spider Spins: Essays on Nietzsche's Critique and Use of Language*, Berlin/Boston: De Gruyter, 197–231.

Constâncio, João (2013) "On Nietzsche's Conception of Philosophy in *Beyond Good and Evil*: Reassessing Schopenhauer's Relevance", in: M.E. Born and A. Pichler (eds.), *Texturen des Denkens: Nietzsches Inszenierung der Philosophie in "Jenseits von Gut und Böse"*, Berlin/Boston: De Gruyter, 145–164.

Constâncio, João (2015) "Struggles for Recognition and Will to Power: Probing an Affinity between Hegel and Nietzsche", in: L.R. Santos and K. Hay (eds.), *Nietzsche, German Idealism and Its Critics*, Berlin/Boston: De Gruyter (forthcoming).

Gemes, Ken (2009) "Nietzsche on Free Will, Autonomy, and the Sovereign Individual", in: K. Gemes and S. May (eds.), *Nietzsche on Freedom and Autonomy*, Oxford: Oxford University Press, 33–49.

Heidegger, Martin (1985) *History of the Concept of Time: Prolegomena*, Bloomington and Indianapolis: Indiana University Press.

Jurist, Elliot L. (2000) *Beyond Hegel and Nietzsche: Philosophy, Culture, and Agency*, Cambridge, MA/London: MIT Press.

Leiter, Brian (2002) *Nietzsche on Morality*, London/New York: Routledge.

Leiter, Brian (2015) *Nietzsche on Morality, Second Edition*, London/New York: Routledge.

Lupo, Luca (2006) *Le Colombe dello Scettico. Riflessioni di Nietzsche sulla Coscienza negli anni 1880–1888*. Pisa: ETS.

Pippin, Robert B. (1999) *Modernism as a Philosophical Problem*, Oxford: Blackwell.

Pippin, Robert B. (2010) *Nietzsche, Psychology, and First Philosophy*, Chicago/London: University of Chicago Press.

Riccardi, Mattia (forthcoming) "Nietzsche on the Superficiality of Consciousness", in: M. Dries (ed.), *Nietzsche on Consciousness and the Embodied Mind*, Berlin/Boston: De Gruyter.

Richardson, John (2012) *Heidegger*, London/New York: Routledge.

Rödl, Sebastian (2007) *Self-consciousness*, Cambridge, MA/London: Harvard University Press.

Stegmaier, Werner (2000) "Nietzsches Zeichen", in: *Nietzsche-Studien* 29, 41–69.

Stegmaier, Werner (2012) *Nietzsches Befreiung der Philosophie. Kontextuelle Interpretation des V. Buches der "Fröhlichen Wissenschaft"*, Berlin/Boston: De Gruyter.

Žižek, Slavoj (2012) *Less Than Nothing*, London: Verso.

Bartholomew Ryan
12 The Plurality of the Subject in Nietzsche and Kierkegaard: Confronting Nihilism with Masks, Faith and *Amor Fati*

> Pur tu, solinga, eterna peregrina,
> Che sì pensosa sei, tu forse intendi,
> Questo viver terreno,
> Il patir nostro, il sospirar, che sia;
> Che sia questo morir, questo supremo
> Scolorar del sembiante,
> E perir dalla terra, e venir meno
> Ad ogni usata, amante compagnia.
> (Giacomo Leopardi)[1]

Introduction

> On my next visit to Germany I propose to take up the psychological problem of Kierkegaard
> (Friedrich Nietzsche, letter to Georg Brandes, Nice, 19.02.1888)[2]

Reflecting on the most creative thinkers of the nineteenth and early twentieth century that rose up in protest and despair to their epoch, Robert B. Pippin concludes one of his books on Nietzsche: "No one, with the possible exception of Heidegger, is more important to and representative of this modernist mood, or 'Stimmung', than Nietzsche."[3] Here we have a case of an established academic philosopher and Hegel and Nietzsche scholar overlooking the relevance and power of Kierkegaard's thought as a mirror and response to the modernist mood as well as being the figure that inspired Heidegger to develop work on such key

---

[1] Leopardi 2010: 196: "Canto Notturno Di Un Pastore Errante Dell'Asia", published in 1831. Translation: "Yet you, eternal solitary wanderer,/you who are so pensive,/understand this life on earth, perhaps/what our suffering and sighing is,/what this death is, this last/paling of the face, and leaving earth behind, deserting all familiar, loving company."
[2] Brandes 1972: 71.
[3] Pippin 2010: 123. Another example of this kind of omission is in Pippin (2005) and also in David Carr's book *The Paradox of Subjectivity* (1999) which does not even mention Kierkegaard once or even give a reason why the Danish philosopher is completely omitted as the author makes his way through Kant, Husserl and Heidegger.

terms as *Stimmung* [*Stemning*], *Wiederholung* [*Gjentagelsen*] and *Angst* [*Angest*], and the impetus to develop the existential concepts *Augenblik* [*Øieblikket*] (from Luther's choice of word in his translation of *1 Corinthians 15:52* in *The New Testament*) and *Geworfenheit*.[4] In modifying Pippin's statement, it would be more correct to insert Kierkegaard's name beside Nietzsche. This article acts as a bridge between section one and two of this book because, on the one hand, while he belongs to a generation earlier than Nietzsche, Kierkegaard's reception comes later. Kierkegaard is a latecomer to idealism[5] and at the tail end or hangover of Romanticism under the rubric of "Tradition and Context". On the other hand, given that the reception of Kierkegaard mostly came after Nietzsche, he is one of the most striking thinkers that confronts the crisis of the subject, and despite being the last great Christian philosopher of modernity, Kierkegaard is also the first and most perplexing existentialist thinker for the twentieth-century movement, and is having a renaissance in the twenty-first century as the complete works are published for the first time so that he can sit comfortably with Nietzsche's remark in the Preface to *The Antichrist* that "Some are born posthumously",[6] despite Leopardi's thought that anyone born in the nineteenth century was born too late.[7]

In approaching this article as a bridge between two sections, I explore Kierkegaard and Nietzsche's reflections and responses to subjectivity under three sections: 1) Transforming subjectivity; 2) Masks via the 'eyes of Argus', 'giving style' and deception; and 3) Confronting nihilism with faith and *Amor Fati*. There are many points of contact between Kierkegaard and Nietzsche such as, for example, their celebration of existential passion in their striking depictions of Dionysian and Christ-like existence; their anti-system stance and unrelenting critique of modern philosophy; the creation of masks and multiple voices; the attack against the bourgeoisie of emerging democratic society and the estab-

---

[4] There is a wonderful expression of the *Geworfenheit* in Kierkegaard's book *Repetition* that captures the poetic and dramatic essence of the idea: "Where am I? What does it mean to say: the world? What is the meaning of that word? Who tricked me into this whole thing and leaves me standing here? Who am I? How did I get into the world? Why was I not asked about it, why was I not informed of the rules and regulations but just thrust into the ranks as if I had been bought from a peddling shanghaier of human beings? How did I get involved in this big enterprise called actuality? Why should I be involved? Isn't it a matter of choice? And if I am compelled to be involved, where is the manager – I have something to say about this. Is there no manager? To whom shall I make my complaint?" (Kierkegaard 1983: 200/SKS 4: 68)
[5] Benjamin 1999: 702.
[6] A Preface/KSA 6: 167.
[7] See for, example: "The best generations are not those to come but those gone by; and there is no hope that the world will change its custom and go backward instead of forward; and, still advancing, it cannot do otherwise than get worse" (Leopardi 2013: 196).

lished church; their solitary existence; their call for honesty; their humour, irony and wit; and their stylistic positioning as dramatic-poetic thinkers at odds with academic philosophical writing.

A number of books have been written and published in the English language (and some influential translations into English) juxtaposing Kierkegaard and Nietzsche over the years such as, for example, from Thomas Miles (2013), Tom P.S. Angier (2006), Alastair Hannay (2003), Thomas Brobjer (2002), James Kellenberger (1997), Gilles Deleuze (1994), Albert Cinelli (1989), John Powell Clayton (1985), Gerd-Gunter Grau (1985), Charles Lewis (1986), Lawrence M. Hinman (1980), Gregor Malantschuk (1962), and Karl Jaspers (1955).[8] Thomas Miles points out in the latest book on Nietzsche and Kierkegaard that most of these books as well as the numerous articles published on Kierkegaard and Nietzsche "are often unaware of the vast body of literature on this topic".[9] The latest book by Miles is by far one of the more thoughtful and balanced analyses in bringing the two thinkers together and ultimately focuses on how to live out the best way of life. In linking the two thinkers' response to subjectivity, I will explore why and how these two thinkers not only prioritize most vehemently individuality or the 'single individual [*Den Enkelte*]' in the face of philosophy, artistic guilds, and political and religious institutions where the "crowd is untruth",[10] but who also set about presenting – rather than a death of the subject – a plurality of the subject in the quest for a unity of the self (in the case of Kierkegaard) and total dilution of the self as subject (in the case of Nietzsche) in the quest for the self as subject. They both know that the crisis of the self also entails a crisis of belief and in their various ways they re-discover the *amor fati* and 'knight of faith [*Troens Ridder*]' respectively – whether in the face of God and need of God for salvation, or in the face of an abyss in the light of the "death of God" which signifies the collapse of the authority of both the ideals of the Enlightenment enterprise and the older institutions of belief.[11]

1 Transforming subjectivity

> However grateful one may go to welcome the *objective* spirit – and who has not been sick to death at least once of everything subjective, with its damned *ipsissimosity*! – nevertheless,

---

8 See bibliography at end of this article for information on these publications.
9 Miles 2011: 263. For a comprehensive list of the literature on Kierkegaard and Nietzsche, see the bibliography in Miles' article (Miles 2011: 288–298).
10 Kierkegaard 1998: 106/SKS 16: 90.
11 Pippin 1999: 145. See Pippin (2005).

in the end we even have to be cautious of our gratitude, and put an end to the exaggerated terms in which people have recently been celebrating the desubjectivization and depersonification of spirit, as if this were some sort of goal in itself, some sort of redemption or transfiguration.

(Friedrich Nietzsche, *Beyond Good and Evil*)[12]

1.1 Georg Brandes as the messenger

Before embarking on this journey proper of the plurality of the subject in this article, I begin with the great Danish critic Georg Brandes as the first one to link Kierkegaard and Nietzsche, who is responsible for their closest point of contact, and who is the first to see them as 'psychologists' in the wake of the crisis of subjectivity on the eve of the twentieth century. Brandes was the first major intellectual to promote and write monographs on both Kierkegaard in 1877 (which was translated into German in 1879) and Nietzsche in 1889. Brandes and Nietzsche maintained a warm and trusting letter correspondence in the two years leading up to Nietzsche's mental collapse. Soon after his encounter with Nietzsche, Brandes quickly set about encouraging him to read Kierkegaard, and wrote to Nietzsche on 11 January 1888 (almost exactly a year before Nietzsche's collapse): "There is one Scandinavian writer whose works would interest you, if only they were translated: Søren Kierkegaard; he lived from 1813 to 1955, and is in my opinion one of the profoundest psychologists that has ever existed".[13] After agreeing with Brandes that he would "take up the psychological problem of Kierkegaard"[14] he lamented to say in another letter that it was a pity he understood neither Danish nor Swedish.[15] Brandes was exceptionally sharp in spotting the most powerful new thinkers and artists of his time who would later make a profound impact on the twentieth century and beyond. Although Nietzsche never ultimately got the chance to read any of Kierkegaard's own works, the emphasis on psychological treatment alongside philosophical analysis in both authors points to the alternative approach to subjectivity that was emerging. As is well known, what Nietzsche admired so much in Dostoevsky was the great psychologist at work in the novels, and what he says about him and Pascal in his final posted letter to Brandes we can imagine what he might have said about Kierkegaard:

---

12 BGE 207/KSA 5: 134.
13 Brandes 1972: 69.
14 Brandes 1972: 71.
15 Brandes 1972: 81.

> I esteem him [Dostoevsky] [...] as the most valuable psychological material I know – I am grateful to him in an extraordinary way, however antagonistic he may be to my deepest instincts. Much the same as my relation to Pascal, whom I almost love, since he has taught me such an infinite amount [...].[16]

Kierkegaard himself wrote in the year Nietzsche was born: "Psychology is what we need, and above all, expert knowledge of human life and sympathy with its interests."[17]

1.2 "The age of disintegration"

Both Kierkegaard and Nietzsche think that Western civilisation has found itself in a landscape that is utterly lost: politically, religiously, ethically, and metaphysically – even if man does not know that yet. Zarathustra declares: "I find man in ruins and scattered as over a battlefield or butcher-field"[18]; and Nietzsche begins *The Antichrist* with these lines: "'I have got lost; I am everything that has got lost,' sighs modern man."[19] Kierkegaard's pseudonym begins perhaps his most perfect work with these two sentences: "Not only in the business world but also in the world of ideas, our age stages *ein wirklicher Ausverkauf* [a real sale]. Everything can be had at such a bargain price that it becomes a question whether there is finally anyone who will make a bid."[20] Reflections on the lost condition of man are rife throughout Kierkegaard's published and unpublished writings, and there is an especially fascinating journal entry from 1848 on the different aspects of the 'age of disintegration' which would speak for a whole generation in the interwar years of the twentieth century. Here is a snippet:

> That it was the age of disintegration – all existence like a vortex in the throes of a vertigo, induced and feverishly intensified by constantly wanting [...] to assist the moment with the momentary, which is to nourish the sickness [...] when what was needed was the very opposite; the eternal and the "single individual". That it was the age of disintegration – an age of crisis, that history was about to take a turn [...].[21]

It is easy to see the crucial differences in Nietzsche and Kierkegaard in seeking a solution for the radical Christian and radical post-Christian position, but we will

---

16 Letter from Turin, 20.11.1888 (Brandes 1972: 94).
17 Kierkegaard 1996: 185 (*Pap.* V B 53: 29, 1844). For more on Kierkegaard as psychologist, see Nordentoft (1972).
18 Z II Redemption/KSA 4: 178.
19 A 1/KSA 6: 169.
20 Kierkegaard 1983: 5/SKS 4: 101
21 Kierkegaard 1996: 350 (*Pap.* IX B 63: 7 1848).

come to that later. Here, we have two examples of the explosive force in which Kierkegaard and Nietzsche depict the 'present age'. What they are both audaciously calling for is a new, polyphonic and paradoxically honest voice that is profoundly thoughtful as well as courageously artistic amidst the collapse of both objectivity and subjectivity. It is no wonder then that James Joyce begins one of the most iconic novels of the twentieth century at the height of the age of disintegration with the ironic declaration by Buck Mulligan that he and Stephan Dedalus are 'Hyperboreans' – consciously echoing Nietzsche from the same paragraph in *The Antichrist* on modern man being lost – before setting off on a revolutionary journey to recycle and restore a cracked epic of Western civilisation, prioritising subversion, humour, love and the human body in literature, while World War I was raging on a continent that was doing its best to propel the human body into oblivion.[22]

Both Kierkegaard and Nietzsche knew that they were standing on a threshold between the afterglow of German Idealism as the golden age in modern European philosophy and the rise of nationalism, mass movements, journalism, population growth and technology. What brings them together is that they go to war with Western culture, at the same time re-igniting the human being with the demand for courage, passion, complexity, radical critique and offence. Out of this endeavour, a new form of subjectivity emerges of which we are only now really beginning to feel the effects of today in that (to repeat), what seemed to be a death of, had become a plurality and multiplicity of the subject.

1.3 The plural and multiple subject

In dealing with the crisis of the subject, both Nietzsche and Kierkegaard create pluralities and multiplicities of the self as subject, sometimes against their original intention – especially in the case of Kierkegaard. Take for example the two authors' 'reports to history': Kierkegaard's *Point of View* and Nietzsche's *Ecce Homo*. Here we have subjectivity transforming into plurality and multiplicity

---

[22] See Joyce 2008: 5. Here is the opening paragraph of *The Antichrist* which includes the Hyperborean, modern man as lost, facing ourselves and the labyrinth – all crucial elements throughout this article: "Let us face ourselves. We are Hyperboreans; we know very well how far off we live. 'Neither by land nor by sea will you find the way to the Hyperboreans' – Pindar already knew this about us. Beyond the north, ice and death – our life, our happiness. We have discovered happiness, we know the way, we have found the exit out of the labyrinth of thousands of years. Who else has found it? Modern man perhaps? 'I have got lost; I am everything that has got lost,' sighs modern man." (A 1/KSA 6: 169)

even when Kierkegaard is determined to have the final say on his 'authorship'. In the process of this attempt to bring unity to his work, the text begins with a few titles with the head-title as *The Point of View for my Work as an Author*, followed by the sub-titles "A Direct Communication" and "Report to History". These are then followed by a motto on the theme of 'weight' – by the bishop Hans Adolph Brorson whose hymn focuses on the greatness and wisdom of God and the weightlessness of the poor words we humans have at our disposal, and then by the dramatic poet Shakespeare via Prince Henry that "in everything the purpose must weigh with the folly". Kierkegaard has a very hard time trying to finish this book which begins the conclusion with an "Epilogue", that is then followed by a "Conclusion", then a "Supplement" containing "Two Notes", a "Preface" and two further points ("No. 1" and "No. 2"), this is then followed by a "Postscript", and finally a "Postscript to the 'Two Notes'"! Of course we have seen the attempt in the dictum "purity of heart is to will one thing [*Hjertets Reenhed er at ville Eet*]"[23] in works by Kierkegaard under his own name, but his love of paradox never subsides, and the presence of the poet manifested in the madness of structures and unrelenting, stumbling self-analysis in his 'report to history' confirms the statement made by Graham Parkes that the "air of paradox dissipates if one regards the poet's self not as something unitary but as inherently multiple".[24] After so much playfulness, irony and humour in his various books, under pseudonyms and his own name, Kierkegaard perhaps failed to see the serious joke that was unfolding in his *Point of View* in the shattering of the self and plurality of the subject in his attempt to unify the poetic thinker. Or perhaps Kierkegaard knew very well what he was doing and what was happening by calling his report to history a *point of view* which is just another particular perspective in his struggle between "the emptying out"[25] of the famous polyphonic, pseudonymous authorship and the deeply philosophical, theological and psychological upbuilding discourses.

Nietzsche is more playfully self-conscious in creating a plurality of the subject in his own 'report to history' in *Ecce Homo* on the eve of his breakdown. The outrageous title brings forth the Messiah from Pontius Pilate's famous uttering from *The Gospel of John 19:5*, and then the reader is taken on a highly entertaining and mesmerising journey through the various deceptions, insights,

---

23 See, for example, Kierkegaard 1993: 25/SKS 8: 24.
24 Parkes 1994: 29.
25 "Emptying out [*at udtømme*]" is an expression Kierkegaard uses in *The Point of View* in explaining the publication of his pseudonymous works between 1843 and 1846 (Kierkegaard 1998: 86/SKS 16: 65).

digressions and hilarious chapter titles of Nietzsche's concise prose and audacious declarations. Nietzsche can be seen to be speaking both for himself and Kierkegaard when he mischievously confesses: "It is my sagacity [*Klugheit*] to have been many things and in many places so as to be able to become *one person* [...]".[26] This is the transformed subjectivity when we are reminded of it as a condition of being a subject – of possessing perspectives, experiences, feelings, beliefs and desires. In approaching *Ecce Homo* like this, Nietzsche's famous comment in paragraph 12 from *Beyond Good and Evil* makes more sense:

> Between you and me, there is no need to get give up "the soul" itself, [...] and thus to renounce one of the most ancient and venerable hypotheses [...] But the path lies open for new versions and sophistications of the soul-hypothesis – and concepts such as the "mortal soul" and the "soul as subject-multiplicity [*Seele als Subjekts-Vielheit*]" and the "soul as a society constructed out of drives and affects" [...].[27]

This soul as subject-multiplicity is for both thinkers the polemical response to the crisis of the subject as a plurality. Before turning to how this is manifested in their distinctive *oeuvre* as dramatic thinkers, it is worth mentioning the famous mantra 'truth is subjectivity', that is declared in Kierkegaard's massive *Concluding Unscientific Postscript*, and how it both relates and is opposed to Nietzsche's thought to conclude this section.

1.4 "Truth is subjectivity"

While Nietzsche's most famous statement is "God is dead" from *The Gay Science*, perhaps (though less dramatic or catchy) Kierkegaard's most famous statement is "Truth is subjectivity"[28] – declared through his most philosophical pseudonym Johannes Climacus. Both focus on the crisis of the subject and see themselves as the interlude [*Mellemspil*] between the Western philosophical tradition of the past and an uncertain, chaotic future. "Truth is subjectivity" is, on the one hand, Kierkegaard's reinstatement of subjectivity against Hegel's system of history, religion, ethics and teleology; and, on the other hand, a celebration of the possibilities and ultimately responsibility of individual perspectives. Like Nietzsche after him, in the wake of the age of disintegration, truth has been blown open for a human being where truth is revealed as that mobile army of

---

[26] EH UM 3/KSA 6: 321.
[27] BGE 12/KSA 5: 27.
[28] Kierkegaard 1992: 189/SKS 7: 173.

metaphors[29] or as synonymous with lunacy[30] and the fixed idea of a Don Quixote, as knight-errant, forever chasing imaginary adversaries along the dusty desert plains of La Mancha,[31] and is both singleminded and ridiculous enough to charge windmills. As Miguel de Unamuno, the enthusiastic Spanish reader of Kierkegaard, put it on reflecting on the literary figure Don Quixote: "But the battered Don Quixote will go on living, because he sought health within himself and dared to charge the windmills".[32] Climacus is more than just a perspective for Kierkegaard, he is probably closer to a picture of Kierkegaard than the 'Kierkegaard' that signs his works, and he is someone that knows Kierkegaard rather better than Kierkegaard knows himself.

At the end of Johannes Climacus' final book *Concluding Unscientific Postscript*, in the insertion by "S. Kierkegaard" – "A First and Last Explanation", the author of the various pseudonyms or 'polyonyms'[33] declares himself to be an "imaginative constructor" and the "poetically actual subjective thinker [*en digterisk-virkelig subjektiv Tænker*]".[34] However, this is also a dramatic statement, much like the various projections and declarations in *Ecce Homo*, which leads me to say that Kierkegaard and Nietzsche are 'dramatic thinkers' (as analogous to the 'dramatic poets' such as, for example, Shakespeare and Fernando Pessoa) as well as being regularly labelled as poetic thinkers because of their elegant and multifarious styles and use of images, figures and stories. This is a way to respond to the age of disintegration and crisis of the subject, and to carry out the unfolding of a multiplicity of the self. While of course there is a difference, in that Nietzsche is far more ruthless with subjectivity, and that Kierkegaard's subjectivity is the attempt to lead one ultimately face to face with God – to rebel

---

29 TL (Nietzsche 1976: 46)/KSA 1: 880.
30 Kierkegaard 1992: 194/SKS 7: 178.
31 Kierkegaard 1992: 195/SKS 7: 179. See also Kierkegaard's journal entry on his idea of a perfected version of Cervantes' *Don Quixote* on the impossibility of Don Quixote's journey ever ending: "It is a sad mistake for Cervantes to Don Quixote by making him sensible and then letting him die. Cervantes, who himself had the superb idea of having him become a shepherd! It ought to have ended there. That is, Don Quixote should not come to an end; he ought to be presented as going full speed, so that he opens vistas upon an infinite series of new fixed ideas. Don Quixote is endlessly perfectible in madness, but the one thing he cannot become (for otherwise he could become everything and anything) is sensible. Cervantes seems not to have been dialectical enough to bring it to this romantic conclusion (that there is no conclusion)" (*Pap*. VIII I A 59, 1847).
32 Unamuno 1976: 58.
33 Kierkegaard writes in "A First and Last Explanation": "My pseudonymity or polyonymity" (Kierkegaard 1992: 625/SKS 7: 569).
34 Kierkegaard 1992: 625/SKS 7: 570.

against or embrace God, or in other words, to succumb to demonic despair or heroic faith. But both are united and hold fast to radical expressions of passion and paradox to which subjectivity is explicitly bound. Perhaps, when reading Kierkegaard it is easier to grasp because, as Climacus explains, "When the eternal truth relates itself to an existing person, it becomes the paradox".[35]

Johannes Climacus will seduce and then bewilder the reader along his repetitive, meandering journey through subjective perspectives of Christianity where the elusive concept inwardness [*Inderlighed*] is at its ungraspable centre: "At its highest, inwardness in an existing subject is passion; truth as a paradox corresponds to passion, and that truth becomes a paradox is grounded precisely in its relation to an existing subject".[36] This 'truth' is both the subject of Nietzsche's critique and the answer to it, as Climacus explains a few pages further: "Here is such a definition of truth: *An objective uncertainty, held fast through appropriation with the most passionate inwardness, is the truth*, the highest truth there is for an *existing* person."[37] However, unlike Nietzsche's canonical targets, Climacus does not claim to be anything other than a loafing, thirty year old student who has found no real vocation in life except to make things more difficult[38] in a world where everything has become more easy. A gesture that Nietzsche would most certainly have sympathized with. And if there was any more doubt about Climacus' intentions regarding subjectivity, after his various philosophical attempts to demonstrate and define subjectivity and inwardness, before Nietzsche can step in to make his critique, Climacus digresses to tell of a time whereby he made one of his usual walks in the graveyard,[39] thereby giving us both an example of the subjective thinker in action, and the subversive exercise of what a philosophical book can be. Here, like the two reports to history in Kierkegaard's *Point of View* and Nietzsche's *Ecce Homo*, thought and existence are intertwined. Our world is our story, or rather, as I have quoted elsewhere from the philosopher John Moriarty: "We say of ourselves that we live in a world, but it would perhaps be truer to say that we live in a tale told".[40]

---

35 Kierkegaard 1992: 209/SKS 7: 192.
36 Kierkegaard 1992: 199/SKS 7: 182.
37 Kierkegaard 1992: 203/SKS 7: 186.
38 Kierkegaard 1992: 186/SKS 7: 171. Climacus writes here: "You must do something, but since with your limited capabilities it will be impossible to make anything easier than it has become, you must, with the same humanitarian enthusiasm as the others have, take it upon yourself to make something more difficult."
39 Kierkegaard 1992: 235/SKS 7: 214.
40 Moriarty 2009: 103. See also my article "Kierkegaard's Fairytale" for more on this idea (Ryan 2013).

After all, if for both Nietzsche and Kierkegaard "the crowd is untruth", then the 'truth' that brings these two thinkers together is not 'the mobile army of metaphors' but rather something pertaining to the 'single individual', the passionate reader, and most of all the attempt to be honest and not hypocritical – difficult tasks indeed. The paradox however intensifies in the issue of subjectivity and honesty, as just when the reader may think that s/he has grasped the author in question, s/he encounters a new mask and distorted mirror. Thus, although Kierkegaard is aiming to make the reader aware of how difficult it is to become a Christian as a riposte to modernity and that subjectivity is truth, what emerges, paradoxically, is an authorship that is full of deceptions, perspectives and polyphonic voices thus confirming a plurality of the subject in Nietzsche and Kierkegaard. This leads me to the second part of the issue of subjectivity in Nietzsche and Kierkegaard, on how they achieve plurality over a death of the subject, which is through exhausting the limits of their creative powers.

2 'The Eyes of Argus', 'Giving Style' and deception

> There is a probably no young person with any imagination who has not at some time been enthralled by the magic of the theatre and wished to be swept along into that artificial actuality in order like a double to see and hear himself and to split himself up into every possible variation of himself, and nevertheless in such a way that every variation is still himself.
>
> (Constantin Constantius)[41]

2.1 The eyes of Argus

What both Nietzsche and Kierkegaard do in confronting the crisis of the subject and in transforming or exploding the idea of subjectivity is famously create a variety of masks and perspectives, and demand that the human as artist in life 'give style' to one's character in coping with celebrating an emotion of multitude. The expression – "emotion of multitude" – is from the poet W.B. Yeats (who is another self-conscious creator of masks) who gives Shakespeare's art an example of this:

---

[41] Kierkegaard 1983: 154/SKS 4: 30.

> We think of King Lear less as the history of one man and his sorrows than as the history of a whole evil time. Lear as shadow is in Gloster, who has ungrateful children, and the mind goes on imagining other shadows, shadow upon shadow till it has pictured the world.[42]

Nietzsche was at least under the influence or in creative conversation[43] with Emerson's "Representative Men" who declares that all great men are a "composition of several persons",[44] and that "He should see that he can live all history in his own person"[45]; and then there is the presence of the sweeping gesture of Walt Whitman's "I contain multitudes".[46] This is not something unusual as many great poets and writers from the latter half of the nineteenth century and first two decades of the twentieth century are doing the same in presenting multiplicities of the self and subject such as not only in Yeats and Whitman, but also Joyce, Pessoa, and Antonio Machado.

But what is new here is that Nietzsche and Kierkegaard are attempting to do this in philosophy what will later happen more explicitly in literature and painting. For Nietzsche, every meaning becomes an interpretation and every work of his becomes a challenge and work in progress to be overcome, or an overcoming of oneself – from *The Birth of Tragedy* and *Untimely Meditations* and his relation and overcoming of his early heroes Wagner and Schopenhauer; to finding a voice amidst the French aphoristic writers and positivists in *Human, All Too Human*; to the scathing, iconoclastic critiques of Western culture in *Beyond Good and Evil*, *Genealogy of Morals*, *Twilight of the Idols* and *The Antichrist*; to the books of joy and embracing the great Nietzschean Yes to the tragic life in *The Gay Science* and *Thus Spoke Zarathustra*; and finally to the masterful autobiography of *Ecce Homo* with its plurality of voices and darkly hilarious, mythic revelations.

Revelling in his finely honed plurality of the subject, Nietzsche's thought reaches new heights in his notes when he declares: "The task: to *see* things *as they are*! *The means*: to be able to see with a hundred eyes, from *many persons*".[47] But the ominous *daemon* taking him down this path is starkly

---

[42] Yeats 1961: 215.
[43] "Creative conversation" is an expression by Edward Clarke in his book *The Later Affluence of W.B. Yeats and Wallace Stevens* (Clarke 2012: 1, 9, 21, 24, 30).
[44] Emerson 1987: 56. This citation is also used as the motto for Graham Parkes' book *Composing the Soul* (1994).
[45] Emerson 2000: 115.
[46] Whitman 1982: 246. Echoing Emerson, Whitman asks: "Do I contradict myself?/Very well then I contradict myself./(I am large, I contain multitudes)."
[47] KSA 9, 11 [65] (translated by Graham Parkes. See Parkes 1994: 303).

evident on the eve of his collapse when he writes in a letter to Jacob Burckhardt: "What is disagreeable and offends my modesty is that at bottom I am every name in history."[48] On the surface, Kierkegaard moves in a different direction in his final days, but there is the point of contact in that he reveals himself to be a direct critic of European culture also in his attack on church and state, selling his pamphlet *Øieblikket* which runs for nine issues cut short by his own collapse and subsequent death shortly after. Kierkegaard's poet connects with the later Nietzsche in calling for a way to see with Argus eyes – the hundred-eyed giant from Greek mythology, whose eyes are changed upon awakening: "The poet is allowed to talk himself out, yet watching with Argus eyes lest the poet trick it and it all becomes a poet".[49] Notice that Nietzsche also conjures up the power of seeing with many eyes again in his later work *Genealogy of Morals*: "the more eyes, different eyes through which we are able to view this same matter, the more complete our 'conception' of it, our 'objectivity', will be."[50] In a section called "Struggles for Multiple Vision" in his compelling book *Composing the Soul*, Graham Parkes points out that we can see this connection of seeing with many eyes with the dramatist and leading to psychological insight that Nietzsche brought to light early on in *The Birth of Tragedy*:

This ability to participate in other souls and see with many eyes, which in *The Birth of Tragedy* is ascribed to the dramatist alone (BT 8), will later come to be the hallmark of the astute philosopher and a trait to be cultivated by anyone who aspires to psychological understanding.[51]

And after *The Birth of Tragedy*, Nietzsche, like Kierkegaard, says it himself in referring to psychological travel and the figure of Argus:

> He who, after long practice in this art of travel, has become a hundred-eyed Argus [...] will rediscover the adventurous travels of his ego [...] in Egypt and Greece, Byzantium and Rome, France and Germany [...] in the Renaissance and the Reformation, at home and abroad, indeed in the sea, the forests, in the plants and in the mountains. Thus self-knowledge will become knowledge of everything with regard to all that is past.[52]

This brings me back to Yeats' emotion of multitude when we think of Nietzsche and Kierkegaard with their eyes of Argus both incorporating drama into their

---

48 Nietzsche 1976: 686.
49 Kierkegaard 1988: 77/SKS 16: 57. An analysis of the metaphor of the 'Argus eyes' in *Point of View* is undertaken by Joakim Garff in his article "The Eyes of Argus: The Point of View and Points of View with respect to Kierkegaard's 'Activity as an author'" (in: Rée/Chamberlain 1997).
50 GM III 12/KSA 5: 365.
51 Parkes 1994: 112.
52 AOM 223/KSA 2: 478.

writings to express the plurality of the subject, thus becoming dramatic thinkers or performing philosophers. The emotion of multitude in writing happens easily in theatre with Shakespeare; the challenge is to bring that into serious philosophy as a way to confront the problem of subjectivity for modernism and postmodernism.

2.2 Giving style

The second aspect of showing and dealing with the transformation of subjectivity in the creative-critical process is Kierkegaard and Nietzsche's demand "to 'give style' to one's character [*Seinem Charakter 'Stil geben'*]".[53] This links them in their response to the crisis of the subject, transforming subjectivity and through the emotion of multitude to give style to one's character. In section 290 of *The Gay Science*, Nietzsche initially writes that 'giving style' is "practiced by those who survey all the strengths and weaknesses of their nature and then fit them into an artistic plan until every one of them appears as art and reason and even weaknesses delight the eye".[54] Here is the aesthetic stance – to create something beautiful and strong, or express life as an aesthetic phenomenon. But it comes with a deeply moral gesture in Nietzsche's thought in that there is the dual goal of offering beauty and sharp thoughts in the aphoristic writings while hammering home the hypocrisies in philosophical and religious 'truths' – sometimes bombastically and sometimes with extreme subtlety. That is Nietzsche's 'giving style' to transforming subjectivity as a creative and dramatic thinker. One can see that Marie Henri Beyle, with his various aliases and voices, better known as Stendhal, provides an appropriately intense inspiration for Nietzsche with the combination of passionate confessions and analytically cool insights and psychological treatment, and with forceful and subtle critiques of his time, framed in sophisticated aesthetic form in works such as *De l'Amour* and *Le Rouge et le Noir*. For Nietzsche, here is a perfect example of an author who is "'giving style' to one's character".

Kierkegaard's Johannes Climacus demands that the "subjective thinker" give style, or more precisely to "have style [*at have Stiil*]":

> One who is existing is continually in the process of becoming; the actually existing subjective thinker, thinking, continually reproduces this in his existence and invests all his think-

---

53 GS 290/KSA 3: 530.
54 GS 290/KSA 3: 530.

ing in becoming. This is similar to having style. Only he really has style who is never finished with something but "stirs the waters of language" whenever he begins, so that to him the most ordinary expression comes into existence with newborn originality.[55]

Note here that for Climacus, having style is in the state of "becoming" – which is always in the pursuit of the self which is always a little out of reach but whose seeking confirms the selfhood of the one struggling and seeking; and it is also connected to the poetic use of language and vocation of our creative state. This description from Kierkegaard's Climacus reaches its peak in *Ecce Homo* – a book whose subtitle is "How One Become what One is" (*Wie man wird, was man ist*), and which is the voice of the subjective thinker who 'stirs the waters' of the German language. Both Nietzsche and Kierkegaard are absolute masters of their native language. In expressing the task for the so-called self as plurality of the subject, Climacus, three quarters of the way through his large and meandering book, challengingly states: "Between poetry and religiousness, worldly wisdom about life performs its vaudeville. Every individual who does not live either poetically or religiously is obtuse [Dum]."[56] Both Nietzsche and Kierkegaard came from a strict religious background, and both react and respond to it in different ways: the former calling for a revival of New Testament teaching and *De Imitatione Christi* where we need to catch up with Christ rather than vice versa; and the latter making an all-out attack on the very idea, belief and grammar of a Judeo-Christian God as a central element in the sickness of Western culture. Both, however, also demand giving style to one's character in doing this – which means living poetically or religiously. Thus, Brandes' subtitle of his monograph on Nietzsche is called "An Essay on Aristocratic Radicalism", which Nietzsche was very pleased about: "The expression *Aristocratic Radicalism*, which you employ, is very good. It is, permit me to say, the cleverest thing I have yet read about myself."[57] Kierkegaard, though equally radical in advocating that one live with passion and paradox – poetically or religiously (or ultimately both, which can be one and the same thing, but that is for another article or book), calls out to "the single individual" who edges closer to the "common man" as his life draws to a close. By the time of his death, his only followers are laymen, the downtrodden and the odd radical (evidenced by his funeral attendance) after his direct assault on the established church of Denmark with handing out his *Øieblikket* pamphlets on the streets. Kierkegaard refuses to accept communion

---

55 Kierkegaard 1992: 86/SKS 7: 85.
56 Kierkegaard 1992: 457/SKS 7: 415.
57 Letter from Nietzsche to Brandes from Nice, 02.12.1887, Brandes 1972: 64.

from a priest (who represents the Danish church which of course is officially connected to the State) on his deathbed but only from a layman, of which he does not receive.

2.3 *Mundus vult decipi*[58]

The last aspect of this section is the issue and use of deception in Kierkegaard and Nietzsche's authorship. Kierkegaard writes in his 'report to history' (published posthumously): "What, then, does it mean 'to deceive'? It means that one does not begin directly with what one wishes to communicate but begins by taking the other's delusion at face value".[59] Here we have the Socratic strategy, of which Kierkegaard sees himself as the Socrates for the modern age: "Popular opinion maintains that the world needs a republic, needs a new social order and a new religion – but no one considers that what the world, confused simply by too much knowledge, needs is a Socrates."[60] Too much knowledge, as for Nietzsche, leads to a much deeper deception, including the worst kind – self-deception. Kierkegaard, under his own name, in *Works of Love*, emphasizes the most dangerous deception as self-deception: "There is also talk about being deceived by life or in life, but the one who in his self-deception deceived himself out of living – his loss is irreparable".[61]

Nietzsche sees this danger also, and they both experiment in psychology to dissect more deeply what it is to be a human being and to expose the deceptions we commit. Robert Pippin has recently explored the ability of psychology to unravel self-deception in the penultimate chapter of his book on Nietzsche as psychologist under the title: "The Psychological Problem of Self-Deception". And Kierkegaard, reflecting on his reception of his authorship in Copenhagen, points out that in general:

> The secret of the deception that indulges the world, which wants to be deceived consists partly in forming a clique and all that goes with it, in joining one or two of those mutual admiration societies whose members assist each other by word and pen for the sake of

---

[58] Translation: "The world wants to be deceived". This is part of a phrase (*Mundus vult decipi ergo decipiatur*), which Kierkegaard inserts in a sentence when discussing deception in *The Point of View*. The expression has been attributed to the Roman satirist Petronius from the first century, Augustine in the *City of God*, and later to Pope Paul IV. See Kierkegaard 1998: 58/SKS 16: 39.
[59] Kierkegaard 1998: 54/SKS 16: 36.
[60] Kierkegaard 1980a: 92/SKS 11: 205.
[61] Kierkegaard 1995: 6/SKS 6: 14.

worldly gain, and partly in hiding from the human throng, never being seen, in order in this way to produce effect on the imagination.⁶²

Hence, the strategies that Nietzsche and Kierkegaard take on are in turning deception in upon itself, so that when in his earlier writings Nietzsche defines truth as a mobile army of metaphors and later goes on to think of truth as a woman – i.e. something appearing as slippery, devious, deceptive and seductive -, he subverts this idea of truth itself (which comes in the form of God, Christianity, nationalism, good and evil, etc.) and makes his own writing just that – slippery, devious, deceptive, and seductive. Witness, for example, the seductive power of *Thus Spoke Zarathustra* or *Beyond Good and Evil*, the devious tone of *Ecce Homo*, and the deceptive critique of *On the Genealogy of Morals*. Nietzsche is constructing one mask after another to show that truth itself is a mask. Kierkegaard has some similar targets such as the 'truth' in the nation-state, Christendom, and bourgeois *Klogskab* (translated as cleverness or sagaciousness) self-satisfaction, and creates more explicit masks through his pseudonyms and elusive voices in the attempt to deceive the reader, to lure him/her in, and to ultimately unsettle him/her.

Both Kierkegaard and Nietzsche are deceivers, concealing in order to reveal. In their revelations, they are concealing and creating more riddles (such as in *Point of View* and *Ecce Homo*). The fundamental distinction between Kierkegaard and Nietzsche is that for Kierkegaard the truth is Jesus Christ. In their sharp awareness of the tenuous position and problem of the subject, both are attempting to speak to the reader (which includes themselves) to become what they are. In essence, this also means to be constantly in a state of both becoming and process of liberating: restless, striving and questioning in the face of knowledge, establishments and groups, but always also with a smile and making space for laughter. In *Point of View*, Kierkegaard states clearly: "In Christendom – to become a Christian is either to become what one is (the inwardness of reflection or the reflection of inward deepening), or it is first of all to be wrested out of a delusion, which again is a category of reflection"⁶³; and that he is "a friend and lover of laughter".⁶⁴ *The Antichrist* begins with the statement: "Let us face ourselves", and Zarathustra declares that what is of great importance in the order of rank amongst philosophers in the capacity for laughter.⁶⁵ Like much of

---

62 Kierkegaard 1998: 58/SKS 16: 39.
63 Kierkegaard 1998: 55/SKS 16: 37.
64 Kierkegaard 1998: 114/SKS 16: 94.
65 BGE 294/KSA 5: 236: "I would go as far as to venture an order of rank among philosophers according to the rank of their laughter – rising to those capable of *golden* laughter."

Climacus' *Concluding Unscientific Postscript*, Nietzsche's statement of facing ourselves is a serious joke in that it sounds like a parody of a Christian sermon while at the same time is a call to literally 'face' our 'selves', which may be an impossible task, but one worth at least trying. Kierkegaard and Nietzsche have provided the creative tools to dealing with the plurality of the subject through the emotion of multitude and offering multiple perspectives with the eye of Argus; of seeking to give style to one's character; and, like all great artists but this time as philosophers and proto-psychologists performing as deceivers, feigners and falsifying selves, deceiving the reader out of the delusion and into the delusion by creating more illusions for the reader (again which also always includes themselves) to do much of the hard work, as the only ultimate gift they can give is to unsettle and awake the reader from what they see as a paradoxically soporific state in the rapidly accelerating present age. As Kierkegaard, in the guise of Johannes Climacus, discloses at one point halfway through *Concluding Unscientific Postscript*: "the most one person can do for another is to unsettle him."[66] Nietzsche almost says the same thing in describing his mission: "To make the individual uncomfortable, that is my task".[67]

3 Confronting nihilism with faith and *amor fati*

> He is cured by faith who is sick of fate [...]
> What cant be coded can be decorded if an ear aye siezs what no eye ere grieved for.
> (James Joyce, *Finnegans Wake* 1939)[68]

Following the transformation of subjectivity and utilising the creative power in expressing the subject as plurality in the unending process of 'becoming oneself', this final section brings up Kierkegaard and Nietzsche's core ideals of the knight of faith and embracing *amor fati* woven into the plurality of the subject to confront the spectre of nihilism that pervades modernity. Both writers were raised in devoutly religious families, and – as is well known – they quickly became deeply suspicious with the Church and the kind of faith that now existed in modernity. They were also deeply aware of a valueless society and age of nihilism that was creeping in. Thus, Nietzsche and Kierkegaard's complex subjectivity includes yet another provocative aspect in their controversially affir-

---

66 Kierkegaard 1992: 387/SKS 7: 352.
67 Nietzsche 1976: 50.
68 Joyce 1992: 482.

mative *amor fati* and knight of faith which can be viewed as the third and final attribute (alongside the transformation and masks of subjectivity) in confronting nihilism. In thinking about *amor fati* and knight of faith in the crisis of the subject, two aspects are explored briefly here: the power of the story and the life of risk with no security.

3.1 Let me tell you a story

The first part of conjuring the knight of faith and being saved by the *amor fati* is the capacity and power to tell the story over and over in new and astonishing ways while always approaching and confronting the apparent indifference and sameness of a nihilistic universe. After his *Stemning* ('Attunement'), the dialectical poet Johannes de silentio begins his "Eulogy on Abraham" with this remarkably Nietzschean vision of the universe which ends with the creation of the poet, speechmaker and the hero. It is worth quoting the passage in full here:

> If a human being did not have an eternal consciousness, if underlying everything there were only a wild, fermenting power that writhing in dark passions produced everything, be it significant or insignificant, if a vast, never appeased emptiness is beneath everything, what would life be then but despair? If such were the situation, if there were no sacred bond that knit humankind together, if one generation emerged after another like forest foliage, if one generation succeeded another like singing of birds in the forest, if a generation passed through the world as a ship through the sea, as wind through the desert, an unthinking and unproductive performance, if an eternal oblivion, perpetually hungry, lurked for its prey and there were no power strong enough to wrench that away from it – how empty and devoid of consolation life would be! But precisely for that reason it is not so, and just as God created man and woman, so he created the hero and the poet or orator [*Taleren*].[69]

This paragraph is important for this article for three reasons: first, in depicting a nihilistic world without storyteller and story-maker; second, the poet's faith in the power of *the story*; and third, the symbiotic relationship that exists between the courageous adventurer and the imaginative poet who recounts the adventure. On the third point, the two roles can be interchanged when we think of Nietzsche and Kierkegaard who see themselves as both adventurers embarking on treacherous waters and as imaginative, philosophical storytellers. This is vital to the plurality of the subject for confronting the crisis of the subject in that their endeavour is that their lives become a work of art, or the life is the art and

---

[69] Kierkegaard 1983: 15/SKS 4: 112.

their art/authorship is their life. This also supports their philosophy as process rather than progress: for Kierkegaard the Christian God is a finished system, but human life is always in a state of becoming; and for Nietzsche, there is no fixed truth to things, and meaning is infinitely interpretable in building and becoming a human being – the key is to think and question differently. Notice how in Kierkegaard's most celebrated book on faith the whole text (*Fear and Trembling*) is framed around different ways to tell a story, and different stories to communicate the same message with an apparent overriding narrative where many other stories unfold. The book is a Pandora's box and labyrinth into the complexity of subjectivity, offering many ways to 'break the silence', and – as Kierkegaard says on more than one occasion – like Scheherazade who kept herself alive by telling fairytales, he keeps himself alive by writing.[70]

Much like Johannes de silentio in *Fear and Trembling*, Nietzsche keeps coming up against the same obstacles again and again, where laughter and acceptance of the absurdity of our lives prompts Zarathustra to learn to laugh, and for Nietzsche to insert a new motto in the 1887 edition of *The Gay Science* which concludes with "I laugh". It is this acceptance that runs alongside the critical struggle with all values, ideas and systems that gives birth to the *amor fati*. In true Nietzschean fashion, the one wish that the aesthete of *Either/Or* asks the gods is to "always have the laughter on my side",[71] to which the gods respond with thunderous laughter and the wish is granted. It is this laughter on their side that Nietzsche and Kierkegaard that frees them from their minds' bondage as they make their hermeneutical journey through a myriad of stories to transform themselves as readers and imagine many possible interpretations in making things more difficult and unsettling for the reader of the future – that, after all, is their ultimate task. And all this has to do with the plurality of the subject in confronting the nihilism of modernity, as the hero and poet leap into existence – living and re-telling the story, repeated again and again with various nuances and transformations. This telling the story is a great "Yes" to life that Johannes de silentio expresses in the extended citation above, which in itself is another aspect of faith – as a belief in affirmation. Hence also, Nietzsche's plural self in his mythical report to history (*Ecce Homo*) declares a faith in *amor fati* after his relentless attack on Western philosophy of which he is a product:

---

[70] Kierkegaard 1996: 342 (*Pap.* IX A 411): "How true, therefore, the remark I have often made concerning myself, that like Scheherazade who saved her life by telling fairy-tales, I save my life, or keep myself alive, by writing."
[71] Kierkegaard 1987: 43/SKS 2: 52.

My formula for greatness in a human being is *amor fati*: that one wants nothing to be other than it is, not in the future, not in the past, not in all eternity. Not merely to endure that which happens of necessity, and on no account still less to dissemble it – all idealism is untruthfulness in the face of necessity – but to *love* it ...[72]

3.2 "Without risk, no faith"[73]

With Kierkegaard as lover of passion and paradox ("The thinker without paradox is like the lover without passion"[74]) and Nietzsche's heroic mantra at the edge of madness of living dangerously (in the search for knowledge),[75] it is no surprise that their answer to the crisis of subjectivity is an isolated striving for an impossible faith and love of a precarious destiny. But as irrational as this may sound, Johannes Climacus's statement that "without risk, no faith" is in fact a rational proposition given that subjectivity is such a slippery concept, and that there cannot be any proofs for belief (hence it would no longer be belief) nor conceited acceptance of fixed truths. If we are go to battle with nihilism and the residues of Western tradition, we must be both aware of the unstable footing we are standing on and the ever-transforming, pluralistic subject that is always in a state of both becoming and shedding in thinking about the crisis of the subject. Hence, Kierkegaard's Johannes Climacus reminds all scientists, theologians, historians and philosophers:

> Is not Venice built upon the sea, even though it was built in such a way that a generation finally came along that did not notice this at all, and would it not be a lamentable misunderstanding if this latest generation was so in error until the pilings began to rot and the city sank? But, humanly speaking, consequences built upon a paradox are built upon the abyss, and the total content of the consequences, which is handed down to the single individual only under the agreement that it is by virtue of a paradox, is not to be passed on like real estate, since the whole thing is in suspense.[76]

And Nietzsche, following his demand "to live dangerously!" in *The Gay Science* in order combat a death of the subject or impending doom of an age of nihilism, declares: "Build your cities on the slopes of Vesuvius! Send your ships into unchartered seas! Live at war with your peers and yourselves!"[77] Loving insecur-

---

72 EH Clever 10/KSA 6: 297.
73 Kierkegaard 1992: 204/SKS 7: 187.
74 Kierkegaard 1985: 37/SKS 4: 242.
75 GS 283/KSA 3: 526.
76 Kierkegaard 1985: 98/SKS 4: 261.
77 GS 283/KSA 3: 526.

ity not certainty, calling out for honesty, living with no teleology, isolating themselves completely to speak for "single individuals" and "for all and none", Nietzsche and Kierkegaard set themselves hard tasks indeed of which they both pay the price knowingly. But like all great artists and revolutionary thinkers, this is their creative practice and strategy of subverting the various patriarchal forces of church, state and knowledge. Thus, the title of one discourse by Kierkegaard is called "Adversity is Prosperity [*Modgang er Medgang*]"[78]; and Nietzsche encourages the reader to embrace the undecided fate of his/her life.

Nietzsche's *amor fati* is enigmatic in that it is loving one's destiny which is somehow equivalent to necessity and determinism, but it is also synonymous with affirmation: "*Amor fati*: let that be my love henceforth! [...] And all in all and on the whole: some day I wish only to be a Yes-sayer."[79] Hence both thinkers are affirming life as it is, as something impermanent,[80] or the certainty is in the glorious uncertainty in Nietzsche's 'fate' and Kierkegaard's 'faith' as pluralistic subjects. This is why Kierkegaard's thinly disguised pseudonym Vigilius Haufniensis is comfortable with the definition of faith (when trying to recall a definition by Hegel) as "the inner certainty that anticipates infinity".[81] Finally then, both thinkers are linked again in their awareness of the gaping abyss that their authorship hovers over and is always on the verge of falling into. Both know their plurality of subjectivity walks a tightrope but flourishes through their various perspectives and styles and their faith in pursuing to continue speaking and writing in the face of the abyss. There is an excellent book called *Kierkegaard and the Self before God: Anatomy of the Abyss* (2011) by Simon D. Podmore from a predominantly theological perspective; one could write a parallel text called *Nietzsche and the Self before Nothing: Anatomy of the Abyss*, and both works would not be so far from each other. Kierkegaard and Nietzsche live and think in risk for they both see the passionate, honest life as risk. But ultimately, for Kierkegaard, as Thomas Miles puts it succinctly, "living by faith is

---

78 Kierkegaard 1997a: 150/SKS 10: 158.
79 GS 276/KSA 3: 521. In *Nietzsche e o enigma do mundo*, João Constâncio argues that Nietzsche's *amor fati* – as a love of immanence – is practically identical to Spinoza's *amor intellectualis Dei* (See Constâncio 2013: 342). This is a very fruitful connection which I will not explore here, but instead I am showing the 'other' side of Nietzsche – if we think of two sides of Nietzsche in the pursuit of the serenity of Spinoza on the one hand, and the striving, suffering spirit of Kierkegaard on the other hand. It would be interesting to compare the often overlooked Kierkegaard discourse on joy (which is linked to faith) as being "present to oneself [*at være sig selv nærværende*]" with *amor fati*. See Kierkegaard 1997b: 39–45/SKS 11: 40–48.
80 Miles 2013: 177.
81 Kierkegaard 1980b: 157/SKS 4: 457.

putting one's trust absolutely in God"[82]; and for Nietzsche, living by *amor fati* is putting one's trust absolutely in necessity. Nietzsche's disregard for faith ("if you wish to strive for peace and pleasure, then believe; if you wish to be a devotee of truth, then inquire [...]"[83]) is not that far from the unceasing, infinite striving of Kierkegaard's conception of faith – which is, however, close to Nietzsche's idea that "all great problems demand *great love*".[84]

Conclusion

> Estar é ser. Fingir é conhecer-se.
> (Álvaro de Campos)[85]

The poetic, existential writings of Nietzsche and Kierkegaard confirm the crisis of the subject in the European tradition for the twentieth and twenty-first century while offering a path beyond the logocentrism and exclusiveness of the Western mind having "its cultural origins in Hebrew prophesy, Greek philosophy and science, and Roman law".[86] Nietzsche's and Kierkegaard's task may be impossible, but like many suspicious, modernist artists and thinkers after them such as Trakl, Kafka, Beckett, Unamuno, Benjamin, and Cioran, etc., the art becomes the passionate endeavour itself.

Kierkegaard and Nietzsche continue to remain writers at the interlude of philosophy and poetry, theology and psychology, revealing the complexity of subjectivity that emerges as a plurality. With Kierkegaard, here is the thinker against philosophy, a Christian against Christendom, and a poet against the aesthete standpoint. And Nietzsche, reflecting on the imminent reaction to his first major work *The Birth of Tragedy*, shows himself also as a figure of the interlude and one who defies categorisation: "I continue to fear that the philologists won't want to read it because of the music in it, the musicians because of the philology, and the philosophers because of the music and the philology, and am thus feeling anxiety and sympathy for my good publisher".[87] Although both thinkers very often are strongly opposed to each other especially by their under-

---

[82] Miles 2013: 41.
[83] Letter to his sister Elisabeth, 11.06.1865 (Nietzsche 1976: 30).
[84] GS 345/KSA 3: 577.
[85] Pessoa 2012: 234 ["Where we are is who we are. To pretend is to know ourselves". Tr. Richard Zenith in Pessoa 2001: 200].
[86] Moriarty 2009: 3.
[87] Letter to Erwin Rohde in November 1871. See Parkes 1994: 84.

standing of figures such as Socrates and Christ; they are however bound together by their extreme individuality in the wake of "the death of god" and collapse of patriarchal authorities, their argument and presentation of a human being that is in flux and restless, their feigning and construction of deceptive masks and multiple perspectives in seeking the elusive self as subject, and finally their pioneering achievement in combining a deeply psychological analysis with a poetic voice into the modern philosophical exploration of subjectivity.

References

Angier, Tom P.S. (2006) *Either Kierkegaard/Or Nietzsche: Moral Philosophy in a New Key*, Aldershot: Ashgate.
Benjamin, Walter (1999) *Selected Writings: Volume 2, 1927–1934*, Cambridge, MA: Harvard University Press.
Brandes, Georg (1972) *Friedrich Nietzsche*, New York: Macmillan.
Brobjer, Thomas (2002) "Nietzsche's Knowledge of Kierkegaard", in: *Journal of the History of Philosophy* 40(4), 251–263.
Carr, David (1999) *The Paradox of Subjectivity*, New York/Oxford: Oxford University Press.
Cinelli, Albert (1989) "Nietzsche and Kierkegaard on Existential Affirmation", in: *Southwest Philosophy Review* 5, 135–141.
Clarke, Edward (2012) *The Later Affluence of W.B. Yeats and Wallace Stevens*, Hampshire: Palgrave MacMillan.
Clayton, John Powell (1985) "Zarathustra and the Stages on Life's Way: A Nietzschean Riposte to Kierkegaard?", in: *Nietzsche-Studien* 14, 179–200.
Constâncio, João (2013) *Arte e Niilismo: Nietzsche e o Enigma do Mundo*, Lisbon: Tinta-da-China.
Emerson, Ralph Waldo (1987) *Representative Men*, Cambridge, MA: Harvard University Press.
Emerson, Ralph Waldo (2000) *The Essential Writings of Ralph Waldo Emerson*, ed. Brooks Atkinson, New York: The Modern Library.
Grau, Gerd-Günter (1985) "Nietzsche and Kierkegaard", trans. Wendy Radar, in: James C. O'Flaherty, Timothy F. Sellner and Robert M. Helm. (eds.), *Studies in Nietzsche and Judeo-Christian Tradition*, Chapel Hill: University of North Carolina Press, 226–251.
Hinman, Lawrence M. (1980) "Temporary and Self-Affirmation. A Kierkegaardian Critique of Nietzsche's Doctrine of the Eternal Recurrence of the Same", in: *Kierkegaardiana* 11, 93–119.
Jaspers, Karl (1955) "The Origin of the Contemporary Philosophical Situation: The Historical Meaning of Kierkegaard and Nietzsche", in: *Reason and Existenz: Five Lectures*, 3rd edition, trans. William Earle. New York: Noonday Press, 19–50.
Joyce, James (1992) *Finnegans Wake*, London: Penguin.
Joyce, James (2008) *Ulysses*, ed. Jeri Johnson, Oxford: Oxford University Press.
Kellenberger, James (1997) *Kierkegaard and Nietzsche*, New York: Macmillan.
Kierkegaard, Søren (1980a) *The Sickness unto Death*, trans. Howard V. Hong and Edna H. Hong, Princeton, NJ: Princeton University Press.

Kierkegaard, Søren (1980b) *The Concept of Anxiety*, trans. Reider Thomte, Princeton, NJ: Princeton University Press.
Kierkegaard, Søren (1983) *Fear and Trembling/Repetition*, trans. Howard V. Hong and Edna H. Hong, Princeton, NJ: Princeton University Press.
Kierkegaard, Søren (1985) *Philosophical Fragments*, trans. Howard V. Hong and Edna H. Hong, Princeton, NJ: Princeton University Press.
Kierkegaard, Søren (1987) *Either/Or: Part I*, trans. Howard V. Hong and Edna H. Hong, Princeton, NJ: Princeton University Press.
Kierkegaard, Søren (1992) *Concluding Unscientific Postscript*, trans. Howard V. Hong and Edna H. Hong, Princeton, NJ: Princeton University Press.
Kierkegaard, Søren (1993) *Upbuilding Discourses in Various Spirits*, trans. Howard V. Hong and Edna H. Hong, Princeton, NJ: Princeton University Press.
Kierkegaard, Søren (1995) *Works of Love*, trans. Howard V. Hong and Edna H. Hong, Princeton, NJ: Princeton University Press.
Kierkegaard, Søren (1996) *Papers and Journals: A Selection*, trans. Alastair Hannay, London: Penguin.
Kierkegaard, Søren (1997a) *Christian Discourses/The Crisis and a Crisis in the Life of an Actress*, trans. Howard V. Hong and Edna H. Hong, Princeton, NJ: Princeton University Press.
Kierkegaard, Søren (1997b) *Without Authority*, trans. Howard V. Hong and Edna H. Hong, Princeton, NJ: Princeton University Press.
Kierkegaard, Søren (1998) *The Point of View*, trans. Howard V. Hong and Edna H. Hong, Princeton, NJ: Princeton University Press.
Leopardi, Giacomo (2010) *Canti*, trans. Jonathan Galassi, London: Penguin.
Leopardi, Giacomo (2013) *Zibaldone: The Notebooks of Leopardi*, eds. Michael Caesar and Franco D'Intino, London: Penguin.
Lewis, Charles (1986) "Kierkegaard, Nietzsche, and the Faith of Our Fathers", in: *International Journal for Philosophy of Religion* 20(1), 3–16.
Malantschuk, Gregor (1962) "Kierkegaard and Nietzsche", trans. Margaret Grieve, in Howard A. Johnson and Niels Thulstrup (eds.), *A Kierkegaard Critique*, Chicago: Regnery, 116–129.
Miles, Thomas P. (2011) "Friedrich Nietzsche: Rival Visions of the Best Way of Life", in: Jon Stewart (ed.), *Kierkegaard and Existentialism, Kierkegaard Research: Sources, Reception and Resources, Volume 9*. Farnham: Ashgate, 263–297.
Miles, Thomas P. (2013) *Kierkegaard and Nietzsche on the Best Way of Life*, New York: Palgrave Macmillan.
Moriarty, John (2009) *Dreamtime*, Dublin: Lilliput.
Nietzsche, Friedrich (1976) *The Portable Nietzsche*, ed. and trans. Walter Kaufmann. New York: The Viking Press.
Nordentoft, Kresten (1972) *Kierkegaard's Psychology*, trans. Bruce Kirmmse, Pittsburgh: Duquesne University Press.
Parkes, Graham (1994) *Composing the Soul: Reaches of Nietzsche Psychology*, Chicago: University of Chicago Press.
Pessoa, Fernando (2001) *The Selected Prose of Fernando Pessoa*, ed. and trans. Richard Zenith, New York: Grove Press.
Pessoa, Fernando (2012) *Prosa de Álvaro de Campos*, edição Jerónimo Pizarro e Antonio Cardiello, colaboração Jorge Uribe, Lisbon: Ática.

Pippin, Robert B. (1999) *Modernism as a Philosophical Problem*, 2nd edition, Oxford: Blackwell.
Pippin, Robert B. (2005) *The Persistence of Subjectivity*, New York: Cambridge University Press.
Pippin, Robert B. (2010) *Nietzsche, Psychology, and First Philosophy*, Chicago/London: University of Chicago Press.
Podmore, Simon D. (2011) *Kierkegaard and the Self before God: Anatomy of the Abyss*, Bloomington: Indiana University Press.
Rée, Jonathan/Chamberlain, Jane (1997) *Kierkegaard: A Critical Reader*, Oxford: Blackwell, 75–102.
Ryan, Bartholomew (2013) "Kierkegaard's Fairytale", in: *Rivista di Filosofia Neo-Scolastica* 3–4, 945–961.
Unamuno, Miguel de (1976) *Our Lord Don Quixote: The Life of Don Quixote and Sancho with related Essays*, trans. Anthony Kerrigan, Princeton: Princeton University Press.
Whitman, Walt (1982) *Collected Poetry and Collected Prose*, New York: The Library of America.
Yeats, W.B. (1961) *Essays and Introductions*, New York: Collier Books.

John Richardson
13 Nietzsche vs. Heidegger on the Self: Which I Am I?

1 Introduction

Each of us is, it seems, many things. I, for example, am an organism, a human being, a deliberating agent, a male, an American . . . and on and on.

Am I, in addition to all of these, also a 'self'? What is my 'self', amongst all of these? Is it just another way of referring to *all* of these things that I am? Or does it pick out some one or some few among them, as most fully or decisively 'me'?

1) One view is that my self is a kind of core or center of me, by comparison with which some of these things 'I am' are secondary, perhaps properties or relationships rather than my 'true' or 'very' self. So the self is as it were a center around which there adhere parts or aspects that are 'mine' but not 'me'.
2) But there's another view: my self lies in how I am 'towards myself', i.e. reflexively refer to myself. It is some feature of this self-referring, and not a prior or independent thing or part. It's this view, I'll argue, that both Nietzsche and Heidegger hold, although in different forms, and as it were from opposite directions.

I'll call this latter view of the self the '*reflexive*' view. It is in its broad lines familiar from a diverse literature, though I will develop it in my own way, with only sporadic mentions of that literature.[1] I will try to introduce, from the simple structure of this view, a framework of terms and relations that can help us to organize Nietzsche's and Heidegger's accounts of the self. This framework

---

[1] Fichte (1982: 34): "It is only through this act [reverting into itself], and first by means of it, . . . that the self *originally* comes to exist for itself." Nozick (1981: 78): "To be an I, a self, is to have the capacity for reflexive self-reference." Velleman (2006: 354): "I don't believe in the self [as] a proper part [of a person] that is both the source of his autonomy and the target of his self-regard because of being the basis of his identity. . . . In my view 'self' is just a word used to express reflexivity . . ."

allows us, I hope, to state the gist of their positions more exactly – or, often, to see where their positions are unsettled or ambiguous. And it lets us see too the main *differences* between their ways of developing this view of the self, and perhaps some comparative strengths and weaknesses.

What they have in common, first, is their rejection of that 'core' view of the self, and especially of one dominant version of that view, which understands the core 'me', my 'true self', to be myself as *subject*, i.e. the subject of consciousness, the thing that thinks and (as also the *agent*) decides. Nietzsche and Heidegger agree in insisting that it is rather our capacity to 'self-relate' that makes us selves, and that this self-relating happens, in the primary case, 'beneath' consciousness. Both make strong use, moreover, of a certain flexibility or play the notion of the self acquires, by being thought of in terms of reflexivity. There is ambiguity, we'll see, just *where* in this reflexivity to locate the self. Moreover, since the self arises by a certain activity, and since this activity can be better or worse carried out, the self can be more or less adequately formed. This reflexive view lies at the bottom of Nietzsche's well-known idea, partly shared by Heidegger, that the self is something one needs to 'create' and 'become'.

When I speak of Heidegger here I'll mean the Heidegger of *Being and Time*. It is the 'existential' aspect of that book that develops the view I'll focus on. Familiarly, though, Heidegger abandons and turns against this existentialism in his later writings, after his 'turn'. The existentialist task of 'becoming a self' comes to seem one more expression of the enframing and technological stance he now attacks. He later favors something more like a Buddhist 'selflessness', in sharp contrast both with Nietzsche, and with his own earlier view.

But although *Being and Time* shares with Nietzsche this idea of selfhood as lying in a self-relation, it comes to the idea from a quite different direction than Nietzsche does, and gives a correspondingly different account of what we need to do, in order to 'become our selves'. The difference is rooted, we'll see, in Nietzsche's naturalism, in contrast with the transcendentalism involved in Heidegger's phenomenology. Thus for Nietzsche the task of achieving selfhood is set us by our biological and social constitution – by their combining and their conflict. It's an historically and personally local task, that requires insight into our historical and personal formation. For Heidegger by contrast the task comes to us from our transcendental structure, as a kind of inbuilt function or aim. It has a supra-historical and supra-personal universality: we realize selfhood by facing our generic structure as Dasein.

Before I turn to Heidegger's and Nietzsche's positions, though, I'd like to introduce some terms and distinctions to use in developing this reflexive view of the self.

2 The reflexive self

Begin with the contrasting 'core view' of the self. This interprets the self as the central part of a more encompassing thing, the part of it that 'I am' above all or in a superlative sense. While the more peripheral parts may be 'mine', they are secondarily so, by the relation in which they stand to this crucial 'me'. This core self is conceived as a *substance*, in the simple sense of being a thing that persists 'beneath' the changing properties and periphera. This innermost self continues steadily as it is, grounding my personal identity through time.

The dominant version of this core view interprets this underlying substance-self as a *subject* – that is, as the subject of consciousness, that 'to which' all one's experience appears. The paradigmatic statement of this view is surely Descartes', when he identifies himself as a thinking thing. This thinking includes, familiarly, all his mental acts and receptions – all that he does in awareness, and all that comes to his awareness. He is the *thing* that thinks, so that this thinking is a first ring around his core, already 'his' but not 'himself'. And his body and its actions are then more peripheral rings, his but still less himself.

By contrast the 'reflexive view' interprets the self in terms of a certain activity – what I will call 'self-meaning' or 'self-referring'. It's what happens when I say, or think, or otherwise mean or intend 'I'. And this view offers the opportunity – which both Nietzsche and Heidegger crave – to treat the self as neither a substance nor a subject. This outcome requires, however, that the reflexive view be filled out carefully, since some plausible versions will license a substance- or subject-self after all. One plausible reading of that view identifies the self as the thing that self-refers, and this might still be something that persists as a substance. And it's also plausible to interpret self-referring to require a consciousness of oneself, so that it's also still the work of a subject. A substance- or subject-self remains an option even once we focus on reflexivity. To avoid slipping back to such a self, Nietzsche and Heidegger must offer some different version of the reflexive view.

Let's call reflexivity 'self-referring', taking this in a very broad sense. It involves three components:

A: what refers
B: the referring
C: what's referred to.

I'll call these, respectively, the self-referrer, the self-referring, and the self-referred. Let's leave it open, for the moment, where among them we are to locate 'the self', and ask some questions about these three elements.

A first key question concerns the nature of B, the referring. How does this happen? In the cases we think of first, it happens both *consciously*, and *in language*. I am aware of myself and describe myself as being such-and-such. But although Nietzsche and Heidegger are of course highly interested in the linguistic and conscious forms of reflexivity, they agree in denying that these forms are basic; our primary self-referring goes on 'beneath' our consciousness, and without words.

They also agree, I suggest, that this non-linguistic and non-conscious referring is still a matter of *intentionality*: a meaning or intending of some content, 'what's meant'. Although Heidegger tends to avoid this Husserlian term, I think the structure he finds in Dasein is all intentional. And it seems to me also what Nietzsche means, when he attributes 'perspective' to us, to our drives, and to all living things. For both, there is a way we 'mean' or 'view' ourselves that is prior to awareness and words. And this is another reason they dispute the idea of the self as a subject.

Another question is whether there are really *three* elements here. For since this is *self*-reference, it seems that A (self-referrer) and C (self-referred) are meant to be identical with one another. If we distinguish them, mustn't it be just as different *aspects* of one single thing, first its aspect 'as referring', and second its aspect 'as referred to'?

But – to be useful for our purposes – C must be more distinct from A than that. We will need it to reflect the way self-referring always happens 'under a description'.[2] That is, one always does two things in saying "I": 1) one points back at the thing that does the pointing, whatever this thing might be, but 2) one also, if often implicitly, points at this thing *as* being some kind of thing. Self-reference involves a *view* of oneself, in which one appears *as* something. I suggest that we think of the C, the self-referred, as what one views oneself as. And this can be more or less different from what the referring thing is. When one tries to point back at oneself, one may not point straight back at what does the pointing, but aside or askew.

Now here we are thinking of the C as (meant as) a kind of hypothesis about the A, but this leaves out a crucial part of the point, for both Nietzsche and Heidegger. It encourages the idea that the real self is the A, and that the C is just (meant in) a more or less false theory about it, and so has no claim to be the self. This would return us to the core notion of the self, the core now being the thing that self-refers. But Nietzsche and Heidegger both treat the C, the self-

---

[2] Thanks to Mattia Riccardi here.

referred, as much more crucial to the self. They will claim that the self *is*, in a manner and to an extent we will need to specify, how it views itself.

But why should the C play this role? To begin with, because this C isn't meant just as a theory or description of the referring thing, but as its aspiration or aim. The reflexivity that makes a self is also active and practical: A refers to C as the who it is trying to be. So the claim is, that in trying to be C, one's self thereby *is* C. The obvious point here is causal: the view of itself as C is to some extent self-fulfilling, for the way A's trying to be C tends to make it more like C. But the crucial claim is constitutional: even before A is changed by its effort, its self is already this C it is trying to be. Its self *is* its aspirations. (This may mean that we're not dealing with a strict reflexivity after all: it's not x relating to x, but x relating to what x is trying to be, or to itself 'in aspiration'.[3] Or, it might still be that x relates to x, but just not to x 'where' it *now* is, but to x where it aspires to be; it would be as if this self-pointing treats its self as a moving target it therefore 'leads'.)

One of my main claims below will be that Nietzsche and Heidegger posit both kinds of self-referring: they think of this reflexive turn back on oneself as operating both theoretically and practically. So on the one hand I 'mean' myself in a way that tries to 'get right' what I already am; this is a project of 'discovery'. But on the other hand I also mean myself in a way that tries to make me as I want to be; here I have the project of 'creating' or 'becoming' myself. But how can my 'self' be given in *both* of these projects? They seem to give me different selves. Sorting out just how Nietzsche and Heidegger connect these two kinds of self-referring, which I will call '*descriptive*' and '*formative*', is crucial for understanding their accounts of the self.

Now where, among A, B, and C, do we find 'the self'? All three are candidates to be identified as this self. But since B, the referring, is an activity, it would involve a certain dislocation to identify it as the self – we take the self to be more a 'thing' than an activity. So perhaps our first options should be A, the self-referrer, and C, the self-referred. Is my self the thing that points back at itself, or is it the thing that's pointed back at? How we answer this question may hang on how we decide between those descriptive and formative views of self-referring. If referring tries to 'get right' what's there, then it seems the self must be what refers, since this *is* already there.[4] If on the other hand referring tries to

---

[3] Compare Velleman (2006: 198) analyzing anticipation: "an intention purports to represent the future from the perspective at which it will arrive to guide action" – so that it will be 'I' doing it.
[4] Nozick (1981: 72): "let us say, as a first approximation, that 'I' refers to that being (entity, x) with the capacity of referring to itself which (who) produces that very token 'I'."

'make' the self, then the latter must be what's referred to, since this comes to be through the referring. Nietzsche and Heidegger, in embracing both the descriptive and formative views, will want 'the self' to be somehow both A and C.[5] And this gives them grounds for turning back to B, the referring, as truly the self despite its not seeming a 'thing'.

We should notice one last feature of this self-referring: it refers back to its 'self'–*in contrast* with everything else, everything other and not-self. So it involves this exclusion or contrast. This exclusion looms large in Nietzsche's and Heidegger's treatments of the self. They are not concerned with my separation of myself from the physical things that adjoin my body. Rather, the 'other' that's especially contrasted with and excluded from self, is for Nietzsche the herd, for Heidegger 'the "they"' (*das Man*). For both the problem will be, that in trying to point to myself, I actually point to this generalized 'other'.

3 Heidegger's self

I want to start, out of order, with Heidegger because his treatment of the self is more conspicuous, and in a certain way simpler than Nietzsche's. As mentioned I'll focus on *Being and Time*, since the idea of the self falls out of favor with later Heidegger: 'self-assertion' (as in the title of his 1933 inaugural address) gets diagnosed as expressing the 'enframing' stance he critiques.

But in *Being and Time* Heidegger gives a central role to the self, developing an unusual but not unprecedented idea of it. I will try to carry us there by steps from a more familiar notion. Each of us is a Dasein, according to that book's analysis. I suggest that Heidegger means by this, principally, an intender or meaner, *for* whom there is meaning or content. But how should we speak of the 'self' of this entity?

1. A first thing we might use 'self' to refer to is simply this entity as entity – the entity 'itself'. In this sense every entity is a self, including everything in the great non-Dasein mass of things. When 'self' occurs in compound personal pronouns such as 'itself', we might say it carries this minimal sense. So we can speak even of 'the rock itself'; it means no more than 'that very rock'.

---

5 Compare James (1992: 174): "the total self of me, being as it were duplex, partly known and partly knower, partly object and partly subject, must have two aspects discriminated in it, of which for shortness we may call one the *Me* and the other the *I*." He says that at least initially we should treat these as *aspects* not *things*, since their identity is "perhaps the most ineradicable dictum of commonsense" (174).

2. A second thing 'self' could refer to is not the entity but a part or aspect that is essential or definitive in it. So we might think of a person's 'true self' as some core or privileged part, perhaps a dominant part. So here 'self' is used as a kind of honorific, for a part within the constitution of an entity. Again this might apply to any entity; I can mean by 'the rock itself' something I consider essential to it, e.g. its molecular structure.
3. However neither of these senses is in the right ballpark for Heidegger, since neither of them makes the self a matter of intentionality. Only something that means, that has (is) a 'there'–a Dasein–can be a self. And this is a third thing 'self' might plausibly refer to: an intender or meaner, a Dasein. It's in this sense that I might refer to my different drives or personae as selves within me–I'm thinking of them as micro-intenders.
4. But this is still missing something crucial: to be a self, the intentionality must also have that reflexive turn upon itself which Heidegger calls 'mineness'. What makes a self is not intending per se, but an intending that intends reflexively, i.e intends itself. It is this reflex in intentionality that Heidegger calls *Jemeinigkeit*–the basis he lays at the very start of the book for selfhood and authenticity. As we'll see, this mineness gets cashed out in the three basic aspects of intentionality–projection, feeling, and talk. So sense 4 is an important part of Heidegger's account of the self.
5. However even this mineness isn't enough to make me a self in Heidegger's full sense. Every Dasein has mineness, but not every Dasein is a self; to be a self I need to carry out or accomplish that mineness in a special way. For it turns out that this reflexive turn is usually corrupted or ruined in the everyday way we all live. This happens because there is something hard or painful about fully or directly intending oneself, and we embrace that everyday stance precisely to avoid this. So my everyday ways of projecting, feeling, and talking fail at 'mineness'. To be a self I must overcome this drift towards avoiding myself. I must intend myself adequately, fully to be a self. This achievement is of course authenticity–being one's own self.

But we need to look at this much more carefully. Let's start with Heidegger's basic notion of 'mineness' [*Jemeinigkeit*], which so clearly announces his reflexive view. "Dasein is an entity which is in each case I myself [*das je ich selbst bin*]; its being is in each case mine [*je meines*]" (SuZ 114).[6] Heidegger builds this mineness into Dasein from the very beginning (in the second sentence of *Being and Time*'s first chapter, and more fully a page later). Mineness is a matter of

---

6 All Heidegger references are to *Being and Time* (SuZ), which I cite by the German pagination.

reflexive reference, and is distinctive of Dasein. "That entity which in its being has this very being as an issue [*um dieses selbst geht*], comports itself towards [*verhält sich zu*] its being as its ownmost [*eigensten*] possibility" (SuZ 42). By contrast, the at-hand (I'll so translate *vorhanden*) lacks mineness because "its being is a matter of indifference to it" (or more precisely, Heidegger thinks, is neither a matter of indifference nor its opposite) (SuZ 42).[7]

He stresses how his analysis rules out the usual interpretations of the self as a substance or subject, which treat it as something at-hand.[8] The self is not some thing that precedes and underlies our self-referring, but an aspect or element in that self-referring itself. It is a way of being of this entity, which seems tantamount to volatilizing the authentic 'core [*Kern*] of Dasein' (SuZ 117)–but this will worry us only if we insist this self must be something at-hand.[9] Heidegger tends strongly to collapse the self-referrer (A) into the activity of self-referring (B).

But just how does Heidegger think this 'self-comporting' works? He claims that it happens in each of the three fundamental aspects of Dasein's intentionality, the three ways it 'means' its world. He treats these in Div. I Ch. 5: *Befindlichkeit*, *Verstehen*, and *Rede*, which I'll translate as 'self-finding', 'understanding', and 'talk'.

Let's start with understanding, since this is primary for Heidegger. We understand the world in our 'know-how', which lies in our 'projecting'. This is the way we press ahead towards ends, and interpret the things we encounter in relation to them. So we encounter things as to-hand [*zuhanden*] rather than at-hand. In projecting towards ends I identify myself with them and pursue them as my own.[10] This happens without any explicit thoughts or representations of those ends, or of them as mine or me. So an 'I' is implicitly attached to our ends, and since things are encountered in relation to those ends (as to-hand for it), we engage them from a first-personal stance.[11] The chair I handle is there for my

---

[7] "Ontologically, Dasein is in principle different from everything that is at-hand or real. Its 'subsistence' is not based on the substantiality of a substance but on the '*self-subsistence*' of the existing self, whose being has been conceived as care." (SuZ 303)

[8] According to the usual view the self is "what maintains itself as something identical through changes in its experiences and ways of behavior" (SuZ 114). He later argues that even Kant falls back into interpreting the I as subject (SuZ 318–320).

[9] "Dasein's selfhood has been defined formally as a *way of existing*, and therefore not as an entity at-hand." (SuZ 267) Cf. SuZ 322.

[10] "[T]he 'for-the-sake-of' always pertains to the being of *Dasein*, for which, in its being, that very being is essentially an *issue*." (SuZ 84)

[11] "Dasein always assigns itself *from* a 'for-the-sake-of-which' *to* the 'with-which' of an involvement; that is to say, to the extent that it *is*, it always lets entities be encountered as at-hand." (SuZ

purposes. By contrast when I view the chair as at-hand I put these aimings 'out of play'; I try to see it out of any relation to myself, i.e. third-personally.

Now how, given the earlier analysis of self-referring, should we understand this way I identify with my ends? Heidegger means, I suggest, a *formative* (rather than descriptive) self-referring. In projecting towards 'possibilities', I identify myself as the ways I can be, the ways I'm pressing to be. "As long as it is, Dasein always has understood itself in terms of possibilities. . . . As projecting, understanding is the kind of being of Dasein in which it *is* its possibilities as possibilities" (SuZ 145). I *am* my possibilities because my projection refers me to them. So these possibilities are, in our earlier term, my 'self-referred' (C). Of course we can see that Heidegger also recognizes, in these passages, a 'self-referrer' (A), though as we've seen he closely identifies this with its activity of self-referring (B). I *am* my possibilities, but I *also am* my projecting at possibilities, and the ambiguity between these is a recurring feature of Heidegger's account. Still, it is chiefly the self-referred, the possibilities I project towards, that he here counts as 'my self'.

The second aspect of being-in is *Befindlichkeit*—which I'll translate, perhaps tendentiously, as 'self-finding' (not 'state-of-mind' as in Macquarrie and Robinson's translation [Heidegger 1962]). For Heidegger stresses this reflexivity in *Befindlichkeit*:

> An entity of the character of Dasein is its there in such a way that, whether explicitly or not, it finds itself [*sich befindet*] in its thrownness. In *Befindlichkeit* Dasein is always brought before itself, it has always already found itself, not as a perceptual finding-itself-before [*Sich-vor-finden*], but as moody self-finding [*gestimmtes Sichbefinden*]. (SuZ 135)

So he links self-finding with mood, and what he means (I suggest) is how things get meaning for us in the way we 'feel' about them. So we mean things not only 'towards' our ends but also 'from' our feeling or mood–as it were 'from the opposite direction'.

So this affective meaning is likewise essentially reflexive: it always involves our first meaning or intending ourselves. It involves my 'finding myself' in my feelings: I am as I've been thrown into feeling, and not just as I project to be. In finding things to be as I feel them, I am always first finding myself. This happens not just in strong and noticed moods, but in all the subtle feelings–self-feelings –that accompany my acts and attitudes. I mean myself so *in* my very feeling, and not in a secondary awareness *of* myself feeling so. (It does not have "the character of a grasping that first turns round and back on itself" [SuZ 136].)

---

86). Since the 'world', as a system of involvements, gets its meaning in relation to my ends, there's a way the whole world is 'mine'.

How does our analysis of self-referring apply here? I refer myself to my feeling, refer myself to it *as* what I've been thrown into (rather than what I'm trying to be). By contrast with the formative reflexivity in projection, I suggest that self-finding is chiefly *descriptive*: I take myself to already be as I feel. And I experience this discrepancy between the self I feel and the self I project, as the difference between the self I already am (have been thrown into being) and the self I'm trying to be.

Heidegger often insists on the authoritative way in which feeling discloses. In mood Dasein "is disclosed to itself *before* all knowing and willing, and *out above* their range of disclosure" (SuZ 136). This disclosure by moods is "originary" (SuZ 134). And it turns out later that the special mood of anxiety, and what it discloses, are crucial to Heidegger's existential story.

The third aspect of being-in is 'talk' or *Rede* ('discourse' in Macquarrie and Robinson). This is the way in which we 'mean' things not via our projects or our feelings, but from or in relation to an articulated system of meanings (*Bedeutungsganze* [SuZ 161]) belonging to our linguistic community. So 'talk' is the stance in which we look, as it were, not ahead towards ends, nor back at our thrownness into moods, but out towards an encompassing social practice – and to other Dasein as sharing in this practice. In this stance of *Rede* we 'mean things' with respect to (in relation to) 'what one says and does' – i.e. to this shared practice. So *Rede* isn't the neutral capacity to use language, nor the capacity to deploy it for our projective ends. It's the capacity to mean out of one's engagement in a community.

And, like projecting and feeling, this involves a certain way of meaning myself.[12] I now identify myself with (I 'mine') not my ends, and not my moods, but the community of talkers who give this dimension of meaning to things. In the usual, everyday case, I mean things simply as that community means: I mean them using its words, and I defer to the meanings it puts on those words.[13] In meaning things *as* an average member of this community, I identify myself as *das Man* ("the 'they'" in Macquarrie and Robinson).[14] And this means, Heidegger famously says, that "[t]he self of everyday Dasein is *das Man-selbst* . . ." ("the 'they'-self") [SuZ 129]. This is the 'who' of my everydayness.

Now by contrast with the other two axes of reflexivity, within projecting and self-finding, Heidegger is clearly judgmental and critical about this third. Some-

---

[12] Admittedly Heidegger does not develop this reflexivity in his principal treatment of *Rede*, in sec. 34. I read the point back from the discussion of *Gerede*, chat, in sec. 35, together with the earlier treatment of *das Man* in sec. 27.
[13] So *das Man* itself "articulates the referential context of significance" (SuZ 129).
[14] "In terms of *das Man*, and **as** *das Man*, I am 'given' proximally to my 'self'." (SuZ 129)

thing usually goes wrong when I mean myself by talking: I *mis*identify myself in meaning things *as das Man*. But is this a failure in description or formation? I think Heidegger treats it both ways. I 'mistake' what I really am, but I also 'mismake' myself. I go astray both theoretically and practically (creatively). But to see this in detail let's turn from Heidegger's account of this 'falling' and 'inauthentic' way of being a 'they-self', to his account how we can correct these flaws and mean ourselves aright.

I think the gist of Heidegger's idea is this. What goes wrong when we fall into *das Man* is that we've failed, first, to turn back and look at ourselves as we are, and that this prevents us, second, from then creating ourselves as we should. So authenticity, 'ownness', involves a 'phase' of self-discovery, and then one of self-formation. These two 'selves' are compatible with one another because, roughly, the former is abstract and the latter concrete: I 'see' my self only in my essence (my existential structure) as Dasein, and by this I then 'make' my self with concrete projects and feelings and words. Indeed, Heidegger is inclined to put it still more forcefully: I discover myself only in negations, *as* a kind of nullity, which is a precondition for then giving myself a positive content. For the key features I find in myself when I'm authentically reflexive are my death and my guilt. I face how my self is (abstractly and negatively) mortal and guilty, and then *choose* a self with (concrete and positive) projects and feelings.

For reasons of space I'll focus on death, and omit the largely parallel story about guilt. Death is a 'possibility', as are all the particular ends in my projection. But it's a distinctive possibility, my 'ownmost' and 'non-relational' possibility; Heidegger stresses how I 'find my self' in it above all. It is ownmost in that in this possibility my "very being is at issue" (SuZ 263). It is non-relational in that I alone can deal with it, so that it "individualizes Dasein down to itself" (SuZ 263). Death is superlatively mine because I have it as my possibility independently of any and all of the social meanings embedded in my language and practices. All my other possibilities I have received from others, and I'm replaceable by others in them. The roles, identities, and aims I pursue all have their meanings by the social-linguistic matrix I inherit and join: that determines what these roles mean and require, not I. And what matters for this matrix is merely that *someone* performs this role, not whether it's I.

But death is a possibility I have by my own essential structure, 'before' my entry into that contingent social domain. I stand in a relation to it that has not been structured by language or by any of the prevailing social practices and outlooks on death. This priority in my relation to death is also shown in how it (partly) motivates and explains my embrace of those social structures. To find myself, in this original relation to death, I must 'look' 'beneath' all those structurings of it, to see how I 'mean' it underneath all the ways I think about it. This is my relation to *my* death – to death as *my* possibility, not a possibility there for anyone else inhabiting that language and practices.

When I turn towards this ownmost possibility in the right way, this takes away my everyday satisfaction with my projects as 'what one does'. Death is a possibility I have from my essential structure: the possibility of my ceasing to exist. And death is 'between me and myself': all that matters is my own effort, and the only help anyone else can give is by inducing or spurring that effort (as phenomenology aims to do). Death brings me back to self-reliance, in relation to my other ends as well; it "individualizes me down to myself" (cf. SuZ 263).

But by this very act of pulling me back from my sociality, into the context of myself, authenticity equips me to choose ends for myself – and here is the second and creative phase of authentic reflexivity. By testing my ends, in my very effort at them, against the possibility of death, by choosing them and shaping them in the midst of this test, I make them 'mine' genuinely. "Becoming free *for* its own death in anticipation, liberates [Dasein] from its lostness in contingently pressing possibilities, so that it can for the first time understand and choose among the factical possibilities that lie before the unattainable [possibility, death]" (SuZ 264). So authenticity involves, as he says in the culminating paragraph, "an impassioned . . . *freedom towards death*" (SuZ 266).

Notice the complexity to Heidegger's account of the self. My self is not an inner core that I need only to discover. There is, in a sense, such a central part, but this is something I have just qua Dasein, and does not include any positive projects or characteristics – nothing distinctive or individual to me. Nevertheless, by being properly related to this – by facing these limits to my structure just as Dasein – I can 'mine', make my own, all the ends, feelings, and words I 'mean'. I can give myself a self (as it were), by my Dasein referring adequately to itself, and willing, feeling, and talking on that basis (in the light of death and guilt).

Notice too how this account is grounded – or claims to be – by Heidegger's distinctive version of phenomenology. By its transcendental move, its claim to infer 'conditions of the possibility' of our observed experience and meaning, it arrives at an a priori structure that is simple and unified – analogous, say, to Kant's categories or schemata.

4 Nietzsche's self

When we turn from Heidegger to Nietzsche we find a much less monolithic and structurally-integrated account, because the empirical component is so much larger. It is larger, indeed, not just in Nietzsche's own theory of the self, but also in what he says that 'I' need to do, in order to become an adequate self. For I must face (not surprisingly!) the same kinds of empirical truths about myself that Nietzsche thinks he has uncovered generally.

Crucially, the self is again understood reflexively, in terms of an attitude of self-relation. But now that self-relating is interpreted as a natural occurrence, something biological and historical. It is a feature of organisms, and of humans by virtue of how they evolved as special organisms. So the story is no longer phenomenological (from the inside out), but naturalistic (from the outside in). This reflexivity is, to be sure, a kind of 'inner' viewpoint or perspective, but we are studying it as happening 'within the world', and not as part of a transcendental event that founds the world (as for Heidegger). So for Nietzsche the challenge is to understand how reflexivity came into the world, i.e. how living things came to be reflexive, and how this reflexivity has developed and evolved.

So Nietzsche treats the 'self' or 'I' according to his usual, distinctive approach to philosophical problems: he puts quotation marks around the topic. He does so not just in the common philosophers' way, of asking "what do we mean by 'X'" as a preliminary to saying what X is. He treats belief in X, i.e. the use of "X" to structure our world as we do, as a psychological condition – and asks how this condition has evolved. This is not to say, however, that he is uninterested in, or has no views about, what X *is*. He allows for *degrees of realism* regarding the Xs he treats in this way. Some are nothing apart from the view that means them – are a kind of delusion. But other notions, he allows, pick out something real – perhaps something *made* real by the view about it. So for example I think he holds *there are* values in the world, *put there* by our positing them. And the same goes for the 'self': selves are made by our positings of them.[15]

Because selves arise by this reflexivity, and because reflexivity always points back at itself 'under a description', there opens that gap we noticed before, between A the self-referrer and C the self-referred. And for Nietzsche too, I suggest, we need to think of the self as involving *both* of these; neither by itself is sufficient to amount to 'the self'. To a certain extent, in viewing myself a given way I *am* that way. The point (we saw above) is partly a causal one: by thinking of myself as having quality C I gradually adjust my attitudes and behavior so that I *become* C. But (we saw) the point is also a constitutive one: I already am this way I interpret myself. Since I act from out of this sense of myself, it has claim to be my very self.

This story about 'the self' is much less conspicuous in Nietzsche than it is in Heidegger. But inspection shows, I think, that it plays a surprisingly important role

---

[15] Here belong Nietzsche's denials that it is the 'I' that thinks; he rather takes "the *I itself as a construction of thinking*" (NL 1885, KSA 11: 526 = WLN, 20); cf. BGE 17.

at key points in his thinking. It's embedded, we'll see, in his idea of will to power. And it's also a part of his pervasive notion of 'values', since he means these as crucially self-referring: our deep values aren't principles held third-personally as right for all, but ambitions a person has *for himself*. The self's importance to Nietzsche is also reflected in his advocacy for 'selfishness' [*Selbstsucht*]. And we find it too in the weight he puts on our *mistakes* in self-reference – in particular our misconception of ourselves as 'egos'. He thinks that this grounds our belief in beings, substances, causes – and many other metaphysical things he rejects. So that faulty self-reference has sweeping consequences (e.g. NL 1885 – 1886, KSA 12: 106).

Thus we find Nietzsche's idea of the self in his account how a sense and concept of the self have arisen by biological-social processes. Let's look in more detail at some of the stages through which this self-referring evolves.

a) **Reflexivity of will to power.** Reflexivity begins at the very simplest level: Nietzsche lodges it within will to power itself, which he claims is the principal character of all living things: they aim deeply at *growth* and *mastery*. Such will to power requires, after all, a distinction between the 'self' or 'own' that's to grow, and the 'other' it's to master and incorporate. A will to power wants not just more, but more of the activity by which it identifies itself: hence its essential 'selfishness'. And it grows by turning the not-me into mine, that is by incorporating what's other and resists it (e.g. D 281, D 285). Note how reflexivity is involved here, for example: "No 'substance', rather something that in itself strives after greater strength, and that wants to 'preserve' itself only indirectly (it wants to *surpass* itself–)" [NL 1887, KSA 12: 392, Kaufmann's translation]. Nietzsche's insistence that will to power is a will to 'self-overcoming' (e.g. Z II Self-Overcoming) brings out its crucial reflexivity, but also the unexpected form he gives to its 'selfishness': it aims also to destroy its current self.

b) **Reflexivity of drives.** The self-reference involved in all will to power is, of course, mainly non-conscious and non-linguistic. We find it at work, Nietzsche claims, in our own bodily drives. Each of these strives, beneath our awareness, and without words, to enhance and develop 'its own' activity – by imposing itself on what is 'other', both within us (other drives) and around us. So, in BGE 6: "every single one of [the basic drives of humans] would like only too well to represent just *itself* as the ultimate goal of existence and the legitimate *master* of all the other drives. For every drive wants to be master . . . ." Every drive is, by this reflexivity, a self of its own, pressing its selfishness against that of other drives.

c) **Reflexivity of drive-complexes and the body.** A person is, to begin with, a complex or synthesis of such selfish drives, whose 'power relations' with one another constitute a relatively stable system that can be treated as having an overall will to power of its own.[16] What lets some set of drives amount to such a unitary will 'of its own' is precisely its reflexivity: that it has a sense of 'itself', of the own that it strives to further by imposition on 'others'. A higher-order will is synthesized once a group of drives begins to operate with a single self-description: it's this above all that constitutes that group as a unity. (Of course this synthetic will may still struggle to keep its constituent drives from breaking out on their own and asserting their narrower self-descriptions against one another as others [NL 1880, KSA 9: 211–213].[17]) It's in this way that Nietzsche thinks of the body as my self: "Behind your thoughts and feelings, my brother, stands a mighty commander, an unknown wise man – his name is Self. In your body he dwells, he is your body" (Z I Despisers of the Body). Although the body lacks words, it is in itself self-relating: the body "does not say I, but does I" (Z I Despisers of the Body).

d) **Reflexivity of consciousness.** But none of this yet concerns what we usually think of as the self. This is that 'I' of conscious and linguistic self-reference, in which I am self-aware and frame my self-description in words. Here selfhood belongs to what we might call the subject or ego or agent. Nietzsche of course rejects such terms, but he recognizes that there is something more going on here than just the drive-synthesis we saw before. The latter happens in animals too; Nietzsche has a story to tell how 'spirit', as he sometimes calls our distinctive capacity, has evolved out of merely animal abilities. By it, a new kind of reflexivity emerges, and with it a new kind of self.

Nietzsche is mainly eager to cut down the pretensions of this conscious self. He stresses its dependence on the drives and body, and often treats it as merely "a small tool and toy" (again Z I Despisers of the Body) of the body-self.[18] At such times he seems to deny that this conscious reflexivity constitutes a self at all, at least one that can effectively press its own interests.[19] How can there be such a

---

16 See Anderson 2012 for a very effective account how this synthesis arises through an interlocking of drives with affects. I give a different suggestion what's key in constituting a unity.
17 The 'selfishness' of every drive also makes it (in another sense) "unegoistic", Nietzsche says, inasmuch as it is prepared to sacrifice the interests of "the whole ego" (NL 1883, KSA 10: 342, Kaufmann's translation).
18 NL 1885, KSA 11: 434 (WLN, 2): "If *I* have anything of a unity within me, it certainly doesn't lie in the conscious I and in feeling, willing, thinking, but somewhere else: in the preserving, appropriating, expelling, watchful prudence of my whole organism, of which my conscious I is only a tool."
19 TI Errors 3: the I "has become a fairy tale, a fiction, a play on words: it has stopped thinking, feeling, and willing altogether!" NL 1887, KSA 12: 398, Kaufmann's translation: "The 'subject' is

self, if consciousness is epiphenomenal? And yet, Nietzsche has a more important complaint against this conscious self: that it's sick and harmful. And for this he needs it to be something real and effective. It is indeed often secretly steered by the drives, but also has a certain independence from them, and indeed antipathy towards them. Its conflict with the drives can only be so damaging to us because it does have effects.[20]

How does Nietzsche think this conscious reflexivity arises? This is the problem of consciousness itself, since this is (in the sense Nietzsche means it) essentially reflexive.[21] It takes the form we can all observe in our own cases. It is a quite particular, highly structured reflexivity that permeates our human experience: my sense of myself as an abiding I whose current thoughts and desires are linked to those I had or will have, hours or days or years behind or ahead in this life I know myself living. This rich phenomenon is far removed from the way the unconscious body acts as a synthesis of drives.[22] So how have we humans come to be self-aware in this characteristic way?

Nietzsche's chief claim about the origin of this conscious selfhood is again a deflating one: that it evolved, paradoxically, in the process of 'socializing' and 'herding' human beings.[23] Human agency was developed under the largely prehistoric "ethic of custom" [*Sittlichkeit der Sitte*] that redesigned these animals so that they could live together in cities and societies. This long harsh training gradually superimposed on our simpler 'animal' drives a layer of social dispositions, which members learn by copying. These new dispositions have been designed by a different kind of selection,[24] with a different structural end: not fitness but social cohesion. Our linguistic and conscious reflexivity – our saying and thinking 'I' – arises within this development.

Perhaps the germ of that self-awareness was the primitive ability to *remember social* rules. It was the habit of recalling, in moments when some stimulus triggers a drive or affect, the verbal formula that preserves the rule: *don't strike!*

---

only a fiction; the ego of which one speaks when one censures egoism does not exist at all." See the *Nachlass* notes collected as WP 481–492 under the heading "Belief in the 'Ego'. The Subject". Gardner (2009: 2–5) assembles much evidence for Nietzsche's "theoretical conception of the self" as "fictive"; he contrasts this with Nietzsche's reliance on the self in his "practical thought".

20 GS 11 presents consciousness as "the latest development of the organic", which is real but "overestimated".

21 See Riccardi (forthcoming).

22 Gardner (2009) forcefully brings out the distance between these.

23 GS 354: "My idea is clearly that consciousness actually belongs not to man's existence as an individual but rather to the community- and herd-aspects of his nature".

24 I call it "social selection" in my *Nietzsche's New Darwinism* (2004).

don't steal! This memory, whose prehistoric development GM tries to sketch, enables members to stretch their reflexivity out through time: in that moment of temptation thoughts of past punishments witnessed and future punishments feared, linked with that rule, oppose their affective force to that of the stimulated drive. The member enjoys a reflexive sense of its own power in its ability to control the drive by this new time-bridging self. But the member's sense of this power has itself been designed to serve social ends: society needs this member to embrace this single and explicit self-identity because this lets it reliably, consistently control its disruptive, antisocial drives.

In the earliest and longest phase of this development, the social character of this new will was overt and insisted upon. Reflexivity initially said (and identified as) not 'I' but 'we'. The rules are understood in the form "we don't steal": as expressing a communal viewpoint in which the member merges. So the socializing will acknowledges itself as a group- or herd-self. Z I Love of the Neighbor: "The you is older than the I; the you has been pronounced holy, but not yet the I". NL 1882, KSA 10: 83: "Originally herd and herd-instinct; the self experienced by the herd as exception, nonsense, madness."

But eventually a subtler form of control emerged – perhaps at this point 'custom' became 'morality'. Humans learned to say 'I' and to think of themselves as individuals separate from the group – yet while not really being such. For under morality it's still a social aim that works in us, even though the member now interprets itself as a free and single agent, master of its own thinking and doing.[25] When I stretch my I out over my past and future thoughts and deeds in the way we saw, this may be *so that* I can enforce the moral restraints on my action that social cohesion wants. The moral agent is a person-type designed by historical processes to fit into and strengthen society. So it's unlike its sense of itself: the self that refers is different from the self it finds. The self-referring will (A) is a behavioral stance designed to align us with our group. But this will conceives of itself (C) as a subject or agent that thinks and acts in each moment by itself and for its own interests. It's in this guise that it distinguishes itself from the bodily drives that it needs (for those social purposes) to oppose and control.

Thus self-consciousness originates with a certain bias and indeed error.[26] It operates under an ideology, of the I as ultimate and autonomous; this ideology

---

[25] Perhaps NL 1882–1883, KSA 10: 220, distinguishes the two phases: "Once the I was hidden in the herd: and now the herd is hidden in the I."

[26] NL 1885, KSA 11: 639, Kaufmann's translation: "The danger of the direct questioning of the subject *about* the subject and of all self-reflection of the spirit lies in this, that it could be useful and important for one's activity to interpret oneself *falsely*. That is why we question the body . . ."

serves the social aim to 'tame' us. It's to serve that social aim that this new reflexive self counts all bodily drives as 'other' to it, as not itself. And it's this utter opposition between the will of this socialized self, and the will of the many bodily appetites and drives, that makes the fatal split and division in us – makes us 'the sick animal'.

When I say 'I', what speaks in me is a herd-self, steered by the manifold moral values I imbibe from my society – values created at varying depths of history, in the interests of various then-ascendent groups. So Nietzsche gets to a point much like Heidegger's about *das Man*, but he arrives there (i.e. he explains it) naturalistically, by a social selective process.

(I've simplified Nietzsche's story. He thinks there are further sources for this conscious-linguistic I. It is also, for example, the first step in a metaphysical picture of the world that makes it manageable by theory. So NL 1885, KSA 11: 526 (WLN 20 – 21): "What separates me most basically from the metaphysicians is: I don't concede to them that it is the 'I' that thinks; much rather I take the *I itself as a construction of thinking* . . .; thus only as *regulative fiction*, with whose help a kind of constancy, hence 'knowability' is laid into, *invented into* a world of becoming.")

e) **Reflexivity of free spirits**. But Nietzsche doesn't think this is the end of the story. Grandly, he claims to inaugurate a major new phase. By this very genealogy, which uncovers how that conscious but moralized I has served foreign interests, I can (in the ideal case) find the path to a more adequate self-reference. This involves a kind of return to my bodily willing – and a redesign of my self-conscious reflexivity to accord with it.

Nietzsche's new reflexivity is a modification of our sense of ourselves as the I of our lifelong thoughts and choices. His new hero, exemplified in Zarathustra, still operates with this claim to be the source – lasting across minutes, days, years, of such thoughts and choices. I don't think we should imagine (as Nietzsche's ideal) a more fragmented self than this, nor one with the unconscious and unworded self-relation of animals. The point is not to give up this personal subjectivity but to modify it in the light of Nietzsche's lessons. These lessons change, in this familiar self-awareness, both the self-referrer and the self-referred.

The self-referrer is no longer – as the moral I is – a 'double agent' set into me (my body) to herd me, but instead a will that has seen through this foreign aim. Think of that typical self-awareness we've noticed, in which each thought is experienced as had by an enduring self: think of this as a dispositional module, developed over many millennia, set into each of us. It is only one element in the overall system of ways we confront the world, many others operating unconsciously. At issue is *what directs* this self-aware module in me. So long as my conscious self-accounts were moralizing, that disposition worked as cultural history had designed it to, so that it was really a herd-self that self-referred, when 'I' thought of myself. But once this aim is laid bare in that very self-awareness, something my (body's) own can take charge of the module – can use it for different ends than the now-exposed herd ends.

The self-referred is now different too. The self freed by genealogy will project a new view of itself. It will project this view, it's important to remember, both descriptively and productively. In seeing itself C, it both (paradoxically) describes itself as C, and also aspires to be C. Nietzsche's new kind of self-relation involves changes in both of these.

Qua descriptive, the new self-referred will have more of the truth. Nietzsche's free spirit will understand itself better, by recognizing its (as a consciousness) own real relation to the body and its drives.[27] It will give up the claim, framed by morality, that its self-awareness has a nonnatural, otherworldly status or source. Seeing its own relation to the body it will tend carefully to the body's best conditions. So EH Clever advocates studying one's body's own needs regarding climate, diet, etc. And TI Skirmishes 47 says that it is crucial "that culture begin in the *right* place – *not* in the 'soul' . . . [but in] the body, gestures, diet, physiology, *everything else* follows from this".[28]

The free spirit's self-understanding will evaluate its own values for their fit with its body and drives. The generalized suspicion against morality's purposes needs to be followed up with detailed scrutiny of the many particular values one finds oneself assuming. We saw how Heidegger calls us to test our projects in the midst of an anxious confrontation with death and guilt; such anxiety has the effect of suspending *das Man* at one blow. Nietzsche envisions a very different kind of test. I must see, by genealogy and psychology, what type of person a value has been designed to favor – and then consider whether I am (in my body) that type. Much of this study will be carried out, I think, by self-psychology – by more honest attention to one's own felt responses to these values as one inhabits them.[29] I must learn to pay attention to a taste in my body, often more reli-

---

27 Z I On The Bestowing Virtue 3: "'Now I bid you lose me and find yourselves'".
28 EH Books D 2: "When you divert seriousness from the self-preservation and energy accumulation of the body, *which is to say: of life*, when you construct an ideal out of anaemia and 'salvation of the soul', out of contempt for the body, what is that if not a *recipe* for decadence?"
29 NL 1886–1887, KSA 12: 232: "My writings speak only of my own experiences [*Erlebnissen*] – fortunately I have experienced much".

able than my deliberated judgments. We can't nullify our herd-self all at once, but must identify it piecemeal and weed it deliberately out of ourselves.[30]

But this is not to say that the free spirit's self-view will be thoroughly true or accurate. For it can't aim just to describe, it must function as aspiration, as an ideal self-image the person tries to inhabit. Its view of itself must see the something better it can be, it must *identify* itself with that better. This stance towards oneself is the one proper to the will to power at the bottom of our body's aims. Its deep purpose is not to preserve what I already am, nor to describe it, but to push always ahead to the me I can be. The free spirit thereby 'creates' itself in this higher image that is already, by this effort, its self.[31] Here we come to the Dionysian character of this self: how it wills to change its self, to overcome itself and pass over into something new.

Let me sum up regarding Nietzsche's new self. It achieves fullest self-relation by the spirit gradually freeing itself from control by received values, and redesigning these values to best serve its own growth. So it achieves an enlightened 'selfishness' contrary to the 'unselfing' by morality. Z III Three Evils 2: "And then it also happened – and truly it happened for the first time! – that his word counted *selfishness* holy, the healthy, sound selfishness that wells out of a powerful soul: – / – out of the powerful soul, to which the elevated body belongs . . .". We should note, finally, how this new self is both narrower and broader than our own.

On the one hand Nietzsche thinks I need to discover myself in my true particularity, in the unique balance of drives and dispositions that make me (this organism) up. I need to align my values with this quite specific self, which means diagnosing and then casting off values designed to 'herd' me, or else designed for types of persons different from myself. Nietzsche harps frequently on the point that no values can be right for all, and that each needs values quite specific to his/her own constitution. So the tendency here is to find a narrow self, and to cast away from it the great mass of values that are 'other' to me.

Yet, on the other hand Nietzsche is attracted an opposite way – to a kind of expansion of the boundaries of me. For he thinks I grow by incorporating other perspectives into my own, and coming to value them *as* my own. So I push the boundary between self and other always outward, as it were, by taking other viewpoints and values into my ever-more comprehensive synthesis. Nietzsche prides himself on this comprehensiveness. And the ideal or ultimate outcome of

---

30 Z III On the Spirit of Gravity 2: "For all that is one's own is well hidden from its owner; and of all treasure hoards it is one's own that is excavated last".
31 See TI Skirmishes 49 on Goethe as self-creating.

this expansion would be, to identify *it all* as myself. In the ideal case I am able to 'say Yes' to it all as also 'me'.

5 Judging Nietzsche's and Heidegger's selves

I now want to explore a little further the difference that has emerged between Nietzsche's and Heidegger's ways of developing this 'reflexive view' of the self. This difference lies in the conditions they set on self-discovery as a precondition for self-formation.

Back at the beginning we noted the tension between thinking of the self as something *discovered*, and thinking of it as something *created* (or chosen). We now see the general strategy, shared by Nietzsche and Heidegger, for combining both. There *is* something 'I' already am, which I need to find out. But in both cases this finding out is only a preliminary to a constructive project: by finding out what I already am, I am able to *become* a self more completely than I already am. I become this fuller self by, in some way, *making* this self.

But both the discovery and the formative sides are different for these two philosophers. They are different together, for the same general reason: Nietzsche's naturalism and empiricism, and Heidegger's transcendental phenomenology. Although each takes a notable step in the other's direction, the general tenor of their views is quite distinct.

Heidegger thinks the self can be discovered by a kind of self-phenomenology. By inspection of my own experience, I have the material to infer and then recognize the deep structure of my intentionality. I discover, in particular, the structural *flaws* that I see I have been *avoiding* recognizing all along. I see also how I have embraced my many particular ends and projects in a manner that avoids facing those flaws, my death and guilt. This discovery alienates me from all those projects, which I view from outside, in the mood of anxiety.

But of course this discovery is only a preliminary. I'm not to wallow in that alienation, but to reembrace ends and projects – though not necessarily the same ones, and certainly not in the same manner. I use the insight into my mortality (or guilt) to *test* my previous projects: can I will them *while aware* (feelingly) that death is not only certain, but possible at *every* time, in every now? Many of the things I now pursue, I just *can't* pursue 'unto death', with death immanently 'in the offing'. But the ones it turns out I *can* pursue in that spirit, will be 'mine' in a fuller sense than was true before. For I will have chosen them from the essential part of me, my facing of death and guilt. Without this, their only authority is that they're 'what one does': they're 'mine' only by being *das*

Man's. My death, in particular, is a kind of touchstone, for Heidegger, that establishes the projects that can help form (make up) an authentic self.

The abstractness of this would offend Nietzsche, I think. The kind of understanding I need, in order to make a real self for myself, is far more detailed and particular. It's not enough to 'face my mortality', to live with this mortality. To become myself I need to 1) peel away all the subversive values and goals that have been imposed on me by social processes, as well as to 2) discover, among the native and ingrained drives of my body, what its main aim or tendency is.

So the 'discovery phase' has two sides, which interact. I need to identify what's 'other', and what's genuinely 'mine'. Genealogy is the principal tool. I apply it to my values – all the ways I care and feel about things. It reveals that some of these values, in particular the *moral* ones, express social interests; they express, in particular, society's interest in 'taming' and 'herding' its members, the better to fit them together into a viable social unit.[32] So these moral values not only constrain my bodily drives, they denounce them as 'evil'. What I need to do is to recognize these suppressed values, the voice of my body, my first self.

Once again, however, this discovery is only preliminary: it makes possible a second and creative phase, which gives me a second self, the self I *become*. Nietzsche insists that his ideal individual – and also he himself! – is someone who 'creates values'. He doesn't just find values already there, even there in his body. He *makes* values. But how is this related to that prior discovery? I think Nietzsche's picture is something like this: the new hero is the one who is able to use the 'healthy taste' of his body to rewrite the moral values general in our culture. Here it is that healthy taste – the interest in power and growth – that is the touchstone (analogous to confronting mortality, for Heidegger). But it only works in conjunction with a genealogy that exposes the real interests of those values. We need to see what these values have been designed to do in us, to judge them by the body's standard of power or growth.

Now I mentioned that each philosophers takes steps in the other's direction. So this difference between them is not utter.

Heidegger *does* find a place for history: the whole second Part of *Being and Time*, unwritten, was planned to give a 'deconstruction' of the history of philosophy, to show how the currently-prevailing misunderstanding of time developed. This looks a bit like a Nietzschean genealogy, but we should note that it comes as an appendage to the phenomenological analysis, and will merely verify the findings reached there. This reflects the way the book encloses Dasein's 'histori-

---

[32] Or, they express the interests of different *types* of people that have, in the past, succeeded in inserting values that serve *them* into the culture's 'table of values'.

city' within its overall, timeless and essentialistic analysis of Dasein's being. History does not bring that Dasein-being into existence; Dasein isn't something that 'evolved'. Phenomenology stays all 'within' Dasein, and refuses the step outside to treat it as science might. And this general point extends to Heidegger's conception how I 'become a self': historical diagnosis plays no role in this.

On the other side, Nietzsche has what we might call a phenomenological aspect, which makes him sometimes inclined to dispense with genealogy, or any detailed study of ourselves as evolving, social organisms. Sometimes he thinks we have a more immediate route into our basic structure – that we can step down into the healthy perspective of will to power itself, and build a healthier self for ourselves solely by attention to this essence. We then see our deep structure as will to power 'from within', similarly to Heidegger's phenomenological grasp of Dasein's structure as being-in. But again I think this is a minority or subordinate viewpoint in him, overshadowed by his sense of the great complexity of the social and historical forces that have made us, and of the need to identify these in order to put them out of play.

So what, very briefly now, are the respective strengths and weaknesses of these two accounts of the self? I confess what may have been evident already, a greater affinity for the more empirical and naturalistic picture of Nietzsche. Heidegger's very neatly structured package of intentional attitudes suffers, I think, when we ask such questions as, how and why it may have happened that creatures with this structure evolved or came to be. Of course Heidegger repeatedly insists on the illegitimacy of such external and non-phenomenological questions about Dasein: it can only be understood 'from within'. By contrast Nietzsche begins with such questions. He tells, I think, a persuasive story how our capacity for conscious self-reference – for saying 'I' – may have evolved. This approach makes his advice what we need to do, to overcome the social forces that now control us, extremely complex and daunting. But it is, I find, a more persuasive story what having a full-fledged *self* might be.

References

Anderson, R.L. (2012) "What is a Nietzschean Self?", in: Janaway/Robertson (2012), 202–233.
Dries, Manuel (ed.) (2013) *Nietzsche on Consciousness and the Embodied Mind*. Berlin/Boston: De Gruyter.
Fichte, Johann Gottlieb (1982) *The Science of Logic*, ed. and tr. P. Heath and J. Lachs, Cambridge: Cambridge University Press.
Gardner, Sebastian (2009) "Nietzsche, the Self, and the Disunity of Philosophical Reason", in: Gemes/May (2009), 1–31.

Gemes, Ken/May, Simon (eds.) (2009) *Nietzsche on Freedom and Autonomy*, Oxford/New York: Oxford University Press.
Heidegger, Martin (1976) [1927] *Sein und Zeit*, Tübingen: Niemeyer. [Gesamtausgabe, vol. 2, Frankfurt a.M.: Klostermann 1977]
Heidegger, Martin (1962) [1927] *Being and Time*, trans. John Macquarrie and Edward Robinson, Oxford/Cambridge: Blackwell.
James, William (1992) *Writings 1878–1899*, New York: Library of America.
Janaway, Christopher/Robertson, Simon (eds.) (2012) *Nietzsche, Naturalism, and Normativity*, Oxford: Oxford University Press.
Nozick, Robert (1981) *Philosophical Explanations*, Cambridge, MA: Harvard University Press.
Riccardi, Mattia (forthcoming) "Nietzsche on the Superficiality of Consciousness", in: M. Dries (ed.), *Nietzsche on Consciousness and the Embodied Mind*, Berlin/Boston: De Gruyter.
Richardson, John (2004) *Nietzsche's New Darwinism*, New York/Oxford: Oxford University Press.
Velleman, J. David (2006) *Self to Self: Selected Essays*, Cambridge: Cambridge University Press.

Sebastian Gardner
14 Nietzsche and Freud: The 'I' and Its Drives

The parallels of Nietzsche with Freud are a matter of common knowledge; much less well appreciated are their differences. My aim in this paper is to underscore and arrive at a better understanding of the latter. I will suggest that the agreement of Nietzsche with Freud regarding certain fundamental matters of human psychology coexists with very deep philosophical disagreement. From one angle Nietzsche and Freud can fairly be described as engaged on a common project. Closer examination reveals that their shared territory is better viewed as the result of a crossing of paths, on the way to different and mutually exclusive destinations. The disagreement of Nietzsche and Freud with one another is, I will suggest, ultimately no less intense than their argument with arch-rationalists such as Kant.

1. Viewed from an appropriate distance – on a canvas sufficiently broad to make salient their common opposition to the Kantian image of human beings – Nietzsche and Freud appear to be seeking the same kind of result: a naturalistic reconstrual of human personality which disabuses us of rationalistic prejudices, destroys illusions of spirituality, and alerts us to the necessity of embarking on a new task of self-understanding, the success of which promises some amelioration of our condition. As the familiar narrative has it, Nietzsche and Freud, following in the path of Spinoza and Hume, are engaged on a common diagnostic and therapeutic enterprise, the crux of which is exposure of the true Nature within us. Ignorance and denial of this buried motivational core is responsible for our present sickness; knowledge of it has the potential to facilitate (though it by no means guarantees) a gain in health.[1] The claims of both thinkers are radical, revisionary, and candidly immodest. Freud does not share Nietzsche's

---

[1] See, famously, BGE 23, regarding the demand that "psychology again be recognized as the queen of the sciences, and that the rest of the sciences exist to serve and prepare for it. Because, from now on, psychology is again the path to the most fundamental problems" (Nietzsche 2002: 24 [KGW VI/2: 33]); and BGE 230: "To translate humanity back into nature; to gain control of the many vain and fanciful interpretations and incidental meanings that have been scribbled and drawn over that eternal basic text of *homo natura* so far; to make sure that, from now on, the human being will stand before the human being, just as he already stands before the rest of nature today, hardened by the discipline of science [...]" (Nietzsche 2002: 123 [KGW VI/2: 175]).

prophetic tone, yet both thinkers regard themselves as preparing for a new stage of modernity, profiting from the gains in knowledge and increased critical awareness accumulated over the course of the Enlightenment but offering unprecedented insight into the underlying dynamics of human existence. The transformation in self-conception urged by Nietzsche and Freud involves not just revising basic beliefs but also conceptual change: cherished notions of individual freedom and rational self-determination are shown to be empty or incoherent, and to stand in need of reconstructive surgery if they are to regain credibility.

The psychological claims on which Nietzsche and Freud concur, and which are of key importance for their shared naturalistic emancipatory ambition, centre on the notion of drive, *Trieb*. The relevant Nietzschean-Freudian conception of drive is that of an enduring motivational state with broad scope which overtakes and subsumes, without displacing, explanation in terms of reasons for action: our ordinary conception of ourselves as doing things because we believe this and desire that, is embedded in a motivational context which outstrips conscious rational awareness and yet *receives expression* through and in the agent's conscious purposes. Human action emerges from drive analysis as having a complex structure in which the end projected by the agent realizes a further end which the agent does not and normally could not recognize, let alone endorse, but in the absence of which their avowed reasons for action would have no force. Understanding agency in drive terms requires therefore a kind of double vision: we continue to see agents as acting for reasons, while also seeing that the ground of the causality of their reasons (the explanation for their having reasons for action at all, and the full explanation for those reasons being determinately thus and not otherwise) is not given within the perspective of rational agency. To invoke drive in the Nietzsche-Freud sense is thus neither to merely postulate a specific origin for desires – as when the aetiology of a want is traced back to a bodily need – nor to merely identify a causal tendency of action extending beyond the agent's awareness – as when social psychology offers functional explanation of individual actions. Drives are neither mere causal antecedents nor mere further effects of actions, but present, realized, in them.

To view agents in these terms is to impute a division within the human subject, between the agent *qua* executor of reasons for action, and the agent *qua* bearer or vehicle or medium of drive. It is natural to conceptualize this contrast in two sets of terms: as a distinction of agency and passivity (the agent is active in the first respect and passive in the second), and as a distinction of psychological appearance from psychological reality (the consciously endorsed reason is the outer shell containing and concealing the true meaning of the action).

Putting the two together, we arrive at the idea that the agent is *active* with respect to psychological *appearances*, but *passive* with respect to psychological *reality*. Devaluation of reflective consciousness, denial of free will, and the conception of intellectual activity as subservient to motivation, are familiar corollaries of the drive model.

This is an abstract, purely formal characterization of the notion of drive. The content that Freud attributes to drives has a distinctively naturalistic character – a close relation to bodily states, intense affective quality, a high degree of indeterminacy as regards its aim, insensitivity to discursive representations, independence from norms, and so forth. Nietzsche too, at some junctures, also characterizes drives in such terms, and when he does so often exhibits striking similarity with Freud. If one were to enter into the detail concerning the convergence of Nietzsche and Freud regarding substantial issues in drive psychology, there are several obvious candidates for inclusion: the similarities of Nietzsche's account of the genesis of human civilization in *On the Genealogy of Morals* with Freud's account in *Civilization and its Discontents*, both emphasizing the sacrifice of instinctual satisfaction required; the thesis that morality, as defined by the phenomenon of guilt and the operations of conscience, has its psychological origin in an act of internalization, whereby outward-directed aggressive impulses are redirected back onto the self; and the notion that, in addition to instinctual repression, a diversion of drives in a new direction, whereby psychic energies are reattached to a new content – sublimation, as Freud calls it – is responsible for the higher products of human culture, including art.[2]

2. The basic respect in which Nietzsche and Freud are of one mind having been stated, let us now turn to what separates them. I start with a historical observation.

Nietzsche is prominent among Freud's precursors as a champion of naturalistic depth psychology, and he undoubtedly has a place among Freud's formative influences, but there is no historical dependence as such. The historical sources of psychoanalytic theory, studies have shown, are multiple and wide-ranging. The precise extent of Freud's knowledge of Nietzsche is hard to determine, but it is unlikely that Freud at any point studied Nietzsche's writings in a systematic fashion, or if he did so, then it was some time after the inception of psychoanalysis. If we are looking for a single precursor for Freud's concept of the unconscious, then it is Schopenhauer who offers the closest approximation:

---

[2] For detailed discussion, see Assoun 2000. Of particular interest, on sublimation, is Gemes 2009.

the central tenets of the drive model are articulated very clearly in *The World as Will and Representation*, and (I will be arguing) the features of Nietzsche's thought which set him apart from Freud are absent from Schopenhauer.

Will is considered by Schopenhauer in various forms: of relevance here is the individuated will of each human subject, which constitutes their essential core – "the primary and substantial thing", "what is real and essential in man", "the radical part of our real nature", our "true self, the kernel of our inner nature".[3] Though itself lacking the power of understanding, the individuated personal will is attached to a particular stock of representations: it makes the individual's decisions and determines her motives, which frequently remain unknown to the intellect, and it is this will, rather than memory, which constitutes personal identity.[4] Only a fraction of its operations are manifest in consciousness and self-consciousness.[5] Many of Schopenhauer's specific psychological hypotheses, concerning the mechanisms by means of which the contents of consciousness are determined by unconscious ends, and the pervasion of motivation by sexuality, have a striking psychoanalytic resonance.[6]

Schopenhauer's concept of will or drive has, of course, sources of its own, and is not be isolated from the broader current of theorizing about human personality which occupied so many Romantic idealists. What distinguishes Schopenhauer from other *naturphilosophisch* psychologists and gives his view a distinctively late modern, proto-Freudian quality, is his forthright denial of purpose and value to the source of human motivation: our drives are not for Schopenhauer the vehicles of providential metaphysical forces, raising the human subject to a higher level of perfection and uniting her with the Absolute, but bare impulsions, no more internally connected to the Good than is the force of gravity. This austere conception carries over straightforwardly to Freud's vision of the psyche as, at the most basic level of its description, a neural mechanism governed by the principle of homeostasis. The blindness of Schopenhauerian will is mirrored in the non-intentionality of pleasure, as Freud con-

---

[3] WWR II, Ch. 19, "On the Primacy of the Will in Self-Consciousness", pp. 205, 215, 219, 239. Schopenhauer generally uses *Wille* where Nietzsche would talk of *Trieb*, tending to reserve *Trieb* for will in organic nature (e.g. the *Trieb* to self-preservation).

[4] WWR II, 209–210 and 238–239, where the relation of the personal will to the individual's intelligible character is indicated. See Janaway 2010.

[5] Schopenhauer (2010 [1839]: 50–51): self-consciousness "is a very limited part of our whole consciousness, dark in its interior, with all of its objective cognitive powers completely externally directed [...] *The outside*, then, lies before its eyes with great brightness and clarity. But inside it is as obscure as a well-blackened telescope."

[6] See my "Schopenhauer, Will and Unconscious", Part I (Gardner 1999: 376–380).

ceives it: there is no more intrinsic purposiveness to the discharge of psychic energy in accordance with Freud's principle of constancy than there is to the objectification of will in the world as representation. For both Schopenhauer and Freud, purposiveness is therefore not a genuine property of human agency as such, but an *appearance* which arises from inside the perspective of the willing subject in consequence of our capacity for abstract representation (which is all that reason amounts to).

If Freud stands in a direct line of descent from Schopenhauer, appropriating the naturalism of his theory of will while discarding its metaphysical aspect, and if Nietzsche's project has at its foundation a critical reaction against Schopenhauer, then Nietzsche's argument with Schopenhauer may be expected to resurface in his relation to Freud. I will return to this in the final section.

3. Having begun to separate Freud from Nietzsche on a historical plane, I now want to draw attention to a vital but neglected difference between their respective psychologies. The drive model described above fits Freud squarely, but in Nietzsche's case there are complications.

Freud's metapsychology draws sharp distinctions between different parts of the mind, characterizing each in discrete functional terms, and apportioning to each a different type of mental content. The result is a clear distinction in psychoanalytic explanation between, on the one side, propositional attitudes and other states of the sort ascribed in ordinary ('folk') psychology, and on the other side, the unconscious items postulated by Freud in order to explain irrational configurations of propositional attitudes and other phenomena (dreams, obsessive-compulsive disorders, etc.) into which ordinary psychology lacks insight. The *explanantia* of psychoanalysis comprise wishes, phantasies, unconscious affects, repressed contents, instinctual representatives, thing-presentations, etc., and these entities are what give substance and determinacy to our unconscious drives. The mental states on which psychoanalytic explanations turn are therefore not propositional attitudes (in so far as they draw content from *Cs.*, it is in a radically altered, degraded form) and their interaction does not conform to the principles of rationality: the formation and transformation of unconscious representations according to the laws of primary process is a form of mental activity not straightforwardly recognizable as thinking. All this marks off the unconscious proper, *Ucs.*, from the mere preconscious, *Pcs.*, the contents of which are of a kind that can be entertained in consciousness but which are contingently inaccessible. Mental life thus divides into two interlocked but separate domains each with its own set of constitutive principles, and which are not to be confused with one another: the representations circulating in *Ucs.* are not of a kind with the beliefs that we consciously entertain about objects in the world; the fantasies entertained in conscious day-dreaming are not the phantasies that give shape to unconscious mental life; the wishes of *Ucs.* are not of the same nature as the wish to drive a fast car or be young again; the exclusion of unwelcome thoughts from consciousness by self-distraction is not the same process as repression; and so on.

In this respect, if in no other, psychoanalysis' claim to the title of *Wissenschaft* should be upheld: Freud's metapsychological writings present a theory of the mind composed of laws and inter-defined theoretical entities, and the psychoanalytic explanation of concrete individuals, evidenced in case histories, gives explicit application to this theory.

Nietzsche is not, and does not pretend to be, *wissenschaftlich* in the same manner. Nietzsche's psychological explanations employ crucially the notion of drive, and the contrast of conscious/unconscious, but nowhere does Nietzsche set out a unified account of mental structure or formulate a basic set of psychological laws, and the various psychological analyses that Nietzsche offers are left unintegrated.[7] Questions that arise when we attempt to coordinate Nietzsche's psychological discussions across his texts are difficult to answer, and it would be hard to maintain that they show a steady growth of psychological doctrine comparable in any way to Freud's continual elaborations and revisions of psychoanalytic thought (narratives of Nietzsche's development focus on many things, but none, to the best of my knowledge, locate its underlying motor in psychological theory as such).

From this it cannot be inferred that Nietzsche regards systematic psychological theory as either impossible or profitless. What is however of significance – and stands in the way of the suggestion that Freud furnishes Nietzsche with the explicit metapsychology that he happens to be missing – is the fact that Nietzsche does not draw distinctions of mental kinds parallel to those drawn by psychoanalysis: Nietzsche does not reserve for unconscious states a special set of properties, and his characterizations of drives are nowise conceptually uniform.[8]

In some contexts Nietzsche's conception of a drive is indeed, as said earlier, in line with Freud's. References to the sexual drive provide obvious examples

---

[7] The doctrine of will to power is, to be sure, some sort of general theory of drives, but whatever we make of it, it does not perform the function of Freud's metapsychology, as I hope to make clear.

[8] This point is argued convincingly and in detail by Thomas Stern, in "Against Nietzsche's Theory of the Drives" (manuscript). On Nietzsche's conception of drives, see Richardson 1996, Ch. 1, Poellner 1995: 213–229, Katsafanas 2013, and Leiter 2002: 91–105.

– "Pity and love of mankind as development of the sexual drive"[9] – and the extended use of cruelty in Essay Two of *On the Genealogy of Morals* parallels, as already noted, Freud's claims concerning the role of aggression in the formation of civilization and morality.[10] It is also true that at certain points, such as the following, Nietzsche makes a general claim about the nature of drives that accords well with Freud's view of the distinctively sub-rational mode of operation of the unconscious:

> As every drive lacks intelligence, the viewpoint of "utility" cannot exist for it [so ist "Nützlichkeit" gar kein Gesichtspunkt für ihn]. Every drive, in as much as it is active, sacrifices force and other drives: finally it is checked; otherwise it would destroy everything through its excessiveness. Therefore: the "unegoistic", self-sacrificing, imprudent, is nothing special – it is common to all the drives – they do not consider the advantage of the whole ego (*because they do not consider at all! [weil sie nicht denken!]*), they act "contrary to our advantage", against the ego and often *for* the ego – innocent in both cases![11]

Nietzsche's practice does not however bear out this conception consistently, and Essay Two of *On the Genealogy of Morals* is not typical: more often than not, Nietzsche attributes to unconscious items the very same kinds of properties possessed by conscious, avowable mental states. This shows itself at every turn. Nietzsche refers to drives directed at "[h]atred, delight in the misfortunes of others, the lust to rob and rule, and whatever else is called evil",[12] to "the drive to appropriate and the drive to submit [*den Aneignungstrieb und den Unterwerfungstrieb*]",[13] and to the virtues of "diligence, obedience, chastity, piety, justice" as drives "mostly harmful to their possessors".[14] A drive is responsible for our believing that our sensations have causes: the "Ursachentrieb" "allows" sensations to appear in consciousness, rendered "meaningful".[15] The drive of the preservation of the species extends in man to "*promoting the faith in life*",

---

[9] WP 255 (1883–84), Nietzsche 1968: 148 [KGW VII/1: 704]. Also relevant are several of the contributions to *Nietzsche on Freedom and Autonomy* (Gemes/May 2009), especially those of Christopher Janaway, Simon May, John Richardson, and Maudemarie Clark and David Dudrick.
[10] GM II 22: "that suppressed cruelty of the animal man who has been frightened back into himself and given an inner life, incarcerated in the 'state' to be tamed, and has discovered bad conscience so that he can hurt himself, after the *more natural* outlet of this wish to hurt had been blocked [...]" (Nietzsche 1994: 63 [KGW VI/2: 348]).
[11] WP 372 (Summer 1883), Nietzsche 1968: 200 [KGW VII/1: 352]. Translation modified.
[12] GS 1, Nietzsche 2001: 27 [KGW V/2: 43]. In §53 Nietzsche refers to the "*Verfeinerung* of the evil drive [den bösen Trieb]", Nietzsche 2001: 63 (KGW V/2: 90).
[13] GS 118, Nietzsche 2001: 116 [KGW V/2: 154].
[14] GS 21, Nietzsche 2001: 43 [KGW V/2: 65].
[15] TI, The Four Great Errors 4, Nietzsche 2005b: 50 [KGW VI/3: 86].

giving rise to "Oughts and Becauses", teachings concerning the purpose and reason for existence.[16] Each drive presents a "one-sided view of the thing or event" but out of their conflict arises "a kind of justice and contract" whereby each "can assert and maintain themselves in existence and each can finally feel it is the right vis-à-vis all the others"; the drives "know very well how to make themselves felt by and how to hurt *each other*" (they may even, for all we know, exhibit "*heroism*").[17] In the unpublished notebooks Nietzsche talks of "our drive to worship [*unserem anbetenden Triebe*] – that continually *proves* itself – by providing guidance",[18] and of the unrest between "opposing value drives [*Werth-Trieben*]";[19] "a single individual contains within him a vast confusion of contradictory valuations and consequently of contradictory drives", implying a correspondence of drives and values;[20] one "seeks a picture of the world in that philosophy in which we feel freest; i.e., in which our most powerful drive feels free to function [*sich frei fühlt zu seiner Thätigkeit*]"[21]; "the will to *logical truth* can be carried through only after a fundamental *falsification* of all events is assumed. From which it follows that a drive rules here that is capable of employing both means, firstly falsification, then the implementation of its own point of view: logic does *not* spring from will to truth."[22] In connection with perspectivism Nietzsche says: "It is our needs that interpret the world; our drives and their For and Against. Every drive is a kind of lust to rule; each one has its perspective that it would like to compel all the other drives to accept as a norm [*jeder hat seine Perspektive, welche er als Norm* ...]."[23]

Drives, or at least some drives, have therefore for Nietzsche a perspective or point of view and a sense of their own freedom, possess and deploy normative conceptions, and direct themselves at complex worldly states of affairs; they differ from full-blown personal agents, as ordinarily conceived, only in so far as each is defined by a single motivational aim (or 'value'). In psychoanalytic eyes, this must be reckoned a mistake, which jeopardizes the coherence of depth psychology: Nietzsche confounds the preconscious, which is merely *descriptively* unconscious, with the *dynamic* unconscious, the contents of which could not come to consciousness in the form in which they exist in *Ucs*. It will be added

---

[16] GS 1, Nietzsche 2001: 28 [KGW V/2: 45].
[17] GS 333, Nietzsche 2001: 185–186 [KGW V/2: 238–239].
[18] WP 253 (Spring 1885), Nietzsche 1968: 146 [KGW VIII/1: 146].
[19] WP 351 (1887–88), Nietzsche 1968: 192 [KGW VIII/2: 366].
[20] WP 259 (1884), Nietzsche 1968: 149 [KGW VII/2: 181].
[21] WP 418 (1883), Nietzsche 1968: 224–225 [KGW VII/1: 352].
[22] WP 512 (1885), Nietzsche 1968: 277 [KGW VIII/3: 366].
[23] WP 481 (1886–87), Nietzsche 1968: 267 [KGW VIII/1: 323].

that Nietzsche fails to individuate mental parts independently of drives: Nietzsche treats each drive as defining (and as all that defines) a different mental part. In consequence of taking drive-identity as the principle of mental partition, and of attributing strategic rationality to drives, Nietzsche's psychology falls into homuncularism, with all of its attendant paradoxes.[24] From all of this a very different relation to ordinary psychology from psychoanalysis emerges: whereas psychoanalysis, conservatively, postulates a *background* to the attributions of common sense psychology which compensates for its limitations, extending and completing our everyday explanations, Nietzsche is engaged in *rewriting* ordinary psychology, contesting and supplanting a significant portion of its attributions.

The orthodox Freudian, sceptical of Nietzschean psychology and wishing to stress the originality of Freud's achievement, will find further grounds for criticism of Nietzsche. In addition to the absence of an explicit metapsychology, and a failure to grasp the qualitative distinctions between the conscious and the unconscious, Nietzsche's psychologizing may be charged with epistemological limitations and a lack of scientific objectivity: Nietzsche does not have, it will be said, the clinical context – the experience of transference and all that follows from it – as a means for close observation of unconscious mental life. Of equal importance is the fact that Nietzsche's psychology is not grounded on a strategy of extension of common sense psychology. Freud proceeds by getting to grips with phenomena that are already constituted as *explananda* before psychoanalysis arrives on the scene: the cast of Freud's case histories are individuals who have already avowed their own failure to understand themselves; ordinary psychology does not pretend to know why we dream about this rather than that, or why we have dreams at all; we plainly lack understanding of group behaviour, moral fanaticism, totemic practices, and so on. The explanatory needs to which psychoanalysis responds are thus fixed independently and antecedently. Nietzsche's psychological constructions are not guided by the same factors. Rather, their direction is determined by Nietzsche's value-driven selection of features of psychological life (the will to power, a hypothesis which finds no echo in Freud, may be cited as evidence of the incursions of an axiological agenda). The upshot, the proponent of psychoanalysis may say, is that even when Nietzsche's speculations do contain some important insight, they fail to meet the strict conditions of psychological knowledge.

---

24 If *Ucs.* shares the same content as *Cs.*, then the unconscious holds beliefs, desires, engages in practical reason, etc., i.e., amounts to a 'second mind'. And this generates paradoxes, as Sartre argued: see my *Irrationality and the Philosophy of Psychoanalysis* (Gardner 1993), Ch. 2.

Whether or not these criticisms hit the mark, an issue which I will not pursue, it should be emphasized that the fact that Nietzsche draws no qualitative distinction between conscious and unconscious mental states is not a conceptual oversight but plays a positive role in relation to his practical concerns. It allows Nietzsche (first) to articulate his psychological analyses in ways that address us at the *personal* level, somewhat in the way the French moralists impugn our integrity and Kierkegaard confronts us with our double-mindedness – as psychoanalytic explanations certainly do not[25]; and (second) it allows drives to be considered as *materials for self-creation*, in a way that psychoanalysis again does not – Nietzsche describes our drives in terms that permit our identification with them, our taking them up in a sense that is not possible for the contents of *Ucs*.[26]

4. I turn now to a second difference between Freudian and Nietzschean psychology.

There is an obvious sense in which the drive model impinges on the unity of the person. Personal unity, as ordinarily conceived, is not threatened by the existence of a mere multiplicity of desires, even when these conflict, so long as their fate stands under the control of a self which determines – blocks, restricts, endorses, etc. – their efficacy. But this controlling self – its omnipotence, if not existence – is exactly what the drive model contests.

The metaphysics of the self do not figure on Freud's agenda, but his metapsychology has clear implications for the 'I', which it reduces to an aspect of ego functioning: apperception registers the discursively formulated, more or less satisfactory outcomes of the ego's negotiations of its relations to the id and superego and of the interaction of its various components with one another, with special attention to their agreement, or lack of it, with social norms.[27] The self, in the sense of what we grasp as the 'I', is merely an ancillary aspect of a substantial entity that lacks any essential I-character, its relation to which the 'I' (constitutively) misrepresents:

> Normally, there is nothing of which we are more certain than the feeling of our self, of our own ego. This ego appears to us as something autonomous and unitary, marked off distinctly from everything else. That such an appearance is deceptive, and that on the contrary the ego is continued inwards, without any sharp delimitation, into an unconscious

---

[25] For an example of a passage in which 'French moralist' critique is interwoven seamlessly with depth psychology, see GS 14.
[26] See for example D 560.
[27] See Tugendhat 1986: 131–132.

mental entity which we designate as the id and for which it serves as a kind of façade – this was a discovery first made by psycho-analytic research.[28]

Freud's view of the 'I' is in line with Schopenhauer's treatment of self-consciousness. In the second chapter of his *Essay on the Freedom of the Will* Schopenhauer offers the following account of the structure of willing.[29] In the most rudimentary case, an object induces a reaction in the subject, a movement of will. At a minimum this comprises a feeling of pleasure or pain, but when the reaction extends to a projected modification of the object, and thus involves bodily movement, we can speak of the object as the motive of an action: the volition is directed at the object, which provides its content. Self-consciousness, Schopenhauer insists, plays no active role in this process: it simply registers the various movements of will. These constitute furthermore the *total content* of self-consciousness in general, according to Schopenhauer: "nothing is present to the so-called inner sense but one's own will".[30] Consciousness of oneself as deciding or resolving is, on Schopenhauer's account, simply a form of consciousness of a movement of will.[31] This minimal account agrees fully with Freud's description of consciousness, in the few places where he says anything about the topic, as merely passive.[32]

Nietzsche's repudiation of the 'I' is well known. In statements such as the following Nietzsche takes a more radical position than either Freud or Schopenhauer, not merely stripping the 'I' of its efficacy, or giving it reduced reality, but denying its existence outright:

> I will not stop emphasizing a tiny little fact that these superstitious men are loath to admit: that a thought comes when "it" wants, and not when "I" want. It is, therefore, a *falsification* of the facts to say that the subject "I" is the condition of the predicate "think". It thinks: but to say the "it" is just that famous old "I" – well that is just an assumption or opinion, to put it mildly, and by no means an "immediate certainty".[33]

> [T]he path lies open for new versions and sophistications of the soul hypothesis; and concepts like the "mortal soul" and the "soul as subject-multiplicity" and the "soul as a society constructed out of drives and affects" want henceforth to have civil rights in the realm of science.[34]

---

28 *Civilization and its Discontents* (henceforth: CD), CD 64–65.
29 Schopenhauer 2010 [1839]: 44.
30 Schopenhauer 2010 [1839]: 51.
31 Schopenhauer 2010 [1839]: 45–48.
32 See for example "A note upon the 'mystic writing-pad'" (1925 [1924]), in Freud, SE 19: 227–234. (Here and hereafter, "Freud, SE" refers to the *Standard Edition of the Complete Psychological Works of Sigmund Freud*.)
33 BGE 17, Nietzsche 2002: 17 [KGW VI/2: 24–25].
34 BGE 12, Nietzsche 2002: 14 [KGW VI/2: 20–21].

According to Nietzsche's new psychology of subjective multiplicity, each of us is "only a society constructed out of many souls [...] All willing is simply a matter of commanding and obeying, on the groundwork, as I have said, of a society constructed out of many 'souls'."[35] Even Schopenhauer's "I will", which, as said, amounts to only an attenuated form of self-consciousness, is classified by Nietzsche as a "superstition".[36]

It is possible to regard Nietzsche as simply following out and making explicit the implications of the drive model as it is formulated by Schopenhauer: if self-consciousness is reduced to a mere power of receptivity in relation to volitions, and if the contribution of transcendental subjectivity to the unity of self-consciousness (which is in any case problematic) is bracketed out, then it is not at all clear that anything remains to give reality to the idea that something identical is present in the multiplicity of acts of will.[37] If so, then the unity of the person reduces to the functional unity of animal individuality: movements of will, or drives, share a common subject just in so far as there is one continuous organismic boundary containing their operations and constraining them to contest one another's efficacy; nothing holds them together on the inside in the way that the 'I' was held to do. If Nietzsche regards this as amounting to elimination rather than reduction, then it is because he has a different, arguably sharper sense of our conceptual investments in the 'I'.

5. This is however another side to Nietzsche's view of the 'I'. Nietzsche's practical philosophy employs a conception of the self which is not warranted by and which appears to contradict the drive model.[38] Nietzsche does not recommend the Schopenhauerian annihilation of selfhood that would result from eliminating the illusion of the *I will*: on the contrary, *I-hood* is integral to the condition of higher life-affirmative existence to which we should aspire. The theme is prominent throughout Nietzsche's writings. In *Daybreak*, II, §105, "*Pseudo-egoism*", Nietzsche endorses an ideal of higher or intensified selfhood: the great majority have no selves to speak of, merely 'phantom' selves ("*das Phantom von ego*")

---

35 BGE 19, Nietzsche 2002: 19–20 [KGW VI/2: 27]. See also the denial that our unity owes anything to consciousness in GS 11; Nietzsche attributes it instead to "the preserving alliance of the instincts" (Nietzsche 2001: 37 [KGW V/2: 56]). And TI Errors 3: "Not to mention the I! That has become a fairy tale, a fiction, a play on words: it has stopped thinking, feeling, and willing altogether!" (Nietzsche 2005b: 178 [KGW VI/3: 85]).
36 BGE 16, Nietzsche 2002: 16 [KGW VI/2: 23].
37 Schopenhauer himself arguably avoids this, but only through his doctrine of the Idea of the individual, as giving necessary unity to the movements of will.
38 See my "Nietzsche, the Self, and the Disunity of Philosophical Reason" (Gardner 2009), section 1.3.

that they have received from others – "no individual among this majority is capable of setting up a real ego, accessible to him and fathomed by him, in opposition to the general pale fiction".[39] In *Daybreak*, II, §108, Nietzsche invokes the self in a reformulation of the Kantian formula of autonomy: once we have disposed of the moral law *qua* something that is "supposed to stand *above* our own likes and dislikes", mankind might "*impose* upon itself a moral law", prompted by feeling but "at its own discretion".[40] A notebook entry confirms Nietzsche in the view that "*I will*" represents a different form of consciousness from mere drive, and one that is axiologically higher: "*Schopenhauer's* basic misunderstanding of the *will* (as if craving, instinct, drive were the *essence* of will) is typical: lowering the value of the will to the point of atrophy. Also hatred against willing; attempt to see something higher, indeed that which is higher and valuable, in willing no more [...]".[41]

Is Nietzsche aware of the rub between his theoretical dissolution of the self and his ethical ideal of substantial individuality? Whether he regards it as a philosophical problem in its own right is hard to determine, but there is evidence that he is at least aware that the self-representation of the practical perspective is discrepant with the theoretical drive model.

In *Daybreak*, II, §109, Nietzsche concerns himself with the available methods of "combating the vehemence of a drive". For the first three quarters of this passage, Nietzsche details a variety of methods, six to be precise, that we may adopt with a view to defeating, or draining of force, a desire that presses on us chronically and that we wish to be rid of. We may, first, weaken the desire by avoiding opportunities for its gratification; second, secure periods of release from its pressure by imposing a regular schedule on its gratification; third, indulge it to the point of disgust and satiety; fourth, forge an association of its fulfilment with some painful experience; fifth, drain its reservoir of mental and physical energy by engaging in other activities; and sixth, generally depress our level of activity to the point of exhaustion through ascetic deprivation.

The stance adopted by Nietzsche in detailing these techniques is the one found in any stoic manual of management of the passions or self-help guide: we *look down* on drives from above, where 'above' means from where *I* am, the *personal* rather than sub-personal standpoint of the judging and willing agent, set to intercede in the goings-on of his or her psychology. From this standpoint, the

---

39 D 105, Nietzsche 1982: 61 [KGW V/1: 90–91].
40 D 108, Nietzsche 1982: 63–64 [KGW V/1: 94]. For passages which leave no doubt concerning the 'I'-centric shape of Nietzschean value, see GS 338 and GS 345.
41 WP 84, (Autumn 1887) [KGW VIII/2: 99]. Translation modified.

drive figures as a would-be usurper: it wishes to "play the master"[42] and can be regarded as suffering from confusion regarding its own proper psychological status (whence its perceived illegitimacy).

Nietzsche draws particular attention to the connection of this top-down perspective with a sense of one's own value:

> The same method is also being employed when a man's pride, as for example in the case of Lord Byron or Napoleon, rises up and feels the domination of his whole bearing and the ordering of his reason by a single affect as an affront: from where there then arises the habit and desire to tyrannise over the drive and make it as it were gnash its teeth. ("I refuse to be the slave of any appetite," Byron wrote in his diary.)[43]

Having exposited the six methods, Nietzsche abruptly – in mid-sentence, without breaking stride – loops back reflexively on the presiding *I*, with the following contention:

> [...]: *that* one *desires* to combat the vehemence of a drive at all, however, does not stand within our own power; nor does the choice of any particular method; nor does the success or failure of this method. What is clearly the case is that in this entire procedure our intellect is only the blind instrument of *another drive* which is a *rival* of the drive whose vehemence is tormenting us: whether it be the drive to restfulness, or the fear of disgrace and other evil consequences, or love. While "we" believe we are complaining about the vehemence of a drive, at bottom it is one drive *which is complaining about another* [...].[44]

The effect is deflating and disorienting: the sensation of Byronic self-mastery which Nietzsche has been stoking is dissipated. We find ourselves dispossessed in a sense in which we were not at the outset, for we began by pitting ourselves against a power that resisted our will, but have learned that whatever we might reckon as an exercise of our will is in truth of the very same order as that which we previously took to be subordinate to it.

So far, so Freudian. But Nietzsche takes one further step. Concluding the passage, Nietzsche observes that, because our suffering from a drive "presupposes the existence of another equally vehement or even more vehement drive", "a *struggle* is in prospect in which our intellect is going to have to take sides [*in welchem unser Intellekt Partei nehmen muß*]".[45] This last clause is crucial. Nietzsche has confronted the first-person practical standpoint of putatively self-

---

42 D 109, Nietzsche 1982: 65 [KGW V/1: 96].
43 D 109, Nietzsche 1982: 64 [KGW V/1: 95]. See also the first paragraph of BGE 257, concerning the inner pathos of distance required for enhancement of the type 'man'.
44 D 109, Nietzsche 1982: 64 [KGW V/1: 96–97].
45 D 109, Nietzsche 1982: 65 [KGW V/1: 97].

determining agency with the third-person theoretical standpoint of sub-personal psychological analysis, and allowed the former to collapse in favour of the latter, but he does not give the third person the last word: in his coda, as we turn to the future, practical necessity returns and our personal status is restored, for we are intellects that are "going to have to take sides".[46]

If we are aware of ourselves as *having to* take sides, it follows that Schopenhauer's analysis of self-consciousness is incomplete. The problem of course is that, at this point, though we are in no doubt that we must *understand ourselves* to have the task of taking sides, we are no longer clear what this amounts to, or in what way it can be true that we have this capacity, since the very notion of 'taking sides' – that is, the concept of a relation to a drive of something that is *not itself* a drive, as distinct from a relation *among* drives – has been shown to make sense only from within a perspective that the drive model eliminates. The puzzle is therefore as follows: Granted the double inescapability of both (1) a first-person practical perspective in which we must take it to be *up to us* what is to be done with and about our drives, and (2) a third-person theoretical perspective in which *drives decide* what happens or is done with us, what mediation is possible? In short, where next?

Nietzsche does not say. Later sections in Book II of *Daybreak* reinforce the perplexing finality of §109. In §119 Nietzsche blocks the supposition that the *Intellekt* could at least cognitively master the drives: they supervene on physiological processes in irrational ways, that we could not hope to grasp, such that there is "no *essential* difference" between the way that drives are expressed in dream and our awareness of them in waking experience[47]; nothing "can be more incomplete" than an individual's "image of the totality of *drives* which constitute his being".[48] Since the tangle of drives cannot be rendered transparent, the notion of a judgement-based, drive-transcendent intervention in one's volitional processes – even if there were a presiding 'I' to undertake it – is empty. And in §129 Nietzsche repeats the exercise in self-alienation of §109, telling us that in certain cases of conflicts of motives, "what I finally *do*" may be the effect of

---

46 As coheres with the broader argument of Book II of *Daybreak*, which has arrived, in the conclusion of the immediately preceding section, at the point where we are to consider *choosing* the moral law. That the self is an illusion is indicated in other passages in the vicinity of §109: mankind confuses "the active and the passive" – it mistakes being *acted upon* for acting (D 120, Nietzsche 1982: 76–77 [KGW V/1: 113]); we naively accord plain truth to "*I will*" (D 124, Nietzsche 1982: 77 [KGW V/1: 114]); "the so-called 'ego' [das sogenannte 'Ich']" is merely one element in the construction of character (D 115, Nietzsche 1982: 72 [KGW V/1: 106]).
47 D 119, Nietzsche 1982: 75 [KGW V/1: 111].
48 D 119, Nietzsche 1982: 74 [KGW V/1:109].

"something quite invisible to us" of which we are "quite unconscious" – all the while sustaining a contrast of "unconscious processes" with the standpoint of an 'I' that anxiously calculates consequences and outcomes, forms a unified "picture of the consequences", and reflects in preparation for the act which it takes itself to have resolved upon.[49]

Now at this point two routes are open. On the one hand we might seek an interpretation that renders Nietzsche's claims consistent. For instance, we might look for an interpretation of the ideal of the 'real ego' that does not presuppose the reality of an effective *Intellekt*,[50] or deny that Nietzsche is obligated to recognize a tension here at all.[51] The alternative is to release Nietzsche's position from the threat of inconsistency by construing it as frankly aporetic – and to then go on to explain why in Nietzsche's terms, that is, with his specific philosophical objectives in view, such a result can be allowed to stand.[52]

I cannot substantiate the claim here, but it seems to me that in Nietzsche's works at large there is no sustained attempt at a positive dissolution of the conflict dramatized in *Daybreak*, II, §109, and that attempts to locate a consistent non-aporetic position in Nietzsche, however ingenious, go against the grain, letter, and spirit of Nietzsche's texts. As a brief indication of the difficulties that lie in wait for such interpretations, it is striking that Nietzsche in *Daybreak*, II, §119, describes the very vocabulary in which he conceives drives – viz., as self-interested homunculi-agents which (or who) desire gratification, exercise and discharge their strength, and seek to fill their emptiness – as "all metaphors [*es ist Alles Bilderrede*]".[53] Nietzsche appears to be saying that our very concept of a drive is conditioned by the 'I' in the sense (first) that drives are grasped as things that figure for the 'I' in so far as it sets itself in relation (resisting, etc.) to them, with the consequence (second) that if we raise up drives and have them supplant the 'I', then we are bound to give them its conceptual character, and so

---

49 D 129, Nietzsche 1982: 129–130 [KGW V/1: 116–118].
50 See Gemes 2009, which interprets Nietzsche's conception of genuine selfhood in terms of subservience to a single "master drive". In my view, Nietzsche is not rigorously third personal and does not suppose it meaningful to attribute 'master' status to a drive and to identify the achievement of selfhood with its hegemony independently from the perspective of self-consciousness. It seems to me, for example, that the passage in *Ecce Homo* (EH, Why I Am So Clever 9) from which Gemes quotes as supporting his view (Gemes 2009: 47) makes sense only when Nietzsche's unconscious (master) drive – to complete the 'task of *revaluing values*' – is viewed in the perspective of what Nietzsche can call *his life* and affirm as such: "Nach dieser Seite hin betrachtet ist mein Leben einfach wundervoll" (KGW VI/3: 292–293).
51 For consideration of this possibility, see Anderson 2013.
52 See my (2009).
53 D 119, Nietzsche 1982: 74 [KGW V/1: 110].

to think of them in terms that are literally false.⁵⁴ Taken at face value, then, Nietzsche's idea, espoused by contemporary eliminativists, seems to be that the conceptual scheme of intentional psychology is incapable of representing the true inner causes of behaviour. And given the mountain of remarks in Nietzsche concerning the superficiality and epistemic incompetence of consciousness, this would hardly be a surprising conclusion for him to have reached; consciousness could not have been expected to determine correctly the nature of the mind.⁵⁵ But if that is so, then Nietzsche's position seems doubly strange: the psychological substrate in favour of which the 'I' was eliminated has turned out to itself have only a limited kind and degree of reality; we seem to be moving sideways, from one fiction to another, rather than out of fiction into psychological truth. Nietzsche hints as much in *Beyond Good and Evil*:

> By putting an end to the superstition that until now has grown around the idea of the soul with an almost tropical luxuriance, the *new* psychologist clearly thrusts himself into a new wasteland and a new suspicion [...] the new psychologist knows by this very token that he is condemned to *invention* – and, who knows?, perhaps to *discovery*.⁵⁶

If only for reasons of this sort, concerning the resistance of Nietzsche's texts to regimentation and the heavy interpolations required in order for Nietzsche to emerge as a thinker with a positive systematic account, it seems to me better to say that what we get (and are meant to get) from Nietzsche is not a solution to the puzzle presented in *Daybreak*, II, §109, but clarified and indeed intensified awareness of the more general conflict which it exemplifies, that of the deliverances of the will to truth and the needs of life: the opposition of theoretical reason and practical reason, I suggest, subsumes the opposition of the drive model and the 'I', of which it is a specific instance; the drive-transcendent perspective of the 'I' belongs with the other fundamental illusions, constitutive

---

54 BGE 17: "It thinks: but to say the 'it' is just that famous old 'I' – well that is just an assumption or opinion, to put it mildly, and by no means an 'immediate certainty'. In fact, there is already too much packed into the 'it thinks': even the 'it' contains an *interpretation* of the process, and does not belong to the process itself. People are following grammatical habits here in drawing conclusions, reasoning that 'thinking is an activity, behind every activity something is active, therefore –'." (Nietzsche 2002: 17–18 [KGW VI/2: 25]). And TI, The Four Great Errors 3: "There are no mental causes whatsoever [gar keine geistigen Ursachen]!" (Nietzsche 2005b: 178) [KGW VI/3: 85].
55 As claimed explicitly in D 115: "*We are none of us* that which we appear to be in accordance with the states for which alone we have consciousness and words [...] we misread ourselves in this apparently most intelligible of handwriting on the nature of ourselves" (Nietzsche 1982: 71–72 [KGW V/1: 105–106]).
56 BGE 12, Nietzsche 2002: 14–15 [KGW VI/2: 21].

errors, that have grown out of the needs of life. Priests and philosophers have however raised this error to a higher power, and their hypostatization and valorization of the 'I' has been internalized. Consequently, there is reason to confront it with the drive model: the 'I' may be ineliminable, but undermining the integrity of the concept of a self-legislating and drive-transcendent 'I' helps to dislodge the (Judeo-Christian, Kantian) modes of evaluation associated with it.[57] Whether the drive model might itself positively assist in value creation – a possibility which Nietzsche seems not to rule out[58] – exposing the conflict of theoretical knowledge and practical existence serves a purpose: it reorientates us towards the needs of life, free from the illusion that our practical problems are amenable to theoretical solutions.[59] I will say some more about this in the next section.

For the narrower purpose of differentiating Nietzsche from Freud, it does not matter ultimately which of the two alternatives is accepted. On either view, Nietzsche is committed to something that is not to be found in Freud: not the existence of a full-blown entity but an ineliminable, quasi-transcendental *neces-*

---

[57] Tom Stern has suggested to me that it also allows us to recapture innocence of a sort, in so far as we shake off the burden of an intrinsically morally characterized self. The return to innocence is hailed in TI, The Four Great Errors 8, where it concludes an extended attack on the will in the name of psychological explanation.

[58] As hinted in the quotation above from BGE 12, concerning the "new psychologist" – which one may read in light of Nietzsche's experimental attitude towards scepticism (GS 51). I am grateful to Tom Stern for drawing my attention to other relevant passages: GS 335 presents a three-part movement: in the name of "physics" Nietzsche (i) decomposes our notion of intellectual conscience into homuncular elements, (ii) turns this conclusion against the categorial imperative, and (iii) refers this result, again in the name of "physics", to the practical perspective, our interest in becoming "those we are" and creators of new values (Nietzsche 2001: 187–188 [KGW V/2: 240–244]). In D 560 Nietzsche (again invoking the personal stance) invites us to contemplate our drives and to recognize that we are at liberty to cultivate them in different ways.

[59] Central to this reorientation is an aesthetic turn, of which we find no equivalent in Freud. It is helpful to compare Nietzsche in this regard with Schiller, who is preoccupied with very similar issues of psychological constitution and personal unity, and whose analysis of human personality in terms of the form-drive and sense-drive in the *Letters on Aesthetic Education* no doubt impressed itself on Nietzsche, its influence being clearly visible in *The Birth of Tragedy*. Schiller recognizes a problematic complexity in the structure of personality which does not appear in Kant, and his conception of a drive is consistently non-psychoanalytic. Schiller however does not think that the complexity of drive-structure impugns the reality of the 'I': it can for Schiller be contained within, and must be understood in terms of, the unity of the 'I' (which is the crux of the transcendental argument for the possibility of the play-drive that he offers in Letters 18–22). And because for Schiller there is no aporia in selfhood as such, wholeness of human personality can in principle be achieved, by aesthetic means. Nietzsche by contrast invokes the aesthetic as compensation for disunity, or so I have argued in Gardner 2013.

sity, that of the first-person practical point of view, incongruent with the theoretical image of the mind.

6. I have argued for two principal differences of philosophical psychology between Nietzsche and Freud. First, Nietzsche does not draw the distinction of psychological parts and corresponding kinds of mental state drawn by Freud. This makes Nietzschean psychology revisionary (in relation to ordinary psychology) in a way that psychoanalysis is not. Second, Nietzsche adopts a complex stand regarding the reality of the 'I', which he excises from the theoretical psychological picture while affirming its ineliminability from the first-person practical point of view, in contrast to Freud, who does not see the 'I' as raising any issues not resolved in his metapsychology. In addition I have indicated the connection of Nietzsche's differences from psychoanalysis with his practical orientation: Nietzsche's psychological analyses are intended to work in concert with his ethical aims. Finally, I have cast doubt on the assumption that Nietzsche regards his drive psychology in unequivocally realist terms, a contrast with Freud that can again be attributed to Nietzsche's practical ambitions, in so far as his new psychology aims ultimately not at true explanation for its own sake, but at therapeutic results.[60] The contrast of Nietzsche with Freud on issues of practical philosophy, their difference of axiology rather than philosophical psychology, is what I want to expand on in this final section.

Nietzsche's contemptuous repudiation of happiness as an ethical value is well known.[61] Freud's theorizing about practical matters – which to be sure does not amount to a moral philosophy, but which involves a commitment to a scale of value – refers to nothing else. Indeed Freud asserts that facts of pain and pleasure, suffering and satisfaction, are the sole considerations to which it makes sense to refer in estimation of the human condition, now that the question of the meaning of life has, with the vanishing of religious belief, itself become meaningless:

> The question of the purpose of human life has been raised countless times; it has never yet received a satisfactory answer and perhaps does not admit of one. Some of those who have asked it have added that if it should turn out that life has *no* purpose, it would lose all value for them. But this threat alters nothing. [...] [O]nly religion can answer the question

---

60 Psychoanalysis aims of course at therapeutic results, but it also aims at theoretical truth for its own sake.
61 E.g., BGE 198, BGE 200, BGE 225, BGE 228. Whether Nietzsche does, or could, find some place for some conception of happiness is not the issue here: the point is just that he rejects it as a value in the (key, intentional object) sense of something *at which* one may aim and *from which* life-affirmation may derive.

of the purpose of life. One can hardly be wrong in concluding that the idea of life having a purpose stands and falls with the religious system.

We will therefore turn to the less ambitious question of what men themselves show by their behaviour to be the purpose and intention of their lives. What do they demand of life and wish to achieve in it? The answer to this can hardly be in doubt. They strive after happiness; they want to become happy and to remain so. This endeavour has two sides, a positive and a negative aim. It aims, on the one hand, at an absence of pain and unpleasure, and, on the other, at the experiencing of strong feelings of pleasure. In its narrower sense the word "happiness" only relates to the last. In conformity with this dichotomy in his aims, man's activity develops in two directions, according as it seeks to realize – in the main, or even exclusively – the one or the other of these aims.

As we see, what decides the purpose of life is simply the programme of the pleasure principle. This principle dominates the operation of the mental apparatus from the start.[62]

Proceeding on this basis, *Civilisation and its Discontents* argues that the suffering which is specifically due to civilization (and which, Freud notes, so many of his contemporaries complain of) is functionally necessary: it is fixed by the invariant psychological constitution of human beings, the quantity and quality of our instinctual input, in conjunction with the objective circumstances of social order, the arrangements required to control aggression, and it is roughly justified on a utilitarian calculus; lifting the restrictions of civilized life would bring no overall gain.

> The programme of becoming happy, which the pleasure principle imposes on us, cannot be fulfilled; yet we must not – indeed, we cannot – give up our efforts to bring it nearer to fulfilment by some means or other. Very different paths may be taken in that direction, and we may give priority either to the positive aspect of the aim, that of gaining pleasure, or to its negative one, that of avoiding unpleasure. By none of these paths can we attain all that we desire. Happiness, in the reduced sense in which we recognize it as possible, is a problem of the economics of the individual's libido.[63]

Some limited scope remains for remedial action, therefore. Freud accordingly criticizes certain institutions as dysfunctional – the norms of modern marriage, he argues, are responsible for an undue level of sexual dissatisfaction,[64] and religion does not deliver on its hedonic promises[65] – but it is not Freud's view that a

---

[62] CD, 74–75.
[63] CD, 82.
[64] " 'Civilized' Sexual Morality and Modern Nervous Illness" [1908], in Freud, SE 9: 177–204.
[65] CD, 83–84: "Its technique consists in depressing the value of life and distorting the picture of the real world in a delusional manner [...] by forcibly fixing them in a state of psychical infantilism and by drawing them into a mass-delusion, religion succeeds in sparing many people an individual neurosis. But hardly anything more."

revision of our values can mitigate significantly the suffering arising from the renunciation of instinctual satisfaction which civilization presupposes, which is bound to remain at a roughly constant level; and since nothing else could give it sense, axiological change is not for Freud a meaningful possibility. There is consequently in Freud no analogue of Nietzsche's non-utilitarian notions of individual and cultural flourishing, or of failure thereof, and Freud does not suggest that we are tending to a nihilistic climax; rather, it is modern warfare, a very material threat, that poses the main danger for Freud.[66] Again, Freud does not follow Nietzsche's critique of modern secular reason: since the comforts of religion were of very limited efficacy, Freud sees nothing to regret in the hegemony of the will to truth. Because Freud's pessimistic, stoical conservativism derives directly from his empirical claims concerning (i) the universal and unalterable laws governing human psychology, and (ii) the social structures which they necessitate,[67] it can be challenged on terms that Freud would accept only by disputing one or both of the latter (as attempted in the Frankfurt School).

What is responsible for this very considerable difference of outlook? No mystery attaches to Freud's utilitarianism, the grounds of which are familiar and transparent, and which can plausibly be viewed as the default position for a naturalist of Freud's sort. The question is rather why Nietzsche, given that he too rejects so much of what is required for any non-utilitarian scheme of values, is so uncompromisingly opposed to Freud's axiological standpoint.

There is an obvious suggestion to be made concerning the root of Nietzsche's anti-hedonism. We may return to Nietzsche's dissatisfaction with Schopenhauer, and observe that the pessimism of Schopenhauer's that Nietzsche resists so fiercely is grounded on hedonic considerations. There is for Schopenhauer an intrinsic wrongness ('injustice') to individuated existence as such, but what converts this metaphysical 'fact' into a motive for denial of the will to live is the phenomenal suffering to which it directly gives rise: the structure of willing, Schopenhauer argues, entails *a priori* the impossibility of happiness, to which the miserable character of human life bears witness *a posteriori*.

Nietzsche does not endorse Schopenhauer's analysis of pleasure and pain, but he does not dispute Schopenhauer's account of the balance sheet of human weal and woe; in those terms Nietzsche allows Silenus the last word. Nietzsche's counter-pessimistic strategy focusses instead on the *reception* of suffering, the way that it is *construed*, and which determines its bearing on the will. A passage

---

[66] "Thoughts for the Times on Death and War" [1915], in: Freud, SE 14: 273–300, esp. Part I, "The Disillusionment of War".
[67] See Deigh 1986.

in *The Gay Science* puts the point in focus. After noting that we moderns have relatively reduced acquaintance with bodily pain, Nietzsche observes that

> 'pain is hated much more now than formerly; one speaks much worse of it; indeed, one can hardly endure the presence of pain *as a thought* and makes it a matter of conscience and a reproach against the whole of existence'.[68]

In this passage Nietzsche implies that our inability to tolerate suffering is mere squeamishness on our part (which we might be cured of by a strong blast of real first-order pain), but his fully developed view, set forth in *On the Genealogy of Morals*, is that suffering has become intolerable to modern man not, or not just, because of the exaggerated delicacy of his sensibility – a simple matter of mental fabric – but because of his unmet demand that suffering *have meaning*, a property that Nietzsche connects closely with rational explanation and justification.[69] The complexity that Nietzsche identifies in suffering sets him in disagreement with Freud, for whom "[in] the last analysis, all suffering is nothing else than sensation".[70]

Now the interesting – and very difficult – question is what Nietzsche makes of this insight, more exactly, what stand he wants to take regarding the need for *Sinn*. The plain therapeutic implication of Nietzsche's diagnosis is that the beliefs and dispositions responsible for our incapacity to tolerate suffering need to be exorcised, and clearly it is a central ambition of Nietzsche's to eradicate the notion that suffering shows existence to be something evil (by inducing us either to interpret suffering in a different way or to desist from interpreting it at all). But two quite opposite rationales for undertaking to eliminate the need for *Sinn* are possible, one of which is entirely consistent with the hedonic axiology of Schopenhauer and Freud. If the problem is simply that we suffer twice over, our second-order suffering weighing on us more heavily than our first-order pain, then there is a *hedonic* reason for targeting the *Sinn*-needing disposition, namely, on account of its disutility. This of course cannot be Nietzsche's view: Nietzsche does not recommend (as Freud well might) that we attempt to cease asking for suffering to have meaning because doing so makes us unhappier than we might otherwise be. But in that case, there is a hard question that

---

68 GS 48, Nietzsche 2001: 61 [KGW V/2: 88].
69 See especially §28 of the Third Essay (discussed in my (2009), section 3.2). That Nietzsche distinguishes mere sensitivity from need-for-*Sinn* in its modern, rationalistically conditioned form is shown by the fact that he attributes the former, but not of course the latter, to the unsocratized Homeric Greeks: BT 3, Nietzsche 1993: 23 [KGW III/1: 32].
70 CD, 77.

Nietzsche must answer, and that appears to expose a tension in his position. In the name of which value(s) does Nietzsche reject utility? Had Nietzsche exposited a positive ethics, equipped with a justification independent of his anti-hedonism, then the question might have a clear answer, but we do not of course find anything so cut and dried in Nietzsche; on the contrary, if we want to determine what Nietzsche's values amount to, then we need to work in the other direction, that is, extrapolate his values from his critiques of hedonism, Kantianism, and so on. Nor is the question answered by the thesis that values are (to be) created, for – aside from the point that it is not clear why desire satisfaction could not be created *as a value* – it is precisely the intelligibility of value-creation that, for the Freudian ethical naturalist, stands in need of explanation and justification: before we can get to the point of positing (say) 'becoming what one is' or 'real ego-hood' as a value, we first need to know that it *makes sense* to envisage anything *other* than hedonic facts as candidates for the Good. To regard Nietzsche in this way, as under pressure to justify his rejection of a hedonic axiology, does not require, note, that we interpret him as a fully committed naturalist: it arises simply from his having apparently stripped out of existence all of the features that would rationalize any conception of value that goes beyond desire-satisfaction. So, to repeat, there is a puzzle: Whence for Nietzsche the freedom from natural fact required in order to espouse values other than desire satisfaction? Or, as it might also be put, whence the very idea of value *as opposed to* fact? In one sense, of course, the answer to the question is plain: *history* has made available to Nietzsche a non-naturalistic conception of value. Nietzsche has as keen a sense as any rationalist of the 'queerness' of value, the spectacular alteration in the order of things effected by the emergence of a value-positing creature, the work of imagination and hallucinations of depth required in order for human beings to experience and interpret the world as an axiological domain. This explains very well why Nietzsche should think that we, having acquired a taste for trans-natural values, cannot be satisfied with mere desire-satisfaction – our problem lies, Nietzsche shows, one step back, in our inability to form desires, our finding no *reason to desire*[71] – but it does not explain why Nietzsche thinks that he is within his rights to, as it were, carry on playing the same game as his anti-naturalistic predecessors, the game that Freud clear-sightedly throws over.

If this is right, then Nietzsche faces a dilemma: either he condemns hedonic axiology on the basis that it does not answer to our need for *Sinn*, in which case he is obliged to grant the latter validity, which seems contrary to Nietzsche's

---

71 See Pippin 2010, Ch. 1.

aim of detaching life affirmation from rational reflection; or he follows Freud in repudiating the need for *Sinn* and treating it purely as an object of psychological and historical explanation, in which case he has no grounds for refusing a hedonic axiology.

The problem reveals itself most acutely when we consider Nietzsche from Freud's perspective, but this does not represent the limit of its interest, for what has been brought to light is the extreme thinness of the line that Nietzsche is trying to walk between, on the one hand, an axiology of the self in the modern (Rousseauian, Kantian, post-Kantian, German Romantic) tradition, which attempts to meet the demands of reflection, and on the other, the naturalistically reduced conceptions of value that are all that appear to remain when the grounds of non-naturalistic conceptions of the Good have been removed.

Earlier I suggested that the Freudian will take a critical view of Nietzsche's depth psychology, and the same, I have just argued, occurs in the sphere of value: viewed psychoanalytically, Nietzsche's project of axiological transformation falls outside the bounds of natural possibility and has nothing to recommend it; we are not defective for life in any way that it makes sense to lament or that could be fundamentally overcome; suffering has *Sinn* enough by virtue of being scientifically explicable; the relief that psychoanalysis brings by showing that our anxieties, neuroses and so on derive from natural sources is as much as can be hoped for. If this leaves existential demands unsatisfied, then these must be reckoned a trick of the light, an optical illusion created by our constitutive introversion and underpinned by two millennia of slave metaphysics. Since Nietzsche knows perfectly well that the needs of the spirit are infected with error – it is his own insight that, with the internalization of the instincts, the inner world expands and becomes populated with fictive entities[72] – the puzzle lies in his refusal to accept that in the cold light of the present day we can no longer justifiably allow our axiological expectations to be conditioned by anything other than hard, scientifically attested psychological fact.

This critique of Nietzsche's axiological project raises many questions which cannot be pursued here, but there is one important point to be made concerning the connection of Nietzsche's rejection of hedonist axiology with his difference from Freud concerning the 'I'. If Nietzsche's diagnosis is correct, then relinquishing the possibility of non-hedonic value comes at a much heavier price than Freud supposes – the implications are, as Schopenhauer supposes, catastrophic,

---

[72] GM II 16. And TI, The Four Great Errors 3: "The 'inner world' is full of illusions and phantasms" (Nietzsche 2005b: 178) [KGW VI/3: 85], and BGE 16, Nietzsche 2002: 16 [KGW VI/2: 23].

and Freud is quite mistaken in thinking that the threat of life's losing all meaning 'alters nothing'. This immediately gives Nietzsche leverage: if our need for *Sinn*, or at any rate, our incapacity to tolerate hard unadorned natural fact, is a fixed parameter, then it is *practically necessary* that we work within it, that is, that we employ (in the spirit of "I *must* go on dreaming lest I perish"[73]) whatever axiological devices are required in order for life to preserve itself. But in appealing at this point to *practical necessity* as a ground for value creation, it is absolutely necessary that Nietzsche *affirm* the value and the *authority* of the standpoint of life – since this is exactly what Schopenhauer will dispute. (What is it to invoke 'practical necessity', Schopenhauer will object, but to repeat, insanely, the error of the *Wille zum Leben* that his philosophy has incontrovertibly exposed?) And it is at this point that we see how important the drive-transcendent 'I' is to Nietzsche, for it is from and *only* from its perspective that the standpoint of life presents itself as valid, and can assert itself as *rightful*, as mere drive cannot. The transcendence of theoretical reason by practical consciousness – the movement whereby life projects itself beyond the facts of suffering – is available only to a self-determining 'I' which, even when theoretical reason has concluded that the game is not worth the candle, can still elect to will.[74] If this is correct, then there is in Nietzsche an echo of Kant's 'primacy of practical reason' and of Fichte's *Thathandlung* – on a very different basis and in a very different form, to be sure, but a recognizably transcendentalist residue nonetheless.[75]

References

Anderson, R. Lanier (2013) "Nietzsche on Autonomy", in Ken Gemes and John Richardson (eds.), *The Oxford Handbook of Nietzsche*, Oxford: Oxford University Press, 432–460.
Assoun, Paul-Laurent (2000) *Freud and Nietzsche*, trans. Richard L. Collier, Jr., London: Athlone.

---

[73] GS 54, Nietzsche 2001: 63 [KGW V/2: 91].
[74] See BGE 56: the "world-affirming individual", who wills eternal recurrence, "needs himself – and makes himself necessary [...] *circulus vitiosus deus*" (Nietzsche 2002: 50–51) [KGW VI/2: 73]. It is no accident that Schopenhauer explicitly declares that philosophy is exclusively theoretical and denies privileges to the 'practical point of view' (it is simply, as explained above, inner theoretical consciousness); see WWR I, 271, 285, and Schopenhauer 2010 [1840], §4. Freud is of the same view, implicitly.
[75] I am grateful for helpful comments to Herman Siemens and others at the conference at the University of Salento where parts of this paper were first presented, and to Tom Stern for stimulating discussion of the issues.

Deigh, John (1986) "Freud's Later Theory of Civilization: Changes and Implications", in: *The Sources of Moral Agency: Essays in Moral Psychology and Freudian Theory*, Cambridge: Cambridge University Press, 94–112.

Gardner, Sebastian (1993) *Irrationality and the Philosophy of Psychoanalysis*, Cambridge: Cambridge University Press.

Gardner, Sebastian (1999) "Schopenhauer, Will and Unconscious", in: Christopher Janaway (ed.), *The Cambridge Companion to Schopenhauer*, Cambridge: Cambridge University Press, 375–421.

Gardner, Sebastian (2009) "Nietzsche, the Self, and the Disunity of Philosophical Reason", in: K. Gemes and S. May (eds.), *Nietzsche on Freedom and Autonomy*, Oxford: Oxford University Press, 1–31.

Gardner, Sebastian (2013) "Nietzsche's Philosophical Aestheticism", in: Ken Gemes and John Richardson (eds.), *The Oxford Handbook of Nietzsche*, Oxford: Oxford University Press, 599–628.

Gemes, Ken (2009) "Freud and Nietzsche on Sublimation", in: *Journal of Nietzsche Studies* 38, 38–59.

Gemes, Ken/May, Simon (eds.) (2009) *Nietzsche on Freedom and Autonomy*, Oxford/New York: Oxford University Press.

Janaway, Christopher (2010) "The Real Essence of Human Beings: Schopenhauer and the Unconscious Will", in: Angus Nicholls and Martin Liebscher (eds.), *Thinking the Unconscious: Nineteenth-Century German Thought*, Cambridge: Cambridge University Press, 140–155.

Katsafanas, Paul (2013) "Nietzsche's Philosophical Psychology", in: K. Gemes and J. Richardson (eds.), *The Oxford Handbook of Nietzsche*, Oxford: Oxford University Press, 727–755.

Leiter, Brian (2002) *Nietzsche on Morality*, London/New York: Routledge.

Nietzsche, Friedrich (1968) *The Will to Power* [Nachlaß 1883–88], trans. Walter Kaufmann and R.J. Hollingdale, ed. Walter Kaufmann, New York: Vintage.

Nietzsche, Friedrich (1982) *Daybreak: Thoughts on the Prejudices of Morality*, trans. R.J. Hollingdale, Cambridge: Cambridge University Press.

Nietzsche, Friedrich (1993) *The Birth of Tragedy Out of the Spirit of Music* [1872], trans. Shaun Whiteside, ed. Michael Tanner, Harmondsworth: Penguin.

Nietzsche, Friedrich (1994) *On the Genealogy of Morals* [1887], trans. Carol Diethe, ed. Keith Ansell-Pearson, Cambridge: Cambridge University Press.

Nietzsche, Friedrich (2001) *The Gay Science* [1882], trans. Josefine Nauckhoff, ed. Bernard Williams, Cambridge: Cambridge University Press.

Nietzsche, Friedrich (2002) *Beyond Good and Evil: Prelude to a Philosophy of the Future* [1886], trans. Judith Norman, ed. Rolf-Peter Horstmann and Judith Norman, Cambridge: Cambridge University Press.

Nietzsche, Friedrich (2005b) *Twilight of the Idols: or How to Philosophize with a Hammer* [1889], in *The Anti-Christ, Ecce Homo, Twilight of the Idols, and Other Writings*, trans. Judith Norman, ed. Aaron Ridley and Judith Norman, Cambridge: Cambridge University Press.

Pippin, Robert B. (2010) *Nietzsche, Psychology, and First Philosophy*, Chicago/London: University of Chicago Press.

Poellner, Peter (1995) *Nietzsche and Metaphysics*, New York: Oxford University Press.

Richardson, John (1996) *Nietzsche's System*, Oxford: Oxford University Press.

Schopenhauer, Arthur (2010) [1839] *Prize Essay on the Freedom of the Will*, in *The Two Fundamental Problems of Ethics*, trans. David E. Cartwright and Edward E. Erdmann, Oxford: Oxford University Press.

Schopenhauer, Arthur (2010) [1840] *Prize Essay on the Basis of Morals*, in *The Two Fundamental Problems of Ethics*, trans. David E. Cartwright and Edward E. Erdmann, Oxford: Oxford University Press.

Stern, Thomas, 'Against Nietzsche's 'Theory' of the Drives', *Journal of the American Philosophical Association*, Volume 1, Issue 1, March 2015, pp. 121–140.

Tugendhat, Ernst (1986) *Self-Consciousness and Self-Determination*, trans. Paul Stern, Cambridge, MA: MIT Press.

Yannick Souladié
15 Nietzsche, Deleuze: Desubjectification and Will to Power

Deleuze was a great admirer and a diligent reader of Nietzsche. He also played a leading role in the reinstatement of the German philosopher during the early 1960s in France. Deleuze combines a very precise knowledge of his philosophy (the noteworthy *Nietzsche and Philosophy*, published in 1962) with a special interest in Nietzsche's life.

This article will examine two aspects of the link between Deleuze and Nietzsche, both related to the problem of subjectivity. It will first focus on Deleuze's interest in how Nietzsche presents himself in his last works. By displaying his own figure in his books, Nietzsche launches a real process of desubjectification. Using the specific example of paragraph 36 from *Beyond Good and Evil*, the paper will then examine how this double process of self-affirmation and self-abolition can be an integral part of the problematic of Nietzsche's most academic texts, and not merely involve the autobiographical works.

1 Desubjectification

Nietzsche and Philosophy offers a meticulous and very complete analysis of the philosopher's works. Despite some obvious mistakes,[1] this interpretation still sets the standard for secondary literature on Nietzsche. Deleuze considerably helped draw attention to Nietzsche in French academic circles. In his interpretation, he insists on the profound importance of the concepts of will to power and eternal return. He claims that their relationship constitutes the very heart of Nietzsche's philosophy.

---

[1] Basing his interpretation on the fake book "*The Will to Power*", Deleuze reads "*innere Wille* (internal will)" instead of "*innere Welt* (internal world)" in the posthumous note 36[31], 1885 (NL 1885, KSA 11: 563, incorrectly transcribed in the "aphorism" 309 of the second book of *La volonté de puissance*, ed. F. Würzbach, trans. G. Bianquis (Nietzsche 1942). Deleuze writes that this passage is "one of the most important texts which Nietzsche wrote to explain what he understood by will to power". He comments then that "the will to power is thus ascribed to force, but in a very special way: it is both a complement of force *and* something internal to it." (Deleuze 1986: 49). See Paolo D'Iorio, "Postface" in Montinari 1997: 143–146; Müller-Lauter 1974: 35f.

15 Nietzsche, Deleuze: Desubjectification and Will to Power — 395

Even if he does not emphasise Nietzsche's *philosophy* in his polemic against philosophies of the subject,[2] Deleuze takes a close interest in Nietzsche's life. Deleuze conceives of the individual as a complex being, and not as a substance or as a conscious, reasonable subject but as "a concentration, an accumulation a coincidence of a certain amount of convergent pre-individual particularities [*singularités préindividuelles convergentes*]".[3] To define the human being as 'subject' misses the complexity of forces which traverse the individual. It also leads to errors about the real nature of desire, as explained in *Anti-Oedipus* and *A Thousand Plateaus*. Borrowing an expression from Whitehead, Deleuze thus qualifies the individual not as "subject [*sujet*]" but as a "superject [*superjet*]".[4]

In cooperation with Félix Guattari during the 1970s, Deleuze asserts the necessity of a process of "desubjectification [*désubjectivation*]".[5] If at this point Deleuze is still concerned with Nietzsche's theoretical texts, after *Nietzsche and Philosophy* we observe how he more frequently focuses on Nietzsche's character, or more precisely on texts in which the philosopher presents himself. But Nietzsche is neither a major historical figure nor a novelist. Deleuze's attention is attracted neither by the events of Nietzsche's private life nor the beauty of his prose. He is interested rather in Nietzsche's talent for self-presentation: the way he presents and directs his role in his philosophical works. He is interested in Nietzsche's self-understanding and how he inscribed himself in his works as a "destiny".

Through writing, Nietzsche found a very special way to conduct a process of desubjectification. Nietzsche has always taken the art of writing very seriously. He becomes really angry when his friend Carl Spitteler characterizes *Thus Spoke Zarathustra* as "a higher stylistic exercise" and does not see that it speaks of "his problems" and has "invented a new gesture of language for these things which are new in every respect". Nietzsche refuses to be regarded as somebody who "commits *literature*", because his *Zarathustra* is "the most profound and decisive event between two millenaries"[6] and because what he writes "will break the history of humanity in two, when it will be understood".[7] Writing has

---

[2] Deleuze actually more often refers to Spinoza and Bergson, as Pierre Montebello (2011) reminds us.
[3] Deleuze 1988: 85, my translation.
[4] Deleuze 1988: 27. See Whitehead 1969: 373.
[5] Deleuze/Guattari 1980: 168, 197, 330. Elisabeth Rigal defines desubjectification in this way: "it is an abolishment of the alienated form under which the individual is constituted in a subject, for the benefit of a subjectivation without subjections." (Rigal 2003: 75, my translation)
[6] Letter to Carl Spitteler, 10.02.1888, KSB 8, nr. 247, my translation.
[7] Letter to Paul Deussen, 14.09.1888, KSB 8, nr. 1111, my translation.

always to be taken seriously; "writing always means becoming something".⁸ Thus, for Deleuze and Guattari,

> A book has neither object nor subject; it is made of variously formed matters, and very different dates and speeds. To attribute the book to a subject is to overlook this working of matters, and the exteriority of their relations. It is to fabricate a beneficent god to explain geological move-ments. In a book, as in all things, there are lines of articulation or segmentarity, strata and territories; but also lines of flight, movements of deterritorialization and destratification.⁹

It seems especially true in Nietzsche's last works, in which according to Deleuze and Guattari the philosopher has mastered the art of both desubjectification and the multiplication of his "conceptual personae [*personnages conceptuels*]".¹⁰ More than any other philosopher, Nietzsche has relied on conceptual personae.¹¹

> The conceptual persona is not the philosopher's representative but, rather, the reverse: the philosopher is only the envelope of his principal conceptual persona an of all the other personae who are the intercessors [...] The philosopher is the idiosyncrasy of his conceptual personae.¹²

The art of writing appears to be the art of desubjectification par excellence. Deleuze and Guattari confess that they have kept their names in *Anti-Oedipus* and *A Thousand Plateaus* only to make themselves "unrecognizable".

> To reach, not the point where one no longer says I, but the point where it is no longer of any importance whether one says I. We are no longer ourselves. Each will know his own. We have been aided, inspired, multiplied.¹³

In the *Abécédaire*, we can find this startling sentence: "if there was someone who was not interested in his childhood, it was Proust." Deleuze also claims that "talking about one's childhood is the opposite of all literature". Proust becomes a child "but it is not his childhood. He becomes a child, yes, but it is no longer his childhood or anyone's childhood, it is the childhood of the world".

---

8 Deleuze 2004, chap. "Enfance", my translation.
9 Deleuze/Guattari 1987: 3.
10 Deleuze/Guattari 1991: 62.
11 "We invoke Nietzsche because few philosophers have worked so much with both sympathetic (Dionysus, Zarathustra) and antipathetic (Christ, the Priest, the Higher Men; Socrates himself becomes antipathetic...) conceptual personae." (Deleuze/Guattari 1994: 65)
12 Deleuze/Guattari 1994: 64.
13 Deleuze/Guattari 1987: 3.

For Deleuze, every great novelist, philosopher or poet only writes because "something of life goes through him".

> Writing activity has nothing to do with one individual situation [*son affaire à soi*]. That doesn't mean that one doesn't put all of one soul into it. Literature, writing is profoundly connected to life. But life is something more than personal.[14]

The novelist or the philosopher does not profess solipsism. On the contrary, he aims to highlight the universal character of certain life events. In the *Abécédaire*, Deleuze explains to Claire Parnet that his own childhood really has little importance, and that speaking about his childhood seems "useless" to him. He just mentions the day when he saw a horse dying in the street. In doing so, he does not intend to lament his own trauma, but to explain that this tragic vision was a gateway to a universal event. He was able to grasp something of the tragedy of life, something of the relationships connecting animals to man (of man's "becoming-animal [*devenir animal*]" in his own words). The living memory of this event takes him back to the description of similar episodes in the novels of Dostoyevsky and also to Nietzsche's collapse, which, at that time, the legend whereby Nietzsche threw his arms around the neck of a horse being beaten in Turin was believed to be authentic. It allows Deleuze to "meet [*rencontrer*]" Nietzsche and be part of the "becoming-animal" of the philosopher as he abandoned the world of the humans.[15]

Writing truthfully means conducting a desubjectification process, thereby merging with the world. In his last texts, Nietzsche melts into multiplicity. "A multiplicity has neither subject nor object, only determinations, magnitudes, and dimensions that cannot increase in number without the multiplicity changing in nature", we read in *A Thousand Plateaus*.[16] The "I" of *Ecce Homo* refers to something which is more than personal. "The subject is not a subject, it is an envelope", writes Gilles Deleuze in *Negotiations*.[17] "Friedrich Nietzsche" is only a figurehead for the multiplicity of voices which expresses themselves in his texts. In his philosophical texts, Nietzsche does not try to isolate the subject "Friedrich Nietzsche" from the world, but on the contrary wants to open the body of the thinker to the world. In Nietzsche's body, writes Pierre Montebello, "the thought grasps itself in the imposition of the world within her (and not in the transcendental isolation of the subject), within a totality which interiorises

---

14 Deleuze 2004, chap. "Enfance", my translation.
15 Deleuze 2004, chap. "Enfance".
16 Deleuze/Guattari 1987: 8.
17 Deleuze 1990: 212, my translation.

and fulfils itself".[18] Nietzsche does not speak to us of his tiny private affairs, but follows the *"main thread of the body"*.[19] Through the experiences of his own life, he tries to seize something of life in general. Nietzsche's life does matter in his own eyes, or in Deleuze's eyes, because his thought appears inevitably linked to his living experience, to his body. The understanding of *Zarathustra* would require that "whole generations catch up with the intimate experiences [*inneren Erlebnisse*], on the basis of whom this work could arise".[20] "The entire organism thinks".[21] "The body philosophises".[22] Telling the story of a thought always means telling the story of a body. *Ecce Homo* is thus the story of Nietzsche's body, of a universal body ("I am every name in history"[23] "*I* rule the word"[24]); a body for every possible experience, a Dionysian body.

A well-known text of *Ecce Homo* seems in this way remarkable:

> I know my lot [*Loos*]. Some day my name will be linked to the memory of something monstrous, of a crisis as yet unprecedented on earth, the most profound collision of consciences, a decision conjured up *against* everything hitherto believed, demanded, hallowed. I am not a man [*Mensch*], I am dynamite. [...] the truth speaks from me. – But my truth is *terrifying*, for lies were called truth so far. – *Revaluation of all values*: that is my formula for the highest act of self-reflection [*Selbstbesinnung*] on the part of humanity, which has become flesh and genius in me.[25]

According to this text, the Inversion of all values would have already happened in Nietzsche's very own body. This inversion is then at once an historic event (who "breaks the history of humanity in two"[26]), a book by Nietzsche (*The Antichrist*), and an experience which has occurred in the body of Nietzsche himself. Nietzsche extends the desubjectification process until he abolishes any distinction between

---

18 Montebello 2003: 40.
19 NL 1885, 36[35], KSA 11: 565, my translation.
20 Letter to Karl Knortz, 21.06.1888, KSB 8, nr. 1050, my translation.
21 NL 1884, 27[19], KSA 11: 279f, my translation.
22 NL 1882–1883, 5[32], KSA 10: 226, my translation.
23 Letter to Jacob Burckhardt, 06.01.1889, KSB 8, nr. 1256, my translation. This letter may indeed have been written earlier than the 6th of January. See Yannick Souladié, note 3 to Nietzsche 2011: 240.
24 Letter to Julius Kaftan, end of December, 1888, KSB 8, nr. 1218, my translation.
25 EH, Warum ich ein Schicksal bin 1, KSA 6: 365; Nietzsche 2012: 88. [For the translations used in this chapter, see *References* below.]
26 EH, Warum ich ein Schicksal bin 8, KSA 6: 373; Nietzsche 2012: 94. See also letters of 1888 to Paul Deussen, 14 September, KSB 8, nr. 1111; to Malwida von Meysenbug, 4 October, KSB 8, nr. 1126; to Franz Overbeck, 18 October, KSB 8, nr.1132; to August Strindberg, 8 December, KSB 8, nr. 1176; to Heinrich Köselitz, 9 December, KSB 8, nr.1181.

his work and himself. Both are the Antichrist. Thus, according to the famous expression of the preface, Nietzsche as well as his work "are born posthumously". It is worth noting that this only concerns *The Antichrist-Inversion of all values*. In *Ecce Homo*, which Nietzsche presents as a "*preparatory* book",[27] a "Preface"[28] to *The Antichrist*, he indeed writes "I am one thing, my writings are another".[29]

Most likely, it was Josef Viktor Widmann who first suggested the analogy with dynamite. In the *Bund* of the 16th–17th September 1886, he had compared *Beyond Good and Evil* to the wagons which carried dynamite for the Saint Gothard tunnel, and marked their dangerous load with a black flag. This sentence is often regarded as a mere one-liner. If dynamite seems rather harmless nowadays compared with all our modern explosives and weapons, it was different at Nietzsche time. Invented in 1867 by Alfred Nobel, dynamite had an unprecedented power of destruction.[30] It was dangerous for both the target and the user. In this way, "I am dynamite" can be linked with this sentence in a letter to Heinrich Köselitz: "I belong among those machines that can *explode!*"[31] Yet, in this time, dynamite also represented *progress*: without it no one could have drilled the Saint Gothard tunnel. "I am dynamite" then means: I am an accumulation of extremely sensitive, explosive and dangerous power which will bring radical change and promises brighter days. Dynamite is an agent of the transvaluation of values; it breaks the history of humanity in two. But at the edge of madness, Nietzsche not only identifies himself with dynamite, but identifies dynamite with himself. He could have written that "the tunnel of Saint Gothard, it's me!"; or "all the big explosions of history, they're me!" Deleuze and Guattari write in regard to Nietzsche: "The abortionists of unity are indeed angel makers, *doctores angelici*, because they affirm a properly angelic and superior unity".[32] Following "the philosopher Dionysus",[33] Nietzsche is constantly abolishing himself in his books in order to reach a superior dimension. He keeps on opening his body to the world. According to Deleuze, this process reaches its climax in his madness.

> There is no Nietzsche-the-self, professor of philology, who suddenly loses his mind and supposedly identifies with all sorts of strange people; rather, there is the Nietzschean

---

[27] Letter to Constantin Georg Naumann, 06.11.1888, KSB 8, nr. 1139, my translation.
[28] Letter to Heinrich Köselitz, 13.11.1888, KSB 8, nr. 1142, my translation.
[29] EH, Warum ich so gute Bücher schreibe 1, KSA 6:298; Nietzsche 2012: 36.
[30] See the draft of letter to Georg Brandes, beginning of December, 1888: "I'm the most terrifying dynamite there is", KSB 8, nr. 1170, my translation.
[31] Letter to Heinrich Köselitz, 14.08.1881, KSB 6, nr. 136, my translation.
[32] Deleuze/Guattari 1987: 6.
[33] GD, Was ich den Alten verdanke 5, KSA 6: 160, my translation.

subject who passes through a series of states, and who identifies these states with the names of history: "every name in history is I...." The subject spreads itself out along the entire circumference of the circle, the centre of which has been abandoned by the ego.[34]

For Deleuze and Guattari, "it is not a matter of identifying with various historical personages, but rather identifying the names of history with zones of intensity on the body without organs" so that each time Nietzsche-as-subject exclaims: "They're me\ So it's me\". On the edge of madness, Nietzsche "consumes all of universal history in one fell swoop".[35]

2 The will to power and the object-world

Deleuze and Guattari write that Nietzsche so often uses conceptual personae that "it might be thought that he renounces concepts". And yet, he doesn't; instead, "he creates immense and intense concepts".[36] The second part of this paper intends to emphasise how this process of desubjectification applies in texts which could be (and have been!) regarded as systematic, such as paragraph 36 of *Beyond Good and Evil*.

Far from giving in to dualism, in this text Nietzsche first intends to abolish the traditional distinction between the three strata of the world: the inorganic (or "pre-organic"[37]), the organic and the mind stratum. Thought (the mind stratum) becomes no more than "a relation between these drives", and "the so-called mechanistic (and thus material) world" (the inorganic stratum) is now defined "as belonging to the same plane of reality as our affects themselves".[38] The differences between these strata are no longer differences in *nature*, but only in *degree*, or to be more precise and use an expression dear to Deleuze:

---

34 Deleuze/Guattari 1977: 21.
35 Deleuze/Guattari 1977: 21. Deleuze and Guattari refer then to *Nietzsche et le cercle vicieux* from Pierre Klossowski: "The vision of the world granted to Nietzsche does not inaugurate a more or less regular succession of landscapes or still lifes, extending over a period of forty years or so; it is, rather, a parody of the process of recollection [*parodie remémorante*] of an event: a single actor will play the whole of it in pantomime in the course of a single solemn day – because the whole of it reaches expression and then disappears once again in the space of just one day – even though it may appear to have taken place between December 31 and January in a realm above and beyond the usual rational calendar." (Deleuze/Guattari 1977: 21f.).
36 Deleuze/Guattari 1994: 65.
37 See NL 1885, 41[11], KSA 11: 687, my translation.
38 JGB 36, KSA 5: 55; Nietzsche 2003: 36.

degrees of differentiation. The same principle would be at work in the inorganic world, in our body and in our thought. Undifferentiated and "contained in a powerful unity" in the inorganic world, this principle would branch off and organize itself in the organic world, and then in the world of mind. This fundamental principle is the will to power. Intellectual life and organic and preorganic life could be understood from this single principle.

> We *must* make the attempt to hypothetically posit the causality of the will as the only type of causality there is. "Will" can naturally have effects only on "will" – and not on "matter" (not on "nerves" for instance –): enough: we must venture the hypothesis [*Hypothese*] that everywhere "effects" are recognized, will is effecting will – and that every mechanistic event in which a force is active is really a force and effect of the will. – Assuming, finally, that we succeeded in explaining our entire life of drives as the organization [*Ausgestaltung*] and outgrowth [*Verzweigung*] of One basic form of will – namely, of the will to power, which is *my* proposition [*wie es* mein *Satz ist*] –; Assuming we could trace all organic functions back to this will to power and find that it even solved the problem of procreation and nutrition – which is a single problem –, then we will have earned the right to clearly designate *all* efficacious force as: *will to power*. The world seen from inside, the world determined and described with respect to its "intelligible character" – would be just this "will to power" and nothing besides [*wäre eben "Wille zur Macht" und nicht außerdem*]. –³⁹

In this paragraph 36 of *Beyond Good and Evil*, Nietzsche imitates the logical sequence of the classic philosophical demonstration, which is quite unusual in his writings. He assumes "our world of appetites and passions" to be a unique and fundamental fact, and comes to draw a conclusion on the general character of the world. Nietzsche derides here the "immediate certainties" of Descartes and Schopenhauer. In paragraph 16, he had previously criticized the way both of them developed their philosophical system from those immediate certainties. Descartes deduced the existence of God and the world from his "*Je pense* [I think]". Schopenhauer established that the will was "the most familiar thing in the world"⁴⁰ from his "*Ich will* [I will]", and developed his conception of the world as will and representation. Both committed the mistake of thinking that the "subject" ("I") was the "cause" of the act of thinking or willing. Nietzsche asked, "What gives me the right to speak about an I, and, for that matter, about an I as cause, and, finally, about an I as the cause of thoughts?"⁴¹

This will, which Nietzsche puts hypothetically as the "only type of causality there is", does not correspond either to Schopenhauer's will (it is not a "will to

---

39 JGB 36, KSA 5: 55; Nietzsche 2003: 36, translation modified.
40 JGB 19, KSA 5: 31–34; Nietzsche 2003: 18–20.
41 JGB 16, KSA 5: 30; Nietzsche 2003: 17.

live" presented as the most familiar thing we can know about ourselves), or to the Cartesian will (it is not the univocal expression of a conscious subject). It is the manifestation of a very complex instinctive world. Nietzsche's will is not the will of a conscious subject. The intentional use of several different words ("instincts [*Instinkte*]", "drives [*Triebe*]", "appetite [*Begierden*]", "passions [*Leidenschaften*]", "affects [*Affekte*]", "penchants [*Hänge*]", "inclinations [*Neigungen*]" and "aspirations [*Streben* or *Verlangen*]") indicates that Nietzsche refuses any simplification of this world, as Patrick Wotling points out.[42] Every entity we call "instinct" or "drive" hosts a very complex and composite reality. The will to power is not immediately accessible to us, as Schopenhauer's will was supposed to be. A certain methodical process is required to attain to the will to power. Paragraph 36 indeed proposes such a process: starting from our complex instinctive world (the only reality we can access), we should try to attain a more primitive form of instinct, a fundamental principle, a unique "causality", which would explain the totality of becoming: the will to power. According to Deleuze and Guattari, by "aborting" the unity of the subject, Nietzsche affirms "a properly angelic and superior unity",[43] that of the will to power.

The published works provide few details about the will to power. The unpubllished drafts are much more revealing. We know that Nietzsche had planned to write his principal work, which would be called *The Will to Power*. Thanks to Montinari, we also know that he abandoned this project for *The Antichrist*.[44] Perhaps Nietzsche intended to reserve the technical aspects of his will to power for his planned principal work? The draft contemporary with *Beyond Good and Evil* specifies that:

> Our drives [*Triebe*] are reducible to *the will to power*. The will to power is the ultimate fact [*letzte Factum*] at which we arrive.[45]

> Movements are symptoms, thoughts are also symptoms: we can detect appetites [*Begierden*] behind them both, and the fundamental appetite is the will to power.[46]

> The derivation [*Ableitung*] of all affects from the only [*dem Einen*] will to power: all identical in essence [*wesengleich*].[47]

---

42 Wotling 1999a: 45f., 77f.
43 Deleuze/Guattari 1987: 6.
44 See Souladié (2007).
45 NL 1885, 40[61], KSA 11: 661, my translation.
46 NL 1885–1886, 1[59], KSA 12: 25, my translation.
47 NL 1887, 10[57], KSA 12: 490, my translation. In NL 1884, 26[273], KSA 11: 221, Nietzsche also characterizes the will to power as the fundamental feeling: "the will to power [...] The development of all feelings from the fundamental feeling [Grundgefühle]."

Nietzsche intends to return to a unique and fundamental form of instinct, from which our most complex drives derive. Nietzsche identifies this fundamental form with an affect. The ultimate fact at which we arrive, the will to power, is "affect".

> That the will to power is the primitive form of affect [*primitive Affekt-Form*], that all other affects are but his arrangements [*Ausgestaltungen*].[48]

The affect–something [*etwas*]'s[49] ability to be attracted–appears as the fundamental fact. There are for Nietzsche no isolated substances, no isolated things; everything, every "something" is taken in a tangle of relations.

> *Phenomenal* is then: the interference of the concept of the number, the concept of the subject, the concept of the motion: we still have our *eye*, our *psychology* in there. Shall we eliminate these additions: there remain no things [*Dinge*], but dynamic quanta, in a relation of tension to all other dynamic quanta: whose essence [*Wesen*] consists in their relation to all other quanta, in their "work" [*Wirken*] on the same – the will to power not a being [*Sein*], not a becoming, but a *pathos* is the most elementary fact [*elementarste Thatsache*] from which only a becoming, a work arises...[50]

The will to power is essentially relational. There is only one fundamental fact, remote action:

> The "remote action" [*actio in distans*] must not be set aside: *something attracts* [heranziehen] *something else, something feels attracted* [gezogen]. This is the fundamental fact [*Grundthatsache*].[51]

As Pierre Montebello writes:

> No force exists separately, there are only struggles of forces, and in these struggles, every force is immediately affectively determined by the relation it has with the other forces. Without this relation, nothing would express itself as will to power; or to be more precise, the will to power would not express itself.[52]

The world "is essentially a relations-world [*Relations-Welt*]"[53]: "there is no being itself [*Wesen an sich*], only relations constitute beings [*Wesen*]".[54] Nietzsche

---

48 NL 1888, 14[121], KSA 13: 300, my translation.
49 Nietzsche uses the expression *etwas* (for example in NL 1885, 34[247], KSA 11: 503) to refer to an entity, in order to indeterminate it as much as possible.
50 NL 1888, 14[79], KSA 13: 259, my translation.
51 NL 1885, 34[247], KSA 11: 504, my translation.
52 Montebello 2001: 24, my translation.
53 NL 1888, 14[93], KSA 13: 271, my translation.
54 NL 1888, 14[122], KSA 13: 303, my translation.

rejects the concept of substance, including for the determination of the ultimate principle of the universe. The human being is not a stable subject; the will to power is no substance identical to itself. As Deleuze writes, "no one extended the critique of all forms of identity further than Nietzsche".[55]

Let us confront these drafts with the way Nietzsche presents the will to power in the previous quotation from paragraph 36 of *Beyond Good and Evil*. The hypothetical nature of the will to power in this text has often been highlighted. What should we think about it? To what purpose does Nietzsche first of all present his determination of the world as the will to power as a "hypothesis", to describe it a few lines further as "*my* proposition" [Nietzsche underlines "*my*"]? Does he simply intend to assert the personal and perspectival nature of this proposition? The latter would then represent only the limited point of view of the subject Friedrich Nietzsche? Would this text propose only an isolated interpretation, which would have no more validity or weight than any other interpretation? Does this text set up a philosophical relativism, intended to assert the impossibility of a universal truth?

This seems to be contradicted, not only by the drafts, but also by the published texts. In Nietzsche's works, the will to power does not have a solely hypothetical nature. Zarathustra says that this principle can be found in the very heart of life:

> Now hear my word, you wisest ones! Test seriously whether I have stolen into the heart of life itself and right down to the roots of its heart! Wherever I found a living thing, there I found the will to power; and even in the will of the servant I found the will to be master.[56]

Beyond Good and Evil itself presents the will to power as a reality and not as a simple hypothesis: paragraph 13 claims that "life itself is will to power",[57] paragraph 186 that the "essence [*Essenz*]" of the world "is will to power",[58] and paragraph 259 that each body, if it is living and not dying,

> will have to be the embodiment of will to power, it will want to grow, spread, grab, win dominance, – not out of any morality or immorality, but because it is *alive*, and because life *is* precisely will to power. [...] it is a result of genuine will to power, which is just the will of life.[59]

---

55 Deleuze (1986), *Nietzsche and Philosophy*, "Preface to the English translation", XI.
56 Z II, Von der Selbst-Überwindung, KSA 4: 147f.; Nietzsche 2003: 87.
57 JGB 13, KSA 5: 27; Nietzsche 2002: 15.
58 JGB 186, KSA 5: 107, my translation.
59 JGB 259, KSA 5: 208; Nietzsche 2002: 153.

Similar propositions can be found in *On the Genealogy of Morality*: it mentions thie "democratic idiosyncrasy" which misunderstands "the essence [*Wesen*] of life, its *will to power*".[60] *The Case of Wagner* also presents "the will to power as the principle of life"[61] Finally in *The Antichrist*, Nietzsche bases his physiological and axiological conceptions on the will to power.[62]

Why does Nietzsche propose the will to power as a hypothesis in BGE 36, while asserting in another paragraph of *Beyond Good and Evil* that "life *is* precisely [*eben*] will to power"[63]? Is his philosophy based on contradiction, as maintained by Jaspers, Granier and Biser,[64] amongst others? As for Deleuze, he refuses this kind of interpretative artifice. According to him, Nietzsche's philosophy "forms an absolute anti-dialectics"[65] and "in fact, to the eye of the genealogist, the labour of the negative is only a coarse approximation to the games of the will to power".[66] Rejecting the "negative premises", the "two negations" which produce "a phantom of affirmation",[67] and which are the very essential feature of resentment, Nietzsche opposes "the affirmation of affirmation" to the "famous negation of the negation".[68] Far from considering that the nature of the will to power is contradictory or simply hypothetical, Deleuze claims that "affirmation remains as the sole quality of the will to power".[69]

Actually, the use of words belonging to the language of logic ("assuming [*gesetzt*]", "given [*Gegeben*]", "suffices [*ausreicht*]", "by definition [*aus ihrer Definition*]", "hypothesis [*Hypothese*]") in paragraph 36 of *Beyond Good and Evil* is rather unusual for Nietzsche, and should warn us to be cautious. Does this terminology indicate that Nietzsche tried to base his determination of the world as the will to power on logic? And that he came to the conclusion that he could only determinate it as a hypothesis? That doesn't really sound like Nietzsche. Would he not rather use this terminology the same way he uses biblical and Christian terminology in *Thus Spoke Zarathustra*? That is to say, as parody? Nietzsche seems to make fun of metaphysics and of the heuristic claims of its logical demonstration. But going beyond parody, this logical terminology under-

---

60 GM II 12, KSA 5: 316, my translation.
61 WA, Epilog, KSA 6: 51, my translation.
62 AC 2, 6, 17, KSA 6: 170, 172, 183.
63 JGB 259, KSA 5: 208; Nietzsche 2002: 153. Nietzsche underlines.
64 Karl Jaspers (1952); Eugen Biser (1985: 97); Jean Granier (1966: 11).
65 Deleuze 1986: 195.
66 Deleuze 1986: 157f.
67 Deleuze 1986: 196.
68 Deleuze 1986: 197.
69 Deleuze 1986: 198.

lines the importance of scientific method, which Nietzsche distinguishes from logical demonstration (he thus underlines the word "method" in this paragraph). "*Methods* are the most valuable insights", he writes in The Antichrist.[70]

In paragraph 36 of *Beyond Good and Evil*, Nietzsche first presents the universality of "the causality of the will" as a "hypothesis [*Hypothese*]". However, a few lines further he affirms that, "explaining our entire life of drives as the organization [*Ausgestaltung*] and outgrowth [*Verzweigung*] of One basic form of will – namely, of the will to power" is "mein *Satz*", that is, "my thesis" or "*my proposition*".

It seems now necessary to dwell on this word "*Satz*". Nietzsche's "*Satz*" refers to the explanation of "our entire life of drives as the organization and outgrowth of One basic form of will – namely, of the will to power", as *his*. In mathematics, the word "*Satz*" can mean "proposition", in some cases "theorem" or even "axiom", but it remains relatively unused.[71] In philosophy, "*Satz*" means "sentence", "proposition", "thesis", "article [of law]" and, more to the point, "principle".

In philosophy, "*die Hypothese*" is usually associated with "*die These*", the former being more cautious, awaiting the confirmation of a theory, while "*die These*" takes its own theory for granted. Nietzsche does not answer this *Hypothese* with a simple *These*, but with *his Satz*. In doing so, he points out that he does not intend to demonstrate the validity of his theory by following the rules of formal logic, from which he ironically borrows the terminology in the beginning of this paragraph. The use of "*Satz*" indicates that Nietzsche defends much more than a simple thesis. "*Satz*", which is often used in the last works, particularly in *The Antichrist*,[72] should be understood as "proposition" or "principle". The word "*Satz*" indicates that the reason why Nietzsche is able to propose the interpretation of the world as the "'will to power' and nothing besides" is only because he himself is also will to power. Or it is only because the will to power is also his own principle, *his Satz*. I, Friedrich Nietzsche, understand the world as the will to power, because the will to power is *my own physiological principle*; because the will to power also constitutes me. I too, Friedrich Nietzsche, am the will to power and nothing besides. Nietzsche writes in a preparatory draft of

---

70 A 13; AC 13, KSA 6: 179, my translation.
71 "*Ausgabe*", "*Theorem*" or "*Lehrsatz*", "*Axiom*" are more usual.
72 See for example: "The weak and the failures should perish: first principle [*Satz*] of *our* love of mankind." (A 2; AC 2, KSA 6: 170, my translation); "Here I will touch on the problem of the *origin* of Christianity. The *first* principle [*Satz*] for solving this problem is [...] The second principle [*Satz*] is [...]" (A 24; AC 24, KSA 6: 191, my translation); and of course the "principles" or "articles" of the "Law against Christianity": "*Erster Satz*", etc. (KSA 6: 254).

paragraph 36 of *Beyond Good and Evil*: "*This world is the will to power – and nothing besides!* And you yourselves are also this will to power – and nothing besides! [*und nicht außerdem*]".[73]

Nietzsche does not claim that his determination of the world as the will to power is a mere hypothesis, one which might be no more valid or true than any other hypothesis, as has sometimes been argued.[74] Nietzsche's assertion of this proposition is the fruit of his most intimate experiences. Its presentation as a hypothesis may be understood as the consequence of a methodological approach: the determination of the world as the will to power is the fruit of an affirmation, not the outcome of a scientific thesis presented as objective. Thus the determination of the world as the will to power is not purely hypothetical. Nietzsche does not write that this determination is "*meine Hypothese*". The determination of the world as the will to power is neither dogmatic, nor simply hypothetical: it is problematic.

Deleuze emphasises the fact that the will to power is an "internal principle of determination",[75] it corresponds to "the world seen from inside".[76] It is not possible to understand the world as the will to power and nothing besides, if you do not feel yourself to be the will to power and nothing besides. Nietzsche's proposition is neither a thesis nor a logical demonstration: it is the fruit of an intimate experience. Being able to assert such a proposition implies that you have yourself felt the affirmative power of the will to power, that you have experimented with this value-creating power on your own body. It implies that your body has itself been the site of a transvaluation of values.

Thus, Nietzsche affirms that the world is the will to power. He does not demonstrate it. Nietzsche does not present himself as the one who has discovered the essence of the world, the will to power. He only sets the fundamentally affirmative nature of the will to power.[77]

What paragraph 36 of *Beyond Good and Evil* suggests is that our understanding of the world, whatever it is, is determined by our own intimate experiences. You can understand the world as the will to power and nothing besides, only if you feel that you are a part of this world; that you are merging with this world.

---

[73] NL 1885, 38[12], KSA 11: 611, my translation.
[74] See for example Wotling 1999b: 81f.
[75] Deleuze 1986: 52. If Deleuze makes an obvious mistake on the will to power (see our first note), he was nevertheless among the firsts to highlight the conceptual importance of this will to power within the philosophy of Nietzsche. See Deleuze 1986: 49–64.
[76] JGB 36, KSA 5: 55; Nietzsche 2002: 36.
[77] See Deleuze 1986: 198.

Conversely, the opposite principle to Nietzsche's *Satz*, its *Gegensatz*, would be to understand this world through something apart from it, outside of it. That would entail either projecting the meaning of this world onto an afterworld, a suprasensible metaphysical world, or even when you have suppressed the metaphysical world, to understand it through the schema of reason, as materialism does. If you cannot achieve an understanding of the world as the will to power and nothing besides, it is because you *feel* this world and its explosions of power as something external. It is because you are yourself an opposite principle, not to the will to power (for everything is will to power), but to the rising will to power, to the intensification of power, because you cannot be at one with this world.

> This world: a monster of energy [*Kraft*], without beginning, without end [...] a sea of forces flowing and rushing together, eternally changing, eternally flooding back, with tremendous years of recurrence, with an ebb and a flood of its forms; out of the simplest forms striving toward the most complex, out of the stillest, most rigid, coldest forms toward the hottest, most turbulent, most self-contradictory, and then again returning home to the simple out of this abundance, out of the play of contradictions back to the joy of concord, still affirming itself in this uniformity of its courses and its years, blessing itself as that which must return eternally, as a becoming that knows no satiety, no disgust, no weariness: this, my *Dionysian* world of the eternally self-creating, the eternally self-destroying, this mystery world of the twofold voluptuous delight [...][78]

Deleuze would say that the reactive forces prevent us from understanding this Dionysian world. In fact it is the morality of resentment that turns us against the world: we understand it from the outside because, from a physiological point of view, we feel this world as a "*Gegenwelt*", as a "counter-world".

> In order to come about, slave morality first has to have an opposing, external world [*Gegen- und Außenwelt*], it needs, physiologically speaking, external stimuli in order to act at all, – its action is basically a reaction. The opposite is the case with the noble [*vornehmen*] method of valuation: this acts and grows spontaneously, seeking out its opposite [*Gegensatz*] only so that it can say "yes" to itself even more thankfully and exultantly, – its negative concept "low", "common", "bad" is only a pale contrast created after the event compared to its positive basic concept, saturated with life and passion, "we the noble, the good, the beautiful and the happy!"[79]

If "the bad ones", the upholders of the morality of resentment, need counter-people ("evil ones") to establish their system of values,[80] they also need a

---

[78] NL 1885, 38[12], KSA 11: 610f.; trans. Kaufman, Hollingdale: WP 1067, p. 550.
[79] GM I 10, KSA 5: 271; Nietzsche 1994: 20.
[80] GM I 10, KSA 5: 270–274.

counter-world. Indeed, they can only determine the world as an *"Außenwelt"*, that is as an external world, and as a *"Gegenwelt"*; that is as a world which they conceive as standing up against them, a hostile world, literally a counter-world. We find here the problem of the subjectivity: *die Gegenwelt* can also be approximated to *der Gegenstand* (the object). As Deleuze and Guattari assert,

> Subject and object give a poor approximation of thought. Thinking is neither a line drawn between subject and object nor a revolving of one around another. Rather, thinking takes places in the relationship of territory and the earth.[81]

The precedence of the subject contributed to the impoverishment of thinking. Thought remained dominated by reactive forces.[82] The philosophies of the subject establish a faulty relationship with the earth, a twisted link to the world. Its thinkers are not able to merge with our world. By understanding themselves as reasonable, conscious subjects, they only conceive of it as an external world that has risen against them, as an "object world".

To conclude, we should note that for Nietzsche, any philosophy which professes a morality of resentment or postulates that thinking is an attribute of a subject[83] is not simply in error but is the expression of "decadence".[84] The human being has for too long inhabited "the dark side of earth".[85]

References

Biser, Eugen (1985) "The Critical Imitator of Jesus", in: James C. O'Flaherty and Timothy F. Sellner (eds.), *Studies in Nietzsche and the Judeo-Christian Tradition*, Chapel Hill/London: The University of North Carolina Press, 86–99.
Deleuze, Gilles (1986) *Nietzsche and Philosophy*, trans. H. Tomlinson, London/New York: Continuum.
Deleuze, Gilles (1988) *Le pli. Leibniz et le baroque*, Paris: Minuit.
Deleuze, Gilles (1990) *Pourparlers 1972–1990*, Paris: Minuit.
Deleuze, Gilles (2004) *L'Abécédaire*, Paris: DVD Editions Montparnasse.
Deleuze, Gilles/Guattari, Félix (1977) *Anti-Oedipus*, trans. R. Hurley, M. Seem and H.R. Lane, Minneapolis/London: University of Minnesota Press.
Deleuze, Gilles/Guattari, Félix (1980) *Mille plateaux*, Paris: Minuit.

---

81 Deleuze/Guattari 1994: 85.
82 See Deleuze 1986: 58–61.
83 Descartes 1992, II: 77.
84 See for example GD, Das Problem der Sokrates 1–2, KSA 6: 67f.
85 See Deleuze 1986: 198. I would like to deeply thank Charles Lomas for his proofreading and his advices.

Deleuze, Gilles/Guattari, Félix (1987) *A Thousand Plateaus*, trans. B. Massumi, Minneapolis/London: University of Minnesota Press.

Deleuze, Gilles/Guattari, Félix (1991) *Qu'est-ce que la philosophie?*, Paris: Minuit.

Deleuze, Gilles/Guattari, Félix (1994) *What is Philosophy?*, trans. H. Tomlinson and G. Burchell, New York: Columbia University Press.

Descartes, René (1992) *Méditations Métaphysiques*, Paris: Flammarion.

Granier, Jean (1966) *Le problème de la vérité dans la philosophie de Nietzsche*, Paris: Editions du Seuil.

Jaspers, Karl (1952) *Nietzsche und das Christentum*, Munich: R. Piper & Co.

Montebello, Pierre (2001) *Nietzsche. La volonté de puissance*, Paris: Presses Universitaires de France.

Montebello, Pierre (2003) *L'autre métaphysique*, Paris: Desclée de Brouwer.

Montebello, Pierre (2011) "Deleuze, Une Anti-Phénoménologie?", in *Chiasmi International* 13 ("Merleau-Ponty Fifty Years After His Death"), 315–325.

Montinari, Mazzino (1997) *"La Volonté de puissance" n'existe pas*, trans. P. Farazzi and M. Valensi, Paris: Editions de l'Eclat.

Müller-Lauter, Wolfgang (1974) "Nietzsches Lehre vom Willen zur Macht", in *Nietzsche-Studien* 3, 1–60.

Nietzsche, Friedrich (1942) *La volonté de puissance*, ed. F. Würzbach, trans. G. Bianquis, Paris: Gallimard.

Nietzsche Friedrich (2003) *Thus spoke Zarathustra*, trans. T. Wayne, New York: Algora Publishing.

Nietzsche, Friedrich (2011) *Dernières lettres*, ed. and trans. Y. Souladié, Paris: Editions Manucius.

Nietzsche, Friedrich (2012) *Ecce Homo. How To Become What You Are*, trans. D. Large, Oxford: Oxford University Press.

Rigal, Elisabeth (2003) "Désubjectivation", in: *Le vocabulaire de Gilles Deleuze*, eds. R. Sasso and A. Villani, *Les Cahiers de Noesis* 3, 75–81.

Souladié, Yannick (2007) "L'*Inversion* contra *La volonté de puissance*", in: Y. Souladié (ed.), *Nietzsche. L'Inversion des valeurs*, Hildesheim: Olms, 4–25.

Whitehead, Alfred North (1969) *Process and Reality*, New York: Free Press.

Wotling, Patrick (1999a) *La pensée du sous-sol. Statut et structure de la psychologie dans la philosophie de Nietzsche*, Paris: Éditions Allia.

Wotling, Patrick (1999b) *Nietzsche et le problème de la civilisation*, Paris: Presses Universitaires de France.

Keith Ansell-Pearson
16 Questions of the Subject in Nietzsche and Foucault: A Reading of *Dawn*

> Perhaps no nineteenth-century thinker or writer has shaped contemporary discussions of selfhood more than Friedrich Nietzsche ... many who declare themselves his disciples emphasize his pioneering and sharp criticism of traditional notions about the self, his powerful denials that the ego is or can be coherent or stable, and that human beings should be regarded as "subjects" in the senses presumed by science, morality, or citizenship. Nietzsche's powerful rejection of such views has provided much ammunition and inspiration for later thinkers who have found reason to announce or welcome the death of the self, the author, or the subject
>
> (Seigel 2005: 537).

> The path towards the self will always be something of an Odyssey
> (Foucault 2005: 249).

1

We have to acknowledge that Foucault's interest in Nietzsche took place under quite specific conditions and is far from being intellectually neutral. These conditions were those of French academic culture in the post Second World War period. As Foucault himself pointed out, those who sought recourse to Nietzsche at this time were looking for a way out of phenomenology (Foucault 1990: 24, 31). For a figure like Foucault the attempt to break free of phenomenology was motivated by the desire to develop an intellectual programme that was not governed – as was seen to be the case with phenomenology – by a philosophy of the subject. In interviews Foucault repeatedly maintained that he was profoundly suspicious of the attempt to ground philosophy on the basis of a sovereign, founding subject, "a universal form of subject to be found everywhere". Foucault says he is not only sceptical of this position but also deeply hostile to it. His contrary belief is that the subject "is constituted through practices of subjection, or, in a more autonomous way, through practices of liberation, as in Antiquity, on the basis, of course, of a number of rules, styles, inventions to be found in the cultural environment" (Foucault 1990: 50 – 51).

With respect to Nietzsche it was his great achievement for Foucault to show that there was a *history* of the subject. It is perhaps for this reason that in one interview Foucault declared, "I am simply Nietzschean" (1990: 251).¹ This, of course, begs the question: just what is it to be Nietzschean? This is especially difficult to work through in the case of a figure like Nietzsche where, with respect to his experimental texts, there is little in the way of settled views or consensus on the meaning of the many topics we encounter in them, including the question of the subject. As Foucault himself admits, "I do not believe there is a single Nietzscheanism ... or that ours is any truer than others" (1990: 31). For his "post-modern" commentators, from Foucault to Vattimo, Nietzsche deconstructs and dissolves the subject. But then we are faced with some problems, and let me mention two: (a) how do we explain Nietzsche's appeal, running throughout his writings, to our becoming those that we are (unique, singular, incomparable, *self-creating, self-legislating*)? (b) how do we account for the interest in the self and the subject shown by Foucault in what we now call his late writings?

As Beatrice Han has done much to point out, it's unclear how the later stress in Foucault on a self-constituting ethical subjectivity is compatible with the genealogical analysis of techniques of subjection and historical constitution of the subject (see Han 2002: 11, 169, 184–185). However this issue is resolved it's clear that Foucault came to regard the constitution of an ethics of the self as an urgent, fundamental, and politically indispensable task (see Foucault 2005: 252). As one commentator has noted, "Given our current political and ethical situation, an ethics of the self would represent one critical point of resistance" (McGushin 2005: 630). Conceptions of the subject and of subjectivity operate on two levels: first, on the discursive or theoretical level and which allows us to comprehend the function of power; and, second, on the practical level in terms of "a tactical intervention in the deployment of resistance to power" (McGushin 2005: 630).

Some commentators, such as Peter Dews, see Foucault's so-called return to the subject as an abrupt turn (Dews 1989), whilst others, notably Deleuze, see no such return at all in his work simply because questions of subjectification have little to do with a subject or persons and more to do with an individuated field of intensities (Deleuze 1995: 92–93, 98–99). Foucault himself said his concern was threefold: How are we constituted as subjects of our own knowledge? How are we constituted as subjects who exercise or submit to power relations? How are we constituted as moral subjects of our own actions? (Foucault 2007: 117) If we turn our attention to Nietzsche we encounter a similarly compli-

---

1 On this statement see Oksala 2005: 183. In an interview with Stephen Riggins, Foucault says that it was Nietzsche, and no-one else, who inspired him to undertake his own personal intellectual work. See Foucault 1997: 125.

cated picture. Nietzsche is well-known for his hermeneutics of suspicion towards free will and the primacy of consciousness. In his writings he does much to show that the ego or self is not master in its own house and to argue that we need to pay closer attention to the body, to the unconscious, and to our drives. And yet, we also find in Nietzsche repeated appeals to self-mastery (and self-overcoming) as the goal of an art of living.

Deleuze is especially helpful, I think, on these points. He acknowledges the new dimension in Foucault's work and asks after its name, "this relation to oneself that is neither knowledge nor power ... the affect of self by self ..." (Deleuze 1995: 106). Foucault's focus, then, is on techniques of the self and how to conceive of an aesthetics of existence (how we fashion ourselves as a work of art). It's widely thought that Foucault turns, and once again, to Nietzsche for inspiration on this point (see Sluga 2003: 235), but what's surprising about the late work on ethics is the lack of references to Nietzsche and to the "witty and graceful texts" of the middle period that so appealed to him (see Foucault 1990: 33). We get only general references to Nietzsche's idea of creating the self as a work of art. However, it is true that for both Nietzsche and Foucault what is at stake is not our finding ourselves or realizing a true or authentic self.

Let me first explore Foucault's appropriation of Nietzsche for the ends of anti-humanism, and then turn for the rest of the essay to this concern with ethical self-formation. Here I shall focus on Nietzsche's *Dawn*, a text of 1881 which I believe can be fruitfully read as a text of ethical resistance to the normalizing tendencies of biopolitical society. This is a possibility Foucault did not see in the text since at the time he was interested in it, around the early 1970s, his main concern was with the destruction of the subject (of knowledge) and not the theme of the care of self.

2

As an anti-humanist thinker *par excellence* Foucault did much in his work of the 1960s and 1970s to dethrone the primacy of the subject within philosophical and scientific discourse. Doing philosophy in the days of his training, the early 1950s, meant doing the history of philosophy where the dominant influences were Hegel and phenomenology. Here the history of philosophy was delimited by, on the one hand, Hegel's theory of systems, and, on the other hand, by a philosophy of the subject. Foucault writes: "I chose not to be a historian of philosophy like my professors and ... I decided to look for something completely different from existentialism" (Foucault 2001: 247). He found this in Nietzscheanism (especially the work of Bataille and Blanchot), which represented for him two things:

(i) an invitation to call into question the category of the subject, namely its foundational function and supremacy.
(ii) Second, converting this operation into an experience that leads to its destruction and explosion.

Here we see Foucault's specific interest in the subject is in the nature of the limit-experience in which the subject is dissolved and even destroyed. In the mid-1970s the interest in the subject shifts as Foucault's focus is on a history of the microphysics of power in terms of a genealogy of the modern soul in which, along with many other things, the primacy of the subject as a foundation of knowledge is abandoned and attention is focused on the constitution of individuals "as correlative elements of power and knowledge" (Foucault 1977a: 194). In a late text Foucault declared that the general theme of his research was not, as commonly supposed, power but the subject, in particular his concern is with how we are transformed into subjects *and* how we transform ourselves into subjects (Foucault 1982: 208). Whatever we think of the status of Foucault's thinking on the subject, it is clear that the topic is at the centre of his concerns. What is difficult to work through and make cohere is the changing fate of the subject in his corpus.

It is clear that Nietzsche occupies a special place in Foucault's intellectual development. There are at least three main phases in his development: first, the interest in the limit-experience; second, the concern with genealogy and the destruction of the subject of knowledge; and third, the interest in the care of self. Let me now focus on the second development. In several of his writings Foucault appeals to Nietzsche to account for an anti-humanist break within the history of modern philosophy. This break centres on the very subject of knowledge. Above all, Foucault wants to show that the subject of knowledge itself has a history in which the relation of the subject to the object, or truth itself, has a history (Foucault 2001: 2). The focus is how social practices engender new domains of knowledge which bring to light not only new objects, new concepts, and new techniques, but also new forms of subjectivity and subjects of knowledge. The key claim is that there is no *given* subject of knowledge. This means that the subject is not foundational with respect to questions of knowledge, including its production, promotion, and advancement. Although Foucault mentions psychoanalysis, and its discovery of the prodigious terrain of the unconscious, as a key theory and practice that has re-evaluated in a quite fundamental way the sacred priority conferred on the subject and established in the Western tradition since Descartes, it is to Nietzsche that Foucault appeals the most. In a key admission he writes:

> ... I would like to pick up again, in a different way, the methodological reflections I spoke of earlier. It would have been possible, and perhaps more honest, to cite only one name, that of Nietzsche, because what I say here won't mean anything if it isn't connected to

Nietzsche's work, which seems to me to be the best, the most effective, the most pertinent of the models that one can draw upon (Foucault 2001: 5).

For Foucault, Nietzsche's significance resides in the fact that he undertakes a historical analysis of the formation of the subject, involving an analysis of the birth of a certain type of knowledge (*savoir*) that does not grant the pre-existence of a subject of knowledge (*connaissance*). Rather, knowledge is invented, it is an *Erfindung*. And to say that it is invented is to say that it is without origin:

> More precisely, it is to say, however paradoxical this may be, that knowledge is absolutely not inscribed in human nature. Knowledge doesn't constitute man's oldest instinct; and, conversely, in human behaviour, the human appetite, the human instinct, there is no such thing as the seed of knowledge (Foucault 2001: 8).

But more than this we can also say that, in addition to not being bound up with human nature, it is also not intimately connected to the world to be known. This means that there is no resemblance or prior affinity between knowledge and the things that need to be known, or, expressed in Kantian terms, we can say that the conditions of experience and the conditions of the object of experience are completely heterogeneous. For Foucault, and I quote:

> This is the great break with the prior tradition of Western philosophy, for Kant himself has been the first to say explicitly that the conditions of experience and those of the object of experience were identical. Nietzsche thinks, on the contrary, that between knowledge and the world to be known there is as much difference as between knowledge and human nature. So one has a human nature, a world, and something called knowledge between the two, without any affinity, resemblance, or even natural tie between them (Foucault 2001: 9).

Foucault cites from *Dawn* 45 and that heralds a "tragic ending for knowledge" (see Foucault 1977b: 164). Here Nietzsche notes that it is human sacrifice that has traditionally served as the means of producing exaltation; this sacrifice has both elevated and exalted the human being. What if mankind were to now *sacrifice itself*: to whom would it make the sacrifice? Nietzsche suggests that it would be the knowledge of truth since only here could the goal be said to be commensurate with the sacrifice, "because for this goal no sacrifice is too great".[2] But this goal remains too distant and lofty; much closer to home is the task of working out the extent to which humanity can take steps towards the advancement of knowledge and ascertaining what kind of knowledge-drive could impel

---

[2] See also on this GM II 7, in which Nietzsche notes that life has always known how to play tricks so as to justify itself, including its "evil", and today, for us moderns and free spirits, this takes the form of "life as a riddle, life as a problem of knowledge".

it to the point of extinction "with the light of an anticipatory wisdom in its eyes". However, we may need the help of other species on other planets in order to pursue the practice of knowledge with enthusiasm:

> Perhaps one day, once an alliance for the purpose of knowledge has been established with inhabitants of other planets and one has communicated one's knowledge from star to star for a few millennia: perhaps then enthusiasm for knowledge will swell to such a high tide! (D 45)

Foucault places the passion of knowledge in the service of a philosophical project that aims at disabusing humanity of its consoling fictions and encouraging it to pursue new truths and a new kind of philosophical wisdom. Foucault writes of this passion in a number of places, perhaps most poignantly and incisively in the Introduction to the second volume of his *History of Sexuality* on the use of pleasure. Foucault speaks of what motivates his intellectual work and declares it to be curiosity – not the curiosity that assimilates what it is proper for one to know but the kind that enables one to get free of oneself. As Foucault asks:

> After all, what would be the value of the passion for knowledge if it resulted only in a certain amount of knowledgeableness and not, in one way or another and to the extent possible, in the knower's straying afield of himself? (Foucault 1985: 8)

The task is to break with accustomed habits of knowing and perceiving, so that one has the chance to become something different than what one's history has conditioned one to be, to think and perceive differently. For Foucault this gives us, in fact, a definition of philosophical activity today, which consists in the critical work that thought brings to bear on itself. Instead, of legitimating what is already known the task is to think differently, and this is an essential part of philosophical activity conceived as an *askēsis*.

In his celebrated essay on "Nietzsche, Genealogy, and History", Foucault puts the passion of knowledge in the service of an anti-humanist intellectual agenda and project. Nietzsche's aim, contends Foucault, is not to capture the essence of things or their purest possibilities and protected identities since this is to assume "the existence of immobile forms that precede the world of accident and succession" (Foucault 1977b: 142). Continuing this anti-Platonic agenda, Foucault writes of a search for what is already there waiting to be uncovered, "the image of a primordial truth fully adequate to its nature" and that requires "the removal of every mask to ultimately disclose an original identity" (Foucault 1977b: 142). Replacing metaphysics with (genealogical) history, Nietzsche finds not timeless and eternal secrets behind things, but the secret that they have no essence or that if such an essence exists it was fabricated in a piecemeal manner from alien forms. The history of reason demonstrates that it was born from chance, so that what is found at the historical beginning of things is not the inviolable identity of their origin but rather disparity. In a radical moment Foucault further contends:

> Genealogy does not resemble the evolution of a species and does not map the destiny of a people. On the contrary, to follow the complex course of descent is to maintain passing events in their proper dispersion; it is to identify the accidents, the minute deviations – or conversely, the complete reversals – the errors, the false appraisals, and the faulty calculations that gave birth to those things that continue to exist and have value for us; it is to discover that truth or being do not lie at the root of what we know and what we are, but the exteriority of accidents (Foucault 1977b: 146).

The history of humanity is a series of interpretations; this history is not one that requires the slow exposure of a meaning hidden in the origin since if it was then only metaphysics could make sense of the development of humanity. Instead we need to conceive interpretation as "the violent or surreptitious appropriation of a system of rules, which in itself has no essential meaning" (Foucault 1977b: 151). When we conceive interpretation in this way it becomes possible to bend it to a new will and impose a different direction. This is to practice what Foucault calls "effective history" that does away with constants, including the constant of humanity and of being ourselves in our identity:

> Knowledge, even under the banner of history, does not depend on "rediscovery", and it emphatically excludes the "rediscovery of ourselves". History becomes "effective" to the degree that it introduces discontinuity into our very being – as it divides our emotions, dramatizes our instincts, multiplies our body and sets it against itself (Foucault 1977b: 154).

This "effective" history, which Nietzsche starts to practice in earnest in *Dawn*, deprives the self of any reassuring stability of life and nature. This is because, as Foucault has it, knowledge is not made so much for understanding as it is for "cutting" (*trancher*). The task is to make ourselves different to what history has, in fact, made us. We need to appreciate that the forces that operate in history do not conform to destiny or are subject to the control of regulative mechanisms: events are singular and even random.

Foucault illuminates this realm of chance as follows: the world that can be known is not one where events are reduced so as to accentuate their essential traits, their final meaning, and their ultimate value. Rather, what is to be encountered in "a profusion of entangled events", in which what appears as profound and meaningful is, in fact, something that begins its existence through a host of errors and phantasms: "We want historians to confirm our belief that the present rests upon profound intentions and immutable necessities. But the true historical sense confirms our existence among countless lost events, without a landmark or a point of reference" (Foucault 1977b: 154). For Foucault, then, history has a more important task than to be a handmaiden to (metaphysical) philosophy, such as recounting the necessary birth of truth and values. Rather, it needs to become a differential knowledge, one of energies and failings, of heights and degenerations of poisons and antidotes; in short, its "task is to become a curative science" (Foucault 1977b: 156).

As we have seen, Foucault takes extremely seriously Nietzsche's insight that the passion of knowledge may entail the perishing of humanity. In short, what is signalled here is the double death of God and of man – that is, of man as *the* very "subject" of knowledge:

> Even in the greatly expanded form it assumes today, the will to knowledge does not achieve a universal truth; man is not given an exact and serene mastery of nature. On the contrary, it ceaselessly multiplies the risk, creates dangers in every area; it breaks down illusory defences; it dissolves the unity of the subject; it releases those elements of itself that are devoted to its subversion and destruction. Knowledge does not slowly detach itself from its empirical roots, the initial needs from which it arose, to become pure speculation subject only to the demands of reason; its development is not tied to the constitution and affirmation of a free subject ...(Foucault 1977b: 163)

What Foucault acutely recognises is that where once religion demanded the sacrifice of our bodies, knowledge now calls for Nietzsche for an experimentation on ourselves, and this requires we "sacrifice" the subject of knowledge.

Two key points emerge from Foucault's rather dense presentation of the claims of the enterprise of genealogy: (a) firstly, inquiry cannot lay claim to a truth that would be detached and timeless, but rather needs to see itself as a practical took for the critique of values; (b) secondly, such a critique of values must destroy the idea of a fixed human identity, so that instead of positing solid identities we learn to engage in a radical experimentation with ourselves (see Sluga 2003: 228). As Nietzsche himself puts it in *Dawn* 453, we *are* experiments and the task is to *want* to be such.

3

This, then, is the critique of the subject we find in Foucault's writings up to the point of his late writing and so-called ethical turn. With this turn the focus of his attention shifts quite dramatically from the production of the subject through regimes of power-knowledge to how the subject produces itself through a form of ethical life and involving technologies of the self. At the outset we can note that his concern is not with the self as "substance" but as "activity". Foucault points out that "self" is a reflexive pronoun that has two meanings: "auto" means the same but also conveys the notion of identity. The latter meaning shifts the question from the essentialist question, what is the self?, to the different question, what is the plateau on which I shall find my identity? We can find the self in a dialectical movement: taking care of the body is not taking care of the self since the self is not clothing, tools, or possessions, so the concern is over the soul or psyche (*psukhē*) and to be conceived, as already pointed out, as activity and not substance. Later in the text Foucault will say: "Theoretically, the cultivation of the self is soul-oriented, but all the concerns of the body take on a considerable importance" (Foucault 1997: 234).

As Johanna Oksala has pointed out, Foucault must be presupposing a subject that enjoys some relative independence with regard to the constitutive power-knowledge network and as a way of positing a subject that is capable of critical self-reflection and ethical work on the self (Oksala 2005: 165; see also 191–192). Here we now have a subject, as Deleuze appreciates, capable of turning back on itself and of critically examining the processes of its own constitution and bringing about changes in them. This, of course, is what Foucault calls an ethics centred on the care of self. It is this new ethical subject, this care of self, that is, I believe, relevant to an appreciation of the moment of *Dawn*, perhaps the most neglected text in Nietzsche's corpus but in my view one of his most fertile and relevant texts today. To date there has been little speculation on how the Foucault of the 1980s would read Nietzsche. As one commentator has it: "Certainly, Nietzsche's work is highly suggestive of a rich array of practices of care of the self. But this is not the place to begin an exploration of that type" (McGushin 2007: 277–278).[3] Before turning to Nietzsche and this text let me outline some principal features of Foucault's conception of the care of self.

For Foucault self-cultivation takes the form of an "art of existence"–a *technē tou biou*–and is guided by the principle that one must "take care of oneself" (Foucault 1986: 43). Foucault claims that care of self (*epimeleia heautou*) is a Socratic notion or one that Socrates "consecrates" (Foucault 1986: 44). However, it only becomes a universal philosophical theme in the Hellenistic period, being promoted by the likes of Epicurus, the Cynics, and Stoics such as Seneca. Foucault insists that taking care of one's self does not simply mean being interested in oneself or having an attachment to or fascination with the self. Rather, "it describes a sort of work, an activity; it implies attention, knowledge, technique" (Foucault 1997: 269).

---

3 For notable work in this area see Urpeth 1998 and Milchman/Rosenberg 2007.

According to Foucault, the Delphic injunction to know one's self was subordinated to self-care. He gives several examples from the literature to vindicate his core thesis, including Epicurus's letter to Menoeceus, a text in which it is stated that it is never too early or too late to occupy oneself with oneself: "Teachings about everyday life were organized around taking care of oneself in order to help every member of the group with the mutual work of salvation" (Foucault 1988: 21; see also 1986: 46). For Foucault it is in Epictetus that we find the highest philosophical development of the theme of care of self. For Epictetus the human is destined to care for itself and is where the basic difference between the human and other creatures resides. Moreover, for Epictetus the care of self "is a privilege-duty, a gift-obligation that ensures our freedom while forcing us to take ourselves as the object of all our diligence" (Foucault 1986: 47). For Foucault the care of self is not constituted as an exercise in solitude but as a "true social practice" (Foucault 1986: 51). He is keen to stress that the "conversion to self" entails the experience of a pleasure that one takes in oneself:

> This pleasure, for which Seneca usually employs the word *gaudium* or *laetitia*, is a state that is neither accompanied nor followed by any form of disturbance in the body or the mind. It is defined by the fact of not being caused by anything that is independent of ourselves and therefore escapes our control. It arises out of ourselves and within ourselves (Foucault 1986: 66).

For Foucault the contrast to be made is with *voluptas* which denotes a pleasure whose origin resides outside us and in objects whose presence we cannot be sure of (a pleasure that is precarious in itself).

As one commentator astutely notes, for Foucault care of self does not simply denote attentiveness to, or even anxiety, about oneself, but is rather "a deliberate practice or set of practices that one uses in order to care for one's existence" (McGushin 2005: 634). Moreover:

> The goal of care was to establish the right, true, or full relation of oneself to oneself. This relation could be defined in terms of self-mastery, tranquillity, harmony, distance, or joy to name just a few possibilities (McGushin 2005: 634).

It's only by establishing and maintaining the right relation to oneself that we have the basis for forming full relations with others: "Care of the self was the preparatory work, the means, to the *telos* of living a noble existence" (McGushin 2005: 637). In all the different schools and developments in antiquity, philosophy is not simply about knowledge but about living a certain kind of life and being a certain type of subject. Knowledge is pursued to the extent that aids this mode of life and taking care of self. However, this tradition has become obscure to us today and we can account for this obscurity in terms of several developments. Foucault notes that there has been a deep transformation in the moral principles of Western society. He elaborates:

> We find it difficult to base rigorous morality and austere principles on the precept that we should give ourselves more care than anything else in the world. We are more inclined to see taking care of ourselves as an immorality, as a means of escape from all possible rules. We inherit the tradition of Christian morality which makes self-renunciation the condition for salvation. To know oneself was paradoxically the way to self-renunciation (Foucault 1988: 22).

Such is our assimilation of this morality of self-denial, to the point where we identify it as the domain of morality in and for itself, that the kind of morality pursued by the ancients strikes us today as an exercise in moral dandyism. As Foucault notes, we have the paradox of a precept of care of self that signifies for us today either egoism or withdrawal, but which for centuries was a positive principle, serving as the matrix for dedicated moralities (Foucault 2005: 13). Christianity and the modern world have based the codes of moral strictness on a morality of non-egoism to the point where we forget that such codes originated in an environment marked by the obligation to take care of oneself. We can note here: Nietzsche, at least in the popular imagination, is taken to be an immoralist in the crude sense identified by Foucault when, on the contrary, he can be fruitfully read as an ethical thinker in the way Foucault thinks we have forgotten ethics.

Foucault wishes, then, to promote an ethics centred on a care of the self, in which the self is not given to itself, and there is a need to fashion a self through practices of freedom. For Foucault ethics concerns itself with how the individual constitutes himself as a moral subject of their own actions, so we have moved from the subject as one constituted by power or power-knowledge to one that aims to constitute itself, and this is the work of freedom. In the Stoics, for example, the experience of the self is not a matter of discovering a truth or the truth hidden inside the self "but an attempt to determine what one can and cannot do with one's available freedom" (Foucault 1997: 276). As an ethicist Foucault is concerned with ethics in its Greek sense of *ethos:*

> The Greeks problematized their freedom, and the freedom of the individual, as an ethical problem. But ethical in the sense in which the Greeks understood it: ethos was a way of being and behaviour. It was a mode of being for the subject, along with a certain way of acting, a way visible to others. A person's ethos was evident in his clothing, appearance, gait, in the calm with which he responded to every event, and so on (Foucault 1997: 286).

Furthermore:

> What strikes me is that in Greek ethics people were concerned with their moral conduct, their ethics, their relations to themselves and to others much more than with religious pro-

blems. For instance, what happens to us after death? What are the gods? Do they intervene or not – these are very unimportant problems for them ... The second thing is that ethics is not related to any social – or at least to any legal – institutional system. For instance, the laws against sexual misbehaviour were very few and not very compelling, The third thing is that what they were worried about, their theme, was to constitute a kind of ethics which was an aesthetics of existence (Foucault 1997: 255).

Foucault wonders if our problem today might not be similar in that "we" no longer believe that ethics is founded on religion and we resist the invasion into our lives of legal control and prohibition. Recent liberation movements for Foucault suffer from the fact that they cannot isolate any principle on which to base an ethics or elaborate a new one: "They need an ethics", he says, "but they cannot find any other ethics than one founded on so-called scientific knowledge of what the self is, what desire is, what the unconscious is, and so on ..." (Foucault 1997: 256) The Greeks don't provide a solution to our problem simply because we cannot find a solution to our problems in another time; but what they do is call into question and relief our moral-Christian inheritance and shows us a different way of being ethical and practising freedom.

4

Before turning to an analysis of Nietzsche on the self, let me say something about the text itself, *Dawn*, and then review the question of the subject in Nietzsche as we might pose it today. Disregarding general claims, we can ask: what does Nietzsche actually say about the self in the text? Might Nietzsche appeal to an ethics of the self in the text as a moment of resistance and, if so, what is he resisting?

Typically, and as witnessed in Roberto Esposito's work, Nietzsche's relevance for biopolitics centres on his late work, that is, *Beyond Good and Evil* and after (see Esposito 2008). However, in the neglected middle period texts we encounter a Nietzsche preoccupied with the care of self and in opposition to the fundamental disciplinary and biopolitical tendencies of modernity. What intrigues me about the book are the rarely examined references in the book to 'commercial society' and 'security'. There is a socio-political backdrop to the work and Nietzsche's attack on the presumptions of morality. I have come to think that Foucault's focus on biopolitics might enable one to get a grasp on the anxieties and concerns Nietzsche expresses in the book. For Foucault biopower is a power of regularization and normalization, and it is this power that Nietzsche appears to be responding to in *Dawn*. Foucault writes:

16 Questions of the Subject in Nietzsche and Foucault: A Reading of *Dawn* — 423

> The normalizing society is a society in which the norm of discipline and the norm of regulation intersect along an orthogonal articulation. To say that power took possession of life in the nineteenth century, or to say that power at least takes life under its care … is to say that it has, thanks to the play of technologies of discipline on the one hand and technologies of regulation on the other, succeeded in covering the whole surface that lies between the organic and the biological, between body and population (Foucault 2003: 253).

As Esposito rightly notes, Nietzsche challenges the idea that the human species is ever given once and for all; rather, it is susceptible, "in good and evil, to being moulded in forms for which we do not have exact knowledge, but which nevertheless constitute for us both an absolute risk and an inalienable challenge" (Esposito 2008: 83). He quotes Nietzsche from 1881 on the selection of the human: "why should we not realize in the human being what the Chinese are able to do with the tree, producing roses on the one side and on the other side pears?" (KSA 9, 11[276]).

In *Ecce Homo* Nietzsche informs his readers that his "campaign" against morality begins in earnest with *Dawn* and he adds that we should not smell gunpowder at work here but, provided we have the necessary subtlety in our nostrils, more pleasant odours. I think Nietzsche is here drawing the reader's attention to something important, namely, the fact that he wants to open up the possibility of plural ways of being, including plural ways of being moral or ethical. His act is not one of simple wanton destruction. The "campaign" against morality centres largely on a critique of what Nietzsche sees as the modern tendency, the tendency of his own century, to identify morality with the sympathetic affects, especially *Mitleid*, so as to give us a definition of morality. Nietzsche has specific arguments against the value accorded to these affects, but he also wants to advocate the view that there are several ways of living morally or ethically and the morality he wants to defend is what we can call an ethics of self-cultivation. With regards to the modern prejudice, which is one of the main foci of his polemic in the book, here there is the presumption that we know what actually constitutes morality: "It seems *to do* every single person *good* these days to hear that society is on the road to *adapting* the individual to fit the needs of the throng and that the *individual's happiness as well as his sacrifice* consist in feeling himself to be a useful member of the whole …" (D 132) As Nietzsche sees it, then, the modern emphasis is on defining the moral in terms of the sympathetic affects and compassion. We can, he thinks, explain the modern in terms of a movement towards managing more cheaply, safely, and uniformly individuals in terms of "*large bodies and their limbs*". This, he says, is "*the basic moral current of our age*": "Everything that in some way supports both this drive to form bodies and limbs and its abetting drives is felt to be *good*" (D 132)

Nietzsche's main target in the book is what he sees as the fundamental tendency of modern "commercial society" and its attempt at a "collectivity-building project that aims at disciplining bodies and selves and integrating them into a uniform whole" (Ure 2006: 88 n. 45). Here "morality" denotes the means of adapting the individual to the needs of the whole, making him a useful member of society. This requires that every individual is made to feel, as its primary emotion, a connectedness or bondedness with the whole, with society, in which anything truly individual is regarded as prodigal, costly, inimical, extravagant, and so on. Nietzsche's great worry is that a healthy concern with self-fashioning will be sacrificed and this, in large part, informs his critique of what he sees as the cult of the sympathetic affects within modernity. For Nietzsche it is necessary to contest the idea that there is a single moral-making morality since every code of ethics that affirms itself in an exclusive manner "destroys too much valuable energy and costs humanity much too dearly" (D 164). In the future, Nietzsche hopes, the inventive and fructifying person shall no longer be sacrificed and "numerous novel experiments shall be made in ways of life and modes of society" (D 164). When this takes place we will find that an enormous load of guilty conscience has been purged from the world. Humanity has suffered for too long from teachers of morality who wanted too much all at once and sought to lay down precepts for everyone (D 194). In the future, care will need to be given to the most personal questions and create time for them (D 196). Small individual questions and experiments are no longer to be viewed with contempt and impatience (D 547). In place of what he sees as the ruling ethic of sympathy, which he thinks can assume the form of a "tyrannical encroachment", Nietzsche invites individuals to engage in self-fashioning, cultivating a self that others can look at with pleasure and giving vent to an altruistic in a subtle and delicate manner:

> *Moral fashion of a commercial society* – Behind the fundamental principle of the contemporary moral fashion: "moral actions are generated by sympathy (*Sympathie*) for others", I see the work of a collective drive toward timidity masquerading behind an intellectual front: this drive desires … that life be rid of *all the dangers* it once held and that *each and every person* should help toward this end with all one's might: therefore only actions aimed at the common security and at society's sense of security may be accorded the rating "good!" – How little pleasure people take in themselves these days, however, when such a tyranny of timidity dictates to them the uppermost moral law (*Sittengesetz*), when, without so much as a protest, they let themselves be commanded to ignore and look beyond themselves and yet have eagle-eyes for every distress and every suffering existing elsewhere! Are we not, with this prodigious intent to grate off all the rough and sharp edges from life, well on the way to turning humanity into *sand*? … In the meantime, the question itself remains open as to whether one is *more useful* to another by immediately and constantly leaping to his side and *helping* him – which can, in any case, only transpire very superficially, provided the help doesn't turn into a tyrannical encroachment and transformation – or by *fashioning* out of oneself something the other will behold with pleasure, a lovely, peaceful, self-enclosed garden, for instance, with high walls to protect against the dangers and dust of the roadway, but with a hospitable gate as well (D 174).

16 Questions of the Subject in Nietzsche and Foucault: A Reading of *Dawn* — 425

The perspective Nietzsche adopts here on commercial society is perhaps a little odd since we typically associate it with an ethic of selfishness and pride. However, this is mistaken. As one commentator notes, those who favoured commercial society, such as the French *philosophes*, including thinkers such as Voltaire and Montesquieu, held that by "establishing bonds among people and making life more comfortable, commerce softens and refines people's manners and promotes humaneness and civility" (Rasmussen 2008: 18). I think it is clear that in this section Nietzsche is expressing an anxiety that other nineteenth-century social analysts, such as Tocqueville, have, namely, that market-driven atomization and de-individuation can readily lead to a form of communitarian tyranny (Ure 2006: 82). Unknown to ourselves we live within the effect of general opinions about "the human being", which is a "bloodless abstraction" and "fiction" (D 105). Even the modern glorification of work and talk of its blessings can be interpreted as a fear of everything individual. The subjection to hard industriousness from early until late serves as "the best policeman" since it keeps everyone in bounds and hinders the development of reason, desire, and the craving for independence. It uses vast amounts of nervous energy which could be given over to reflection, brooding, dreaming, loving and hating and working through our experiences: "… a society in which there is continuous hard work will have more security: and security is currently worshipped as the supreme divinity" (D 173).

In *Dawn* Nietzsche employs what we can call a care of self as a way of taking to task what he identifies as some worrying developments in modern society. We can describe both Nietzsche and Foucault as modern-day virtue ethicists who seek "to liberate the capacity of individual self-choice and personal self-formation from oppressive conformism …" (Ingram 2003: 240). Let me now explore questions of the subject in the text.

5

On the face of it, it's not an easy task to claim that Nietzsche has an intimate concern with the fate of the subject in *Dawn*. Today notions of autonomy and sovereign individuality have been placed under suspicion in many quarters of philosophy and in some quarters of Nietzsche-studies.[4] Sometimes it is flatly stated that Nietzsche denies the self without further investigation or any deep appreciation of his oeuvre (Sorabji 2006: 17). In fact, a suspicion about the

---

4 For a sceptical treatment of the sovereign individual, which contests the claim that it represents Nietzsche's ideal, see Acampora 2006. See also Rakgaber 2012.

subject in Nietzsche dates back to an essay Gianni Vattimo published in Italian in 1979. Vattimo argued that Nietzsche's critique of morality is not conducted, "in the name of the free and responsible subject, for such a subject is likewise a product of neurosis, a thing formed in illness" (Vattimo 2006: 164).

As Arthur Danto has noted, the psychology in *Dawn* is dazzling and precocious. Nietzsche's psychology, he argues, is resolutely anti-Cartesian and has to be inasmuch as his critique of morality entails the view that we do not really know what we are, while Cartesianism is precisely the view that what we essentially are is something immediately present to consciousness, and nothing is true of us psychologically of which we are not directly and noninferentially aware (Danto 2005: 249). Here several aphorisms in book two of *Dawn* are especially significant. In aphorism 115 on the "so-called 'ego'" (*Ich*), Nietzsche draws attention to the prejudices of language, noting that they hinder a properly rich and subtle understanding of inner processes and drives. We seem to have words that exist only for the "*superlative* degrees" of these processes and drives: "Wrath, hate, love, compassion, craving, knowing, joy, pain – these are all names for *extreme* states." This would not be important were it not for the fact, Nietzsche thinks, that it is the milder middle degrees, as well as the lower ones, which elude us and yet "collaborate … in the formation of our character and destiny". In D 116 on the "unknown world of the 'subject' (*Subject*)", Nietzsche startles us with his shocking assertion that from the most distant times of the past to the present day what has been so difficult for us to comprehend is our ignorance of ourselves: "The age old delusion that one knows, knows just exactly in every instance *how human action comes about*, lives on." We superstitiously believe we know what we want, that we are free and can freely assume responsibility for ourselves and hold others responsible for their actions, and so on. He urges us to recognize that actions are never what they appear to be: "It took so much effort for us to learn that external things are not what they appear to us – now then! It is just the same with the inner world!" In this regard it is necessary to work against both metaphysical and moral "realism" (D 116). Finally, in aphorism 128 of the book Nietzsche challenges the Oedipal fantasy we might have of ourselves in which we exist as our own mother and father. Nietzsche's suggestion is that we are responsible neither for our dreams nor our waking life and that the idea of freedom of the will "has human pride and feeling of power for its mother and father" (D 128).

It is perhaps on the basis of a reading of aphorisms like these that Vattimo claims, to repeat, that Nietzsche's critique of morality in *Dawn* is not conducted, "in the name of the free and responsible subject" since this subject is "a product of neurosis, a thing formed in illness" (Vattimo 2006: 164). He contends that because there is an inextricable connection between internal or internalized conscience, *including the "individual in* revolt", and social morality, the appeal to freedom in Nietzsche cannot be made in the name of "the sovereignty of the individual" (Vattimo 2006: 162–163). He rightly notes that Nietzsche unmasks morality as a set of principles not intended for the utility or the good of the individual on whom they are imposed but for the preservation of society, even to the detriment of individuals; but he also infers that Nietzsche's aim is not to defend the individual against the claims of the group. The reason, he argues, is not because, metaphysically speaking, it is necessary to prefer the claims of determinism over the belief in freedom, "but simply because there is no subject of such actions. Not: the subject is not free, but simply: the subject is not" (Vattimo 2006: 161).

It is true that Nietzsche has done much in the text to deconstruct the fiction of some ontologically given or fixed unified self. However, this does not mean he has no concern with the "ego" or self. In aphorism 105, for example he paints a contrast between one's "phantom ego" (*Phantom von ego*), which is formed in the heads of those around us and then communicated to us, and makes sure we live "in a fog of impersonal, half-personal opinions", as well as arbitrary and fictitious evaluations, and one's "self-established, genuine ego" (*ergründetes ego*), an ego that Nietzsche invites us to juxtapose to the "common, pallid fiction" of the "human being" (D 105). It would seem that for Nietzsche this "self-established ego" is a construction and work in progress, centred on the cultivation of the drives. As he puts it in a note from the end of 1880:

> It is a myth to believe that we will find our authentic self (*eigentliches Selbst*) once we have left out or forgotten this and that. That way we pick ourselves apart in an infinite regression: instead, the task is to *make ourselves*, to *shape* a form all the elements! The task is always that of a sculptor! A productive human being! *Not* through knowledge but through practice and an exemplar do we become *ourselves*! Knowledge has, at best, the value of a means! (KSA 9, 7[213]).

Similarly, Foucault appeals to "creativity" over "authenticity": "From the idea that the self is not given to us, I think there is only one practical consequence: we have to create ourselves as a work of art" (Foucault 1997: 262).

Whilst it is true that Nietzsche exposes the extent to which the I or ego is the subject *of* its drives and affects (it is not the master in its own house we might say, looking ahead to Freud), it is manifestly clear that he is *perturbed* by this fact, that is, troubled by the extent to which the self is little more than a contingency or mere happenstance. In aphorism 119 he explores the drives and notes that no matter how much we struggle for self-knowledge nothing is more incomplete to us than the image of the totality of our drives. It is not only that we cannot call the cruder ones by name, but also more worryingly that their number and strength, their ebb and flow, and most of all the laws of their alimentation remain completely unknown to us:

> This alimentation thus becomes the work of chance: our daily experiences toss willy-nilly to this drive or that drive some prey or other which it seizes greedily, but the whole coming and going of these events exists completely apart from any meaningful connection to the alimentary needs of the sum drives: so that the result will always be two-fold: the starving and stunting of some drives and the overstuffing of others (D 119).

Our experiences, then, are types of nourishment; the problem is that there is a deficit of knowledge on our part as to the character of our experiences. The result is that we live as contingent beings:

> … as a consequence of this contingent alimentation of the parts, the whole, the fully-grown polyp turns out to be a creature no less contingent (*Zufälliges*) than its maturation (D 119).

The ethical task in Nietzsche, it would seem, is not to allow oneself to be this mere happenstance. We need to experience dissatisfaction with ourselves and assume the risk of experimenting in life, freely taking the journey through our wastelands, quagmires, and icy glaciers. The ones who don't take the risk of life will, "never make the journey around the world (that you yourselves are!), but will remain trapped within yourselves like a knot on the log you were born to, a mere happenstance" (D 343). This is not to deny that the self or subject is not something contingent for Nietzsche: his whole point in *Dawn* is to show the contingencies of our moral formation and deformation and to disclose to the self that it is something other than what it takes itself to be (fixed and stable) and that it may become something more fluid and dynamic, in short, that it may cultivate a becoming of what it is.

To suppose, as Vattimo does, that the "subject" is by definition something neurotic is to fail to make a distinction between autonomy and heteronomy, a distinction that can be drawn in Nietzschean and not just Kantian terms (see Sachs 2008), and to rule out *tout court* the possibility of an ethic of self-cultivation. For Nietzsche the focus is to be on the cultivation of the drives, and an initial step on the path to self-enlightenment and self-liberation is to know that here we do enjoy a certain liberty:

> One can handle one's drives like a gardener and, though few know it, cultivate the shoots of one's anger, pity, musing, vanity as fruitfully and advantageously as beautiful fruit on espaliers; one can do so with a gardener's good or bad taste and, as it were, in the French or English or Dutch or Chinese style; one can also let nature have her sway and only tend to a little decoration and cleaning-up here and there; finally, one can, without giving them any thought whatsoever, let the plants, in keeping with the natural advantages and disadvantages of their habitat, grow up and fight it out among themselves – indeed, one can

take pleasure in such wildness and want to enjoy just this pleasure, even if one has difficulties with it. We are free to do all this: but how many actually know that they are free to do this? Don't most people *believe in themselves* as completed, *fully-grown facts*? Haven't great philosophers, with their doctrine of the immutability of character, pressed their seal of approval on this prejudice? (D 560)

The focus, then, is on the drives in which the self is not conceived metaphysically for there is no self independent of the structuring and organisation of the drives. For Nietzsche what we call the "self" just is a site or agent of structuring, ordering, and organising. In a note from autumn 1880 he insists that the intellect is the tool of our drives, "it is *never free*". What it does is to sharpen itself in the struggle with various drives and thereby refines the activity of each individual drive. But he also insists that: "The will to power (*der Wille nach Macht*), to the infallibility (*Unfehlbarkeit*) of our person, resides in our greatest justice and integrity (*Redlichkeit*): scepticism just applies to all authority, we do not want to be duped, not even by *our drives*! But what does not *want*? A drive, certainly!" (KSA 9, 6[130]; see also D 109) So, although we cannot escape the drives in any absolute sense we can gain a distance from them so that we are not "duped" by them. And although we share drives with animals, our increase in integrity makes us less dependent on the stimulus of the drives (KSA 9, 6[234]).

6

As Ruth Abbey has pointed out, an ethics of care of self in Nietzsche centres on a concern for quotidian minutiae, attention to individualized goods, and an awareness of the close connection between psyche and physique (Abbey 2000: 102). For Nietzsche the small, daily practices of care of self are undervalued. In modern culture we can detect, Nietzsche writes, a "feigned disrespect for all the things which men in fact take most seriously, *for all the things closest to them*" (WS 5). As Abbey notes, in devaluing the small, worldly matters Christian and post-Christian sensibility, "puts people at war with themselves and forbids a close study of which forms of care of the self would be most conducive to individual flourishing" (Abbey 2000: 99). As Nietzsche notes, most people see the closest things badly and rarely pay heed to them, whilst "*almost all the physical and psychical frailties* of the individual derive from this lack … being *unknowledgeable in the smallest and everyday things* and failing to keep an eye on them – this it is that transforms the earth for so many into a 'vale of tears'" (WS 6). Our understanding of existence is diverted away from the smallest and closest things:

> Priests and teachers, and the sublime lust for power of idealists of every description ... hammer even into children that what matters is something quite different: the salvation of the soul, the service of the state, the advancement of science, or the accumulation of reputation and possessions, all as the means of doing service to mankind as a whole; while the requirements of the individual, his great and small needs within the twenty four hours of the day, are to be regarded as something contemptible or a matter of indifference. (WS 6)

Nietzsche goes on to name here Socrates as a key figure in the history of thought who defended himself against this "arrogant neglect" of the human for the benefit of the human race (D 9).[5] Nietzsche argues: "Our continual offences against the most elementary laws of the body and the spirit reduce us all ... to a disgraceful dependence and bondage ... on physicians, teachers and curers of soul who lie like a burden on the whole of society" (WS 5). All the physical and psychical frailties of the individual derive form a lack of knowledge about the smallest and most everyday things, such as what is beneficial to us and what is harmful to us in the institution of our mode of life, in the division of the day, eating, sleeping, and reflecting, and so on (WS 6).

The Stoic Epictetus is especially admired by Nietzsche in *Dawn* on account of his dedication to his own ego and for resisting the glorification of thinking and living for others (D 131). Of course, this is a partial and selective appropriation of Epictetus on Nietzsche's part. Although his chief concerns are with integrity and self-command, Epictetus is also known for his Stoic cosmopolitanism in which individuals have an obligation to care for their fellow human beings, and Nietzsche is silent about this aspect of Stoic teaching.[6] Nevertheless, it is true that the ethical outlook of Epictetus does invite people "to value their individual selves over everything else" (Long 2002: 3),[7] and for Nietzsche he serves as a useful contrast to Christian thinkers such as Pascal, who considered the ego to be something hateful:

> If, as Pascal and Christianity claim, our ego (*Ich*) is always *hateful*, how might we possibly ever allow or assume that someone else could love it – be it God or a human being! It

---

[5] In *Dawn* section 9 Socrates is said to be one of those (rare) moralists who offer the individual a morality of self-control and temperance and as a means to their own advantage or a personal key to happiness. For further insight into the different depictions of Socrates we find in Nietzsche see Nehamas 1998: 128–156. See also Hadot 1995: 147–179.

[6] Thomas Brobjer suggests that Nietzsche did not read the extended *Discourses* and was only familiar with Epictetus's short 'Manual' or *Enchiridion*, and this might account for the somewhat one-sided portrait of him we get from Nietzsche's appraisal. See Brobjer (2003: 430). For a full picture of Epictetus see Long (2002).

[7] Long also notes that Epictetus devotes more thought to the care of the self than he does to what is incumbent on human beings as members of society (2002: 30).

16 Questions of the Subject in Nietzsche and Foucault: A Reading of *Dawn* — 431

> would go against all decency to let oneself be loved knowing full well that one only *deserves* hate – not to mention other feelings of repulsion. – "But this is precisely the kingdom of mercy". – So is your love-thy-neighbour mercy? Your compassion mercy? Well, if these things are possible for you, go still one step further: love yourselves out of mercy – then you won't need your God any more at all, and the whole drama of original sin and redemption will play itself out to the end in you yourselves (D 79).

Nietzsche wishes to replace morality, including the morality of compassion, with a care of self. We go wrong when we fail to attend to the needs of the "ego" and flee from it:

> Let's stick to the idea that benevolence and beneficence are what constitute a good person; only let's add: "provided that he is first benevolently and beneficently disposed *towards himself!*" For *without this* – if he runs from himself, hates himself, causes injury to himself – he is certainly not a good person. Because he is rescuing himself from himself *in others* ... to run from the ego (*ego*) and to hate it and to live in others, for others – has, heretofore, been called, just as unreflectedly as assuredly, "*unegotistical*" *and consequently* "*good*"! (D 516)

Such passages clearly indicate, I think, that Nietzsche has what I am crediting him with in *Dawn*, namely, an intimate concern with the fate of the self and centred on a care of it.

Dawn is a text in which Nietzsche positions himself in important ways in relation to the history of philosophy. One of the most significant is his appeal throughout the text to various enlightenment traditions, including ancient and modern. Nietzsche seems keen to revitalize neglected and forgotten aspects or tendencies within the development of philosophy. If we focus our attention on questions of the ethical subject in Nietzsche, it is clear that he is breaking with modern conceptions and seeking to revive interest in an ancient care of self. There are key references to the likes of Epicurus and Epictetus in the text and these are figures that play a crucial role in Foucault's history of the care of self. Nietzsche was inspired by Epicurus's conception of friendship and the ideal of withdrawing from society and cultivating one's own garden. In a letter to Peter Gast of 1883 Nietzsche writes that Epicurus "is the best negative argument in favour of my challenge to all rare spirits to isolate themselves from the mass of their fellows" (KGB III/1: 418). In a note from 1881 Nietzsche states that he considers the various moral schools of antiquity to be "experimental laboratories" containing a number of recipes for the art of living and holds that these experiments now belong to us as our legitimate property: "we shall not hesitate to adopt a Stoic recipe just because we have profited in the past from Epicurean recipes" (KSA 9, 15[59]).

Taken as a whole the text *Dawn* perhaps represents Nietzsche's most avowedly Epicurean moment. A great deal of the thinking contained within the book is an attempt to revitalize for a modern age ancient philosophical concerns, notably a teaching for mortal souls who wish to be liberated from the fear and anguish of existence, as well as from God, the metaphysical need, and who are able to affirm their mortal conditions of existence. Here one might adopt Hadot's insight into the therapeutic ambitions of ancient philosophy which was, he claims, "intended to cure mankind's anguish" (for example, anguish over our mortality) (Hadot 1995: 265–266). This is evident in the teaching of Epicurus which sought to demonstrate the mortality of the soul and whose aim was, in the words of a recent commentator, "to free humans from 'the fears of the mind'" (Wilson 2008: 7) Similarly, Nietzsche's teaching in *Dawn* is for mortal souls. In *Dawn* 501, which is entitled "Mortal Souls", Nietzsche writes that, "So far as the promotion of knowledge is concerned, humankind's most useful achievement is perhaps the abandonment of its belief in an immortal soul" (D 501).

For Foucault the principle of the care of self allows for variation: in Plato's Alcibiades care of self "refers to an active political and erotic state" (Foucault 1988: 24), but, according to Foucault, in the Hellenistic and Roman periods the care of self has become a universal principle and politics is left to one side as so "to take better care of the self" (1988: 31). How does *Dawn* fit into this schema as a nineteenth-century work of resistance? The philosophical and ethical therapy Nietzsche is proposing in *Dawn* appears to be directed at those solitary free spirits who exist on the margin of society and seek to cultivate or fashion new ways of thinking and feeling, attempting to do this by taking the time necessary to work through their experiences. It is certain that Nietzsche sought to found a philosophical school modelled on Epicurus's garden. As he wrote to Gast in 1879 (26 March), "*Where* are we going to renew the garden of Epicurus?". For some commentators, such as Horst Hutter, Nietzsche's ultimate goal is the shaping of the future of European humanity and society, and on this conception of his philosophy the retreat into an Epicurean-inspired community of friends is merely a temporary expedient in which free spirits work on themselves so as to become philosophical legislators of a future culture. As Hutter writes, "such fraternities of free spirits would be necessary to traverse the period of nihilism until a future point in time, when direct political action would again become possible" (Hutter 2006: 5).

7

In this essay I have sought to clarify some important aspects of Foucault's work on the subject and at the same time explore Nietzsche's text of 1881, *Dawn*, as a site of ethical resistance to normalization and the biopolitical tendencies of modernity. *Dawn* is a heavily neglected text in Nietzsche's corpus, and here I have sketched one possible appropriation of it. The text has been admired in recent years for its ethical naturalism (see Clark/Leiter 1997) and even for its anticipation of phenomenology (see Safranski 2002). I am claiming it for a specific tradition within the history of philosophy and that I believe Nietzsche regarded as a neglected one in his own time, and one that he sought to employ for critical effect.

Neither Nietzsche nor Foucault advocates an ahistorical return to the ancients. In the case of *Dawn* Nietzsche highlights the teaching of Epictetus, for example, as a way of indicating that what we take to be morality today, where it is taken to be coextensive with the sympathetic affects, is not a paradigm of some universal and metahistorical truth. If we look at history we find that there have been different ways of being ethical, and this in itself is sufficient, Nietzsche thinks, to derail the idea that there is a single moral-making morality. Both thinkers seek to work against the construction of moral necessities out of historical contingencies. A key difference from the ancients is that Nietzsche is developing a therapy for the sicknesses of the soul under specifically modern conditions of social control and discipline. As such, he offers *Dawn* as a work of ethical resistance. Nietzsche's ethical ambition in *Dawn* is clear and it centres on the experiment of the human being and working against its closure. Let me end with a citation from Nietzsche's *Nachlass* of 1880:

> My morality (*Moral*) would be to take the general character of man more and more away from him ... to make him to a degree non-understandable to others (and with it an object of experiences, of astonishment, of instruction for them) ... Should not each individual (*Individuum*) be an attempt to achieve a *higher species than man* through its most individual things? (KSA 9, 6[158])

References

Abbey, Ruth (2000) *Nietzsche's Middle Period*, Oxford: Oxford University Press.
Acampora, Christa Davis (2006) "On Sovereignty and Overhumanity: Why It Matters How We Read Nietzsche's Genealogy II: 2", in: Christa Davis Acampora (ed.), *Nietzsche's on the Genealogy of Morals: Critical Essays*, Lanham/Oxford: Rowman & Littlefield, 147–163.
Brobjer, Thomas (2003) "Nietzsche's Reading of Epictetus", in: *Nietzsche-Studien* 32, 429–435.
Clark, Maudemarie/Leiter, Brian (1997) "Introduction" to F. Nietzsche, *Daybreak: Thoughts on the Prejudices of Morality*, trans. R.J. Hollingdale, Cambridge: Cambridge University Press.
Danto, Arthur C. (2005) *Nietzsche as Philosopher*, expanded edition, New York: Columbia University Press.

Deleuze, Gilles (1995) *Negotiations 1972–1990*, trans. Martin Joughin, New York: Columbia University Press.
Dews, Peter (1989) "The Return of the Subject in the Late Foucault", in *Radical Philosophy* 51, 37–41.
Esposito, Roberto (2008) *Bios: Biopolitics and Philosophy*, trans. Timothy Campbell, Minneapolis: University of Minnesota Press.
Foucault, Michel (1977a) *Discipline and Punish*, trans. Alan Sheridan, Harmondsworth: Penguin.
Foucault, Michel (1977b) "Nietzsche, Genealogy, History", in *Language, Counter-Memory, and Practice: Selected Essays and Interviews*, trans. Donald F. Bouchard and Sherry Simon, Oxford: Basil Blackwell, 139–165.
Foucault, Michel (1982) "The Subject and Power", in: Hubert L. Dreyfus and Paul Rabinow (eds.), *Michel Foucault: Beyond Structuralism and Hermeneutics*, Brighton: Harvester Press, 208–227.
Foucault, Michel (1985) *The Use of Pleasure: The History of Sexuality* volume 2, trans. Robert Hurley, Harmondsworth: Penguin.
Foucault, Michel (1986) *The Care of the Self: The History of Sexuality* volume 3, trans. Robert Hurley, Harmondsworth: Penguin.
Foucault, Michel (1988) "Technologies of the Self", in: Luther H. Martin et al (eds.), *Technologies of the Self: A Seminar with Michel Foucault*, London: Tavistock, 16–50.
Foucault, Michel (1990) *Politics, Philosophy, Culture: Interviews and Writings 1977–84*, trans. Alan Sheridan and others, London: Routledge.
Foucault, Michel (1997) *Ethics: The Essential Works 1*, ed. Paul Rabinow, Harmondsworth: Penguin.
Foucault, Michel (2001) *Power: The Essential Works 3*, ed. James D. Faubion, Harmondsworth: Penguin.
Foucault, Michel (2003) *Society Must Be Defended: Lectures at the College de France 1975–76*, trans. David Macey, Harmondsworth: Penguin.
Foucault, Michel (2005) *The Hermeneutics of the Subject: Lectures at the College de France 1981–82*, trans. Graham Burchell, New York: Palgrave Macmillan.
Foucault, Michel (2007) "What is Enlightenment?", in: *The Politics of Truth*, trans. Lysa Hochroth and Catherine Porter, Los Angeles: Semiotext(e), 97–121.
Hadot, Pierre (1995) *Philosophy as a Way of Life*, trans. Michael Chase, Oxford: Basil Blackwell.
Han, Beatrice (2002) *Foucault's Critical Project: Between the Transcendental and the Historical*, Stanford: Stanford University Press.
Hutter, Horst (2006) *Shaping the Future: Nietzsche's New Regime of the Soul and its Ascetic Practices*, Lanham, MD: Lexington.
Ingram, David (2003) "Foucault and Habermas", in: Gary Gutting (ed.), *The Cambridge Companion to Foucault*, 2nd edition, Cambridge: Cambridge University Press, 240–284.
Long, A.A. (2002) *Epictetus*, Oxford: Clarendon Press.
McGushin, Edward (2005) "Foucault and the Problem of the Subject", in: *Philosophy & Social Criticism* 31(5/6), 623–648.
McGushin, Edward F. (2007) *Foucault's Askēsis: An Introduction to the Philosophical Life*, Evanston: Northwestern University Press.
Milchman, Alan/Rosenberg, Alan (2007) "The Aesthetic and Ascetic Dimensions of an Ethics of Self-Fashioning: Nietzsche and Foucault", in: *Parrhesia* 2, 44–65.

Nehamas, Alexander (1998) *The Art of Living: Socratic Reflections from Plato to Foucault*, London/Berkeley: University of California Press.

Oksala, Johanna (2005) *Foucault on Freedom*, Cambridge: Cambridge University Press.

Rakgaber, Matthew (2012) "The 'Sovereign Individual' and the 'Ascetic Ideal': On a Perennial Misreading of the Second Essay of Nietzsche's *On the Genealogy of Morality*", in: *Journal of Nietzsche Studies* 43(2), 213–240.

Rasmussen, Dennis C. (2008) *The Problems and Promise of Commercial Society: Adam Smith's Response to Rousseau*, University Park, PA: Penn State University Press.

Sachs, Carl B. (2008) "Nietzsche's *Daybreak*: Toward a Naturalized Theory of Autonomy", in: *Epoché* 13(1), 81–100.

Safranski, Rüdiger (2002) *Nietzsche. A Philosophical Biography*, trans. Shelley Frisch, New York: Norton.

Seigel, Jerrold (2005) *The Idea of the Self: Thought and Experience in Western Europe since the Seventeenth Century*, Cambridge: Cambridge University Press.

Sluga, Hans (2003) "Foucault's Encounter with Heidegger and Nietzsche", in: Gary Gutting (ed.), *The Cambridge Companion to Foucault*, 2nd edition, Cambridge: Cambridge University Press, 210–240.

Sorabji, Richard (2006) *Self. Ancient and Modern Insights about Individuality, Life, and Death*, Oxford: Oxford University Press.

Ure, Michael (2006) "The Irony of Pity: Nietzsche contra Schopenhauer and Rousseau", in: *Journal of Nietzsche Studies* 32, 68–92.

Urpeth, James (1998) "Noble Ascesis: Between Nietzsche and Foucault", in: *New Nietzsche Studies* 2(3/4), 65–93.

Vattimo, Gianni (2006) *Dialogue with Nietzsche*, trans. William McCuaig, New York: Columbia University Press.

Wilson, Catherine (2008) *Epicureanism at the Origins of Modernity*. Oxford: Oxford University Press.

Jaanus Sooväli
17 Gapping the Subject: Nietzsche and Derrida

1

Jacques Derrida has given extensive analysis to Plato, Freud, Husserl, Heidegger and Levinas, but only relatively small pieces exclusively on Nietzsche.[1] At the same time, Nietzsche's name comes up often, in most of his works and, as one might argue, in quite focal or critical points. When Richard Beardsworth asked him in an interview why he had not written longer analyses on Nietzsche's thinking, he replied that he has "found it difficult to bring together or stabilize, within a particular configuration, a 'thought' of Nietzsche".[2] Due to the irreducible multiplicity of voices in Nietzsche's work, Derrida did not think it was possible to organize his thinking "around a guiding meaning, a fundamental project, or even a formal feature".[3] It is this multiplicity that, according to Derrida, should be strictly respected and taken into account. But Derrida's treatment of other authors does precisely that: it tries to demonstrate that a multiplicity of "voices" can also be found in Plato, Husserl and Heidegger. What does Nietzsche's specificity consist in then as Derrida asks? Perhaps the point is that Nietzsche, unlike Husserl, Freud or even Heidegger, does not pretend to build a unified system of thought; rather, he seems to have discharged his thinking without any "mediation", "premeditation" – it is as if his different voices spoke without any "master" pretending to be present. In other words, the various voices in Nietzsche do not have to be pulled out from the text, nor pointed out or written out; they are not the result of deconstructive reading. Nietzsche's work, one could perhaps claim, would be an example of an open and constant self-deconstruction. Derrida himself puts it slightly differently though: "he is perhaps, of them all, the most mad!"[4]

---

[1] Derrida has published only two short stand-alone texts on Nietzsche: *Spurs – Nietzsche's Styles* (1979) and *Otobiographies* (1985a). There is also a short essay called *Interpreting Signatures (Nietzsche/Heidegger): Two Questions* (1986). A relatively long discussion on Nietzsche can be found in his book *Politics of Friendship* (1997b). In addition, there is one quite extensive interview with Richard Beardsworth "Nietzsche and the Machine" (2002). Shorter discussions are scattered around everywhere in Derrida's corpus.
[2] Derrida 2002: 216.
[3] Derrida 2002: 216.
[4] Derrida 2002: 217.

Thus, one can already draw some general conclusions regarding the concept of the "subject" in Nietzsche and Derrida. Firstly, Derrida seems to point out in his reading or interpretation of Nietzsche that the latter did not only have a discourse on the subject as a multiplicity of drives, forces etc.,[5] but that his whole philosophical corpus is a multiplicity of voices bearing witness to the multiplicity of Nietzsche himself as a subject. Nietzsche refers to this multiplicity in himself on several occasions as well.[6] This, on the other hand, is directly related to madness: Nietzsche seems to have no *ultimate* control over this multiplicity of voices with which he speaks in his work; he is also a bit lost here, as Derrida puts it in *Les Styles de Nietzsche* with regard to Nietzsche's plurality of views on women.[7] A rational person is usually thought to be somebody who has conscious knowledge of and control over his own actions, he listens to the reasons his rational deliberations have provided him with and acts according to those reasons; the mad one, on the contrary, seems to be somebody who is determined by "forces" he cannot *completely* control and have no clear knowledge of. The mad one speaks in tongues, to use a biblical expression. In this sense, the whole of Nietzsche's work – that is, his different styles, voices, philosophical perspectives etc. – testifies to the irreducible multiplicity of the subject.

This multiplicity of Nietzsche as a subject can also be related to Derrida's discussion on the proper name. The proper name is normally thought to be something that marks one's identity and individuality by picking out a unique referent in the world; it seems to be important for our sense of individuality and identity. The proper name also marks (legal) ownership: when we read a book or a letter signed by Nietzsche, for instance, then we know that this book belongs to Nietzsche, it is the very property of the unique individual called Nietzsche, and the only person who is supposed to answer for (take responsibility of) what is written in the book is nobody else than Nietzsche himself as some sort of identity. However, Derrida argues that the proper name is not as proper as it seems, in fact, it can never simply refer to some identity and be an exclusive

---

[5] Cf. NL 1884–85, 40[42], KSA 11: 650 (my translation): "The assumption of *one subject* is perhaps not necessary; perhaps it is just as well allowed to assume a multiplicity of subjects whose interplay and struggle is the basis of our thinking and our consciousness in general? [...] *My hypothesis*: subject as multiplicity [...]."

[6] For instance in *Ecce Homo*, Nietzsche writes: "[...] and considering that I have an extraordinary number of inner states, I also have a lot of stylistic possibilities – the most multifarious art of style that anyone has ever had at his disposal." (EH, Why I Write Such Good Books 4)

[7] Cf. Derrida (1979: 101): "Nietzsche too is a little lost there. [...] Nietzsche might well be a little lost in the web of his text, lost much as a spider who finds he is unequal to the web he has spun."

property of a person it names.[8] The proper name, as Niall Lucy puts it, "is made up of common signifying elements which do not belong to anyone".[9] In other words, a proper name, being composed of iterable elements and forming a part of the general system of language, is improper, as it has very little to do with the identity and uniqueness that it is supposed to pick out and refer to. Insofar as a person understands his identity and individuality through his name, his is already non-identical with himself. And Nietzsche, by signing some of his late letters, for instance, with various proper names (Nietzsche Caesar, Dionysius, the Crucified),[10] seems to exemplify the fact that the proper name 'Friedrich Nietzsche' does not refer to some sort of unique identity.[11]

2

At this point, it is perhaps also worth mentioning that for Derrida (and actually for Nietzsche as well[12]) the concept of the subject belongs to a whole series of metaphysical terms which, taken all together, builds a certain system, a relatively determined way of perceiving the world. In this sense, this particular concept has no priority within this metaphysical terminology; it is just one among others. Hence, all the metaphysical terms like substance, essence, subject, soul, truth, and consciousness are just different designations for some kind of *centre* or *origin* from which everything else could be determined, and refer more specifically to the determination of "Being as *presence* in all senses of this word".[13] Thus, by deconstructing the notion of truth or the notion of being,

---

8 Cf. Derrida (1985b: 107): "However, if an idiom effect or an effect of absolute properness can arise only within a system of relations and differences with something else that is either near or far, then the secret proper name is right away inscribed – structurally and a priori – in a network where it is contaminated by common names."
9 Lucy 2004: 104.
10 Cf. KSB 8, nr. 1256 (my translation): "What is unpleasant and a strain on my modesty is that in fact I am all the names in the history".
11 Cf. Anderson 2003: 82–83.
12 In BGE 20/JGB 20, Nietzsche interestingly writes: "That individual philosophical concepts are not arbitrary and do not grow up on their own, but rather grow in reference and relation to each other; that however suddenly and randomly they seem to emerge in the history of thought, they still belong to a system just as much as all the members of the fauna of a continent do: this is ultimately revealed by the certainty with which the most diverse philosophers will always fill out a definite basic scheme of *possible* philosophies."
13 Derrida 2009b: 353.

for instance, one is in some sense already also *decentralizing* other concepts that make up this system, like the concept of the subject. In this sense, Nietzsche's criticism of metaphysics in general, that is, his criticism of Platonism, his emphasis on becoming instead of being, his project to write a genealogy of supposedly unhistorical philosophical concepts and moral values is, according to Derrida, already a certain deconstruction of the subject – that is, decentralization of the centre, undermining of the idea of being as presence. Quite often, when Derrida acknowledges the work of Nietzsche, he does not explicitly refer to the latter's work on the concept of the subject (sometimes, Freud seems to be a more obvious reference when he speaks specifically about this), but to his criticism of other aspects of metaphysics. For example, in *Structure, Sign and Play in Discourses of Human Sciences*, Derrida writes[14]:

> [...] if we wished to choose several "names," as indications only, and recall those authors in whose discourses this occurrence [that is, decentring of the centre – J.S.] has kept most closely to its most radical formulation, we doubtless would have to cite the Nietzschean critique of metaphysics, the critique of the concepts of Being and truth, for which were substituted the concepts of play, interpretation, and sign (sign without present truth); the Freudian critique of self-presence, that is, the critique of consciousness, of the subject, of self-identity and of self-proximity or self-possession; [...] and the Heideggerian destruction of metaphysics [...].[15]

What Derrida states here about Freud's critique of the subject could have easily been said about Nietzsche's work as well, and maybe even more justifiably so. But perhaps more important is the fact that what he does write here about Nietzsche's contribution – the substitution of truth for interpretation and play etc. – also has a direct and quite essential consequence for, and bearing on, the concept of the subject.

This consequence consists in the fact that since there are, according to Nietzsche, only interpretations and evaluations,[16] since knowledge always

---

14 Cf. Derrida's words about Nietzsche's main contribution from *Of Grammatology* (1997a: 19): "Radicalizing the concepts of interpretation, perspective, evaluation, difference, and all the 'empiricist' or non-philosophical motifs that have constantly tormented philosophy throughout the history of the West, and besides, have had nothing but the inevitable weakness of being produced in the field of philosophy, Nietzsche, far from remaining simply (with Hegel and as Heidegger wished) within metaphysics, contributed a great deal to the liberation of the signifier from its dependence or derivation with respect to the logos and the related concept of truth or the primary signified, in whatever sense that is understood."
15 Derrida 2009b: 354.
16 Cf. NL 1885–1887, 7[60], KSA 12: 315, my translation: "Against positivism which stays with the phenomena 'there are only facts', I would say: No, facts are precisely what there is not, only inter-

involves some perspective,[17] some determined and more or less narrow point of view, there can never be a final truth about the subject;[18] in Derrida's terminology, there is no simple truth present, neither about the subject nor about anything else. One can recount different narratives about the subject and attribute various interpretations to it without ever being able to reach the true account of the subject, for there is no truth, as Nietzsche claims.[19] And this obviously means that also Nietzsche's own account of the subject as a multiplicity of drives is nothing more than a conceptual description and interpretation. In other words, the subject (or we, the subjects) does not have a true essence, it is to a great extent constructed through the stories we tell about it (about ourselves). But that clearly does not mean that all the interpretations are equally good or that one can invent and construct arbitrarily everything. If this was the case, then Nietzsche could not call the Cartesian narrative, for instance, a fiction and a falsification (see below). One still has to justify what one says, provide arguments, interpretations do have to be supported by different kind of (textual) evidence even if there can never be final justifications and grounds that would settle the matter once and for all. For Derrida as well, for instance, there does seem to be some other 'outside' language that guides our interpretations, they cannot be completely random.[20] Moreover, every narrative belongs to a certain context in which it makes sense, or as Enwald writes by summarizing Derrida's position: "There can be different inventions, narratives and fables of subjectivity, but these narratives cannot be made outside a social and discursive context because they would not have any meaning."[21] This point seems to imply that every attempt to reinterpret and reinvent the subject and subjectivity must begin by including itself in the specific philosophical context, by in some way taking into account and criticising the dominating view(s) about it; the reinterpretation of the subject cannot come out of nothing, *ex nihilo*. And both Nietzsche's and

---

pretations. We cannot establish any fact 'in itself': Maybe it is absurd to want something of the sort. 'Everything is subjective', you say: But already that is an interpretation, the 'subject' is not something given, but something added and invented, something put behind what there is."
17 Cf. NL 1885–1887, 7[60], KSA 12: 315, my translation: "In so far as the word 'knowledge' [*Erkenntnis*] has any meaning, the world can be known; but it can be interpreted otherwise, it has no meaning behind itself, but countless meanings. 'Perspectivism.'"
18 Cf. Anderson (2003: 80): "If there is no absolute truth but only interpretation and evaluation, then his idea of multiple interpretations – through which the subject as a state of becoming appears – permeates his writings. Nietzsche is claiming that the subject is not 'fixed' but in its changing, its shifting, its fleetingness, is perpetually becoming."
19 Cf. NL 1885–1887, 2[108], KSA 12: 114.
20 Cf. Derrida 2007: 1–47.
21 Enwald 2004: 237.

Derrida's accounts of the subject start precisely by treating it as a problem, by 'deconstructing' the traditional views about it.

3

Another important aspect to emphasize in this context is that Derrida, similarly to Nietzsche,[22] does not really want to 'liquidate' and destroy the subject. In a certain 'discourse of opinion', as Derrida calls it, there has been and there still is a wide-spread view that a whole series of authors, sometimes disdainfully called postmodernists, poststructuralists or deconstructionists, wanted to completely liquidate and do away with the subject and the self. To those authors, some of them directly influenced by Nietzsche, belong, among others, Freud, Marx, Heidegger, Lacan, Derrida and Foucault. In this respect, for example, Derrida has sometimes interestingly been accused of being too Nietzschean in his approach. Derrida is explicitly trying to counter and undermine this *doxa* or "discourse of opinion" in his interview with Jean-Luc Nancy in the influential book *Who Comes after the Subject* (1991) by pointing out that none of the authors mentioned above does really want to liquidate or eliminate the subject. In this interview with Nancy, he says:

> For these three discourses (Lacan, Althusser, Foucault) and for some of the thinkers they privilege (Freud, Marx, Nietzsche), the subject can be re-interpreted, restored, re-inscribed, it certainly isn't "liquidated". The question "who", notably in Nietzsche, strongly reinforces this point. This is also true of Heidegger, the principal reference or target of the *doxa* we are talking about. The ontological question that deals with the *subjectum*, in its Cartesian and post-Cartesian forms, is anything but a liquidation.[23]

But Derrida does not only counter the supposed 'death of the subject'; he also tries to disperse the idea of there being *one* and the *same* concept of the subject in the whole of metaphysics of Modernity (in the thinking of, for example, Descartes, Kant, Fichte, Hegel, etc.) – the concept that, according to the mentioned *doxa*, those poststructuralists now supposedly and *jointly* – as if they all had

---

[22] Cf. BGE 12/JGB 12: "Between you and me, there is absolutely no need to give up 'the soul' itself, and relinquish one of the oldest and most venerable hypotheses – as often happens with naturalists: given their clumsiness, they barely need to touch 'the soul' to lose it. But the path lies open for new versions and sophistications of the soul hypothesis – and concepts like the 'mortal soul' and the 'soul as subject multiplicity' and the 'soul as a society constructed out of drives and affects' want henceforth to have civil rights in the realm of science."
[23] Derrida 1991: 97.

agreed upon what this classical subject is all about – wanted to 'liquidate'. Derrida seems to be rather calling for a more detailed and elaborate history or genealogy of the subject that would not retrospectively try to homogenize and equalize, but also takes very rigorously into account the differences between various Modernist thematizations of the subject,[24] as well as differences between its various 'deconstructions'. But by drawing attention to that fact, Derrida does not mean that the classic discourse on the 'subject' does not have common roots or that there are no evident similarities, analogies or shared characteristics between different Western conceptualizations of the 'subject'. Rather, at least partly, his own argument depends on those analogies, on a certain more or less direct continuity in Western philosophy. But even though there seems to be a certain classical – but perhaps not as homogenous and unitary as imagined – concept and discourse on the subject, and even though Derrida does explicitly deconstruct it from different angles in his work, he is very far from wanting to liquidate the subject altogether. He seeks rather to resituate it, and he is very explicit on that point:

> I have never said that the subject should be dispensed with. Only that it should be deconstructed. To deconstruct the subject does not mean to deny its existence. There are subjects, "operations" or "effects" (*effets*) of subjectivity. This is an incontrovertible fact. To acknowledge this does not mean, however, that the subject is what it says it is. The subject is not some meta-linguistic substance or identity, some pure *cogito* of self-presence; it is always inscribed in language. My work does not, therefore, destroy the subject; it simply tries to resituate it.[25]

Hence, according to Derrida, the subject is not "some meta-linguistic substance or identity, some pure cogito of self-presence" (one can interpret Derrida as naming here some of those common characteristics and analogies that make up the "classical discourse"), and it seems that it is not that because, above all, "it is always inscribed in language". Since this claim seems to be very similar to Nietzsche's position, one can assume that the latter has directly influenced Derrida in this respect. It is mainly by – but not *only* – analysing language, by paying more attention to the system of language, that Nietzsche as well as Derrida deconstruct and undermine the Cartesian concept of the subject.

---

[24] Cf. Simon Critchley (1996: 22): "Has there ever existed a unified conscious subject, a watertight Cartesian ego? Or is the subject some phantasy or abstraction that is retrospectively attributed to the past that one wants either to exceed, betray or ignore? That is to say, is not the subject a fiction that Kant finds in Descartes, without it being in Descartes, what Heidegger finds in Kant without it being in Kant, or that Derrida finds in Husserl without it being in Husserl?"
[25] Derrida 1982: 125.

4

Nietzsche and Derrida both agree that the self-present, immediately self-aware, self-sufficient, autonomous, self-identical rational 'subject'–let us call this the 'classical discourse' on the subject–is nothing more than a linguistic description, just one interpretation among others, moreover, quite a bad interpretation, and Nietzsche even repeatedly calls it a fiction, a falsification or a fable. In *Twilight of the Idols*, for example, Nietzsche claims that "the inner world is full of illusions and phantasms" and that the I (the 'subject') "has become a fairy tale, a fiction, a play on words" (TI, The Four Great Errors 3/GD, Die vier grossen Irrthümer 3). What Nietzsche means by that, as it becomes clear from the context of the aphorism, is that the idea of some self-conscious subject as the cause of our thoughts and actions has become entirely incredible in his historical context. Along the same lines, Nietzsche supposes that the "I" is rather a "perspectival illusion", "an apparent unity, in which, as in the horizon line, everything gets amalgamated".[26] In *Beyond Good and Evil*, Nietzsche expresses his astonishment that people still believe in immediate certainties:

> There are still harmless self-observers who believe in the existence of "immediate certainties," such as "I think," or the "I will" that was Schopenhauer's superstition: just as if knowledge had been given an object here to seize, stark naked, as a "thing-in-itself," and no falsification took place from either the side of the subject or the side of the object. But I will say this a hundred times: "immediate certainty," like "absolute knowledge" and the "thing in itself" contains a *contradictio in adjecto*. For once and for all, we should free ourselves from the seduction of words! (BGE 16/JGB16)

This passage is followed by Nietzsche's critique of Descartes' "I think" which, far from being the absolute basis for all knowledge, is said to involve "a whole set of bold claims that are difficult, perhaps impossible, to establish".[27] For instance,

> that *I* am the one who is thinking, that there must be something that is thinking in the first place, that thinking is an activity and the effect of a being who is considered the cause, that there is an "I," and finally, that it has already been determined what is meant by

---

[26] NL 1885–1887, 2[91], KSA 12: 106, my translation.
[27] It seems that the target of Nietzsche's criticism of the 'I' and 'I think' is not only Descartes but also Spir and Teichmüller, cf. Dickopp 1970. That would also explain why Nietzsche's criticism of Descartes is not completely justified or does not bear on him in every respect. One could perhaps say that Nietzsche attacks a certain wider narrative regarding the subject which Descartes indeed initiated but which is not completely identical with his thinking on the subject.

> thinking, – that I *know* what thinking is. Because if I had not already made up my mind what thinking is, how could I tell whether what had just happened was not perhaps "willing" or "feeling"? Enough: this "I think" presupposes that I *compare* my present state with other states that I have seen in myself, in order to determine what it is: and because of this retrospective comparison with other types of "knowing," this present state has absolutely no "immediate certainty" for me. (BGE 16/JGB 16)

Nietzsche makes here several important points. By analysing the sentence "I think", he discovers a number of unjustified metaphysical claims. This sentence does not simply correspond to some matter of facts; it rather *creates* an impression of certain matter of facts. Similarly to the aphorism from *Twilight of the Idols* that I just referred to, Nietzsche firstly puts into doubt the idea that the subject "I" is the condition of the predicate "think". The thought, as Nietzsche claims in the following aphorism, comes when it wills, not when I will: "It is, therefore, a *falsification* of the facts to say that the subject 'I' is the condition of the predicate 'think'" (BGE 17/JGB 17). For Nietzsche, this illusion that the 'I' causes our thoughts (and actions), that every happening is an act and that every act presupposes a doer,[28] goes back to the basic grammar of Indo-European languages: to the subject/predicate structure of the sentence.[29] However, in relation to Nietzsche's putative influence on Derrida, perhaps more interesting in the quotation from BGE 16/JGB 16 is the point that Nietzsche makes about how to determine what thinking really is. Approximately at the time of writing *Beyond Good and Evil*, Nietzsche had noted in the *Nachlass*: "[...] in *cogito* lies not only some occurrence [*Vorgang*] which is simply being recognized – this is absurd! – but a judgment that it is this particular occurrence, and who, for example, did not know how to differentiate between thinking, feeling and wanting, could not establish the occurrence at all."[30] Hence, Nietzsche claims that one can only know what thinking is if one compares and relates it to other states one has experienced in oneself. In other words, thinking is something only by having a reference to other

---

[28] NL 1885–1887, 2[83], KSA 12: 101–103; cf. GM I 13.
[29] Cf. Nietzsche has noted for himself in the *Nachlass*: "Let us be more careful than Cartesius who got caught up in the snare of words. *Cogito* is, of course, just a word but it means something multiple (several things are multiple and we coarsely grab after them, firmly believing that they are one). Behind that famous *cogito* there is, firstly, it thinks, secondly, I believe that I am the one there that thinks, thirdly, supposing that this second point remains suspended as a matter of belief, also that first 'it thinks' contains yet another belief: namely, that thinking is an action for which a subject, at least an 'it', must be thought: and further, the *ergo sum* means nothing! But this is the belief in the grammar which posits 'things' and their 'actions', and we are quite far from any immediate certainty" (NL 1884–1885, 40 [23], KSA 11:630–640, my translation).
[30] NL 1884–1885, 40[24], KSA 11: 640–641, my translation.

mental states, that is, in being different, in differing from other states one has experienced in oneself. There is no thinking without this "being different from" something else, thinking is never present as such, there is no thinking in itself; it not only involves a detour, a relation to the other, but becomes what it is only by way of this detour. And that applies, of course, not only to thinking but to all the mental states one can experience, for instance, willing, feeling, loving, desiring, understanding, hating, perceiving, imagining etc. Furthermore, Nietzsche refers in the above quotation from BGE 16/JGB 16 to the complication of *time*, that is, this comparison of different mental states is always *retrospective*, one has to trust one's memory, to *re-call* and *re- present* other mental states (like feeling and willing) in order to be able to compare them with the "present" one (which, as said, is not really present either, since it "is" something distinguished and determined only by means of the comparison, or a certain differential relationship, with mental states that have to be re-called and re-presented). Taking all that into account, we are very far, as Nietzsche states, from that "immediate certainty" and evidence Descartes and others were looking for.

Now, to experience something as thinking, willing or feeling, one has to have seen these states several times, what is experienced as appearing only once is nothing determinate at all and remains completely unrecognizable *as* something; in other words, one can distinguish and determine a mental state if one not only compares it to other mental states, but also to the earlier occurrences of the same mental state; one has to be able to experience a certain equality between what one experiences now and what one experienced yesterday, for instance. But what guarantees (besides memory which can be easily fallible) that what I experienced yesterday as thinking is exactly the same what I experience now as thinking? Nietzsche indeed thinks that such equality is created and constructed. For instance in the *Nachlass*, he has noted for himself the following: "'Subject' is a fiction, as if many *equal* states in us were an effect of a substratum: but *we* have first created the 'equality' of these states; the *making* equal and *fixing* up of these states is the *case* and *not* the equality (–this should rather be *denied*)."[31] Let us not analyse here what this 'we' refers to. In any case, Nietzsche is fully aware that these kinds of expressions like "we think" or "we create" bring us back to the old Cartesian idea that there is some separate entity that thinks or creates–and precisely this idea is under attack.[32]

According to Nietzsche, as we saw, the view of there being certain unified self-present subject or substratum that produces equal mental states, intentions

---

31 NL 1885–1887, 10[19], KSA 12: 465, my translation.
32 NL 1885–1887, 10[158], KSA 12: 549-550.

and actions, goes back, at least partly (there might also be other reasons why this 'illusion' emerged, like the slave revolt in morality), to the grammar which already posits 'things' and their 'actions' [*Thätigkeiten*].³³ But what, more specifically, is responsible for this process of 'making equal' [*Gleichsetzen*] of various mental states? Why do they seem to be equal? It seems that, according to Nietzsche, language has an important role to play in this process (though not necessarily only language). In *On Truth and Lie in a Non-Moral Sense*, Nietzsche writes explicitly that every word originates through the process of making equal what is not really equal (TL 1/WL 1). In the aphorism "The so-called 'Ego'" from *Daybreak*, Nietzsche somewhat similarly argues that "words really exist only for superlative degrees" of inner processes: "the milder, middle degrees, not to speak of the lower, degrees which are continually in play, elude us, and yet it is they which weave the web of our character and our destiny" (D 115/M 115). But more importantly, he implies in the same aphorism that there is really no exact thinking without words and language (in the *Nachlass*, he claims more directly that we can "only think in the form of language"³⁴); we are unable to perceive accurately (or perhaps not at all) when we run out of words, running against the limits of language. As Nietzsche puts it, we "are none of us that which we appear to be in accordance with the states for which alone we have consciousness and words [...]". (D 115/M 115). Hence, we perceive ourselves by the help of general and common language and what we see in this way is far from what we (or our mental states) 'really' are. On the contrary, language seems rather in some sense to create and construct the self as well as the unity of various mental states. So it seems that the 'thinking' Nietzsche spoke about in JGB 16/ JGB 16 is experienced as a more or less unitary state that can be compared to other states mainly because of language. The same idea is conveyed in an aphorism "On 'the genius of the species'" from *The Gay Science* where Nietzsche argues that "conscious thinking takes place in words, that is, in communication symbols, and this fact discloses the origin of consciousness" (GS 354/FW 354).³⁵ In principal, one can never reach the subtleties of one's inner states and 'movements' since the origin of the consciousness lies in the general and common language which has very little to do with some sort of singularity or 'individuality'.³⁶ This also implies that consciousness and language tend to construct the self (the image of self) as well as the apparent unity of inner states through

---

33 NL 1884–1885, 40 [23], KSA 11: 639-640.
34 NL 1885–1887, 5[22], KSA 12: 193.
35 Cf. Constâncio 2012.
36 Sooväli 2012.

abstractions or generalities and never really express and capture the possible singularity of the person. In general and particularly in this aphorism, Nietzsche is very far from understanding conscious thinking and consciousness as being the absolute form of existence or some pure origin of thoughts, decisions and actions, but more like a superficial effect of language and different non-present drives and forces, differences of forces.[37]

5

Hence, from Nietzsche's treatment of the subject, precisely the same thing seems to follow what Derrida said about it in the above quotation, namely that "the subject is not some meta-linguistic substance or identity, some pure *cogito* of self-presence" and that "it is always inscribed in language". Let us try to determine a little more precisely what Derrida means by this last formulation. But firstly, it should be emphasized that Derrida's historical-intellectual context was obviously slightly different than Nietzsche's. That is, besides Nietzsche, Derrida also draws on other, more contemporary sources, and not only those strictly belonging to philosophy. In his deconstruction of the subject, he also takes developments in linguistics, particularly Saussure's work, rigorously into account. Bearing that in mind, let us look a little closer at Derrida's article *Différance*.

Following Saussure, he claims there that language is a system of differences, that is, the sign – its material side, the signifier, as well as its conceptual side, the signified – is constituted solely by the differential relations to other terms of the language. This system obviously involves generality (*iterability*), or as Derrida puts it elsewhere: "as soon as there is language, generality has entered the scene".[38] In this system of differences, no linguistic element is simply present to itself: "Every concept is necessarily and essentially inscribed in a chain or a system, within which it refers to another and to other concepts, by a systematic play of differences."[39] Derrida's famous term *différance* refers precisely to this movement, process or play of differing and deferral: "What we note as *différance* will thus be the movement of play that 'produces' (and not by something that is simply an activity) these differences, these effects of difference."[40] No concept, even 'thinking' for instance, refers only to itself or is purely

---

[37] Cf. Lupo 2012.
[38] Derrida 1995: 200.
[39] Derrida 1973a: 140.
[40] Derrida 1973a: 141.

identical with itself. Concepts are all woven by the differential relationships, and this reminds us quite directly of what Nietzsche said about 'thinking' in BGE 16/JGB 16.

According to Derrida, what is the relation of the subject to the language as a general system of differences? Derrida argues in the same article that "the subject (self-identical or even conscious of self-identity, self-conscious) is inscribed in language, that it is a 'function' of the language. He becomes a *speaking* subject only by conforming his speech [...] to the system of linguistic prescriptions taken as the system of differences [...]."[41] Hence, Derrida uses here again the expression that "the subject is inscribed in language". By this, he refers to the fact that the self-conscious subject is not the master of language: for example, somebody who just makes use of this system of differences, but essentially remains untouched and undisturbed by it. The subject is a "function" of (or is "produced" by) language, the subject is caught in differential relationships that exclude simple self-presence and are governed by language.[42] In other words, there is no self-conscious subject who speaks and uses the language, somebody who simply directs and guides his speech; rather, it is language itself that produces the appearance of the self-conscious subject as an effect. This idea (that the self-conscious subject is an effect of the *general system* of language), as we saw, can already explicitly be found in its pre-Saussurean form in Nietzsche's work, and it is precisely this kind of argumentation that is behind the famous slogan of the "death of the author" (that is, death of a some supposed original subjectivity of an author) by Roland Barthes[43] (although Derrida, as he clearly claims, does not believe in any "deaths",[44] neither in that of the "subject", nor in that of the "author"; as "effects", "subject" as well as "author" still remain important and undeniable, as something that can be investigated).

Having argued that the self-conscious subject is a "function" of the system of language, Derrida raises in *Différance* a possible objection to what he has just said: it is certainly evident that the subject "becomes a signifying subject only by entering into the system of differences"; hence, "the speaking or signifying subject would not be self-present [...]. But can we not conceive of a presence and

---

41 Derrida 1973a: 145–146.
42 Cf. Derrida's words from *Positions* (1981: 29) where he notes the following: "[...] the subject, and first of all the conscious and speaking subject, depends upon the system of differences and the movement of *différance* [...] the subject is not present, nor above all present to itself before *différance* [...] the subject is constituted only in being divided from itself, in becoming space, in temporizing, in deferral [...]."
43 Cf. Barthes 1977: 142–148.
44 Cf. Derrida 1981: 6.

self-presence of the subject before speech or its signs, a subject's self-presence in a silent and intuitive consciousness?"[45] According to Derrida, this question supposes two interrelated things: firstly, that before and outside the realm of signs something like consciousness might be possible; and secondly, that before the distribution of its signs, "consciousness can gather itself up in its own presence".[46] Thus, we should ask: can we not conceive of Descartes' *cogito* before language and signification? One could perhaps argue, that he might have grasped the "I think" and its evident truth in his intuitive consciousness and only afterwards, by speaking with himself in a soliloquy, for instance, or by writing it down, by communicating it to others, entered in the system of differences?

According to Derrida, this privilege accorded to pre-linguistic consciousness and presence belongs to the very 'essence' of metaphysics. By questioning the privilege of the presence, this epoch of presence in general, Derrida comes to see, as it already became clear, "presence"–and, in particular, consciousness, the being-next-to-itself of consciousness–no longer as the absolutely matrical form of being but as "a 'determination' and an 'effect' [...]".[47] And it is exactly at this point where he explicitly refers to Nietzsche (but, again, among Freud and Heidegger) and his criticism of consciousness. Thus, Derrida writes:

> I shall only recall that for Nietzsche "the important main activity is unconscious" and that consciousness is the effect of forces whose essence, ways, and modalities are not peculiar to it. Now force itself is never present; it is only a play of differences and quantities. [...] Is not the whole thought of Nietzsche a critique of philosophy as active indifference to difference, as a system of reduction or adiaphoristic repression? [...] In Nietzsche, there are so many themes that can be related with the kind of symptomatology that always serves to diagnose the evasions and ruses of anything disguised in its *différance*. [...] We shall therefore call *différance* this "active" (in movement) discord of the different forces and of the differences between forces which Nietzsche opposes to the entire system of metaphysical grammar.[48]

We see here that Derrida directly relates his notion of *différance* to several themes in Nietzsche's work; for Derrida, it is Nietzsche, among others, who has demonstrated that there is no self-presence of the subject in some silent and intuitive consciousness. More generally, Nietzsche, according to Derrida, has shown with his whole *corpus* that there are no pure, self-identical terms, con-

---

45 Derrida 1973a: 146.
46 Derrida 1973a: 147.
47 Derrida 1973a: 147.
48 Derrida 1973a: 148–149.

cepts and states, or in Nietzsche's own words, there are no pure oppositions. This point is "present" almost everywhere in Nietzsche's thinking, but most clearly in BGE 2/JGB 2, where he famously states: "The fundamental belief of metaphysicians is the *belief in opposition of values*." Hence, Nietzsche, as Derrida put it in the quotation, has diagnosed "the evasions and ruses of anything disguised in its *différance*".

At this point, a possible confusion should be clarified. We have written a great deal about language and the differences within language, but neither for Nietzsche nor for Derrida is language *in a strict sense* everything there is. In the above quotation, Derrida refers to the differences of forces in Nietzsche and not specifically linguistic differences. When analysing BGE 16/JGB 16, we brought language in via interpretation, by evoking other pertinent passages in Nietzsche's work, but Nietzsche did not directly speak about language there, rather about mental states. For Derrida, the flow of experience is not 'essentially' something linguistic in the strict sense. The point is that Derrida's notion of *différance* does not confine itself to the language (and semiolinguistic differences); *différance* applies to the whole field of 'experience'. This means that the same properties that characterize language – generality, iterability, absence, differential relations, and mediation – can also be found in the flow of experience itself.[49] With regard to that fact, one could speak of 'language' in a broad sense, of language before or preceding language. Derrida himself uses the phrase "originary writing" (*arche-écriture*) which is neither speech nor writing in the common-sense and implies that there is no unmediated experience, no unmediated mental state. Every experience or mental state involves retentions (there is always a blind spot), re-presentations, repetitions and differences. And this is precisely what Nietzsche claimed regarding Descartes' *cogito* in BGE 16/JGB 16. Derrida himself explicitly says in the essay *Signature, Event, Context* that the traits of the classical concept of writing (iterability, absence, differential relations, mediations etc.) "are valid not only for all orders of 'signs' and for all languages in general, but moreover, beyond semio-linguistic communication, for the entire field of what philosophy would call experience, even the experience of being or the above-mentioned 'presence'".[50] One of Nietzsche's general but at the same time most direct, constant and consistent influences on Derrida seems exactly to be the fact that mediation, detour, difference and some form of 'impurity' go all the way down.

---

[49] Derrida demonstrates that in a detailed manner in his *Speech and Phenomena* (1973) by analysing Husserl's phenomenology of time consciousness.
[50] Derrida 1988: 9.

6

For Derrida, this mediation and *différance* mean that some putative interiority of the subject is always contaminated by some outside; more precisely still, the interiority of the Cartesian, Kantian or Husserlian transcendental ego is not only contaminated by some outside, but it is constituted through the relation to some (mundane) exteriority, to some outside or other: to the world, body, language, social space, differences of forces, as in Nietzsche etc.[51] For Derrida, in so far as the inside has always already been invaded and penetrated by the outside, his conception of the subject has no doubt naturalistic and materialistic tendencies,[52] and it opens up the possibility of naturalistic conceptions of the subject, soul (as Nietzsche, for instance, wants to reinterpret soul in a naturalistic way, see BGE 12/JGB 12) and other concepts. These naturalistic tendencies are most clearly visible in his text *Freud and the Scene of Writing.* Having that in mind, it is somewhat strange and out of place that Brian Leiter opposes Nietzsche as a "naturalist" to "postmodernists" like Foucault and Derrida by writing in his *Nietzsche on Morality*: "This book joins cause with some recent literature in arguing that, rightly understood, Nietzsche belongs not in the company of postmodernists like Foucault and Derrida, but rather in the company of naturalists like Hume and Freud [...]."[53] This quotation creates an impression, as if there was some serious incompatibility between Humean-Freudian naturalism and Derrida's or Foucault's discourses.

However, Derrida is certainly not a *scientistic* naturalist, that is, somebody who completely relies on the sciences. He does draw on them, especially in his early work (such as *Of Grammatology*), but does not blindly follow them and their self-understanding (in some sense, his analysis touches upon the conditions of possibility of sciences). Richard Schacht has demonstrated exactly the same thing with regard to Nietzsche's naturalism.[54] But despite these obvious similarities and relations between Nietzsche and Derrida with respect to the naturalistic understanding of the subject, it has to be emphasized as well that Derrida is quite far from putting such an enormous emphasis on the body,

---

[51] Cf. Derrida (2009a: 285): "The 'subject' of writing does not exist if we mean by that some sovereign solitude of the author. The subject of writing is a *system* of relations between strata: [...] the psyche, society, the world. Within that scene, on that stage, the punctual simplicity of the classical subject is not to be found."
[52] Cf. Roden 2004: 96–100.
[53] Leiter 2002: 2.
[54] Cf. Schacht 2012.

instincts, and drives as Nietzsche does. In short: body, instincts, drives, and physiology in general play a much bigger role in Nietzsche's thinking on the subject than in Derrida's. Whereas Derrida exposes and discloses those blind spots and margins where the mundane (the worldly, body, instincts) has already crept into some supposed ideality and interiority of the subject, Nietzsche traces the latter quite directly back to the body and its mechanisms.

References

Anderson, Nicole (2003) "The Ethical Possibilities of Subject as Play: In Nietzsche and Derrida", in: *The Journal of Nietzsche Studies* 26, 79–90.

Barthes, Roland (1977) "The Death of the Author", in: *Image–Music–Text*, ed. and trans. S. Heath, New York: Hill and Wang, 142–148.

Constâncio, João (2012) "Consciousness, Communication, and Self-Expression. Towards an Interpretation of Aphorism 354 of Nietzsche's The Gay Science", in: J. Constâncio and M.J. Mayer Branco (eds.), *As the Spider Spins: Essays on Nietzsche's Critique and Use of Language*, Berlin/Boston: De Gruyter, 197–231.

Critchley, Simon (1996) "Prolegomena to Any Post-Deconstructive Subjectivity", in: S. Critchley and P. Dews (eds.), *Deconstructive Subjectivities*, Albany, NY: State University of New York Press.

Derrida, Jacques (1973a) "Différance", in: *Speech and Phenomena and Other Essays on Husserl's Theory of Signs*, trans. D.B. Allison, Evanston: Northwestern University Press, 129–160.

Derrida, Jacques (1973b) "Speech and Phenomena", in: *Speech and Phenomena and Other Essays on Husserl's Theory of Signs*, trans. D.B. Allison, Evanston: Northwestern University Press, 1–104.

Derrida, Jacques (1979) *Spurs. Nietzsche's Styles/Éperons. Les Styles de Nietzsche*, trans. B. Harlow, Chicago/London: University of Chicago Press.

Derrida, Jacques (1981) *Positions*, trans. A. Bass, Chicago: University of Chicago Press.

Derrida, Jacques (1982) "Deconstruction and the other" (interview with Richard Kearney), in: Richard Kearney (ed.), *Dialogues with Contemporary Continental Thinkers*, Manchester: Manchester University Press, 105–126.

Derrida, Jacques (1985a) "Otobiographies", in: *The Ear of the Other: Otobiography, Transference, Translation*, ed. C.V. McDonald, trans. A. Ronell and P. Kamuf, New York: Schocken Books, 1–38.

Derrida, Jacques (1985b) "Roundtable on Translation", in: *The Ear of the Other: Otobiography, Transference, Translation*, ed. C.V. McDonald, trans. A. Ronell and P. Kamuf, New York: Schocken Books, 91–161.

Derrida, Jacques (1986) "Interpreting Signatures (Nietzsche/Heidegger): Two Questions", in: Diane Michelfelder and Richard Palmer (eds. and trans.), *Dialogue and Deconstruction: The Gadamer-Derrida Encounter*, New York: SUNY Press, 57–74.

Derrida, Jacques (1988) "Signature Event Context", in: *Limited Inc*, trans. S. Weber, Evanston: Northwestern University Press, 1–25.

Derrida, Jacques (1991) "Eating Well, or the Calculation of the Subject", in: E. Cadava, P. Connor and J-L. Nancy (eds.), *Who Comes After the Subject*, New York: Routledge, 96–119.
Derrida, Jacques (1995) "There is no *One* Narcissism (Autobiophotographies)", in: *Points... Interviews, 1974–1994*, Stanford: Stanford University Press, 196–215.
Derrida, Jacques (1997b) *Of Grammatology*, trans. G. Spivak, Baltimore: The Johns Hopkins University Press.
Derrida, Jacques (1997) *Politics of Friendship*, trans. G. Collins, London: Verso Books.
Derrida, Jacques (2002) "Nietzsche and the Machine", in: *Negotiations: Interventions and Interviews 1971–2001*, ed. and trans. E. Rottenberg, Stanford: Stanford University Press, 215–256.
Derrida, Jacques (2007) *Psyche. Inventions of the Other*, vol. 1, Stanford: Stanford University Press.
Derrida, Jacques (2009a) "Freud and the Scene of Writing", in: *Writing and Difference*, trans. A. Bass, London/New York: Routledge, 246–291.
Derrida, Jacques (2009b) "Structure, Sign and Play in the Discourse of Human Sciences", in: *Writing and Difference*, trans. A. Bass, London/New York: Routledge, 351–370.
Dickopp, Karl-Heinz (1970) "Zum Wandel von Nietzsches Seinsverständnis–African Spir und Gustav Teichmüller", in: *Zeitschrift für philosophische Forschung* 24, 50–71.
Enwald, Marika (2004) *Displacements of Deconstruction: The Deconstruction of Metaphysics of Presence, Meaning, Subject and Method*, Diss., Tampere: Tampereen Yliopistopaino Oy Juvenes Print.
Leiter, Brian (2002) *Routledge Philosophy Guidebook to Nietzsche on Morality*, London/New York: Routledge.
Lucy, Niall (2004) *A Derrida Dictionary*, Oxford: Blackwell.
Lupo, Luca (2012) "Drives, Instincts, Language, and Consciousness in Daybreak 119: 'Erleben und Erdichten'", in: J. Constâncio and M.J. Mayer Branco (eds.), *As the Spider Spins: Essays on Nietzsche's Critique and Use of Language*, Berlin/Boston: De Gruyter, 179–195.
Roden, David (2004) "The Subject", in: J. Reynolds and J. Roffe (eds.), *Understanding Derrida*, New York/London: Continuum, 93–102.
Schacht, Richard (2012) "Nietzsche's Naturalism", in: *The Journal of Nietzsche Studies* 43(2), 185–212.
Sooväli, Jaanus (2012) "The Absence and the Other. Nietzsche and Derrida against Husserl", in: J. Constâncio and M.J. Mayer Branco (eds.), *As the Spider Spins: Essays on Nietzsche's Critique and Use of Language*, Berlin/Boston: De Gruyter, 161–177.

Maria João Mayer Branco
18 Questioning Introspection: Nietzsche and Wittgenstein on "The Peculiar Grammar of the Word 'I'"

> Mais vous qui doutez de tout et ne pouvez douter de vous-même, qui êtes-vous?
> (René Descartes, *La recherche de la vérité*)

1

In spite of considerable differences in their thought, Nietzsche and Wittgenstein share a philosophical interest in common problems and an "unconventional" way of treating them that justifies approaching these thinkers together. In his Introduction to the *Cambridge Companion to Wittgenstein*, Hans Sluga speaks of Wittgenstein in terms that could easily apply to Nietzsche, highlighting "the unconventional cast of his mind, the radical nature of his philosophical proposals, and the experimental form he gave to their expression".[1] Sluga goes on to compare Wittgenstein's reception with Nietzsche's, arguing that "both have been acclaimed as new starting points in philosophy and both have been dismissed as not really being philosophers at all".[2]

It is certainly true, as Robert B. Pippin has recently emphasized, that "both Ludwig Wittgenstein and Nietzsche were trying to say something about what it might mean for philosophy itself to come to an end, for a culture to be 'cured' of philosophy".[3] According to this view, there is a close affinity between the two thinkers in that they agree that "there is no such thing as philosophical theory", although there could still be philosophers and attempts at "conventional restatements" of their thinking are "understandable".[4] Their work can in fact be said to constitute an effort to "avoid doctrines",[5] particularly every doctrine's main metaphysical assumption: the assumption of a conceptual "supra-individuality" or

---

1 Sluga 1996: 1.
2 Sluga 1996: 29.
3 Pippin 2010: xiv. Pippin refers to Bernard Williams paper *"Nietzsche's Minimalist Moral Psychology"*, published in Schacht 1994: 237–247.
4 Pippin 2010: xiv.
5 See Stegmaier 1995.

universality, immune to the conditions of communication, that is to say, the assumption that a theory could ever use concepts that might be neutral and independent from their use and users. Moreover, both thinkers refuse to build systems (Nietzsche: "I distrust all systematizers and avoid them. The will to a system is a lack of integrity", TI, Arrows and Epigrams 26), they both renounce all theory (Wittgenstein: "The difficulty of renouncing all theory: One has to regard what appears so obviously incomplete, as something complete", RPP §723), and by doing this they both conceive of philosophy as the manifestation of a "continuousness of critical energy, never itself quite housed within theses and doctrines".[6]

Bringing these two philosophers together from this perspective implies situating them within a precise moment of the history of philosophy. It requires recognizing that their philosophical proposals belong to the moment where the status of metaphysics as 'first philosophy' was questioned and where philosophy proved once again to be a problem for itself. This critical moment corresponds to the interrogation of what grounds philosophical activity and to what extent its existence still makes sense and contributes for the development of Western culture. Nevertheless, when it comes to their understanding and expectations in regard to philosophy, Nietzsche's and Wittgenstein's positions seem quite distant from each other, or at least show differences that can by no means be diminished. In fact, while Nietzsche worries about the threat that modern nihilism and philistinism represent for the "philosophers of the future" (e.g., BGE 42) and hence still considers philosophy to be a means for the overcoming of cultural diseases, Wittgenstein speaks of his work as "one of the heirs of the subject that used to be called philosophy" (*Blue Book* – BLBK, 28), thereby indicating that he understands philosophical anxieties as something of the past and philosophers of today as beings whose task, experiences and problems are infinitely more modest, more prosaic or less "tragic" than what Nietzsche expected or hoped for.[7]

---

[6] Eldridge 1997: 14–15.

[7] This seems to be clear in one of the rare occasions in which Wittgenstein's writings explicitly mention Nietzsche: "There are problems I never tackle, which do not lie in my path or belong to my world. Problems of the intellectual world of the West which Beethoven (& perhaps Goethe to a certain extent) tackled & wrestled with but which no philosopher has ever confronted (perhaps Nietzsche passed close to them). [...] In this world (mine) there is no tragedy & with that all the endlessness that gives rise to tragedy (as its result) is lacking/It is as though everything were soluble in the ether; there are no harnesses/This means that hardness & conflict do not become something splendid but a *defect*/Conflict is dissipated in much the same way as is the tension of a spring in a mechanism that you melt (or dissolve in nitric acid). In this solution tensions no longer exist." (CV, 11–12)

The affinities and differences between Nietzsche and Wittgenstein certainly deserve more attention than they have received so far, as comparative studies of these philosophers remain scarce.[8] It is certainly true, as Marco Brusotti has recently and convincingly shown, that we cannot speak of a direct influence of Nietzsche on Wittgenstein.[9] Textual references to Nietzsche or quotations from his work do not abound in Wittgenstein's writings. Those that exist clarify Wittgenstein's position regarding the ideas that he attributes to Nietzsche, as well as his evaluation of Nietzsche's historical significance and importance in the intellectual atmosphere of his age, particularly within the Vienna Circle. However, the absence of a direct influence of one thinker over another does not necessarily imply that comparing their views on specific themes cannot be philosophically valuable.

The aim of this chapter is to contribute to a comparative study of these philosophers by focusing on the concrete topic of subjectivity. Underlying this aim there are two main ideas. The first is that despite the fact that they are both highly critical of the philosophical tradition – which is manifest in Nietzsche's positions against his predecessors and in Wittgenstein's rare references to the history of philosophy, writing almost as if he was the first philosopher on Earth[10] –, their thought should be understood in the light of their specific historical-philosophical contexts. This is not to suggest that their work must be "incorporated into traditional philosophical theory",[11] but it does imply that their critical positions with regard to traditional answers to certain philosophical problems are a way of coming to terms with them. Despite their originality and unconventionality, it remains true that their work emerges from a dialogue and engagement with the work of previous philosophers, particularly from the (anti-)Cartesian tradition. The first assumption of this article is hence that Nietzsche's and Wittgenstein's views on the problem of subjectivity involve an

---

[8] Although it is possible to find references to Nietzsche in work done by Wittgenstein scholars – e.g., Sluga (1996); Cavell (1979, rep. 1999) and, more recently, Cavell in Day/Krebs (2010: 86); Mulhall (2007: 109, 113–114); Schulte (2013) –, a substantial comparative study of both is still missing (to our knowledge, Gordon Bearn's *Waking to Wonder* (1997) and Glen T. Martin, *From Nietzsche to Wittgenstein: The Problem of Truth and Nihilism in the Modern World* (1989) are some of the (not so recent) and rare works that discuss Nietzsche's and Wittgenstein's philosophical views). Nevertheless, we can find recent work by Wittgenstein scholars on Nietzsche – Sluga in Young (2015); Mulhall in May (2011) and in Came (2014) and Mulhall (2013) – but less on Wittgenstein by Nietzsche scholars, apart from the recent and valuable work done by Marco Brusotti (2009 and 2014).
[9] Brusotti 2009.
[10] According to Cavell, "The call upon history will seem uncongenial with Wittgenstein. He seems so ahistorical. – He is ahistorical the way Nietzsche is atheistical." Cavell (1979, rep. 1999: 370).
[11] Pippin 2010: xv.

engagement with the philosophical tradition, even if this engagement is fundamentally critical and the views they put forward are fundamentally new.

The second idea underling this article concerns the theme that suggests a greater affinity between Nietzsche and Wittgenstein, which is language. Wittgenstein's interest in Nietzsche was mostly focused on Nietzsche's approach to ethical and cultural questions and it is doubtful whether he had any interest in Nietzsche's critique of language.[12] Nevertheless, it is undeniable that there are crucial similarities in their understanding of language and these similarities concern aspects of their thought that determine the whole of their philosophical inquiries and, particularly, their views on subjectivity.

I shall start by briefly summarizing the Cartesian conception of the self in order to clarify Nietzsche's and Wittgenstein's common point of departure. I shall then analyze, in separate sections, their criticisms of Cartesianism by focusing mainly on sections of Nietzsche's *Daybreak*, *Beyond Good and Evil*, *Twilight of the Idols* and *The Gay Science* and on Wittgenstein's famous 'private language argument' (PI, Part I, §§ 243–315), as well as on crucial passages from his *Blue Book*. By showing that those criticisms are grounded on the attention both thinkers pay to language, I shall try to clarify the reasons for their rejection of introspection. These are at the basis of the proposals that they put forward in opposition to the traditional understanding of subjectivity. More precisely, I shall argue that the experience of immediacy and self-coincidence of the subject, which both Nietzsche and Wittgenstein analyze through the example of the experience of suffering or of being in pain, is not a moment where the truth about who we are reveals itself, but a moment where we can lose track of what such 'truth' might signify. By focusing in the experience of suffering, both Nietzsche and Wittgenstein show that in it the subject comes to realize, not the 'truth' about his identity, but rather the degree in which the latter depends on the existence of other subjects. In the final part of the chapter, I conclude by comparing Nietzsche's and Wittgenstein's views on the possibility of self-knowledge.

2

Nietzsche's and Wittgenstein's reflections on the modern conception of the subject or of the 'I'[13] can be said to have the same philosophical starting point.

---

12 Brusotti 2009.
13 The specific sense of each of these terms will not be distinguished here since Nietzsche and Wittgenstein seem to use them indistinctively when dealing with questions of subjectivity (also resorting

As has been already claimed, they both belong to "a kind of brotherhood of modern anti-Cartesians"[14] since they question the philosophical treatment of the self as a truth or the truth upon which it might be possible to ground the totality of knowledge. In other words, they question the (*ego*) *cogito* as a self-grounded, immediate certainty, as knowledge supposed to be free from all doubt that makes the 'I' correspond to the truth, or to true being.

Descartes famously introduced this conception of the self by arguing that "this proposition, 'I am, I exist', whenever it is uttered by me, or conceived in the mind, is necessarily true".[15] Descartes contrasted the certainty of the subject's self-knowledge with the doubtfulness of knowledge about external realities. While knowledge of phenomena belonging to the outer world is dependent on the mediation of the senses and thus remains always uncertain, the thinking subject can perceive itself immediately, that is, by introspective insight or intuition, being, therefore, beyond doubt. Thus, according to Descartes, introspection guarantees epistemological certainty and it provides what he considers to be 'first knowledge', that is to say, the foundation or the ground for any other kind of knowledge. Furthermore, introspection presupposes that the subject is capable of somehow withdrawing from the external world in order to achieve a state of self-consciousness independent from his physical or bodily existence. In other words, the Cartesian *(ego) cogito* is a metaphysical reality devoid of extension and hence distinguished from the *res extensa*, it is self-sufficiently and immediately self-conscious, and it is fundamentally characterized by the capacity to think. The 'I' corresponds, therefore, to a thinking subject that exists separately from the external world. The latter cannot be reached without mediation and its existence is thus doubtful. Self-knowledge, by contrast, is certain, immediate and self-grounded, and this certainty amounts to truthfulness: "I am therefore, speaking precisely, only a thinking thing, that is, a mind, or a soul, or an intellect, or a reason [...]. I am therefore a true thing, and one that truly exists [...]".[16]

What the "brotherhood of anti-Cartesians" to which Nietzsche and Wittgenstein belong mainly criticize in Cartesianism[17] is, in the first place, the ontologi-

---

to the words 'ego', 'consciousness', 'self' and 'soul', for example). This does not, of course, imply that all these terms have equivalent meanings or that they don't deserve further and more careful examination, but rather that they will be here treated as variations of the general topic at stake.

14 Pippin 2010: 77. See also Pier 2015. On such "brotherhood" and Nietzsche's explicit place on it, see Sluga 1996: 327.

15 Descartes 2008: 13–17.

16 Descartes 2008: 19.

17 It is worth noticing two things about what I call here "anti-Cartesianism", namely that in spite of their criticisms 'anti-Cartesians' owe, of course, a great deal to Descartes (concerning

cal conception of the subject that transforms the self into a metaphysical substance completely transparent to itself and detached from the world in which it lives.[18] This conception of the self not only denies the self's bodily and physical constitution by conceiving it as a pure interiority that can only be grasped through inward intuition. It also allows for the conception of the world as will and representation, as in the philosophy of Arthur Schopenhauer (who, as is well-known, was a decisive influence on both Nietzsche and Wittgenstein, such that Nietzsche's thought can be seen as a long-term attempt to overcome Schopenhauer's pessimism,[19] and Wittgenstein's thought a long-term attempt to overcome Schopenhauer's solipsism[20]). Secondly, anti-Cartesianism rejects another important consequence of Descartes's solipsistic views of the self, namely the ego's self-sufficiency. Anti-Cartesianism questions the epistemology of Cartesian self-knowledge by criticizing the way it draws the line between subject and world and renders not only the existence of physical objects doubtful, but also the existence of other minds, from which, according to Descartes, the existence of the thinking subject is considered to be completely independent. Against this view of an 'I' that is absolutely isolated from other selves, the anti-Cartesian conception of the 'I' argues for a self"; "I shall argue that Nietzsche's and Wittgenstein's main criticism that is constituted in relation to others and has a fundamentally constitutive social dimension.[21] In the case of the authors here at stake, this dimension is mainly considered through the analysis of the role that language plays in the constitution of the subject. Both for Nietzsche and Wittgenstein there is a fundamental (and also problematic) linguistic or conceptual connection between the individual subject and an intersubjective linguistic common space that Descartes failed to acknowledge, but whose epistemological importance, they argue, can by no means be neglected and allows for a different, non-Cartesian account of what is at stake in what we call the 'I'.

I shall argue that Nietzsche's and Wittgenstein's main criticism addresses Descartes's claim that there is immediate access of the subject to itself, i.e. the

---

Nietzsche and Descartes, see Isabelle Wienand's chapter in this volume), and that "Cartesianism" here corresponds to a generalization of Descartes's philosophical views that is not completely fair to the author because, as Garry L. Hagberg has correctly pointed out, it means a set of "metaphysically dualistic views" that were not explicitly advanced by Descartes. See Hagberg 2008, *"Introduction: The Cartesian Legacy"*, p. 3.
18 See Lacoue-Labarthe 2012: 7–21.
19 See Constâncio 2011 and Sousa's and Faustino's chapter in this volume.
20 See Hagberg 2008, chapter 1 and Glock 1996: 348–352.
21 For a development of the social dimension of Nietzsche's views on the self, see Cristina Fornari's and Herman Siemens' chapters in this volume.

supposed immediacy involved in the experience of introspection, as well as the presupposition that such an experience is the ground of all specifically human relationships with an external world. The rejection of immediate introspection entails several other criticisms that the authors develop with different consequences, but that nevertheless present some affinities. In effect, if, as Nietzsche and Wittgenstein argue, the I is not immediately available to itself, than it is not prior to any other experience and the refusal of its immediacy entails the rejection of its anteriority, as well as of its foundational and unconditioned status. On the other hand, the rejection of immediacy also entails a questioning of the self's transparency to itself, that is to say, of the possibility of a direct, neutral, access of ourselves to ourselves. Hence, by rejecting introspective immediacy, both Nietzsche and Wittgenstein propose that the 'I' is not an object of immediate intuition, that is to say, that it cannot know itself instantaneously by means of a peculiar inward vision. They both conceive of the 'I' as emerging from a process that requires time and reject that it can be immediately present in introspective moments and reveal itself as an immutable, self-coincident entity. This, in turn, implies that they both put to question not only the self's immediacy, anteriority, transparency, and instantaneity, but also its interiority. Thus, both for Nietzsche and for Wittgenstein, the 'I' is not a hidden or concealed entity, an inner, invisible and inexpressible substance available only to itself. By questioning the self's epistemological immediacy, transparency and interiority, they will insist on the possibility that self-knowledge is rather an indirect, mediated access of the 'I' to itself in which language plays a decisive role. Consequently, they will convert the Cartesian ontology of the ego and its epistemological claims into a linguistic or grammatical question that brings to light the opaque but also public nature of selfhood.

On the other hand, by showing Descartes's disregard for the constitutive role played by language in the very process of philosophical thinking, both Nietzsche and Wittgenstein clarify the reasons why that negligence made Descartes overlook the limitations of his own account of the thinking subject. As their criticisms make clear, the Cartesian views on the 'I' were determined by Descartes's rather naive reliance on linguistic transparency. By shifting the perspective towards the linguistic "prejudices" (Nietzsche) or "bewilderments" (Wittgenstein) that led to the Cartesian account of the self, they bring the question of subjectivity back to its starting point and make the 'I' a philosophical problem yet to be resolved. By doing so, they propose new ways of dealing with it that are grounded on the conviction that the human subject has an irrevocable linguistic constitution and is, therefore, inextricably linked to the existence of other subjects.

3

Nietzsche's criticisms of the Cartesian subject are often expressed in his writings from the year of 1885 and they become explicit in Part I of *Beyond Good and Evil*, titled "On the Prejudices of Philosophers". In BGE 16, without naming Descartes, Nietzsche writes:

> There are still harmless self-observers who believe in the existence of "immediate certainties," such as "I think" [...]: just as if knowledge had been given an object here to seize, stark naked, as a "thing-in-itself," and no falsification took place from either the side of the subject or the side of the object. But I will say this a hundred times: "immediate certainty," like "absolute knowledge" and the "thing in itself" contains a *contradictio in adjecto*. For once and for all, we should free ourselves from the seduction of words! (BGE 16)

These lines present Nietzsche's two main claims against the Cartesian *cogito*. They develop, firstly, a refutation of its epistemological immediacy, of the "immediate certainty" or "nakedness" of the "I think". Nietzsche refuses the supposed transparency of the thinking subject by arguing that the *cogito* is not an immediate object to himself because it is given in language and language 'falsifies'. And this entails a second claim: introspection does not give evidence of the existence of the I as a simple and stable unity, so that the 'I' is in fact given as complex and opaque. Contrary to what the word 'I' seems to indicate, the 'I' is only given as a dynamic complexity. The linguistic concept 'I' abstracts from this complexity, thereby convincing us of a simplicity and unity that are false, that are linguistic falsifications. This is Descartes's "naiveté" regarding the word 'I', a naiveté that made him accept without further questioning a set of pre-conceptions about the "I think" that are "difficult, perhaps impossible, to establish" (BGE 16), namely:

> that *I* am the one who is thinking, that there must be something that is thinking in the first place, that thinking is an activity and the effect of a being who is considered the cause, that there is an "I," and finally, that it has already been determined what is meant by thinking, – that I *know* what thinking is. (BGE 16/JGB 16)

Hence, Nietzsche's questioning of the immediacy and simplicity or unity of the 'I think' entails the questioning of the very existence of a stable entity that thinks and that is the condition of the act of thinking or, in logical terms, its cause. In other words, by questioning the unity and simplicity of the Cartesian 'I', Nietzsche ends up questioning its causality, that is to say, the precedence of a neutral and permanent substance that is supposed to be the cause of all thoughts. By doing this, Nietzsche undermines Descartes' demand for certainty, that is, for an indubitable ground of all knowledge to be found by self-observation. He casts doubt onto the radicality with which Descartes led his entire philosophical inquiry, accusing him of being "superficial" (BGE 191)[22] because he did not draw the ultimate consequences of his own methodological proposal.[23] Descartes was a victim of the "prejudices of philosophers", namely because he was a-critically seduced by the simplicity of the word "I"[24] and because he simply established without further questioning that "the subject 'I' is the condition of the predicate 'think'" (BGE 16).[25]

Nietzsche's more general point is that the Cartesian conception of the self suffers from the tendency to establish a "logical-metaphysical postulate" such as "when there is thinking, there ought to be something that 'thinks'" that is nothing but "an expression of our grammatical habit which adds a doer to every deed" (NL 1887, 10[158], KSA 12: 549, my translation; see also BGE 17). In *Twilight of the Idols*, Nietzsche further develops the consequences of these "grammatical habits" for philosophy by arguing that they force us "to make use of unity, identity, permanence, substance, cause, objectification, being" (TI Reason 5). They are a result of the "presuppositions of the metaphysics of language", which

> sees doers and deeds all over; [...] it believes in the "I", in the I as being, in the I as substance, and it *projects* this belief in the I-substance onto all things – this is how it creates the concept "thing" in the first place ... Being is imagined into everything – pushed under everything – as a cause; the concept of "being" is only derived from the concept of "I" ... (TI Reason 5)

Nietzsche's claim is that language is an "advocate for error" (TI Reason 5), that it fosters, among other errors, the "error of false causation" (TI Errors 3) accord-

---

[22] See also NL 1885, 40[10], KSA 11: 632: "Descartes is not radical enough for me. In the face of his demand for certainty and his 'I do not want to be deceived', it is necessary to ask 'why not?' [...]" (my translation).
[23] As Nietzsche puts it in 1887, following Descartes's path "one does not reach something absolutely certain, but only a very strong belief" (NL 1887, 10[158], KSA 12: 549, my translation).
[24] See NL 1884–1885, 40[23], KSA 11: 639–640, where Nietzsche mentions Descartes's falling into "the trap of words" not realizing that "*cogito* is just a word but it means something multiple".
[25] On the "fictions" of causality and unity denounced in BGE 16, see Patrick Wotling's analysis in *La pensée du sous-sol. Statut et structure de la psychologie dans la philosophie de Nietzsche*, Wotling 1999: 26ff. See also Giuliano Campioni's chapter in this volume, which shows the important influence of French authors such as Bourget, Stendhal, Taine and Ribot and of the theory of the '*petits faits vrais*' on Nietzsche's critique of the "atomism of the soul" (BGE 12), a critique, moreover, that is crucial for Nietzsche's diagnosis of European nihilism and *décadence*. Campioni extensively develops this reading in Campioni 2001.

ing to which the "realm of 'inner facts'" is a realm of causes (consciousness being the cause of actions and the 'I' the cause of thoughts – TI Errors 3). But for Nietzsche this realm of 'inner facts' that we place beyond doubt has not at all been proven to exist. In fact, it is "full of illusions and phantasms" and has become "a fiction, a play on words"[26] (TI Errors 3). So, Descartes's *cogito* corresponds to an "objectification" (TI Reason 5) of the 'I' that results from linguistic prejudices and not from an immediate (self-)knowledge that could guarantee epistemological certainty. In fact, an immediate knowledge of the 'I' is not at all possible precisely because knowledge is always mediated by language, including the knowledge of our 'inner world'. Accordingly, we can refer to 'inner facts' only by using "the words that lie to hand" (D 257), and we should doubt that words adequately represent such 'inner' reality.

In the famous aphorism of *Daybreak* titled "The so-called 'ego'" (D 115), Nietzsche had already called attention to the fact that

> language and the prejudices upon which language is based are a manifold hindrance to us when we want to explain inner processes and drives: because of the fact, for example, that words only exist for superlative degrees of these processes and drives; and where words are lacking, we are accustomed to abandon exact observation because exact thinking there becomes painful [...] We are none of us that which we appear to be in accordance with the states for which alone we have consciousness and words [...]. (D 115)

Three things deserve discussion in this passage: i) Nietzsche treats language as a "hindrance", ii) he states that where words lack exactness, thinking becomes painful, and iii) he equates consciousness with words. Let me start by this third aspect which is perhaps the most crucial for understanding Nietzsche's counter-proposal to the Cartesian *cogito*. He develops it at length in section 354 of *The Gay Science*, the text where Nietzsche more extensively develops his conception of consciousness, and where he concludes with the assertion that his interest in consciousness has nothing to do with "the opposition between subject and object":

> I leave that opposition to those epistemologists who have got tangled up in the snares of grammar (or folk metaphysics). Even less am I concerned with the opposition between "thing in itself" and appearance: for we "know" far too little to even be entitled to *make* that distinction. We simply have no organ for *knowing*, for "truth" [...]. (GS 354)

---

[26] On Nietzsche's scepticism regarding knowledge of the inner world and Lange's decisive influence on Nietzsche in this respect, see Gori's, Jensen's and Constâncio's chapters in this volume. For a discussion of the three chapters, see the Introduction.

Thus, Nietzsche refuses conceiving of consciousness as a 'thing', as an object for a knowing subject.[27] On the other hand, as already seen, he also does not conceive of consciousness as a metaphysical substance, as a thing in itself located beyond worldly appearances and that could only be reached by a special kind of 'organ for knowing'. He presents his interpretation of consciousness as an "extravagant conjecture" (GS 354) according to which "our becoming conscious of our sense impressions, our power to fix them and, as it were, to place them outside of ourselves, has increased in proportion to the need to convey them *to others* by means of signs" (GS 354).[28] In other words, Nietzsche's "extravagant" view is that consciousness cannot be reduced to the subject's withdrawal into himself, or into silent concentration and inward-observation, and in fact involves the capacity to externalize 'inner facts' by finding a *medium* to convey them, i.e. involves the *"ability to communicate"* (GS 354). Put differently, Nietzsche's suggestion is that consciousness corresponds not to one's effort of becoming transparent to oneself, but rather to the effort of becoming understandable to others – and only then to oneself. Consciousness therefore depends on communication, and to a very important degree, on language.

This dependence, however, raises the first problem mentioned above, namely that "language and the prejudices upon which language is based are a manifold hindrance to us when we want to explain inner processes" (D 115). More precisely, it raises several problems which Nietzsche dealt with in his earlier writings and that are at the basis of his criticisms of language.[29] The first of these criticisms is that words are abusive generalizations that treat different things as if they were identical. Nietzsche analyzed this difficulty in *On Truth and Lying in a Non-Moral Sense*, where he showed that words fix in general abstractions the incommensurable multiplicity of what exists, taking what is different to be identical. By unifying distinct and irreducible things in identical

---

[27] Consciousness is, according to Nietzsche, more a "process" than an "entity", as João Constâncio points out in his reading of GS 354, calling attention to the fact that GS 354 explicitly refers to the gradual becoming aware of oneself and of one's inner states ("Sich-Bewusst-Werden"). See Constâncio 2012: 197–231.

[28] In his work *Le colombe dello scettico. Riflessioni di Nietzsche sulla coscienza negli anni 1880–1888*, Luca Lupo develops a careful analysis of GS 354 insisting on the relation between consciousness, language and experience and clarifying the views that Nietzsche puts forward in that text through the reading of important notes from the *Nachlass* of the same period. See Lupo 2012, esp. pp. 185–202.

[29] I have developed this problem elsewhere, and here I shall only summarize some of the points made in Branco (2012) in Constâncio/Branco (eds.) 2012: 233–253. On Nietzsche's views on language, see Constâncio/Branco 2011 and Constâncio/Branco 2012.

terms and naming each individual object with words that apply to several objects, i.e. with words that are general or common, language fails to do justice to each thing or object and, therefore, "lies". But in addition to preventing the apprehension of singular objects, language also hinders the expression of human individuality.[30] By "overlooking what is individual (*das Uebersehen des Individuellen*)" (TL 1), words presuppose "similar experiences" in different individuals (BGE 268). Therefore, by expressing what is "similar" or "common" ("base", *gemein* – BGE 268), words "falsify and corrupt" what Nietzsche designates as the most "personal" aspect of ourselves (NL 1885 – 1886, 1[202], KSA 12: 56, my translation). For this reason, he claims,

> [...] all communication by words is shameless; words dilute and make stupid; words depersonalise (*entpersönlicht*); words make the exceptional (*das Ungemeine*) base (*gemein*) (NL 1887, 10[60], KSA 12: 493, Kaufmann's translation, modified).

Thus language falsifies because it equates different objects and because it de-individualizes us. Additionally, Nietzsche also identifies a third problem. Language is not just a moving away or deviation from things. By corrupting singularities and falsifying what is unique it creates a new reality, or rather, it creates appearances which are later taken to be truths. Insisting on the discrepancy between language and reality, between language and truth, Nietzsche highlights the absence of neutrality that is characteristic of the first: words are human creations with a history and a context, such that prejudices are implicitly sedimented in them. The problem is that the passing of time makes us inattentive to that fact. We forget that we invented those words on the basis of particular experiences and perspectives and use them as if language restored things to us in a neutral way. Therefore, Nietzsche dismisses the idea of a coincidence between language and reality and conceives of their relation not as one of adequacy, but rather as a creative one involving what he calls "errors", "falsities", "fictions" or "lies". Words do not restore things, they create them (GS 58); and this is why, in spite of the many objections Nietzsche raises against language, he does not understand its inadequacy only as a failure, or only the impossibility of expressing things, an assertion of the ultimate unutterability of what is. What Nietzsche's philosophy shows is that there is no "truth" beyond linguistic articu-

---

30 In a recent paper, John Richardson analyzes Nietzsche's critical judgments on language and distinguishes Nietzsche's two "complaints" against it: the first is a general "epistemic" complaint that has to do with language's "referential use" regarding objects (it equates different objects); the second is an "existential" one, that concerns language's "expressive use" and regards the way words "harm our individuality" by "commonizing" it. See Richardson 2015.

lation and that *"what things are called* is unspeakably more important than what they are" (GS 58). The problem is that

> the reputation, name, and appearance, the worth, the usual measure and weight of a thing – originally almost always something mistaken and arbitrary [...] – has, through the belief in it, and its growth from generation to generation, slowly grown onto and into the thing and has become its very body: what started as appearance in the end nearly always becomes essence and *effectively acts* as its essence! (GS 58)

As initially mentioned, this is one of Nietzsche's main criticisms of Descartes' *(ego) cogito* and it brings us back to *Daybreak* 115 and to the idea that "language and the prejudices upon which language is based are a manifold hindrance to us when we want to explain inner processes" and that "where words are lacking, we are accustomed to abandon exact observation". Nietzsche's first point is that we live in the reality created by language, in the linguistic illusions that we no longer perceive as such because we cling to them and become habituated to them as if they told the truth, even about the most irreducible of facts, the 'inner facts' that constitute what we take to be our singularity, the uniqueness of our individuality. His second point, however, is that outside or beyond that linguistically created reality, that is to say, "where words are lacking", we abandon "exact observation (*genau zu beobachten*)" (D115). Even more precisely, his idea is that we abandon exact observation "because exact thinking there becomes painful (*weil es peinlich ist, dort noch genau zu denken*)" (D 115). Simply put, where words are lacking thinking becomes difficult. The lack of words prevents "exact thinking", which means that it promotes its opposite, i.e. impreciseness, confusion or obscurity, uncomfortable situations that put us in a "painful" state from which we feel the need to free ourselves. Hence, if it is true that language equates what is different, and if it furthermore vulgarizes our individuality and fosters prejudice and habit, it is also true that where language fails we are faced not with the ideal transparency of thought that words are supposed to hinder, but with the impossibility to think clearly. Put differently, where words are lacking, and particularly where they are lacking and "we want to explain inner processes" (D 115), we must deal with a painful state of confusion that precludes precise articulation and communication – with the state, that is, of isolation.

Nietzsche describes this state in the text that immediately precedes the one just quoted and which is dedicated to "the knowledge acquired through suffering" (D 114). There he considers suffering as a state of immediate self-presence where the subject cannot fail to identify his "inner facts" because the sufferer "lies there before himself stripped of all colour and plumage" (D 114). It is therefore a state that recalls Nietzsche's description of Descartes's thinking subject and where this subject presents itself to itself "stark naked, as a 'thing-in-itself'" (BGE 16), as well as a state about which no doubt can be raised. However, according to Nietzsche, this state is not desirable, but intolerable. It is the state of extreme individuation where the subject coincides with itself but finds such self-coincidence unbearable. Suffering "separates", as Nietzsche claims (BGE 270), it distinguishes and awakens a "silent arrogance" in the sufferer, as well as the "certainty" that he knows what nobody else can know (BGE 270, D 114). Nevertheless, however valuable and "noble" (BGE 270) this state may be – and there certainly is an abundance of texts in which Nietzsche claims that this state has a crucial differentiating and ennobling effect on the human body and soul –, it demands "relief" (D 114). Its "antidote" is "to become estranged from ourself and depersonalised, after pain (*der Schmerz*) has for too long and too forcibly made us *personal*" (D 114).

Pain is where we experience the most radical transparency to ourselves, where we become more "personal" or more individualized, more distinct from any other individual. Precisely for this reason, it is the state where we most clearly feel that words are lacking, such that there seems to be an almost absolute coincidence between what we feel and what we are. This is what makes that state so difficult to communicate, so difficult to share with someone else. When we are suffering, we cannot be mistaken about the pain that we feel. Error and illusion seem almost impossible here, so that we seem to have reached precisely the kind of immediate knowledge that words were supposed to hinder. And yet we do not want to remain in this state. In other words, in this situation where it seems that we finally achieve direct, immediate access to ourselves and to our 'inner world', we wish for "depersonalisation", for "disguises" or "masks" (BGE 270) that may protect us from the painful state of being totally exposed – and totally lost or detached from the rest of the world, totally separate from every other individual. Nietzsche claims in BGE 289 that "every word is a mask", meaning that it conceals or protects at the same time that it communicates or speaks. Language hides and hinders, but it does not hide a meta-linguistic secret essence; it hides what it reveals, because it is a medium, something that impedes direct access but that, at the same time, connects (a "net" – as in GS 354). Language separates what it binds together, i.e. each individual from others and the individual from itself[31] allowing it to distance itself from what is happening to it in order to see and think more exactly.

Hence, in spite of his criticisms of language, Nietzsche seems to admit of situations where linguistic falsification and the commonality or depersonaliza-

---

[31] See Hamacher 1986.

tion that it promotes are not only desirable, but highly valuable because they serve an imperative need. For this reason, if Nietzsche conceives of consciousness as a development of the "*ability to communicate*", Nietzsche also stresses that "the ability to communicate, in turn, [developed from] to *need to communicate*" (GS 354). Extreme situations of suffering as the one mentioned in D 114 are analogous to the ones from which consciousness developed and which are described in GS 354, i.e. painful situations of danger and vulnerability, situations where human survival is at stake. Accordingly, Nietzsche writes that

> as the most endangered animal, [man] *needed* help and protection, he needed his equals; he had to express his neediness and be able to make himself understood – and to do so, he first needed "consciousness", i.e. even to "know" what distressed him, to "know" how he felt, to "know" what he thought. (GS 354)

The painful state of not being able to think "exactly" which Nietzsche refers in *Daybreak* can thus be considered a state of self-coincidence and transparency, but one that reveals not the subject's auto-sufficiency, but rather its need, its dependence on a shared medium even when it wants to know his most individual feelings and thoughts. We need words that separate us from ourselves and through which we gain distance from and become conscious of our own ('inner') experiences. This is why Nietzsche conceives of consciousness, not as the capacity to know by identifying something that lies, so to speak, silently within our minds, but as a development of the need to "place outside" our 'inner facts', to communicate them – "consciousness is really just a net connecting one person with another" (GS 354). Nietzsche's conclusion is thus twofold: on the one hand, "the development of language and the development of consciousness […] go hand in hand", and, on the other hand, "only as a social animal did man learn to become conscious of himself" (GS 354). This, however, raises the problem of knowing what does self-knowledge amount to if Nietzsche does not reduce it to painful states in which the becoming personal becomes intolerable. Put differently, if consciousness depends on the mediation of language and is achieved, not in isolation, but socially, not by means of introspection, but by means of communication, and given that Nietzsche does not give up on the idea that we should nevertheless strive for the preservation of our inalienable individuality, how are we supposed, not only to protect it, but to effectively get to know it – to know who we are? In Nietzsche's philosophy, self-knowledge certainly constitutes a key-problem with which he constantly must deal with. In GS 354 he identifies this problem by writing that

> My idea is clearly that consciousness actually belongs not to man's existence as an individual but rather to the community- and herd-aspects of his nature; that accordingly, it is

finely developed only in relation to its usefulness to community or herd; and that consequently each of us, even with the best will in the world to *understand* ourselves as individually as possible, "to know ourselves", will always bring to consciousness that which is "non-individual", that which is "average" [...] At bottom, all our actions are incomparably and utterly personal, unique, and boundlessly individual, there is no doubt; but as soon as we translate them into consciousness *they no longer seem to be* ... (GS 354)

I shall briefly come back to this problem after turning now to Wittgenstein.

4

Wittgenstein's views on the self suffer considerable modifications throughout his work. In the *Tractatus* he presents a defense of solipsism that he will afterwards gradually put into question in order to grasp both the meaning of the concept of the 'I' and the linguistic constitution of the subjective realm of inner experience. In doing so, Wittgenstein relentlessly interrogates the traditional philosophical understanding of the subject and maintains, from beginning to end, a clear anti-Cartesian position.[32] Arguing against the existence of "the thinking subject" (TLP 5.631), of a "bodiless" *cogito, ergo sum* (BLBK, 69) and of "the soul" (TLP 5.5421) in his earlier writings, he will end up proposing a clarification of the "grammatical fiction" (PI, Part I, §307, pp. 102–103) that grounded the conception of the *(ego) cogito* and by revaluating his own Tractarian account of the self. His account of subjectivity can therefore be characterized as a transference of the Cartesian substantive and individuated self onto a linguistic plane.[33]

Underlying the anti-Cartesian views of Wittgenstein's earlier writings is the conviction that "the I is not an object" (NBs, 80)[34] and that empiricism, physicalism and mentalism consist of objectivist views of human subjectivity that are simply philosophically insufficient. The I is neither an external, nor an interior object because "the I objectively confronts every object. But not the I". (NBs, 80). Thus, it cannot become an object either to science, or to itself, which makes Wittgenstein assert in a note from his wartime diary: "The I, the I is what is

---

32 On Wittgenstein's "enduring hostility to the idea of an individuated, substantive self" and on the anti-Cartesianism of his positions, see Hans Sluga (1996: 320–353). Sluga relates Wittgenstein's anti-Cartesianism to the anti-objectivism and anti-referencialism that characterize his proposals concerning subjectivity, and we will closely keep to his arguments in this article.
33 See Glock 1996, "I/Self", pp. 160–164.
34 *Notebooks 1914–1916*, 7.8.1916.

deeply mysterious" (NBs, 80).³⁵ According to the metaphysics of the *Tractatus*, science cannot solve this mystery that lies outside of the world (TLP 5.631). The philosophical 'I' is not an object but a "metaphysical subject", meaning that it cannot be found within the physical world describable by natural science (TLP 5.633). The "philosophical self", Wittgenstein argues, is "a limit – not a part – of the world" (TLP 5.641): it consists of "a contraction, a point without extension" that embraces or circumscribes external reality (TLP 5.64). Accordingly, it cannot be seen or observed, or objectively confronted, and therefore it cannot become an object of knowledge.

But although the subject of experience cannot be part of experience, he is logically presupposed in every experience, because belonging to a subject is a logical feature of every experience. Therefore, the connection between I and world is logical and not a constructive or creative relation where the I might be causally efficacious and intervene in empirical reality.³⁶ As Wittgenstein writes, "the world is independent of my will" (TLP 6.373).³⁷ Nevertheless, the reduction of the subject to a limit of the world makes it coincide with the point outside the world where meaning happens and from where the very existence of the world ultimately depends (TLP 6.431). This dependence is, as already mentioned, logical and it entails a model of metaphysical adequacy that has important consequences for the understanding of language. In effect, the Tractarian solipsistic view is connected with the idea that there must be a correspondence between the logical form of meaningful sentences and the logical structure of the facts which they refer to – that is to say, that "there must be something identical in a picture [i.e. in a proposition] and what it depicts to enable the one to be a picture of the other at all" (TLP 2.161). In other words, in order to be meaningful, the structure of propositions should correspond to one and the same logical structure – the hidden, metaphysical structure of the world. The latter, however, cannot be named. It is beyond "the limits of language" (TLP 5.6). It shows itself in the world, but, just like the "mysterious", metaphysical I, it is not a part of the world and cannot be part of the propositional world. Hence, not only the 'I' cannot be known, it also cannot be designated or described. Since it is not an object of knowledge because it is not a part of the world, it can neither be

---

35 *Notebooks 1914 – 1916*, 11.8.1916.
36 Sluga distinguishes Wittgenstein's and Nietzsche's proposals on the self referring precisely to this crucial point. See Sluga 1996: 329.
37 On the mystical attitude proposed in the *Tractatus* and the "ideal of thought and speech and action" that it supports – and in contrast with Sluga's interpretation –, see Eldridge 1997: 112 – 117. On Schopenhauer's influence on the Tractarian solipsistic view, see Glock 1996, "Solipsism", pp. 348 – 352.

pointed at nor referred to. Thus by rejecting objectivism, Wittgenstein's solipsism at the same time rejects both the possibility of introspective self-knowledge and the application of a linguistic referential model to a subject, for this subject lies beyond the limits of language.

Wittgenstein's early solipsism is grounded on the assumption that meaning is linguistic, so that the solipsist's "godlike self-consciousness"[38] is in fact already conceived of as a "discursive consciousness".[39] This aspect has several consequences in Wittgenstein's post-Tractarian approach to subjectivity. It leads, in particular, to the famous discussion of the 'private language argument' in the *Philosophical Investigations*. This discussion had already been prepared in the *Philosophical Remarks* (PR 57–58)[40] where Wittgenstein presented the hypothesis of a language from which the first-person pronoun was eliminated, a mono-centered language from which the word 'I' was suppressed. The presup-

---

38 See James C. Edwards quoted by Eldridge (1997: 114).
39 See Eldridge 2010: 162–179.
40 See Stern 2010: 178–196. Stern uses the second edition of the *Philosophical Remarks* in his paper: Wittgenstein, Ludwig, *Philosophical Remarks*, ed. Rush Rhees, trans. Raymond Hargreaves and Roger White [Second Edition 1975], Oxford Blackwell 1998 (PR). Wittgenstein's text runs as follows:

"We could adopt the following way of representing matters: if I, L.W., have tooth ache, then that is expressed by means of the proposition 'There is toothache.' But if that is so, what we now express by the proposition 'A has toothache', is put as follows: 'A is behaving as L.W. does when there is toothache.' Similarly we shall say 'It is thinking' and 'A is behaving as L.W. does when it is thinking'. (You could imagine a despotic oriental state where the language is formed with the despot as its centre and his name instead of L.W.) It's clear that this way of speaking is equivalent to ours when it comes to questions of intelligibility and freedom from ambiguity. But it's equally clear that this language could have anyone at all as its centre.

Now, among all the languages with different people as their centres, each of which I can understand, the one with me as its centre has a privileged status. This language is particularly adequate. How am I to express that? That is, how can I rightly represent its special advantage in words? This can't be done. For, if I do it in the language with me as its centre, then the exceptional status of the description of this language in its own terms is nothing very remarkable, and in the terms of another language my language occupies no privileged status whatever. The privileged status lies in the application, and if I describe this application, the privileged status again doesn't find expression, since the description depends on the language in which it's given. And now, which description gives just that which I have in mind depends again on the application.

Only their application really differentiates languages; but if we disregard this, all languages are equivalent. All these languages represent only a single incomparable and cannot represent anything else. (Both these approaches must lead to the same result: first, that what is represented is not one thing among others, that it is not capable of being contrasted with anything; second, that I cannot express the advantage of my language.)"

position of this hypothesis is that the word 'I' is redundant when we speak of "immediate experiences" (PR 57), as in the case of pain experiences. The idea at stake is that sentences like 'I am in pain' are not open to ignorance or doubt and thus seem to convey irrefutable truths. Wittgenstein thus seems to give up the earlier idea according to which language serves the single purpose of depicting or representing objects of external reality. Language now seems rather more suitable for expressing inner or private processes, whose certainty confers an almost unquestionable authority to the speaker.[41] This authority, however, is grounded on the impossibility of comparing the special kind of objects that inner, private experiences are. It is, therefore, a very questionable authority precisely because it relies on the subject's self-sufficiency and it does not admit comparison, it cannot be contrasted.

It is exactly this argument that Wittgenstein uses against the alleged privacy of subjective experiences in the *Philosophical Investigations*. It leads to the conclusion that "an 'inner process' stands in need of outward criteria" (PI §580). In order to reach this conclusion, Wittgenstein recurs once again to an anti-objectivist and anti-referentialist interpretation of the self by developing the typical linguistic or grammatical view adopted in his later works. Instead of the suppression of the word 'I', the idea is now that the philosophical and particularly the metaphysical "use" of that word has to be questioned or interrogated:

> When philosophers use a word – "knowledge", "being", "object", "I", "proposition", "name" – and try to grasp the *essence* of the thing, one must always ask oneself: is the word ever actually used this way in the language which is its original home?
>
> What *we* do is to bring words back from their metaphysical to their everyday use. (PI §116)

It is this procedure that is at stake in the famous private language argument developed in §§243–315 of the *Philosophical Investigations*, which Wittgenstein introduces as follows:

> A human being can encourage himself, give himself orders, obey, blame and punish himself; he can ask himself a question and answer it. We could even imagine human beings who spoke only in monologue; who accompanied their activities by talking to themselves. – An explorer who watched them and listened to their talk might succeed in translating their language into ours. (This would enable him to predict these people's actions correctly, for he also hears them making resolutions and decisions.)

---

[41] As Eldridge argues, "One of the first things to be recognized about the fantasy of having knowledge of inner experiences and how they lie behind, explain, and justify one's public performances is that it is a fantasy about the acquisition of authority." See Eldridge 1997: 243.

> But could we also imagine a language in which a person could write down or give vocal expression to his inner experiences – his feelings, moods, and the rest – for his private use? – Well, can't we do so in our ordinary language? – But that is not what I mean. The individual words of this language are to refer to what can only be known to the person speaking; to his immediate private sensations. So another person cannot understand the language. (PI §243)

A private language would thus be the opposite of an "ordinary", public or common language, that is to say, it would be a language "for private use" and a language that could not be shared. It would correspond to the language that a Cartesian *cogito* would speak in order to refer to its "inner experiences" and "immediate private sensations". It would, therefore, not only rely on the mentalist assumption according to which psychological words stand for phenomena that occur in a private mental theatre only accessible to the subject himself; it would also presuppose a referentialist conception of language according to which the meaning of words is given by what they stand for.[42] The supposed privacy of such phenomena further implies both the idea of their exclusive ownership by the subject and an epistemological privacy, that is to say, that their knowledge is exclusive to their owner.[43] Accordingly, no one else can have my sensations, my thoughts, my pains, or know what I feel when I experience them, but also no one else except me can understand what I mean when I say 'pain', for example.

The possibility of a private language raises the discussion about "how do words refer to sensations" (PI §244), as well as about the effective privacy of sensations. It serves to interrogate the linguistic referentialist model and to propose a new conception of inner phenomena that defies the model 'object and designation' (PI §293), i.e. the idea that there are inner objects that can be designated by a (private) sensation language. For these reasons, the private language argument is directed "against the objectivism embedded in the Cartesian conception of the mind".[44] Wittgenstein puts forward imaginary situations that exemplify a private linguist's conception of language and of himself, such as giving a name to one's own pain (PI §244, §253), keeping a diary about a recurring sensation (PI §258) or playing a game by oneself (PI §248), whereby he will once again interrogate the possibility of introspective self-knowledge, i.e. its alleged immediacy, transparency, certainty, identity, interiority, and self-sufficiency.

---

42 See Glock 1996, "Private Language Argument", pp. 309–315, and also Sluga 1996.
43 See Glock 1996, "Privacy", pp. 304–309.
44 See Sluga 1996.

Wittgenstein starts with the example of the way a child learns to express pain. In asking the question "how does a human being learn the meaning of the names of sensations? – of the name 'pain', for example" (PI §244), he advances the possibility of words being connected with primitive, natural expressions of sensation and being used in their place, as when a child learns linguistic "pain-behaviour" that replaces cries.[45] The first thing that this example stresses is that an inner phenomenon like pain is not necessarily invisible, inaccessible to the gaze of others and only reachable by inward observation. Furthermore, pain is not an object that appears among other objects and to which a name is made to correspond, as if this name could only be given by the subject who is suffering. The name, in this case, is something we learn from others (in this case, our parents; see also PI §257). Consequently, even the meaning of those words that refer to the most intimate of sensations, pain, is something acquired or for which we need instruction and mediation, not something we ourselves immediately attribute to our inner experiences, as if it could only be understood by individual introspection. In addition, this example does not at all imply a contrast between cries and words. On the contrary, it implies a connection between them, as PI §245 confirms.[46] What is at stake is not an ascription of linguistic terms to something that is not linguistic, but a replacement of natural, non-linguistic expressions or manifestations of sensations by linguistic expressions. Wittgenstein is interested here in how parents teach their children "new pain-behaviour" when they cry, that is to say, he is interested in the variety of possibilities of pain expression. Designating pain by using the word "pain" is only one among other such possibilities.

As it becomes clear in the other examples that Wittgenstein gives, he is here engaging in a discussion about, on the one hand, the idea that words refer to sensations as names designate objects and, on the other hand, the idea according to which sensations are private phenomena that do not manifest themselves or are

---

[45] "How do words refer to sensations? – There doesn't seem to be any problem here; don't we talk about sensations every day, and give them names? But how is the connexion between the name and the thing named set up? This question is the same as: how does a human being learn the meaning of the names of sensations? – of the word "pain" for example. Here is one possibility: words are connected with the primitive, the natural, expressions of the sensation and used in their place. A child has hurt himself and he cries; and then adults talk to him and teach him exclamations and, later, sentences. They teach the child new pain-behaviour.

'So you are saying that the word 'pain' really means crying?' – On the contrary: the verbal expression of pain replaces crying and does not describe it." (PI §244)

[46] "For how can I go so far as to try to use language to get between pain and its expression?" (PI §245)

inexpressible, and cannot therefore be perceived from the 'outside' of the thinking-feeling subject. Throughout this discussion, Wittgenstein questions the privacy of inner experiences, i.e. the idea that "only I can know whether I am really in pain; another person can only surmise it", as the private linguist puts it in PI §246. The latter insists that, even if "very often" other people know he is in pain, they do not know it "with the certainty with which I know it myself!" (PI §246) The argument is, of course, Cartesian, in that my inner experience is beyond doubt and it is only accessible to me. And if others can know about it, their knowledge of it is knowledge of an external fact, a knowledge that remains uncertain because it is mediated by sense impressions, a knowledge that is the opposite of the immediate, introspective knowledge, which guarantees epistemological certainty. So, the private linguist's conclusion is that "it makes sense to say about other people that they doubt whether I am in pain; but not to say it about myself" (PI §246). Wittgenstein's refutation of this certainty is grounded, firstly, on the rejection of the privacy of inner sensations, of the idea that they are placed within a subjective, and somehow secret, interiority. This does not mean that he is here arguing for a purely bodily location of pain, as it becomes clear in PI §286,[47] but rather that he is again proposing the possibility raised in the example of the crying child. Pain, being a sensation, is expressive and manifests itself through visible, outer or public phenomena. This being so, others can know that I have a sensation because it is not necessarily hidden and available only to the subject – even if he can, of course (although only within certain limits), conceal it.[48]

So, privacy corresponds less to metaphysical isolation than to our capacity to isolate ourselves if we choose to do so (by controlling the expression of our sensations or by pretending to have sensations we do not have).[49] Nevertheless, the private linguist does not give up his idea. In another imaginary example

---

[47] "What sort of issue is: Is it the *body* that feels pain? – How is it to be decided? What makes it plausible to say that it is *not* the body? – Well, something like this: if someone has a pain in his hand, then the hand does not say so (unless it writes it) and one does not comfort the hand, but the sufferer: one looks into his face." (PI §286)

[48] And even so, we must consider that concealing is – like pretending or lying – already "a language-game that needs to be learned like any other one" (PI §249). See also PI §250.

[49] This suggestion is made by Mulhall (2007: 60). Mulhall also points out that, considered from this perspective, the comparison between the propositions "Sensations are private" and "One plays patience with oneself" (PI §248) brings to light that even a game that involves only one player can be played in a space that is shared with other people, under the eyes of other people, if the player so decides. It is, moreover, this possibility that makes it a game, i.e. that enables us to give it rules and therefore to learn and teach how to play it and how to follow it when another is playing. The comparison makes clear that the privacy of sensations does not imply that they are beyond the public sphere, beyond the reach of words. See Mulhall 2007: 59ff.

Wittgenstein presents a dialogue about someone who intends to keep a diary about a recurring sensation to which this person refers to with the sign 'S' (PI §258). In response to the objection that this sign's definition cannot be formulated at all, the private linguist's says that "I can give one [definition] to myself as a kind of ostensive definition!" Wittgenstein rejects this possibility asking whether it is really possible to "point to the sensation". The diarist's answer summons up the traditional, Cartesian, metaphysical use of the word 'I' that the private language argument tries to bring back to its everyday use:

> How? Can I point to the sensation? – Not in the ordinary sense. But I speak, or write the sign down, and at the same time I concentrate my attention on the sensation – and so, as it were, point to it inwardly. – But what is this ceremony for? For that is all it seems to be! A definition serves to lay down the meaning of a sign, doesn't it? – Well, that is done precisely by concentrating my attention; for in this way I commit to memory the connection between the sign and the sensation. – But "I commit it to memory" can only mean: this process brings it about that I remember the connection *correctly* in the future. But in the present case, I have no criterion of correctness. One would like to say: whatever is going to seem correct to me is correct. And that only means that here we can't talk about "correct". (PI §258)

Thus, while the Cartesian-private-linguist insists that the meaning of the sign or word is given by means of inward concentration or introspection, its anti-Cartesian opponent argues that such inner "ceremony" does not provide any "criterion of correctness" for relating words and object-sensations. Put differently, Wittgenstein emphasizes that solitary "inward pointing" is not sufficient to establish or determine the meaning of a word because it simply indicates an act of self-referentialism, a reference of the self to himself comparable only to the self-giving act in which the right hand gives money to the left one (PI §268).[50] Furthermore, this "pointing-into-yourself" or "pointing with your attention" (PI §275) is not what the subject understands he is doing when he expresses his private experiences, the ones that putatively belong only to him. As Wittgenstein claims, "the essential thing about private experience is really not that each person possesses his own exemplar, but that nobody knows whether other people also have *this* or something else" (PI §272). In fact, a private experience is an experience one considers as "something quite definite" (PI §276), that is to say, so irreducible or "'specific'" (PI, Part II, xi, p. 224) that it can only be defined by inward pointing or pointing to oneself.[51] But the problem is that

---

[50] A procedure, moreover, whose model is again the relation with others, as Mulhall points out (Mulhall 2007: 122).
[51] For a discussion of the assumption that the word 'specific' refers to and defines private experiences, see Schulte 2003: 50ff. Schulte argues that "the specificity of any experience can only be

when one speaks about the irreducible specificity of his experiences, one is not offering "an intersubjectively helpful criterion for testing the relevant statements"; consequently, "other people will not know how to deal with my statements" but also "I myself" will have no means of testing them and so they will also be nonsensical to me.[52]

Self-referentialism, private ostensive definition or inward, introspective pointing are therefore rejected because they presuppose the same auto-sufficiency that was already at stake in the passage of the *Philosophical Remarks* mentioned above. They are based on the allegedly indisputable authority of the thinking subject – "whatever is going to seem correct to me is correct" (PI §258) – which, according to Wittgenstein, is highly problematic. Wittgenstein's opposition to the private linguist is based on the fact that an ostensive definition already implies linguistic rules that cannot be individually determined. Even more precisely, what he shows is that any 'private' ostensive definition implicitly depends not on introspective insights, but on the existence of a language that is not created by a single individual and could never be intelligible only to himself. It is rather a 'public' language, in fact a language that exists previously to the existence of each individual (therefore, individuals receive it from other individuals instead of giving it to themselves, as was already the case with the crying child). This idea becomes clear in the following remarks:

> What reason have we for calling "S" the sign for a *sensation*? For "sensation" is a word of our common language, not of one intelligible to me alone. So the use of this word stands in need of a justification which everybody understands. – And it would not help either to say that it need not be a *sensation*; that when he writes "S", he has *something* – and that is all that can be said. "Has" and "something" also belong to our common language. (PI §261)

Wittgenstein's conclusion is that the idea of a private language is incoherent because such a language would still have to rely on the existence of a common language. The incoherence of the idea of a private language is furthermore proved by the fact that it presupposes a conception of what language is: an activity guided by rules that determine the correct use of words in order for them to be understood or have meaning. A private language would not obey any

---

elucidated within appropriated circumstances" and that "it is necessary to find or bring out a situation in which the person in question can learn to apply the word concerned", that is to say, "whatever appears specific in an experience will have its basis in the relevant language game" (p. 51). For this reason, Wittgenstein concludes that "the expression 'specific psychological phenomenon' corresponds to that of the private ostensive definition" (RPP I §200).
52 Schulte 2003: 60–61.

rules – the idea of a private rule is nonsensical – and so its words would be meaningless. Hence, it would prevent effective communication, but even more importantly it would not be intelligible for his only speaker. The latter would still have to use words like "sensation" or "pain" whose meaning is public and does not depend on inner mental phenomena available only to one individual's introspective insight. Consequently, any meaningful account of subjective experiences is necessarily structured by language or conceptually constituted. Even more precisely, to gain consciousness of oneself and of one's inner processes always involves gaining a "discursive consciousness"[53] that is not achieved immediately by means of self-observation, but always through the mediation of others. The solipsist is thus forced to recognize that he is not a metaphysical subjectivity isolated from the empirical world and skeptical about the existence of other minds, but one human being among others of whom he depends, even – and perhaps above all – whenever he tries to know who he is.

Thus, Wittgenstein's discussion of the private language argument does not, as it becomes clear, propose another philosophical meaning for the philosophical words that "try to grasp the *essence* of the thing": "knowledge", "being", "object", "I", "proposition", "name" (PI §116). It rather contests the traditional philosophical conception of these words by paying attention to "their everyday use" (PI §116) and shows, in particular, that they raise misunderstandings about subjectivity that must be clarified. This is particularly the case with the meaning and use of the word 'I', or with the self-reference that we associate with it. According to Wittgenstein, in order to clarify what is at stake in such self-referentialism it is necessary to analyze "the peculiar grammar of the word 'I', and the misunderstandings this grammar is liable to give rise to" (BLBK, 66). The peculiarity consists in that the first-person pronoun can have a "use as object" and a "use as subject" (BLBK, 66).[54] In the first case, it is used to speak of the human body and its physical characteristics (e.g., "My arm is broken" or "I have grown six inches"); in the second case, it is used to speak about mental states and sensations, like the feeling of pain. If, in the first case, its use is referential because it is meant to designate an object, in the second case no object is referred to, so that in the sentence "I have pain" no description is made. Hence, contrary to the traditional, Cartesian and referentialist assumption, first-person propositions are not descriptions of (inner) objects and they can even fail to have any referential function at all. And this means that the problem with Cartesian referentialism is not so much that it corresponds to an epistemological error

---

53 See Eldridge 2010.
54 On this distinction, see Sluga 1996.

as rather that it is grounded on a misunderstanding of grammar: "we feel that in the case in which 'I' is used as subject, we don't use it because we recognize a particular person by his bodily characteristics; and this creates the illusion that we use this word to refer to something bodiless, which, however, has its seat in our body" (BLBK, 69).

Wittgenstein's effort, of which the private language discussion is exemplary, is thus to clarify "one of the great sources of philosophical bewilderment: a substantive makes us look for a thing that corresponds to it" (BLBK, 1). What he intends to prove is that this tendency prevents us from considering the possibility that a sentence like 'I am in pain' could stand, not as the description of an experience, but as its utterance or expression. To understand this, it is also necessary to attend to the "behavior" of the speaker (PI §281). But to the question whether Wittgenstein is "saying that everything except human behaviour is a fiction" he replies: "If I speak of a fiction, then it is of a *grammatical* fiction." (PI §307)[55] In other words, his concern is to do away with the ontological distinction between inner and outer, mind and body, I and others by showing that it really consists of a grammatical question. The grammatical fiction is grounded on the confusion between the two possible ways of using the word 'I' and on the idea that language merely serves one purpose, "to convey thoughts – which may be about houses, pains, good and evil, or anything else you please" (PI §304). Both behaviorism and its apparent opposite, Cartesian mentalism, suffer from the effects of this misunderstanding because they both assume that words always have meaning by standing for something. In order to fight this grammatical illusion, Wittgenstein suggests that more attention should be paid to the assumption that the subject and its inner experiences must be considered as objects and that nouns and pronouns are names or descriptions of objects.[56]

---

55 Wittgenstein's insistence on behaviour does not commit him to a behaviourist conception of the self and he clarifies that if behaviour stands as an outer criteria that enables ascribing inner experiences, then "there is a difference between pain-behaviour accompanied by pain and pain-behaviour without any pain" (PI §304). See Sluga 1996 and Schulte 2003.

56 It is precisely this assumption that is depicted in the imaginary example of the beetle in the box: "If I say of myself that it is only from my own case that I know what the word 'pain' means – must I not say the same of other people too? And how can I generalize the *one* case so irresponsibly?

Now someone tells me that *he* knows what pain is only from his own case! – Suppose everyone had a box with something in it: we call it a 'beetle'. No one can look into anyone else's box, and everyone says he knows what a beetle is only by looking at *his* beetle. – Here it would be quite possible for everyone to have something different in his box. One might even imagine such a thing constantly changing. – But suppose the word 'beetle' had a use in these people's language? – If so it would not be used as the name of a thing. The thing in the box has

The model of 'object and designation' (PI §293) must therefore be definitely rejected with regard to what modern philosophy called the "subject". In addition to all the misunderstandings it creates – about the I's certainty, immediacy, privacy etc. –, it also fosters the illusion of a permanent and stable identity that the example of the beetle in the box denounces ("One might even imagine such a thing constantly changing" and "the box might even be empty"). Insisting on the constitutive role of language for the way in which we can eventually come to know ourselves, the private language discussion hence discards the idea that the 'I' is a secret substance, protected within the walls of an inner realm (within a 'box') and transformed into a "thing" about which only the subject himself can speak. To speak of myself in terms that no one else understands is the same as uttering "inarticulate sounds" (PI §261) – as inarticulate as the cry of a child in pain and whose meaning the child herself cannot fully grasp until she is capable of achieving a perspective on herself, that is to say, the capacity for what can properly be called selfhood. Being constitutionally linguistic such perspective threatens the idea of an original self-sufficiency, of the individual's absolute independence and self-possession. In other words, it brings "an inevitable sense of dispossession: the loss of a certain possible ideal of philosophical self-coincidence and self-assurance, of the self's transparency to itself, beyond any allegiance to the common ground of human life, and the everyday words that thread through it".[57] To recognize that our relation with ourselves is mediated by language thus implies accepting that it presupposes a connection to something that lies, so to speak, beyond or outside the self itself. Moreover, this is something that the subject cannot achieve merely by himself and for the acquisition of which he shall always depend on others.

5

This is how Wittgenstein sees the problem of self-knowledge – the problem that was raised above with respect to Nietzsche. The truth is that neither of them provides a straightforward answer for this problem, although they both agree that introspection is not the way to deal with it. As already seen, they both consider

---

no place in the language-game at all; not even as a *something*: for the box might even be empty. – No, one can 'divide through' by the thing in the box; it cancels out, whatever it is.

That is to say: if we construe the grammar of the expression of sensation on the model of 'object and designation' the object drops out of consideration as irrelevant." (*PI* §293)

57 Mulhall 2007: 101.

that Descartes's introspective method relies on an objectification of the 'I' and on a referentialist model that fosters "grammatical habits" (Nietzsche) or a "grammatical fiction" (Wittgenstein) whereby the self remains unknown. On the other hand, insisting on the role played by linguistic mediation in the self's relation with itself, they underline that whatever the 'I' may be, it is not a silent or mute entity that lingers in a secret place waiting for the only eye that is capable of finding it, i.e. its own. For both Nietzsche and Wittgenstein, the 'I' is not absolutely incommunicable and any possibility of self-knowledge must rely on communication and expression. Communication and expression provide us with a perspective on ourselves fostering, not a coincidence, but a differentiation of distinct moments and states that cannot be reduced to a single, simple, substantive entity. By doing this, they enable us to distance ourselves from our sensations, thoughts or emotions, from their presence and potential control over us. They allow us to articulate our 'inner states' and to recognize their transience, to compare them with other moments of our experience, thereby displacing or freeing us from being overwhelmed by the state in which we provisionally are.

According to Nietzsche and Wittgenstein, selfhood does not therefore depend on the absolute concentration of the 'I' on itself (i.e., on introspection, self-presence, self-coincidence, etc.). It is rather achieved through a process of self-differentiation, through our ability to separate ourselves from what we feel and think, thereby realizing that we are not immersed or enclosed within our present condition. Nietzsche called this possibility "pathos of distance" (BGE 257), considering it not as a form of knowledge, but as an affect that demands "new expansions of distance within the soul itself" (BGE 257) and incites the capacity to recognize differences "inside the same person even, within a single soul" (BGE 260). He conceives of it as a sign of nobility, that is to say, the opposite of vulgarity or commonness that language always entails, because it allows for a continual differentiation that escapes being fixed in the words which it nevertheless cannot fail to use and say. The pathos of distance is probably at the root of Nietzsche's "unconquerable distrust in the possibility of self-knowledge" and of his "kind of revulsion against believing anything definite about myself" (BGE 281). His idea that "we are unknown to ourselves" (GM Preface 1) must not be understood as his conclusion regarding the problem of self-knowledge, but as this problem's starting point, which Nietzsche also formulates as follows: "each is furthest from himself" (GM Preface 1).

As regards Wittgenstein, it can also be said that in all the examples that show the attempts to constitute a private language its speaker is conceived as always already divided, being on the one hand the one that feels, and on the other hand, the one that points to or names what is being felt, thereby implicitly acknowledging the process of self-differentiation that he must go through, as well as "the internal relation between the acquisition of language and the acquisition of selfhood".⁵⁸ This relation is also explicitly proposed by Nietzsche in GS 354, as discussed above, although he nowhere raises the possibility of a private language. Nietzsche certainly addresses the question of the difficulty of being understood by others (e.g., GS 381, BGE 290, GM Preface 1) and, as was also pointed out, his writings constantly give voice to the tension between the individual quality of experiences and the public dimension of their linguistic account. His complaints about language bring to light a degree of resistance to the linguistic formulation of thoughts and experiences that can, therefore, be compared with the private linguist's resistance to use public terms to refer to inner phenomena. The text where Nietzsche seems to be more aware of the private linguist's aversion for common language is the following:

> We stop valuing ourselves when we communicate. Our true experiences are completely taciturn. They could not be communicated even if they wanted to be. This is because the right words for them do not exist. The things we have words for are also the things we have already left behind. There is a grain of contempt in all speech. Language, it seems, was invented only for average, mediocre, communicable things. People vulgarize themselves when they speak a language. – Excerpts from a morality for the deaf-mutes and other philosophers. (TI Skirmishes 26)

My suggestion is that the last line of this text seems to make Nietzsche's position clear, which is that a solipsistic insistence on the 'specificity' of experiences and on the impossibility of restoring them by means of a language that is not our own is adequate only to "deaf-mutes". A deaf-mute is someone deprived of the capabilities that allow for linguistic contact with other human beings. The deaf-mute is (more or less) incapable of receiving and using verbal language, and he is therefore isolated from the "net" that connects one person to another, as isolated, we could add, as the Cartesian ego "and other philosophers".

Nietzsche's irony in this passage seems thus to allow for an interpretation of the first sentences that reads them as meaning the opposite of what they say: we start to value ourselves only when we communicate (as only then do we become conscious of ourselves), our true experiences are loquacious (we feel the need to communicate them), the words for them are "the words that lie to hand" (D 257) (the common words), and the things we have words for are the things that constitute our world (the human world of appearances created by language). But we could even risk a bit more in the reading of the last lines of TI Skirmishes 26 and conclude that for Nietzsche there is an increase in self-esteem in speaking,

---

58 Mulhall 2007: 113.

that language was also invented for the exceptional things, and that people are able to ennoble themselves when they speak a language.

We shall conclude the comparison between Nietzsche and Wittgenstein by focusing precisely on this last idea. Is it really possible to sustain such an interpretation of Nietzsche's words? Is he not saying the opposite?

In order to understand the reading I am proposing, one has to be reminded that both for Nietzsche and for Wittgenstein consciousness, self-knowledge or self-awareness is something acquired that allows for degrees. This is the idea that Nietzsche puts forward in GS 354 and that Wittgenstein also subscribes, considering that self-awareness can be more or less perfect, more or less developed. Accordingly, each of us can fail to understand the inner phenomena to which we give nevertheless expression, as is the case in Wittgenstein's examples of the child and the diarist. In other words, we can be unknown to ourselves even if we are not aware of that (as in the case where someone "thinks he understands" and attaches "some meaning to the word, but not the right one" – PI §269). For Wittgenstein, as seen above, this can also be the case of someone who is in pain precisely because he is overwhelmed by his suffering. And this being the case, that person can eventually be better known and understood by someone who is not in his position, who is not suffering or having that experience. Hence, one can counter the private linguist's certainty about his inner states of which "only I can know whether I am really in pain; another person can only surmise it" (PI §246) with the possibility that the very expression of pain consists not in an identification or a register of an inner fact, but rather in the attempt to be acknowledged. In other words, the alleged certainty brought about by the state of pain can correspond instead to the expression of one's ignorance and incapacity for dealing with the actual state of one's inner life, that is to say, to the possibility of one not (or not yet) being able to understand this life and expressing it in ways that are not understandable to others and to oneself – so much so that one can conceive of the possibility of inventing a private, 'specific' language in order to deal with it. Furthermore, with this possibility, Wittgenstein opens up space for a reversion of the idea according to which knowing oneself is something guaranteed while knowing another corresponds to an impossibility. His proposal is that self-knowledge must necessarily rely on the way others can help us understand ourselves, an idea that he summarizes thus:

> It is correct to say "I know what you are thinking", and wrong to say "I know what I am thinking". (A whole cloud of philosophy condensed into a drop of grammar.) (PI, Part II, xi, p. 222)

Nietzsche's idea is not exactly the same, but it ultimately manifests something in common with what Wittgenstein was trying to point at. But it does that to a different degree. While suspecting of the possibility of consummate self-knowledge, Nietzsche nevertheless insists in our capacity for exercising it as a continuous process.[59] He also admits of degrees of self-awareness or consciousness and seems to reserve the higher ones to the most noble and distinguished of men, those spirits who are freer than common or vulgar human beings, and also more free from the constraints of language. These free spirits are not solipsists, they do not dismiss common language as being inadequate to their experiences and they do not dispense with the need to communicate with others. On the contrary, while expressing their extreme individuality, they address common words to a wide human community. Nietzsche sees them belonging to the "genius of communication" (TI Skirmishes 24) and he is thinking of artists and philosophers, who are not interested in inventing a private language, but in creating a "new language" (BGE 4) that becomes a "new convention" (WS 122) whereby many individuals can continue to develop consciousness and self-understanding, and find "new expansions of distance within the soul itself" (BGE 257). Nietzsche certainly includes himself within this group of individuals, considering his works and his philosophical concepts as a contribution to Western community and society and believing that the community of his readers will expand in future generations, enabling him to be born again, "posthumously".[60] Therefore, according to Nietzsche's most personal and peculiar grammar of the word 'I', the latter will only become transparent through his writings, of which he says:

> "I" am in them, together with everything that was inimical to me, *ego ipisissimus*, indeed, if a yet prouder expression be permitted, *ego ipsissimum*. (AOM Preface 1)

References

Branco, Maria João Mayer (2011) "The Spinning of Masks. Nietzsche's Praise of Language", in: Constâncio, João/Branco, Maria João Mayer (eds.) (2012) *As the Spider Spins. Essays on Nietzsche's Critique and Use of Language*, Berlin/Boston: De Gruyter, 233–253.
Brusotti, Marco (2009) "Wittgensteins Nietzsche. Mit vergleichenden Betrachtungen zur Nietzsche-Rezeption im Wiener-Kreis", in: *Nietzsche-Studien* 38, 335–362.
Brusotti, Marco (2014) *Wittgenstein, Frazer und die "ethnologische Betrachtungsweise"*, Berlin/Boston: De Gruyter.

---

[59] Such an exercise, of course, has a decisive genealogical element that is not developed in this paper, in spite of its importance for Nietzsche's counter-proposal to introspective knowledge. On this important topic, see Paul Katsafanas' chapter in this volume.
[60] On Nietzsche's creation of "new commons" that aim to impact "wider communities" and even "changing society (even, grandly, human history)", see again Richardson (2015).

Campioni, Giuliano (2001) *Les lectures françaises de Nietzsche*, Paris: PUF.
Cavell, Stanley (1979) *The Claim of Reason. Wittgenstein, Skepticism, Morality and Tragedy*, Oxford/New York: Oxford University Press (reprinted with a new preface in 1999).
Cavell, Stanley (2010) "The Touch of Words", in: W. Day and V. Krebs (eds.), *Seeing Wittgenstein Anew*, New York: Cambridge University Press, 81–98.
Constâncio, João (2011) "On Consciousness. Nietzsche's Departure from Schopenhauer", in: *Nietzsche-Studien* 40, 1–42.
Constâncio, João (2012) "Consciousness, Communication, and Self-Expression. Towards an Interpretation of Aphorism 354 of Nietzsche's The Gay Science", in: J. Constâncio/ M.J. Mayer Branco (eds.), *As the Spider Spins: Essays on Nietzsche's Critique and Use of Language*, Berlin/Boston: De Gruyter, 197–231.
Constâncio, João/Branco, Maria João Mayer (eds.) (2011) *Nietzsche on Instinct and Language*, Berlin/Boston: De Gruyter.
Constâncio, João/Branco, Maria João Mayer (eds.) (2012) *As the Spider Spins. Essays on Nietzsche's Critique and Use of Language*, Berlin/Boston: De Gruyter.
Descartes, René (2008) *Meditations on First Philosophy*, Oxford/New York: Oxford University Press.
Eldridge, Richard (1997) *Leading a Human Life. Wittgenstein, Intentionality and Romanticism*, Chicago/London: University of Chicago Press.
Eldridge, Richard (2010) "Wittgenstein on Aspect-Seeing, the Nature of Discursive Consciousness, and the Experience of Agency" in: William Day/Victor J. Krebs (eds.), *Seeing Wittgenstein Anew. New Essays on Aspect-Seeing*, Cambridge: Cambridge University Press, 162–179.
Glock, Hans-Johann (1996) *A Wittgenstein Dictionary*, Oxford: Blackwell, 348–352.
Hagberg, Garry L. (2008) *Wittgenstein and Autobiographical Consciousness*, Oxford: Clarendon Press.
Hamacher, Werner (1986) "Disagregation des Willens. Nietzsche über Individuum und Individualität", in: *Nietzsche-Studien* 15, 306–336.
Lacoue-Labarthe, Philippe (2012) *La réponse d'Ulysse et autres textes sur l'Occident*, Paris: Nouvelles Éditions Lignes.
Lupo, Luca (2006) *Le Colombe dello Scettico. Riflessioni di Nietzsche sulla Coscienza negli anni 1880–1888*. Pisa: ETS.
Lupo, Luca (2012) "Drives, Instincts, Language, and Consciousness in Daybreak 119: 'Erleben und Erdichten'", in: J. Constâncio/M.J. Mayer Branco (eds.), *As the Spider Spins: Essays on Nietzsche's Critique and Use of Language*, Berlin/Boston: De Gruyter, 179–195.
Mulhall, Stephen (2007) *Wittgenstein's Private Language. Grammar, Nonsense, and Imagination in Philosophical Investigations §§243–315*, New York: Oxford University Press.
Mulhall, Stephen (2011) "The Promising Animal: The Art of Reading *On the Genealogy of Morality* as Testimony", in: Simon May (ed.), *Nietzsche's on the Genealogy of Morality. A Critical Guide*, Cambridge: Cambridge University Press, 234–264.
Mulhall, Stephen (2013) *The Self and its Shadows. A Book of Essays on Individuality as Negation in Philosophy and the Arts*, Oxford/New York: Oxford University Press.
Mulhall, Stephen (2014) *"Orchestral Metaphysics:* The Birth of Tragedy *between Drama, Opera, and Philosophy"*, in: Daniel Came (ed.), *Nietzsche on Art and Life*, Oxford/New York: Oxford University Press, 107–126.
Pier, Jens (2015) "The 'I' and the 'We'. Wittgenstein, Strawson, and the Way Back to Hegel", in: *inter.culture.philosophy* 1/2015.

Pippin, Robert B. (2010) *Nietzsche, Psychology, and First Philosophy*, Chicago/London: University of Chicago Press.
Richardson, John (2015) "Nietzsche, Language, Community", in: Julian Young (ed.), *Individual and Community in Nietzsche's Philosophy*, New York: Cambridge University Press, 214–243.
Schulte, Joachim (2003) *Experience and Expression. Wittgenstein's Philosophy of Psychology*, Oxford/New York: Oxford University Press.
Schulte, Joachim (2013) "Wittgenstein on Philosophy as Poetry", in: M.F.M Molder, D. Soeiro/ N. Fonseca (eds.), *Morphology. Questions on Method and Language*, Bern: Peter Lang, 347–369.
Sluga, Hans (1996) "Ludwig Wittgenstein: Life and Work. An Introduction", in: Hans Sluga/ David G. Stern (eds.), *The Cambridge Companion to Wittgenstein*, Cambridge: Cambridge University Press, 1–33.
Sluga, Hans (1996) "'Whose House is That?' Wittgenstein on the Self", in: Hans Sluga/ David G. Stern (eds.), *The Cambridge Companion to Wittgenstein*, Cambridge: Cambridge University Press, 320–353.
Sluga, Hans (2015) "'The Time is Coming When One Will Have to Relearn about Politics'", in: Julian Young (ed.), *Individual and Community in Nietzsche's Philosophy*, New York: Cambridge University Press, 31–50.
Stegmaier, Werner (1995) "Philosophieren als Vermeiden einer Lehre. Inter-individuelle Orientierung bei Sokrates und Platon, Nietzsche und Derrida", in: J. Simon (ed.), *Distanz im Verstehen. Zeichen und Interpretation II*, Frankfurt a.M.: Suhrkamp, 214–239.
Stern, David (2010) "Another Strand in the Private Language Argument", in: Arif Ahmed (ed.), *Wittgenstein's Philosophical Investigations. A Critical Guide*, New York: Cambridge University Press, 178–196.
Williams, Bernard (1994) Nietzsche's Minimalist Moral Psychology, in: Richard Schacht (ed.), *Nietzsche, Genealogy, Morality: Essays on Nietzsche's On the Genealogy of Morals*, Berkeley: University of California Press, 237–247.
Wotling, Patrick (1999) *La pensée du sous-sol. Statut et structure de la psychologie dans la philosophie de Nietzsche*, Paris: Éditions Allia.

Werner Stegmaier
19 Subjects as Temporal Clues to Orientation: Nietzsche and Luhmann on Subjectivity

This chapter is written by a German-speaking author, who orientates himself by the *use of the concept of the subject* in the German language. In German, just as in English, French, Spanish, Portuguese, Italian, and so on, the concept 'subject' is used in philosophical and scientific language, as well as in everyday language, and mostly refers to persons. But in legal language it is also used to refer to non-human, legal and economic subjects, and in grammar it also refers to an 'object' (*Gegenstand*) about which something is predicated. In German everyday language it can also be used pejoratively ('*ein übles Subjekt*'), but not, as for example in English or French, as synonymous with 'citizen' ('Her Majesty's subjects'), or with serf, vassal ('a loyal subject'), or 'medical patient', 'guinea pig', 'volunteer' ('the subject did trials'), and also not for the 'topic' of a text or work of art ('the subject of this book'), unless it is used as a foreign word. In these various uses what is preserved is not the Greek meaning of 'substrate' (*hypokeímenon*), but rather the Latin meaning of 'being subjected to' – being that which passively accepts what happens to it. Whereas the French tradition, shaped by Rousseau, used the word in a productive way – such that in the concept of *volonté générale* the sovereign subject is immediately connected with the subject that is subjected to the law –, in the German tradition, strongly shaped by Kant, the passive use of the concept was abandoned: a subject ought first and foremost to be the ground responsible for its own actions. In all languages mentioned above, the adjective 'subjective' incorporates from the subject only its personal, varying, individual character. It is inescapably associated with its opposite, 'objective', whereas the substantive has a meaning also without the opposite 'object'.[1]

---

[1] Balibar/Cassin/Libera (2004) work out how the strands of meaning 'substrate', 'subordinate' and 'individual' partly ran next to each other and partly were interlocked with one another in the Middle Ages and Modernity, then finally, with Rousseau, fused into one single meaning and in the twentieth century (with Levinas, Derrida and Foucault, among others) headed to their self-destruction. They see the strongest break in the history of the concept of the subject in Nietzsche. And whereas he speaks of "commanding and obeying" as the structure of the will, without using the concept of the subject (BGE 19), *nolens volens* the French translation uses the word anyway

Striking paradoxes follow from this in the *modern philosophical concept of the subject*, as developed from Descartes to Kant. In the Enlightenment, the concept of the subject liberated the individual from his bond to God and his traditional social relationships, thus radically handing him back to himself – as autonomous thinker. In this process, the peculiarity, that is, the inequality, of his thought (as in the adjective 'subjective') was recognized, but at the same time the equality of common structures of thought (in which he can be 'objective') was postulated: he (or she) is supposed to be *simultaneously unequal and equal*. The paradox deepens when 'the subject' becomes the object of description, for he/she is then converted into its opposite, 'the object', and hence cannot be described *as* subject at all. This became the paradoxical starting-point of all attempts to endeavor such a description, above all in the case of Husserl's transcendental phenomenology. Paradoxes warn against accepting concepts as if that about which they speak existed outside of them – in this case, against the assumption that the word 'subject' names something really observable and describable. One can therefore hardly expect tenable answers to the question on what is the subject and what constitutes its essence, its 'subjectivity'. The concept of the subject is a means for description, not an object of description. Also Descartes and Kant conceived of the subject (although Descartes did not yet use the term) as *the condition of possibility* of objective knowledge. But Nietzsche and Luhmann suspended this conception of the subject as well. They faced the paradoxes of the concept of the subject, and instead of asking what a 'subject' is, they looked for the *function* or functions the concept has fulfilled in European philosophy – functions which in the meantime may already have changed and become superfluous.[2]

(1243). Conversely, they argue that in German (as the case of Habermas makes particularly clear) it would be very difficult to explore the concept of the subject in the same way as in French, but that would be perfectly acceptable in English (1251).

2 On the complex history of the concept cf. the articles Subjekt (B. Kible/J. Stolzenberg/T. Trappe/U. Dreisholtkamp), Subjekt, transzendentales (W. Halbfass), Subjekt/Objekt, subjektiv/objektiv (S.K. Knebel/M. Karskens/E.-O. Onnasch), Subjekt/Prädikat (R. Rehn/G. Schenk/E. Elling), Subjektivität (H. Clairmont/A. Beelmann/P. Cosmann), Subjektivität, transzendentale (U. Claesges) in: *Historisches Wörterbuch der Philosophie* (Gründer 1998: 373–473). Nietzsche is here constantly treated in a very abbreviated way; Luhmann is not treated at all. On the concept of intersubjectivity, which Luhmann strongly attacked and which we will have to leave aside here, cf. Oswald Schwemmer (1995), Arnim Regenbogen (2010). Luhmann's repeatedly delivered critique is also not mentioned here. For the philosophical qualities of Luhmann's sociological systems theory are until now yet barely known. Cf. Jean Clam 2000. On Luhmann's philosophical rank cf. Robert Spaemann (1990) and Werner Stegmaier (2011). So far as I can see, Luhmann's

1 The function of the concept of the subject in Descartes and Kant: Conceivability of a foothold [Halt] in science and ethics

We shall start by recapitulating a few things that are more or less known, in order to clarify what Nietzsche and Luhmann drew on from their innovations.[3] According to the current understanding, what represents the *transition from Middle Ages to Modernity* is the fact that the human being became doubtful about its place in the world. Whereas in the Middle Ages there was no doubt that the human being stood between the animal and God and was responsible for the preservation of the order that God created. Now it has become doubtful on how God himself related to this order – whether He left it once He had created it, or continues to intervene in it, or is constantly creating it anew as a whole. That brought new questions about whether and in which sense one could ascribe reason and will to God, as one ascribes to human beings, and if yes, to what extent are divine reason and divine will accessible to human beings. One became less and less certain of one's relation to God and became more and more aware that one was under the compulsion to orientate oneself by something that one did not know and could not know sufficiently. One found oneself in an irritating and, so to speak, paradoxical double blind, which fueled doubt, triggered a growing disorientation and finally led to a revolutionary reflexion on the orientation that prevailed hitherto as self-evident. This was a process of reorientation that lasted several centuries, and in which the triumph of the sciences played the crucial role of helping develop a peculiar "Legitimacy of Modern Age" (Blumenberg), which was increasingly liberated from theology. The necessary foothold (*Halt*) was found in the concept of the subject, even if people did not call it that at that time. People orientated themselves by their reason and will, and it was doubt that gave the subject its structure.

As Hegel would later make clear, the very fact that *Descartes started with doubt* gave a new structure to thought as such. Descartes no longer defined it as

---

relation to Nietzsche and the relation from Luhmann's theory to Nietzsche's philosophy until now has not been investigated at all.

3 We rely mostly on Hans Blumenberg, *Die Legitimität der Neuzeit* (1966), *Der Prozess der theoretischen Neugierde* (1973), *Die Genesis der kopernikanischen Welt* (1975). Blumenberg has, in turn, following Ernst Cassirer's *Substanzbegriff und Funktionsbegriff* (1910) shifted from a substantialist understanding of the history of mind to a functional one. Like Blumenberg, Niklas Luhmann also remains sceptical of the concept of secularization (cf. Luhmann 2000: 278–319).

something positively determining or truly representing, but rather as negation and self-reference: to doubt means to think that something (apparently self-evident) is not (self-evident); thinking does not simply determine or represent anymore, but rather *decides* what is and what is not. It can thus lead to disorientation, as Descartes shows in his First Meditation, but it can also lead out of it again. At the beginning of the Second Meditation, Descartes presents the image of a vortex triggered by thought with its doubts, a vortex which drags thought down and threatens to drown it, and from which thought must now by its own strength literally 'bolt out', and 'work its way up' (*enîti*). *No longer self-evident, this thought which is only certain in its self-reference and which is capable of autonomy, becomes the modern 'subject'.*

This subject first became plausible psychologically, as a *consciousness* (*conscientia*) with its constantly changing ideas (*ideae*). While all ideas may be doubtful, it is not doubtful that one is or can become conscious of them. However, when one is conscious of them, consciousness is also–self-referentially–conscious of itself. Then, secondly, the concept of the subject also became historically plausible. 'Subject', the translation of the Aristotelian *hypokeímenon*, signified also for Descartes the 'substrate' [*das Zugrundeliegende*], now a substrate of unremittingly changing ideas. But this substrate was itself no longer a permanent being equally accessible to everyone and hence 'external'. It was observable only by itself and hence 'internal'. It was itself an idea, and ideas can be different for each person. With that Descartes took the decisive step of Modernity from 'being' to 'consciousness', from ontological metaphysics to the philosophy of consciousness. 'Being', the Aristotelian *ousía*, in Latin *substantia*, in which the world of experience had its thinkable foothold, is now only given in ideas of consciousness, which are as such fleeting and possibly different for each consciousness. Consciousnesses are *separated* from each other. Since consciousnesses cannot compare their ideas either with being or with each other's ideas and thus can never determine if their ideas are 'true' in the old sense (for once again consciousnesses have only their own ideas of being and of each other), they *totally lose every foothold*.

Thus the foothold of the world *for* consciousness and its own foothold *in* the world become the most urgent problem. Since it is no longer evidently given, it must first be created by the 'subject', which thereby can now only hold on to itself. It must thus step out of the passivity of a mere substrate and become *active*, in current language: creative or constructive. After this, there is no longer an order of things in itself (*ordre des choses*) for consciousness. The subject must create an order of reasons for itself (*ordre des raisons*). This can be just an order of its ideas. As we know, Descartes' suggestion regarding the sciences was: decide the rules of a *method*, and then follow them consistently. ('Morals', the good customs for the everyday life – in which the rules were embedded – he left 'provisorily' open). If different consciousnesses do that equally, a common order comes about, and with it a stable stock in their ideas. This results neither from correspondence with external beings, nor from coincidence of ideas among different consciousnesses, but rather from the consistency with which the rules are followed. Through thinking as an ordering of one's ideas, consciousness, which is only certain in its self-reference, creates for itself its *own foothold in the world*.

In order for consciousness – as subject of its own ideas – to hold on to the rules of a method, it must, however, be itself stable, or constant over time. Through mere self-reference, which, as Descartes stresses in the Second Meditation, is a mere temporal performance ("*quamdiu* me aliquid esse cogitabo", "ego sum, ego existo, *quoties* a me profertur", my italics), a foothold is not guaranteed, but, on the contrary, is put into question. For that reason, Descartes went back, once more, to the metaphysical concept of substance and, in accordance with the old Aristotelian metaphysics, designated *conscientia* as a *res cogitans*, a 'thinking thing' that allowed him to simultaneously separate consciousness from the body and guarantee the immortality of the soul afresh. In this way, the subject gained and offered a *new timeless, absolute foothold*.

However, one cannot know such a substance. One can only imagine it. *Kant* (and Hume before him) detects this inconsistency in the course of his critique of metaphysics. The subject loses its status as a substance, but Kant still manages to maintain the Cartesian timeless foothold by providing the subject with 'transcendental' *a prioris*, universal and timeless 'forms'. These are more than mere rules that one can decide to follow or not, for they are supposed to have been rather always already given to the 'mind' (*Gemüt*).[4] That is how Kant preserves the idea of transcendence: it is no longer God's transcendence, which has become even more doubtful, but only the transcendence of the subject itself. He thereby follows Descartes, for he still deems the 'transcendental method' the condition of possibility of the objectivity of science. However, if the subject does not have to *decide* on transcendental *a prioris*, it must nonetheless *distinguish* between them and, in fact, it once again has to do this in itself, that is, among its fleeting ideas. The subject itself must draw a boundary in its consciousness, separate in itself the 'empirical subject' from the 'transcendental subject' and, as long as science is at stake, it shall always have to hold on to the transcendental side of this divide. In this way, as Nietzsche and Luhmann would later point

---

4 On the paradoxical construction of these forms cf. Werner Stegmaier, "Immanuel Kant: Kritik der reinen Vernunft", in Stegmaier 1997: 15–60.

out,⁵ already as a scientific subject it becomes a moral subject. And it becomes then recognizably paradoxical: in order to be able to think the objectivity of objects in its empirical consciousness, with the help of transcendental a prioris that transcend the empiricity of its consciousness, the subject has to desubjectify itself. Kant thinks objects as desubjectified subjects, and since his concept of the subject includes both the empirical and the transcendental subjects, he simultaneously conceals the paradox. That is why one could and still can today think of objectivity without being disturbed by the paradox.

In fact, the concealed paradox made the concept of the subject shimmer in a new light. One can assume with plausibility that there is consciousness, that consciousness observes its ideas, and that it also observes that different consciousnesses can have different ideas. However, a transcendental subject, which is pure from everything empirical, cannot in a strict sense – according to the criteria of the *Critique of Pure Reason* which establishes that what is real must also be given sensorily – be real. 'There is', in the common sense of the term, no transcendental subject; the 'transcendental subject' is and was also for Kant only a theoretical concept, a conceived condition of possibility of the universality of scientific and moral judgments.⁶

Kant was correct in establishing the rule that 'subjects' in the plural are empirical subjects.⁷ Existing empirical subjects are also what is at stake in action (where they affect each other), that is, in *practical philosophy*. However, as moral agents subjects ought also to desubjectify themselves. Kant followed here the method of transcendentalization. The starting point of actions are subjective ideas of the empirical subject; when such ideas are made fixed they are called 'habits', and these are called 'maxims' when made conscious and explicit. In order to determine whether these 'maxims' can be thought of as general laws, one will have to test them according to the categorical imperative. The empirical subject must also differentiate between empirical and 'pure' motives of his/her actions, and here it becomes evident how difficult and almost hopeless that is, because (as constantly shown anew since the French moralists up until Nietzsche) for every selfless fulfillment of a duty one can always find a hidden selfish interest; this was well known especially to protestants. Therefore, the

---

5 Cf. FW 345, and also Stegmaier 2012: 161–191, Luhmann (1981), Wie ist soziale Ordnung möglich?, in: Niklas Luhmann, Gesellschaftsstruktur und Semantik. Studien zur Wissenssoziologie der modernen Gesellschaft, vol. 2, Frankfurt a.M.: Suhrkamp, 195–285, 243.
6 This is shown in Kant's texts by Simon 2003: 46–55.
7 Cf. for example KrV B 322 and B 849; KpV, AA 5: 58; KU § 33, AA 5: 285, and § 36, AA 5: 288. Cf. also the very sophisticated monograph by Poljakova, Ekaterina (2013) *Differente Plausibilitäten. Kant und Nietzsche, Tolstoi und Dostojewski über Vernunft, Moral und Kunst.*

demand becomes both rigorous and full of pathos. According to Kant, the moral command indicates "constraint for the subject that is sensibly affected", and demands "*submission*" and "sacrifice". If it succeeds, which nevertheless can never be ascertained, the subject becomes "*holy*" as "subject of the moral law" (KpV, AA 5: 80, 83, 87). That is something one can only hope for.

But Kant also opened up a new view over the subject. He replaced the internal- with the external-view. For now the issue is no longer the internal, and hard to observe, delimitation of boundaries among affects and forms independent of affects in the field of cognition, or among needs and norms in the field of action. Indeed, the issue regards this field, but is now the *imputation* of actions or deeds, an imputation which is external and can be clearly observed. Kant writes:

> An action is called a *deed* insofar as it comes under obligatory laws and hence insofar as the subject, in doing it, is considered in terms of the freedom of his choice. By such an action the agent is regarded as the *author* of its effect, and this, together with the action itself, can be *imputed* to him, if one is previously acquainted with the law by virtue of which an obligation rests on these.[8]

Kant says explicitly that the subject is here "considered in terms of the freedom of his choice", his deed "can be *imputed* to him", and not that *there is* such a free subject. This imputation may be justified or not, but in any case it is an observable fact. This observable fact entails free will and (again paradoxically) compulsory submission to a moral law, all of which Nietzsche will consequently count among the "perhaps most indispensable [...] fictions" (BGE 4). Luhmann will call the "convention of imputation" a "normal illusion" (Luhmann 1990: 11, 619).

2 Nietzsche's replacement of the concept of the subject with the concept of perspectives: Conceivability of a foothold in life

Nietzsche is known for having massively criticized the concept of the subject.[9] But he has also developed its function or functions further in the European

---

8 Immanuel Kant, Die Metaphysik der Sitten, Einleitung IV: Vorbegriffe zur Metaphysik der Sitten, AA 6: 223, translated by Mary J. Gregor, in: Kant 1996: 378.
9 Cf. Salehi 2000: 334f., and Goedert 2011: 367f. Nietzsche criticized precisely the "metaphysics of subjectity (Subiectität)" which Martin Heidegger (1961: 382) ascribed to him. On the most

history of the spirit. In his critique, he uncovered the paradoxes that had arisen with Descartes' and Kant's uses of the concept of the subject and with that he thought he unmasked it and made it collapse (Luhmann will be the first to see that differently). He declared what Kant had sensed but didn't say – that the concept of a desubjectified subject was no proof of there being a subject: "*Kant essentially wanted to prove that the subject cannot be proven on the basis of the subject – and neither can the object. The possibility that the subject [...] has a merely apparent existence might not always have been foreign to him*" (BGE 54).[10] Nietzsche denounced the transcendental or free subject as "superstition" (BGE Preface) and dovetailed this denunciation with his critique of the "violence" of language (BGE 268): language (at least in the Indo-European language-circle) seduces into the concept of a free or transcendental concept because it ascribes to every event a subject as "doer" or, "agent" (BGE 16f., GM I 13). Thus Nietzsche gave the subject a new foundation – in language.

From the nineteenth century onwards, the transcendental *a prioris* were softened or abandoned and the concept of the subject gradually became synonymous with the concepts of 'person' and 'human being' (*Mensch*), Nietzsche also criticized these concepts, likewise the concepts of 'consciousness' and 'I'. The *function* of all these concepts was *to create unity and order over time in the chaos of ideas of individuals and among individuals* – and Nietzsche saw this, no less than both Descartes and Kant did. However, he insisted that it was precisely with this chaos that one had to cope (cf. GS 109), no longer concealing, obscuring and belittling it through the kind of transcendentality and normativity whereby one had limited the horizon of philosophy to (mathematical) science and (normative) ethics. Conceived of without transcendental *a prioris*, the subject becomes a mere individual, which is different from any other individual and which in its own subjectivity cannot reach the subjectivity of another subject. Subjects remain separated, no matter how much they manage to desubjectivize themselves. They are, in a word, perspectives. Because this otherness, separation, and perspectivity cause fear – a fear of insuperable loneliness, as Nietzsche thought –, one pre-

---

recent – also mostly new-Kantian – research on the relation between Nietzsche and Kant cf. the collection of essays by Hartwig Frank (2006), Tom Bailey (2006), and Mattia Riccardi (2009). See there further references to the research tradition.

10 In fact, Kant introduced "the paradox" in his discussion about the transcendental subject, namely when he deals with the subject's self-observability (KrV B 152f.). As an observable subject, it must be empirical, and in the "inner sense" that Kant introduced for this purpose, he distinguished an "active" and a "passive" subject, that is, a simultaneously subjective and objective subject, which is a paradoxical subject once again. In this way, he 'unfolded' or 'displaced', as Luhmann will call it, the paradox.

ferred to hold on to the paradox of a selfless self, which is presupposed by science and morality (cf. GS 345). Given that right and morality need to ascribe guilt, it was difficult to get rid of such a selfless self anyway (cf. GM I 13).

In fact, however, the search for the reasons of an event, including good and bad actions, could be carried further *ad infinitum*, with the consequence that, in the end, nobody could be held responsible for an action (cf. WS 23). From this point of view, the function of the concept of the subject is *to break the genealogical investigation for practical* aims. A subject is declared the definitive starting point of an event and thus of *his* actions. Whereas others may stop here, philosophers are challenged to carry the genealogy further. Nietzsche tried to do that by widening the philosophical horizon of the thinking and acting subject to *'life'*. 'Life' in the philosophical understanding thwarts in its indissoluble contingency and temporality all the attempts to organize it permanently. It is always different from what one can grasp of it; literally, 'life' cannot be 'established' or 'fixated'.

For this reason, a reflection on 'life' must also stop somewhere. Nietzsche's terminus is no longer our thinking, for he intentionally chooses to stop precisely at the terminus which Descartes had separated and excluded from our thinking, namely the *body*. We obviously cannot think without the body, and Nietzsche made it his 'guiding thread'. He inverted the relation between the two and tried to conceive of thinking from the perspective of the body. It is even less plausible that one denies the existence of the body than that of thinking. In the body, thinking experiences the contingency and temporality of life 'in its own skin'. In the late posthumous notes he experimented with conceiving of *subjectivity as the vitality of the body* (*Lebendigkeit des Leibes*) and with replacing the former with the latter.The biological body, which can autonomously move and look after itself in its environment, appears as a self-referential unity, but precisely "*only* as *organization and interplay*", as "a *formation of rule*, which *means* 'one' but *is* not one" (NL 1885, 2[87], KSA 12: 104), something which is interpreted as a unity, without being in itself a unity. The body drives the 'I', 'reason', 'spirit' – which are all only "something sticking to the body" ("*etwas am Leibe*", not "*im Leibe*", Z I, On the Despisers of the Body) – into a double perspective. As long as the body works well, they take it for an unproblematic unity that they can forget about, and yet they know at the same time that the body is an ultimately inscrutable multiplicity, whose functioning always remains uncertain. If it stops working, if it gets sick, they will be reminded of it and experience the fact that it is also difficult or even impossible to understand the body. The healthy, spiritual-bodily subject lives, thus, in a systematic self-deception – he believes that he is independent of the body, but is in fact dependent on its aproblematic functioning, its health: "The danger in all direct questioning of the subject about the subject, and all self-contemplation of the mind, is that it could be useful and important for the subject's activity to misinterpret itself" (NL 1885, 40[21], KSA 11: 639).[11]

A subject, which should be essentially self-assurance and yet must continuously deceive itself about itself, is paradoxical, and the paradox seemed obviously so annoying to Nietzsche that he didn't immediately go public with it.[12] It is equally paradoxical "to assume a multiplicity of subjects on whose interplay and struggle our thinking and our consciousness in general is based" (NL 1885, 40[42], KSA 11: 650; cf. NL 1885, 37[4], KSA 11: 576–579). This interplay would also then have to have a subject, but it would be a contradiction in the concept of the subject that a subject could underlie other subjects. And that also applies to the attempt to think the subject as something that can be fragmented in multiplicities of subjects or appropriate other subjects: "The sphere of a subject constantly becoming *larger* or *smaller* – the centre of the system constantly *shifting*" (NL 1887, 9[98], KSA 12: 391f.). *The recourse to the concept of life makes the problems with the concept of the subject clear, but does not solve them.* The concept of life eventually exhausts the concept of the subject.

However, in the texts that were published or intended for publication, Nietzsche radicalizes the *uniqueness and singularity* of the subject (thereby acting as a subject that does *not* desubjectify itself). He demands, at least from philosophers and their "spirituality" (*Geistigkeit*), the courage to individuality and solitude, and makes of this courage the criterion for the order of rank among them. As representative of mankind, a philosopher shall make of himself the experiment of resolutely resisting the need for a foothold on others and other things, and shall have the courage to live with a complete lack of a foothold [*Haltlosigkeit*], leading to ultimate disorientation and nihilism (cf. TI, Maxims and Arrows 2).[13] With the fiction of the subject that paradoxically desubjectifies itself, Nietzsche shall no longer accept as evident any kind of unity, duration, distinction, opposition, valuation or object whatsoever. However, in order to dare to go on with this experiment, he must already have a hold in himself or, as Nietzsche says, "have a firm grip on himself" ["*fest auf sich selber sitzen*", (GS 345)]. The problem is, then, how can both things be compatible.

Nietzsche solves the problem with *an intrinsically 'lively' terminology* for what previously was established [*fest-gestellt*] as 'subject' and 'object'. Instead of definitely determining the meaning of concepts, he creates metaphors that leave leeways [*Spielräume*] for meanings and keep them in motion. Water and

---

11 Cf. Bertino 2011: 96–101.
12 See the evidence for this in Bertino 2011.
13 On nihilism in this sense cf. Stegmaier 2012: 319–338.

the flux of a river are his primal metaphors here. Accordingly, the possibility of regulating and organizing the involuntarily emerging and vanishing ideas must not be presupposed from the start; on the contrary, the possibility of such regulation and organization requires – not only, but especially in science – a particular discipline or, as Wittgenstein was not the first to point out, requires 'training' (*Abrichtung*).[14] Such training or restraint of the living use of signs and concepts does not originate in the individual, but rather in the society where the individual grows up and gradually takes on certain tasks. It relies on communication and ascesis. Thus, consciousness can be understood in a different way: no longer as a subject of its ideas, but rather as a function of social communication (cf. GS 354).[15] According to Nietzsche's conjecture, consciousness was able to evolve as an easier and faster way of mutual understanding based on the use of common signs, which means that consciousness evolved before it was necessary to resort to self-observation in the use of those signs (especially when they were misunderstood) and, therefore, before the kind of introspection and reflection that one later connected with the concept of a subject.

If one asks further, to whom shall be ascribed the conventional use of language, whether to outstanding personalities that are superior to others in power of speech, or precisely to ordinary, average human beings who rely on conventionality, Nietzsche's answer is the following: to the struggle of both with one another. In his published writings he places himself on the side of the great solitary individuals, even if for himself he may have acknowledged a more balanced state of affairs. Instead of "subjectity", as Heidegger and Luhmann will say,[16] he relies thus on *agonality*. When the relation to the other does not rely on aprioristic similarities, but is simply a relation of otherness, the only alternative which remains (besides indifference) is between friendship and antagonism, and Nietzsche wants to see adversaries even in friends (Z I, On the Friend). The agonality leads, in turn, to the *semantics of enhancement*: the enhancement of 'life' beyond its mere preservation, the 'overman' (*Übermensch*) upstaging 'mankind' (*Menschheit*), the 'overfullness' (*Überfülle*) of meaning overtrumping the 'fullness' (*Fülle*) of sense. Nietzsche's concept for that is 'will to power', a concept which is at first glance

---

14 WB 5; GD, Was den Deutschen abgeht 5; Ludwig Wittgenstein, *Philosophische Untersuchungen* (*Philosophical Investigations*), PI § 6.
15 See García 2011, Constâncio 2012, and Stegmaier 2012: 262–288. On the untenability of the thesis of Peter V. Zima (2000: 131), according to which Nietzsche has tried "*in extremis* to save the solitary subject" and the equally untenable thesis of Udo Tietz (2000), according to which Nietzsche got stuck in the paradigm of the philosophy of consciousness of German idealism, cf. Axel Pichler (2010: 256 and 138f.).
16 Cf. Heidegger 1950: 236 et al., Luhmann 1984: 145, and Luhmann 1997: 1028 et al.

aggressive, but at second glance is multilayered and complex. 'Will to power' is a will that wants to go beyond itself to something which it does not yet know and which in its contingency it cannot know, a will that experiences itself precisely by grappling with other wills to power, and thus overcomes the concept of the subject. In this way, the semantics of enhancement culminates in the *semantics of experimentation and adventure*. Adventures are uncontrollable experiments, experiments made under the fundamental condition of uncertainty. In this uncertainty Nietzsche also disallows the absolute self-certainty of the subject.

However, Nietzsche reunites the strands of his constructive critique of the subject with the *semantics of orientation*. Although he does not use the term 'orientation', this is in fact the semantics through which he makes plausible his critique of the subject. Nietzsche replaces the concept of the subject with the concepts of standpoint, horizon and perspective, which were already familiar to Kant and before him Leibniz, and he frees these concepts from the theologically pre-established harmony and the transcendental *a priori*. As perspective, the subject has no free, synoptic, and unlimited view over the world, no ideas of the world from a standpoint from above the world. It is rather limited in his view of the world by a standpoint and horizon within the world; it is only inside these limits, which include logical, ontological and linguistic "schemata" (cf. NL 1886–87, 5[22], KSA 12: 193f.), that the subject can ever relate to any objects. What a perspective finds in its limits is also a foothold, a foothold in its life and perspectivity. A perspective in Nietzsche's sense is a 'lively' subject. It can widen or straighten its horizon and displace its standpoint, and thereby adapt both its horizon and its standpoint to its current life situation. But it always remains bound to a standpoint and horizon, it cannot arbitrarily abandon them (therefore, there is also no danger of a relativism of arbitrariness). Nevertheless, it can–even if always only from its own perspective (and hence again paradoxically)–place itself in the perspectives of others, and in this way increase the amplitude of its possibilities of perception; objectivity becomes then conceivable as multiperspectivity (cf. GM III 12). The semantics of enhancement and experimentation is then finally converted into the *semantics of sovereignty*: sovereign is the one who is able to change perspectives quickly and easily (cf. MA I Vorrede 6; GM III 12).[17] This sovereignty is no longer bound to consciousness; on the contrary, it achieves its certainty by becoming an *instinct*. 'Instinct' is the non-conscious certainty of orientation.[18] An individual sure of its orientation

---

[17] The semantics of sovereignty in the concept of the subject will be made particularly strong by Georges Bataille. Cf. Balibar/Cassin/Libera 2004: 1244.
[18] Cf. Constâncio/Branco (2011).

remains totally on its own, just like the metaphysical and the transcendental subject, but it is now in the middle of 'life' and deals with life.

3 Luhmann's replacement of the concepts of subject and perspective with the concept of observation: Conceivability of a foothold in social communication

Most likely deterred by Nietzsche's metaphorical, aphoristic and agonistic style, Luhmann has intentionally avoided him. He wanted his science and sociology to be grounded on a conceptual, systematic, verifiable theory, indeed a theory capable of being true or false, but also embedded in time and evolution. In order to describe modern society in sufficiently complex terms, he structured his science as a "system theory", and this system theory went so deep that it included the whole history of the European spirit and hence also philosophy. A system theory demands a fundamental philosophical reorientation of our way of thinking and, therefore, unlike many Nietzsche texts, it doesn't seem immediately plausible. But it can give Nietzsche's philosophy a new plausibility.

Luhmann shares with Nietzsche (and Kant and Descartes and their concept of the subject) first of all the *starting point in self-reference*. But he now applies it also to society: society exists only insofar as in society one speaks of society – society exists only in social communications. It consists in such communications, and not in the human beings, persons or subjects that are normally identified (again in social communications) as the authors of such communications. To borrow the terminology of critical philosophy, the conditions of possibility of communication in society are the same as the conditions of possibility of philosophy, and Nietzsche had already insisted on that. But Luhmann draws from that a clear 'constructivist' consequence: whatever is said to exist exists only on this very condition, namely that it is said to exist, such that in other communications other worlds shall be distinguished (which does not entail that one can arbitrarily change the conditions of communication – also here there is no danger of relativism qua arbitrariness). With this, Luhmann comes so close to Nietzsche that one can dare say that *he shares his philosophical fundamental decisions, but makes them apt for theory*.

In Luhmann, the concepts 'thinking', 'consciousness', 'human being', etc become mere distinctions made in the context of social communications, distinctions that could also have been made differently. They are all 'constructions' or 'constructs', like everything else. They exist only on the condition that someone, no matter who, constructs them. Precisely like Nietzsche, Luhmann no longer asks for the 'agents' or 'subjects' of those constructions; for they would only be other constructions. With the concept of construction (or '*Begriff des Konstrukt*', the concept of 'the construct'), Luhmann offers "an alternative formulation of the concept of concept" (1990: 515): a construct does not purport either to correspond to a pre-given object or to apprehend it, to 'represent' it. The construct validates itself only by being able to lead to further constructions. That is how it makes itself 'true', or is 'verified'. Whenever necessary, a construct can also be replaced and, in this sense, falsified. That is how constructs can become theories. With his decision to commit himself to the concept of construct and to his constructivism, Luhmann transforms into a theory Nietzsche's fundamental philosophical decision of committing himself to perspectivism.

Luhmann's sociological system theory[19] also includes an *additional philosophical critique of the subject*. He has dedicated a particular essay to it, titled "*Die Tücke des Subjekts und die Frage nach dem Menschen*", that is, the 'cunning' or 'slyness' of the subject.[20] "The cunning of the subject – that is its way to appear human, to ingratiate itself as a human being" (Luhmann 1995: 157)–, its way to make itself easily plausible. For, as follows from what was said above, the subject is not at all something that simply is. The "subject", which in its Aristotelian sense "underlies itself and everything else", and which in its Kantian sense "distinguishes itself in its freedom from all empirical causations", is certainly "the most demanding title that humanity has ever given itself" (Luhmann 1995: 162). In its "freedom" "all that is unknown and uncertain [...] was accommodated", and the subject could then (ultimately by Sartre) be made responsible for all that is unknown and uncertain – just as before only God had been (Luhmann 1995: 161). As one can easily see in Descartes and Kant, with the concept of the subject religious transcendence was transferred to the human being. But when a semantics has such a huge success as the semantics of the subject, its significance cannot be merely internal to philosophy. It must also have a function in society as a whole.

According to Luhmann, the function of a concept should be recognized not so much in what it (positively) delimits, but rather in what it (negatively)

---

19 For an introduction cf. preferably Luhmann's own posthumously published introductory lecture-course: *Einführung in die Systemtheorie* (2004). It includes a comprehensive chapter on the critique of the subject under the title "Beobachten" (Luhmann 2004: 141–166).

20 Luhmann 1995. The critique of the subject extends through Luhmann's whole work. Cf. in particular: Luhmann 1989, Luhmann 1990: 11ff. et al., Luhmann 1997: 866–878, 1016–1036.

excludes, in short, in the fact that it distinguishes. According to Luhmann's thesis, the concept of the subject had the function of excluding other subjects and, thus, society as such: "If 'subject' means to underlie itself and thus the whole world, then there cannot be any other subject" (Luhmann 1995: 158). In this way, considered from a sociological point of view, the concept of the subject liberated not only from the privileges of the old hierarchical society, but also from privileges such as property, education and natural talent. Thus the concept of the subject helped make thinkable the idea of reconstructing society from its ground, of reconstructing it by transforming a stratified, hierarchic differentiation into a functional differentiation regulated exclusively by performance or accomplishment. Thus the concept of the subject worked in early modernity as *a semantics of transition*: through it 'freedom' and 'equality' could be ascribed to everyone.

However, the philosophical concept of the subject did not only help make room for a new conception of society. Precisely because it formulated self-reference in such a way that it made the external reference, the reference to other subjects, more difficult, at the same time it *blocked* a new conception of society. This "paradox of self-affirmation" (Luhmann 1995: 160), the paradox that put the subject against other subjects who were supposed to be as equal and free as itself and establish with it a new society, could not have been solved by such concepts as Nietzsche's concept of life and will to power. For as unities that should not be grasped as unities, as something that had to be determined but eluded any determination, life and will to power were again unintentionally paradoxical and continued to bar the path to a theory of society.

Nevertheless, with those concepts Nietzsche made a first step towards a transference of the paradox from the subject itself to its relation with others and to the others, thereby connecting the independence of the subject with dependence, its autonomy with heteronomy, its self-reference with reference to the other (here Kant had already made some preparatory work by defending that in knowledge thought is dependent on sensual perceptions, although he still used his transcendental structures to protect the independency of the subject itself). Thus Nietzsche promoted the functionalization of the concept of the subject and in the process took a deeply new epistemological decision – even if only to a certain extent. Only in this regard did Luhmann concede him a certain role as predecessor. That was the decision to no longer let oneself be scared by logical paradoxes, but rather use them resolutely for the development of theories.[21] The

---

[21] See the end of JGB 22, which is famous precisely on account of this end and is still intensely discussed: "Gesetzt, dass auch dies [dass alle Gesetzlichkeit Interpretation sei] nur Interpretation ist – und ihr werdet eifrig genug sein, dies einzuwenden? – nun, um so besser"; and see Luhmann

very concept of 'distinguishing' or 'distinction' [*Unterscheidung*] already involves a paradox, for it is simultaneously identity (the unity of the distinction made) and difference (what is thereby distinguished), or operation (the execution of the distinction) and the result of the operation (what has been distinguished), and hence Luhmann decided to understand the development of theories as 'development of paradoxes', a decision which aims to finally avoid all forms of metaphysics, transcendental philosophy, and mysticism.[22]

He replaced the unintentionally paradoxical concepts of subject and perspective with the explicitly paradoxical concept of *observation* and the unintentionally paradoxical unity of life with the explicitly paradoxical distinction between *system and environment*. In order to do this, he carried out, in his own formulation, "four semantic revolutions" (Luhmann 1995: 163f.):

1. An approach based on *temporal operations*, and no longer on supposedly timeless objects. Thus he understood the subject no longer as object, but rather as a temporal operation of its self-reference.
2. The adoption of *recursive* operations, which repeat themselves under recourse to their own results and are no longer independent from one another. Whereas the subject is supposed to constitute itself at once and forever, recursive operations are continuously generating something new (*autopoiesis*).
3. The insistence on strict *observability*: whereas the transcendental subject is supposed to be a 'pure' subject, an observer that was able to observe empirically but was not itself empirically observable, now all the observers, including the theoretician of observation, become observable. The concept of observation no longer distinguishes, as it was common from Plato onwards, according to 'faculties' of the 'subject', – for example, sensibility and understanding, which Kant used to make a further distinction between the empirical and the transcendental. The concept of observation now distinguishes according to self-reference and external reference. An observation observes something other than itself; but in order to distinguish this other thing from itself, it must also observe itself ("are these now only my ideas or not?"). It refers simultaneously to the outside and to the inside, and nevertheless it cannot observe different things at the same time, that is, other things and

---

(1990: 94): "Man muß [...] im Stile Nietzsche/Heidegger/Derrida mit der Paradoxie von sich selbst negierenden Unterscheidungen arbeiten und die expressiven Möglichkeiten des Vertextens nutzen, um genau dies mitzuteilen." See also Luhmann 1992: 219f., Luhmann 1997: 91.

[22] On the productive handling of paradoxes cf. especially Luhmann 1990: 537–541, Luhmann 1991, Luhmann 2011: 127–131.

itself. It is, thus, structurally paradoxical. The paradox is overcome when time is taken into account. The observation changes temporally back and forth between external reference and self-reference, it 'oscillates' between them (whereby the paradox lands up in time, which in turn is simultaneously always the same and always another). However, one can also observe one's own observation in such a way that one observes how other observers observe it (for example, that they are irritated when my observations are false for them). One can also oscillate between these possibilities of direct and indirect self-observation. In both cases, an external reference is incorporated in the self-reference and a self-reference is incorporated in the external reference; in this way, a "radically difference-theoretical [*differenztheoretischer*] starting point" is won. Luhmann's name for the leading difference is 'system and environment': 'system' precisely because the observation must refer to itself, 'close' itself in a system, in order to – as the metaphor of the perspective had already made clear – observe other things, and open itself to other things; 'environment' [*Umwelt*] (and not 'world' [*Welt*]) because the system observes the apparently given world always only in its own specific way and hence always only *its* environment, the environment as is self-evident to it.

4. The fact that a system in Luhmann's sense is simultaneously closed and open – or the fact that the system, according to him, is "the difference between system and environment" and, thus, simultaneously identity and difference (as already distinguishing is identity and difference at the same time) – makes it a paradox too. As paradox, it cannot be an object. The fourth and last semantic revolution that Luhmann mentions here is, thus, the *'self-foundation' of system theory in paradox*. Paradoxes can be the foundation of theories precisely because they make logical thought – which aims at timeless determinations and is committed to consistency – oscillate between two equally legitimate but not simultaneously executable alternatives (for example, self-reference and external reference, identity and difference). If logical thought oscillates, if it becomes undecidable, it doesn't go further, it blocks (for example, a sentence like 'I lie' states a truth that is a lie). But precisely in this blockage it then also has a 'foothold' from which it can 'proceed', a 'starting point' for a theory. In this way, the philosophical concept of foundation also becomes paradoxical; it simultaneously is a foundation and not a foundation, because it is itself 'only' a paradox of thought. However, as one can now see, it was precisely such a paradoxical foundation that was at stake in modern philosophy's concept of the subject.

The further consequences that Luhmann derives from this correspond well to Nietzsche. He sustains that "autopoietic systems" are "always individual (in-dividual) systems", "systems which are subsumed under general concepts are *for each other environment* and, in fact, for each other *always different environments*" – like Nietzsche's will to power. The "radically individualistic theory" of autopoietic self-differentiating systems opens up, as Nietzsche wanted, "new possibilities of description of the richness of the world". However, since each system distinguishes from itself *its* environment – or, in the old language, each subject distinguishes from itself *its* objects – and we therefore replace the old "subject with the observer and define observers as systems, which create themselves through the sequential practice of their distinctions, there is no longer any formal guarantee for objects" (Luhmann 1997: 878) and, as already for Nietzsche, objectivity becomes multiperspectivity. In the network of observers there are, according to Luhmann, "plenty of options to choose a reference system" (Luhmann 1995: 165f.).

With the concept of the system of observation, Luhmann only captures the *formal* structure of the subject, its self-reference (completing it with the external reference). In such a way, he can relate it not only to the old human subjects but also to non-human social systems of observation, on the one hand, and to biological systems of observation, on the other. He calls the social systems of observation "function systems" of social communication, insofar as since early modernity they have "differentiated" themselves via a conversion from "segmentary differentiation" (groups) and "stratified differentiation" (classes) into "functional differentiation" of social communication. That is, they developed themselves into autonomous systems of observation, which are limited in their structure only by their environment and by the systems of observation that depend on individual human observers, so that one can speak of '*the* economy', '*the* political arena', '*the* law', '*the* education system', '*the* science', '*the* art', and '*the* media' as if these were agents, acting subjects. In this way, human subjects become the environment of the function systems of social communication – a fact which is still "so unwelcome and so adamantly rejected" (Luhmann 1995: 167).[23] Luhmann distinguishes them as "conscious" or "psychic systems", in opposition to the biological or "physical systems", their corresponding bodies. The *separation of humans in particular systems of observation* is well justified. For, as Nietzsche had already emphasized (cf. GS 11 and Z I, On the Despisers of the Body), only a minimal part of the functions of the physical system becomes conscious in the psychic system, and only a minimal part of the functions of the

---

23 Against the "humanist burdensome legacy" Luhmann tactfully adds that it is "incomprehensible why the place in the environment of the system of society should be such a bad place. I at least wouldn't like to change." (Luhmann 1995: 167)

psychic system is articulated in the function systems of social communication (cf. BGE 268 and GS 354). They are 'structurally linked' only by narrow bridges.

On the other hand, however, the differentiated function systems of social communication, which use their specific 'codes' (such as true/false in science, fair/unfair in law, and solvent/non-solvent in economy), are also the environment for the psychic system; in the old language, they are 'objects', which the psychic system perceives 'subjectively' or 'in perspective'. In its observation of this environment, the psychic system can, voluntarily or involuntarily, choose codes and switch between them (for example, in a case of corruption, the psychic system may cease to consider it judicially or economically and consider it morally instead). If the psychic system takes the perspective of a function system, it must desubjectify itself in order to do justice to the function of that system (most obviously in science); but it remains 'subjective' in the *decision for this code or another*.

But the modalities of 'subjective' or 'perspectival' decisions – not only of the decision to adopt one of those codes instead of another, but also to adopt any distinctions in general – are no longer *the focus of the sociological system theory*. Therefore, the sociological system theory cannot have the philosophical last word on the question about the current meaning of subjectivity.[24] Hence, we will finally return to the semantics of orientation, just like Nietzsche (who nevertheless avoided the concept of orientation itself, probably because his declared opponent Eugen Dühring had favored it). The semantics of orientation can grasp the physical, psychic and social systems of observation as a unity which differentiates itself, without bringing it back again to the unity of an underlying entity in the sense of the old subject.[25]

4 Integration of the concepts of subject, perspective and observation in the concept of orientation: Conceivability of a foothold in general – temporarily

The recognizably metaphorical concept of orientation was introduced in philosophy by Kant ("What Does It Mean to Orient Oneself in Thinking?") at the sug-

---

24 Besides, as Luhman himself has noticed, with his approach society falls into the conceptual situation of the old subject. It also doesn't have a subject next to it, with which it could communicate. Cf. Luhmann 1997: 874f.
25 For a closer examination of this point, see Stegmaier 2008, Stegmaier 2010.

gestion of Mendelssohn. Then it has become indispensable in the philosophical, scientific and everyday language (Luhmann has also constantly made use of it). It designates the capacity to find one's way in a given situation, in order to find possibilities of action that may allow one to master the situation. It incorporates in itself (A.) Luhmann's concepts of observation and system, Nietzsche's concept of perspective, and Kant's concept of subject, and (B.) goes beyond them.

A. Orientation has the function of a system of observation. With the distinction between orientation and situation, orientation can be said to be, like the *Luhmannian system of observation*, simultaneously a unity and a difference. Orientation is always orientation in a situation, which orientation (like the Luhmannian system) distinguishes from itself as its environment. Orientation operates recursively, autopoietically, in that each orientation incorporates the results of previous orientations, creates a new situation (a situation in which one is orientated is clearly different from one in which one is not orientated), and thereby again a new need for orientation. It is observable in the success or failure of one's own or another's orientation. It is based on a paradoxical self-reference: in the face of a success or a failure of orientations there is nothing one can do but orientate oneself again. Orientation is not limited to consciousness. Biological, living, and physical systems also must and can orientate themselves (and animals often orientate themselves a lot better than humans). Each orientation must be able to distinguish between right and left, above and below, front and back, but these references are, as Kant saw, neither perceivable nor definable; one must have them, as people say, by 'feeling' or 'instinct' (with regard to right and left individuals may sometimes fail). On the other hand, the function systems of social communication also 'orientate themselves', for example economics by politics, and vice-versa. But the orientation itself has no other foundation besides itself, nor does it have a particular subject that could be identified within it as its driving-center. Like the brain, orientation can differentiate itself in many levels and distinguish within itself [*ausdifferenzieren*] different operating regions, which remain nonetheless connected in networks. That is how orientation operates: always as a whole, and yet with internally differentiated weights. If one wants to talk of orientation in terms of an agent or a subject of action, one realizes that orientation is so difficult to restrain within the traditional determinations of the subject as is the system in Luhmann's sense.

In their standpoints, horizons, and perspectives, orientations *in Nietzsche's sense* are individual. When they are understood as modes of orientation, perspectives are not fixed in themselves, as the previously so-called 'perspectives' (telescopes), but rather allow ceaseless movements of standpoints and horizons and thus also of themselves. They are operations, not states; they remain, in

Nietzsche's metaphorical semantics, continuously in flux. In order to cope with more demanding situations, orientations must enhance and differentiate themselves. Then they have to simplify themselves again into an overview. They must be 'wills to power' in order to 'master' and continually 'control' those situations. In doing that they can always fail. They are, thus, always experiments. Ultimately, they may be considered sovereign if they can easily 'master' even surprising and dangerous situations in which others fail.

In Descartes' sense, orientation is driven by doubt. In an environment which is constantly changing, it can never be completely certain of itself. However, orientation attains stability not first by the use of scientific methods, but already through everyday routines, in which what was once difficult becomes easy, and what was once difficult to understand becomes self-evident. But every self-evidence can quickly be disturbed again. Then, new orientation is needed.

B. The *peculiarity of orientation* in contrast to the Kantian-Cartesian subject, the Nietzschean perspective, and the Luhmannian system is, first of all, *its universality*. All distinctions, including the subject, the perspective, and the system, are *orientation decisions*, and one can take such decisions in one way or the other. In doing this one can orientate oneself by this or that, decide for or against communication, and in communication decide oneself for one or the other function system. One decides according to the current relevance in the current situation. The relevance is, in turn, a function of the constantly possible disorientation, which is always to be avoided. Disorientation is unbearable uncertainty or, in terms of the metaphor we have been using here, the 'lack of a foothold' [*Haltlosigkeit*]. Disorientation is by itself the need of orientation and drives to orientation.

Thus, orientation creates certainty within continuous uncertainty, *a foothold within the lack of foothold* (the paradox involved here no longer needs to be characterized specifically). Orientation creates this foothold by holding on to 'clues' [*Anhaltspunkten*] that stand out, 'clues' that vary from case to case and that orientation can provisionally get hold of and use to look around for further clues, until it believes to have gotten enough 'support' [*Rückhalt*] for acting. The orientations of others can also become clues for one's own action, both the orientations of other individuals and the orientations that are offered by society's functioning systems of communication; in contrast to the concept of the subject, the concept of orientation can be readily pluralized. For orientation is always orientation *by* ... X, and this will be first and foremost other orientations – corporal or linguistic, intentional or non-intentional signs, which emanate from those orientations.

In the '*by* ... X' lies the second prominent peculiarity of orientation. When one orientates oneself by something, one does not 'submit' or 'subject' oneself to that, one does not accept it as a binding rule, but rather reserves for oneself a *leeway* [*Spielraum*] in which one decides if and how far one should follow it (Wittgenstein's rule-following paradox). Simultaneously, one also evaluates the relevance of the rule. The leeways can be larger or smaller, one can work to widen them or else let them become narrower, for example in legal terms, but especially in pragmatic, inter-individual and moral ways of behaving. Leeways are observable freedoms (again in plural), freedoms deprived of metaphysical and transcendental protections (for these are unobservable and thus difficultly tenable in case of doubt). Leeways can also unexpectedly close themselves (not only when one experiences some form of violence, but also when, for example, one 'falls madly in love'). They are, like all the processes of orientation, temporal. If time is the original source of every paradox (because, as mentioned, it is simultaneously always the same and always another) and if everything has its time and is infected with the paradoxicality of time, then orientation designates the accomplishment of being able to cope with time, to create a *temporary foothold*. A temporary foothold is enough. In the orientation, one can still distinguish a subject, but does not have to.

References

Bailey, Tom (2006) "After Kant: Green and Hill on Nietzsche's Kantianism", in: *Nietzsche-Studien* 35, 228–262.
Balibar, Étienne/Cassin, Barbara/Libera, Alain de (2004) "Art. Sujet", in: Barbara Cassin (ed.), *Vocabulaire européen des philosophies. Dictionnaire des intraduisibles*, Paris: Seuil, 1233–1254.
Bertino, Andrea Christian (2011) *"Vernatürlichung". Ursprünge von Friedrich Nietzsches Entidealisierung des Menschen, seiner Sprache und seiner Geschichte bei Johann Gottfried Herder* (Monographien und Text zur Nietzsche-Forschung, vol. 58), Berlin/Boston: De Gruyter.
Blumenberg, Hans (1966) *Die Legitimität der Neuzeit*, Frankfurt a.M.: Suhrkamp Verlag.
Blumenberg, Hans (1973) *Der Prozess der theoretischen Neugierde*, Frankfurt a.M.: Suhrkamp.
Blumenberg, Hans (1975) *Die Genesis der kopernikanischen Welt*, Frankfurt a.M.: Suhrkamp.
Cassirer, Ernst (1910) *Substanzbegriff und Funktionsbegriff*, Berlin: Bruno Cassirer.
Clam, Jean (2000) "Unbegegnete Theorie. Zur Luhmann-Rezeption in der Philosophie", in: Henk de Berg and Johannes Schmidt (eds.), *Rezeption und Reflexion. Zur Resonanz der Systemtheorie Niklas Luhmanns außerhalb der Soziologie*, Frankfurt a.M: Suhrkamp, 296–321.
Constâncio, João (2012) "Consciousness, Communication, and Self-Expression. Towards an Interpretation of Aphorism 354 of Nietzsche's The Gay Science", in: J. Constâncio and M.J. Mayer Branco (eds.), *As the Spider Spins: Essays on Nietzsche's Critique and Use of Language*, Berlin/Boston: De Gruyter, 197–231.
Constâncio, João/Branco, Maria João Mayer (eds.) (2011) *Nietzsche on Instinct and Language*, Berlin/Boston: De Gruyter.

Frank, Hartwig (2006) "Nietzsche und Kant", in: *Nietzsche-Studien* 35, 311–320.
García, André Luiz Muniz (2011) "'Vermoralisirung' e 'Entmoralisirung'. Da linguagem da moral ao caráter extra-moral da linguagem: as diretrizes de Nietzsche para um novo modo de pensar e escrever em filosofia", Doctoral thesis, Campinas.
Goedert, Georges (2011) "Art. Subjekt", in: Christian Niemeyer (ed.), *Nietzsche-Lexikon*, 2nd, revised and expanded edition, Darmstadt: WBG, 367–368.
Gründer, Karlfried (ed.) (1998) *Historisches Wörterbuch der Philosophie*, ed. Joachim Ritter et al., vol. 10, Basel/Darmstadt: Schwabe Basel.
Heidegger, Martin (1950) "Nietzsches Wort 'Gott ist tot'", in: Martin Heidegger (ed.), *Holzwege*, Frankfurt a.M.:Klostermann.
Heidegger, Martin (1961) *Nietzsche*, vol. 2, Pfullingen: Neske.
Kant, Immanuel (1996) "The Metaphysics of Morals", trans. Mary J. Gregor, in: I. Kant (ed.), *Practical Philosophy*, ed. Mary J. Gregor, Cambridge: Cambridge University Press.
Luhmann, Niklas (1981) *Gesellschaftsstruktur und Semantik. Studien zur Wissenssoziologie der modernen Gesellschaft*, vol. 2, Frankfurt a.M: Suhrkamp.
Luhmann, Niklas (1984) *Soziale Systeme. Grundriß einer allgemeinen Theorie*, Frankfurt a.M.: Suhrkamp.
Luhmann, Niklas (1989) "Wie ist soziale Ordnung möglich; Individuum, Individualität, Individualismus", in: Niklas Luhmann (ed.), *Gesellschaftsstruktur und Semantik. Studien zur Wissenssoziologie der modernen Gesellschaft*, vol. 3, Frankfurt a.M.: Suhrkamp, 207–212.
Luhmann, Niklas (1990) *Die Wissenschaft der Gesellschaft*, Frankfurt a.M.: Suhrkamp.
Luhmann, Niklas (1991) "Sthenographie und Euryalistik", in: Hans Ulrich Gumbrecht and K. Ludwig Pfeiffer (eds.), *Paradoxien, Dissonanzen, Zusammenbrüche. Situationen offener Epistemologie*, Frankfurt a.m: Suhrkamp, 58–82.
Luhmann, Niklas (1992) *Beobachtung der Moderne*, Opladen: Westdeutscher Verlag.
Luhmann, Niklas (1995) "Die Tücke des Subjekts und die Frage nach dem Menschen", in: Niklas Luhmann (ed.), *Soziologische Aufklärung 6: Die Soziologie und der Mensch*, Opladen: Westdeutscher Verlag, 155–168.
Luhmann, Niklas (1997) *Die Gesellschaft der Gesellschaft*, Frankfurt a.M.: Suhrkamp.
Luhmann, Niklas (2000) *Die Religion der Gesellschaft*, Frankfurt a.M: Suhrkamp.
Luhmann, Niklas (2004) *Einführung in die Systemtheorie*, ed. Dirk Baecker, Darmstadt: WBG.
Luhmann, Niklas (2011) *Organisation und Entscheidung*, 3rd edition, Wiesbaden: VS Verlag für Sozialwissenschaften, 127–131.
Pichler, Axel (2010) *Nietzsche, die Orchestikologie und das dissipative Denken*, Vienna: Passagen.
Poljakova, Ekaterina (2013) *Differente Plausibilitäten. Kant und Nietzsche, Tolstoi und Dostojewski über Vernunft, Moral und Kunst* (Monographien und Texte zur Nietzsche-Forschung Bd. 63), Berlin/Boston: De Gruyter.
Regenbogen, Arnim (2010) "Art. Intersubjektivität", in: Hans Jörg Sandkühler (ed.) *Enzyklopädie Philosophie*, 2nd edition in 3 vols., Hamburg: Meiner, 1152–1156.
Riccardi, Mattia (2009) *"Der faule Fleck des Kantischen Kriticismus". Erscheinung und Ding an sich bei Nietzsche* (Beiträge zu Friedrich Nietzsche, vol. 14), Basel.
Salehi, Djavid (2000) "Art. Subjekt", in: Hennig Ottmann (ed.), *Nietzsche-Handbuch. Leben – Werk – Wirkung*, Stuttgart/Weimar: Metzler.
Schwemmer, Oswald (1995) "Art. Intersubjektivität", in: Jürgen Mittelstraß (ed.) *Enzyklopädie Philosophie und Wissenschaftstheorie*, vol. 2, Stuttgart/Weimar: Metzler, 282–284.

Simon, Josef (2003) *Kant. Die fremde Vernunft und die Sprache der Philosophie*, Berlin/New York: De Gruyter.
Spaemann, Robert (1990) "Niklas Luhmanns Herausforderung der Philosophie", in: *Niklas Luhmann, Paradigm lost: Über die ethische Reflexion der Moral. Rede anläßlich der Verleihung des Hegel-Preises 1989*, Frankfurt a.M.: Suhrkamp, 49–73.
Stegmaier, Werner (in cooperation with Hartwig Frank) (1997) *Interpretationen. Hauptwerke der Philosophie. Von Kant bis Nietzsche*, Stuttgart: Reclam.
Stegmaier, Werner (2008) *Philosophie der Orientierung*, Berlin/New York: De Gruyter.
Stegmaier, Werner (2010) "Die Freisetzung einer Philosophie der Orientierung durch Friedrich Nietzsche", in: Joachim Bromand and Guido Kreis (eds.), *Was sich nicht sagen lässt. Das Nicht-Begriffliche in Wissenschaft, Kunst und Religion*, Berlin: Akademie Verlag, 355–367.
Stegmaier, Werner (2011) "Niklas Luhmann als Philosoph", in: Christina Gansel (ed.), *Systemtheorie in den Fachwissenschaften. Zugänge, Methoden, Probleme*, Göttingen: Vandenhoeck & Ruprecht, 11–32.
Stegmaier, Werner (2012) *Nietzsches Befreiung der Philosophie. Kontextuelle Interpretation des V. Buches der "Fröhlichen Wissenschaft"*, Berlin/Boston: De Gruyter.
Stegmaier, Werner (2012) "Wie leben wir mit dem Nihilismus? Nietzsches Nihilismus aus der Sicht einer aktuellen Philosophie der Orientierung", in: *Tijdschrift voor Filosofie 74*, 319–338.
Tietz, Udo (2000) "Phänomenologie des Scheins. Nietzsches sprachkritischer Perspektivismus", in: *Nietzscheforschung 7*, 215–242.
Zima, Peter V. (2000) *Theorie des Subjekts. Subjektivität und Identität zwischen Moderne und Postmoderne*, Tübingen/Basel: UTB.

Sofia Miguens
20 Three Senses of Selfless Consciousness: Nietzsche and Dennett on Mind, Language and Body

> Leib bin Ich ganz und gar, und Nichts ausserdem; und Seele ist nur ein Wort für ein etwas am Leibe. Der Leib ist eine grosse Vernunft, eine Vielheit mit einem Sinne.
> (*Also Sprach Zarathustra*, Von den Verächtern des Leibes)

In his description of the project that gave rise to this volume – the FCT research project, "*Nietzsche and the contemporary debate on the Self*" – João Constâncio asked whether Nietzsche's critique of subject and language could be said to foreshadow Dennett's Multiple Drafts Model of consciousness and the doing away with the Cartesian Theatre.[1] I will begin at this point.[2] The idea is that there is something like a common anti-Cartesian and naturalizing move, in Nietzsche's as in Dennett's theory of consciousness. The move is towards what I will call a 'selfless consciousness'. Nietzsche would certainly agree with Dennett's claim that although there is consciousness in nature there is no Central Meaner, no Central Intender, no Observer, no presence of self to itself or natural unity of a self.[3] Rejecting the naturalness of an *Einheit* of the subject, and endorsing multiplicity (*Vielheit*) are essential components of Nietzsche's own anti-Cartesianism and naturalism. For him, a human being is body, and consciousness is a phenomenon of body and brain ("the latest development of the organic" – GS 11).[4] Naturally, if consciousness is a phenomenon of the body, and the body itself is seen as a multiplicity of reasons (*Grunde*) and drives (*Triebe*), something like a

---

[1] Dennett 1991.
[2] This means that I will not consider here the whole cognitivist reception of Nietzsche, a general task João attributed to me at the beginning of the research project mentioned above. Although Dennett's functionalist models of consciousness do classify as proposals within a cognitivist model of mind, a more comprehensive review of the cognitivist reception of Nietzsche should include not only debates on consciousness and the self but also debates on free will and morality.
[3] See Dennett 1991, in particular Chapters 5 ("Multiple Drafts versus the Cartesian Theater"), 8 ("How Words Do Things With Us"), 9 ("The Architecture of the Human Mind") and 13 ("The Reality of Selves").
[4] "Das Bewusstsein. – Die Bewusstheit ist die letzte und späteste Entwicklung des Organischen [...]."

unified 'I' (the '*Ich als syntetischer Begriff*'[5]) can only be regarded as coming into the picture at a later stage. This is precisely the case: the '*Ich als syntetischer Begriff*' involves for Nietzsche, the use of language, and its status may in a certain sense be regarded as fictional. Dennett would agree with all this.

In fact, Dennett and Nietzsche share even more: they share an idea of personal identity as self-creation.[6] But I will not explore this aspect here, since I am not so much interested in personal identity as in consciousness and the self. So what I will do is compare and contrast Nietzsche's and Dennett's positions on mind and language first and then on mind and body.

As I already mentioned, as readers and interpreters of both Nietzsche and Dennett, we are entitled to see a common move towards a selfless consciousness in their theories of consciousness. But let us now try to put Nietzsche's and Dennett's approaches in perspective. Why do we want such a selfless consciousness? Do we in fact want it? What difference would the '*full naturalization*'[7] of consciousness, resulting in a selfless consciousness, make for philosophical pursuits in general? One might as well ask directly: *What is a theory of consciousness a theory of*, after all? Now, this is a quite difficult question to answer.[8] Not necessarily only because there are so many competing theories of content and consciousness in analytic philosophy of mind and language, and philosophy of perception, but especially if we think of how plausible different answers may be. We may, for instance, take a theory of consciousness to be about the brain. Or we may take it to be about the self, or about thoughts and thinking, and thought's relation to the world. So, which one is it? Is consciousness a specific topic for philosophy of mind, and cognitive science? Is a theory of consciousness ultimately a position on mind-brain-body relations in a human being? Or is that a position on consciousness bears in a much stronger way on one's general metaphysical conception of thought-world relations? I believe one problem with both Nietzsche and Dennett is that they seem to want it all here. It is with this in mind that I will try to put forward some distinctions.

---

5 "insofern wir andererseits die Gewohnheit haben, uns über diese Zweiheit vermöge des synthetischen Begriffs 'ich' hinwegzusetzen" (JGB 19).
6 Dennett's views on self-creation are built around a notion of the self as 'narrative centre of gravity'. His non-absolutist conception of personhood, which he formulates in terms of 'conditions of personhood', involves a condition of 'Nietzschean self-evaluation' (he was influenced by Charles Taylor here) (cf. Miguens 2002, 4.4.3 "Do eu à personalidade" [From self to personhood] and 4.4.4. "Quererei eu realmente ser aquilo que sou?" [Do I really want to be what I am?]).
7 This is João Constâncio's term. See Constâncio 2011.
8 See Miguens/Preyer 2012.

1 *Vielheit* and *Intermittenzen*.⁹ How does natural language make for a conscious mind? Nietzsche and Dennett on mind and language: A deflationary view of the self

I assume Nietzsche's theory of consciousness[10] is better known to Nietzsche scholars, so I first will give more attention to Dennett's. I should say that I think Nietzsche's 'critique of the subject' is a more general and ambitious project than a mere view of the self in relation to consciousness and the body. But let us start with the fact that it involves a deflationary view of the self. By this I mean that Nietzsche – after e.g. Leibniz and Schopenhauer – conceives of our minds as not essentially conscious, and also as not essentially unified or centred. Consciousness is not the kernel of our being. This means, for him, among many other things, that humans could think and act without consciousness. The question then becomes why did consciousness come into existence, if it seems superfluous. One answer to this question is to be found in *The Gay Science* §354. Here, Nietzsche puts forward the idea that consciousness developed under the pressure of the need for communication. In saying that, he acknowledges that language, and the publicity associated with it, is a necessary condition for there to be consciousness and selves in beings such as ourselves. Yet such beings could think and act in their absence.[11] Not surprisingly, it is precisely this very well-

---

9 "Man hält die Bewusstheit für eine feste gegebene Grösse! Leugnet ihr Wachsthum, ihre Intermittenzen! Nimmt sie als 'Einheit des Organismus'!" ["One takes consciousness to be a given determinate magnitude! One denies its growth and intermittences! One takes it to be the 'unity of the organism'!"] (FW 11).

10 Here I relied mostly on Katsafanas (2005), "Nietzsche's Theory of Mind: Consciousness and Conceptualization", Constâncio (2011) "On Consciousness – Nietzsche's Departure from Schopenhauer", and Riccardi (forthcoming), "Nietzsche on the Superficiality of Consciousness".

11 I take two of the most important aphorisms on consciousness to be BGE 268 and GS 354 ("Wir könnten nämlich denken, fühlen, wollen, uns erinnern, wir könnten ebenfalls 'handeln' in jedem Sinne des Wortes: und trotzdem brauchte das Alles nicht uns 'in's Bewusstsein zu treten' (wie man im Bilde sagt). Das ganze Leben wäre möglich, ohne dass es sich gleichsam im Spiegel sähe: wie ja thatsächlich auch jetzt noch bei uns der bei weitem überwiegende Theil dieses Lebens sich ohne diese Spiegelung abspielt –, und zwar auch unsres denkenden, fühlenden, wollenden Lebens, so beleidigend dies einem älteren Philosophen klingen mag. Wozu überhaupt Bewusstsein, wenn es in der Hauptsache überflüssig ist? – Nun scheint mir, wenn man meiner Antwort auf diese Frage und ihrer vielleicht ausschweifenden Vermuthung Gehör geben will, die Feinheit und Stärke des Bewusstseins immer im Verhältniss zur Mittheilungs-Fähigkeit eines Menschen (oder

known aphorism from *The Gay Science* that Dennett quotes more than once in his work on consciousness.[12] So the first thing I want to do is to show that Dennett's reference to Nietzsche makes sense. I believe their approaches do converge, so I will try to explore how is it exactly that they might be seen as converging. My main idea in what follows, then, is that they converge in relating the very unity of a conscious mind, as well as the nature of particular conscious mental states, to language and thus to publicity (in the sense that a language, in contrast with a brain, or a body, is public and shared).

I will consider the functionalist models of consciousness of *Brainstorms* (1978) and *Consciousness Explained* (1991). The fact that the first model[13] is relatively crude helps to bring out what matters in the discussion. One thing to keep in mind is that such models – which are a fundamental part of Dennett's approach to consciousness although definitely not all there is to it[14] – are closer to cognitive science (e.g. to B. Baars' 1988 global workspace model) than to philosophers' discussions. These are models of cognitive architecture, not arguments. And philosophers, in particular analytic philosophers, are much more likely to approach the issue of consciousness by means of arguments, e.g. arguments about phenomenal consciousness or epiphenomenalism. Yet it is in the context of the functionalist models that one should understand Dennett's proposals about the status of the self and of higher-order mental states. The two

---

Thiers) zu stehn, die Mittheilungs-Fähigkeit wiederum im Verhältniss zur Mittheilungs-Bedürftigkeit: letzteres nicht so verstanden, als ob gerade der einzelne Mensch selbst, welcher gerade Meister in der Mittheilung und Verständlichmachung seiner Bedürfnisse ist, zugleich auch mit seinen Bedürfnissen am meisten auf die Andern angewiesen sein müsste. Wohl aber scheint es mir so in Bezug auf ganze Rassen und Geschlechter-Ketten zu stehn: wo das Bedürfniss, die Noth die Menschen lange gezwungen hat, sich mitzutheilen, sich gegenseitig rasch und fein zu verstehen, da ist endlich ein Ueberschuss dieser Kraft und Kunst der Mittheilung da, gleichsam ein Vermögen, das sich allmählich aufgehäuft hat und nun eines Erben wartet, der es verschwenderisch ausgiebt [...] Gesetzt, diese Beobachtung ist richtig, so darf ich zu der Vermuthung weitergehn, dass <u>Bewusstsein überhaupt sich nur unter dem Druck des Mittheilungs-Bedürfnisses entwickelt hat</u>, – dass es von vornherein nur zwischen Mensch und Mensch (zwischen Befehlenden und Gehorchenden in Sonderheit) nöthig war, nützlich war, und auch nur im Verhältniss zum Grade dieser Nützlichkeit sich entwickelt hat. Bewusstsein ist eigentlich nur ein Verbindungsnetz zwischen Mensch und Mensch". See also Emden 2005. Dennett quotes GS 354; Dennett's focus is on cognitive architecture and evolution, but the point is similar to Nietzsche's.

12 See namely Dennett 1978a (*Brainstorms*): 285 and Dennett 1991 (*Consciousness Explained*): 227.
13 See Baars 1988, *A Cognitive Theory of Consciousness*.
14 In order to be fully charitable to Dennett, one should consider at least three different components in his approach to consciousness: the functionalist models of cognitive architecture, a higher-order theory of the status of conscious states in a cognitive system and, finally, his (more well-known) arguments for '*quining*' (i.e. eliminating) qualia. See Miguens 2002.

aspects are essential for understanding consciousness' relation to language and publicity and to understand the convergence with Nietzsche's claims.

Six boxes in the 1978 model (see Fig. 20.1) stand for the functional subcomponents of a cognitive system such as a human being – the subcomponents are perception, memory, problem solving, attention, control and 'public relations'. The arrows represent computational accesses among these subcomponents as well as the system's output. Dennett's proposal is that being a self simply is being this functional organization. In other words, a self is nothing but the global access that a cognitive system which has such functional organization (at the sub-personal level) has to itself (at the so-called 'personal level'). That there be a self in such a system is thus a matter of what we may regard as global self-monitoring by the system. What makes Dennett's model close to Baars' conception of consciousness as a global workspace is the idea that what is globally accessible to the system is 'publicly available', i.e. it is available to the system as a whole. This contrasts with information processing going on in the subsystems, which is available for controlling the behaviour of the system, but is not 'centrally' available, i.e. it is not available to the self. Let us now take Nagel's question about consciousness and ask "*what is it like to be such a system?*" One might be sceptical here and doubt that it could be like anything – nothing is being captured in the model about the 'essence of consciousness', only cognitive workings, one might think. This is in fact the position most analytic philosophers dealing with consciousness take towards Dennett's type of approach. Yet Dennett's claim is that there is no other way to get something in nature for which 'it

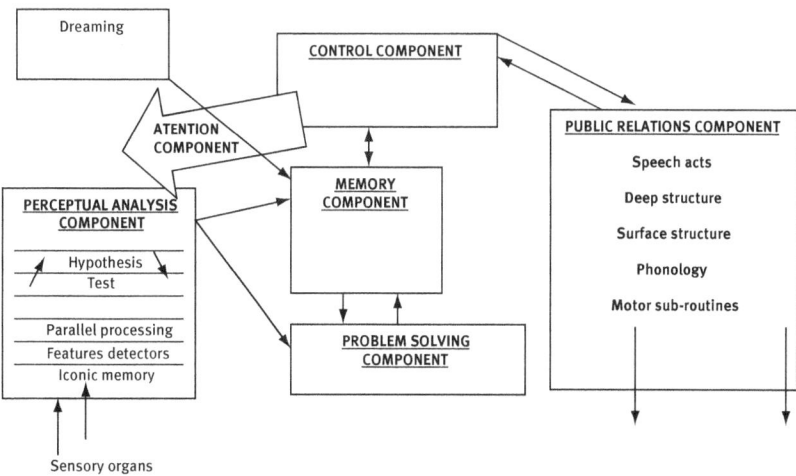

Fig. 20.1: *Brainstorms*, "Toward a Cognitive Theory of Consciousness", p. 155

is like something to be'. Having an inner life is a matter of functional organization,[15] nothing else. Being a self simply is appearing to oneself by means of self-monitoring within such a cognitive architecture. This means, of course, that much more is going on in the system that is not accessible to the self.

In Dennett's own words what he is doing is constructing a full-fledged 'I' from sub-personal parts, by exploiting the notion of access (Dennett 1978c). Let me be then more specific about this notion of access. The notion has to be conceived in relation to Dennett's uses of 'consciousness' and 'awareness' (he distinguishes them). There are three types of access involved in the construction of a full-fledged 'I', according to the model: besides the so-called *personal access* (the global access the system has to itself) there are two types of sub-personal access, computational access and so-called 'public access'. 'Personal access' is Dennett's term for global access, for that of which I am aware (i.e. that of which *I* am aware). This (and only this) is what he calls 'consciousness', i.e. proper consciousness. The 'I', the self, is the subject of consciousness, i.e. the subject of personal level awareness. This type of awareness (proper consciousness) is characteristic of human beings only. Human beings, because they have such personal level access to themselves, are capable of a kind of awareness very different from any other animal's. When personal access takes place, the 'subject' of awareness is the person, not 'parts of the person'. Now, awareness in general (as it is involved in behaviour control, and which humans have in common with other animals) exceeds this, and consists in sub-personal accesses (i.e. forms of *computational access*, i.e. access among information–processing sub-personal parts of the agent). In the case of humans, because they are linguistic creatures, there is also, according to Dennett, another type of access, a sub-personal access, which connects computational accesses and personal access. In the 1978 model he calls it '*public access*'. This is sub-personal access for (linguistic) publicizing by the cognitive system as whole of some of its dealings with 'content'. Sub-personal public access makes available that which is available for being reported, as the system uses language. Now, besides being a matter of (global) personal access of the system to itself, proper consciousness requires language, i.e. it happens only when and if there are such linguistic reports by human agents. Then the global agent might speak (i.e. perform personal level speech acts) and say for instance "I am Sofia", or "This is a bottle". And this is a kind of awareness very different from that of other (non-linguistic) animals. It is important to underline the fact that the so-called public access is, for Dennett, also sub-personal. In other words, it concerns the role of language in the cognitive archi-

---

[15] Dennett 1978c: 164–165, 171. As John McDowell once put it, it would be quite unexpected to find jelly in the inside.

tecture of humans. In the terms of the 1978 model, it concerns the Public Relations component in the model. The Public Relations component "takes as input orders to perform speech acts [...] and executes these orders" (Dennett 1978c: 156).[16] This means, of course, that the 'subject' of such sub-personal public access is not the person, the 'I'. In fact, there is no subject at this level – the idea is that something like a sub-personal role of language is needed to make for a subject, a person, a conscious human, as a linguistic creature. The subject, a person, an 'I', is something which exists only at the personal level, for the system, as it takes itself globally. Nietzsche's *Ich als syntetischer Begriff* is simply not there at the sub-personal level.

One immediate consequence of this is that we ourselves do not have access to 'content-bearers' at the sub-personal level.[17] Whichever selection of sub-personal information I become aware of (e.g. in order to say "I am Sofia" or "This is a bottle") this is not something I can search and find out through introspection. What goes on at the sub-personal level is not within reach for 'me', for the 'I' – it is rather a topic for cognitive theory. What goes on in the brain, or within the cognitive architecture, is not accessible from a first-person perspective. When I find myself saying "This is a bottle", I am not reporting on something that I observe inside myself. What happens is rather that if I am consciously aware of something, the Public Relations, i.e. the sub-personal component for language, must have made such content available for me. And only when there is such global availability *I* am there.

Thus, 'consciousness' (*proper consciousness*) is not an on-off, all or nothing, question but rather a question of *Intermittenzen*. It is explained in the context of a functionalist model in terms of awarenesses and accesses. There is one more important point here, which ultimately paves the way for Dennett's elimination of qualia (i.e. for his well-known rejection of the very idea of phenomenal consciousness[18]). In Dennett's terminology from the period I am considering, there is awareness-1 (*availability for behavioural control*) and awareness-2 (*availability for linguistic reporting*). Both are sub-personal. Awareness-2 makes 'personal access' (i.e. consciousness, the personal access a linguistic creature has to herself) possible and marks its conceptual shape. According to this picture, there is continuity between (unconscious) awareness involved in sub-personal accesses and consciousness. And, one should add, this exhausts consciousness; this is all there is

---

[16] This PR component is on par with the Perception, Memory, Control and Problem Solving components in the description of the architecture of the agent.
[17] In his 1994 article on Dennett, John McDowell praises this view.
[18] See Miguens 2002, 6.4 "A natureza e o seu interior. Consciência fenomenal ou ilusão do utilizador de uma máquina virtual" ["Nature and its interior. Phenomenal consciousness or user-illusion in a virtual machine"].

to it. There is no 'awareness-3', which would be something completely different from awareness-1, awareness-2 and of an on-off nature, and 'phenomenal'. All there is besides availability for behavioural control and availability for linguistic reporting is the linguistic reporting itself, by a self, if and when it takes place. In other words, proper consciousness is personal access and personal access only. In other words, it is just another type of access, not the 'something completely different' that the defenders of qualia and phenomenal consciousness have in mind.

So, where am I or what, as David Hume would ask? Am I real?[19] How can I be real if it is language that somehow makes up the important characteristics of the self I conceive of myself as being? How can I be real if it is language that makes for myself as a unity? How can my being conscious be 'real' if it is language that makes for my conceptual awareness of the ways things are in the world? Dennett's answer to Hume's question would be the following. I am an entity which conceives of itself as one, from a global point of view upon itself, at the personal level. There a self exists; that is what a self is. Only in such conditions I am conceptually aware of the world. All this, of course, depends on language. When I say "This is a bottle", or "I am Sofia" there is flow of information and specialized agents dealing with it at the sub-personal level and definitely no 'Cartesian natural unity or centre stage' there. The unified I who speaks is itself an achievement, a result, which exists at the personal level only. So language plays a doubly important role: there can be no centre without a self and there is no self without language. Also, without language there could be no conceptual awareness of the way things are in the world, as opposed to behaviour-controlling awareness. In Dennett's metaphor for his Multiple Drafts Model (Dennett 1991), in the brain of animals such as ourselves, language gives rise to an inner political miracle – it makes a commander of the agents possible. From a cognitive point of view, minds simply are the putting together of many specialised agents. Such agents are busy dealing with their 'private' affairs, producing multiple drafts, i.e. sub-personal content-fixations; they do not 'mind' other agents. Marvin Minsky's *Society of Mind* view of the mental is a clearly acknowledged inspiration of the Multiple Drafts Model model here (Dennett 1991). But we are also definitely not far from Nietzsche, when he says "I am a herd and a shepherd".[20] That we are, according

---

[19] As Lewis Carroll once formulated it: "Tweedledum: You're only one of the things in his dream! You know very well you are not real! – I am real! – said Alice and began to cry" (*Through the Looking Glass*; Carroll 1995: 116).

[20] "Aber der Erwachte, der Wissende sagt: Leib bin ich ganz und gar, und Nichts ausserdem; und Seele ist nur ein Wort für ein Etwas am Leibe. Der Leib ist eine grosse Vernunft, eine Vielheit mit Einem Sinne, ein Krieg und ein Frieden, eine Heerde und ein Hirt." (Z I Verächtern).

to Dennett, conscious creatures only in as far as we are linguistic creatures, makes us profoundly different from other sensient creatures. What's more, and this is yet another convergence with Nietzsche, that 'we' are as described – a multitude of agents, which, in the absence of language, would go on with their business in a non-communicating way – is what makes us the appropriate material for the all-important Nietzschean operations of self-moulding and self-exhorting.[21]

I mentioned that both self and higher-order mental states were essential for understanding the implications of Dennett's cognitive models in his view of consciousness. So now I want to say something about higher-order mental states. It is important to remember that at the output end of the 1978 model there is the Public Relations component. Its input are 'semantic intentions', i.e. it gets orders to perform speech acts and acts on such orders. It gets orders from the executive component (the Control-Component, CC), and accesses information only through a memory storage (Memory-Component, MC). In such circumstances, an introspection routine occurs the following way: the Control-Component 'decides' to initiate the introspection sub-routine, and addresses a question to the Memory-Component. When the answer arrives, is may access it (censor it, interpret it, infer from it) or pass it on to the Public Relations component. The result is a speech command to the Public Relations component, which acts according to it, i.e produces a speech act (e.g. "I am Sofia", or "This is a bottle"). In *Consciousness Explained* the status of such speech acts and their importance for consciousness is explained in terms

---

[21] One should notice here that thinking about language Dennett is thinking of *natural language*. One of his main aims is to distance himself from a Fodorian Language of Thought hypothesis, for reasons having to do with a critique of a Cartesian Theatre. In *Brain Writing and Mind Reading* (Dennett 1978b) this is clearly stated by saying that there is no language 'deeper' than the one we use 'on the outside'; any claim to the contrary would amount to infinite regress. One may want to agree with this, and with the reason given for it: mentalese, Dennett says, is "a hopeless answer. It is hopeless not because there couldn't be any such system to be found in the internal goings on in people's brains. Indeed there could be [...] it is hopeless as an answer to the question we posed, for it merely postpones the question. Let there be a language of thought. How do you know what your sentences in the language of thought mean? This problem comes into sharper focus if we contrast the language of thought hypothesis with its ancestor and chief rival, the picture theory of ideas. Our thoughts are like pictures, runs this view; they are about what they are because, like pictures they resemble their objects" (Dennett 1996: 52). But how is one to tell? Who is there to tell? No one – and that is Dennett's point. But one should notice also that the dispute about the status of natural language in a cognitive system is not just a dispute around the representational theory of mind, which is the arena of Dennett's opposition to Fodor: it also reflects on conceptions of personal identity and personhood. In particular, this is the link between the cognitive models and the question of self-creation: linguistic self-moulding and self-exhortation are the (cognitive) means for self-evaluation (which is, for Dennett, as I said before, a 'condition of personhood').

of a *higher-order theory*. This is a third component of Dennett's approach to consciousness, besides the functionalist models and the arguments for eliminating qualia. According to Dennett 'creature consciousness' takes place if and when higher-order mental states (i.e. mental states which are about other mental states) take place. These higher-order states are, according to Dennett, beliefs, and not perceptions, as in other higher-order theories. In this proposal Dennett is close to, and in a way, follows, David Rosenthal.[22] Like Rosenthal, he explains creature consciousness appealing to higher-order mental states. He believes the fact that one reports on one's own mental states by expressing higher-order mental states is crucial for (creature) consciousness. He disagrees with Rosenthal only in that Rosenthal sees his own higher-order theory as an exercise of conceptual analysis of consciousness. For Dennett, in contrast, a higher-order theory is a conception of cognition. The point anyway is that consciousness requires that higher-order beliefs about one's own beliefs be linguistically formulated. Besides their linguistic (and thus conceptual) nature the most important thing to notice about higher-order states is that Dennett is not saying that there are salient and independent higher-order mental states in one's mental life due to something like inner observation. What he is saying is that only the linguistic framing itself, i.e. the linguistic prompting of the system by the system, constructs them.

Again, only this is proper consciousness, and such consciousness is characteristic of linguistic creatures only. We, human beings, are like that. In fact, if a self is in place and linguistically expressed higher-order mental states take place we may say that the illusion of the Cartesian Theatre is perfectly real. In this sense there *is* a cartesian theatre, i.e. there is self-presentation or self-appearing in the cognitive system. The fact that other animals are not like that is what makes them, in Dennett's words, very much unlike us: in his words, "they are not beset by the illusion of the Cartesian Theatre" (Dennett 1998b: 346).

I will make just two more points about the 1991 Multiple Drafts Model. As the 1978 model, the 1991 model aims at explaining consciousness in terms of cognitive architecture. Yet now there is a new focus: Dennett is keen on explaining the unity and continuity of phenomenological experience in cognitive systems such as ourselves, in which at the hardware level there is distributed parallel processing of information and at the functional level there are competing 'agents', producing multiple drafts (Dennett now refers to these multiple drafts as *microtakings or microjudgements*). In other words, we are again confronted with Nietzschean multiplicity at the sub-personal level and with the need to explain the unity at the personal level. Only now it is not only the unity of a self that is at stake but also the

---

[22] Rosenthal 1997, *A Theory of Consciousness*.

unity of the flow of consciousness. Both the level of distributed parallel processing of information and the functional level of competing 'agents' are sub-personal levels. Inasmuch as the 1991 Multiple Drafts Model is about this sub-personal level, it is a cognitive model. But it also prepares the ground for Dennett's positions on what we may regard as formal features of personal level conscious experience such as its unity, centeredness, sense of the present or presence and sense of control. Such positions got him involved in discussions about phenomenology (discussions in which he introduced the strangely named 'heterophenomenology', which I will not consider here). Explaining such features in terms of a cognitive architecture, as the model purports to do, is explaining how we appear to ourselves as mental. Now according to Dennett in *Consciousness Explained*, all the features above are virtual features. By this he means that they exist at the level of a 'cognitive interface'. Still, they are fully real for us, i.e. fully real from within. In fact, the level of interface is the only level in which there is any 'us'. One last important difference between the 1991 model and the 1978 model brings Dennett even closer to Nietzsche, and adds to the meaning of Nietzschean *Intermittenzen*. Even if the role of language in personal access remains at the centre of the theory Dennett now stresses that there is no such thing as an 'awareness *line*' as still he proposed there was in the 1978 model, and the crossing of which marked proper consciousness. All there is are sub-personal levels of multiple drafts and linguistic promptings which intermittently constitute proper consciousness. This, in spite of the reality from within of self-presentation and thus of a certain 'cartesian theatre', is one more step in doing away with a certain other conception of the Cartesian Theatre.

2 *Unterseelen*.[23] Nietzsche and Dennett on mind and body (or on mind being embodied and thus 'owned')

> When you make a mind, the materials matter.
> (Daniel Dennett)[24]

'Selfless consciousness' in the first sense I have been considering implies that according to the functionalist models (selfless) awareness precedes and exceeds

---

23 BGE 19. "Der Wollende nimmt dergestalt die Lustgefühle der ausführenden, erfolgreichen Werkzeuge, der dienstbaren 'Unterwillen' oder Unter-Seelen – unser Leib ist ja nur ein Gesellschaftsbau vieler Seelen – zu seinem Lustgefühle als Befehlender hinzu."
24 Dennett 1996: 76.

proper consciousness which is (1) consciousness of a self and (2) linguistic, and thus, conceptual awareness of ways things are. Selves and conceptual awareness are language-based achievements, the result of sub-personal processes in a cognitive architecture. They are not there by essence, nor from the start. Now I want to move on to a second sense of selfless consciousness, a sense in which we might *not* want a selfless consciousness. We may take the following line (this is actually a criticism the neuroscientist Antonio Damasio addressed to Dennett[25]). All that I have said until now (about personal access as global availability, about virtual unity and centeredness as being perceived from within as fully real), tells us only about the 'film', i.e. about consciousness as a flow and some of its formal characteristics, including its very unity. We are told nothing whatsoever about the characteristic *mine-ness of consciousness*, i.e. about our own sense of ownership of our consciousness. Dennett's functionalist models are first and foremost about natural language and the mind-brain, not about phenomenology (although, as I said before, exploring the consequences of the models for a view of consciousness ended up getting him involved in discussions with phenomenologists about 'phenomenology'). It is in the context of cognitive models anyway that consciousness is explained appealing to language, self-reference and higher-order thoughts. Body, body proper, its organic nature, or other, is (as it is to be expected from 'classical functionalism') indifferent for the explanation. We are speaking, as it were, of mental life implemented and characterizing it on the side of the mental, not on the side of 'body'. That on which the mental is implemented, is not *per se* relevant. Obviously this upsets Damasio, as an advocate of the brain. We could put his point thus. Although Dennett is making space for a self through language, and thus (at least partly) explaining consciousness, nothing is said about the ownership of such a consciousness, whether it is mine or yours, or someone else's. In other words, Dennett's consciousness comes off as a selfless consciousness. Now, we know (we know phenomenologically, one might say) that a sense of ownership goes with our consciousness – I experience my consciousness as owned by me, i.e. as mine. In his work[26] Damasio himself defends a conception of self or consciousness according to which self or consciousness simply is "*having the body – body*

---

[25] In fact I am borrowing the expression 'selfless consciousness' from Damasio. According to Damasio Dennett's model gives us a theory of a selfless consciousness – a linguistic self may be there but it is still in Damasio's sense, self-less. Damasio meant it as a criticism; part of what I want to do in this article is to consider whether this is necessarily a bad thing.
[26] See especially Damasio 2010; see Damasio 1992, 1994, 1999, 2003.

proper–in mind".²⁷ The fact that we are embodied conscious beings, and not Cartesian souls, shows in the fact that our consciousness is such that we always have the self in mind. This is what 'subjectifies' consciousness, what makes my consciousness mine, different from yours. Understanding how embodiment makes for such mine-ness is, for instance, crucial for thinking about self and emotion. And self and emotions is Damasio's territory, as it is Nietzsche's. Does Dennett have anything to say for himself here? The fact is, although there are many different things going on in Dennett's theory of consciousness, Damasio is right that functionalist accounts such as the Multiple Drafts Model might, while accounting for the status of the self, and of higher-order mental states, and for characteristics of the flow of consciousness, still leave us with a de-subjectified consciousness in hands. Materialistic as the models may be, *embodiment* is indeed, in a sense, missing. Now neither Nietzsche nor Dennett want consciousness to be self-less in this sense, i.e. in the sense that our minds seem to be conceivable as clean-cut separable from a particular body proper, as a Cartesian soul might be clean-cut separable from a particular body proper (this would bring back all problems about personal identity that Cartesian souls carried with them). Let us call the question at stake here *the question of the ownership of the flow of consciousness*. What accounts for such ownership if there is no natural unity over and above body and brain? Who is the owner of the flow? How and why does the flow (i.e. conscious experience) appear to me as being owned by me?

In *Kinds of Minds* (1996), Dennett makes some interesting suggestions which I think converge with Nietzsche's idea of *Unterseelen* (sub-souls), which Nietzsche himself formulates for drives (*Triebe*). Quoting the famous passage from Zarathustra's "The Despisers of the Body", Dennett (1996: 78–89) ultimately reads Nietzsche's words ("Body is a great reason" and "There is more reason in your body than in your best wisdom") as the idea that evolution embodies information in all parts of one's body.²⁸

---

27 This gave rise to harsh criticism. Cf. e.g. Colin McGinn: "What has really happened is that Damasio has made an elementary confusion, and that infects his entire discussion. It is true that whenever there is a change in our mental state there is a change in the state of our body, and that this bodily state is the ground or mechanism that makes the mental state possible. But it is a gross non sequitur to infer that the mental state is about this bodily state. When I see a bird in the distance my retina and cortex are altered accordingly; however, that doesn't mean that I don't really see the bird but only my retina and cortex. The body is indeed the basis of my mind's ideas, but it is not their object. Once again Damasio has neglected the intentionality of mental states, with grotesque consequences." (McGinn 2003)
28 Cf. Constâncio 2011, note 30, on Nietzsche against Schopenhauer on the smartness of instincts.

In doing this he is distancing himself from the classic dis-embodied (and, as it were, 'dis-embrained') functionalism, inspired by Artificial Intelligence. In particular he is trying to deal with the fact that "*When you make a mind, materials matter*". He does not hide Damasio's influence here. Ultimately, classical functionalism is simply the idea that in order to be naturalizable, intelligence should be made of non-intelligent parts. This is not something Dennett wants to drop; in that sense he is definitely still a functionalist. What he now sees differently is the status of the parts, of the 'homunculi', the 'components of mind'. These are not just sub-minds, dis-embodied sub-functional components; rather they are now sub-bodies. And this is an important reason why it is not possible to separate *me* from *my body* leaving a clean border, as philosophers have sometimes assumed.[29] In other words, in a very literal sense, what matters is what a mind is made of. The materials of a minded portion of matter *matter*. Our organic body, unlike peripheral devices of classic computers, is not a mere auxiliary for abstract information gathering, bringing it into a nervous system also to be thought of as an abstract control system, the body coming back into the picture only when action is about to be performed. Although functionalism is anything but absurd, there are problems with the fact that the specifics of physical implementation of mental functions is not indifferent. In other words, even if the key idea of multiple realizability makes sense in relation to central processing (central belief fixation as Jerry Fodor once put it[30]), it does not make sense when it comes to information gathering or implementation of action: there the physical composition of transducers and effectors is dictated by the job they have to do. Thus, embodiment matters. Matter matters. This does not mean that there is something wrong in thinking of mind in terms of multiplicity or sub-parts (I must say I very much appreciate Nietzsche's term 'sub-souls', as I appreciate the fact that Nietzsche does not drop the term 'soul'; we certainly do not have to do that, just because we drop Cartesian immaterialism).

Anyway the interesting point about the idea of 'subsouls of the body' is that it helps counter a certain kind of mind-body dualism which may very well persist at the heart of materialist reductionist approaches to mind and personal identity (think for instance of Derek Parfit's formulations and recent reformulations of his reductionist view of personal identity; Parfit 2012). The very distinction between that which is implemented and the materials which implement it does not go well with the idea of a body's multiple minds, or subsouls. We may go on saying, as Dennett does, that:

---

29 Dennett himself included (cf. e.g. "Where am I?", in Dennett 1998a, 310–323).
30 Namely in *The Modularity of Mind* (Fodor 1983).

There is no more anger or fear in adrenalin than there is foolishness in a bottle of whisky. These substances are per se, as irrelevant for the mental as gasoline or carbon dioxide. It is only when their abilities to function as components of larger functional systems depend on their internal composition that their so called intrinsic nature matters. (Dennett 1996: 76)

But embodiment by sub-souls adds something to self-reference and self-representation: it results in my flow of consciousness appearing to me as mine. Only through it is there mine-ness of consciousness, myself as more than just unity, formal self-reference and self-attribution of mental states. And this is one more meaning for Nietzsche's *"Leib bin Ich gar und ganz"*.

3 Is that all? *Warheit* and *Wissenschaft*

I have now explored the first and the second senses of selfless consciousness, comparing Dennett and Nietzsche. Yet as we know, Nietzsche is not just interested in self and language, self and body. He is also interested in thought's most elaborate products, such as systems of morality, or science. His philosophy trades in 'truths' and their valuing. This means that in discussing Nietzsche's views on consciousness, issues very different from the ones I have been considering do naturally come up. Until now I tried to isolate questions regarding self, language and body. I think that Nietzsche's orientations concerning such questions are very much alive and fruitful. But Nietzsche's ideas regarding the thinking of linguistic thoughts are a different department. It is here, namely, that observations regarding simplification (the 'simplifying apparatus inseparable from language'),[31] falsification, or generality as vagueness appear. I believe such questions do not have the same status as the discussions about self, body and language,[32] they are not all on the same footing. Hence my initial suggestion that we should be extremely careful in distinguishing the very different pursuits that go under a 'theory of consciousness'.

The first thing I think is worth pointing out is that if one speaks of consciousness as 'falsification', there must have been some claim to truth in the

---

[31] Nietzsche's talk of 'vagueness' or 'simplification' given that 'thoughts are signs' is itself too vague. The nature of articulation, compositionality, context, has to be considered for thought and for language prior to any such general qualifications. My point here is just that Nietzsche's views on the role of natural language in our psychology are not by themselves a conception of language, or of thought-language relations.

[32] See Katsafanas 2005 and Riccardi (forthcoming). The question should be: simplification of what? What complexity was there before? Short of an already intellectualized conception of the world *an sich*, it is not even possible to say such thing.

first place. In other words, there must be some conception of truth at play, and there was nothing like that in the *Einheit/Vielheit* issues regarding mind and language, and mind and body that I have discussed until now. Such conception belongs rather in Nietzsche's sensualist-perspectivist-empiricist views of *Wahrheit* and *Wissenschaft*. The issues there are quite distinct from Nietzsche's insights on body, language and self. So what I want to do to finish this article by suggesting what the differences might be.

Again, I will look for a starting point in Dennett. Looking at Dennett's models of consciousness we were mostly looking at Dennett's 'cog-sci persona'. It is there where we found parallels with Nietzsche – the task was explaining the difference natural language and embodiment make for certain kinds of minds from a cognitive viewpoint. Yet is it the case that it is a viewpoint on cognition that is at stake whenever we discuss consciousness? In the context of discussing his Intentional Stance Theory, Dennett says the following:

> The intentional stance presupposes [...] the rationality and hence the unity of the agent – the intentional system – while the Multiple Drafts Model opposes this central unity all the way. Which [...] is the right way to conceive of a mind? It all depends on how far you are. The closer you get the more the disunity, multiplicity and competitiveness stand out as important. (Dennett 1991: 458)

What I want to suggest is that if it is not cognition that we are focusing on, we do not have to go too close, to zoom in, go into the brain, and make the unity disappear, as we have been doing in for thinking of body, self and language. Especially not when the issue is thought-world relations. If we are concerned with thought-world relations and thus truth, and truths, we might, namely, want to consider that the appropriate units for pursuing an investigation are thoughts, propositions or judgements, and not selves. In other words, the unity that matters in thinking thoughts about the world (such as '2+2=4', 'I am Sofia' or 'This is a bottle') is not the same unity we have been discussing until now.

So the suggestion is that these two unities should not be conflated. The first concerns mind representing (this) mind-body to itself as one-ness, centred-ness and mine-ness, self-agency and self-control. That is the self I have been speaking about in this article – its relation to language, and its relation to the body. It is in addressing these questions that I believe is wise that we take from Nietzsche, in the contemporary debate, the *Intermittenzen*, the achieved *Einheit*, the *Unterseelen*. The viewpoint of the theory of cognition may, admittedly, have an impact on philosophy. But if we pose the metaphysical question about thought-world relations, we deal with thinkers thinking thoughts and questions of truth enter the picture. And this is a different territory. Such issues cannot be approached by thinking about the brain from the viewpoint of cognition, or centring on consciousness' selflessness due to multiplicity and bodily nature. Why not? To put it crudely, the trouble starts when we say that thoughts are mental states – do we really want to do that? One might argue that there are very good reasons not to.

On the other hand, Nietzsche on truth is a complicated subject, first of all because of his own mixed feelings in regard to it. No sooner is he calling all truths metaphorical, than Nietzsche, the eager reader of natural science of his time, is evoking natural science to make us see 'clear, hard to take, truths'. We may say that he does want to keep some truths after all, some more than others. And so he wants to stick to truth and truths. This is precisely what should make us carefully consider the nature of Nietzsche's philosophical pursuits. Nietzsche is, as he himself would claim, and that is his great strength, a philosopher-psychologist-physiologist, a *moraliste* in the French sense he so much praises. Thus, much of his critique of subject and language is about psychology, cognition, and morals, and not so much about thought (issues to which new approaches were rising in the German-speaking philosophical world in his time in the hands of Husserl and Frege). For Nietzsche the philosopher-psychologist-physiologist-*moraliste*, the self-lessness of consciousness is no problem; it is rather a very valuable discovery. In fact it might be what we still want today. Yet mind-body-brain is not all we want to think of when we think about thinking and about how thought and world relate, or else we risk psychologistic confusions (along the lines of the one Colin McGinn accused Damasio of). So we should be careful namely in mixing together the concept truth with assumptions and value judgements regarding appearance-reality relations introduced in the discussions of mind-body-self-consciousness relations. Basically, saying that all thinking is fiction or falsification does not naturally come out of accepting the non-naturalness of the unity of the self. In fact, accepting the non-naturalness of the *Einheit* of the self is not even the same thing as saying that the unity of self – apparent as it may be – is not fully real for us. Nietzsche's own view on consciousness as falsification at least sometimes seem to be nothing but over-indulgence, in its 'romantic pessimism' and condemnation of the world. And in doing that he seems to forget his own criticisms of the devaluing of appearances in *The Birth of Tragedy*.

In conclusion, do we want a selfless consciousness or not? One first answer is Yes, if that means that there is mind and consciousness in nature and there are no 'given' unities, such as Cartesian souls. Dennett and Nietzsche are together there. What we have are intermittences and achievement, and no unity as given. The second answer is No, if selfless consciousness means dis-embodied minds, and being oblivious to the sense of ownership that characterizes our kind of consciousness. We do not want it because our minds simply are not like that, they are not 'dis-owned'. Nietzsche and Dennett are together there as well. Finally, one third answer is Yes: we might want a selfless consciousness in the sense that we may want to carefully distinguish the issues surrounding the self at stake in the theory of cognition, in its relation to philosophy of mind and moral philosophy, from the issues at stake in metaphysical (and epistemological) discussions of thought-world relations. In his 'critique of the subject' Nietzsche tries to do it all – being a physiologist-psychologist-*moraliste*, a critic of culture and of the history of philosophy, and also sometimes a philosopher in the more 'conservative' sense of dealing with thought-world relations. It is altogether natural that he is not equally successful on all fronts.[33] Trying to do it all is also a temptation for Dennett. In other words, Nietzsche and Dennett are also together here – but they are not right.

References

Ansell Pearson, Keith (2009) *A Companion to Nietzsche*, Oxford: Blackwell.
Baars, Bernard (1988) *A Cognitive Theory of Consciousness*, Cambridge: Cambridge University Press.
Block, Ned (1994) "What is Dennett's Theory a Theory of?", in: *Philosophical Topics* 22, 23–40.
Block, Ned (1997) "On a confusion about the function of consciousness", in: N. Block, O. Flanagan and G. Guzeldere (eds.), *The Nature of Consciousness*, Cambridge, MA: MIT Press.
Carroll, Lewis (1995) *Through the Looking Glass*, Ware/Hertfordshire: Wordsworth.
Constâncio, João (2011) "On Consciousness. Nietzsche's Departure from Schopenhauer", in: *Nietzsche-Studien* 40, 1–42.
Damasio, Antonio (1992) "The Selfless Consciousness", in: *Behavioral and Brain Sciences* 15, 208–209.
Damasio, Antonio (1994) *O Erro de Descartes*, Lisbon: Europa América.
Damasio, Antonio (1999) *The Feeling of What Happens: Body and Emotion in the Making of Consciousness*, New York: Harcourt Brace.
Damasio, Antonio (2003) *Ao Encontro de Espinosa – as emoções sociais e a neurologia do sentir*, Lisbon: Europa-América.
Damasio, Antonio (2010) *Self Comes to Mind – Constructing the Conscious Brain*, London: Random House.
Dennett, Daniel (1978a) *Brainstorms – Philosophical Essays on Mind and Psychology*, Cambridge, MA: MIT Press.
Dennett, Daniel (1978b) "Brain Writing and Mind Reading", in: Daniel Dennett (ed.), *Brainstorms*, Cambridge, MA: MIT Press, 39–50.

---

[33] This brings us to a very important hermeneutic issue for Nietzsche studies: is it really the same author continental and analytical philosophers are interested in when they are interested in Nietzsche, *in particular where a critique of the subject is concerned*? I would not go that far.

Dennett, Daniel (1978c) "Towards a Cognitive Theory of Consciousness", in: Daniel Dennett (ed.), *Brainstorms*, Cambridge, MA: MIT Press, 149–173.
Dennett, Daniel (1986) [1969] *Content and Consciousness*, 2nd edition, London: Routledge and Kegan Paul.
Dennett, Daniel (1991) *Consciousness Explained*, Boston: Little Brown.
Dennett, Daniel (1995) *Darwin's Dangerous Idea–Evolution and The Meanings of Life*, New York: Touchstone. [Portuguese translation: *A Ideia Perigosa de Darwin*, Lisbon: Círculo de Leitores 2000]
Dennett, Daniel (1996) *Kinds of Minds, Toward an Understanding of Consciousness*, New York: Basic Books.
Dennett, Daniel (1998a) *Brainchildren–Essays on Designing Minds*, London: Penguin.
Dennett, Daniel (1998b) "Animal Consciousness", in: Daniel Dennett (ed.), *Brainchildren*, London: Penguin, 337–350.
Emden, Christian J. (2005) *Nietzsche on Language, Consciousness and the Body*, Chicago: University of Illinois Press.
Fodor, Jerry (1983) *The Modularity of Mind*, Cambridge MA: MIT Press.
Hofstadter, Douglas/Dennett, Daniel (1981) *The Mind's I–Fantasies and Reflections on Self and Soul*, New York: Bantam Books.
Katsafanas, Paul (2005) "Nietzsche's Theory of Mind: Consciousness and Conceptualization", in: *European Journal of Philosophy* 13, 1–31.
Magnus, B./Huggins, K. (eds.) (1996) *The Cambridge Companion to Nietzsche*, Cambridge: Cambridge University Press.
McDowell, John (1994) "The Content of Perceptual Experience", in: *Philosophical Quarterly* 44, 190–205. [Reprinted in: John McDowell, *Mind, Value, and Reality*, Cambridge MA: Harvard University Press 1998]
McGinn, Colin (2003) "Review of A. Damásio, 'Looking for Spinoza': The Source of Emotion", in: *New York Times*, 23 February 2003.
Miguens, Sofia (2002) *Uma Teoria Fisicalista do Conteúdo e da Consciência–D. Dennett e os debates da filosofia da mente*, Porto: Campo das Letras.
Miguens, Sofia (2008) *Será que a minha mente está dentro da minha cabeça? Da ciência cognitiva à filosofia*, Porto: Campo das Letras.
Miguens, Sofia/Preyer, Gerhard (eds.) (2012) *Consciousness and Subjectivity*, Frankfurt: Ontos.
Parfit, Derek (2012) "We Are Not Human Beings", in: *Philosophy* 87(1), 5–28.
Riccardi, Mattia (forthcoming) "Nietzsche on the Superficiality of Consciousness", in: M. Dries (ed.), *Nietzsche on Consciousness and the Embodied Mind*, Berlin/Boston: De Gruyter.
Richardson, John (1996) *Nietzsche's System*, Oxford: Oxford University Press.
Rosenthal, David (1997) "A Theory of Consciousness", in: Ned Block, Owen J. Flanagan and Güven Güzeldere (eds.), *The Nature of Consciousness–Philosophical Debates*, Cambridge, MA: MIT Press, 729–753.

Part III: **Current Debates – From Embodiment and Consciousness to Agency**

Mattia Riccardi
21 Nietzsche on the Embodiment of Mind and Self

1 Introduction[1]

One of the most celebrated and most frequently quoted passages from Nietzsche's *Thus Spoke Zarathustra* stems from the speech entitled "On the Despisers of the Body".

> "Body am I and soul" – thus talks the child. And why should one not talk like children?
>
> But the awakened one, the one who knows, says: Body am I through and through, and nothing besides; and soul is merely a word for something in the body.
>
> The body is a great reason, a manifold with one sense, a war and a peace, a herd and a herdsman.
>
> A tool of the body is your small reason too, my brother, which you call "mind" [*Geist*], a small tool and toy of your great reason.
>
> "I" you say, and are proud of this word. But the greater thing – in which you do not want to believe – is your body and its great reason: it does not say I, but does I.
>
> (Z I, On the Despisers of the Body, translation changed)

Some of the things Zarathustra says here are easier to make sense of than others. For instance, it seems plain that he is suggesting that we are creatures whose mind (*Geist*) is in some sense embodied. Less straightforward is how we are to understand the claim that the body is, or has, a "great reason" of which what we usually call "reason" – or, again, "mind" – is but a "tool". Even less clear is what role the reference to our practice of "proudly" uttering the word "I" is supposed to play in this context. And why should one think that Zarathustra's words convey a picture of mind and self which is, if not in tune with our naïve intuitions, at least intriguing and perhaps even philosophically attractive?

---

[1] I have benefited from discussing earlier drafts of this paper in São Paulo, Lisbon and London. In particular, I would like to thank João Constâncio, Ken Gemes, Pietro Gori, and Paolo Stellino for pointing out some important weaknesses in the earlier versions.

At the very end of this paper I shall come up with my own answers to these questions. To get there, however, we first need to work out in some detail Nietzsche's view on the embodiment of mind and self.

2 Two notions of embodiment

Different notions of embodiment have been appealed to by philosophers concerned with the nature of the mind and the self. Thus, in order to fruitfully illuminate Nietzsche's own view on such subject matters, it will be helpful to sort out the ways in which we can talk of the mind and of the self as being embodied. In particular, I shall introduce a distinction put forward by Barry Dainton, which seems to me especially suited to provide us with a congenial way of framing further explorations of Nietzsche's position.

Dainton's distinction can be illustrated by considering two different questions we may ask about a certain being's embodiment. On the one hand, we could ask whether it is "effectively embodied", i.e., whether, "as a matter of actual fact, it has a body" (Dainton 2008: 205). Similarly, we could ask whether its mind *de facto* depends, in some fundamental sense, on the kind of body it happens to have. Following Dainton, I shall refer to this notion of embodiment as *effective embodiment*. On the other hand, we can ask whether the being in question is presented to itself as being embodied and, again in the same spirit, whether it experiences its own mental life as in some sense shaped by the kind of body it happens to have. Here, the relevant dimension is purely phenomenological. Accordingly, the label suggested by Dainton is *phenomenal embodiment*.

Obviously, the two notions of embodiment just sketched are closely related. There is, however, a remarkable asymmetry in how they interconnect. On the one hand, though effective embodiment is not entailed by phenomenal embodiment, the case of a being that is presented to itself in experience as an embodied cognitive self, but that is not in fact embodied, should strike us as a remote possibility.[2] On the other hand, the case of a being which is effectively, but not phenomenally, embodied seems something we can much more easily make sense of. For instance, if we assume that to experience oneself as being such-and-such requires a minimum of cognitive sophistication, it follows that most animals, though arguably embodied in the effective sense, fail to satisfy a necessary con-

---

[2] Were you a brain-in-a-vat, you would be a being of that kind. Let us grant, however, that this is indeed a quite remote possibility.

dition for phenomenal embodiment. More strikingly, according to Nietzsche, *we are beings of the latter kind*, or so I shall argue.

3 Nietzsche's position: An initial sketch

That Nietzsche thinks that we are effectively embodied cognitive selves, I take it, should be agreed upon by most scholars. At least, this seems to be one of the only few points one can straightforwardly read out from what Zarathustra tells us in the passage on the "Despisers of the Body" quoted at the very beginning of this paper. Much more controversial, and surely in need of some persuasive illustration, is on the contrary to attribute to him the view that we lack, in some substantial respect, phenomenal embodiment.

Let me start by considering a *Nachlass* passage belonging to the set of preliminary notes Nietzsche wrote down as he was working on *Thus Spoke Zarathustra*:

> Behind your thoughts and feelings there is your body and your self within the body [*dein Selbst im Leibe*]: the terra incognita. What do you have *these* thoughts and feelings *for*? Thereby your self within the body [*dein Selbst im Leibe*] *wants* something. (NL 1882, 5[31], KSA 10: 225)

This passage touches upon aspects which are relevant for both notions of embodiment previously introduced. On the one hand, the claim that we have the "thoughts" and "feelings" we happen to have because of our body's hidden purposes suggests that at least mental states of this sort are – in some sense still to be clarified – "brought about" by the body. Nietzsche seems to be claiming thus that the mind is effectively embodied. Moreover, Nietzsche's talk of the "self within the body [*Selbst im Leibe*]" clearly indicates that, in his view, there is something like an effectively embodied self.

On the other hand, Nietzsche's characterization of the body as a "terra incognita" suggests that we lack some kind of relevant epistemic access to it. At first sight, this claim may strike one as hardly plausible, for it seems obvious that we hold a privileged access to (some of) the states of our own body. For instance, I do not need to look at my arm to know that it is stretched out. Facts of this kind regarding my body we typically know in a direct, non-inferential way. This is precisely what motivates Schopenhauer's definition of the body as the only "*immediate object*" (Schopenhauer 1819: § 18, 124) we may encounter in experience. Should then Nietzsche's characterization of the body as a "terra incognita" be read as a denial of the apparently undisputable facts substantiating Schopenhauer's view of the body as the immediately given?

This would be an overhasty conclusion. Rather, I propose to understand Nietzsche as pointing out that what we lack is epistemic access to a certain range of facts concerning the way in which the body shapes mind and self. More precisely, my thesis is Nietzsche thinks that, in some important sense, we are not presented to ourselves as embodied selves, nor does our mental life look to us as intimately constituted by the kind of body we happen to have. If this is true, it seems thus fair to interpret Nietzsche as suggesting that we are not phenomenally embodied.

Still, in order for Nietzsche's position to sound somewhat plausible, we need to narrow the scope of his claim that we lack phenomenal embodiment, so as not to entail that we lack any kind of privileged awareness whatsoever of our own body. For Nietzsche's view of the body as a "terra incognita" would otherwise deny those basic facts Schopenhauer appeals to in describing the body as the unique *"immediate object"* of experience. My proposal is therefore to understand Nietzsche's claim that we lack phenomenal embodiment as restricted to a certain class of psychological states, namely, to that of propositionally[3] articulated conscious attitudes (like beliefs, desires, emotions, volitions, etc.). Importantly, the scope of the claim is not intended to include so-called raw feelings, i.e. purely phenomenal states (like pains) or qualities (like sensory qualities). Thus, I propose that we understand Nietzsche as claiming that we lack epistemic access to the constitutive relation obtaining between certain bodily facts and one's attitudes. Similarly, I submit, he claims that we are not presented to ourselves as the embodied bearers of states of this kind.

To my eyes, Nietzsche's endorsement of these restricted claims about our lacking phenomenal embodiment are deeply rooted in his view on introspection. More precisely, he thinks that the way in which we introspectively access conscious attitudes is such that, in experiencing ourselves as the bearer of such attitudes, we take ourselves to be, in a relevant sense, non-embodied beings. This feature of our self-experience is nicely expressed by Sydney Shoemaker, who notes that "when one is introspectively aware of one's thoughts, feelings, beliefs and desires, one is not presented to oneself as a flesh and body person" (1984: 102). Thus, at least as long as we are concerned with conscious attitudes like those listed by Shoemaker, Nietzsche takes what is usually called the *Cartesian* picture of mind and self[4] to accurately capture the conception we naïvely form

---

3 Nietzsche does not believe in the existence of propositions conceived of as abstract entities. Thus, "proposition" refers here to the basic grammatical structure of sentences of a given natural language. In this sense, "propositional" is somewhat equivalent to "linguistic".
4 What I call the "Cartesian picture" is not meant to reproduce all the details of Descartes's own view. It is just a handy label.

of ourselves as thinkers and agents. It is this conception of self-experience which, in turn, substantiates Nietzsche's qualification of the body as a terrain which remains unknowable to the subject. Of course, all this needs some substantial unpacking, and that is the main focus of this paper.

4 Nietzsche on effective embodiment

Let us start with Nietzsche's view on effective embodiment. To be effectively embodied requires a being's mental life to essentially depend on its specific bodily constitution. According to Nietzsche, this is true of us. In his writings, he points out different ways in which our mind is shaped by our being the kind of organism we are. For the purposes of the present paper, I shall focus on his claim that mind and self are, so to speak, spread throughout the entire organism. I shall refer to this as the *distributed* view (of the mind and self). The task of this section is to spell out Nietzsche's understanding of it.

Let us start by considering the evidently interrelated descriptions of the body and of the soul Nietzsche offers in *Beyond Good and Evil*. First, he suggests that the "soul" should be conceived of as "a society constructed out [*Gesellschaftsbau*] of drives and affects" (BGE 12). Later on in the book, he then states that "our body is, after all, only a society constructed out [*Gesellschaftsbau*] of many souls" (BGE 19). Taken together, these two passages are naturally read as claiming that the body is constituted by souls which are, in turn, constituted by drives (and affects). However, this way of putting things is at best misleading, for Nietzsche actually thinks there is no substantial difference between what he calls "body" and what he calls "soul": as he puts it in the passage from *Zarathustra* I have started with, "soul is only the name of something in the body" (Z I, On the Despisers of the Body). If we take "soul" to be a broad notion somehow embracing those of "mind" and "self" – as it seems natural to do – it follows that these two terms are to be understood, too, as referring to "something in the body". We can therefore conclude that mind and self are for Nietzsche effectively embodied.

Unfortunately, as soon as we look back at the descriptions Nietzsche offers of the body and of the soul by keeping in mind that he sees no substantial difference between the two, those descriptions start looking quite puzzling. The first problem is how to make sense of his claim that the body is constituted by "many souls", as he writes in BGE 19. A plausible suggestion is that the "many souls" Nietzsche refers to there are in fact just the "drives" he claims the body is constituted by in BGE 12. In the light of this suggestion, we should read him as saying that the body as well as the soul are constituted by the drives – an interpretation which nicely fits with his further claim according to which there is no substantial difference between body and soul. However, this raises a second problem. For why does Nietzsche then use the term "soul" instead of "drive" in BGE 19?

To start answering this question, note that – if we assume the reasoning so far to be correct – what is constituted by the drives can be referred to either as the "body" or as the "soul". This seems to indicate that the drives can be described in physical or physiological as well as in mental or psychological terms. As Nietzsche takes the soul to be just "something in the body", it seems natural to conclude that he conceives the drives as something essentially physical. It is less clear, however, in which sense they qualify as mental. To my eyes, a plausible proposal is to consider Nietzsche as holding that the drives are mental *qua* intentional, i.e. *qua* directed towards certain aspects of reality. As he writes in an unpublished note, "each 'drive' is the drive to 'something good', as seen from a certain standpoint; there's valuation [*Werthschätzung*] in it" (NL 1884, 26[72], KSA 11: 167). Thus, a rationale for Nietzsche's referring to the drives as "souls" in BGE 19 could be that there he is primarily concerned with their mental, rather than with their physical features, i.e. with their intentionality.[5]

How does all this relate to the distributed view of mind and self? A quick answer to this question is that, according to Nietzsche, mind and self are realized by the relations the multiple drives have with each other. For instance, in another aphorism from *Beyond Good and Evil* Nietzsche writes that "thinking is only a relation between the drives" (BGE 36). Here, I submit, "thinking" should be taken to broadly cover, if not the entirety, at least the vast majority of our psychological states.[6] Hence, states of this kind all result from relations obtaining between one's drives. Of course, in order to better spell out what this claim

---

[5] Richardson argues that drives should not be conceived as mental. He contends that it would be wrong to think of them not only as "conscious", but also as " 'previewing' or 'preconceiving' their outcomes unconsciously" (2004: 36). Rather, he suggests that we should understand the drives as selected dispositions. Just some brief considerations, as I cannot address his argument in detail here. My view is that the mere fact that Nietzsche talks of the drives as being unconscious suffices to ascribe to them some sort of mentality, given that the realm of the unconscious is usually taken to be part of the mind. Thus, to this extent the disagreement may be purely terminological. A more substantial point may regard the question of whether drives are in some – perhaps minimal – sense representational. I think that Nietzsche's evaluative talk suggests that they are. Be it as it may, it is important to note that holding the drives to be representational is compatible with Richardson's convincingly argued main thesis that they are a product of natural selection.

[6] See also GS 333, where Nietzsche argues, in a similar vein, that knowledge derives from the certain interplay of certain drives.

exactly means, we need to know more about Nietzsche's conception of the drives.

Maudemarie Clark and David Dudrick (2012) have argued for a homuncularist reading inspired, in particular, by the work of Daniel Dennett. Dennett defends (a certain variety of) homuncularism as the proper approach to most cognitive and, in general, psychological puzzles. The main strategy, he suggests, consists in "breaking the single-minded agent down into miniagents and microagents" (1991: 458), which display much simpler patterns of behaviour, thus becoming empirically tractable. Accordingly, the personal-level behaviour of the agent is to be explained as resulting from the interplay of such sub-personal cognitive systems.[7]

Surely, we find places in Nietzsche's *corpus* – in particular, in his unpublished notes – which are most naturally interpreted as putting forward a homuncularist model. In an unpublished note from 1884 he writes, for instance: "By following the thread of the body we recognize the human being as a multiplicity of living beings which – partly fighting one another, partly hierarchized and subordinated to one another – by affirming their individual existence involuntarily also affirm the whole" (NL 1884, 27[27], KSA 11: 282). The variety of homuncularism emerging from this passage seems far less sober than that of Dennettian brand. Were we to look for a contemporary counterpart of it, a better option would probably be Francisco Varela's view that a minimal form of selfhood can be sensibly ascribed even to the simplest living systems (Varela 1991; see also Thompson 2007, in particular chs. 3, 5 and 6). Accordingly, each "living being" which is part of our organism would be an instance of such a minimal self.

However, if we zoom in on Nietzsche's notion of drive, we also find something in the vicinity of Dennett's idea of a sub-personal cognitive system. In another unpublished note, he describes the drives as "*higher organs [höhere Organe]*" constituted by some kind of coalescence of "actions, sensations and feelings" (NL 1883, 7 [198], KSA 10: 304). Though it is hard to make sense of what he might have in mind here, it seems fair to read this note as suggesting that the drives are to be identified in somewhat functional terms, i.e. in terms of the "actions, sensations and feelings" they typically involve, or something along

---

[7] The homuncularist model has been criticized by Katsafanas (2013), who has instead put forward a dispositionalist reading of Nietzsche's conception of the drives. In my view, both proposals capture important aspect of Nietzsche's view. Nor do I see them as necessarily incompatible approaches. Thus, my suggestion would be to pursue a conciliatory strategy – something I have to leave to another occasion. Richardson (2004), too, offers a dispositionalist definition of drives. On Nietzsche's homuncularism see also Lopes (2012).

these lines. More obscure is the meaning that the expression "higher organ" might have in this context. In another note from the same notebook, he gives an example which helps us to better grasp what he thereby means: "The hand of the pianist, the wiring [*Leitung*] there and a region of the brain form together an organ [...]. *Separate parts of the body telegraphically connected – i.e. a drive*" (NL 1884, 7[211], KSA 10: 308). If we follow the lead offered by this example, Nietzsche seems to conceive of the drives as sub-systems, which are physiologically realized by a kind of network connecting different parts of the body. Accordingly, the term "higher organ" refers to such networks.

If we try to put things together, it looks that Nietzsche's conception of the drives consists of three main claims. First, the drives are sub-personal systems to be primarily individuated in functional terms. As such, a drive is identified by the pattern of actions it typically produces in association with certain phenomenal states – sensations and feelings, as Nietzsche has it. For instance, hunger is identified by food-searching actions and unpleasant bodily sensations localized in the stomach. The drive toward cruelty is identified by pain-inflicting actions and, say, by the excitement and pleasant feeling of domination associated with them. Second, different parts of the organism contribute to the physiological realization of the sub-personal system a given drive is. They are embodied networks, one could say. Third, to resume a point made earlier, drives are in some – perhaps minimal – sense intentional, as they substantiate an evaluative stance which directs the organism towards certain objects. As such, they impact the way in which the world appears to us. For instance, as Katsafanas (2013) notes, a certain drive makes that determinate features of the environment become salient. Hunger makes me notice the restaurant on the opposite side of the busy square. The drive towards cruelty makes that lizard look as something on which pain can be inflicted.

We are now in a position to appreciate Nietzsche's distributed view of the mind and the self. On the one hand, he believes that (most of) our psychological states result from the interplay between the drives, which he conceives of as sub-personal cognitive systems. The physiological realization of such systems requires that different parts of the body cooperate. This means that the cognitive processes underlying our mental life are spread over, and depend on, the entire organism. This is the very point Nietzsche makes in assuming "that the entire organism thinks, that all organic formation [*Gebilde*] participates in thinking, feeling, willing – consequently, that the brain is only an enormous centralisation apparatus" (NL 1884, 27[19], KSA 11: 279 – 280). On the other hand, and similarly, one's self is constituted by the relations in which one's drives stand to each other. This is why we should conceive of the "soul as subject-multiplicity", as Nietzsche suggests (BGE 12).

5 Nietzsche on phenomenal embodiment

In the previous section, I have argued that, according to Nietzsche, what we usually refer to when we talk about mind and self is in fact constituted by, or results from, the interplay of the drives, which he conceives of as physiologically realized sub-personal systems. This, however, is not how things look to us in introspection, for we do not take psychological states like beliefs, desires and emotions to result from the workings of a cognitive network distributed over our entire organism. More generally, it is part of the intuitive conception we have of ourselves as thinkers and agents that our being in states of this kind does not essentially depend on our being "a flesh and body person", as Shoemaker has it. The philosophical outlook of this intuitive conception is the Cartesian picture that Nietzsche critically targets on several occasions. Nonetheless, Nietzsche grants that the Cartesian picture accurately captures important features of the way in which we are presented to ourselves. He just holds it to be wrong. To put it differently, he thinks that, despite our being effectively embodied cognitive selves, there is a relevant sense in which we lack phenomenal embodiment. More precisely, the embodied character of propositionally articulated attitudes, on the one hand, and of the self which is the bearer of such states states, on the other hand, does not figure into the conception we intuitively have of mind and self. This means that the experience we have of ourselves is, in some way, profoundly misleading. But in which way is it so?

Typically, we experience ourselves as having a *unified* mental life. Moreover, we usually take this unity to reflect the fact that each of us is the bearer of the psychological states constituting her or his own mental life. *I* am the source of the *unity* of my mental life – this is how each of us thinks of herself or himself. In some rough approximation, we could say that the Cartesian picture is but a sophisticated articulation of precisely this aspect of such a naïve self-conception.

As we have seen, Nietzsche argues – contrary to this – that our mental life has no real unity as it is constituted, or results from, the workings of several sub-personal systems. Thus, the unified character we take it to have is fictitious. In his writings, Nietzsche offers a diagnosis of why we have come to have such a fallacious self-conception. This diagnosis aims at debunking the idea that introspection provides us a secure grip on the nature of our mind and our self – the very idea from which the Cartesian story's derives its intuitive force.[8]

---

[8] I offer a more detailed account of Nietzsche's skeptical take on introspection in Riccardi (2015).

To start with, and in order to spell out Nietzsche's diagnosis, we need to briefly consider his account of consciousness. To this purpose, I shall focus on some of the claims put forward in aphorism 354 of *Gay Science*, where he provides the most articulated treatment of consciousness to be found in his published works.[9] The first thing to note is that Nietzsche's way of talking suggests that the kind of consciousness he is concerned with is actually something close to *self*-consciousness. Support for this reading comes, *inter alia*, from his claim that consciousness is intimately related to language. As he has it, "the development of language and the development of consciousness [...] go hand in hand" (GS 354). Of course, most of the meanings in which the term "consciousness" might be used are such that this statement would turn out to be deeply puzzling, if not evidently false. If we read consciousness as self-consciousness, however, the problem does not surface. For one, self-consciousness arguably requires the ability to self-refer. Since this capacity is usually understood as depending on one's mastery of terms like "I" and "mine", it seems reasonable to conclude that self-consciousness is language-dependent.[10]

Nietzsche, however, also holds the converse of this statement to be true: unconscious cognition is non-linguistic in nature. From this, some points flow which are relevant for our discussion. First, note that for Nietzsche the working of the drives is to be situated at the unconscious level. This means that the cognitive processes going on in such systems do not involve linguistically articulated contents. On the contrary, such contents are to be found exclusively at the conscious level. Second, according to Nietzsche this implies that, in turning conscious, the content of psychological states undergoes a significant conversion: whatever kind of structure it may have, this structure is traded in for propositional articulation. Third, from this Nietzsche draws the conclusion that "all becoming conscious involves a vast and thorough corruption, falsification, superficialization, and generalization" (GS 354). This is not the place to try to spell out this claim in detail. In the remainder of this section, I shall focus on just one language-dependent trait which typically characterizes the way in which we are conscious of our own psychological states. This trait, I shall argue, figures prominently in the naïve conception we have of our mind and our self as essentially unified as well as in the Cartesian picture which further elaborates on such a conception.

The feature I have in mind has already been mentioned at the very end of the previous paragraph: it is, namely, the self-referential employment of the

---

9 Here, I take up a reading more carefully defended in Riccardi (forthcoming).
10 From now on, I shall use the term "conscious" as referring to this kind of self-consciousness.

word "I". To appreciate its role, we first need to focus on some general features of propositionally articulated attitudes such as beliefs, desires, volitions, emotions, etc. (Recall that states of this kind are precisely those with regard to which Nietzsche believes that we lack phenomenal embodiment.) Here, two aspects are crucial. On the one hand, as we have seen, Nietzsche holds that states of this sort are realized by the interplay of various sub-personal systems – the drives – whose cognitive workings occur at the unconscious level and do not operate on linguistically articulated contents. On the other hand, as soon as they become conscious, mental states acquire the linguistic shape under which we introspectively know them. Thus, the way in which we experience ourselves as cognitive selves is shaped by the intrinsically language-mediated access we have to our own psychological states. This is true, in particular, of the experience we have of ourselves as having a unified mental life that does not essentially depend on our being (effectively) embodied.

The general form of a first-person propositional attitude encompasses three elements: the first-person pronoun, a mental verb, and a sentence embedded in a that-clause. Suitable examples are: "I think that Lisbon is in Portugal", or "I hope that Benfica will lose the next game". Nietzsche's concern is, in particular, with the first two elements of such attitudes. Given its unique philosophical pedigree, he focuses specifically on the instance "I think". However, most of what he says easily generalizes to other examples of "I + mental verb" constructions. In a famous aphorism he writes:

> When I dissect the process expressed in the proposition "I think", I get a whole set of bold claims that are difficult, perhaps impossible, to establish, – for instance, that *I* am the one who is thinking, that there must be something that is thinking in the first place, that thinking is an activity and the effect of a being who is considered the cause, that there is an "I", and finally, that it has already been determined what is meant by "thinking"[.] (BGE 16)

Here, Nietzsche points out several different beliefs we supposedly endorse as a consequence of our naïve understanding of expressions like "I think". The main point of the aphorism is to rebut a view which considers such beliefs to be "immediate certainties" (BGE 16), since – Nietzsche argues – they could at best arrived at only via complicated inferential patterns. However, other passages from his work suggest that he does not think that we are mistaken solely with regard to their epistemic status. Rather, he seems to maintain that the beliefs in question are, as such, false. To see this, let us take a closer look at the three most relevant among the "bold claims" he refers to.

The first claim concerns the way in which the token-referential use of the term "I" shapes the conception we have of ourselves. On the one hand, the usage of the first-person pronoun in expressions like "I think" inclines us to believe that there is something to which the word "I" refers and which is, in some sense, the bearer of the relevant mental state. On the other hand, as the following passage makes explicit, we are also inclined to believe that this "something" does not coincide with the body:

> People used to believe in "the soul" as they believed in grammar and the grammatical subject: people said that "I" was a condition and "think" was a predicate and conditioned – thinking is an activity, and a subject *must* be thought of as its cause. (BGE 54)

Thus, Nietzsche argues that our conception of ourselves as disembodied selves – as "souls", or "subjects" – is a kind of folk-metaphysical conclusion we derive from our naïve understanding of expressions like "I think". Interestingly, a famous passage by Wittgenstein provides a quite similar diagnosis:

> We feel then that in the cases in which "I" is used as subject, we don't use it because we recognize a particular person by his bodily characteristics; and this creates the illusion that we use this word to refer to something bodiless, which, however, has its seat in our body. In fact, *this* seems to be the real ego, the one of which it was said "Cogito, ergo sum". (Wittgenstein 1965: 69)

Second point is this: our taking the term "I" to pick out "something bodiless", as Wittgenstein puts it, is reflected in the way in which we conceive of ourselves as unified selves. However, as soon as we discover that we are effectively embodied beings, such a unified character reveals itself as merely apparent.

> To start from the *body* and from physiology: why? – We attain the right view about our kind of subject-unity, namely as that of a regent at the top of a community and not as "souls" or "vital forces", as well as about the dependence of these regents from those they reign on and about the conditions of rank and labor division as enabling both the individuals and the whole. (NL 1885, 40[21], KSA 11: 638)

Thus, whereas the experience we have of ourselves as mediated by the self-referential use of "I" prompts the belief that we are souls, or subjects, characterized by some kind of primitive unity, empirical investigation shows that we are in fact constituted by multiple sub-personal systems – the drives –, the interplay of which gives shape to our self.

The third claim concerns our self-conception as the bearers of our mental states. In the passage from BGE 16 quoted above, Nietzsche stresses how expressions like "I think" suggests that the mental verb in question – in the example, "think" – designates a kind of "activity" which the "I" is supposed to be causing. Put in different words, he argues that we most naturally tend to read "I think" as something along these lines: "There is some kind of thoughtful activity and I am the cause thereof". This, again, is an erroneous belief we come to have as a result of the token-referential usage we make of the term "I" – or, as Nietzsche has it, as a result of our taking grammar at face value.[11]

Let me briefly recapitulate where we have gone so far. Nietzsche argues that, by the process in virtue of which they turn conscious, mental states become propositionally articulated. Given that the domain of introspection only encompasses conscious states, the access we have to our own mind is confined to propositionally articulated states – for all and only conscious states have propositional content. From this, it follows for Nietzsche that the naïve conception we have of ourselves as thinkers and agents is shaped by such a peculiar language-mediated access we have to our own mind. In particular, he argues that the self-referential use of "I" plays thereby a crucial role due to the disembodied mode of presentation associated with it. Here is where the conception of ourselves as "souls" or "subjects" originates, which confers to the Cartesian picture of the mind and of the self its typical intuitive appeal.

6 Zarathustra's speech

We are now in a position to address the relation between body, mind, and self as it emerges from the Zarathustrian speech "On the Despisers of the Body", which served as an *incipit* to my paper. Let us start by bringing his very words back to mind.

The quoted passage starts by contrasting the "child's" way of talking about the body and the soul with that of the "awakened one". Whereas the child is presented as claiming to be body and soul alike, the "one who knows" conceives of himself, on the contrary, as being body "through and through". Soul, he adds, is "just a word for something in the body". As Gerhardt notes, a first point con-

---

[11] Some considerations, which are sympathetic to Nietzsche's own reasoning, have been recently put forward by John Campbell. To start with, Campbell notes that "our pattern of use of the first person is heavily invested in the idea that the self is causally significant" (2012: 373), a point which resembles Nietzsche's third claim. Key to the notion of causation involved in our usage of the first-person, he goes on, is the commonsensical idea of a "mechanism" sustaining certain "counterfactual structures" (2012: 374). Thus, as we conceive of the person as causally efficacious in this sense, we come to believe that "there must be a single concrete thing" which is the relevant mechanism (375). Then, as "[t]here seems to be no physical object that could sustain that role, [...] we are driven to suppose that it must be a non-physical thing, the soul" (375). Here, Campbell makes a point similar to that made by Nietzsche – his first claim – and Wittgenstein, though he provides a more substantial story about why the causal self-conception embedded in the pattern of use of "I" leads us to assume that we are disembodied subjects.

veyed by Zarathustra's speech is that "the distinction between body and soul is [...] portrayed as the expression of a naïve kind of consciousness". Conversely, it also suggests that, "[i]n the awakened light of mature consciousness and the perspective of knowledge, the difference between body and soul is evidently no longer defensible" (2006: 282).

In a recent paper, Christine Daigle has questioned Gerhardt's reading of this passage. It would be wrong, she argues, to read the "child's" way of talking to express some kind of naïve dualism, as implied by Gerhardt's rendering. She proposes instead to understand the "child" as saying that body and soul are just two aspects of the same entity – a "body-soul", as Daigle puts it. Accordingly, there is no real opposition between the two points of view: "[t]he enlightened man knows that 'Seele' is only a word and that it refers to a bodily thing and not to something beyond or separate from the body. So the enlightened man is introduced here to bring a word of caution" (Daigle 2011: 237). This line of argument does not seem compelling, however. First, Gerhardt's reading is arguably the most natural one. Second, Daigle's own interpretation faces some exegetical shortcomings, at least to my eye. For instance, it seems to flow from the very dialectic of Nietzsche's text that the two alternative ways of talking – that of the "child" and that of the "one who knows" – are in tension with one another.[12] This textual aspect, however, though nicely reflected by Gerhardt's reading, does not harmonize with her interpretation.

Be it as it may, the point that is relevant to our present concern and that is agreed upon by both scholars is that the view Zarathustra ends up endorsing amounts to the claim that there is no substantial difference between what we usually call "body" and what we usually call "soul". Notably, this goes hand in hand with how the relation between "body" and "soul" is characterized in *Beyond Good and Evil*,[13] a book which is supposed to provide, in Nietzsche's own words, an "introduction to the background of Zarathustra".[14]

After contrasting the "child's" point of view and that of the "one who knows", Nietzsche introduces his famous description of the body as a "great reason".[15] The "mind" (*Geist*), on the contrary, is said to constitute but a "small

---

[12] Zarathustra's question "And why should one not speak like children?" is only *prima facie* a rhetorical invitation to endorse the "child's" point of view. For the dialectical context of the passage is such that the question is immediately followed by the introduction of the contrasting point of view held by the "one who knows".
[13] See section 4 above.
[14] Letter to E.W. Fritzsch, 07.08.1886, KSB 7: 224.
[15] The description of the body goes on as follows: "a multiplicity with one sense, a war and a peace, one herd and one shepherd". I shall not consider these further characterizations, for to my

reason" which is actually "a tool of your body", "a small tool and toy of your great reason". In light of the proposed reading, the qualification of the body as a "great reason" is best understood as the claim that cognition is distributed over the entire organism. Furthermore, the claim that what we usually call the "mind" – that for which Nietzsche uses the term "*Geist*" – is but a "small reason" and, as such, a "tool" of the body should be interpreted as expressing the fact that one's psychological states result, in fact, from the interplay between one's drives. In other words, the conscious states constituting one's mental life are dependent on certain bodily facts.

In order to address what comes next, it is worth reading Nietzsche's text afresh.

> "I" you say, and are proud of this word. But the greater thing – in which you do not want to believe – is your body and its great reason: it does not say I, but does I. (Z I, On the Despisers of the Body)

Different points are here condensed in a few lines. First, Zarathustra refers to our common usage of the first person pronoun in a somewhat disqualifying tone. But how are we to make sense of his saying that we are "proud of this word"? To start answering this question, recall that according to him the access we have to our own mind is mediated by the self-referential employment of the word "I". This fact is responsible – to briefly resume the points made in the previous section – for our intuitive belief that we are the disembodied bearers of our psychological states. Thus, as the experience we have of our mental life is shaped by the disembodied mode of presentation associated with the first-personal pronoun, it seems reasonable to say, as Zarathustra does, that we are "proud" of the word "I". For, to put it in different terms, the conception we have of ourselves as cognitive selves is governed by the self-referential use we make of it.

Completely absent from this picture is, on the contrary, the "great reason" which is our body, Zarathustra goes on. Although our mind and self are constituted by the body's "great reason" – the cognitive states and processes distributed over the entire organism – we normally fail to become aware of this fact. The main reason for this is that such states and processes, which Nietzsche conceives of as resulting from the working of, and interplay between, our drives, occur at the unconscious level. Thus, we simply lack any kind of direct access to them. Of course, we do become conscious of many of our psychological states. However, such conscious and thus introspectable states are for Nietzsche

---

eye, they have to do with the conception Nietzsche has of the drives as building a hierarchical structure – a view which is not immediately relevant to the topic of the present paper.

always propositionally articulated and, consequently, already involve the self-referential pronoun "I". (Recall that we are here concerned with attitudes of the form "I+mental verb+'that'-clause".) Hence, in introspecting one's conscious psychological states, one is presented to oneself as the kind of disembodied soul, or subject, to which we usually take the word "I" to refer. We are therefore in no position to access the unconscious goings-on of our drives, which are doomed to remain – as Nietzsche wrote in the *Nachlass* note quoted earlier – a "terra incognita" hidden behind those propositionally articulated states to which we do have introspective awareness.[16] Notably, a revised version of this passage was interpolated by Nietzsche into the published text of Zarathustra's speech, just a few lines below:

> Behind your thoughts and feelings, my brother, stands a mighty commander, an unknown wise man – is name is Self. In your body he dwells, he is your body. (Z I, On the Despisers of the Body)

References

Campbell, John (2012) "Lichtenberg and the Cogito", in: *Proceedings of the Aristotelian Society* 112(3), 361–378.
Daigle, C. (2011) "Nietzsche's Notion of Embodied Self: Proto-Phenomenology at Work?", in: *Nietzsche-Studien* 40, 226–243.
Dainton, B. (2008) *The Phenomenal Self*, Oxford: Oxford University Press.
Dennett, Daniel (1991) *Consciousness Explained*, New York: Back Bay Books.
Gerhardt, Volker (2006) "The Body, the Self and the Ego", in: Keith Ansell Pearson (ed.), *A Companion to Nietzsche*, Oxford: Blackwell, 273–296.
Katsafanas, Paul (2013) "Nietzsche's Philosophical Psychology", in: K. Gemes and J. Richardson (eds.), *The Oxford Handbook of Nietzsche*, Oxford: Oxford University Press, 727–755.
Lopes, R. (2012) "Das politische Triebmodell bei Nietzsche", in: J. Georg and C. Zittel (eds.), *Nietzsches Philosophie des Unbewussten*, Berlin/New York: De Gruyter.
Maudemarie Clark and David Dudrick (2012) *The Soul of Nietzsche's Beyond Good and Evil*. Cambridge: Cambridge University Press.
Nietzsche, Friedrich (2005b) *Twilight of the Idols*, in F. Nietzsche, *The Anti-Christ, Ecce Homo, Twilight of the Idols and Other Writings*, ed. A. Ridley and J. Norman, trans. J. Norman, Cambridge: Cambridge University Press.

---

[16] One might worry that thereby Nietzsche's view drifts perilously towards some unrecommendable version of epiphenomenalism about consciousness. In Riccardi (forthcoming) I defend that Nietzsche holds, indeed, a version of epiphenomenalism. However, I also try to show that, given the notion of consciousness he is concerned with, his epiphenomenalism is less radical than it might appear at first sight, though admittedly still unpalatable to many.

Riccardi, Mattia (2015) "Inner Opacity. Nietzsche on Introspection and Agency", in: *Inquiry* 58(3), 221–243 (Special Issue: Nietzsche's Moral Psychology, ed. by B. Leiter).

Riccardi, Mattia (forthcoming) "Nietzsche on the Superficiality of Consciousness", in: M. Dries (ed.), *Nietzsche on Consciousness and the Embodied Mind*, Berlin/Boston: De Gruyter.

Richardson, John (2004) *Nietzsche's New Darwinism*, New York/Oxford: Oxford University Press.

Schopenhauer, Arthur (1819) *The World as Will and Representation. Volume I*, trans. and eds. J. Norman, A. Welchman and C. Janaway, Cambridge: Cambridge University Press 2010.

Shoemaker, Sydney (1984) "Personal Identity: A Materialist's Account", in: S. Shoemaker and R. Swinburne (1984) *Personal Identity*, Oxford: Basil Blackwell, 67–132.

Thompson, E. (2007) *Mind in Life. Biology, Phenomenology, and the Sciences of Mind*, Cambridge, MA: Harvard University Press.

Varela, F. (1991) "Organism: A Meshwork of Selfless Selves", in: A.I. Tauber (ed.), *Organism and the Origins of Self* (Boston Studies in the Philosophy of Science, vol. 129), 79–107.

Wittgenstein, Ludwig (1965) *The Blue and Brown Books*, New York: Harper & Row.

Paolo Stellino
22 Self-Knowledge, Genealogy, Evolution

> Mirrors should reflect a little before throwing back images.
> (Jean Cocteau, *The Blood of a Poet*)

It is widely known that, at least from the period of *Human, All Too Human*, Nietzsche is profoundly sceptical about the possibility of self-knowledge. There are several reasons that explain this attitude and several passages which show how firm this attitude is. However, given deeper scrutiny, the situation becomes more complex. In particular, Nietzsche seems to be open to the possibility that self-knowledge can be attained through indirect means. Even the language he uses sometimes betrays the conviction that different attempts to know or observe the self can be compared with each other and judged as more or less accurate. For example, in the posthumous fragment 11[113] from November 1887–March 1888, Nietzsche criticizes the explanation of the process of thinking given by theorists of knowledge as the result of a *false* self-observation. Against this explanation, Nietzsche opposes his own account of the self, which he obviously considers as better or *truer*. However, Nietzsche's better or *truer* self-observation seems to lead him to a paradox: given that the phenomenalism of the inner world is inevitable (among other reasons), the only conclusion we can draw from a better or *truer* self-knowledge is that we cannot know ourselves.

Part of this paper is devoted to the solution of this paradox which is solved once we clarify the use Nietzsche makes of the word "self-knowledge" or other related terms in his writings and notes. Thus, I will distinguish between different conceptions of the self (the object) and different kinds of self-knowledge (the methodology). My claim is that Nietzsche thinks he provides a better or *truer* self-observation because he relies on a different, indirect methodology based on three distinct, but complementary, disciplines, namely physiology, psychology and genealogy. By focusing on the sections BGE 32 and GS 335 and by giving particular attention to genealogy, I will show how these three disciplines work together in order to make possible a renewed insight into the human self, an insight which, in Nietzsche's view, plays a pivotal role in both the overcoming of morality and the creation of new tables of values, as well as in the creation of the self.

Finally, the last part of the paper will be devoted to the strategy Nietzsche deploys in both BGE 32 and GS 335. Here Nietzsche anticipates the very same strategy which will be at work in the *Genealogy*: light is shed on the *origin* of *x* (be it our model of agency as in BGE 32 or our moral judgments as in GS 335) in order to call into question its *value* or to spoil its *emotional appeal*. This strategy is far from being obsolete or anachronistic. On the contrary, as I will argue, there are several reasons for considering Nietzsche's genealogical philosophy as an anticipation of more recent attempts to provide a critique of morality on the grounds of its evolutionary genealogy.

1

There is little doubt that many readers might find the very beginning of the *Preface* to the *Genealogy of Morality* somewhat puzzling: "We are unknown to ourselves", Nietzsche writes, "we knowers: and with good reason. We have never looked for ourselves,–so how are we ever supposed to *find* ourselves?" (GM Preface 1).[1] How can Nietzsche possibly write that men of knowledge are unknown to themselves because they never sought themselves? What about the well-known injunction "know thyself" which was engraved on the temple of Apollo at Delphi? And how could we forget the passage from Plato's *Phaedrus* (229e) where Socrates says that he seems to him ridiculous to investigate irrelevant things when he is not yet able to know himself?

In the passage from the *Genealogy*, Nietzsche seems initially to ascribe the lack of self-knowledge to insufficient seriousness (*Ernst*) and time in interpreting one's own "experiences" (*Erlebnisse*). Apparently, every effort in knowing oneself has failed out of *superficiality*: "I fear we have never really been 'with it' in such matters: our heart is simply not in it–and not even our ear!". The imagery of the ears calls to mind the later preface to *Twilight of the Idols* where Nietzsche makes clear that, in order to hear the hollow sound of the idols, one must be a psychologist and have "ears even behind his ears" (TI, Foreword). In the *Genealogy* the sound heard is that of the twelve strokes of the bell which surprises and disconcerts just in the same way as our experiences do. They surprise and disconcert us because we fail to understand them and we inevitably ask what *really* was that which we experienced and who we *really* are. The first section of the *Preface* thus ends with the reiteration of the initial point:

> We remain strange to ourselves out of necessity [*nothwendig*], we do not understand ourselves, we *must* [*müssen*] confusedly mistake who we are, the motto "everyone is furthest

---

[1] The translations used in this paper are from the Cambridge Edition of Nietzsche's works. One exception is Duncan Large's translation of *Twilight of the Idols* (Oxford University Press), which I find to be more faithful to the original text. For the *Nachlass*, I have used – when available – either the Cambridge Edition (*Writings from the Late Notebooks*) or Kaufmann's and Hollingdale's translation of *The Will to Power*. Posthumous fragments are however identified with reference to the Colli and Montinari standard edition.

from himself" applies to us for ever, – we are not "knowers" when it comes to ourselves ... (GM Preface 1)

The use of the adjective *nothwendig* together with the verb *müssen* seems to suggest, however, that Nietzsche's claim is stronger than it initially appeared: every effort of knowing oneself has failed not merely out of superficiality, but rather out of *inadequacy*. This claim will not surprise those who are familiar with Nietzsche's profound scepticism about the possibility of human self-knowledge. Similar sceptical claims can be found in great number in both Nietzsche's published works and posthumous fragments. The entry on "consciousness" in the *Nietzsche-Wörterbuch* (van Tongeren et al. 2004: 342–344) lists eleven different ways in which Nietzsche defines the limits of human consciousness. The phenomenalism of the inner world, the mediation of language, the unknown multiplicity of affects and drives, and the social, non-individual character of consciousness are only a few of the several reasons for which, for Nietzsche, human beings cannot achieve self-knowledge and thus remain strange to themselves.

As Schlimgen (1998: 134–136) points out, Nietzsche rejects the traditional view according to which self-knowledge would provide us with a privileged or immediate access to the inner world. The phenomenalist position endorsed by Nietzsche in GS 354 applies not only to our experience of the external world, but also to that of the inner one.[2] It would be therefore wrong to assume that the inner world is more easily known because it is more familiar to us. On the contrary: "The familiar is what we are used to, and what we are used to is the most difficult to 'know' – that is, to view as a problem, to see as strange, as distant, as 'outside us' ..." (GS 355) As Nietzsche shows, this widespread assumption has its roots in the belief in the so-called "facts of consciousness" (*Thatsachen des Bewusstseins*), that is, the belief in a pure and direct knowledge of the inner world which consciousness would disclose to us. According to Nietzsche, there are no such facts: what is known through consciousness is always something mediated, cognized as through a mirror.[3] We cannot avoid phenomenalism in self-observation.[4]

---

2 As Nietzsche plainly puts it in the posthumous fragment NL spring 1888, 14[152], KSA 10: 334–335=WP, 264: "One must not look for phenomenalism in the wrong place: nothing is more phenomenal (or, more clearly): nothing is so much *deception* as this inner world which we observe with the famous 'inner sense'." On this, see Abel 2001: 27.
3 See NL autumn 1885–autumn 1886, 2[87], KSA 12: 104 and 2[204], KSA 12: 166–167; NL end 1886–spring 1887, 7[1], KSA 12: 247–250. As Lupo (2007: 32) points out, there are two common elements in the imagery used by Nietzsche when trying to "grasp" consciousness: the element of mediation/transformation (organ, tool, hand) and that of boundary/limit (surface, mirror).
4 See NL autumn 1885–autumn 1886, 2[204], KSA 12: 166–167.

The inevitable phenomenalism of the inner experience and the impossibility of achieving an immediate knowledge of the inner world have relevant consequences for the possibility of self-knowledge. Nietzsche makes them clear in section 16 of *Beyond Good and Evil*:

> There are still harmless self-observers who believe in the existence of "immediate certainties," such as "I think," or the "I will" that was Schopenhauer's superstition: just as if knowledge had been given an object here to seize, stark naked, as a "thing-in-itself," and no falsification took place from either the side of the subject or the side of the object. But I will say this a hundred times: "immediate certainty," like "absolute knowledge" and the "thing in itself" contains a *contradictio in adjecto*. For once and for all, we should free ourselves from the seduction of words! (BGE 16)[5]

Nietzsche's scepticism towards the possibility of self-observation, which is undoubtedly patent in the works of the late period, can be traced back at least to the period of *Human, All Too Human*, if not to the unpublished essay *On Truth and Lying in a Non-Moral Sense*, written in 1973.[6] It would be, therefore, hardly wrong to say that throughout his work Nietzsche's attitude towards self-knowl-

---

[5] See also the even more explicit passage from BGE 281.
[6] See the following passage (TL 1): "What do human beings really know about themselves? Are they even capable of perceiving themselves in their entirety just once, stretched out as in an illuminated glass case? [...] Nature has thrown away the key, and woe betide fateful curiosity should it ever succeed in peering through a crack in the chamber of consciousness, out and down into the depths, and thus gain an intimation of the fact that humanity, in the indifference of its ignorance, rests on the pitiless, the greedy, the insatiable, the murderous – clinging in dreams, as it were, to the back of a tiger." It is, however, from the period of *Human, All Too Human* on, that Nietzsche visibly assumes a critical stance towards self-knowledge (see HH I 32, HH I 491 and HH II 223). According to Müller-Buck (2002: 98), the "unconquerable distrust in the *possibility* of self-knowledge" shown by Nietzsche in *Beyond Good and Evil* (BGE 281) became a deep-rooted conviction after the reading of Dostoevsky's *Notes from Underground* during the winter 1886–87. Nietzsche read a French adaptation of the *Notes* (the second part of *L'esprit souterrain*) and described it as "a stroke of psychological genius, a sort of self-ridicule of the *gnōthi sautón*" (letter to Overbeck of 23 February 1887, KSB 8: 28=Nietzsche 1996: 261) and as "a true stroke of genius in psychology – a frightening and cruel piece of mockery of *gnōthi sautón*, but done with such a light audacity and joy in his superior power, that I was drunk with delight" (letter to Gast of 7 March 1887, KSB 8: 41=my translation; see also the letter to Overbeck of 13 May 1887, KSB 8: 75). There is little doubt that the reading of the *Notes* strengthened Nietzsche's critical attitude towards self-knowledge. As shown, however, Nietzsche's scepticism was already a prominent feature of his philosophy at the time of his discovery of Dostoevsky. In this sense, I would rather say that part of Nietzsche's enthusiastic reaction to the reading of the *Notes* can be precisely explained by his previous scepticism towards self-knowledge. On Nietzsche's reading of the *Notes*, see Stellino 2015.

edge has been *almost* always critical.[7] Nonetheless, as much as this picture may be correct, it is *incomplete*. To see why this is so, consider the posthumous fragment 11[113] of November 1887–March 1888, which focuses on the phenomenalism of the inner world.

In the final part of this note, by recurring to a similar argumentation of GM I 13 Nietzsche criticizes as essentially wrong the explanation of the process of thinking given by theorists of knowledge. In order to explain this process, theorists of knowledge have erroneously posited a doing (the thinking) and a doer (the mind, i.e. something that *does* the thinking). However, Nietzsche claims, both are simply fictions. Indeed, the thinking is obtained by arbitrarily "selecting one element from the process and subtracting all the others, an artificial trimming for the purpose of intelligibility …" Once thinking is posited, an entity (the mind) which performs this act is added, a subject-substratum which we take as the origin of every act of thinking. Nevertheless, Nietzsche claims, this entity is a pure fiction.

What is interesting to notice about Nietzsche's conception of the mind – as derivative from a prior postulation of the act of thinking – is that this conception is described as a consequence of a "*false* self-observation" (my italics). Similarly, within the same posthumous fragment, the assumption of an immediate, causal bond between thoughts is denounced as "the consequence of the *crudest* and *clumsiest* observation" (my italics). As the use of the adjectives "false" (*falsch*), "crude" (*grob*) and "clumsy" (*plump*) seems to suggest, for Nietzsche, in order to gain a more accurate picture of the inner world a better or *truer* self-observation is needed. This, however, leads to the paradox that was mentioned above: given that the phenomenalism of the inner world is inevitable (among other reasons), the only conclusion we can draw from a better or *truer* self-knowledge is that we cannot know ourselves. How could this be possible?

---

[7] In *The Birth of Tragedy*, Apollo appears as "the magnificent divine image of the *principium individuationis*" (BT 1), the deification of the same principle which "knows just one law: the individual, which is to say, respect for the limits of the individual, *measure* in the Hellenic sense" (BT 4). Opposing every kind of excess and exaggeration, Apollo exacts measure of his disciples and, in order to maintain it, he requires self-knowledge. It is in this sense that Nietzsche defines him as an "ethical deity" who demands his disciples to know themselves. In *On the Uses and Disadvantages of History for Life* the Delphic maxim has a positive connotation: as the ancient Greeks learned through it to organize the chaos of forms and concepts inherited by foreign cultures (they concentrated on themselves, that is, on their genuine needs and let the pseudo needs die out), similarly, in Nietzsche's view, in order to recover from his historical disease, the modern man should recall to his mind the Delphic imperative and learn to organize the chaos within him.

2

In order to solve this (apparent) paradox, we clearly need to make some distinctions between (i) a different conception of the self (what is to be known), and (ii) different kinds of self-knowledge (that is, different methodologies to achieve knowledge of the self). In what follows, I will focus my attention on both points.

(i) The first distinction we need to make concerns the *object* of self-knowledge, that is, the *cognoscendum*. In fact, when Nietzsche uses the words "self-knowledge" (*Selbsterkenntnis*) and "self-observation" (*Selbstbeobachtung*), he has in mind two very different conceptions of the self. In the first case, the self to be known (S1) is the inner world of thoughts, motives, affects, drives, and so on. In Nietzsche's opinion, the effort of attaining this kind of self-knowledge is nearly hopeless because, among other reasons, consciousness operates as a kind of surface and skin – "which, like every skin, reveals something but *conceals* even more" (BGE 32). In the second case, the self to be known (S2) is not the *content* of the inner world, but rather its *functioning*, that is, such heterogeneous, but interconnected things as the processes of thinking or willing or knowing, the model of agency and the nature of the moral act.[8] As the posthumous fragment 11[113] shows, Nietzsche sometimes defines the attempt to achieve an insight into such processes as "self-knowledge", "self-observation" or even "self-contemplation" (*Selbstbesinnung*).

(ii) The second distinction we need to make concerns the *methodology* of self-knowledge, that is, the *modus cognoscendi*. Nietzsche absolutely rejects any attempt to know both S1 and S2 through *direct* self-observation. In the case of S1, we have already seen that, according to Nietzsche, the thinking which becomes conscious is merely the smallest, the shallowest, the most superficial and superfluous, and the less individual part of our whole thinking. The phenomena of consciousness are final phenomena (only the peak of an iceberg), last links in a chain which we erroneously believe to be known to us.[9] We are not even sure about the true nature of this chain (whether the relation between different thoughts is causal or associative).[10] All we have is the illusion that "the

---

8 To borrow a term from Janaway (2007: 11), we could say that S2 is the object of a "generic psychology" whose aim is not to decipher the singular self of a person *x*, but rather to uncover the universal processes which regulate human phenomena such as thinking, willing, knowing, etc. I thank Paul Katsafanas for having drawn my attention to Janaway's term. To avoid any misunderstanding, notice that Janaway uses the term in a completely different sense from the one I mean here.
9 See NL end of 1886 – spring 1887, 7[1], KSA 12: 247–250.
10 On this, see Lupo (2007: 119–120). According to Lupo, Nietzsche seems to be inclined for an associative relation.

succession of thoughts, feelings, ideas in consciousness" is a causal one and upon this illusion *"we have founded our whole notion of mind, reason, logic*, etc." (NL November 1887–March 1888, 11[145], KSA 13: 68=WLN, 228). In short, we do not have any immediate access to the multiplicity of thoughts which constitutes the core of our unconscious thinking. Conscious thinking is only a *final* thinking. This is why every effort of knowing S1 through direct self-observation is doomed to be superficial and incomplete:

> Distrust of self-observation. That a thought is a cause of a thought cannot be established. On the table of our consciousness there appears a succession of thoughts, as if one thought were the cause of the next. But in fact we don't see the struggle going on under the table – – (NL autumn 1885–autumn 1886, 2[103], KSA 12: 112=WLN, 78)

In the case of S2 as well, Nietzsche believes that direct self-observation is clearly inadequate. To see why this is so, consider Nietzsche's critique of Kant's and Schopenhauer's belief in the existence of "immediate certainties". As already mentioned, Nietzsche judges this belief to be wrong because of the inevitable phenomenalism of the inner experience. In particular, for Nietzsche, Kant's and Schopenhauer's mistake consists in having taken the inner world as a fixed, stable, metaphysical entity accessible to us through direct self-observation, as if the self were a common object.[11] As Nietzsche puts it in a posthumous fragment from spring 1880:

> Erkenntnißtheorie ist die Liebhaberei jener scharfsinnigen Köpfe, die nicht genug gelernt haben und welche vermeinen, hier wenigstens könne ein Jeder von vorne anfangen, hier genüge die "Selbstbeobachtung." (NL spring 1880, 3[57], KSA 9: 63)

Notice however that Nietzsche's sceptical position is not that of adopting an attitude of *epoché* towards S2. In other words, Nietzsche is not claiming that it is impossible for us to achieve any knowledge of S2, but rather that the direct approach is clearly inadequate. Indeed, there is little doubt that Nietzsche puts forward his own account of S2 and that he considers his account more accurate than the one which, for instance, makes use of metaphysical entities. This can be clearly seen in Nietzsche's critique of free will in BGE 19. In this section, Nietzsche criticizes the way in which "philosophers tend to talk about the will as if it were the most familiar thing in the world" (the reference here is to Schopenhauer). This superficial attitude has led them to formulate "*erroneous* conclusions and, consequently, *false* evaluations" (my italics) about the will. In fact, misled by "the syn-

---

[11] See Gerhardt (2011: 184): "Was dieses "Selbst" ist, steht weder von Anfang an noch für eine gewisse Zeit und schon gar nicht in einer über alle Zeit hinausreichenden Weise fest. *Das Selbst ist weder metaphysisch noch empirisch eine feste Größe*."

thetic concept of the 'I'", they have failed to understand the whole complexity of every act of willing which, according to Nietzsche, is composed of a plurality of feelings, a commandeering thought and the affect of the command.

Here we can see that to an erroneous, false and prejudicial explanation of the will, Nietzsche opposes his own interpretation, which he obviously considers as more realistic and truthful. The same logic is at work in the posthumous fragment 11[113] mentioned above, where Nietzsche considers the explanation of the process of thinking given by theorists of knowledge as consequence of a "false self-observation". This explanation is replaced by Nietzsche's more accurate interpretation of the process of thinking as a continuum of thoughts between which there are "*all sorts of affects* at play".

Taking into account all these considerations, it is easy now to see why the paradox mentioned above is only an *apparent* paradox. Recall the paradox: Nietzsche's rejection of the postulation of the mind (the subject-substratum which *does* the thinking) as a consequence of a *false* self-observation seems to suggest that in order to gain a more accurate picture of the inner world we need a better or *truer* self-observation. And Nietzsche does indeed provide (or, at least, he thinks he provides) a better or *truer* self-observation: he gives his own interpretation of the process of thinking and considers his interpretation as better and more accurate than the previous one. The problem, however, is that this better and truer self-observation only confirms the initial scepticism towards self-knowledge, and this is the paradox: thanks to a better or *truer* self-knowledge we discover that the phenomenalism of the inner world is inevitable and, therefore, self-knowledge is a chimera.

To solve this apparent paradox, it suffices to introduce the distinction made above between S1 and S2. Indeed, when Nietzsche thinks that a better or *truer* self-observation must replace the previous, *false* self-observation, he is making reference to S2, that is, the *cognoscendum* is here the *functioning* of the inner world. However, a better knowledge of S2 leads Nietzsche to assume a sceptical position about the possibilities of knowing S1, that is, about the possibility to achieve an insight into the *content* of the inner world. Nietzsche therefore does not find himself stuck in a paradox when he thinks that a better, or *truer* self-knowledge (S2) leads us to conclude the impossibility of self-knowledge (S1).

3

Does Nietzsche really think that we can *never* achieve knowledge of S1? And why does he believe that his account of S2 is *truer* or more accurate than the one given by theorists of knowledge? Let us consider each question in turn. First of all, notice that Nietzsche is certainly sceptical about the possibility to achieve knowledge of S1 *through direct self-observation*. However, this does not imply that knowledge of S1 can be achieved *through indirect means*. Consider, for instance, section 491 of *Human, All Too Human*:

> *Self-observation.* – Man is very well defended against himself, against being reconnoitred and besieged by himself, he is usually able to perceive of himself only his outer walls. The actual fortress is inaccessible, even invisible to him, unless his friends and enemies play the traitor and conduct him in by a secret path. (HH I 491)

Here Nietzsche clearly thinks that the direct approach to the self is useless and that for us it is impossible to achieve knowledge of S1 unless we take an indirect path to it.

Now, consider a second, more interesting example to which Lupo (2007: 227) draws attention. In section 223 of the second part of *Human, All Too Human*, Nietzsche understands self-knowledge as "universal knowledge with all that is past":

> Direct self-observation is not nearly sufficient for us to know ourselves: we require history, for the past continues to flow within us in a hundred waves; we ourselves are, indeed, nothing but that which at every moment we experience of this continued flowing. (HH II 223)[12]

This passage confirms an essential element of the analysis presented above: Nietzsche rejects the direct approach to the self as inadequate and unsuccessful because, among other reasons, the self is not a fixed, immutable entity, but rather a "continued flowing", something that is fluid, constantly changing and becoming, so that

> when we desire to descend into the river of what seems to be our own most intimate and personal being, there applies the dictum of Heraclitus: we cannot step into the same river twice. (HH II 223)

The only way to attain knowledge of S1 is, once again, by means of an indirect approach, identified this time by Nietzsche with history.

As these two examples clearly show, although Nietzsche considers direct self-observation an inadequate path to S1, he nonetheless thinks that knowledge of S1 can be achieved through indirect means such as interpersonal interaction

---

[12] Compare this with the following passage from the posthumous fragment 23[48], from the end of 1876 – Summer 1877: "Die moralische *Selbstbeobachtung* genügt jetzt keineswegs, Historie und die Kenntniß der zurückgebliebenen Völkerschaften gehört dazu, um die verwickelten Motive unseres Handelns kennen zu lernen." (KSA 8: 421)

or history.[13] Thus, as one can see, his scepticism towards the possibility of self-knowledge (S1) is not as radical as a superficial reading may lead one to believe. On the other hand, it is important to stress that, as Pippin (2010: 101) points out, this kind of knowledge is "not observational but interpretative and, let us say, always promissory, futural, as complexly interpretive as the interpretive question of just what it is that is being done".

Let us now consider the second question of why Nietzsche considers his own account of S2 *truer* or more accurate than the one given by philosophers and theorists of knowledge. My hypothesis is that Nietzsche thinks he is in the position of claiming privilege for his own account of S2 because he relies on a different, indirect methodology based on three different, but complementary disciplines, namely physiology, psychology and genealogy. In what follows, I will briefly focus the attention on each of them.

The relevance of physiology for self-knowledge is evident in Nietzsche's intention from the period 1884/85 of using "the guiding thread of the body" (*Leitfaden des Leibes*) to understand the inner world. In a posthumous fragment from this period, Nietzsche clearly states that self-reflection is not nearly sufficient to grasp all the spiritual processes of the inner world and that, to this end, is necessary to follow the guiding thread of the body:

> Aus der Selbstbespiegelung des Geistes ist noch nichts Gutes gewachsen. Erst jetzt, wo man auch über alle geistigen Vorgänge sich am Leitfaden des Leibes zu unterrichten sucht z.B. über Gedächtniß, kommt man von der Stelle. (NL summer–autumn 1884, 26[374], KSA 11: 249)[14]

The reference to the body has a clear *anti-metaphysical* and *anti-substantialist* function: on the light of several, different readings from his time (above all, Wilhelm Roux's *Der Kampf der Theile im Organismus*) and in clear contraposition to the body/soul dualism of the philosophical tradition, Nietzsche conceives of the human being as a multiplicity of affects and drives.[15] From now on, any correct interpretation of the psychological processes cannot avoid making refer-

---

13 Schlimgen (1998: 136) is, therefore, wrong in claiming that Nietzsche sees in intoxication (*Rausch*) and frenzy (*Ekstase*) the *sole* possibility to know the self.
14 See also the posthumous fragment 26[432] from the same period: "Wenn ich an meine philosophische Genealogie denke, so fühle ich mich im Zusammenhang mit der antiteleologischen, d.h. spinozistischen Bewegung unserer Zeit, doch mit dem Unterschied, [...] daß ich alles Ausgehen von der Selbstbespiegelung des Geistes für unfruchtbar halte und ohne den *Leitfaden des Leibes* an keine gute Forschung glaube." (KSA 11: 266)
15 NL 27[27], summer–autumn 1884, KSA 11: 282: "Am Leitfaden des Leibes erkennen wir den Menschen als eine Vielheit belebter Wesen, welche theils mit einander kämpfend, theils einander

ence to the physiological *substratum* of the psyche, i.e. the body. Psychology is thus reinterpreted as a "physio-psychology" (BGE 23).

The value of this new methodology does not consist, however, in freeing psychology only from the metaphysical and substantialist prejudice, but also from the *moral* one. In fact, it is only because it has freed itself from the tyranny of morality that the new psychology can gain a refined outlook on "the human soul and its limits, the scope of human inner experience to date, the heights, depths, and range of these experiences, the entire history of the soul *so far* and its still unexhausted possibilities" (BGE 45).[16] Thus, the "*new* psychologist" puts an end to the belief (i.e. the superstition) in the *atomism of the soul*. The soul is now reinterpreted as "subject-multiplicity" or as a "society constructed out of drives and affects" (BGE 12). Nietzsche denies that we have any right whatsoever to believe in the existence of "immediate certainties" or to hypostasize a metaphysical subject as the cause of our thoughts (BGE 16, BGE 17), nor can we ignore the complexity hidden behind the single word "will" (BGE 19) or fail to see the whole naivety of the opposition free will/un-free will (BGE 21). As a consequence of the self-contemplation (*Selbstbesinnung*) brought about by the renewed and refined psychology, all these concepts and many others become a fable and a fiction. As Nietzsche puts it in *Twilight of the Idols*: "We have thought better of all this [*uns besser besonnen*]. Nowadays we no longer believe a word of it." (TI, The Four Great Errors 3)

The last discipline in which S2 relies in order to achieve an insight into the inner world is genealogy. We have already seen that, according to Nietzsche, history and the genealogical method can be one of the indirect paths which lead one to achieve some knowledge of S1. However, when it comes to S2, Nietzsche concedes a much more important role to genealogy. As I will show in what follows, this is evident in the analysis Nietzsche develops of the model of agency in BGE 32 and of the nature of the moral act in GS 335. In both sections Nietzsche anticipates the very same strategy which will be at work in the *Genealogy*: in order either to call into question the *value* of x or to spoil its *emotional appeal*, Nietzsche launches an investigation on the *origin* of x (e.g. on the origin of our model of agency, as in BGE 32, or on the origin of our moral judgments, as in GS 335).

---

ein- und untergeordnet, in der Bejahung ihres Einzelwesens unwillkürlich auch das Ganze bejahen."

16 The reason for which Nietzsche rejects the old psychology is not only for its superficiality, but also primarily for having put itself "under the dominance of morality" (BGE 47). Indeed, its superficiality is understood by Nietzsche precisely as a direct consequence of its having been stuck in "moral prejudices and fears": "the power of moral prejudice has deeply affected the most spiritual world [...] and the effect has been manifestly harmful, hindering, dazzling, and distorting." (BGE 23)

However, before we turn to the analysis of both sections, a very relevant aspect of self-knowledge must be brought to light (S2). As mentioned, Nietzsche relies on physiology, psychology and genealogy in order to reject the account of S2 given by philosophers and theorists of knowledge, and to put forward his own, superior account. For Nietzsche, this improvement in self-knowledge is relevant not only for what concerns the theoretical understanding of the self, but also and above all for what concerns the *practical consequences* this new understanding is supposed to bring about (this is what we might call the "performative character" of Nietzsche's self-knowledge). To make this point clearer, consider what Katsafanas points out regarding the relevance of genealogy for Nietzsche's self-knowledge.[17]

According to Katsafanas, using genealogy, Nietzsche would show that our conception of agency determines the way in which I experience my action. In this sense, were my conception of agency different, I would experience, understand and perceive my action in a completely different way. As Katsafanas puts it, "the conceptual scheme through which I view the world structures my perception of the world".[18] In this sense, Katsafanas continues, "were my conception of agency different [...] I would not perceive my own thinking in the same way".

What the analysis of BGE 32 can add to this is that the insight into our conception of agency determines not only the way in which I experience my action, but also and more importantly the way in which I act. In this sense, were my conception of agency different, not only would I not perceive my action as usual, but I would also not act in the same way as I do, nor would I make the same moral judgments I make. On the contrary, a different conception of agency would force me to overcome the Christian morality I so fervently revere and persuade myself to create my own, distinct values. As I will show in what follows, this is precisely what Nietzsche has in mind when in BGE 32 and GS 335 he relates the renewed self-contemplation his philosophy has brought with the overcoming of morality.

4

Consider, first of all, section 32 of *Beyond Good and Evil*. Here Nietzsche presents a concise moral history of humanity which he divides into three main periods: a

---

[17] I here make reference to Katsafanas' paper "Kant and Nietzsche on Self-Knowledge" contained in this volume.
[18] Katsafanas makes this point clear by reference to Nietzsche's distinction between the modern and the ancient conception of agency in GM I 13.

pre-moral, a *moral* and an *extra-moral* one. What should be noticed here is that these three different periods coincide with three distinct stages in the evolution of human self-knowledge. During the longest epoch of human history (the *pre-moral* period), the value of an action was derived from its consequences; the action itself and its origin were ignored. According to Nietzsche, "the imperative 'know thyself!' was still unknown". The *pre-moral* period is followed by a *moral* period (the last ten thousand years), during which a "refinement [*Verfeinerung*] of outlook and criterion" makes possible a reversal of perspective where the attention is shifted from the consequences to the origin of an action. As Nietzsche puts it, "this marks the first attempt at self-knowledge". This first effort of self-knowledge is nevertheless compromised by "a disastrous new superstition", for the origin is interpreted in a very peculiar way, as origin out of an *intention*. The result is a "morality of intentions [*Absichten-Moral*]" (the morality we have had up to now) which opens the door to concepts morally loaded, such as free will, responsibility and guilt. The origin of every action is located in consciousness: thus, as Nietzsche puts it in *Twilight of the Idols*, "the *most fundamental* piece of counterfeiting *in psychologicis* became the principle of psychology itself" (TI, The Four Great Errors 7).

It is precisely "a renewed self-contemplation [*Selbstbesinnung*] and deepening of humanity" (BGE 32) that makes possible the transition to the third period, the *extra-moral*, on the threshold of which we should be standing. This transition is motivated by the suspect, if not the awareness, that "the decisive value is conferred by what is specifically *unintentional* about an action, and that all its intentionality, everything about it that can be seen, known, or raised to 'conscious awareness,' only belongs to its surface and skin". If this is so, the very presupposition on which morality is built is erroneous: being based on an "*essentially flawed* self-observation" (NL spring–summer 1883, 7[268], KSA 10: 323=my translation), morality, as it has been understood so far, is rejected as mere prejudice and put it on the same level as astrology and alchemy.[19]

What role does genealogy exactly play here? As Katsafanas puts it, "genealogy helps me to see that my conception of agency is *optional*: it supplanted an early form, and could be supplanted by another". In other words, genealogy would make us discover that our conception of agency is *historically contingent*: we began by attributing value to the consequences of an action, then, to the

---

[19] See D 103: "I deny morality [*Sittlichkeit*] as I deny alchemy, that is, I deny their premises." In the same section Nietzsche claims that morality "is among the coarser or more subtle deceptions (especially *self-deception*) which men practise" (my italics). For a reading of Nietzsche as a Presupposition Error-Theorist, see Hussain 2013.

intentions and, lastly, to what is unintentional. Now, Katsafanas is certainly right in stressing that, according to Nietzsche, our conceptual schemes are historically contingent. Nonetheless, the way in which Nietzsche presents this concise moral history of humanity (as a progress in self-knowledge) clearly shows that he is here making a stronger point: he is claiming that although conceptual schemes are historically contingent, nevertheless, they can be compared by reference to a standard such as *accuracy* or, to use a more Nietzschean term, *truthfulness*. In other words, although Nietzsche thinks that both models of agency of the moral and the extra-moral period are only different *interpretations* of human agency, he clearly considers his conception (or the one which corresponds to the extra-moral period) as more accurate and truthful than that of the moral period. This conviction is no longer supported by genealogy, but rather by the insight into S2 which, as shown, Nietzsche thinks he has achieved with the help of physiology and a moraline-free psychology.

What follows from this "renewed self-contemplation" or, as Gerhardt (2011: 175) puts it, from this "refinement of *self-reflection*", is in Nietzsche's opinion nothing less than the overcoming of morality, which brings with it both the possibility and necessity "to effect a reversal and fundamental displacement of values", that is, in other words, a transvaluation of values.[20] To prepare for humanity's *Selbstbesinnung* and "*great noon*" thus becomes Nietzsche's task, the far-reaching importance of which is highlighted in the following passage from EH, Daybreak 2:

> My task, preparing for humanity's moment of highest self-examination [*Selbstbesinnung*], a *great noon* when it will look back and look out, when it will escape from the domination of chance and priests and, for the first time, pose the question "why?", the question "what for?" *as a whole* –, this task follows necessarily from the insight that humanity has *not* put itself on the correct path, that it has absolutely *no* divine governance, that instead, the instinct of negation, of corruption, the decadence-instinct, has been seductively at work, and precisely under humanity's holiest value concepts. The question of the origin of moral values is a question of the *first rank* for me because it determines the future of humanity.

5

That the renewed self-contemplation and self-knowledge of humanity has practical consequences and a performative character is even more clearly shown in

---

[20] See EH, Why I Am a Destiny 1: "*Revaluation of all values*: that is my formula for an act of humanity's highest self-examination [*Selbstbesinnung*], an act that has become flesh and genius in me."

section 335 of *The Gay Science*. This insight, brought by a better self-observation, into how moral judgments come into existence has the double function of, on the one hand, purifying our moral opinions and value judgments, and on the other hand, of impelling us towards the creation of new tables of what is good and which are our own. Let us focus our attention on both aspects.

The section begins with Nietzsche's usual and familiar scepticism towards self-knowledge:

> So, how many people know how to observe? And of these few, how many to observe themselves? 'Everyone is farthest from himself' – every person who is expert at scrutinizing the inner life of others knows this to his own chagrin; and the saying, 'Know thyself', addressed to human beings by a god, is near to malicious. (GS 335)

The sceptical tone and the saying "everyone is furthest from himself" inevitably call to mind the later *Preface* to the *Genealogy*. Indeed, in both cases, the existence of moral prejudices is linked with a wrong or superficial self-knowledge. However, in the section from the *Gay Science*, this link is clearer and more explicit. Here Nietzsche claims that the bad state in which self-observation is, is confirmed by the "quick, willing, convinced, talkative manner" in which nearly everyone speaks of the nature of the moral act. According to Nietzsche, the usual explanation of the moral act given by popular psychology begins with a judgment ("*x* is right"), continues with an inference ("*x* must come about") and ends with the act itself (*a* does *x*). No matter how common this explanation might be, in Nietzsche's opinion it is wrong. For it fails to see, among other things, that what we have here is three separate acts of a very different nature (even the judgment "*x* is right" is an act, Nietzsche claims).

The incorrect explanation popular psychology gives of the moral act is only an example of the bad state in which, for Nietzsche, self-observation is. However, it makes plain how superficially and without any further questioning we tend to accept our belief about how moral judgments come into existence. The same happens, for instance, with the judgments of our conscience which, according to Nietzsche, we take as invariably true and right, ignoring that we do so because we were taught to do so since our childhood or disregarding the fact that every single judgment has "a prehistory in your drives, inclinations, aversions, experiences, and what you have failed to experience" (GS 335).

As expressions like "never having thought much about yourself" or "your blindly having accepted [...]" indicate, this self-confidence in our moral judgments stems from superficial and inadequate self-observation. That this is the case is also shown by Nietzsche's critique of Kant's categorical imperative in the same section. According to Nietzsche, no one who considers his own judgment a universal law "has yet taken five steps towards self-knowledge" (GS 335). For, had he done so, he would know that every act is unique and unrepeatable; that every moral prescription relates only to the rough exterior of an action; that every action is inscrutable and every act unknowable; and so on. What popular psychology and Kant's categorical imperative have in common is, therefore, their being the result of an insufficient self-knowledge and self-observation. To use the expression from BGE 23, they have attended only to the surface of things and have not "ventured into the depths". In other words, they have failed to see the whole complexity of our inner world, they did not understand it.

What we now need in Nietzsche's view is a better self-knowledge, that is, a deeper insight into the making of moral judgment. This insight is, at the same time, physiological (it takes into consideration the role of the body), psychological (it considers inclinations and aversions) and genealogical (it takes into account the history of our experiences). As in the case of the "renewed self-contemplation" mentioned in BGE 32, this insight brings with it inevitable consequences on a practical level:

> [...] had you reflected more subtly, *observed better* [my italics], and studied more, you would never continue to call this 'duty' of yours and this 'conscience' of yours duty and conscience. Your insight into *how such things as moral judgments could ever have come into existence* would spoil these emotional words for you [...]. (GS 335)

The insight (*Einsicht*) into the real formation of moral judgments, brought by a better self-observation, spoils the emotional appeal that moral concepts have, thus causing a "purification of our opinions and value judgments" (GS 335). Likewise, the awareness of the absurdity of a universal law, based on the ignorance of the uniqueness and inscrutableness of every action, impels us towards the "*creation of tables of what is good that are new and all our own*" (GS 335). As Zarathustra puts it: "But he will have discovered himself [*sich selber entdeckt*] who speaks: 'This is *my* good and evil.' With this he has silenced the mole and dwarf who says: 'Good for all, evil for all.'" (Z III, On the Spirit of Gravity 2) As one can see, these passages could not bring to light in a clearer and more evident way the practical consequences which derive from Nietzsche's renewed and refined self-knowledge.

6

As the conclusion of GS 335 clearly shows, self-knowledge (S2) plays a pivotal role not only in the creation of new, autonomous tables of value, but also in the creation of the self. What is surprising, however, is that, according to Nietzsche, in order to achieve this creation we need to know *physics*, we must become *physicists*:

> We, however, want to *become who we are* – human beings who are new, unique, incomparable, who give themselves laws, who create themselves! To that end we must become the best students and discoverers of everything lawful and necessary in the world: we must become *physicists* in order to be *creators* in this sense – while hitherto all valuations and ideals have been built on *ignorance* of physics or in *contradiction* to it. So, long live physics! And even more long live what *compels* us to it – our honesty! (GS 335)

The enthusiastic exclamation "long live physics!", which is also the title of the section, could seem to be completely out of place in a section dedicated to the origin of moral judgments. What is the relation between both the creation of the self and the creation of values and ideals, on the one side, and physics, on the other side? And why does Nietzsche claim that all valuations and ideals so far have ignored or contradicted physics? An answer to these questions can be found in the posthumous fragment 24[18] of Winter 1883–1884 which, even if it follows chronologically the composition of *The Gay Science*, can be nonetheless helpful in explaining Nietzsche's reference to physics.

In this note, Nietzsche claims that science and morality so far carried out a similar function: that of enlightening the external and the inner world, respectively. Whereas science tried to remove "the perfect confusion of things" by reference to hypotheses which aimed to explain everything, morality attempted to represent figuratively the inner world by using a scheme, thus presenting the human being as something known and familiar. In both cases, the common aim was to overcome "the intellect's aversion to chaos". However, the annihilation of morality, operated by Nietzsche's philosophy, brings about a change in this situation. The human being is again something strange, unfamiliar: "We have become again *completely obscure* to ourselves! I know that I know nothing *about myself*." (NL 1883–1884, 24[18], KSA 10: 656=my translation)

As one can see, we have the same picture as the one given above: having been freed from the tyranny of morality, Nietzsche's philosophy is able to bring a new insight into the human being, namely, that – to use the expression from the *Genealogy* – we are unknown to ourselves. The only possible answer to the Delphic maxim is, therefore, a slight variation of the Socratic paradox: I know that I know nothing ... about myself. However, this profound scepticism is mitigated by the new role played by science and, particularly, physics: "*Physics* proves to be a *relief* for the spirit: science (as the way to *knowledge*) acquires a new fascination after the abolition of morality." (*ibid.*)

Once morality has been abolished, the *true* investigation of the self (self-knowledge in the sense of S2) can begin, this time with a non-prejudicial attitude. This task is assigned by Nietzsche not only to physiology, psychology and genealogy, as we have already seen, but also to science because of its distrustfulness (GS 33), honesty (GS 107) and severity ("this inexorability in matters great and small, this swiftness in weighing, judging, and passing judgment"; GS 293). Among the different branches of science, Nietzsche mentions precisely physics, which he understands in its etymological sense as the knowledge of nature (*phúsis*), human nature being a part of it. This mention clearly betrays Nietzsche's anti-metaphysical intentions. Indeed, against the metaphysical baggage upon which the understanding of the self by the old, popular psychology rests ("morality translated into metaphysics as force, cause, goal", as Nietzsche puts it in EH, Why I Am a Destiny 3), Nietzsche endorses the study and the discovery of "everything lawful and necessary in the world" (GS 335). For, as he puts it in D 130, perhaps there is only the realm of chance and necessity, "perhaps there exists neither will nor purposes, and we have only imagined them".

The study of nature becomes the indispensable prerequisite of the creation of the self. Thus, a new task lies ahead of the human being:

> To translate humanity back into nature; to gain control of the many vain and fanciful interpretations and incidental meanings that have been scribbled and drawn over that eternal basic text of *homo natura* so far; to make sure that, from now on, the human being will stand before the human being, just as he already stands before the *rest* of nature today, hardened by the discipline of science, – with courageous Oedipus eyes and sealed up Odysseus ears, deaf to the lures of the old metaphysical bird catchers who have been whistling to him for far too long: "You are more! You are higher! You have a different origin!" (BGE 230)

The creation of the self is possible only if the human being previously gets rid of the many false, metaphysical interpretations which have been given about the self throughout the centuries and replaces them with more accurate, anti-metaphysical, moraline-free, genealogical hypotheses. Viewed in this particular light, we can thus say with Gerhardt (2011: 184) that "self-knowledge is always self-determination [*Selbstbestimmung*]".

It would therefore be wrong (or at least inaccurate) to assume that in the 1880s Nietzsche completely dismisses self-knowledge in favour of self-creation. Certainly, his scepticism towards the possibility of self-knowledge leads him to focus his attention from the knowledge of the self to the creation of the self. As the posthumous fragment 7[213] of this period clearly shows, this tendency appears as early as the end of 1880.[21] It then grows stronger, to the point that in

---

21 In this note, Nietzsche claims that the task is not to know oneself – something which, given the fact that the self is constantly becoming, would be simply impossible – but rather to give form, to shape, to mould one's self. See the whole note: "Es ist Mythologie zu glauben, daß wir unser eigentliches Selbst finden werden, nachdem wir dies und jenes gelassen oder vergessen

Ecce Homo self-knowledge represents the greatest danger for the one who aims to become who he is.²² However, as GS 335 clearly shows, this scepticism is directed towards S1, whereas S2 is considered on the contrary as a previous, necessary step towards self-creation. In order to "*become who we are*", Nietzsche claims in the section from *The Gay Science*, we need the knowledge of nature, particularly, of our human nature. The "will to self-determination, to evaluating on one's own account" (HH I, Preface 3) would be blind if it were not supported by a prior knowledge of the self. Self-knowledge (S2) is, therefore, necessary in order to make self-creation possible.

7

Let us recapitulate the picture which emerges from the analysis developed so far. As it is well known, Nietzsche maintains a profound scepticism about the possibility of self-knowledge. This scepticism – which can be traced back at least to the period of *Human, All Too Human*, if not to *On Truth and Lie in Non-Moral*

---

haben. So dröseln wir uns auf bis ins Unendliche zurück: sondern *uns selber machen*, aus allen Elementen eine Form *gestalten* – ist die Aufgabe! Immer die eines Bildhauers! Eines produktiven Menschen! *Nicht* durch Erkenntniß, sondern durch Übung und ein Vorbild werden wir *selber*! Die Erkenntniß hat bestenfalls den Werth eines Mittels!" (NL 1880, 7[213], KSA 9: 7)

22 See EH, Why I Am so Clever 9: "Becoming what you are presupposes that you do not have the slightest idea *what* you are. [...] where *nosce te ipsum* is the recipe for decline, then forgetting yourself, *misunderstanding* yourself, belittling, narrowing yourself, making yourself mediocre would be the essence of reason." As Heit (2013: 176) has pointed out, it is not clear whether the *Ecce Homo* formula "wie man wird, was man ist" should be read as a *descriptive* or *prescriptive* formula. In the first case, the phrase would describe the result of a process in which – according to the Aristotelian-Hegelian tradition – potentiality passes into actuality. The formula could be then paraphrased as "how one finally became, what one in reality had always been" (as Heit (p. 177) puts it: "Wie man schließlich wurde, was man in Wirklichkeit schon immer war"). In this way, we would ascribe to Nietzsche a kind of *essentialism of the subject* (Subjekt-Essentialismus), according to which self-becoming (Selbst-Werdung) is interpreted as self-realization (Selbst-Verwirklichung). This seems to be the kind of reading proposed by Leiter (1998 and 2002: 81–87; for a critique, see Owen and Ridley (2003) and Leiter's reply to their critiques (2007: 6–7)). On the contrary, those interpretations which read the formula as being prescriptive usually tend to lay emphasis on the process of self-creation (see, for instance, Nehamas 1983). Heit proposes to interpret this process in a genealogical way as the consequence of contingent events and circumstances which have led to the actual state (*Zustand*), a situation which represents an unstable equilibrium, not a final outcome. Thus, what one is, would be neither determined in advance, nor something whose essence is finally disclosed in the outcome of the process: on the contrary, the (momentary) outcome of the process *is* what one is.

Sense – is motivated by several reasons, among which the phenomenalism of the inner world. According to Nietzsche, it is wrong to assume that we have a privileged, direct access to this world and that we know the so-called "facts of consciousness". On the contrary, the inner world is as much as phenomenal, and therefore deceptive, as the external world.

Alongside the many passages in which Nietzsche shows his scepticism, there are, nonetheless, other passages which indicate a considerably different view. In particular, Nietzsche's rejection of the postulation of the mind – the subject-substratum which *does* the thinking – as a consequence of a false self-observation in a note from the late notebook, seems to suggest that a better or *truer* self-observation is not only possible, but it can also give us a more accurate picture of the inner world. This picture confirms, however, the initial scepticism towards self-knowledge, so that we have the following, paradoxical result: thanks to a better or *truer* self-knowledge we discover that the phenomenalism of the inner world is inevitable and, therefore, self-knowledge is a chimera.

To solve this apparent paradox, I have proposed to distinguish between two different meanings of "self" which can be found in Nietzsche's writings. In the first meaning of the term (S1), the word "self" refers to the content of the inner world (the whole plurality of thoughts, motives, affects, drives, and so on). In Nietzsche's opinion, the effort of attaining this kind of self-knowledge is nearly hopeless, but not impossible. In the second meaning of the term (S2), the word "self" refers to the functioning of the inner world (processes of thinking, willing, knowing, model of agency, etc.). Nietzsche's view on the possibility to achieve knowledge of the self so understood is less sceptical. Indeed, knowledge of S2 becomes possible thanks to three main ways strictly interconnected with each other: physiology (and physics), psychology and genealogy. If we take into account this distinction between S1 and S2, it becomes clear that the paradox mentioned above is not a real paradox, for Nietzsche is simply claiming that one of the consequences brought about by a better self-knowledge (S2) is that (direct) self-knowledge (S1) is unsuccessful.

The other, more relevant consequence which self-knowledge (S2) brings or should bring about is not of a theoretical, but rather of a practical kind. Indeed for Nietzsche, as sections BGE 32 and GS 335 show, the renewed self-knowledge has a clear performative character, leading to the overcoming of morality and to the creation of new tables of values. Section GS 335 particularly shows how, according to Nietzsche, physiology, psychology and genealogy are meant to work together. In fact, it is by considering the (physiological, psychological and genealogical) origin of a particular moral judgment that Nietzsche calls into question its value. In this sense, it is possible to claim that section GS 335 moves along the same path as that on which Nietzsche's "historical philosophy"

(HH I 1) moves, a path which leads from the investigation and the study of the origin (and evolution) of moral values to its critique. As Nietzsche famously puts it in the *Genealogy* (GM Preface 6): "we need a *critique* of moral values, *the value of these values should itself, for once, be examined* – and so we need to know about the conditions and circumstances under which the values grew up, developed and changed."

Whether this kind of reasoning falls foul of what is commonly known as the genetic fallacy is a complex question which I must leave open here.[23] Instead, I want to draw attention to the fact that Nietzsche's genealogical strategy is very far from being anachronistic or obsolete, as a superficial critic could be led to believe. On the contrary, as Dennett (1995: 182) puts it in his influential book on the theory of evolution, Nietzsche's *Genealogy* can be considered as "one of the first and still subtlest of the Darwinian investigations of the evolution of ethics". Let me conclude this paper by briefly explaining why I think that Dennett's emphatic claim can be taken seriously.

First of all, notice that genetic reasonings which attempt to support or discredit a belief on the grounds of its causal or historical genesis are not always fallacious. Indeed, although the charge of genetic fallacy still remains one of the favourite means to which critics of genetic reasoning tend to resort, it is safe to say with Klement (2002: 383) that "it is now often recognized that the causal history of a belief or position is sometimes relevant to its epistemic status and even its truth or falsity". In this sense, it would be clearly erroneous to believe that a "genealogical debunking" of morality is condemned *a priori* to failure. As Joyce (2006: 179) points out:

> Every belief has a causal history and it would be a ridiculous theory that implied that knowledge of a belief's etiology automatically undermines the confidence one should have in that belief. Yet it is clear that on some occasions knowledge of a belief's origins can undermine it.[24]

---

[23] For a discussion of this question, see Loeb 1995. Section GS 345, however, clearly shows that Nietzsche was aware that, as Geuss (2005: 158) puts it, genealogy "does not automatically imply the rejection of what is subjected to genealogical analysis".

[24] Joyce (2006: 179) makes his point clear with the help of the following thought experiment: suppose that there were a pill which makes us believe that x (Napoleon won Waterloo). Imagine that one day we discover that our belief that x was caused by having taken such a pill. Should this discovery undermine our faith in our belief that x? Joyce answer is that, "of course it should". Notice that Joyce is not claiming that our belief that x is *false*, but rather that our faith in it is undermined.

Secondly, Nietzsche was one of the first philosophers to understand the importance of a historical approach to philosophy.[25] In the *Twilight of the Idols* (TI Reason 1), he deemed the philosophers' tendency to *"dehistoricize [enthistorisiren]"* a concept, that is, to consider it *"sub specie aeterni"*, as one of their most dangerous idiosyncrasies. The historical approach, on the contrary, allowed Nietzsche to look at concepts not as fixed, immutable entities, but rather as originated at a certain moment of human history and, then, evolved. In other words, to paraphrase Prinz (2007: 242), the historical stance altered his epistemic stance towards concepts in the same way as the genealogical stance altered his epistemic stance towards moral values. I believe it is precisely this intuition about the potentially ground-breaking role of genealogy that makes Nietzsche's philosophy still so relevant nowadays. As Prinz puts it:

> Genealogy is a powerful critical tool, because it forces us to see held convictions in a new light. We tend to think fairly superficially about our moral values. We take our values to be obvious or received truths. We regard immoral behaviour as unnatural. When we adopt a historical stance we alter our epistemic stance toward value. (Prinz 2007: 242)

Thirdly and lastly, whereas Nietzsche-scholars have widely researched Nietzsche's stance towards Darwin or Darwinism, as well as the influence of this theory on his philosophy,[26] less attention has been given to how Nietzsche's philosophy could contribute to the contemporary debate on philosophy of biology or evolutionary ethics.[27] I will offer here only one, but telling example: Nietzsche's strategy of calling into question moral values through their genealogy can be considered as, *mutatis mutandis*, the very same strategy which philosophers such as Ruse (1986) and Joyce (2006) have deployed in order to defend an evolutionary anti-realist account in metaethics.[28] Obviously, whereas Ruse's and Joyce's genealogies seek to explain from a primarily *biological* perspective

---

25 For the role played by the reading of Rée's *The Origin of the Moral Sensations* and the "English psychologists" (GM I 1), see particularly Fornari 2006 (also available in German translation).
26 See, among many others, Stegmaier 1987, Moore 2002, Richardson 2004, Fornari 2006, Johnson 2010.
27 An exception is represented by Small 2007.
28 With this, I do not mean to overlook the important differences which differentiate the three accounts. Joyce himself (2006: 188) distinguishes his own strategy by that of Ruse. Prinz (2007) compares Ruse's attempt to discredit morality to Nietzsche's own attempt, and points out that "Ruse differs from Nietzsche in two key respects. First, he uses history (of our species) to argue that moral values are good for us, whereas Nietzsche uses history (of our culture) to argue that moral values are bad for us. Second, Ruse is trying to show that moral beliefs are false, whereas Nietzsche can be interpreted as a moral realist – moral rules are social constructions that are true in the way that social facts, such as economic facts, are true." Needless to say, the interpretation

why and how morality evolved, Nietzsche rather resorts to a *psychological* explanation. However, the aim is one and the same, namely that of showing that our moral beliefs are best explained by our evolutionary history or a slave revolt caused by resentment, rather than by a mysterious, human capacity to track moral truths. From this point of view, I believe, Nietzsche, Ruse and Joyce can be said to share a similar strategy and an analogous goal. In short, as one can see, there are several reasons for taking Dennett's claim (mentioned above) seriously and considering Nietzsche's genealogical work to be still relevant and actual in the panorama of philosophy today. [29]

References

Abel, Günter (2001) "Bewußtsein–Sprache–Natur. Nietzsches Philosophie des Geistes", in: *Nietzsche-Studien* 30, 1–43.
Dennett, Daniel (1995) *Darwin's Dangerous Idea. Evolution and the Meanings of Life*, London: Penguin.
Fornari, Maria Cristina (2006) *La morale evolutiva del gregge. Nietzsche legge Spencer e Mill*, Pisa: ETS.
Gerhardt, Volker (2011) "Selbstbegründung. Nietzsches Moral der Individualität", in: Volker Gerhardt (ed.), *Die Funken des freien Geistes. Neuere Aufsätze zu Nietzsches Philosophie der Zukunft*, eds. J.-C. Heilinger and N. Loukidelis, Berlin/New York: De Gruyter. [Originally published in *Nietzsche-Studien* 21 (1992), 28–49].
Geuss, Raymond (2005) *Outside Ethics*, Princeton: Princeton University Press.
Heit, Helmut (2013) "'…was man ist'? Zur Wirklichkeit des Subjekts bei Nietzsche", in: *Nietzscheforschung* 20, 173–192.
Hussain, Nadeem J.Z. (2013) "Nietzsche's Metaethical Stance", in: K. Gemes and J. Richardson (eds.), *The Oxford Handbook of Nietzsche*. Oxford: Oxford University Press, 389–414.
Janaway, Christopher (2007) *Beyond Selflessness. Reading Nietzsche's Genealogy*. Oxford: Oxford University Press.
Johnson, Dirk R. (2010) *Nietzsche's Anti-Darwinism*, Cambridge: Cambridge University Press.
Joyce, Richard (2006) *The Evolution of Morality*, Cambridge, MA: MIT Press.
Klement, Kevin C. (2002) "When Is Genetic Reasoning Not Fallacious?", in: *Argumentation* 16, 383–400.
Leiter, Brian (1998) "The Paradox of Fatalism and Self-Creation in Nietzsche", in: C. Janaway (ed.), *Willing and Nothingness. Schopenhauer as Nietzsche's Educator*. Oxford: Clarendon Press.

---

of Nietzsche as a moral realist is much more problematic and debated than Prinz seems to be aware of.
29 For their comments on earlier versions of this paper, I am indebted to João Constâncio and Paul Katsafanas.

Leiter, Brian (2002) *Nietzsche on Morality*, London/New York: Routledge.
Leiter, Brian (2007) "Nietzsche's Theory of the Will", in: *Philosophers' Imprint* 7, 1–15.
Loeb, P.S. (1995) "Is There a Genetic Fallacy in Nietzsche's Genealogy of Morals?", in: *International Studies in Philosophy* 27(3), 125–141.
Lupo, Luca (2007) *Le colombe dello scettico. Riflessioni di Nietzsche sulla coscienza negli anni 1880–1888*, Pisa: ETS.
Moore, Gregory (2002) *Nietzsche, Biology and Metaphor*, Cambridge: Cambridge University Press.
Müller-Buck, Renate (2002) "'Der einzige Psychologe, von dem ich etwas zu lernen hatte': Nietzsche liest Dostojewskij", in: *Dostoevsky Studies, New Series* 6, 89–118.
Nehamas, Alexander (1983) "How One Becomes What One Is", in: *The Philosophical Review* 92(3), 385–417.
Nietzsche, Friedrich (1996) *Selected Letters of Friedrich Nietzsche*, Indianapolis: Hackett.
Owen, David/Ridley, Aaron (2003) "On Fate", in: *International Studies in Philosophy* 35(3), 63–78.
Pippin, Robert B. (2010) *Nietzsche, Psychology, and First Philosophy*, Chicago/London: University of Chicago Press.
Plato (1914) *Euthyphro, Apology, Crito, Phaedo, Phaedrus*, Cambridge, MA: Harvard University Press.
Prinz, Jesse (2007) *The Emotional Construction of Morals*, Oxford: Oxford University Press.
Richardson, John (2004) *Nietzsche's New Darwinism*, New York/Oxford: Oxford University Press.
Ruse, Michael (1986) *Taking Darwin Seriously*, New York: Blackwell.
Schlimgen, Erwin (1998) *Nietzsches Theorie des Bewußtseins*, Berlin/New York: De Gruyter.
Small, Robin (2007) "Nietzsche's Evolutionary Ethics", in: G. von Tevenar (ed.), *Nietzsche and Ethics*. Bern: Peter Lang. pp. 119–135.
Stegmaier, Werner (1987) "Darwin, Darwinismus, Nietzsche. Zum Problem der Evolution", in: *Nietzsche-Studien* 15, 264–287.
Stellino, Paolo (2015) "Notas sobre la lectura nietzscheana de *Apuntes del subsuelo*", in: *Estudios Nietzsche* 11, 113–125.
Van Tongeren, Paul et al. (2004) *Nietzsche Wörterbuch*. Vol. 1, Berlin/New York: De Gruyter.

Brian Leiter
23 Moralities Are a *Sign-Language of the Affects*[1]

1 Sign-languages and symptoms

My title comes from section 187 of Nietzsche's *Beyond Good and Evil*, though the theme in question – that moralities are "a sign-language of the affects" – is a pervasive one in Nietzsche's work throughout the 1880s and central to his moral psychology. In *Daybreak*, he declares that "our moral judgments and evaluations … are only images and fantasies based on a physiological process unknown to us" (D 119). In *The Gay Science*, he suggests that, "Answers to the questions about the *value* of existence … may always be considered first of all as the symptoms of certain bodies" (GS Preface 2). Again, in *Beyond Good and Evil*, he tells us that a philosopher's "morality" simply bears "decisive witness to … the innermost drives of his nature" (BGE 6). In the *Genealogy*, Nietzsche famously claims that "our … values … grow from us with the same inevitability as fruits borne on the tree" (GM Preface 2). In *Twilight of the Idols*, Nietzsche remarks that "[J]udgments of value … have value only as symptoms" (TI Socrates 2). And in a *Nachlass* note of 1885–86, he says "Moral judgments [are] symptoms and sign languages which betray the process of physiological prosperity or failure" (WP 258).

Nietzsche has two main metaphors for describing moralities or systems of value – that of *sign-language* (*Zeichensprache*) and of *symptom* (*Symptome*) – and two main idioms in which to explain the referent of the sign-language or cause of the symptom, one psychological involving affects (*Affekten*), feelings (*Gefühle*), or drives (*Triebe*), and the other physiological. The physiological idiom is undoubtedly important to Nietzsche, influenced as he was by the German Materialist movement in Germany in the mid-nineteenth century,[2] but it seems equally clear that, apart from calling attention to the possibility of physiological explanations for evaluative orientations, Nietzsche makes no real intel-

---

[1] This chapter is a reprint (with permission of Cambridge University Press) of Brian Leiter's article, "Moralities Are *a Sign-Language of the Affects*", *Social Philosophy & Policy* 30: 1/2 Winter 2013, pp. 237–258. Brian Leiter presented a first version of this article in March 2012 at the Universidade Nova de Lisboa, Faculdade de Ciências Sociais e Humanas, within the context of the research project, "Nietzsche and the Contemporary Debate on the Self". [*Editors' note*]
[2] See Leiter (2002: 63–71).

lectual contribution to this kind of explanation.³ Like Freud, Nietzsche plainly thinks that some class of mental phenomena are physically explicable, though, unlike Freud, he was fairly explicit in rejecting any type-identity of mental and physical states of the person.⁴ But Nietzsche is like Freud in another respect, namely, that the explanatory idiom in which he does most of his work is a *psychological* one, and it is on that idiom we shall focus here.

What could it mean to diagnose particular evaluative judgments, or whole systems of value, as a "sign-language" or "symptom"? The idea of a "symptom" presents the more straightforward case. Consider: my *sore throat* is the symptom of a *viral infection*. That means: the symptom (the soreness of the throat) is *caused by* the virus. So if moral judgments are *symptoms* of certain psychological states, that means those states are *causes* of the moral judgments. Of course, the relationship is not *simply* causal: rather the symptoms count as *evidence* for their cause, because they reveal something about the psychological states that give rise to them.

Sign-languages are, at first blush, a bit different. A sign-language is some system of symbols or signs that have semantic content, that is, have some *meaning* in virtue of *representing* something else.⁵ If I raise just my pointer and middle finger, that *means* either peace or victory. The referent of a sign with representational content need not, however, be the cause of that content, though there is certainly one familiar, contemporary view of semantic content in which that would be the case. But like a symptom, the sign does stand in some kind of meaningful inferential relation with its referent (or cause): in both cases, the referent, or cause, is expressed by the symptom or sign. Since Nietzsche uses the metaphors of "symptom" and "sign-language" interchangeably, and since there is no evidence he had a well-developed semantic view, it is natural to understand them the same way. Thus, in what follows, I will assume that the claim that a morality is a "symptom" or "sign-language" of X means that X is the *cause* of the morality (or the cause of some person making a particular evaluative or moral judgment) and, moreover, it is a cause whose existence can be correctly inferred from the symptom or sign.⁶

---

3 He acknowledges as much in the "Note" at the end of GM I when he calls for a prize to encourage physiologists and doctors to study the effects of different values on persons.
4 Leiter (2002: 24–25).
5 There are non-representationalist views of semantic content (think Robert Brandom or Huw Price, for example), but there is no reason, of course, to think Nietzsche had such a view in mind, or, indeed, that he had loyalty to any particular theory of meaning. It is thus best to interpret his remarks in the most natural, 'ordinary-language' way that still allows us to make sense of his terminology.
6 I will thus assume that to the extent a symptom or sign *expresses* a meaning, it does so in virtue of how it is caused by the underlying item of which it is a sign or symptom.

What, then, of the psychological causes on offer? Nietzsche refers, as noted above, to just three: affects, feelings, and drives. I take *affects* and *feelings* to refer usually to the same kind of mental state for Nietzsche,[7] while I will construe drives, following Katsafanas (2013), as *dispositions to have affective responses under certain conditions*. We will consider each of these in turn, before taking up the reasons for thinking that, suitably construed, moralities *really are* symptomatic of our affects.[8]

2 Feelings and affects

In *Daybreak*, "moral feelings" (*Moralische Gefühle*) are said to be inculcated when "children observe in adults inclinations for and aversions to certain actions and, as born apes, *imitate* these inclinations [*Neigungen*] and aversions [*Abneigungen*]; in later life they find themselves full of these acquired and well-exercised affects [*Affekten*] and consider it only decent to try to account for and justify them" (D 34). We may bracket for the moment the astute concluding observation – about the impulse to supply post-hoc rationalizations for evaluative judgments produced by a non-rational mechanism – in order to focus for now on what this passage tells us about Nietzsche's conception of affects and moral judgment.

Moral feelings or affects, in the passage under consideration, are equated with "inclinations for and aversions to certain actions", or, more precisely, with the mental state, whatever it is, that motivates one to perform certain actions or avoid certain other actions.[9] Nietzsche's ontology of the mind thus includes (unsurprisingly) mental states that are *motivationally effective*, at least in the sense that they produce what I will call henceforth *motivational oomph* (or *push*), that is, they incline towards or avert away from certain acts, even if they

---

[7] There are occasional exceptions, e.g., BGE 19, but these are somewhat anomalous.
[8] Of course, many different things might be symptomatic of our affects: e.g., our facial expressions, our behaviors. Nietzsche thinks, however, that moralities reveal things about our affects and drives that are especially important and which we would not otherwise recognize *unless* we interpreted moral judgments as expressive of affects. This will become clearer in the discussion that follows, below.
[9] There is a certain affinity here to aspects of Stoic moral psychology, with which Nietzsche, as a classicist, was certainly familiar, though he rejects the ultimately rationalist elements of the Stoic view. Brennan (2003) is a useful overview. The relationship between Nietzsche's view and that of the Stoics requires independent treatment.

are not ultimately successful in producing action. In this respect, Nietzsche's usage is quite intelligible to us: we typically presume that *affects* or *feelings* are characterized, in part, by their ability to produce *motivational oomph*, and, indeed, the fact that they do so is one of the main points thought to count in favor of meta-ethical views that understand moral judgments to involve essentially the expression of feelings (a point to which we will return).

It is equally a part of ordinary usage to take feelings to have another crucial characteristic: namely, that they are phenomenologically distinctive. There is something *it feels like* to be inclined to stop the child from sticking his hand in the fire, and there is something *it feels like* to be inclined to avoid killing a child. A *non-cognitivist* view of affects claims that they can be fully individuated by their distinctive phenomenal feel; a cognitivist view denies that, claiming, instead, that to individuate the affect one also needs to consider some aspect of its *cognitive* (i.e., truth-evaluable) content, such as a belief. Cognitivist views of emotions, notoriously, are forced to deny that human infants can have emotions, since they lack the concepts necessary for having truth-evaluable judgments (cf. Deigh 1994). That infants cannot have emotions might seem a *reductio* of the cognitivist position, at least to anyone who has ever cared for an infant. But less anecdotally, cognitivism about the emotions runs up against a large body of psychological research showing that, as Jesse Prinz puts it, "emotions can arise without judgment, thoughts, or other cognitive mediators" (2007: 57). While it may be doubtful that qualitative feel can distinguish all emotional states (Prinz's example is differentiating "anger" from "indignation" [2007: 52]), that is not necessarily pertinent to Nietzsche's concerns. For Nietzsche locates the *affective* source of moral judgment, in the first instance, in fairly basic or simple mental states of *inclination* and *aversion*, and it seems quite plausible that there is something it feels like to be *inclined towards* X or *averted away from* Y, even if the relevant *qualia* might be thought inadequate to pick out all conceptual nuances we might want to apply to such cases. It is also possible, of course, that our conceptually nuanced distinctions between, say, *anger* and *indignation* are explanatorily otiose with respect to the *motivational oomph* associated with the feeling in question. (The crucial moral emotion of "guilt" presents a special case, however, to which we will return shortly.)

Perhaps more pertinent is the other problem that is supposed to afflict non-cognitivist views of feelings or affects, namely, how to account for our propensity to think emotional responses can be assessed as warranted or not (cf. Prinz 2007: 60ff.). Even in infants, of course, emotional responses have causal triggers: the infant *sees* a scary monster and reacts by crying in fear. The infant's *fear* has an *intentional content*: it is *about* something, namely, the scary monster. We might believe the infant is wrong to be afraid (i.e., what the infant sees is not dangerous, since it is only make-believe), but that does not change the fact that the infant experiences upset and fear. I believe that a child is about to stick his hand in the flame, and so I *feel inclined* to stop him. "Feel inclined" understates the character of the feeling, of course: *I feel I must* stop him. But the fact that there is a causal relationship between a mental state with cognitive content and an affective response, does not show that to *identify* the affect one must understand it to be constituted, in whole or even in part, by a *cognitive* component. We need to account for the *intentionality* of emotions, to be sure, but that does not mean we have to identify emotions with *judgments* or, more generally, with propositional attitudes like belief and desire. It might suffice to introduce a kind of explanatorily primitive mental state, as Peter Goldie (2002: 19) famously proposes, like "feeling towards", one that captures both the *intentionality* of emotional states *and* their distinctive qualitative character.

So feeling inclined to do X or averse to doing Y can have a distinctive phenomenal character, even if the causal trigger for the feeling is a false belief of the agent with the distinctive feeling. When we criticize the resulting emotion, perhaps, then, we are making a different normative judgment, something like: a correct belief about the facts ought not cause such an affective response. Consider: the infant falsely perceives (without any conceptual content) the family dog as dangerous, and so bursts into tears. We think the infant is *mistaken*, because we know that the family dog is not dangerous. But we don't criticize the infant for having an unwarranted affective response, rather we console the infant. Why? Perhaps because we don't think the infant is *epistemically responsible* for its false cognition of the family dog as dangerous. But when I react with anger to a perceived slight by the store clerk that, in reality, was nothing of the kind, I can be criticized not because anger is anything other than non-cognitive, and not because my "belief that I've been slighted" is a causal trigger for my anger, but because I am epistemically culpable for having a false belief, one that produces unhappy consequences (my anger, a fight with the clerk at the store, an unpleasant scene, etc.).

Yet it seems I can also be criticized for responding with anger even when my belief was correct, i.e., when the store clerk *really was* rude. How can that criticism make sense if the cognitive belief is just a causal trigger for an evaluative/affective response that has no cognitive content? The obvious answer is that such judgments are, themselves, the expression of other non-cognitive attitudes or feelings, such as an inclination towards non-aggressive responses to insults or an aversion to aggressive ones (we might call the latter the "Christian attitude"). Of course, if we view such criticism as making a cognitive, rather than non-cognitive, claim, then we will be forced towards an error-theoretic interpretation of such judgments (that is, we will have to interpret all such judgments as false). But on the general Nietzschean view, it is surely natural to treat such normative criticisms as, themselves, yet more expressions of affects or feelings.[10]

I belabor these points because I want to argue that Nietzsche's view of affects or feelings is basically *non-cognitivist*: he thinks our basic affects of inclination and aversion are marked by a distinctive conscious, qualitative feel. And he thinks such qualitatively distinctive *feels* are the causal root of our moral judgments, even if those fully articulated judgements are influenced by other factors, to which we will turn momentarily. Given that Nietzsche focuses mainly on *inclination* and *aversion towards* as the crucial affective states, the claim that they can be individuated in non-cognitive terms is especially plausible. But we can now also see how the social practice of assessing such feelings as warranted or unwarranted can be compatible with the non-cognitive character of the feeling: to deem them warranted or unwarranted is either (1) to render an epistemic judgment about the cognitive judgment that is the causal trigger for the non-cognitive state, or (2) to express a meta-affect (i.e., an affect *about* an affect) about someone else's affective response to a causal trigger.

3 Drives

The other key element of Nietzsche's ontology of the mind, for purposes of explaining motivation and action, is the notion of a *drive*, which, following Katsafanas (2013), we will treat as a *disposition to have a particular affective response under certain circumstances*. Thus, the sex drive would be a disposition to become sexually aroused in the presence of an attractive member of the opposite or same sex.[11] The important relationship between drives and affects is usefully illustrated by this passage from *Daybreak*:

> The same drive evolves into the painful feeling of *cowardice* under the impress of the reproach custom has imposed upon this drive; or into the pleasant feeling of *humility* if it happens that a custom such as the Christian has taken it to its heart and called it *good*. That is to say, it is attended by either a good or a bad conscience! In it itself it has, *like every drive*, neither this moral character nor any moral character at all, nor even a definite

---

10 As I discuss below, I actually think we should resist ascribing any *semantic* view to Nietzsche, so the claims in this paragraph should, strictly speaking, be treated as *explanatory* of moral judgment, rather than as part of a semantics of moral judgment.
11 The discharge of that drive would then involve acting on the sexual arousal or urge, but the drive can manifest itself in an affective response, even when it is not satisfied.

attendant sensation of pleasure or displeasure: it acquires all this, as its second nature, only when it enters into relations with drives already baptized good or evil or is noted as a quality of beings the people has already evaluated and determined in a moral sense.... (D 38)

In the particular example on offer from Nietzsche, the same *drive* is said to have the potential to give rise to two different moral feelings, that of *cowardice* (which has an unpleasant valence) or *humility* (a pleasant valence), depending on the cultural context. The drive in question must be something like, *a disposition to avoid offending dangerous enemies*, which, if experienced by a Homeric Greek would then give rise to feelings of self-contempt for being a coward and, if experienced by a Christian, would be experienced as the admirable virtue of humility. Cultures, partly through the mechanisms of parental inculcation already noted (as well as concurrent social pressures), teach individuals to have particular affective responses to the very same drive. Notice, however, that we now have two layers of affects here: first, there is the affect of *aversion towards offending dangerous enemies* which is produced by the drive itself, but *then* there is the distinctively *moral affect* of feeling ashamed (as the Homeric Greek does) or proud (as the Christian does) of that affective response. The *moral affect*, then, is more complicated than what I will henceforth call "the basic affect" of inclination or aversion. The *feeling of being a coward*, on this account, represents the combination of a *feeling of aversion towards offending a dangerous enemy*, conjoined with a meta-feeling of contempt or disgust for having that original feeling. The meta-feeling is, at bottom, a feeling of aversion away from the basic affect, though perhaps to individuate it correctly we will need to add some kind of *belief* about why that basic feeling of aversion is contemptible: e.g., the belief that Homeric men slay their offending enemies, rather than cower before them. Perhaps this is also what Nietzsche is getting at when he writes: "[B]ehind feelings there stand judgments [*Urtheile*] and evaluations [*Werthschätzungen*] which we inherit in the form of feelings (inclinations, aversions). The inspiration born of a feeling is the grandchild of a judgment – and often of a false judgment!" (D 35). So, for example, the Christian judges that a good person *chooses* to display humility, a trait admirable in the eyes of God, and thus when the Christian experiences the basic affect of aversion towards offending a dangerous enemy, he then experiences the meta-affect of a positive inclination or valence towards that basic affect: he is proud of his humility. The Christian then inculcates those same affective responses in his children, so that their feelings of inclination and aversion are traceable back to a false judgment, i.e., the judgment that there is a God who thinks humility is a virtuous trait, as well as the false belief that the "humility" of the Christian is a free choice, rather than a reaction he can not avoid having.¹² As Nietzsche observes, "we are all irrational" in that we "still draw the conclusions of judgments we consider false, of teachings in which we no longer believe – our feelings make us do it" (D 99), a claim well-supported by the recent empirical literature on "moral dumbfounding", which finds that people will often remain attached to a moral judgment, even when all their reasons for it are defeated (cf. Haidt 2001). (We will return to that literature at the end.)

If to individuate the meta-affect correctly, we need to take account of the cognitive judgment that informs it, then our picture would be complicated somewhat: we would have non-cognitivism about basic affects, and a cognitivist view about meta-affects. On the other hand, it might suffice for causal explanation of behavior to individuate only the meta-affect of aversion or inclination towards the basic affect. In other words, what might matter for explaining the behavior of the Homeric Greek afflicted with the basic affect of aversion towards giving offense to dangerous enemies is that he feels a motivational push *against* acting on that basic affect, i.e., he feels aversion towards his basic aversion towards offending dangerous enemies. His cognitive beliefs may be causal triggers for the meta-affect, but we need only understand the meta-affect to understand his behavior.

Is that right? When the Homeric agent judges his aversion towards offending a stronger enemy as "cowardice", and feels "shame" or "guilt" about it, that judgment is a symptom of his basic affect of aversion towards offending dangerous enemies and his meta-affect of aversion towards the basic affect. But is it really explanatorily idle whether or not that meta-affect is one of "guilt" or "shame"? Take a slightly different Greek example. Recall that Oedipus, upon realizing he has killed his father and married his mother, gouges out his eyes, because he is overwhelmed with *shame* and so does not want to look into anyone's eyes again. Of course, Oedipus did not freely and intentionally choose to kill his father and marry his mother, so his overriding moral emotion is not one of guilt – but what if it were? Eliminating the possibility of human eye contact would not relieve the pain of *guilt*, since guilt, as usually construed,

---

12 Recall GM I 13: "When out of the vengeful cunning of powerlessness the oppressed, downtrodden, violated say to themselves: 'let us be different from the evil ones, namely good! And good is what everyone is who does not do violence, who injures no one, who doesn't attack, who doesn't retaliate, who leaves vengeance to God, who keeps himself concealed, as we do, who avoids all evil, and in general demands very little of life, like us, the patient, humble, righteous' – it means, when listened to coldly, and without prejudice, actually nothing more than: 'we weak ones are simply weak; it is good if we do nothing *for which we are not strong enough.*'"

does not require an observer. The agent who experiences the meta-aversion (of "guilt") to the basic aversion of not marrying one's mother or killing one's father would believe he was *responsible* for having done this and thus blameworthy for his lapse of judgment. But, of course, Oedipus doesn't believe any of that, since he did not freely do what he did; he was fated to do so, which is why his meta-aversion is that of shame rather than guilt. So his meta-affective aversion towards his aversion towards killing his father and marrying his mother is of a particular kind: it is *ashamed aversion*, which can be blunted by eye-gauging, rather than *guilty aversion*, which could not be. It thus seems that *sometimes* the distinctively moral emotion is constituted in part by a particular cognitive content (for example, the one–whatever it is precisely–that separates shame from guilt), and so Nietzsche can not be a thorough-going non-cognitivist about the affects underlying moral judgment, even if he is a non-cognitivist about basic affects.

That conclusion would, however, explain why Nietzsche holds out the hope that attacking the falsity of the judgments that are the "grandparents" of the meta-affects could make a difference: "We have to *learn to think differently* [umzulernen]–in order at least, perhaps very late on, to attain even more: *to feel differently* [umzufühlen]" (D 103). To be sure, it could be that correcting such mistaken judgments could make a difference to even non-cognitive affects, insofar as those judgments *happen to be* causally connected to the affects. But if such judgments are partly constitutive of the meta-affects, then the attack on the truth of the metaphysical presuppositions about agency (such as free will) that I have argued elsewhere (2002: 87–101) is a key part of Nietzsche's critique of morality would be especially relevant.

None of the preceding considerations affect my basic thesis, however: namely, that for Nietzsche, moral judgments are produced by affective responses. The complication we have noted is that drives give rise to feelings of inclination or aversion, but *not* to moral affects proper, the latter arising from the influence of culture (e.g., Homeric Greece vs. Christian) which yield meta-affective responses to the basic affects of inclination and aversion. Moral judgments are *still* symptoms of the affects, but the affects now have two different sources: there is the affect of inclination or aversion towards particular actions or things or persons in the world, and then there are affective responses to those basic affects–where the latter are largely inculcated by the local culture and *perhaps* also individuated by their cognitive content. The latter observation also explains why Nietzsche expresses the optimistic view that revising our beliefs might actually lead to a revision of our feelings, i.e., those meta-affects or meta-feelings whose object is partly individuated by the cognitive judgment in question.

Someone might object, of course, that if moral judgments are indeed symptoms of *affects,* but some of these affects (the meta- ones) are either contingently or perhaps constitutively (in the case of, say, guilt vs. shame) tied to beliefs, then moral judgments are not *only* the causal products of affective responses: they do depend on what people *believe*, not simply how they *feel*. That might suggest that Nietzsche's view of moral judgment would have to be tempered to say that moralities are symptoms of *affects, but not only affects*. I actually think Nietzsche has available a more ambitious response, since he also seems to hold the view that what I will call "belief fixation"–that is, the doxastic state in which an agent *takes a belief seriously enough that he will act on it*–is itself dependent on affective investment in the belief (think, e.g., of his explanation of how a desire to punish motivates belief in free will). I will not be able to defend that view here, and it will suffice for the rest of the paper if the reader is persuaded that moralities are symptomatic of affects, even if in some cases, they are symptomatic of affects *plus certain beliefs*.

4 Affects, drives, and the doctrine of types

How does the preceding picture of affects and drives, and their role in moral judgment, fit with what I have called Nietzsche's "Doctrine of Types" (Leiter 2002: 8–10), that is, his view that each person has some relatively stable set of psycho-physical traits that figure centrally in the explanation of his behaviors and values? The *psychological* component of a person's type consists of *drives*, as suggested by the famous passage on "great" philosophers in *Beyond Good and Evil*, which concludes that the "morals" of a philosopher "bear decided and decisive witness to *who he is*–which means, in what order of rank the innermost drives of his nature stand with respect to each other" (BGE 6). Yet, as we learned from *Daybreak*, drives stand in some relationship to both *basic* and *moral* affects (D 38, D 109), and the latter reflect–given the account in *Daybreak*–the influence of parental and cultural conditioning.[13] Yet, as I have argued in previous work (Leiter 2002: 26), Nietzsche is not shy about ascribing *essential* aspects to humans, as when he refers to "the weakness of the weak ...–I mean [their] *essence* [*Wesen*]" (GM I 13) or when he writes in 1886 that "assuming that one is

---

13 See, e.g., D 10: "[W]e arrive [at our evaluation, which causes actions] as *children*, and rarely learn to change our view; most of us are our whole lives long the fools of the way we acquired in childhood of judging our neighbors (their minds, rank, morality, whether they are exemplary or reprehensible) and of finding it necessary to pay homage to their evaluations."

a person, one *necessarily* [*nothwendig*] has the philosophy that belongs to that person" (GS Preface 2). A philosophy would only *necessarily* belong to a particular person if there were facts about that person – such as facts about his drives – that necessitated certain moral views, which, in turn, necessitated a certain philosophical position in their service. The impression that at least some part of the individual's psychic make-up is "hard-wired" (as the contemporary metaphor has it) is reinforced by Nietzsche's Lamarckianism, that is, his embrace of the view (widely accepted at the time) that culturally acquired traits of the parents can then be inherited by the offspring (cf. GS 143; BGE 213). The irony, from the standpoint of the early twenty-first century, is that while we now know Lamarck was wrong, the *heritability* of characterological traits – such as a propensity towards violence (or "aggressive antisocial behavior" as psychologists usually call it) – is, in fact, well-established in behavioral genetics (see Knobe/Leiter 2007).[14] Of course, such traits naturally have a certain culturally specific component that might seem to lend support to Lamarckianism, yet they are not actually *inherited*, since the trait itself has no gene. But such traits can be *heritable*, and thus mimick the Lamarckian result, because of the interplay of genetically determined traits and cultural milieu. Let me explain.

Here is a simple example:[15] a gene for having a large nose can be inherited, but in a cultural environment where large noses are objects of ridicule (such that their possessors end up being quite shy), shyness, as a character trait, will turn out to be *heritable*, not because of a "shyness gene" but because of a "large nose gene" conjoined with a stable cultural environment which interacts with the inherited phylogenetic features of human organisms to produce the psychological attribute. If, like Lamarck, you do not know that genes are the mechanism by which evolution by natural selection operates, one might well think that culturally acquired traits can be inherited.

Nietzsche knew as little about the difference between inheritance and heritability as Lamarck, but that is not the point here. The point is that it is not crazy to think of even character traits as among the type-facts about a person, at least against the background of a particular cultural environment. So, to return to our

---

14 Typically, these studies are conducted either by looking at twins (comparing monozygotic to dizygotic) or by looking at adopted children. One study, for example, using 1,523 pairs of twins found a heritability of aggressive antisocial behavior of 70% (Eley/Lichtenstein/Stevenson 1999). Other studies yield percentages that are lower but still surprisingly high – for example, 60% (Edelbrock/Rende/Plomin/Thompson 1995) and 49% (Deater-Deckard/Plomin 1999). These huge effect sizes cannot plausibly be ascribed to experimental artifacts or measurement error, as opposed to genetic influences.

15 And a memorable one, which I owe to Jesse Prinz.

earlier example, if the drive to avoid dangerous enemies is inherited – in the sense that an aversion towards such enemies is "hard-wired" or part of a person's type – and the cultural environment is more-or-less stable in its Christian values, then it will certainly *appear* that "humility" is a "hard-wired" part of the slavish type of person.

Of course, the crucial idea here is that Nietzsche thinks certain affective responses are either inherited or heritable, such that they are facts about an agent over which the agent has no control. In the case of drives that give rise to basic affects, they can be simply inheritable; in the case of meta-affects, as long as they are heritable, the situation will be the same for the agent. I think it is clear that something like this is Nietzsche's view – not a surprising view in the nineteenth century, of course – but it is worth emphasizing that it is also not, in light of subsequent research, an implausible view.[16]

---

16 A different kind of question can also be raised about Nietzsche's picture of moral psychology: namely, why should we think drives exist in the first place? In many passages, after all, Nietzsche notes how ignorant persons are about the drives that constitute them: "However far a man may go in self-knowledge, nothing however can be more incomplete than his image of the totality of *drives* which constitute his being", as he puts it in *Daybreak* (119). Since drives are not identified directly by their conscious, qualitative feel, the grounds for positing their presence must amount to something like an inference to the best explanation of observable behavior and conscious feelings. Yet Nietzsche is notoriously promiscuous with his ontology of drives; in *Daybreak* alone he refers to "the drive to restfulness, or the fear of disgrace and other evil consequences" (D 109); the hunger drive (D 119); "moral ... drives" (D 119); "our drive to tenderness or humorousness or adventurousness or ... our desire [*Verlangen*] for music and mountains" (D 119); "the drive to praise or blame" (D 140); the drive to feel sorrow or sadness (when triggered by music) (D 142); and "the drive to attachment and care for others (the 'sympathetic affection')" (D 143). On top of that, Nietzsche also claims that drives vary in their degree of *strength* or *vehemence* (*Heftigkeit*) (D 109) – that is, how badly they need to be satisfied – and that this quality of drives is important to their role in explaining moral judgment and action (cf. D 119).

How are we to appraise Nietzsche's promiscuous ontology of drives? There is not even the pretense of demonstrating the explanatory need for some of the drives he posits, many of which are on a par with Moliere's doctor's explanation that opium makes one sleep because of its dormitive power! It is worth bearing in mind, however, that the interest of Nietzsche's hypothesis about the role of drives in moral judgment does *not* depend on any specific hypothesis about particular drives; it turns, rather, on the correctness of the basic model of the mind. We may view some of the specific claims simply as "placeholders" for a more adequate psychology, and it is reasonable to think some of the specific drives Nietzsche posits are explanatorily otiose and would drop out of a more systematic account. (I am indebted here to Roger Eichorn.)

Drives for Nietzsche are (per Katsafanas's formulation) "dispositions that induce affective orientation in the agent". These affective orientations structure how the world appears to us evaluatively: they influence, for example, "perceptual salience", the features of a situation that come to the fore for the agent (because the drive focuses attention on them). (Cf. D 119.

5 Is it true that moralities are just a sign-language of the affects?

We have now given a systematic exposition of Nietzsche's idea that moral judgments are symptoms or sign-languages of the affects, in the sense that moral judgments are caused by affects and meta-affects, which are the joint product of nature and culture, as it were. This is, I have argued, Nietzsche's view, but the more pressing philosophical question is: why should we accept it?

The idea that moral judgments are caused by affective responses has three kinds of evidence in its favor: first, sincere moral judgments – not the lip-service to morality that is the stuff of so much public life – motivate action (or at least produce what we earlier called *motivational oomph*); second, it is a view of moral judgments compatible with one plausible metaphysics of morality, namely, anti-realism (the view that there are no objective moral facts), a view Nietzsche himself explicitly endorses; and third, it squares best with existing empirical research on the psychology of moral judgment and moral disagreement. The latter two considerations are not decisive, of course, since it might turn out that Nietzsche held false views, if it happened that moral realism were true or that empirical psychology gave us a different account of moral judgment and disagreement. But if there is good textual evidence that Nietzsche held a view that also seems to be true, then that seems an additional reason of interpretive charity to ascribe it to him. Let us take these considerations up in turn.

First: sincere moral judgments motivate action or, at least, produce motivational oomph. If I genuinely judge that X is morally wrong or Y is morally right, I feel motivated, respectively, to prevent X or bring about Y, even if I fail to do either – cowardice, weakness of will, timidity and so on may all intervene to prevent people from acting on their moral judgments. But what is striking is that

---

Humeans also have a similar view: see, e.g., Sinhababu (2009: 469–470), discussing the "attention-direction" aspect of desire.) Katsafanas also argues that Nietzschean drives share two features of drives on the Freudian view (unsurprisingly given Freud's interest in Nietzsche). First, drives have a kind of constancy that particular desires do not. The music you desired to listen to in your 20s may no longer appeal in your 40s; but the hunger drive keeps coming back whether you are 20 or 40. Second, drives do not depend on an external stimulus to be aroused. External stimuli can give rise to a desire to eat or to have sex, to be sure, but those same desires can simply arise in the absence of any stimuli. It is particularly useful to distinguish, as Freud does (33), between the *Ziel* (aim) of the drive (e.g., sex, eating) and the *Objekt* of the drive (e.g., this woman, this bit of food). Insofar as a drive is aroused not by an external stimulus, it will then seek out an object for its realization – and in so doing impose a "valuation" on the object.

those who sincerely affirm a moral judgment at least feel a motivational tug in its direction. That fact has long been thought to be one of the strongest reasons in favor of anti-realist views of moral judgment. More precisely, it has been thought to count in favor of *non-cognitivist* views of moral judgments, according to which such judgments simply express motivationally effective mental states, such as desires and feelings, rather than mental states like belief that only represent aspects of the world. Nietzsche, as I have argued previously (Leiter 2000), does not have a considered view about the semantics of moral judgment, which is hardly surprising given that the issue was not a live one prior to the twentieth century, and given that it is one that turns on such subtle linguistic considerations that many philosophers have now gravitated towards "hybrid" views in which the correct analysis of the semantics is thought to incorporate both cognitivist and non-cognitivist elements.[17] I suggest we prescind from these issues, both for interpretive reasons (Nietzsche has no real view on them) and philosophical ones. On the philosophical front, remember that the primary consideration thought to militate against a non-cognitivist interpretation of the semantics has always been the Frege-Geach problem, the problem of how to explain the truth-preserving properties of inferences involving moral propositions embedded in the antecedents of conditionals (e.g., "If stealing is wrong, then it is wrong to encourage John to steal"; but "stealing is wrong"; so "it is wrong to encourage John to steal"). But it would be mad to let our metaphysics – our most plausible account of what really exists – be driven by linguistic practices: why let the semantic tail wag the metaphysical dog? As Crispin Wright observed twenty years ago, if metaphysical anti-realism about moral facts conjoined with non-cognitivism about the semantics of moral judgments had "absolutely no prospect of a satisfactory construal of conditionals with moral antecedents that could hardly be decisive. Rather, whatever case there was for [this kind of anti-realist view] would become potentially revisionary of our ordinary and moral linguistic practice...." (Wright 1988: 31). If we do not want to "bite the bullet" on such "radical revisionism" (as Wright aptly calls it), then there remain two main options on the semantic front: first, there are highly technical non-cognitivist solutions to the Frege-Geach challenge, like Gibbard's; and second, we can adopt a minimalist approach to truth, such that the propriety and intelligibility of certain assetoric idioms in evaluative language is enough to warrant cognitivism, with the issue between moral realists and anti-realists located elsewhere (for example, in the conception of objectivity).[18]

---

[17] For doubts about these, see Schroeder (2009).
[18] Wright (1992) is the *locus classicus* for this kind of view.

Even if we bracket the semantics, and view the thesis that moral judgments are a "sign-language" of the affects as primarily a causal hypothesis – which is how I have suggested we take it – then the considerations just adduced that count in favor of non-cognitivist semantics will also count in favor of Nietzsche's actual hypothesis. For if agents making sincere moral judgments are motivated to act in accordance with those judgments (whether or not they follow through on the motivation), then it counts in favor of any hypothesis about the causes of moral judgments that it should explain why such judgments produce motivational oomph. But the hypothesis that moral judgments are caused by affective responses is precisely that kind of hypothesis, since everyone agrees that affective or emotional responses put causal pressure on action. So the first reason to believe that moral judgments really are just "sign-languages of the affects" is that it explains why moral judgments motivate their makers, that is, cause them to feel inclined to or averted from certain actions, even if they do not actually act upon those feelings.

Second: any acceptable view of moral judgment ought to be consistent with a plausible account of the metaphysical status of moral facts, and any plausible view of moral judgment ascribed to Nietzsche should, in particular, be compatible with his own view about the metaphysical status of moral facts. I have argued elsewhere (Leiter 2002: 146–150; Leiter 2014) that Nietzsche's metaphysical view, following the pre-Socratics, is clear: there are no objective facts about what is morally right and wrong. Nature is, as he says in *The Gay Science*, "always value-less, but has been given value at some time, as a present – and it was we who gave and bestowed it" (GS 301). Such a metaphysical picture fits neatly with the idea that our judgments about moral value are not responsive to the pre-existing evaluative features of the world, but rather caused by non-cognitive affective states of the judger.[19]

Let us look at two illustrative statements of Nietzsche's view from *Daybreak*, his first 'mature' work as it were. Early on in Book I (D 3), he compares the way "man has ascribed to all that exists a connection with morality [*Moral*] and laid an *ethical significance* [*ethische Bedeutung*] on the world's back" to the earlier, and now discredited, "belief in the masculinity or femininity of the sun". Later, in Book II of the same work (D 100), he compares the way "wise and noble men

---

[19] I concede it is possible that someone might claim that affective responses are epistemically reliable ways of tracking the truth about what morality requires. That is plainly not Nietzsche's own view, and, given the overwhelming evidence of the ways in which emotional responses are epistemically unreliable in so many other contexts, it would be surprising, indeed, were they to turn out to be epistemically superior in this domain.

still believe in the 'moral significance [*sittliche Bedeutung*] of existence'" to the way they previously "believed in the music of the spheres", which is "no longer ... audible to them". (The switch to *sittliche Bedeutung* probably reflects the fact that the theme of the "morality of custom [*Sitte*]"–i.e., *Sittlichkeit*–was introduced in Book I.)

Passages like these invite both a metaphysical and an epistemological interpretation (I put aside the possible semantic reading, for the reasons already given). On the *metaphysical* reading, Nietzsche is saying that *there do not exist objective moral properties in the world*, just as there do not exist gendered properties of the sun, or musical properties of the heavenly bodies. To be sure, at one time, humans "perceived" the sun and the heavenly bodies as having gendered and musical properties, but those entities did not really (objectively) have them. Nietzsche's view thus seems to be a kind of *projectivism,* in particular, an instance of what Peter Kail (in discussing Hume) calls *explanatory projection* according to which "some feature of our mentality explains how the world appears to us". In a case of *explanatory projection,* "The thinker is not responsive to the world in a way whereby their beliefs, concepts and experience reflect their object. In a slogan: explanatory projection is non-detective [or non-detecting] explanation" (Kail 2007: xxix–xxx.).[20] On the e*pistemological* interpretation, which I think Nietzsche probably also intends, our purported *knowledge* of objective moral facts is an illusion, an unsurprising upshot of the metaphysical reading. As Nietzsche puts it, once again in *Daybreak* (D 2): "it is a prejudice of the learned that *we now know better* than any other age ... what is good and evil".

Now the ascription of moral anti-realism in Nietzsche's case is complicated by the fact that he does not seem to make the mistake of some earlier twentieth-century anti-realists, like A.J. Ayer and Charles Stevenson, who simply assumed that the metaphysical status of moral norms was different in kind from the status of epistemic norms. After all, as we have already seen, it is nature "that is value-less", and *all* value (*Werthe*) is "bestowed" by humans onto this value-free nature. But judgments about what we *ought* to believe in light of the evidence also depend on *values*–"epistemic norms" as we usually say nowadays–and it is hard to see why those values should be exempt from Nietzschean anti-realism. All knowing is, after all, as Nietzsche argues in the famous *Genealogy*

---

20 The contrast is with what Kail calls "feature projection", which he also finds in Hume, and which is central to the Freudian concept of projection: "In features projection, features of our mentality become represented as features of some other object (I project my hate in thinking that someone else hates me)".

passage on perspectivism (GM III 12), animated by *affects* (or interests), but if those are, as I have argued, non-cognitive, then it is hard to see how they could be deemed epistemically reliable or special. The point is even more explicit in the late discussion of perspectivism in *The Gay Science* (in Book V, added in 1886), when Nietzsche says that "we 'know' (or believe or imagine) exactly as much as is *useful* to the interests of the human herd, to the species: and even what is here called 'usefulness' is finally also just a belief, an imaginary construct ..." (GS 354).[21] These passages are important, in this context, not because they express doubts about truth or its existence, but because their target is explicitly *epistemic*, suggesting that norms of epistemic warrant answer to interests and affects that, themselves, have no independent standing as reliable trackers of the truth.

The conjunction of an apparent global anti-realism about value and specifically moral anti-realism can appear perplexing, and has confused some Anglophone philosophers.[22] On the one hand, Nietzsche seems to deny the metaphysical objectivity of values on the basis of broadly naturalistic considerations, considerations that themselves suppose certain epistemic norms, the norms in virtue of which we deem nature to have the non-moral characteristics it has. Yet Nietzsche seems to have no reason to exempt epistemic values from his value skepticism. How then should we understand his position?

There is no reason, in my view, to think Nietzsche had a clear handle on this philosophical issue. Like a lot of intellectuals self-taught in philosophy, he tended to make a mess of certain philosophical problems, especially those related to knowledge and truth. Yet the problem his meta-normative skepticism presents is one that has become familiar in the second-half of the twentieth century, one that figures in the work of Quine and McDowell, among other leading philosophers of the past half-century. Let me propose, then, a resolution that may or may not have been one Nietzsche had in mind, but which makes good philosophical sense of his position (and, indeed, seems to me a sensible position).

Suppose one thinks, with Nietzsche (and arguably others), that no values, moral or epistemic, can claim any special metaphysical standing, that nature is really "value-less", meaning, among other things, that nature does not settle what moral values to accept or what *epistemic* values to accept. Various lessons

---

[21] "[W]ir 'wissen' (oder glauben oder bilden uns ein) gerade so viel als es im Interesse der Menschen-Heerde, der Gattung, nütlizch sein mag: und selbst, was hier 'Nütlizchkeit' gennant wird, ist zulezt auch nur ein Glaube, eind Einbuildung...."
[22] Hilary Putnam (2004) on the fact-value distinction is a good example.

from twentieth-century philosophy certainly push in that direction. First, from the famous Duhem-Quine thesis (Duhem 1914; Quine 1975, 1990) about the under-determination of scientific theories by evidence, we know that there are not even any scientific hypotheses that are epistemically obligatory, in the sense of required by the norms of logic and evidence.[23] This is because any recalcitrant evidence elicited in a test of an hypothesis is compatible with the hypothesis as long as we are willing to give up the background assumptions such a test requires. In choosing among competing hypotheses and background assumptions, we must always fall back on evaluative considerations that "nature" does not adjudicate among, considerations such as theoretical simplicity, methodological conservatism, and consilience (cf. Quine/Ullian 1978). Second, unless there were a plausible *substantive* conception of rationality (there does not appear to be one, alas), then rationality, including any internalist norm of epistemic warrant, is itself instrumental, imposing normative constraints only on the means chosen to realize our ends, whatever they may happen to be. Thus, even norms for belief are hostage to ultimate ends, and so particular beliefs are unwarranted (that is, irrational) only relative to the believer's ends (see Railton 1986). That would hardly be surprising to Nietzsche, who clearly appreciated the extent to which theoretical questions were driven by practical ends and interests (BGE 3–9).

Why, then, think there is a special metaphysical problem for *moral* values? The idea of a "special" problem for metaphysical realism about moral values is ambiguous, however, between a problem *in kind* as opposed to one *of degree*. One upshot of the preceding considerations is that there may be no metaphysical difference *in kind* between moral and epistemic values, but that is still compatible with a radical difference in degree between them, and I think that is the key to making sense of Nietzsche's view. Let us call a "Global Humean" about epistemic values someone who notices that creatures like us generally converge on epistemic norms because those norms do so well at meeting widely shared human needs and interests. Consider epistemic norms like the following: treat as *prima facie* veridical perceptual evidence, honor logical inferences, and employ the inductive method in empirical inquiry. These epistemic norms seem to facilitate successful navigation of the world and prediction of the future

---

[23] I acknowledge that the inveterate dogmatic realist may think this is merely an *epistemic* point, not a metaphysical one: there could still be *real epistemic values*, after all, we just do not know what they are or how to apply them. That is a logically possible position, but I am with Quine in thinking that if the *actual successful sciences* do not disclose such epistemic values, then it is dubious that reality demands any particular set of them.

course of experience. Something like this, I suspect, was Hume's own view, though unlike Hume, Nietzsche doesn't think natural dispositions converge as well in the ethical case. That would explain why the great insight Nietzsche attributes to the Sophists concerns "the multiplicity (the geographical relativity) of the moral value judgments [*Moralischen Werthurtheile*]" (WP 428), not *all* value judgments, in other words, but the distinctively moral ones.

Third and finally: Nietzsche's view that moralities are a sign-language of the affects in something like the sense I have articulated here fits well with the empirical evidence about moral judgment and motivation. We should acknowledge, of course, that the evidence is ambiguous, but it certainly tends in the Nietzschean direction. Recall, for example, Nietzsche's claim, discussed earlier, that "moral feelings" (*Moralische Gefühle*) are inculcated when "children observe in adults inclinations for and aversions to certain actions and, as born apes, *imitate* these inclinations [*Neigungen*] and aversions [*Abneigungen*]; in later life they find themselves full of these acquired and well-exercised affects [*Affekten*] and consider it only decent to try to account for and justify them" (D 34). That point fits nicely with Jonathan Haidt's famous work on the "social intuitionist" model of moral judgment (Haidt 2001) according to which in most ordinary situations, moral judgments are produced by emotional or affective responses, the reasons adduced in their support being post-hoc: they do not explain the judgment, as evidenced by the resilience of the judgment even in the face of the defeat of the preferred reasons. Haidt, himself, is somewhat confused about the import of these empirical findings, for, contrary to Haidt, they state no dispute with a philosophical rationalist about moral judgment like Kant, since Kant is not committed to *either* the claim that most people actually arrive at their moral judgments through the exercise of practical reason *or* that most people arrive at moral judgments that can be justified, even after the fact, by the correct exercise of practical reason. The Kantian rationalist is committed, I take it, only to the claim that rational agents can, in principle, revise their moral judgments in light of practical reason, but nothing in Haidt's research rules out that possibility – indeed, he acknowledges that sometimes reasoning can result in a revision of moral judgments. But Nietzsche needs for his purposes only the descriptive thesis – that affective or emotional responses ordinarily determine moral judgment – since he has independent arguments for skepticism about practical reason against the moral rationalist like Kant that do not depend on the actual causal process by which people ordinarily arrive at moral judgments.

Recent empirical work on moral psychology also lends support to Nietzsche's view of moral judgments as sign-languages of the affects. As a recent literature survey notes, individuals "with selective deficits in emotional processing" due to disease or injury to the brain render different moral judgments about hypothetical situation like the Trolley cases, than most emotionally normal subjects to hypothetical situations (Cushman/Young/Greene 2010: 53–54), suggesting that the affective responses are causes of the moral judgments. Psychologist and philosopher Joshua Greene (2007) has argued that emotional responses loom larger in deontological than consequentialist moral judgments, the latter demanding more "controlled cognition", but in more recent work even Greene has acknowledged that "affect supplies the primary motivation to view harm as a bad thing" in the first place, so that even consequentialist reasoning has "an affective basis" (Cushman/Young/Greene 2010: 54; 62).[24]

In a recent review of the empirical literature, Timothy Schroeder, Adina Roskies and Shaun Nichols found that the view they dub "sentimentalism" – namely, the view that "the emotions typically play a key causal role in motivating moral behavior" (Schroeder/Roskies/Nichols 2010: 77) – is well-supported by the "evidence from psychology and neuroscience" (Schroeder/Roskies/Nichols 2010: 98), and that while "motivation derived [exclusively] from higher cognitive centers independently of desire is possible ... the only known model of it is pathological" involving Torrette syndrom (Schroeder/Roskies/Nichols 2010: 94). Such empirical findings do not rule out the possibility that moral judgments are not causal products of the affects, of course, but they suggest that the evidential burden must be borne by views that deny that causal role to affective responses.

Nietzsche's account of moral judgments as sign-languages of the affects seems, in short, to have the empirical evidence on its side, and this is not the first time a Nietzschean hypothesis has turned out to win support from subsequent empirical psychology, as I have argued elsewhere (Knobe/Leiter 2007; Leiter 2007). But that fact raises a question of its own, which I would like to address in concluding. Any reader of Nietzsche knows that he is not primarily concerned to report the findings of psychological "research" or to establish, through conventional methods of argumentation and the mustering of evidence, the truth of particular empirical hypotheses. His work is suffused with psychological and empirical claims, to be sure, but his aims are always much more

---

24 More precisely, "affect supplies the primary motivation to regard harm as bad. Once this primary motivation is supplied, reasoning proceeds in a currency-like manner ["currency emotions are designed to participate in the process of practical reasoning"]" (Cushman/Young/Greene 2010: 63). "[A]larm-bell emotions are designed to circumvent reasoning" (*id.* at 62) and, arguably, this is "the origin of the welfare principle", namely "in "Parkinson disease appears to show that intrinsic desires are necessary to the production of motivation in normal human beings, and this would seem to put serious pressure on the cognitivist position" (93).

polemical: to transform the consciousness of at least some readers about the morality they take for granted, and thus, at the same time, to change their affective orientation towards their lives. Nietzsche's psychological claims are always subservient to these rhetorical aims, but this does not alter the fact that Nietzsche makes psychological claims, ones that admit of empirical study and confirmation, and many of which may, as recent research suggests, be true. But, how one might wonder, could Nietzsche have been so right about so much of moral psychology without employing the methods of contemporary empirical psychology?

To start, we must remember that the best account of the psychology of human agency, moral and otherwise, is on a clear continuum with ordinary "folk" psychological explanations of behaviour, in a way that contemporary physical science is *not* derivable from "folk" physics, that is, from the ordinary categories we use to make sense of our observations about the physical world around us. Atoms, molecules, and invisible forces do not play an obvious role in my observation that if I drop the sofa on my toe, it will hurt, but contemporary empirical psychology avails itself of basically the same ontology–beliefs, desires, traits, bodily movements–that are the very stuff of unsystematic folk psychology.

To be sure, empirical psychology has plainly evolved methods for testing and confirming hypotheses that were not in use in the nineteenth century, but that does not mean Nietzsche lacked *evidence* on which to base his speculative moral psychology. Speculation by geniuses based on limited evidence has always played a major role in scientific progress, and it should hardly be surprising if psychology were any different. Nietzsche's own evidence appears to have been of three primary kinds. First, there were his own observations, both introspective and of the behaviour of others. Second, Nietzsche was an avid consumer of the psychological observations recorded by others, in a wide array of historical, literary and philosophical texts over long periods of time, observations which, in some respects, tended to reinforce each other (consider, for example, the realism about human motivations detailed by Thucydides in antiquity and, in the modern era, in the aphorisms of La Rochefoucauld, both authors whom Nietzsche admired). Finally, there was Nietzsche's extensive reading about contemporaneous scientific developments in the 1850s and 1860s, most of which–even if amateurish or simply wrong by today's standards–did represent systematic attempts to bring scientific methods to bear on the study of human beings and many of which, in at least some of their broad outlines, have been vindicated by subsequent developments. By the standards of contemporary methods in the human sciences, we would not deem insights based on this evidence to be well-confirmed, but that certainly does not mean such evidence is not, in the hands of a genius like Nietzsche, adequate for insights that survive scrutiny by our contemporary methods. This is precisely one of the reasons why Nietzsche, like Hume, is a great *speculative* naturalist in the history of philosophy: with unsystematic data and methods he could nonetheless arrive at hypotheses – including the hypothesis that moral judgments are sign-languages of the affects – that turn out to be supported by the more systematic data and methods the scientific study of human beings relies on today.[25]

References

I have drawn on English translations by Walter Kaufmann, R.J. Hollingdale, or Maudemarie Clark and Alan Swensen, and then made modifications based on Friedrich Nietzsche, *Sämtliche Werke: Kritische Studienausgabe in 15 Bänden* (KSA); where there is no existing English edition, the translation is my own.

Brennan, Tad (2003) "Stoic Moral Psychology", in: B. Inwood (ed.), *The Cambridge Companion to the Stoics*, Cambridge: Cambridge University Press, 257–294.

Cushman, Fiery/Young, Liane/Greene, Joshua D. (2010) "Multi-system Moral Psychology", in: *Doris* (2010), 47–71.

Deater-Deckard, K./Plomin, R. (1999) "An Adoption Study of the Etiology of Teacher Reports of Externalizing Problems in Middle Childhood", in: *Child Development* 70, 144–154.

Deigh, John (1994) "Cognitivism in the Theory of the Emotions", in: *Ethics* 104, 824–854.

---

[25] I have benefitted from discussion of the issues treated in this paper with the participants in the Spring 2011 seminar on "Nietzsche and Moral Psychology" at the University of Chicago: Nir Ben-Moshe, Jaime Edwards, Roger Eichorn, Guy Elgat, Michael Forster, Simon Gurofsky, Peter Kail, Alex Langlinais, and David Showalter. Teaching Nietzsche's *Genealogy* with Peter Kail at Oxford in autumn 2011 was also very helpful in clarifying my thoughts on several issues treated here. An earlier version of this paper was presented as the Bernd Magnus Lecture to the Department of Philosophy at the University of California at Riverside on 7 March 2012. I am grateful to the audience there for helpful questions and discussion; I should mention in particular David Glidden, Pierre Keller, Samantha Matherne, Jozef Müller, and Howard Wettstein. The current version benefitted from critical discussion with João Constâncio and his colleagues and students at the Nietzsche International Lab at the New University of Lisbon; from discussion with Justin Coates and with participants at the "New Essays in Moral Philosophy" conference in Tucson in January 2013; from the comments of an anonymous referee for this journal and from the editor, David Schmidtz; and from written commentary by Maudemarie Clark and David Dudrick, and discussion with them and the audience at an invited session on "Nietzsche, Moral Psychology and Empirical Psychology" at the Central Division meeting of the American Philosophical Association in February 2013.

Doris, John M./The Moral Psychology Research Group (eds.) (2010) *The Moral Psychology Handbook*, Oxford: Oxford University Press.
Duhem, Pierre (1914) *La Theorie Physique: Son Objet et sa Structure*. Paris: Marcel Riviera & Cie.
Edelbrock, C./Rende, R.D./Plomin, R./Thompson, L.A. (1995) "A Twin Study of Competence and Problem Behavior in Childhood and Early Adolescence", in: *Journal of Child Psychology and Psychiatry* 36, 775–785.
Eley, Thalia/Lichtenstein, Paul/Stevenson, Jim (1999) "Sex Differences in the Etiology of Aggressive and Nonaggressive Antisocial Behavior: Results from Two Twin Studies", in: *Child Development* 70, 155–168.
Goldie, Peter (2002) *The Emotions: A Philosophical Exploration*, Oxford: Oxford University Press.
Greene, Joshua (2007) "The Secret Joke of Kant's Soul", in: W. Sinnott-Armstrong (ed.), *Moral Psychology*, vol. 3, Cambridge, MA: MIT Press, 35–117.
Haidt, Jonathan (2001) "The Emotional Dog and Its Rational Tail: A Social Intuitionist Approach to Moral Judgment", in: *Psychological Review* 108, 814–834.
Hussain, Nadeem (2007) "Honest Illusion: Valuing for Nietzsche's 'Free Spirits'", in: Leiter/Sinhababu (2007), 157–191.
Kail, Peter (2007) *Projection and Realism in Hume's Philosophy*, Oxford: Oxford University Press.
Katsafanas, Paul (2013) "Nietzsche's Philosophical Psychology", in: K. Gemes and J. Richardson (eds.), *The Oxford Handbook of Nietzsche*, Oxford: Oxford University Press, 727–755.
Knobe, Joshua/Leiter, Brian (2007) "The Case for Nietzschean Moral Psychology", in: Leiter/Sinhababu (2007), 83–109.
Leiter, Brian (2000) "Nietzsche's Metaethics", in: *European Journal of Philosophy* 8, 277–297.
Leiter, Brian (2002) *Nietzsche on Morality*, London/New York: Routledge.
Leiter, Brian (2007) "Nietzsche's Theory of the Will", in: *Philosophers' Imprint* 7, 1–15.
Leiter, Brian (2014) "Moral Skepticism and Moral Disagreement in Nietzsche".
Leiter, Brian/Sinhababu, Neil (eds.) (2007) *Nietzsche and Morality*. Oxford: Oxford University Press.
Prinz, Jesse (2007) *The Emotional Construction of Morals*, Oxford: Oxford University Press.
Putnam, Hilary (2004) *The Collapse of the Fact/Value Dichotomy and Other Essays*, Cambridge, MA: Harvard University Press.
Quine, W.V.O. (1975) "On Empirically Equivalent Systems of the World", in: *Erkenntnis* 9, 313–328.
Quine, W.V.O. (1990) "Three Indeterminacies", in: R.B. Barrett and R.F. Gibson (eds.), *Perspectives on Quine*, Cambridge, MA: Blackwell.
Quine, W.V.O./Ullian, Joseph (1978) *The Web of Belief*, 2nd edition, New York: Random House.
Railton, Peter (1986) "Facts and Values", in: *Philosophical Topics* 14, 5–31.
Schroeder, Mark (2009) "Hybrid Expressivism: Virtues and Vices", in: *Ethics* 119, 257–309.
Schroeder, Timothy/Roskies, Adina L./Nichols, Shaun (2010) "Moral Motivation", in: Doris (2010), 72–109.
Sinhababu, Neil (2009) "The Humean Theory of Motivation Reformulated and Defended", in: *Philosophical Review* 118, 465–500.
Wright, Crispin (1988) "Realism, Antirealism, Irrealism, Quasi-Realism", in: P. French et al. (eds.), *Midwest Studies in Philosophy*, Notre Dame: University of Notre Dame Press, 25–49.
Wright, Crispin (1992) *Truth and Objectivity*, Cambridge, MA: Harvard University Press.

Ken Gemes and Imogen Le Patourel
24 Nietzsche on Consciousness, Unity, and the Self

Introduction[1]

The importance of unconscious drives is a central theme of much of Nietzsche's work. A corollary of this theme is his disparagement of the traditional high estimation of the importance of consciousness. On these issues he is clearly a follower of Schopenhauer and a precursor of Freud. These facts naturally lead to the question of how Nietzsche conceived of the relation between conscious and unconscious mental activity. In his description of the origins of 'bad conscience' in *On the Genealogy of Morality* he discussed one scenario in which the clash of consciousness and instinctual demands produced devastating results:

> ... the poor things were reduced to relying on thinking, inference, calculation ... that is, to relying on their "consciousness", that most impoverished and error-prone organ! ... and meanwhile, the old instincts had not suddenly ceased to make their demands! ... all those instincts of the wild, free, roving man were turned backwards, *against man himself*.... man impatiently ripped himself apart, persecuted himself, gnawed at himself.... as the result of a forcible breach with his animal past ... (GM II 16)[2]

This violent inner conflict memorably culminates in the fundamental self-contradiction of "the worst and most insidious illness ... man's sickness of ... *himself*" (GM II 16). This pathological state is brought about by an undue reliance on conscious thought in tandem with a repression of certain strong instincts (those of the "wild, free, roving man"). We might naturally speculate that, given the horrifying result of this rupture, Nietzsche's aim would be to overcome such inner conflict by bringing about some form of amity or reunification between conscious thought and the instincts.

---

[1] Thanks are due to Gudrun von Tevenar, Sebastian Gardner, Tom Stern, Paul Katsafanas, Andrew Huddleston and Mark Little for helpful comments on earlier drafts, and to Charlie Huenemann for help with footnote 22.
[2] Note, some of the quoted passages from translations cited in the bibliography have been modified where the translations were deemed to be inadequate to the original German. Occasionally we have preferred literal to more stylistically elegant translations where the latter might be deemed contentious.

There is certainly evidence that the unity of the self was of great concern to Nietzsche. His hero Goethe "took as much as possible ... within himself", yet "disciplined himself to a whole" (TI Skirmishes 49); whereas lamentably "[m]ost men present pieces and fragments of man: one has to add them up for a complete man to appear" (KSA 12: 520). Against such fragmentation Zarathustra declares that "this is all my composing and striving, that I compose into one and bring together what is fragment and riddle and cruel coincidence" (Z II Redemption).

What might this sought-after wholeness or completeness consist in? Paul Katsafanas (2011) has argued that Nietzschean unity refers to a relation of harmony between drives and conscious thought. This construal of unity might seem well-placed to offer a solution to the problem of self-division and self-persecution described in GM II 16. Katsafanas proffers this reading of unity against the prevalent interpretation, which he calls the 'predominance model'. According to the predominance model "unity obtains when one drive predominates and imposes order on the other drives" (Katsafanas 2011: 87).[3] This latter model does not seem to offer any special role to consciousness in the achievement of a unified self and may possibly even render it superfluous. On the 'predominance' reading, where Nietzsche talks in GM about people "relying on their 'consciousness'", we need not conclude that the instincts are in total abeyance here. Rather, we would suggest that in certain enervated states, particular instincts (for instance, the instincts to sociability or caution) utilise consciousness as an effective (and in biological terms, relatively recent) tool against the more primitive, aggressive animal instincts. In what follows, we aim to give our reasons for preferring this reading. In order to do this, we will first need to clarify what Nietzsche in fact means by the 'self' and how he characterises the role of consciousness. We will then consider his notion of the *unity* of the self and examine this notion in the context of the Nietzschean ideals of self-creation and of becoming what one is.

Part 1 below looks at how we might conceive of the Nietzschean self. It argues for a pronounced distinction between the self and the I or ego. In the

---

3 In the works of those authors who emphasise Nietzsche's drive psychology, for instance Katsafanas (2011), Richardson (1996) and Gemes (2009b), there is little register of any difference between Nietzsche's use of the terms *Instinkt* (instinct) and *Trieb* (drive). Arguably this is a reasonable position since it is not clear that Nietzsche himself uses these terms to mark a significant difference. To our modern ears the notion of instinct may have a stronger suggestion of something hard-wired and non-malleable than does the notion of a drive, for example, but more work would be needed to substantiate any claim that Nietzsche's respective usage of the two terms picks out any such particular resonances.

extreme, Nietzsche is sceptical about the I's or ego's very existence, though we will argue that his considered view involves only scepticism about its importance for self, action and agency. It is argued that for Nietzsche the self and the core of one's agency are to be located primarily in the activity of the unconscious drives, and that Nietzsche has a largely deflationary account of the role of consciousness.

Part 2 considers what the Nietzschean self looks like through examining the two alternative models of unity referred to above: unity according to the predominance model – achieved when a 'master drive' organises or sublimates the other drives into hierarchical relations to itself – or unity as a harmony between the drives and conscious reflection. We will conclude that the predominance model best captures the Nietzschean position. On this reading Nietzsche's overriding concern is to re-establish the drives in what he took to be their rightful pre-eminent place. We go on to elaborate some implications of this view of the importance of the drives over conscious thought for mental activity such as the process of deciding between competing motives. We will argue that for Nietzsche it is always the drives rather than consciousness that are the root causal determinants of our actions and the formation of the self, and that where consciousness does have a role, it is essentially as a tool of the drives.

1 Ego, I, consciousness and self

1.1 Paradoxes of self-creation

The first question we must consider is the array of different views that Nietzsche seemingly expresses about selfhood. Sebastian Gardner (2009) has puzzled over the tension, if not outright contradiction, between Nietzsche's theoretical claims that there is no I or ego and his practical injunctions which seem to be aimed at that very I: injunctions commending self-creation, becoming what one is, and self-overcoming. If there is no I, no ego, then to whom is Nietzsche addressing these injunctions, and who is capable of fulfilling or even responding to them?

It is worth noting that in the case of self-creation it is unnecessary to go so far as to contrast the above theoretical and practical commitments to raise the spectre of paradox. The very injunction to engage in self-creation suggests a kind of paradox. If one has a self, then it is clear who is being addressed by the injunction, but its command then seems empty – for the self already exists and therefore does not need to be created. One gets a suggestion of this type of problem from Nietzsche's enigmatic phrase "become what you are". If one is already X there seems to be no task of becoming X. Analogously, if there is a self, there is no task of becoming a self. On the other hand, if there is no self, then, again, who is being enjoined to undertake this act of self-creation? Who is being enjoined to become what one is? How would it be possible to obey these commands? This puzzle is also apparent when Nietzsche proclaims approvingly that Goethe "disciplined himself to a whole, he *created* himself …" (TI Skirmishes 49). Here Nietzsche simultaneously invokes the ideals of wholeness *and* self-creation – suggesting that to create oneself might mean precisely to bring about this state of wholeness. Yet if one is not already whole, who is there to create a self that *is* whole? Prior to that creation one is presumably multiple or conflicted – and therefore not likely to be in a position to 'discipline' oneself, an activity which seems to require some pre-existing unity of purpose and function?

Perhaps a resolution to these paradoxes might be achieved by giving a weaker interpretation of the injunction to create a self. On such a reading, the injunction assumes that a somehow inadequate or defective self is already in play as the basis for further development, and exhorts the creation of a *better* (more cohesive) self. By the same token the injunction to become what you are would be understood as the injunction to activate some potentiality in oneself. The task would be to move from being a merely potential X, for instance a potential unified self, to becoming an actual X. Even if such a reading is provisionally accepted, the problem remains that there are various passages where Nietzsche seemingly denies the very existence of the I or ego, and also passages where Nietzsche incisively derides the supposed efficacy of consciousness. Such passages seem to leave little room for a project of conscious self-creation. This suggests that we must in all likelihood look elsewhere to understand how he conceives of the self and of self-creation.

1.2 Scepticism about the I versus scepticism about the self

Nietzsche famously debunks notions of the I. Thus he writes disparagingly of

> … the metaphysics of language … that believes in the I, in the I as being, in the I as substance … (TI Reason 5)[4]

Such scepticism about the I is also expressed in other passages:

---

[4] Note where Nietzsche uses the term *ich* in this passage and others quoted below Hollingdale typically translates it as 'ego'. In the case of Freud there has been criticism of Strachey's systematic translation of Freud's term *Ich* as 'ego' (see Bettelheim 1982).

24 Nietzsche on Consciousness, Unity, and the Self — 601

> In Christianity ... nothing but imaginary causes ("God", "soul", I, "spirit", "free will" – or "unfree will") (A 15)

> When I analyse the process that is expressed in the sentence, "I think," I find a whole series of daring assertions that would be difficult, perhaps impossible, to prove: for example, that it is I who thinks ... that thinking is an activity and operation on the part of a being who is thought of as a cause, that there is an "I" ... What gives me the right to speak of an "I", and even of an "I" as cause, and finally of an I as the cause of thought? (BGE 16)

> ... this multifarious thing [the will] that the common people call by one word alone. In any given case, we both command *and* obey ... we are in the habit of ignoring or overlooking this division by means of the synthetic concept I. (BGE 19)

The I is here characterised as a *synthetic* concept in opposition to the common tendency to posit a persisting 'monadic', unitary, I that autonomously generates our conscious thoughts. In place of this conventional picture Nietzsche posits a bundle of diverse forces in complex power relations of command and obedience. Our linguistic and conceptual habits gloss over the complexity and multiplicity of the forces at work. The I of conscious reflection, far from being self-evident, is for Nietzsche an artificial construct or oversimplification, one that elides the complex relations between internal forces and mislocates true causal efficacy.

Nietzsche's scepticism towards the I is of a piece with his warnings on the limitations of conscious introspection and self-knowledge:

> We are none of us that which we appear to be in accordance with the states for which alone we have consciousness and words ... those cruder outbursts of which alone we are aware make us misunderstand ourselves ... we misread ourselves in this apparently most intelligible of handwriting on the nature of our self [*selbst*]. (D 115)

> However far a man may go in self-knowledge, nothing however can be more incomplete than his image of the totality of drives which constitute his being [*sein Wesen*]. He can scarcely name even the cruder ones: their number and strength, their ebb and flood, their play and counterplay among one another, and above all the laws of their nutriment remain wholly unknown to him. (D 119)

For Nietzsche our self-conscious experience (what we appear to ourselves to be) is but a small part of what we actually are, and to interpret ourselves only on the basis of that self-conscious component leads to misunderstanding of the (actual) self. In D 119, he locates the lacuna in our self-knowledge: it is the *drives* that we do not have introspective access to, but "which constitute [our] being".[5]

---

[5] One can of course ask (as Tom Stern notably does in a unpublished manuscript "Against Nietzsche's Theory of Drives") how Nietzsche can at one and the same time forcefully assert both our lack of knowledge about the interplay of the drives *and* notions of the self which depend on precisely that interplay. Given that following this statement in D 119 he immediately goes on to

Passages explicitly evincing scepticism towards the ego, that is passages which explicitly employ sceptical use of the term *ego* rather than *Ich*, are less common. The most notable case is the following from his unpublished notes:

> The "subject" is only a fiction, there is no ego, from which one talks when one blames egoism. (KSA 12: 398)

Hereafter we will take Nietzsche's use of the terms 'ego' and 'I' to be equivalent as we can find no textual basis for a separation. This I, or ego, is for Nietzsche the locus of consciousness.

By contrast to his I (and ego) scepticism, it is hard to find passages where Nietzsche expresses outright scepticism towards the notion of the *self* (*selbst*). There is an important reason why it would be strange for Nietzsche to reject the notion of self in an equivalent way: he is a philosopher who repeatedly calls for self-creation.[6] It is noteworthy that he does not extol a project of creating the I or ego.[7] What all this suggests is that rather than collapsing the notion of self on one hand and the notion of ego or I on the other, we should pay careful attention to the distinction.

From the foregoing we can expect Nietzsche's view of the self to downplay the I that is the locus of conscious awareness and to emphasise the role of the (largely unknown) unconscious drives. In the following passage Nietzsche's

---

make some very specific claims about the activity of the drives, one wonders whether perhaps he thought that his characterisation of our general ignorance did not apply to himself as psychologist *par excellence*.

6 One might also be tempted here to reference his use of the notion of self-overcoming (*Selbstüberwindung*). However, as Nietzsche uses this term not simply in the context of application to individuals, but also to morality (EH, Why I am a Fate 3) and to Europe (GM III 27), it is not clear that self-overcoming literally involves the presence of an actual self. Here the sense relayed by 'selbst' in 'Selbstüberwindung' is that of the reflexive 'itself', as in morality overcomes itself, where the 'itself' presumes no actual self. Similarly, a bridge can be self-identical or collapse on itself without it having an actual self.

7 Of course, and as emphasised by Janaway (2007), Nietzsche, in his polemics against the morality of compassion championed by both Schopenhauer and Christianity, typically commends a robust egoism. The crucial point here is that this lauded egoism does not extol or even concern the conscious I or ego that is the topic of discussion above. Rather egoism in the relevant sense is self-cultivation, as in paying proper respect to one's own needs, one's own drives. The opposition between compassion and egoism is for Nietzsche not the conventional opposition between a conscious care for my conscious ego (including my conscious desires) and a conscious care for the egos of others (including their conscious desires). Rather, it is an opposition between a regimen of suppression of one's drives in order to meet the needs of others and a robust cultivation of one's own drives. Nietzsche contrasts this healthy egoism with the pathological self-obliteration of the morality of compassion and selflessness.

mouthpiece Zarathustra specifically extols the importance of the self over the importance of the I:

> Behind your thoughts and feelings, my brother, stand a mighty commander, an unknown sage [*Weiser*] – his name is Self [*Selbst*]. In your body he dwells, he is your body ... Your Self laughs at your I [*dein Ich*] and its proud leapings. "What are these leapings and soarings of thought to me?" it says to itself. "A detour to my purpose. I am the leading-string of the I [*des Ich's*] and the prompter of its conceptions." (Z I Despisers of the Body)

In this passage Zarathustra describes the self as standing *behind* (*hinter*) our conscious thoughts and feelings – indeed here, the self "is your body" – it is not to be equated with the I of conscious experience. What is more, Nietzsche characteristically rebukes the misplaced pride of conscious reflection; this pride is ridiculed by the self. Conscious thoughts and feelings are demoted in status, as of instrumental use to the unknown self (a 'detour' to its purpose) and largely determined by the self, which is the 'leading-string' and 'mighty commander'.

This passage from *Zarathustra* suggests a picture where Nietzsche identifies the I, as does the modern tradition from Descartes, with conscious thoughts and feelings. However, unlike that tradition, Nietzsche rejects the identification of the *self* with the I and consciousness. It is the unknown self that is the real engine of our actions and even of our conscious thoughts. In the Cartesian tradition, the self, ego and I are identical and are fully open to conscious introspection. Nietzsche not only directly challenges the assumptions of Cartesianism, but carves out a new model of the self.[8]

1.3 The downgrading of consciousness

As we saw above, for Nietzsche we cannot deduce the nature of the self by examining only the conscious states which we are able to describe – indeed we are inevitably lured into error concerning our own nature by the *apparent intelligibility* of these states (D 115). He claims that consciousness, as a 'surface', has a dual character. It reveals but, more characteristically, it also *conceals*:

> ... do we not suspect that all of an action's intentionality, everything that can be seen or known about it, that can be "conscious" about it, is still part of its surface and skin – which, like all skin, reveals something, but *hides* even more? (BGE 32)

---

[8] Nietzsche himself realises that others before Schopenhauer, specifically Leibniz, had already claimed that "what we call consciousness constitutes only one state of our physical and spiritual world (and possibly a pathological one) and *not by any means the whole of it*" (GS 357).

At his most strident, he famously calls into question the very value of consciousness and self-consciousness:

> The problem of consciousness (more correctly, of becoming self-conscious) confronts us only when we begin to comprehend how we could dispense with it ... the whole of life would be possible without, as it were, seeing itself in a mirror. Even now for that matter, the greatest part of life actually take place without this mirror effect; and this is true even of our thinking feeling and willing life; however offensive this many sound to older philosophers. For what purpose any consciousness at all when it is in the main superfluous? (GS 354; translation altered)

Here we see that Nietzsche, prefiguring Freud, allows that there is non-conscious thinking, feeling and willing. Moreover, he even claims that the majority of human mental activity is in fact unconscious.[9] As he goes on to say in GS 354:

> Man, like every living being, thinks continuously without knowing it; the thinking that rises to consciousness is only the smallest part of it – the most superficial and worst part of it.

So if (contra the Cartesian tradition) thinking, feeling and willing are not wholly the provenance of consciousness, what is it that characterises consciousness for Nietzsche? In D 115 he spoke of "the states for which alone we have consciousness and words". This suggestive equation of consciousness with that which is available to be expressed in public language is given fuller expression in the key GS 354 passage:

---

[9] Nietzsche's conjecture that consciousness is largely 'superfluous' can lead to the view that he believes it is purely epiphenomenal. Such a view is developed in Leiter (2002) and defended in Riccardi (forthcoming); however the latter takes Nietzsche's claims about the epiphenomenal nature of consciousness (*Bewusstsein*) to refer only to self-conscious mental states, that is, mental states whose objects are our own mental states. Katsafanas (2005) cogently argues against Leiter's strong epiphenomenalist reading. The strong epiphenomenalist reading is hard to square with the drama of GM as sketched in the introduction to this paper – where over-reliance on consciousness leads to a desperately damaging alienation from, and blocking of, 'wild' or 'animal' instincts. Similarly, it is hard to square with related passages where Nietzsche writes negatively of the effects of consciousness, for instance: "in all productive men it is instinct that is the creative-affirmative force and consciousness acts critically and dissuasively" (BT 13). We would argue, then, that consciousness must have *some* causal efficacy for Nietzsche, despite the scepticism expressed in, for example, BGE 16 about I as cause, and in GS 354 towards the necessity of consciousness. Constâncio (2011) emphasises that Nietzsche repeatedly describes consciousness as a tool (*Werkzeug*); for instance D 109 emphasises that consciousness is a tool of the drives in their struggle for dominance over each other. As Constâncio observes, it is hard to reconcile the notion of a tool with the notion of having no causal powers.

> I may now proceed to surmise that consciousness has developed only under the pressure of the need for communication ... Consciousness is really only a net of communication between human beings.[10]

Consciousness is necessitated by our need to be intelligible to one another as social beings; but in claiming that the content of our conscious thought is the "most superficial and worst part", Nietzsche raises the provocative question of whether the development of consciousness is in fact largely detrimental to us. Part of the "problem of consciousness" lies in the fact that it is at a relatively early and unstable stage in its evolution, Nietzsche believes:

> *Consciousness* – Consciousness is the latest development of the organic, and hence also its most unfinished and unrobust feature ... If the preserving alliance of the instincts were not so much more powerful ... humanity would have to perish with open eyes of its misjudging and its fantasising ... in short, of its consciousness ... Before a function is fully developed and mature, it constitutes a danger to the organism ... Thus, **consciousness is properly tyrannised** – and not least by one's pride in it! One thinks it constitutes the *kernel* of man, what is abiding, eternal, ultimate, most original in him! ... One denies its growth and intermittences! **Sees it as "the unity of the organism"**! This ridiculous overestimation and misapprehension of consciousness has the very useful consequence that an all-too-rapid development of consciousness was *prevented* ... so far we have incorporated only our *errors* and ... all of our consciousness refers to errors! (GS 11; bold emphasis ours)

Nietzsche here explicitly argues that consciousness is anything but the enduring essence ('kernel') of the human being. Nor is it even the most powerful element in the human being; by far, that element is the "preserving alliance of the instincts".

Nietzsche's analysis is historically situated: he is talking about a particular stage in the evolution of consciousness, at which it is still fragile, unreliable and unfinished; *so far* we have only incorporated errors[11] – but he does not say these are inevitable and permanent features of consciousness. In fact, he says that we have incorporated only errors *because* we have grossly overestimated conscious-

---

10 This might suggest that Nietzsche is committed to a specific account of the essence of consciousness; namely, a conscious state (for instance, a conscious thought) is a state that is expressed in language (perhaps in a language of thought, à la Fodor) or, alternatively, a conscious state is a state that is expressible in a public language. Katsafanas (2005) and Constâncio (2011) claim that for Nietzsche a conscious state is a conceptual state, and that unconscious states, for instance unconscious thoughts, are non-conceptual. We do not wish to attribute such fine-grained accounts as we feel the text is too thin to adequately support them. Nietzsche's decided emphasis is on the significance rather than the constitution of consciousness.
11 We do well here to recall passages such as BGE 4 where Nietzsche points out that errors, falsehoods and illusions are sometimes necessary and life-supporting.

ness to date. The intriguing question left unaddressed here, then, is that of what consciousness might be like when it is more 'mature', when it *is* fully developed (or, more immediately, when we accept a more accurate and modest estimation of it). Indeed he says that "Before a function is fully developed and mature ... it is a good thing for it to be properly tyrannised in the meantime" – which leaves some hope that when it *is* mature it will no longer need to be tyrannised. However, given Nietzsche's frequent emphasis on the pernicious effects of consciousness, it seems unlikely on his view that in becoming fully developed consciousness would thereby shed all its detrimental features.

1.4 Drives and selves: Two possibilities

Whereas consciousness is largely 'superfluous' (GS 354), the drives (*Triebe*) seem to be the obvious contenders to be the real seat of the self: in D 119, the totality of a man's drives "constitute his being"; in BGE 12 Nietzsche's mission is to "kill off ... *the atomism of the soul* ... the belief that holds the soul to be something ... indivisible, a monad, an atom ...", and promote instead the "soul as the social construct of drives and emotions".

One possibility here is that one's 'self' is simply to be identified with the totality of one's drives, as the wording of D119 seems to suggest. We might call this the 'egalitarian' reading since it entails that each human's collection of drives constitutes a self.[12] A second possibility is that the self is located in a *particular arrangement* of one's drives. The second reading is suggested by Nietzsche's talk of the soul as a social construct and his injunctions to self-creation. That is to say, behind Nietzsche's injunctions may lie the convictions that most human beings are constituted by a haphazard, fragmented, or unproductive arrangement of drives; and that to self-create might be to bring about a particular, more desirable relation between those drives – a result which not everyone achieves. We might call this the 'elitist' reading: if the created self involves a certain configuration of drives, those human beings whose totality of drives does not constitute such an arrangement will fail to have genuine selves.

---

12 In fact the text says that the totality of his drives constitutes his being (*Wesen*), not his self (*Selbst*). So one might read D 119 as simply saying that each human is constituted by their totality of drives. On this reading D 119 takes no stand on whether each human counts as a self. In fact it is the Zarathustra passage quoted above (Z I Despisers of the Body), which identifies the self with the body, that implicitly gives most credence to the egalitarian reading – though, as Andrew Huddleston has pointed out, the claim that your self is your body does not itself entail that each body constitutes a self.

In fact we know of no passage where Nietzsche explicitly says that there are humans who do not have *selves*, though Nietzsche's general disparagement of most humans as merely members of the herd and his talk of humans being mere fragments such that "one has to add them up for a complete man to appear" support the elitist reading. Further support comes from his occasional analogous claim that most humans do not constitute *persons*:

> Nothing is rarer than a personal act [*Handlung*]. A state, a rank, a race, an environment, an accident – all these are expressed in a deed or doing [*einem Werke oder Thun*] rather than a person. b) One should not at all assume that most humans [*Menschen*] are "persons" [*Personen*]. Indeed, many are multiple people, and most are not people at all. Where the average qualities dominate in order that a type continues, it would be a waste or a luxury to ask for a person. They [average humans] are carriers, transmission tools. c) The person is a relatively isolated fact. (KSA 12: 491)[13]

The implication is that most actions are herd actions rather than expressive of individual identity: human beings are more or less passive vehicles for "average qualities". The genuine, unique, *creative* individual is Nietzsche's rare ideal.

The above claim from 1887 that most humans are not persons echoes an earlier claim from his notebooks:

> Most humans show clearly enough that they do not regard themselves as individuals: their lives indicate this ... There are only three forms of existence in which a human remains an individual: as philosopher, saviour, and artist. But just let us consider how a scientific human bungles his life: what has the teaching of Greek particles to do with the sense of life? – Thus we can also observe how innumerable humans merely live, as it were, as preparation for a genuine person [eines *wirklichen Menschen*]: for example, the philologist as preparation for the philosopher, who in his turn knows how to utilise his [the philologist's] ant-like work to pronounce some opinion upon the value of life. When such ant-like work

---

13 It is easy to focus in on the startling claim here that not even some, but *most*, humans do not qualify as persons at all. However Nietzsche makes another claim which might get overlooked in comparison: that "many are multiple people". If to fail to be a 'person' is to have a chaotic relation between drives, we might venture to characterise someone who is 'multiple people' as someone who has more than one drive of sufficient strength to 'recruit' other drives to sub-personal centres of power that are able to generate significant goals, but do not *win out* over the others to result in one overall, coherent, unifying goal. The alternative to this – where no person is present at all – would mean that no drives have emerged as relatively stable foci of power, and there is just a general inchoate struggle. If this interpretation is correct, it maintains a link between personhood (in the sense of unique individuality) and the type of organisation that prevails amongst the drives (and therefore dictates the manner of their expression).

is not carried out under any special direction the greater part of it is simply nonsense and superfluous. (KSA 8: 31–32)[14]

In this passage it is notable that Nietzsche equates individuality with what we might call three vocations or callings: philosopher, saviour and artist. This is a remarkably exclusive group capable of achieving authentic individuality – not even the scientist or philologist qualifies. Where the latter seem to fall short is in accepting a role that makes of them a mere means to an end, which Nietzsche links to the failure to be driven by an overall goal (a 'special direction') which relates to life's *value*. This puts an extreme limitation on who can consider themselves to be a genuine individual. Note that here Nietzsche's explicit criterion revolves, not around a particular type of internal arrangement per se, but around what one does with one's life – one's overarching goal or purpose. We will argue in sections 1.5 and 2.2 however that only certain internal arrangements of drives would make it possible for someone to fulfil such vocations on Nietzsche's account.

Here we come to the heart of Nietzsche's practical injunctions about the self:

> The man who does not wish to belong to the mass needs only to cease taking himself easily; let him follow his conscience, which calls to him: "Be yourself! All you are now doing, thinking, desiring, is not you yourself." (SE 1)

Nietzsche's texts suggest the following picture: For many humans their doings are to be explained not by elements of their individuality but by their passive herd-like participation in some external group. Thus consider a fan participating in a crowd chant at a football match. Where some would want to say that the fan is committing the action of chanting, Nietzsche seems inclined to suggest that it is the crowd that is committing the act of chanting – the individual chanter is here just a "transmission tool" of the crowd. In a sense the individual chanter is not acting at all, as more conventional philosophers would say that when you choose to lift a book, though your hand is involved in the lifting, it is your action and not that of your hand. Arguably, the notion of agent is tied to a normative notion of causation, so that part of what is involved in describing someone or something as an agent behind a given action is giving them a special causal significance in the performance of the action.[15]

---

14 This high valuation of the philosopher, saviour and artist is not confined simply to Nietzsche's unpublished works but also occurs in published texts, for instance SE 5.

15 Nietzsche, like Hume, is one of those philosophers who enigmatically both expresses a good deal of scepticism about causation, yet at the same time gives causal, indeed genealogical,

Nietzsche's injunctions to selfhood and self-creation are in some manner concerned with the ability to express one's own values, as opposed to those of the 'herd' or 'mass' – those who simply follow the majority, custom and tradition. The iconic GS 335 passage voices a call to this ideal:

> We, however, want to *become who we are* – human beings who are new, unique, incomparable, who give themselves laws, who create themselves! (GS 335)

Self-creation, becoming who we are – both formulations used, apparently interchangeably, here – involve rejecting the very concept of 'universal law' and creating personal ideals to live by. Such injunctions in themselves seem to tell us very little about the internal constitution that is necessary for self-creation. However we can link this concern with personal ideals to Nietzsche's condemnation of consciousness as being intrinsically superficial and general, precisely because of its function in facilitating communication. Consciousness arises out of our social nature, which Nietzsche distrusts as fostering in the weak majority an inauthentic, 'herd' mentality:

> ... In short, the development of language and the development of consciousness (*not* of reason but strictly of the way in which we become conscious of reason) go hand in hand ... only as a social animal did man learn to become conscious of himself – he is still doing it, and he is doing it more and more. [...] each of us, even with the best will in the world to *understand* ourselves as individually as possible, "to know ourselves", will always bring to consciousness precisely that in ourselves which is "non-individual", that which is "average" [...] At bottom, all our actions are incomparably and utterly personal, unique, and boundlessly individual, there is no doubt; but as soon as we translate them into consciousness, *they no longer seem to be*... [...]the world of which we can become conscious is merely a surface- and sign-world, a world turned into generalities and thereby debased to its lowest common denominator ... everything which enters consciousness thereby *becomes* shallow, thin, relatively stupid, general ... In the end, the growing consciousness is a danger; and he who lives among the most conscious Europeans even knows it is a sickness. (GS 354)

Nietzsche contends that the supposed self-knowledge that is available to consciousness actually fails to reveal who we really are specifically because the

---

stories of a wide range of human phenomena, including, for instance, how we come to our very understanding of causation. One way to reconcile this tension in both philosophers is to argue that their scepticism is towards wholly objectivist accounts of causation. In Hume's case that scepticism is expressed in his claim that the necessity of causation lies in a certain propensity of the mind. It may be argued that in Nietzsche's case one relevant claim concerns an essential normative dimension in judgements of causation. However this difficult issue is beyond the scope of this paper.

consequence of the partial and simplified picture provided by the conscious 'surface-world' is to *make that which is unique and individual appear common and general*. This line of thought also suggests that to engage successfully in self-creation or becoming what one is cannot be, at root, a conscious process.[16]

1.5 Consciousness's proper role

Nietzsche wants the genuine individual to be *possible*. Indeed he even claims in GS 354 that at root our actions *already are* "boundlessly individual" – but consciousness makes it seem otherwise; it strips them of their uniqueness.[17] It is striking in this passage that Nietzsche even denies that reason is the preserve of consciousness: we have only become conscious, in a particular way, *of* reason. This reflects the view presented by Zarathustra who divides a "lesser" conscious reason from a "greater" unconscious reason:

> The body is a great reason, a manifold with one sense, a war and a peace, a herd and a herdsman. A tool of the body is your small reason too, my brother, which you call "spirit", a small tool and toy of your great reason. "I" you say, and are proud of this word. But the greater thing – in which you do not want to believe – is your body and its great reason: it does not say I but it does I. (Z I Despisers of the Body).

Both GS 11 and GS 354 emphasise that relying on consciousness is inimical to the quest to understand what is personal and individual about ourselves: more

---

[16] It might be objected that the tenor of GS 335 – its concern with self-knowledge and intellectual conscience, with "reflect[ing] more subtly", its claim that "we must become *physicists* in order to be creators in this sense" (i.e. to be those who can create themselves and their own personal ideals) – instead points to the centrality of conscious reflection and knowledge in self-creation and becoming who you are. We would argue, however, that this reflection and knowledge need not be at a *conscious* level. As GS 333 has just asserted, "by far the greatest part of our mind's activity proceeds unconscious"; GS 354 repeats the claim that "man ... is constantly thinking but does not know it", and that self-knowledge is actually hampered by the process of becoming-conscious. One best develops a personal ideal *before* becoming consciously aware of it (as EH Clever 9 illustrates).

[17] This might seem to point towards the egalitarian reading described in 1.4 above – selfhood simply resides in the totality of one's (unconscious) drives – suggesting that the issue in GS 354 is not so much to do with the real nature of this totality but in the way that it appears and relates to consciousness. However, as we have said, the injunction to self-creation is a mysterious one if everyone already has a self simply in virtue of the existence of this totality; and as noted above Nietzsche says "there are only three forms of existence in which a man remains an individual" (KSA 8: 31–32). The uniqueness referred to in GS 354 is best understood as the uniqueness that separates each human from the other, but not the type of uniqueness that characterises a genuine self.

than that, growing consciousness is a danger and a sickness. We have become dangerously unbalanced, increasingly estranged from ourselves.[18] This emphasis on the danger of growing consciousness actually points to an alternative to Katsafanas' formulation of the role of consciousness: *pace* Katsafanas, unity is not achieved through establishing a harmonious relation between consciousness and the drives, but rather, one in which consciousness is 'properly tyrannised' (GS 11) – so that its ability to obscure individual uniqueness is minimised. But what does 'properly tyrannised' mean here? Our suggestion is that consciousness is properly tyrannised when it is used by drives that are capable of using it to positive effect; in particular, the positive effect of integrating the other drives. Conversely consciousness is improperly tyrannised when it is used by some drives to effect the repression of other drives. It is in this pathological internalisation, the result of the improper tyrannisation of some drives by others, that Nietzsche sees consciousness as a tool for self-evisceration, hence as a danger and a sickness (as described in GM II 16 – see also section 2.2 below).

This gives us a way of explaining what Nietzsche himself is trying to do in GM. Note there is a prima facie problem of reconciling Nietzsche's polemical ends (he subtitles GM "A Polemic") with views that downplay the significance of consciousness. Our understanding of GM is arguably a largely conscious understanding.[19] But if consciousness is in itself basically ineffective and/or counterproductive how does Nietzsche hope that such understanding will have any salutary effect? One could argue that in writing GM Nietzsche cares little for such "downstream effects" and that he simply wanted to make available certain truths, truths about the historical development of morality[20] – in which case the project would, ironically enough, be an example of the ascetic ideal in its manifestations as the will to truth (for its own sake) that Nietzsche seems bent on exposing in the third essay of GM. Alternatively, we could see GM as providing ammunition which can be used to lessen the dominance of certain drives, the drives that typically resonate with Christian morality, for instance drives towards acceptance and sociability. In the war of drives against each other, each drive attempts to grab what weapons it can, typically through its influence on the vast reservoir of our unconscious thinking – in another work Nietzsche graphically described how a "drive seized the event as its prey" (D 119). GM, then, is a weapon to be used to loosen the grips of certain drives. Nietzsche's

---

18 For more on this see Gemes 2006.
19 Katsafanas draws attention to this point in discussing how the genealogical method functions (2011: 107).
20 However, see GM Preface 5 where he explicitly rejects this motive.

motive for wanting to loosen the grip of those drives, for instance those that have latched on to the ascetic ideal, is that, as GM itself argues, those drives have come to dominate at the price of a severe, indeed pathological, repression of other drives. Seen in this light, part of the point of GM would be to weaken the grip of those repressive drives so that other drives might come to the fore, drives which in ascendancy are more likely to 'properly tyrannise' – that is to effect an integration, rather than suppression, of antithetical drives.[21]

Given that the role of consciousness for Nietzsche is generally harmful (for example, becoming a danger and a sickness when used as a tool of repression; promoting our 'herd' nature at the expense of our individuality), its role in unified selfhood by the same token seems to be a largely negative one (it is properly tyrannised). However, there are hints that its role need not be entirely detrimental:

> Language and the prejudices upon which language is based are a manifold hindrance to us when we want to explain inner processes and drives ... and *yet it is they which weave the web of our character and our destiny ... Our opinion of ourself, however, which we have arrived at by this erroneous path, the so-called "I", is thenceforth a fellow worker in the construction of our character and our destiny.* (D 115; italics added. Note the heading of the passage reads "The so-called 'I'".)

Our "character and destiny" are largely determined, then, by subterranean "inner processes and drives" which we cannot understand through our words and concepts. However, the "so-called 'I'" – i.e. our misunderstanding of ourselves, brought about by the fact that we are only able to fathom ourselves on the basis of the unrepresentative, distorted and inadequate translation into conscious thought of the workings of the drives – then becomes a *"fellow worker in the construction of our character"*. This is a very suggestive passage, indicating as it does that our conscious sense of self, in spite of or perhaps in consequence of its erroneous and distorting nature, itself contributes to our ongoing self-development – interacting with the drives in some way to do so. This idea again recalls Nietzsche's claims about the value of some errors and falsehoods. Nietzsche's main point in the passage is that the I is not what we usually think it is; but the term 'fellow worker' suggests that the illusions and errors of the conscious I do not prevent it from playing some kind of potentially helpful role in shaping the nature of the individual.

There seems to be no doubt, nevertheless, that if we want to "create ourselves" or "become who we are", to become genuine, unique persons, we

---

[21] This interpretation of the function of GM is elaborated in Gemes (2006).

cannot look to our *conscious* sense of ourselves to provide the key to this. This suspicion is confirmed if we look at Nietzsche's famous description of 'how one becomes what one is', as this trajectory occurred in his own life:

> ... For assuming that the task, the vocation, the *destiny* of the task exceeds the average measure by a significant degree, there would be no greater danger than to catch sight of oneself *with* this task. That one becomes what one is presupposes that one does not have the remotest idea *what* one is. ... The entire surface of consciousness – consciousness *is* a surface – has to be kept clear of any of the great imperatives ... [there is] a danger that the instinct will "understand itself" too early. In the meantime the organising "idea" destined to rule grows and grows in the depths – it begins to command ... it prepares *individual* qualities and abilities which will one day prove themselves indispensable as a means to achieving the whole – it constructs the *ancillary* capacities one after the other before it gives any hint of the dominating task, of the "goal", "objective", "meaning".... For the task of a *revaluation of values* more capacities perhaps were required than have dwelt together in one individual, above all antithetical capacities which however are not allowed to disturb or destroy one another. Order of rank among capacities; distance; the art of dividing without making inimical; mixing up nothing, "reconciling" nothing; a tremendous multiplicity ... – no trace of *struggle* can be discovered in my life.... [22] (EH Clever 9).

Consciousness again is a *surface*, but here its concealing nature is actually helpful insofar as the instinctual process must not rise to the surface too soon; the instinct's, the organising idea's, crucial work and commanding power must be well advanced long before it reaches conscious awareness. The "organising 'idea'" here, then, is not meant in the ordinary sense of a conscious concept (hence in Nietzsche's text 'idea' is in quotation marks) but rather in the sense of the aim of the drive or instinct, or of an unconscious idea supplied by the rele-

---

[22] This complex passage raises several interpretative challenges. Nietzsche's claim that there is "no trace of struggle" might seem probative in favour of the harmony interpretation of unity. But it is a highly implausible claim and arguably amounts to a rhetorical device or form of bravado on Nietzsche's part. More accurate is his private letter to Franz Overbeck in which he confesses "The daily struggle against my head trouble and the laughable complexity of my distresses demand so much attention that I am in danger of becoming *petty* in this regard" and talks of "the highflying drives that so rule me"(KSB 6: 49). See also KSB 6: 135, 138 where he refers to his daily struggles ("Jeder Tag ein Kampf"). In GS Preface 3 he tell us "[o]nly great pain, the long, slow pain that takes its time – on which we are burned, as it were, with green wood – compels us philosophers to descend into our ultimate depths". In the *Ecce Homo* passage he says antithetical capacities do not "disturb" one another, but then neither are they to be "reconciled" – a point highlighted by Harcourt (2011: 278 – 279), who argues that the Nietzschean ideal of individuality centres on the "shape" of one's character, or its "form". He considers that the notion of "form" might be interpreted as an aesthetic ideal of unity, or as an ideal of health, in which conflicting drives are not disowned or repressed. Harcourt takes this ideal to be fundamentally distinct from an ideal of harmony.

vant instinct. Indeed in his own case Nietzsche gives all credit to "the secret labour and artistic working of my instinct" (EH Clever 9).

Another crucial point should be noted: the task is a rare and exceptional one – it "exceeds the average measure by a significant degree". This task is the revaluation of values,[23] and thus 'becoming what one is' is described chiefly in terms of the dominating *task* – again, he is not focusing explicitly on a certain internal arrangement as an end in itself, but in order to be capable of enacting a life's goal. Thus Nietzsche presents himself as an example of that rarefied category of human being we met in the quotation given above from KSA 8: 31–32 – the philosopher, artist or saviour – and in *this* sort of case he considers it crucial that an "organising 'idea'" prepares the conditions for achieving the task below the level of consciousness before coming to 'understand itself'. Here we also learn that the internal constitution associated with such truly creative vocations consists of an unusually diverse multiplicity of capacities which coexist and are ordered in a particular way. 'Becoming what one is', as described in this passage, presupposes a certain level of internal complexity, a range of capacities that, through a largely unconscious process of ordering, are put in service of an exceptional and creative goal.[24]

---

[23] On Katsafanas's reading, Nietzschean freedom is related to the capacity for critical reflection. He takes it that Nietzsche's discussions of freedom focus on "'revaluating', creating new values, questioning traditional values" (2011: 93): i.e. he takes freedom to be demonstrated by the ability to rise above, or at least reflectively call into question, the moral values of the society in which one is raised, and to live by new and different values. Yet in the *Ecce Homo* passage, where Nietzsche describes what makes his own "revaluation of values" possible, he takes pains to emphasise that the preconditions for achieving this task were largely unconscious and that if they had entered consciousness too soon this would have endangered the task or rendered its realisation impossible. The task is attributed instead to "the protracted secret labour … of my instinct". If this is a paradigm example of Nietzschean freedom, it is not a freedom primarily concerned with the ability to consciously deliberate. (See also TI Skirmishes 38 – where "the free man is a *warrior*" in whom the *instincts* for "war and victory" have "gained mastery over the other instincts".) Gemes (2009b) gives a less cognitive account of what Nietzschean freedom consists in.

[24] One might here raise the objection that the Greek masters of GM Essay I seem fairly simple non-conflicted beings devoid of such creative goals, unless, in the words of GM I 11, "schoolboy pranks" of "a hideous succession of murder, arson rape and torture" are to count. Yet surely, runs the objection, the Greek masters count as persons, as having selves. First, it is worth noting that the masters of GM are also configured as "beasts of prey" and "blond beasts", that is, lions (*ibid*). Neither we, nor Nietzsche, normally equate persons with beasts – would Nietzsche be happy to equate his favourite candidate for full personhood, namely Goethe, with a beast? Second, and more to the point, the portrait of the Greek masters in GM I is a deliberately simplified caricature deployed for rhetorical purposes and not Nietzsche's considered view of the

2 Unity and the predominance model

2.1 Two models of unity

In section 1.4 we hypothesised that given Nietzsche's views on consciousness (1.3), and his differing treatment of the (conscious) I/ego and the *self* (1.2), the arrangement of the (largely unknown, non-conscious) drives must be pivotal to his conception of the self. This led us to consider a possible 'elitist' reading concerning the desirable arrangement of the drives that is required for a genuine self, namely that this arrangement is one of *wholeness* or *unity*; on this reading, most modern human beings would be in some sense fragmented or disunified, whereas the rare few achieve a coherent organisation of the drives and their competing aims. We then related this idea to Nietzsche's views on personal uniqueness – which seem to both lend some credence to the 'elitist' interpretation, and to underline Nietzsche's problematisation of consciousness. Finally, we looked at how a coherent organisation of drives achieved through a largely unconscious process can underpin the ideal of "becoming what one is".

It remains to look more closely at how we are to understand Nietzschean unity. Gemes (2009b) argued that Nietzsche's aim is to foster the development of genuine persons, those who are unified or whole; and, furthermore, *that this occurs when the various drives are hierarchically organised under the aegis of a ruling or master drive*, which prevails over the others sufficiently to create order and direction from relative formlessness. This is the 'predominance model' challenged by Katsafanas (2011). According to this model each drive has its own aim and is constantly pressing for expression in order to attain that aim. Thus drives are brought into a power conflict with one another, insofar as they cannot all be simultaneously directly satisfied, either for merely practical reasons or – more acutely – where they are inherently contradictory in nature and so pull in opposing, incompatible directions[25]:

---

ancient Greeks. In the earlier *The Birth of Tragedy* Nietzsche gave his more considered view that in fact the ancient Greeks were incredibly complex and conflicted but through the use of tragedy they were able to reconcile, for instance, their sophisticated pessimistic realisation that life is irredeemably painful with their will to affirm life. For more on this, especially on the above-mentioned rhetorical purposes of GM, see Gemes 2006.

25 The force of 'directly' here will become apparent soon enough. The point is that drives often have conflicting aims that can't simply be directly and simultaneously satisfied. For instance, the drive to dominate and the drive to be accepted by others are prima facie in such conflict. But if a drive can be diverted from its primary aim it may in its diverted form find a satisfaction without

> ... all the instincts have practised philosophy, and ... each one of them would like only too well to represent *itself* as the ultimate aim of existence and as the legitimate *master* of all other instincts. For every instinct is tyrannical ... (BGE 6)

> Every drive is a kind of attempt to dominate; each has its own perspective, which it wants to force as a norm on the other drives. (KSA 12: 315)

Constituted by a number of competing drives, each human being might either be a formless chaos of conflicting impulses, *or* might be unified (to some degree or other) under the rule of some predominant drive – a rule which enables that drive's imperative aim to be consistently and effectively pursued. Thus in EH Clever 9, we learned that "the organising 'idea' destined to rule begins to command ... it prepares *individual* qualities and abilities ... as a means to achieving the whole". Here, 'becoming what one is' seems to be characterised as involving a process of predominance.[26]

Against the predominance model Katsafanas offers a harmony model. He argues that unity is achieved "when the parts [drives and conscious thought] relate to each other in a harmonious way, rather than when one part dominates the other parts" (2011: 102).[27] He claims this reading has some significant advantages over the predominance model.[28] Katsafanas points out that there is an

---

thereby impeding the satisfaction of other drives that its direct satisfaction would naturally thwart.

[26] In Z I Despisers of the Body, Zarathustra also proclaims that "Always the Self listens and seeks: it compares, compels, conquers, destroys. It rules and is also the I's ruler".

[27] Katsafanas (2011) is careful to acknowledge Nietzsche's claim that "... most of a philosopher's conscious thinking is secretly guided and channelled ... by his instincts" (BGE 3), and that Nietzsche "denies that there is any self over and above the drives" and is "deeply sceptical ... of the idea that reflective choice is anything more than a precipitate of drives" (2011: 89). Nevertheless these observations are strangely at odds with the main thrust of his central claim about Nietzschean unity, which appears to give the role of conscious reflection and judgement at least equal prominence to that of the drives.

[28] Katsafanas argues against the predominance view on the basis that Nietzsche characterises Wagner as one who has diverse drives that are co-ordinated under a ruling passion or drive yet Nietzsche also characterises Wagner as being "a paradigm of *disunity*" (2011: 100). But this is in no way probative since the text that Katsafanas uses to show that Nietzsche sees Wagner as having a predominating sublimating master drive is taken from Nietzsche's early work of 1876 "Wagner in Bayreuth", whereas the characterisation that suggests that Wagner was a paradigm of disunity comes from a much later work of 1888, *The Case of Wagner*. In the earlier work Nietzsche was still attempting to establish Wagner as a paradigm of the great individual, the genius, who is the engine of cultural renewal; he characterises Wagner in terms of "the rule of a single inner law" (RWB 2). In stark contrast, the later work attempts to establish Wagner as a paradigm of modern sham culture; he characterises Wagner in terms of his "multiplicity, abundance and arbitrariness" (CW 10). Between the 1876 work and the 1888 work Nietzsche came to

apparent discrepancy between Nietzsche's valuing of unity, on the one hand, and his tendency to champion the cultivation of internal conflict or tension on the other – as evidenced in such passages as the following:

> We adopt the same attitude towards the "enemy within" ... there too we have grasped its *value*. One is *fruitful* only at the cost of being rich in contradictions ... (TI Morality 3)

Katsafanas concludes that these Nietzschean attitudes are not mutually contradictory if we understand "fruitful" conflict as obtaining amongst the drives, while unity is a relation that should obtain between the drives *and conscious thought*:

> Nietzsche is not inconsistent when he praises individuals with conflicting drives, for Nietzschean unity is *not* unity between particular drives, but unity between drives and other parts of the individual. (Katsafanas 2011: 103)

But it is not clear that this solves the problem. The question remains: unity between *which* drives and conscious thought? Given that the drives are in conflict with each other, at best a harmonious relation could presumably only exist between some subset of drives and conscious reflection on this account.

2.2 Unity through sublimation

The root problem here is that Nietzsche seems to extol both internal conflict and unity. He valorises a kind of agonal struggle between the drives, each trying to be master of all the others, yet also values a certain kind of unity. Gemes (2009a) argued that this tension is reconcilable though proper attention to the distinction between repression and sublimation:

> Sublimation is what happens when a drive's primary aim is substituted for by a secondary aim that allows for expression of the drive in a manner consonant with the master drive. As John Richardson succinctly puts it, "[D]rive A rules B insofar as it has turned B towards A's own end, so that B now participates in A's distinctive activity" (1996: 33). Repression is what happens when a drive is denied its immediate aim and is then split off from other drives in the sense that its aims are not integrated with the aims of other drives and it must battle, often unsuccessfully, for any opportunity to achieve expression. (Gemes 2009a: 48)

A classic case of sublimation is where an artist reconciles his sexual drive with his drives for social acceptability and creativity by producing art with a certain

---

completely revise his (public) assessment of Wagner. So this provides no evidence that Nietzsche *at one and the same time* held Wagner as constituting a case of diverse drives being co-ordinated under a ruling drive and as a paradigm of disunity.

amount of erotic content. Here his sexual drive is not repressed but redirected towards an end that is both creative and socially acceptable.

Sublimation, then, allows that the unifying activity of the ruling drive will still allow other drives some (controlled, organised) expression, whilst sufficiently marshalling their energy to enable achievement of its overall goal.[29] This model allows for the continuing agonal struggle between drives because sublimated drives will always be disposed to return to pursue their primary aim. Given the opportunity, for instance through the weakening of a one-time predominant drive that has forced them for some time to pursue secondary aims, they will try to revert to their primary aim and, indeed, seek dominance of the formerly ascendant drive.

Arguably, then, Nietzsche does not actually understand 'unity' to mean harmony; he does not claim that the predominant drive is entering into a 'harmonious' relation with those it organises; after all it has by some means to impose and maintain its rule. What matters to Nietzsche is that the ruling drive is able to bring about a *cohesive* organisation of internal forces directed towards a clear (ideally creative) goal and without simply annihilating the competition. In GM Nietzsche is clearly concerned about the damaging effects of instinctual repression, which he presents as inimical to a flourishing life. Clearly the type of internal conflict described in GM II 16 is not desirable.[30] It seems safe to conclude that a suitable model of predominance is incompatible with this kind of debilitating repression. However, equally, this does not equate predominance achieved through sublimation with an absence or resolution of all internal conflict.[31]

The fact that ongoing agonal struggle is consistent with unity through sublimation may also be helpful when considering a related issue that Katsafanas

---

[29] One might reasonably worry that, while sublimation might work in specific instances such as the case of the artist's production of work with erotic content, it is of a different order to expect that it could in practice successfully reconcile all the range of opposing instincts in a complex individual. For more on this see Le Patourel (2012).

[30] For Nietzsche not all internalization of instincts is bad; after all, it is such internalization that gives us depth. Here we need to distinguish between those forms of suppression that are a step towards later integration and those forms of severe repression that Nietzsche identifies with pathological moralization. For more on this see Gemes 2009a.

[31] Le Patourel (2012) similarly argues against a reading that equates Nietzschean unity with harmony, for example noting such passages as GS 266 and A 57, where Nietzsche advocates severity and even cruelty towards oneself. However Le Patourel ultimately finds it hard to reconcile Nietzsche's positions on unity and on internal conflict, and proposes that while unity remains a powerful Nietzschean ideal it is perhaps not fully realisable in the modern individual who is subject to particularly deep internal contradictions.

suggests is problematic for the predominance model, namely that the ruling drive has no particular 'right' to rule, i.e. does not especially express or represent the whole self (2011: 98). On the elitist reading we have outlined, however, until the ruling drive brings about the requisite internal ordering, there is no 'self' to represent. This would help to explain why the issue of the ruling drive's 'right' to rule does not appear to trouble Nietzsche, who seems quite comfortable with the idea of a powerful drive seizing control and imposing its own aims. Indeed he often characterises our instincts as 'tyrants':

> Our most powerful instinct, the tyrant in us, subjugates not only our reason, but also our conscience ... (BGE 158)

In BGE 6, *every instinct is tyrannical* in that it seeks power, it seeks to bend resources to its goal. Recall also that consciousness, at least in its current state, is *properly tyrannised* (GS 11).[32] 'Tyranny' for Nietzsche has a necessary place in the dynamics of the self:

> Overcoming of the affects? No, if that means their weakening and annihilation. But instead employing them; which may mean a long tyrannising of them ... At last they are confidently given freedom again: they love us as good servants and happily go wherever our best interests lie. (KSA 12: 39)

Here, a passage often cited as highlighting his concern with sublimation of the affects (they must not be annihilated) nevertheless describes an initial long *tyrannising* of them *before* they can be allowed freedom (and then, only as obedient servants – not as equals). Such a tyrannising, and the tyrannised drives' eventual 'freedom' as good servants, do not suggest that these affects are able to directly pursue their own aims.

In response to Katsafanas' concerns regarding the 'credentials' of the ruling drive, it is furthermore worth noting that the account of sublimation provided above is so far merely formal. It specifies sublimation as the mastery of one drive over others through redirecting those other drives to ends congruent with that of the master drive. This might suggest that any drive is capable of such mastery.[33] However, it is clearly Nietzsche's view that some drives by the very

---

32 Thus, while the repression/sublimation distinction is often described in terms of 'tyranny' versus 'mastery' respectively, we should remember that Nietzsche himself does not always use 'tyranny' disapprovingly.
33 Gemes (2009a and 2009b), cited in Katsafanas (2011) as exemplifying the predominance view, strongly emphasises the necessity of, not mere dominance, but ordering and organising, which can only be achieved through sublimation and not repression. The case of the recluse whose pre-

nature of their aims gain mastery though repression rather than the re-directing of other drives. A drive for sociability or a drive for contentment is a drive that typically masters at the expense of repressing rather than sublimating other drives. For Nietzsche it is clearly drives such as the drive to creativity or to philosophise that are suitable candidates for the role of a sublimating master drive.[34]

2.3 The Nietzschean self, conscious judgement and decision-making

Nietzsche talks of a "drive to reflection" (D 119) and claims that "the largest part of conscious thinking has to be considered an instinctual activity" (BGE 3). It is the misplaced pride of consciousness that mistakenly regards itself as functioning autonomously. (Recall that Zarathustra calls the unknown self "the leading-string of the [conscious] I and the *prompter of its conceptions*".)

Thus, Nietzsche makes the repeated claim (e.g. D 109, BGE 117) that what we usually take to be conflict between our conscious reflection and our drives is ultimately a conflict between various drives:

> ... inner struggles and crises in which a man is torn back and forth by various motives until he finally decides for the most powerful – as is said (in truth until the most powerful decides about us). (HH I 107)

Here Nietzsche's aside ("in truth") marks his considered belief that one's decision is the product of motives over which one has little conscious control. This is of a piece with his claim

---

dominant drive is to collect stamps is used to argue that not any drive is suited for this role (Gemes 2009a, footnote 23).

34 Katsafanas (2011: 98) suggests that the case of a high-functioning masterful alcoholic, whose drive to drink manages to sublimate all his other drives, provides a refutation of the unity through predominance view. It seems more likely however that such a drive would achieve mastery at the cost of a severe repression of at least some of the other drives, for instance the drive to health. But if we were to accept the possibility of the sublimating alcoholic we might go one step further and think of the masterful alcoholic whose consciousness has been so dominated by his drive to consume alcohol that, after initially resisting, his conscious reflection now approves of his alcoholic inclinations. Here we would have the type of harmony between conscious reflection and drives that Katsafanas seems to approve of. Would this extra bit of dominance be sufficient to produce genuine freedom and agency? Why should we identify the so-called "voice of the agent" with this "weak overpowered element" (2011: 98) of past resistance and present compliance?

I have no idea what I am doing! I have no idea what I should do. You are right, but have no doubt: *you will be done* [*du wirst gethan*]. (D 120)

Here, the 'I' who has no idea, the 'you' who will be done, is presumably the 'I' of conscious reflection. On our interpretation, D 120 suggests that where we fail to form a satisfactory conscious conception of what we are doing, or fail to deliberate successfully so as to make a conscious decision about how to act, the drives nevertheless bring about action. The striking formulation 'you will be done' implies both that the source of the action remains largely unknown to consciousness, and that consciousness has a largely passive role. This characterisation is not confined to those cases where conscious deliberation evidently founders. Nietzsche's typical formulations of selfhood – e.g. "*who he is* – that is, in what hierarchy the innermost drives of his nature are arranged" (BGE 6); the "soul as the social construct of drives and emotions" (BGE 12) – conspicuously do not depend on the role of conscious reflection. We must also remember that in Zarathustra, the self *laughed* at the pride of the conscious I; and even more strongly (as we saw in section 1.3 above) in GS 11 Nietzsche claims that "consciousness is properly tyrannised [*tüchtig tyrannisiert*]" and explicitly says that we are mistaken in seeing consciousness as "the unity of the organism".[35]

How does this demotion of conscious reflection fit in with the much referenced passage where Nietzsche talks of Goethe disciplining himself (TI Skirmishes 49)? A crucial point to note here is that Nietzsche does not say that Goethe *consciously* disciplined himself. A reading which conflates these two merely shows an attachment to the Cartesian view rejected by Nietzsche that the self is to be identified with the conscious I. Goethe may have fashioned himself, but that does not mean the fashioning was a self-conscious project.

With this in mind, we can consider what is happening more generally when a person decides between various conflicting motives. Consider the example of a married person who is torn between the desire to have an affair, on the one hand, and the desire to stay loyal to their spouse and keep their marriage vows, on the other. Suppose that this person judges that it is better to remain faithful and, despite powerful temptation, succeeds in doing so. We might characterise this as an admirable example of self-control and say that the person did not 'give in' to the temptation. Note however that if they had 'given in' despite the conscious judgement that staying faithful is better, we would be implying that

---

35 To claim that consciousness *alone*, in itself, fails to constitute the unity of the organism is admittedly not the same as denying that unity could be achieved by some harmonious relation of consciousness *with* the instincts. However, it also seems undeniable that the instincts have by far the greater role to play, and that tyranny and harmony are far apart.

'they' were relatively passive in the face of an overwhelming desire. That is to say, however, that we would have construed the example in the standard Platonic/Kantian way. This way of viewing the matter can be so customary, so automatic, that it can be difficult to keep hold of the startling Nietzschean proposition that it need not be so construed. The conscious judgement that it would be better not to have the affair is implicitly aligned with the 'real' locus of the self, such that acting in accordance with that judgement, even in the face of powerful contradictory drives, is to genuinely *act*. Yet as we have seen for Nietzsche, famously, when these inner struggles take place,

> While "we" believe we are complaining about the vehemence of a drive, at bottom it is one drive *which is complaining about another* ... in this entire procedure our intellect is only the blind instrument of *another drive* which is a *rival* of the drive whose vehemence is tormenting us ... (D 109)

Thus, when the married person resists having the affair, the source of this behaviour is ultimately a rival drive which is in conflict with the drive to be unfaithful – for instance, perhaps, a drive to stay within the bounds of socially acceptable behaviour or to preserve a stable relationship – and it is this rival drive which *produces* the conscious judgement that staying faithful is better. This is still ultimately a relation *between* drives (in which the intellect is only a "blind instrument"), not a relation between the drives and conscious judgement. Nietzsche does indeed say "a *struggle* is in prospect in which our intellect is going to have to take sides" (D 109). But this 'taking sides' is neither the definitive part of the process, nor something it does autonomously from the influence of the drives; rather, it is a reflection of the "order of rank" within our drives.

A key concern raised about the predominance model, as we saw in 2.2, is that if one allows that one may be ruled by a master drive, possibly a master drive that one does not consciously identify with, then when one does something one is being overcome by an (internal) force, rather than expressing the self. This echoes Kant's claim that being overpowered by a drive is heteronomy, as opposed to autonomy.[36] On such a view, any 'doing' produced in such a situation is not an exhibition of true agency. Thus, if the married person in our example had actually had the affair, despite their conscious disapproval of doing so, on this view they would typically be described as having been 'overcome' by a strong wayward desire. Now if a drive were to assume *total* mastery then presumably no other

---

[36] Korsgaard (2009) expresses similar concerns about being overcome by an internal force as incompatible with acting as a unified whole. Gemes (2009b) explicitly argues that autonomy of a Nietzschean kind is to be explained in terms of a certain rank order of the drives.

drive would be able to supply the conscious I with an alternative motive, hence internal conflict would not occur. Of course on the predominance model defended earlier other drives can still have primary aims that are in conflict with the aim of the master drive, but as such drives would be sublimated towards a secondary aim congruent with that of the master drive, those conflicting aims would not enter into consciousness. Still, presumably, such total mastery is rare, even among great individuals. The crucial point here is that in this case we have domination *of the conscious I* by the master drive, not domination of the *self*. The view that takes this to be a case of one's not acting but being acted upon, as being merely passive, is a view that in the Cartesian and Kantian manner implicitly, if not explicitly, identifies the self with the I.[37] For Nietzsche your self is acting in such cases even if the conscious I is not the controlling force, or simply does not approve of the action – recall here Nietzsche's claim mentioned above, "you will be done [*du wirst gethan*]", and likewise Zarathustra's claim "Your Self laughs at your I [*dein Ich*] and its proud leapings. 'What are these leapings and soarings of thought to me?' it says to itself."[38] Zarathustra locates the self as the greater reason and herdsman and the I as a lesser reason and as part of the herd (Z I Despisers of the Body), not (like Descartes and Kant) the other way round.

As we saw with D 109, which is about *"self-mastery"*, the combating of a vehement drive is not achieved by the authority of the conscious ego, but *by another drive*. The struggle between the drives, rather than a process of conscious reflection, similarly takes centre stage in Nietzsche's discussion of "what knowing means":

> ... what is this *intelligere* other than ... [a] result of the different and conflicting impulses to laugh, lament, and curse? Before knowledge is possible, each of these impulses must first have presented its one-sided view of the thing or event; then comes the fight between these one-sided views, and occasionally out of it a mean, an appeasement, a concession to all three sides, a kind of justice and contract; for in virtue of justice and a contract all these impulses can assert and maintain themselves in existence and each can finally feel it is in the right vis-à-vis all the others. Since only the last scenes of reconciliation and final accounting at the end of this long process rise to consciousness, we suppose that *intelligere* must be something conciliatory, just, and good – something that stands essentially opposed to the instincts, when in

---

37 Katsafanas, despite his earlier acknowledging that "Nietzsche does not accept the distinction between being an agent and being a locus of forces" (2011: 90), shows his implicit commitment to the Cartesian/Kantian view when he says of an alcoholic whose conscious judgement against drinking is overridden by his cravings that "the voice of the agent seems to reside in the weak, overpowered element of resistance" (2011: 98).

38 Note this is not to say that the self *is* simply the dominating drive: the self is the unity achieved under the influence of the dominating drive.

> fact *it is only a certain behaviour of the drives towards one another.* For the longest time, conscious thought was considered thought itself. Only now does the truth dawn on us that by far the greatest part of our mind's activity proceeds unconscious and unfelt ... precisely philosophers are most easily led astray about the nature of knowledge. (GS 333)

Nietzsche is making various claims in this passage which are by now familiar: the primacy of drive activity; rejection of the idea that conscious judgement is autonomous, or more powerful and important than the instincts; each drive has its own characteristic ('one-sided') demand, and thus conflicts with and 'fights' the others; what arrives in consciousness is only the final outcome of this process. Note that when a kind of 'justice' or 'reconciliation' occurs between the drives' conflicting claims, this is not due to the adjudication of conscious judgement, and does not represent a harmony *between* the drives and conscious judgement. Conscious thought does not bring about the conciliation; we mistakenly think it does only because it is only the conciliation itself, not the underlying struggle, which rises to consciousness. Nietzsche clearly locates the decisive activity producing understanding in the conflict between drives; this *fight* is presented as the condition of the possibility of knowledge. He goes on to describe conscious thought as the "least vigorous" and "calmest" kind of thought. It is for this reason we are inclined to misconstrue conscious understanding as a form of impartial observation that transcends, reflects on and can control conflicting impulses.

Given this quintessentially Nietzschean view, with its scepticism about traditional accounts of objective knowledge, its foreshadowing of the perspectivism of GM III, its insistence on the role of unconscious conflict, it is hard to be convinced by any interpretation of Nietzschean selfhood that allocates a pivotal role to conscious reflection and places an emphasis on harmony.[39] The battlefield of the unconscious drives in their relentless agonal struggle is more important to Nietzsche than what presents itself belatedly in consciousness as a more or less harmonious outcome of the battle.

Conclusion

We have argued that the Nietzschean self is not to be equated with the I or ego of consciousness. Instead, the self is to be found most essentially in the interre-

---

[39] In line with the general overestimation of the role of consciousness and reflection in Nietzsche, most commentators take perspectivism to be a claim about truth or knowledge, thus assuming that perspectives concern propositions we might believe or entertain. Gemes (2013), following Richardson (1996), argues that for Nietzsche it is essentially drives that have perspectives.

lation between the drives. We discussed whether the self is simply to be identified with any given individual's collection of drives (the egalitarian version) or with only select, unified sets of drives (the elitist version). Emphasising the latter view, we argued that becoming what one is, being a genuine individual, involves having an internal order that is imposed by a predominant drive, marshalling one's capacities in the service of a creative vocation or task (one which deals in values) that is supplied by that drive. In Katsafanas's alternative model, unity hinges on conscious reflection being in harmony with the drives. We argued that Nietzsche, the champion of agonal struggle and the great sceptic of the power and function of conscious reflection, should not be domesticated in this manner as an apologist for a traditional valorisation of harmony between instincts and reason.

We have seen that Nietzsche is drawn to consider the "problem of consciousness" (GS 354), concluding that consciousness is something that belongs to the individual's "social or herd nature" and not to her "individual existence". In GM, the problem centres on internal alienation, the repression of instinctual life that can occur when conscious thought is over-privileged. In *The Gay Science*, the problem is the loss of individuality that occurs when we take at face value what we appear to be when viewed through the distorting filter of consciousness, which reduces our uniqueness to the average and the generic. While the problems in each case are different, the overestimation of consciousness is key to both. Katsafanas' account of unity might at first sight seem to offer a possible solution to the problem of consciousness by showing how it might be reconciled with the drives; we have argued that this cannot be Nietzsche's solution.

In this essay we have more or less explicitly identified a range of notions found in Nietzsche's texts – becoming what you are, having a self, becoming a genuine individual, being a person – with that of achieving a unity of drives under the sublimating hegemony of a master drive. Alternatively, one might wish to argue that such unity is for Nietzsche only a prerequisite of becoming a self and/or becoming what you are, and/or becoming a genuine individual, and/or being a person; and to provide an account that differentiates between these ideas. Or, inversely, one might claim that being a person, and/or having a self, is a precondition for establishing unity. Nietzsche's texts are arguably not precise or detailed enough to provide a definitive basis for strict distinctions of this kind. But there is an important point that needs to be made here. Wilfred Sellars has rightly observed that the notion of being a person is as much a normative as a descriptive notion – a point with which Nietzsche would presumably agree. Thus, for Sellars (1966) part of saying X is a person is to take on the commitment that X should not merely be treated as a thing (in Kant's terminology it is to recognise them as a member of the Kingdom of Ends). Given the centrality, we would say primacy, of normative ends in Nietzsche project/s, taking an elitist stance which identifies genuine unity with the desired outcomes of being a person, having a self, being a genuine individual, becoming what you are, expressly reflects both his philosophical tone and normative commitments. Those of a more egalitarian disposition might of course say that in this case Nietzsche's use of such terms is an honorific use and that there is a perfectly acceptable, pared down, modest notion of, say, being a person that is applicable to all human beings. The crucial point here is that this "acceptability" is not a matter of descriptive fact – say, the alleged descriptive fact that even seriously disunified individuals are persons. Rather the acceptability of such modest claims itself is a matter of, a reflection of, one's own (non-Nietzschean) normative commitments.

Returning to the paradoxes of self-creation discussed at the beginning of Part 1: we have argued that it is not the conscious I or ego that does the self-creation. If anything, consciousness is typically inimical to such a task. Where it does participate in self-creation it is not an instigator but a tool or, at best, a co-worker. The real engine of self-creation is a ruling drive with the strength to create a hierarchy and an organisation of the other drives; a ruling drive that sublimates the other drives, allowing them some form of expression rather than bringing about their repression or extirpation.[40] Such a drive taken singly is no self – it lacks the requisite complexity. However, when successful, it is the instigator of rank order among the drives; it is this rank order that constitutes a self (the elitist reading). While this self exhibits unity, the lower members of the rank order are ever waiting the opportunity to struggle to improve their rank. So this unified self does not prohibit agonal struggle between the drives. The ultimate addressee of the call to self-creation, then, is neither the I of consciousness nor a pre-existent self – even if sometimes, as in the case of those who are inspired by Nietzsche's writings to find their true vocation, that message is first filtered through the conscious I.[41]

---

[40] This might suggest that the master drive, indeed all drives, are for Nietzsche some kind of homunculi – a worry exacerbated by Nietzsche's talk of drives "complaining" about each other (D109, as quoted above), drives "fighting" each other (GS 333, as quoted above), etc. While this is a real worry, Gemes (2009a) attempts to provide a non-homuncular account of how drives may function in the construction of a self. Katsafanas (2013) contains the most detailed and nuanced discussion of the nature of Nietzsche's notion of the drives, with express focus on the homunculi problem.

[41] The conscious I may *filter* Nietzsche's message, but as we have said this is not equivalent to its being the addressee of the injunction to self-create. The effect of Nietzsche's texts, on this view, would be to weaken certain drives and empower others (see section 1.5 above). If the conscious I understands his message, this is understanding more in the sense of GS 333 – the 'final accounting' available to conscious thought of the battle of the drives.

References

Acampora, Christa Davis (ed.) (2006) *Nietzsche's On the Genealogy of Morals: Critical Essays*, Lanham/Oxford: Rowman & Littlefield.
Bettelheim, Bruno (1982) *Freud and Man's Soul*, London: Chatto & Windus.
Constâncio, João (2011) "On Consciousness. Nietzsche's Departure from Schopenhauer", in: *Nietzsche-Studien* 40, 1–42.
Gardner, Sebastian (2009) "Nietzsche, the Self, and the Disunity of Philosophical Reason", in: Gemes/May (2009), 1–31.
Gemes, Ken (2006) "'We Remain of Necessity Stranger to Ourselves': The Key Message of Nietzsche's *Genealogy*", in: Christa Davis Acampora (ed.), *Nietzsche's On the Genealogy of Morals: Critical Essays*. Lanham & Oxford: Rowman & Littlefield, 191–208.
Gemes, Ken (2009a) "Freud and Nietzsche on Sublimation", in: *Journal of Nietzsche Studies* 38, 38–59.
Gemes, Ken (2009b) "Nietzsche on the Sovereign Individual, Free Will and Autonomy", in: Gemes/May (2009), 33–50.
Gemes, Ken (2013) "Life's Perspectives", in: Gemes/Richardson (2013), 553–575.
Gemes, Ken/May, Simon (eds.) (2009) *Nietzsche on Freedom and Autonomy*, Oxford/New York: Oxford University Press.
Gemes, Ken/Richardson, John (eds.) (2013) *The Oxford Handbook on Nietzsche*, Oxford: Oxford University Press.
Harcourt, Edward (2011) "Nietzsche and the 'Aesthetics of Character'", in: May (2011), 265–284.
Huenemann, Charlie (2013) "Nietzsche's Illness", in: Gemes/Richardson (2013): 63–80.
Janaway, Christopher (2007) *Beyond Selflessness. Reading Nietzsche's Genealogy*, Oxford: Oxford University Press.
Katsafanas, Paul (2005) "Nietzsche's Theory of Mind: Consciousness and Conceptualization", in: *European Journal of Philosophy* 13, 1–31.
Katsafanas, Paul (2011) "The Concept of Unified Agency in Nietzsche, Plato and Schiller", in: *Journal of the History of Philosophy* 49, 87–113.
Katsafanas, Paul (2013) "Nietzsche's Philosophical Psychology", in: Gemes/Richardson (2013), 727–755.
Korsgaard, Christine M. (2009) *Self-Constitution: Agency, Identity and Integrity*, Oxford: Oxford University Press.
Lehrer, Keith (ed.) (1966) *Freedom and Determinism*, New York: Random House.
Leiter, Brian (2002) *Nietzsche on Morality*, London/New York: Routledge.
Le Patourel, I. (2012) "Nietzschean Selfhood: Inner Conflict and Unification", MPhilStud thesis, Birkbeck, University of London.
May, Simon (ed.) (2011) *Nietzsche's On the Genealogy of Morality: A Critical Guide*, Cambridge: Cambridge University Press.
Nietzsche, Friedrich (1966) *Beyond Good and Evil*, trans. W. Kaufmannn, New York: Vintage.
Nietzsche, Friedrich (1968) *Twilight of the Idols* in: *Twilight of the Idols and the Antichrist*, trans. R.J. Hollingdale, London: Penguin.
Nietzsche, Friedrich (1969a) *Ecce Homo* in: *On the Genealogy of Morals and Ecce Homo*, trans. W. Kaufmann and R.J. Hollingdale, New York: Vintage.

Nietzsche, Friedrich (1969b) *On the Genealogy of Morals*, in: *On the Genealogy of Morals and Ecce Homo*, trans. W. Kaufmann and R.J. Hollingdale, New York: Vintage.

Nietzsche, Friedrich (1974) *The Gay Science*, trans. W. Kaufmann, New York: Vintage Vintage

Nietzsche, Friedrich (2005) *Thus Spoke Zarathustra*, trans. G. Parkes, Oxford: Oxford University Press.

Riccardi, Mattia (forthcoming) "Nietzsche on the Superficiality of Consciousness", in: M. Dries (ed.), *Nietzsche on Consciousness and the Embodied Mind*, Berlin/Boston: De Gruyter.

Richardson, John (1996) *Nietzsche's System*, Oxford: Oxford University Press.

Sellars, Wilfrid (1966) "Fatalism and Determinism", in: Lehrer (1966), 141–174.

Stern, Thomas, "Against Nietzsche's Theory of the Drives" (manuscript).

Herman Siemens
25 Nietzsche's Socio-Physiology of the Self[1]

Introduction

At issue in this essay is the notion of the individual or person that is presupposed by liberal contract theory in general and by John Rawls in specific, in the so-called 'original position' set out in his well-known *Theory of Justice*[2]. I will examine Nietzsche's thought on the social and historical sources of the self, an area of his thought that has not received sufficient attention, and reconstruct it as a counter-argument against the liberal concept of the individual. In specific, I will set it up against two well-known charges that have been levelled against Rawls by his critics. They are that the notion of the individual deployed in the original position presupposes that:

1. the person is *antecedently individuated*: a person is what it is as a person independently of the ends or values it freely chooses; the ends I choose are not constitutive of my identity or who I am.
2. the person is *asocial*: a person's ends are formed prior to, or independently of, society; society does not inform a person's identity, values or ends, but is rather the outcome of a contract between individuals whose ends are already given.

The validity of these charges, as criticisms of Rawls, has been much debated,[3] but for my purpose that is of secondary importance. In the first place, these notions have a long history in political and moral thought, especially the kinds of democratic liberalism, contract theory and morality that Nietzsche was famil-

---

[1] This essay is based on the work I have done on the political implications of Nietzsche's thought, and especially his critique of liberal-democratic values (Siemens 2006 and 2009a), as well as my article *Empfindung* for the *Nietzsche-Wörterbuch* (Siemens 2011). I would like to thank João Constâncio for the opportunity to present and discuss an early version of this essay at a workshop in Lisbon.
[2] Rawls (1971, esp. §§ 4 and 24). My understanding of Rawls's notion of the self and Nietzsche's opposition to it is much indebted to David Owen's account in Owen 1995: 133–138.
[3] For an account of the debate and a critical assessment of these charges, see Mulhall/Swift (1992) and (2003: 460–487). After *Theory of Justice*, Rawls's position takes account of these criticisms. On the later Rawls, see Owen (1995: 154–164), Mouffe (1996: 248–255) and Mulhall/Swift (2003).

iar with, as we will see. Secondly, they continue to inform our everyday, pre-philosophical self-understanding as moral and political agents. And most importantly, they are often ascribed to Nietzsche himself by those who see him as a champion of autarkic or aristocratic individualism. These are the principal targets of the Nietzschean counter-argument against the liberal concept of the individual I will set out in this essay.

The Nietzschean counter-argument is both critical and constructive. Nietzsche offers both a powerful critique of the asocial, antecedently individuated concept of personhood, and an alternative positive conception of personhood. On one side are arguments to the effect that the individual or person is inseparable from its ends or values, which in turn are socially constituted, and that our capacities as individuals, especially for sovereign agency, are the product of a long social history and pre-history. On the other side is the constructive counter-claim that the maintenance and cultivation of our capacities (for autonomous reflection and agency) is dependent on relations of measured antagonism both between and within us as individuals, or rather: dividua. In what follows these arguments will be developed along four main lines of thought:

1. on the social origins and character of (self-)consciousness;
2. on the (pre-)history and social constitution of our capacities as sovereign individuals;
3. on the social origins of moral phenomena (as internalisations of communal norms); and
4. the physiological destruction of the substantial moral subject, coupled with the physiological reconstruction of the subject as dividuum.

Most of the texts to be examined are from the *Nachlass* of 1880–1882 (KSA 9), especially notebook 11 (= M III I from early 1881), and are pitched at a physiological level, as my title indicates. It is a characteristically Nietzschean 'category mistake' to discuss moral and political issues in physiological terms, and it is important to understand his rationale for doing so. A key impulse in Nietzsche's thought, from early to late, is to undermine the autonomy of the normative sphere and collapse the self-understanding of morality as sovereign onto the plane of immanence through what he calls the "naturalisation of morality"[4] or "moralistic naturalism":

---

[4] For "naturalisation of morality" see NL 1886, 9[8], KSA 12: 342: "An Stelle der moralischen Werthe lauter naturalistische Werthe. Vernatürlichung der Moral [...]". See also "naturalism of morality" in NL 1888, 15[5], KSA 13: 403: "Kritik der Philosophie. [...] Die Philosophen als Moralisten: sie untergraben den Naturalismus der Moral".

I can designate the tendency in these considerations as moral<istic> nat<uralism>: my task is to translate the apparently emancipated moral values that have become nature-less back into their nature – i.e. into their natural 'immorality' (NL 1886, 9[86], KSA 12: 380).⁵

Clearly the naturalisation of moral values requires a naturalised understanding of the human being, the task famously described in BGE 230 as "translating the human back into nature", so as to expose "the terrifying underlying text *homo natura*". These tasks cannot, however, be engaged directly, since the underlying problem is that our concept of nature, especially human nature, has been thoroughly moralised. In Nietzsche's view, the "idealisation" or "de-naturalisation" (*Entnatürlichung*) of morality has gone hand-in-hand with the moralisation of nature.⁶ To translate morality and the human being back into nature is pointless if it means translating them into a moralised nature. That is why Nietzsche writes of the "natural 'immorality'" of our values (KSA 12, 9[86]) and "the terrifying underlying text *homo natura*" (BGE 230): the nature in question is one that has been de-moralised and regained its innocence and ferocity. There are, then, two moves that must be co-ordinated in the project to naturalise morality: to translate values and the human being back into nature, and to translate morality out of (human) nature: the *Vernatürlichung der Moral* goes hand-in-hand with an *Entmoralisierung der Natur*.⁷ In the texts that follow we will see examples of both.

All translations are mine, although I have leaned on R.J. Hollingdale (*Beyond Good and Evil*, R.J. Hollnigdale (tr.), London: Penguin, 1974) for *JGB* and Kate Sturge (*Writings from the Late Notebooks*, R. Bittner (ed.), K. Sturge (tr.), Cambridge: CUP, 2003) for some of the *Nachlass*.
5 "Ich darf die Tendenz dieser Betrachtungen als moral<istischen> Nat<uralismus> bezeichnen: meine Aufgabe ist, die scheinbar emancipirten und naturlos gewordenen Moralwerthe in ihre Natur zurückzuübersetzen – d.h. in ihre natürliche 'Immoralität'".
6 Note NL 1886, 9[86], KSA 12: 380 above speaks of "[...] dem souverain gemachten Sittengesetz, losgelöst von seiner Natur (– bis zum Gegensatz zur Natur –)/Schritte der 'Entnatürlichung der Moral' (sog. 'Idealisirung')". Nietzsche here plans to reconstruct this process of de-naturalisation, step by step.
7 For "Entmoralisierung", see NL 1883–4, 24[7], KSA 10: 647: "unser Bedürfniß ist jetzt die Welt zu entmoralisiren: sonst könnte man nicht mehr leben [...]". See also NL 1888, 16[16], KSA 13: 487: "Wir Wenigen oder Vielen, die wir wieder in einer entmoralisirten Welt zu leben wagen, wir Heiden dem Glauben nach [...]"; and as part of a book plan, NL 1887, 10[57], KSA 12: 485: "Geschichte der Vermoralisirung und Entmoralisirung."; cf. NL 1888, 12[1], KSA 13: 203. Closely related to "Entmoralisirung" is the term "Entmenschung" (and "entmenschlichen"), since the moralisation of nature is often conceived as a process of anthropomorphisation (e.g. FW 109). See e.g. NL 1881, 11[211], KSA 9: 525: "Meine Aufgabe: die Entmenschung der Natur und dann die Vernatürlichung des Menschen, nachdem er den reinen Begriff 'Natur' gewonnen hat." Also NL 1881, 11[238], KSA 9: 532: "Die Menschen und die Philosophen haben früher in die Natur hinein den Menschen gedichtet – entmenschlichen wir die Natur!"

1 On the social origins and character of (self-)consciousness

I begin by sketching Nietzsche's views on the social origins and social character of (self-)consciousness, and the kinds of problems they raise. I will do so on the basis of two well-known texts: FW 354 *Vom "Genius der Gattung"*; and JGB 268 *Was ist zuletzt die Gemeinheit?* Both texts are polemical reformulations or deflations of Schopenhauer's doctrine of the 'Genius der Gattung', which guides the selection of sexual partners, unbeknownst to them, for the *Gattung*'s end of reproducing its specific character or 'type' in the next generation (WWV II §44). In both texts, the argument revolves around the history and development of language. In FW 354 Nietzsche argues that the development of (self-)consciousness is bound up with communicative needs: with the selective or survival value of the ability to communicate on the part of human animals. Language, consciousness and conscious thought therefore pertain to common or shared needs and overlapping interests – to the interests of the group or herd, and not to what is distinctive, different or unique to each individual. (Self-)consciousness cannot therefore be consciousness of what is unique or distinctive in each of us; it takes not the particular perspective of individuals, but the herd-perspective confined to common needs and overlapping interests; it is a kind of individuated collective consciousness.

This argument forms part of Nietzsche's broader critique of consciousness in favour of the body, understood as a social body: one that is embedded in social relations, formed by them and regulated by the kind of 'reason' that governs social interactions. We will see more of this in §§ 2–4. But already we can see that this argument militates against the liberal concept of a pre-social or asocial individual. For the implication of the argument concerning the social origins and functions of (self-)consciousness is that we are (self-)conscious individuals only insofar as we are social individuals.

In JGB 268 Nietzsche returns to the social origins of language and its consequences. Here the focus is not on consciousness, but on common or shared needs, with the thesis that language (words) signifies shared sentiments or clusters of sentiments (*Empfindungen/Empfindungs-Gruppen*); that is to say: non-unique inner experiences (*Erlebnisse*) and needs (*Bedürfnisse*). Nietzsche goes on to argue that that the most important and urgent needs are the first to find linguistic expression and as such, they come to define our fundamental values (*Rangordnung der Werthe, Gütertafel*). But if, as he has argued, it is our common and recurrent needs and experiences that are the most urgent and important, it follows that the (self-conscious) individual will advance the values corresponding to common and recurrent needs, that is, the fundamental values, or table of values of the community or society to which it belongs. Combining both texts, we can reconstruct the following argument: Insofar as individual (self-)consciousness is itself a product of language (FW 354), and insofar as language signifies the shared or common needs that determine the values of the community (JGB 268), it follows that the (self-)conscious individual is inseparable from values, and specifically, from the fundamental values of the community to which it belongs. Clearly this implication militates against the liberal concept of the individual as asocial and antecedently individuated. For on this argument, a person *cannot* be understood independently of its ends or values; they are constitutive of personhood. Nor are these fundamental values freely chosen; they are the social or communal values that articulate the common needs of the society or community to which the individual belongs.

On the other hand, these arguments also raise serious problems for Nietzsche's own communicative practice and our engagement with language. For they imply that language, consciousness and thought are inadequate to the particularity of persons. If language is confined to what is common, how then to speak of and to needs, feelings and thoughts that are not common – other [*anders*] and particular? What kind of engagement with language would allow particularity to be thought and said?

In a *Nachlass* note that begins (first paragraph) with a condensed summary of the argument in JGB 268, Nietzsche writes:

> Words are phonetic signs for concepts: but concepts are more or less stable groups of recurring conjoined sensations [*Empfindungen*]. For understanding one another it is not enough to use the same words: one must also use the same words for the same inner experiences [*innere Erlebnisse*] – and one must have these **in common** [...] Which groups of sensations stand in the foreground determines the evaluations: but the evaluations are the consequence of our innermost needs. –
>
> This is said in order to explain why it is difficult to understand writings such as mine: the inner experiences, evaluations and needs are other [*anders*] in my case. For years I have had social intercourse with people and I have taken self-denial and politeness so far as never to speak of things that were close to my heart. Indeed, it is virtually only in this way that I have lived with people. – (NL 1885, 34[86], KSA 11: 448)[8]

---

8 "Worte sind Tonzeichen für Begriffe: Begriffe aber sind mehr oder weniger sichere Gruppen wiederkehrender zusammen kommender Empfindungen. Daß man sich versteht, dazu gehört noch nicht, daß man dieselben Worte gebraucht: man muß dieselben Worte auch für dieselbe Gattung innerer Erlebnisse brauchen – und man muß diese **gemeinsam** haben. [...] Welche Gruppen von Empfindungen im Vordergrund stehn, das bedingt nämlich die Werthschätzungen: die Werthschätzungen aber sind die Folge unserer innersten Bedürfnisse. / – Dies ist gesagt, um zu erklären, warum es schwer ist, solche Schriften wie die meinigen zu verstehen: die inneren Erlebnisse, Werthschätzungen und Bedürfnisse sind bei mir anders. Ich habe Jahre lang mit

Against the background of his theoretical restriction of language to what we have in common, Nietzsche here describes his own confinement to the level of common needs (*gemeinsame Bedürfnisse*) and experiences in his intercourse with other people over the years. This makes it hard to see how we could understand Nietzsche's inner experiences in their otherness, let alone how he could communicate them. But in JGB 268, there is also a hint at how he sought to communicate the otherness of his own particular experiences and needs:

> The people who are more similar [to one another], the more ordinary people were and are still at an advantage, the more select, finer, more unusual, the ones more difficult to understand easily remain alone, succumb to accidents more easily in their isolation and rarely propagate themselves. One must summon tremendous counter-forces in order to cross this natural, all too natural progressus in simile, the continued formation of the human being into the similar, the ordinary, the average, the herd-like – into the common [or base: *Gemeine*]. (BGE 268)[9]

For the "schwerer Verständlichen" like Nietzsche the task is "to cross" the progressive similitude of persons mediated by language. So perhaps the key to thinking and saying what is particular is to "cross" different discourses or language games, to 'cross-breed' diverse discourses into a text that would 'cross out' or at least resist the rule of similitude governing each one. If so, we have another clue to the Nietzschean 'category mistake' of discussing moral and political issues in physiological terms, to which I now turn.

2 On the (pre-)history and social constitution of our capacities as sovereign individuals

In NL 11[182] (KSA 9: 509, 1881) Nietzsche offers a naturalistic account of the history and social constitution of our capacities as sovereign individuals (the second criticism of liberalism). The text begins with an organismic model of sovereignty in which our capacities are conceived as qualities or 'functions' of the organism, where the organism (following Roux: see Müller-Lauter 1978,

---

Menschen Verkehr gehabt und die Entsagung und Höflichkeit so weit getrieben, nie von Dingen zu reden, die mir am Herzen lagen. Ja ich habe fast nur so mit Menschen gelebt. – ".

9 "Die ähnlicheren, die gewöhnlicheren Menschen waren und sind immer im Vortheile, die Ausgesuchteren, Feineren, Seltsameren, schwerer Verständlichen bleiben leicht allein, unterliegen, bei ihrer Vereinzelung, den Unfällen und pflanzen sich selten fort. Man muss ungeheure Gegenkräfte anrufen, um diesen natürlichen, allzunatürlichen progressus in simile, die Fortbildung des Menschen in's Ähnliche, Gewöhnliche, Durchschnittliche, Heerdenhafte – in's Gemeine! – zu kreuzen."

1999) is characterised above all by processes of internal organisation and self-regulation:

> A strong free human being feels the qualities of the **organism** towards [*gegen*] everything else
> 1) self-regulation: in the form of fear of all alien incursions, in the hatred towards [*gegen*] the enemy, moderation etc.
> 2) overcompensation: in the form of acquisitiveness the pleasure of appropriation the craving for power
> 3) assimilation to oneself: in the form of praise reproach making others dependent on oneself, to that end deception cunning, learning, habituation, commanding incorporating [*Einverleiben*] judgements and experiences
> 4) secretion and excretion: in the form of revulsion contempt for the qualities in itself which are no longer of use to it; communicating [*mittheilen*] that which is superfluous goodwill
> 5) metabolic power: temporary worship admiration making oneself dependent fitting in, almost dispensing with the exercise of the other organic functions, transforming oneself into an "organ", being able to serve
> 6) regeneration: in the form of sexual drive, pedagogic drive etc. (NL 1881, 11[182], KSA 9: 509f.)[10]

These capacities cannot, however, be *presupposed* as somehow intrinsic to human beings, as they are in liberal contract theory. Rather, they are the very late fruit of a long social history which Nietzsche then recounts. He does so from a *socio-physiological* perspective in which the social origins of the sovereign individual are focused not on our reason (emphasised by liberal contract theories), but on our affects and drives. The thesis is that our drives are not 'natural', but learnt and assimilated from society or the state.

In the first phase of Nietzsche's story we are but organs of a larger, self-regulating social organism to which we belong ("society"/"the state"). In the second phase, sovereign individuals are formed when the organs cease to be organs and become instead autonomous organisms (in place of society or the state).

---

10 "Ein starker freier Mensch empfindet gegen alles Andere/die Eigenschaften des **Organismus**/ 1) Selbstregulirung: in der Form von Furcht vor/allen fremden Eingriffen, im Haß gegen den Feind,/im Maaßhalten usw./2) überreichlicher Ersatz: in der Form von Habsucht/Aneignungslust Machtgelüst/3) Assimilation an sich: in der Form von Loben Tadeln/Abhängigmachen Anderer von sich, dazu Verstellung/List, Lernen, Gewöhnung, Befehlen Einverleiben von/Urtheilen und Erfahrungen/4) Sekretion und Excretion: in der Form von Ekel/Verachtung der Eigenschaften an sich, die ihm nicht mehr/nützen; das Überschüssige mittheilen Wohlwollen/5) metabolische Kraft: zeitweilig verehren bewundern sich/abhängig machen einordnen, auf Ausübung der anderen/organischen Eigenschaften fast verzichten, sich zum/"Organe" umbilden, dienen-können/6) Regeneration: in der Form von Geschlechtstrieb, Lehrtrieb/usw.[...]"

This transition, Nietzsche argues, is made possible by a process of learning, assimilation or incorporation (*Einverleibung*). In the first phase, where human beings are organs, their actions and impulses are determined by the needs of the organism to which they belong: they feel the "affects of society towards [*gegen*] other societies and single beings [...] and not as individuals"; there are *only* public enemies. But as an organ, the human being also assimilates the interests, needs, the "experiences and judgements" of the organism, so that later "when the ties of society break down", it is able to reorganise itself into an autonomous individual or organism. Nietzsche speaks of the "reorganisation and assimilation excretion of drives" needed to transform the human being from an organ into an organism.

In a central passage of the note Nietzsche takes issue with liberal assumptions on three accounts:

> [1.] Society first educates the single being [*das Einzelwesen*], pre-forms it into a half- or whole individual, it is **not** formed out of single beings, not out of contracts among them! Rather, an individual is needed at most as a focal point (a leader) and this one will only be "free" in relation to the lower or higher level of the others. So: [2.] the state does not in its origins somehow oppress the individuals: these do not even exist! [3.] It [the state] makes the existence of human beings at all possible, as herd-animals. Our drives affects are first taught to us from there: there is nothing originary about them! There is no "state of nature" for them! As parts of a whole we take part in the conditions of existence and functions of the whole and incorporate [*einverleiben uns*] the experiences and judgements made in that process. (NL 1881, 11[182], KSA 9: 511)[11]

Nietzsche's criticisms of liberal contract theory are, then:

1. Society is not formed out of pre-existing individuals by way of a contract; rather it is society that educates and forms individuals, so that they are the product of society.
2. Since individuals are the product of the society or state to which they belong, the state cannot be understood as a threat to pre-existing indivi-

---

[11] "[...] Die Gesellschaft erzieht erst das Einzelwesen, formt es zum Halb- oder Ganz-Individuum vor, sie bildet sich **nicht** aus Einzelwesen, nicht aus Verträgen solcher! Sondern höchstens als Kernpunkt ist ein Individuum nöthig (ein Häuptling) und dieser auch nur im Verhältniß zu der tieferen oder höheren Stufe der Anderen 'frei'. Also: der Staat unterdrückt ursprünglich nicht etwa die Individuen: diese existiren noch gar nicht! Er macht den Menschen überhaupt die Existenz möglich, als Heerdenthieren. Unsere Triebe Affekte werden uns da erst gelehrt: sie sind nichts Ursprüngliches! Es giebt keinen 'Naturzustand' für sie! Als Theile eines Ganzen nehmen wir an dessen Existenzbedingungen und Funktionen Antheil und einverleiben uns die dabei gemachten Erfahrungen und Urtheile.[...]"

duals. In particular, the liberal concept of individual freedom as a primordial power or 'natural right' of individuals in need of protection against the artificial construct of the state is ruled out.
3. Nietzsche's socio-physiology forbids the abstraction of our capacity to reason from our affective, embodied existence. Not only are our "experiences and judgements" incorporated and learnt from the state; so too are our very affects and drives. Together, they are pre-formed by the interests and functions of the social organism to which we originally belong. This rules out not only those liberal contract theories that presuppose our capacity for reason or autonomous reflection (e.g. Rawls), but also those that presuppose primordial affects and drives on the individual's part, such as Hobbes' fear of death and desire for self-preservation.[12]

Clearly, all of this implies a critique of the liberal notion of freedom as the right to choose one's concept of the good, where this right is attached to an asocial, antecedently individuated person. But it also raises the question: What sense of individual freedom or sovereignty does Nietzsche's socio-physiology leave open? That Nietzsche wishes to advance a viable alternative to the liberal concept of freedom is clear from the organismic model of sovereignty that opens the text. A full examination of this account of sovereignty goes beyond the scope of this paper. Nevertheless, Nietzsche's socio-physiology in this and related texts does provide some important clues in the form of necessary conditions for sovereign individual agency. They are 1. that sovereignty requires a radically individual ethos of self-legislation; and 2. that sovereignty requires a maximisation of antagonism or struggle among the drives or powers constitutive of the individual. The second point will be addressed in the context of Nietzsche's physiological reconstruction of the individual as dividuum in § 4. For the moment I will concentrate on the first point, which comes almost as an afterthought in his account of the emergence of the individual out of the social organism.

In this, the second phase of Nietzsche's story, "when the ties of society break down", the first experimental individuals or "*Versuchs-Individuen*" assert themselves as sovereign. This process involves the transformation of an organ

---

12 See the closing paragraph of *Leviathan* Ch. XIII. In Nietzsche's text Hobbes's war of all against all is recast as the phase in which individuals suffer the dysfunctions that accompany the breakdown of the social organism and must secure their own existence as individual organisms (not just organs) by re-ordering their drives and functions.

into an autonomous organism, a painful and difficult "reorganisation and assimilation excretion of drives":

> The times when they emerge are those of de-moralisation [Entsittlichung], of so-called corruption, that is, all drives now want to go it alone and, since they have not until now adapted to that personal utility [i.e. the vital interests of the individual – HS], they destroy the individual through excess [Übermaaß]. Or they lacerate it in their struggle [Kampfe] with one another. (NL 1881, 11[182] KSA 9: 511f.)[13]

The destructive conflict of drives unleashed by their emancipation from bondage to the social organism moves the first moral philosophers to save the individual by commending a reactionary path of bondage:

> The ethicists [Ethiker] then come forward and seek to show human beings how they can still live without suffering so from themselves – mostly by commending to them the old conditioned way of life under the yoke of society, only that in place of society it is [the yoke of] a concept – they are reactionaries. But they preserve many, even if they do so by recurring back to bondage [Gebundheit]. Their claim is that there is an eternal moral law [ewiges Sittengesetz]; they will not acknowledge the individual law [das individuelle Gesetz] and call the effort to attain it immoral and destructive. – (NL 1881, 11[182], KSA 9: 512)[14]

The individual is hereby saved and saved from suffering, but *not* its sovereignty. The ethos of self-subjection to the concept of the moral law enables the nascent individual to impose measure and peace among its drives, but it does so at the cost of bondage and conformism.

If self-subjection to the moral law, conceived as universal and eternal, is the path of bondage, then the path to sovereignty is a form of *self-legislation* that is *radically individual*, what Nietzsche here calls "das individuelle Gesetz".[15] This thought, which appears en passant in the above note, is central to another note

---

13 "[...] Die Zeiten, wo sie entstehen, sind die der Entsittlichung, der sogenannten Corruption d.h. alle Triebe wollen sich jetzt persönlich versuchen und nicht bis dahin jenem persönlichen Nutzen angepaßt zerstören sie das Individuum durch Übermaaß. Oder sie zerfleischen es, in ihrem Kampfe mit einander. [...]"
14 "[...] Die Ethiker treten dann auf und suchen dem Menschen zu zeigen, wie er doch leben könne, ohne so an sich zu leiden – meistens, indem sie ihm die alte bedingte Lebensweise unter dem Joche der Gesellschaft anempfehlen, nur so daß an Stelle der Gesellschaft ein Begriff tritt – es sind Reaktionäre. Aber sie erhalten Viele, wenn gleich durch Zurückführung in die Gebundenheit. Ihre Behauptung ist, es gebe ein ewiges Sittengesetz; sie wollen das individuelle Gesetz nicht anerkennen und nennen das Streben dahin unsittlich und zerstörerisch. – [...]"
15 On radically individual self-legislation, see Gerhardt (1992: 28 – 49); also Siemens (2008) and (2009b).

from the same notebook, in which Nietzsche takes up the question of the individual's relation to the species as a whole:

> Are the goals of the individual <u>necessarily</u> the goals of the species? No. Individual morality: as the consequence of a random throw of the dice, a being is there, which seeks <u>its</u> conditions of existence – let us take this seriously and not be fools who <u>make sacrifices for the unknown!</u> (NL 1881, 11[46], KSA 9: 458f.)[16]

Here Nietzsche warns us against self-subjection or -sacrifice to the unknown – such as the "the eternal moral law" – in favour of a radically individual morality. Of importance is the naturalistic reasoning behind this position: the call for a radically individual morality is grounded in the naturalistic concept of value as the means for a given life-form to meet its conditions of existence[17] and in the presupposition of an originary plurality of life-forms, each of which is unique and subject to its own conditions of existence. We are each, as Nietzsche writes in SE, "ein Unicum", a "seltsamer Zufall", a "wunderlich buntes Mancherlei" thrown together into "Einerlei", whose task is "nach eignem Maass und Gesetz zu leben" (SE 1 KSA 1: 338f.). When compared with these earlier expressions, the 1881 *Nachlass* note displaces the Romantic metaphysics of the *Unzeitgemässe Betrachtungen* with a (post-)Darwinian naturalism focused on conditions of existence or life (*Existenzbedingungen, Lebensbedingungen*). As such this note illustrates how the 'category mistake' of discussing morality in physiological terms can serve Nietzsche as a textual strategy for 'crossing out' or at least resisting the rule of similitude in language, so as to say particularity: particularity, as the ground of the demand for radically individual morality, is itself grounded in conditions of existence specific to each unique form of life. At the same time, this note also throws some light on Nietzsche's organismic concept of sovereignty (NL 1881, 11[182], KSA 9; see p. 635 above) as a model for individual social agency. Nietzschean sovereignty is non-sovereign in the sense that it depends on cultivating certain relations with others; it is deeply embedded and thoroughly relational in character. But it is sovereign in the sense that those relations are determined *from within* by the specific life-form ("organism") in search of the of optimal conditions of existence unique to it and by the kind of self-reg-

---

[16] "Sind die Zwecke des Individuums <u>nothwendig</u> die Zwecke der Gattung? Nein. Die individuelle Moral: in Folge eines zufälligen Wurfs im Würfelspiel ist ein Wesen da, welches <u>seine</u> Existenzbedingungen sucht – nehmen wir <u>dies</u> ernst und seien wir nicht Narren, zu <u>opfern für das Unbekannte!</u>"

[17] See NL 1887–8, 11[118] KSA 13: 56; NL 1888, 14[158], KSA 13:343. In JGB 3 Nietzsche refers the concept of value to the physiological demands for the preservation of a specific form of life.

ulation this requires. Nietzsche's turn to physiology, then, or the physiological turn in Nietzsche's account of sovereignty, enables him to rethink self-determination in relational and radically individual terms: Sovereignty requires that an individual determine its actions towards others in response to those conditions that best enable it to meet its needs and flourish as a unique form of life.

It remains unclear, however, whether sovereignty in this sense is attainable or just a naturalistic moral ideal. In the note in question, it is ascribed to the "strong free human being" (*starker freier Mensch*) who is posited at the end of Nietzsche's socio-physiological history as "the human who has become free" (*freigewordener Mensch*). Yet in the closing lines he writes of us ("wir") as *deformed beings* [*Mißgestalten*] and of our *malaise* [*Mißbehagen*] as "individuals in the process of becoming free [*frei werdenden Individuen*]".[18] If self-subjection to the universal and eternal moral law, as commended by moral philosophers, is the path of bondage, how can radically individual freedom be realised, if at all? How can the individual be saved from the destructive conflict of drives in a way that *advances* sovereignty? We will return to these questions in § 4.

3 On the social origins of moral sentiments

As part of the project to naturalise morality, Nietzsche's socio-physiology translates the human being back into nature in a way that undermines the liberal notion of freedom as the right to choose on the part of an asocial, antecedently individuated person. But as we saw in the introduction, nature and human nature in particular have been thoroughly moralised in the long history of morality and must be de-moralised if the naturalisation of morality is to make sense. In this section I turn to a number of texts in which Nietzsche seeks to de-moralise human nature and recover its innocence by arguing that our moral sentiments are not natural, but the consequence of internalising social norms. By highlighting the social origins of our moral ends and values, these texts further undermine the liberal claims that personhood is separate from the ends and values it freely chooses independently of society.

In one such text, Nietzsche takes issue with conscience (*das Gewissen*) as an inner norm that we can fall back on as a gold standard for evaluating action and

---

[18] "[...] Aber wir sind lange Mißgestalten, und dem entspricht das viel größere Mißbehagen der frei werdenden Individuen – im Vergleich zur älteren abhängigen Stufe und das massenhafte Zugrundegehen."(NL 1881, 11[182], KSA 9: 512)

opinions. He does so by first reducing conscience to a set of moral sentiments (*Empfindungen*) and then reducing these to mere sentiments of inclination or aversion (*Zu- und Abneigung*) that have been imitated (*nachgeahmt*) from those who have moral authority over us:

> That humans have within themselves the norm according to which they have to act – this extraordinary stupidity is still believed today! Conscience! It is a sum of sentiments of inclination and aversion in relation to actions and opinions, <u>imitated</u> sentiments which we came across in parents and teachers! (NL 1880, 5[13], KSA 9: 103)[19]

The naturalistic reduction of the inner voice of conscience to a set of imitated sentiments (*Summe von nachgeahmten Empfindungen*) of inclination/aversion clearly robs it of its unquestioned normative authority. But the actual mechanism of imitation or *internalisation* as Nietzsche describes it also has the effect of freeing human nature from any moral sentiments or qualities whatsoever. This can be seen in a note in which Nietzsche analyses the judgement concerning "an evil action" in socio-physiological terms:

> Of themselves the drives are neither good nor evil to our sentiments. [...] When a drive is <u>always</u> satisfied with a feeling of prohibition and anxiety, an <u>aversion</u> grows towards it: we now hold it to be <u>evil</u>. We have attached an accompanying sentiment inseparably to it, a new unity has emerged. "An evil action." (NL 1880, 6[204], KSA 9: 251)[20]

At issue here are our negative moral judgements concerning our own impulses or drives. The notion of "an evil action" is referred back to the linking of a given drive, or rather: its satisfaction, with an accompanying sentiment of aversion. But how does a sentiment of aversion come to be attached to drive-satisfaction? The idea that this might be a result of inner moral sentiments towards our drives is dismissed in favour of a process of socialisation: aversion towards drive-satisfaction is felt when a social prohibition is internalised as a "feeling of prohibition and anxiety" that accompanies its satisfaction. As Nietzsche writes in another note: "To have a drive and to feel repugnance at its satisfaction is the

---

19 "Die Menschen hätten in sich schon die Norm, nach der sie zu handeln hätten – die ungeheure Albernheit ist bis auf heutigen Tag noch geglaubt! Das Gewissen! Es ist eine Summe von Empfindungen der Zu- und Abneigung in Bezug auf Handlungen und Meinungen, <u>nachgeahmte</u> Empfindungen, die wir bei Eltern und Lehrern antrafen!"
20 "An sich sind die Triebe weder gut noch böse für die Empfindung. [...] Wenn ein Trieb <u>immer</u> mit dem Gefühl des Verbotenen und der Angst befriedigt wird, so entsteht eine <u>Aversion</u> vor ihm: wir halten ihn nun für <u>böse</u>. Wir haben eine Nebenempfindung untrennbar an ihn geknüpft, es ist eine Einheit entstanden. 'Eine böse Handlung.' [...]"

"moral" phenomenon".[21] The moralisation of our drives through processes of internalisation is best described in a note in which the social or relational character of our drives is spelled out clearly:

> What drives would we have that did not bring us from the start into a disposition towards others, nutrition e.g., sex-drive? That which others teach us, want from us, tell us to fear or pursue, is the original material of our mind: alien judgements about things. They give us our image of ourselves, according to which we measure ourselves, are well- or ill-satisfied with ourselves! Our own judgement is only an extension [*Fortzeugung*] of combined alien [judgements]! Our own drives appear to us under the interpretation of others: while at bottom they are all pleasant [*angenehm*], they are so mixed with unpleasant accompanying feelings [*unangenehmen Beigefühlen*] through the inculcated judgements concerning their value, indeed some are now felt to be bad drives: "it takes me where it ought not to [*nicht sollte*]" – whereas bad drive is actually a contradictio in adjecto. – (NL 1881, 6[70], KSA 9: 212f.)[22]

In themselves our drives are not morally good or bad. In themselves, they are not even felt [*empfunden*] to be good or bad by us. Rather, when we judge a drive to be bad, it is just because the pleasure of its satisfaction is mixed with unpleasure or aversion. And we feel unpleasure towards drive-satisfaction as a result of internalising the interpretations, judgements or prohibitions of others in our social milieu. The effect of this account of the moralisation of our drives is to de-moralise our drives: the concept of a bad drive is contradictory, since drive-satisfaction is neither good nor bad; of itself it is simply agreeable (*angenehm*). But this account also shows how deep the process of socialisation goes for Nietzsche. The arguments for the social character of individual (self-)consciousness from language reviewed in § 1 are here reinforced in terms of the internalisation of others' moral interpretations or judgements. Not only are others' moral judgements the source of our moral judgements; they are the original material or content of our mind and give us our very image or understanding

---

[21] "Einen Trieb haben und vor seiner Befriedigung Abscheu empfinden ist das 'sittliche' Phänomen" (NL 1880, 6[365], KSA 9: 290).
[22] "Welche Triebe hätten wir, die uns nicht von Anfang an in eine Stellung zu anderen Wesen brächten, Ernährung z.B., Geschlechtstrieb? Das, was Andere uns lehren, von uns wollen, uns fürchten und verfolgen heißen, ist das ursprüngliche Material unseres Geistes: fremde Urtheile über die Dinge. Jene geben uns unser Bild von uns selbst, nach dem wir uns messen, wohl und übel mit uns zufrieden sind! Unser eigenes Urtheil ist nur eine Fortzeugung der combinirten fremden! Unsere eigenen Triebe erscheinen uns unter der Interpretation der Anderen: während sie im Grunde alle angenehm sind, sind sie doch durch die angelernten Urtheile über ihren Werth so gemischt mit unangenehmen Beigefühlen, ja manche werden als schlechte Triebe jetzt empfunden: 'es zieht hin, wohin es nicht sollte' – während schlechter Trieb eigentlich eine contradictio in adjecto ist. – [...]"

of ourselves. The distance separating this account from the asocial, self-interested individual presupposed by liberal contract theories is spelled out clearly in this same note, when Nietzsche writes:

> To refer all social relations back to egoism? Good: but for me it is also true that all egoistic inner experiences [*innere Erlebnisse*] are to be referred back to our habituated inculcated dispositions towards others. (NL 1881, 6[70], KSA 9: 212)[23]

The internalised, social character of the self and our self-relation is central to Nietzsche's critical destruction of the substantial moral subject and his attempt to reconstruct the subject as dividuum, to which I now turn.

4 Against the subject as unified substance

The critique of substance ontology in favour of a dynamic, pluralistic interpretation of reality is one of the great themes that cuts across Nietzsche's entire oeuvre.[24] A good deal of this is directed against the concept of the subject, often seen as the source of our projected belief in enduring things or substances around us. In these contexts, the critique of substance ontology takes the form of a physiological destruction of the substantial moral subject, coupled with a physiological reconstruction of the subject as dividuum. The subject is hereby pluralised and dynamised in Nietzsche's concept of the "life-system" or organism, and our belief in a substantial moral subject, indeed our very "feeling of subjectivity" (*Subjekt-Empfindung*), is reduced to a "means of preservation", "a condition of life for organic existence" (NL 1881, 11[270], KSA 9: 545). But Nietzsche also looks to formulate a prescriptive counter-ideal to the liberal ideal of subjective autonomy, a physiological, dynamic and pluralistic account of sovereignty. As I will argue, Nietzsche's texts suggest an agonal ideal of an *inner* plurality of drives in measured, productive conflict, sustained by and inter-

---

[23] "[...]–Alle socialen Beziehungen auf den Egoismus zurückzuführen? Gut: für mich ist aber auch wahr daß alle egoistischen inneren Erlebnisse auf unsere eingeübten angelernten Stellungen zu Anderen zurückzuführen sind. [...]"
[24] For an extended treatment of Nietzsche's critique of substance ontology, see Aydin 2003. Nietzsche's earliest recorded critique of Schopenhauer from 1868 focuses on the concept of unity and charges that unity is projected from the phenomenal to the noumenal realm by Schopenhauer (*Zu Schopenhauer*, dated Oktober 1867–April 1868, in: BAW 3: 352–370 (452–453 for *Nachbericht*). See also Katrin Meyer on Nietzsche's sustained epistemological assault on the concepts of being, substance etc. born of his youthful engagement with the pre-Socratics (Meyer 1998: 8–38).

locked with an *outer* plurality of sovereign beings or organisms engaged in measured, productive conflict with one another.

Nietzsche's critique of substance ontology confronts him with the task of explaining in naturalistic terms how we come to take substances – the existence of enduring things, including the subject – to be fundamental and self-evident truths. Typically, he argues that they are of selective or survival value, as means for the preservation of organic life, but not therefore true. Time and again, he insists that the selective value of a belief is logically independent of its truth-value. Thus:

> It is in the way the first organic forms [*Bildungen*] sensed stimuli and judged the outside that the life-preserving principle must be sought: that belief prevailed, preserved itself, through which continued existence became possible; not the most true belief, but the most useful. "Subject" is the condition of life for organic existence, hence not "true"; rather, subject-feeling [*Subjekt-Empfindung*] can be essentially false, but as the only means of survival. Error [is] the father of living beings [...]. (NL 1881, 11[270], KSA 9: 545; cf. NL 1881, 11[268], KSA 9: 543f.)[25]

"Subject-feeling" (*Subjekt-Empfindung*) is not an originary truth of human existence, but a derivative error formed in response to the conditions of existence for all organic life. This primordial protoplasmic lie lives on, Nietzsche argues, in our political belief in the state as an enduring whole, for the same physiological reason that all organic life-forms perceive "enduring things" around them: to facilitate processes of assimilation and subordination:

> In the most developed conditions we still commit the oldest error: e.g. we represent the state to ourselves as something whole enduring real as a thing and accordingly submit ourselves to it, as a function [thereof]. Without the protoplasm's representation of an "enduring thing" outside itself there would be no submission, no assimilation (NL 1881, 11[270], KSA 9: 545).[26]

In other contexts, Nietzsche warns against conflating the supposed "individual" with the real "life-system" that we are:

---

[25] "In der Art, wie die Erstlinge organischer Bildungen Reize empfanden und das Außer-sich beurtheilten, muß das lebenserhaltende Princip gesucht werden: derjenige Glaube siegte, erhielt sich, bei dem das Fortleben möglich wurde; nicht der am meisten wahre, sondern am meisten nützlichen Glaube. 'Subjekt' ist die Lebensbedingung des organischen Daseins, deshalb nicht 'wahr', sondern Subjekt-Empfindung kann wesentlich falsch sein, aber als einziges Mittel der Erhaltung. Der Irrthum Vater des Lebendigen! [...]"

[26] "[...] In den entwickeltsten Zuständen begehen wir immer noch den ältesten Irrthum: z.B. stellen wir uns den Staat als Ganzes Dauerndes Wirkliches als Ding vor und demgemäß ordnen wir uns ihm ein, als Funktion. Ohne die Vorstellung des Protoplasma von einem 'dauernden Dinge' außer ihm gäbe es keine Einordnung, keine Assimilation".

> But I distinguish: the imaginary individuals and the true "life-systems" which we are each and every one of us – they are conflated, whereas "the individual" is but a sum of conscious feelings [*Empfindungen*] and judgements and errors, a <u>belief</u>, a small part of the true life-system or several small parts conceived together and confabulated [*zusammengedacht und zusammengefabelt*], a "unity" that does not hold up. [...] To learn step-by-step to cast off the <u>supposed individual</u>! To expose the errors of the ego! To see <u>egoism</u> as <u>error</u>! But not to mistake altruism for its opposite! That would only be love for <u>other supposed</u> individuals! No! To go **beyond** "me" and "you"! **To feel cosmically** [*Kosmisch empfinden*]! (NL 1881, 11[7], KSA 9: 443)[27]

Whatever exactly "cosmic feeling" means, it entails a way of relating to oneself and to others beyond the false unities of "me" and "you", and it is part of a prescriptive programme announced in this note to shake off the error of the individual. In the context of Nietzsche's critique of substance ontology this involves redescribing our self-relation *without* presupposing an underlying unity or identity, starting out instead from an originary multiplicity. Thus in the above note, the substantive moral subject is described as a false unity that is in fact "confabulated" [*zusammengefabelt*] out of a multiplicity of "feelings", "judgements", "errors" or "parts" of the real life-system. And Nietzsche's *prescriptive* task is to formulate a viable form of self-relation that does not falsify, but does justice to the multiplicity that we are. As we would expect from the texts considered in § 3, this 'inner' multiplicity is given form through the internalisation of social mores. Since, as Nietzsche writes, "wir haben die 'Gesellschaft' in uns verlegt", we relate to ourselves in thoroughly socialised terms:

> We direct all the good and bad habitual drives against ourselves: in thinking about ourselves, in feeling for and against us [*Empfinden für und gegen uns*], the struggle in us – we never treat ourselves as an individual, but as a twosome or multiplicity; we exercise towards ourselves all social practices (friendship revenge envy) properly. The naive egoism of the animal has been completely altered by our <u>social</u> integration: we just can no longer feel a singularity [*Einzigkeit*] of the ego, <u>we are always among many</u>. We have split and continue to divide ourselves again and again. The <u>social</u> drives (like enmity envy hatred) (which presuppose a plurality) have transformed us: we have displaced "society" within

---

[27] "Ich unterscheide aber: die eingebildeten Individuen und die wahren 'Lebens-systeme', deren jeder von uns eins ist – man wirft beides in eins, während 'das Individuum' nur eine Summe von bewußten Empfindungen und Urtheilen und Irrthümern ist, ein <u>Glaube</u>, ein Stückchen vom wahren Lebenssystem oder viele Stückchen zusammengedacht und zusammengefabelt, eine 'Einheit', die nicht Stand hält. [...] Schrittweise lernen, das <u>vermeintliche</u> <u>Individuum</u> abzuwerfen! Die Irrthümer des ego entdecken! Den <u>Egoismus</u> als <u>Irrthum</u> einsehen! Als Gegensatz ja nicht Altruismus zu verstehen! Das wäre die Liebe zu den <u>anderen vermeintlichen</u> Individuen! Nein! Über <u>'mich'</u> und <u>'dich'</u> **hinaus**! **Kosmisch empfinden!**"

ourselves, compressed it, and to retreat into oneself is not a flight from society, but often a discomforting <u>dreaming-on and interpreting</u> of the processes in us according to the scheme of earlier experiences. [...] (NL 1881, 6[80], KSA 9: 215)[28]

Even in the retreat to solitude – often taken as symptomatic of Nietzsche's autarkic individualism – we practise social relations towards ourselves and bring with us all our social habits and drives. But what is striking in this account is not just the redescription of our self-relation as an internalisation of social relations, but the emphasis on struggle and self-division ("for and against"). In this note, it is hard to make out the exact tenor – descriptive and/or prescriptive – of this claim. But in other notes, the prescriptive element is unmistakable:

> Whoever has the capacity for deep feelings must also suffer the vehement struggle between them and their opposites. One can, in order to be perfectly calm and without inner suffering, just wean oneself from deep feelings, so that in their weakness they arouse only weak counter-forces: they can then, in their sublimated rarity, be <u>overlooked</u> and give human beings the impression that they are quite in harmony with themselves ... – Just so in social life: if everything ought to proceed altruistically, then the oppositions among individuals must be reduced to a sublime minimum: so that all inimical tendencies and tensions, through which the individual maintains itself as individual [*durch welche das Individuum sich als Individuum erhält*] can barely be perceived, that means: individuals must be reduced to the thinnest tonality of individuality! So, equality predominating by far! That is euthanasia, completely unproductive! [...] (NL 1880, 6[58], KSA 9: 207f.)[29]

---

[28] "[...] Wir wenden alle guten und schlechten gewöhnten Triebe gegen uns: das Denken über uns, das Empfinden für und gegen uns, der Kampf in uns – nie behandeln wir uns als Individuum, sondern als Zwei- und Mehrheit; alle socialen Übungen (Freundschaft Rache Neid) üben wir redlich an uns. Der naive Egoismus des Thieres ist durch unsere <u>sociale Einübung</u> ganz alterirt: wir können gar nicht mehr eine Einzigkeit des ego fühlen, <u>wir sind immer unter einer Mehrheit</u>. Wir haben uns zerspalten und spalten uns immer neu. Die <u>socialen Triebe</u> (wie Feindschaft Neid Haß) (die eine Mehrheit voraussetzen) haben uns umgewandelt: wir haben 'die Gesellschaft' in uns verlegt, verkleinert und sich auf sich zurückziehen ist keine Flucht aus der Gesellschaft, sondern oft ein peinliches <u>Fortträumen und Ausdeuten</u> unserer Vorgänge nach dem Schema der früheren Erlebnisse. [...]" See also NL 1880, 6[70], KSA 9: 212: "We treat ourselves as a multiplicity and bring to these 'social relations' all the social habits which we have towards humans animals places things".

[29] "Wer tiefer Empfindungen fähig ist, muß auch den heftigen Kampf derselben gegen ihre Gegensätze leiden. Man kann, um ganz ruhig und leidlos in sich zu sein, sich eben nur die tiefen Empfindungen abgewöhnen, so daß sie in ihrer Schwäche eben auch nur schwache Gegenkräfte erregen: die, in ihrer sublimirten Dünne, dann wohl <u>überhört</u> werden und dem Menschen den Eindruck geben, er sei ganz mit sich im Einklange. – Ebenso im socialen Leben: soll alles altruistisch zugehn, so müssen die Gegensätze der Individuen auf ein sublimes Minimum reduzirt werden: so daß alle feindseligen Tendenzen und Spannungen, durch welche das Individuum sich als individuum erhält, kaum mehr wahrgenommen werden können, das heißt: die Indivi-

On the assumption (contra substance ontology) of an originary plurality of feelings (*Empfindungen*) in conflict, there can be no such thing as genuine peace, harmony or agreement with oneself. One can, however, *overlook* the antagonism among one's feelings and mistake this for peace or harmony, through strategies that weaken one's feelings and so reduce their vehement discord with their opposites. This is a clear reference to the Socratic ideal of agreement with oneself[30] and the eudemonistic tendency Socrates introduced into philosophy.[31] It is important to see that, according to Nietzsche, this strategy for inner peace or harmony goes hand in hand with the strategy of self-subordination to the "sovereign concept"[32] (the moral law) ascribed to the first moral philosophers (*Ethiker*) in Nietzsche's socio-physiology (NL 1881, 11[182], KSA 9) discussed in § 2. Both strategies, as Socrates, saw, have the advantage of saving the individual from suffering by imposing measure (*Maass*) on the excess (*Übermaas*) of individual drives, so as to reduce the tension or struggle between them (NL 1881, 11[182], KSA 9; see p. 638 above). Yet they carry a high cost. Nietzsche writes in the above note of the loss of human diversity and richness in favour of unifor-

---

duen müssen auf den blassesten Ton des Individuellen reduzirt werden! Also die Gleichheit weitaus vorherrschend! Das ist die Euthanasie, völlig unproduktiv! [...]"
30 Gorgias 482c: "It would be better for me [...] that multitudes of men should disagree with me rather than that I, being one, should be out of harmony with myself." In "Philosophy and Politics" Hannah Arendt's version is: "it is much better to be in disagreement with the whole world than *being one*, to be in disagreement with myself" (Arendt 1990: 87). In this essay, she defends this position against the divisiveness of the agonal spirit in Greece and denies that Socratic oneness or harmony with oneself excludes pluralism. Nietzsche's position, as we will see, is that disagreement or a measure of conflict is necessary for genuine pluralism.
31 See NL 1873, 19[20], KSA 7: 422: "Nach Sokrates ist das allgemeine Wohl nicht mehr zu retten, darum die individualisirende Ethik, die die Einzelnen retten will". But already in 1869 Nietzsche writes: "Euripides hat von Sokrates die Vereinzelung des Individuums gelernt" (NL 1869, 1[106], KSA 7: 41). See also NL 1872–3, 23[35], KSA 7: 555: "Sokrates bricht mit der bisherigen Wissenschaft und Kultur, er will zurück zur alten Bürgertugend und zum Staate". See also the notes on "Wissenschaft und Weisheit und im Kampfe" from KSA 8 (1875): NL 1875, 6[13], KSA 8: 102 "Von Sokrates an: das Individuum nahm sich zu wichtig mit einem Male"; NL 1875, 6[15], KSA 8: 103: on the pre-Socratic philosophers: "Bei ihnen hat man nicht 'die garstige Pretension auf Glück', wie von Sokrates ab. Es dreht sich doch nicht alles um den Zustand ihrer Seele: denn über den denkt man nicht ohne Gefahr nach"; and equally NL 1875, 6[15], KSA 8: 103: "sie [die ältere Philosophie–HS] ist nicht so individuell-eudämonologisch, ohne die garstige Pretension auf Glück". In NL 6[26] (KSA 8: 108, 1875) he accuses Socrates of tearing the individual out of his historical context and in NL 6[21] (KSA 8: 106, 1875) he characterises Socrates' position with the words: "da bleibt mir nichts als ich mir selbst; Angst um sich selbst wird die Seele der Philosophie."
32 See NL 1871–2, 16[17], KSA 7: 399: "Socrates. Liebe und Bildung. Der souveräne Begriff".

mity, and the loss of productive power: a living death or "euthanasia". In NL 11[182] (KSA 9, 1881), as we saw, he writes of conformism and bondage along the path of the moral philosophers. We can now take up the question raised in that context: If inner peace and measure through self-subjection to the universal and eternal moral law is the path of bondage, how then can radically individual freedom be realised, if at all? How can the individual be saved from the destructive conflict of drives in a way that *advances* sovereignty? From the above text it is clear that Nietzsche favours the vehement antagonism of our drives, not their diminution into a lukewarm 'peace', as the key to a plurality of vibrant productive individuals. The same can be said of his socio-physiology, where Nietzsche formulates a prescriptive ideal of sovereignty centred on conflict. In another, related note on socio-physiology he distinguishes sharply between the path to bondage inaugurated by the first moral philosophers, as the history of the "herd-animal" that has come to dominate in modernity, and the history of solitary singular beings, as the path to sovereignty:

> – The development of the herd- animals and social plants is an entirely other one to that of the solitary [or singular: *einzeln lebend*] beings. (NL 1881, 11[130], KSA 9: 488)[33]

In the first case, Nietzsche emphasises the prevalence of self-subordination (*Unterordnung*) today (to the state, family, church etc.) and its long pre-history in our existence as pre-individual organs of a social organism. In the latter case, he emphasises the increasing complexification of the individual through the incorporation of social structures, but also the difficulties of the transition from organ to self-regulating organism:

> – Solitary [*Einzeln lebend*] humans, if they do not go to ground, develop into societies, a number of domains of work is developed, and much struggle of the drives for nutrition space time as well. (NL 1881, 11[130] KSA 9: 488)[34]

But struggle is not just a feature of the emergence of singular individuals; it is also central to the ideal of sovereignty with which the note ends:

> The freest human has the greatest <u>feeling of power</u> over itself, the greatest <u>knowledge</u> about itself, the greatest <u>order</u> in the necessary <u>struggle</u> of its powers, the relatively greatest <u>independence</u> of its single powers, the relatively greatest <u>struggle</u> within itself: it is the

---

33 "– Die Entwicklung der Heerden-Thiere und gesellschaftlichen Pflanzen ist eine ganz andere als die der einzeln lebenden".
34 "– Einzeln lebende Menschen, wenn sie nicht zu Grunde gehen, entwickeln sich zu Gesellschaften, eine Menge von Arbeitsgebieten wird entwickelt, und viel Kampf der Triebe um Nahrung Raum Zeit ebenfalls."

most divisive being and the most changeable and the one who lives longest and the extravagantly desirous one, [extravagantly] self-nourishing, the one who eliminates the most and regenerates itself [the most].(NL 1881, 11[130] KSA 9: 488)[35]

In this portrait, several of the self-regulating functions in Nietzsche's organismic model of sovereignty (NL 1881, 11[182] KSA 9; cited on p. 635 above) can be recognised:

- "the extravagantly desirous one" refers to "2) overcompensation: in the form of *acquisitiveness* the pleasure of appropriation the craving for power";
- the "[extravagantly] self-nourishing" one refers to "3) assimilation to oneself: in the form of praise reproach making others dependent on oneself, to that end deception cunning, learning, habituation, commanding incorporating [*Einverleiben*] judgements and experiences";
- the "one who *eliminates* the most" refers to "4) secretion and excretion: in the form of revulsion contempt for the qualities in itself which are *no longer* of use to it; communicating [*mittheilen*] that which is superfluous goodwill"; and
- the one who "*regenerates itself*" refers to "6) regeneration: in the form of sexual drive, pedagogic drive etc."

All of these functions fall under self-regulation, or the achievement of "*the greatest order*" and the resultant "*feeling of power*" over oneself. Inner order by means of effective self-regulation is, then, the key to Nietzsche's concept of sovereignty. But as this note makes clear, the achievement of inner order is inseparable from what resists order, namely: the antagonism or struggle among one's forces. And just as the vehement antagonism of our feelings must be maximised for there to be a plurality of vibrant individuals (NL 1880, 6[58], KSA 9 above), so here the greatest sovereignty comes from maximising the antagonism of forces and the feeling of power over oneself that comes from being able to order them. We can therefore say, sovereignty requires that we sustain the tension between maximal antagonism and maximal order among the plurality of forces or drives that constitute each of us.

With this ideal, Nietzsche clearly intends a counter-ideal to both the liberal ideal of subjective autonomy and the Socratic ideal of inner peace or agreement

---

35 "–Der freieste Mensch hat das größte Machtgefühl über sich, das größte Wissen über sich, die größte Ordnung im nothwendigen Kampfe seiner Kräfte, die verhältnißmäßig größte Unabhängigkeit seiner einzelnen Kräfte, den verhältnißmäßig größten Kampf in sich: er ist das zwieträchtigste Wesen und das wechselreichste und das langlebendste und das überreich begehrende, sich nährende, das am meisten von sich ausscheidende und sich erneuernde."

with oneself, the moral law and conformism. The dynamic, pluralised social ontology, in which Nietzsche's concept of sovereignty is grounded, undercuts the substance-metaphysics on which the asocial, antecedently individuated person rests. As argued earlier in § 2, the physiological turn in Nietzsche's discourse not only naturalises but also singularises the concept of sovereignty by referring self-determination to the processes of self-regulation that best enable a given life-form to meet the conditions of existence unique to it as a singular being. And as we saw in NL 11[182] (KSA 9, 1881) sovereignty in this sense, as *radically individual self-legislation*, is specifically opposed to self-subjection to the concept of universal and eternal moral law, to the conformism and loss of human diversity this implies. Finally, the ideal of maximising inner antagonism is clearly opposed to the Socratic ideal of peace or agreement with oneself and the weakening of affects on which it rests. Nietzsche's opposition to both liberal and Socratic ideals rests to a large extent on the thesis that there can be no genuine pluralism or freedom without a measure of conflict. But one can then ask what the right measure of conflict is and how it is determined. What is the measure for maximising the antagonism of our drives without dis-integrating the individual altogether under the pressure of unmeasured drives in conflict? Indeed, how can measure or limits be found at all for our drives, if their conflict is to be maximised?

If the problem is how to avoid the dis-integration or explosion of individuals under the (outward) pressure of a maximal conflict of drives, the solution would seem to involve the exercise of *inward pressures* from the outside, pressures that neither overpower and absorb the individual, nor are overpowered by it, but would be *more-or-less equal* to the outward expansionist pressure exerted by the individual's powers. In other words, the measure for maximising inner antagonism consistent with the unity of the individual is given by social, inter-subjective or *political relations of approximate equality*. This thought is broached in NL 6[58] (KSA 9, 1880) discussed above, when Nietzsche describes the socio-political correlate of the Socratic strategy of minimising the discord of our feelings:

> –Just so in social life: if everything ought to proceed altruistically, then the oppositions among individuals must be reduced to a sublime minimum: so that all inimical tendencies and tensions, through which the individual maintains itself as individual [*durch welche das Individuum sich als Individuum erhält*] can barely be perceived, that means: individuals must be reduced to the thinnest tonality of individuality! So, equality predominating by far! That is euthanasia, completely unproductive! [...] (NL 1880, 6[58], KSA 9: 207f.)[36]

---

36 "[...] – <u>Ebenso</u> im socialen Leben: soll alles altruistisch zugehn, so müssen die Gegensätze der Individuen auf ein sublimes Minimum reduzirt werden: so daß alle feindseligen Tendenzen und

If these lines describe the history of the herd-animal that has come to dominate in modernity, Nietzsche also intimates an alternative. When he writes of the "inimical tendencies and tensions, through which the individual maintains itself as individual", he is connecting strong inner antagonism with outer, interpersonal antagonism as its condition. It is through relations of tension and antagonism with others that the antagonism of inner drives is best contained, so that the dividuum can attain unity, or maintain itself as an individual with the maximum of inner tension required for sovereignty. The level or measure of maximal inner antagonism consistent with individual existence is determined by relations of tension *between* individuals who are more-or-less equal in power, so that none are overpowered and absorbed by others. And since the maximisation of inner antagonism consistent with individual integrity is the condition for a plurality of sovereign and productive human types, we can say that Nietzsche's socio-physiology suggests a politics of equality, not in the sense of universal equal rights that protect us from conflict and incursion, but a politics of enmity among more-or-less equal powers that allows a plurality of individuals to be productive dividua while maintaining their unity as individuals and exercising sovereignty in their relations with others.

Aspects of this political ideal can be made out in the kinds of relations Nietzsche describes in his organismic model of sovereignty (see p. 635 above). Under the rubric 1) of self-regulation, *antagonism* appears in the form *of "fear* of all alien incursions" and "*hatred* towards [*gegen*] the enemy". But self-regulation also entails the crucial moment of "moderation" or *measure*: "Maaßhalten". Under rubrics 2) and 3) – overcompensation and assimilation – *antagonism* takes the forms of "*acquisitiveness*", "appropriation", "the craving for power", "making others dependent on oneself" and "commanding". Yet this is then balanced by "goodwill" under rubric 4) secretion, and by obeying under rubric 5) metabolic power: "temporary worship admiration making oneself dependent fitting in, [...] being able to serve". Relations between more-or-less *equal powers* are here regulated by reciprocal dependencies, reciprocal commanding-and-obeying, goodwill-and-hatred, taking-and-giving.

In conclusion, Nietzsche's socio-physiological texts of 1881 develop not just a powerful critique of the liberal concept of individual personhood and its metaphysical presuppositions; they also formulate an alternative concept of person-

---

Spannungen, durch welche das Individuum sich als individuum erhält, kaum mehr wahrgenommen werden können, das heißt: die Individuen müssen auf den blassesten Ton des Individuellen reduzirt werden! Also die Gleichheit weitaus vorherrschend! Das ist die Euthanasie, völlig unproduktiv! [...]"

hood and on its basis suggest a counter-concept of sovereign agency that turns on singularity (/diversity) and the maintenance of a maximal but measured inner antagonism through a measured external antagonism with others. Against the Socratic claim that the conflict that we each are can only be measured (moderated) by eliminating (or at least reducing) our inner antagonism, Nietzsche suggests that our inner antagonisms can be contained through outer relations of measured antagonism with equals. In place of the Socratic ideal of inner peace or harmony: the elimination of conflict, Nietzsche's texts point to the possibility of transforming *unmeasured destructive conflict* – the mutual destruction of competing drives, and with them the individual they inhabit – into *productive measured conflict*. What institutional conditions are needed to maintain the measured productive conflict between sovereign beings, upon which this depends, remains an open question.

References

Arendt, Hannah (1990) "Philosophy and Politics", in: *Social Research* 57(1), 73–103.
Aydin, Ciano (2003) *Zijn en Worden. Nietzsches omduiding van het substantiebegrip*, Maastricht: Shaker.
Gerhardt, Volker (1992) "Selbstbegründung. Nietzsche's Moral der Individualität", in: *Nietzsche-Studien* 21, 28–49.
Meyer, Katrin (1998) *Ästhetik der Historie: Fr. Nietzsches "Vom Nutzen und Nachteil der Historie für das Leben"* (Epistemata Würzburger Wissenschaftliche Schriften, Reihe Philosophie, vol. 238), Würzburg: Königshausen & Neumann.
Mouffe, Chantal (1996) "Democracy, Power and the 'Political'", in: Seyla Benhabib (ed.), *Democracy and Difference: Contesting the Boundaries of the Political*, Princeton: Princeton University Press, 245–256.
Mulhall, Stephen/Swift, Adam (1992) *Liberals and Communitarians*. Oxford: Blackwell.
Mulhall, Stephen/Swift, Adam (2003) "Rawls and Communitarianism", in: S. Freeman (ed.), *The Cambridge Companion to Rawls*, Cambridge: Cambridge University Press, 460–487.
Müller-Lauter, Wolfgang (1978) "Der Organismus als innerer Kampf. Der Einfluss von Wilhelm Roux auf Fr. Nietzsche", in: *Nietzsche-Studien* 7, 189–223.
Müller-Lauter, Wolfgang (1999) "Der Organismus als innerer Kampf. Der Einfluss von Wilhelm Roux auf Fr. Nietzsche", in: *Über Werden und Wille zur Macht, Nietzsche-Interpretationen I*, Berlin/New York: De Gruyter, 97–140.
Owen, David (1995) *Nietzsche, Politics & Modernity*, London: Sage.
Plato *Gorgias*, Benjamin Jowett (tr.), Project Gutenberg.
Rawls, John (1971) *A Theory of Justice*. Oxford: Oxford University Press.
Siemens, H.W. (2006) "Nietzsche Contra Liberalism on Freedom", in: Keith Ansell-Pearson (ed.), *A Companion to Nietzsche*, Oxford/Malden, MA: Basil Blackwell, 437–454.
Siemens, H.W. (2008) "Nietzsche and the Temporality of Self-Legislation", in: Manuel Dries (ed.), *Nietzsche on Time and History*, Berlin/New York: De Gruyter, 191–210.

Siemens, H.W. (2009a) "Nietzsche's Critique of Democracy", in: *Journal of Nietzsche Studies* 38, 20–37.
Siemens, H.W. (2009b) "(Self-)legislation, Life and Love in Nietzsche's Philosophy", in: Isabelle Wienand (ed.), *Neue Beiträge zu Nietzsches Moral-, Politik- und Kulturphilosophie*, Fribourg: Press Academic Fribourg, 67–90.
Siemens, H.W. (2011) "Empfindung", in: *Nietzsche-Wörterbuch*, Nietzsche Online (NO), De Gruyter (ed.), Berlin/Boston: De Gruyter. DOI: 10.1515/NO_W017186_0080.

Robert Pippin
26 The Expressivist Nietzsche

1

In a 2010 book, *Nietzsche, Psychology, & First Philosophy*, I argued for the importance of the French *moralistes* for any attempt to understand why Nietzsche should have said in *Beyond Good and Evil* that "psychology" might now (that is, because of him, Nietzsche) once again become the "queen of the sciences", and so once more the "path to the fundamental problems". Among other things, this led to a characterization of Nietzsche on agency that could be considered "expressivist". My intention here is to clarify that notion in more detail.

My purpose in invoking the tradition of Pascal, La Rochefoucauld, and above all Montaigne, aside from the fact that Nietzsche's frequent praise of that tradition and identification with it has gone relatively unnoticed, was two-fold. First, the book is based on earlier lectures that were originally given in a *cours* at the *Collège de France* in 2004[1] and anyone who knows anything about twentieth-century French philosophy and especially French appropriations of Nietzsche will know of the enormous influence of Heidegger on that tradition. My somewhat ironic intention was to remind my audience that from the point of view of Nietzsche, he is unquestionably better understood as a French *moraliste* than the German metaphysician of Heidegger's influential lectures from the 1930s and 1940s.[2] But this historical association raises the philosophical question. Granted, one might concede, Nietzsche admired these people and described what he was doing as psychology in a way that called them to mind, but what does that tell us? What, viewed this way, *is* psychology?

This is the question the book tries to answer from a number of different perspectives, but the core issue is the one that chiefly interested Nietzsche: the problem of self-knowledge and the relation between that problem and knowledge of others' actions and words, and especially the unique kind of difficulty one faces in attempting to know such things as why one (or anyone) did what one did, what it actually was that one (or anyone) did; what one (or some other) truly values; why one values what one does; could one come to know what sort

---

[1] Published as *Nietzsche, moraliste français: La conception nietzschéenne d'une psychologie philosophique* (Pippin 2006).
[2] Heidegger 1991.

of a life one might truly affirm, and if so how?³ It is clear everywhere in his texts that Nietzsche did not think that this question could be answered by any manner of introspection, inner observation of any kind, anything like a natural science, and such self-knowledge is certainly not to be had by a priori philosophizing about *the* basic structure of the human soul, as in Plato's theory of the tri-partite soul. It would at least be fair to say that the most prominent Nietzschean characterization of claims to self-and other-knowledge is that it is *extremely* difficult to arrive at such self- and other-knowledge, partly because it is neither empirical nor a priori knowledge, partly because the soul is not an object in the usual sense, but mostly because in his treatments such putative self- and other-knowledge is almost always an expression of some self-deception that must be overcome. (We should expect this to be the same problem, subject to the same nearly ubiquitous self-deception, even if we take Nietzsche to have some sort of "self-fashioning" theory of the self, as if an aesthetic product, a work of art. The question just becomes *what* "self" I have "fashioned" or "created". The questions of what it is I have fashioned in "fashioning myself" and whether it was really *my* fashioning, whether it is as I take myself to have fashioned it, just begin with any aesthetic conception of a subject's relation to her activities and practices; that conception alone does not resolve them.)⁴

This is not to say that there is no such thing as self- or other-knowledge properly understood, but to suggest that the truth in such a realm does not have as its opposite falsity in the propositional sense, but a kind of fraudulence in what one reports about oneself or claims about another.⁵ Understanding this, the *moralistes,* for Nietzsche, offered observations on the sort of questions posed above, not by relying on a general theory that provided instances, but by finding ways to characterize how the human soul typically works (how such questions as those above are posed and pursued) in ways true to the unstable, variable, situation dependent, self-interested contexts in which they arise. There

---

3 Why the pursuit of such questions should be understood not as a sub-field or part of philosophy but as "first philosophy" or "queen of the sciences" (as opposed say to the conventional queen, metaphysics), is an even more difficult question. It turns on what appears to be Nietzsche's view on the role of some evaluative stance, mattering, or erotic attachment and commitment, in the possible intelligibility of anything at all, in any possible intentional relation to an object. This *does* tie him to Heidegger but to the Heidegger of *Being and Time* and the role of "care" or *Sorge* in any "horizon" of intelligibility, but that is a complicated separate topic. It will emerge a bit below with the issue of "depth commitments".
4 I raise several more objections to the self-fashioning view in Chapter Six of the book (Pippin 2010: 105ff.), several relevant to Alexander Nehamas's well-known interpretation.
5 See EH Vorwort 3: "Irrthum ... ist nicht Blindheit, Irrthum ist Feigheit".

is no way to summarize the "method" they used to do this because there is no such method, anymore than there is any method that can be invoked to show how "I knew not only that she was lying but that she knew I knew she was lying and didn't care". We *do* know those things and saying that we know them by "inferences from cues", say, gets us nowhere. One might as well ask what method Shakespeare (another of Nietzsche's heroes) used in coming to understand human beings like Macbeth or Othello (or ambition or jealousy) so well.

Here is a summary passage on the dangers of a philosophical psychology that, I argued in the book, should be adopted as some sort of publication hurdle: nothing can appear on Nietzsche unless consistent with the remarks. It is in the "Assorted Opinions and Maxims" section of *Human, All Too Human*. Nietzsche is describing what he calls the "original sin" of philosophers, who, he says have always appropriated and ruined the views of the *Menschenprüfer*, the evaluators of the human and the *moralistes*, because

> they have taken them for *unqualified* propositions and sought to demonstrate the absolute validity of what these moralists intended merely as approximate signposts or even as no more than truths possessing tenancy only for a decade – and through doing so thought to elevate themselves above the latter. (AOM 5)

The example of such an original sin he gives is Schopenhauer on the will. Nietzsche claims that Schopenhauer was in reality, without appreciating the fact himself, a "moralist", who rightly used the term "will" loosely, and in a way that referred broadly to a meaning common to many different human situations and merely filled a gap in language and so earned the right to "speak of the will as Pascal had spoken of it". Unfortunately though "the philosophical rage for universality" turned such a moraliste *façon de parler* into a metaphysical claim about the omnipresence of the will in all of nature (a claim some have attributed to Nietzsche, but that he calls a piece of "mystical mischief", "*mystischen Unfuge*") and so ended up turning everything into a false reification, "*zu einer falschen Verdinglichung*" (AOM 5; Nietzsche 1996: 215–216).

2

The crucial passage for the interpretation I present is GM I 13.

> To demand of strength that it should not express itself as strength, tha it should not be a desire to overcome, a desire to throw down, a desire to become master, a thirst for enemies and resistances and triumphs, is just as absurd as to demand of weakness that it should express itself as strength. A quantum of force is equivalent to a quantum of drive, will, effect – more, it is nothing other than precisely this very driving, willing, effecting, and

only owing to the seduction of language (and of the fundamental errors of reason that are petrified in it) which conceives and misconceives all effects as conditioned by something that causes effects, by a "subject" can it appear otherwise. For just as the popular mind separates the lightning from its flash and takes the latter for an *action*, for the operation of a subject called lightning, so popular morality also separates strength from expressions of strength, as if there were a neutral substratum behind the strong man, which was *free* to express strength or not to do. But there is no such substratum; there is no "being" behind doing, effecting, becoming: the "doer" is merely a fiction added to the deed – the deed is everything. (Nietzsche 2006)

The passage is highly literary, enigmatic and not at all systematic. However fascinating, it does not give us a lot to work with and much of the interpretive task consists in determining what Nietzsche could have meant, given what else he says (and manifests) about psychological explanation. The idea that Nietzsche is indirectly proposing here that the doer is "expressed" in the deed and in that sense is not "behind" it as a separate cause, opens the door to very large issues prominent in Spinoza (on a substance's non-temporal, *nunc stans* expression in its attributes and modes), and similar issues in everyone from Leibniz to Schelling to Böhm, as Deleuze has argued (Deleuze 1990). But more directly and from the outset, one might entertain immediate doubts that, to explain the passage, we need to commit Nietzsche to that *different* relation between doer and deed than an ex ante causal origin, with the deed as a result. Why not, as the passage seems to suggest, "*no* relation"? No doer at all?

Admittedly, the most startling formulation in the GM passage is an analogy: just as there is no lightning behind, and causing as a result, the flash (as might be suggested by "the lightning flashed"), so there is no doer behind the deed (as might be suggested by "John hit the ball"); such a substratum is a fiction added on; the deed is all there is, everything, *alles* (as if really we should say, I suppose, "there are just ball-hitting-events going on"). As noted, I argued that this passage should be understood as a quick sketch of an "expressivist" theory of action one can find throughout Nietzsche; that is, that he remains committed to the distinction between action and event, and is proposing a way to make the distinction different from voluntarism, spontaneity theories, intention-causal theories.[6] That difference involves noticing that Nietzsche is only denying that there is a doer "behind" and separate from the deed. The language of doer-deed is not dropped; a strong person's "strength" is *expressed* in "a desire to over-

---

6 Given the use of the notion of "expressivism" in logical positivism's characterization of value judgments, this is perhaps not the most felicitous of terms, but it is the term Nietzsche wants us to use to understand the relation between strength and its manifestation ("*sich äussern*") and I trust the difference with the positivist use is clear.

come, a desire to throw down, a desire to become master, a thirst for enemies and resistances and triumphs…" The various bodily movements involved in each of these activities would be unintelligible, mere bodily movements in space and time, were we not able to understand them in their *psychological meaning*, as expressions of strength, as motivated by a strength that wants expressing. If deeds are reduced to mere bodily movements like natural events, we won't have any way of distinguishing identical bodily movements that are differently motivated and so are different deeds. There would be many such problems. However, the "no substratum", nothing-"behind"-the-deed language prohibits us from thinking of psychological motives or even their neuro-biological counterparts, as causes of separate deeds, and we must keep this in mind when Nietzsche gives his own psychological explanations (and I wouldn't know how to characterize those explanations except as psychological) of pity, humility, the desire for equality, for the slave revolt in morality and so forth. Hence my suggestion that Nietzsche is trying to get us to see the doer "in" the deed, rather than "behind it" and the point of that is to deflate our reliance on our own ex ante formulations of intention to account for what happens. Such formulations, while necessary (again, there wouldn't be deeds unless such mindedness could be attended to as such), are only *provisional*, are *realized* (or not) only in the deed that reveals what in fact we are committed to doing, what we "really" intended. Nietzsche does not go any further in the passage (or elsewhere) so, as noted, the task is filling out such a view in ways consistent with other things Nietzsche says (like the Schopenhauer/*moraliste* passage just quoted, or his own psychological explanations).

Now, I should say, there is a perfectly ordinary sense in which we want to call the intention that explains what the deed is and why it was done simply "what the agent had in mind to do", *ex ante*. Sometimes this intention is implicit and unformulated, but it is easily available at any point if I am asked what I am doing and why. We can certainly imagine this mental state occurring some time "before" the bodily movement begins, and so can say easily that such an intention and the agent who holds it can be understood as before and so behind the deed that is eventually performed. Likewise, there is nothing in what Nietzsche is suggesting to imply that there are not conditions that have to be met for the deed to qualify as mine alone. I have to be able to exercise some control over the events, not be coerced or duped and manipulated. I see no Nietzschean reason to deny that persons can come to understand themselves this way and can attempt to "live out" the implications of such a self-image. It is the correct analysis of this way of speaking that is at issue.

So the Nietzschean account need not deny that *there are* such ex ante formulations, as if they couldn't exist. His model just holds them to be *provisional*, most often, in ordinary doings, actually and unproblematically manifested in the deed, but it is only "there" that the provisional becomes actual. They *are* realized, made real in what we are willing actually to do. And they need to be considered provisional because in a surprisingly large number of significant cases, what we are willing to avow as our intention is a fantasy, largely self-deluded, and not consistent with what we do.[7]

In the passage, in other words, Nietzsche still refers to "deeds" and not events, and with that, as far as I can see, the question of how and why the deed was produced, and with *that*, the problem of the "doer", is unavoidably raised. So I presume that everyone would agree that Nietzsche shows no tendency to treat a plant's phototropism or iron ore rusting as explicable in the same way as human activities. There is perhaps some analogous or metaphorical way to say that the plant's turning toward the sun "expresses" its need for light, but there is nothing in that that refers to *the plant's view of what it needs and why*, nothing "psychological". As indicated in the examples cited above – Nietzsche's explanation of such things as the slave revolt, pity, humility, egalitarianism – a reference to the mindedness inherent in such activities is essential to their individuation and explanation. If we simply try to do justice to the fact that Nietzsche's explanations of such phenomena are everywhere psychological (an attempt to determine *what* mindedness is *really* expressed in the deed), the issue of how he understands the relation between the doer's mindedness and deed is unavoidable. He rejects "behind" and "before"; and I suggested he is thinking of "in" and as a process of realization. Things get complicated quickly because Nietzsche is deeply suspicious of the avowed, self-ascribed motivations provided by agents, but he always suggests, as what truly motivates, other psychological phenomena, like *ressentiment* or fear or self-hatred.[8]

---

7 This raises a problem similar to one discussed recently in epistemology, called "disjunctivism". Here the issue would be: why, in trying to understand the role of mindedness in some bodily movements, take one's bearing from odd or failed or infrequent instances, such as not actually doing what I sincerely avow I intend to do? That is too large an issue to address here, but at least in this case, the instances at issue, if unusual, are not thereby marginal or insignificant, especially given the prevalence of self-deception in Nietzsche's genealogies. We can be just as easily lulled into complacency about the form of action by the standard cases as we can be misled by unusual ones.

8 There is no indication that Nietzsche thinks that ultimately such phenomena are to be explained by factors "outside" the psychological, as if *ressentiment* were some discrete sort of drive-quanta, pushing an agent into something. *Ressentiment* is what the slave feels, experiences (and denies to himself) and that requires that he understand the meaning of his situation in a way, all of which must be "inside" the psychological.

And, although in this passage, Nietzsche suggests that strength cannot but express itself as strength, that claim must be made consistent with a variety of things he says about such dispositions. There is the issue of what *counts* as the expression of strength, much easier to say in the case of birds of prey than human expressions. (The ascetic might regard his activities, refraining from expressions of strength, as the highest manifestation of strength.) Then there are contexts in which strength is not allowed its expression, and the strong can be said to rub themselves raw on the bars of self-imposed cages.[9] There is strength that can be said to turn against itself as strength. Distinguishing any of these will require the depth psychology Nietzsche is proposing.

Still, one might say, while agreeing that Nietzsche does not tie any notion of individual responsibility to a spontaneous causal power to initiate bodily movements, any continuing to talk of a doer even in the deed betrays a lingering reluctance to break more completely with the essentially moral notions of responsibility, agent, and accountability, a truly revolutionary break many suspect may be the sort Nietzsche intended. But it is not clear where such a radical break would land us. I made use of Nietzsche's invocation of Spinoza to show why, for him, agent regret is not regret that I could have done otherwise, but sadness that I turned out to be other than I had imagined. Such a suggestion requires much more filling out, but any such extension must be consistent with the fact that, first, Nietzsche clearly *wants* some sort of account of agent regret. That is why he turned to Spinoza. And, second, Nietzsche's rhetoric is everywhere hortatory and condemnatory. In some sense or other he expects or at least hopes that we can overcome nihilism, largely by listening to, being gripped by, him, a transformation that may produce what we now are not – sovereign individuals. All these notions continue and deepen the question of the right understanding between an agent and her deeds; it does not avoid or dismiss the question as if there is no such distinction.

And at this point, there are several things to be said about the "expressivist logic", let us say, of inner and outer, in, first, failed actions. They are the first sorts of cases often raised as objections, but they do not bear on Nietzsche's claims. Someone, Lanier let us say, did everything he could to arrive on time for Joshua's party but some intervening contingency prevented him. But surely he intended to arrive on time. Must an expressivist account say otherwise? No. Lanier took several steps toward the outer realization of the intention, there is plenty of evidence from other actions that he is always polite and conscientious about such things, that he values Joshua's friendship, and there is no way he

---

9 See, for example, GM I 16.

could have *gotten himself* stuck in the traffic jam. He was well on the way, and there is plenty of "outer" manifesting his "inner", even if not completely. The situation would change if we imagine Lanier's wife saying, "Why do you always come this way to go to Joshua's? You know it *always* makes us late, and you know there is a better way." Or if we imagined Lanier at home, thinking, "There's plenty of time to get there, but I always have bad luck with traffic, so I might as well not even go since I'll arrive so late. But at least I intended to go until I remembered this."

Moreover, the fact that the doer must be understood to be expressed in the deed need not entail either that *everything* in the agent's ex ante mindedness must be expressed for the movement to count as a deed (that the doer is wholly identified with the deed in that sense; there can be degrees of expression that can be authentic expressions), or that that *expression* alone warrants the agent's *affirmation* of the deed.

On the former issue: the position I want to attribute to Nietzsche is not wildly indifferent to contingencies. I begin to sculpt and a small insignificant chisel mark cracks the entire stone into pieces. One should not say that I must have intended this pile of rubble, that I must be identified with what happens. That is the key: *something happened*; the result was not a deed, an expression of any aspect of my mindedness. (Just as Lanier's getting stuck in traffic is not something, we assume, he did, but something that happened to him.) Again, the situation changes if we imagine someone warning our sculptor: "You take too many risks always chiseling like that; so many of your marbles crack." So on my account the relation between doer and deed is not some form of identity. Something can count as a deed, even if not *the* deed I self-deceptively and self-servingly insist it is. The deed can be mine even if a lot remains undetermined for me and others about what I actually intended by doing it. We might have to wait and see what else I am willing to do in order to be more determinate. There can be a great deal of interpretive play and so indeterminacy (for me and for others affected) in what it is I have done. There can be a lot of imprecision in trying to draw a line between what happens because of me but is not something I did, and what I did.

On the latter, expression/affirmation issue, there are clearly two senses at work of "the deed being mine". The first might be called a merely forensic sense, an answer to the question, "whose deed is this?" This deed was brought about, but by whom? This is the sense in which the law wants to know "whose deed?", "whose murder?" The butler's; the mistress's? Etc. Then there is another sense much more difficult to answer. The answer turns on the very elusive issue of the Nietzschean theory of freedom. Nietzsche was obviously concerned that the power of modern conformism would render *any* expression of anyone's mindedness some sort of distortion, and so some sort of social pathology. But a distortion of what? Of what the agent would have intended had he not been subject to these conforming powers? Would have intended if we imagine him free *ab initio* to be whomever he wants to be? That is clearly an idle fantasy for Nietzsche. No one could ever be in such a position. This latter sense of "genuinely" or "authentically" mine is extremely difficult and a long-standing problem (from the "happy slaves" issue to Rousseau and Kant on self-legislation to Emerson on self-reliance to Heidegger on *Eigentlichkeit*). And I don't think that some notion of one's "struggling to overcome some obstacle in the outer" will get us very far on this issue. People can struggle very hard to express a canned and wholly inherited and manipulated sense of themselves. A few minutes observing American politics can make that point. I think that all the evidence is that Nietzsche thought *he* knew how to make this distinction between mine in the purely forensic or factual sense (not someone else's) and "truly" mine, all without a "true self" ontology, but he did not make it easy for commentators to state the nature of this distinction. So, there is still much to be done.

3

Here is another component any "psychological" reading of Nietzsche must face. Bernard Williams praised Nietzsche's "minimalist" psychology. He was aligning himself with what he took to be Nietzsche's suspicions of accounts of the human soul that were already committed to some moral or ethical ideal, and then postulated the faculties or capacities necessary to make the pursuit of such ideals look possible and coherent. The divided soul, the free will, conscience, moral sense, would all be examples of such a mistake. The relation, Nietzsche and Williams in effect argued, should go the other way. If we wanted to explain the possibility and coherence of the pursuit of such ideals, we ought to be constrained in doing so by an account of capacities and faculties available in non-moral actions. In the book my emphasis on "the erotic Nietzsche" was meant to do justice to this constraint.[10]

Having introduced that notion, my aim was to associate it in its generality with the kinds of things the Platonic Socrates invokes eros to account for, from art to philosophy to love of good laws to friendship. The idea in such a generality was first to notice the signal importance of what Nietzsche sometimes called

---

[10] This is an invocation (eros) that begins early in Nietzsche's work and stays late, especially in the musings on himself as Dionysus in late works. See EH Vorwort 2, or in frequent asides, as in the quotation from Ovid in §3.

"esteeming", *schätzen*, valuing. Nietzsche considers asserting a claim or recommending an action, I argued, as expressions of some commitment to a value, something like promises to keep faith with and to be able to justify what was claimed, to remain committed to the implications of what one was recommending. (So the claim is *quite* general; it is that the domain of intentional intelligibility itself is the domain of value, self-subsumption under norms.) For Nietzsche, famously, these values are values because they are valued, not in themselves, although that intimation of a "projection" of value misleadingly suggests "acts" of projection at punctated moments of time, "conferring" value. That is not the case. The claim is: there would not be such values were humans not to have come to value them, but that process is collective, sustained over time, mediated in many institutional, religious and artistic practices, and inherited; *very rarely* open to revision. Nietzsche thinks we are living through such a potentially revolutionary time, comparable to the end of the "tragic age of the Greeks". Making use of John Haugeland's "Truth and Rule-Following" article,[11] I went on to distinguish everyday commitments to various values, which are frequently subject to revision, expansion, abandonment, and, by contrast, "depth" commitments, the loss of which would leave us near literally lost, disoriented; so they are almost impossible to imagine giving up. In undertaking these depth commitments we are not fulfilling some *other* commitment, as if there could be a universal obligation to undertake some depth commitments. That would obviously start an infinite regress. But there must be a hierarchical relation between thin and depth commitments. In making a claim or recommending an action we commit ourselves to a variety of obligations that cannot all be fulfilled and we need some orienting concern, some general sense of what is more or less important to us if we are to resolve such conflicts. We might say that this issue concerns what matters to us; which things matter because others do, and things that simply matter, that we could not imagine not mattering.[12] Since we do not *decide* what ought to matter, and thereby have it matter (even though we can do what we think ought to be significant to do, even without it actually mattering to us more than that), and since things can matter to us that we think ought not to matter, we have to call such commitments pre-reflective and pre-volitional; or, I suggested, erotic attachments. (We do not decide whom or what to love;

---

[11] In Haugeland 2000: 305–362.
[12] This is much closer to the semantic field of "the erotic", and so less volitional than "valuing". One does not, cannot, will what ought to matter to one; one can come to have a belief that some goal is important, and yet still find it doesn't much matter to one; one can be ashamed of what does matter to one.

whom or what to care about.) This is all as mysterious in its way as the appearance and disappearance of an inspiring eros.

In our actions and inactions, we can be said to express what matters and what does not (much more reliably than by what we avow), and in certain rare "crisis" moments, a "depth commitment" can be at stake and the extent of such depth can be revealed. Now this does not commit Nietzsche to any "inner self". He is a well known critic of that notion. For one thing, there is no assumption about some underlying, permanent set of such commitments or bearer of such commitments. Things come to matter to someone in this critical way, and they can cease to matter, or matter in a different sense. The qualitative difference in the degree of the importance of the commitment, and the role of that commitment in ordering one's actions need not entail any inner self ontology. Some critical deed may be critical because what it is at stake is what matters the most, but only at that time, in that context. The spatial relation at issue is actually not rightly captured by notions like underlying or deep, but rather "highest", as in "highest values".

Now, I argued in the book and elsewhere that it was important to see things this way in order to understand that Nietzsche's diagnosis of nihilism was that it was not a crisis of credible belief or of strength of will, but the failure of desire, the failure of mattering. This, admittedly, immediately gives the impression that the signal manifestation of this problem is "failure" in the sense of collapse; nothing mattering enough to be worth any investment or sacrifice. Boredom would be an example. This *is* of course a clear manifestation and Nietzsche does appeal to the failure of desire in this sense. But there are lots of things that "the last men", paradigmatic nihilists, *care about*; and they might even desire what they desire, however trivial, with passionate intensity. (Nietzsche's descriptions of "last men" and "pale atheists" do not suggest this, but he says nothing that would definitively rule it out.) The even more paradoxical thought is that Nietzsche seems to think that one particularly catastrophic manifestation of nihilism is *contentment*, bovine satisfaction in the low and base, caring about the wrong things, not "not caring".

Clearly we need a more general notion of "failure", more than just collapse or absence, if we are to understand nihilism as a failure of desire. We need something like: certain pathological *manifestations* of desire (not its absence) can also count as its "failure", as in obsessive and so forever unsatisfiable desire, desires for unreasonable, unattainable objects, and an old standby in Nietzsche, self-deceived self-destructive desires.[13] One thought would be to pay

---

[13] I am much indebted to Ken Gemes for extensive correspondence about his issue. I don't regard myself as having provided yet an adequate answer to Geme's questions about "failure" and pathology. These are only some suggestions.

attention to the fact that Nietzsche does not say that nihilism is the collapse of *anything* worth caring about, of all values. Nihilism is defined by the event: the *highest* values devalue themselves. We might have lost the distinction between highest and lowest; might cease to care about it; to care only for what we happen to want. So the last men might care about all sorts of ends, but be without an orienting sense of the highest, that which matters most, worth sacrifice. This disorientation is treated by Nietzsche as a kind of failure. They drift instead from pleasure to pleasure, timid, unwilling to take any risks for the sake of something worth taking risks for. This would count as a pathology if we can imagine such a life, without begging any questions, as inevitably threatening some form of self-contempt, practical incoherence, conflicts that cannot be resolved, or as possible at all without these effects only by massive self-deceit. We could point to these *self*-defeating effects as a defense against the charge that we are inventing a capacity (for depth commitment) in order to defend an ethical ideal, contra Williams' minimalism. I don't suggest that it is obvious that Nietzsche thinks this, but just want to propose that this is the answer suggested by many of Nietzsche's formulations.

4

A final issue for the expressivist, psychological interpretation. It is how to understand the frequent Nietzschean emphasis on the value of "self-overcoming" (which he virtually equates with his understanding of freedom) and such remarks in GM as "every good thing on earth" eventually overcomes ["sublates"] itself, or later in GM when Nietzsche proclaims what he calls the "law of life", "the law of the necessity of self-overcoming in the nature of life" (where he uses both the Hegelian *Selbstaufhebung* and *Selbstüberwindung*) (GM III 27); and to do justice to the appearance of "constantly" (*beständig*) in remarks like,

> How is freedom measured, in individuals as in nations? By the resistance which has to be overcome, by the effort it costs to stay aloft. One would have to seek the highest type of free man where the greatest resistance is *constantly being overcome*. (TI Skirmishes 38; Nietzsche 2005; my emphasis)

Does this emphasis on Nietzsche's praise of self-overcoming skew the interpretation in favor of some sort of "priority" of self-dissatisfaction, as if only such endlessly unsatisfied individuals are worthy of Nietzsche's praise? I don't see why that should be the case. Here is my first attempt at a summary of what the self-overcoming passages show:

One initial, still quite crude summary of what he is getting at in these passages would simply be that achieved freedom involves achieving a capacity both to sustain a whole-hearted commitment to an ideal (an ideal worth sacrificing for, that provides the basis for a certain hierarchical unity among one's interests and passions), and what appears at first glance to be a capacity in some tension with such wholeheartedness – a willingness to overcome or abandon such a commitment in altered circumstances or as a result of some development. To be unable to endure the irresolvable dynamic of what Nietzsche calls an ideal's or a goal's or a value's constant self-overcoming, to remain dogmatically attached to an already overcome form of life... all these are treated as forms of unfreedom. If I am going to be upbraided for too "Hegelian" a reading of Nietzsche (as I frequently am), I might as well get the benefit too: a dialectical tension in the Nietzschean desiderata, not an unbalanced "priority".

Secondly, is it a consequence of this expressivism that it counts what should be, and is treated by Nietzsche as, a rare and very difficult achievement – seeing oneself expressed in one's deeds in a whole-heated affirmation – as a normal, everyday occurrence? But as emphasized before, there are two separate questions here that must be kept distinct. "Expressivism" is a claim that shares an assumption with all accounts of actions as such – that there are bodily movements or mental happenings that stand in a relation to a subject's mindedness – and it argues for a kind of relation different from all causal, compatibilist and voluntarist, free-will accounts. There are then all sorts of *further* questions one can ask *about such expressed mindedness*, including whether the deed actually expresses what the agent avows, and whether the agent's mindedness can be said to reflect *her*, or is itself the product of a coercive conformism. (So, to jump to another point, the "weak" types can certainly be said to express themselves in their, say, vengeful, moralistic acts of punishment. But what they avow as their intention is self-deceived, and because of that, they can be said to be engaged in a self-defeating pattern of valuation. Their acts express a motivation that they disavow (even to themselves, if they are self-deceived and not hypocrites), making holding together the deception and the psychic satisfaction from realizing their real intentions, more and more difficult, especially in a religion that insists on honesty about intentions). Or, without self-deception, one could say: teaching that course on "ethics for bureaucrats" is *what I did*, is my deed. My intention to teach the course is expressed in what I do; my preparation, my showing up on time, all express my intention to do a good job. But this job I found at East Podunk Technical Teacher's College is the only one I could find after Princeton, and the activity is not an expression of my highest values, or what I would have chosen, or what I believe ought to be taught, etc. I can be said to see some aspect of myself in the deeds (say, my willingness to do whatever it takes to keep teaching some sort of philosophy), but certainly not the self I would whole-heartedly affirm. Nothing I attribute to Nietzsche is inconsistent with such a characterization.

References

Deleuze, Gilles (1990) *Expressionism in Philosophy: Spinoza*, trans. Martin Joughin, New York: Zone Books.
Haugeland, J. (2000) *Having Thought: Essays in the Metaphysics of Mind*, Cambridge: Harvard University Press.
Heidegger, Martin (1991) *Nietzsche*, Vols. 1, 2, 3 and 4, trans. David Farrell Krell, New York: Harper & Row.
Nietzsche, Friedrich (1996) *Human, All Too Human*, ed. and trans. R.J. Hollingdale, Cambridge: Cambridge University Press.
Nietzsche, Friedrich (2005) *The Anti-Christ, Ecce Homo, Twilight of the Idols, and Other Writings*, eds. Aaron Ridley and Judith Norman, trans. Judith Norman, Cambridge: Cambridge University Press.
Nietzsche, Friedrich (2006) *On the Genealogy of Morality*, ed. Keith Ansell-Pearson, trans. Carol Diethe, Cambridge: Cambridge University Press.
Pippin, Robert B. (2006) *Nietzsche, moraliste français. La conception nietzschéenne d'une psychologie philosophique*, trans. I. Wienand, Paris: Odile Jacob.
Pippin, Robert B. (2010) *Nietzsche, Psychology, and First Philosophy*, Chicago/London: University of Chicago Press.

Complete Bibliography

Abbey, Ruth (2000) *Nietzsche's Middle Period*, Oxford: Oxford University Press.
Abel, Günter (1984) *Die Dynamik der Willen zur Macht und die ewige Wiederkehr*, Berlin/New York: De Gruyter. [2nd edition 1998].
Abel, Günter (1999) *Sprache, Zeichen, Interpretation*, Frankfurt a.M.: Suhrkamp.
Abel, Günter (2001) "Bewußtsein–Sprache–Natur. Nietzsches Philosophie des Geistes", in: *Nietzsche-Studien* 30, 1–43.
Abel, Günter (2004) *Zeichen der Wirklichkeit*, Frankfurt a.M.: Suhrkamp.
Abel, Günter (2012) "Die Aktualität der Wissenschaftsphilosophie Nietzsches" in: H. Heit, G. Abel and M. Brusotti (eds.), *Nietzsches Wissenschaftsphilosophie*, Berlin/Boston: De Gruyter, 481–530.
Acampora, Christa Davis (2006) "Naturalism and Nietzsche's Moral Psychology", in: Keith Ansell-Pearson (ed.), *A Companion to Nietzsche*, Oxford: Blackwell, 314–333.
Acampora, Christa Davis (2006) "On Sovereignty and Overhumanity: Why It Matters How We Read Nietzsche's Genealogy II: 2", in: Christa Davis Acampora (ed.), *Nietzsche's On the Genealogy of Morals: Critical Essays*, Lanham/Oxford: Rowman & Littlefield, 147–163.
Acampora, Christa Davis (ed.) (2006) *Nietzsche's On the Genealogy of Morals: Critical Essays*, Lanham/Oxford: Rowman & Littlefield.
Acampora, Christa Davis (2008) "Forgetting the subject", in: S.V. Hicks and A. Rosenberg (eds.), *Reading Nietzsche at the Margins*, West Lafayette: Purdue University Press, 34–56.
Anderson, Nicole (2003) "The Ethical Possibilities of Subject as Play: In Nietzsche and Derrida", in: *The Journal of Nietzsche Studies* 26, 79–90.
Anderson, R. Lanier (2012) "What is a Nietzschean Self?", in: C. Janaway and S. Robertson (eds.), *Nietzsche, Naturalism, and Normativity*, Oxford: Oxford University Press, 202–233.
Anderson, R. Lanier (2012) "The Will to Power in Science and Philosophy", in: H. Heit, G. Abel and M. Brusotti (eds.), *Nietzsches Wissenschaftsphilosophie*, Berlin/Boston: De Gruyter, 55–71.
Anderson, R. Lanier (2013) "Nietzsche on Autonomy", in: Ken Gemes and John Richardson (eds.), *The Oxford Handbook of Nietzsche*, Oxford: Oxford University Press, 432–460.
Angier, Tom P.S. (2006) *Either Kierkegaard/Or Nietzsche: Moral Philosophy in a New Key*, Aldershot: Ashgate.
Ansell Pearson, Keith (2009) *A Companion to Nietzsche*, Oxford: Blackwell.
Apel, Karl-Otto (1975) "Das Leibapriori der Erkenntnis: Eine erkenntnisanthropologische Betrachtung im Anschluß an Leibnizens Monadenlehre", in: H.-G. Gadamer and P. Vogler (eds.), *Neue Anthropologie. Siebenter Band: Philosophische Anthropologie. Zweiter Teil*, Munich/Stuttgart: DTV/Thieme, 264–288.
Arendt, Hannah (1990) "Philosophy and Politics", in: *Social Research* 57(1), 73–103.
Arendt, Hannah (1994) [1946] "French Existentialism", in: *Essays in Understanding 1930–1954*, New York: Harcourt, 188–193.
Assoun, Paul-Laurent (2000) *Freud and Nietzsche*, trans. Richard L. Collier, Jr., London: Athlone.
Atwell, John E. (1990) *Schopenhauer: The Human Character*, Philadelphia: Tempel University Press.
Atwell, John E. (1995) *Schopenhauer on the Character of the World: The Metaphysics of Will*, Berkeley/Los Angeles: University of California Press.

Aydin, Ciano (2003) *Zijn en Worden. Nietzsches omduiding van het substantiebegrip*, Maastricht: Shaker.
Baars, Bernard (1988) *A Cognitive Theory of Consciousness*, Cambridge: Cambridge University Press.
Bailey, Tom (2006) "After Kant: Green and Hill on Nietzsche's Kantianism", in: *Nietzsche-Studien* 35, 228–262.
Banks, Erik C. (2003) *Ernst Mach's World Elements. A Study in Natural Philosophy*, Dodrecht: Kluwer.
Barbera, S./Campioni, G. (2010) *Il genio tiranno. Ragione e dominio nell'ideologia dell'Ottocento: Wagner, Nietzsche, Renan*, Pisa: ETS.
Barthes, Roland (1977) "The Death of the Author", in: *Image–Music–Text*, ed. and trans. S. Heath, New York: Hill and Wang, 142–148.
Bayertz, K./Gerhard, M./Jaeschke, W. (eds.) (2007) *Weltanschauung, Philosophie und Naturwissenschaft im 19. Jahrhundert*, vol. 3: *Der Ignorabimus-Streit*, Hamburg: Meiner.
Benjamin, Walter (1999) *Selected Writings: Volume 2, 1927–1934*, Cambridge, MA: Harvard University Press.
Berlin, Isaiah (1958) *Two Concepts of Liberty*, in: I. Berlin (1969), *Four Essays on Liberty*, Oxford: Oxford University Press.
Bertino, Andrea Christian (2011) *"Vernatürlichung". Ursprünge von Friedrich Nietzsches Entidealisierung des Menschen, seiner Sprache und seiner Geschichte bei Johann Gottfried Herder* (Monographien und Text zur Nietzsche-Forschung, vol. 58), Berlin/Boston: De Gruyter.
Bettelheim, Bruno (1982) *Freud and Man's Soul*, London: Chatto & Windus.
Biser, Eugen (1985) "The Critical Imitator of Jesus", in: James C. Flaherty et al. (eds.), *Studies in Nietzsche and the Judeo-Christian Tradition*, Chapel Hill/London: University of North Carolina Press.
Blackmore, John T. (1972) *Ernst Mach. His Work, Life, and Influence*, Berkeley/Los Angeles: University of California Press.
Block, Ned (1994) "What is Dennett's Theory a Theory of?", in: *Philosophical Topics* 22, 23–40.
Block, Ned (1997) "On a Confusion About the Function of Consciousness", in: N. Block, O. Flanagan and G. Guzeldere (eds.), *The Nature of Consciousness*, Cambridge, MA: MIT Press.
Blumenberg, Hans (1966) *Die Legitimität der Neuzeit*, Frankfurt a.M.: Suhrkamp.
Blumenberg, Hans (1973) *Der Prozess der theoretischen Neugierde*, Frankfurt a.M.: Suhrkamp.
Blumenberg, Hans (1975) *Die Genesis der kopernikanischen Welt*, Frankfurt a.M.: Suhrkamp.
Bodei, Remo (2002) *Destini personali. L'età della colonizzazione delle coscienze*, Milan: Feltrinelli.
Bornedal, Peter (2010) *The Surface and the Abyss*, Berlin: De Gruyter.
Bourget, Paul (1885) *Nouveaux Essais*, Paris: Lemerre.
Bourget, Paul (1912) *Pages de critique et de doctrine*, tome I, Paris: Plon.
Bourget, Paul (1928) L'irréparable, Paris: Plon.
Bourget, Paul (1993) *Essais de psychologie contemporaine. Etudes littéraires*, ed. A. Guyaux, Paris: Gallimard.
Branco, M.J. Mayer (2013) "Musicofobia, musicofilia e filosofia: Kant e Nietzsche sobre a música", in: *Kriterion: Revista de Filosofia* 54/128, 497–512.
Brandes, Georg (1906) *Samlede Skrifter*, tome XVI, Copenhagen: Gyldendal.
Brandes, Georg (1972) *Friedrich Nietzsche*, New York: Macmillan.
Brennan, Tad (2003) "Stoic Moral Psychology", in: B. Inwood (ed.), *The Cambridge Companion to the Stoics*, Cambridge: Cambridge University Press, 257–294.

Brentano, Franz (1874) *Psychologie vom empirischen Standpunkt*, Leipzig: Dunker & Humblot.
Brobjer, Thomas (2002) "Nietzsche's Knowledge of Kierkegaard", in: *Journal of the History of Philosophy* 40(4), 251–263.
Brobjer, Thomas (2003) "Nietzsche's Reading of Epictetus", in: *Nietzsche-Studien* 32, 429–435.
Brobjer, Thomas (2008) *Nietzsche and the English: The Influence of British and American Thinking on His Philosophy*, New York: Humanity Books.
Brobjer, Thomas (2008) *Nietzsche's Philosophical Context*, Urbana: University of Illinois Press.
Brown, Deborah J. (2006) *Descartes and the Passionate Mind*, Cambridge: Cambridge University Press.
Brusotti, Marco (2009) "Wittgensteins Nietzsche. Mit vergleichenden Betrachtungen zur Nietzsche-Rezeption im Wiener-Kreis", in: *Nietzsche-Studien* 38, 335–362.
Brusotti, Marco (2014) *Wittgenstein, Frazer und die "ethnologische Betrachtungsweise"*, Berlin/Boston: De Gruyter.
Burckhardt, Jacob (1990) [1878] *The Civilization of the Renaissance in Italy*, London: Penguin.
Buzon, Frédéric de (1992) "L'homme et le langage chez Montaigne et Descartes", in: *Revue philosophique de la France et de l'étranger* 1, 451–466.
Campbell, John (2012) "Lichtenberg and the Cogito", in: *Proceedings of the Aristotelian Society* 112(3), 361–378.
Campioni, Giuliano (1979) "Individuo e comunità nel giovane Nietzsche", in: *Prassi e teoria* 1, 145–177.
Campioni, Giuliano (1987) "'Wohin man reisen muss': Über Nietzsches Aphorismus 223 aus Vermischte Meinungen und Sprüche", in: *Nietzsche-Studien* 16, 209–226.
Campioni, Giuliano (2001) *Les lectures françaises de Nietzsche*, Paris: PUF.
Campioni, Giuliano (2009) *Der französische Nietzsche*, trans. R. Müller-Buck and L. Schröder, Berlin/New York: De Gruyter.
Campioni, Giuliano (2010) "Gaya scienza und gai saber in Nietzsches Philosophie", in: Chiara Piazzesi, Giuliano Campioni and Patrick Wotling (eds.), *Letture della Gaia Scienza – Lectures du Gai Savoir*, Pisa: ETS, 15–38.
Campioni, G./D'Iorio, P./Fornari, M.C./Fronterotta, F./Orsucci, A. (eds.), in collab. with Müller-Buck, Renate (2003) *Nietzsches persönliche Bibliothek*, Berlin: De Gruyter.
Canziani, G. (1999) "La métaphysique et la vie. Le sujet psychosomatique chez Descartes", in: K. Sang Ong-Van-Cung (ed.), *Descartes et la question du sujet*, Paris: Presses Universitaires de France, 67–91.
Carr, David (1999) *The Paradox of Subjectivity*, New York/Oxford: Oxford University Press.
Cassin, Barbara (ed.) (2004) *Vocabulaire européen des philosophies. Dictionnaire des intraduisibles*, Paris: Seuil.
Cassirer, Ernst (1902) *Leibniz' System in seinen wissenschaftlichen Grundlagen*, Marburg: Elwert'sche Buchhandlung.
Caton, Hiram (1973) *The Origin of Subjectivity: An Essay on Descartes*, New Haven/London: Yale University Press.
Cavaillé, J.-P. (1994) "'Le plus éloquent philosophe des derniers temps'. Les stratégies d'auteur de René Descartes", in: *Annales. Histoire, Sciences Sociales* 49(2), 349–367.
Cavell, Stanley (1979) *The Claim of Reason. Wittgenstein, Skepticism, Morality and Tragedy*, Oxford/New York: Oxford University Press (reprinted with a new preface in 1999).
Cavell, Stanley (2010) "The Touch of Words", in: W. Day and V. Krebs (eds.), *Seeing Wittgenstein Anew*, New York: Cambridge University Press, 81–98.

Cavell, Stanley (1990) *Conditions Handsome and Unhandsome: The Constitution of Emersonian Perfectionism*, Chicago/London: University of Chicago Press.
Cinelli, Albert (1989) "Nietzsche and Kierkegaard on Existential Affirmation", in: *Southwest Philosophy Review* 5, 135–141.
Clam, Jean (2000) "Unbegegnete Theorie. Zur Luhmann-Rezeption in der Philosophie", in: Henk de Berg and Johannes Schmidt (eds.), *Rezeption und Reflexion. Zur Resonanz der Systemtheorie Niklas Luhmanns außerhalb der Soziologie*, Frankfurt a.M.: Suhrkamp, 296–321.
Clark, Maudemarie/Leiter, Brian (1997) "Introduction" to F. Nietzsche, *Daybreak: Thoughts on the Prejudices of Morality*, trans. R.J. Hollingdale, Cambridge: Cambridge University Press.
Clayton, John Powell (1985) "Zarathustra and the Stages on Life's Way: A Nietzschean Riposte to Kierkegaard?", in: *Nietzsche-Studien* 14, 179–200.
Constâncio, João (2011) "Instinct and Language in Nietzsche's *Beyond Good and Evil*", in: J. Constâncio and M.J.M. Branco (eds.), *Nietzsche on Instinct and Language*, Berlin/Boston: De Gruyter, 80–116.
Constâncio, João (2011) "On Consciousness. Nietzsche's Departure from Schopenhauer", in: *Nietzsche-Studien* 40, 1–42.
Constâncio, João (2012) "Consciousness, Communication, and Self-Expression. Towards an Interpretation of Aphorism 354 of Nietzsche's The Gay Science", in: J. Constâncio and M.J. Mayer Branco (eds.), *As the Spider Spins: Essays on Nietzsche's Critique and Use of Language*, Berlin/Boston: De Gruyter, 197–231.
Constâncio, João (2012) "A Sort of Schema of Ourselves: On Nietzsche's 'Ideal' and 'Concept' of Freedom", in: *Nietzsche-Studien* 41, 127–162.
Constâncio, João (2013) *Arte e Niilismo: Nietzsche e o Enigma do Mundo*, Lisbon: Tinta-da-China.
Constâncio, João (2013) "On Nietzsche's Conception of Philosophy in *Beyond Good and Evil*: Reassessing Schopenhauer's Relevance", in: M.E. Born and A. Pichler (eds.), *Texturen des Denkens: Nietzsches Inszenierung der Philosophie in "Jenseits von Gut und Böse"*, Berlin/Boston: De Gruyter, 145–164.
Constâncio, João (2013) "'Quem tem razão, Kant ou Stendhal?' uma reflexão sobre a crítica de Nietzsche à estética de Kant", in: *Kriterion: Revista de Filosofia* 54/128, 475–495.
Constâncio, João (2014) "'O que somos livres para fazer?' Reflexão sobre o problema da subjectividade em Nietzsche", in: Scarlett Marton, Maria João Mayer Branco and João Constâncio (eds.), *Sujeito, Décadence e Arte. Nietzsche e a Modernidade*, Lisbon/Rio de Janeiro: Tinta-da-China, 159–196.
Constâncio, João (2015) "Struggles for Recognition and Will to Power: Probing an Affinity between Hegel and Nietzsche", in: L.R. Santos and K. Hay (eds.), *Nietzsche, German Idealism and Its Critics*, Berlin/Boston: De Gruyter (forthcoming).
Constâncio, João (forthcoming) "Nietzsche on Consciousness, Will, and Choice: Another Look at Nietzschean Freedom" in: Manuel Dries (ed.), *Nietzsche on Consciousness and the Embodied Mind*, Berlin/Boston: De Gruyter.
Constâncio, João/Branco, Maria João Mayer (eds.) (2011) *Nietzsche on Instinct and Language*, Berlin/Boston: De Gruyter.
Constâncio, João/Branco, Maria João Mayer (eds.) (2012) *As the Spider Spins. Essays on Nietzsche's Critique and Use of Language*, Berlin/Boston: De Gruyter.
Couturat, Louis (1901) *La logique de Leibniz d'après des documents inédits*, Paris: Alcan.
Cox, Christoph (1997) "The 'Subject' of Nietzsche's Perspectivism", in: *Journal of the History of Philosophy* 35(2), 269–291.

Cox, Christoph (1999) "Naturalism and Interpretation", online: http://publishing.cdlib.org/ucpressebooks/view?docId=ft5x0nb3sz&chunk.id=d0e7331&toc.depth=1&toc.id=d0e6849&brand=ucpress
Critchley, Simon (1996) "Prolegomena to Any Post-Deconstructive Subjectivity", in: S. Critchley and P. Dews (eds.), *Deconstructive Subjectivities*, Albany, NY: State University of New York Press, 13–46.
Cushman, Fiery/Young, Liane/Greene, Joshua D. (2010) "Multi-system Moral Psychology", in: Doris (2010), 47–71.
Daigle, C. (2011) "Nietzsche's Notion of Embodied Self: Proto-Phenomenology at Work?", in: *Nietzsche-Studien* 40, 226–243.
Dainton, B. (2008) *The Phenomenal Self*, Oxford: Oxford University Press.
Damasio, Antonio (1992) "The Selfless Consciousness", in: *Behavioral and Brain Sciences* 15, 208–209.
Damasio, Antonio (1994) *O Erro de Descartes*, Lisbon: Europa América.
Damasio, Antonio (1999) *The Feeling of What Happens: Body and Emotion in the Making of Consciousness*, New York: Harcourt Brace.
Damasio, Antonio (2003) *Ao Encontro de Espinosa – as emoções sociais e a neurologia do sentir*, Lisbon: Europa-América.
Damasio, Antonio (2010) *Self Comes to Mind – Constructing the Conscious Brain*, London: Random House.
Danto, Arthur C. (2005) *Nietzsche as Philosopher*, expanded edition, New York: Columbia University Press.
Deater-Deckard, K./Plomin, R. (1999) "An Adoption Study of the Etiology of Teacher Reports of Externalizing Problems in Middle Childhood", in: *Child Development* 70, 144–154.
Deigh, John (1986) "Freud's Later Theory of Civilization: Changes and Implications", in: John Deigh (ed.), *The Sources of Moral Agency: Essays in Moral Psychology and Freudian Theory*, Cambridge: Cambridge University Press, 94–112.
Deigh, John (1994) "Cognitivism in the Theory of the Emotions", in: *Ethics* 104, 824–854.
Deleuze, Gilles (1986) *Nietzsche and Philosophy*, trans. H. Tomlinson, London/New York: Continuum.
Deleuze, Gilles (1988) *Le pli. Leibniz et le baroque*, Paris: Minuit.
Deleuze, Gilles (1990) *Expressionism in Philosophy: Spinoza*, trans. Martin Joughin, New York: Zone Books.
Deleuze, Gilles (1990) *Pourparlers 1972–1990*, Paris: Minuit.
Deleuze, Gilles (1994) *Difference and Repetition*, trans. Paul Patton, New York: Columbia University Press.
Deleuze, Gilles (1995) *Negotiations 1972–1990*, trans. Martin Joughin, New York: Columbia University Press.
Deleuze, Gilles (2004) *L'Abécédaire*, Paris: DVD Editions Montparnasse.
Deleuze, Gilles/Guattari, Félix (1977) *Anti-Oedipus*, trans. R. Hurley, M. Seem and H.R. Lane, Minneapolis/London: University of Minnesota Press.
Deleuze, Gilles/Guattari, Félix (1980) *Mille plateaux*, Paris: Minuit.
Deleuze, Gilles/Guattari, Félix (1987) *A Thousand Plateaus*, trans. B. Massumi, Minneapolis/London: University of Minnesota Press.
Deleuze, Gilles/Guattari, Félix (1991) *Qu'est-ce que la philosophie?* Paris: Minuit.
Deleuze, Gilles/Guattari, Félix (1994) *What is Philosophy?* trans. H. Tomlinson and G. Burchell, New York: Columbia University Press.

Della Rocca, Michael (2008) *Spinoza*, London: Routledge.
Dennett, Daniel (1978) "Brain Writing and Mind Reading", in: Daniel Dennett (ed.), *Brainstorms*, Cambridge, MA: MIT Press, 39–50.
Dennett, Daniel (1978) "Towards a Cognitive Theory of Consciousness", in: Daniel Dennett (ed.), *Brainstorms*, Cambridge, MA: MIT Press, 149–173.
Dennett, Daniel (1981) [1978] *Brainstorms–Philosophical Essays on Mind and Psychology*, Cambridge, MA: MIT Press.
Dennett, Daniel (1986) [1969] *Content and Consciousness*, 2nd edition, London: Routledge and Kegan Paul.
Dennett, Daniel (1991) *Consciousness Explained*, Boston: Little Brown.
Dennett, Daniel (1995) *Darwin's Dangerous Idea–Evolution and The Meanings of Life*, New York: Touchstone. [Portuguese translation: *A Ideia Perigosa de Darwin*, Lisbon: Círculo de Leitores 2000]
Dennett, Daniel (1996) *Kinds of Minds, Toward an Understanding of Consciousness*, New York: Basic Books.
Dennett, Daniel (1998) "Animal Consciousness", in: Daniel Dennett (ed.), *Brainchildren*, London: Penguin, 337–350.
Dennett, Daniel (1998) *Brainchildren–Essays on Designing Minds*, London: Penguin.
Derrida, Jacques (1973) "Différance", in: *Speech and Phenomena and Other Essays on Husserl's Theory of Signs*, trans. D.B. Allison, Evanston: Northwestern University Press, 129–160.
Derrida, Jacques (1973) "Speech and Phenomena", in: *Speech and Phenomena and Other Essays on Husserl's Theory of Signs*, trans. D.B. Allison, Evanston: Northwestern University Press, 1–104.
Derrida, Jacques (1979) *Spurs. Nietzsche's Styles/Éperons. Les Styles de Nietzsche*, trans. B. Harlow, Chicago/London: University of Chicago Press.
Derrida, Jacques (1981) *Positions*, trans. A. Bass, Chicago: University of Chicago Press.
Derrida, Jacques (1982) "Deconstruction and the other" (interview with Richard Kearney), in: Richard Kearney (ed.), *Dialogues with Contemporary Continental Thinkers*, Manchester: Manchester University Press, 105–126.
Derrida, Jacques (1985a) "Otobiographies", in: *The Ear of the Other: Otobiography, Transference, Translation*, ed. C.V. McDonald, trans. A. Ronell and P. Kamuf, New York: Schocken Books, 1–38.
Derrida, Jacques (1985b) "Roundtable on Translation", in: *The Ear of the Other: Otobiography, Transference, Translation*, ed. C.V. McDonald, trans. A. Ronell and P. Kamuf, New York: Schocken Books, 91–161.
Derrida, Jacques (1986) "Interpreting Signatures (Nietzsche/Heidegger): Two Questions", in: Diane Michelfelder and Richard Palmer (eds. and trans.), *Dialogue and Deconstruction: The Gadamer-Derrida Encounter*, New York: SUNY Press, 57–74.
Derrida, Jacques (1988) "Signature Event Context", in: *Limited Inc*, trans. S. Weber, Evanston: Northwestern University Press, 1–25.
Derrida, Jacques (1991) "Eating Well, or the Calculation of the Subject", in: E. Cadava, P. Connor and J-L. Nancy (eds.), *Who Comes After the Subject*, New York: Routledge, 96–119.
Derrida, Jacques (1995) "There is no *One* Narcissism (Autobiophotographies)", in: *Points... Interviews, 1974–1994*, Stanford: Stanford University Press, 196–215.
Derrida, Jacques (1997) *Of Grammatology*, trans. G. Spivak, Baltimore: Johns Hopkins University Press.
Derrida, Jacques (1997) *Politics of Friendship*, trans. G. Collins, London: Verso Books.

Derrida, Jacques (2002) "Nietzsche and the Machine", in: *Negotiations: Interventions and Interviews 1971–2001*, ed. and trans. E. Rottenberg, Stanford: Stanford University Press, 215–256.
Derrida, Jacques (2007) *Psyche. Inventions of the Other*, vol. 1, Stanford: Stanford University Press.
Derrida, Jacques (2009) "Freud and the Scene of Writing", in: *Writing and Difference*, trans. A. Bass, London/New York: Routledge, 246–291.
Derrida, Jacques (2009) "Structure, Sign and Play in the Discourse of Human Sciences", in: *Writing and Difference*, trans. A. Bass, London/New York: Routledge, 351–370.
Des Chene, D. (2001) *Spirits and Clocks. Machines and Organism in Descartes*, Ithaca: Cornell University Press.
Descartes, René (1996) *Œuvres*, eds. Ch. Adam and P. Tannery, 11 vols., Paris: Vrin.
Descartes, René (2008) *Meditations on First Philosophy*, Oxford/New York: Oxford University Press.
Descartes, René (2008) *The Philosophical Writings of Descartes*, trans. J. Cottingham, R. Stoothof and D. Murdoch, 3 vols., Cambridge:Cambridge University Press.
Descartes, René (2015) *Der Briefwechsel mit Elisabeth von der Pfalz* [und mit Christina von Schweden sowie Pierre Chanut], French-German, ed. I. Wienand, O. Ribordy, trans. I. Wienand and O. Ribordy, B. Wirz with the collaboration of A. Schiffhauer, Hamburg: Meiner.
Dews, Peter (1989) "The Return of the Subject in the Late Foucault", in: *Radical Philosophy* 51, 37–41.
Dickopp, Karl-Heinz (1970) "Zum Wandel von Nietzsches Seinsverständnis–African Spir und Gustav Teichmüller", in: *Zeitschrift für philosophische Forschung* 24, 50–71.
Dillinger, Jakob (2012) "Bewusstsein als Krankheit. Eine Anspielung auf Dostojewskij in Die fröhliche Wissenschaft Nr. 354?", in: *Nietzsche-Studien* 41, 333–343.
Doris, John M./The Moral Psychology Research Group (eds.) (2010) *The Moral Psychology Handbook*, Oxford: Oxford University Press.
Dries, Manuel (ed.) (forthcoming) *Nietzsche on Consciousness and the Embodied Mind*, Berlin/Boston: De Gruyter.
Drossbach, Maximilian (1884) *Über die scheinbaren und die wirklichen Ursachen des Geschehens in der Welt*, Halle: C.E.M. Pfeffer.
Du Bois-Reymond, Emile (1974) "Leibnizische Gedanken in der neueren Naturwissenschaft" (1870), in: S. Wollgast (ed.), *Vorträge über Philosophie und Gesellschaft*, Hamburg: Meiner, 25–53.
Du Bois-Reymond, Emile (1886) "Über die Grenzen des Naturerkennens", in: *Reden von Emil Du Bois-Reymond*, Leipzig: Veit, 106–130.
Duhem, Pierre (1914) *La Theorie Physique: Son Objet et sa Structure*. Paris: Marcel Riviera & Cie.
Dühring, Eugen (1873) *Kritische Geschichte der Philosophie von ihren Anfängen bis zur Gegenwart*, 2nd edition, Berlin: Heimann's.
Edelbrock, C./Rende, R.D./Plomin, R./Thompson, L.A. (1995) "A Twin Study of Competence and Problem Behavior in Childhood and Early Adolescence", in: *Journal of Child Psychology and Psychiatry* 36, 775–785.
Eldridge, Richard (1997) *Leading a Human Life. Wittgenstein, Intentionality and Romanticism*, Chicago/London: University of Chicago Press.
Eldridge, Richard (2010) "Wittgenstein on Aspect-Seeing, the Nature of Discursive Consciousness, and the Experience of Agency", in: William Day and Victor J. Krebs (eds.), *Seeing*

Wittgenstein Anew. New Essays on Aspect-Seeing, Cambridge: Cambridge University Press, 162–179.
Eley, Thalia/Lichtenstein, Paul/Stevenson, Jim (1999) "Sex Differences in the Etiology of Aggressive and Nonaggressive Antisocial Behavior: Results from Two Twin Studies", in: *Child Development* 70, 155–168.
Emden, Christian J. (2005) *Nietzsche on Language, Consciousness and the Body*, Chicago: University of Illinois Press.
Emerson,Ralph Waldo (1858) *Versuche (Essays: First and Second Series)*, trans. G. Fabricius, Hannover: Carl Meyer.
Emerson,Ralph Waldo (1862) *Die Führung des Lebens*, trans. E. S. von Mühlberg, Leipzig: Steinacker.
Emerson,Ralph Waldo (1876) *Neue Essays (Letters and Social Aims)*, trans. J. Schmidt, Stuttgart: Auerbach.
Emerson, Ralph Waldo (1971–) *The Collected Works*, ed. A.R. Ferguson, 4 vols., Cambridge: Harvard University Press.
Emerson, Ralph Waldo (1987) *Representative Men*, Cambridge, MA: Harvard University Press.
Emerson, Ralph Waldo (2000) *The Essential Writings of Ralph Waldo Emerson, ed. Brooks Atkinson*, New York: The Modern Library.
Enwald, Marika (2004) *Displacements of Deconstruction: The Deconstruction of Metaphysics of Presence, Meaning, Subject and Method*, Diss., Tampere: Tampereen Yliopistopaino Oy Juvenes Print.
Esposito, Roberto (2008) *Bios: Biopolitics and Philosophy*, trans. Timothy Campbell, Minneapolis: University of Minnesota Press.
Fechner, Gustav (1860/1966) *Elements of Psychophysics*, vol. 1, Engl. trans., New York: Holt, Rinehart and Winston.
Fichte, Johann Gottlieb (1982) *The Science of Logic*, ed. and trans. P. Heath and J. Lachs, Cambridge: Cambridge University Press.
Figl, Johann (1982) *Interpretation als philosophisches Prinzip: Friedrich Nietzsches universale Theorie der Auslegung im späten Nachlass*, Berlin/New York: De Gruyter.
Fischer, Kuno (1865) *Geschichte der neuern Philosophie*, vol. 1, part 2: *Baruch Spinoza*, Heidelberg: Bassermann.
Fischer, Kuno (1867) *Geschichte der neuern Philosophie*, vol. 2: *Leibniz und seine Schule*, 2nd edition, Heidelberg: Bassermann.
Fleming, Marie (2012) "Nietzsche on Science and Consciousness", in: H. Heit, G. Abel and M. Brusotti (eds.), *Nietzsches Wissenschaftsphilosophie*, Berlin/Boston: De Gruyter, 333–344.
Fodor, Jerry (1983) *The Modularity of Mind*, Cambridge, MA: MIT Press.
Fornari, M. C. (2006) *La morale evolutiva del gregge. Nietzsche legge Spencer e Mill*, Pisa: ETS.
Fornari, M. C. (2009) "Beiträge zur Quellenforschung", in: *Nietzsche-Studien* 38, 320.
Foucault, Michel (1971) "*Nietzsche, La généalogie, l'histoire*", in: *Hommage à Jean Hyppolite*, Paris: PUF, 145–172.
Foucault, Michel (1977) *Discipline and Punish*, trans. Alan Sheridan, Harmondsworth: Penguin.
Foucault, Michel (1977) "Nietzsche, Genealogy, History", in: *Language, Counter-Memory, and Practice: Selected Essays and Interviews*, trans. Donald F. Bouchard and Sherry Simon, Oxford: Basil Blackwell, 139–165.

Foucault, Michel (1982) "The Subject and Power", in: Hubert L. Dreyfus and Paul Rabinow (eds.), *Michel Foucault: Beyond Structuralism and Hermeneutics*, Brighton: Harvester Press, 208–227.
Foucault, Michel (1984) *The Foucault Reader*, ed. Paul Rabinow, New York: Pantheon Books.
Foucault, Michel (1985) *The Use of Pleasure: The History of Sexuality* volume 2, trans. Robert Hurley, Harmondsworth: Penguin.
Foucault, Michel (1986) *The Care of the Self: The History of Sexuality* volume 3, trans. Robert Hurley, Harmondsworth: Penguin.
Foucault, Michel (1988) "Technologies of the Self", in: Luther H. Martin et al (eds.), *Technologies of the Self: A Seminar with Michel Foucault*, London: Tavistock, 16–50.
Foucault, Michel (1990) *Politics, Philosophy, Culture: Interviews and Writings 1977–84*, trans. Alan Sheridan and others, London: Routledge.
Foucault, Michel (1997) *Ethics: The Essential Works 1*, ed. Paul Rabinow, Harmondsworth: Penguin.
Foucault, Michel (2001) *Power: The Essential Works 3*, ed. James D. Faubion, Harmondsworth: Penguin.
Foucault, Michel (2003) *Society Must Be Defended: Lectures at the College de France 1975–76*, trans. David Macey, Harmondsworth: Penguin.
Foucault, Michel (2005) *The Hermeneutics of the Subject: Lectures at the College de France 1981–82*, trans. Graham Burchell, New York: Palgrave Macmillan.
Foucault, Michel (2007) "What is Enlightenment?", in: *The Politics of Truth*, trans. Lysa Hochroth and Catherine Porter, Los Angeles: Semiotext(e), 97–121.
Frank, Hartwig (2006) "Nietzsche und Kant", in: *Nietzsche-Studien* 35, 311–320.
Freud, Sigmund (1953–74) *Standard Edition of the Complete Psychological Works of Sigmund Freud*, 24 vols., trans. under the general editorship of James Strachey, in collaboration with Anna Freud, assisted by Alix Strachey and Alan Tyson, London: Hogarth Press and Institute of Psycho-Analysis.
Frothingham, Octavius B. (1959) *Transcendentalism in New England*, New York: Harper & Brothers. [Reprint of: New York, Putnam's Sons 1876]
García, André Luiz Muniz (2011) "'Vermoralisirung' e 'Entmoralisirung'. Da linguagem da moral ao caráter extra-moral da linguagem: As diretrizes de Nietzsche para um novo modo de pensar e escrever em filosofia", Doctoral thesis, Campinas. Tese de Doutorado Campinas 2011.
Gardner, Sebastian (1993) *Irrationality and the Philosophy of Psychoanalysis*, Cambridge: Cambridge University Press.
Gardner, Sebastian (1999) "Schopenhauer, Will and Unconscious", in: Christopher Janaway (ed.), *The Cambridge Companion to Schopenhauer*, Cambridge: Cambridge University Press, 375–421.
Gardner, Sebastian (2009) "Nietzsche, the Self, and the Disunity of Philosophical Reason", in: K. Gemes and S. May (eds.), *Nietzsche on Freedom and Autonomy*, Oxford: Oxford University Press, 1–31.
Gardner, Sebastian (2013) "Nietzsche's Philosophical Aestheticism", in: Ken Gemes and John Richardson (eds.), *The Oxford Handbook of Nietzsche*, Oxford: Oxford University Press, 599–628.
Gawoll, Hans-Jürgen (2001) "Nietzsche und der Geist Spinozas", in: *Nietzsche-Studien* 30, 44–61.

Gemes, Ken (2006) "'We Remain of Necessity Stranger to Ourselves': The Key Message of Nietzsche's *Genealogy*", in: Christa Davis Acampora (ed.), *Nietzsche's On the Genealogy of Morals: Critical Essays*. Lanham & Oxford: Rowman & Littlefield, 191–208.
Gemes, Ken (2009) "Freud and Nietzsche on Sublimation", in: *Journal of Nietzsche Studies* 38, 38–59.
Gemes, Ken (2009) "Nietzsche on Free Will, Autonomy, and the Sovereign Individual", in: Gemes/May (2009), 33–49.
Gemes, Ken (2013) "Life's Perspectives", in: Gemes/Richardson (2013), 553–575.
Gemes, Ken/May, Simon (eds.) (2009) *Nietzsche on Freedom and Autonomy*, Oxford/New York: Oxford University Press.
Gemes, Ken/Richardson, John (eds.) (2013) *The Oxford Handbook on Nietzsche*, Oxford: Oxford University Press.
Gerhardt, Volker (1996) *Vom Willen zur Macht: Anthropologie und Metaphysik der Macht am exemplarischen Fall Friedrich Nietzsches*, Berlin/New York: De Gruyter.
Gerhardt, Volker (2006) "The Body, the Self and the Ego", in: Keith Ansell Pearson (ed.), *A Companion to Nietzsche*, Oxford: Blackwell, 273–296.
Gerhardt, Volker (2011) "Selbstbegründung. Nietzsches Moral der Individualität", in: Volker Gerhardt (ed.), *Die Funken des freien Geistes. Neuere Aufsätze zu Nietzsches Philosophie der Zukunft*, eds. J.-C. Heilinger and N. Loukidelis, Berlin/New York: De Gruyter, 169–192. [Originally published in *Nietzsche-Studien* 21 (1992), 28–49]
Geuss, R. (2005) *Outside Ethics*, Princeton: Princeton University Press.
Gilson, E. (1925) "Commentaire", in: René Descartes (ed.), *Discours de la méthode*, Paris: Vrin.
Glock, Hans-Johann (1996) *A Wittgenstein Dictionary*, Oxford: Blackwell, 348–352.
Gödde, G./Loukidelis, N. (eds.) (2016) *Nietzsche und die Lebenskunst*, Stuttgart/Weimar: Metzler.
Goedert, Georges (2011) "Art. Subjekt", in: Christian Niemeyer (ed.), *Nietzsche-Lexikon*, 2nd revised and expanded edition, Darmstadt: WBG, 367–368.
Goldie, Peter (2002) *The Emotions: A Philosophical Exploration*, Oxford: Oxford University Press.
Goncourt, Edmond and Jules de (1864) *Renée* Mauperin, Paris: Charpentier.
Goncourt, Edmond and Jules de (1887) *Journal*, vol. II, Paris: Charpentier.
Goncourt, Edmond de (1882) *La Faustin*, Paris: G. Charpentier.
Gori, Pietro (2009) "The Usefulness of Substances. Knowledge, Metaphysics and Science in Nietzsche and Mach", in: *Nietzsche-Studien* 38, 111–155.
Gori, Pietro (2012) "Nietzsche as Phenomenalist?", in: Helmut Heit, Günter Abel and Marco Brusotti (eds.), *Nietzsches Wissenschaftsphilosophie*, Berlin/Boston: De Gruyter, 345–356.
GORI, Pietro/PIAZZESI (2012) Chiara, Crepuscolo degli idoli, Introduzione, traduzione e commento, Roma: Carocci.
Granier, Jean (1966) *Le problème de la vérité dans la philosophie de Nietzsche*, Paris: Editions du Seuil.
Grau, Gerd-Günter (1985) "Nietzsche and Kierkegaard", trans. Wendy Radar, in: James C. O'Flaherty, Timothy F. Sellner and Robert M. Helm (eds.), *Studies in Nietzsche and Judeo-Christian Tradition*, Chapel Hill: University of North Carolina Press, 226–251.
Green, Michael Steven (2002) *Nietzsche and the Transcendental Tradition*, Urbana: University of Illinois Press.
Greene, Joshua (2007) "The Secret Joke of Kant's Soul", in: W. Sinnott-Armstrong (ed.), *Moral Psychology*, vol. 3, Cambridge, MA: MIT Press, 35–117.
Gründer, Karlfried (ed.) (1998) *Historisches Wörterbuch der Philosophie*, eds. Joachim Ritter et al., vol. 10, Basel/Darmstadt: Schwabe/WBG.

Günzel, Stephan (2001) "Leibniz heute noch gefährlich: Die Theodizee als moderne Denkfigur – Über das implizite und explizite Fortwirken von Leibniz bei Nietzsche", in: H. Poser (ed.), *Nihil sine ratione – Mensch, Natur und Technik im Wirken von G.W. Leibniz (VII. Internationaler Leibniz-Kongress)*, Berlin: Gottfried Wilhelm Leibniz Gesellschaft, 434–440.

Guzzardi, Luca (2010) *Lo sguardo muto delle cose*, Milan: Raffaello Cortina.

Habermas, Jürgen (1985) "Nachwort (1968): Zu Nietzsches Erkenntnistheorie", in: *Zur Logik der Sozialwissenschaften*, Frankfurt a.M., 505–528.

Habermas, Jürgen (1987) *Philosophical Discourse of Modernity*, trans. Frederick Lawrence, Cambridge, MA: MIT Press.

Hadot, Pierre (1995) *Philosophy as a Way of Life*, trans. Michael Chase, Oxford: Basil Blackwell.

Hagberg, Garry L. (2008) *Wittgenstein and Autobiographical Consciousness*, Oxford: Clarendon Press.

Haidt, Jonathan (2001) "The Emotional Dog and Its Rational Tail: A Social Intuitionist Approach to Moral Judgment", in: *Psychological Review* 108, 814–834.

Hamacher, Werner (1986) "Disagregation des Willens. Nietzsche über Individuum und Individualität", in: *Nietzsche-Studien* 15, 306–336.

Han, Beatrice (2002) *Foucault's Critical Project: Between the Transcendental and the Historical*, Stanford: Stanford University Press.

Hannay, Alastair (2003) "Nietzsche/Kierkegaard: Prospects for Dialogue?", in: Hannay, Alastair (eds.), *Kierkegaard and Philosophy: Selected Essays*, London: Routledge, 207–217.

Harcourt, Edward (2011) "Nietzsche and the 'Aesthetics of Character'", in: May (2011), 265–284.

Haugeland, J. (2000) *Having Thought: Essays in the Metaphysics of Mind*, Cambridge: Harvard University Press.

Heidegger, Martin (1950) "Nietzsches Wort 'Gott ist tot'", in: Martin Heidegger (ed.), *Holzwege*, Frankfurt a.M.: Klostermann.

Heidegger, Martin (1961) *Nietzsche*, 2 vols., Pfullingen: Neske.

Heidegger, Martin (1962) [1927] *Being and Time*, trans. John Macquarrie and Edward Robinson, Oxford/Cambridge: Blackwell.

Heidegger, Martin (1976) [1927] *Sein und Zeit*, Tübingen: Niemeyer. [*Gesamtausgabe*, vol. 2, Frankfurt a.M.: Klostermann 1977]

Heidegger, Martin (1985) *History of the Concept of Time: Prolegomena*, trans. Theodore Kisiel, Bloomington/Indianapolis: Indiana University Press.

Heidegger, Martin (1991) *Nietzsche*, Vols. 1, 2, 3 and 4, trans. David Farrell Krell, New York: Harper & Row.

Heidelberger, Michael (1996) *Die innere Seite der Natur: Gustav Theodor Fechners wissenschaftlich-philosophische Weltauffassung*, Frankfurt a.M.: Klosterman.

Heit, Helmut (2013) "'…was man ist'? Zur Wirklichkeit des Subjekts bei Nietzsche", in: *Nietzscheforschung* 20, 173–192.

Helmholtz, Herman von (1904) *Populäre Vorträge*, ed. Daniel Shumway, Boston: Heath & Co.

Helmholtz, Herman von (1962) [1867] *Treatise on Physiological Optics*, 3 vols., trans. James P.C. Southall, 3rd edition, New York: Dover.

Helmholtz, Herman von (1977) *Epistemological Writings: The Paul Hertz/Moritz Schlick Centenary Edition of 1921*, trans. Malcolm F. Lowe, Dordrecht/Boston: D. Reidel.

Helmholtz, Herman von (1995) *Science and Culture: Popular and Philosophical Lectures*, ed. D. Cahan, Chicago: University of Chicago Press.

Hill, R. Kevin (2003) *Nietzsche's Critiques: The Kantian Foundations of his Thought*, Oxford: Oxford University Press.
Himmelmann, Beatrix (ed.) (2005) *Kant und Nietzsche im Widerstreit*, Berlin/New York: De Gruyter.
Hinman, Lawrence M. (1980) "Temporary and Self-Affirmation. A Kierkegaardian Critique of Nietzsche's Doctrine of the Eternal Recurrence of the Same", in: *Kierkegaardiana* 11, 93–119.
Hofstadter, Douglas/Dennett, Daniel (1981) *The Mind's I—Fantasies and Reflections on Self and Soul*, New York: Bantam Books.
Huenemann, Charlie (2013) "Nietzsche's Illness", in: Gemes/Richardson (2013), 63–80.
Hussain, Nadeem (2007) "Honest Illusion: Valuing for Nietzsche's 'Free Spirits'", in: Leiter/Sinhababu (2007), 157–191.
Hussain, N.J.Z. (2013) "Nietzsche's Metaethical Stance", in: K. Gemes and J. Richardson (eds.), *The Oxford Handbook of Nietzsche*. Oxford: Oxford University Press, 389–414.
Hutter, Horst (2006) *Shaping the Future: Nietzsche's New Regime of the Soul and its Ascetic Practices*, Lanham, MD: Lexington.
Ijsseling, I. (1997) *Over Voorwoorden. Hegel, Kierkegaard, Nietzsche*, Amsterdam: Boom.
Ingram, David (2003) "Foucault and Habermas", in: Gary Gutting (ed.), *The Cambridge Companion to Foucault*, 2nd edition, Cambridge: Cambridge University Press, 240–284.
Itaparica, André Luís Mota (2014) "Crítica da modernidade e conceito de subjetividade em Nietzsche", in: Scarlett Marton, Maria João Mayer Branco and João Constâncio (eds.), *Sujeito, décadence e arte. Nietzsche a modernidade*, Lisbon/Rio de Janeiro: Tinta da China, 39–60.
James, William (1992) *Writings 1878–1899*, New York: Library of America.
Janaway, Christopher (1989) *Self and World in Schopenhauer's Philosophy*, New York/Oxford: Oxford University Press.
Janaway, Christopher (1991) "Nietzsche, the Self, and Schopenhauer", in: Keith Ansell Pearson (ed.), *Nietzsche and Modern German Thought*, London: Routledge, 119–142.
Janaway, Christopher (2006) "Nietzsche on Free Will, Autonomy, and the Sovereign Individual", in: *Aristotelian Society Supplementary Volume* 80, 339–357.
Janaway, Christopher (2007) *Beyond Selflessness. Reading Nietzsche's Genealogy*, Oxford: Oxford University Press.
Janaway, Christopher (2010) "The Real Essence of Human Beings: Schopenhauer and the Unconscious Will", in: Angus Nicholls and Martin Liebscher (eds.), *Thinking the Unconscious: Nineteenth-Century German Thought*, Cambridge: Cambridge University Press, 140–155.
Janaway, Christopher/Robertson, Simon (eds.) (2012) *Nietzsche, Naturalism, and Normativity*, Oxford: Oxford University Press.
Jaspers, Karl (1952) *Nietzsche und das Christentum*, Munich: R. Piper & Co.
Jaspers, Karl (1955) "The Origin of the Contemporary Philosophical Situation: The Historical Meaning of Kierkegaard and Nietzsche", in: *Reason and Existenz: Five Lectures*, 3rd edition, trans. William Earle. New York: Noonday Press, 19–50.
Jensen, Anthony (2013) *Nietzsche's Philosophy of History*, Cambridge: Cambridge University Press.
Johnson, D.R. (2010) *Nietzsche's Anti-Darwinism*, Cambridge: Cambridge University Press.
Joyce, James (1992) *Finnegans Wake*, London: Penguin.
Joyce, James (2008) *Ulysses*, ed. Jeri Johnson, Oxford: Oxford University Press.
Joyce, Richard (2006) *The Evolution of Morality*, Cambridge, MA: MIT Press.

Jurist, Elliot L. (2000) *Beyond Hegel and Nietzsche: Philosophy, Culture, and Agency*, Cambridge, MA/London: MIT Press.
Kail, Peter (2007) *Projection and Realism in Hume's Philosophy*, Oxford: Oxford University Press.
Kant, Immanuel (1996) "The Metaphysics of Morals", trans. Mary J. Gregor, in: I. Kant (ed.), *Practical Philosophy*, ed. Mary J. Gregor, Cambridge: Cambridge University Press.
Kant, Immanuel (1996) *The Metaphysics of Morals*, ed. Mary Gregor, New York: Cambridge University Press.
Kant, Immanuel (1998) *Critique of Pure Reason*, trans. Paul Guyer, Cambridge: Cambridge University Press.
Kant, Immanuel (1998) *Groundwork of the Metaphysics of Morals*, ed. Mary Gregor, New York: Cambridge University Press.
Kant, Immanuel (1999) *Critique of Practical Reason*, eds. Paul Guyer and Allen Wood, New York: Cambridge University Press.
Kant, Immanuel (1999) *Critique of Pure Reason*, eds. Paul Guyer and Allen Wood, New York: Cambridge University Press.
Kant, Immanuel (1999) *Religion within the Boundaries of Mere Reason*, eds. Allen Wood and George di Giovanni, New York: Cambridge University Press.
Kant, Immanuel (2006) *Anthropology from a Pragmatic Point of View*, ed. Robert Louden, New York: Cambridge University Press.
Kateb, Georg (1992) *The Inner Ocean: Individualism and Democratic Culture*, Ithaca, NY: Cornell University Press.
Kateb, Georg (1995) *Emerson and Self-reliance*, Thousand Oaks: Sage.
Katsafanas, Paul (2005) "Nietzsche's Theory of Mind: Consciousness and Conceptualization", in: *European Journal of Philosophy* 13, 1–31.
Katsafanas, Paul (2011) "The Concept of Unified Agency in Nietzsche, Plato and Schiller", in: *Journal of the History of Philosophy* 49, 87–113.
Katsafanas, Paul (2013) "Nietzsche's Philosophical Psychology", in: K. Gemes and J. Richardson (eds.), *The Oxford Handbook of Nietzsche*, Oxford: Oxford University Press, 727–755.
Katsafanas, Paul (2013) "Value, Affect, Drive", in: Peter Kail and Manuel Dries (eds.), *Nietzsche on Mind and Nature*. Oxford: Oxford University Press.
Katsafanas, Paul (in progress) "The Moral Significance of Perceptual Experience".
Kaulbach, Friedrich (1979) "Nietzsche und der monadologische Gedanke", in: *Nietzsche-Studien* 8, 127–156.
Kaulbach, Friedrich (1980) *Nietzsches Idee einer Experimentalphilosophie*, Cologne: Böhlau.
Kaulbach, Friedrich (1990) *Philosophie des Perspektivismus: Erster Teil. Wahrheit und Perspektive bei Kant, Hegel und Nietzsche*, Tübingen: Mohr.
Kellenberger, James (1997) *Kierkegaard and Nietzsche*, New York: Macmillan.
Kierkegaard, Søren (1980) *The Concept of Anxiety*, trans. Reider Thomte, Princeton, NJ: Princeton University Press.
Kierkegaard, Søren (1980) *The Sickness unto Death*, trans. Howard V. Hong and Edna H. Hong, Princeton, NJ: Princeton University Press.
Kierkegaard, Søren (1983) *Fear and Trembling/Repetition*, trans. Howard V. Hong and Edna H. Hong, Princeton, NJ: Princeton University Press.
Kierkegaard, Søren (1985) *Philosophical Fragments*, trans. Howard V. Hong and Edna H. Hong, Princeton, NJ: Princeton University Press.

Kierkegaard, Søren (1987) *Either/Or: Part I*, trans. Howard V. Hong and Edna H. Hong, Princeton, NJ: Princeton University Press.
Kierkegaard, Søren (1992) *Concluding Unscientific Postscript*, trans. Howard V. Hong and Edna H. Hong, Princeton, NJ: Princeton University Press.
Kierkegaard, Søren (1993) *Upbuilding Discourses in Various Spirits*, trans. Howard V. Hong and Edna H. Hong, Princeton, NJ: Princeton University Press.
Kierkegaard, Søren (1995) *Works of Love*, trans. Howard V. Hong and Edna H. Hong, Princeton, NJ: Princeton University Press.
Kierkegaard, Søren (1996) *Papers and Journals: A Selection*, trans. Alastair Hannay, London: Penguin.
Kierkegaard, Søren (1997) *Christian Discourses/The Crisis and a Crisis in the Life of an Actress*, trans. Howard V. Hong and Edna H. Hong, Princeton, NJ: Princeton University Press.
Kierkegaard, Søren (1997) *Without Authority*, trans. Howard V. Hong and Edna H. Hong, Princeton, NJ: Princeton University Press.
Kierkegaard, Søren (1998) *The Point of View*, trans. Howard V. Hong and Edna H. Hong, Princeton, NJ: Princeton University Press.
Kierkegaard, Søren (2013) *Søren Kierkegaards Skrifter*, 28 text volumes and 28 commentary volumes, eds. Niels Jørgen Cappelørn, Joakim Garff, Jette Knuden, Johnny Kondrup and Alastair McKinnon. Copenhagen: Gad Publishers.
Klement, K.C. (2002) "When Is Genetic Reasoning Not Fallacious?", in: *Argumentation* 16, 383–400.
Klossowski, Pierre (1975) *Nietzsche et le cercle vicieux*, Paris: Mercure de France.
Klossowski, Pierre (1997) *Nietzsche and the Vicious Circle*, Chicago: University of Chicago Press.
Knobe, Joshua/Leiter, Brian (2007) "The Case for Nietzschean Moral Psychology", in: Leiter/Sinhababu (2007), 83–109.
Köhnke, K.C. (1986) *Entstehung und Aufstieg des Neukantianismus: Die deutsche Universitätsphilosophie zwischen Idealismus und Positivismus*, Frankfurt a.M.: Suhrkamp.
Korsgaard, Christine M. (2009) *Self-Constitution: Agency, Identity and Integrity*, Oxford: Oxford University Press.
Lacoue-Labarthe, Philippe (2012) *La réponse d'Ulysse et autres textes sur l'Occident*, Paris: Nouvelles Éditions Lignes.
Lampert, L. (1993) *Nietzsche and Modern Times: A Study of Bacon, Descartes, and Nietzsche*, New Haven: Yale University Press.
Lange, Friedrich Albert (1866) *Geschichte des Materialismus und Kritik seiner Bedeutung in der Gegenwart*, Iserlohn: Baedeker.
Lange, Friedrich Albert (1880) [1875] *The History of Materialism and Criticism of its Present Importance*, vol. 2/3, English translation by Ernest Chester Thomas, Boston: Houghton, Mifflin & Co.
Lange, Friedrich Albert (1881) [1875] *The History of Materialism and Criticism of its Present Importance*, vol. 3/3, English translation by Ernest Chester Thomas, Boston: Houghton, Mifflin & Co.
Lange, Friedrich Albert (1887) [1875] *Geschichte des Materialismus*, 2nd edition, Iserlohn/Leipzig: J. Baedeker.
Lange, Friedrich Albert (1902) [1866] *Geschichte des Materialismus und Kritik seiner Bedeutung in der Gegenwart*, 2 vols., ed. Hermann Cohen, Leipzig: Baedeker.

Lange, Friedrich Albert (1974) *Geschichte des Materialismus und Kritik seiner Bedeutung in der Gegenwart*, Book I, Frankfurt a.M.: Surkamp [Reprint of 2nd edition, Iserlohn: Baedeker 1873].
Lange, Friedrich Albert (2006) [1875] *Geschichte des Materialismus und Kritik seiner Bedeutung in der Gegenwart*, Book II, Leipzig: Elibron Classics.
Leary, David E. (1980) "The Historical Foundations of Herbart's Mathematization of Psychology", in: *Journal of the History of Behavioral Sciences* 16, 150–163.
Lehmann, Gerhard (1987) "Kant im Spätidealismus und die Anfänge der neukantische Bewegung", in: Hans L. Ollig (ed.), *Materialien zur Neukantianismus-Diskussion*, Darmstadt: WBG, 44–65.
Lehrer, Keith (ed.) (1966) *Freedom and Determinism*, New York: Random House.
Leiter, Brian (1998) "The Paradox of Fatalism and Self-Creation in Nietzsche", in: C. Janaway (ed.), *Willing and Nothingness. Schopenhauer as Nietzsche's Educator*, Oxford: Clarendon Press, 217–257.
Leiter, Brian (2000) "Nietzsche's Metaethics", in: *European Journal of Philosophy* 8, 277–297.
Leiter, Brian (2002) *Nietzsche on Morality*, London/New York: Routledge.
Leiter, Brian (2002) *Routledge Philosophy Guidebook to Nietzsche on Morality*, London/New York: Routledge.
Leiter, Brian (2007) "Nietzsche's Theory of the Will", in: *Philosophers' Imprint* 7, 1–15.
Leiter, Brian (2014) "Moral Skepticism and Moral Disagreement in Nietzsche".
Leiter, Brian/Sinhababu, Neil (eds.) (2007) *Nietzsche and Morality*. Oxford: Oxford University Press.
Leiter, Brian (2015) *Nietzsche on Morality, Second Edition*, London/New York: Routledge.
Leopardi, Giacomo (2010) *Canti*, trans. Jonathan Galassi, London: Penguin.
Leopardi, Giacomo (2013) *Zibaldone: The Notebooks of Leopardi*, eds. Michael Caesar and Franco D'Intino, London: Penguin.
Le Patourel, I. (2012) "Nietzschean Selfhood: Inner Conflict and Unification", MPhilStud thesis, Birkbeck, University of London.
Lewis, Charles (1986) "Kierkegaard, Nietzsche, and the Faith of Our Fathers", in: *International Journal for Philosophy of Religion* 20(1), 3–16.
Liebmann, Otto (1865) *Kant und die Epigonen: Eine kritische Abhandlung*, Stuttgart: Schober.
Loeb, P.S. (1995) "Is There a Genetic Fallacy in Nietzsche's Genealogy of Morals?", in: *International Studies in Philosophy* 27(3), 125–141.
Long, A.A. (2002) *Epictetus*, Oxford: Clarendon Press.
Lopes, Rogério (2012) "Das politische Triebmodell bei Nietzsche", in: J. Georg and C. Zittel (eds.), *Nietzsches Philosophie des Unbewussten*, Berlin/New York: De Gruyter, 147–156.
Loukidelis, Nikolaos (2005) "Quellen von Nietzsches Verständnis und Kritik des Cartesischen *cogito, ergo sum*", in: *Nietzsche-Studien* 34, 300–309.
Loukidelis, Nikolaos (2006) "Nachweis aus Otto Liebmann, *Zur Analysis der Wirklichkeit*", in: *Nietzsche-Studien* 35, 302–303.
Loukidelis, Nikolaos (2007) "Nachweise aus Otto Liebmann, *Gedanken und Thatsachen* (1882)", in: *Nietzsche-Studien* 36, 391–396.
Loukidelis, Nikolaos (2013) *Es denkt: Ein Kommentar zum Aphorismus 17 aus "Jenseits von Gut und Böse"*, Würzburg: Königshausen & Neumann.
Loukidelis, Nikolaos (2014) "Nietzsche und die 'Logiker'", in: H. Heit and L. Heller (eds.), *Handbuch Nietzsche und die Wissenschaften*, Berlin/Boston: De Gruyter, 222–241.
Lucy, Niall (2004) *A Derrida Dictionary*, Oxford: Blackwell.

Luhmann, Niklas (1981) *Gesellschaftsstruktur und Semantik. Studien zur Wissenssoziologie der modernen Gesellschaft*, vol. 2, Frankfurt a.M.: Suhrkamp.
Luhmann, Niklas (1984) *Soziale Systeme. Grundriß einer allgemeinen Theorie*, Frankfurt a.M.: Suhrkamp.
Luhmann, Niklas (1989) "Wie ist soziale Ordnung möglich; Individuum, Individualität, Individualismus", in: Niklas Luhmann (ed.), *Gesellschaftsstruktur und Semantik. Studien zur Wissenssoziologie der modernen Gesellschaft*, vol. 3, Frankfurt a.M.: Suhrkamp, 207–212.
Luhmann, Niklas (1990) *Die Wissenschaft der Gesellschaft*, Frankfurt a.M.: Suhrkamp.
Luhmann, Niklas (1991) "Sthenographie und Euryalistik", in: Hans Ulrich Gumbrecht and K. Ludwig Pfeiffer (eds.), *Paradoxien, Dissonanzen, Zusammenbrüche. Situationen offener Epistemologie*, Frankfurt a.M.: Suhrkamp, 58–82.
Luhmann, Niklas (1992) *Beobachtung der Moderne*, Opladen: Westdeutscher Verlag.
Luhmann, Niklas (1995) "Die Tücke des Subjekts und die Frage nach dem Menschen", in: Niklas Luhmann (ed.), *Soziologische Aufklärung 6: Die Soziologie und der Mensch*, Opladen: Westdeutscher Verlag, 155–168.
Luhmann, Niklas (1997) *Die Gesellschaft der Gesellschaft*, Frankfurt a.M.: Suhrkamp.
Luhmann, Niklas (2000) *Die Religion der Gesellschaft*, Frankfurt a.M.: Suhrkamp.
Luhmann, Niklas (2004) *Einführung in die Systemtheorie*, ed. Dirk Baecker, Darmstadt: WBG.
Luhmann, Niklas (2011) *Organisation und Entscheidung*, 3rd edition, Wiesbaden: VS Verlag für Sozialwissenschaften, 127–131.
Lupo, Luca (2006) *Le Colombe dello Scettico. Riflessioni di Nietzsche sulla Coscienza negli anni 1880–1888*. Pisa: ETS.
Lupo, Luca (2012) "Drives, Instincts, Language, and Consciousness in Daybreak 119: 'Erleben und Erdichten'", in: J. Constâncio and M.J. Mayer Branco (eds.), *As the Spider Spins: Essays on Nietzsche's Critique and Use of Language*, Berlin/Boston: De Gruyter, 179–195.
Mach, Ernst (1863) "Vorträge über Psychophysik", in: *Österreichische Zeitschrift für praktische Heilkunde* 9, 146–148, 277–279, 294–298, 316–318, 335–338, 352–354, 362–366.
Mach, Ernst (1886) *Beiträge zur Analyse der Empfindungen*, Jena: Fischer.
Mach, Ernst (1914) *The Analysis of Sensations*, Eng. trans. Chicago/London: Open Court.
Mach, Ernst (1976) [1905] *Knowledge and Error. Sketches on the Psychology of Enquiry*, Eng. trans., Drodrecht: Reidel.
Magnus, B./Huggins, K. (eds.) (1996) *The Cambridge Companion to Nietzsche*, Cambridge: Cambridge University Press.
Malantschuk, Gregor (1962) "Kierkegaard and Nietzsche", trans. Margaret Grieve, in Howard A. Johnson and Niels Thulstrup (eds.), *A Kierkegaard Critique*, Chicago: Regnery, 116–129.
Marion, J.-L. (2013) *Sur la pensée passive de Descartes*, Paris: PUF.
Martinelli, Riccardo (1999) *Misurare l'anima. Filosofia e psicofisica da Kant a Carnap*, Macerata: Quodlibet.
Maudemarie Clark and David Dudrick (2012) *The Soul of Nietzsche's Beyond Good and Evil*. Cambridge: Cambridge University Press.
May, Simon (ed.) (2011) *Nietzsche's On the Genealogy of Morality: A Critical Guide*, Cambridge: Cambridge University Press.
McDowell, John (1994) "The Content of Perceptual Experience", in: *Philosophical Quarterly* 44, 190–205. [Reprinted in: John McDowell, *Mind, Value, and Reality*, Cambridge, MA: Harvard University Press 1998]
McGushin, Edward (2005) "Foucault and the Problem of the Subject", in: *Philosophy & Social Criticism* 31(5/6), 623–648.

McGushin, Edward F. (2007) *Foucault's Askēsis: An Introduction to the Philosophical Life*, Evanston: Northwestern University Press.
Melamed, Yitzhak (2013) *Spinoza's Metaphysics: Substance and Thought*, Oxford: Oxford University Press.
Meyer, Julius Robert (1845) *Die organische Bewegung im Zusammenhang mit dem Stoffwechsel*, Heilbronn: C. Drechsler'sche Buchhandlung.
Meyer, Katrin (1998) *Ästhetik der Historie: Fr. Nietzsches "Vom Nutzen und Nachteil der Historie für das Leben"* (Epistemata Würzburger Wissenschaftliche Schriften, Reihe Philosophie, vol. 238), Würzburg: Königshausen & Neumann.
Miguens, Sofia (2002) *Uma Teoria Fisicalista do Conteúdo e da Consciência–D. Dennett e os debates da filosofia da mente*, Porto: Campo das Letras.
Miguens, Sofia (2008) *Será que a minha mente está dentro da minha cabeça? Da ciência cognitiva à filosofia*, Porto: Campo das Letras.
Miguens, Sofia/Preyer, Gerhard (eds.) (2012) *Consciousness and Subjectivity*, Frankfurt a.M.: Ontos.
Milchman, Alan/Rosenberg, Alan (2007) "The Aesthetic and Ascetic Dimensions of an Ethics of Self-Fashioning: Nietzsche and Foucault", in: *Parrhesia* 2, 44–65.
Miles, Thomas P. (2011) "Friedrich Nietzsche: Rival Visions of the Best Way of Life", in: Jon Stewart (ed.), *Kierkegaard and Existentialism, Kierkegaard Research: Sources, Reception and Resources, Volume 9*. Farnham: Ashgate, 263–297.
Miles, Thomas P. (2013) *Kierkegaard and Nietzsche on the Best Way of Life*, New York: Palgrave Macmillan.
Montaigne, Michel de (1962) *Œuvres complètes*, ed. M. Rat, Paris: Gallimard.
Montebello, Pierre (2001) *Nietzsche. La volonté de puissance*, Paris: Presses Universitaires de France.
Montebello, Pierre (2003) *L'autre métaphysique*, Paris: Desclée de Brouwer.
Montebello, Pierre (2011) "Deleuze, Une Anti-Phénoménologie?", in: *Chiasmi International* 13 ("Merleau-Ponty Fifty Years After His Death"), 315–325.
Montinari, Mazzino (1997) *"La Volonté de puissance" n'existe pas*, trans. P. Farazzi and M. Valensi, Paris: Editions de l'Eclat.
Moore, G. (2002) *Nietzsche, Biology and Metaphor*, Cambridge: Cambridge University Press.
Moore, G. (2002) "Nietzsche, Spencer and the Ethics of Evolution", in: *The Journal of Nietzsche Studies* 23, 1–20.
Moriarty, John (2009) *Dreamtime*, Dublin: Lilliput.
Mouffe, Chantal (1996) "Democracy, Power and the 'Political'", in: Seyla Benhabib (ed.), *Democracy and Difference: Contesting the boundaries of the political*, Princeton: Princeton University Press, 245–256.
Mulhall, Stephen (2007) *Wittgenstein's Private Language. Grammar, Nonsense, and Imagination in Philosophical Investigations §§243–315*, New York: Oxford University Press.
Mulhall, Stephen (2011) "The Promising Animal: The Art of Reading *On the Genealogy of Morality* as Testimony", in: May Simon (ed.), *Nietzsche's On the Genealogy of Morality. A Critical Guide*, Cambridge: Cambridge University Press, 234–264.
Mulhall, Stephen (2013) *The Self and its Shadows. A Book of Essays on Individuality as Negation in Philosophy and the Arts*, Oxford/New York: Oxford University Press.
Mulhall, Stephen (2014) "Orchestral Metaphysics: *The Birth of Tragedy* between Drama, Opera, and Philosophy", in: Daniel Came (ed.), *Nietzsche on Art and Life*, Oxford/New York: Oxford University Press, 107–126.

Mulhall, Stephen/Swift, Adam (1992) *Liberals and Communitarians*, Oxford: Blackwell.
Mulhall, Stephen/Swift, Adam (2003) "Rawls and Communitarianism", in: S. Freeman (ed.), *The Cambridge Companion to Rawls*, Cambridge: Cambridge University Press, 460–487.
Müller, Johannes (1822) *Dissertatio inauguralis physiologica sistens Commentarios de Phoronomia Animalium*, Bonn: Thormann.
Müller-Buck, R. (2002) "'Der einzige Psychologe, von dem ich etwas zu lernen hatte': Nietzsche liest Dostojewskij", in: *Dostoevsky Studies, New Series* 6, 89–118.
Müller-Lauter, Wolfgang (1971) *Nietzsche. Seine Philosophie der Gegensätze und die Gegensätze seiner Philosophie*, Berlin/New York: De Gruyter.
Müller-Lauter, Wolfgang (1974) "Nietzsches Lehre vom Willen zur Macht", in: *Nietzsche-Studien* 3, 1–60.
Müller-Lauter, Wolfgang (1978) "Der Organismus als innerer Kampf. Der Einfluss von Wilhelm Roux auf Fr. Nietzsche", in: *Nietzsche-Studien* 7, 189–223.
Müller-Lauter, Wolfgang (1999) "Das Problem des Gegensatzes in der Philosophie", in: *Über Werden und Wille zur Macht. Nietzsche-Interpretationen I*, Berlin/New York: De Gruyter, 1–24.
Müller-Lauter, Wolfgang (1999) "Der Organismus als innerer Kampf. Der Einfluss von Wilhelm Roux auf Fr. Nietzsche", in: *Über Werden und Wille zur Macht, Nietzsche-Interpretationen I*, Berlin/New York: De Gruyter, 97–140.
Müller-Lauter, Wolfgang (1999) *Über Freiheit und Chaos*, Berlin/New York: De Gruyter.
Nehamas, Alexander (1983) "How One Becomes What One Is", in: *The Philosophical Review* 92(3), 385–417.
Nehamas, Alexander (1985) *Nietzsche: Life as Literature*, Cambridge, MA: Harvard University Press.
Nehamas, Alexander (1998) *The Art of Living: Socratic Reflections from Plato to Foucault*, London/Berkeley: University of California Press.
Nietzsche, Friedrich (2005b) *Twilight of the Idols*, in F. Nietzsche, *The Anti-Christ, Ecce Homo, Twilight of the Idols and Other Writings*, ed. A. Ridley and J. Norman, trans. J. Norman, Cambridge: Cambridge University Press.
Nietzsche, Friedrich (2011) *Dernières lettres*, ed. and trans. Y. Souladié, Paris: Editions Manucius.
Nordentoft, Kresten (1972) *Kierkegaard's Psychology*, trans. Bruce Kirmmse, Pittsburgh: Duquesne University Press.
Nozick, Robert (1981) *Philosophical Explanations*, Cambridge, MA: Harvard University Press.
Oksala, Johanna (2005) *Foucault on Freedom*, Cambridge: Cambridge University Press.
Orsucci, A. (1992) *Dalla biologia cellulare alle scienze dello spirito. Aspetti del dibattito sull'individualità nell'Ottocento tedesco*, Bologna: Il Mulino.
Owen, David (1995) *Nietzsche, Politics & Modernity*, London: Sage.
Owen, David (2009) "Autonomy, Self-Respect, and Self-Love: Nietzsche on Ethical Agency", in: Ken Gemes and Simon May (eds.), *Nietzsche on Freedom and Autonomy*, New York/Oxford: Oxford University Press, 197–221.
Owen, David/Ridley, Aaron (2003) "On Fate", in: *International Studies in Philosophy* 35(3), 63–78.
Parfit, Derek (2012) "We Are Not Human Beings", in: *Philosophy* 87(1), 5–28.
Parkes, Graham (1994) *Composing the Soul: Reaches of Nietzsche Psychology*, Chicago: University of Chicago Press.

Pessoa, Fernando (2001) *The Selected Prose of Fernando Pessoa*, ed. and trans. Richard Zenith, New York: Grove Press.
Pessoa, Fernando (2012) *Prosa de Álvaro de Campos*, ed. with an introduction and notes by Jerónimo Pizarro and Antonio Cardiello, Lisbon: Ática.
Pfeffer, Rose (1972) *Nietzsche: Disciple of Dionysus*, Lewisburg: Bucknell University Press.
Piazzesi, C. (2007) "Pathos der Distanz et transformation de l'expérience de soi chez le dernier Nietzsche", in: *Nietzsche-Studien* 36, 258–295.
Pichler, Axel (2010) *Nietzsche, die Orchestikologie und das dissipative Denken*, Vienna: Passagen.
Pier, Jens (2015) "The 'I' and the 'We'. Wittgenstein, Strawson, and the Way Back to Hegel", in: *inter.culture.philosophy* 1/2015.
Pippin, Robert B. (1996) "Nietzsche's Alleged Farewell", in: *Cambridge Companion to Nietzsche*, Cambridge: Cambridge University Press, 252–278.
Pippin, Robert B. (1999) *Modernism as a Philosophical Problem*, Oxford: Blackwell.
Pippin, Robert B. (2005) *The Persistence of Subjectivity*, New York: Cambridge University Press.
Pippin, Robert B. (2006) *Nietzsche, moraliste français. La conception nietzschéenne d'une psychologie philosophique*, trans. I. Wienand, Paris: Odile Jacob.
Pippin, Robert B. (2010) *Nietzsche, Psychology, and First Philosophy*, Chicago/London: University of Chicago Press.
Plato (1914) *Euthyphro, Apology, Crito, Phaedo, Phaedrus*, Cambridge, MA: Harvard University Press.
Podmore, Simon D. (2011) *Kierkegaard and the Self before God: Anatomy of the Abyss*, Bloomington: Indiana University Press.
Poellner, Peter (1995) *Nietzsche and Metaphysics*, New York: Oxford University Press.
Poellner, Peter (2006) "Phenomenology and Science in Nietzsche", in: Keith Ansell-Pearson (ed.), *A Companion to Nietzsche*, Oxford: Blackwell, 297–313.
Poljakova, Ekaterina (2013) *Differente Plausibilitäten. Kant und Nietzsche, Tolstoi und Dostojewski über Vernunft, Moral und Kunst* (Monographien und Texte zur Nietzsche-Forschung Bd. 63), Berlin/Boston: De Gruyter.
Prinz, Jesse (2007) *The Emotional Construction of Morals*, Oxford: Oxford University Press.
Putnam, Hilary (2004) *The Collapse of the Fact/Value Dichotomy and Other Essays*, Cambridge, MA: Harvard University Press.
Quine, W.V.O. (1975) "On Empirically Equivalent Systems of the World", in: *Erkenntnis* 9, 313–328.
Quine, W.V.O. (1990) "Three Indeterminacies", in: R.B. Barrett and R.F. Gibson (eds.), *Perspectives on Quine*, Cambridge, MA: Blackwell.
Quine, W.V.O./Ullian, Joseph (1978) *The Web of Belief*, 2nd edition, New York: Random House.
Railton, Peter (1986) "Facts and Values", in: *Philosophical Topics* 14, 5–31.
Rakgaber, Matthew (2012) "The 'Sovereign Individual' and the 'Ascetic Ideal': On a Perennial Misreading of the Second Essay of Nietzsche's *On the Genealogy of Morality*", in: *Journal of Nietzsche Studies* 43(2), 213–240.
Rasmussen, Dennis C. (2008) *The Problems and Promise of Commercial Society: Adam Smith's Response to Rousseau*, University Park, PA: Penn State University Press.
Rawls, John (1971) *A Theory of Justice*, Oxford: Oxford University Press.
Rée, Jonathan/Chamberlain, Jane (1997) *Kierkegaard: A Critical Reader*, Oxford: Blackwell, 75–102.

Regenbogen, Arnim (2010) "Art. Intersubjektivität", in: Hans Jörg Sandkühler (ed.), *Enzyklopädie Philosophie*, 2nd edition in 3 vols., Hamburg: Meiner, 1152–1156.
Rethy, R. (1976) "The Descartes Motto to the First Edition of *Menschliches, Allzumenschliches*", in: *Nietzsche-Studien* 5, 289–297.
Riccardi, Mattia (2009) *"Der faule Fleck des Kantischen Kritizismus". Erscheinung und Ding an sich bei Nietzsche* (Beiträge zu Friedrich Nietzsche, vol. 14), Basel: Schwabe.
Riccardi, Mattia (2010) "Nietzsche's Critique of Kant's Thing in Itself", in: *Nietzsche-Studien* 39, 333–351.
Riccardi, Mattia (2014) "Nietzsche und die Erkenntnistheorie und Metaphysik", in: H. Heit and L. Heller (eds.), *Handbuch Nietzsche und die Wissenschaften*, Berlin/Boston: De Gruyter, 242–264.
Riccardi, Mattia (2015) "Inner Opacity. Nietzsche on Introspection and Agency", in: *Inquiry* 58(3), 221–243 (Special Issue: Nietzsche's Moral Psychology, ed. by B. Leiter).
Riccardi, Mattia (forthcoming) "Nietzsche on the Superficiality of Consciousness", in: Manuel Dries (ed.), *Nietzsche on Consciousness and the Embodied Mind*, Berlin/Boston: De Gruyter.
Richardson, John (1996) *Nietzsche's System*, Oxford: Oxford University Press.
Richardson, John (2004) *Nietzsche's New Darwinism*, New York/Oxford: Oxford University Press.
Richardson, John (2012) *Heidegger*, London/New York: Routledge.
Richardson, John (2015) "Nietzsche, Language, Community", in: Julian Young (ed.), *Individual and Community in Nietzsche's Philosophy*, New York: Cambridge University Press, 214–243.
Richardson, Robert D. (1995) *Emerson: The Mind on Fire*, Berkeley/Los Angeles/London: University of California Press.
Rigal, Elisabeth (2003) "Désubjectivation", in: *Le vocabulaire de Gilles Deleuze*, eds. R. Sasso and A. Villani, *Les Cahiers de Noesis* 3, 75–81.
Roden, David (2004) "The Subject", in: J. Reynolds and J. Roffe (eds.), *Understanding Derrida*, New York/London: Continuum, 93–102.
Rödl, Sebastian (2007) *Self-consciousness*, Cambridge, MA/London: Harvard University Press.
Rosen, Stanley (1989) *The Ancients and the Moderns: Rethinking Modernity*, New Haven: Yale Press.
Rosenthal, David (1997) "A Theory of Consciousness", in: Ned Block, Owen J. Flanagan and Güven Güzeldere (eds.), *The Nature of Consciousness – Philosophical Debates*, Cambridge, MA: MIT Press, 729–753.
Ruse, Michael (1986) *Taking Darwin Seriously*, New York: Blackwell.
Russell, B. (1900) *A Critical Exposition of the Philosophy of Leibniz*, Cambridge: Cambridge University Press.
Ryan, Bartholomew (2013) "Kierkegaard's Fairytale", in: *Rivista di Filosofia Neo-Scolastica* 3–4, 945–961.
Sachs, Carl B. (2008) "Nietzsche's *Daybreak*: Toward a Naturalized Theory of Autonomy", in: *Epoché* 13(1), 81–100.
Sachs-Hombach, Klaus (1993) *"Der Geist als Maschine. Herbarts Grundlegung der naturwissenschaftlichen Psychologie"*, in: Jörg F. Maas (ed.), *Das sichtbare Denken*, Amsterdam: Rodopi, 91–111.
Safranski, Rüdiger (2002) *Nietzsche. A Philosophical Biography*, trans. Shelley Frisch, New York: Norton.

Salaquarda, Jorg (1978) "Nietzsche und Lange", in: *Nietzsche-Studien* 7, 236–253.
Salaquarda, Jorg (2007) "Leib bin ich ganz und gar ... Zum dritten Weg bei Schopenhauer und Nietzsche", in: Konstantin Broese, Matthias Koßler and Barbara Salaquarda (eds.), *Die Deutung der Welt. Jorg Salaquardas Schriften zu Arthur Schopenhauer*, Würzburg: Königshausen & Neumann.
Salehi, Djavid (2000) "Art. Subjekt", in: Hennig Ottmann (ed.), *Nietzsche-Handbuch. Leben–Werk–Wirkung*, Stuttgart/Weimar: Metzler.
Scandella, Maurizio (2012) "Did Nietzsche Read Spinoza? Some Preliminary Notes on the Nietzsche-Spinoza Problem, Kuno Fischer, and Other Sources", in: *Nietzsche-Studien* 41, 308–332.
Schacht, Richard (1995) Making Sense of Nietzsche, Urbana: University of Illinois Press.
Schacht, Richard (2012) "Nietzsche's Naturalism", in: *The Journal of Nietzsche Studies* 43(2), 185–212.
Schlimgen, Erwin (1998) *Nietzsches Theorie des Bewußtseins*, Berlin/New York: De Gruyter.
Schopenhauer, Arthur (1969) *The World as Will and Representation* [1819/1844], 2 vols., trans. E.F.J. Payne, New York: Dover.
Schopenhauer, Arthur (1974) *On the Fourfold Root of the Principle of Sufficient Reason*, trans. E. Payne, La Salle, IL: Open Court.
Schopenhauer, Arthur (1977) *Zürcher Ausgabe*, 10 vols., eds. Arthur Hübscher et al., Zurich: Diogenes.
Schopenhauer, Arthur (1999) *Prize Essay on the Freedom of the Will*, ed. Günter Zöller, trans. E. Payne, Cambridge: Cambridge University Press.
Schopenhauer, Arthur (2009) *The Two Fundamental Problems of Ethics*, ed. Cristopher Janaway (The Cambridge Edition of the Works of Schopenhauer),Cambridge: Cambridge University Press.
Schopenhauer, Arthur (2010) [1819] *The World as Will and Representation. Volume I*, trans. and eds. J. Norman, A. Welchman and C. Janaway. Cambridge: Cambridge University Press.
Schopenhauer, Arthur (2010) *Prize Essay on the Freedom of the Will* [1839], in: *The Two Fundamental Problems of Ethics*, trans. David E. Cartwright and Edward E. Erdmann, Oxford: Oxford University Press.
Schopenhauer, Arthur (2010) *Prize Essay on the Basis of Morals* [1840], in: *The Two Fundamental Problems of Ethics*, trans. David E. Cartwright and Edward E. Erdmann, Oxford: Oxford University Press.
Schrift, A.D. (2001) "Rethinking the Subject: Or How One Becomes-Other than What One Is", in: Richard Schacht (ed.), *Nietzsche's Postmoralism. Essays on Nietzsche's Prelude to Philosophy's Future*, Cambridge: Cambridge University Press, 47–62.
Schroeder, Mark (2009) "Hybrid Expressivism: Virtues and Vices", in: *Ethics* 119, 257–309.
Schroeder, Timothy/Roskies, Adina L./Nichols, Shaun (2010) "Moral Motivation", in: Doris (2010), 72–109.
Schulte, Joachim (2003) *Experience and Expression. Wittgenstein's Philosophy of Psychology*, Oxford/New York: Oxford University Press.
Schulte, Joachim (2013) "Wittgenstein on Philosophy as Poetry", in: M.F.M Molder, D. Soeiro and N. Fonseca (eds.), *Morphology. Questions on Method and Language*, Bern: Peter Lang, 347–369.
Schwemmer, Oswald (1995) "Art. Intersubjektivität", in: Jürgen Mittelstraß (ed.), *Enzyklopädie Philosophie und Wissenschaftstheorie*, vol. 2, Stuttgart/Weimar: Metzler, 282–284.
Seigel, Jerrold (2005) *The Idea of the Self: Thought and Experience in Western Europe since the Seventeenth Century*, Cambridge: Cambridge University Press.

Sellars, Wilfrid (1966) "Fatalism and Determinism", in: Lehrer (1966), 141–174.
Shapiro, L. (ed.) (2007) *The Correspondence between Princess Elisabeth of Bohemia and René Descartes*, Chicago: University of Chicago Press.
Shoemaker, Sydney (1984) "Personal Identity: A Materialist's Account", in S. Shoemaker and R. Swinburne (1984) *Personal Identity*, Oxford: Basil Blackwell.
Siemens, H.W. (2006) "Nietzsche Contra Liberalism on Freedom", in: Keith Ansell-Pearson (ed.), *A Companion to Nietzsche*, Oxford/Malden, MA: Basil Blackwell, 437–454.
Siemens, H.W. (2008) "Nietzsche and the Temporality of Self-Legislation", in: Manuel Dries (ed.), *Nietzsche on Time and History*, Berlin/New York: De Gruyter, 191–210.
Siemens, H.W. (2009) "Nietzsche's Critique of Democracy", in: *Journal of Nietzsche Studies* 38, 20–37.
Siemens, H.W. (2009) "(Self-)legislation, Life and Love in Nietzsche's Philosophy", in: Isabelle Wienand (ed.), *Neue Beiträge zu Nietzsches Moral-, Politik- und Kulturphilosophie*, Fribourg: Press Academic Fribourg, 67–90.
Siemens, H.W. (2011) "Empfindung", in: *Nietzsche-Wörterbuch*, Nietzsche Online (NO), De Gruyter (ed.), Berlin/Boston: De Gruyter. DOI: 10.1515/NO_W017186_0080.
Siemens, H.W. (2013) "Travando uma Guerra contra a Guerra: Nietzsche contra Kant acerca do conflito", in: *Kriterion: Revista de Filosofia* 54/128, 419–437.
Simon, Josef (1984) "Das Problem des Bewusstseins bei Nietzsche und der traditionelle Bewusstseinsbegriff", in: M. Djuric and J. Simon (eds.), *Zur Aktualität Nietzsches*, vol. 2, Würzburg: Königshausen & Neumann, 17–33.
Simon, Josef (1995) "Verstehen ohne Interpretation?: Zeichen und Verstehen bei Hegel und Nietzsche", in: *Distanz im Verstehen: Zeichen und Interpretationen II*, Frankfurt a.M.: Suhrkamp.
Simon, Josef (2003) *Kant. Die fremde Vernunft und die Sprache der Philosophie*, Berlin/New York: De Gruyter.
Sinhababu, Neil (2009) "The Humean Theory of Motivation Reformulated and Defended", in: *Philosophical Review* 118, 465–500.
Sleinis, E.E. (1999) "Between Nietzsche and Leibniz: Perpectivism and Irrationalism", in: B.E. Babich and R.S. Cohen (eds.), *Nietzsche, Theories of Knowledge, and Critical Theory. Nietzsche and the Sciences I*, Dordrecht/Boston/London: Kluwer, 67–76.
Sluga, Hans (1996) "Ludwig Wittgenstein: Life and Work. An Introduction", in: Hans Sluga David G. Stern (eds.), *The Cambridge Companion to Wittgenstein*, Cambridge: Cambridge University Press, 1–33.
Sluga, Hans (1996) "'Whose House Is That?' Wittgenstein on the self", in: Hans Sluga and David G. Stern (eds.), *The Cambridge Companion to Wittgenstein*, Cambridge: Cambridge University Press, 320–353.
Sluga, Hans (2003) "Foucault's Encounter with Heidegger and Nietzsche", in: Gary Gutting (ed.), *The Cambridge Companion to Foucault*, 2nd edition, Cambridge: Cambridge University Press, 210–240.
Sluga, Hans (2015) " 'The Time is Coming When One Will Have to Relearn about Politics' ", in: Julian Young (ed.), *Individual and Community in Nietzsche's Philosophy*, New York: Cambridge University Press, 31–50.
Small, Robin (2001) *Nietzsche in Context*, Aldershot/Burlington/Singapore/Sydney: Ashgate.
Small, Robin (2007) "Nietzsche's Evolutionary Ethics", in: G. von Tevenar (ed.), *Nietzsche and Ethics*. Bern: Peter Lang.

Sooväli, Jaanus (2012) "The Absence and the Other. Nietzsche and Derrida against Husserl", in: J. Constâncio and M.J. Mayer Branco (eds.), *As the Spider Spins: Essays on Nietzsche's Critique and Use of Language*, Berlin/Boston: De Gruyter, 161–177.
Sorabji, Richard (2006) *Self. Ancient and Modern Insights about Individuality, Life, and Death*, Oxford: Oxford University Press.
Souladié, Yannick (2007) " *Nietzsche. L'Inversion des valeurs*, Hildesheim: Olms.
Spaemann, Robert (1990) "Niklas Luhmanns Herausforderung der Philosophie", in: *Niklas Luhmann, Paradigm lost: Über die ethische Reflexion der Moral. Rede anläßlich der Verleihung des Hegel-Preises 1989*, Frankfurt a.M.: Suhrkamp, 49–73.
Spinoza, Baruch de (1996) *Ethics*, trans. Edwin Curley, New York: Penguin.
Spir, Afrikan (1877) *Denken und Wirklichkeit. Versuch einer Erneuerung der kritischen Philosophie, Erster Band. Das Unbedingte*, Leipzig: Findel.
Springmann, Simon (2010) *Macht und Organisation: Die Machtkonzeption bei Friedrich Nietzsche und in der mikropolitischen Organisationstheorie*, Berlin: Duncker & Humblot.
Stack, George (1983) *Lange and Nietzsche*, Berlin: De Gruyter.
Stack, George (1992) *Nietzsche and Emerson. An elective affinity*, Athens: Ohio University Press.
Stambaugh, Joan (1994) *The Other Nietzsche*, Albany: SUNY Press.
Stegmaier, Werner (1987) "Darwin, Darwinismus, Nietzsche. Zum Problem der Evolution", in: *Nietzsche-Studien* 15, 264–287.
Stegmaier, Werner (1995) "Philosophieren als Vermeiden einer Lehre. Inter-individuelle Orientierung bei Sokrates und Platon, Nietzsche und Derrida", in: J. Simon (ed.), *Distanz im Verstehen. Zeichen und Interpretation II*, Frankfurt a.M.: Suhrkamp, 214–239.
Stegmaier, Werner (in cooperation with Hartwig Frank) (1997) *Interpretationen. Hauptwerke der Philosophie. Von Kant bis Nietzsche*, Stuttgart: Reclam.
Stegmaier, Werner (2000) "Nietzsches Zeichen", in: *Nietzsche-Studien* 29, 41–69.
Stegmaier, Werner (2004) "'Philosophischer Idealismus' und die 'Musik des Lebens': zu Nietzsches Umgang mit Paradoxien", in: *Nietzsche-Studien* 33, 90–128.
Stegmaier, Werner (2008) *Philosophie der Orientierung*, Berlin/New York: De Gruyter.
Stegmaier, Werner (2010) "Die Freisetzung einer Philosophie der Orientierung durch Friedrich Nietzsche", in: Joachim Bromand and Guido Kreis (eds.), *Was sich nicht sagen lässt. Das Nicht-Begriffliche in Wissenschaft, Kunst und Religion*, Berlin: Akademie Verlag, 355–367.
Stegmaier, Werner (2011) "Niklas Luhmann als Philosoph", in: Christina Gansel (ed.), *Systemtheorie in den Fachwissenschaften. Zugänge, Methoden, Probleme*, Göttingen: Vandenhoeck & Ruprecht, 11–32.
Stegmaier, Werner (2012) *Nietzsches Befreiung der Philosophie. Kontextuelle Interpretation des V. Buches der "Fröhlichen Wissenschaft"*, Berlin/Boston: De Gruyter.
Stegmaier, Werner (2015) "Wie leben wir mit dem Nihilismus? Nietzsches Nihilismus aus der Sicht einer aktuellen Philosophie der Orientierung", in: *Tijdschrift voor Filosofie* 74, 319–338.
Stellino, Paolo (2015) "Notas sobre la lectura nietzscheana de *Apuntes del subsuelo*", in: *Estudios Nietzsche* 11, 113–125.
Stern, David (2010) "Another Strand in the Private Language Argument", in: Arif Ahmed (ed.), *Wittgenstein's Philosophical Investigations. A Critical Guide*, New York: Cambridge University Press, 178–196.
Stern, Thomas, 'Against Nietzsche's 'Theory' of the Drives' (manuscript).
Taine, Hippolyte (1864) *Le positivisme anglais. Étude sur Stuart Mill*, Paris: Baillière.

Taine, Hippolyte (1870) *English Positivism. A Study on John Stuart Mill*, London: Williams and Norgate.
Taine, Hippolyte (1870) *De l'intelligence*, vol. II, Paris: Hachette.
Taine, Hippolyte (1906) *Préface* a *De l'intelligence*, Paris: Hachette.
Taine, Hippolyte (1914) *De l'intelligence*, 3rd edition, Paris: Hachette.
Taine, Hippolyte (1945) *Appunti su Parigi. Vita e opinioni di Federico Tommaso Graindorge*, Milan: Domus.
Taine, Hippolyte (1863–1864) *Histoire de la littérature anglaise*, vol. 4, Paris: Hachette.
Taine, Hippolyte (1877) *Notes sur Paris. Vie et opinions de M. Frédéric-Thomas Graindorge*, Paris: Hachette
Taine, Hyppolite (1878) *Geschichte der englischen Literatur*. Erster Band: Die Anfänge und die Renaissance-Zeit der englischen Literatur. Bearbeitet und mit Anmerkungen versehen von Leopold Katscher, Leipzig: E. J. Günther [BN].
Taine, Hippolyte (1907) *Sa vie et sa correspondance*, 4 Bde., hg. von Victor Giraud, Paris: Hachette.
Taylor, Charles (1992) *Sources of the Self: The Making of the Modern Identity*, Cambridge: Harvard University Press.
Thompson, E. (2007) *Mind in Life. Biology, Phenomenology, and the Sciences of Mind*, Cambridge, MA: Harvard University Press.
Tietz, Udo (2000) "Phänomenologie des Scheins. Nietzsches sprachkritischer Perspektivismus", in: *Nietzscheforschung* 7, 215–242.
Tugendhat, Ernst (1986) *Self-Consciousness and Self-Determination*, trans. Paul Stern, Cambridge, MA: MIT Press.
Überweg, Friedrich (1866) *Grundriss der Geschichte der Philosophie von Thales bis auf die Gegenwart. Dritter Theil. Die Neuzeit*, Berlin: Mittler & Sohn.
Ulfers, Friedrich/Cohen, Mark Daniel (2007) "Nietzsche's Amor Fati: The Embracing of an Undecided Fate", in: *The Nietzsche Circle Journal*, June 2007, 1–14.
Unamuno, Miguel de (1976) *Our Lord Don Quixote: The Life of Don Quixote and Sancho with related Essays*, trans. Anthony Kerrigan, Princeton: Princeton University Press.
Ure, Michael (2006) "The Irony of Pity: Nietzsche Contra Schopenhauer and Rousseau", in: *Journal of Nietzsche Studies* 32, 68–92.
Urpeth, James (1998) "Noble Ascesis: Between Nietzsche and Foucault", in: *New Nietzsche Studies* 2(3/4), 65–93.
Vaihinger, Hans (1916) *Nietzsche als Philosoph*, 4th edition, Berlin: Reuther & Reichard.
Vaihinger, Hans (1922) *Die Philosophie des Als Ob: System der theoretischen, praktischen und religiösen Fiktionen der Menschheit*, 7th edition, Leipzig: Meiner.
Van Tongeren, Paul et al. (2004) *Nietzsche Wörterbuch*. Vol. 1, Berlin/New York: De Gruyter.
Varela, F. (1991) "Organism: A Meshwork of Selfless Selves", in: A.I. Tauber (ed.), *Organism and the Origins of Self* (Boston Studies in the Philosophy of Science, vol. 129), 79–107.
Vattimo, Gianni (2000) "La saggezza del superuomo", in: G. Vattimo (ed.), *Dialogo con Nietzsche. Saggi 1961–2000*, Milan: Garzanti.
Vattimo, Gianni (2006) *Dialogue with Nietzsche*, trans. William McCuaig, New York: Columbia University Press.
Velleman, J. David (2006) *Self to Self: Selected Essays*, Cambridge: Cambridge University Press.
Vivarelli, Vivetta (1994) "Montaigne und der freie Geist", in: *Nietzsche-Studien* 23, 79–101.
Ware, Owen (2009) "The Duty of Self-Knowledge", in: *Philosophy and Phenomenological Research* 79(3), 671–698.

Wellek, René (1965) *Confrontations: Studies in the Intellectual and Literary Relations Between Germany, England, and the United States During the Nineteenth Century*, Princeton, NJ: Princeton University Press.
Whitehead, Alfred North (1969) *Process and Reality*, New York: Free Press.
Whitlock, Greg (1996) "Roger Boscovich, Spinoza, and Nietzsche: The Untold Story", in: *Nietzsche-Studien* 25, 200–220.
Whitman, Walt (1982) *Collected Poetry and Collected Prose*, New York: The Library of America.
Wienand, I./Ribordy, O. (2013) "Public and Private Objections to the Cartesian Thesis of Mind-Body Union: The Divergent Replies in Descartes' Letters", in: *Society and Politics* 7, 2/14, 142–159.
Williams, Bernard (1993) *Shame and Necessity*, Berkeley/Los Angeles: University of California Press.
Williams, Bernard (1994) Nietzsche's Minimalist Moral Psychology, in: Richard Schacht (ed.), *Nietzsche, Genealogy, Morality: Essays on Nietzsche's On the Genealogy of Morals*, Berkeley: University of California Press, 237–247.
Wilson, Catherine (2008) *Epicureanism at the Origins of Modernity*, Oxford: Oxford University Press.
Wilson, Margaret D. (2007) "Spinoza's Theory of Knowledge", in: Don Garret (ed.), *Cambridge Companion to Spinoza*, Cambridge: Cambridge University Press, 89–141.
Wittgenstein, Ludwig (1958) *Philosophical Investigations*, trans. G.E.M. Anscombe, 2nd edition, Oxford: Blackwell.
Wittgenstein, Ludwig (1965) *The Blue and Brown Books*, New York: Harper & Row.
Wittgenstein, Ludwig (1998) *Culture and Value*, Oxford: Blackwell.
Wittgenstein, Ludwig (1998) *Notebooks 1914–1916*, eds. G.E.M. Anscombe and G.H. von Wright, trans. G.E.M. Anscombe, Oxford: Blackwell. [2nd edition 1979]
Wittgenstein, Ludwig (1998) *Philosophical Remarks*, ed. Rush Rhees, trans. Raymond Hargreaves and Roger White, Oxford: Blackwell. [2nd edition 1975]
Wittgenstein, Ludwig (1998) *Preliminary Studies for the "Philosophical Investigations"*, Generally Known as The Blue and Brown Books, Oxford: Blackwell. [2nd edition 1969]
Wittgenstein, Ludwig (1998) *Remarks on the Philosophy of Psychology, Volume I*, eds. G.E.M. Anscombe and G.H. von Wright, trans. G.E.M. Anscombe, Oxford: Blackwell. [1st pub. 1980]
Wittgenstein, Ludwig (2001) *Tractatus Logico-Philosophicus*, trans. D.F. Pears and B.F. McGuinness with an introduction by Bertrand Russell, London/New York: Routledge.
Wollenberg, David (2013) "Nietzsche, Spinoza, and the Moral Affects", in: *Journal of the History of Philosophy* 51(4), 617–649.
Wood, Allen (2003) "Kant and the Problem of Human Nature", in: Allen Wood (ed.), *Essays on Kant's Anthropology*, Cambridge: Cambridge University Press.
Wotling, Patrick (1999) *La pensée du sous-sol. Statut et structure de la psychologie dans la philosophie de Nietzsche*, Paris: Éditions Allia.
Wotling, Patrick (1999) *Nietzsche et le problème de la civilisation*, Paris: Presses Universitaires de France.
Wotling, Patrick (2011) "What Language do Drives Speak?", in: J. Constâncio and M.J. Mayer Branco (eds.), *Nietzsche on Instinct and Language*, Berlin: De Gruyter.
Wright, Crispin (1988) "Realism, Antirealism, Irrealism, Quasi-Realism", in: P. French et al. (eds.), *Midwest Studies in Philosophy*, Notre Dame: University of Notre Dame Press.
Wright, Crispin (1992) *Truth and Objectivity*, Cambridge, MA: Harvard University Press.

Wurzer, William (1975) *Nietzsche und Spinoza* (Monographien zur philosophischen Forschung, vol. 141), Meisenheim am Glan: Anton Hain.
Yeats, W.B. (1961) *Essays and Introductions*, New York: Collier Books.
Yovel, Yirmiyahu (1992) *Spinoza and Other Heretics*, vol. 2., Princeton: Princeton University Press.
Zavatta, Benedetta (2013) "Historical Sense as Vice and Virtue in Nietzsche's Reading of Emerson", in: *Journal of Nietzsche Studies* 44(3), 372–397.
Zima, Peter V. (2000) *Theorie des Subjekts. Subjektivität und Identität zwischen Moderne und Postmoderne*, Tübingen/Basel: UTB.
Žižek, Slavoj (2012) *Less Than Nothing*, London: Verso.

List of Contributors/Affiliations

Isabelle Wienand
Universität Basel

David Wollenberg
University of Chicago

Nikolaos Loukidelis
Berlin-Brandenburgische Akademie der Wissenschaften

Christopher Brinkmann
Technische Universität Berlin

Paul Katsafanas
Boston University

Luís de Sousa
Universidade Nova de Lisboa/Faculdade de Ciências Sociais e Humanas

Marta Faustino
Universidade Nova de Lisboa/Faculdade de Ciências Sociais e Humanas

Pietro Gori
Universidade Nova de Lisboa/Faculdade de Ciências Sociais e Humanas

Anthony Jensen
Providence College

Giuliano Campioni
University of Pisa

Maria Cristina Fornari
University of Salento

Benedetta Zavatta
École Normale Supérieure de Paris/CNRS/ITEM

João Constâncio
Universidade Nova de Lisboa/Faculdade de Ciências Sociais e Humanas

Bartholomew Ryan
Universidade Nova de Lisboa/Faculdade de Ciências Sociais e Humanas

John Richardson
New York University

Sebastian Gardner
University College London

Yannick Souladié
Université de Toulouse

Keith Ansell-Pearson
University of Warwick

Jaanus Sooväli
University of Tartu

Maria João Mayer Branco
Universidade Nova de Lisboa/Faculdade de Ciências Sociais e Humanas

Werner Stegmaier
Universität Greifswald

Sofia Miguens
Universidade do Porto/Faculdade de Letras/Instituto & Departamento de Filosofia/MLAG (Mind Language Action Group)

Mattia Riccardi
Universität Bonn

Paolo Stellino
Universidade Nova de Lisboa/Faculdade de Ciências Sociais e Humanas

Brian Leiter
University of Chicago

Ken Gemes
Birkbeck College London

Imogen Le Patourel
Birkbeck College London

Herman Siemens
Leiden University/UDP (adjunct)

Robert B. Pippin
University of Chicago

Index

Actio in distans (see *also* Pathos of distance) 9, 96, 98, 104, 403
Action/ Deed(s) 1, 9, 11, 18, 27, 40, 43–44, 53, 69–70, 75, 79, 86, 96, 98, 104, 111–115, 117–118, 120–121, 126–127, 132, 139, 144, 150, 153–164, 166, 185, 187, 216, 246, 250–251, 260, 263–264, 273, 347, 359, 368, 377, 403, 408, 426, 462, 492–493, 495, 506–507, 524, 561–563, 564–565, 576–577, 579, 585–586, 588, 599, 603, 608, 621, 623, 640–641, 656–663, 666–667
Actor 24, 309–310, 312, 400
Adaptation 21, 244–245, 247, 249, 553
Adequacy/ Adequation (see also Correspondence) 16–17, 88–93, 208, 210–211, 465, 470
Adualism 2, 10, 53, 150
Affect(s)/affection(s) 3–5, 8, 11, 18, 29, 39–40, 65, 67–83, 89–93, 103, 117–118, 120, 124–125, 144, 149, 152–153, 160–161, 186, 193, 197, 207, 236, 250, 256, 265, 273, 279, 280, 282–283, 286, 291, 294, 303, 308, 324, 357–358, 371, 377, 380, 400, 402–403, 405, 413, 423, 427, 433, 441, 481, 492–493, 537, 552, 555, 557, 559–560, 569, 574–595, 619, 635–637, 650
Affirmation (of Life) 8, 23, 28–29, 35, 66, 71, 74, 77, 81–89, 92–93, 104, 285, 299, 315, 334–337, 338, 378, 385, 389–390, 407, 604
Agency/agent 1, 3, 5, 7, 27–28, 34, 40–42, 55, 119–120, 126–128, 144, 153, 156–157, 159–161, 183, 185, 187, 190–193, 196, 213, 255, 260, 262, 272, 280, 282–283, 287, 300, 307–308, 343–344, 357–360, 368–369, 371, 379, 381, 399, 429, 493–494, 506, 516–517, 526, 539, 550, 555, 560–563, 569, 578, 581–583, 585, 594, 599, 608, 620, 622–623, 630, 637, 639, 652, 654, 658–662, 666
Agonism 8, 69, 80, 199, 499
Althusser, L. 285, 441

Altruism *see* Egoism/Altruism
Amiel 221
Amor fati 24, 67, 70, 77, 84–85, 88–89, 92–93, 258, 270, 317–319, 334, 335–336, 338
Analogy 49, 96, 98–99, 104, 137–138, 147, 160, 189, 399, 657
Andreas-Salomé, L. 68
Animality 7, 54–55, 111–112, 148, 154–155, 162, 236, 237, 244, 290–292, 294, 305, 357–358
Anthropomorphism(s) 72, 98, 231, 282, 631
Anti-humanism 30, 413
Anti-realism 15, 16–17, 28, 36, 38, 40, 198, 206, 209–211, 571, 586–587, 589–590
Apperception 1, 9–10, 111–116, 119–122, 129–130, 376
Arendt, H. 313–314, 647
Aristotle 95, 102, 201, 302–304
Art/artists 20, 29, 40, 60, 66, 75, 143, 219, 221, 223, 225, 228, 231, 236, 259, 271, 293, 298, 304, 309–310, 313, 327, 329–330, 335, 339, 369, 395–396, 413, 419, 427, 431, 437, 487, 504, 607–608, 613–614, 617–618, 655, 662
Asceticism/ascetic ideal 117, 219, 225, 229, 287–288, 291, 311, 611–612
Assimilation, *see* Incorporation
Atomism 3, 5, 20, 183, 192, 286, 290, 294, 462, 560, 606
Authenticity 27, 30, 33, 41, 307, 349, 353–354, 427, 662
Autobiography 50, 57, 60–61, 221, 328
Autonomy 179, 190, 249–250, 343, 359–360, 373, 379, 425, 428, 442–443, 490, 501, 565, 622, 630, 636–638, 643, 649
Avenarius, R. 173, 205

Bacon, F. 50
Bagehot, W. 236–238
Balzac, H. de 56–57, 223, 228, 231
Barthes, R. 280, 448
Bataille, G. 413, 498

Baudelaire, C. 221
Beckett, S. 339
Becoming What/Who one is 22, 40, 261, 264–265, 267, 331, 333, 389, 568, 598–600, 610, 614–616, 625
Benjamin, W. 318, 339
Berkeley, G. 242
Berlin, I. 240
Bilderrede 28, 382
Biopolitics 422
Blanchot, M. 413
Body 11, 34, 37, 140–141, 144, 147, 287, 357, 495, 504, 522–523, 533, 535, 537, 545, 547–548, 603, 606, 610, 616, 623
Body without organs 400
Boscovich, R. 9, 198
Bourget, P. 19–20, 42–43, 219–233, 286, 294, 462
Brandes, G. 24, 220, 223, 225, 317, 320–321, 331, 399
Brentano, F. 12, 168, 171, 304
Buddhism 232, 344
Burckhardt, J. 311, 329, 398
Byron, Lord 270, 380

Campos, A. de 339
Camus, A. 24, 55, 313–314
Care 27, 29–31, 313, 350, 364, 413–414, 419–425, 429–432, 655, 663–665
Carey, H. 236, 238
Cartesianism 1–2, 7–8, 11, 32, 35, 37–38, 44, 49–62, 132, 133, 135, 141, 157, 158, 285, 289, 307, 402, 426, 440–441, 443, 445, 451, 457–463, 469, 511, 603
Cassirer, E. 97, 205, 489
Causality/causation/ causal efficiency 2, 9, 12, 16–18, 22, 27, 39, 41, 52–53, 71–79, 84, 88–93, 96, 118–119, 126, 128, 133, 135–138, 140, 144, 154, 157–161, 166–167, 169, 174–176, 183, 186–189, 191–192, 199, 200–201, 209–210, 259, 262–264, 283, 294, 302–303, 347, 355, 368, 401–402, 406, 443, 461–463, 470, 500, 543-545, 554–556, 560, 567, 570, 574–575, 577–579, 581–583, 588, 592–593, 598–599, 601, 604, 608–609, 657, 660, 666

Chaos 34, 72, 86–90, 93, 251, 295–296, 314, 494, 554, 566, 616
Character 1, 11, 22–23, 26, 31, 51, 60, 102, 117, 124, 127, 135, 146, 153–156, 159–163, 254–275, 309, 327, 330–331, 334, 370, 381, 401, 426, 429, 446, 487, 584, 612, 613
Christianity 3, 25, 31, 85, 133, 167, 192, 219, 223, 279, 289, 292–293, 311, 321, 326–327, 331, 333–334, 339, 384, 406, 421, 429–431, 561, 578–580, 582, 601–602, 611
Cioran, E. 339
Civilization (see *also* Culture) 227, 238, 321–322, 369, 373, 377, 386, 387
Cogito/I think 1, 24, 32–33, 49–50, 52, 57, 61–62, 111, 128, 132, 134–135, 138–139, 141, 153, 166–167, 183, 186, 189, 191, 192, 279, 312, 401, 442–444, 447, 449–450, 458, 461–463, 466, 469, 473, 543–544, 553, 601
Cognition *see* Knowledge
Cohen, H. 202
Communication 4, 6, 34–35, 203, 304–308, 323, 446, 450, 455, 464–465, 478, 481, 484, 497, 499, 504–507, 513, 605, 609
Community 21–22, 127, 160, 169, 235–236, 239, 241, 247–248, 280, 289, 291, 306, 310, 312–313, 352, 358, 432, 469, 484, 544, 633
Compassion (see *also* Pity) 120, 240, 260, 274, 291, 423, 426, 431, 602
Concepts/Conceptualization 4, 6, 15–16, 18, 31–32, 35–36, 101, 119, 148, 153, 197–198, 200, 203, 207, 210–211, 214, 282, 305–307, 400, 448, 488, 497, 513, 571, 589, 612, 633
Conscience 71, 122–125, 167, 219, 291, 294, 296, 299, 369, 373, 388, 424, 427, 564–565, 579, 597, 608, 610, 619, 640–641, 662
Consciousness 1–5, 9–11, 12–19, 20, 24, 26–27, 33–36, 40–41, 53–54, 100, 104–105, 111–119, 131–160, 172, 187–188, 191, 196–217, 226–228, 236, 242–243, 246, 279–309, 312–315, 335, 344–346, 357–360, 369–375, 377–379,

381–383, 413, 425, 437–439, 446–450, 458, 463–464, 468–471, 478, 483–484, 490–494, 496–498, 499, 511–528, 546, 548, 552, 553, 555–556, 562, 597–626, 630, 632–633
- as 'accidens of representation' 9, 105, 152, 199
- as 'mirror' 9, 18, 29, 102, 145–147, 152, 199–201, 212, 217, 280, 302, 552, 604
- as 'net'/'connecting-net' 4, 24, 33, 199, 280, 306, 312, 467–468, 482, 514, 605
- as 'surface' 2–4, 11, 27, 29, 36, 118, 120, 121, 129, 131, 146–147, 188, 199–201, 207–211, 217, 280, 282, 293, 301, 307, 312, 515, 552, 555, 562, 565, 603–604, 609–610, 613
- as 'tool' 11, 18, 27, 29, 41, 131, 145, 147–149, 199, 201, 210, 212, 217, 280, 287, 303–304, 306, 429, 533, 547, 552, 599, 604, 610, 626
- as 'superfluous' 17–18, 146, 301–303, 604, 606
Constructivism 500
Continuum 10, 106, 118, 149, 153, 196, 212, 280, 594
Correspondence (see *also* Adequacy) 80, 138, 204, 374, 470, 491
Couturat, L. 97
Culture (see *also* Civilization) 40, 66, 202, 216, 229–230, 232, 248, 269, 292, 298, 339, 361, 387, 411, 455–457, 580, 583–585, 616

Damasio, A. 35, 522–524, 527
Darwin, C. 237, 571
Darwinism 21, 70, 234, 236–237, 358, 570–571, 639
Dasein 27, 84, 304, 344, 346, 348–354, 364–365
Death 68, 314, 353–354, 363–364, 422, 637, 648
Death of God 6, 19–20, 23–24, 58, 172, 281, 285, 288–289, 298, 300–301, 311–312, 313, 319, 339, 418
Death of the Subject/Man/Author 23–24, 280–281, 288–289, 319, 322, 327, 337, 441, 448

Décadence/Decadence 19–20, 219, 221–223, 228–233, 265, 285–286, 294–295, 311, 361, 409, 462, 563
Decentred Subjectivity/Decentredness 23–24, 279–316
Deconstruction 31, 131, 364, 412, 427, 436–447
Deed(s) *see* Action
Deleuze, G. 28–29, 319, 394–409, 412–413, 419, 657
Dennett, D. 32, 34–35, 38, 511–528, 539, 570, 572
Derrida, J. 31, 436–452, 487, 502
Descartes, R. 1, 3, 7, 16, 24, 33, 42, 49–62, 81, 98, 107, 131–133, 139, 142, 166–167, 183, 220–221, 279–280, 282, 307, 312, 345, 401, 409, 414, 442–443, 445, 449–450, 454, 458–463, 466, 481, 488–491, 494–495, 499–500, 507, 536, 603, 623
Desubjectification 28, 492, 496, 505
Deussen, P. 133, 395, 398
Différance 31, 447–451
Dionysian/Dionysus 23, 25, 84, 89, 275, 318, 362, 396, 398–399, 408, 438, 662
Doctrine of types 39–40, 196–197, 206, 583–584
Dostoevsky, F. M. 19, 220, 222–223, 320–321, 397, 553
'Double aspect' *see* Parallelism
Drive for causality: *see* Ursachentrieb
Drive/Trieb 3–5, 9–11, 15, 17–18, 27–28, 39–41, 69–70, 83, 87, 90, 96, 103–104, 118, 120, 126, 131, 138, 142–163, 188, 190, 193, 196–201, 207–216, 226, 235–236, 239–240, 244, 247, 256, 258–264, 268, 274, 280–284, 286, 291, 294–295, 299, 303, 306, 308, 324, 346, 349, 356–364, 367–391, 400–403, 406, 413, 415, 423–429, 437, 440–441, 447, 452, 463, 511, 523, 537–548, 552, 555, 559–560, 564, 569, 574–576, 579–587, 597–626, 635–652, 656, 659
Drossbach, M. 9–10, 15, 97, 99–100, 103, 106, 205
Du Bois-Reymond, E. 12, 99, 172–173, 177, 205

Dualism 1-3, 9–11, 149, 153, 157, 167, 183, 187, 190, 279–81, 400, 459, 524, 546, 559
Dühring, E. 53, 68, 99, 249, 505

Ego 11, 23, 25–26, 31–32, 40, 52, 55, 128, 133, 136–137, 140, 142, 145, 148, 181–185, 187, 199, 207, 215, 236, 241, 247, 250–251, 260, 271, 273–274, 329, 356–358, 373, 376, 378–379, 381–382, 389, 400, 411, 413, 426–427, 430–431, 442, 446, 451, 458, 459–460, 463, 466, 469, 482, 484, 491, 544, 598–600, 602–603, 615, 623–626, 645–646
Egoism/altruism 21, 66, 69, 79, 235, 239–240, 249–251, 260, 357–358, 373, 378–379, 421, 602, 643, 645–646
Eliminism 3–4, 33
Elisabeth of Bohemia 53-54
Embodiment 2, 5–6, 35–36, 38, 132, 138–140, 196, 251, 521–528, 533–548, 637
Emerson, R. W. 22–23, 215, 254–275, 328, 662
Emotions (see *also* Affects) 37, 39, 73, 121, 139, 174, 240, 271–272, 327, 417, 424, 481, 523, 536, 541, 550, 560, 565, 577–578, 581–582, 588, 592–593, 606, 621
Empfindung (see *also* Sensation) 9, 100, 105, 179, 205, 290, 629, 630–633, 635, 641–647
Enlightenment 33, 65, 281, 292, 319, 368, 431, 488
Epictetus 31, 420, 430–431, 433
Epiphenomenalism 2, 5–6, 13, 16–18, 41, 160, 188, 196–201, 211–212, 302–303, 358, 514, 548, 604
Espinas, A. 235, 246–247, 249
Esposito, R. 422–423
Essence 55, 72, 78, 87–89, 142, 154–155, 161, 163, 245, 254, 260–262, 318, 353, 365, 379, 402–405, 407, 416, 438, 440, 449, 466–467, 472, 478, 488, 515, 522, 568, 583, 605
Euripides 647
Evaluation(s) *see* Valuations

Evolution(ism) (see *also* Darwinism) 2, 5, 17–18, 21–22, 24, 35–36, 38, 50, 131, 143, 234–252, 280, 283, 301–304, 417, 499, 523, 550–551, 570–572, 584, 605
Existential(ism) 6, 8, 19–21, 23–26, 28, 36, 67, 187, 279–315, 318, 339, 344, 352–353, 390, 413, 465, 626
Expressivism 5, 11, 26, 33, 42–43, 75, 91, 158, 161–162, 215, 465, 475, 654–667

Falsification 62, 128, 135, 191–192, 250, 296, 374, 377, 440, 443, 461, 467, 525, 527, 542, 553
Fatalism 84–85, 88, 155–156, 163, 229, 255
Fechner, G. 12, 166, 168–172, 178–181
Feré, C. 231
Fichte, J. G. 26, 28, 280, 314–315, 343, 391, 441
Fictions 1–2, 11–13, 23, 26, 104, 138, 157, 185–191, 206, 213, 243, 280, 298, 312, 357–358, 360, 378–379, 383, 390, 416, 425, 427, 440, 442–443, 445, 462–463, 465, 469, 479, 481, 493, 496, 512, 527, 541, 554, 560, 602, 657
First-Person/First-Personal Perspective 1–2, 4–7, 12–15, 19–20, 24, 26, 29, 32, 37–38, 44, 49–50, 55–62, 140, 281–285, 300, 308, 315, 350–351, 356, 380–381, 385, 471, 478, 517, 543–545, 547
Fischer, K. 8, 15, 67–83, 85, 87–88, 91–92, 99, 238
Flaubert, G. 227
Foucault, M. 29–30, 69, 245, 280, 411–423, 425, 427, 431–433, 441, 451, 487
Fouillée, A. 221, 235, 246–247, 249
Free spirit 7, 22, 27, 50, 59, 222, 224, 266, 288–289, 299, 309, 360–362, 415, 432, 484
Freedom 24, 27, 41–42, 68–69, 75, 78, 81–82, 84, 127, 153, 156–158, 160–161, 163, 209, 246, 256, 258–260, 262–264, 272, 299, 301, 311–313, 354, 359, 361–362, 368–369, 374, 389, 418, 420–422, 426, 427, 429, 432, 484, 493–494, 500–501, 508, 562, 580–583, 600–601, 614, 619–620, 629, 633, 635–640, 648, 650, 657, 661–662, 665–666

French *Moralistes* 42–43, 286, 328, 376, 462, 492, 527, 654–656, 658
French Psychologists 19, 20, 42, 219–233, 243, 286, 462
Freud, S. 27–28, 31, 367–391, 427, 436, 439, 441, 449, 451, 575, 586, 589, 597, 600, 604
Functionalism 35, 38, 511, 514–517, 520–524

Genealogy 5, 10, 17, 20, 38, 61, 126–129, 215–216, 227, 229, 243, 245, 361, 364–365, 412, 416–418, 439, 442, 495, 550–572, 608–609, 611, 659
Genius 236, 391, 553, 563, 594–595, 616
Genius of the Species 306–307, 446, 632
Gerber, G. 198
German Idealism *see* Idealism
Gersdorff, C. von 202–203, 207, 211
Goethe, J.W. von 68, 84, 220, 229, 241, 255–256, 273–274, 362, 455, 598, 600, 614, 621
Goncourt, E. and J. 225, 230–232
Grammar 13, 32, 53, 86, 121, 133, 136–138, 167, 183, 281, 283, 331, 383, 444, 446, 449, 454–484, 487, 536, 544–545
Guilt 27, 39, 156, 354, 361, 363, 369, 424, 495, 562, 577, 581–583
Guyau, J.-M. 235, 246–248

Habermas, J. 65, 107, 488
Habit 50–53, 136, 138, 183, 220, 238, 274, 310, 358, 380, 383, 416, 428, 462, 466, 481, 492, 601, 635, 643, 645–646, 449
Hadot, P. 430, 432
Hartmann, E. von 216, 221
Health 18, 58, 61, 162, 216, 223, 227–229, 233, 265, 269, 288, 294, 300, 325, 362, 364–367, 495, 602, 613, 620
Hegel, G. W. F. 26, 157, 221, 242, 280, 314–315, 317, 324, 338, 413, 439, 441, 489
Hegelianism 24, 216, 285, 313, 565–666
Heidegger, M. 25–27, 31, 42, 49–50, 157, 304, 317–318, 343–365, 436, 439, 441–442, 449, 493, 497, 502, 654–655, 662
Helmholtz, H.L. von 13, 15, 196–217
Heraclitus 213, 271, 558

Herbart, J.F. 169–171, 177–178, 185
Herd/Herd-Perspective/Herd-Instinct 21–22, 27, 31, 147, 162, 234, 239, 246, 248–250, 266, 280, 288–294, 298, 300, 306–308, 312–313, 348, 358–364, 468–469, 518, 533, 546, 590, 607–612, 623, 625, 632, 634, 636, 648, 651
Heritability (see *also* Inheritance) 39, 584–585
Higher Men/Higher Individuals/Higher Types 21–22, 60, 162, 249–250, 260, 292, 294, 396, 433, 484, 623
Historical sense 273, 293, 295, 300, 418
Hobbes, T. 248, 637
Honesty 25, 57, 117, 124, 281, 284, 297, 314, 319, 322, 327, 338, 361, 414, 429, 566–567, 666
Horace 219
HOT (High Order Thoughts) 303-304, 519–523
Hume, D. 88, 132, 242, 367, 451, 491, 518, 586, 589, 591–592, 595, 608–609
Husserl, E. 31, 34, 36, 304, 317, 346, 436, 442, 450–451, 488, 527
I (see *also* Self, Subject, Apperception, Consciousness, and *Cogito/I think*) 26, 40–41, 57, 111, 115, 128, 132–142, 147, 167–193, 226–228, 232, 234–235, 240, 241, 243, 250–251, 279, 281–283, 286–287, 307, 315, 328, 344–365, 367, 376–385, 391, 396–401, 406, 443, 444, 454, 457–463, 469–484, 512, 516–519, 534, 542–545, 547–548, 557, 578, 599–606, 610, 612, 615, 621, 624–626, 660–662
— The I of apperception 1
— The I of consciousness 26, 41, 147, 307, 601, 603, 626
"I think", see *Cogito/ I think*
I of apperception, *see* Apperception and I
Idealisation 22, 292, 311, 631
Idealism 4–6, 102, 170, 202–203, 207–208, 220, 224, 318, 337, 370, 430, 452
— German Idealism 24, 26, 255, 322, 497
'Immediate Certainty'/ 'Immediate Certainties' 52, 62, 128, 136, 141–142, 166–167, 189, 192, 281–282, 284, 296,

307, 377, 383, 401, 443, 444–445, 458, 460–461, 543, 553, 556, 560
In-itself, *see* Thing in-itself
Incorporation 61, 302, 356, 362, 605, 635–638, 644, 648–649, 651
Individual/individuality/individuation 1, 20–22, 27–28, 31–34, 40–42, 72–73, 75, 78, 87–88, 135, 138, 140, 148, 150, 152–164, 167, 180–182, 186, 209, 216, 221, 223, 227, 235–252, 255–275, 280, 289, 291, 294–295, 299–300, 306–309, 310–315, 319, 321, 327, 331, 334, 338, 340, 353–354, 358–359, 364, 370, 372, 374, 378–379, 381, 387, 391, 395, 412, 414, 421–425, 427, 429–430, 433, 437–438, 446, 454, 459, 465–469, 477–478, 480, 484, 487, 488, 494, 496, 497, 504, 506, 539, 540, 544, 554, 556, 577, 579–582, 584, 607–610, 611–613, 616–618, 625–626, 639, 646, 650, 659
Inheritance (see *also* Heritability) 39, 584–585
Inner Sense 110, 112–116, 122, 128, 139–140, 142, 146, 186, 494, 552
Instinct 3, 5, 7, 15, 18, 41, 50, 61, 65, 90, 131, 143, 150–153, 160–162, 163, 183, 190, 198, 207, 212, 214–216, 231–232, 235–236, 238–241, 244, 246, 248, 250, 251, 265, 271, 273, 279–280, 289–295, 298–300, 306–307, 314, 321, 359, 369, 371, 378, 379, 386–387, 390, 402–403, 415, 417, 452, 498, 506, 523, 563, 597–598, 604–605, 613–614, 616, 618–621, 623–625, 629–652, 659–660, 665
Intellectual Conscience *see* Conscience
Intentionality 4–5, 26, 44, 157, 304–306, 346, 349–350, 363, 365, 383, 523, 526, 538, 540, 577–578, 655, 663
Intermittence/Intermittenzen 35, 513, 517, 521, 526–527, 605
Intersubjectivity 4–6, 24, 32–33, 44, 148, 203, 281, 306, 309, 315, 459, 477, 488, 650
Introspection (see *also* Self-observation) 5, 13, 17, 32–33, 37–38, 43, 111–112, 116–119, 121–125, 129, 139, 141, 267, 282–284, 307–308, 454–484, 497, 517,

519, 536, 541, 543, 545, 547–548, 594, 601, 603, 655
Intuition 112–114, 206, 458–460, 571, 592
Irony 25, 228, 251, 299, 319, 323, 482, 584
Irrationality 36, 79, 82, 90, 111, 144–145, 149, 154, 160, 264, 337, 371, 375, 381, 581, 591

Jaspers, K. 24, 319, 405
Jesus 25, 219–220, 229, 331, 333, 340, 396
Joyce, J. 38, 322, 328, 334
Judgement 36, 39–40, 78, 81, 112–113, 115–116, 119–123, 129, 139, 153, 189, 197, 214, 238–239, 251, 381, 526, 551, 560, 564–569, 575–595, 616, 620–624, 635–637 641–642, 645, 649, 657

Kafka, F. 339
Kant, I. 1, 10, 12, 16, 24, 28, 62, 71, 95, 97–98, 103, 110–129, 132–140, 145, 154, 166, 169–170, 202–203, 205–206, 280, 314, 317, 350, 354, 367, 384, 391, 415, 441–442, 487–488, 491–494, 498–502, 505–506, 556, 561, 564–565, 592, 622–623, 625, 662
Kepler, J. 177
Kierkegaard, S. 24–25, 317–340, 376
Knowledge/ Cognition (see *also* Self-knowledge) 5, 7, 10, 12, 17, 30, 32–33, 35, 37, 43, 49, 54, 58–59, 65, 67, 69 75, 77, 80–93, 99, 103, 104, 107, 111–116, 119, 121–122, 124, 126, 128–129, 132, 134–135, 137, 139–140, 144–145, 146, 153–154, 158, 160, 168–173, 177, 183, 184–185, 190–191, 193, 201, 203–204, 206–207, 210, 215–216, 219–220, 222, 228, 233, 244–245, 255, 261, 268, 270–273, 282–285, 297, 299–302, 304–305, 307, 321, 329, 332, 337–338, 368, 375, 384, 413–422, 423, 427, 428, 430, 432, 437–439, 440, 443, 458, 461–463, 466–467, 470, 472–473, 475, 478, 481, 484, 493, 501, 520, 526–528, 538, 542, 546, 550, 553–554, 557, 561, 566-568, 570, 589–590, 601, 610, 623–624, 648, 655
Kopernicus, N. 177

Index — 703

La Rochefoucauld, F. de 42, 221, 286, 594, 654
Lacan, J. 24, 300, 308, 441
Lamarck, J.B. 257, 584
Lamarckianism 39–40, 584
Lange, F.A. 7, 12–15, 16–17, 20, 23, 28, 31, 38, 43, 68, 99, 166, 168, 170–171, 173–179, 182, 184–187, 190–191, 193, 197–198, 202–214, 216, 241, 260, 282–285, 296, 306, 308, 314, 463
Language 3, 6, 31, 32–33, 34–35, 37, 101, 104, 119, 137, 148, 156, 183, 186, 205, 216, 280, 282–283, 296, 305–307, 313, 331, 352–354, 426, 438, 440, 442, 444, 446–452, 457, 459, 460–461, 465, 467–484, 494, 511–521, 522, 525–527, 536, 542–543, 552, 600, 604–605, 609, 612, 632–634, 639, 642, 657
Last Man 249, 288, 292, 298, 312, 664–665
Leibniz, G.W. 8–9, 16, 95–100, 102, 104–107, 152, 199, 280, 498, 513, 603, 657
Leopardi, G. 270, 317–318
Levinas, E. 436, 487
Lichtenberg, G.C. 182–183
Liebmann, O. 9–10, 15, 70, 97–99, 103–106, 170, 198
Locke, J. 242
Logic 185–186, 189, 242, 406, 556, 591, 660
Lubbock, J. 236
Luhmann, N. 32–34, 488–489, 491–494, 497, 499–506
Lukács, G. 24
Luther, M. 318

Mach, E. 12, 20, 168, 171–173, 178–186, 190–191, 193, 198, 204
Machado, A. 328
Madness 29, 117, 323, 325, 337, 399–400, 437
Marx, K. 441
Mask 24, 25, 225, 266, 296, 309–314, 317–318, 327, 333, 335, 340, 416, 467
Materialism 168, 174, 176, 191–192, 201, 226, 408, 451, 523–524, 574
Metaethics 38, 571, 577
Metaphor(s) 18, 28, 143, 151, 174, 199–200, 210, 232, 255, 257, 280, 302–304, 324–325, 329, 333, 382, 496–497, 499, 503, 505–507, 518, 527, 574–575, 659

Metaphysics 12–14, 19–20, 23, 32, 35, 42–43, 50, 53, 55, 66–67, 83, 85, 89–90, 95, 101, 106, 111, 128, 138, 157, 166–193, 219–221, 225–226, 234, 242, 246, 260, 262, 272, 281, 285, 287, 356, 360, 376, 405, 408, 416–418, 426–427, 432, 438–439, 441, 444, 449–450, 455, 458–459, 462–464, 470, 472, 475, 476, 478, 490–491, 502, 508, 512, 526, 528, 544, 556, 559–560, 567, 582, 586–591, 600, 639, 650, 654–656
Miles, T.P. 319, 338–339
Mill, J.S. 238, 242, 247
Modern philosophy 1, 3–4, 7, 23–25, 33–34, 44, 49–50, 54–55, 99, 106, 127, 132–133, 138–139, 167, 279–282, 284–285, 289, 318, 340, 390, 414, 457, 480, 487–488, 503, 561, 603
Modernism 25, 317, 330, 339, 442
Modernity 6, 20, 23–25, 28, 30–31, 132–133, 220, 223, 227, 231–232, 235, 238, 269, 279–286, 289–295, 298, 300, 308, 309–315, 318, 321–322, 327, 330, 332, 334, 336, 368, 370, 386–388, 415, 421, 422–425, 429–433, 455, 487, 489–490, 499, 501, 594, 615–616, 618, 648, 651, 661
Monads/Monadology 8–10, 95–96, 99–102, 107, 193, 294, 601, 606
Monism 12, 168, 178–179, 182
Montaigne, M. 42–43, 54–56, 654
Montesquieu, C.-L. de Secondat, Baron de 425
Moral Judgement(s) 561, 564, 579, 582, 586, 593
Morality 3, 21, 35–36, 38–40, 42–43, 51–52, 56, 58, 66, 69–70, 74–75, 86, 111, 113–114, 119, 122–124, 126, 156–157, 159, 167, 219, 223–224, 227, 230–231, 234–236, 240–241, 243–251, 255–256, 262–265, 274, 279, 286, 289–293, 296–297, 330, 359–362, 364, 369, 373, 375, 379, 381, 384–386, 404, 408–409, 411–412, 421–422–428, 430–431, 433, 439, 446, 482, 490–493, 495, 505, 508, 511, 525, 527–528, 550–551, 555, 560, 561–572, 574–595, 602, 611, 614, 618, 629–631, 634, 638–643, 645, 647–648, 650, 657–658, 660, 662, 666

Moral Values *see* Values
Moriarty, J. 326, 339
Müller, J. 170, 175, 198, 205
Müller-Lauter, W. 96, 209, 394, 634
Music 257, 294, 339, 585–586, 589
Myth/ Mythology 171, 176, 187, 202, 209, 221, 236, 262, 328–329, 336, 427, 467

Nagel, T. 515
Natorp, P. 202
Natural selection 21, 303, 538, 584
Naturalism 7, 12, 19–20, 26, 28, 198, 344, 363, 371, 433, 451, 511, 630–631, 639
Neo-Kantianism 12, 15, 43, 97, 197–198, 201–202, 205, 282, 284
Nerves/Nervous System 171, 175–176, 177, 182, 196, 203–204, 208–209, 228, 231, 242–243, 298, 401, 425, 524
Neurosis 386, 390, 426
Newton, I. 98–99
Newtonian Mechanics/ Physics 73, 172
Nihilism 6, 19, 20, 24, 40, 81, 224–225, 228, 250, 268, 285–288, 291–292, 298–299, 301, 312–315, 317–318, 334–337, 378, 387, 432, 455, 462, 496, 660, 664–665
Nobel, A. 399
Nobility/Noble 32, 51, 75, 237, 240, 290, 293, 295, 300, 408, 420, 467, 481, 483–484, 588
Norms 36, 40, 42, 44, 369, 374, 376, 386, 493, 589–591 630, 640–641, 663
Normativity 6, 21, 23, 285, 289, 374, 494, 578, 590–591, 608, 625–626, 630, 641
Nozik, R. 26

Objectivity 20, 102, 229, 268, 273, 281, 298, 322, 329, 375, 491–492, 498, 504, 587, 590,
Ontology 32, 42, 83, 86, 88–89, 142, 179, 460, 576, 579, 585, 594, 643–645, 647, 650, 662, 664
Order of Rank (*Rangordnung*) 5, 290, 294, 496, 583, 613, 622, 626, 632
Organism 11, 17–18, 40, 42, 87, 101, 129, 142, 144–148, 160, 171, 179, 187–188, 190, 201, 204, 206, 211–212, 214, 238–239, 245, 247–249, 256, 258, 260, 264, 302, 304, 306–307, 343, 355, 357, 362, 365, 378, 398, 513, 537, 539–541, 547, 559, 584, 605, 621, 634–639, 644, 648–649, 651
Orientation 33-34, 487–508
Overman (*Übermensch*) 235, 246, 249, 251, 267, 497

Pain (*see also* Suffering) 23, 32–33, 139, 182, 229, 237, 269, 270, 377, 379, 385–388, 426, 457, 463–469, 472–475, 478–480, 483, 536, 540, 579, 613, 615
Paradox 33–34, 168, 297, 317, 323, 326–327, 331, 337, 488–489, 491–496, 498, 501–503, 506–508, 554–555, 557, 566, 569, 599–600, 626, 664
Parallelism 2, 12–14, 180, 184, 495
Paralysis of Will *see* Will
Pascal, B. 42, 273, 320–321, 430, 654, 656
'Passion for knowledge' (*Leidenschaft derErkenntnis*) 30, 59, 68, 270, 337, 415–416
Pathos of distance 33, 294, 380, 481, 484
Perspectivism 4–5, 8–10, 95–96, 101–103, 206, 210, 307, 309, 440, 494–495, 498, 500, 504, 562, 571, 589–590, 624, 632, 635
Pessimism 61, 227–228, 231, 269–270, 298, 315, 387, 459, 527, 615
Pessoa, F. 325, 328, 339
'petits *faits vrais*' 20, 225, 228–229, 462
Phenomenalism 4–5, 15, 146, 282, 307, 309, 539, 550, 552–554, 556–557, 569
Phenomenology 2, 34, 344, 354, 363, 365, 411, 413, 433, 450, 488, 521, 522, 577
Philosophy of Mind 34–35, 37, 512, 528
Phrenology 174–175, 177, 256
Physicalism 1–2, 285, 469
Physiognomy: 197, 202–208, 214, 246
Physiology 2, 7, 9, 10, 12–16, 38, 41–42, 50, 54–55, 75, 104, 155, 168, 170, 173–178, 184–185, 187–191, 206, 214, 220, 223, 226–227, 229, 231–232, 235, 243, 245, 283, 298, 361, 381, 405–406, 408, 452, 527, 528, 538, 540–541, 544, 550, 559–561, 563, 565–566, 569, 575–576,

629–630, 634–635, 637, 639, 640–641, 643–644, 647–648, 650–651
— Socio-Physiology 41–42, 635, 637, 640–641, 647–648, 651
Physio-psychology 12, 38, 283, 560
Pity (*see also Compassion*) 117, 120–121, 289, 291–292, 373, 428, 458, 659
Plasticity 23, 233, 274, 290, 293–294, 296–297, 300
Plato 3, 23, 92, 202, 262, 272–273, 279, 281, 287–288, 432, 436, 502, 551, 655
Platonism 4, 416, 439, 662
Pleasure 20, 59, 76, 139, 160, 182, 220, 269, 298, 339, 370, 377, 386–387, 416, 420, 424, 429, 580, 635, 642, 649, 665
Podmore, S.D.: 338
Poincaré, H. 172
Postmodernity 2, 6, 24, 34, 280, 281, 283, 285, 315, 330, 441, 451
Power (see also Will to Power) 2–3, 5, 7–9, 15–18, 23, 30, 41, 51, 54, 59, 65–67, 69–91, 96, 98, 100–101, 103–104, 118, 121, 142–144, 150–151, 160, 162, 198–199, 207, 209, 212, 214, 216, 228, 240, 245, 249–251, 256, 259, 261, 264, 266–267, 270, 272, 274, 284, 291–292, 299, 314, 356–357, 359, 362, 364–365, 372, 374–375, 380, 395, 400–409, 412–414, 418–419, 421–423, 426, 429–430, 497–498, 501, 504, 507, 551, 601, 605, 607, 613
Private language 32, 33, 457, 471–484
Problem of Subjectivity 1, 2, 5–6, 9, 12–13, 15–16, 19–23, 28, 32, 36, 40, 44, 166, 279, 280–281, 283–286, 288, 290, 297, 307, 314, 394
Proust, M. 396
Psychoanalysis 308, 367–391, 414
Psychology 7–10, 12, 13, 15–16, 19–20, 27, 35–40, 42–44, 51, 55, 67, 69–73, 75–77, 83, 103–104, 113, 125–126, 134, 143, 155, 166–170, 173–179, 181–192, 196, 210, 215, 219–233, 240–243, 245–246, 249–250, 264, 283, 286, 302, 308, 317, 320–321, 329, 332, 334, 339–340, 361, 367–391, 403, 426, 473, 477, 490, 527–528, 550–551, 553, 555, 559–567,
569, 571–572, 574, 576–577, 583–586, 593–595, 598, 602, 654, 656–660, 662, 665
— French Psychology see French *Moralistes* and French Psychologists
— Moral Psychology 39, 191, 241, 243, 454, 574, 576, 585–586, 592, 594
– 'Psychology Without a Soul' 12, 14, 166, 168, 169, 171, 178, 185
— Scientific Psychology 12, 14, 171, 173–178, 191, 243
Psychophysics 12, 14, 168–169, 171, 178–181

Qualia 514, 517–518, 520, 577

Rank-order see Order of rank
Rationalism 27, 65, 107, 367, 389, 576, 592
Rationality 2, 3, 5, 8, 77–93, 128, 131, 150, 154, 160, 206, 264, 281, 368, 371, 375, 388, 390, 437, 526, 576, 591–592
Rawls, J. 629, 637
Reason 11, 13, 79–80, 90, 93, 128, 134, 136–137, 144, 159, 166, 169, 283, 378, 462–463, 571, 600
Rée, P. 21, 68, 234, 329, 571
Reflexivity see Self-reflection
Relativism 206, 236, 404, 498–499
Religion 60, 68, 85, 167, 223, 225, 229, 232, 265, 292, 324, 332, 385, 386, 418, 422, 666
Renan, E. 219, 224–225
Representation (*Vorstellung*) 4, 9, 15–16, 100, 105, 111–115, 134–135, 138, 140, 144, 148, 152, 167, 197–199, 201, 205–206, 208, 210–212, 214–215, 240, 251, 302, 304–305, 350, 369–371, 379, 401, 459, 471–472, 490, 519, 526, 538, 566, 575, 644
Responsibility 153, 156–157, 239, 246, 262, 264, 292, 324, 426, 437, 562, 582, 660
Ressentiment 119, 125, 220, 659
Revaluation/Transvaluation of Values (see also Valuation(s) and Values) 193, 219, 246, 274, 281, 295, 398–399, 407, 414, 469, 563, 613–614
Ribot, T. 19–20, 220, 226, 231–232, 243, 462
Riemann, B. 172

Ritschl, F. 198
Romanticism/Romantic 220, 224, 227, 318, 325, 370, 390, 527, 639
Rousseau, J.J. 390, 487, 662
Roux, W. 238, 245, 559, 634
Russell, B. 97, 180

Sainte-Beuve, C.-A. 224–225, 230
Sartre, J.P. 24, 314, 375, 500
Scepticism 5, 13–17, 19, 23, 28, 31, 38, 40, 41, 52, 56, 112, 122, 133, 167, 201, 268, 282–285, 296–301, 306, 308, 314, 375, 384, 411, 429, 463, 478, 541, 550, 552–553, 556, 557–559, 564, 566–569, 590, 592, 599–602, 604, 608–609, 616, 624
Schelling, F.W.J. 221, 179, 657
Schema/Schematism 101, 263, 295, 354, 408, 498, 646
Schiller, F. 384
Schopenhauer, A. 1–2, 4, 10–11, 16–18, 22, 24, 37, 43, 68, 128, 131–164, 197, 199–201, 203, 221–222, 234, 240, 260–262, 265, 270, 280, 282, 284–285, 291, 302, 328, 369–371, 377–379, 381, 387–388, 390–391, 401–402, 443, 459, 470, 513, 523, 535–536, 553, 556, 597, 602–603, 632, 643, 656, 658
Science 3, 12, 14, 15, 20, 24–25, 28, 29, 33, 38, 42, 43, 52, 54, 58, 66, 76, 83, 86, 95, 96, 99, 117, 153, 168–185, 191–192, 203, 205–206, 219, 223–226, 229, 230, 234–236, 240–243, 245, 248, 256, 260, 269, 271, 281, 286, 298, 339, 365, 367, 375, 377, 390, 406, 407, 411, 413, 418, 422, 430, 441, 451, 469 470, 487, 489, 491–492, 494–495, 497, 499, 504–507, 512–514, 525, 527, 566–567, 625
Self (see also I and Subject) 1, 2, 5, 7, 10–11, 13, 16–18, 22–44, 49–55, 61–62, 131–164, 196–201, 207, 209, 211–213, 214–217, 239, 242, 244–246, 250–251, 258, 262–267, 272, 275, 280, 287, 300, 307, 319, 322–323, 325, 328, 331, 336, 340, 343–365, 369–370, 379, 390, 411, 413–414, 417–422, 425, 427–429, 431, 432, 441, 446, 469, 457–460, 469–470, 472, 476, 511–528, 533–548, 550, 566, 567, 569, 574, 597, 599, 600–603, 606–610, 615–626, 629–652
Self-consciousness 1, 11, 13, 16–18, 33, 35, 41, 53, 69, 111–112, 139–140, 144, 279, 282, 302–303, 307, 315, 323, 327, 370, 377–382, 448, 458, 483–484, 542, 601, 604, 621, 630, 632–634, 642
Self-creation 21–22, 156, 295, 300, 376, 408, 412, 424, 567, 598–600, 606, 609–610, 626
Self-critique 20
Self-cultivation 31, 255, 419, 423, 428, 602
Self-deception 20, 23, 43, 81, 110, 114–117, 119, 122–124, 296–298, 332, 495, 562, 655, 659, 661, 664–666
Self-expression 313
Self-interest 117, 382, 643
Self-knowledge 5, 6, 10, 13, 16–17, 23, 31–33, 37–39, 43, 110–129, 139, 210, 269, 271, 282–284, 296–297, 306, 329, 427, 457–459, 463, 468, 471, 473, 480–481, 483–484, 550–569, 585, 601, 609, 610, 654–655
Self-legislation 42, 384, 412, 637–638, 662
Self-mastery 380, 430, 623
Self-narration/Self-narratives 58–61
Self-observation (see also Introspection) 13–14, 52, 34, 114, 116, 121, 128, 141, 146, 190, 200, 205, 270, 282, 443, 461–462, 494, 497, 553–558, 564–565, 569
Self-overcoming 356, 413, 599, 602, 665–666
Self-preservation 71, 72, 76–77, 91–92, 143, 236, 239, 311, 637
Self-reference/ Self-referentiality 4–5, 23, 38, 58, 288, 343–348, 350–352, 355, 359–360, 294–297, 477–478, 490–491, 499, 502–503, 525, 542–543, 547, 643, 645
Self-reflection/Reflexivity 1, 4–5, 26, 30, 33, 37, 294–296, 300, 302, 304–307, 314, 343–360, 363, 380, 398, 419, 559, 563, 602
Semper, K. 245

Sensation (see also Empfindung) 5, 9–10, 33, 100, 129, 169–171, 175–176, 178–183, 186–188, 190, 204, 241–243, 251, 257–258, 271, 290, 293, 304–305, 373, 380, 388, 473–478, 480, 539–540, 580, 633
Senses 15, 54, 68, 168, 170, 176, 204, 206, 207–208, 305–306, 464, 475
Shakespeare, W. 220, 308, 323, 325, 327, 330, 656
Sickness (see also Illness) 19, 61, 227–228, 321, 331, 367, 433, 597, 609, 611–612
Sign-Language(s) 39–40, 574–595
Signs 4, 15–17, 188–189, 204, 207, 211, 213–215, 282, 304–308, 313, 439, 447, 449–450, 464, 476–477, 497, 507, 525, 575, 609, 633
Socialization 248, 290–291, 641–642
Society of actors 24, 309–314
Society/sociability/sociality/social 3–5, 18, 21–22, 24, 27, 30, 33–34, 41–42, 70, 79, 125, 127, 148, 223, 227, 229, 234–252, 264–266, 279–281, 290–291, 300, 303, 305–308, 310, 313, 344, 352–354, 356, 358–360, 364–365, 368, 376, 386–387, 414, 420, 422, 427, 433, 440, 451, 459, 468, 488, 497, 499, 504–506, 552, 571, 579–580, 592, 605–606, 609, 617, 618, 621–622, 625, 629–652, 661–662
Socrates 3, 25, 279, 295, 299, 332, 340, 396, 419, 430, 551, 574, 647, 662
Solipsism 4, 20, 397, 459, 469, 470–471, 478, 482, 484
Soul 2–5, 7, 12, 14, 20, 35, 38, 43, 54–55, 70, 73, 90, 105, 107, 131, 133, 135, 139–143, 147, 151–152, 160, 166–193, 207, 209, 216, 225–229, 240, 242–243, 245–246, 258, 262, 271–273, 279, 283, 286–290, 292–297, 304, 324, 329, 361–362, 377–378, 383, 397, 414, 419, 430, 432–433, 438, 441, 451, 458, 462, 467, 469, 481, 484, 491, 523–525, 527, 533, 537–538, 540, 544–545, 548, 559–601, 606, 621, 655, 662
Sovereignty/Sovereign individual 22, 41, 42, 240, 272, 311, 425, 427, 487, 498, 507,
630, 634–635, 637–640, 643–644, 647–652, 660
Spencer, H. 21, 234–235, 242, 244–246, 248–249
Spinoza, B. de 7–8, 12, 16, 65–93, 107, 230–231, 238, 273, 280, 338, 367, 395, 657, 660
Spir, A. 53, 68, 99, 198, 443
Spirit (Geist) 3–4, 7, 19, 21–23, 24, 27, 50, 52, 54, 56, 59, 61, 84, 86, 104, 142, 152, 168, 171, 179, 181, 187, 192, 210, 220–224, 242, 249, 255, 258, 266, 268, 274, 279, 287–296, 298–301, 309, 311–314, 319–320, 338, 357, 359–362, 367, 382, 390–391, 415, 430–432, 484, 494, 495, 499, 559, 566, 601, 603, 610, 647
Spirituality 367, 496
Spiritualization 190
Stendhal [M.-H. Beyle] 19–20, 42, 220, 221–222, 224–225, 228–229, 330, 462
Stimuli (see also Nerves/nervous system) 148, 272, 274, 408, 586, 644
Stoicism/Stoics 31, 379, 387, 419, 421, 430, 431, 576
Strindberg, A. 398
Subject 1–8, 10–12, 16, 23–34, 36, 38–39, 42, 49, 52, 57, 62, 66, 95, 103–104, 107, 113, 114, 126, 128, 131–142, 144–145, 149, 153–154, 156–157, 160, 164, 166, 169, 174, 177, 182–183, 185, 187, 189–192, 201, 204, 214, 225, 227, 234–235, 240–251, 279–290, 299, 308–309, 315, 317–319, 322–328, 330–331, 333–340, 344–346, 348, 350, 357–359, 368, 370–371, 377–378, 395–397, 400–404, 409, 411–415, 417–422, 425–428, 431–432, 436 441–445, 447–449, 451–452, 455, 457–464, 466–480, 487–502, 504–508, 511, 513, 516–517, 527–528, 537, 544–545, 548, 553–554, 557, 560, 568–569, 602, 630, 643–645, 655, 657, 666
Subject-multiplicity (Subjekts-Vielheit) 3–4, 21–22, 38, 193, 226, 287, 289, 296, 300, 308, 324, 378, 540

Subjectivity (*see also* Problem of Subjectivity) 1–9, 11–26, 28–29, 31–34, 36, 38–40, 44, 49–50, 67, 69, 134, 141, 153, 158, 166–167, 186–187, 193, 197–198, 206–207, 309, 215, 226, 236, 243, 245–246, 272, 279–290, 293, 296–298, 300, 307–308, 314–315, 319–320, 322, 324–326, 330, 334–340, 360, 377–378, 440, 456–457, 469–471, 497, 505, 540, 560
Sublimation 41, 369, 599, 616–620, 623, 625, 626, 646
Substance 1, 4–5, 11, 14, 20, 29–30, 32, 42, 52–53, 86, 95, 102, 122, 135–138, 157, 161, 163, 166, 169, 174, 177, 179, 186, 192, 199, 231, 243, 261, 345, 350, 356, 371, 395, 403–404, 419, 438, 442, 447, 460–462, 464, 480, 491, 525, 600, 643–645, 647, 650, 657
Suffering (see *also* Pain) 19, 32–33, 140, 229, 232, 239, 269–270, 273, 290–292, 317, 338, 365, 380, 385–388, 390–391, 422, 424, 457, 462, 466, 467–468, 474–475, 483, 638, 646
Symptoms 17, 39–40, 96, 99, 118, 159, 176, 210, 229, 231, 402, 574–575, 582–583, 586

Taine, H. 19–20, 220, 222–232, 241–243, 286, 462
Taylor, C. 127, 512
Teichmüller, G. 9–10, 15, 43, 97, 101–103, 106, 443
Teleology 66, 69–70, 75, 85, 93, 245, 324, 338
Thathandlung 28, 391
Thing in-itself 98, 137, 146, 154, 181, 183–184, 203, 216, 282, 443, 461, 467, 553
Thucydides 594
Tocqueville, A. 425
Tolstoy, L. 232, 492
Tragedy/tragic 133, 313, 328, 397, 415, 455, 527, 615, 663
Trakl, G. 339
Truth 16–17, 25, 28, 33, 35, 51, 56, 58–59, 80, 83, 87, 90, 92, 123, 126, 189, 193, 206, 209, 210, 223, 225–226, 242, 268, 274, 281, 287– 288, 296, 310, 324, 326, 330, 333, 336–337, 339, 361, 374, 383, 385, 398, 404, 414–418, 421, 433, 438, 439–440, 446, 449, 457–458, 463, 465–466, 472, 502, 525–527, 570–572, 577, 582, 588, 590, 593, 611, 624, 644, 655–656
— 'figurative truths' 209
— 'truth is subjectivity' 25, 324, 327
— Will to Truth 28, 287, 299, 374, 383, 387, 611
Truthfulness 172, 397, 458, 563
Tylor, E.B. 236
Types/type-facts: *see* 'Doctrine of types'

Ueberweg, F. 53, 198
Umwelt 503
Unamuno, M. 325, 339
Unconsciousness/Unconscious 1, 3, 9–11, 13, 15–17, 18, 20, 22, 27, 20, 40, 51, 110, 119, 126, 131, 138, 144–145, 148–152, 161, 189, 192, 196–201, 204, 206, 210–214, 216, 227, 232, 250, 256, 263, 265, 280, 282, 284, 296, 287, 294, 301–302, 305, 358, 369–376, 382, 413–414, 422, 449, 517, 538, 542–543, 547–548, 556, 597, 602, 604–605, 610, 611–615, 624
Undeterminedness 23, 127, 285, 296–297, 300, 313–314, 661
Ursachentrieb 373
Utilitarianism 21, 28, 78–79, 244, 246–247, 386–387

Valuation(s) (see *also* Revaluation/Transvaluation of Values and Values) 5, 21, 49, 79, 103, 120, 148, 150–151, 162, 193, 219, 222, 224, 227, 229, 232, 239, 246, 274, 281, 290, 294–295, 361, 374, 384, 398–399, 407–408, 414, 427, 439–440, 456, 469, 496, 512, 519, 538, 540, 556, 563, 566, 568, 574–575, 578–583, 586–588, 591, 608, 613–614, 633, 640–641, 655–656, 666
Values (*see also* (E)valuation(s) and Revaluation/Transvaluation of Values) 21, 23, 25, 28, 41, 43, 52, 74–75, 125, 150–152, 219, 221, 229, 232, 234–236, 240, 246, 251–252, 264–265, 267, 269, 274, 281, 290, 294–295,

299–300, 311–312, 236, 355–356, 360–362, 364, 374, 382, 384, 387, 389, 398–399, 407–408, 418, 439, 450, 550, 561, 563, 566, 569, 570–571, 574–575, 583, 585, 589–591, 609, 613–614, 617, 625, 629–633, 640, 654, 660, 663–665
— Moral Values 360, 364, 439, 563, 570–571, 591, 614, 631
Vellemen, J.D. 26, 343, 347
Virchow, R.C. 241
Voltaire 270, 425

Wagner, R. 67, 219, 229, 232, 236, 265, 328, 405, 616–617
Wagnerism 221, 232,
Weakness of Will *see* Will
Whitehead, A.N. 395
Whitman, W. 328
Will 9, 14, 29, 66, 67, 81, 98, 120, 126–127, 131–132, 139–140, 143–145, 147, 149, 152, 155, 158–160, 176, 201, 224, 227 232–233, 242–243, 298–300, 360, 264, 370, 371, 377–379, 384, 387, 401–402, 406, 426, 487, 556–557, 601, 656

— Disease/Degeneration of the Will 224, 232, 268
— Freedom of the Will/Free Will 69, 260, 426
— Paralysis of Will 24, 285, 298–300, 308
— Reflexivity of Will 356
— Strength of Will 300, 664
— Weakness of Will 227, 230, 300, 586
Will to Know/Will to Knowledge 87, 149, 229, 418
Will to Power 8, 9, 28–29, 75, 76–77, 85–86, 90–91, 96, 98, 100, 142–143, 209, 245, 250, 284, 299, 356–357, 362, 365, 372, 375, 395, 400–409, 429, 497–498, 501, 504, 507, 551
Will to Truth *see Truth*
Williams, B. 127, 454, 662, 665
Wittgenstein, L. 31–33, 157, 454–484, 497, 508, 544–545
Wundt, W. 176

Yeats, W.B. 327–329

Zeller, E. 198
Žižek, S. 308